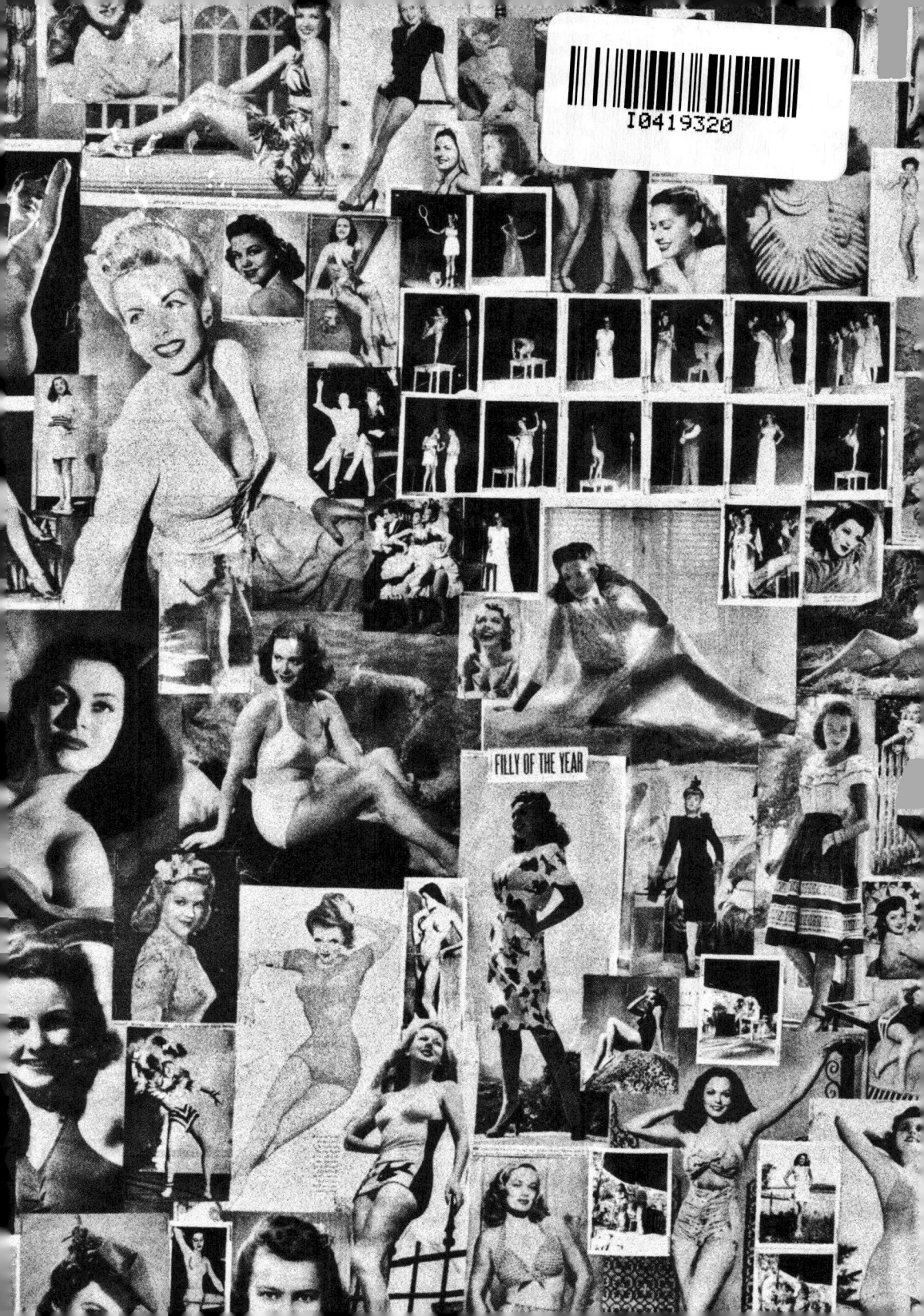

FILLY OF THE YEAR

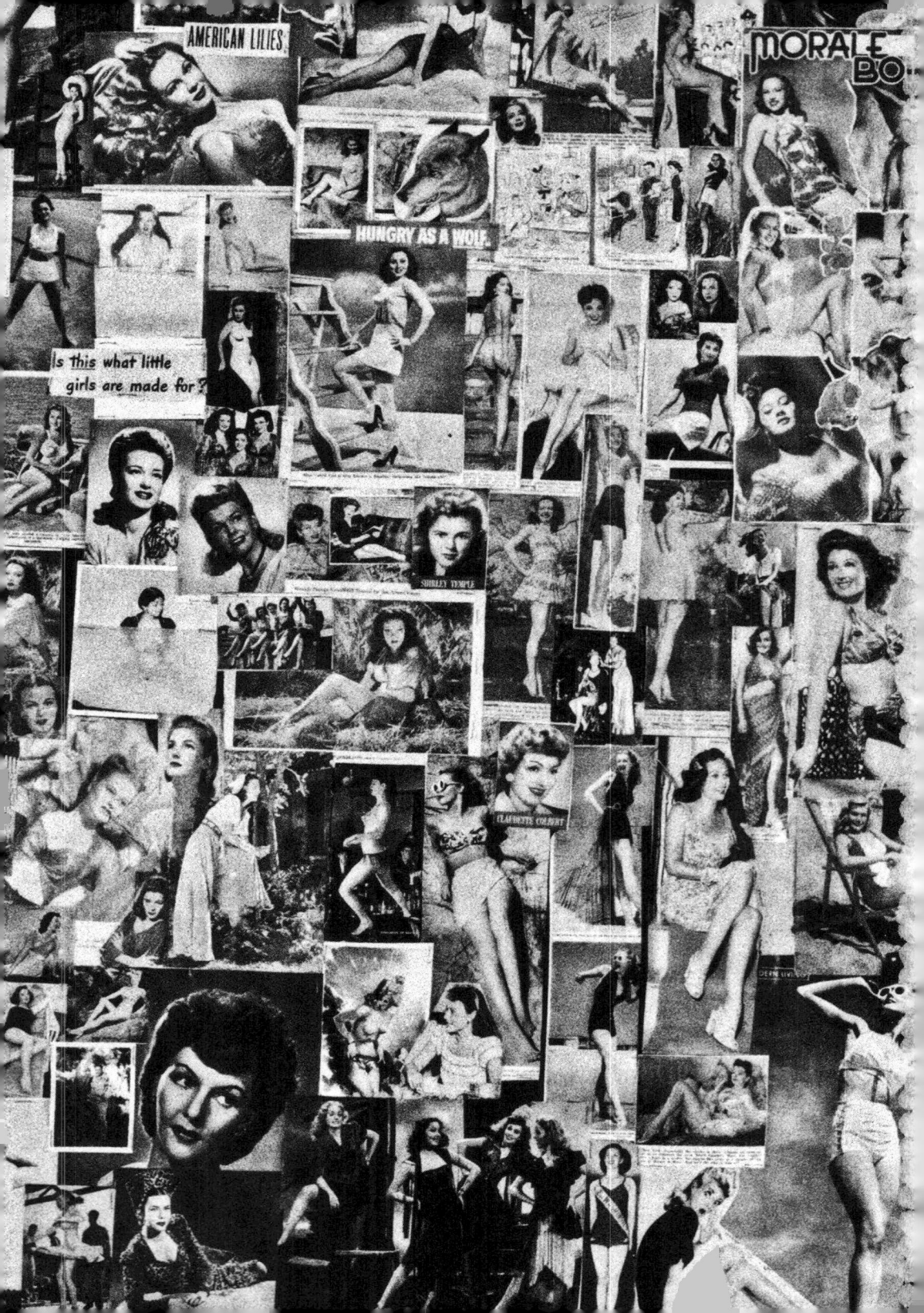

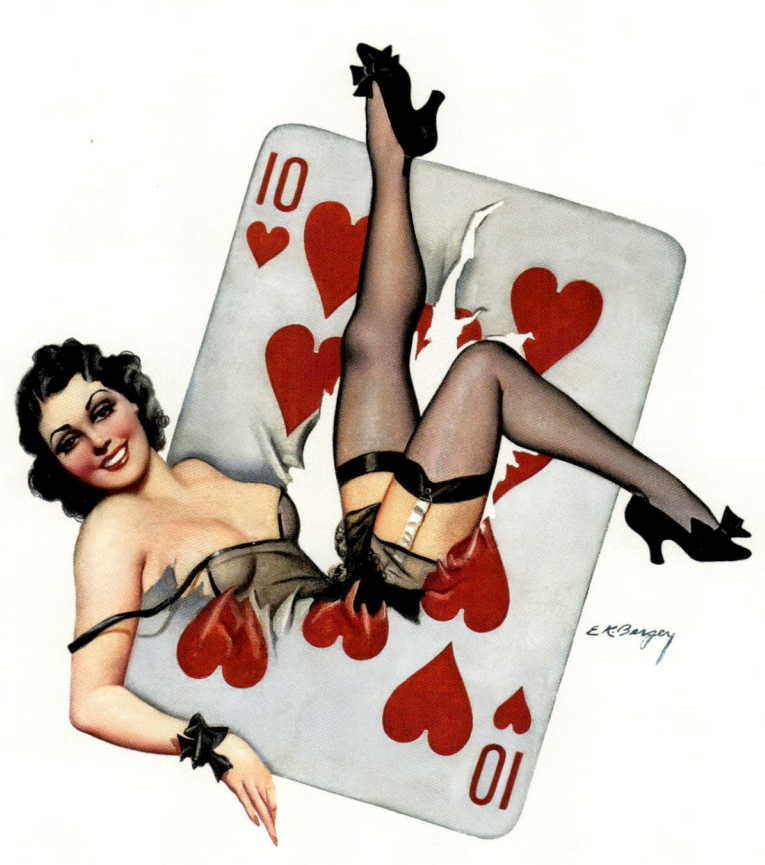

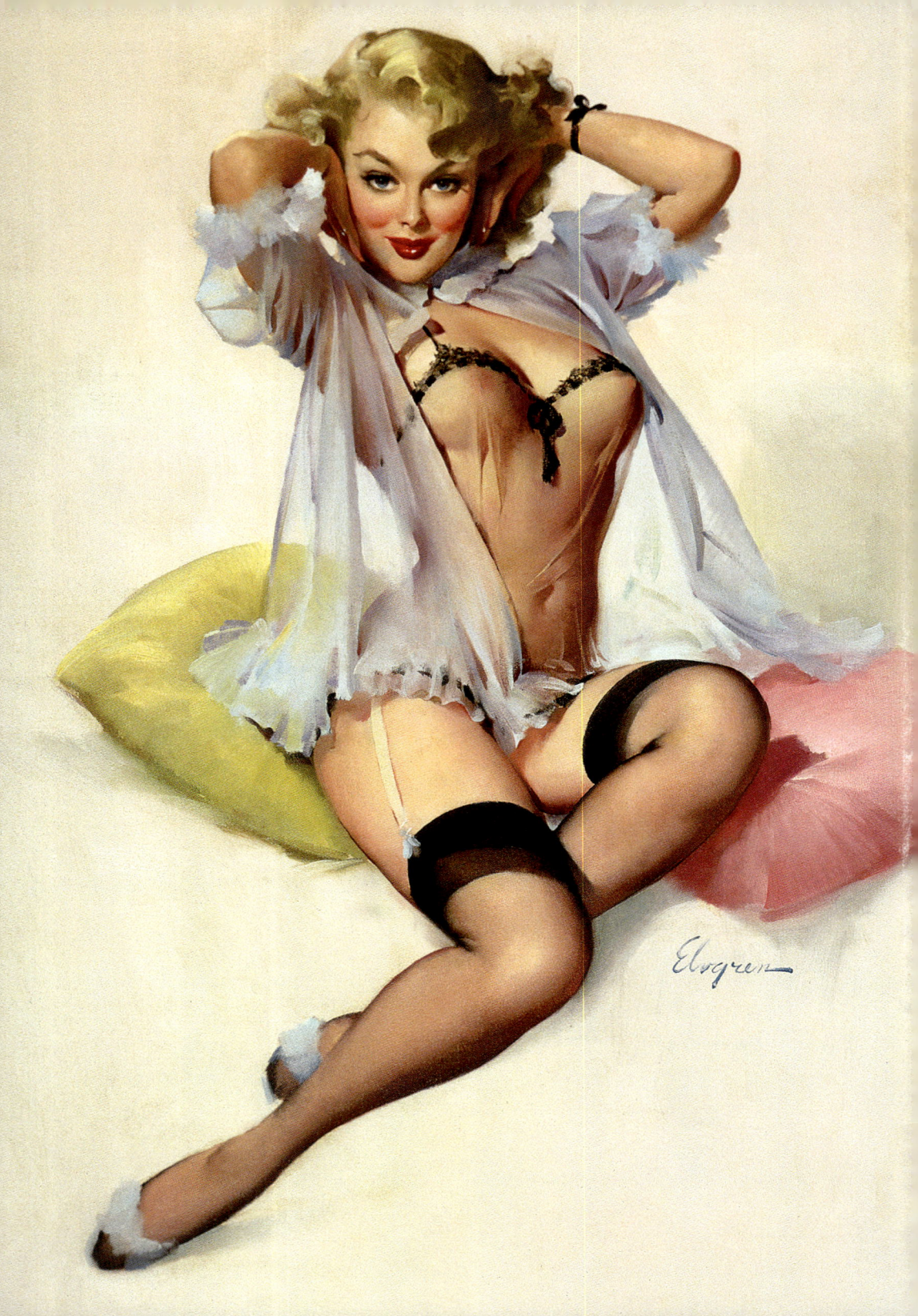

DIAN HANSON

WITH LOUIS K. MEISEL
AND SARAHJANE BLUM

THE ART OF
PIN-UP

TASCHEN

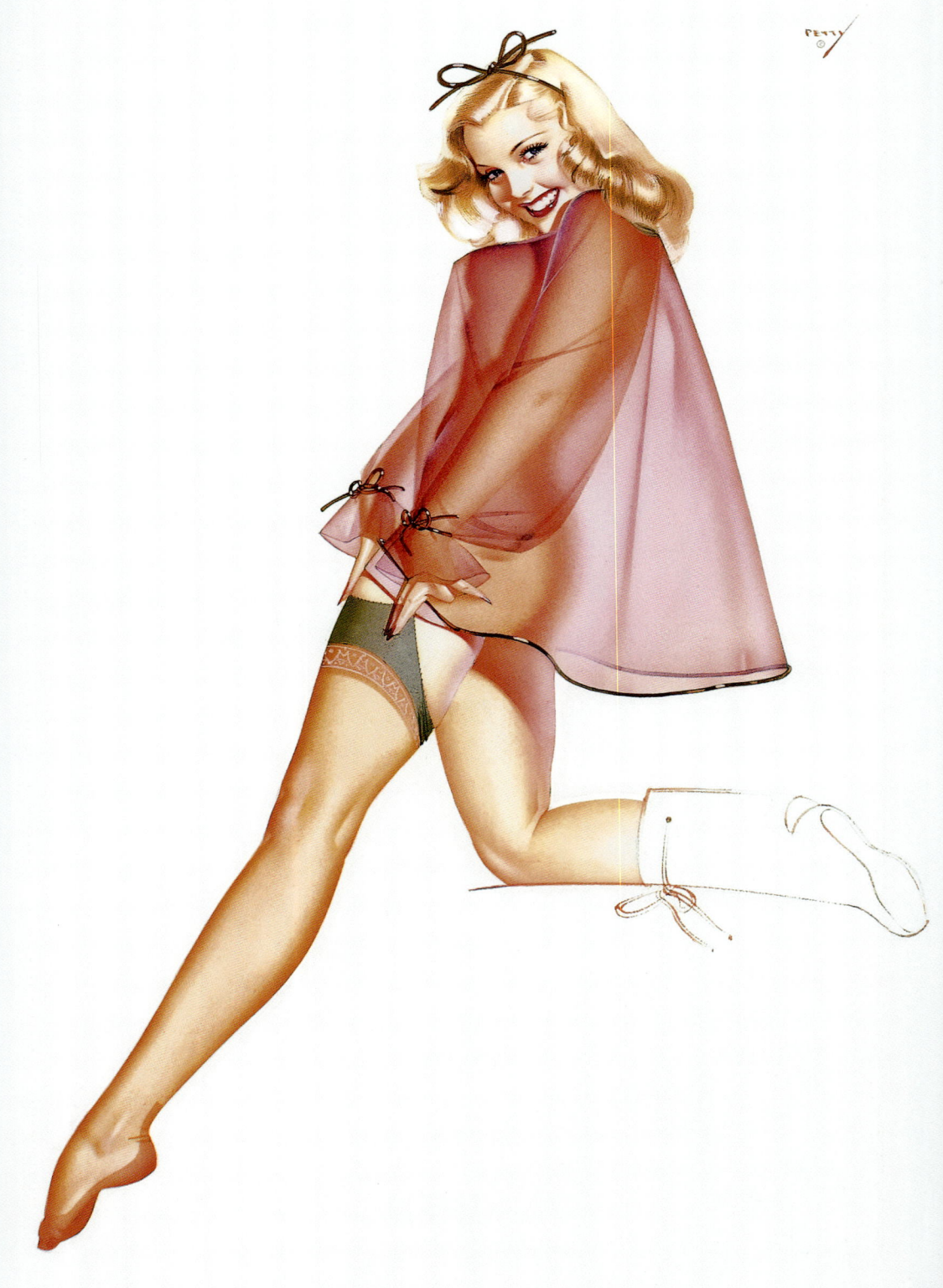

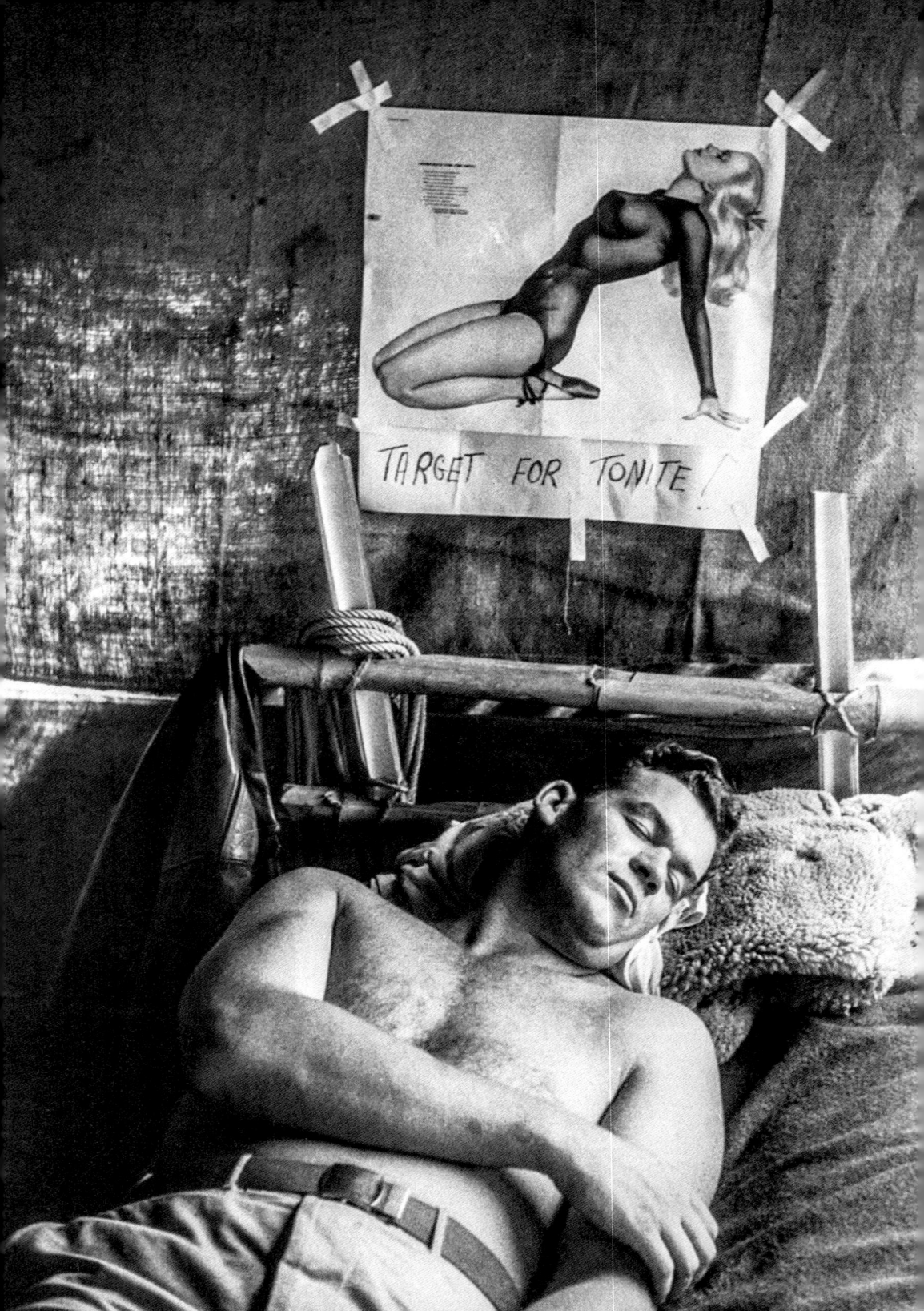

PIN-UP: A HIGHLY BIASED HISTORY

BY DIAN HANSON

Blame the economy, global warming, or ubiquitous porn: Many long for simpler times. Less modern misery and more Eisenhower innocence, please. Take us back to those halcyon days when cigarettes were nifty, red meat was neato, and cocktails were swell, before red states and blue states, big oil and big government, autism and Alzheimer's, factory farms and factory layoffs, the death of the seas and the death of the bees, when modernist meant Picasso instead of cuisine and when women had more — and showed it less.

Back in 1970 sex seemed new; we wanted to see it all. But now that Google offers two billion results for "porn," we're turning back to pin-up, something flirty that can stay on the wall when Mom comes to visit. What was risqué in 1945 is now not only acceptable, but fashionable. Amy Schumer channeled Marilyn Monroe for the May 2016 cover of *Vanity Fair*, while Billie Eilish's pin-up cover for the June 2021 issue of *Vogue* scored record sales to men and women alike. Bettie Page has never been bigger; Dita Von Teese has brought back burlesque; and Gil Elvgren's iconic pin-ups decorate everything from handbags to Christmas ornaments to tattooed biceps. Often female biceps.

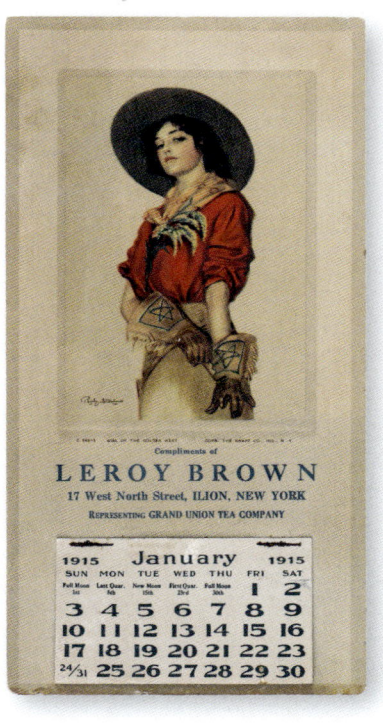

Why wouldn't women love pin-up as much as men? It's all about the girl, and it owes its very existence to women's liberation, which arrived in 1890 on bicycle wheels.

In the 1800s most Western women stayed close to home. When they traveled it was on foot to the local market or in the carriages of fathers and husbands. Layers of petticoats and skirts made travel for pleasure difficult, and sport was out of the question. Then along came the bicycle, more specifically the "safety" bicycle, with a rear chain drive and pneumatic tires

Opposite: American B-24 pilot Captain R. N. Skipper, stationed in Darwin, Australia, 1943, naps beneath his "target for tonite!": *Esquire*'s June 1943 centerfold by legendary pin-up artist Alberto Vargas. © Bettmann/ Getty Images.

Above: The Girl of the Golden West, modeled by actress Olive Thomas for this 1915 calendar. Olive was

Hollywood's first wild child, a wide-eyed beauty who began as a 20-year-old artist's model in 1914, when this illustration was made, joined the Ziegfeld Follies in 1915, and moved on to film in 1916. She died in Paris in 1920, at 25, after drunkenly mistaking her husband's topical syphilis medicine for more booze. 12 x 4.5 inches.

that made it physically, if not morally, acceptable for women to ride. Doctors and ministers railed against the "wheel," claiming that bouncing over cobblestones damaged delicate female organs, while the friction of the seat aroused immoral passions. Suffragists called it a "freedom machine," allowing women to travel far and wide without male escort, which was the men's real complaint.

Riding outfits quickly followed, comprised of knee-length bloomers, stockings, and high boots. For the first time in centuries, women's legs were revealed, and though still well covered, this "bifurcation" served up equal measure of outrage and delight. Women were becoming men! Women were becoming whores! Women, at last, were becoming interesting!

By demanding a place in the masculine world, women freed men to look at them and appraise them in an exciting, new way.

The first artist to celebrate the new woman was Charles Dana Gibson, who began illustrating for *Life* magazine, a small humor digest, in 1886. In 1887 his first "girl" cover was published, showing an hourglass torso rising from the center of a flower, with petals peeled back by cherubs. By 1895, when Gibson married into an elegant old Virginia family, a recognizable Gibson Girl was in place. By observing his wife and her imperious sisters, he refined his creation into the Girl America loved, the one who became a weekly centerfold in *Life*.

The Gibson Girl was beautiful, bosomy, and headstrong, her dark hair piled carelessly high, her lips full, her eyes heavy-lidded and sensual. She was often portrayed surrounded by hapless

Below: The Gibson Girl hardly looks like a feminist in her corset and voluminous skirts. While an object of lust, she *was* portrayed as in control and indifferent to her many suitors, as in this pen-and-ink sketch titled *Stepped On.*

Opposite: In the 1910s trousers were the insignia of female rebellion and women usurping the male role, as seen on this woman on her way to a women's suffrage parade in Chicago, 1916. At the same time, trousers were highly eroticised by men who had never seen the outlines of female legs displayed in public. © Corbis Images.

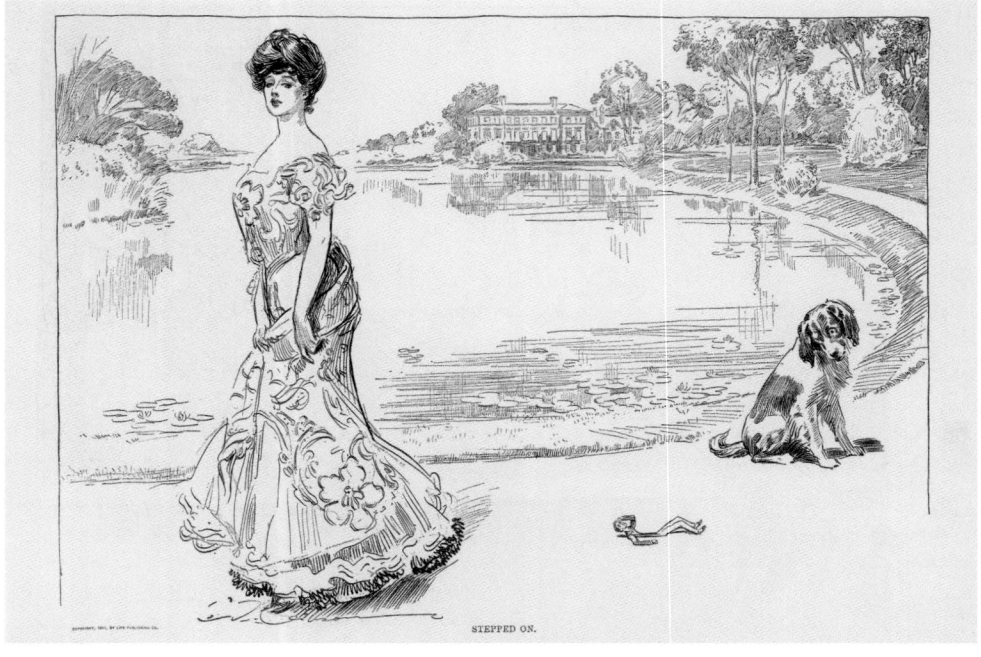

STEPPED ON.

THE ART OF PIN-UP

suitors, whom she confidently ignored. In one 1901 drawing, *Stepped On*, a doll-sized man lies crushed on the ground as the Gibson Girl walks on unconcerned, casting a steamy glance at the viewer. She was strong yet feminine, never salacious, entirely independent; a woman who couldn't be categorized as wife or whore. Being both ladylike and sexy, while eternally single, she became the first dream girl, the archetype of good girl art. Her September 18, 1902, *Life* centerfold was a collage of Gibson's achingly beautiful female faces, staring limpidly at the viewer, captioned "Wallpaper for Bachelors." There is no doubt that some pinned it up.

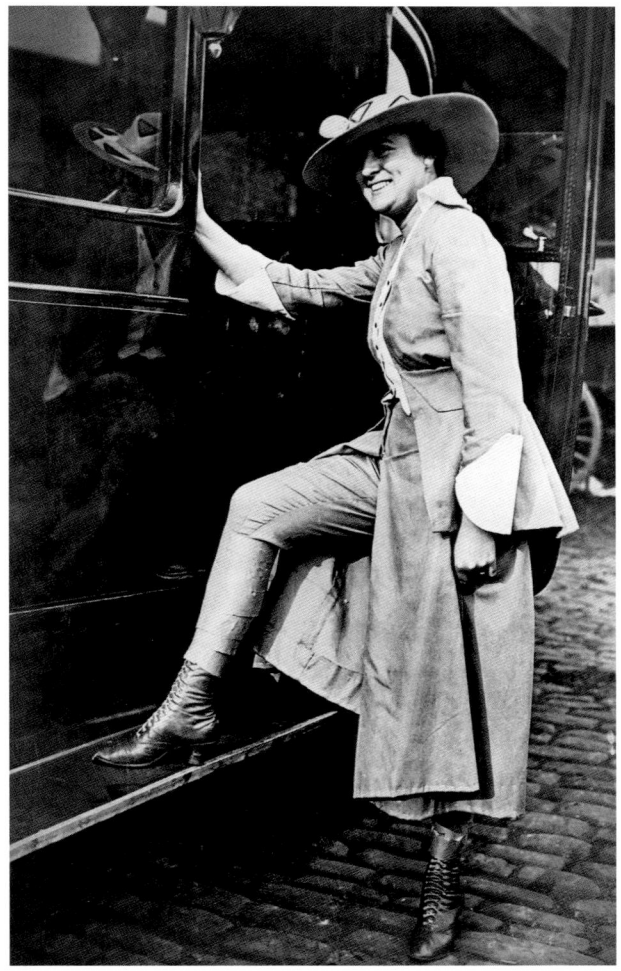

Every success brings imitators, and Gibson inspired many. Howard Chandler Christy's Christy Girl debuted in *The Century* magazine in 1895, and thereafter appeared frequently in *Scribner's*. Like the Gibson Girl, she was beautiful, regal, and aloof; unlike her, Christy's girl evolved with the times. As she advanced into the 1910s, she went sporty, even bobbing her hair in 1921.

Puck magazine, a competitor of *Life,* wanted its own girl, and got her from Harrison Fisher. Naturally, she was called the Fisher Girl, and her beauty was more homespun. Fisher described her as "genuine, gracious, tender when need be, buoyant when occasion calls, and feminine always." She proved more popular with women than men and appeared on the cover of *Cosmopolitan* magazine from 1912 until 1934.

A crucial step toward true pin-up came with World War I. The concept of propaganda was born with this war, drawn from Freud's new science of social psychology. Germany, England, and the United States all produced propaganda during the Great War, aimed at demoralizing the enemy, stirring up patriotism at home, and urging its troops to fight. American President Woodrow Wilson formed the Division of Pictorial Publicity in 1917, and its director enlisted Charles Dana Gibson to recruit poster artists. Christy, Fisher, and Montgomery Flagg, another early "girl" artist, created the first posters linking pretty girls to military victory, a manipulation that would be perfected for the next war. Christy's contribution was most memorable.

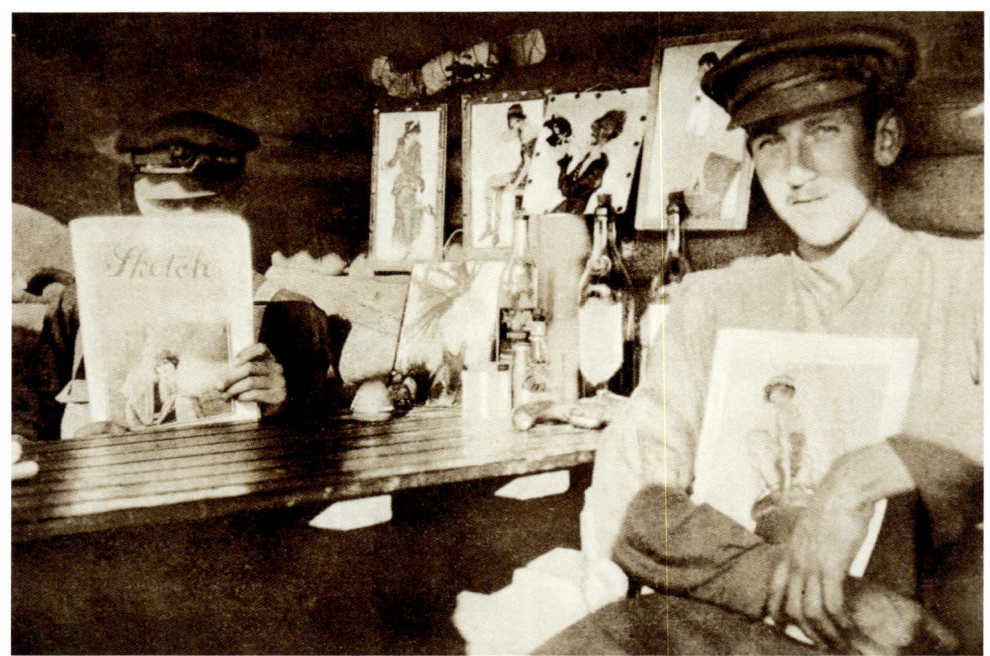

His iconic girls, dressed in flimsy, revealing gowns and military uniforms, exhorted men: *If You Want to Fight! Join the Marines*, *Fight or Buy Bonds*, and *Gee!! I Wish I Were a Man. I'd Join the Navy*, subtitled with the unsubtle *Be a Man and Do It*. The posters were saved and cherished—and, yes, pinned up.

In *The Great American Pin-Up*, published by TASCHEN in 1996, the late Charles Martignette described a pin-up image as "one that shows a full-length view of its subject and characteristically of a theme or some kind of story. The woman in a pin-up is usually dressed in a form-revealing outfit, either one that may be worn in public, such as a bathing suit, swimsuit, or skimpy dress, or one that is more provocative and intimate, such as lingerie. Sometimes, a pin-up may be shown in the nude, but this is more the exception than the rule." He goes on to separate pin-up from "glamour art," describing the latter as "generally attired in an evening gown, fancy dress, or some other attire that is less revealing than that of a pin-up." He labeled a third category "pretty girl" art: "a term used to refer to painting of a glamour-art nature that was done by mainstream illustrators. It found its audience among popular magazines like *The Saturday Evening Post* and *Cosmopolitan* and in the world of advertising."

Above: A rare photo of World War I British soldiers in a dugout near Ypres, France, with pin-ups pulled from *La Vie Parisienne* and *Le Sourire*, early risqué magazines not available back home in Britain. One reads *The Sketch*, the English society magazine that first published Agatha Christie. Private Collection/The Stapleton Collection/The Bridgeman Art Library.

Opposite: Pastel on paper, 1912, by Rolf Armstrong. This image by Armstrong, known as the "Father of American Pin-up," was one of his earliest commercial works, commissioned for the November 17, 1912, cover of the *American Sunday* newspaper supplement. Armstrong was just out of art school when this piece was completed, but the figure's face already shows the cool confidence that would become his trademark in the 1920s and '30s. 28 x 22.5 inches. Courtesy Heritage Auctions.

THE ART OF PIN-UP

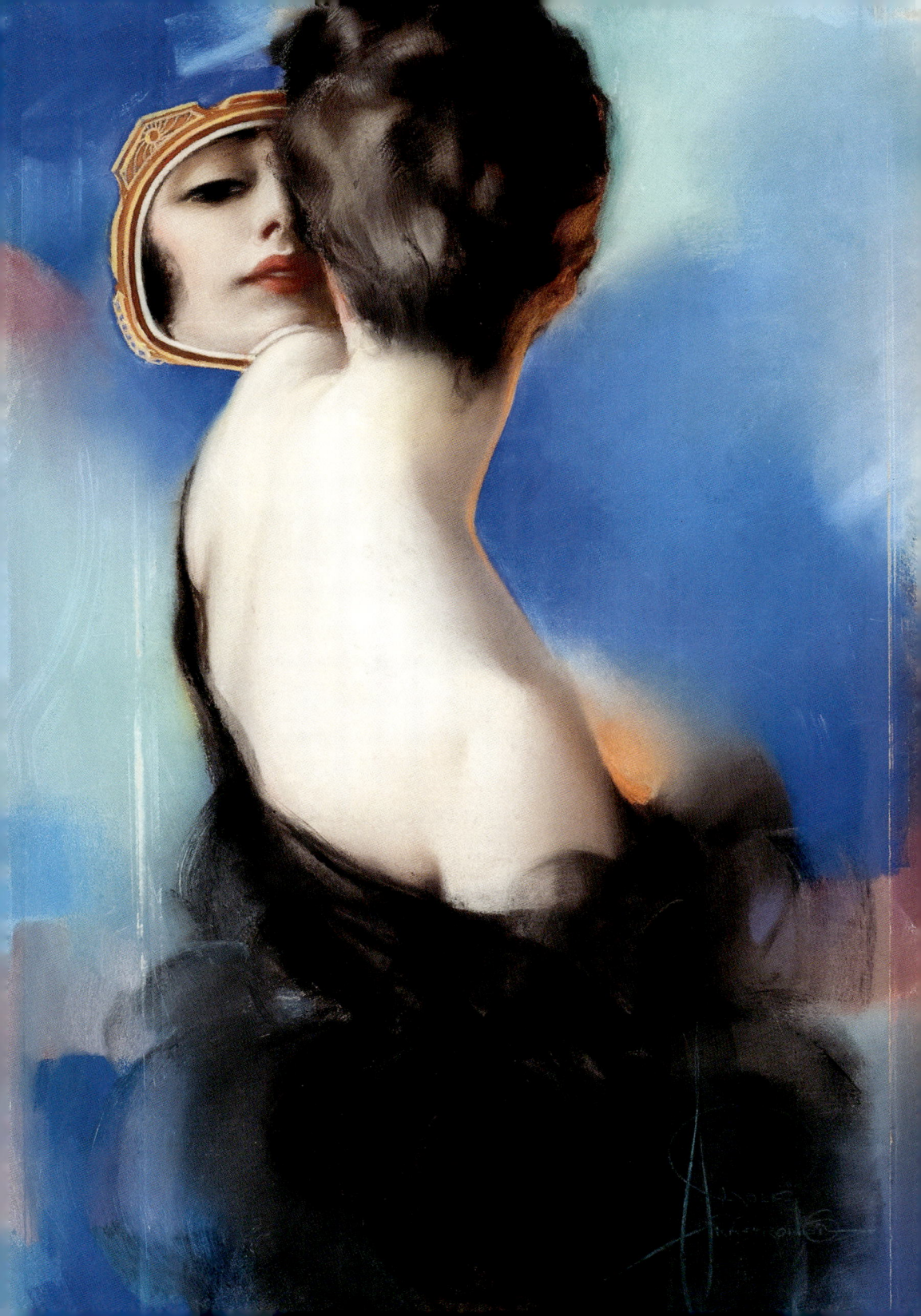

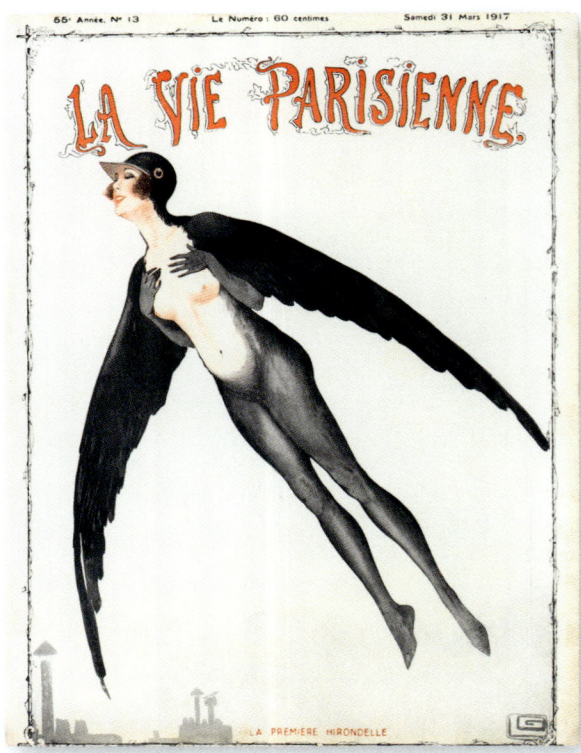

LA VIE PARISIENNE

LA PREMIÈRE HIRONDELLE

There are no footnotes telling where Martignette found these rules; most likely he made them up, based on his lifelong study of American illustration. Today, when everything pin-up is so desirable, and all of it seems equally modest, a new definition is in order. At auction, any girl by Gil Elvgren, Zoë Mozert, George Petty, or Alberto Vargas, in bathing suit or evening gown, is called a pin-up, as that appellation increases its value. It's true that an Elvgren nude such as his 1947 *Gay Nymph*, sold by Heritage Auctions in 2011 for a record-breaking $286,800, will always bring more than his modest Miss Sylvanias, but the Miss Sylvania buyer still reckons he's got a pin-up, and he counts himself lucky.

For this book, I'll define pin-up as a provocative but never explicit image of an attractive woman created specifically for public display in a male environment. If nude, it must be modest: The average observer shouldn't view it as masturbation material, though men have undoubtedly used pin-up this way. The alternate term "good girl art" says it all. A pin-up girl is not a slut. Her sexiness is natural and uncontrived, and her exposure is always accidental: A fishhook catches her bikini top, an outboard motor shreds her skirt, a spunky puppy trips her up, or the ever-present playful breeze lifts her hem, revealing stocking tops and garter straps but never the whole enchilada.

Gil Elvgren's late-career *Still Life*, the title a tongue-in-cheek reference to a bowl of fruit in the foreground of a torrid harem scene, never saw mainstream distribution due to the shocking presence of pubic hair. This was not a pin-up. When Hugh Hefner insisted that Alberto Vargas add pubic hair to his *Playboy* pin-ups in 1971, the artist consented only for fear of losing his job. Alberto knew his fan base better than Hef: These explicit paintings are less popular because they break the rules of pin-up. Even Art Frahm, whose damsels suffered the double indignity of falling panties and wayward winds, shielded the viewer from what the strategically placed men in his paintings enjoy. He understood the parameters: Pin-ups must stay pure.

Above: La Vie Parisienne (Paris Life) was the original French risqué weekly magazine. Founded in 1863, it blended humor, gossip, the arts, nightlife, and fashion with beautiful, frequently nude, illustrations by leading artists of the day. The original title existed until 1970, but the magazine was at its peak during WWI and was a favorite souvenir for American soldiers. This issue is dated March 31, 1917.

Opposite: Le Sourire (The Smile) was a French humor magazine loosely patterned on *La Vie Parisienne*, featuring jokes, short stories, and racy illustrations of scantily clad women. It began in the 1910s and persisted until WWII. This issue is January 8, 1931.

With the end of the Great War, the United States saw rapid social change. Though the death toll was low compared to Europe's loss, more than a quarter million young men were killed or injured, and all had seen things previously undreamed of—though not all bad. Those serving in France discovered cabaret and risqué magazines such as *La Vie Parisienne* and *Le Sourire*. They returned restless and dissatisfied with provincial America, preferring drinking and dancing to jobs and marriage. The women they came home to had changed as well. The jobs many held during the war had provided a taste of financial freedom. They bobbed their hair and indulged in lipstick, silk stockings, and high-heeled tango shoes. When the 18th Amendment passed in 1919, banning the sale of alcohol, it just fanned the flames of youth rebellion. Flappers and flippers—their male counterparts—swapped the tango palace for the speakeasy and augmented illegal liquor with marijuana, cocaine, and opiates. The usual parties complained, but most were fascinated by this wild youth, especially by the free-spirited women, and the media rushed to cash in.

Rolf Armstrong's sultry flappers first appeared on movie magazine covers around 1920. He'd already seen success with his demure *Dream Girl* calendar, released by Midwest calendar company Brown & Bigelow in 1919, but it was a pastel flapper with defiant kohl-rimmed eyes and red-lacquered lips, titled *Betty*, created in '24 for a 1926 calendar, that made Armstrong a star.

As Armstrong completed *Betty*, Enoch Bolles painted a lean flapper brandishing a whip for the cover of *Film Fun* magazine. At her feet, tiny men race around an oversized wedding ring. Her triumphant stance indicates that none has a chance of winning her heart. Contemporaries Ruth Eastman, Guy Hoff, John Held Jr., McClelland Barclay, Walter Dean Goldbeck, and Frank Leyendecker, brother of J. C., painted equally liberated women for the covers of *Life*,

Judge, and *College Humor*. A number of lesser humor titles, including *Capt. Billy's Whiz Bang*, *Hot Dog*, *Smokehouse Monthly*, *Burten's Follies*, *Old Bob Edwards' Calgary Eye Opener*, and *Cap'n Joey's Jazza Ka Jazza*—the title referencing "jazz" as a synonym for sex—featured more risqué flapper covers, often by anonymous artists.

Back at the calendar companies, richly colored art deco fantasy—heavy on exotic locale and barely dressed beauties—joined the flappers in the late '20s. Indian maidens, Egyptian queens, Hawaiian savages, and feral nymphets characterized the work of Henry Clive, Edward Eggleston, Mabel Rollins Harris, Gene Pressler, and William Fulton Soare. Though lush and highly detailed, the exoticism in these early works was superficial, largely confined to the brief

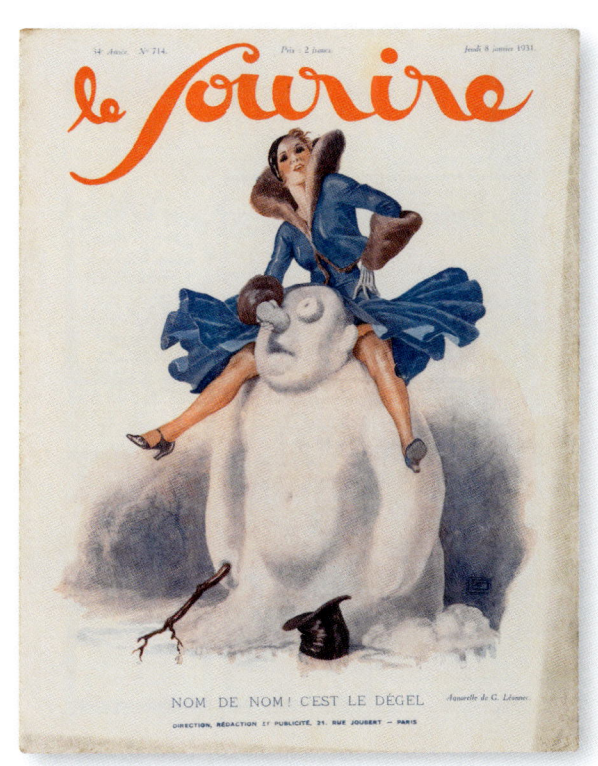

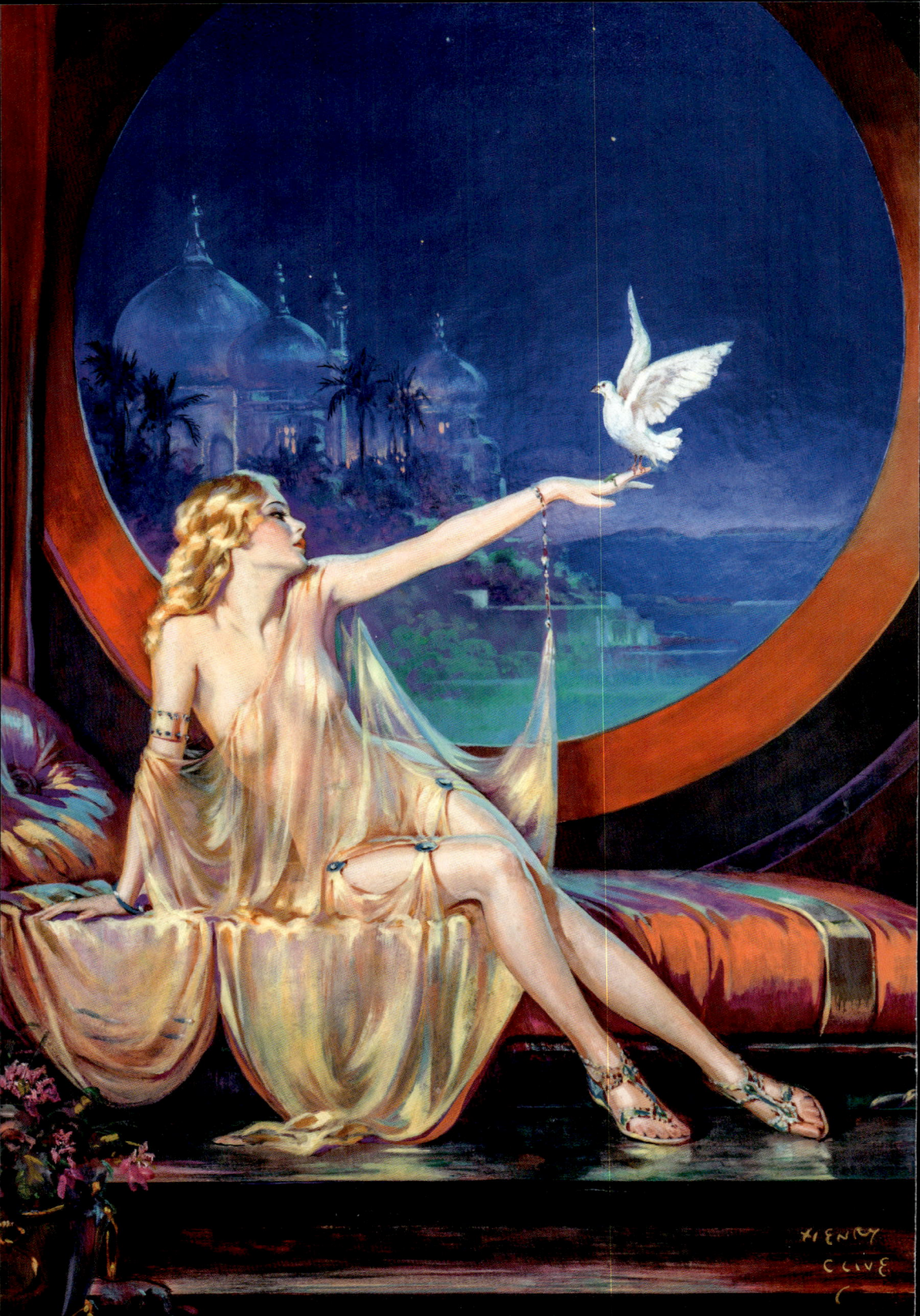

native costumes, as the calendar companies expected their pin-ups to be white. Joseph C. Hoover & Sons of Philadelphia and Thomas D. Murphy of Red Oak, Iowa, printed some of the best Deco pin-up calendars, but Brown & Bigelow of St. Paul, Minnesota, was rising fast and preparing for world domination in the next decade.

In 1889 Thomas Murphy and Edmond Osborne printed the first calendar with advertising beneath the image. It proved a brilliant concept: A calendar stays on the wall for a year, and every time you check the date you see the advertiser's message. Competitors quickly followed, including McCleery-Cummings, Kemper-Thomas, John Baumgarth, Gerlach-Barklow, Joseph C. Hoover & Sons, Louis F. Dow, Skinner-Kennedy, C. Moss, Goes Lithograph, and Shaw-Barton, but none would be as successful, or as synonymous with pin-up, as Brown & Bigelow.

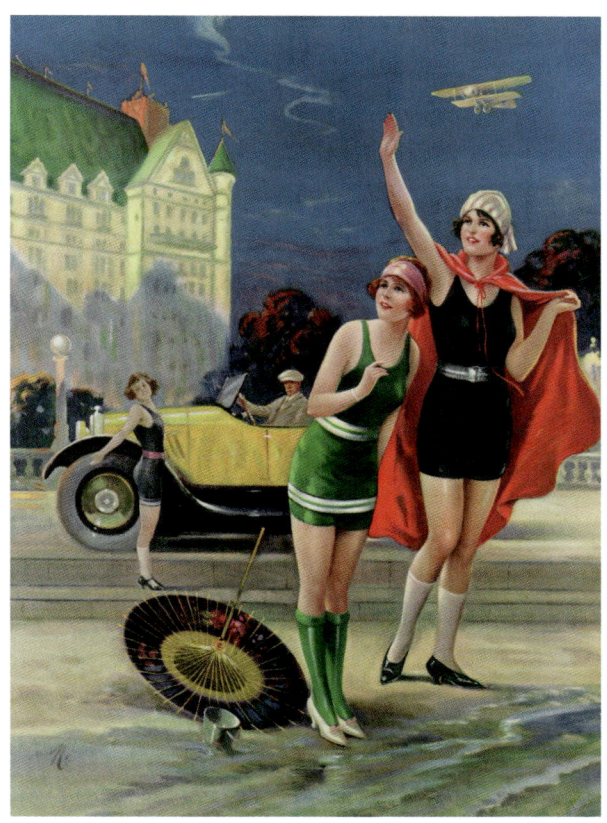

B&B, as it's known, didn't just make pin-up calendars, but its pin-ups were the best and the biggest — created by top artists, who were groomed in-house, then rewarded with contracts unequaled for generosity. These artists included Rolf Armstrong, Al Buell, Earl MacPherson, Bill Medcalf, Earl Moran, Zoë Mozert, Knute Munson, Edward Runci, and, most notably, the great Gil Elvgren, who worked exclusively for B&B from 1945 until 1971. Curiously, this empire was built neither by Mr. Brown, who died in 1904, nor by Mr. Bigelow, who followed him in 1933, but by a diamond-studded, gold-toothed gangster named Charlie Ward. An ex-resident of Leavenworth penitentiary, his life story reads like a Hollywood film script. In fact, a movie based on Ward's life was in development at the time of his death in 1959, when his wife called it off. It's said she feared the facts going public, and well she might. Here, a short history:

In 1896 young salesman Herbert Huse Bigelow tried to interest St. Paul, Minnesota, printer Hiram D. Brown in buying some Osborn-Murphy calendars. Brown suggested that

Opposite: Sultana, oil on board, circa 1925, is Henry O'Hara Clive's best known pin-up, created as a calendar illustration for the Louis F. Dow Company. 30 x 23.75 inches.

Above: A calendar lithograph, circa 1928, demonstrates the wonders of the liberated 1920s: private automobiles that gave young people freedom to travel, and a place to "court"; a biplane to free them from earth's bonds; and most prominent, free-spirited flappers ready to fulfill a man's fantasies.

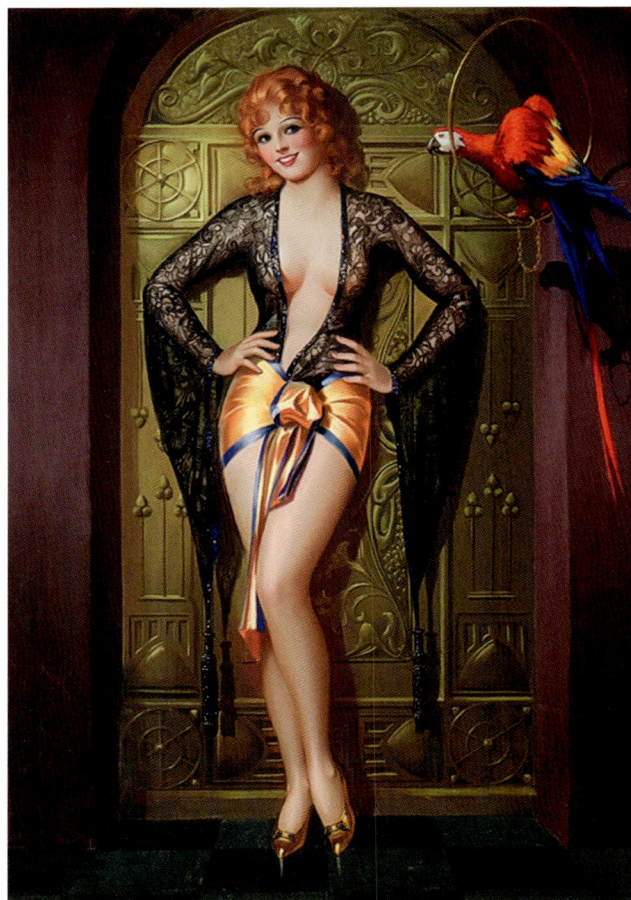

he and Bigelow form their own calendar company, with Brown supplying capital and lithographic prints, while Bigelow did the selling. Their first calendar featured George Washington and made a modest profit. Within three years the two had branched out into caps, aprons, change pouches, and horse covers, all bearing promotional slogans. In 1903 B&B introduced its first girl calendar, *Cosette,* by artist Angelo Asti. It revealed no more than a hint of cleavage, but it proved so profitable that B&B was able to move into new, bigger quarters.

The company further expanded following Brown's death, printing the first four-color calendars, adding wildlife and adventure artists—and more girls. Bigelow came up with the slogan "Remembrance Advertising" to describe his company's products, and men certainly remembered Brown & Bigelow pin-up calendars, which became staples in every male hangout. Herbert Bigelow was forward-thinking, and quick to adopt the latest print advances, but he was also aloof and arrogant, with a well-developed sense of privilege. These shortcomings led to his conviction for tax evasion in 1923 and a two-year stretch in Leavenworth federal prison.

Enter Charles Ward, destined for Leavenworth from birth. He was born in 1886 at the rough Bremerton Navy Yard, near Seattle, and was running errands for local saloons at age 14. At 16 he trained a fighting dog that killed the navy's top dog in an arranged match, winning him $1,000. He spent half this comparative fortune on a gold tooth for the dog, thereafter

Above: *Miss Glory* is one of Gene Pressler's best-known works, an impressive large pastel, circa 1932. 43.5 x 31.5 inches.

Opposite left: *Bathing Beauty,* pen and ink on board, by James Montgomery Flagg, circa 1928. Flagg was a competitor to Charles Gibson, known for his illustrations for *Judge, Liberty, Cosmopolitan,* and *College Humor* magazines from 1900 to 1950. He is best known for his

1917 recruitment poster of Uncle Sam, captioned "I Want YOU for U.S. Army." 26.5 x 20.5 inches.

Opposite right: The 1920s were a time of disinhibition and reckless stunts performed by newly liberated young women. In 1926 these flappers danced the Charleston on the roof ledge of Chicago's Sherman Hotel. © Underwood & Underwood/Corbis Images.

THE ART OF PIN-UP

called Goldie. Over the following decades, Charlie emulated his dog, having all of his teeth, top and bottom, capped in gleaming gold: the prototypical grill.

Gold was Ward's god. In 1903 he chased it to Arizona, then joined the rush to Alaska in 1906, and in 1910 ended up in National, Nevada, a mining town as rough as its gold was plentiful. Here, Ward smuggled ore out of company mines to finance a trip to Mexico, where he and a friend joined Pancho Villa's revolution. Ward cared nothing for the peasant's cause, but he admired flamboyant Villa, who let him have the hides off the cattle he rustled to feed his troops. Ward sold the hides in Texas, making $70,000 in three years. He left Mexico when his friend was killed in 1916, and he began spending his money. Ward partied for two years, ending up in Denver, where he was arrested and charged with trafficking in cocaine. He fought the charge until his money was gone; the judge gave him 10 years in maximum-security prison.

When Bigelow got to Leavenworth, Ward was a trustee, a powerful prison player with many friends and special privileges. Ward heard that the rich businessman was being bullied by other inmates and connived to have Bigelow transferred to his cell. There he offered the terrified man a deal: protection in prison in exchange for a job when he got out. Bigelow gratefully accepted, and Charlie kept him safe until his release in 1925.

Bigelow wasn't eager to honor the bargain when Ward showed up in St. Paul shortly after. He tried to buy Charlie off and, when that failed, gave him a backbreaking menial job. To Bigelow's surprise, Ward proved a hard worker with innovative ideas who rose rapidly in the company. He always stayed close to Bigelow, claiming him as his best friend. How the effete Bigelow felt about a best buddy with gold teeth who said "dem" for "them" and "dose" for "those" was not recorded, but by 1930 Ward was director and vice president of the company.

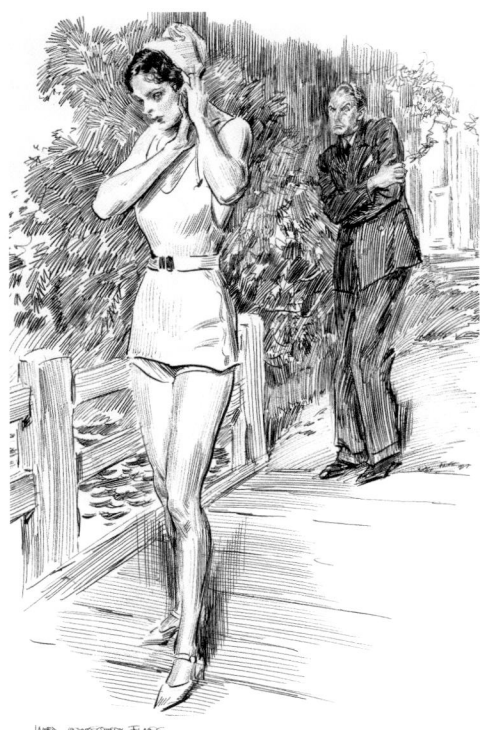

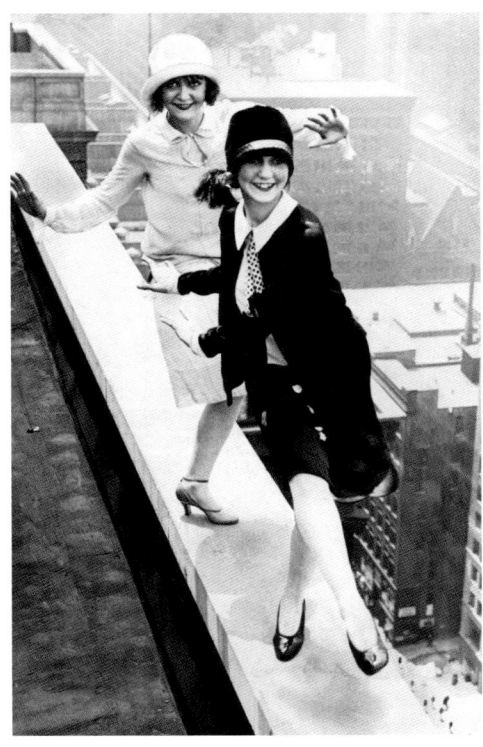

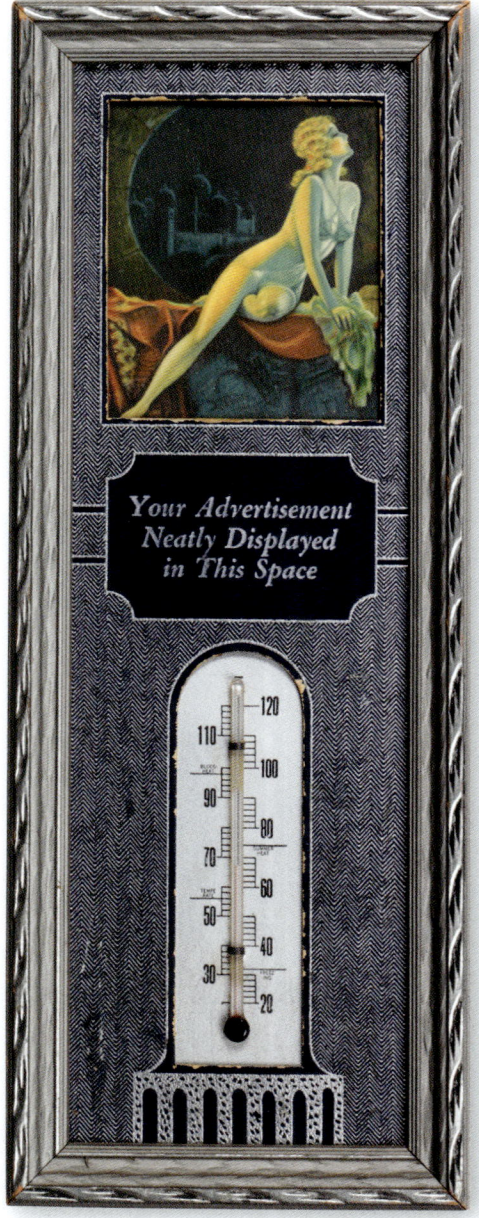

It was Charlie who made Rolf Armstrong the best-paid pin-up artist in America; Charlie who signed Earl Moran in 1937 at $10,000 a year, plus studio rent and model fees; and Charlie who lured Gil Elvgren away from Louis F. Dow in 1944 with the bait of $2,000 a painting. Contrary to persistent rumors, it was *not* Charlie who upset Herbert Bigelow's canoe on Basswood Lake on September 19, 1933, and left him to drown while his guide swam to shore with his companion, the wife of the company's top salesman. It *was* Charlie who inherited the company, however, and a third of Bigelow's fortune, in a will drawn up shortly before the accident.

Who hired Bigelow's guide was never explored.

So began the reign of Ward and the golden age of Brown & Bigelow. Charlie immediately established a policy of hiring ex-cons and secretly helped men still in prison. In the book *John Dillinger Slept Here*, author Paul Maccabee states that in 1933 Ward gave gangster Bugsy Siegel $100,000 in an attempt to spring two Murder Inc. hit men from a Minnesota prison. Given the year, it's tempting to link this to Bigelow's fatal accident, but no connection can be made. To his credit, Ward treated his cons like any other employee, pushing all relentlessly, rewarding high achievers with bonuses and original pin-up art and firing the rest. B&B's turnover was so high that ex-employees became its biggest competitors: Several left to form the Shaw-Barton calendar company.

Hard as he was on salesmen, Ward paid his artists more than any other calendar company and far outstripped the magazines. In 1939 George Petty was making $100

Above: A salesman's sample wall thermometer, circa 1930, with art deco pin-up. Pin-up flourished during the Great Depression, most examples featuring exotic escapist fantasies of wealth and vague Orientalism.

Opposite: Eugene Pressler was a master of the art deco pastel. His colors were rich, his locations exotic, and his subjects always in danger of losing their clothes. Pastel on board, circa 1920, 40 x 30 inches. Courtesy Heritage Auctions.

THE ART OF PIN-UP

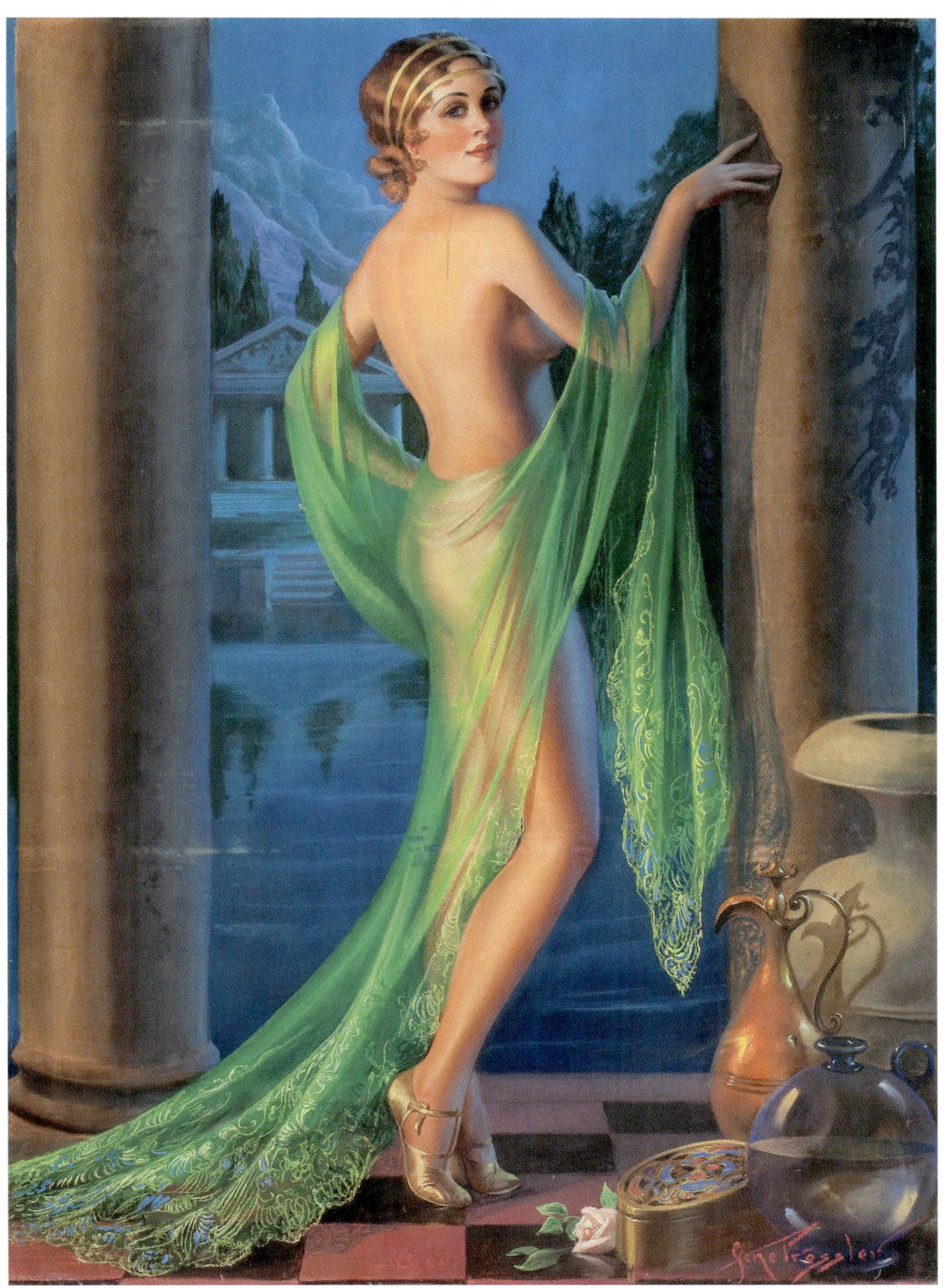

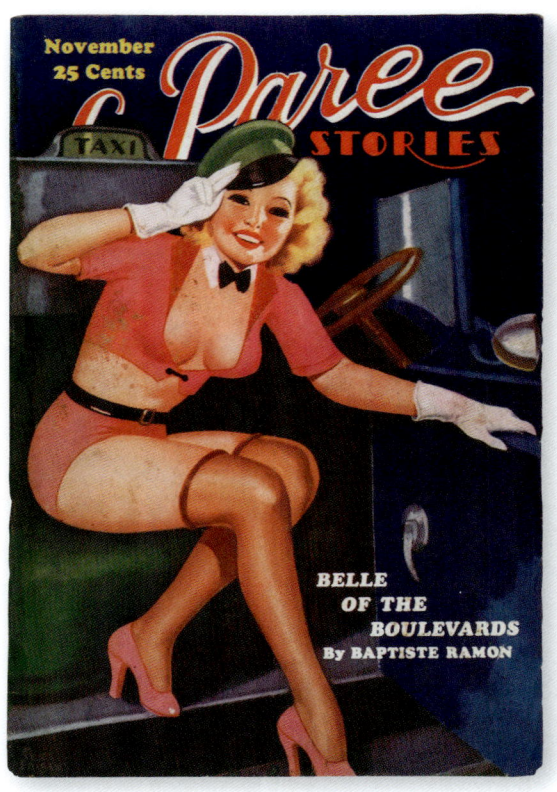

a centerfold at *Esquire,* while B&B paid $1,000 for a comparable painting. Little wonder every pin-up artist hoped to land a contract with Brown & Bigelow. Ward also gave so conspicuously to charity that *Life* magazine named him the "World's Most Generous Man." Those privy to B&B's finances countered that Charlie Ward was his own favorite charity, estimating that it cost the company $1 million a year to maintain his lifestyle in 1955. His indulgences included multiple estates — a 2,000-acre farm in Wisconsin with a herd of buffalo, an 80,000-acre ranch in Arizona, and a California beach house for nude sunbathing — a retinue of servants and personal assistants who traveled with him everywhere; a fleet of exotic cars fitted with bulletproof glass and custom gun holsters; weekly parties for hundreds of guests, featuring rare game and costly gifts; a pocketful of gold cigarette lighters inscribed with his name, used to tip waiters and bellhops; and more diamond and gold jewelry than a '90s rap star.

Just in case the grill wasn't bling enough.

Ward's ultimate extravagance was the company's Diamond Jubilee of 1956. In the largest civilian airlift in American aviation history, he flew 1,800 salesmen, artists, and their families to St. Paul for a four-day bacchanalia. They dined on roast pig, pheasant, and buffalo and sipped champagne from ever-flowing fountains — but for all the show, things were not well at B&B.

Ward had taken the company public in 1948, and by the mid-'50s his expensive lifestyle was draining profits and driving down stock values. When he died in his sleep in a Beverly Hills hotel room on May 26, 1959, aged 73, his autocratic rule left no one fit to run the company. Fearing its stock would fall further, B&B quickly sold out to Standard Packaging Corporation, which downsized drastically, then sold the company on to Saxon Industries in 1970. It was during the Saxon rule that a catalog was compiled of all the company-owned pin-up art, over 1,000 Armstrongs, Buells, Elvgrens, MacPhersons, Morans, Mozerts, Munsons, and Runcis, with

Above: La Paree Stories, November 1937, with cover by Peter Driben. This was a spicy fiction title – risqué stories printed on cheap pulp paper with a pin-up cover to draw in buyers – that started publication in 1930 and ceased at the end of 1938. Earle Bergey illustrated many early covers, but he was replaced by the prolific Peter Driben in December 1936.

Opposite: Rise and Shine, mixed media on canvas, 1933, by Earle Bergey for the February 1934 cover of *Snappy* magazine. The clock is a photographic image collaged into the painting. Bergey was a top pulp magazine cover artist in the 1930s, with paintings appearing on detective, adventure, romance, western, and so-called spicy publications. 31 x 22 inches.

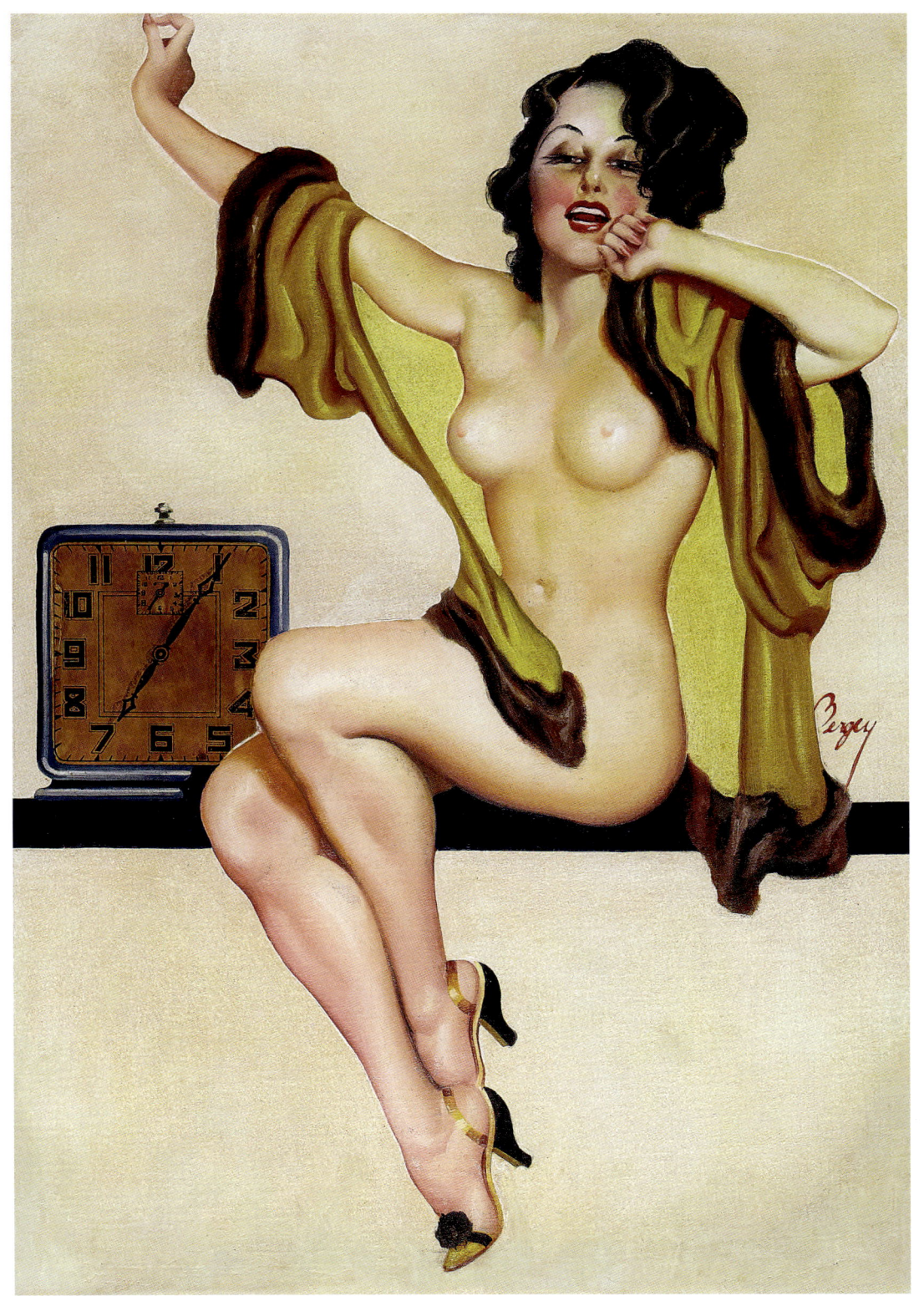

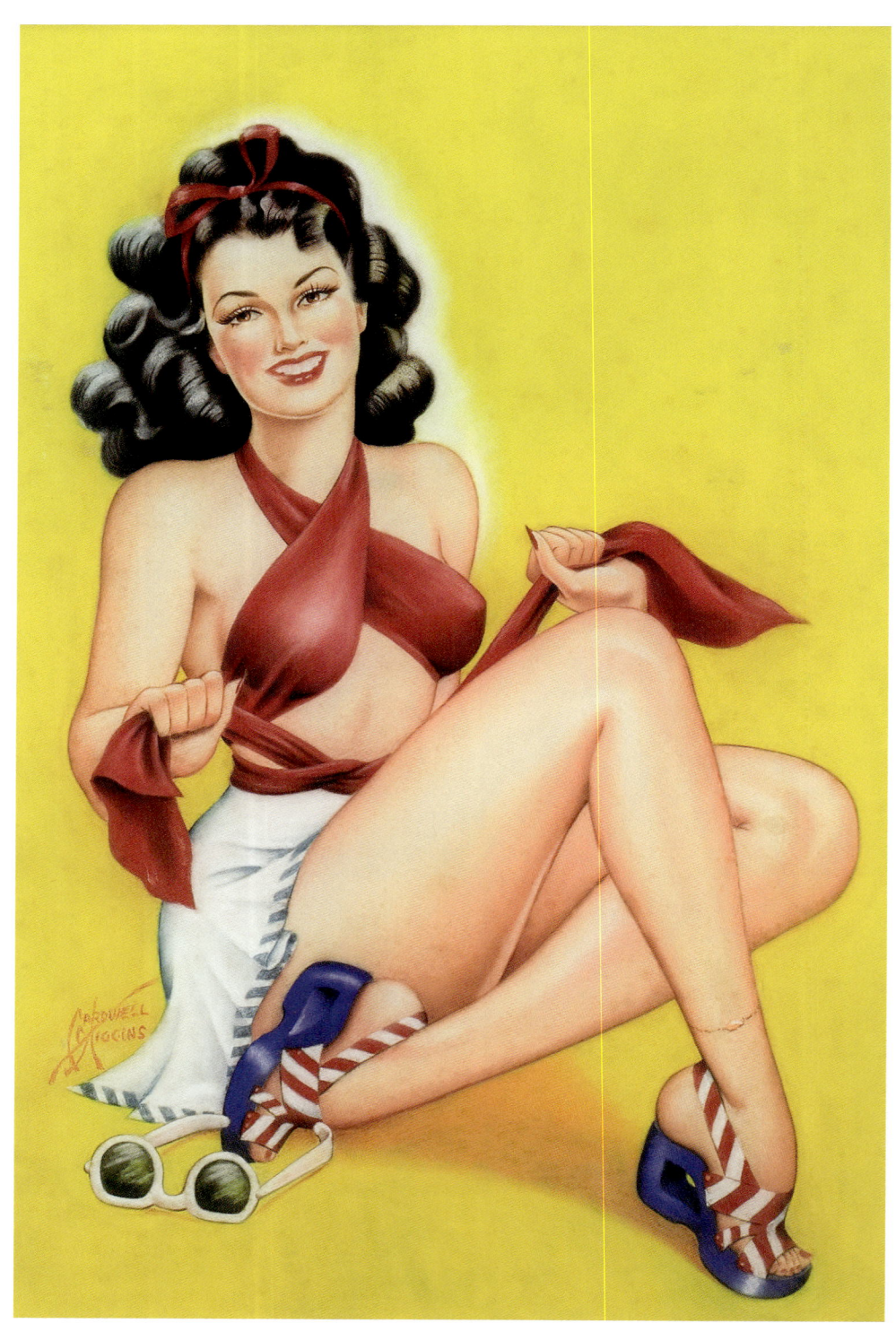

prices ranging from $25 to $300. One by one they went, and when sales slacked off the remainder were sold at 10 for $100.

Saxon declared bankruptcy in 1983, and the company languished until 1988, when William Smith Sr., one of Charlie Ward's old salesmen, bought it. Smith's two sons now run the company. Though the art is gone and calendars are no longer the company's main product, the Smiths have preserved the vast Brown & Bigelow calendar archive and maintain the attendant copyrights, licensing usage for images by Gil Elvgren, Earl Moran, Rolf Armstrong, Zoë Mozert and others.

It's like digging for gold in the Brown & Bigelow vault — a simile Charlie Ward would have appreciated. There are two or three 40-pound boxes for each year, and the pin-ups are mixed in with Boy Scout, baseball, cute-baby and duck-hunting calendars. You turn

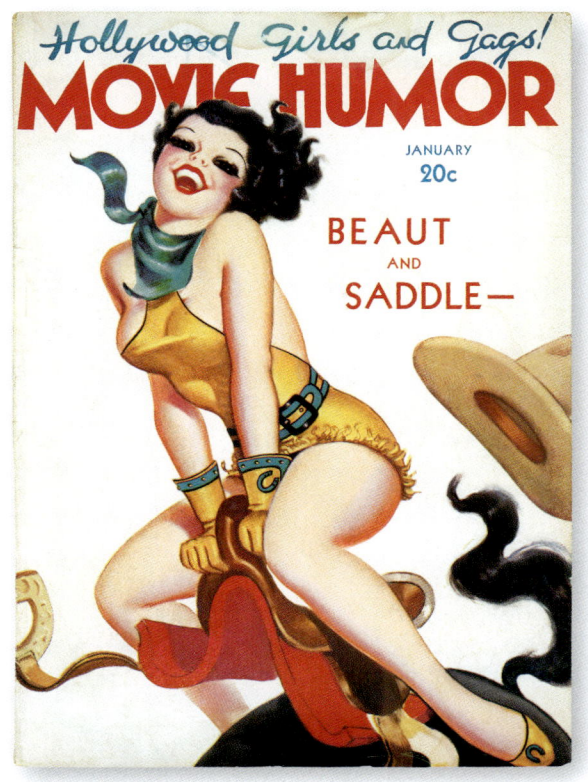

them over one by one, 100 or more in a box, to find the treasure: a stunning Gene Pressler in a multilayered, heavily embossed art deco frame; an elegant Armstrong flapper flanked by wolfhounds in an uncommon horizontal format; twenty little Enoch Bolles blotters; then, finally, Earl Moran's first calendar, 1935, precontract, rare as anything in pin-up. *Miss St. Paul,* as she's titled, is neither art deco nor flapper but moving toward the Depression-era escapism of Hollywood glamour. Beautiful as these carefully crafted calendars are, they weren't actually the leading edge of pin-up in the 1930s; the breaking news was — where else? — at the newsstand.

The perceived knowledge is that erotica is recession-proof, that people cling to small pleasures in times of economic downturn — and the pleasures men cling to tightest are sexual. This was the case during the Great Depression, when a flood of titillating film and fiction magazines appeared. *Film Fun,* featuring stunning Enoch Bolles covers from 1923, inspired several imitators in the '30s, all wanting that Bolles look. George Quintana and Peter Driben delivered it, illustrating covers for *Movie Humor, Movie Fun, Movie Merry-Go-Round, Real Screen Fun,* and

Opposite: Pastel on board, circa 1935, by Cardwell Higgins. The 1930s saw a sharp increase in risqué and detective magazines, a cheap escape for men mired in the Great Depression. Higgins was a popular cover artist for second-tier titles including *Expose Detective, Amazing Detective Cases, The Stocking Parade, Silk Stocking Stories,* and *Real Screen Fun.* 34 x 24 inches.

Above: George Quintana was an Enoch Bolles imitator employed to create covers for *Film Fun* movie magazine competitors. One of his best covers adorns this January 1937 issue of *Movie Humor.* All of the '30s film magazines had a similar content of stills provided by the motion picture studios, with an emphasis on leggy starlets in lingerie.

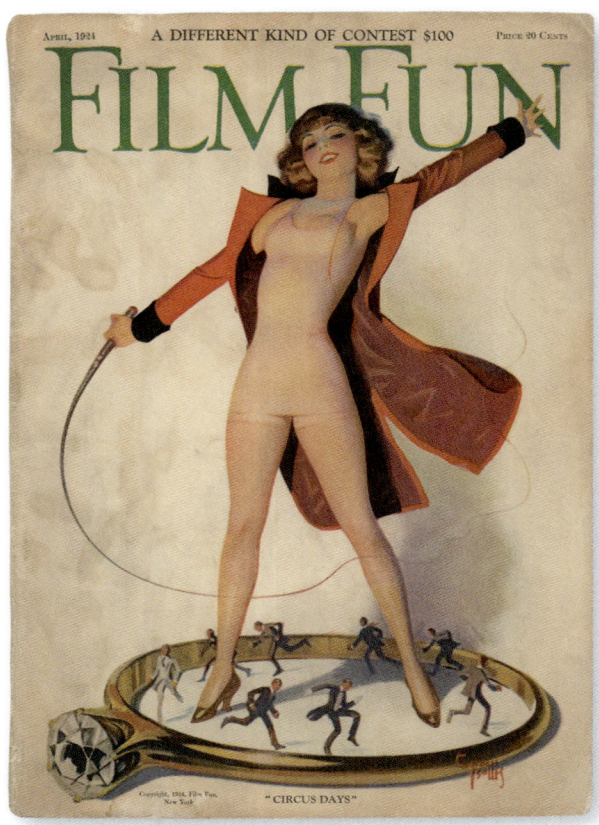

Reel Humor through the 1930s. The lurid fiction digests, with titles including *Broadway Nights*, *Paris Nights*, *Gay Parisienne*, *Pep Stories*, *French Follies*, *Tattle Tales*, *Snappy Stories*, and *La Paree*, had pin-up covers by Oscar Greiner, Earle Bergey, Cardwell Higgins, the mysterious Moskowitz, and prolific Driben. In the late '30s *Gay Book* and *High Heel Magazine* appeared, full-sized glossies with articles, fiction, and photos of partially dressed women on the inside, wrapped in pin-ups by Bolles, Bergey, and Driben. Surprisingly, the template for these magazines was the same one Hugh Hefner would choose 20 years later for *Playboy,* the launching pad for two of history's three greatest pin-up artists.

When *Esquire* magazine premiered in October 1933, it borrowed from 1905 *Life* and put its pin-ups on the inside. George Petty provided two cartoons for that first issue, both of women with men. Readers responded so positively to his women, and so negatively to the men, that Petty replaced the latter with telephones and let the women's one-sided conversations form the punch line. Readers soon salivated at the mere sight of the phone, and the punch lines were dropped. What remained was the pin-up perfected: free of distracting text and protected inside the magazine until pulled out and tacked up. By sequestering pin-ups within a respectable package, *Esquire* sold far more copies than *Gay Book,* making Petty a star while Bolles worked himself to exhaustion and into the Greystone mental asylum. Petty, too, was overworked by the end of the decade, but advertising supported him nicely after he passed the pin-up work to Alberto Vargas, just in time for World War II.

Forty-five years of pin-up prequel climaxed with the Second World War; even the term "pin-up" dates to this time, when fighting men were urged, en masse, to pin up images of pretty women for moral support. The U.S. government had refined its understanding of male psychology since its crude propaganda efforts of World War I. When American President Franklin

Above: This 1924 cover illustration by Enoch Bolles celebrates the independent spirit — and irresistible allure — of the flapper. Her tiny male victims race round and round, driven by her lash. Her only interest, we presume, is who can supply the biggest ring. Bolles was the sole cover artist for *Film Fun* from 1923 until 1941, even after taking up residence in a New Jersey mental institution.

Opposite: Edward Eggleston was a master of art deco pin-up, creating calendars featuring harem girls and sexy pirates through the 1930s. This large poster, from an oil on canvas, is one of a series he created for the Pennsylvania Railroad, circa 1935, all featuring pin-ups.

Delano Roosevelt created the Office of War Information in 1942, he instructed it to coordinate all media, to provide a consistent message of optimism and encouragement to American troops. Instead of whipping up hatred for the enemy, American propaganda concentrated on safeguarding home, family, and the American way of life. Pictures of pretty girls — the imagined sweethearts — were considered essential reminders of what men were fighting for, and magazine and calendar companies happily provided them — by the millions.

Photos of World War II barracks show them papered with pin-ups, often up the walls and over the ceilings. Pin-ups were found on ships and in submarines; in Quonset huts, tents, and tanks; in the cockpits of troop transports and as nose art on bombers. Men carried them in their wallets and backpacks, and some even pasted them inside their helmets. There are heartbreaking stories of dead soldiers found clutching pin-ups, intent that some Vargas or Petty be the last mortal thing they would see. Pin-ups were equally popular with our English and Russian allies, and filmmaker Russ Meyer — a U.S. Army cameraman during WWII — claimed that German troops searched American bodies for pin-ups, while the Americans searched the Germans for nude photos. "We had pin-ups, but the Germans had the best porn," he alleged.

Esquire's publisher anticipated the United States entering the war in 1940, hastening his decision to replace the increasingly troublesome George Petty with amenable Alberto Vargas. Petty's last *Esquire* pin-ups appeared in 1941, leaving Vargas to see men through the war. Alberto accommodated with girls in abbreviated military attire — and in tropical sarongs, for the benefit of those serving in the Pacific theater. In 1944 *Esquire* issued a special military edition, sold at cost to the government, with the advertising removed, and with an additional Vargas pin-up on the back cover. The magazine's foresight made Vargas the most popular pin-up artist of the 1940s, though Petty's '41 centerfolds adorned plenty of Air Force bombers.

While *Esquire* provided monthly painted pin-ups, *Yank,* the U.S. Army's official magazine, included photographic pin-ups in each weekly issue. Most were American starlets, in bathing suits and lingerie, supplied to the military by Hollywood studios. Linda Darnell, Deanna Durbin, Susan Hayward, Rita Hayworth, Marie McDonald, Jane Russell, and the Radio City Music Hall Rockettes were a few among the hundreds.

The studios also sent millions of pin-ups directly to troops overseas — three million copies of Betty

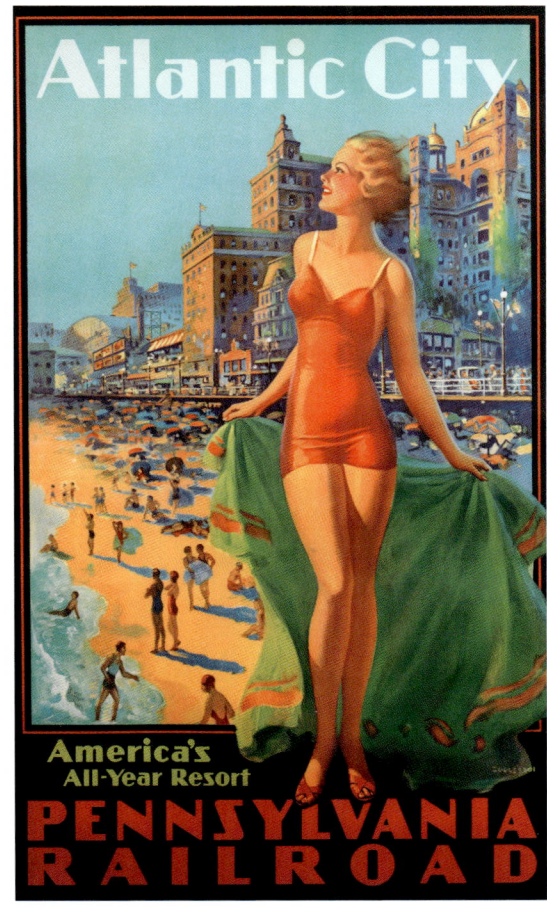

Grable's iconic back view alone — and enterprising glamour photographers printed pin-up catalogs for servicemen, offering hundreds of clothed yet provocative choices at reduced shipping rates. More pin-up photos came from a glut of new men's magazines, including *Who's Your Pin-up Girl?*, *War Laffs, Jest, Sleek, Snap, Show,* and the revamped *Gay Book,* all featuring photographic covers and centerfolds. The choice of photos over art was largely economic: A photograph was $25 vs. $250 for a painting — if you could find an artist. Vaughan Bass, Edward D'Ancona, Harry Ekman, Art Frahm, Earl MacPherson, Bill Medcalf, and Edward Runci all served in the war. Fortunately for *Esquire,* 46-year-old Vargas was exempt; fortunately for the calendar companies, so were Rolf Armstrong, Gil Elvgren, Earl Moran, and Zoë Mozert. Fortunately for all, the long-term impact of all those photographs was still a decade away.

Armstrong, Elvgren, Moran, and Mozert were for Brown & Bigelow and Louis F. Dow what Vargas was for *Esquire.* Moran and Mozert painted dozens of patriotic subjects for pocket-sized Mutoscope cards, while Armstrong created propaganda posters and calendars. Louis F. Dow printed a series of 9.2-7.2-inch booklets titled *Pin-Ups,* promising "12 Gorgeous Glamour Girls" by artist Gil Elvgren. These books recycled Elvgren's best-known paintings for Dow, printed on thin, lightweight paper, with pages perforated for easy removal, all contained in

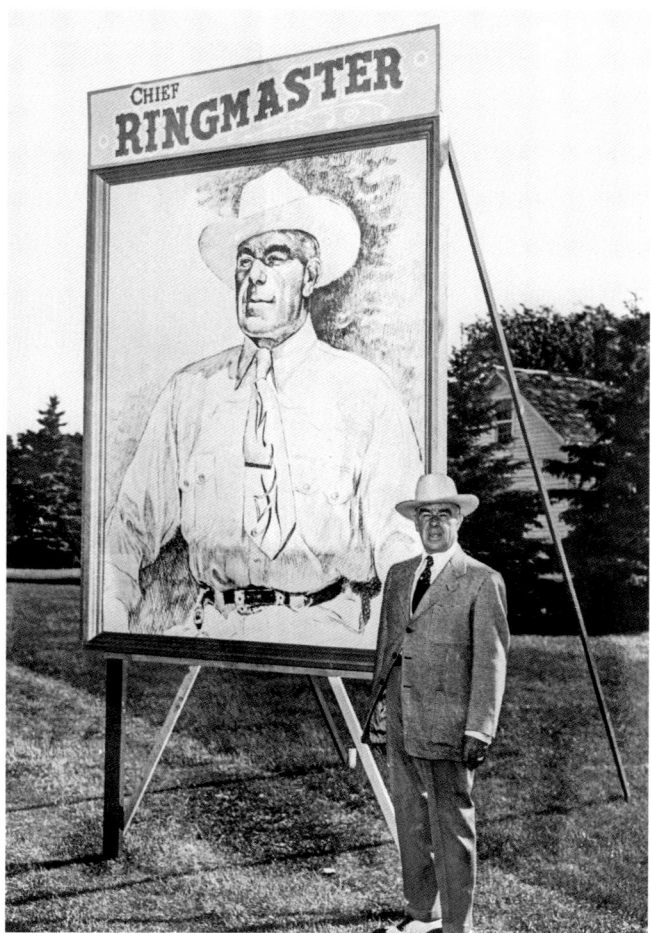

a mailer ready to stamp and post to anywhere in the world for just three cents. Brown & Bigelow countered with a smaller booklet of Mozert pin-ups that shipped even cheaper. Zoë referred to these as V-mail, or Victory Mail, booklets. True V-mail was a method of transmitting single-page military letters on microfilm, to save space in mailbags, so it's likely her reference was simply to the small size, cheap postage, and morale-boosting content of the booklets.

After 1942 the calendar companies boosted profits further with contracts from the War Advertising Council, an organization conceived to mobilize the ad industry to produce propaganda. Both Rosie the Riveter and Smokey the Bear were conceived by this council: Rosie to encourage women to take defense jobs, Smokey in fear that Japanese shelling

THE ART OF PIN-UP

of the American West would spark forest fires. Brown & Bigelow held its own War Advertising Conferences in 1943 and '44 to develop new patriotic themes, with Armstrong, Mozert, Moran—and models—in attendance. Armstrong introduced his muse Jewel Flowers at the first conference, dressed in a brief red, white, and blue costume, and B&B sales brochures linked their new pin-ups to military success, announcing the 1944 Earl MacPherson *Sketch Pad* with "Wherever you read…it's war maneuvers. On our sales front…it's womaneuvers…Maneuvering in the right direction means victory."

Charlie Ward wasn't the only one to conflate pin-up with patriotism; it was irresistible to the entire advertising industry. All knew that sex sold product, but with pin-up suddenly a national obsession, the brakes were off. Pretty girls could flog virtually anything as long as the accompanying text connected the product to winning the war. These ads were a warm-up for Madison Avenue's aggressive tactics of the '50s and '60s, when the War Advertising Council became simply the Advertising Council.

The pin-up push of World War II had wide-ranging effects on American popular culture. Consider bosom king Russ Meyer, trained as a photographer and filmmaker by the army. When the war ended, he first pursued a career in glamour photography, then in sexploitation films, paving the way for America's $10-billion-a-year porn industry. Meyer was inspired partly by pin-ups, partly by French bordellos, and he got his first big break shooting centerfolds for fellow vet Hugh Hefner.

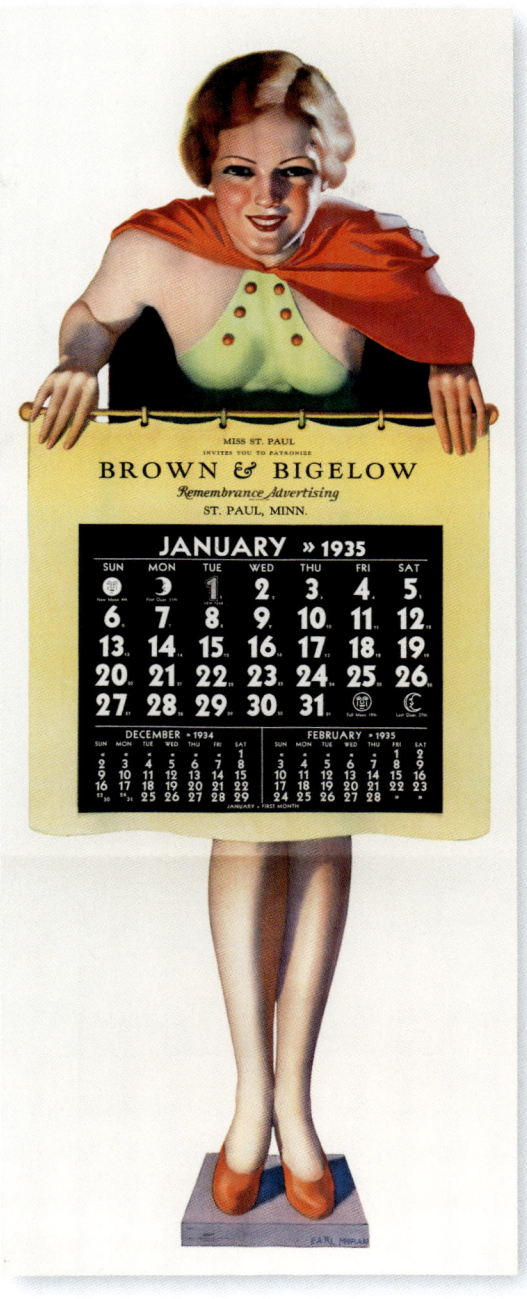

Opposite: Flamboyant ex-con Charlie Ward ran Brown & Bigelow, America's foremost calendar company, from 1933, following Mr. Bigelow's mysterious death, until his own death in 1959. He was known for his extravagant parties, exotic cars, and solid gold teeth.

Above: Pin-up master Earl Moran's first calendar for Brown & Bigelow. The pastel original was created in 1933, the year the company stole him away from calendar competitor Thomas D. Murphy and signed him to an exclusive contract.

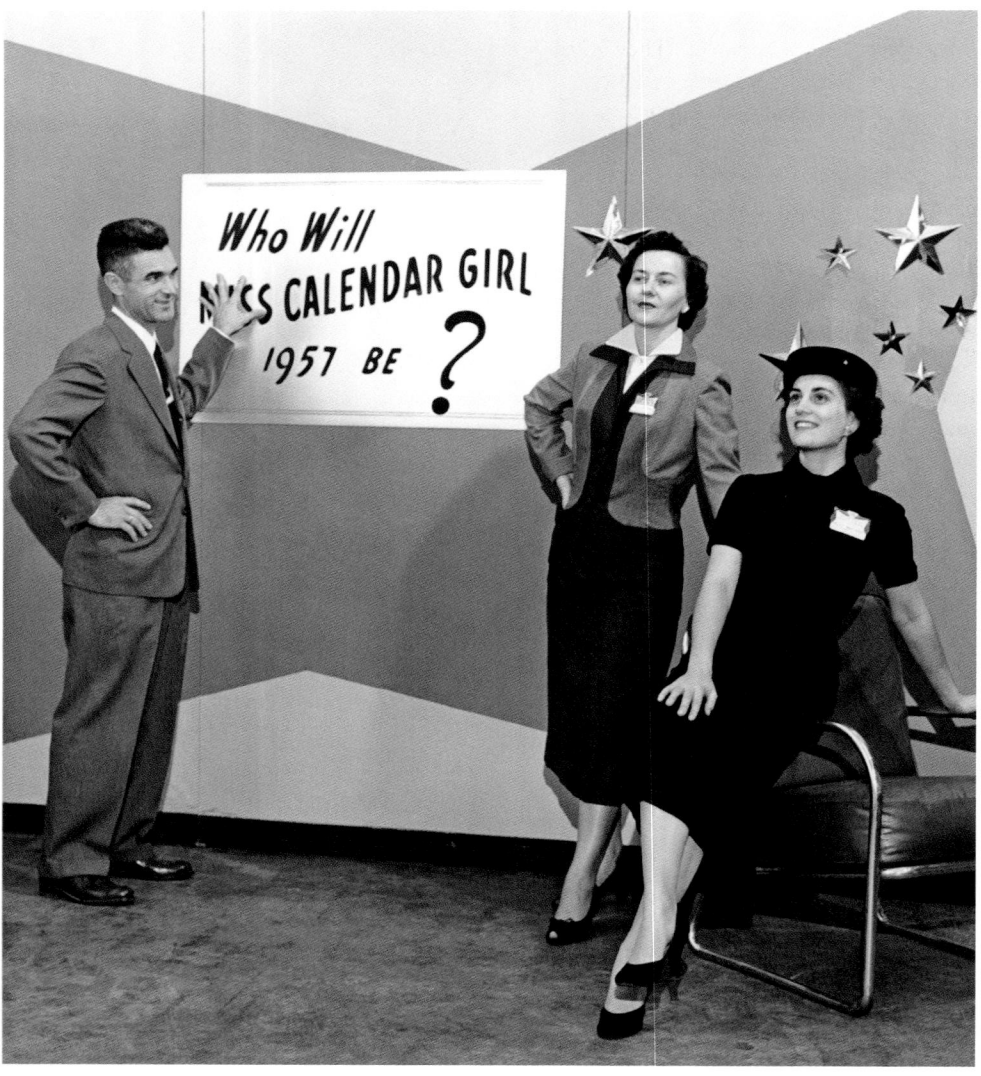

Hef served his time as a stateside clerk, but he loved pin-ups, and *Esquire,* as much as any combat soldier. When he got out he scored a job there; when *Esquire* moved to New York in 1950, Hef stayed behind in Chicago to launch *Playboy* in 1953. The magazine was conceived as an updated *Esquire* for young vets.

While Russ and Hef studied the pin-up girls, Frederick Mellinger studied their outfits. This garment worker returned from war with pin-up-inspired designs for women's lingerie. New York newspapers refused to take ads for his scandalous creations, so he moved to Los

Above: Here salesmen's wives pose in a set reserved for pin-up models competing to appear on 1957 Brown & Bigelow calendars. The unnamed man covers the word "Miss" in deference to the women's married status.

Opposite: By 1956 many of B&B's pin-up calendars were photographic rather than illustrated. Here a model poses with her calendar at the Diamond Jubilee.

THE ART OF PIN-UP

Angeles and opened Frederick's of Hollywood. In 1982 Mellinger told me that fellow G.I.s had been his real inspiration. "They all said they wished their wives and girlfriends dressed like pin-ups," he said. "I designed my clothes to save those marriages."

The pin-ups that inspired these men were largely photographic, thanks to the wartime deluge. Hefner loved *Esquire's* Vargas paintings and employed Vargas to produce pin-ups for *Playboy* between 1960 and 1977, but he recognized that the future was in photographs. Robert Harrison's *Beauty Parade, Wink, Titter, Eyeful,* and *Whisper* were the last American magazines with great pin-up covers, delivered by Billy DeVorss, Earl Moran, and, mostly, Peter Driben. Harrison launched *Beauty Parade* in 1942, when pin-up was at its peak. In 1955, when the magazines ended their run, every American men's magazine looked a lot like *Playboy,* and illustrated pin-ups were found only on calendars, in *Esquire,* and, occasionally, on the great covers of *Motor Age* magazine.

In 1945 this future was unforeseeable, unthinkable. Companies that had geared up for wartime production were not about to let the pin-up die. The artists returned from war and all found work. Brown & Bigelow seduced Gil Elvgren away from Louis F. Dow and entered its most productive era. Shaw-Barton not only stole MacPherson from B&B, they stole the *Sketch Pad* concept and launched 10 years of MacPherson *Artist's Sketch Books.* Haddon Sundblom

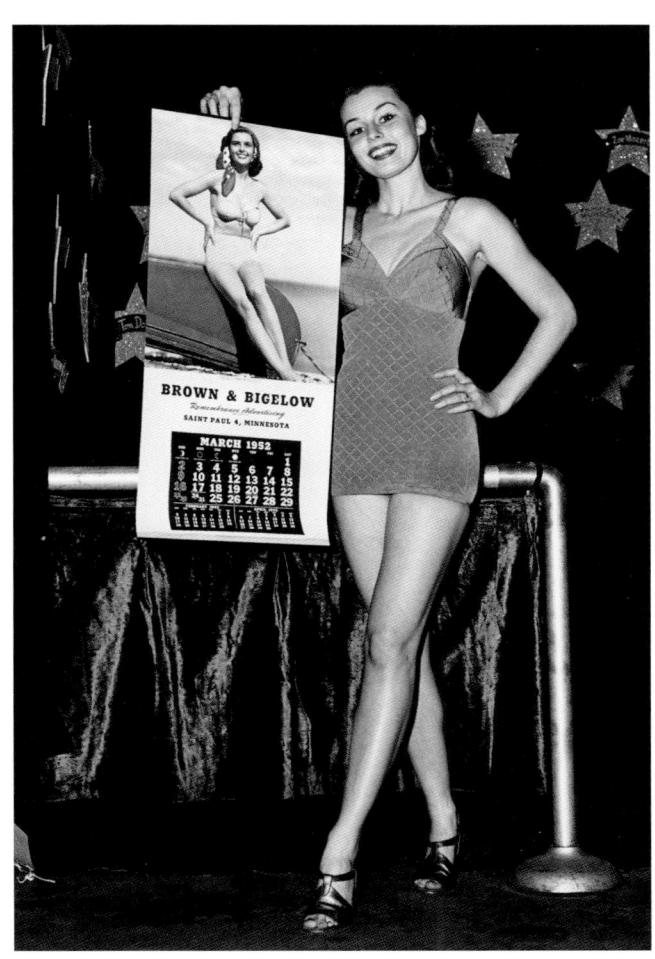

formed his fourth studio, and the Art Institute of Chicago, alma mater to more pin-up artists than any other school, continued matriculating hopeful future Elvgrens. Over all, between 1945 and 1950, artists and publishers produced as if there were still 15 million servicemen eager for anything pin-up. And since men had grown used to seeing pin-ups everywhere, this worked, and calendar companies entered the '50s confident of continued success.

The first hint of trouble appeared in late 1953. The December 30 issue of *People Today,* a men's digest, wrote that "fetching females are no longer America's top calendar favorites...B&B's biggest orders for '54 are for their official Boy Scout Calendar, by Norman Rockwell...Among the leading subjects for '54 only one is a girl, B&B reports. Five years ago, there were 6 girls among

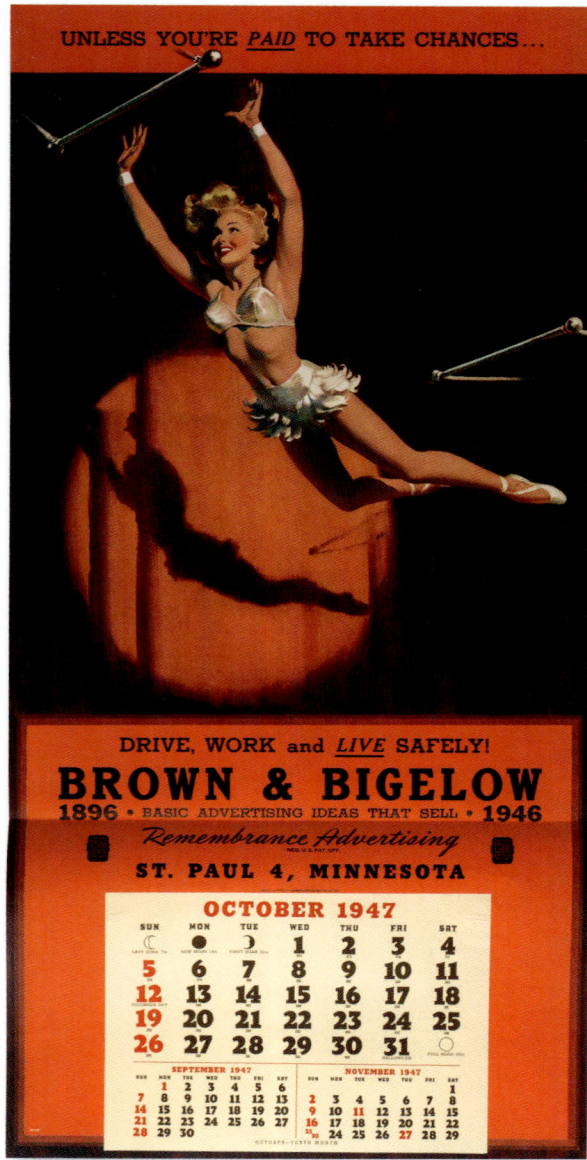

UNLESS YOU'RE *PAID* TO TAKE CHANCES...

DRIVE, WORK and *LIVE* SAFELY!

BROWN & BIGELOW
1896 • BASIC ADVERTISING IDEAS THAT SELL • 1946
Remembrance Advertising
ST. PAUL 4, MINNESOTA

OCTOBER 1947

the top 12...This year Brown & Bigelow bought the Western Litho Co. of Los Angeles, publisher of the calendar with the famous Marilyn Monroe nude. B&B says bare Marilyn was dropped immediately." Ward attributed these changes to an increased client demand for calendars as giveaways to housewives, with fewer going to "meeting places for males."

The baby boom had dropped. And what irony that pin-up began when women left the home and ended with their return.

As new fathers abandoned the old male hangouts, Brown & Bigelow responded with more family-friendly pin-ups. Zoë Mozert complained that the company began rejecting her nudes in 1954. Elvgren, who'd painted *Gay Nymph*, *Vision of Beauty*, *Perfection*, *Fascination*, *Fascinating Figures*, and other nudes for B&B in the late '40s and early '50s, produced just two after 1953. Moran also stopped painting nudes in the '50s, though he returned with a vengeance in retirement.

Meanwhile, men's magazines introduced more nudity, all of it photographic. The environment had changed, but not men. They still wanted to see pretty girls, but could no longer pin them up

Above: "Drive, Work and Live Safely!" was a strange directive from Brown & Bigelow's Charlie Ward, who drove, worked, and lived as recklessly as any man alive. This rare 1947 Gil Elvgren calendar, from the B&B archive, appeared in the 1951 film *A Streetcar Named Desire*, visible in the scene where Blanche's admirer Mitch confronts her about her tawdry past. 46 x 22 inches.

Opposite: A model for *Silk Stocking Stories* reads a copy of the magazine, circa 1937. In the mid-'3Cs leg art magazines began displacing the spicy fiction pulps. Printed on better paper, in larger format, *Silk Stocking Stories* and *High Heel Magazine* included seminude photos and pin-up covers by Peter Driben anc Earle Bergey. Photo by George Marks/Retrofile/ Getty Images.

over the bed. Magazines were more easily concealed, and once the dream girl went from the wall to a crate in the garage, there was no reason to maintain her innocence. As men's magazines now seem archaic, chaste pin-ups looked dated in the *Playboy* era.

Inevitably, calendar companies tried to compete by issuing photo calendars. At first, models were posed to resemble painted pin-ups, sometimes exact replicas of existing artwork, but companies soon learned this wasn't necessary. Those buying photo calendars didn't want or expect them to look like art. Real women lacked the mile-long legs, nipped waists, and buoyant breasts of painted pin-ups, but they were actual women, actually naked, and that has its own timeless appeal.

And so, between 1955 and '65, contracts were cut back, and most pin-up artists turned to advertising, book cover illustration, fine art, or simply retired. Magazines flourished and calendars declined. Louis F. Dow closed in the late 1960s. Shaw-Barton bought Gerlach-Barklow in 1959 and shut down the plant. Charlie Ward died that same year, and Brown & Bigelow was sold. The new owners kept making pin-up calendars, and a few top artists, notably Gil Elvgren, chose to keep illustrating them. It probably helped that B&B provided him contract work for the National Automotive Parts Association and Ditzler auto paints. Car repair was one of the last male bastions, and NAPA commissioned painted pin-ups through the 1960s, while Ditzler persevered into the '80s with a variety of artists. Elvgren kept refining his style until the end, producing some of his best work in the 1960s, but demand still dwindled: In 1968 he

created eight paintings for Brown & Bigelow; from '69 through '71 it was just two per year. Both he and Zoë Mozert delivered their last pin-ups in 1971. Fritz Willis held on another year, selling 12 paintings for future calendars in '72, while Mayo Olmstead sold a single pin-up to B&B in 1973. After that, the only active pin-up artist at Brown & Bigelow was Duane Bryers, who continued his chubby *Hilda* character into the early '80s.

Esquire, where the painted foldout originated, maintained its pin-ups until 1957, cultivating a unique stable of artists. When Vargas bailed in 1946, the magazine introduced its Gallery of Glamour, featuring work by Ernest Chiriacka, Joe De Mers, Thornton Utz,

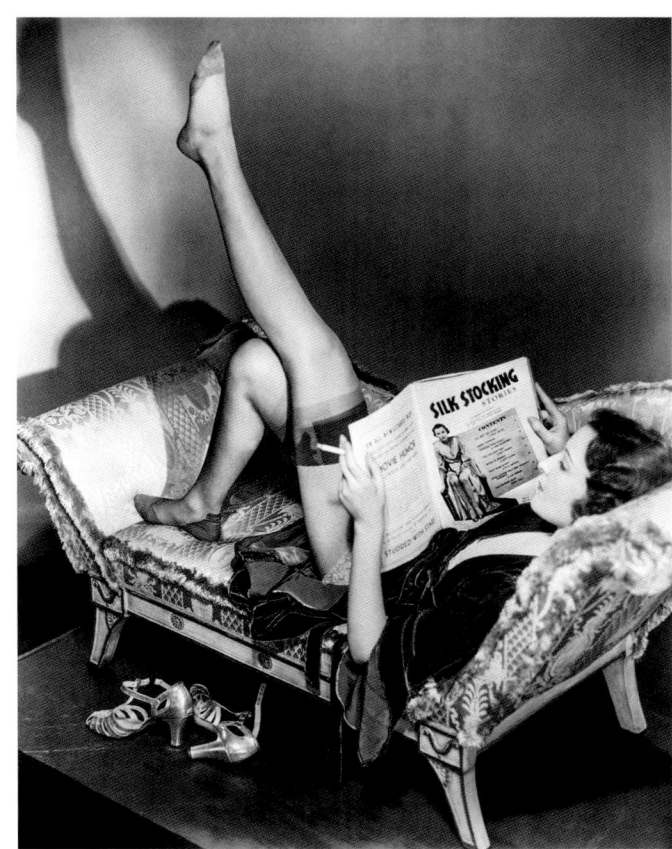

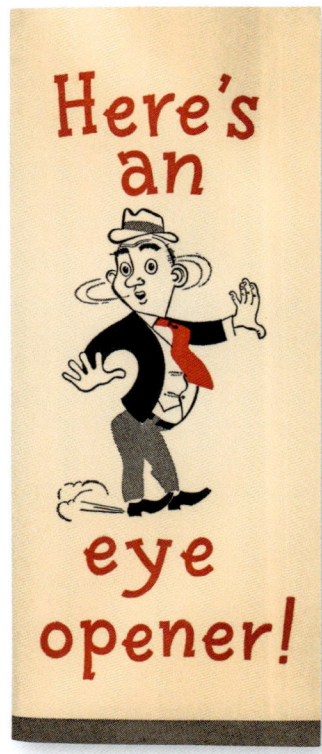

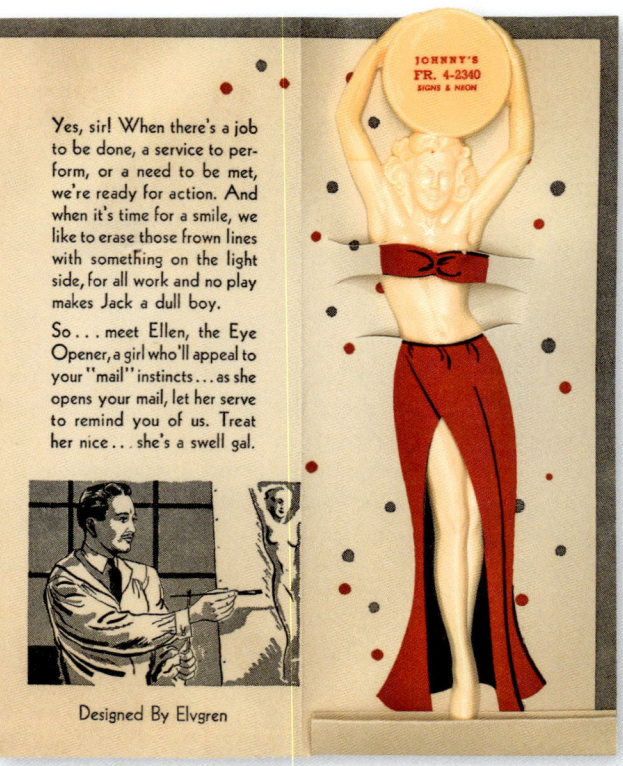

Here's an eye opener!

Yes, sir! When there's a job to be done, a service to perform, or a need to be met, we're ready for action. And when it's time for a smile, we like to erase those frown lines with something on the light side, for all work and no play makes Jack a dull boy.

So . . . meet Ellen, the Eye Opener, a girl who'll appeal to your "mail" instincts . . . as she opens your mail, let her serve to remind you of us. Treat her nice . . . she's a swell gal.

Designed By Elvgren

JOHNNY'S
FR. 4-2340
SIGNS & NEON

Al Moore, Eddie Chan, Mike Ludlow, Ben-Hur Baz, and J. Frederick Smith. Contract arrangements are unknown, but the only place outside *Esquire* their pin-ups appeared was in Brown & Bigelow's 1953 *Ballyhoo* calendar. These artists' originals seldom come to market, as *Esquire* purchased all rights and passed the paintings on to the University of Kansas as part of a tax write-off in 1980: At the school's Spencer Museum of Art, 164 Vargas originals and 23 Chiriackas can be seen, while hundreds of other works languish in a sealed shipping container, waiting—for more than 40 years now—for a federal arts grant to finance sorting and identifying the contents.

After 1960 *Playboy* was the only magazine still publishing pin-ups—first Vargas, then Don Lewis and Olivia De Berardinis. Hefner, whose photographic centerfolds hastened the art form's demise, kept the flame feebly burning in the years when most had lost interest. These were the years when Charles Martignette amassed the world's largest pin-up collection.

Secretive, obsessive, eccentric, Martignette coveted pin-up from age eight, when he saw his first calendar on a barbershop wall. He acquired his first Elvgren in 1978, at 27, and spent the '80s buying up everything he could find. This began with driving to all the existing calendar companies, because the standard practice had been to buy artwork outright and store

Above: Brown & Bigelow made many promotional items under their "Remembrance Advertising" banner. This letter opener was advertised as "Designed by Elvgren" to take advantage of the company's most popular pin-up artist. The card opens to reveal the pin-up-shaped opener seemingly dressed in bra and skirt. When slipped out of the card, she is nude.

it—or give it away—after printing the calendar. Martignette saved hundreds of paintings from destruction by convincing the dying companies to sell him what they had. He also tracked down artists. His personal correspondence shows how he tried to charm Norman Rockwell, who soon lost patience with his requests for autographs and friendship. Martignette saved every rejection letter, even as the refusals grew harsher. Lastly, he chased the owners of known works, bombarding them with phone calls and letters, pushing and pleading until he got what he wanted. His Florida apartment was crowded with crates in packrat fashion, but most of his 4,300-piece collection of pin-up and illustration art was stored in nearby warehouses, securely wrapped and never exhibited. He'd visit these only at night, armed with a pistol, for fear of robbery. As Martignette always needed money to acquire new art, he placed ads offering pin-ups for sale, but he priced them so high few could afford to buy, since he didn't really want to part with anything.

As the '80s progressed, a few others joined Martignette in unearthing this forgotten art. Louis Meisel curated his first pin-up exhibition in 1982, and Marianne Ohl Phillips began selling vintage prints and calendars in 1988. Interest increased in the '90s, particularly after publication of *The Great American Pin-Up* in 1996. By the time Charles Martignette died of a heart attack in 2008, at 57, pin-up was in full renaissance, and the demand for original art was high. Though Martignette's death was a shock to all, collectors rejoiced when his 4,300 works passed into the hands of Heritage Auctions in Dallas, Texas.

It took three 53-foot-long trucks to haul away Martignette's treasure and 14 auctions over five years to disperse it. Records were set along the way, with prices topping even those imposed by Martignette, while Gil Elvgren, whose talent Charles insisted would one day be recognized as equal to Rockwell's, emerged as America's most important, and valuable, pin-up artist. As Heritage Senior Vice President Ed Jaster said of Elvgren at the close of a 2012 auction: "His talent continues to be the benchmark by which most every other illustrator is measured. Collectors consider him the Gold Standard…"

In *The Great American Pin-Up* Charles Martignette bragged that he owned most of the surviving original pin-up art. He was very nearly right, and while his collection, as a piece, was magnificent, getting all those sketches, paintings, and pastels out of their wrappers and into the world is the best thing that's happened to pin-up and its appreciators since World War II. This art is intended to be seen, as its name declares, not hidden in the warehouses of Louis F. Dow, Shaw-Barton, Kemper-Thomas, Gerlach-Barklow, Joseph C. Hoover, Brown & Bigelow—or Charles Martignette. We owe a debt of gratitude to Charles for collecting and preserving the work and hearty thanks to Heritage for selling it off to hundreds of fans who heretofore had seen pin-up only on prints and calendars, blotters and Mutoscope cards, or in the pages of *The Great American Pin-Up*.

Dismantling the Martignette collection also made this book possible. Even though much of the art featured in *The Great American Pin-Up* belonged to Charles, unwrapping and photographing the originals was so daunting that prints and calendars were often substituted. For this volume, I had better access to original paintings and high-quality photographs of paintings, making it feasible, for the first time, to produce a book of this scale on pin-ups.

Now that all these Elvgrens, Pettys, Vargases, Morans, Armstrongs, Dribens, Mozerts, Ballantynes, Bolleses, and Buells have seen the light, we can only hope that the new owners will resist the temptation to hoard their new treasures in storage facilities and will hang them in their homes or galleries, for personal enjoyment and to inspire new fans. Pinned up, as nature intended.

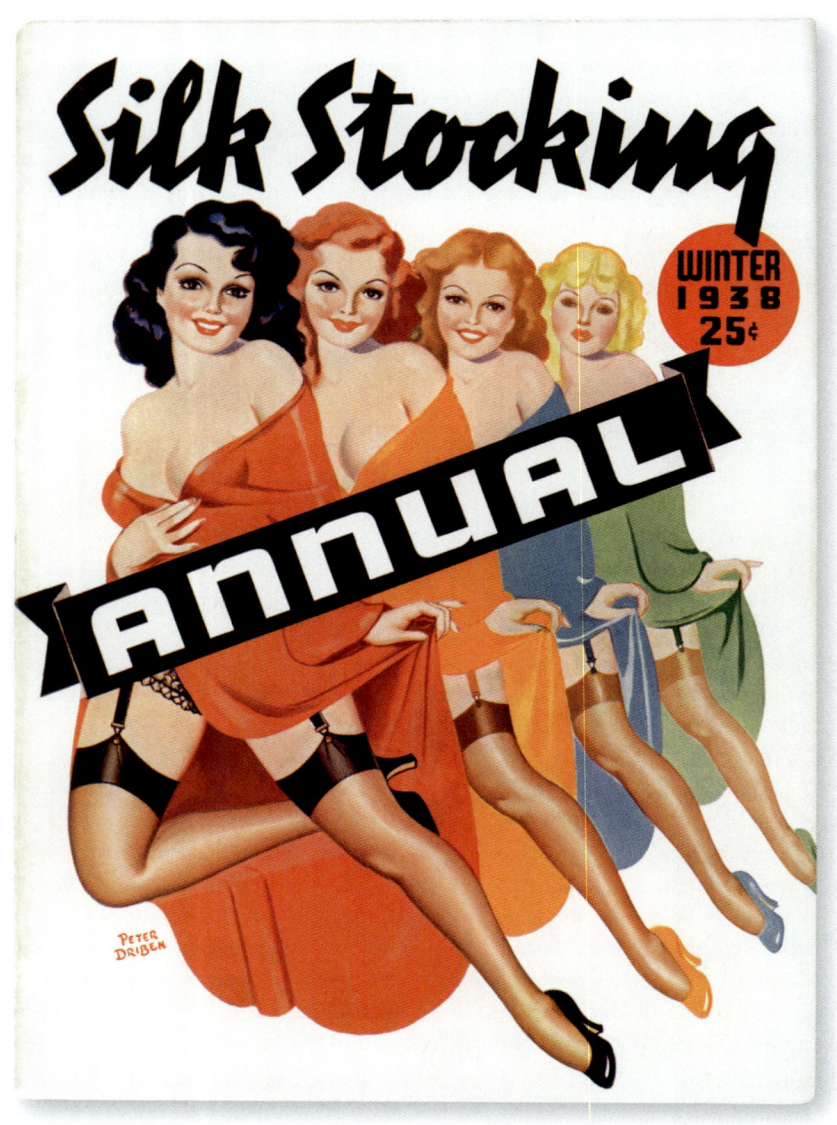

Above: Silk Stocking Annual, winter 1938, with Driben cover. Peter Driben would soon put his leg art experience to good use illustrating covers for Robert Harrison's magazines.

Opposite: Brown & Bigelow was sold following the death of Charlie Ward in 1959, and sold again in 1970,

to a company with no appreciation for the hundreds of original pin-up paintings in the company vault. Binders of photocopied sheets were circulated in the late 1970s, showing paintings and prices. The going price for an Elvgren oil on canvas was $300. Collectors claim that after the most desirable paintings were sold, the remainders went for as little as $10.

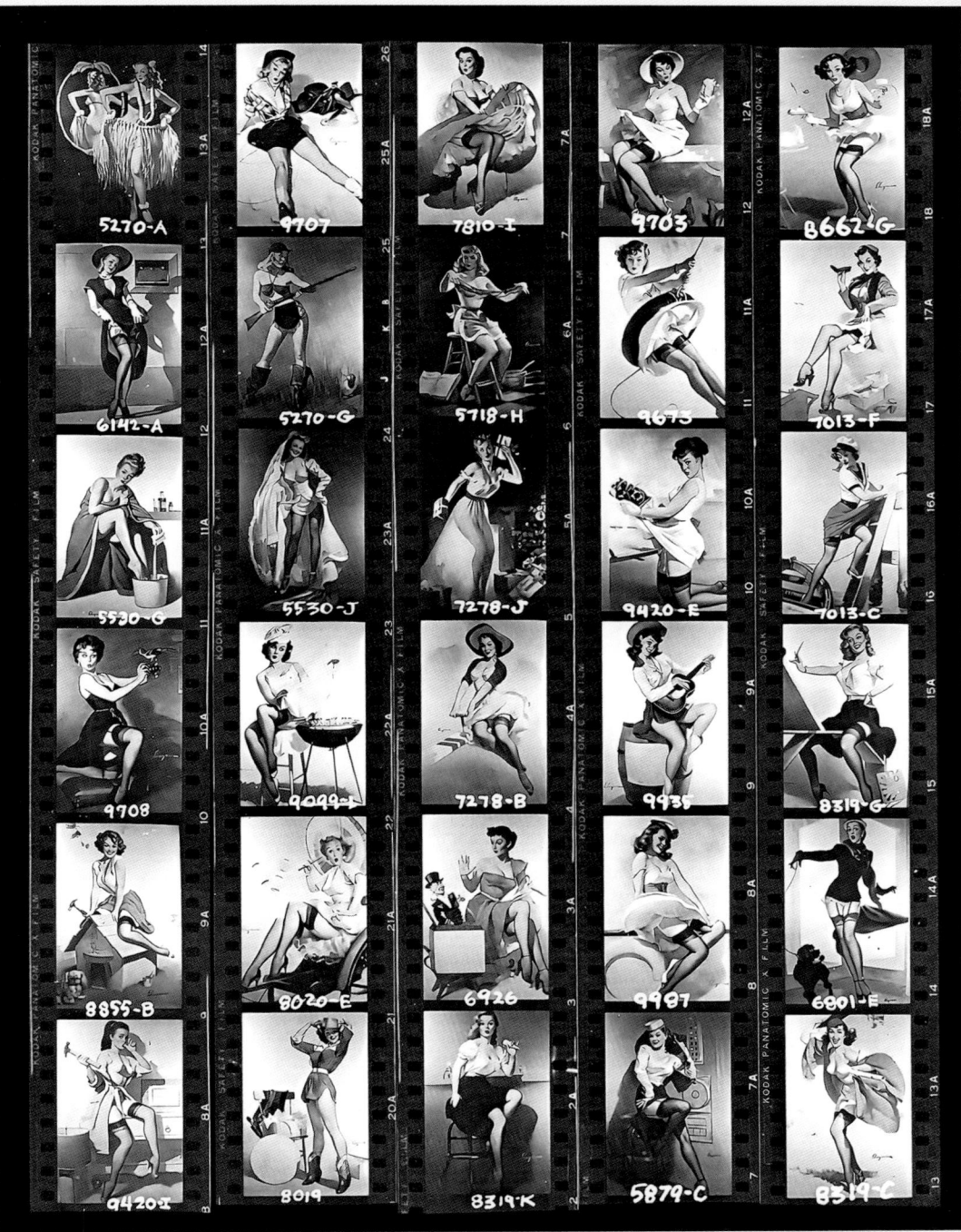

ELVGREN

#13

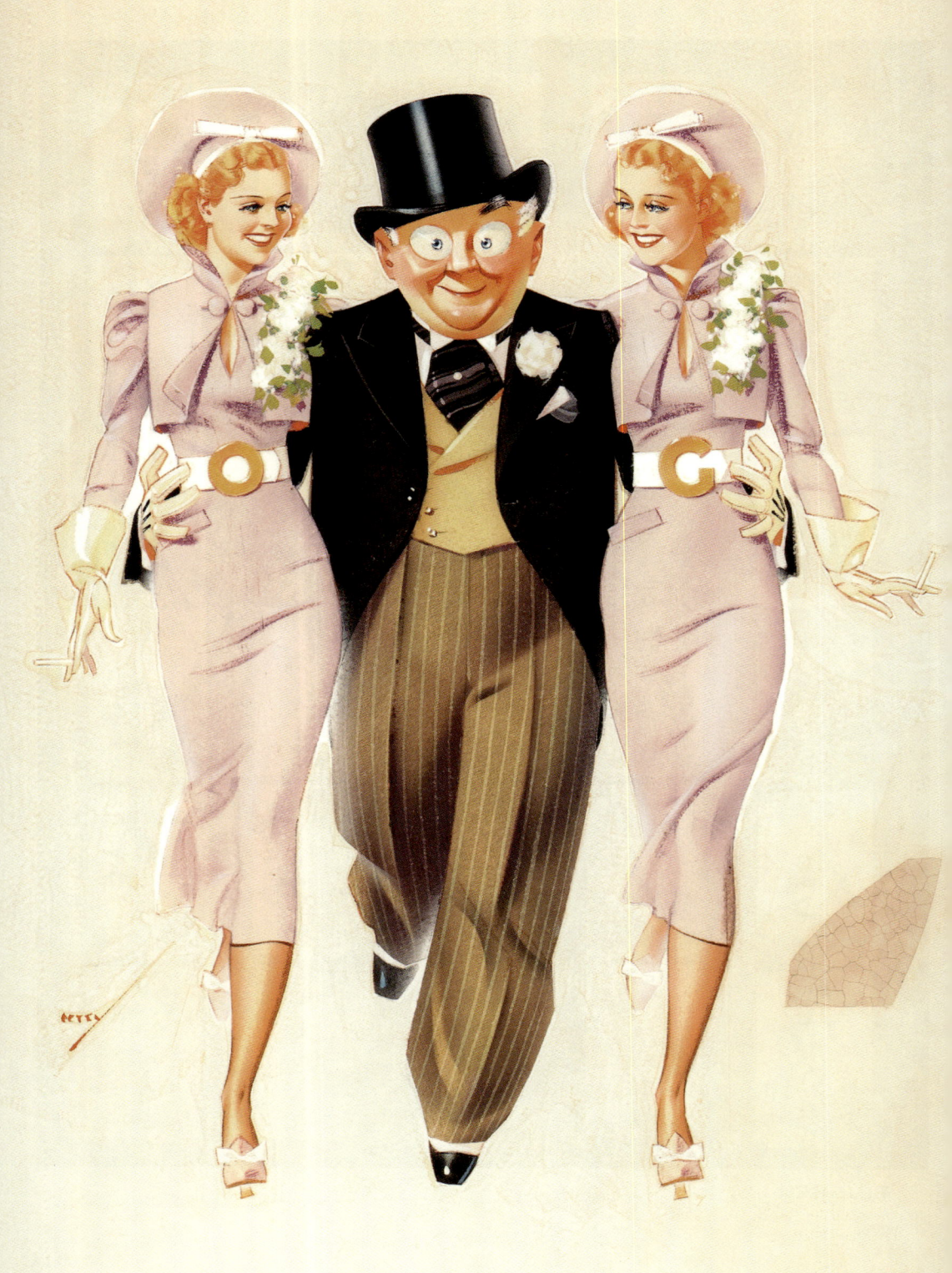

PIN-UPS: EINE SUBJEKTIVE BETRACHTUNG

VON DIAN HANSON

Die Wirtschaftslage, die globale Erwärmung oder die allgegenwärtige Pornografie sind daran schuld: Viele sehnen sich nach einfacheren Zeiten. Bringt uns zurück in jene Zeiten, als Zigaretten noch schick, dunkles Fleisch exquisit und Cocktails famos waren, bevor mächtige Ölkonzerne und Regierungen, industrielle Farmbetriebe und Massenentlassungen noch nicht an der Tagesordnung waren, bevor Meere und Bienen starben, als der Begriff modernistisch noch Picasso beschrieb und nicht eine Kochkunst und Frauen noch mehr zu bieten hatten – und weniger zeigten.

1970 schien Sex etwas Neues zu sein; alles wollten wir sehen. Doch heute, da uns Google beim Stichwort „Porno" zwei Milliarden Treffer bietet, wenden wir uns wieder Pin-ups zu, koketten Bildern, die an der Wand hängen bleiben können, wenn Mama zu Besuch kommt. Was 1945 gewagt war, ist heute nicht nur akzeptabel, sondern schick. Amy Schumer verwandelte sich für das Cover der *Vanity Fair* im Mai 2016 in Marilyn Monroe, während das

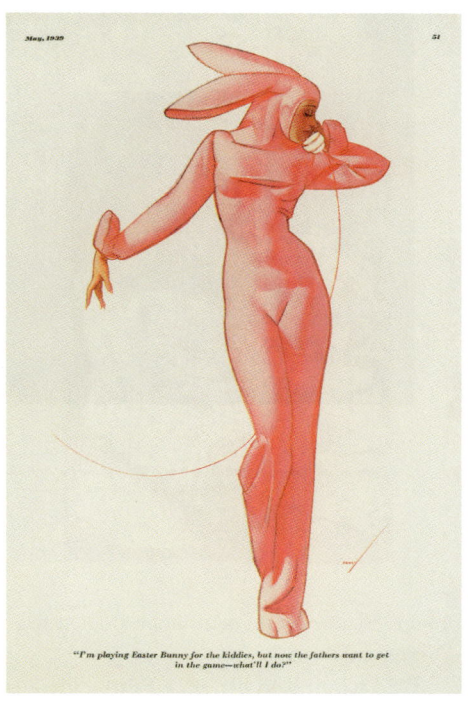

Pin-up-Cover von Billie Eilish für die Juni-Ausgabe 2021 der *Vogue* sowohl bei Männern als auch bei Frauen Rekordumsätze erzielte. Noch nie war Bettie Page angesagter; Dita von Teese hat Burleskes zurückgebracht, und Gil Elvgrens kultige Pin-ups zieren alle möglichen Objekte bis hin zu tätowierten Bizepsen. Oft einen weiblichen Bizeps.

Opposite: George Petty's first illustrations for *Esquire* magazine were captioned cartoons, as seen here, circa 1935. The old gentleman is Esky, *Esquire*'s octogenarian mascot, but the "O" and "G" belt buckles on the twins flanking him indicate that this watercolor on board was recycled as an ad for Old Gold cigarettes, a campaign that ran in 1935 and '36. Petty was a master at re-purposing art, which helped him become one of the richest pin-up artists ever. 26 x 19.5 inches. Courtesy Heritage Auctions.

Above: "I'm playing Easter Bunny for the kiddies…" Petty pin-up from the May 1939 issue of *Esquire*, wherein the artist proves that a woman clothed head to toe can be just as sexy as a nude. In fact, the prominence of her pubic mound caused a bit of controversy.

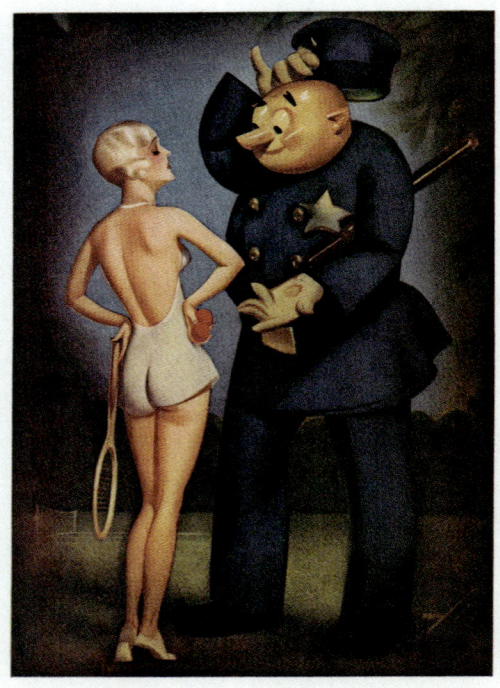

"Pardon me, miss, I didn't see the tennis racket—I thought you had forgotten something"

Warum sollten Frauen an Pin-ups nicht genauso viel Gefallen finden wie Männer? Auf einem Pin-up steht die Frau im Mittelpunkt, und seine Existenz ist der Frauenbefreiung zu verdanken, die 1890 auf Fahrrädern anrollte.

Im 19. Jahrhundert blieben die meisten Frauen im Westen in der Nähe ihres Hauses. Wenn sie reisten, dann zu Fuß oder in den Kutschen von Vätern und Ehemännern. Mehrere Schichten von Unterkleidern und Röcken machten Reisen schwierig und Sport unmöglich. Doch auf einmal gab es das Fahrrad, genauer gesagt, das Niederrad mit Kettenantrieb am Hinterrad und Luftbereifung, das es Frauen rein körperlich, wenn auch nicht gesellschaftlich akzeptiert, ermöglichte, selbst zu fahren. Ärzte und Minister behaupteten, das Geholpere über Kopfsteinpflaster würde empfindliche weibliche Organe schädigen und die Reibung am Sitz unmoralische Lustgefühle erwecken. Die Suffragetten nannten das Fahrrad eine „Freiheitsmaschine", die es Frauen erlaube, ohne männliche Begleitung – und das war das eigentliche Problem der Männer – herumzufahren.

Bald schon kam die erste Fahrradkleidung auf den Markt, zu der knielange Pluderhosen, Strümpfe und hohe Stiefel gehörten. Zum ersten Mal seit Jahrhunderten zeigten Frauen Bein, zwar noch immer gut bedeckt, doch diese „Gabelung" sorgte für ebenso viel Entrüstung wie Entzücken. Frauen wurden zu Männern! Frauen wurden zu Huren! Letztendlich wurden Frauen interessant! Sie forderten einen Platz in der Männerwelt ein und ermöglichten Männern so, sie fortan auf erregend neue Art zu begutachten.

Above: One of two George Petty cartoons to appear in the premier issue of *Esquire* magazine, fall 1933. Petty was forced by the editor to include men—generally old, bald, and hefty—in his paintings through 1934. Readers' letters asking for the girls without the guys finally convinced management that Petty, who had never wanted the men, was right all along.

Opposite: "I know what he wants for Father's Day, but I'm going to give him something to wear," was the caption for this 1939 *Esquire* pin-up. Done in airbrushed watercolor, a technique young Petty learned retouching photographs in his father's portrait studio, this is a classic example of his "telephone girls." The telephone replaced the old men of his early cartoons to give the girls a voice, and a reason for a caption, while eliminating distractions. 13 x 9 inches. Courtesy Heritage Auctions.

THE ART OF PIN-UP

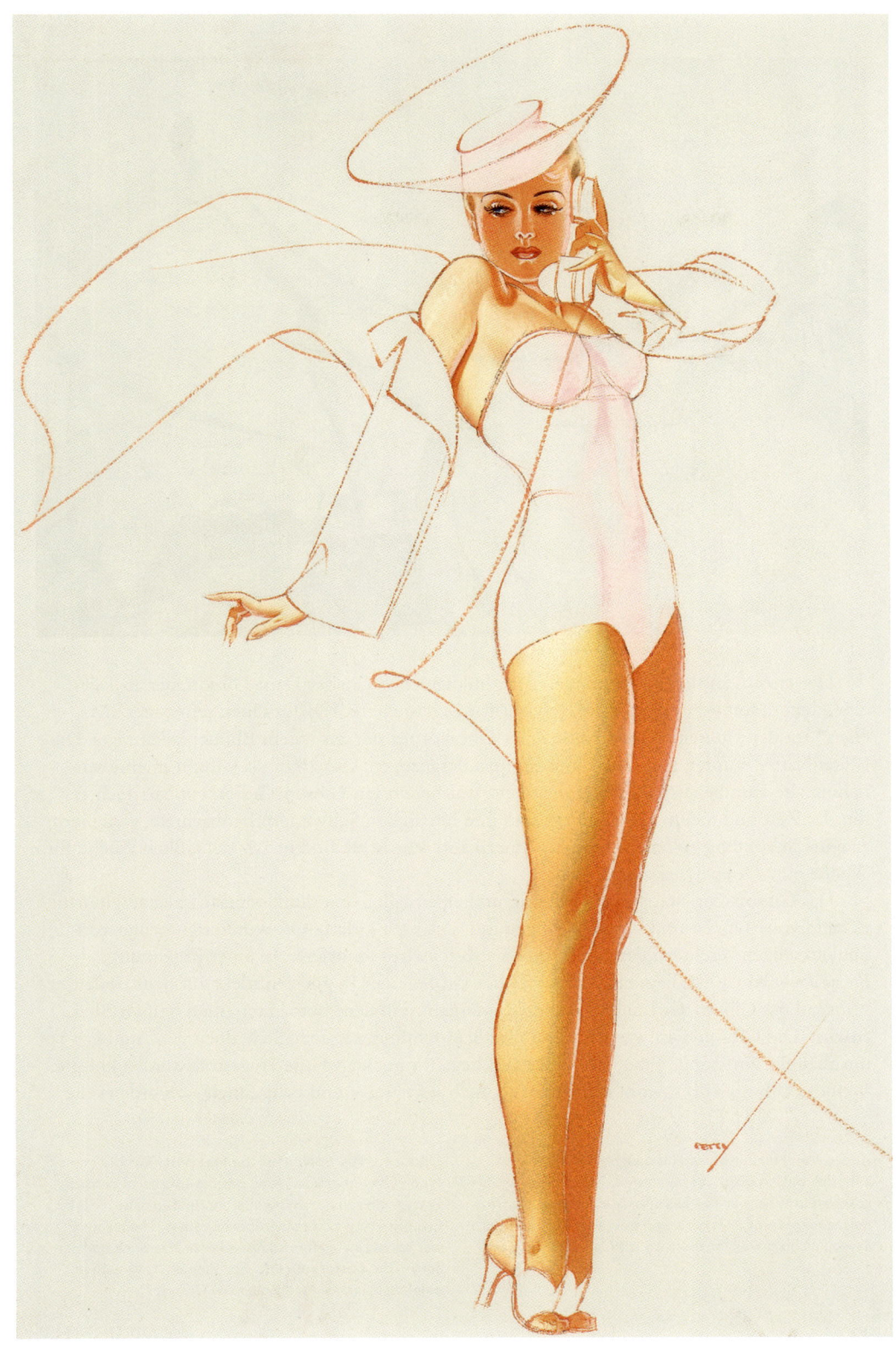

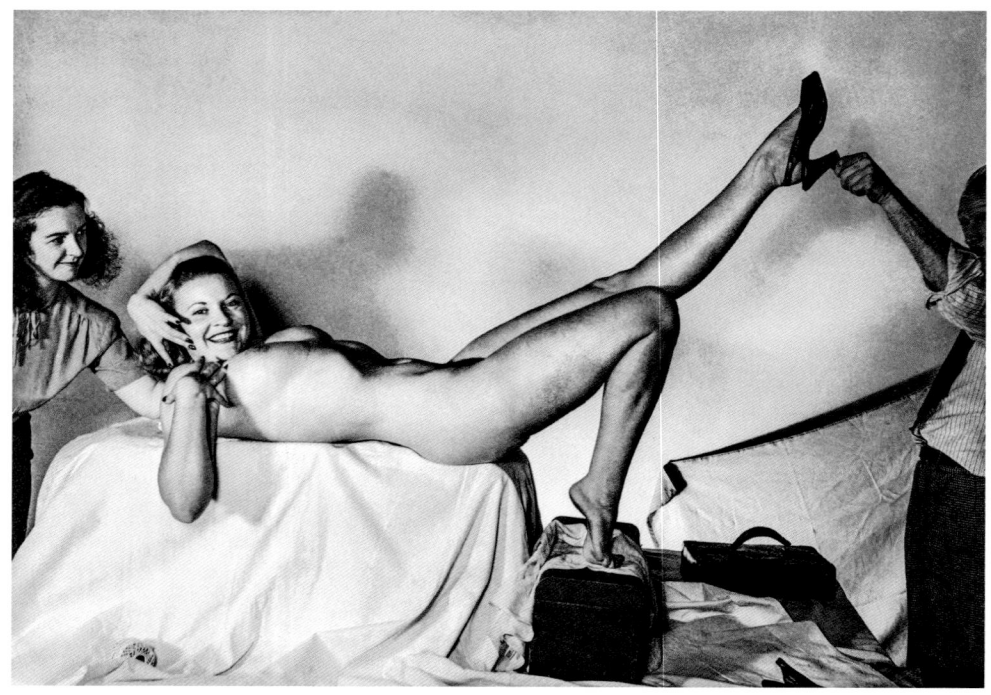

Der erste Künstler, der der neuen Frau huldigte, war Charles Dana Gibson, der ab 1886 eine kleine Humorbeilage für die Zeitschrift *Life* illustrierte. 1887 erschien sein erstes „Mädchen" auf der Titelseite: ein kurvenreicher Oberkörper, der aus einem Blumenkelch ragte. Die Blütenblätter wurden von Cherubim auseinandergezogen. Um 1895, als Gibson in eine vornehme alte Familie aus Virginia einheiratete, war bereits ein Gibson-Girl erkennbar, doch erst mit der Zeit und indem er seine Frau und ihre herrischen Schwestern beobachtete, verfeinerte er seine Schöpfung zu jenem Girl, das Amerika so sehr liebte und in *Life* schließlich Woche für Woche eine Doppelseite zierte.

Das Gibson-Girl war schön, vollbusig und eigenwillig, sein dunkles Haar lässig aufgetürmt, es hatte volle Lippen und sinnliche Augen mit schweren Lidern. Oft wurde es umringt von unglückseligen Verehrern dargestellt, die es selbstbewusst ignorierte. In einer Zeichnung, *Stepped On* von 1901, liegt ein Mann von der Größe einer Puppe zerdrückt auf dem Boden, während das Gibson-Girl unbekümmert weitergeht und dem Betrachter einen heißen Blick zuwirft. Das Gibson-Girl war stark und trotzdem feminin, nie anzüglich, doch ganz und gar unabhängig, eine junge Frau, die weder als Ehegattin noch als Hure eingestuft werden konnte. Weil das Gibson-Girl sowohl damenhaft als auch sexy war – und ewig Single –, wurde es die

Above: Petty famously used his daughter Marjorie as a model, but he used others as well. This model, photographed in 1944, was the basis for a number of the *True* magazine pin-ups Petty created between 1945 and 1947, as well as his cover for the 1948 Ice Capades program.

Opposite: The poster for the 1941 Betty Grable comedy *Moon Over Miami* has long been a source of controversy, with some claiming the uncredited artwork is by George Petty, others by Alberto Vargas. The mystery was solved as I gathered material for this book and came across the poster for *Hotel For Women*, 1939, with a painting clearly signed Bradshaw Crandell.

THE ART OF PIN-UP

erste Traumfrau und zum Urbild der guten Mädchen in der Pin-up-Kunst. Die Doppelseite der *Life*-Ausgabe vom 18. September 1902 bot eine Collage von Gibsons schönen Frauengesichtern, die den Betrachter mit ihren Blicken durchbohrten. „Tapete für Junggesellen" lautete die Überschrift. Zweifellos hat sich so mancher die Abbildung an die Wand gepinnt.

Jeder Erfolg bringt Nachahmer hervor, und Gibson inspirierte viele. Howard Christy Chandlers Christy-Girl debütierte 1895 in der Zeitschrift *The Century* und tauchte anschließend häufig in *Scribner's* auf. Wie das Gibson-Girl war es schön und unnahbar, doch anders als jenes entwickelte sich Christys Mädchen mit der Zeit. In den 1910er-Jahren wurde die junge Frau sportlich, und 1921 ließ sie sich gar eine Bobfrisur verpassen.

Die Zeitschrift *Puck*, ein Konkurrent von *Life*, wollte ihr eigenes Mädchen haben und bekam es von Harrison Fisher. Natürlich wurde dieses Geschöpf Fisher-Girl genannt, und es war eher von schlichter Schönheit. Fisher beschrieb sein Mädchen als „authentisch, anmutig, zartfühlend, wenn nötig, beschwingt, wenn erforderlich, doch stets weiblich". Bei Frauen war diese Figur beliebter als bei Männern, und von 1912 bis 1934 erschien sie auf Titelseiten von *Cosmopolitan*.

Ein entscheidender Schritt zum echten Pin-up wurde im Ersten Weltkrieg getan. Mit diesem Krieg wurde das Konzept der Propaganda geboren, das sich aus Freuds neuer Wissenschaft der Sozialpsychologie ableitete. Während des Ersten Weltkriegs betrieben alle Länder – Deutschland, England und die USA – Propaganda, die darauf abzielte, den Feind zu demoralisieren, in der Heimat den Patriotismus anzustacheln und die eigenen Truppen für den Kampf zu motivieren. 1917 rief der amerikanische Präsident Wilson die Abteilung für Bildwerbung ins Leben, deren Direktor Charles Dana Gibson damit beauftragte, Plakatkünstler zu rekrutieren. Christy, Fisher und Montgomery Flagg, ein weiterer früher „Mädchen"-Maler, schufen die ersten Poster, auf denen hübsche Mädchen mit militärischen Siegen in Verbindung gebracht wurden, eine Manipulation, die für den nächsten Krieg perfektioniert werden sollte.

Christys Beitrag war der denkwürdigste. Seine legendären Mädchen in hauchdünnen, gewagten Kleidern und militärischen Uniformen ermahnten die Männer: „Wenn du kämpfen willst, schließ dich den Marines an!" – „Kämpfe oder kaufe Anleihen, und los!" – „Ich wünschte, ich wäre ein Mann. Dann würde ich zur Marine gehen." Darunter die eindeutige Aufforderung: „Sei ein Mann und tu es." Die Plakate wurden aufbewahrt und geschätzt – und ja, auch gepinnt.

Im 1996 von TASCHEN veröffentlichten Band *The Great American Pin-Up* beschrieb

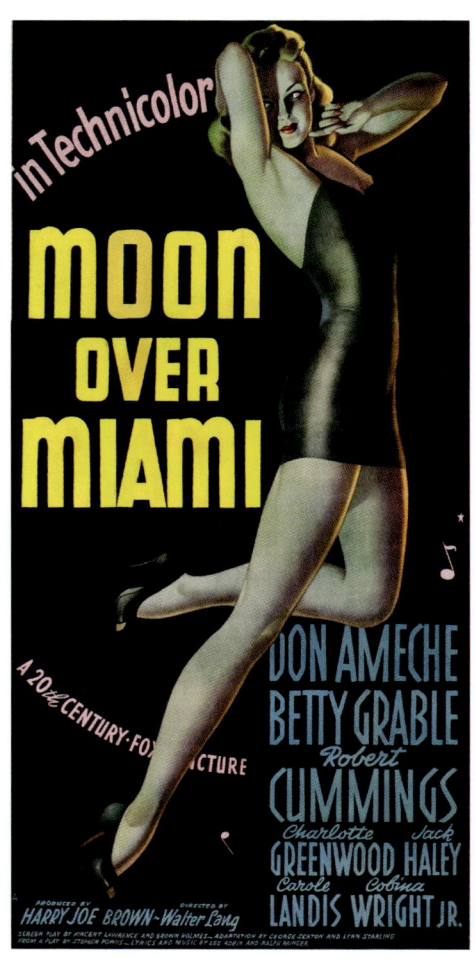

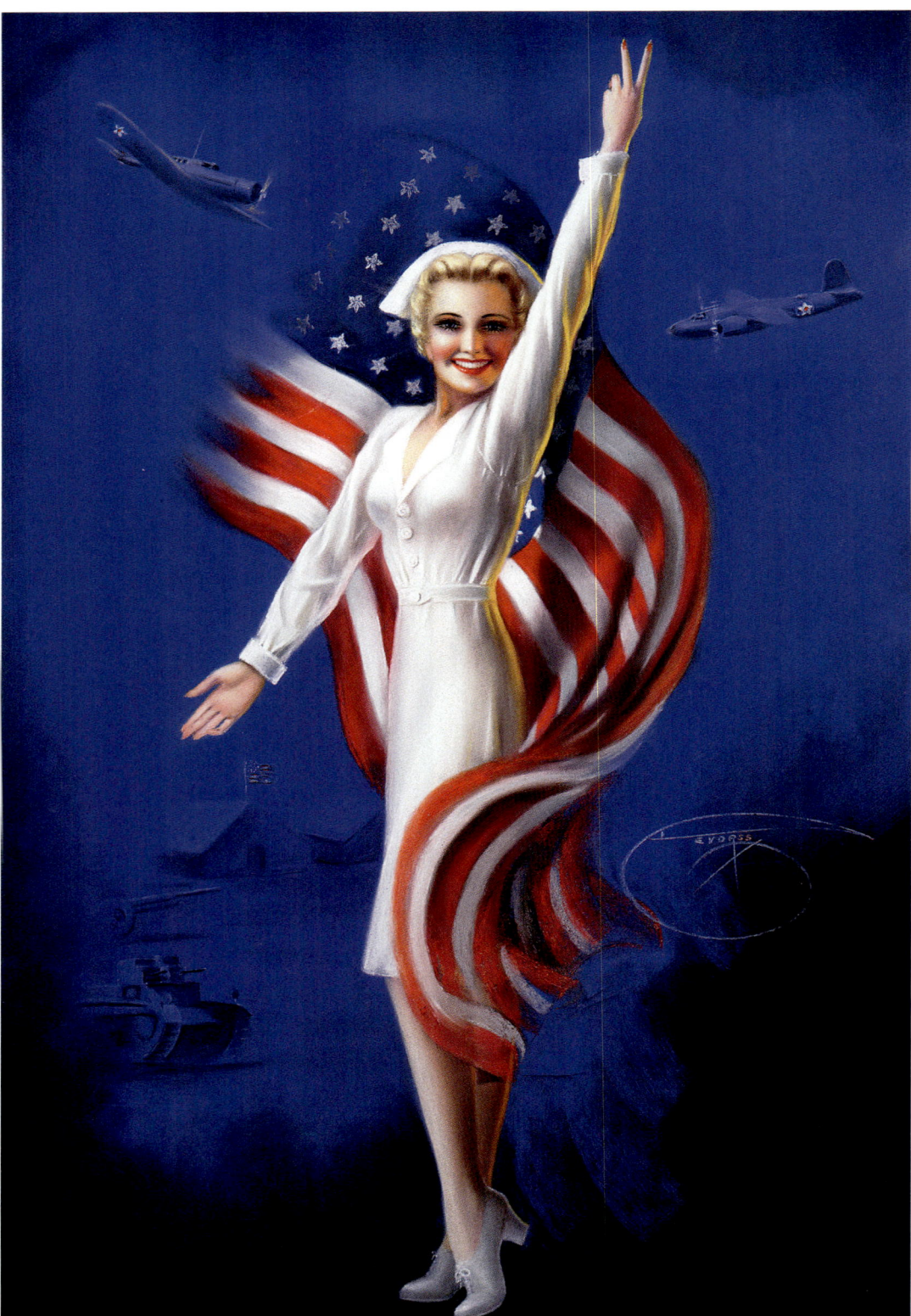

Charles Martignette ein Pin-up als „ein Bild, das eine Ganzkörperansicht der Dargestellten zeigt und in charakteristischer Weise ein Thema oder eine Geschichte wiedergibt. Die Frau auf einem Pin-up trägt meist figurbetonte Kleidung – entweder solche, die man öffentlich tragen kann, wie einen Badeanzug oder ein Kleidchen, oder Sachen, die provokativer und intimer sind, wie Dessous. Manchmal kann ein Pin-up auch eine nackte Frau zeigen, doch das ist eher die Ausnahme." Dann unterscheidet er Pin-ups von „Glamourkunst", bei der die Frau „im Allgemeinen eine Abendrobe, ein fantasievolles Kostüm oder irgendein anderes Kleidungsstück trägt, das weniger preisgibt als die auf einem Pin-up". Schließlich führt er noch eine dritte Kategorie an, die „Pretty Girl"-Kunst, „ein Begriff, der sich auf ein Bildwerk bezieht, das von seiner Eigenart her Glamourkunst ist, aber von einem Illustrator geschaffen wurde, der Gebrauchsgrafiken macht. Solche Bilder fanden ihr Publikum bei populären Zeitschriften wie *The Saturday Evening Post*, *Cosmopolitan* und in der Welt der Werbung."

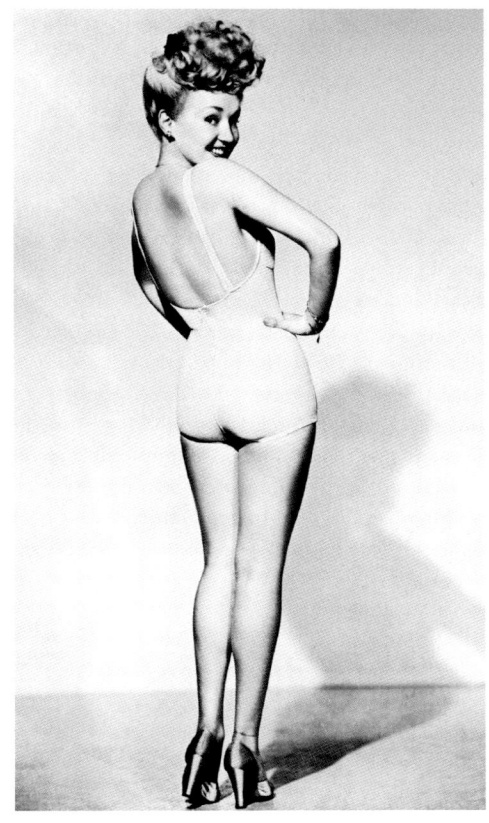

Es gibt keine Fußnoten, die erläutern, woher Martignette diese Definitionen hat; vermutlich hat er sie auf der Grundlage seiner lebenslangen Beschäftigung mit amerikanischen Illustrationen aufgestellt. Heute, da alles, was nach Pin-up aussieht, so begehrenswert ist und alles doch gleichermaßen sittsam zu sein scheint, ist eine neue Definition erforderlich. Auf Auktionen wird jedes von Gil Elvgren, Zoë Mozert, George Petty oder Alberto Vargas geschaffene Mädchen im Badeanzug oder Abendkleid als Pin-up aufgeführt, da diese Bezeichnung seinen Wert steigert. Es stimmt, dass eine Nackte von Elvgren, wie die 1947 entstandene und 2011 von Heritage Auctions für die Rekordsumme von 286.800 Dollar verkaufte *Gay Nymph*, stets mehr einbringen wird als seine züchtigen *Miss Sylvania*-Bilder, doch der Käufer einer *Miss Sylvania* meint immer noch, er hätte ein Pin-up erstanden und schätzt sich glücklich.

Opposite: This Billy DeVorss pastel, titled *Patriot Girl*, circa 1942, is reminiscent of Edward Eggleston's *Let's Go America*, with its deep blue background and airplanes, though here the message is a call to arms, urging American men to join the war effort. Rolf Armstrong, Knute Munson, Zoë Mozert, and Earl Moran also mined the sexy nurse theme during World War II, when young men often needed an angel of mercy more than a pin-up girl.

Above: This Betty Grable pin-up, shot by Frank Powolny as part of the publicity campaign for *Moon Over Miami*, was sent by Grable's Hollywood studio to over three million servicemen, making it the most common, and thus most popular, photographic pin-up of World War II.

Für dieses Buch will ich das Pin-up als ein provokantes, jedoch nie sexuell freizügiges Bild einer attraktiven Frau definieren, das für die öffentliche Zurschaustellung in einer männlichen Umgebung geschaffen wurde. Ist es ein Akt, muss er zurückhaltend sein: Der durchschnittliche Betrachter sollte das Bild nicht als Masturbationsvorlage sehen, obgleich Pin-ups sicherlich für diesen Zweck benutzt wurden. Der alternative Begriff „Good Girl Art" (Brave-Mädchen-Kunst) sagt alles. Ein Pin-up-Mädchen ist keine Schlampe. Sein Sexappeal ist natürlich und ungekünstelt. Stellt es etwas zur Schau, dann immer rein zufällig: Ein Angelhaken verfängt sich an seinem Bikini-Oberteil, ein Außenbordmotor zerfetzt das Kleid, ein verspieltes Hündchen lässt es stolpern, oder ein Windhauch weht den Saum seines Kleides hoch und legt Strumpf-band und Strapse bloß, doch nie alles.

Gil Elvgrens Spätwerk *Still Life* fand wegen der schockierenden Abbildung von Scham-haaren nie weite Verbreitung. Das war kein Pin-up mehr. Als Hugh Hefner 1971 darauf bestand, dass Alberto Vargas seine Pin-ups für den *Playboy* mit Schamhaaren darstellte, gab der Künstler nur nach, weil er fürchtete, seinen Job zu verlieren. Alberto kannte seine Fans besser als Hefner: Diese expliziten Malereien waren nicht beliebt, weil sie die Regeln für Pin-ups brachen. Selbst Art Frahm, dessen Mädchen sowohl mit rutschenden Höschen als auch unberechenbaren Winden zu kämpfen hatten, schirmte den Betrachter von dem ab, was die auf seinen Bildern dargestellten Männer sehen können. Ihm waren die Rahmenbedingungen klar: Pin-ups müssen rein bleiben.

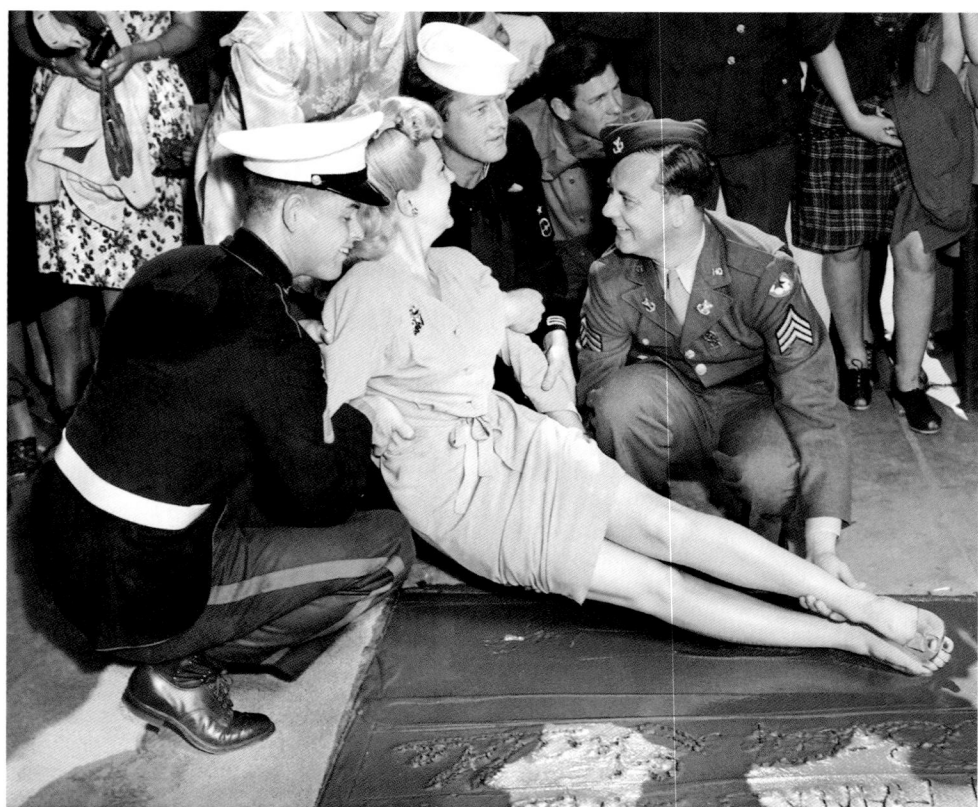

THE ART OF PIN-UP

Mit dem Ende des Ersten Weltkriegs setzten in den USA rasante gesellschaftliche Veränderungen ein. Verglichen mit der Zahl der toten Europäer war der Blutzoll niedrig, doch mehr als eine Viertel Million junger Männer wurden getötet oder verletzt, und alle hatten sie unvorstellbare Dinge gesehen – nicht nur Schlechtes. Jene, die in Frankreich zum Einsatz kamen, entdeckten das Varieté und pikante Zeitschriften wie *La Vie parisienne* und *Le Sourire*. Sie kehrten ruhelos und unzufrieden über das provinzielle Amerika zurück und gingen lieber trinken und tanzen, statt zu arbeiten und zu heiraten. Auch die Frauen, zu denen sie zurückkehrten, hatten sich verändert. Viele hatten während des Krieges gearbeitet, was sie auf den Geschmack finanzieller Freiheit gebracht hatte. Sie trugen Bobfrisuren, frönten Lippenstiften, Seidenstrümpfen und hochhackigen Tangoschuhen. Als 1919 der 18. Zusatzartikel zur Verfassung der USA ratifiziert wurde, der den Verkauf von Alkohol verbot, heizte das die Flammen der Jugendrebellion nur noch an. Flapper und Flipper – ihr männlicher Gegenpart – suchten statt Kneipen nun Tangopaläste auf und ergänzten illegale Alkoholika um Marihuana, Kokain und Opiate. Die üblichen Verdächtigen beklagten sich, doch die meisten waren von dieser wilden Jugend – vor allem den offenherzigen Frauen – fasziniert. Die Medien beeilten sich, damit Kasse zu machen.

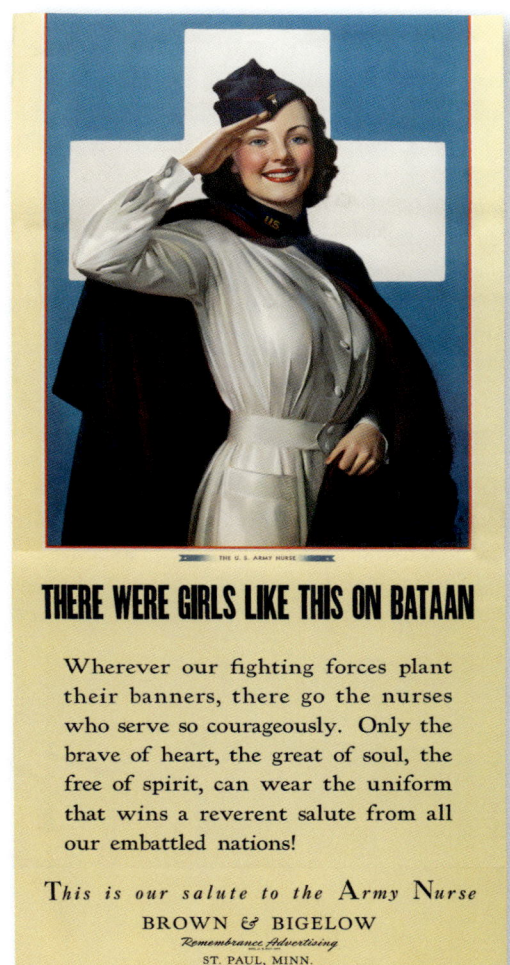

Rolf Armstrongs sinnliche Flapper erschienen zum ersten Mal um 1920 auf den Titelseiten von Filmzeitschriften. Armstrong hatte mit seinem züchtigen *Dream Girl*-Kalender, den die im Mittleren Westen beheimatete Kalenderfirma Brown & Bigelow 1919 verlegte, bereits einen gewissen Erfolg, doch als er 1924 ein Pastell für einen Kalender des Jahres 1926 schuf, das ein Flapper-Mädchen namens Betty mit herausfordernden, kajalbetonten Augen und rot glänzenden Lippen zeigte, wurde er zum Star.

Opposite: An American soldier, sailor, and marine help place Betty Grable's legs in wet cement in front of Grauman's Chinese Theater in Hollywood, February 17, 1943. The theater's forecourt is decorated with hand- and footprints of Hollywood stars. Since Betty famously had the best legs in America, and was the most popular pin-up, it was deemed appropriate to immortalize her most famous part. © Bettmann/Corbis Images.

Above: The U.S. Army Nurse, 1943, by Rolf Armstrong, was part of Brown & Bigelow's war effort. The company's contract artists were required to contribute art for recruitment.

Während Armstrong noch an Betty arbeitete, malte Enoch Bolles für das Cover einer Filmzeitschrift ein Flapper-Mädchen, das eine Peitsche schwang. Zu seinen Füßen rannten winzige Männer um einen übergroßen Ehering herum. Die triumphierende Haltung des Mädchens deutet an, dass niemand eine Chance hat, sein Herz zu gewinnen. Auch Zeitgenossen wie Ruth Eastman, Guy Hoff, John Held Jr., McClelland Barclay, Walter Dean Goldbeck und Frank Leydecker, der Bruder von J. C. Leydecker, malten befreite Frauen für die Titelseiten von *Life*, *Judge* und *College Humor*. Eine Reihe von Publikationen, die nicht unbedingt zu den Humor-Magazinen zählten, wie *Capt. Billy's Whiz Bang*, *Hot Dog*, *Smokehouse Monthly*, *Burten's Follies*, *Old Bob Edwards' Calgary Eye Opener* und *Cap'n Joey's Jazza Ka Jazza* – der Titel spielte auf „Jazz" als Synonym für Sex an –, brachte gewagtere Flapper-Titelbilder, die oft von anonymen Künstlern stammten.

Die Kalenderverlage brachten in den späten 1920er-Jahren bunte Art-déco-Fantasien heraus, deren knapp bekleidete Schönheiten an exotischen Schauplätzen sich nun zu den Flappers gesellten. Junge indische Frauen, ägyptische Königinnen, Ureinwohnerinnen aus Hawaii und wilde Nymphen charakterisierten die Werke von Henry Clive, Edward Eggleston, Mabel Rollins Harris, Gene Pressler und William Fulton Soare. Diese frühen Bilder waren zwar opulent und detailliert ausgearbeitet, der Exotismus beschränkte sich im Wesentlichen jedoch auf knappe Trachten fremder Völker, denn die Frauen dieser Pin-ups mussten weiß sein. Joseph C. Hoover and Sons in Philadelphia und Thomas D. Murphy in Red Oak, Iowa, druckten einige der besten Pin-up-Kalender im Art-déco-Stil, doch Brown & Bigelow in St. Paul, Minnesota, wuchs schnell

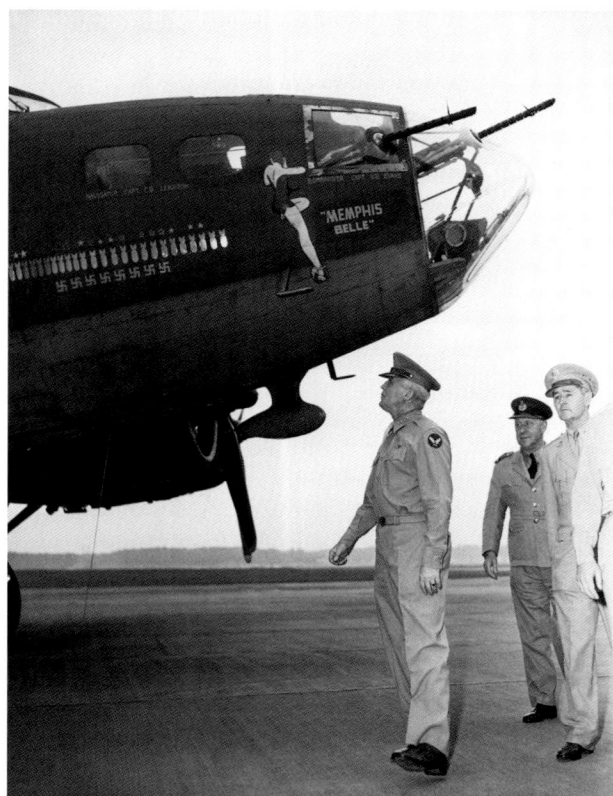

und bereitete sich darauf vor, während der nächsten Dekade in dieser Branche die Vormachtstellung zu übernehmen.

1889 druckten Thomas Murphy und Edmond Osborne den ersten Kalender mit Werbung unter den Bildern. Dies erwies sich als brillantes Konzept: Der Kalender hängt ein Jahr an der Wand, und jedes Mal, wenn der Betrachter auf den Kalender schaut, sieht er die Werbung. Bald schon trat Konkurrenz auf den Plan, darunter McCleery-Cummings, Kemper-Thomas, John Baumgarth, Gerlach-Barklow, Joseph C. Hoover and Sons, Louis F. Dow, Skinner-Kennedy, C. Moss Goes Lithograph und Shaw-Barton, doch kein Unternehmen wurde so sehr mit Pin-ups identifiziert wie Brown & Bigelow.

B & B, wie sie genannt wurden, produzierte nicht einfach

THE ART OF PIN-UP

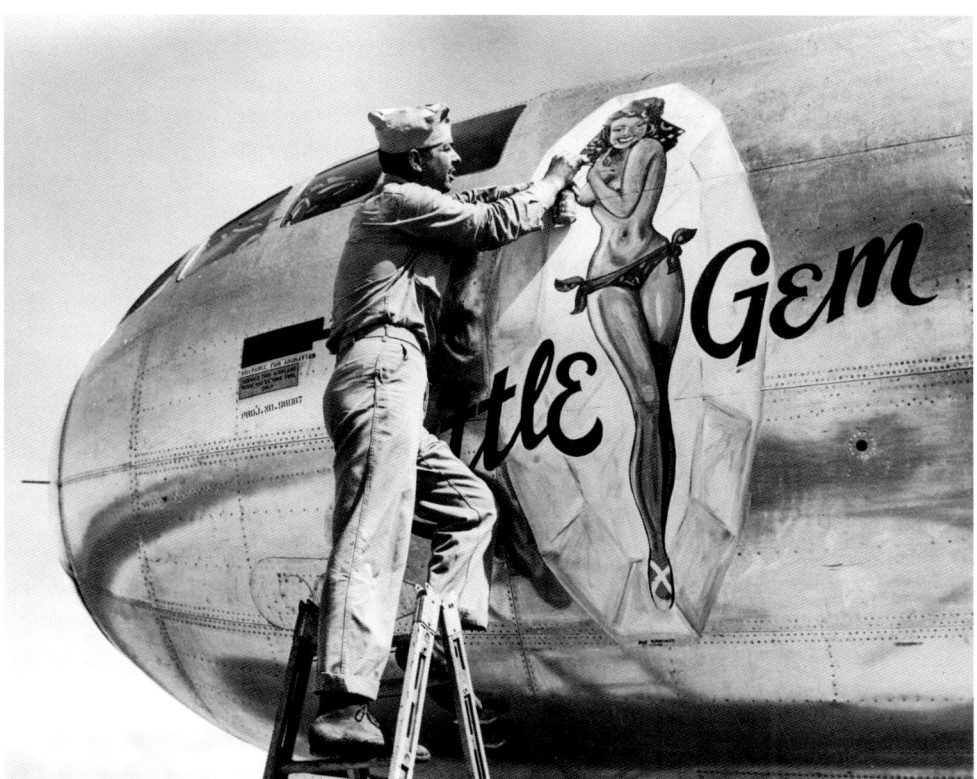

nur Pin-up-Kalender, ihre Pin-ups waren die besten und die größten – geschaffen von Top-künstlern, die im eigenen Hause aufgebaut und dann unübertroffen großzügige Verträge erhielten. Zu diesen Künstlern gehörten Rolf Armstrong, Al Buell, Earl MacPherson, Bill Medcalf, Earl Moran, Zoë Mozert, Knute Munson, Edward Runci und vor allem der grandiose Gil Elvgren, der von 1944 bis 1971 exklusiv für B & B arbeitete. Seltsamerweise wurde dieses Imperium weder von Mr. Brown aufgebaut, der 1904 verstorben war, noch von Mr. Bigelow, der ihm 1933 folgte, sondern von einem Gangster namens Charlie Ward, Ex-Insasse der Strafanstalt Leavenworth, der sich mit Diamanten und Goldzähnen schmückte. Seine Lebensgeschichte liest sich wie ein Hollywood-Drehbuch. Tatsächlich gab es nach seinem Tod 1959 solch ein Filmprojekt, doch seine Ehefrau gebot der Sache Einhalt. Es heißt, sie habe befürchtet, dass gewisse Dinge an die Öffentlichkeit kämen. Eine Kurzfassung der Unternehmenschronik liest sich wie folgt:

Opposite: General H.H. Arnold, Chief of U.S. Army Air Force, looks at the nose art copied from George Petty's April 1941 *Esquire* pin-up on the heavy bomber Memphis Belle, just arrived from England after eight months in Europe. The bombs painted on the side indicate 25 missions completed without losing a single crew member, and the swastikas the eight Nazi planes the crew shot down. © Bettmann/Corbis Images.

Above: U.S. Marine Randall Sprenger, stationed in Saipan, Marianas Islands, 1945, completing the nose art on a B-29 bomber. Little Gem's inspiration was Miss July 1944, from Brown & Bigelow's *Artist's Sketch Pad* by Earl MacPherson.

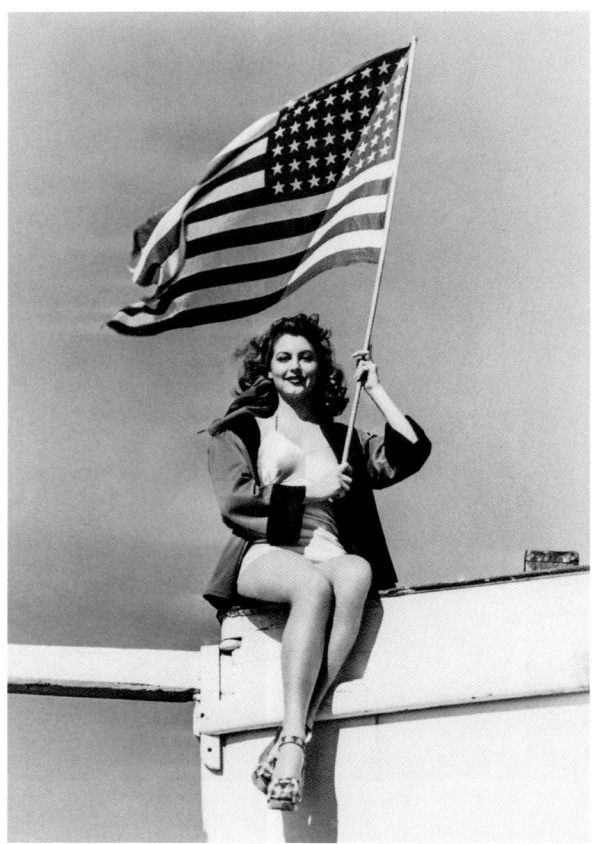

1896 versuchte der junge Händler Herbert Huse Bigelow den in St. Paul, Minnesota, ansässigen Drucker Hiram D. Brown dafür zu gewinnen, ein paar Kalender von Osborn-Murphy zu kaufen. Brown schlug ihm vor, eine eigene Kalenderfirma zu gründen. Er, Brown, würde das Kapital und die lithografischen Drucke einbringen, während Bigelow sich um den Verkauf kümmern könnte. Ihr erster Kalender zeigte Bilder von George Washington und brachte bescheidenen Gewinn ein. Im Laufe der nächsten drei Jahre erweiterten die beiden ihr Angebot um Mützen, Schürzen, Kleingeldbeutel und Pferdedecken, die alle Werbeslogans trugen. 1903 stellte B & B seinen ersten Mädchen-Kalender, *Cosette*, vor, den der Künstler Angelo Asti gestaltet hatte. Gerade mal eine Andeutung von Dekolleté war darauf zu sehen, doch der Kalender war so profitabel, dass B & B ein neues und größeres Domizil beziehen konnte.

Auch nach Browns Tod expandierte das Unternehmen weiter, druckte die ersten Vierfarbkalender und erweiterte das Programm um Künstler, die Wildtiere und Abenteuerszenen – und noch mehr Mädchen – malten. Bigelow prägte, um die Produkte seiner Firma zu beschreiben, den Begriff „Erinnerungswerbung", und an die Pin-up-Kalender von Brown & Bigelow erinnerten sich Männer ganz gewiss, denn die gehörten bald schon zur Grundausstattung jeder Männerbude. Herbert Bigelow war ein vorausschauender Mensch, er übernahm stets schnell die neuesten Errungenschaften der Drucktechnik. Allerdings war er auch distanziert, arrogant und elitär. Dies führte 1923 zu seiner Verurteilung wegen Steuerhinterziehung und einer Haft von zwei Jahren in Leavenworth.

Nun betrat Charles Ward, der von Geburt an für Leavenworth bestimmt war, die Bühne. Er kam 1886 im rauen Milieu der Bremerton-Marinewerft bei Seattle auf die Welt und machte bereits mit 14 Botengänge für örtliche Kneipen. Mit 16 trainierte er einen Kampfhund, der den besten Kampfhund der Marine bei einem Wettspiel besiegte, was ihm 1 000 Dollar einbrachte.

Above: Ava Gardner didn't have the pin-up popularity of Grable and Hayworth, but she did her bit with this 1944 Fourth of July pin-up distributed by MGM studio.

Opposite: Barbara Britton, a Paramount Studios contract player, in a 1944 pin-up distributed to troops. The bombs reference the newly passed Serviceman's Readjustment Act, providing education and housing funds to WWII veterans. Courtesy Heritage Auctions.

THE ART OF PIN-UP

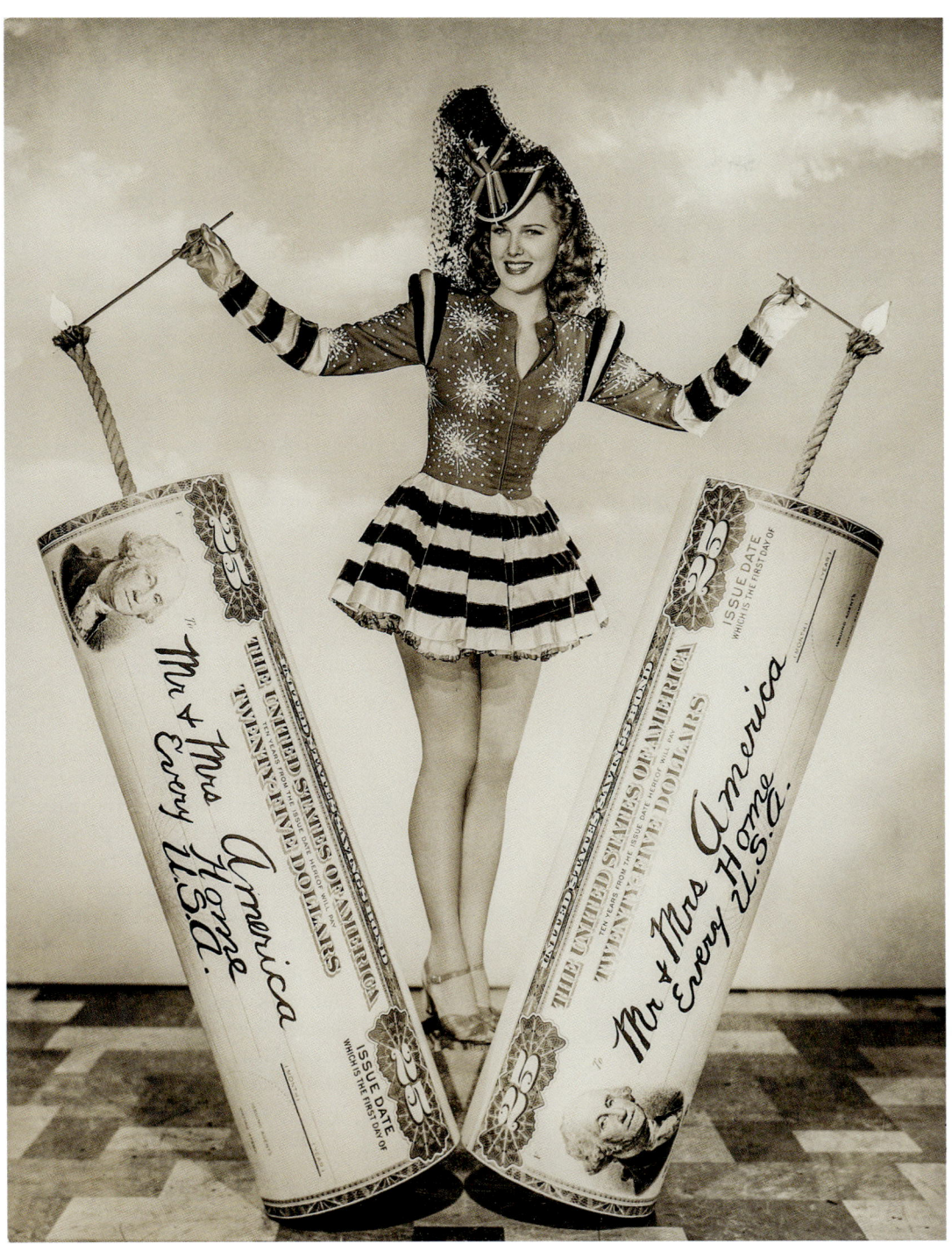

Die Hälfte dieses Gewinns gab er für einen Goldzahn im Maul des Hundes aus, den er danach Goldie nannte. Im Laufe der nächsten Jahrzehnte eiferte Charlie seinem Hund nach und ließ sich all seine Zähne mit Gold überkronen.

Gold war Wards Gott. 1903 jagte er ihm in Arizona nach, folgte dann dem Rausch 1906 nach Alaska und landete schließlich in National, Nevada, einer Goldgräberstadt, in der es, den reichhaltigen Vorkommen entsprechend, ziemlich rau zuging. Hier schmuggelte Ward Erz aus den Minen von Bergbaugesellschaften, um eine Reise nach Mexiko zu finanzieren, wo er sich gemeinsam mit einem Freund dem Kampf von Pancho Villa anschloss. Die Probleme der Bauern interessierten Ward nicht, doch er bewunderte den extravaganten Villa, der ihm die Häute des Viehs überließ, das er stahl, um seine Truppen zu ernähren. Ward verkaufte die Tierhäute in Texas und verdiente so 70 000 Dollar in drei Jahren. Als sein Freund 1916 getötet wurde, verließ er Mexiko und gab sein Geld aus. Zwei Jahre lang ließ er die Puppen tanzen, dann wurde er in Denver verhaftet und wegen Kokainhandels angeklagt. Er widersetzte sich der Anklage, bis er all sein Geld verpulvert hatte. Der Richter verurteilte ihn zu zehn Jahren im Hochsicherheitsgefängnis.

Als Bigelow in Leavenworth eingeliefert wurde, war Ward Vertrauensmann im Knast, hatte viele Freunde und besondere Privilegien. Ward bekam zu Ohren, dass andere Insassen den reichen Geschäftsmann schikanierten und sorgte dafür, dass Bigelow in seine Zelle verlegt wurde. Nun bot er dem verängstigten Mann einen Handel an: Schutz im Gefängnis gegen einen Job, wenn er wieder rauskam. Dankbar akzeptierte Bigelow das Angebot, und Charlie nahm ihn bis zu dessen Entlassung 1925 unter seine Fittiche.

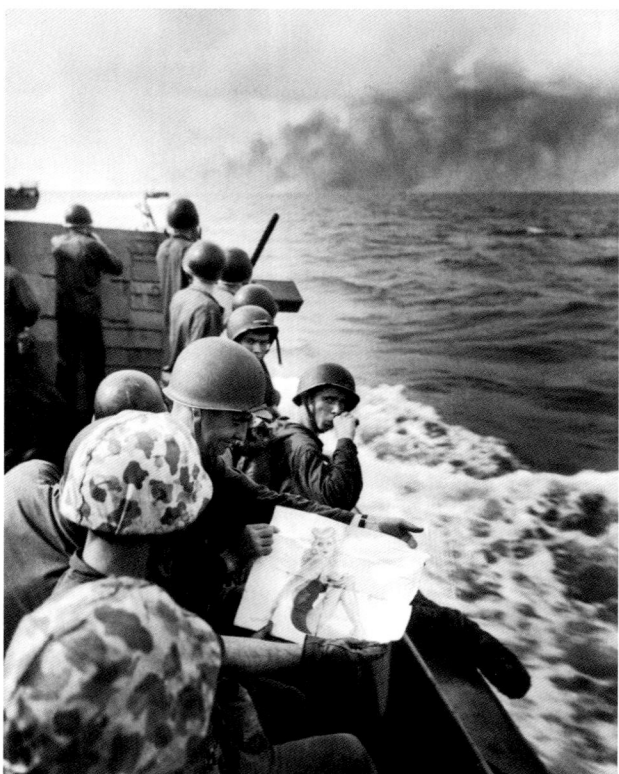

Als Ward dann kurze Zeit später in St. Paul auftauchte, war Bigelow nicht sonderlich begeistert. Er versuchte, Charlie mit Geld abzufinden, doch als dies misslang, gab er ihm einen Knochenjob. Zu Bigelows Überraschung erwies sich Ward als fleißiger Mitarbeiter mit innovativen Ideen. Er stieg im Unternehmen rasch auf, hielt sich stets in der Umgebung Bigelows auf und bezeichnete ihn als seinen besten Freund. Was der verweichlichte Bigelow für den Kumpel mit Goldzähnen empfand, der „dem" statt „them" sagte und „dose" statt „those", ist nicht überliefert, aber um 1930 war Ward Direktor und stellvertretender Geschäftsführer des Unternehmens. Es war Charlie, der dafür sorgte, dass Rolf Armstrong der bestbezahlte Pin-up-Künstler

Amerikas wurde; er war es, der Earl Moran 1937 für 10 000 Dollar pro Jahr plus Ateliermiete und Modellhonorare verpflichtete, und es war Charlie, der Gil Elvgren 1944 mit dem verführerischen Angebot von 2 000 Dollar pro Bild von Louis F. Dow abwarb. Entgegen hartnäckiger Gerüchte war es allerdings nicht Charlie, der am 19. September 1933 Herbert Bigelows Kanu auf dem Basswood-See zum Kentern brachte und ihn absaufen ließ, während der Führer mit seiner Begleitung, der Gattin des Topverkäufers des Unternehmens, ans sichere Ufer schwamm. Allerdings erbte Charlie die Firma und ein Drittel von Bigelows

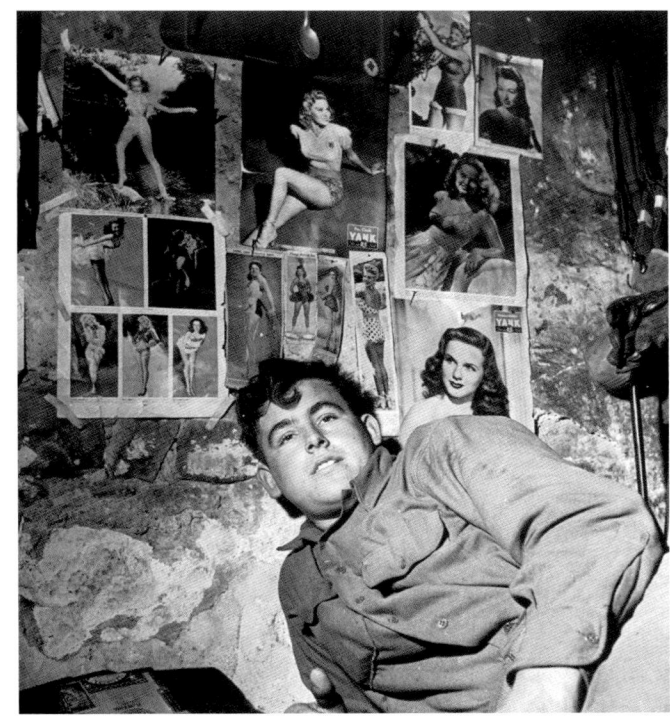

Vermögen. So bestimmte es ein Testament, das kurz vor dem Unfall aufgesetzt worden war. Wer Bigelows Führer angeheuert hatte, ist nie hinterfragt worden.

So begann die Herrschaft von Ward und das Goldene Zeitalter von Brown & Bigelow. Charlie fing sofort an, Ex-Häftlinge einzustellen, und half insgeheim Männern, die noch im Gefängnis saßen. In seinem Buch *John Dillinger Slept Here* legte der Autor Paul Maccabee dar, dass Ward 1933 dem Gangster Bugsy Siegel 100 000 Dollar für einen Versuch gab, zwei wegen Mordes angeklagte Männer aus einem Knast in Minnesota zu holen. Bedenkt man, in welchem Jahr sich dies abspielte, ist man leicht geneigt, die Sache mit Bigelows tödlichem Unfall in Verbindung zu bringen, doch dafür gibt es keine Hinweise. Zu Wards Gunsten muss allerdings gesagt werden, dass er seine Ex-Knackis wie jeden anderen Angestellten behandelte. Schonungslos trieb er allesamt an, belohnte Spitzenkräfte mit Bonuszahlungen und Pin-up-

Opposite: Marines aboard a landing barge approaching the south seas island of Tarawa take a last inspirational look at *Esquire*'s August 1943 Varga Girl — the magazine dropped the "s" from Vargas's name. The American postmaster general declared Vargas's September 1943 centerfold obscene and sued *Esquire* in an attempt to make the magazine discontinue its pin-ups. In response a navy lieutenant in the Pacific wrote his congressman that *"Esquire* magazine is an aid to morale among fighting men," citing a young man under his command who was killed in a foxhole and found clutching a picture of a Varga girl. "He had not wanted to risk leaving his

picture in his tent for fear the enemy would get it," the letter went on. "These boys have so little; they have and hold foremost their memories…" © Bettmann/ Corbis Images.

Above: American private first class Robert Brestow has decorated the stone walls of an Italian farmhouse in the Appenine Mountains with his dream girls. Along with actresses from *Yank* magazine are works by Rolf Armstrong, Zoë Mozert, and Earl Moran. March 31, 1945, by Margaret Bourke-White/Time Life Pictures/ Getty Images.

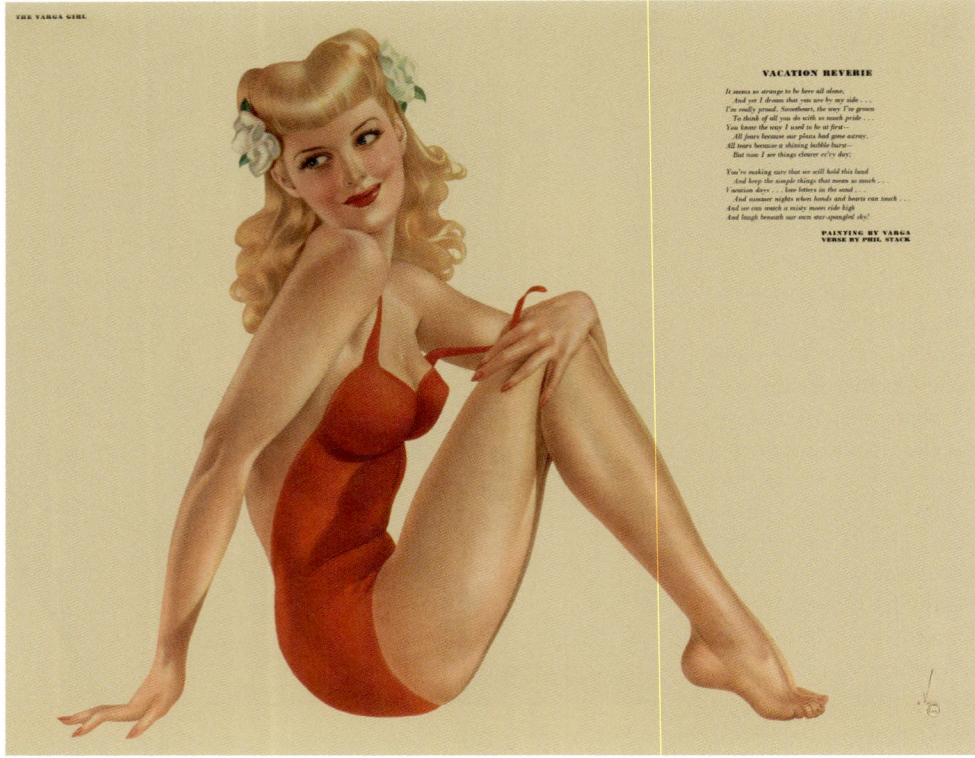

VACATION REVERIE

It seems so strange to be here all alone,
And yet I dream that you are by my side . . .
I'm really proud, Sweetheart, the way I've grown
To think of all you do with so much pride . . .
You know the way I used to be at first—
All fears because our plans had gone astray,
All tears because a shining bubble burst—
But now I see things clearer ev'ry day;

You're making sure that we will hold this land
And keep the simple things that mean so much . . .
Vacation days . . . love-letters in the sand . . .
And summer nights when hands and hearts can touch . . .
And we can watch a misty moon ride high
And laugh beneath our own star-spangled sky!

PAINTING BY VARGA
VERSE BY PHIL STACK

Originalen und feuerte den Rest. Die Umsätze von B & B waren so hoch, dass Ex-Ange-stellte Charlies größte Konkurrenten wurden: Einige nahmen den Hut und gründeten den Shaw-Barton-Kalenderverlag.

So unnachgiebig Ward auch als Geschäftsmann war, seinen Künstlern zahlte er mehr als jeder andere Kalenderverlag, ganz zu schweigen von den Zeitschriften, deren Honorare er weit überbot. 1939 erhielt George Petty für eine Doppelseite in der Zeitschrift *Esquire* 100 Dollar, während B & B für ein vergleichbares Bild 1 000 Dollar hinblätterte. Kein Wunder, dass jeder Pin-up-Künstler einen Vertrag mit B & B schließen wollte. Ward spendete auch so auffällig für wohltätige Zwecke, dass *Life* ihn als den „großzügigsten Mann der Welt" bezeichnete. Diejenigen, die mit den finanziellen Verhältnissen von B & B vertraut waren, setzten dem entgegen, dass Charlie Ward am liebsten sich selbst gegenüber spendabel war, und schätzten, dass das Unternehmen für das Jahr 1955 eine Million Dollar aufwenden musste, um den Lebensstil seines Chefs aufrechtzuerhalten. Zu seinem Luxusleben gehörten diverse Anwesen, darunter eine 810 Hektar große Farm in Wisconsin samt Büffelherde, eine 32.375 Hektar große Ranch in Arizona und ein Strandhaus in Kalifornien, in dem man nackt sonnenbaden konnte. Ein ganzes Gefolge von Dienern und persönlichen Assistenten reiste mit ihm überall hin. Er verfügte über

Above: Esquire magazine's August 1943 foldout by Alberto Vargas. American propaganda concentrated on reminding men of what they must protect at home, in this case the all-American girl.

Opposite: In this Rolf Armstrong lithograph, circa 1944, his muse Jewel Flowers makes dates with a soldier and a sailor at the same time. This was called supporting the troops.

eine Flotte außergewöhnlicher Autos, die alle mit kugelsicherem Glas und speziell angefertigten Pistolenhalftern ausgestattet waren, veranstaltete wöchentlich Partys für Hunderte von Gästen, auf denen es seltenes Wild und aufwendige Geschenke gab, und hatte in seinen Taschen stets goldene Feuerzeuge, auf denen sein Name eingraviert war und die er in der Regel Kellnern und Hotelpagen als Trinkgeld in die Hand drückte. Mit Diamanten- und Goldschmuck war er besser ausgestattet als jeder Rapper der 1990er-Jahre – offenbar waren die goldenen Zahnreihen noch nicht Klunker genug.

Die größte Extravaganz leistete sich Ward zum 60. Firmenjubiläum 1956. Mit der größten zivilen Luftbrücke der amerikanischen Luftfahrtgeschichte ließ er 1.800 Verkäufer, Künstler und ihre Familien zu vier Tage andauernden Bacchanalien nach St. Paul einfliegen. Man speiste Schweinebraten, Fasan und Büffel und schlürfte Champagner – doch hinter den glänzenden Fassaden sah es für B & B gar nicht gut aus.

Ward hatte das Unternehmen 1948 an die Börse gebracht, und Mitte der 1950er-Jahre fraß sein teurer Lebensstil die Gewinne auf und trieb die Aktienwerte nach unten. Als er am 26. Mai 1959 mit 73 Jahren in einem Hotelzimmer in Beverly Hills im Schlaf verstarb, hatte er mit seinem autokratischen Führungsstil dafür gesorgt, dass kein Nachfolger in der Lage war, das Unternehmen zu leiten. Aus Furcht, die Aktienwerte könnten noch tiefer fallen, verkauften die Verantwortlichen B & B schnell an die Standard Packaging Corporation, die drastische Einschnitte vornahm und das Unternehmen 1970 an Saxon Industries weiterverkaufte.

Während jener Saxon-Jahre wurde ein Katalog sämtlicher Pin-up-Kunstwerke erstellt, die im Besitz des Unternehmens waren: Mehr als 1 000 Armstrongs, Buells, Elvgrens, MacPhersons, Morans, Mozerts, Munsons und Runcis wurden mit Preisen von 25 bis 100 Dollar bewertet. Ein Pin-up nach dem anderen wurde verkauft, und als die Verkäufe ins Stocken gerieten, wurden die restlichen Bilder im Zehnerpack für 100 Dollar verscherbelt.

1983 meldete Saxon Insolvenz an. Bis 1988 dämmerte die Firma noch dahin, dann wurde sie von William Smith Sr., einem von Charlie Wards ehemaligen Verkäufern, aufgekauft. Smith betreibt die Firma mit seinen beiden Söhnen noch immer. Die Kunstwerke sind zwar weg und Kalender sind nicht mehr das Hauptprodukt des Unternehmens, doch haben die Smiths das umfangreiche Kalenderarchiv von Brown & Bigelow

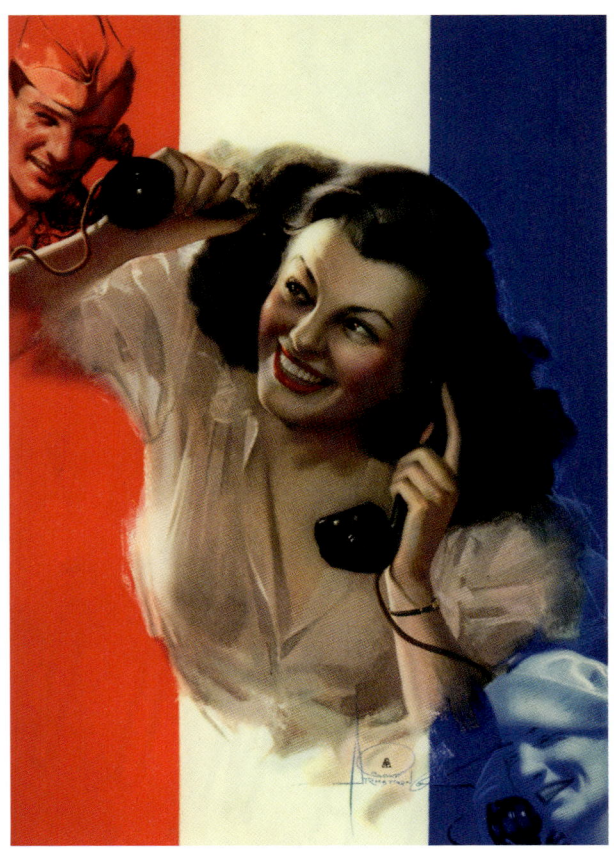

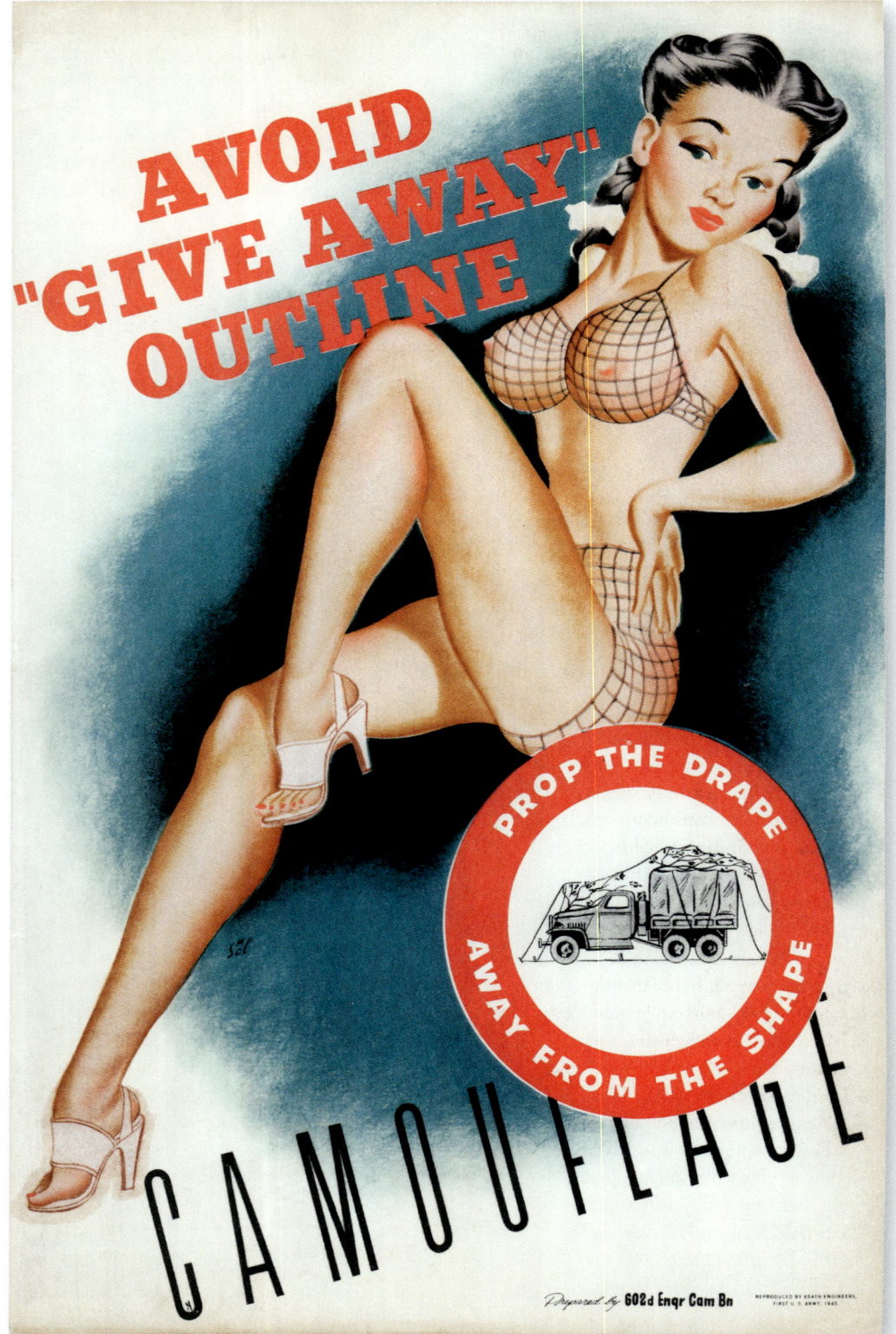

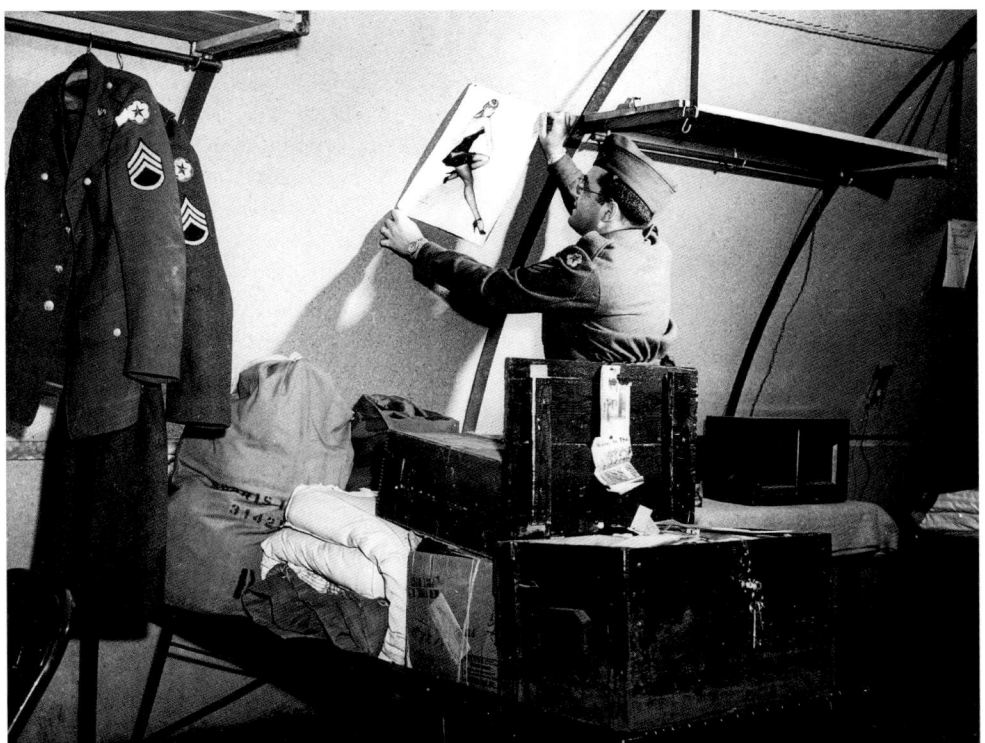

und das dazugehörige Copyright bewahrt. So verkaufen sie nun Lizenzen zum Abdruck von Bildern von Gil Elvgren, Earl Moran, Rolf Armstrong, Zoë Mozert und anderen.

In der Schatzkammer von Brown & Bigelow kommt man sich vor wie ein Goldgräber. Für jedes Jahr gibt es zwei oder drei fast 20 kg schwere Schachteln, in denen die Pin-ups zusammen mit Pfadfinder-, Baseball-, Baby- und Entenjagdkalendern aufbewahrt werden. Geht man die Kalender einzeln durch – in einer Schachtel sind 100 oder mehr – stößt man auf wahre Schätze: einen verblüffenden Gene Pressler in einem breiten Art-déco-Rahmen, einen eleganten, von Wolfshunden flankierten Armstrong-Flapper in einem ungewöhnlichen horizontalen Format, 20 kleine Enoch-Bolles-Löschpapiere und schließlich auf Earl Morans ersten Kalender, den er 1935, noch bevor er unter Vertrag genommen wurde, gestaltet hatte – eine absolute Pin-up-Rarität. Miss St. Paul, wie die entsprechende Kalenderschönheit betitelt wird, ist weder im Art-déco-Stil gehalten noch als Flapper dargestellt. Sie kommt bereits dem Eskapismus des Hollywood-Glamours der Depressionszeit nahe. So schön wie diese sorgsam gearbeiteten Kalender auch sind, so waren sie in den 1930er-Jahren doch schon nicht mehr die Speerspitze des Pin-ups. Das Neueste war – wo sonst? – am Zeitungskiosk zu haben.

Erotika galten als konjunktursicher. Menschen klammern sich in wirtschaftlich schwierigen Zeiten an kleine Vergnügungen – und die Vergnügungen, an die sich Männer am engsten

Opposite: During World War II, the American military incorporated pin-up into many of its training aids and posters.

Above: An American sergeant takes down his pin-up from the barracks wall as he packs his belongings for the return to America at the end of the war, May 25, 1945. Popperfoto/Getty Images.

klammern, sind sexueller Natur. So war es auch in der Großen Depression, als eine Flut aufreizender Film- und Unterhaltungsmagazine auf den Markt kam. *Film Fun*, eine Zeitschrift, die seit 1923 mit fantastischen Titelbildern von Enoch Bolles erschien, inspirierte in den 1930er-Jahren verschiedene Nachahmer, die alle diesen Bolles-Look haben wollten. Den lieferten George Quintana und Peter Driben, die während der 1930er-Jahre Titelseiten für *Movie Humor*, *Movie Fun*, *Movie-Merry-Go-Round*, *Real Screen Fun* und *Reel Humor* illustrierten. Reißerische Digests wie *Broadway Nights*, *Paris Nights*, *Gay Parisienne*, *Pep Stories*, *French Follies*, *Tattle Tales*, *Snappy Stories* und *La Paree* warteten mit Pin-up-Cover von Oscar Greiner, Earle Bergey, Cardwell Higgins, dem geheimnisvollen Moskowitz und dem produktiven Driben auf. In den späten 1930er-Jahren erschienen *Gay Book* und *High Heel Magazine*, großformatige Hochglanzzeitschriften mit Artikeln, Geschichten und Fotos von teilweise bekleideten Frauen auf den Innenseiten und außen mit Pin-ups von Bolles, Bergey und Driben. Erstaunlicherweise nahm Hugh Hefner das Vorbild dieser Magazine 20 Jahre später als Muster für den *Playboy* – und es war die Startrampe für zwei der drei bedeutendsten Pin-up-Künstler.

Als im Oktober 1933 die erste Ausgabe der Zeitschrift *Esquire* erschien, übernahm sie eine *Life*-Idee von 1905 und brachte die Pin-ups auf den Innenseiten. Für diese erste Nummer lieferte George Petty zwei Cartoons, auf beiden waren Frauen mit Männern zu sehen. Die Leser reagierten auf seine Frauenfiguren so positiv und auf die Männer so negativ, dass Petty die Kerle künftig durch Telefone ersetzte und aus den einseitigen Gesprächsbeiträgen der Frauen die Pointe destillierte. Bald geiferten die Leser schon beim bloßen Anblick der Telefone, also wurden die Pointen weggelassen. Was blieb, war das vollendete Pin-up: ohne Text und im Innern des Heftes gut aufgehoben, bis es herausgelöst und aufgehängt wurde. *Esquire* räumte Pin-ups in einem ansehnlichen Gesamtprodukt einen Sonderplatz ein, verkaufte so weit mehr Exemplare als *Gay Book*, machte aus Petty einen Star, während Bolles bis zur Erschöp-

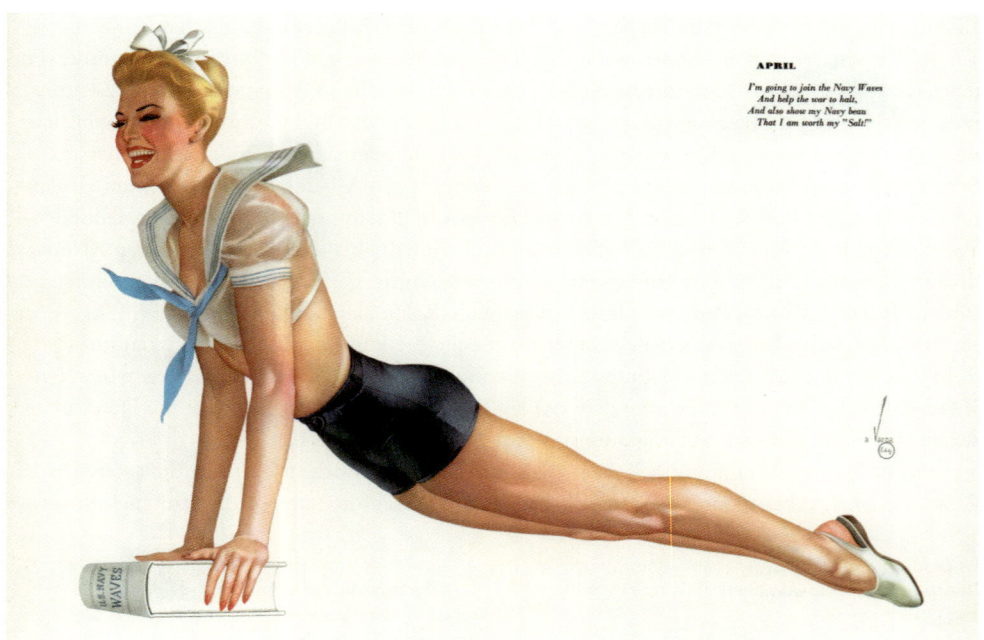

fung rackerte und schließlich in der Greystone-Psychiatrie landete. Auch Petty war gegen Ende des Jahrzehnts überarbeitet, doch nachdem er die Pin-up-Malerei, gerade rechtzeitig vor dem Zweiten Weltkrieg, Alberto Vargas überlassen hatte, konnte er von Werbung gut leben.

Mit dem Zweiten Weltkrieg erreichten die Pin-ups nach 45 Jahren Vorgeschichte den Höhepunkt; selbst der Begriff Pin-up stammt aus jenen Tagen, in denen die kämpfenden Männer fast genötigt wurden, zur moralischen Unterstützung Bilder schöner Frauen aufzuhängen. Seit den anfänglichen Propagandabemühungen im Ersten Weltkrieg hatte die US-Regierung ihre Erkenntnisse zur männlichen Psychologie verfeinert. Als Präsident Franklin Delano Roosevelt 1942 das Office of War Information einrichten ließ, instruierte er die Verantwortlichen, alle Medien so zu koordinieren, dass sie den amerikanischen Truppen stets optimistische und ermutigende Botschaften vermittelten. Statt den Hass auf den Feind anzustacheln, konzentrierte sich die US-Propaganda darauf, den Schutz von Heimat, Familie und des amerikanischen Lebensstils hervorzuheben. Bilder von hübschen Mädchen – der imaginären Liebsten – dienten als unerlässliche Erinnerung an das, wofür

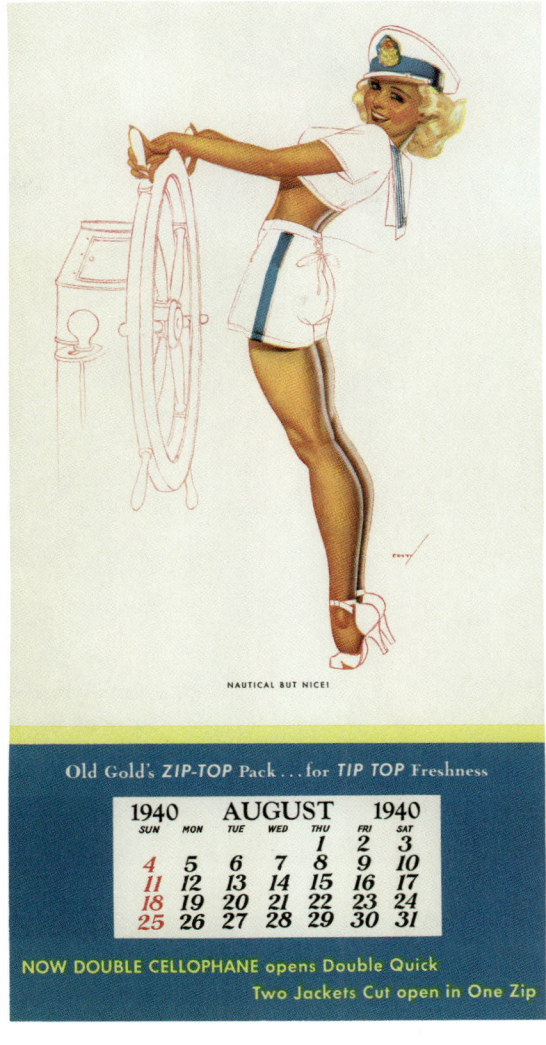

NAUTICAL BUT NICE!

Old Gold's *ZIP-TOP* Pack ... for *TIP TOP* Freshness

1940	AUGUST	1940
SUN	MON	TUE	WED	THU	FRI	SAT
				1	2	3
4	5	6	7	8	9	10
11	12	13	14	15	16	17
18	19	20	21	22	23	24
25	26	27	28	29	30	31

NOW DOUBLE CELLOPHANE opens Double Quick
Two Jackets Cut open in One Zip

Männer kämpften, und Zeitschriften- und Kalenderverlage lieferten derlei – in millionenfacher Auflage – aus.

Fotos von Kasernen im Zweiten Weltkrieg zeigen mit Pin-ups dekorierte Räume, in denen nicht nur die Wände, sondern manchmal auch die Decken beklebt waren. Pin-ups hingen in Schiffen und U-Booten, in Zelten und Panzern sowie in Cockpits, und sie schmückten sogar den Bug von Flugzeugen. Die Männer trugen sie in ihren Brieftaschen und Rucksäcken, und manche klebten sich die Bilder sogar in den Helm. Es gibt Geschichten über Soldaten, die, als sie tot aufgefunden wurden, ein Pin-up umklammerten. Bei den britischen und russischen

Opposite: Miss April, from *Esquire*'s 1944 Varga Girl calendar.

Above: Nautical But Nice!, 1940 Old Gold cigarette calendar with a George Petty lithograph. Calendar measures 17 x 6 inches.

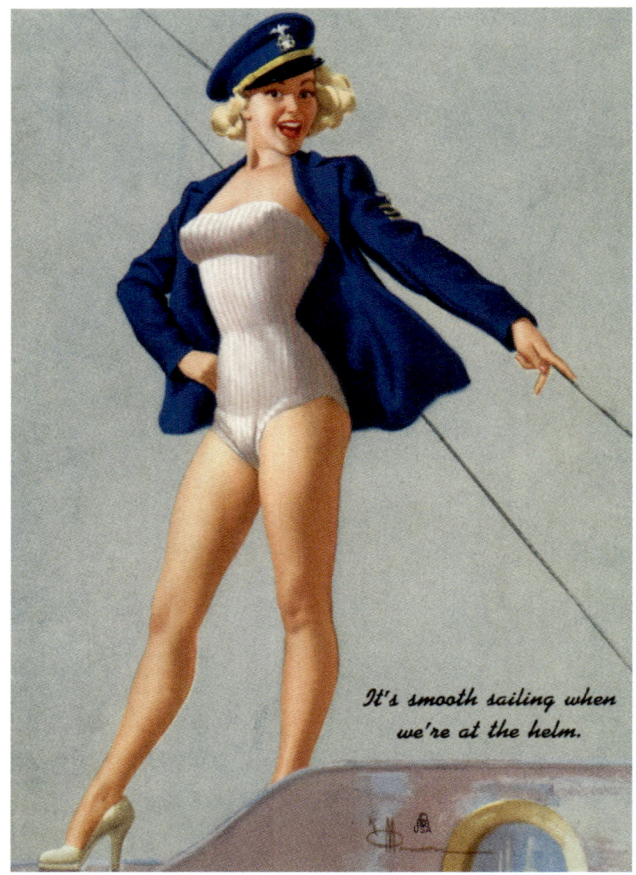

It's smooth sailing when we're at the helm.

Truppen waren Pin-ups gleichermaßen beliebt, und der Filmemacher Russ Meyer – im Zweiten Weltkrieg Kameramann der U.S. Army – behauptete, deutsche Truppen hätten amerikanische Leichen nach Pin-ups durchsucht, während die Amerikaner bei den Deutschen nach Nacktfotos schauten. „Wir hatten Pin-ups, aber die Deutschen hatten die besten Pornos", behauptete er.

Der Verleger von *Esquire* ahnte, dass die USA 1940 in den Krieg eingreifen würden, und beschleunigte sein Vorhaben, den zunehmend problematischen George Petty durch den umgänglicheren Alberto Vargas zu ersetzen. Pettys letzte Pin-ups für *Esquire* erschienen 1941, so fiel Vargas die Rolle zu, die Männer durch den Krieg zu begleiten. Alberto tat dies mit Mädchen in knapper Militäruniform und in tropischen Sarongs – für die Männer, die auf Schauplätzen im Pazifik dienten. 1944 gab *Esquire* auf Kosten der Regierung eine Sonderausgabe für das Militär heraus. Das Heft enthielt keine Anzeigen, dafür aber auf der Umschlagrückseite ein zusätzliches Pin-up von Vargas. Durch den Weitblick der Redaktion wurde Vargas zum populärsten Pin-up-Künstler der 1940er-Jahre, obgleich Pettys doppelseitige Pin-ups von 1941 zahlreiche Bomber der Air Force schmückten.

Während *Esquire* jeden Monat gemalte Pin-ups bot, brachte *Yank*, das Magazin der U.S. Army, Pin-up-Fotos in den wöchentlichen Ausgaben. Meist waren es Fotos von amerikanischen Starlets in Badeanzügen oder Dessous, die dem Militär von den Hollywood-Studios zur Verfügung gestellt wurden. Linda Darnell, Deanna Durbin, Susan Hayward, Rita Hayworth, Marie McDonald, Jane Russell und die Rockettes, die Tanzkompanie der Radio City Music Hall, waren nur einige unter den Hunderten von Frauen.

Above: It's smooth sailing when we're at the helm, blotter lithograph by Knute "KO" Munson, circa 1944. Blotters were popular pin-up items in the days of fountain pens, to soak up excess ink. The pin-up and some advertising material were printed on the top side, and the absorbent blotter was on the bottom.

Opposite: A small navy-themed lithograph, circa 1944, by an anonymous artist.

Die Studios schickten den Truppen auch direkt Millionen von Pin-ups – allein drei Millionen Abbildungen der legendären Rückenaufnahme von Betty Grable –, und geschäftstüchtige Glamourfotografen druckten Pin-up-Kataloge für Soldaten und boten dabei eine Auswahl Hunderter bekleideter, doch provokativer Pin-ups zu ermäßigten Versandkosten. Noch mehr Pin-up-Fotos kamen über eine Fülle neuer Männermagazine auf den Markt, darunter *Who's Your Pin-up Girl?*, *War Laffs*, *Jest*, *Sleek*, *Snap*, *Show* und das aufpolierte *Gay Book*. Die Entscheidung zugunsten von Fotos statt der gemalten Pin-ups war vor allem wirtschaftlich begründet: 25 Dollar für ein Foto gegen 250 Dollar für ein Bild – wenn man überhaupt einen Künstler fand. Vaughan Bass, Edward D'Ancona, Harry Ekman, Art Frahm, Earl MacPherson, Bill Medcalf und Edward Runci waren zum Militär eingezogen worden. *Esquire* hatte das Glück, dass der 46-jährige Vargas vom Kriegsdienst befreit war. Auch für Rolf Armstrong, Gil Elvgren, Earl Moran und Zoë Mozert, die für Kalenderverlage arbei-

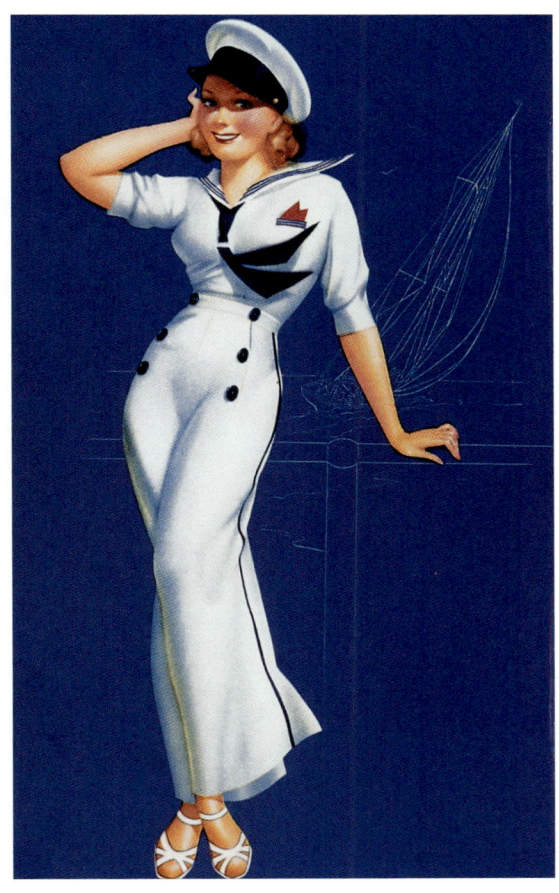

teten, galt das Gleiche. Doch es sollte noch ein Jahrzehnt dauern, bis sich das Foto durchsetzte.

Armstrong, Elvgren, Moran und Mozert waren für Brown & Bigelow und für Louis F. Dow das, was Vargas für *Esquire* war. Moran und Mozert malten Dutzende patriotischer Motive für Mutoskop-Karten im Taschenformat, während Armstrong Propagandaplakate und -kalender entwarf. Louis F. Dow druckte eine Serie von 23 x 18 cm großen Broschüren mit dem Titel *Pin-Ups*, die „12 traumhafte Glamourgirls" des Künstlers Gil Elvgren versprachen. Mit diesen Broschüren wurden Elvgrens bekannteste für Dow angefertigte Bilder recycelt, gedruckt auf dünnem, leichtem Papier und mit perforierten Seiten, die einfach herausgetrennt werden konnten. Sie waren in Umschlägen verpackt, die für zwölf Cent in jeden Winkel der Erde verschickt werden konnten. Brown & Bigelow konterte mit einer kleineren Broschüre, die Mozert-Pin-ups enthielt und noch billiger im Versand war. Zoë nannte diese Hefte V-Mail oder Victory-Mail-Broschüren. Die echte V-Mail war eine Methode, Militärbriefe auf Mikrofilm zu übermitteln, um in Postsäcken Platz zu sparen. So scheint Zoës Bezeichnung sich schlicht auf das preiswert zu versendende Kleinformat und den die Moral hebenden Inhalt der Broschüren zu beziehen.

Nach 1942 steigerten die Kalenderverlage ihre Gewinne durch Verträge mit dem War Advertising Council, einer Organisation, die die Werbeindustrie für die Produktion von

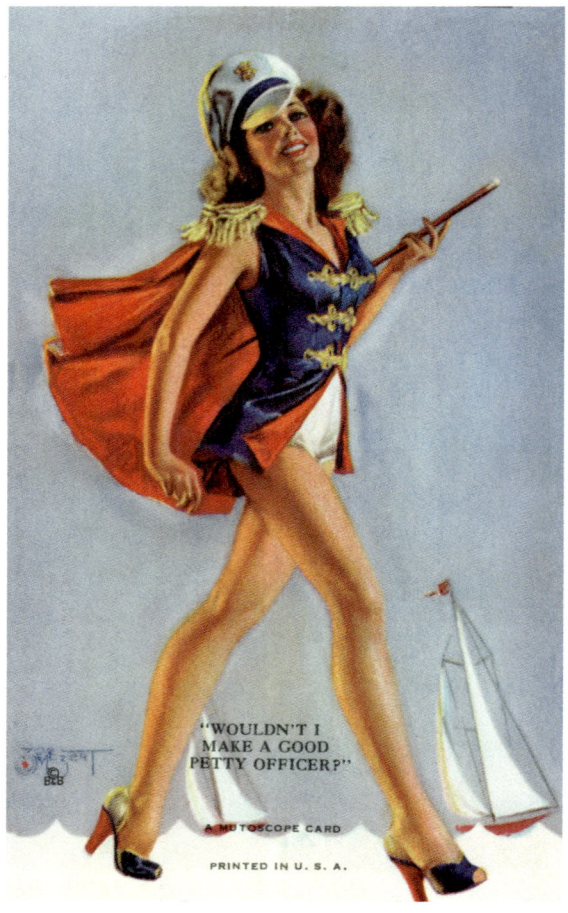

"WOULDN'T I MAKE A GOOD PETTY OFFICER?"

A MUTOSCOPE CARD

PRINTED IN U. S. A.

Propaganda mobilisieren sollte. Sowohl Rosie the Riveter (Rosie, die Nietpistole) als auch Smokey the Bear (Smokey, der Bär) wurden von diesem Gremium entworfen: Rosie, um Frauen zu ermutigen, Jobs in der Kriegsindustrie anzunehmen, Smokey aus Sorge, dass der japanische Beschuss des amerikanischen Westens Waldbrände auslösen könnte. Brown & Bigelow hielt 1943 und 1944 in Anwesenheit von Armstrong, Mozert, Moran sowie der Modelle seine eigenen Kriegsanzeigen-Konferenzen ab, um neue patriotische Themen zu entwickeln. Auf der ersten Konferenz stellte Rolf Armstrong seine Muse Jewel Flowers vor, die ein knappes rot-weiß-blaues Kleidchen trug. In Verkaufsprospekten von B & B wurden die neuen Pin-ups mit militärischem Erfolg verknüpft. So wurde 1944 das *Sketch Pad* von Earl MacPherson folgendermaßen angekündigt: „Wo auch immer du das liest …, es ist ein Kriegsmanöver. An unserer Verkaufsfront … ist es ein *Frauen*över … In die richtige Richtung zu manövrieren bedeutet Sieg."

Charlie Ward war nicht der Einzige, der Pin-ups mit Patriotismus verknüpfte; die gesamte Werbebranche erlag dieser Versuchung. Allen war klar, dass Sex verkaufsfördernd wirkt, doch nun, da Pin-ups mit einem Mal zu einer nationalen Obsession wurden, gab es keine Grenzen mehr. Hübsche Mädchen konnten buchstäblich alles verhökern, solange der zugehörige Werbetext das Produkt mit einem militärischen Sieg verband. Diese Werbemaßnahmen waren ein Warmlaufen für die aggressiven Werbestrategien, die die US-Werbebranche in den 1950er- und 1960er-Jahren pflegte, als aus dem War Advertising Council schlicht der Advertising Council wurde.

Der Pin-up-Schub während des Zweiten Weltkriegs hatte weitreichende Auswirkungen auf die amerikanische Popkultur. Der Busenkönig Russ Meyer beispielsweise, der in der Armee

Above: *"Wouldn't I make a good petty officer?"* Mutoscope card by Zoë Mozert, circa 1942. 5.25 x 3.25 inches. The collectible cards were made by the International Mutoscope Reel Company and dispensed by machines for a penny apiece in the 1940s.

Opposite: *"…so take my advice and just bet your shirt,"* gatefold by George Petty from the July 1941 issue of *Esquire* magazine. Petty left *Esquire* at the end of 1939 and agreed to return for one year in 1941 to do large foldout pin-ups at $1,000 apiece. Meanwhile, *Esquire* had hired Alberto Vargas to replace him, and in '41 pin-ups by both artists ran in each issue.

zum Fotografen und Filmemacher ausgebildet wurde, war nach dem Krieg zunächst Glamour-fotograf, dann machte er kommerzielle Sexfilme. Meyer war teils von Pin-ups, teils von fran-zösischen Bordellen inspiriert und hatte seinen ersten großen Durchbruch mit Aufnahmen für die aufklappbaren Mittelseiten, die er im Auftrag seines ehemaligen Kriegskameraden Hugh Hefner schoss.

Hef diente seine Militärzeit als Schreibkraft in den Staaten ab, doch er liebte Pin-ups und *Esquire* genau so sehr wie alle Soldaten der Kampftruppen. Nach seinem Militärdienst ergatterte er einen Job beim *Esquire*, und als der *Esquire* nach New York zog, blieb Hef zurück in Chicago, um den *Playboy* zu gründen. Dieses Männermagazin war als eine Art aufgefrischter *Esquire* für junge Veteranen konzipiert.

Währenddessen studierte Frederick Mellinger die Outfits der Pin-ups. Der Kleidermacher entwarft nach dem Krieg Dessous, die von Pin-ups inspiriert waren. Da die New Yorker Zei-tungen es ablehnten, Anzeigen für seine skandalösen Kreationen abzudrucken, zog er nach Los Angeles und eröffnete sein Geschäft Frederick's of Hollywood. 1982 erzählte mir Mellinger, dass ihn eigentlich seine GI-Kameraden inspiriert hätten. „Alle erzählten, sie wünschten sich, ihre Frauen und Freundinnen würden sich wie Pin-ups kleiden", sagte er. „Ich habe meine Mode entworfen, um diese Ehen zu retten."

Die Pin-ups, von denen diese Männer sich anregen ließen, waren dank der Bilderflut in Kriegszeiten größtenteils Fotos. Hefner liebte die Bilder von Vargas im *Esquire* und engagierte Vargas, um zwischen 1960 und 1977 für den *Playboy* Pin-ups zu malen. Doch er erkannte,

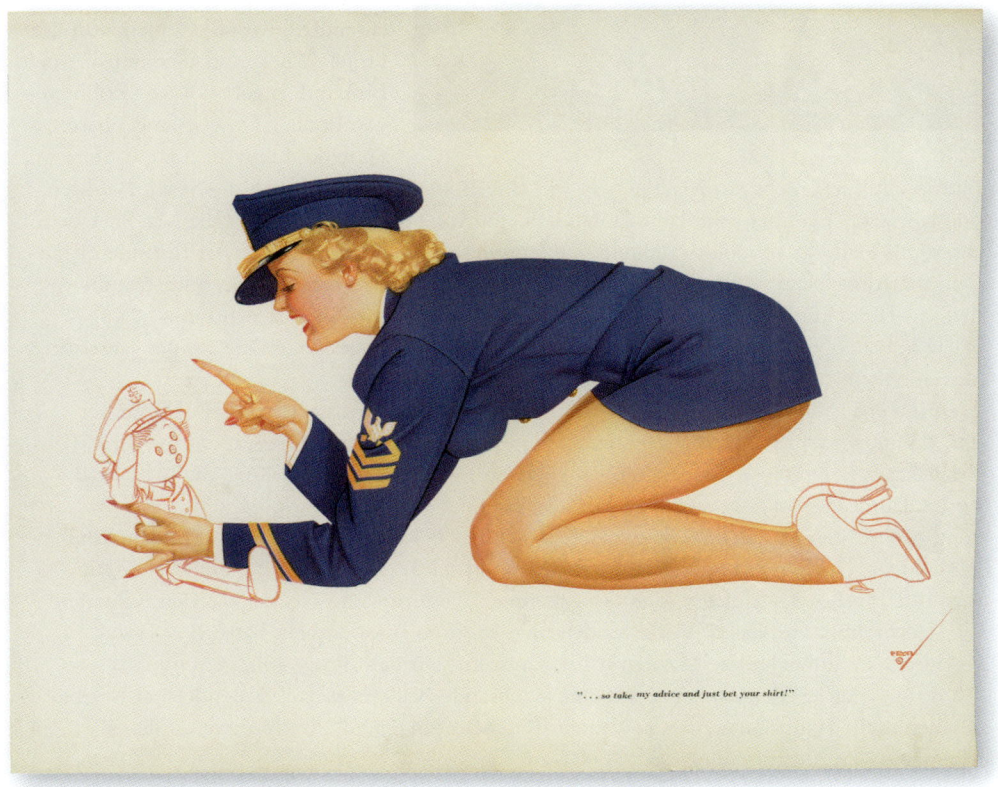

"... so take *my advice and just bet your shirt!*"

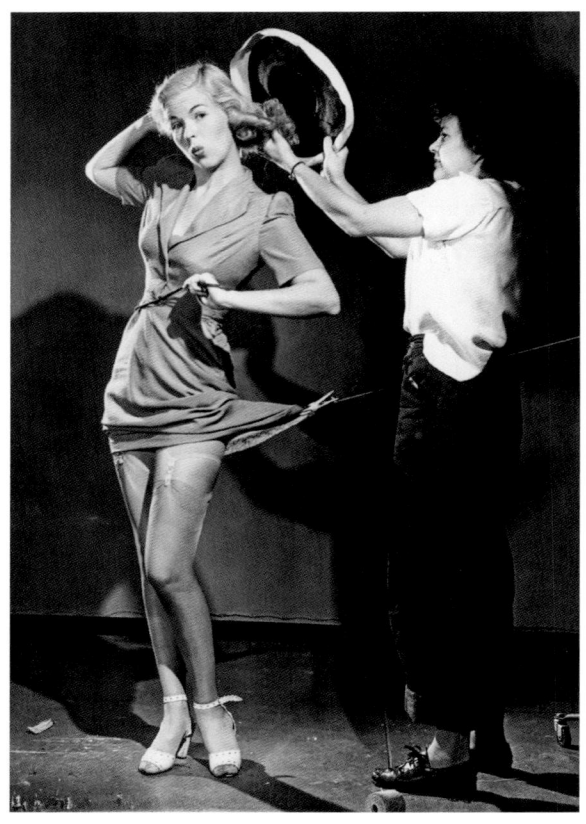

dass die Zukunft dem Foto gehörte. Robert Harrisons *Beauty Parade*, *Wink*, *Titter*, *Eyeful* und *Whisper* waren die letzten amerikanischen Magazine mit großen Pin-up-Titelseiten, die Billy DeVorss, Earl Moran und vor allem Peter Driben lieferten. Harrison hatte *Beauty Parade* 1942 auf den Markt gebracht, als Pin-ups ihren Höhepunkt erreicht hatten. 1955, als diese Zeitschriften ausliefen, sah jedes amerikanische Männermagazin dem *Playboy* sehr ähnlich, und gemalte Pin-ups waren nur noch auf Kalendern, im *Esquire* und gelegentlich auf den großen Titelseiten der Zeitschrift *Motor Age* zu sehen.

1945 war diese Zukunft unvorhersehbar, undenkbar. Firmen, die für die Kriegsproduktion zudem einen Gang höher geschaltet hatten, wollten das Pin-up nicht sterben lassen. Die Künstler kamen von der Front zurück, und alle fanden Arbeit. Brown & Bigelow warb Gil Elvgren von Louis F. Dow ab und läutete seine produktivste Ära ein. Shaw-Barton entführte nicht nur MacPherson von B & B, sondern klaute auch die *Sketch Pad*-Idee und lancierte eine über zehn Jahre laufende Reihe von *Artist's Sketch Books*, die MacPherson anfertigte. Haddon Sundblom richtete sich sein viertes Atelier ein, und das Art Institute of Chicago, Alma Mater von mehr Pin-up-Malern als jede andere Kunstschule, immatrikulierte fleißig weitere künftige Elvgrens. Und da die Männer mit dem Anblick von Pin-ups aufgewachsen waren, funktionierte das auch, und die Kalenderverlage gingen die 1950er-Jahre im Vertrauen auf stetig erfolgreiche Geschäfte an.

Eine erste Warnung zeichnete sich Ende 1953 ab. In der Ausgabe vom 30. Dezember der Männerzeitschrift *People Today* stand zu lesen, dass „attraktive Frauen nicht mehr zu Amerikas beliebtesten Kalendermotiven gehören … die größte Bestellung, die bei B & B für das Jahr 1954 einging, war der Pfadfinderkalender von Norman Rockwell … Unter den begehrtesten Motiven, berichtet B & B, ist für 1954 nur ein Mädchen zu finden. Fünf Jahre zuvor schafften es noch sechs Mädchen unter die Top zwölf … In diesem Jahr kaufte B & B das in Los Angeles ansässige Unternehmen Western Litho Co. auf, das den Kalender mit den berühmten Nacktbildern von Marilyn Monroe veröffentlicht hatte. B & B lässt verlauten, die unbekleidete Marilyn habe man sofort aus dem Programm genommen." Ward führte diese Veränderungen auf eine wachsende Nachfrage nach Kalendern als Werbegeschenke für Hausfrauen zurück. Weniger Kalender gingen an „Treffpunkte, an denen Männer zusammenkommen".

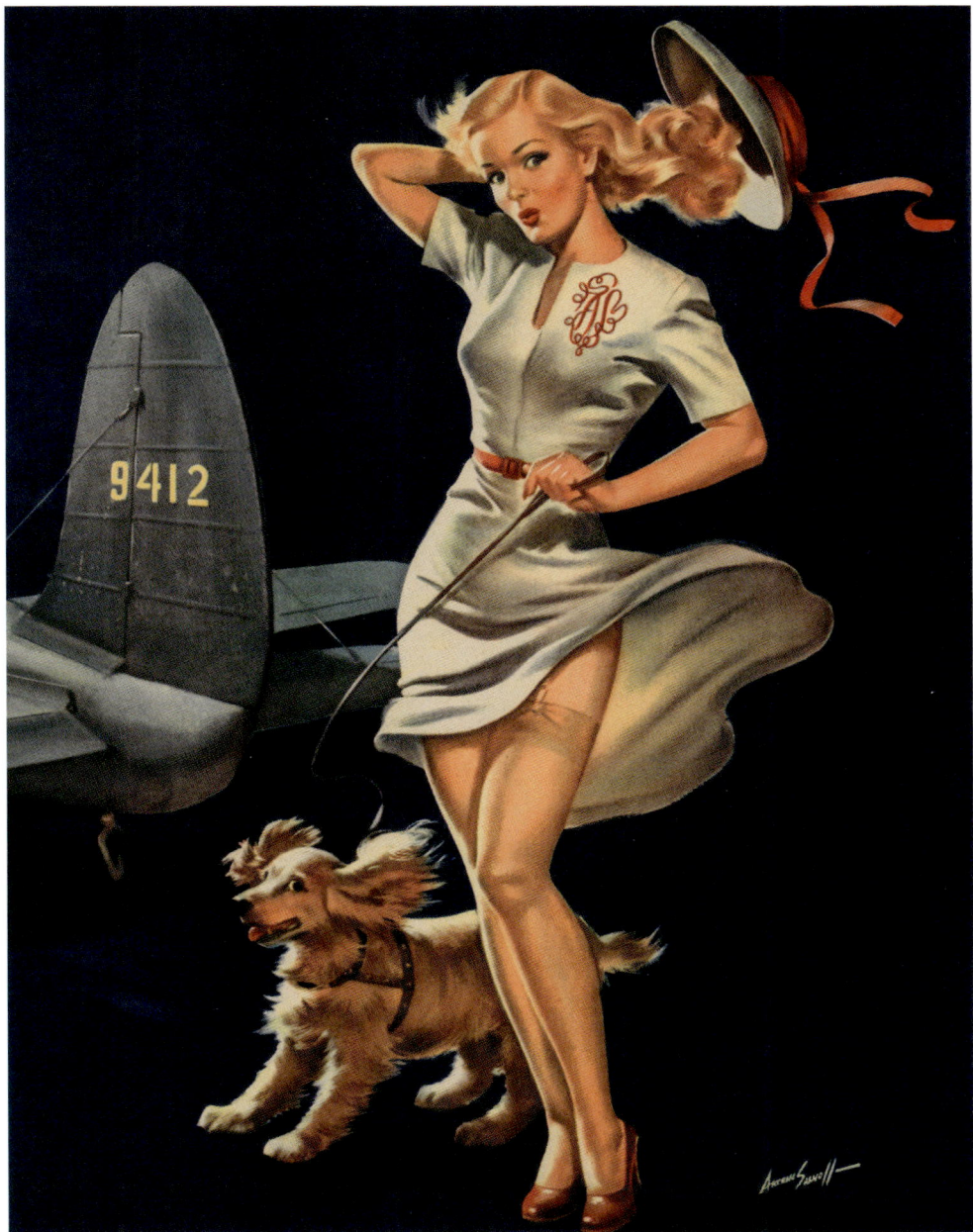

Opposite: An assistant for illustrator Arthur Saron Sarnoff holds a model's hair and hat in place.

Above: Visibility Good, lithograph, by Arthur Saron Sarnoff, from a 1947 calendar. The lead time between when original art was commissioned and when a calendar went on sale was typically two years, meaning that in 1946, when this calendar went on sale, companies had a big backlog of military-themed pin-ups to use up. Sarnoff, an accomplished illus-trator of many themes, makes an interesting reference to Nathaniel Hawthorne's *Scarlet Letter* in this Kemper-Thomas Company illustration.

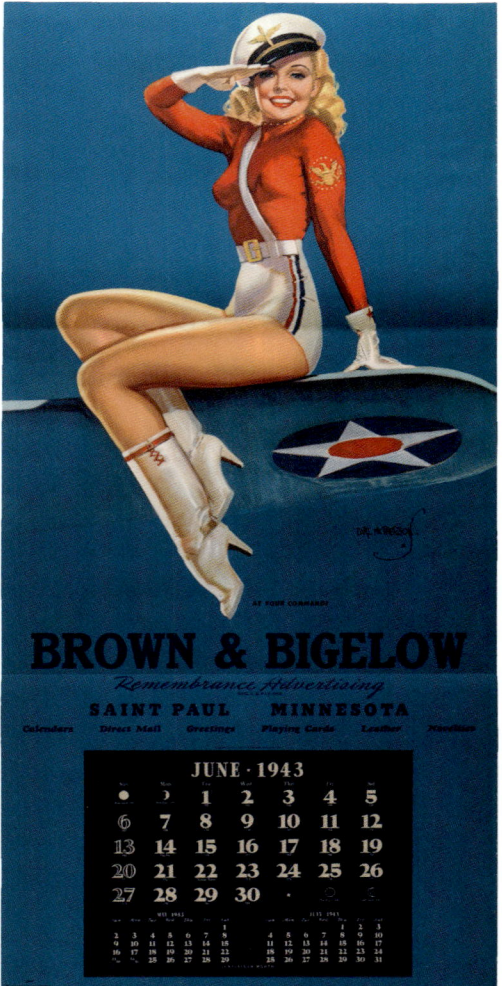

Der Babyboom hatte nachgelassen. Und welche Ironie, dass der Aufstieg des Pin-ups begann, als die Frauen den heimischen Herd verließen, und endete, als sie zurückkehrten.

Weil die neuen Väter die alten Männertreffs aufgaben, reagierte Brown & Bigelow mit familienfreundlicheren Pin-ups. Zoë Mozert beklagte, dass der Verlag ab 1954 ihre Akte ablehnte. Elvgren, der in den späten 1940er- und in den frühen 1950er-Jahren für B & B *Gay Nymph*, *Vision of Beauty*, *Perfection*, *Fascination*, *Fascinating Figures* und andere Akte gemalt hatte, produzierte nach 1953 nur noch zwei Aktbilder. Auch Moran hörte in den 1950ern auf, Akte zu malen, allerdings rächte er sich, als er im Ruhestand war.

Inzwischen sah man immer mehr Nacktes in den Männermagazinen, doch ausnahmslos Fotos. Die Welt hatte sich verändert, nicht die Männer. Sie wollten nach wie vor hübsche Mädchen sehen, konnten sie aber nicht mehr über ihrem Bett aufhängen. Magazine konnten besser versteckt werden, und als das Traummädchen erst einmal von der Wand in eine Kiste in der Garage gestiegen war, gab es keinen Grund mehr, seine Unschuld zu wahren. Die sittsamen Pin-ups wirkten in der *Playboy*-Ära überholt.

Die Kalenderverlage trugen folglich ihren Konkurrenzkampf mit Fotokalendern aus. Zuerst mussten die Modelle so posieren wie auf den gemalten Pin-ups, manchmal wurden exakte Repliken der Pin-ups angefertigt. Doch die Unternehmen erkannten bald, dass dies nicht nötig war. Diejenigen, die Fotokalender kauften, erwarteten nicht, dass die Fotos wie gemalte Kunst aussahen. Den echten Frauen fehlten die langen Beine, die superschmale Taille und die drallen Brüste der gemalten Pin-ups, aber es waren echte Frauen, sie waren tatsächlich nackt, und das hat seinen eigenen, zeitlosen Reiz.

Above: At Your Command!, 1941, by Earl MacPherson, on a 1943 Brown & Bigelow calendar. Earl MacPherson worked almost four years for Brown & Bigelow until he was drafted into the navy in late 1943. When he got out, he signed with competitor Shaw-Barton to escape B&B's policy that all artists had to live near company headquarters in St. Paul, Minnesota. Calendar measures 46 x 22 inches.

Opposite: Miss Liberty, a 1944 Earl Moran sample calendar by Brown & Bigelow, combining patriotism with cheesecake. The whereabouts of this stunning original art are unknown. Calendar measures 46 x 22 inches.

So kam es, dass zwischen 1955 und 1965 immer weniger Pin-up-Künstler unter Vertrag standen, und die meisten wandten sich nun der Werbung, der Buchcovergestaltung und dem Kunstbetrieb zu oder gingen in den Ruhestand. Die Nachfrage nach Magazinen stieg, die nach Kalendern ging zurück. Louis F. Dow stellte seine Aktivitäten in den späten 1960er-Jahren ein. Shaw-Burton kaufte 1959 Gerlach-Barklow auf und schloss den Betrieb. Im gleichen Jahr starb Charlie Ward, und Brown & Bigelow wurde verkauft. Die neuen Besitzer produzierten weiterhin Pin-up-Kalender, und ein paar der Topkünstler, vor allem Gil Elvgren, malten weiterhin Pin-ups. Hilfreich war vermutlich, dass B & B ihm Auftragsarbeiten vom Verband für Automobilzubehör (NAPA) und Autolackunternehmen Ditzler vermittelte. Autowerkstätten gehörten zu den letzten männlichen Bastionen. Die NAPA gab noch während der 1960er-Jahre Pin-up-Gemälde in Auftrag, und Ditzler blieb dieser Tradition noch bis in die 1980er-Jahre mit vielen Künstlern treu. Bis zuletzt arbeitete Elvgren an der Verfeinerung seines Stils und produzierte in den 1960er-Jahren einige seiner besten Arbeiten, doch die Nachfrage ging weiter zurück: 1968 malte er für Brown & Bigelow acht Bilder; von 1969 bis 1971 waren es nur noch zwei pro Jahr. Sowohl Elvgren als auch Zoë Mozert lieferten 1971 ihre letzten Pin-ups. Fritz Willis blieb noch ein Jahr länger am Ball und verkaufte 1972 zwölf Bilder für Kalender, während Mayo Olmstead 1973 an B & B ein einziges Pin-up verkaufte. Danach war Duane Bryers bei Brown & Bigelow der einzige aktive Pin-up-Künstler, der die Figur seiner molligen Hilda bis in die frühen 1980er-Jahren weiterleben ließ.

Esquire, jene Zeitschrift, bei der das gemalte Ausklappbild seinen Ursprung hatte, behielt bis 1957 die Pin-ups bei und förderte damit eine einzigartige Truppe von Künstlern. Als Vargas 1946 abtrat, führte das Magazin seine „Gallery of Glamour" ein, in der Werke von Ernest Chiriaka, Joe De Mers, Thornton Utz, Al Moore, Eddie Chan, Mike Ludlow, Ben-Hur Baz und J. Frederick Smith präsentiert wurden. Das einzige Medium, in dem neben dem *Esquire* noch Pin-ups dieser Künstler erschienen, war der *Ballyhoo*-Kalender von Brown & Bigelow für 1953. Originale dieser Künstler finden sich heute selten auf dem Markt, denn *Esquire* hatte sämtliche Rechte an

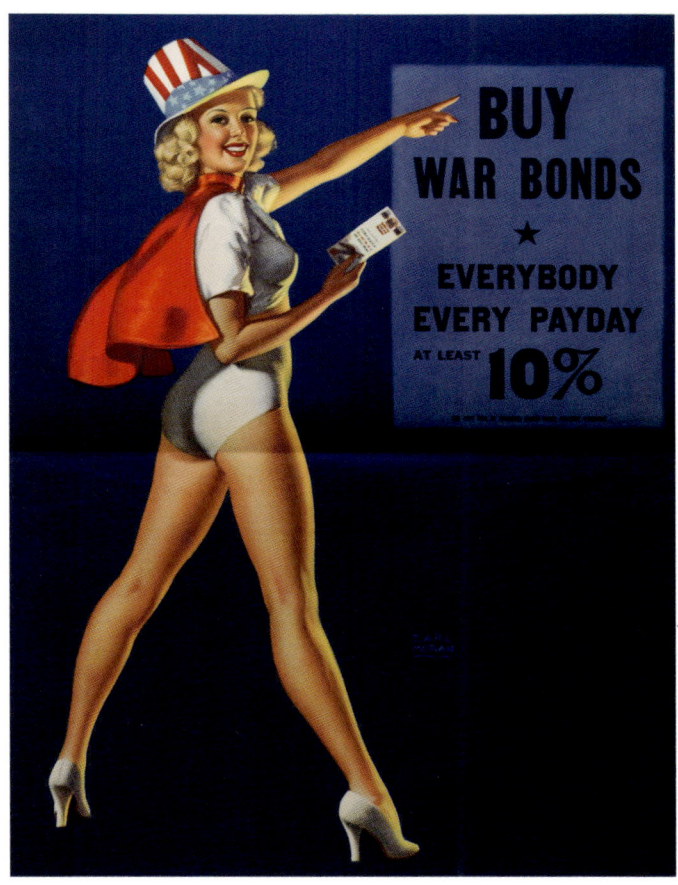

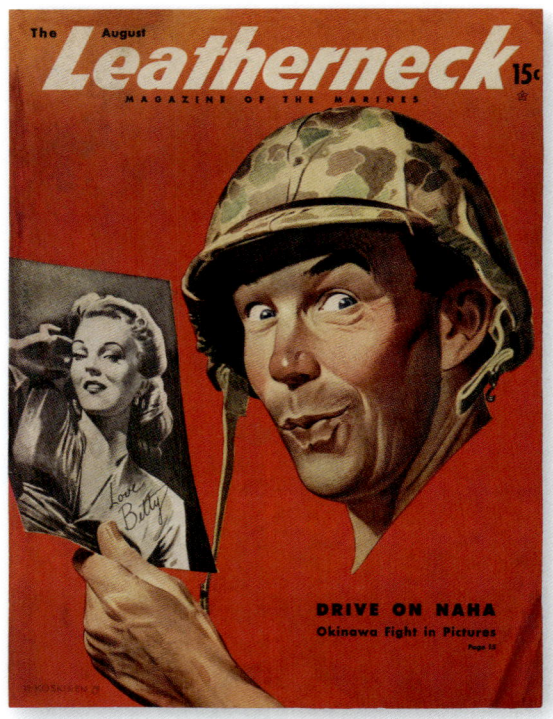

den Werken erworben und gab die Bilder 1980 als Teil einer Steuerabschreibung an die Universität von Kansas weiter: Im Spencer-Museum der Universität sind 164 Originale von Vargas und 23 Chiriakas zu sehen, während Tausende andere Werke in 26 versiegelten Schiffscontainern – inzwischen seit mehr als 30 Jahren – auf eine Bundeshilfe zur Kunstförderung warten, mit der das Einordnen und Protokollieren des Inhalts finanziert werden soll.

Nach 1960 war der *Playboy* das einzige Magazin, das noch Pin-ups veröffentlichte, zunächst Bilder von Vargas, dann von Don Lewis und heute Werke von Olivia De Berardinis. Hefner, dessen Foto-Ausklappbilder den Niedergang jener Kunstform beschleunigten, hielt die Flamme in all den Jahren, in denen die meisten das Interesse daran verloren hatten, immerhin noch am Lodern. Das waren genau die Jahre, in denen Charles Martignette die umfangreichste Pin-up-Sammlung der Welt zusammentrug.

Martignette, verschwiegen, obsessiv und exzentrisch, war bereits seit seinem achten Lebensjahr hinter Pin-ups her, nachdem er einen Kalender mit diesen Bildern zum ersten Mal in einem Friseursalon gesehen hatte. 1987, mit 27 Jahren, erwarb er sein erstes Elvgren-Original, dann kaufte er in den 1980er-Jahren jedes Bild, das er finden konnte. Er fuhr zu sämtlichen noch existierenden Kalenderverlagen, denn üblicherweise hatten diese nicht nur die Rechte an den Bildern, sondern gleich die Werke gekauft, aufbewahrt oder weitergegeben. Indem er die vor dem Aus stehenden Firmen überzeugte, ihm alles zu verkaufen, was sie hatten, rettete Martignette Hunderte von Werken vor der Zerstörung. Auch einige der Künstler spürte er auf. Seine private Korrespondenz belegt, wie er versuchte, Norman Rockwell zu umgarnen, der

Above: As the Aarmy had *Yank*, the marines had *Leatherneck* magazine, founded in 1917 at the Marine Corps base in Quantico, Virginia. During World War II, *Leatherneck* was largely staffed by combat correspondents. Though *Leatherneck* did not feature regular pin-ups, it was a higher-quality magazine than *Yank*, published monthly rather than weekly. This issue is dated August 1945, with cover art by H. Koskinen.

Opposite left: United States Navy seaman L. P. Dowell, stationed in North Carolina, shows off the pin-up girl tattooed on his chest, April 1959. © The Mariners' Museum/Corbis Images.

Opposite right: Staff Sergeant Allen Blake of Defiance, Ohio, following a daring air raid on Nazi targets in France, January 1944, credited the lucky pin-up girl on his jacket for his safe return. Named Flossie, after his wife, the template was a George Petty *Esquire* pin-up. © Corbis Images.

bald schon von Martignettes Anfragen nach Autogrammen und persönlichem Kontakt genervt war. Martignette bewahrte jeden ablehnenden Brief auf. Zu guter Letzt jagte er den Eigentümern bekannter Werke hinterher, bombardierte sie mit Anrufen und Briefen, drängte und flehte, bis er bekam, was er wollte. Seine Wohnung in Florida war vollgestellt mit Kisten, doch den Großteil seiner Sammlung mit 4.300 Pin-ups und ähnlichen Kunstwerken hatte er verpackt in Lagerhallen deponiert. Da Martignette stets Geld benötigte, um neue Kunstwerke zu kaufen, schaltete er Anzeigen und bot Pin-ups zum Verkauf an, setzte die Preise jedoch so hoch an, dass nur wenige Bilder verkauft wurden. Eigentlich wollte er ja mit niemandem teilen.

Im Laufe der 1980er-Jahre fingen neben Martignette noch andere an, diese vergessene Kunstform auszugraben. 1982 kuratierte Louis Meisel seine erste Pin-up-Ausstellung, und 1988 begann Marianne Ohl Phillips, Vintagedrucke und -kalender zu verkaufen. In den 1990er-Jahren, vor allem nach der Veröffentlichung von *The Great American Pin-Up* 1996, nahm das Interesse zu. Als Charles Martignette 2008 mit nur 57 Jahren an einem Herzinfarkt starb, erlebten Pin-ups gerade eine Renaissance, und die Nachfrage nach Originalen war hoch. Obgleich Martignettes Tod alle schockierte, frohlockten Sammler, als dessen 4.300 Werke bei Heritage Auctions in Dallas, Texas, eingereicht wurden.

Drei 16 m lange Lkws waren notwendig, um Martignettes Schatz abzutransportieren, und zwölf Auktionen über vier Jahre, um ihn unter die Leute zu bringen. Gil Elvgren, dessen Talent nach Charles fester Überzeugung eines Tages mit dem von Rockwell verglichen würde, erwies sich als Amerikas bedeutendster und wertvollster Pin-up-Künstler. So bemerkte Ed Jaster, Senior Vice President bei Heritage, nach einer Auktion 2012, dass „sein Talent nach wie vor

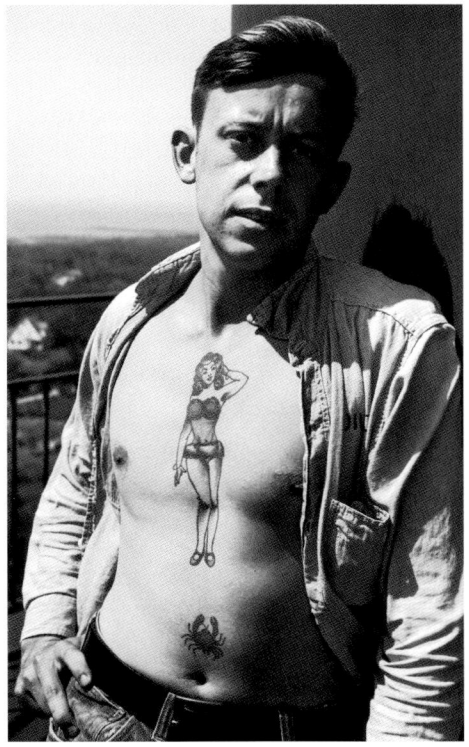 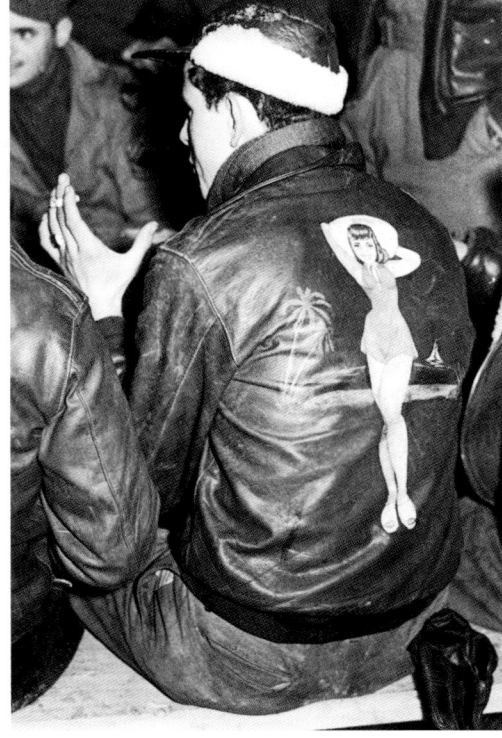

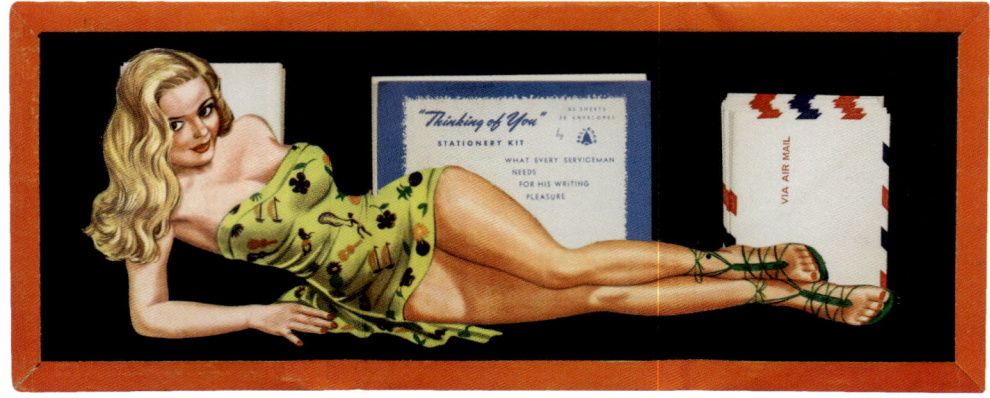

die Bezugsgröße ist, an der fast alle anderen Pin-up-Künstler gemessen werden. Die Sammler betrachten ihn sozusagen als den Goldstandard …"

In *The Great American Pin-Up* prahlte Charles Martignette, er besäße die meisten der noch existierenden originalen Pin-up-Werke. Damit hatte er eigentlich recht. Seine Sammlung war als Ganzes überwältigend, doch der Umstand, dass diese Skizzen, Gemälde und Pastelle aus ihren Hüllen befreit und über die Welt verstreut wurden, ist das Beste, was den Pin-ups und ihren Liebhabern seit dem Zweiten Weltkrieg passieren konnte. Diese Kunst sollte – wie es auch ihre Bezeichnung anklingen lässt – gesehen und nicht in Lagerhallen von Louis F. Dow, Shaw-Barton, Kemper-Thomas, Gerlach-Barklow, Joseph C. Hoover, Brown & Bigelow – oder eben Charles Martignette – verborgen bleiben. Wir schulden Charles Dank dafür, dass er diese Werke gesammelt und bewahrt hat, aber unser Dank gilt auch Heritage Auctions, die diese Bilder an Hunderte von Fans verkauft haben, die die Pin-ups bis dahin nur als Abdrucke in Kalendern, auf Löschpapieren, Mutoskop-Karten oder den Seiten von *The Great American Pin-up* kannten.

Die Auflösung der Sammlung Martignette hat auch dieses Buch ermöglicht. Viele Werke, die in *The Great American Pin-Up* zu sehen waren, gehörten Charles, doch erwies sich das Auspacken und Fotografieren der Originale damals als so entmutigend, dass oft Drucke und Kalender als Vorlage herangezogen wurden. Für diesen Band hatte ich besseren Zugang zu Originalbildern und zu qualitätvollen Aufnahmen der Werke, sodass zum ersten Mal ein Buch dieser Größenordnung über Pin-ups produziert werden kann. Jetzt, da all diese Bilder von Elvgren, Petty, Vargas, Moran, Armstrong, Driben, Mozert, Ballantyne, Bolles und Buell ans Tageslicht gekommen sind, ist zu hoffen, dass die neuen Besitzer ihre Schätze nicht in Lagerstätten horten, sondern öffentlich zeigen, um sich und den Fans Freude zu machen. Aufgepinnt, so wie es der Natur dieser Objekte entspricht.

Above: This trifold stationery kit for the World War II military man meaures 9 x 7 inches when closed and an impressive 21 inches across. When opened it reveals a die-cut, sarong-draped pin-up girl holding notepaper and envelopes. Most Americans knew little if anything about the Pacific Islands before the war.

Opposite: I Hope the Boys Don't Draw Straws Tonight, 1946, by Gil Elvgren for Brown & Bigelow. Oil on canvas, 30 x 24 inches. Courtesy Heritage Auctions.

THE ART OF PIN-UP

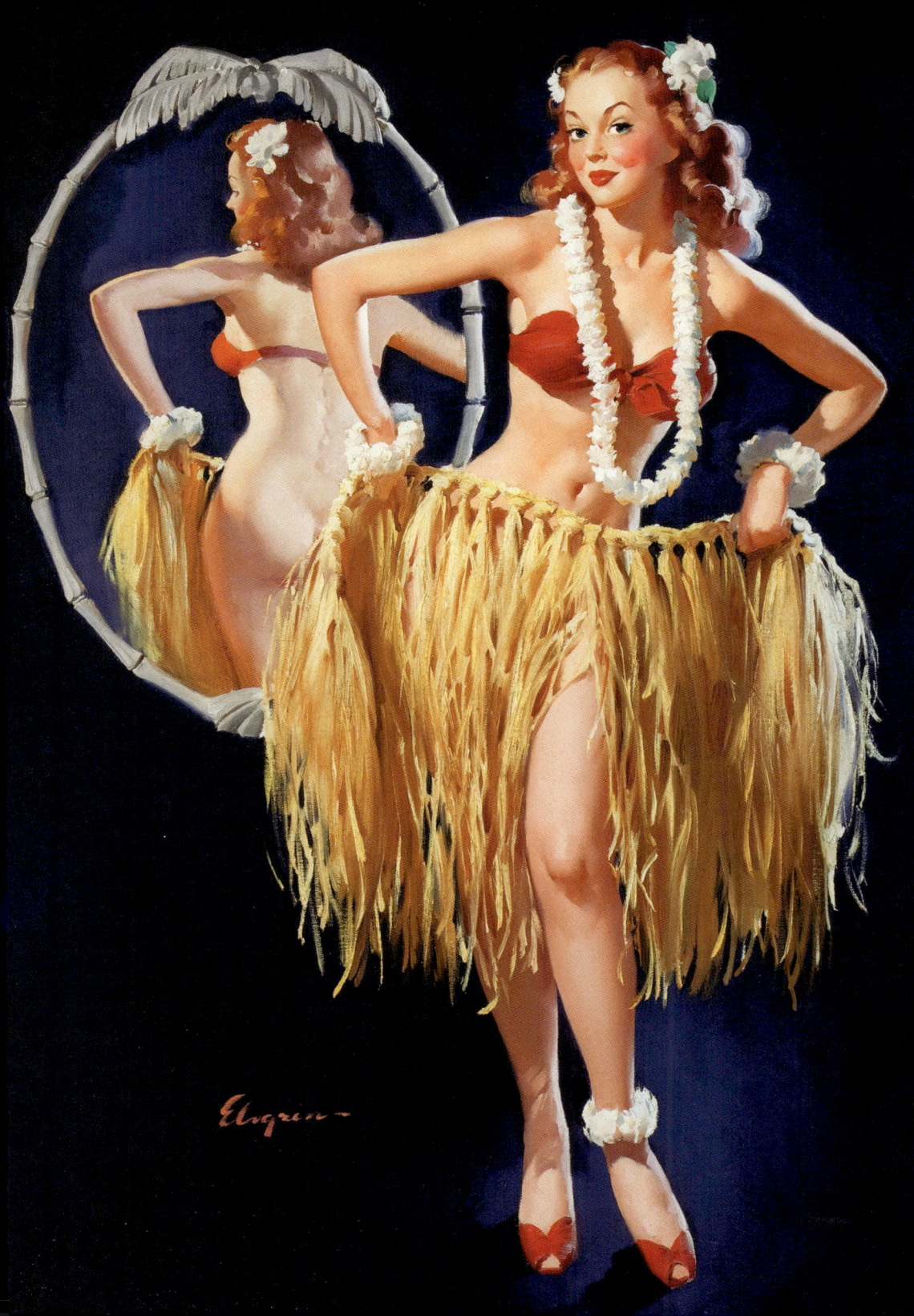

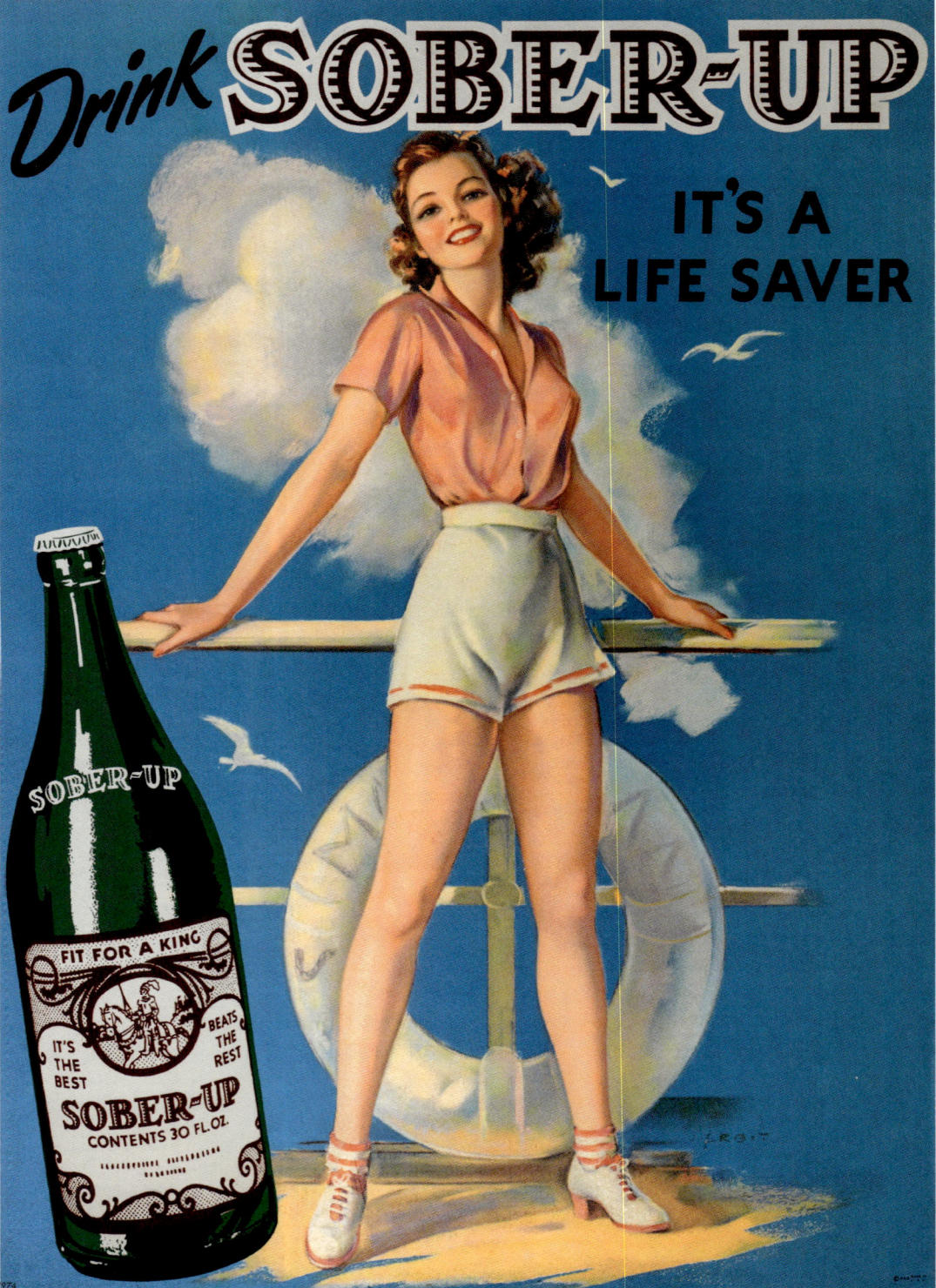

PIN-UP : UNE HISTOIRE TRÈS PARTISANE

PAR DIAN HANSON

La faute à la crise, au réchauffement climatique ou à l'omniprésence de la pornographie : beaucoup d'entre nous aspirent à plus de simplicité. Donnez-nous moins de misère moderne et plus d'innocence bon enfant, s'il vous plaît. Ramenez-nous aux jours heureux où fumer était chic, la viande rouge bath et les cocktails épatants ; avant la foire d'empoigne politicienne, les intérêts pétroliers et la corruption ; l'autisme et Alzheimer ; les poulets de batterie et les licenciements ; le pourrissement des océans et la mort des abeilles ; quand le terme « modernisme » évoquait Picasso et non un courant culinaire ; quand les femmes étaient girondes et en montraient moins.

Dans les années 1970, le sexe semblait être une nouveauté : on voulait tout voir. Aujourd'hui, alors que le terme « porno » déclenche deux milliards de résultats sur Google, on redécouvre les pin-up, des images sexy qu'on n'a pas besoin de décrocher du mur quand maman vient à la maison. Ce qui était osé en 1945 est désormais non seulement acceptable mais à la mode. Amy Schumer a incarné Marilyn Monroe pour la couverture de *Vanity Fair* en mai 2016, tandis que la couverture de pin-up de Billie Eilish pour le numéro de juin 2021 de *Vogue* a enregistré des ventes record auprès des hommes et des femmes. Dita Von Teese a fait renaître l'art de l'effeuillage. On utilise les créatures de Gil Elvgren pour décorer tout et n'importe quoi, des sacs à main aux boules de Noël en passant par les biceps tatoués. Souvent des biceps de femme.

Pourquoi les femmes n'aimeraient-elles pas les pin-up ? Elles sont étroitement associées à leur libération, arrivée en 1890 sur une bicyclette.

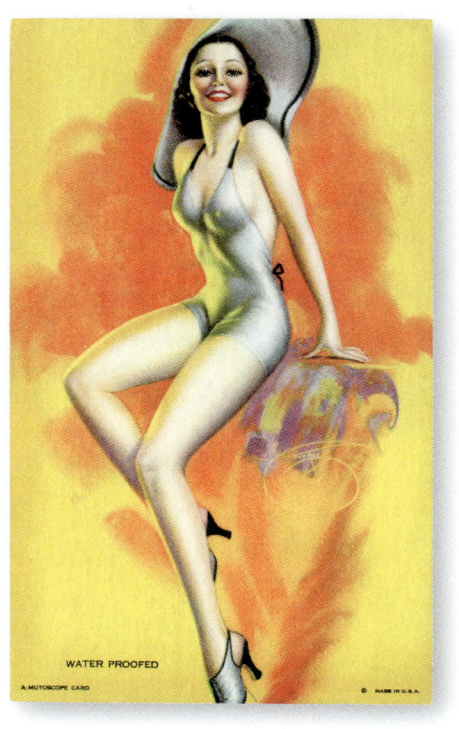

WATER PROOFED

A. MUTOSCOPE CARD   © MADE IN U.S.A.

Opposite: The unsubtly named Sober-Up soda, "Fit for a King," was introduced in the early 1940s and survived into the 1960s. In the 1930s and '40s, pin-up girls commonly flogged soda; this 1940s ad was created by artist Jules Erbit.

Above: Water Proofed Mutoscope card by Billy DeVorss.

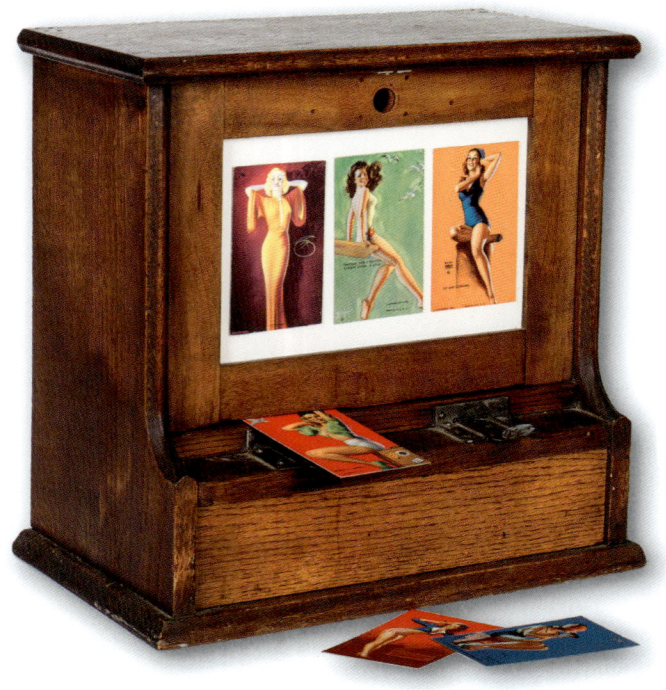

Au XIXᵉ siècle, la plupart des Occidentales s'aventuraient rarement loin de chez elles. Si elles se déplaçaient, c'était à pied jusqu'au marché local ou dans les voitures de leur père ou de leur mari. Leurs nombreux jupons entravaient leurs mouvements et le sport était inconcevable. Puis vint la bicyclette, ou plus précisément la « bicyclette de sécurité », avec une transmission par chaîne et des pneumatiques qui les rendaient acceptables d'un point de vue physique (à défaut de moralement) pour les femmes. Les médecins et les prêtres se récrièrent : les secousses sur les pavés endommageaient les délicats organes féminins tandis que le frottement de la selle déclenchait des pulsions immorales. Les suffragettes la baptisèrent « la machine de la liberté », car elle permettait aux femmes d'aller à leur guise sans une escorte masculine, précisément ce que les hommes ne voulaient pas.

Des tenues adéquates suivirent bientôt, comprenant des culottes descendant jusqu'aux genoux, des bas et de hautes bottes. Pour la première fois depuis des siècles, les jambes des femmes étaient visibles, même si elles restaient couvertes. Cette « enfourchure » suscita autant d'indignation que d'extase. Les femmes se masculinisaient ! Elles se comportaient en putains ! Elles devenaient enfin intéressantes ! En exigeant leur place dans le monde masculin, elles libérèrent le regard des hommes, le laissant les apprécier différemment.

Le premier artiste à célébrer cette nouvelle femme fut Charles Dana Gibson, dont les illustrations pour *Life*, un petit digest humoristique, commencèrent à paraître en 1886. En 1887, sa « girl » fit la couverture : son torse à la taille de guêpe surgissait d'une fleur dont les pétales étaient retroussés par des chérubins. En 1895, il épousa une jeune femme de la grande bourgeoisie de Virginie. Sa Gibson Girl était déjà reconnaissable, mais c'est surtout en observant son épouse et ses impérieuses sœurs qu'il raffina sa création pour en faire celle que toute l'Amérique aimait et attendait chaque semaine dans les pages centrales de *Life*.

La Gibson Girl était belle, avait du caractère et un buste généreux. Ses cheveux noirs étaient remontés en un chignon lâche ; elle avait des lèvres pleines et ses paupières lourdes lui donnaient

Above: The Mutoscope card dispenser, circa 1945, worked via a mechanism similar to a gumball machine's. The 5.25-by-3.25-inch cards were stacked inside, a penny was inserted in a sliding carrier, pushed in, and when the empty carrier was pulled back a single card was dispensed through a slot. Machines were made of metal or wood and could be found from 1925 to the 1950s in amusement park, bars, and tobacco shops.

THE ART OF PIN-UP

un regard sensuel. Elle était souvent entourée de prétendants qu'elle ignorait royalement. Dans un dessin de 1901, *Stepped On*, une Gibson Girl marche sans le voir sur un bonhomme minuscule tout en lançant un regard langoureux vers le spectateur. Forte mais féminine, jamais lubrique, indépendante, on ne pouvait la ranger ni parmi les épouses ni parmi les putains. À la fois élégante et sexy, éternellement célibataire, elle devint la première fille de rêve, l'archétype du *Good Girl Art*. Le numéro du 18 septembre 1902 de *Life* contenait un collage de superbes visages féminins regardant droit vers le spectateur, accompagné de la légende « Papier peint pour célibataires ». Il décora plus d'une garçonnière.

Chaque réussite entraîne son lot d'imitateurs et Gibson n'en manqua pas. La Girl de Howard Chandler Christy fit ses débuts dans *The Century* en 1895, puis apparut fréquemment dans *Scribner's*. Comme la Gibson Girl, elle était belle, royale et distante ; contrairement à elle, elle évoluait avec son temps. Elle devint sportive dans les années 1910, arborant même une coupe au carré en 1921.

Le magazine *Puck*, un concurrent de *Life*, voulut lui aussi sa Girl et la commanda à Harrison Fisher. La Fisher Girl était moins sophistiquée. Son créateur la décrivit comme étant « authentique, gentille, tendre quand il le faut, pleine d'entrain quand l'occasion s'y prête, toujours féminine ». Elle était plus appréciée des femmes que des hommes et fit la couverture de *Cosmopolitan* de 1912 à 1934.

La Grande Guerre et le recours aux nouvelles méthodes de propagande inspirée par la psychologie sociale donnèrent un élan crucial à l'apparition de la vraie pin-up. L'Allemagne, le Royaume-Uni et les États-Unis s'en donnèrent à cœur joie, chacun cherchant à démoraliser l'ennemi, à réveiller le patriotisme de ses concitoyens et à galvaniser ses troupes. En 1917, le président américain Woodrow Wilson créa la Division of Pictorial Publicity et son directeur demanda à Charles Dana Gibson de recruter des illustrateurs. Christy, Fisher et Montgomery Flagg réalisèrent les premières affiches associant de jolies filles à la victoire militaire.

La contribution la plus mémorable fut celle de Christy.

Ses girls, vêtues de robes légères et moulantes ou d'uniformes, exhortaient les hommes : « *Vous voulez vous battre ? Rejoignez les Marines !* » ; « *Battez-vous ou achetez des bons !* » ; « *Ah, si j'étais un homme, je m'enrôlerais dans la Marine !* » Ce dernier slogan s'accompagnait du sous-titre peu subtil : « *Soyez un homme ! Soyez Marine* » Ces affiches très populaires étaient décollées et se retrouvaient, bien souvent, accrochées chez les particuliers.

Dans *L'Âge d'or de la pin-up américaine*, publié par TASCHEN en 1996, le regretté Charles Martignette décrit la pin-up comme « un portrait en pied de jolie femme présentant un élément thématique ou évoquant implicitement une histoire. La pin-up porte généralement une tenue qui révèle ses formes avantageuses, soit un vêtement qui peut être porté en public, comme un maillot de bain, un short ou une robe légère, soit un vêtement plus intime et provocant tel que de la lingerie fine. Il arrive que la pin-up soit entièrement nue mais cela reste l'exception qui confirme la règle ». Il distingue ensuite la pin-up de « l'art glamour » dont le sujet « porte une robe du soir, une tenue de gala ou quelque autre vêtement généralement moins provocant que celui de la pin-up ». Enfin, il établit une troisième catégorie, celle de la « *pretty girl* » : « un portrait glamour exécuté par un illustrateur de magazine à grand tirage comme *The Saturday Evening Post* et *Cosmopolitan*, ou destiné aux publicités ».

Martignette ne nous dit pas où il a trouvé ces critères. Il les a probablement inventés après avoir consacré sa vie à étudier l'histoire de l'illustration américaine. Aujourd'hui, alors que les pin-up ont à nouveau le vent en poupe, une nouvelle définition s'impose. Dans les ventes aux enchères, toute représentation d'une jolie fille en maillot de bain ou en robe du soir peinte par

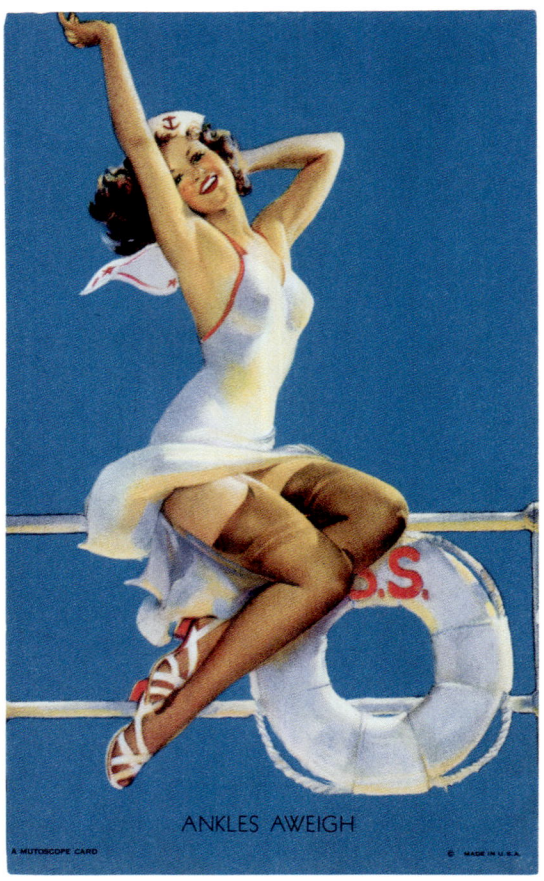

ANKLES AWEIGH

A MUTOSCOPE CARD © MADE IN U.S.A.

Gil Elvgren, Zoë Mozert, George Petty ou Alberto Vargas est qualifiée de pin-up, ce qui augmente sa valeur. Il est vrai qu'un nu d'Elvgren, comme *Gay Nymph* de 1947, vendu en 2011 par Heritage Auctions pour la somme record de 286 800 dollars, vaudra toujours plus que ses chastes *Miss Sylvania*. Néanmoins, celui qui parvient à mettre la main sur une de ces dernières peut se targuer de posséder une vraie pin-up.

Dans ce livre, je définirai la pin-up comme l'image provocante sans être explicite d'une jolie fille conçue spécialement pour être montrée dans un environnement masculin. Si elle est nue, elle doit être pudique : le spectateur moyen ne doit pas voir en elle un support de masturbation (même si elle peut aussi servir à ça). Le terme alternatif de *Good Girl Art* (« l'art de la brave fille ») est éloquent. La pin-up n'est pas une traînée. Elle est naturellement sexy et, si elle s'exhibe, c'est par accident : un hameçon s'accroche au soutien-gorge de son bikini, le moteur d'un hors-bord déchire sa jupe, un chiot la fait trébucher, ou la brise, toujours coquine, soulève ses jupes, révélant le haut de ses bas et des jarretelles mais jamais toute sa panoplie.

La torride scène de harem de *Still Life*, peinte par Elvgren à la fin de sa carrière, ne parut jamais dans un magazine grand public en raison de la présence choquante de poils pubiens. Ce n'est pas une pin-up. Lorsque Hugh Hefner insista pour qu'Alberto Vargas ajoute une toison à ses pin-up pour *Playboy* en 1971, l'artiste n'accepta que par peur de perdre son travail. Vargas connaissait ses admirateurs mieux qu'Hefner : ses images plus explicites ont moins de succès car elles contreviennent aux règles de la pin-up. Même Art Frahm, dont les demoiselles subissent la double indignité de perdre leur culotte et de subir les assauts d'une bourrasque lubrique, cachait au spectateur ce que voient les hommes stratégiquement placés dans ses compositions. Il connaissait la chanson : les pin-up doivent rester pures.

Above: Ankles Aweigh Mutoscope card by Gil Elvgren, oil on canvas, done for the Louis F. Dow Company in 1939. The International Mutoscope Reel Company contracted with all the major calendar companies in the 1940s to reprint their most popular pin-ups on Mutoscope cards.

Opposite: Station Wow, another Elvgren Mutoscope card copied from a calendar illustration done for Louis F. Dow, circa 1940. The cards are as collectible today as they were during World War II, and since they were printed on sturdy cardboard, many thousands survive.

THE ART OF PIN-UP

La fin de la guerre entraîna de rapides changements sociaux aux États-Unis. Si le nombre de victimes était beaucoup plus faible qu'en Europe, plus d'un quart de million de jeunes hommes avaient été tués ou blessés. Tous avaient vu des scènes jusque-là impensables, mais pas que des scènes d'horreur. Ceux qui avaient servi en France avaient découvert le cabaret et les revues libertines comme *La Vie parisienne* et *Le Sourire*. De retour au pays, ils se sentaient frustrés par la vie provinciale, préférant boire et danser plutôt que de chercher du travail et se marier. Les Américaines avaient changé elles aussi. Beaucoup avaient occupé des emplois durant la guerre et pris goût à leur indépendance financière. Elles coupaient leurs cheveux, mettaient du rouge à lèvres, des bas en soie et des chaussures de tango à hauts talons. En 1919, le 18e amendement de la Constitution américaine interdisant la vente d'alcool attisa les flammes de la rébellion. Les *flappers* et les *flippers*, comme on appelait alors les jeunes dans le vent, abandonnèrent les salons de tango pour les bars clandestins et, à l'alcool prohibé, ajoutèrent la marijuana, la cocaïne et l'opium. Les bien-pensants s'insurgèrent, naturellement, mais la plupart étaient fascinés par cette jeunesse extravagante, notamment par les *flappers*, ces garçonnes émancipées, et les médias en firent leurs choux gras.

Les *flappers* sensuelles de Rolf Armstrong apparurent vers 1920 en couverture des magazines de cinéma. L'illustrateur avait déjà rencontré un certain succès avec son sage calendrier *Dream Girl*, publié par Brown & Bigelow en 1919. Ce fut néanmoins Betty, son pastel d'une garçonne aux yeux bordés de khôl et aux lèvres laquées de rouge, créée en 1924 pour un calendrier paru en 1926, qui fit de lui une star.

Pendant qu'Armstrong mettait les dernières touches à Betty, Enoch Bolles peignait une *flapper* brandissant un fouet pour la couverture du magazine *Film Fun*. À ses pieds, de petits bonshommes courent autour d'une alliance géante. À l'allure triomphante de la fille, il est clair qu'aucun n'a une chance d'emporter son cœur. D'autres illustrateurs comme Ruth Eastman, Guy Hoff, John Held Jr., McClelland Barclay, Walter Dean Goldbeck et Frank Leyendecker (frère de J. C.) représentaient également des femmes émancipées pour les couvertures de *Life*, *Judge* et *College Humor*. D'autres journaux satiriques moins importants, dont *Capt. Billy's Whiz Bang*, *Hot Dog*, *Smokehouse Monthly*, *Burten's Follies*, *Old Bob Edwards' Calgary Eye Opener* et *Cap'n Joey's Jazza Ka Jazza* présentaient des *flappers* plus osées, souvent peintes par des artistes anonymes.

Les éditeurs de calendriers, dont les créations de style Art déco faisaient la

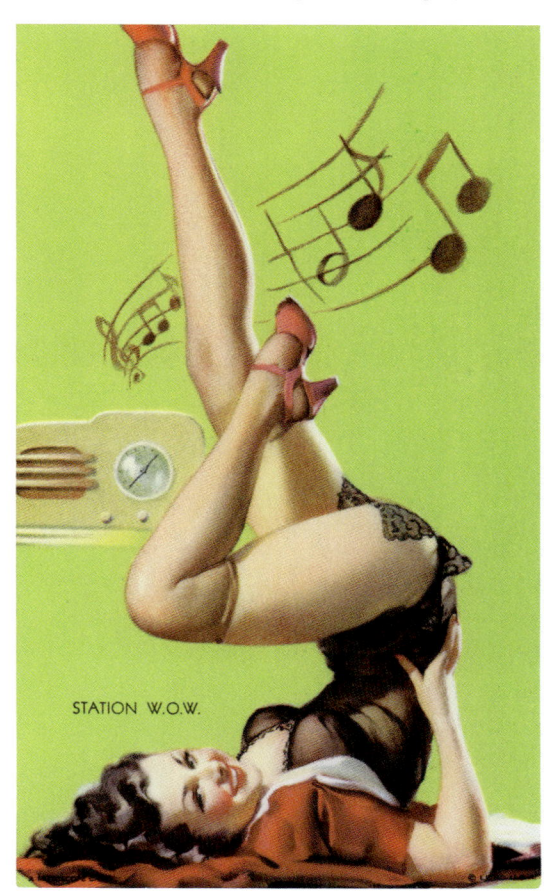

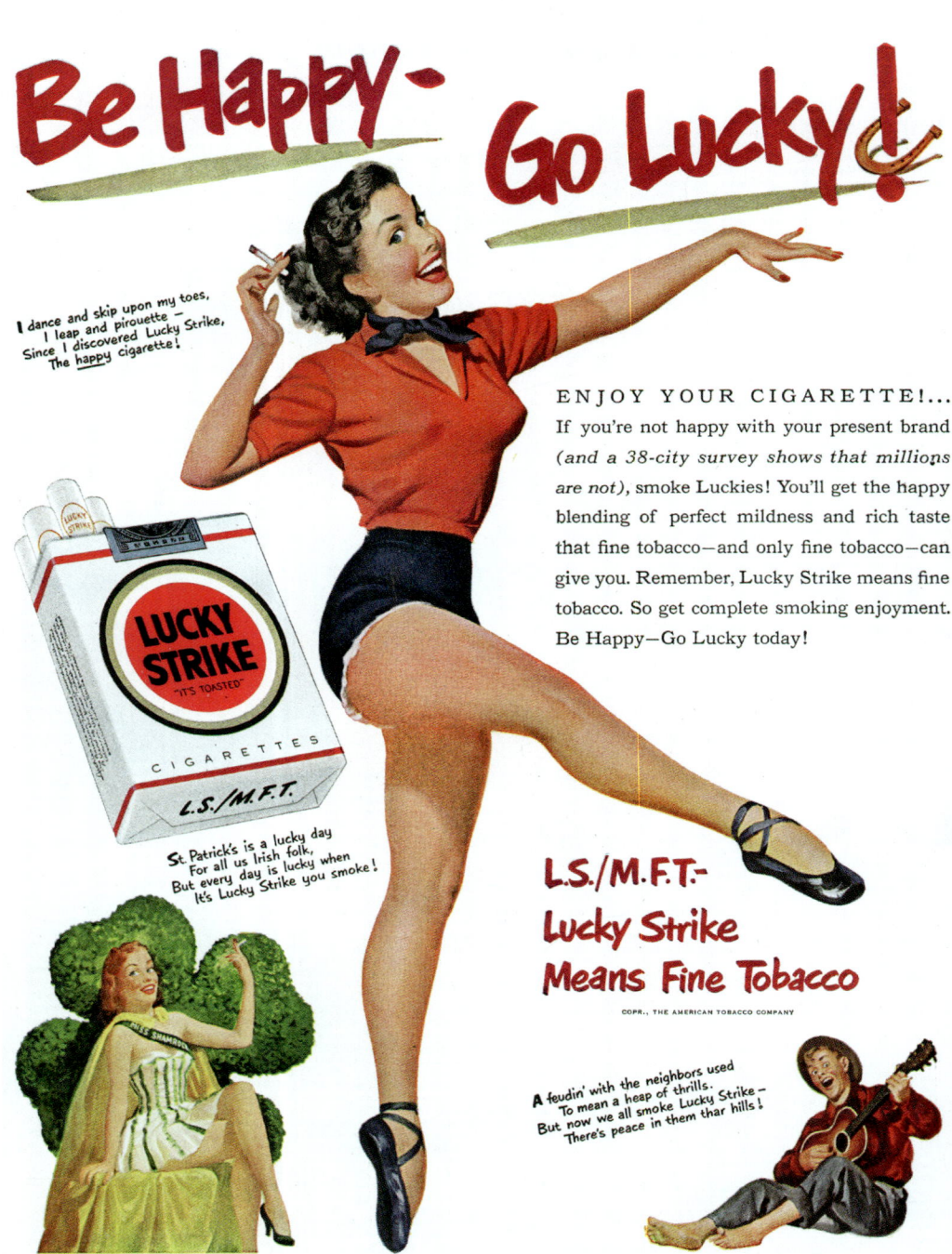

Be Happy - Go Lucky!

I dance and skip upon my toes,
I leap and pirouette —
Since I discovered Lucky Strike,
The happy cigarette!

ENJOY YOUR CIGARETTE!...
If you're not happy with your present brand
(*and a 38-city survey shows that millions
are not*), smoke Luckies! You'll get the happy
blending of perfect mildness and rich taste
that fine tobacco—and only fine tobacco—can
give you. Remember, Lucky Strike means fine
tobacco. So get complete smoking enjoyment.
Be Happy—Go Lucky today!

LUCKY STRIKE
"IT'S TOASTED"

CIGARETTES

L.S./M.F.T.

St. Patrick's is a lucky day
For all us Irish folk,
But every day is lucky when
It's Lucky Strike you smoke!

L.S./M.F.T.- Lucky Strike Means Fine Tobacco

COPR., THE AMERICAN TOBACCO COMPANY

A feudin' with the neighbors used
To mean a heap of thrills.
But now we all smoke Lucky Strike—
There's peace in them thar hills!

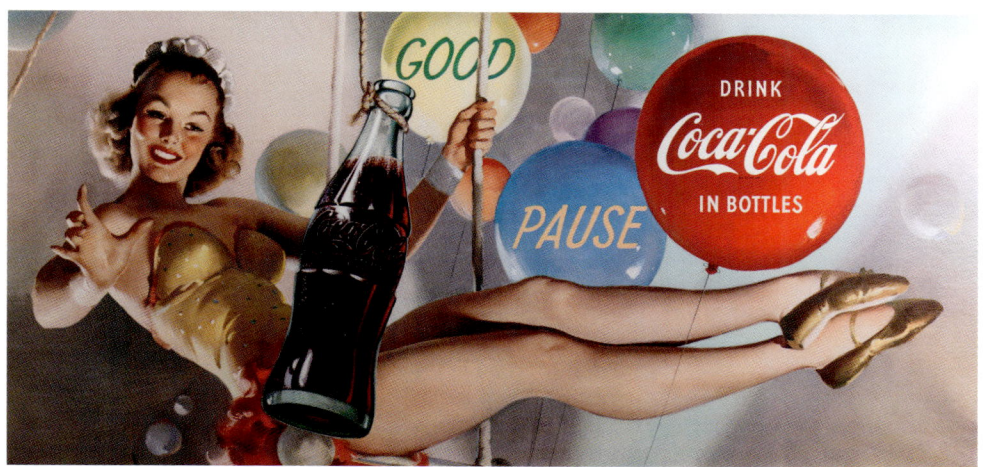

part belle aux décors exotiques et aux beautés peu vêtues, s'emparèrent des *flappers* à la fin des années 1920. Henry Clive, Edward Eggleston, Mabel Rollins Harris, Gene Pressler et William Fulton Soare dessinaient de chastes squaws, des reines égyptiennes, des sauvageonnes hawaiiennes et de farouches nymphettes. Bien que luxueux et détaillé, l'exotisme de ces images était superficiel et se limitait en grande partie à un minicostume indigène, les éditeurs ne pouvant concevoir que leurs pin-up ne soient pas blanches. Joseph C. Hoover and Sons, à Philadelphie, et Thomas D. Murphy, à Red Oak dans l'Iowa, publièrent certains des plus beaux calendriers de pin-up Arts déco, mais Brown & Bigelow, basé à Saint Paul, dans le Minnesota, avait le vent en poupe et se préparait à dominer le monde.

En 1889, Thomas Murphy et Edmond Osborne publièrent le premier calendrier avec de la publicité sous l'image. C'était une idée brillante : un calendrier reste sur votre mur pendant un an et, chaque fois que vous regardez la date, vous voyez le message de l'annonceur. Les concurrents leur emboîtèrent rapidement le pas, notamment McCleery-Cummings, Kemper-Thomas, John Baumgarth, Gerlach-Barklow, Joseph C. Hoover and Sons, Louis F. Dow, Skinner-Kennedy, C. Moss, Goes Lithograph et Shaw-Barton, mais aucun ne connaîtrait un succès équivalent à celui de Brown & Bigelow.

Les pin-up de B&B, comme on les appelait, étaient les meilleures et les plus belles, créées par les plus grands illustrateurs, lesquels étaient formés sur place puis récompensés avec des contrats d'une générosité inédite. Ils inclurent Rolf Armstrong, Al Buell, Earl MacPherson, Bill Medcalf, Earl Moran, Zoë Mozert, Knute Munson, Edward Runci et, surtout, le grand Gil Elvgren qui travailla exclusivement pour cet éditeur de 1944 à 1971. Étrangement, cet empire ne fut pas bâti par M. Brown, qui mourut en 1904, ni par M. Bigelow, qui le suivit en 1933, mais par un gangster couvert de diamants et la bouche bardée d'or : Charlie Ward, ex-pensionnaire du pénitencier de Leavenworth et dont le parcours ressemble à un film noir. D'ailleurs, à l'époque de sa mort en

Opposite: A print ad from 1950 featuring a pin-up by Jack Wittrup, extolling the virtues of Lucky Strike, the "happy" cigarette.

Above: This was Gil Elvgren's most impressive advertising commission for Coca-Cola. The oil on canvas was reproduced as a massive sign for display in soda fountains, mounted in an accompanying Coke-themed frame. Date of the painting's creation is unknown, but the sign is dated 1959. Coca-Cola issued a second version of the sign with the figure and large red balloon silhouetted and the background removed. 62.5 x 35 inches.

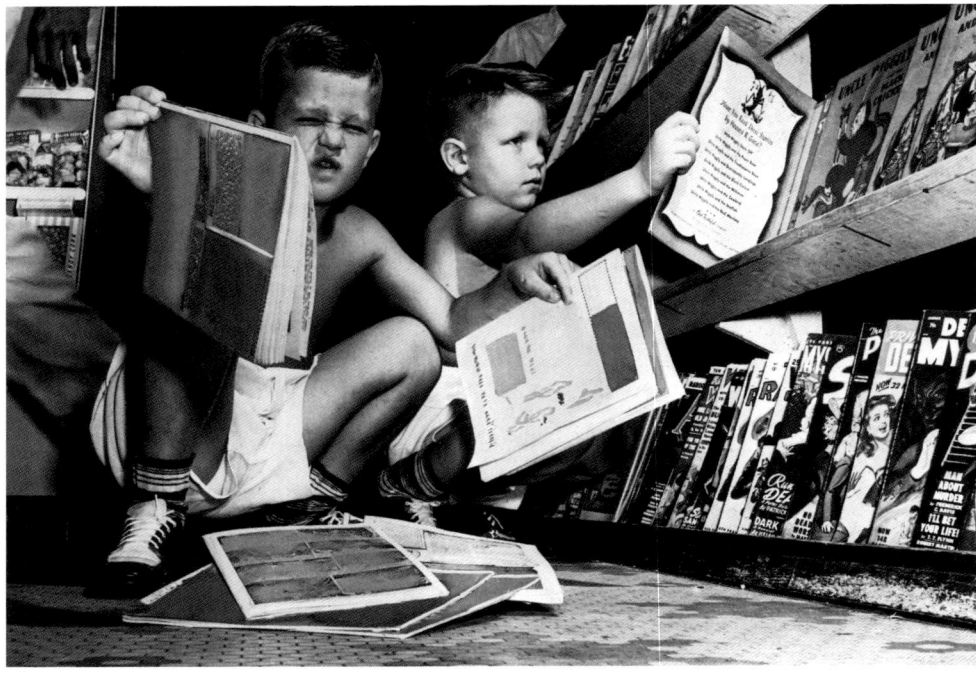

1959, un scénario basé sur sa vie était en projet. Sa femme le fit annuler, ce que l'on peut comprendre. En voici un résumé :

En 1896, un jeune représentant nommé Herbert Huse Bigelow tenta de vendre des calendriers d'Osborn-Murphy à un imprimeur de Saint Paul, Hiram D. Brown. Ce dernier lui proposa plutôt de former leur propre société. Il fournirait le capital et les presses, tandis que Bigelow se chargerait de la vente. Leur premier calendrier représentait George Washington et se vendit mal. Au cours des trois années suivantes, ils se diversifièrent, commercialisant des casquettes, des tabliers, des porte-monnaie et des plaids, tous portant des slogans publicitaires. En 1903, ils éditèrent leur premier calendrier de charme, *Cosette*, réalisé par Angelo Asti. On n'y voyait qu'un soupçon de décolleté, mais il se vendit si bien que B&B put emménager dans de nouveaux locaux plus vastes.

La compagnie s'agrandit encore après la mort de Brown, imprimant les premiers calendriers en quadrichromie et enrichissant son catalogue avec des paysages sauvages, des scènes d'aventures… et toujours plus de filles. Bigelow voyait loin et savait exploiter rapidement les progrès dans l'imprimerie, mais il était également froid et arrogant, avec un sens très développé du privi-

Above: With the war's end, young Americans rushed into marriage and childbearing, resulting in the baby boom of the late 1940s and early '50s. This domesticity led to conservatism, resulting in a sharp decline in pin-up sales and concerns about sex and violence on American newsstands. Retailers were initially instructed to remove objectional magazines and comic books from their inventory, before the comic book industry formed the Comics Code Authority to police and censor its own product in 1954. Here the young sons of a Memphis, Tennessee, drugstore owner examine controversial comic books in 1948.
© Bettmann/Corbis Images

Opposite: Imaginative Tales #2, 1954, with pin-up cover by Harold McCauley. *Imaginative Tales*, folded after 28 issues and was published by Earl Kemp's Greenleaf Publishing, which went on to produce erotic paperbacks, and the infamously banned *Illustrated Presidential Report of the Commission on Obscenity and Pornography* in 1970, earning Kemp a prison sentence for obscenity.

THE ART OF PIN-UP

lège. Cela lui valut une condamnation pour évasion fiscale en 1923 et une peine de deux ans au pénitencier de Leavenworth.

C'est ici qu'entre en scène Charles Ward, destiné à Leavenworth depuis sa naissance. Né en 1886 dans le quartier chaud de l'arsenal de Bremerton, près de Seattle, il rendait des menus services pour des bars locaux à 14 ans. À 16 ans, il entraîna un chien de combat qui tua le champion de la Marine dans un combat truqué, lui rapportant 1 000 dollars. Il en dépensa la moitié pour offrir un croc en or à son chien. Au fil des ans, il en fit de même pour lui, jusqu'à arborer un étincelant râtelier complet.

Ward vénérait l'or. En 1903, il en chercha en Arizona, avant de participer à la ruée vers l'or en Alaska en 1906 et de se retrouver en 1910 à National, dans le Nevada, une ville minière où l'or était aussi abondant que les malfrats. Là, il vola du précieux minerai aux compagnies minières pour s'offrir un voyage au Mexique, où, accompagné d'un ami, il rejoignit la révolution de Pancho Villa. La cause paysanne était le dernier de ses soucis, mais il admirait l'extravagant Villa qui lui laissait les peaux du bétail qu'il volait pour nourrir ses troupes. Ward les revendait au Texas, empochant 70 000 dollars en trois ans. Il quitta le Mexique à la mort de son ami, en 1916, et se mit à claquer son argent. Il fit la fête durant deux ans, atterrissant à Denver, où il fut arrêté et accusé de trafic de cocaïne. Il dépensa jusqu'à son dernier sou pour sa défense. Le juge le condamna à dix ans dans une prison à sécurité maximale.

Lorsque Bigelow arriva à Leavenworth, Ward y était bien installé, un caïd avec de nombreux amis et privilèges. En apprenant que le riche homme d'affaires était malmené par ses codétenus, il le fit transférer dans sa cellule. Là, il lui offrit un marché : il le protégerait en échange d'un travail à sa sortie. Terrifié, Bigelow accepta sur-le-champ et Charlie le prit sous son aile jusqu'à sa libération en 1925.

Lorsque Ward se présenta chez lui à Saint Paul un peu plus tard, Bigelow ne fut pas ravi de le voir. Il tenta de s'en débarrasser en lui offrant de l'argent puis, comme Charlie ne voulait rien entendre, lui proposa un poste subalterne et éreintant. À sa surprise, Ward travailla dur et apporta des idées innovantes. Il gravit rapidement les échelons. Il ne quittait pas Bigelow, déclarant à qui voulait l'entendre qu'il était son meilleur ami. On ne saura jamais ce que pensait Bigelow d'être flanqué d'un tel acolyte mais, en 1930, Ward était devenu directeur et vice-président de la société. Ce fut Charlie qui fit de Rolf Armstrong l'artiste de pin-up le mieux payé des États-Unis ; lui qui, en 1937, embaucha Earl Moran avec un salaire de 10 000 dollars par an, plus la location de son atelier et les honoraires de ses modèles ; lui qui débaucha Gil Elvgren de chez Louis F. Dow en 1944, l'attirant avec la somme de 2 000 dollars par peinture. Contrairement aux rumeurs, ce ne fut pas lui qui fit chavirer le canoë d'Herbert Bigelow sur le lac Basswood le

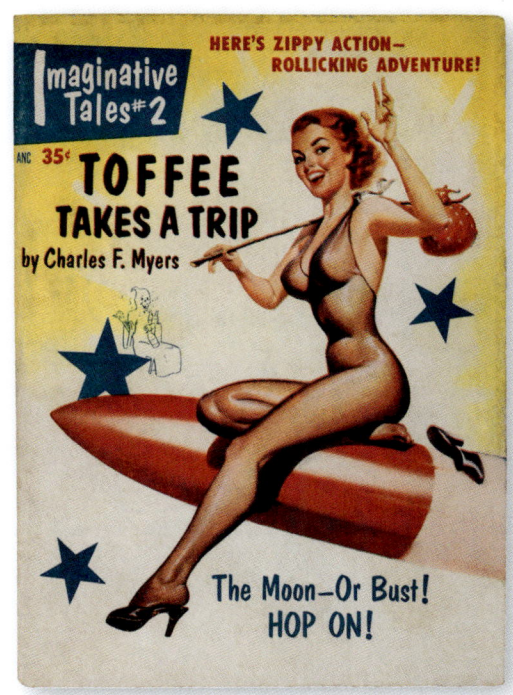

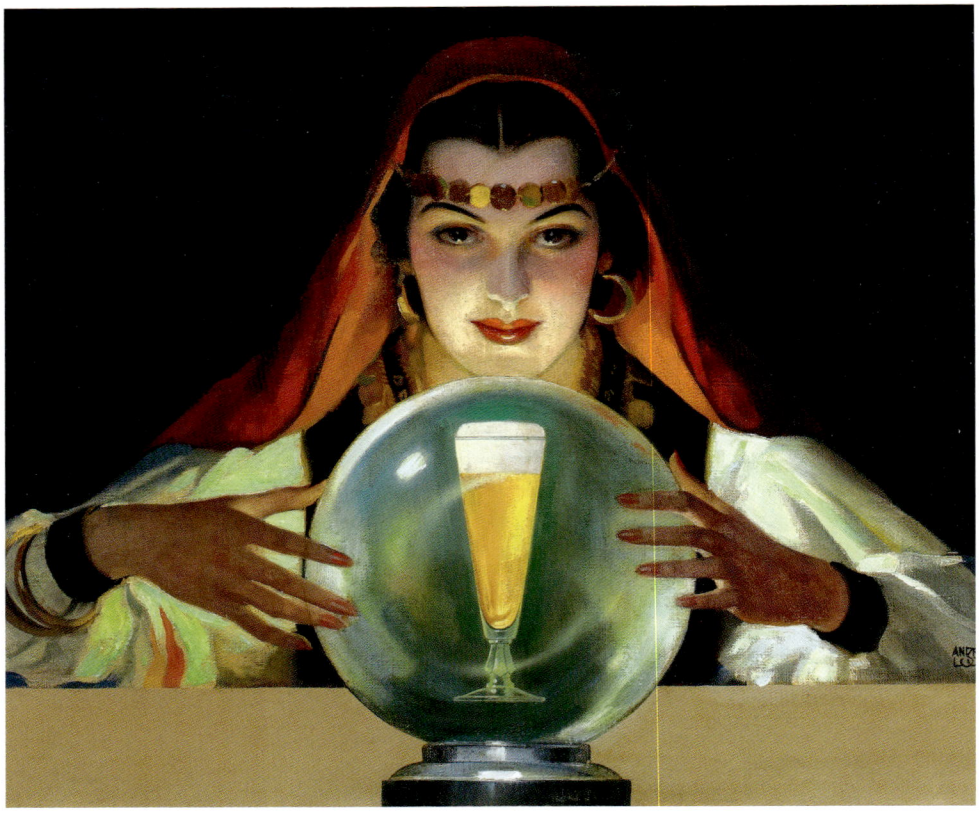

19 septembre 1933, le laissant se noyer pendant que son guide nageait jusqu'à la rive. Ce fut toutefois Charlie qui hérita de la société et d'un tiers de la fortune de Bigelow, conformément à un testament rédigé peu avant l'accident.

On ne sut jamais qui avait recruté le guide de Bigelow.

Ainsi débutèrent le règne de Ward et l'âge d'or de B&B. Charlie se mit aussitôt à recruter d'anciens détenus et aidait secrètement des hommes en prison. Dans son livre *John Dillinger Slept Here*, Paul Maccabee raconte qu'en 1933, Ward donna au gangster Bugsy Siegel 100 000 dollars pour aider deux tueurs de la mafia à s'évader d'une prison du Minnesota. Compte tenu del'année, on ne peut s'empêcher de faire un rapprochement avec l'accident fatal de Bigelow. À son honneur, Ward traitait les ex-détenus comme les autres employés, les harcelant sans cesse, récompensant les plus performants avec des primes et des peintures de pin-up originales, virant les autres. Le personnel se renouvelait tellement vite que ses anciens employés devinrent ses plus grands concurrents : plusieurs d'entre eux s'associèrent pour former la compagnie Shaw-Barton.

Above: This beautiful oil on canvas by Andrew Loomis was commissioned by the Budweiser Brewing Company in the mid-'30s. The ungainly title is *Drink Budweiser, America's Social Companion.* 30.5 x 21.5 inches

Opposite: Harold McCauley was more a sci-fi pulp illustrator than a pin-up artist, but he was known for including sexy girls whenever possible, as in this oil on board for the cover of *Imaginative Tales* #5, May 1955. Following publication of Frederic Wertham's *Seduction of the Innocent* in 1954, condemning sex and violence in American comic books, pin-up covers on magazines popular with children came under fire as well.

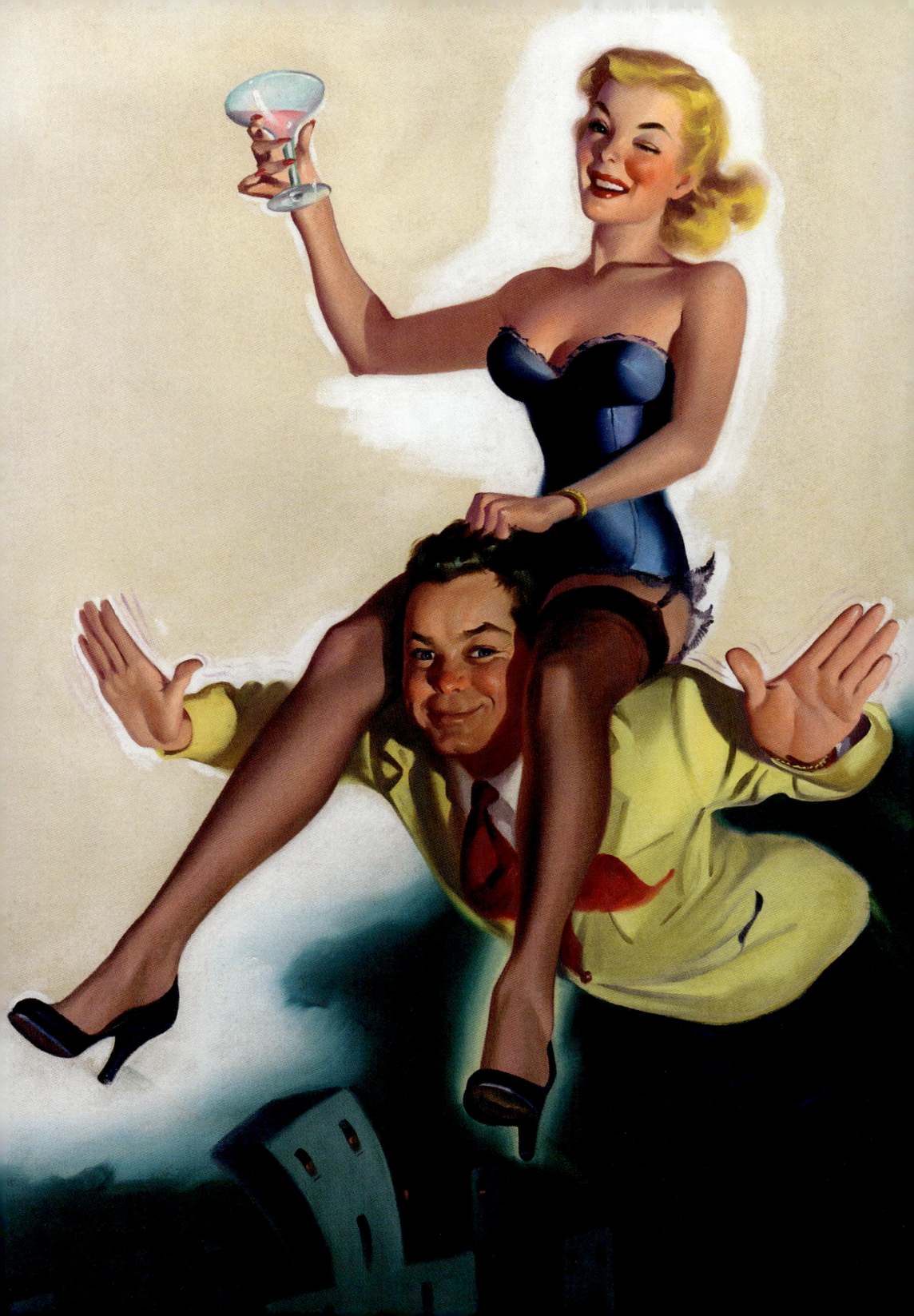

S'il était impitoyable avec ses représentants, Ward payait ses artistes plus que n'importe quel autre éditeur, dépassant de loin les magazines. En 1939, George Petty recevait 100 dollars par pin-up publiée dans *Esquire*, alors que B&B le payait 1 000 dollars pour une peinture similaire. On comprend alors pourquoi tous les illustrateurs rêvaient de signer chez B&B. Ward donnait également d'une manière si ostentatoire à des organismes caritatifs que le magazine *Life* le baptisa « l'homme le plus généreux du monde ». Ceux au fait de la comptabilité de B&B rétorquèrent que Charlie Ward était d'abord généreux envers lui-même, estimant en 1955 que son train de vie coûtait un million de dollars par an à la compagnie. Il possédait plusieurs propriétés, dont une ferme de 810 hectares dans le Wisconsin avec un troupeau de bisons, un ranch de 32 375 hectares en Arizona et une maison au bord de la mer en Californie pour bronzer nu. Il voyageait partout avec un entourage de domestiques et d'assistants. Il possédait une collection de voitures de luxe équipées de vitres pare-balles ; des holsters faits sur mesure ; donnait des fêtes pour des centaines d'invités qu'il couvrait de cadeaux précieux et nourrissait de gibier rare ; avait des briquets en or plein les poches, gravés de son nom, qu'il distribuait aux serveurs et aux grooms en guise de pourboire ; portait plus de bijoux en or et de diamants qu'une star du rap des années 1990.

Au cas où son sourire ne serait pas assez clinquant.

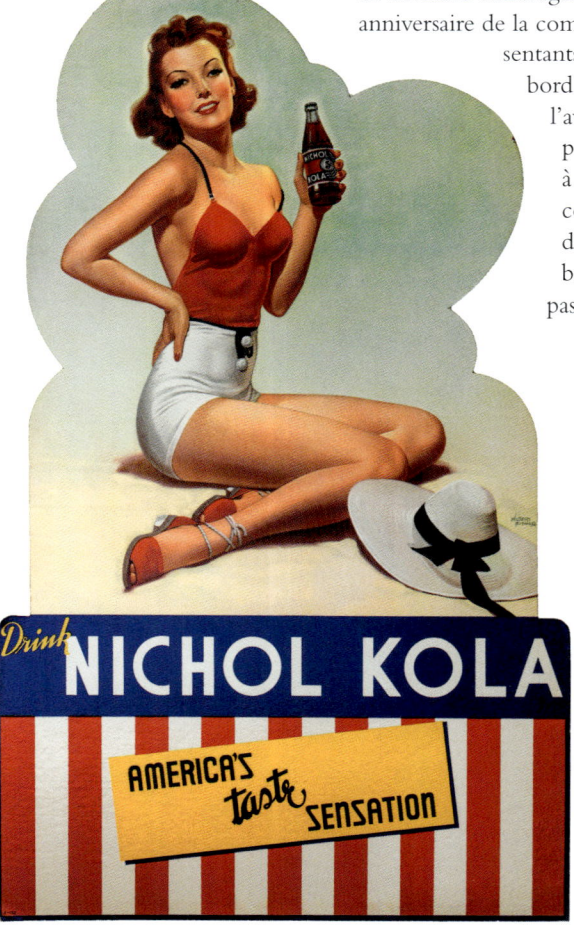

Sa dernière extravagance fut la célébration du soixantième anniversaire de la compagnie en 1956. Quelque 1 800 représentants, artistes et leurs familles grimpèrent à bord du plus gros avion civil de l'histoire de l'aviation américaine pour une bacchanale de quatre jours à Saint Paul. Les fontaines à champagne coulaient à flots tandis que les invités dînaient de cochon rôti, de faisan et de bison. Pourtant, les affaires ne marchaient pas fort pour B&B.

Ward avait fait entrer la société en bourse en 1948. Quelques années plus tard, son train de vie ruineux fit chuter les valeurs de B&B. Lorsqu'il mourut dans son sommeil dans une chambre d'hôtel de Beverly Hills le 26 mai 1959, à l'âge de 73 ans, il n'y avait personne pour assurer la relève de son règne autocratique. Craignant que ses actions ne sombrent encore plus, B&B se vendit rapidement à la Standard Packaging Corporation, qui effectua un dégraissage draconien avant de la revendre à Saxon Industries en 1970. Cette dernière fit établir un catalogue de toutes les peintures de pin-up que possédait la société. Plus de

1 000 œuvres signées Armstrong, Buell, Elvgren, MacPherson, Moran, Mozert, Munson et Runci furent mises en vente à des prix allant de 25 à 300 dollars. Quand les ventes se tarirent, le reste fut bradé à 100 dollars le lot de dix.

Saxon se déclara en faillite en 1983 et la compagnie végéta jusqu'en 1988, quand elle fut rachetée par William Smith Sr., un ancien représentant de Ward. Smith dirige toujours B&B avec ses deux fils. Bien que les originaux soient partis et que les calendriers ne soient plus le produit principal de la société, les Smith ont conservé ses archives ainsi que les droits d'auteur correspondants, délivrant des autorisations d'utilisation des images de Gil Elvgren, Earl Moran, Rolf Armstrong, Zoë Mozert et d'autres.

Fouiller dans les archives de B&B est une véritable chasse au trésor. Il y a deux ou trois caisses de 20 kilos par année. Les pin-up y sont mélangées avec des boy-scouts, des joueurs de base-ball, des bébés joufflus et des scènes de chasse au canard. Il faut sortir les calendriers un à un (ils sont plus de cent par caisse) pour dénicher le magot : un superbe Gene Pressler dans un cadre Art déco gaufré ; une élégante

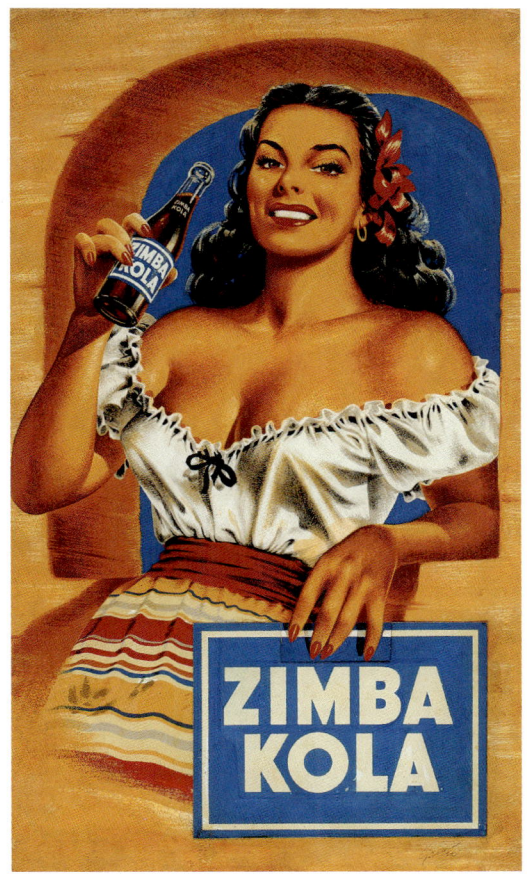

flapper d'Armstrong flanquée de chiens-loups dans un format horizontal inhabituel ; vingt petits buvards d'Enoch Bolles ; puis, enfin, la perle rare : le premier calendrier d'Earl Moran, datant de 1935, avant qu'il ne soit sous contrat. Intitulé *Miss St. Paul*, il évoque le glamour hollywoodien qui faisait tant rêver en cette période de Grande Dépression. Ces calendriers superbement réalisés sont beaux, mais ils ne représentent pas la pointe de l'art de la pin-up des années 1930. Pour cela, il faut plutôt chercher du côté des magazines.

On dit que l'érotisme résiste à la crise ; que, quand les temps sont durs, les gens se consolent avec de petits plaisirs et que les plaisirs auxquels les hommes se raccrochent le plus sont sexuels. Ce fut le cas durant la Grande Dépression qui vit fleurir un grand nombre de films et de magazines émoustillants. *Film Fun*, dont les couvertures étaient réalisées par Enoch Bolles depuis 1923, fit de nombreux émules. George Quintana et Peter Driben reprirent le flambeau tout au long

Opposite: Albert Fisher pin-up on a Nichol Kola point-of-purchase die-cut advertising sign, circa 1945. This heavy cardboard sign was designed with an easel back to stand on a store counter. 29 x 18 inches.

Above: Mixed media on board, circa 1950, by Rudy Garcia for a Zimba Kola sign. Zimba was a regional soft drink made by the Southern Beverage Company of North Carolina, but a notation on the back of this painting says the sign was made for the Cuban market. 25 x 17 inches.

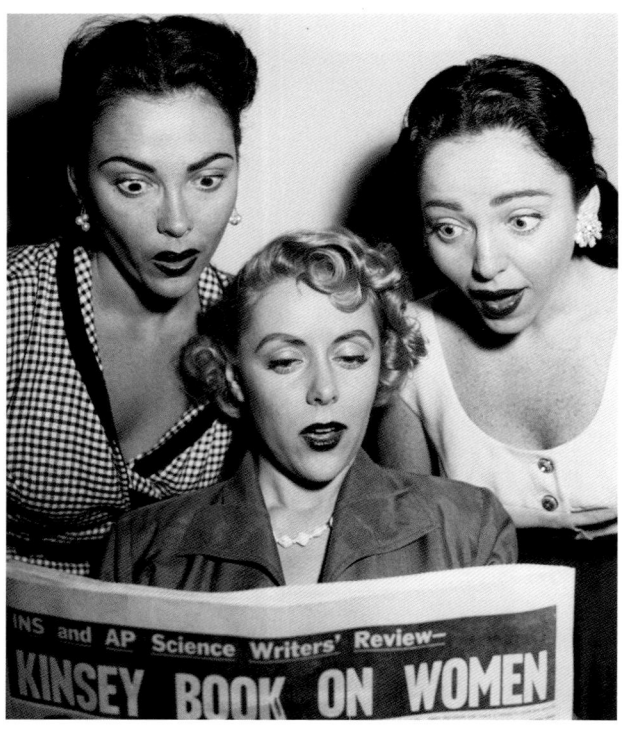

des années 1930, illustrant les couvertures de *Movie Humor, Movie Fun, Movie Merry-Go-Round, Real Screen Fun* et *Reel Humor*. Les *digests* à sensation, dont *Broadway Nights, Paris Nights, Gay Parisienne, Pep Stories, French Follies, Tattle Tales, Snappy Stories* et *La Paree* arboraient en couverture des pin-up signées d'Oscar Greiner, d'Earle Bergey, de Cardwell Higgins, du mystérieux Moskowitz et du prolifique Driben. À la fin des années 1930 parurent *Gay Book* et *High Heel Magazine*, des revues à grand format sur papier glacé, remplies d'articles, de fiction, de photos de femmes légèrement vêtues et, en couverture, des pin-up de trois grands artistes : Bolles, Bergey et Driben. Vingt ans plus tard, ce modèle serait repris par Hugh Hefner pour son *Playboy*.

Lorsque le premier numéro d'*Esquire* parut en octobre 1933, il s'inspirait du *Life* de 1905 et cachait ses pin-up à l'intérieur du magazine. Pour ce numéro, George Petty avait réalisé deux dessins humoristiques montrant des femmes avec des hommes. Les lecteurs réagirent si bien aux femmes et si mal aux hommes qu'il remplaça ces derniers par des téléphones, les héroïnes délivrant leur réplique comique dans le combiné. Bientôt, les répliques furent abandonnées à leur tour et il ne resta plus que la pin-up améliorée : sans texte pour détourner l'attention et attendant sagement à l'intérieur du magazine d'être détachée et punaisée sur le mur. En plaçant ses pin-up dans un emballage respectable, *Esquire* vendit beaucoup plus d'exemplaires que *Gay Book*, faisant de Petty une star pendant que Bolles se tuait à la tâche au point de finir dans un asile psychiatrique. À la fin de la décennie, Petty était lui aussi surmené. Il passa le relais à Alberto Vargas pour se consacrer à la publicité. Juste à temps car la guerre venait d'éclater.

Après avoir mûri pendant quarante-cinq ans, la pin-up atteignit son apogée durant la Seconde Guerre mondiale. Le terme pin-up (« punaisée ») date de cette époque. Les soldats étaient incités à s'entourer d'images de jolies femmes pour soutenir leur moral. Depuis la Grande Guerre, le gouvernement américain avait affiné sa compréhension de la psychologie masculine.

Above: The Barry Sisters, popular American Yiddish language singers of the 1950s, and actress Barbara Lawrence, center, read about Alfred Kinsey's *Sexual Behavior in the Human Female* on "K-Day," August 20, 1953, the date Kinsey set for all publicity about the book to be released. When the book was released on September 14, it quickly climbed the bestseller list, arousing public furor, and titillation, for its detailed statistics on female masturbation, infidelity, premarital sex, and lesbianism, among other things. © Bettmann/ Corbis Images.

Opposite: They're Easy to Handle, also known as *A Cut-Out Doll*, oil on canvas, 1959, 30 x 24 inches. By Edward Runci. Courtesy Heritage Auctions.

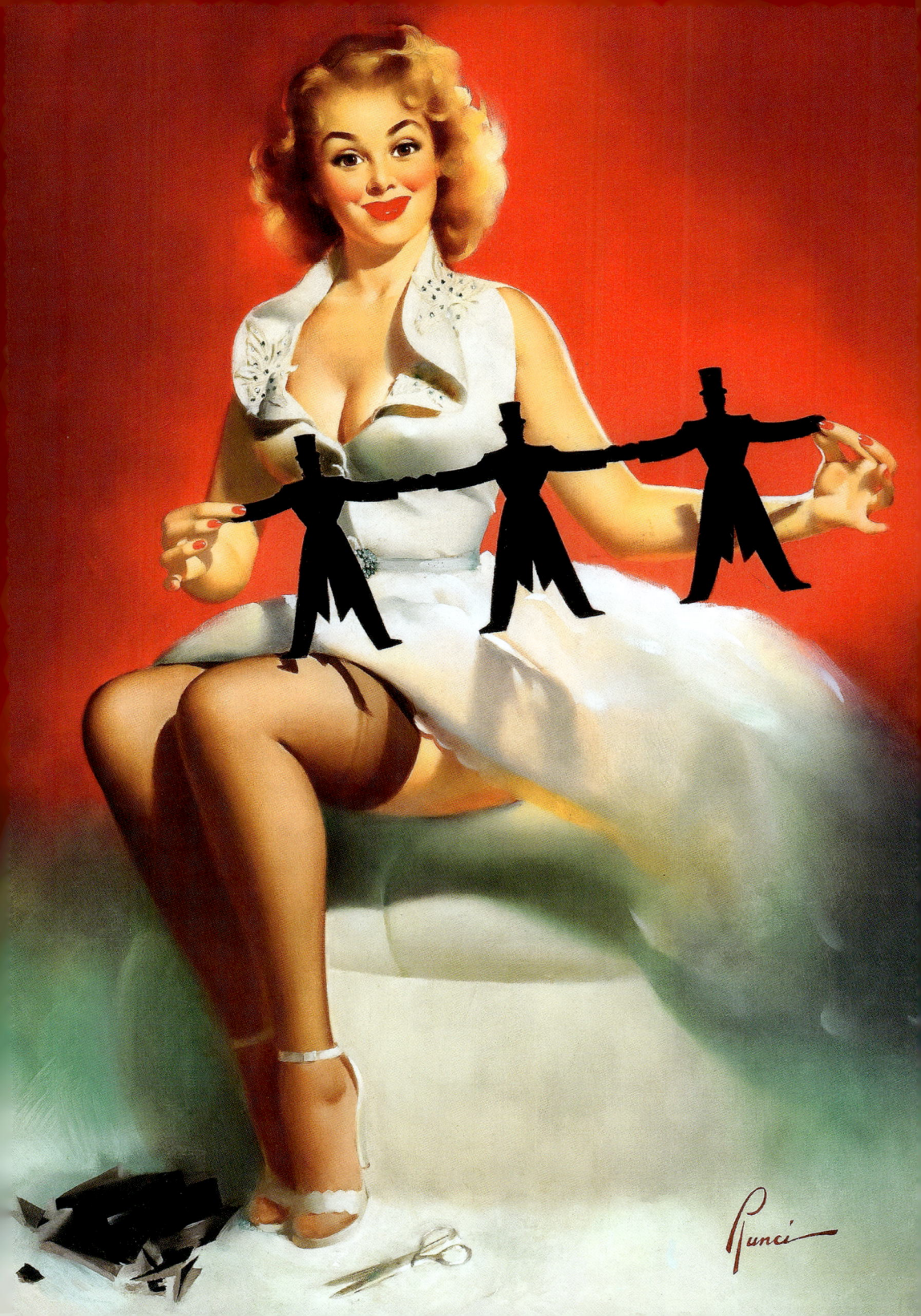

Le président Franklin Delano Roosevelt créa l'Office of War Information en 1942 et lui demanda de coordonner tous les médias afin d'envoyer des messages positifs et encourageants aux troupes. Plutôt que de susciter la haine de l'ennemi, l'accent fut mis sur la protection de la mère patrie, de la famille et du rêve américain. Les images de jolies filles, de petites amies fantasmées, étaient censées rappeler aux hommes pourquoi ils se battaient. Les magazines et les éditeurs de calendrier leur en fournirent par millions.

Les photos des casernes les montrent tapissées de pin-up. Il y en a parfois même jusque sur le plafond. On en trouvait dans les bateaux, les sous-marins, les baraques préfabriquées, les cockpits de transporteurs de troupes et sur le fuselage des bombardiers. Les hommes en conservaient dans leur portefeuille et leur paquetage. Certains les collaient même à l'intérieur de leur casque. On raconte des histoires déchirantes de cadavres de soldats serrant une pin-up dans leur poing, comme s'ils avaient voulu voir une dernière fois une Vargas ou une Petty avant de mourir. Les pin-up étaient également très appréciées des Anglais et des Russes. Le cinéaste Russ Meyer, qui fut caméraman dans l'armée US, a raconté que les soldats allemands fouillaient les cadavres américains en quête de pin-up. De leur côté, les Américains fouillaient les corps allemands à la recherche de photos de filles nues. « Nous avions des pin-up mais les Allemands avaient de la bonne pornographie », a-t-il déclaré.

En 1940, l'éditeur d'*Esquire* anticipa l'entrée en guerre des États-Unis en remplaçant George Petty, toujours plus incontrôlable, par le plus maniable Alberto Vargas. Les dernières pin-up de

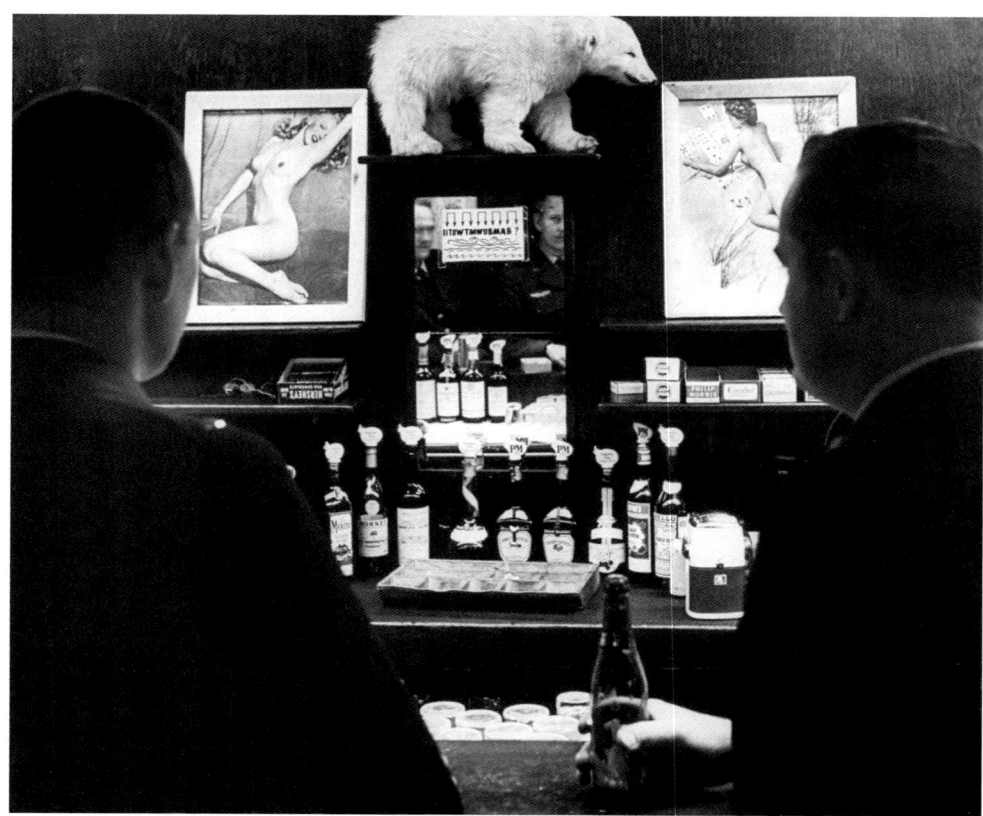

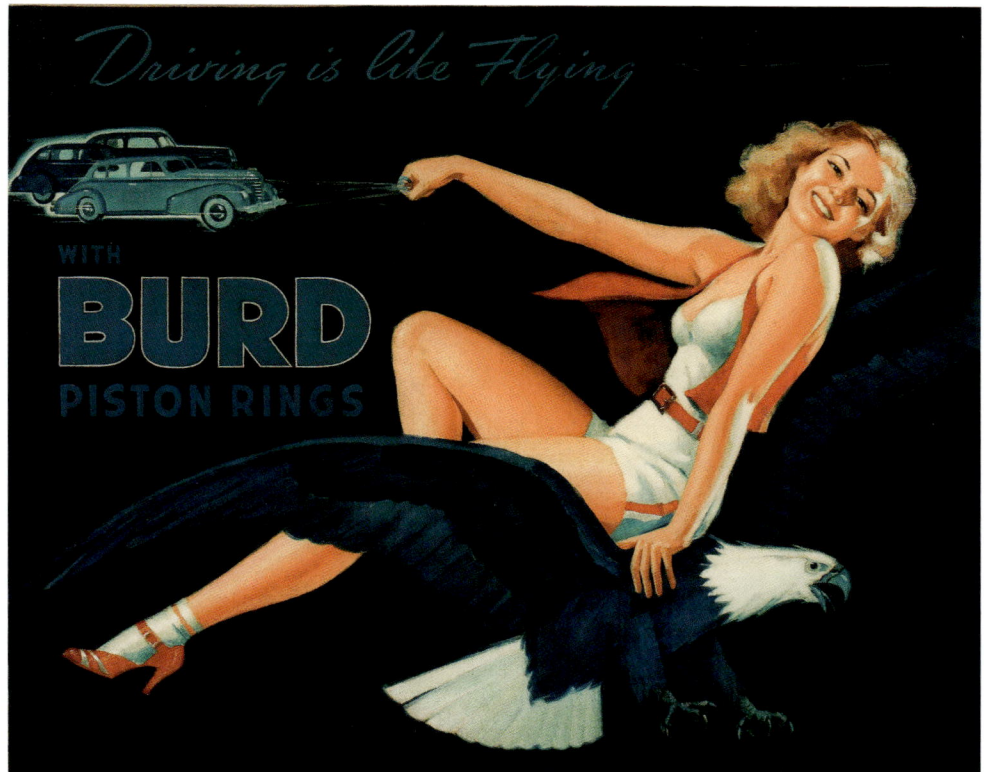

Petty pour *Esquire* parurent en 1941 avant de laisser le champ libre à Vargas pour accompagner les troupes. Celui-ci releva le défi en proposant des girls en uniforme (ou en sarong pour ceux basés dans le Pacifique). En 1944, *Esquire* publia un numéro spécial militaire, vendu à prix coûtant au gouvernement sans les publicités et avec des pin-up de Vargas supplémentaires au dos de la couverture. La prévoyance du magazine fit de Vargas l'illustrateur de pin-up le plus populaire des années 1940, même si celles créées par Petty en 1941 ornèrent bon nombre de bombardiers (voir encadré).

Pendant qu'*Esquire* offrait chaque mois des illustrations de pin-up, *Yank*, le magazine officiel de l'armée américaine, publiait chaque semaine des pin-up photographiques. La plupart étaient des starlettes en maillot de bain ou en petite tenue mises à la disposition de l'armée par les studios d'Hollywood : parmi elles se trouvaient Linda Darnell, Deanna Durbin, Susan Hayward, Rita Hayworth, Marie McDonald, Jane Russell et les Rockettes du Radio City Music Hall.

Les studios envoyèrent également des millions de pin-up directement aux troupes stationnées à l'étranger (dont trois millions d'exemplaires de la célèbre vue de dos de Betty Grable). Des

Opposite: The famous nude calendar photo of Marilyn Monroe hangs next to a taxidermied polar bear cub in the officer's club at Thule Air Force base, 1953. Thule is the United States' most northerly base, situated outside Thule, Greenland. © George Silk/Time Life Pictures/ Getty Images.

Above: This oil on canvas by an unknown artist was a commission by the Burd piston ring company, one of many auto parts suppliers to use pin-ups in promoting their products. From the late 1930s through the '50s Burd commissioned works by Haddon Sundblom and Bill Medcalf, as well as by uncredited artists. 34 x 27 inches.

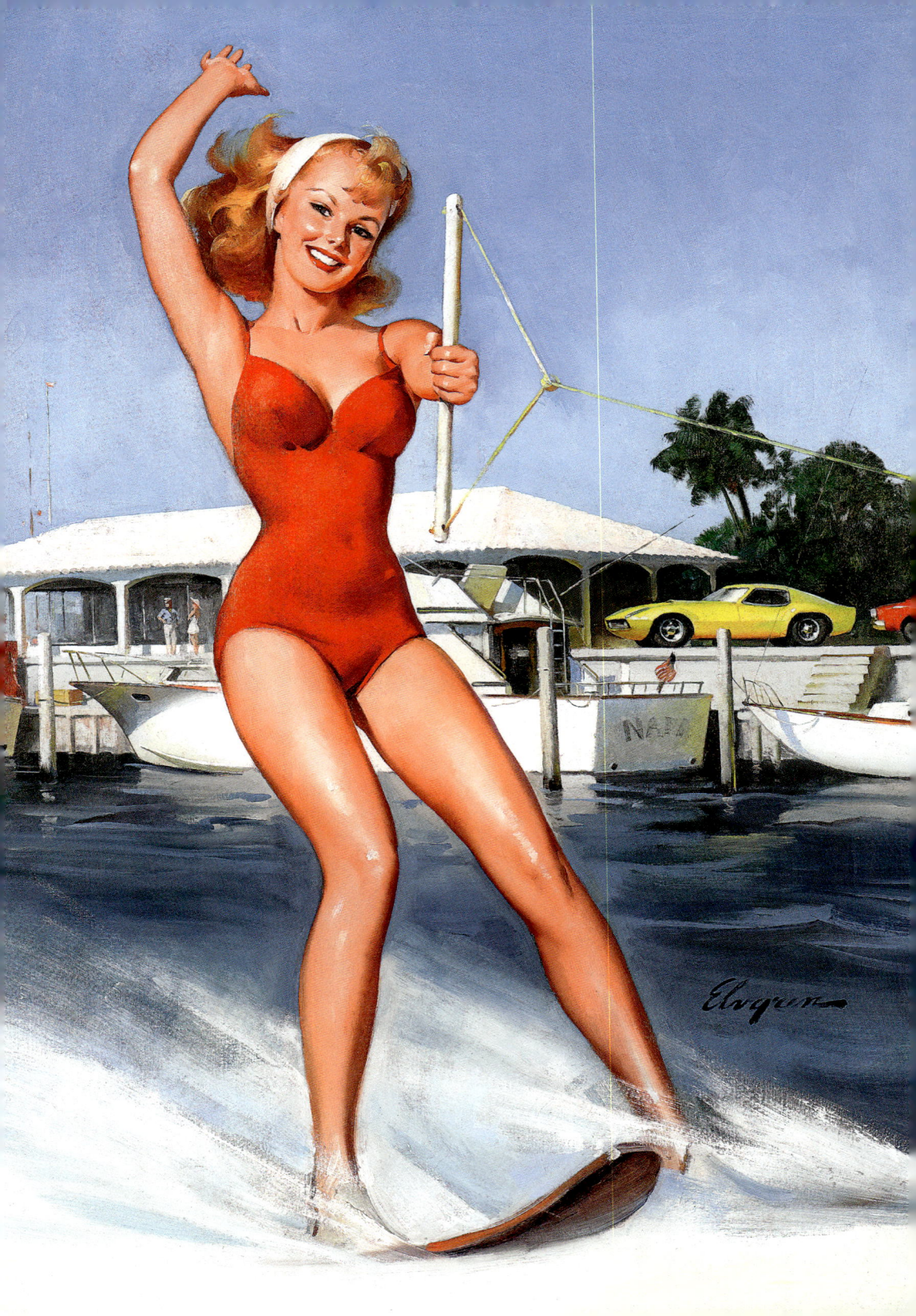

photographes entreprenants impri-
mèrent des catalogues destinés aux soldats, proposant des centaines de jolies
filles habillées mais provocantes avec
des frais de port réduits. Une flopée
de nouveaux magazines pour hommes
parurent, dont *Who's Your Pin-up Girl?*,
War Laffs, *Jest*, *Sleek*, *Snap*, *Show* et une
nouvelle version de *Gay Book*, tous
offrant des photos de pin-up et des
posters centraux. Le choix de photographies plutôt que d'illustrations était
avant tout économique : une photo
coûtait à l'éditeur 25 dollars, une
peinture 250. Encore fallait-il trouver
un illustrateur. Vaughan Bass, Edward
D'Ancona, Harry Ekman, Art Frahm,
Earl MacPherson, Bill Medcalf et
Edward Runci avaient tous été mobili-
sés. Heureusement pour *Esquire*, Vargas,
âgé de 46 ans, était exempté. De même,
les éditeurs de calendriers pouvaient
compter sur Rolf Armstrong, Gil
Elvgren, Earl Moran et Zoë Mozert.

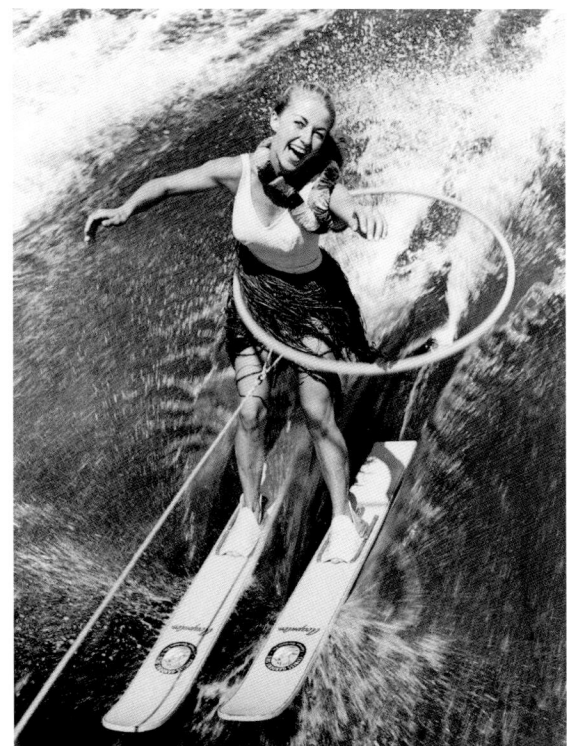

Armstrong, Elvgren, Moran et
Mozert étaient à B&B et Louis F. Dow ce que Vargas était à *Esquire*. Moran et Mozert peignirent
des douzaines de sujets patriotiques sur de petits formats destinés au Mutoscope (voir encadré).
Armstrong, lui, créait des affiches et des calendriers de propagande. Louis F. Dow imprima une
série de petits livrets intitulés *Pin-Ups* et contenant « 12 superbes Girls glamour » signées Gil
Elvgren. Il s'agissait d'images recyclées des plus célèbres pin-up d'Elvgren pour Dow, impri-
mées sur un papier léger et perforé afin que les pages puissent s'enlever facilement, le tout dans
une pochette pouvait être postée n'importe où dans le monde pour 12 cents seulement. B&B
contre-attaqua avec un livret plus petit de Mozert qui était acheminé pour encore moins cher.
Mozert appelait ce système V-mail. Le véritable V-mail ou « courrier de la victoire » consistait
à transmettre des lettres de soldats par microfilm afin de gagner de l'espace dans les sacs postaux,
si bien qu'elle faisait sans doute allusion par là à la petite taille des livrets, à leurs frais postaux
réduits et à leur contenu qui regonflait le moral des troupes.

Après 1942, les éditeurs de calendriers augmentèrent encore leurs profits grâce à des contrats
avec le War Advertising Council, un organisme chargé d'inciter le secteur de la publicité à produire de la propagande. Il créa, entre autres, les personnages de Rosie la Riveteuse (Rosie the
Riveter) et de l'ours Smokey (Smokey the Bear) : Rosie pour encourager les femmes à travailler

Opposite: A wholesome pin-up by Elvgren
for a NAPA calendar.

Above: The hit toy of 1958 was the Hula-Hoop, conceived
and patented by two Californians in their garage. Twenty

million hoops were sold for $1.98 by their company,
Wham-O, in the first six months. Here, a young lady
in Cypress Gardens, Florida, uses one while water
skiing. © Bettmann/Corbis Images.

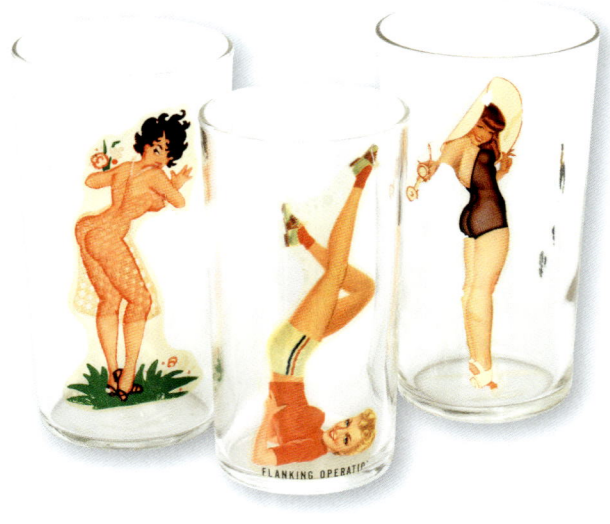

dans l'armement et Smokey de crainte que les bombes japonaises sur la côte ouest ne provoquent des incendies de forêt. B&B organisa ses propres conférences en 1943 et 1944 afin de développer de nouveaux thèmes patriotiques, y faisant intervenir Armstrong, Mozert, Moran et des modèles. Lors de la première, Rolf Armstrong présenta sa muse Jewel Flowers vêtue d'un tout petit costume aux couleurs de la bannière étoilée. Les brochures publicitaires de B&B établissaient un lien direct entre ses nouvelles pin-up et la réussite militaire.

Charlie Ward n'était pas le seul à conjuguer pin-up et patriotisme. Pour le secteur de la publicité, l'attrait était irrésistible. On savait déjà que le sexe faisait vendre mais, les pin-up étant devenues une obsession nationale, les jolies filles pouvaient écouler n'importe quoi à partir du moment où le message associait le produit à la victoire militaire. Ces publicités annonçaient déjà les campagnes accrocheuses des agences de Madison Avenue dans les années 1950 et 1960, lorsque le War Advertising Council devint simplement l'Advertising Council.

Cette explosion de pin-up durant la Seconde Guerre mondiale eut des effets considérables sur la culture populaire américaine. Russ Meyer, le roi des poitrines opulentes, avait été photographe et cinéaste dans l'armée. Après la guerre, il poursuivit sa carrière dans la photographie glamour puis dans les films de « sexploitation », préparant le terrain pour l'industrie américaine du porno qui rapporte aujourd'hui 10 milliards de dollars par an. Meyer s'inspirait des pin-up et des maisons closes françaises ; il se fit connaître en photographiant des posters centraux pour Hugh Hefner.

Hefner était resté au pays durant le conflit, effectuant son service dans l'administration. Néanmoins, comme tous les soldats, il aimait les pin-up et *Esquire*. Il parvint à s'y faire engager après la guerre. Lorsque le journal déménagea à New York en 1950, il resta à Chicago où il lança *Playboy* en 1953. Le magazine était censé être un *Esquire* plus moderne destiné aux jeunes vétérans.

Pendant qu'Hefner et Meyer examinaient l'anatomie des pin-up, Frederick Mellinger étudiait leurs tenues. Ancien ouvrier dans la confection, il revint du front avec des idées de dessous féminins inspirés des pin-up. Les journaux de New York refusant de publier des publicités pour ses créations scandaleuses, il s'installa à Los Angeles où il ouvrit Frederick's of Hollywood. En 1982,

Above: Following the invention of the water-mount decal process in 1936, permanent decals were frequently applied to glassware, with pin-ups the most popular subject. George Petty glasses (one seen here) were marketed in a set of six for $1.98 in 1948.

Opposite: Gouache on board, circa 1955, by Bill Randall. Randall worked with the French underground during World War II by creating illustrations for Resistance propaganda. Upon his return, he became a regular contributor to *Esquire*'s post-Vargas Gallery of Glamour pin-up feature. 16 x 11.5 inches.

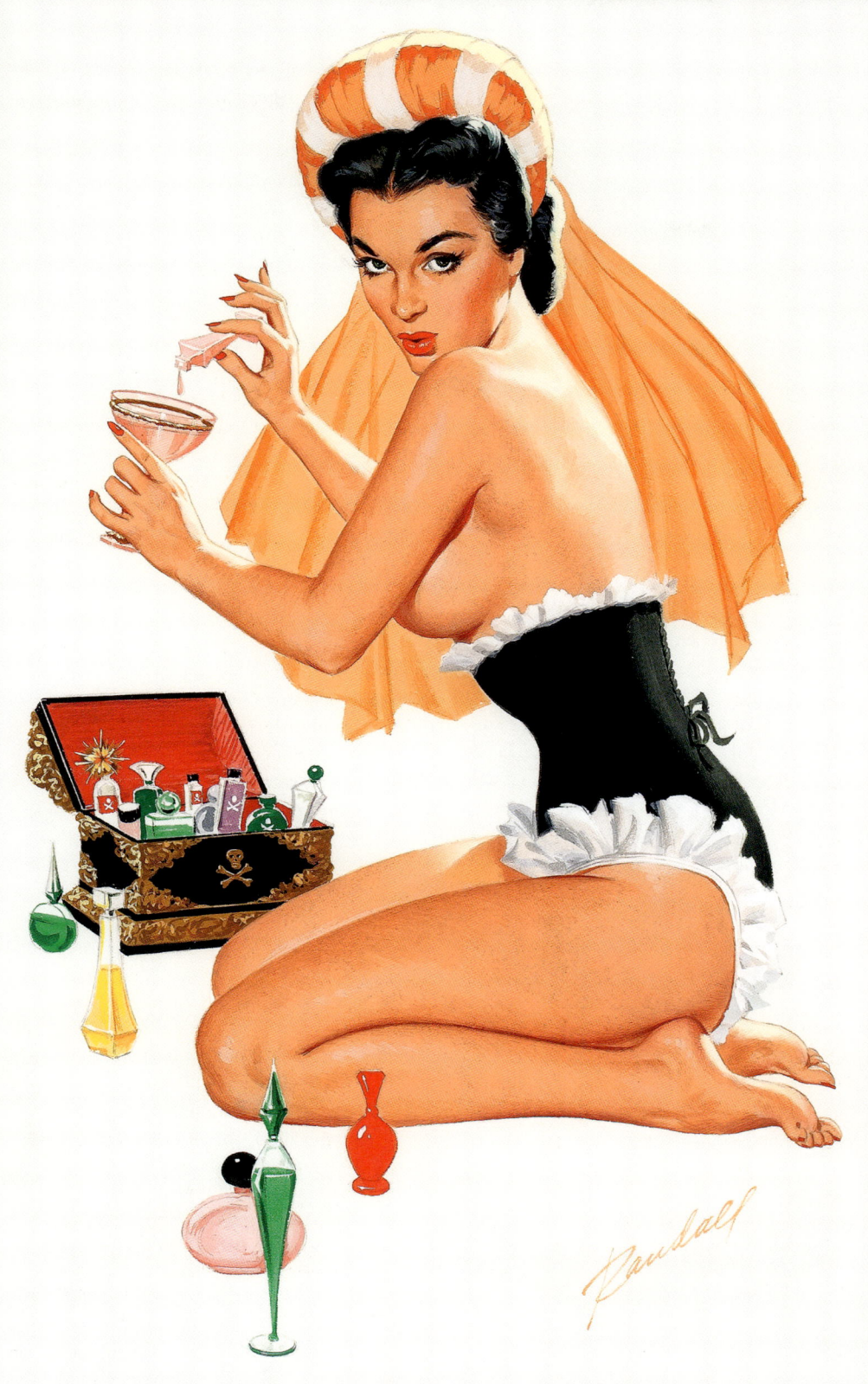

Mellinger m'a confié que sa motivation première lui avait été fournie par ses camarades G.I. :
« Ils disaient tous qu'ils auraient aimé voir leurs épouses et leurs petites amies s'habiller comme des pin-up. J'ai créé ces vêtements pour sauver leur mariage. »

Hefner adorait les peintures de Vargas dans *Esquire*. De 1960 à 1977, il lui fit réaliser des pin-up pour *Playboy*, mais il savait que l'avenir était dans la photographie. Les magazines de Robert Harrison, *Beauty Parade*, *Wink*, *Titter*, *Eyeful* et *Whisper*, furent les derniers à arborer de belles couvertures de pin-up peintes par Billy DeVorss, Earl Moran et, surtout, Peter Driben. Harrison lança *Beauty Parade* en 1942, alors que la pin-up était à son apogée. En 1955, lorsque ses publications cessèrent de paraître, toutes les revues pour hommes ressemblaient à *Playboy* et on ne trouvait plus d'illustrations de pin-up que sur les calendriers, dans *Esquire* et, parfois, sur les superbes couvertures du magazine *Motor Age*.

En 1945, cette évolution était imprévisible et impensable. Les compagnies qui devaient leur prospérité aux pin-up durant la guerre n'étaient pas prêtes à les laisser mourir. Les artistes rentrèrent du front et trouvèrent tous du travail. B&B parvint à arracher Gil Elvgren à Louis F. Dow et entama sa période la plus productive. Shaw-Barton vola MacPherson à B&B ainsi que son concept de l'Artist Sketch Pad, et devait réaliser les *MacPherson Artist's Sketch Books* durant dix ans. Haddon Sundblom créa son quatrième atelier, et l'Art Institute of Chicago continua à former des émules d'Elvgren. Entre 1945 et 1950, les artistes et les éditeurs produisirent comme s'il y avait encore 15 millions de soldats réclamant des pin-up à cor et à cri. Dans la mesure où les hommes s'étaient habitués à en voir partout, cela fonctionna. Les éditeurs de calendriers entamèrent donc les années 1950 confiants en leur avenir.

Les premiers problèmes apparurent à la fin de 1953. Dans le numéro du 30 décembre de *People Today*, il était écrit : « Les calendriers de jolies femmes n'ont plus les faveurs des Américains… La meilleure vente de B&B pour 1954 est le calendrier de boy-scouts de Norman Rockwell. Parmi les sujets les plus populaires cette année, il n'y a qu'un seul calendrier de pin-up. Il y a cinq ans, il en avait six parmi les douze les plus vendus. Cette année, B&B a racheté la Western Litho Co. de Los Angeles, éditeur du célèbre calendrier où Marilyn Monroe apparaît nue. B&B déclare avoir décidé de ne pas le republier. » Ward attribuait ce changement au fait que les hommes offraient de plus en plus de calendriers à leurs épouses et en plaçaient de moins en moins dans les lieux où ils se retrouvaient « entre eux ».

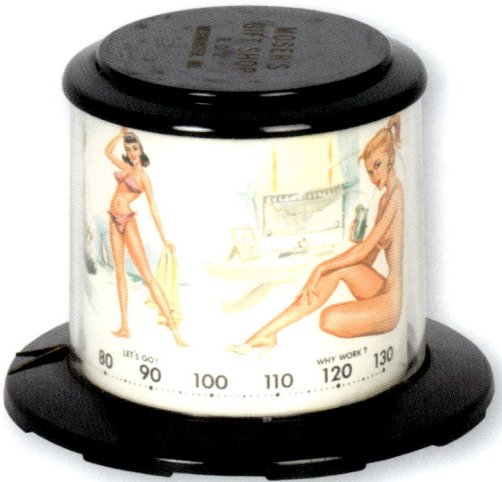

Le baby-boom prenait fin. La pin-up était née quand les femmes avaient quitté le foyer et finissait avec leur retour.

À mesure que les nouveaux pères délaissaient les repaires de célibataires, B&B produisait plus de calendriers orientés vers la famille. En 1954, Zoë Mozert se plaignit que l'éditeur rejetait ses nus. Elvgren, auteur de *Gay Nymph*, *Vision of Beauty*, *Perfection*, *Fascination*, *Fascinating Figures* et d'autres nus pour B&B entre la fin des années 1940 et le début des années 1950, n'en produisit plus que deux après 1953. Moran cessa lui aussi de peindre des nus dans les années 1950,

même s'il se rat-
trapa plus tard une
fois à la retraite.

De leur côté,
les magazines pour
hommes conte-
naient de plus en
plus de nudité,
mais en photo.
Le contexte avait
changé, mais pas
les hommes. Ils
voulaient toujours
voir de jolies filles,
mais ne pouvaient
plus les punaiser
au-dessus de leur
lit. Les magazines
étaient plus faciles
à dissimuler et,
une fois la créature
de rêve rangée dans
une caisse dans le

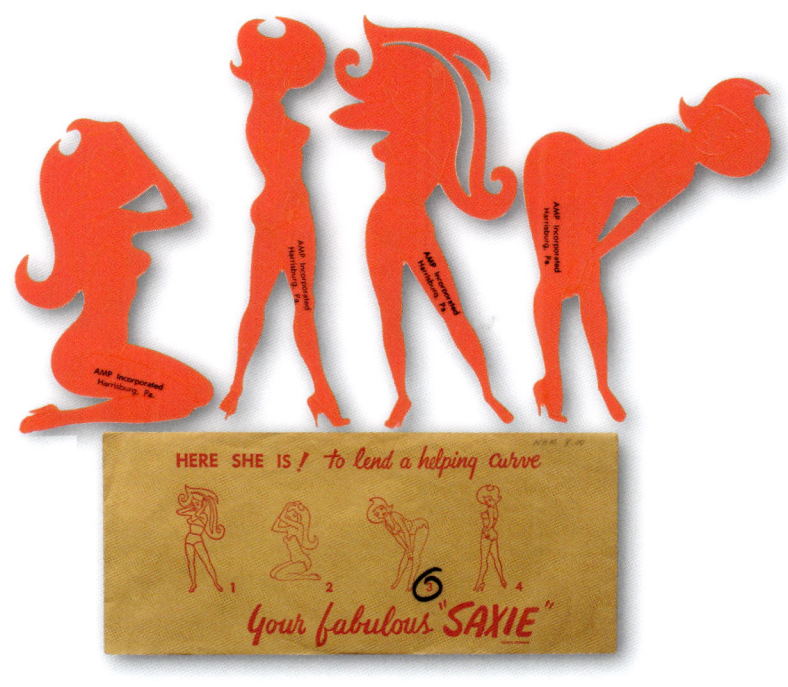

garage, il n'y avait plus de raison de préserver son innocence. Les pin-up paraissaient désormais
vieux jeu.

Inévitablement, les éditeurs de calendriers ripostèrent en recourant aux photographies. Les
premiers temps, les modèles prirent des poses de pin-up peintes, mais les éditeurs se rendirent vite
compte que c'était inutile. Ceux qui achetaient ces calendriers ne demandaient pas à ce que les
modèles ressemblent à des œuvres d'art. Les filles sur les photos n'avaient pas les jambes intermi-
nables, les tailles de guêpe et les poitrines insolentes des pin-up peintes, mais elles étaient réelles,
et nues de surcroît, ce qui a son propre attrait atemporel.

Ainsi, entre 1955 et 1965, les contrats ne furent pas renouvelés et les illustrateurs de pin-up
se tournèrent vers la publicité, les couvertures de livres, les beaux-arts, ou prirent simplement leur
retraite. Les magazines se multiplièrent et les calendriers déclinèrent. Louis F. Dow mit la clef sous
la porte à la fin des années 1960. Shaw-Barton racheta Gerlach-Barklow en 1959 et ferma ses
ateliers. La même année, Charlie Ward mourut et B&B fut racheté. Les nouveaux propriétaires
continuèrent à produire des calendriers de pin-up et quelques-uns des meilleurs artistes continuèrent à les illustrer, notamment Gil Elvgren. B&B lui fit avoir des commandes de la National
Automotive Parts Association (NAPA) et du fabricant de peintures pour automobile Ditzler.

Opposite: A rotating thermometer, circa 1955. As the
temperature rises, the inner sleeve turns, revealing
pin-ups in ever-briefer costumes, until at 130 degrees
Fahrenheit the model is completely nude. Artist
unknown.

Above: Before the computer, draftsmen relied on French
curves, flat plastic tools with smooth edges along which
a pen or pencil could be traced to create specific curves.
The term French curve made men think of women's
bodies, though, and many variations on the pin-up
French curve were produced as novelty items in the
1950s, including "Your fabulous 'Saxie.'"

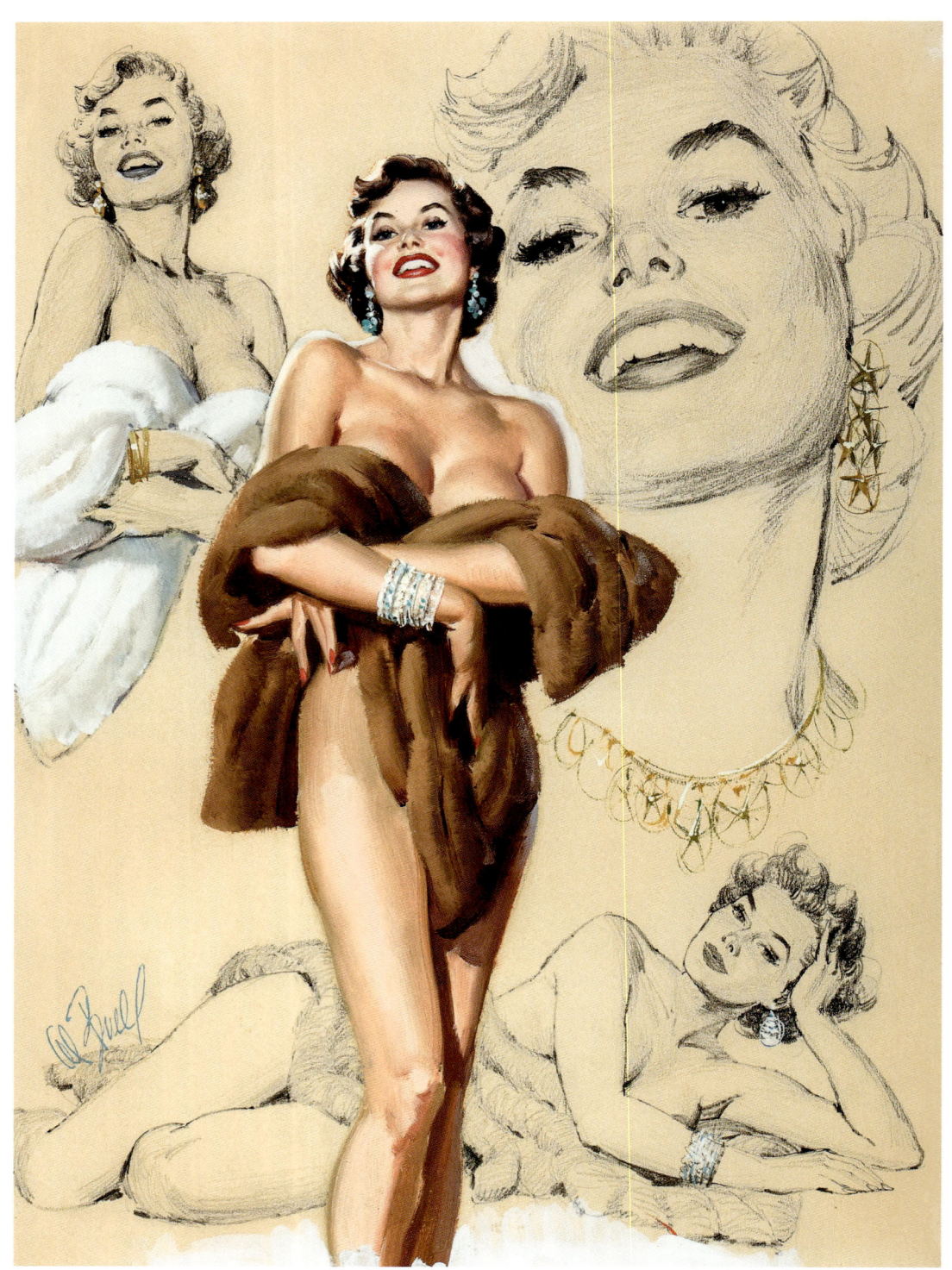

La réparation automobile était l'un des derniers bastions masculins ; la NAPA commanda des pin-up peintes tout au long des années 1960 et Ditzler persévéra jusque dans les années 1980 avec différents artistes. Elvgren continua de peaufiner son style, produisant certaines de ses plus belles pièces dans les années 1960, mais la demande ne cessait de baisser. En 1968, il créa huit œuvres pour B&B ; de 1969 à 1971, il n'en réalisa plus que deux par an. Zoë Mozert et lui livrèrent leurs dernières pin-up en 1971. Fritz Willis tint bon encore un an, vendant douze œuvres pour de futurs calendriers en 1972, tandis que Mayo Olmstead ne vendit qu'une seule pin-up à B&B en 1973. Après cela, il ne resta plus que Duane Bryers qui continua à peindre son personnage de pin-up potelée Hilda jusqu'au début des années 1980.

Esquire, qui avait inventé le concept du poster central, conserva ses pin-up jusqu'en 1957, entretenant une écurie remarquable d'artistes. Lorsque Vargas jeta l'éponge en 1946, le magazine lança sa *Gallery of Glamour*, avec des œuvres d'Ernest Chiriacka, Joe De Mers, Thornton Utz, Al Moore, Eddie Chan, Mike Ludlow, Ben-Hur Baz et J. Frederick Smith. On ignore sous quels arrangements contractuels mais le seul autre endroit à part *Esquire* où ces pin-up parurent fut dans *Ballyhoo*, un calendrier de 1953 de B&B. Les originaux de ces artistes apparaissent rarement sur le marché. *Esquire* détenait tous les droits et, en 1980, transmit les œuvres à l'Université du

Opposite: Mixed media on board, circa 1960, by Al Buell for *Al Buell's Beauties Sketch Pad*, 1961. Buell produced pin-ups for a variety of calendar companies from 1940. He left to do paperback covers in 1951 and returned to pin-up in 1958 with a far more sophisticated style, seen here. 19.5 x 14.5.

Below: A Moment of Pleasure, oil on canvas, circa 1968, by Fritz Willis. Willis is a controversial figure in pin-up, seen by some as the last great talent to emerge, taking over Brown & Bigelow's *Artist's Sketch Pad* calendar series in 1961 with his Willis Girl. Others see him as not quite a pin-up artist at all. His style was distinctively modern, his women more jaded than innocent, and as seen here, he was not afraid of pubic hair. 31.5 x 22 inches.

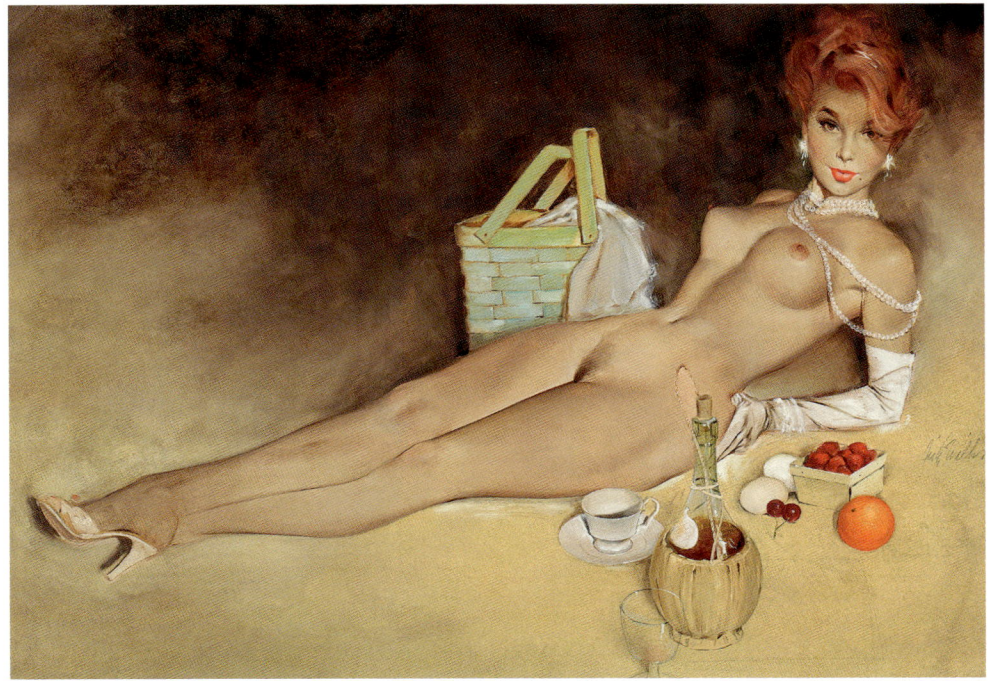

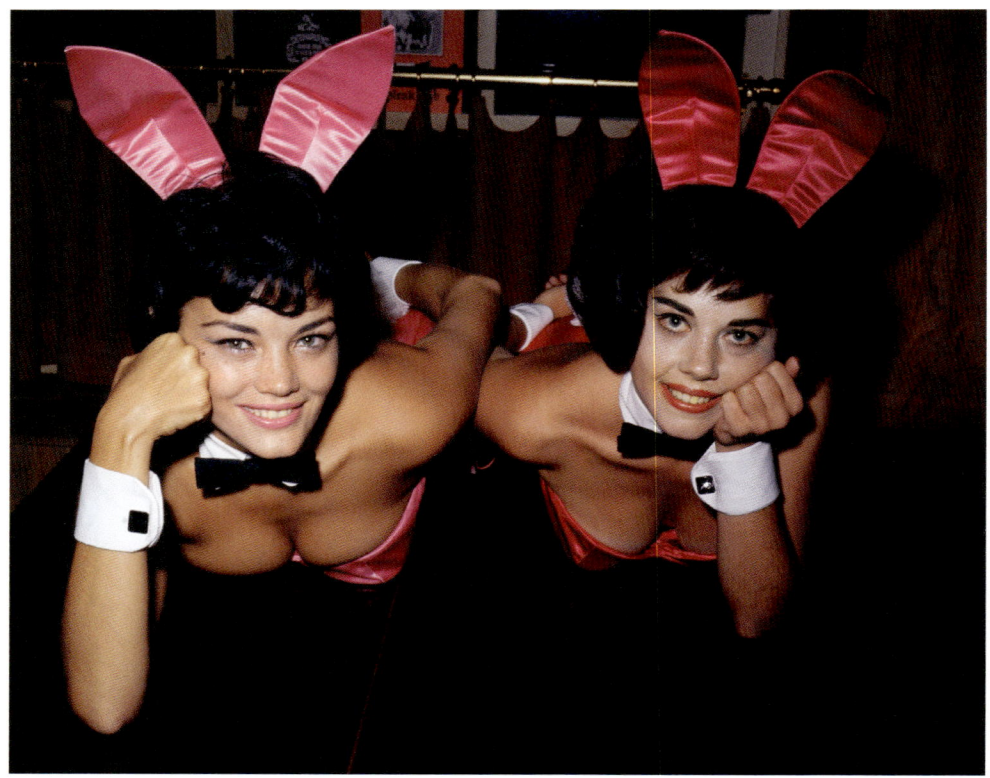

Kansas afin de bénéficier d'une déduction fiscale : 164 Vargas et 24 Chiriackas sont exposés au Spencer Museum de l'Université pendant que des milliers d'autres originaux sont stockés dans 26 conteneurs scellés, attendant depuis plus de trente ans une subvention fédérale permettant de les trier et de les identifier.

Après 1960, *Playboy* resta le seul magazine à publier des pin-up, d'abord des Vargas, puis des Don Lewis et, à présent, des Olivia De Berardinis. Hefner, dont les photographies ont hâté la fin de la pin-up artistique, a entretenu la flamme au fil des ans quand la plupart des autres ne s'y intéressaient plus. Pendant ce temps, Charles Martignette amassait la plus grande collection de pin-up au monde.

Secret, obsessionnel, excentrique, Martignette était fasciné par les pin-up depuis que, à l'âge de 8 ans, il en avait vu une sur le mur d'un coiffeur. Il acheta son premier Elvgren en 1978, à 27 ans, et passa les années 1980 à acquérir tout ce qu'il pouvait. Il commença par se rendre en personne chez tous les éditeurs de calendriers. D'ordinaire, après avoir acheté une œuvre,

Above: Playboy and its pictorial centerfolds had pushed aside *Esquire* and its illustrated pin-ups as America's number-one men's magazine in 1962. Churece Charbonneau and Sandra Gatz were picked from hundreds of applicants to be Bunny hostesses at the New York Playboy Club, the fifth of 40 clubs opened between 1960 and 1984. At the height of *Playboy*'s success there, were clubs in places as diverse as Manchester, England; Nagoya, Japan; and Lansing, Michigan, with members paying $25 a year for the privilege of being served by young women in custom-fitted satin suits, stiletto heels, and bunny ears. The chain closed in 1991, though three new clubs were opened in the 2000s. Bettmann/Corbis Images.

Opposite: Room 206, watercolor on paper, circa 1965, by Don Lewis for the *Playboy Club VIP* magazine. Lewis created a series of popular pin-ups for *Playboy* in the 1960s. 20.5 x 10 inches. Courtesy Heritage Auctions.

ces derniers l'archivaient ou la donnaient une fois le calendrier publié. Martignette sauva des centaines d'œuvres de la destruction en convainquant les éditeurs moribonds de lui vendre tout ce qu'il leur restait. Il traqua également les artistes. Sa correspondance avec Norman Rockwell montre comment il tenta de le séduire, jusqu'à ce que l'artiste perde patience devant ses demandes d'autographes et d'amitié. Martignette conserva toutes ses lettres de rejet, même les plus virulentes. Enfin, il recherchait les propriétaires d'œuvres, les harcelant de coups de téléphone et de lettres jusqu'à ce qu'il obtienne satisfaction. Son appartement en Floride était rempli de caisses mais le plus gros de sa collection de 4 300 illustrations et représentations de pin-up était conservé dans des entrepôts voisins, soigneusement emballé et jamais montré. Il ne s'y rendait que la nuit, armé d'un revolver par peur des voleurs. Comme il avait toujours besoin d'argent pour acheter plus d'œuvres, il mettait des annonces pour vendre des pin-up mais à des prix prohibitifs. Il ne pouvait se résoudre à s'en séparer.

Au cours des années 1980, d'autres s'attelèrent à faire renaître cet art oublié. Louis Meisel organisa sa première exposition de pin-up en 1982 et Marianne Ohl Phillips commença à vendre des reproductions et des calendriers anciens en 1988. L'intérêt s'accrut dans les années 1990, surtout après la publication de *L'Âge d'or de la pin-up américaine* en 1996. Quand Martignette mourut en 2008 à l'âge de 57 ans, la pin-up renaissait de ses cendres et la demande d'œuvres originales était forte. Les collectionneurs se frottèrent les mains lorsque ses 4 300 œuvres furent mises en vente par Heritage Auctions à Dallas, dans le Texas.

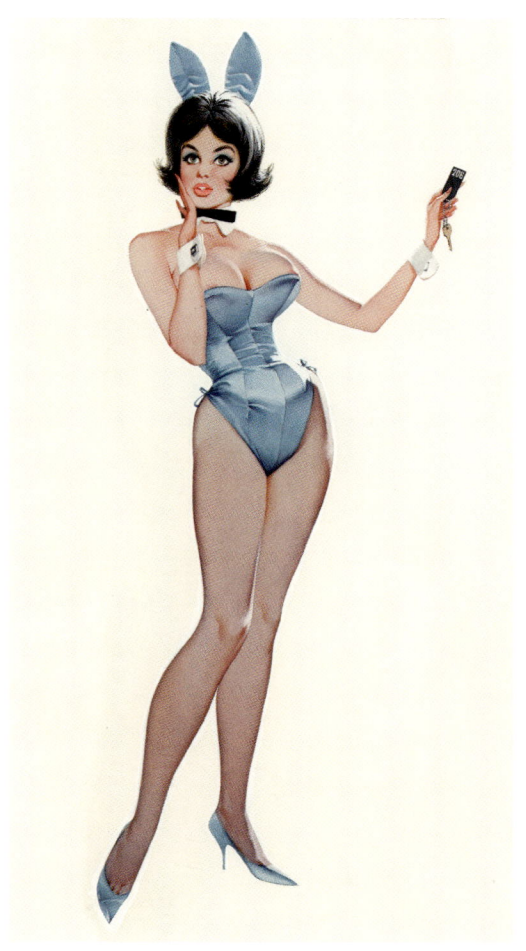

Il fallut trois camions de 16 mètres de long pour transporter le trésor de Martignette, et douze ventes aux enchères étalées sur quatre ans pour le disperser. Des records de prix furent battus, dépassant même ceux imposés par Martignette. Gil Elvgren, dont Charles disait qu'il serait un jour considéré comme l'égal de Rockwell, en émergea comme le créateur de pin-up le plus cher des États-Unis. Comme le déclara Ed Jaster, vice-président d'Heritage, à la fin d'une vente en 2012 : « […] son talent continue d'être la référence avec laquelle on mesure tous les autres illustrateurs. Les collectionneurs le considèrent comme l'étalon or… »

Martignette s'enorgueillissait de posséder pratiquement toutes les pin-up originales restantes. Il avait presque raison, et si sa collection en soi était magnifique, de pouvoir déballer tous ces croquis, ces tableaux et ces pastels et de les disséminer dans le monde est ce qu'il pouvait arriver de mieux à la pin-up et à ses admirateurs. C'est un art conçu pour être vu, comme son nom l'indique, et non caché dans des entrepôts. Nous devons toute notre gratitude à Charles Martignette pour avoir rassemblé et préservé ces œuvres, et toute notre reconnaissance à Heritage pour les avoir vendues à des centaines d'amateurs qui n'avaient jusque-là vu des pin-up qu'en reproduction sur des calendriers, des buvards, des cartes pour Mutoscope ou encore dans *L'Âge d'or de la pin-up américaine*.

Le démantèlement de la collection de Martignette a également rendu ce livre possible. Bien que la plupart des œuvres présentées dans *L'Âge d'or* lui appartenaient, déballer et photographier les originaux représentait une tâche si colossale qu'ils furent souvent remplacés par des reproductions. Pour cet ouvrage, j'ai eu un meilleur accès aux œuvres et à des photographies de haute qualité, ce qui a nous permis de réaliser pour la première fois un livre de cette ampleur sur les pin-up.

Maintenant que tous ces Elvgren, Petty, Vargas, Moran, Armstrong, Driben, Mozert, Ballantyne, Bolles et Buell voient à nouveau la lueur du jour, on ne peut qu'espérer que leurs nouveaux propriétaires résisteront à la tentation de cacher leur trésor et qu'ils les accrocheront dans leurs demeures ou galeries afin d'en profiter pleinement et d'inspirer de nouveaux admirateurs. Punaisées, telles que la nature les a voulues.

Below: Watercolor on board, circa 1975, by Alberto Vargas, presumably for *Playboy* but never published. After *Playboy* began showing pubic hair on Playmates with the January 1971 issue, Vargas was pushed to get onboard. His first pubicly complete pin-up appeared in the June 1971 issue, but he never grew comfortable with the notion. The Max Vargas Collection.

Opposite: Swim, Anyone?, oil on canvas, 1969, by Gil Elvgren. The original painting revealed the figure's breasts below the shirt she is stripping off; obscuring fabric was added later, by Elvgren or a house artist at Brown & Bigelow. 30 x 24 inches.

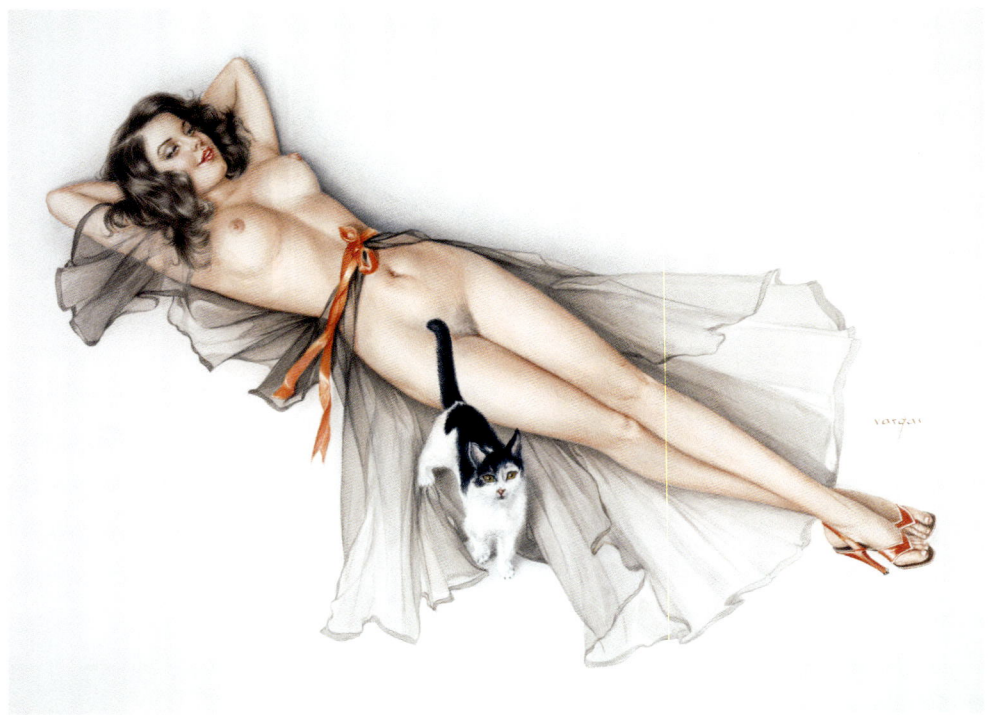

THE ART OF PIN-UP

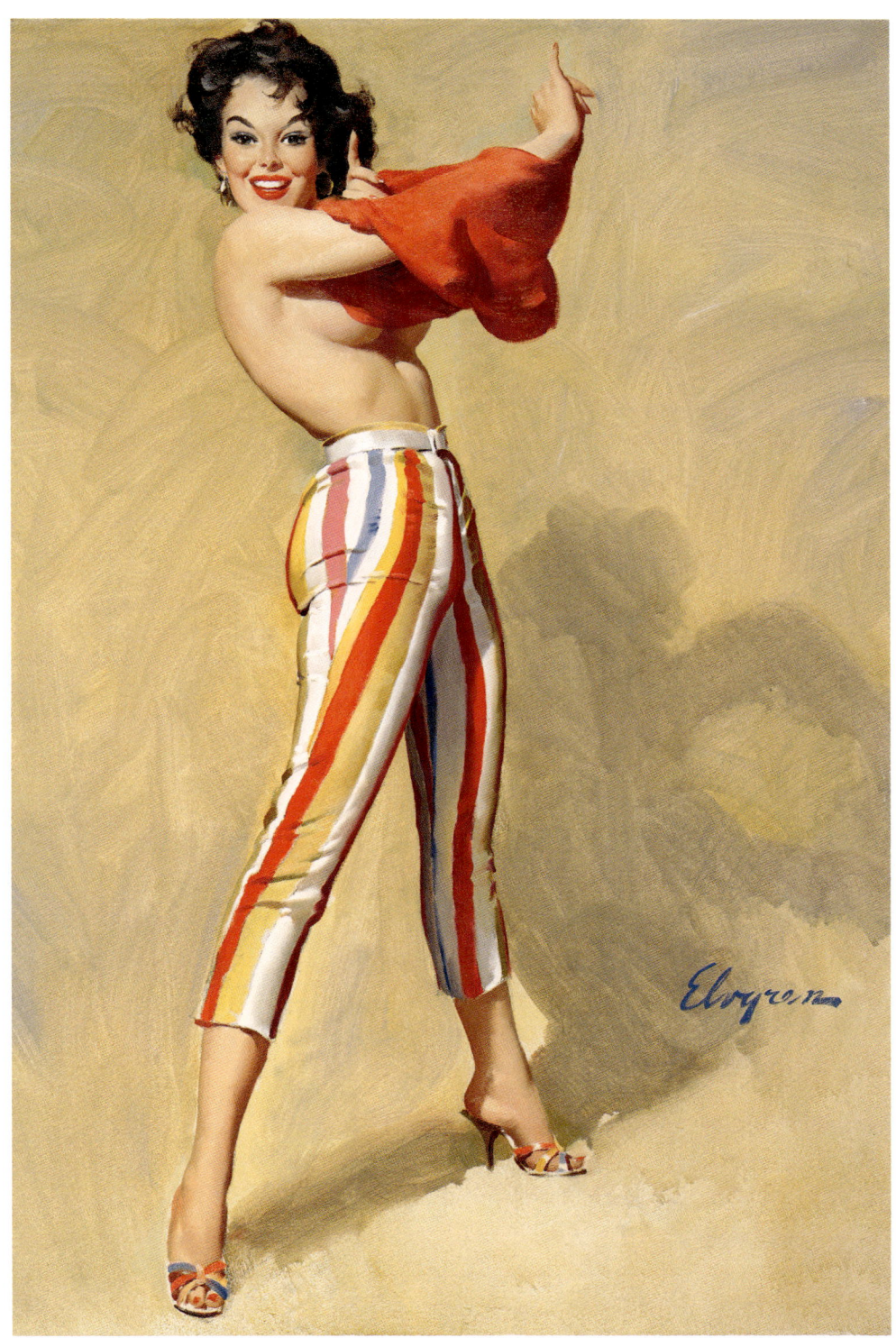

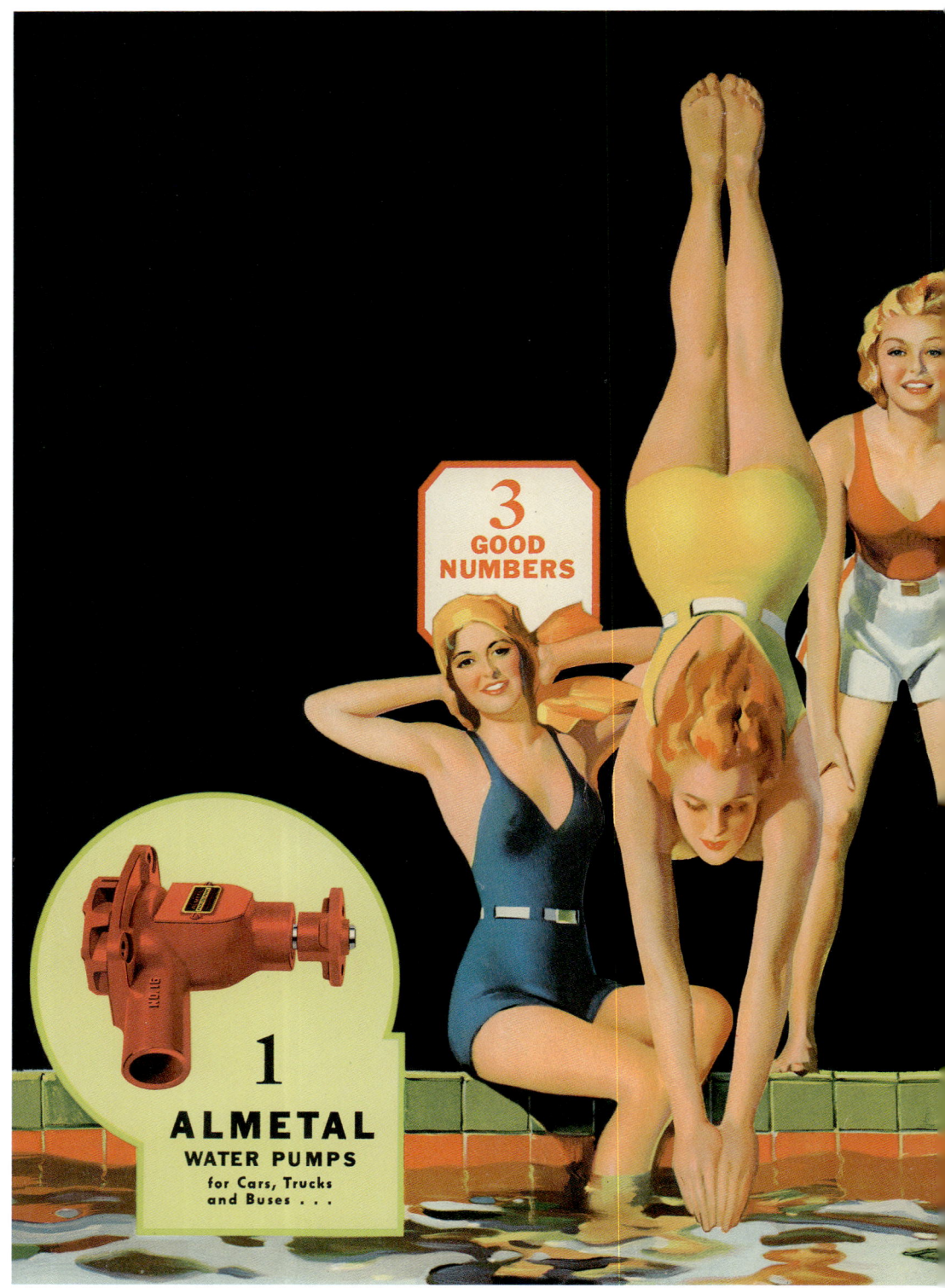

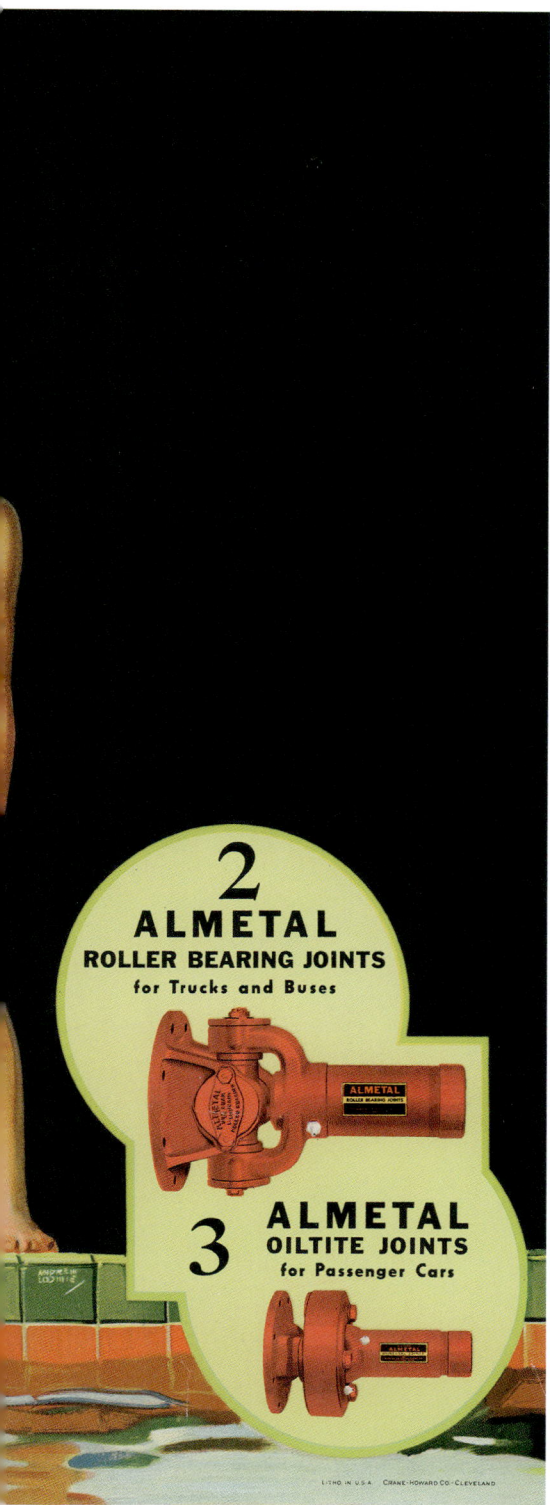

Left: A huge calendar-top lithograph for Almetal automotive parts, circa 1940, by Andrew Loomis. Auto parts manufacturers were one of the biggest supporters of pin-up art, given that garages are notoriously gendered spaces. 19.75 x 16.75 inches.

JOHN SCOTT
"ROLF" ARMSTRONG

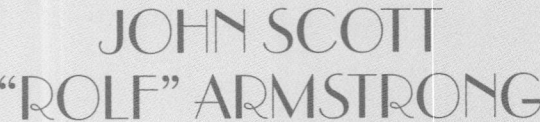

1889–1960

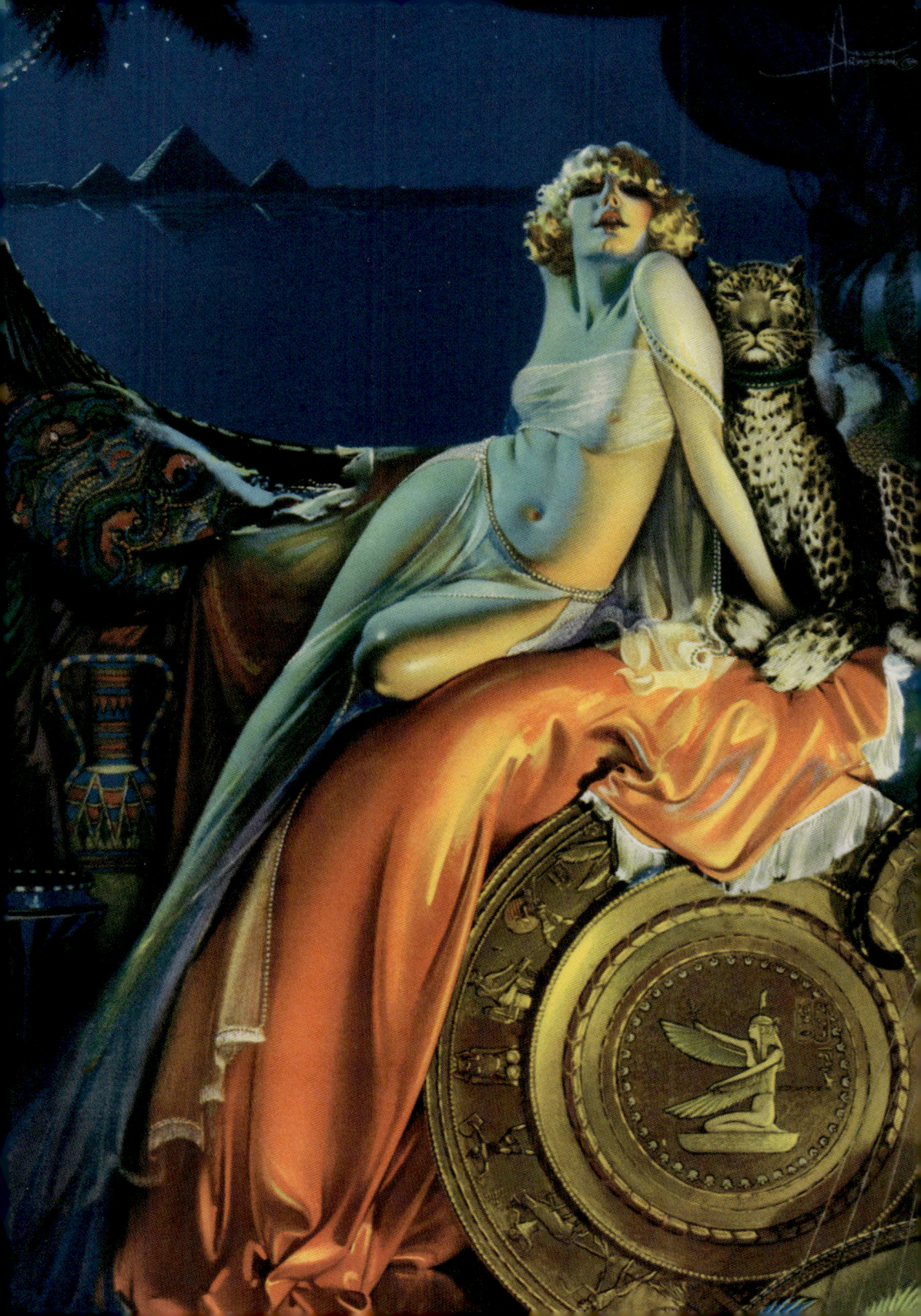

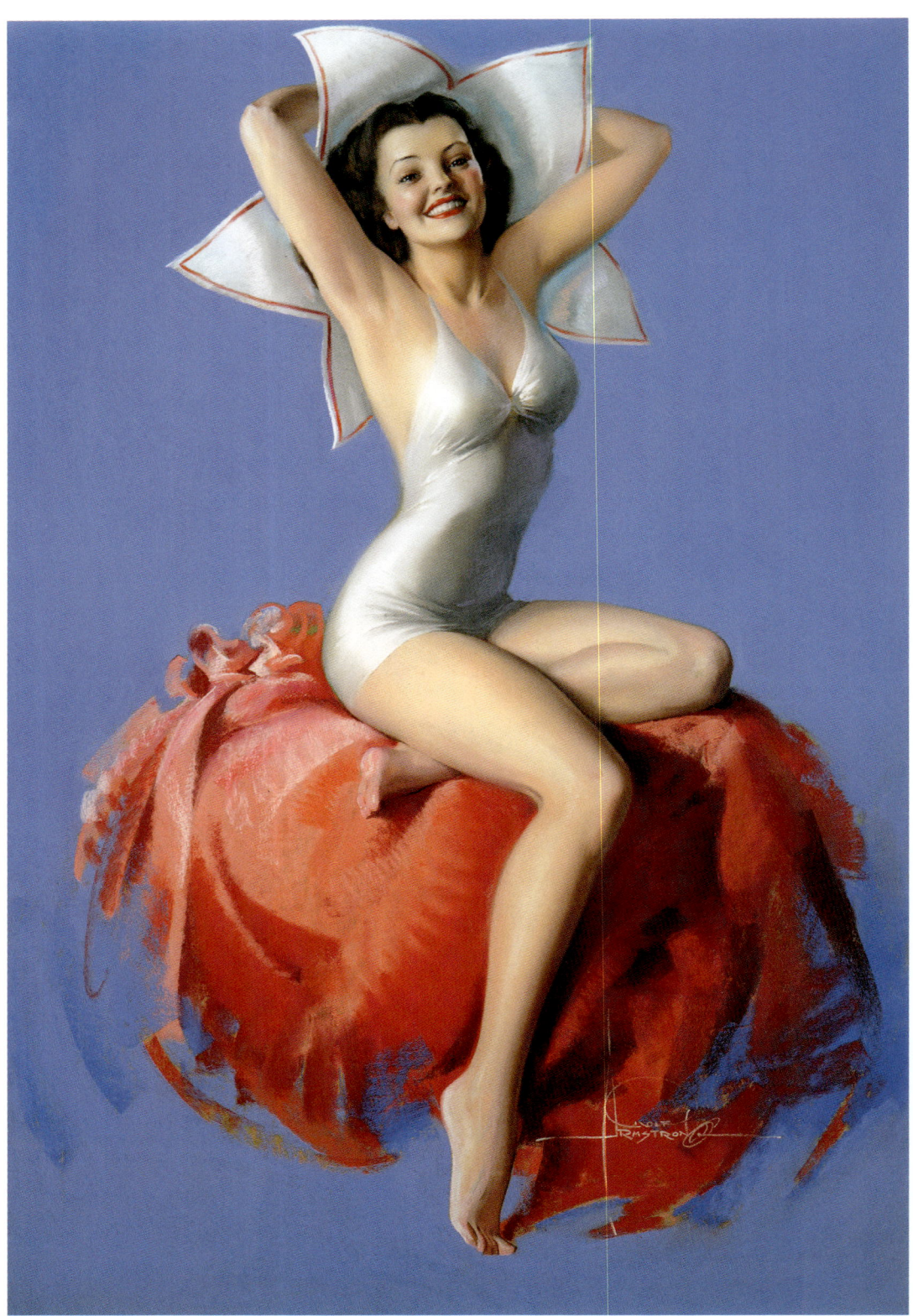

Rolf Armstrong, born in Michigan, 1889, the son of a tugboat captain, quit school after eighth grade to earn money as an amateur boxer and dockworker, and to sketch the nightlife of the gritty port city of Seattle. At 18 he returned to the Midwest to attend the School of the Art Institute of Chicago (SAIC). There, he lived in a one-room apartment with, among others, Thomas Hart Benton. Though the school's purpose was to train working illustrators, Armstrong graduated feeling uneasy about commercial art.

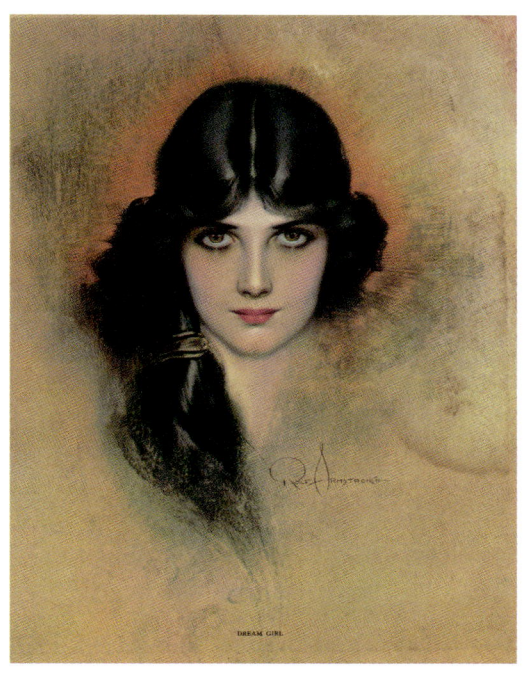

A 1920 article describes the artist as "a young giant, massive shoulders towering above a slim waist wrapped in a Apache sash …[suggesting] the great woods of the Northwest—the prize ring." Armstrong explains the difference between him and common illustrators: "Some, with a rudimentary knowledge of the craft, have been able to juggle a few superficial tricks until they have produced a type of saccharine, feminine prettiness acceptable to the public. This they turn out with the mechanical regularity with which the celebrated Mr. Heinz produces his pickles—but without any of the 'fifty-seven varieties.'"

Armstrong's roundabout attack on the Gibson Girl school of illustration that predominated from 1900 to 1920 was followed by an explosion of sultry Armstrong girls on sheet music, magazine covers, and in advertising, pushing everything from condoms to root beer. Armstrong's coy, mysterious flappers both reflected and influenced the seismic change in feminine ideals during the Jazz Age. He was one of the first artists to show American women sporting kohl-rimmed eyes, faux beauty marks, rouge, and red lipstick—the signature look of flappers. His illustrations

Page 103: Cleopatra was Rolf Armstrong's first monumental work, a rare oil on canvas measuring 7 x 5 feet, painted in 1924 for this 1926 Brown & Bigelow calendar.

Opposite: Pastel on board of Jewel Flowers, circa 1945.

Above: Dream Girl, pastel on board, 1915, was Armstrong's first calendar published by Brown & Bigelow, in 1919. The portrait was originally commissioned for *American Magazine's* September 1915 cover.

JOHN SCOTT "ROLF" ARMSTRONG

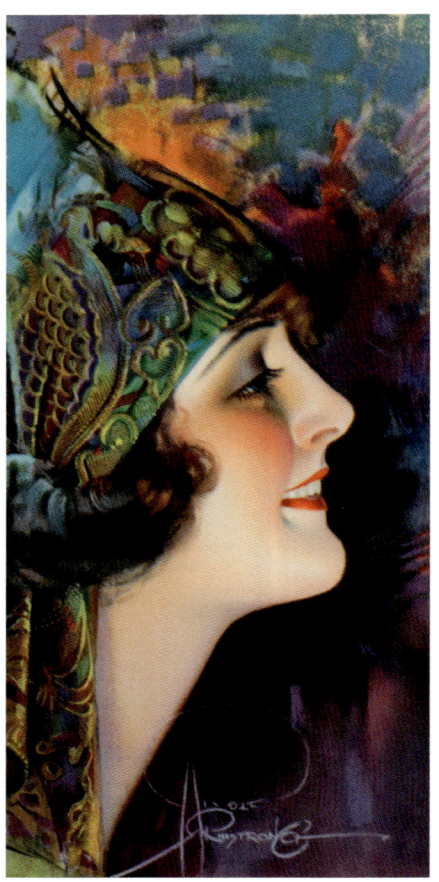

of exotic, defiant girls were tacked up in dressing rooms by those attempting to perfect Armstrong's erotically forward, outrageously made-up new vision of femininity. So far-reaching was the influence of his heavy-lidded, bow-lipped floating heads and long-limbed, sinuous figures that Armstrong became known as the "father of American pin-up," achieving true celebrity in the 1920s.

No illustrator was more photographed than Armstrong, and the photos show a man who made himself into a work of art. His studio was a continual party populated by beautiful models, since he always worked from life. He loved to pose standing in profile with his oversized palette of pastels, his chest thrust out, his waist tightly cinched, a Hemingway with a touch of girlishness. Ample records exist of his well-appointed studios, sailing trophies, cherished Duesenberg sportster, signature ascots and berets, well-muscled arms, and stylish flapper wife, Louise — who later left Armstrong to marry his nephew, the character actor Robert Armstrong. Armstrong took even that as a sophisticate: After a brief display of hurt feelings, he accepted his cuck-oldry, and the three remained "as one family."

But then, the marriage had been unconventional from the start. The couple didn't live together until several months after their 1919 wedding. Two years later, when Armstrong was just beginning to acquire a name as an illustrator, he suspended his contracts to take Louise on an extravagant yearlong trip to Paris. There he emulated the 19th-century salon painters, creating an epic-scaled nude of his half-masked wife. Upon their return to the United States, he began designing and building a dream house on the shores of Long Island, pouring in endless time and money before its completion in 1931. For all of his pre-tensions to pure art, the folly of his dream home turned Armstrong cutthroat in business dealings. He would alter small details on previously completed pastels to resell the images as new, earning additional income with little additional work. This, though he was making $1,000 an image from Brown & Bigelow by the early 1930s, with a contract that guaranteed him the comparative fortune of $30,000 a year.

By the mid-'30s, full-body pin-ups were supplanting Armstrong's signature floating heads that had reproduced so well on magazine covers and in advertising. He struggled to adapt. Some of his work in these years stands the test of time, but it was his least successful period. In 1936 he and Louise followed Robert Armstrong out to Los Angeles (which may have been a warning

Above: This portrait of actress Martha Mansfield was originally commissioned for the July 1920 cover of *Photoplay* magazine. It became a calender in 1927 and is seen here reprinted on a box cover.

Opposite: Twinkle Toes, pastel on board, 1948, for a 1950 Brown & Bigelow calendar. Modeled by Jewel Flowers. 38 x 28.5 inches. Courtesy Heritage Auctions.

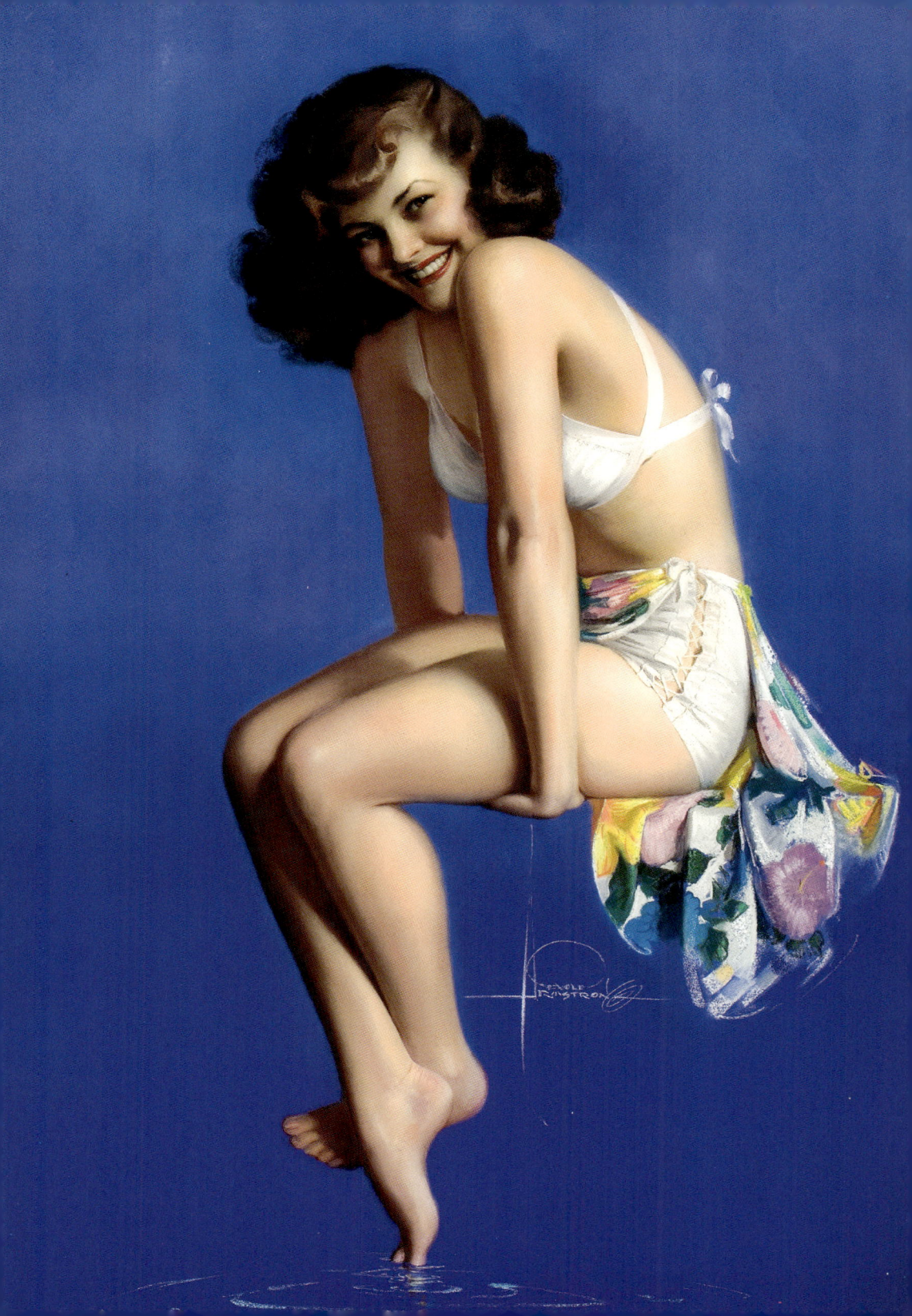

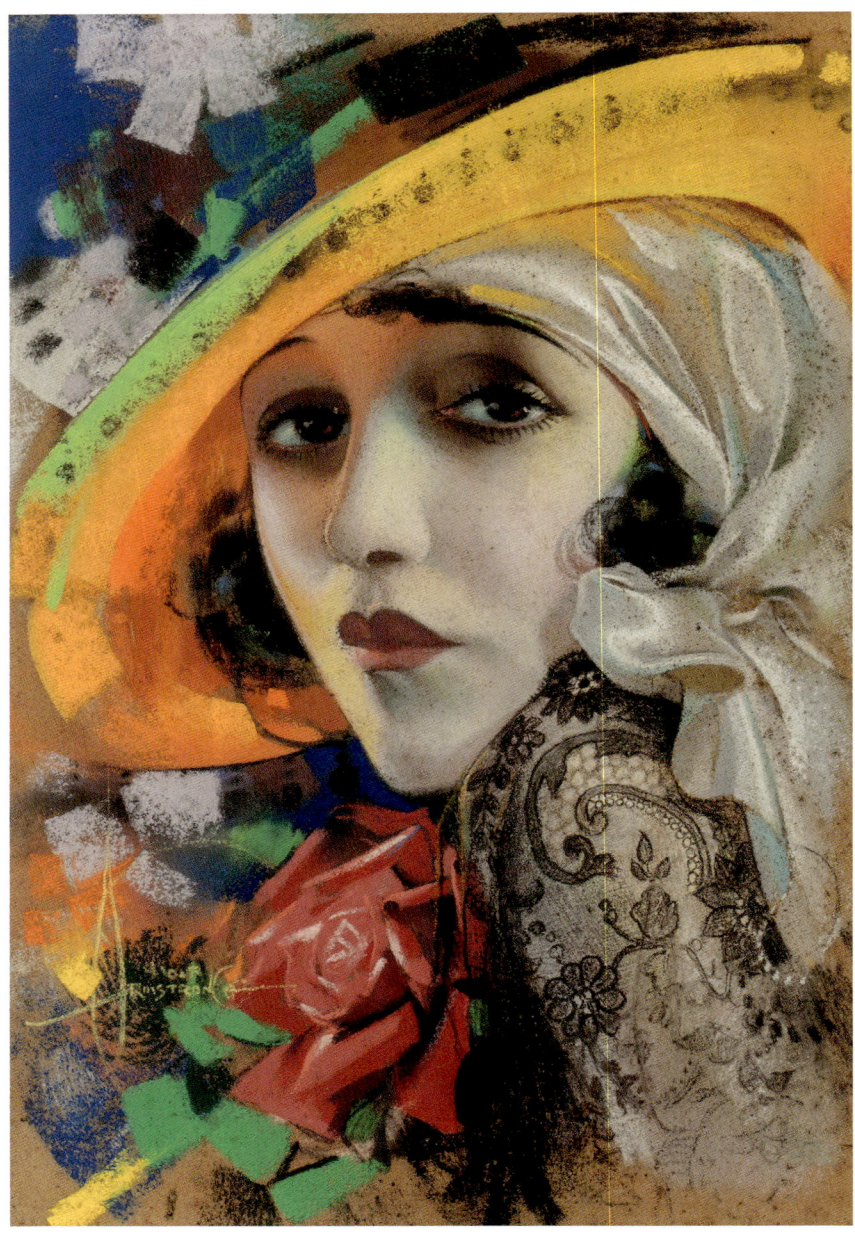

Above: Actress Bebe Daniels for the cover of *Photoplay* magazine, August 1921. Daniels was a child actor being recast as a glamour girl at age 20. Pastel on board, 1921, 15 x 10.5 inches. Courtesy Heritage Auctions.

Opposite: The consummate flapper adorning this 1930 art deco calendar, titled *Thinking of You,* was created as a cover commission for the March 1927 issue of *College Humor* magazine. Calendars were conceived as works of art in the 1920s and '30s, made of sturdy cardboard with the calendar element reduced to its smallest readable size.

sign as to where his relationship was headed), after Robert went west to pursue acting. Armstrong staged one-man shows, marketing reproductions of what he considered his finest efforts, and befriended potential Hollywood portrait clients like Jimmy Cagney, while still working as Brown & Bigelow's top pin-up artist. When both his marriage and hoped-for career as a celebrity portraitist failed, Armstrong returned to New York, setting up shop in the Hotel des Artistes, home to that other great Gibson successor, Howard Chandler Christy.

Once ensconced, Armstrong advertised in *The New York Times* for an artist's model. Small-town beauty queen Jewel Flowers answered his ad and became his quintessential muse. Brown & Bigelow had created a cult of personality around many of Armstrong's previous models, but Flowers was the first to surpass the artist in popularity. A tiny spitfire with an improbably wide smile and dramatic curves—plus that precious name—Flowers proved the perfect pin-up girl for war-torn America. Though early depictions lengthened her legs and played down her curves to give Flowers the streamlined look Armstrong favored, her personality overrode his vision, and he soon realized that her fans preferred a faithful reproduction.

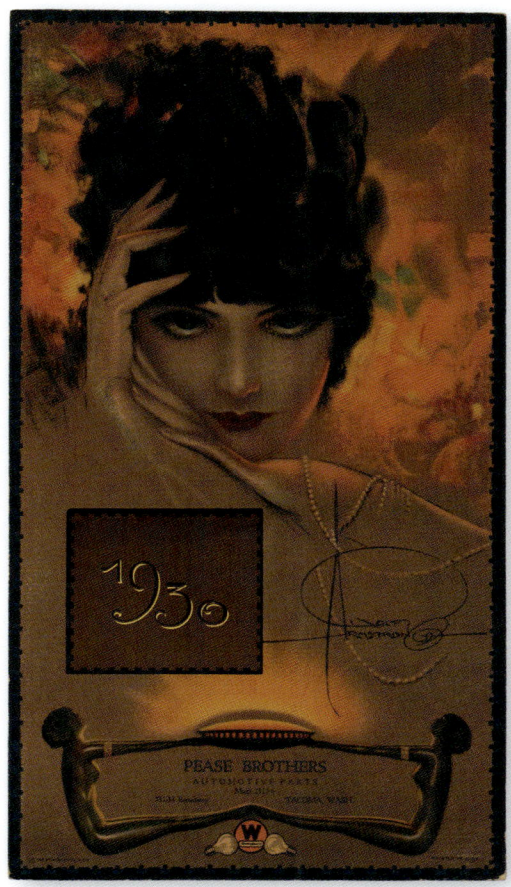

Flowers was introduced as a living pin-up at the 1943 War Advertising Conference. There, standing 4-foot-10 in her Yankee Doodle girl outfit beside Armstrong and his over-the-top patriotic pastel, few noticed the artist, flamboyant as he was. After that, Brown & Bigelow began using Flowers's photos to promote her pin-ups and her provocative association with Armstrong. Her calendars sold well, and servicemen were soon writing her lovestruck letters. Working with Flowers turned Armstrong, the self-styled sophisticate, into a chronicler of wholesome girlhood. Gone was the penetrating stare of the challenging, independent modern woman. In her place, Armstrong developed a personal obsession with depicting Flowers as a cowgirl, as intense and inscrutable as George Petty's fixation on ballet shoes.

Armstrong and Flowers worked together for over 15 years—far longer than the careers of most artists' models—and during those years she became his surrogate daughter, secretary, and occasional escort. When Armstrong moved to Hawaii in the 1950s to enjoy semiretirement, he campaigned for Flowers to relocate with her husband and young son, just to keep her close. And upon Armstrong's death in 1960, Flowers and Louise shared the duty of disposing of his estate and keeping the memory of the father of American pin-up alive.

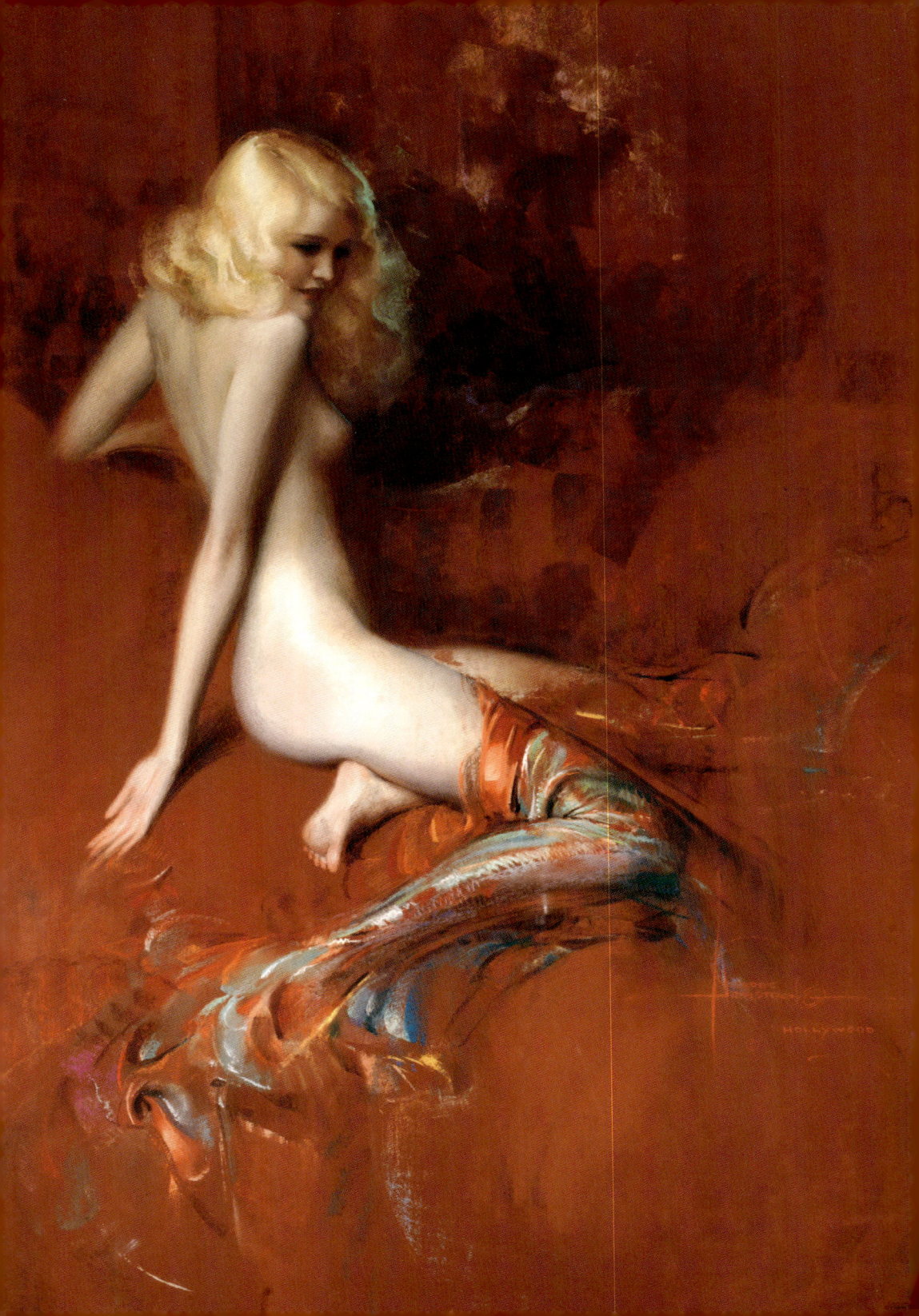

„Der Einfluss seiner Darstellungen … war so weitreichend,
dass Armstrong nicht nur als ‚Vater der amerikanischen Pin-ups‘ gilt,
sondern in den 1920er-Jahren auch echte Berühmtheit erlangte."

Rolf Armstrong, der 1889 in Michigan
geborene Sohn eines Schleppdampfer-
kapitäns, verließ die Schule nach der
achten Klasse, um als Amateurboxer und
Dockarbeiter Geld zu verdienen und das
Nachtleben der Hafenstadt Seattle in Bildern festzuhalten. Mit 18 kehrte er in den
Mittleren Westen zurück und besuchte
das Art Institute of Chicago (SAIC). Er
lebte dort in einer Einzimmerwohnung,
unter anderen mit Thomas Hart Benton.
Das Institut bildete eigentlich Grafiker
für Gebrauchsgegenstände aus, und so
machte Armstrong mit Unbehagen einen
Abschluss in kommerzieller Kunst.

In einem Artikel von 1920 wird der
Künstler als „junger Riese mit breiten
Schultern, die hoch über einer schmalen,
von einer Apacheschärpe umschlungenen
Taille ragen" beschrieben, als Typ, der
„an die weiten Wälder des Nordwestens"
oder an „einen Boxring" denken lässt.

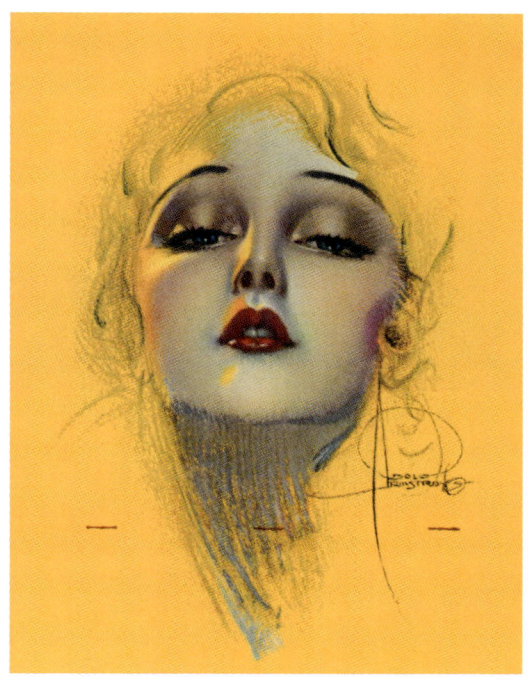

Armstrong erklärt den Unterschied zwischen ihm und gewöhnlichen Illustratoren: „Manchen,
die nur über rudimentäre handwerkliche Kenntnisse verfügen, ist es gelungen, mit ein paar
oberflächlichen Tricks einen Typ von zuckersüßer weiblicher Schönheit hervorzubringen, der
für das Publikum annehmbar ist. Sie fahren mit jener mechanischen Regelmäßigkeit fort, mit
der der berühmte Mr. Heinz seine Soßen produziert – doch ohne dessen ‚57 Variationen‘."

Armstrongs Rundumschlag gegen die Gibson-Girl-Schule, die von 1900 bis 1920 dieses
Genre dominierte, folgte ein wahres Feuerwerk sinnlicher Armstrong-Mädchen auf Notenblät-
tern, Zeitschriftentiteln und in der Werbung, die alles – von Kondomen bis Wurzelbier –

Opposite: Rosalie, also known as *Hollywood Venus*, pastel on board, 1933, was created for a Brown & Bigelow
calendar, circa 1935. It is one of four blonde nudes
created by Armstrong in the mid-'30s, all posed by the
same model. It was one of Armstrong's favorite works
and hung in his studio for 20 years. 41 x 29.5 inches.

Above: Cherie, pastel on board, 1930, for a 1932
Brown & Bigelow calendar.

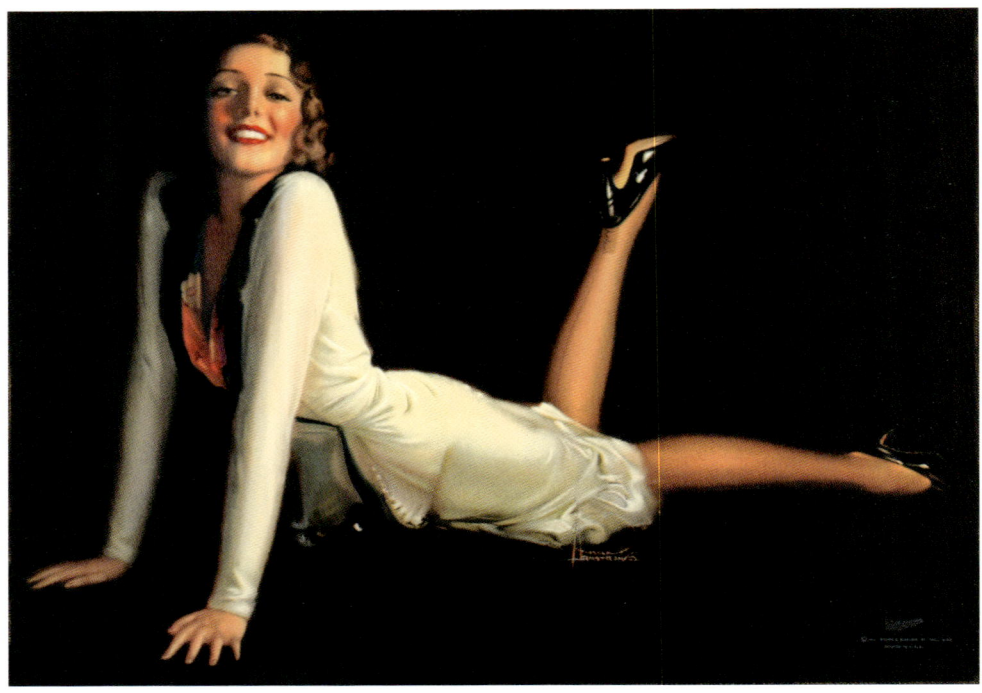

anpriesen. Armstrongs kokette, geheimnisvolle Flappers reflektierten und beeinflussten die seismischen Veränderungen des weiblichen Ideals im Zeitalter des Jazz. Er war einer der ersten Künstler, die amerikanische Frauen mit kajalumrandeten Augen, falschen Schönheitsflecken, Rouge und Lippenstift darstellten – dem Erkennungslook der Flappers. Seine Bilder exotischer, herausfordernder Mädchen wurden von jenen in Umkleidekabinen an die Wand geheftet, die Armstrongs erotisch fortschrittliche, schamlos erfundene neue Vision der Weiblichkeit perfektionieren wollten. Der Einfluss seiner Darstellungen, die schlanke Mädchen mit schweren Lidern, schmollenden Lippen, schwerelos bewegenden Köpfen und geschmeidigen Körpern zeigten, war so weitreichend, dass Armstrong nicht nur als „Vater der amerikanischen Pin-ups" gilt, sondern in den 1920er-Jahren auch echte Berühmtheit erlangte.

Kein Illustrator wurde häufiger fotografiert als Rolf Armstrong: Die Fotos zeigen einen Mann, der sich selbst zu einem Kunstwerk stilisierte. In seinem Atelier herrschte fortwährend Partystimmung, hier tummelten sich schöne Frauen, denn er arbeitete stets nach Modell. Gerne posierte er im Profil mit seiner überdimensionierten Farbpalette, die Brust herausgestreckt, die Taille eng gegurtet, wie ein Hemingway mit einem Hauch Mädchenhaftigkeit. Von allem, was ihn umgab, gibt es reichlich Aufnahmen – von seinen gut ausgestatteten Ateliers, Segeltrophäen, dem geliebten Duesenberg-Sportwagen, seinen Markenkrawatten und -baretten, von seinen muskulösen Oberarmen und seiner modebewussten Flapper-Frau Louise –, die ihn später verließ, um seinen Neffen, den Charakterdarsteller Robert Armstrong zu heiraten. Selbst das nahm Rolf als mondäne Angelegenheit hin: Nach einer kurzen Phase der Zurschaustellung

Above: You'd Be Surprised, lithograph for a 1932 Brown & Bigelow calendar.

Opposite: Girl on Cushion, usage unknown. Pastel on paper, circa 1940, 38 x 24.5 inches. Courtesy Heritage Auctions.

THE ART OF PIN-UP

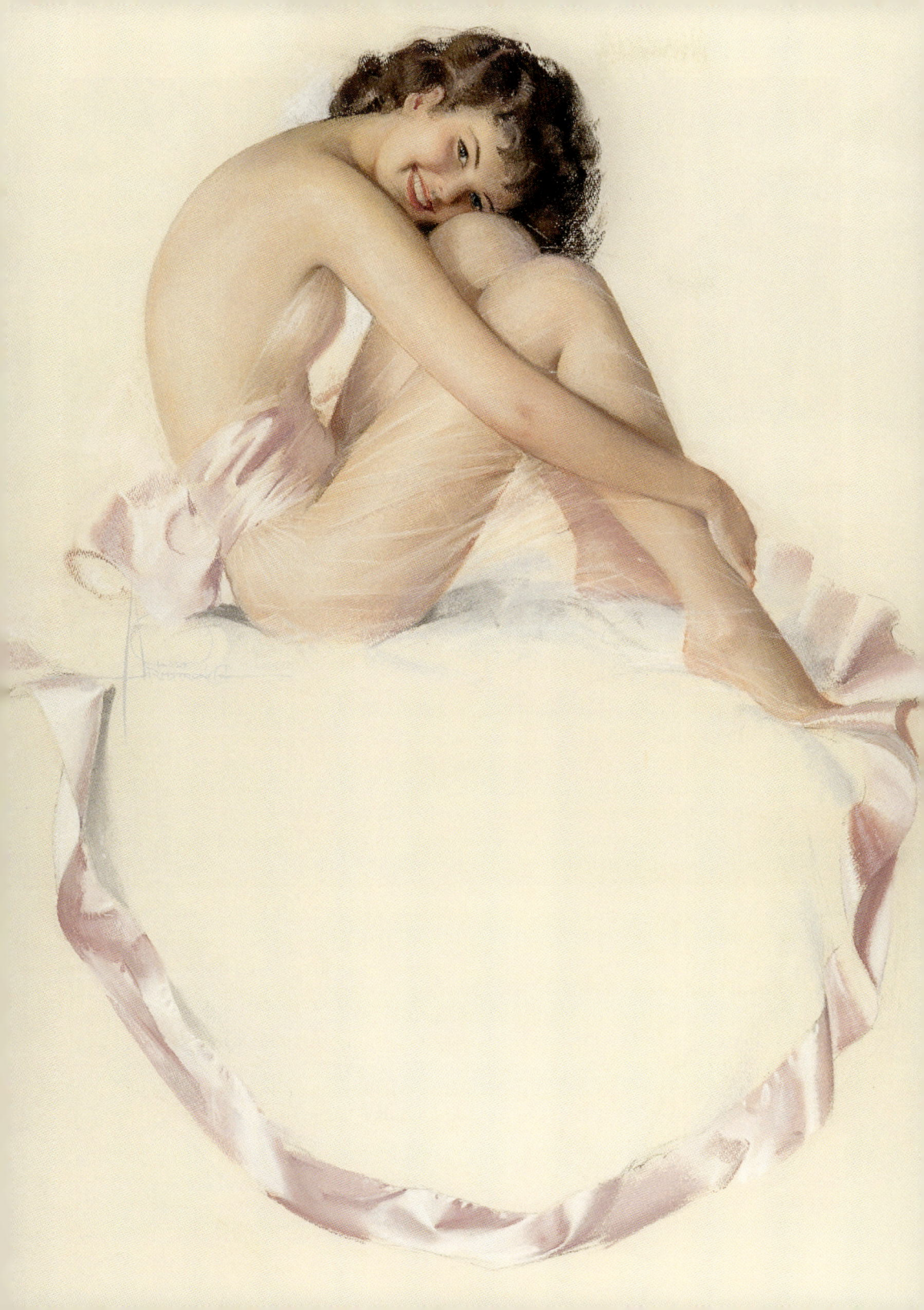

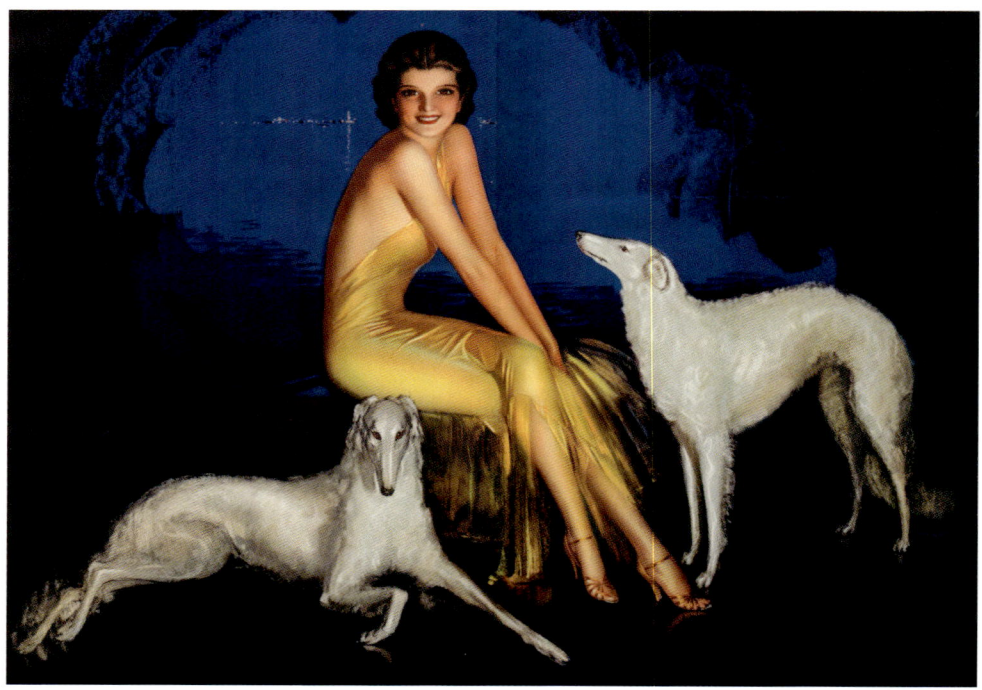

verletzter Gefühle akzeptierte er seine Rolle als betrogener Ehemann, und die drei blieben „als Familie" zusammen.

Seine Ehe war ohnehin von Anfang an unkonventionell. Das Paar zog erst mehrere Monate nach der 1919 gefeierten Hochzeit zusammen. Zwei Jahre später – er war gerade auf dem besten Wege, sich als Künstler einen Namen zu machen – kündigte Armstrong seine Verträge, um sich mit Louise einen extravaganten einjährigen Aufenthalt in Paris zu gönnen. Dort eiferte er den Salonmalern des 19. Jahrhunderts nach und schuf ein riesig dimensioniertes Aktbild seiner halb maskierten Frau. Zurück in den USA begann er, an der Küste von Long Island ein selbst entworfenes Traumhaus zu errichten, in das er bis zur Fertigstellung 1931 endlos viel Zeit und Geld investierte. Trotz seines Anspruchs, ein ernst zu nehmender Künstler zu sein, ließ dieser Prunkbau Armstrong in geschäftlichen Dingen unseriös werden. So änderte er zum Beispiel an älteren Pastellen kleine Details, verkaufte diese Motive dann erneut als neu und verschaffte sich so mit wenig Arbeit zusätzliche Einkünfte, und das, obwohl er in den frühen 1930er-Jahren von Brown & Bigelow für jedes Bild 1 000 Dollar erhielt und ihm vertraglich 30 000 Dollar pro Jahr garantiert waren, damals ein stattliches Vermögen.

Mitte der 1930er-Jahre verdrängten Ganzkörper-Pin-ups Armstrongs dynamisch schwebende Mädchenköpfe vom Markt. Sie waren sein Markenzeichen gewesen, das auf Zeitschriftencover und in Anzeigen so gut angekommen war. Er kämpfte, um sich den neuen Verhältnissen anzupassen. Manche seiner Arbeiten aus jenen Jahren haben die Zeiten

Above: Good Evening, 1936, for a 1938 Brown & Bigelow calendar.

Opposite: Ripplin' Rhythm, for a 1948 Brown & Bigelow calendar. Pastel on paper laid on board, 1947, 40.5 x 29 inches. Courtesy Heritage Auctions.

THE ART OF PIN-UP

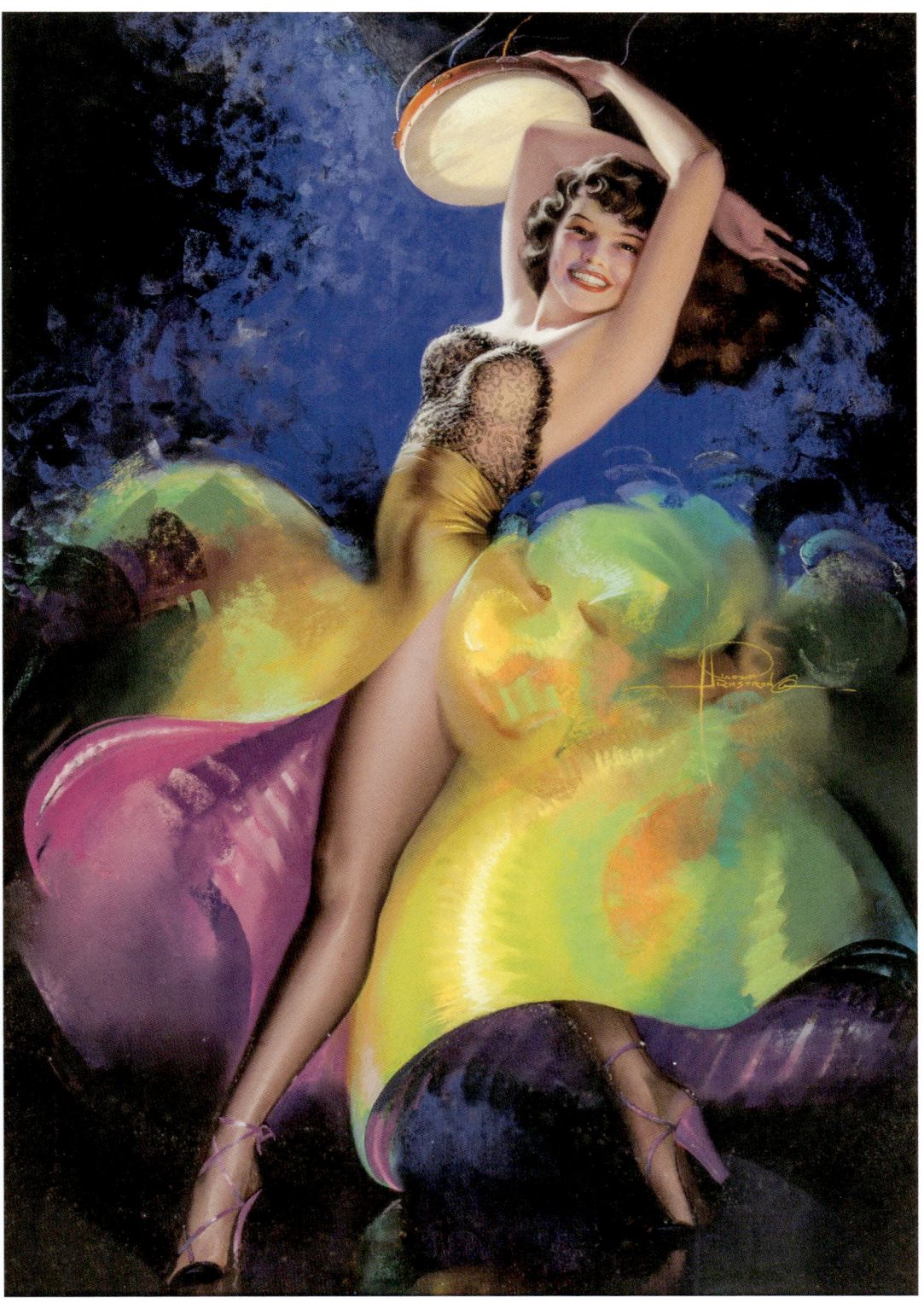

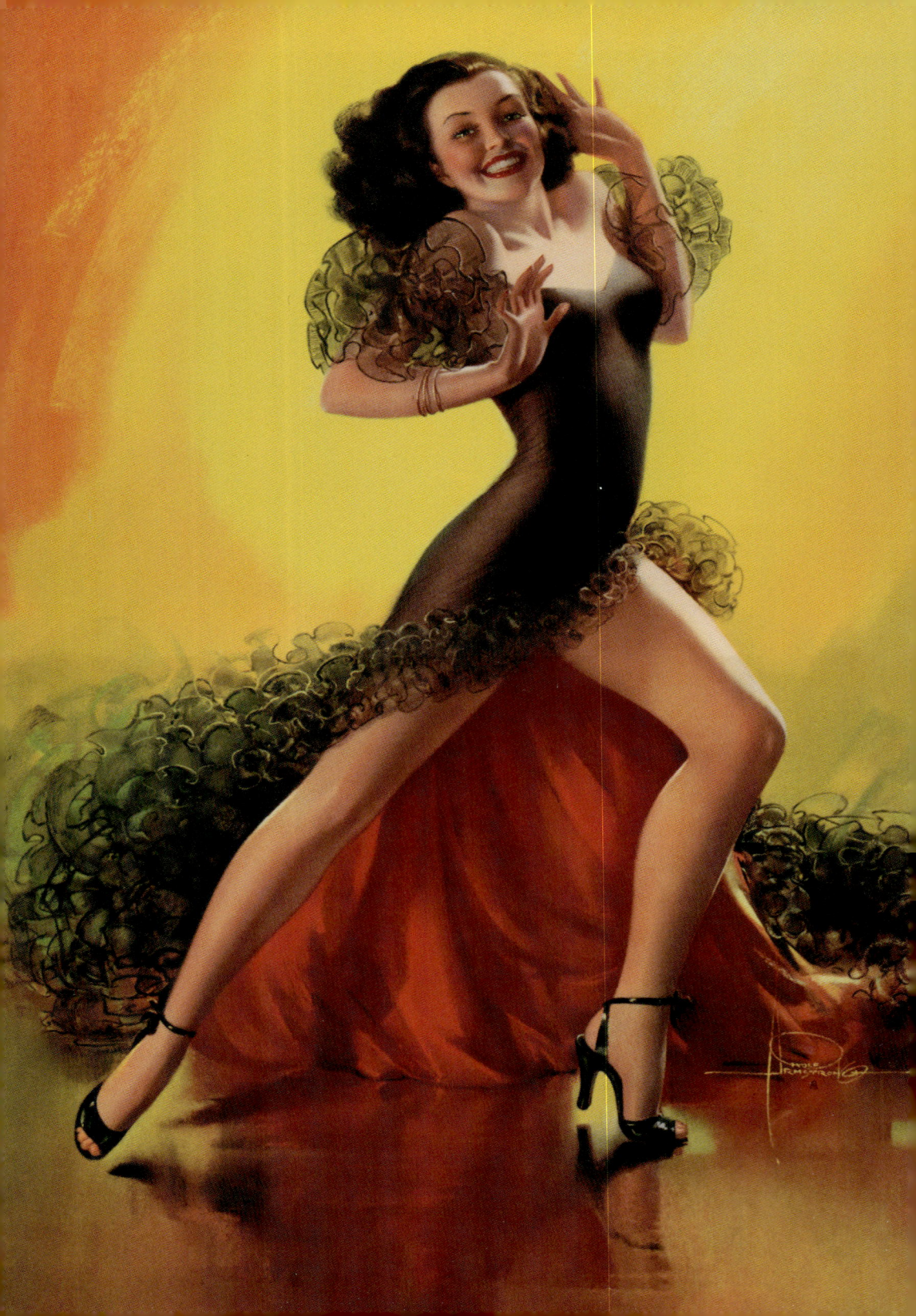

überdauert, doch es war keine erfolgreiche Periode. 1936 folgten er und Louise Robert Armstrong nach Hollywood (eigentlich ein Warnsignal, in welche Richtung sich seine Ehe entwickelte), da Robert sich wegen seiner Schauspielkarriere nach Westen aufgemacht hatte. Armstrong veranstaltete Einzelausstellungen, vermarktete Reproduktionen von Werken, die er als seine besten Arbeiten betrachtete, und befreundete sich mit potenziellen Porträtkunden in Hollywood, wie Jimmy Cagney. Zugleich war er noch als Top-Pin-up-Künstler für Brown & Bigelow tätig. Nachdem sowohl seine Ehe wie auch seine erhoffte Karriere als Porträtmaler von Stars gescheitert waren, kehrte Armstrong nach New York zurück und richtete sich sein Geschäft im Hotel des Artistes ein, in dem auch ein anderer bedeutender Gibson-Nachfolger zu Hause war, und zwar Howard Chandler Christy.

Dann gab Armstrong – auf der Suche nach einem Modell – in der *New York Times* eine Anzeige auf. Jewel Flowers, eine Kleinstadtschönheit, bewarb sich bei ihm und wurde seine vollkommene Muse. Brown & Bigelow hatte schon um viele frühere Armstrong-Modelle einen Kult geschaffen, doch Jewel war das erste Mädchen, das den Künstler an Popularität übertraf. Jewel Flowers, ein zierliches Hitzköpfchen mit einem unglaublich breiten Lächeln und dramatischen Rundungen, das dazu noch diesen kostbaren Namen hatte, erwies sich als das perfekte Pin-up-Mädchen für das kriegsgeplagte Amerika. In frühen Darstellungen hatte Jewel die für Armstrong typischen lang gezogenen Beine und abgeflachten Rundungen, doch Armstrong merkte bald, dass Jewels Fans eine wirklichkeitsgetreue Darstellung des Modells bevorzugten.

Auf der War Advertising Conference von 1943 wurde Jewel als lebendes Pin-up vorgestellt. Als die kaum 1,50 m große Jewel in Yankee-Doodle-Mädchenkleidung neben Rolf und seinem etwas übertrieben patriotischen Pastell stand, beachteten nur wenige den ziemlich extravaganten Künstler. Danach setzte Brown & Bigelow Fotos von Jewel ein, um ihre Pin-ups zu promoten und ihre Verbindung zu Armstrong zu unterstreichen. Ihre Kalender verkauften sich gut, und bald schon schrieben ihr Soldaten Liebesbriefe. Die Arbeit mit Jewel sorgte dafür, dass Armstrong, der selbst ernannte Dandy, zu einem Chronisten mustergültiger Mädchenjahre wurde. Der durchdringende Blick anspruchsvoller, unabhängiger Frauen war nun nicht mehr gefragt. Stattdessen entwickelte Armstrong die ganz persönliche Obsession, Jewel als Cowboy-Mädchen darzustellen, eine Besessenheit, die genau so intensiv und unerklärlich war wie George Pettys Fixierung auf Ballettschuhe.

Armstrong und Jewel Flowers arbeiteten mehr als 15 Jahre zusammen – weit länger, als die Karrieren der meisten Modelle überhaupt dauern –, und im Laufe dieser Jahre wurde sie für ihn Ersatztochter, Sekretärin und gelegentliche Begleiterin. Als Armstrong in den 1950er-Jahren nach Hawaii zog, um seine Altersteilzeit zu genießen, engagierte er sich dafür, dass Jewel mit ihrem Mann und ihrem kleinen Sohn nachzog, nur um sie in seiner Nähe zu haben. Und nachdem Armstrong 1960 gestorben war, übernahmen Jewel und Louise gemeinsam die Verpflichtung, sich um sein Erbe zu kümmern und die Erinnerung an den Vater des amerikanischen Pin-ups lebendig zu halten.

Opposite: Let's Go, 1945, on a 1947 calendar lithograph,
was one of a series of dance-themed calendar illustrations
created for Brown & Bigelow between 1942 and 1950,
all modeled by Jewel Flowers. Calendar measures
26 x 22 inches.

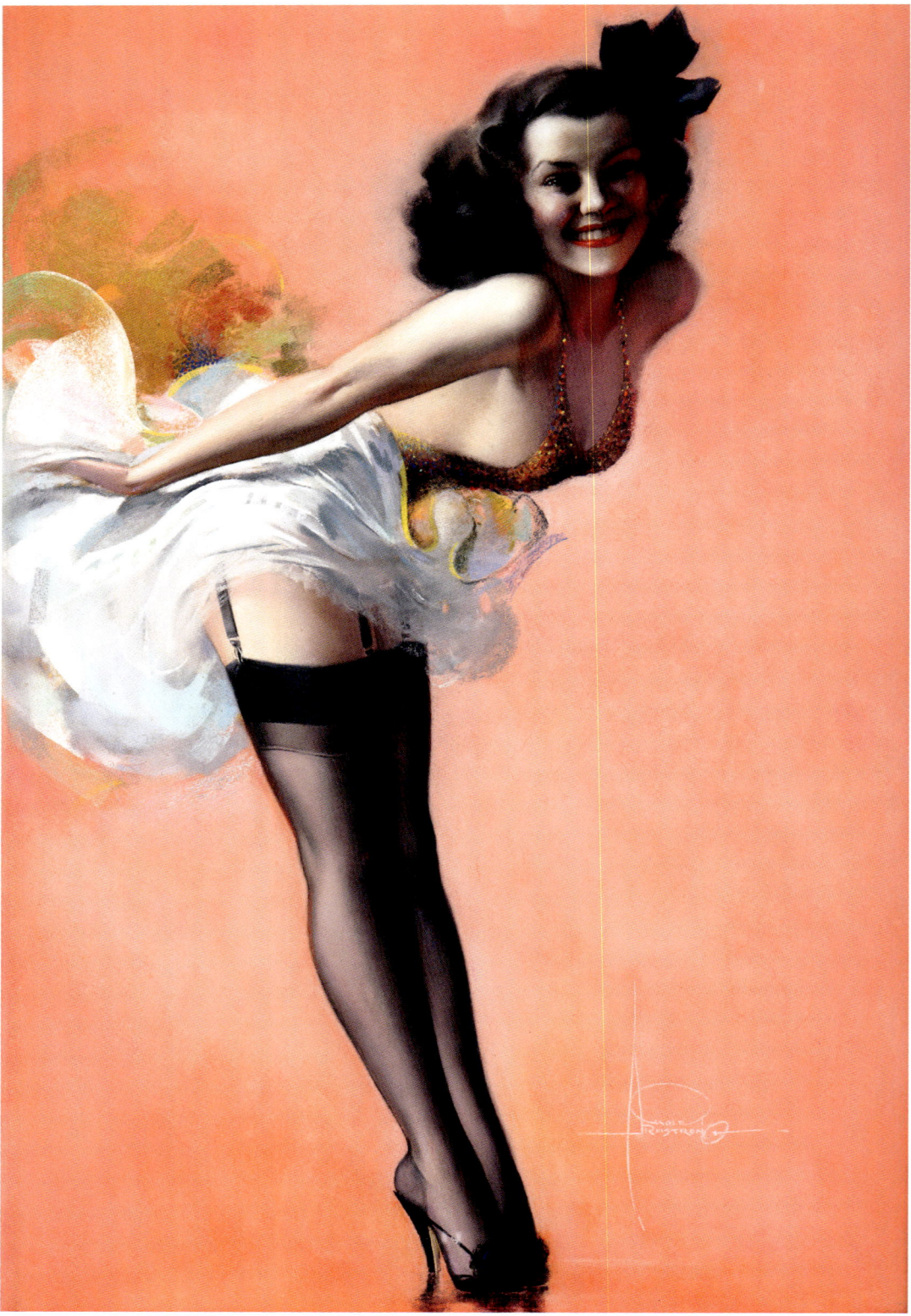

« Ses visages flottants de femmes aux paupières lourdes et aux
lèvres très dessinées, ainsi que ses silhouettes gracieuses aux longues
jambes exercèrent une telle influence qu'il devint le "père
de la pin-up américaine". »

Né en 1889 dans le Michigan, fils d'un capitaine
de remorqueur, Rolf Armstrong quitta l'école
avant l'âge de 15 ans pour gagner sa vie comme
boxeur amateur et docker à Seattle. Déjà, il réalisait
des esquisses de la vie nocturne dans le port.
À 18 ans, il s'inscrivit à l'Art Institute de Chicago.
Il partageait un petit appartement avec, entre
autres, Thomas Hart Benton. Bien que le but de
l'école soit de former des illustrateurs, Armstrong
n'était pas à son aise avec l'art sur commande.

Un article de 1920 le décrit comme « un
géant, avec des épaules massives et une taille fine
ceinte d'une écharpe apache […] semblant tout
droit sorti des forêts du Nord-Ouest ou du ring ».
Armstrong expliqua lui-même ce qui le distin-
guait des autres illustrateurs : « Certains, avec des
connaissances rudimentaires, parviennent à maîtriser quelques procédés superficiels pour produire un
ersatz de joliesse acceptable pour le grand public.
Ensuite, ils pondent leurs images avec la même
régularité mécanique que M. Heinz ses fameux
cornichons, mais sans aucune des "57 variétés". »

Cette critique acerbe de l'école de la Gibson
Girl qui prédominait depuis 1900 fut suivie d'un
déferlement d'Armstrong Girls sur des partitions,
des couvertures de magazine et des publicités van-
tant toutes sortes de produits, des préservatifs aux
sodas. Ses beautés sensuelles, mystérieuses et fausse-

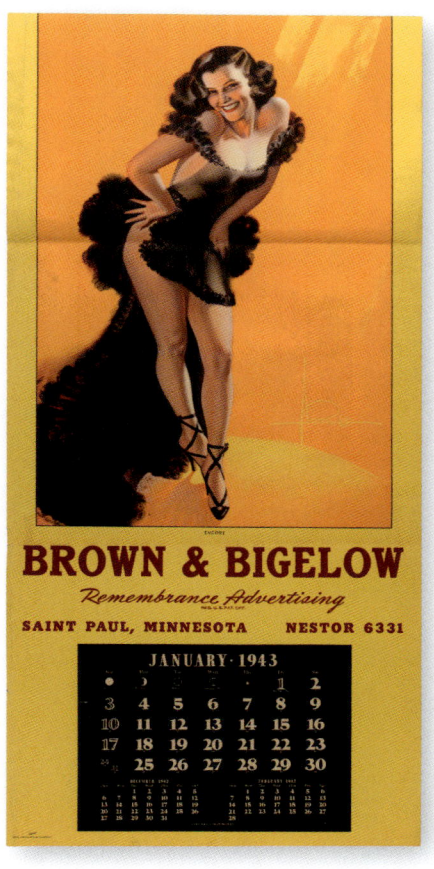

ment timides reflétaient les changements radicaux de l'idéal féminin dans les années 1920 autant
qu'elles les influencèrent. Il fut l'un des premiers à montrer des garçonnes américaines aux
yeux bordés de khôl, arborant des mouches, du fard à joues et des lèvres rouges. Ses images de
femmes provocantes étaient punaisées dans les loges de celles qui tentaient d'imiter sa vision

Opposite: Toast of the Town, pastel on paper, 1942,
posed by Jewel Flowers, for a 1945 calendar. 41 x 28 inches.

Above: Encore, circa 1941, was an attempt to cash
in on the popularity of *How Am I Doing?*, using Flowers
in the same black rhumba dress and ankle-wrap shoes.
Calendar measures 46 x 22 inches.

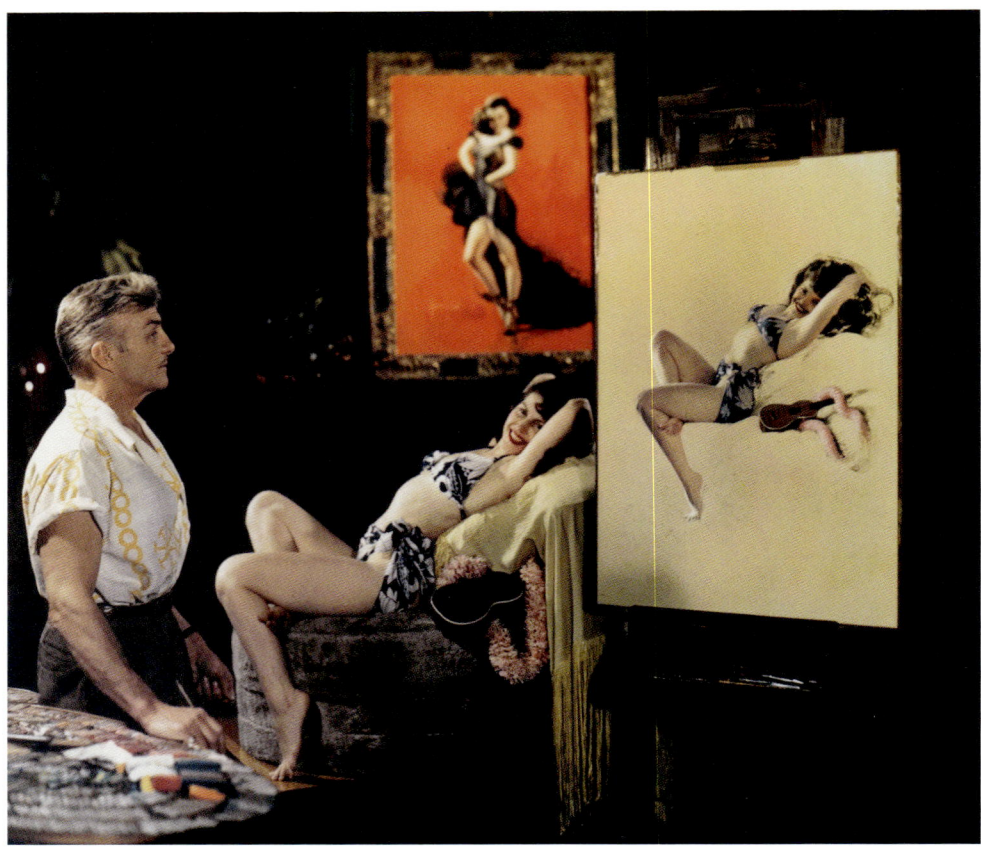

d'une féminité charnelle et outrageusement fardée. Ses visages flottants de femmes aux paupières lourdes et aux lèvres très dessinées, ainsi que ses silhouettes gracieuses aux longues jambes exercèrent une telle influence qu'il devint le « père de la pin-up américaine ».

Aucun illustrateur ne fut autant photographié que Rolf Armstrong, un artiste qui fit de lui-même une œuvre d'art. Son atelier était peuplé de jolies filles, car il ne travaillait que d'après nature. Il aimait poser de profil, la taille serrée, bombant le torse et tenant sa grande palette de pastels, une sorte d'Hemingway avec une touche de féminité. On trouve d'innombrables photos de ses ateliers richement meublés, ses trophées de pêche, sa chère *sportster* Duesenberg, ses lavallières et ses bérets, ses gros biceps et son élégante épouse, Louise, qui le quitta plus tard pour son neveu, l'acteur Robert Armstrong. Là encore, Rolf prit la chose avec élégance : après avoir

Above: Rolf Armstrong and Jewel Flowers in a posed photograph showing his technique of working from life models. *How Am I Doing?* hangs in the background.

Opposite: How Am I Doing?, 1940, was Armstrong's first and favorite pastel of his muse, Jewel Flowers. The title came from her incessant need for reassurance throughout the posing session. The image first appeared on a 1942 calendar and was Brown & Bigelow's bestseller

of the year, so it was rereleased in this costly frame-style calendar with tipped-in print the next year. When Grapefruit Moon gallerists Dan Murphy and Sarahjane Blum acquired Flowers's archive after her death, they found a box of wrinkled and tattered costumes that included the *How Am I Doing?* dress. The sad reality of this cheap gauzy rag proves Armstrong's power of imagination.

THE ART OF PIN-UP

brièvement exprimé ses sentiments meurtris, il accepta son rôle de cocu et le trio forma « une famille unie ».

Cela dit, leur ménage n'avait jamais été conventionnel.

Le couple n'emménagea ensemble que quelques mois après leur mariage en 1919. Deux ans plus tard, alors qu'Armstrong commençait tout juste à se faire un nom dans le monde de l'illustration, il interrompit tous ses contrats pour emmener Louise pendant un an à Paris. Là, il imita les peintres académiques du XIXᵉ siècle, réalisant des nus monumentaux de Louise masquée. Lorsqu'ils rentrèrent aux États-Unis, il dessina les plans d'une demeure de rêve sur les berges de Long Island, y consacrant un temps et des sommes considérables jusqu'à son achèvement en 1931. Ce projet fit de lui un véritable requin en matière de négociations commerciales. Il altérait de légers détails de ses pastels antérieurs pour les revendre comme de nouvelles œuvres. Il vendait chaque image 1 000 dollars à Brown & Bigelow au début des années 1930, avec un contrat qui lui garantissait 30 000 dollars par an, une petite fortune à l'époque.

Au milieu des années 1930, les pin-up en pied commencèrent à supplanter les visages flottants d'Armstrong qui avaient eu tant de succès sur les couvertures des magazines et les publicités. Il s'efforça de s'adapter. Certaines de ses œuvres de cette époque ont résisté à l'épreuve du temps mais ce fut néanmoins sa période la moins réussie. En 1936, Louise et lui suivirent Robert à Los Angeles. Armstrong organisa des expositions personnelles, commercialisa des repro-

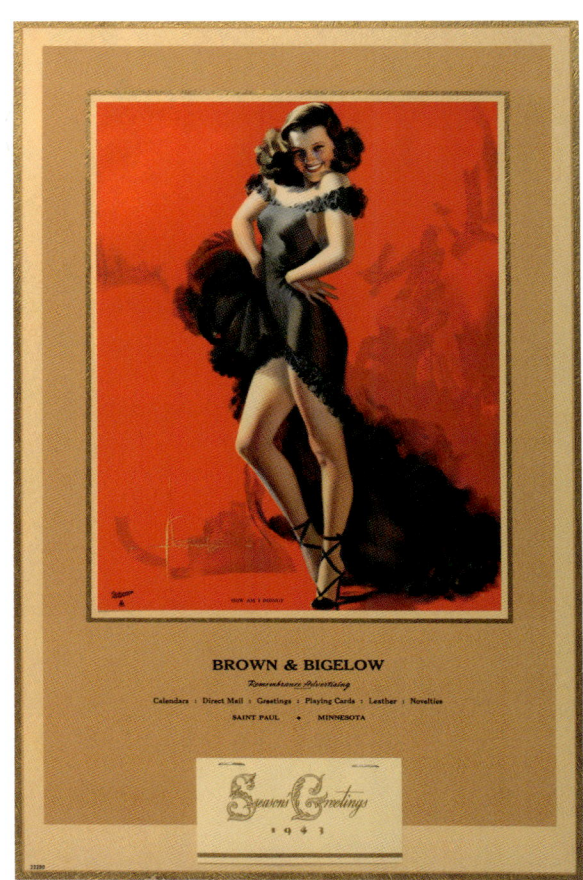

ductions de ce qu'il considérait comme ses meilleures œuvres et fréquenta d'éventuels clients de portraits comme James Cagney, sans cesser de réaliser des pin-up pour B&B. Lorsque son mariage et ses tentatives de devenir portraitiste de stars échouèrent, Armstrong rentra seul à New York et s'installa à l'Hôtel des Artistes, où logeait un autre grand successeur de Gibson, Howard Chandler Christy.

Là, Armstrong posta des petites annonces dans le *New York Times* pour trouver des modèles. Une ex-reine de beauté d'une petite ville de province lui répondit, Jewel Flowers. Elle devint sa muse. B&B avait déjà érigé en icônes de nombreux anciens modèles d'Armstrong mais Jewel fut la première à surpasser l'artiste en popularité. Petite créature volcanique avec un immense sourire et des courbes spectaculaires, elle était la pin-up rêvée pour une Amérique déchirée par la guerre. Dans ses premières toiles, Armstrong lui rallongea les jambes et atténua ses courbes pour lui donner l'allure élancée qu'il avait toujours privilégiée. Cependant, la personnalité de la jeune femme l'emporta sur sa vision et il se rendit vite compte que ses admirateurs la préféraient telle qu'elle était.

Jewel fut présentée comme pin-up vivante lors de la War Advertising Conference de 1943. Le petit bout de femme de moins de 1,50 mètre drapée dans une tenue aux couleurs du drapeau américain éclipsa Rolf et son tableau outrageusement patriotique. B&B commença à utiliser des photos d'elle pour promouvoir ses pin-up. Les calendriers où elle figurait partaient comme des petits pains et les soldats lui envoyaient des lettres d'amour. Sous son influence, Armstrong changea de registre pour peindre des filles débordantes de santé. Adieu le regard pénétrant de la garçonne émancipée. À sa place, il développa une obsession pour Jewel déguisée en cow-girl, une fixation aussi impénétrable que celle de George Petty pour les chaussons de danse.

Armstrong et Flowers collaborèrent pendant plus de quinze ans, plus que la carrière de la plupart des modèles d'artistes. Durant cette période, elle devint sa fille, sa secrétaire et, occasionnellement, sa compagne. Lorsqu'il emménagea à Hawaii à la fin des années 1950 pour y vivre une semi-retraite, il fit des pieds et des mains pour que Jewel et son mari l'y suivent. À sa mort en 1960, Jewel et Louise se partagèrent sa succession et veillèrent à maintenir vivante la mémoire du père de la pin-up américaine.

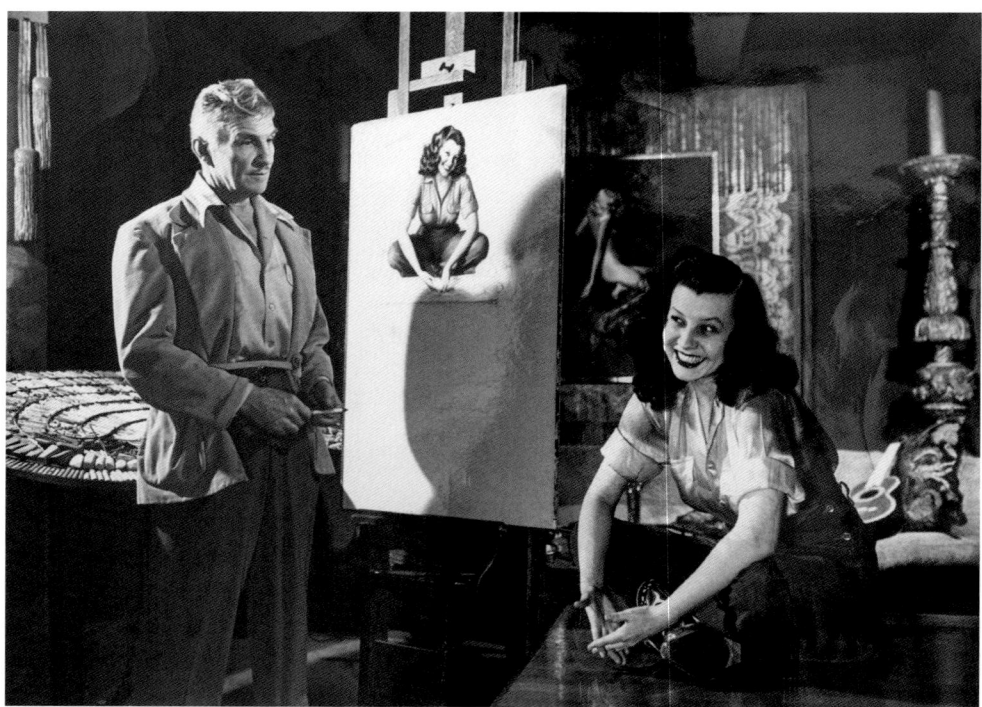

Above: Armstrong working on *Here We Go*, with Flowers in position and *Rosalie* hanging in the background.

Opposite: Pastel on board, circa 1950, for the Brown & Bigelow Jewel Flowers bathing suit calendar series, all created between 1945 and 1952. Flowers sat for approximately 60 Armstrong pastels between 1940 and 1960. Her husband endured Armstrong's obsession with his wife, but the marriage ended in 1961, the year after Armstrong's death.

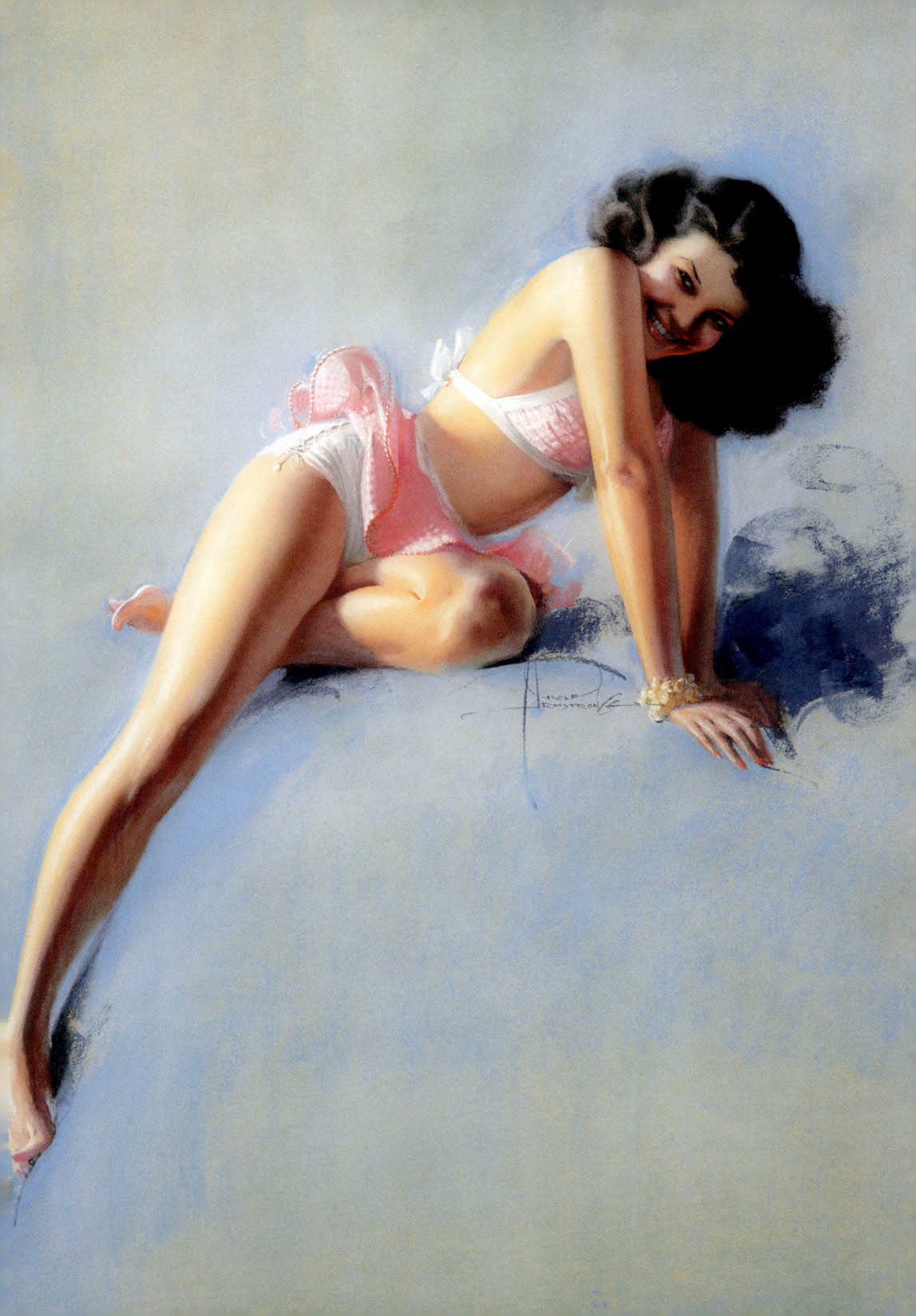

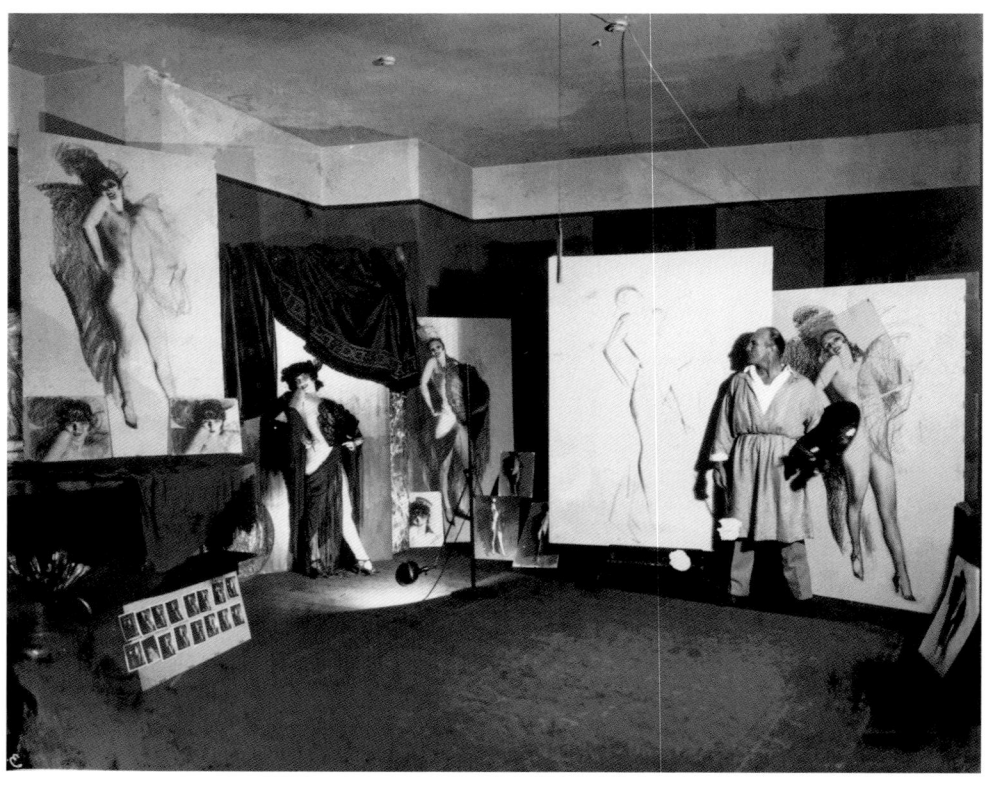

Above: Armstrong reveals his technique with his many life-size preparatory sketches for *Carmen*, as well as the finished oil on canvas, and an appropriately dressed model.

Opposite: Carmen, oil on canvas, 1929. Not only were the completed paintings in this series larger than life-sized, the preliminary sketches were in the same scale. 80 x 60 inches.

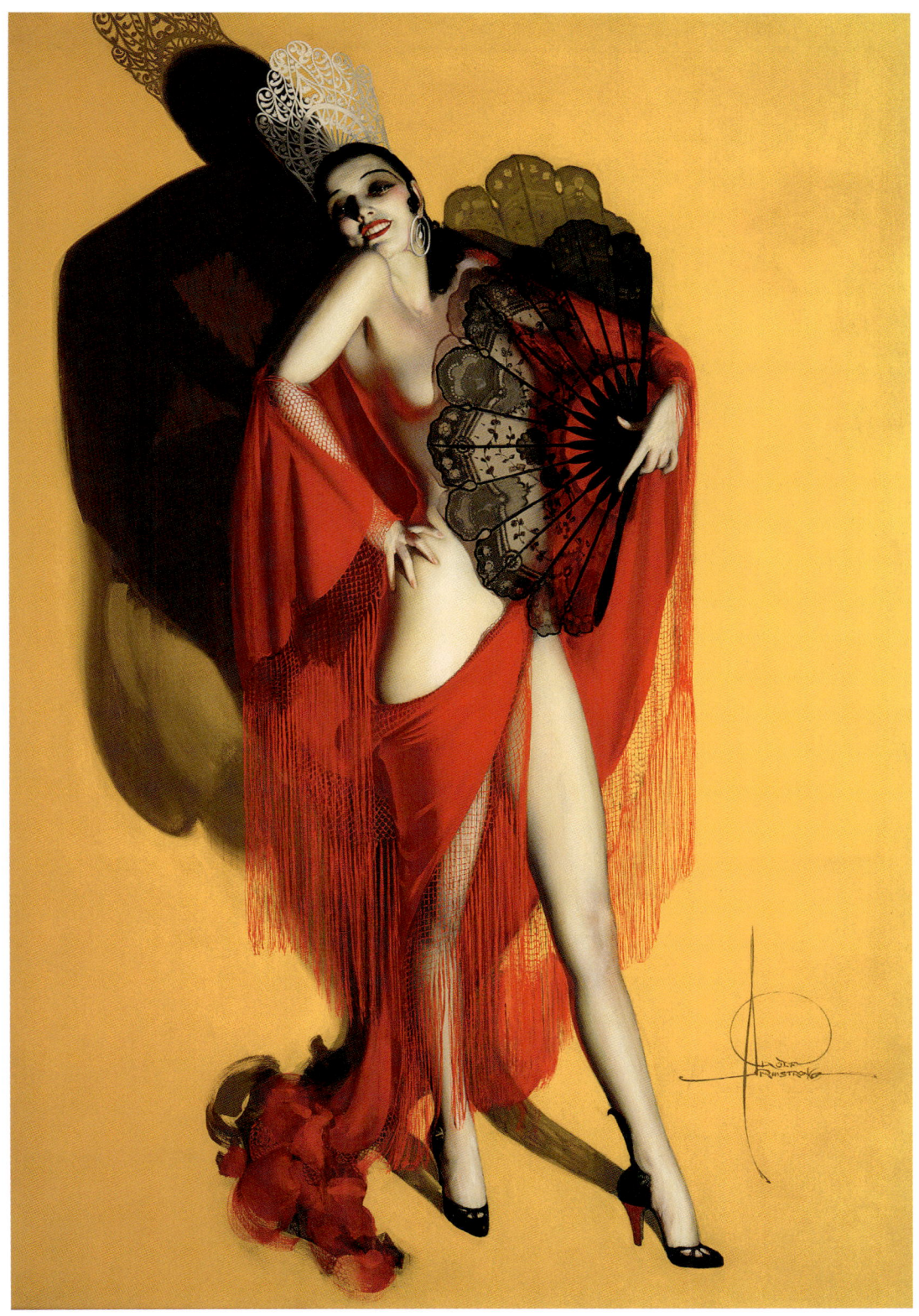

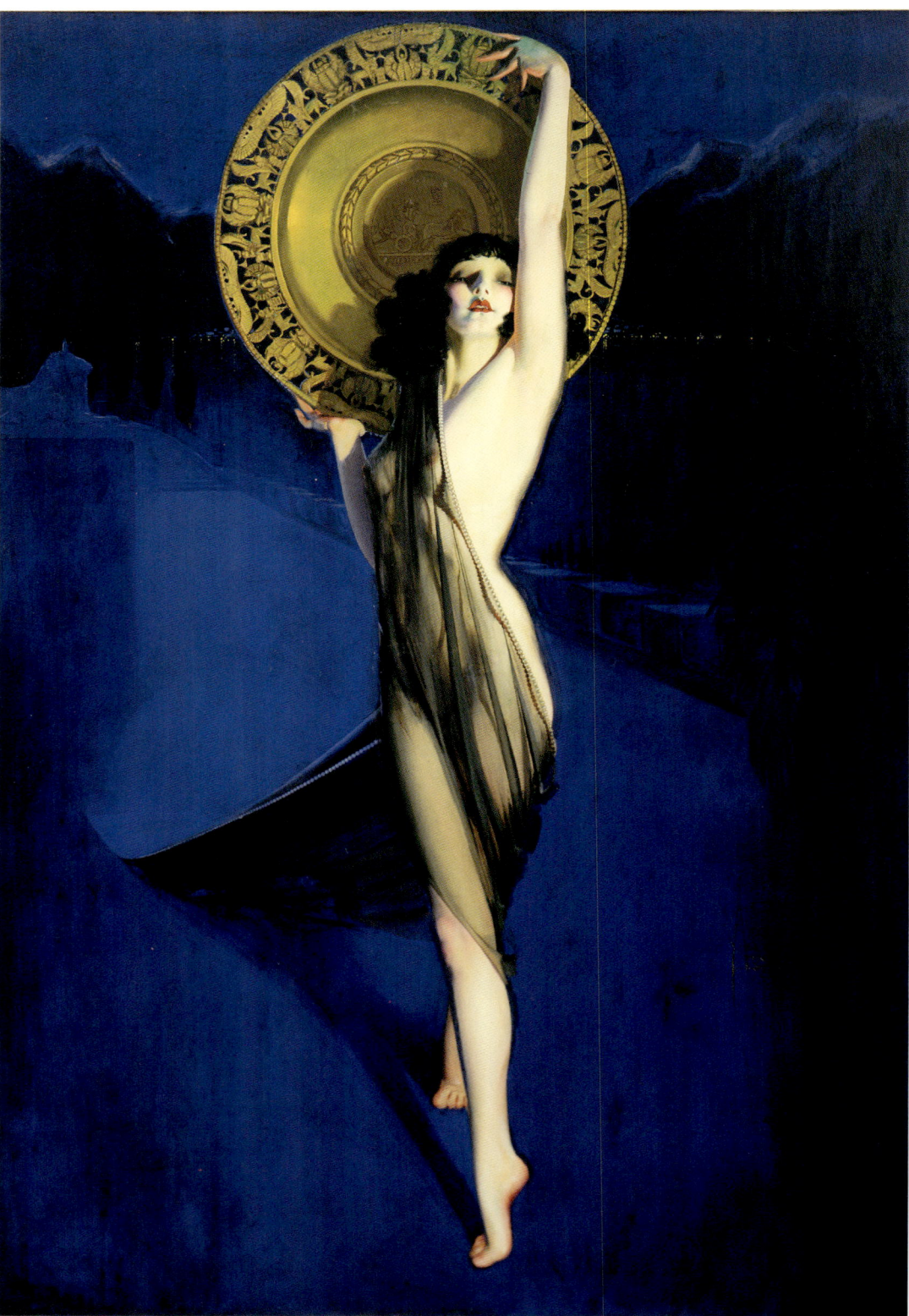

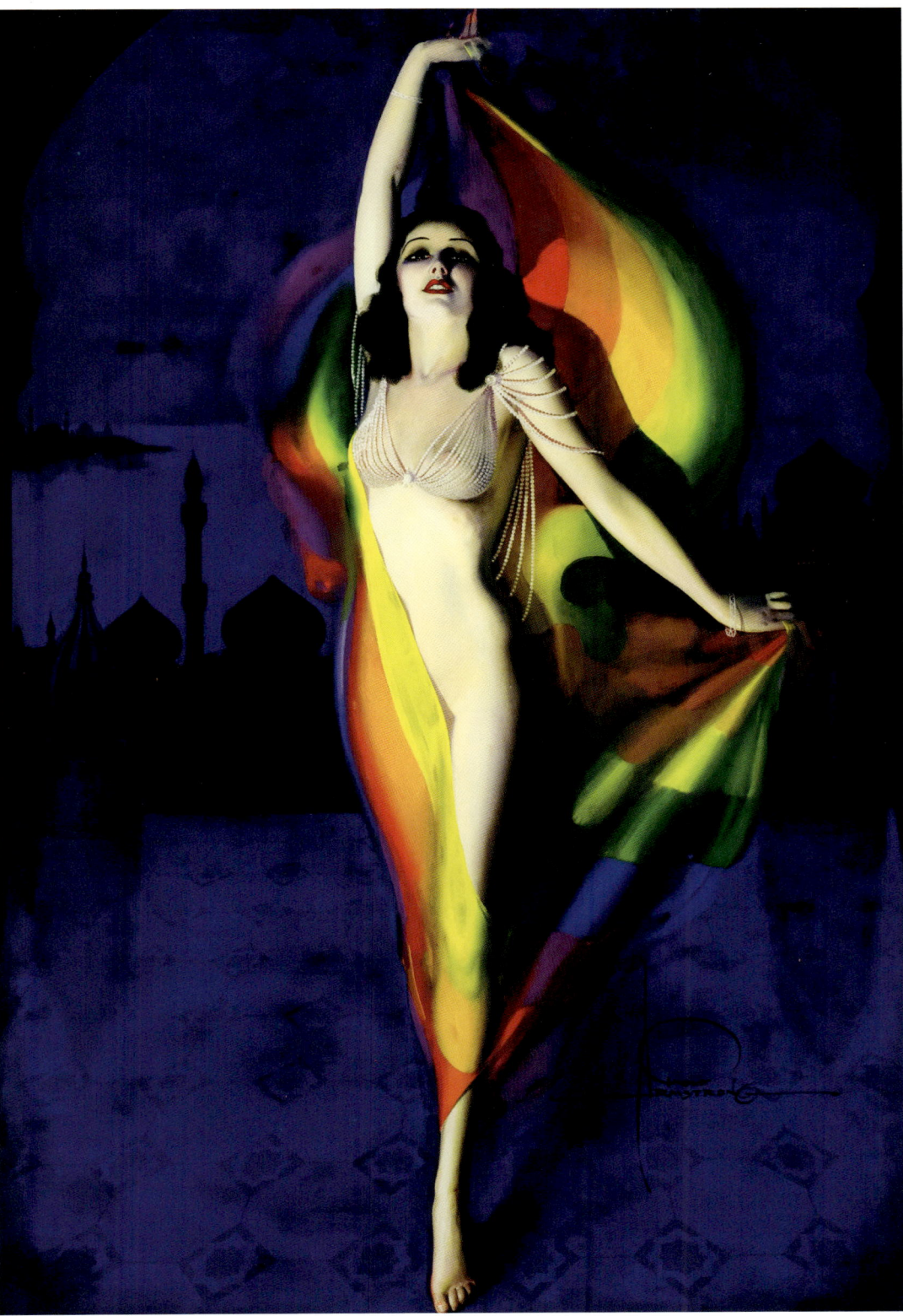

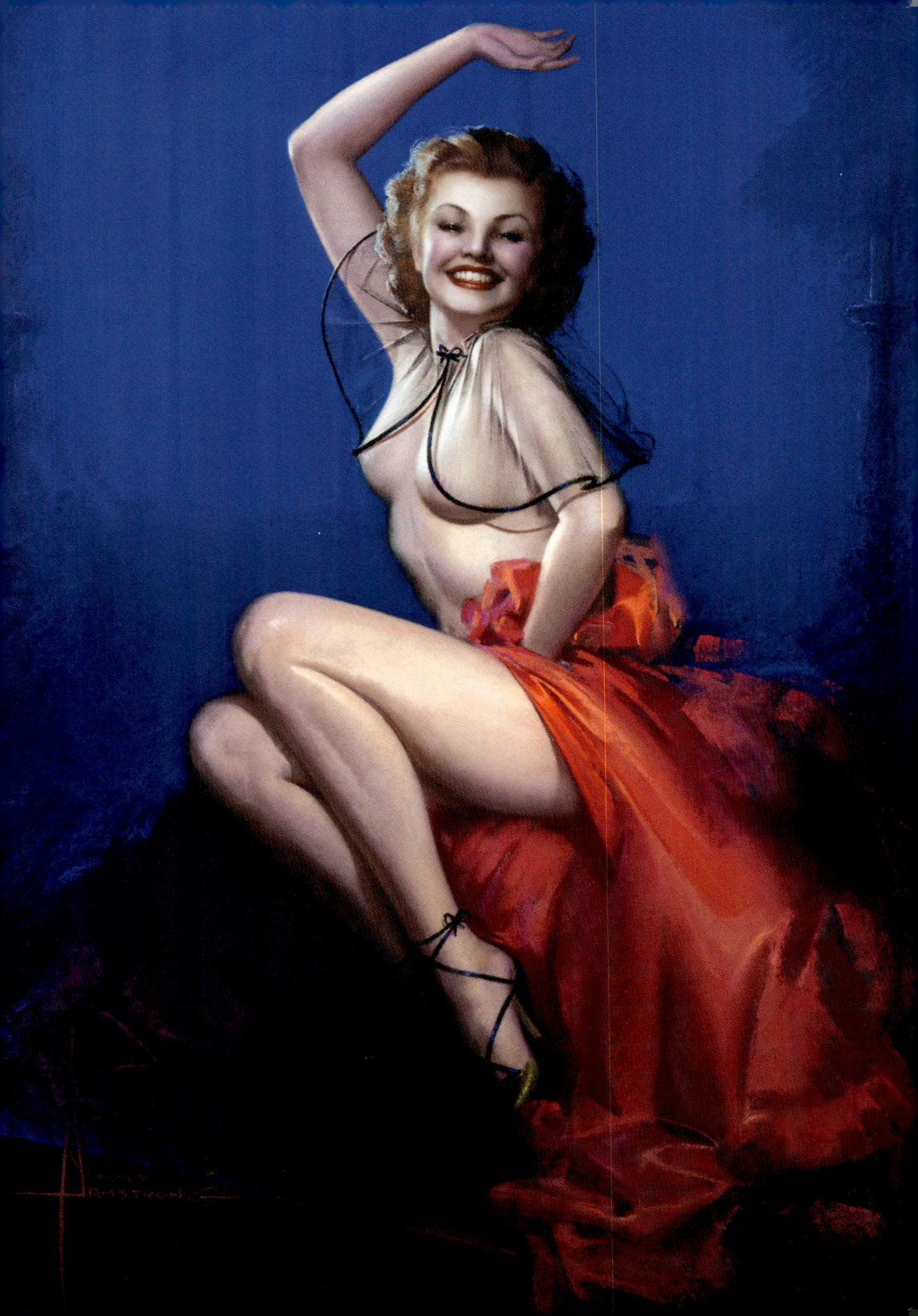

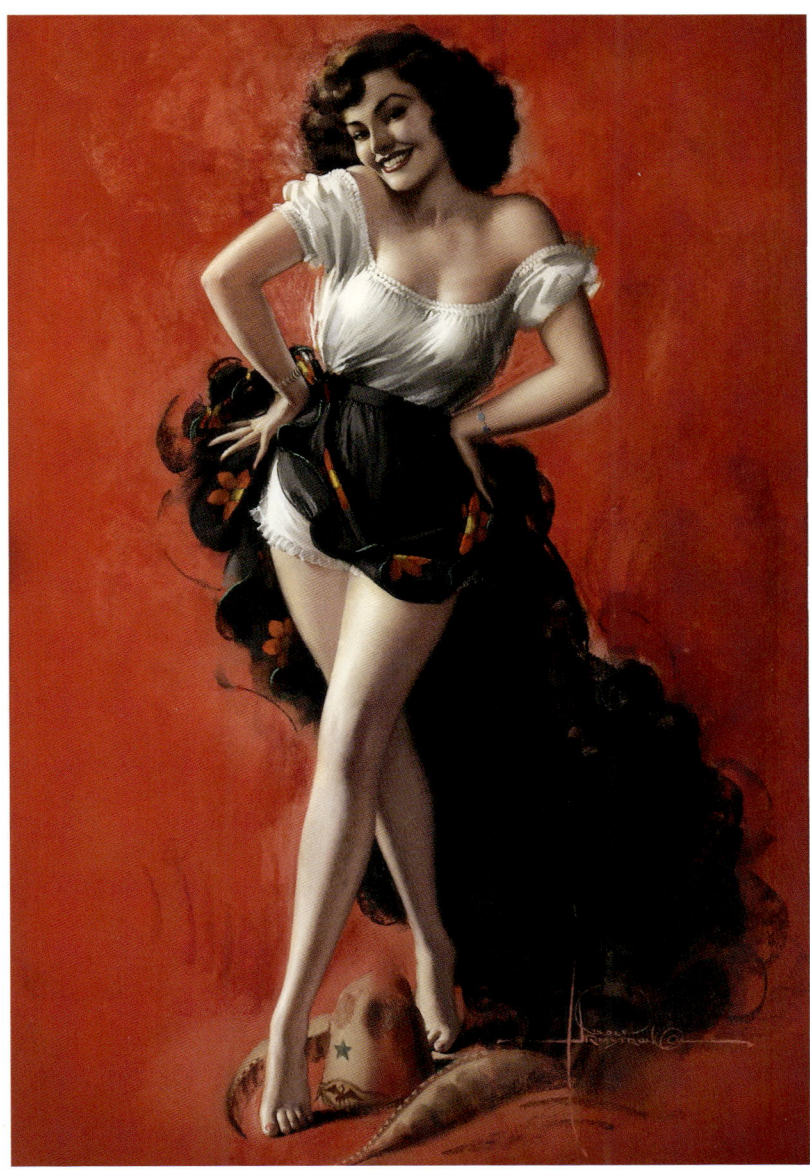

Previous left: The Enchantress, oil on canvas, 1927,
80 x 60 inches.

Previous right: Song of India, 1931, was the last of
Armstrong's four monumental oils on canvas created
between 1927 and '31. The series was inspired by his
Cleopatra, 1926. All were 80 x 60 inches in dimension
and created for Brown & Bigelow calendars. The paintings were thought lost until 1990, when the grandchildren

of a deceased Armstrong friend found all four rolled up
in the attic. Only *Arabian Nights* was damaged beyond
repair. Courtesy Heritage Auctions.

Opposite: The Crinoline Girl, pastel on board, 1939,
is a rare partial nude by Armstrong. 30 x 40 inches.

Above: Hat Dance, pastel on paper, circa 1940,
36.5 x 26 inches. Courtesy Heritage Auctions.

JOHN SCOTT "ROLF" ARMSTRONG

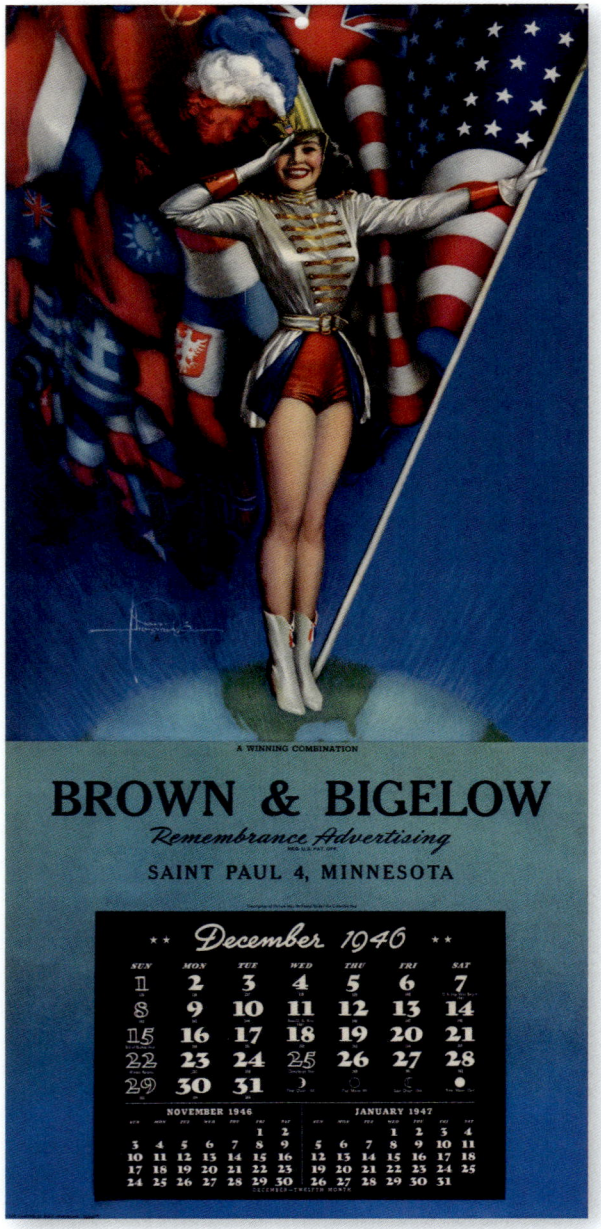

Above: *A Winning Combination*, created in 1945 for this 1946 calendar, celebrated the defeat of the Axis powers and the end of World War II. Armstrong jumbled in the flags of many nations, with the United States, Britain, and Russia predominant, but with Australia, Cuba, the former Czechoslovakia, France, Greece, Holland, Norway, Poland, and Taiwan also discernible. Calendar measures 46 x 22 inches.

Opposite: Hi, Neighbor!, pastel on board, 1943, 42 x 30 inches for a 1944 Brown & Bigelow calendar. Courtesy Heritage Auctions.

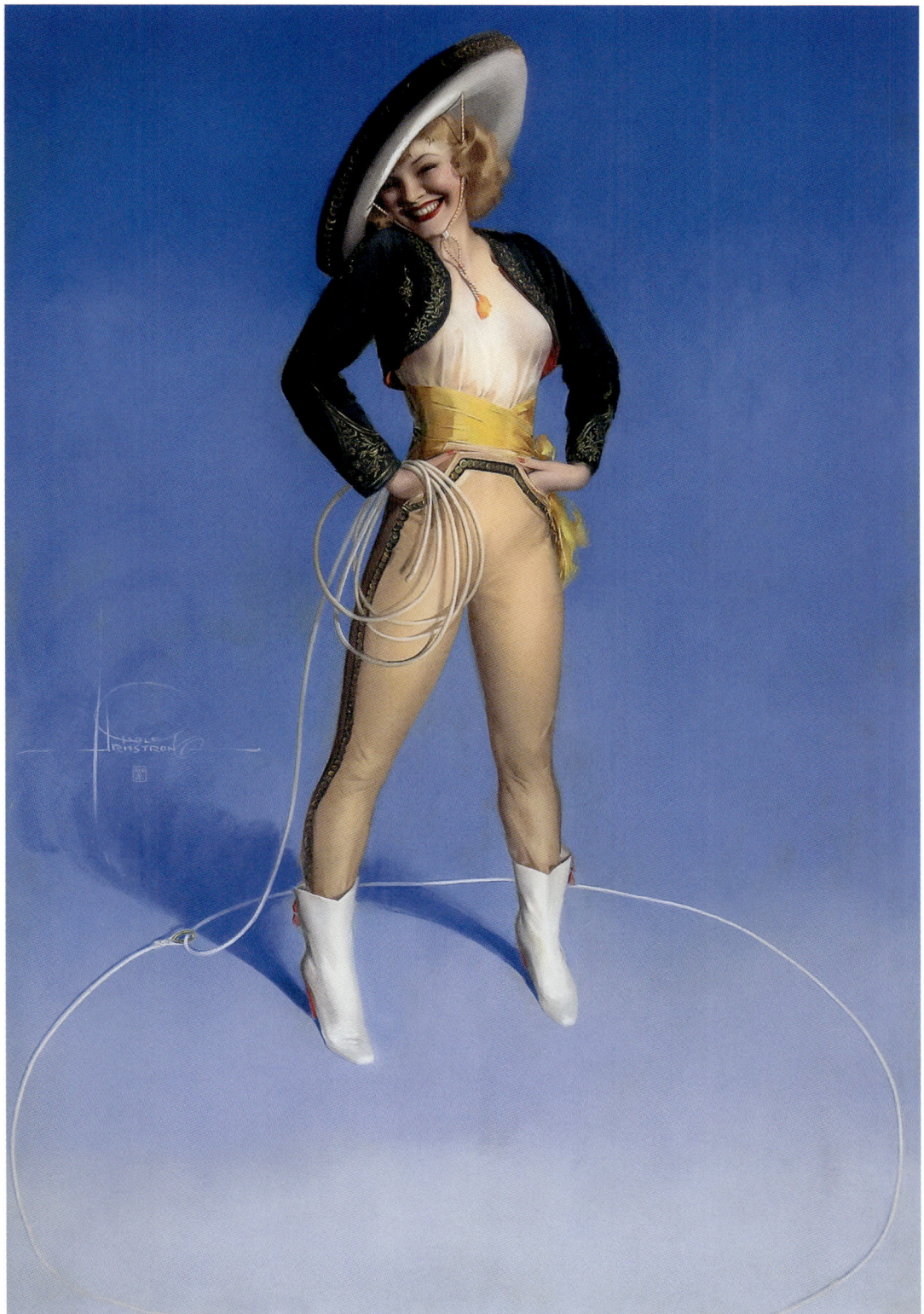

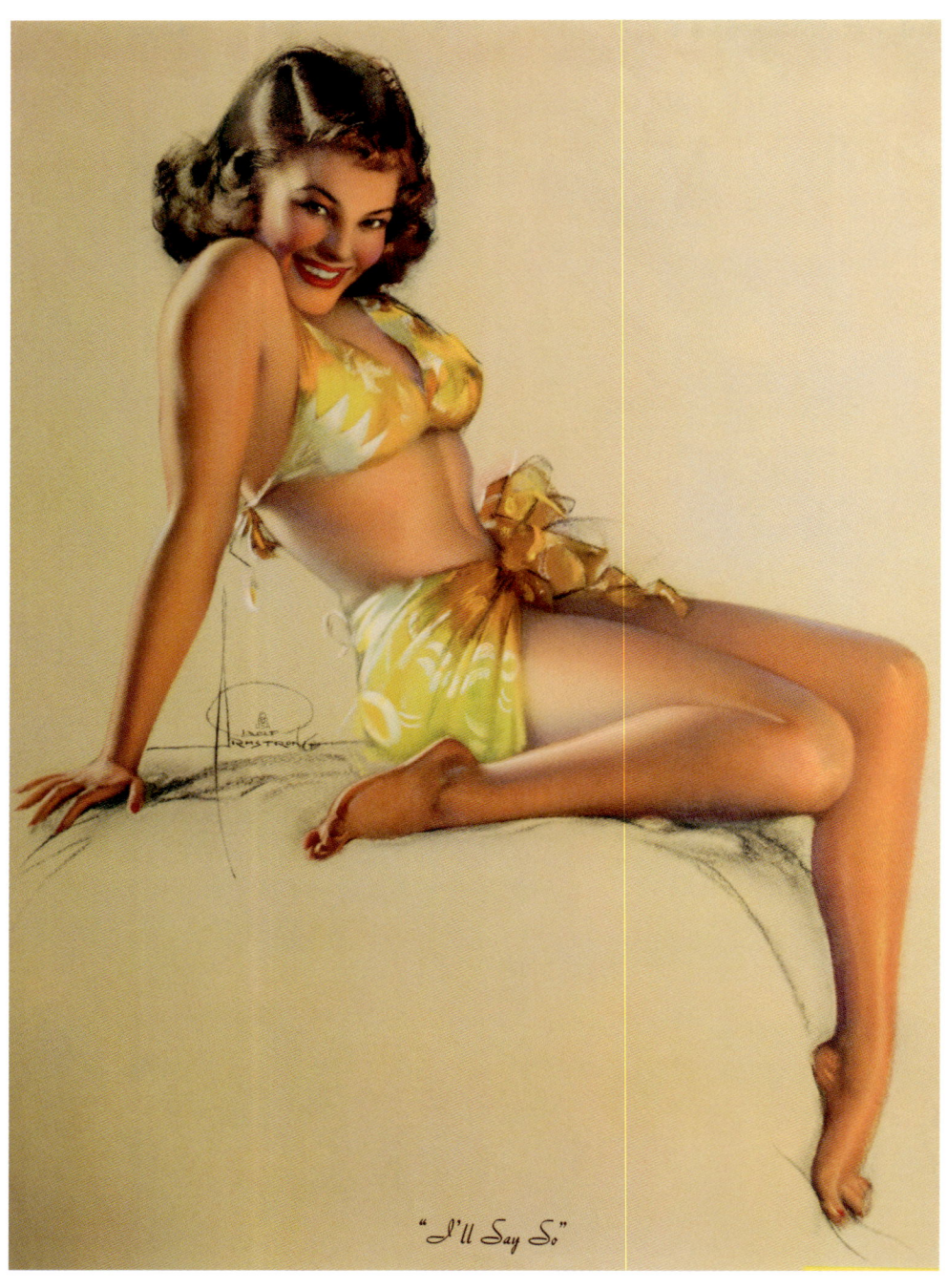

"I'll Say So"

*Above: I'll Say So, 1948, pastel on paper
of Jewel Flowers.*

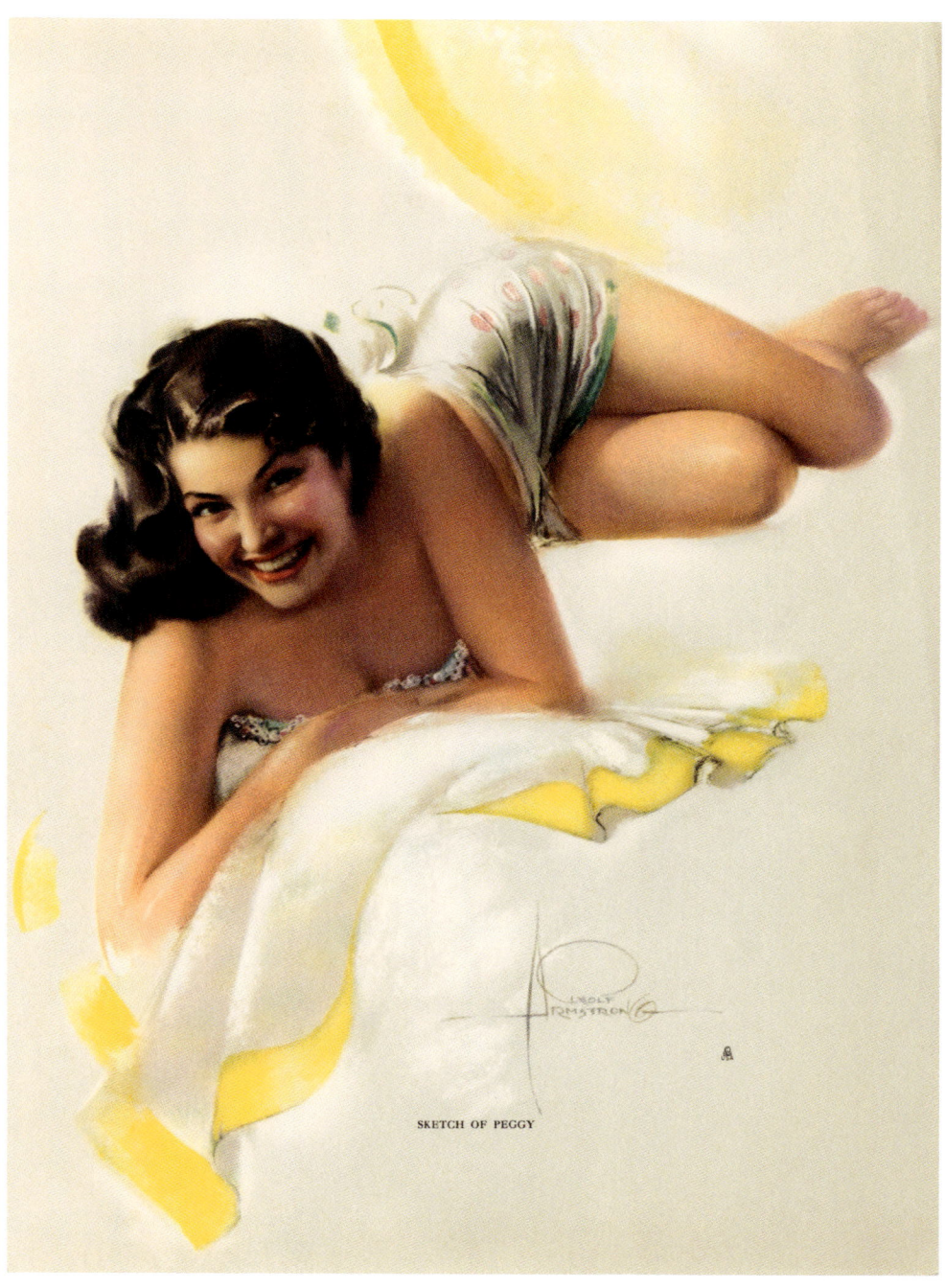

SKETCH OF PEGGY

Above: Sketch of Peggy, a calendar lithograph
circa 1950.

JOHN SCOTT "ROLF" ARMSTRONG

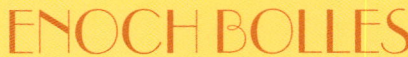

ENOCH BOLLES

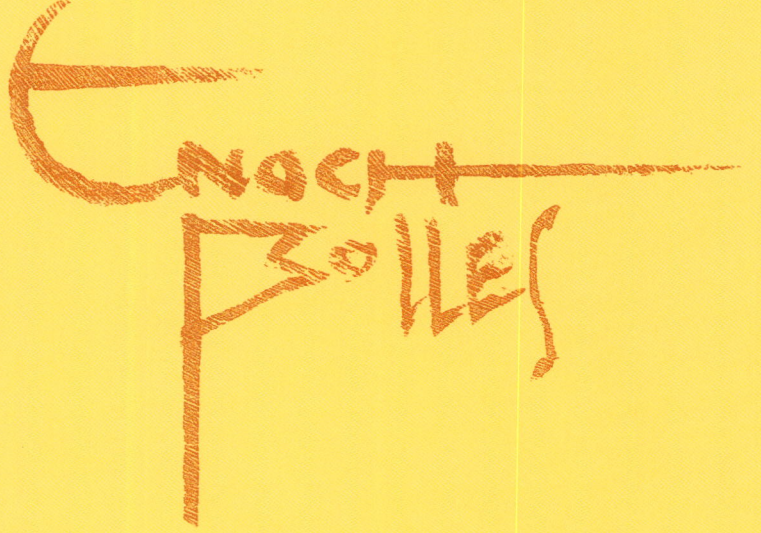

1883–1976

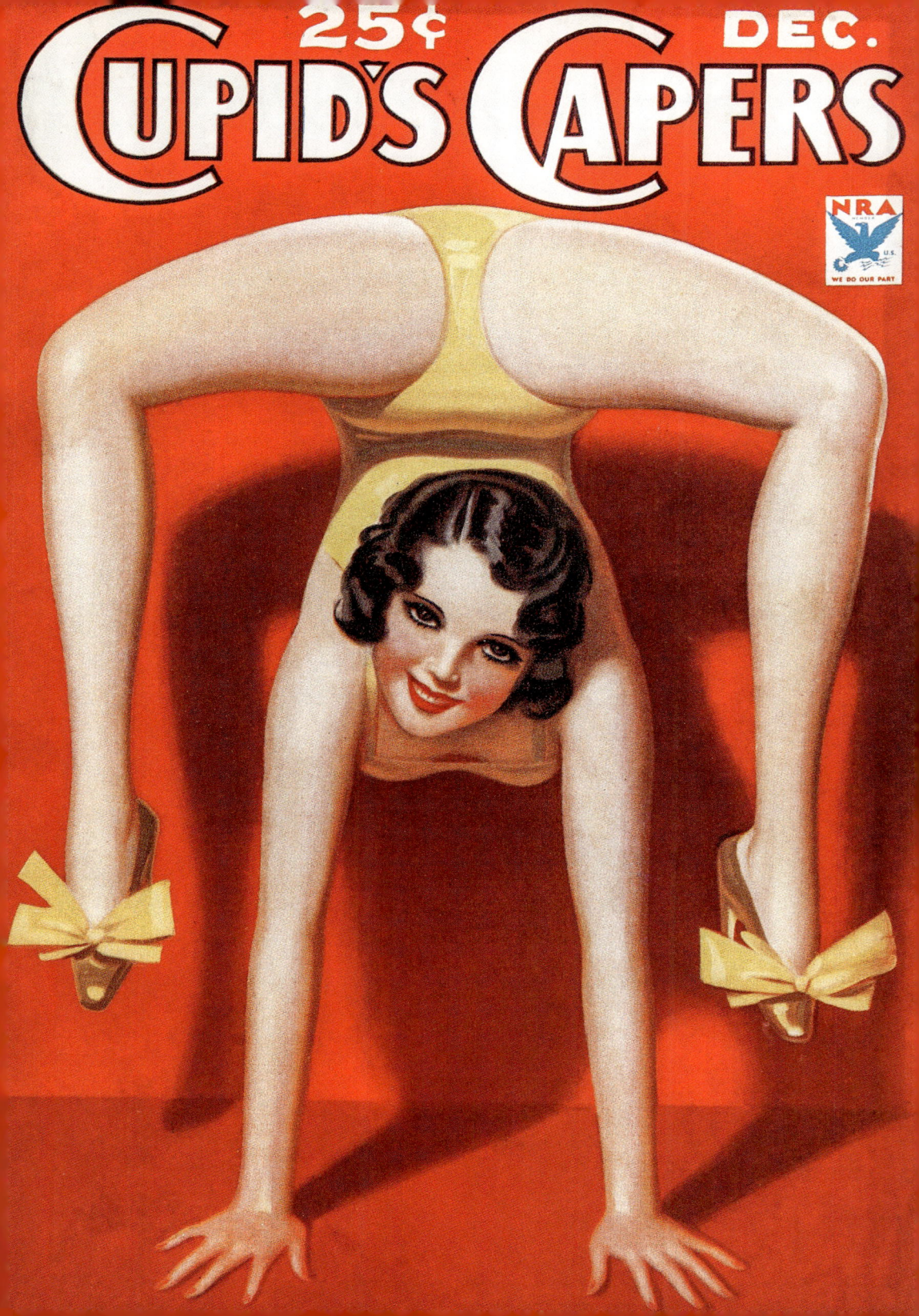

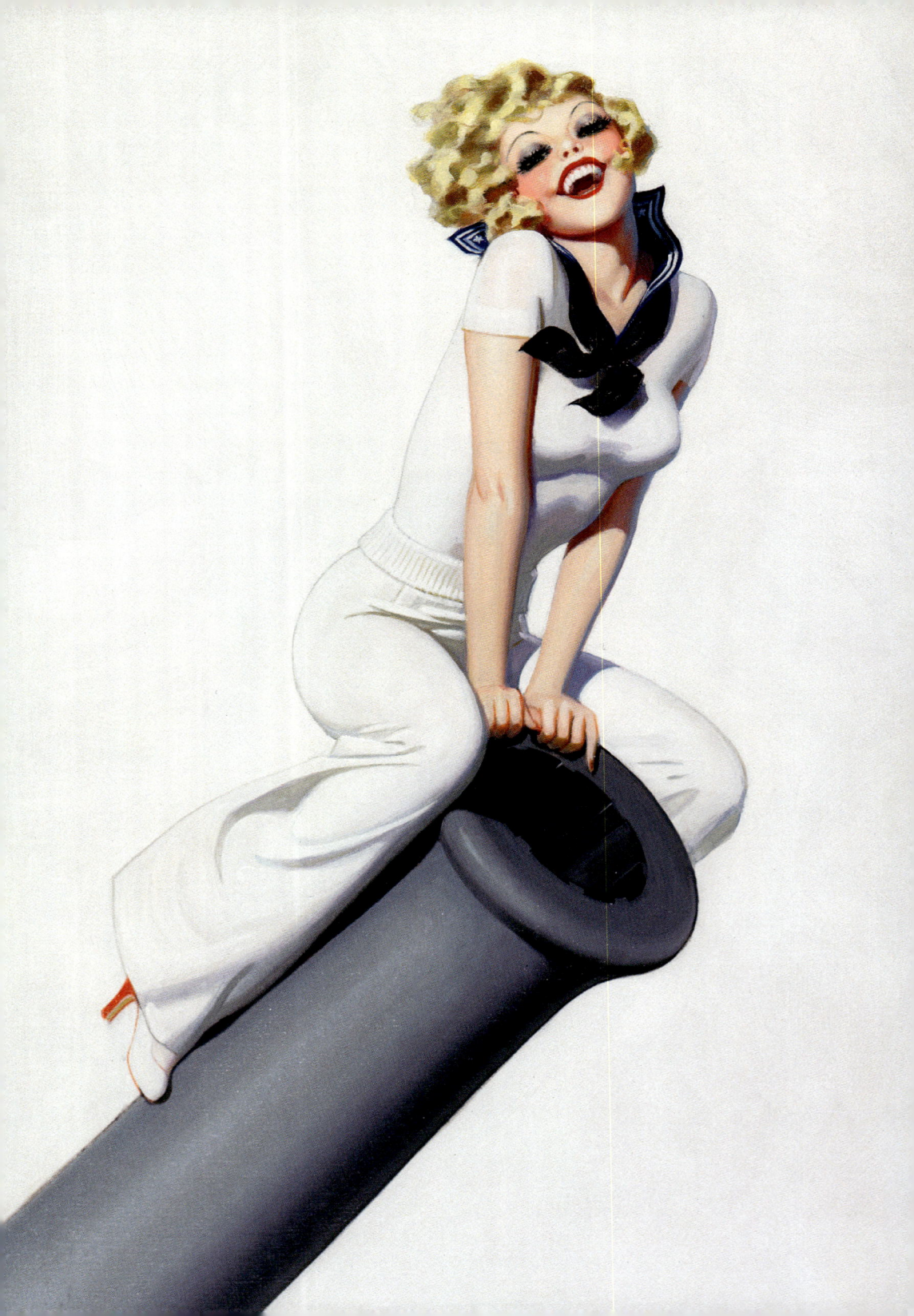

"Bolles' covers celebrated a dynamic and sometimes unsettling vision of the flapper waif. These *Film Fun* girls were young, thin, reckless, and always in motion."

Born in 1883, Enoch Bolles spent his early years among a genteel and comfortable family that owned and operated citrus groves in central Florida. When he was 10, the sudden death of his father and grand-father, coupled with a devastating freeze that crippled the orange industry, forced the Bolles family to move north, where they were taken in as poor relations. For most of his subsequent adolescence, Bolles lived in tenement apartments in New York City and Newark, New Jersey. The jarring shift from a stable life in the rural South to a hand-to-mouth struggle in the densely populated, infinitely diverse urban North created the peculiar vertigo that pervades Bolles's work.

In 1903 Bolles married Clara Kaufman, and for the next four years he worked to support his mother, sister, wife, and child through various tradesman's jobs. Census records conflict as to when their first child was born—it was either shortly before their marriage, or three

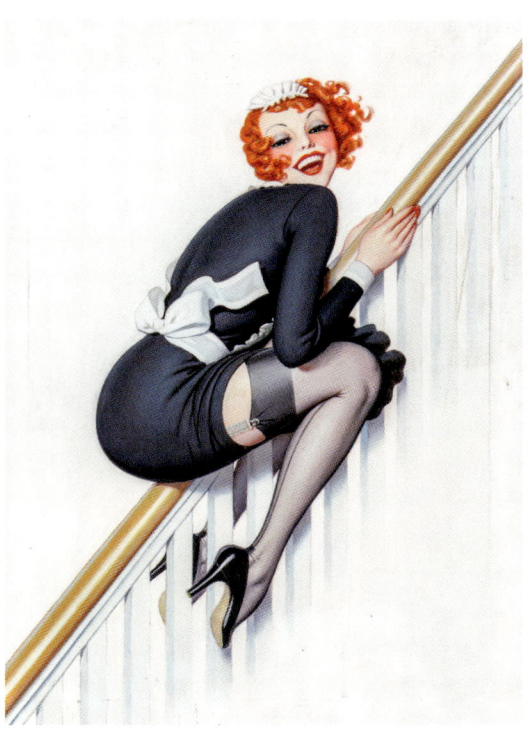

years after—but the couple would go on to have seven more. Seeking stable income, the young father enrolled in art school in 1907 and found work illustrating trolley car advertisements. He went on to study under Robert Henri, a noted member of the Ashcan School—an early 20th- century art movement focused on the seamy underbelly of emerging cities. Their unsett-ling vigorous realism influenced Bolles. His early covers for *Judge* and *Puck* magazines evoke the burlesque paintings of Ashcan artist Everett Shinn, and even as Bolles developed his own

Page 135: Cupid's Capers magazine cover, December 1933, by Enoch Bolles. Courtesy Heritage Auctions.

Opposite: Sure to Make a Hit, oil on canvas, for the cover of *Film Fun* magazine, October 1935. 30 x 22 inches.

Above: There's No Stopping Her!, for the cover of *Film Fun,* May 1936. Oil on canvas, 1936, 28 x 20 inches. Courtesy Heritage Auctions.

innovative style he remained transfixed by the beauty hidden in hard living. In 1923 Bolles became the sole cover artist for *Film Fun* magazine — a campy precursor of men's magazines comprised of provocative stills from Hollywood films. His work for *Film Fun* was never lucrative enough to fully support his family, but his association with the magazine would come to define him as an artist. Throughout the 1920s, Bolles's covers celebrated a dynamic and sometimes unsettling vision of the flapper waif. These *Film Fun* girls were young, thin, reckless, and always in motion. As the carefree Jazz Age careened into the Depression, and as Bolles struggled under ever-growing workloads to make ends meet, the women he painted became both larger and more menacing. The '30s was a period of tremendous anxiety for American men, who often had to rely on wives and mothers for support. The superhuman vixens on the covers of 1930s *Film Fun* — seen taming bears, riding cannons, even masquerading as Santa Claus (St. Nick is surely the greatest provider in history) — reflect the American man's sense of being overtaken by independent women. Their skin, bright and shiny as lamination, enhances the sense that Bolles's women are an entirely new species. The pulp covers Bolles executed for magazines even less reputable than *Film Fun* amplified this dangerous, aggressive new sexuality. In his work for *Bedtime Stories* and *Stolen Sweets*, Bolles returned to the grit of burlesque, depicting coquettish teasers with cigarettes and beckoning, blackened eyes. The increasing frenzy and darkness of his work reflected Bolles's own unstable state of mind. In 1938 Bolles served his first stint in New Jersey's Greystone Park — a state-run mental asylum. He continued to contribute covers for various pulps until 1943, painted both in his hospital-provided studio, and during intermittent trips home, but his work became more sporadic and less inspired. He would be institutionalized for the better part of 30 years, undergoing the invasive medical treatments popular at the time for treating schizophrenia, his contested diagnosis. In 1969, as this treatment model went out of fashion, Bolles was released into the care of his family. He died in 1976.

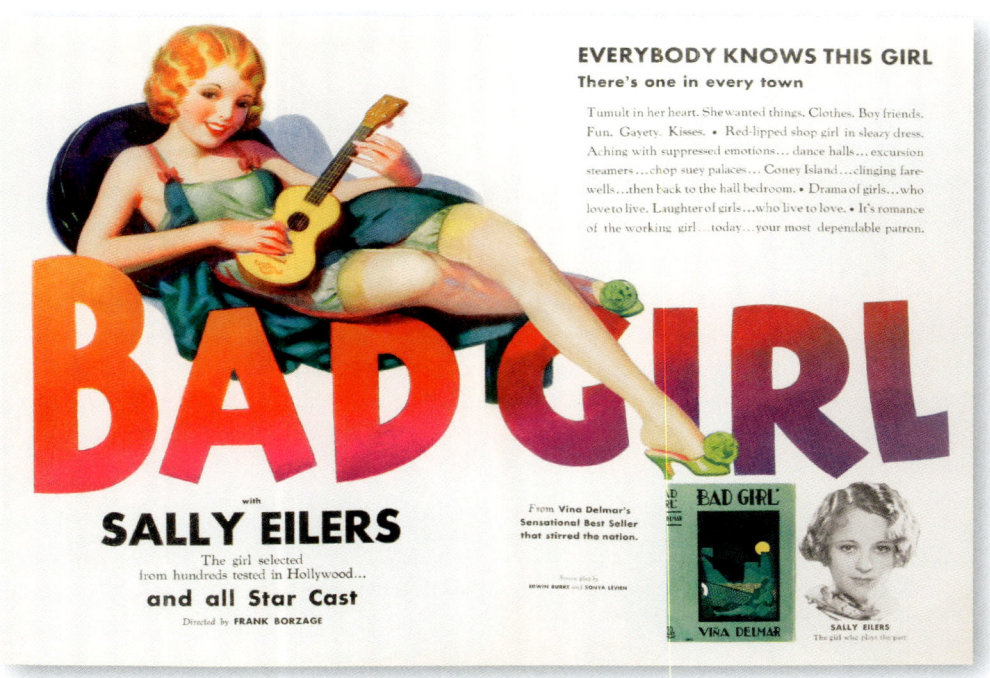

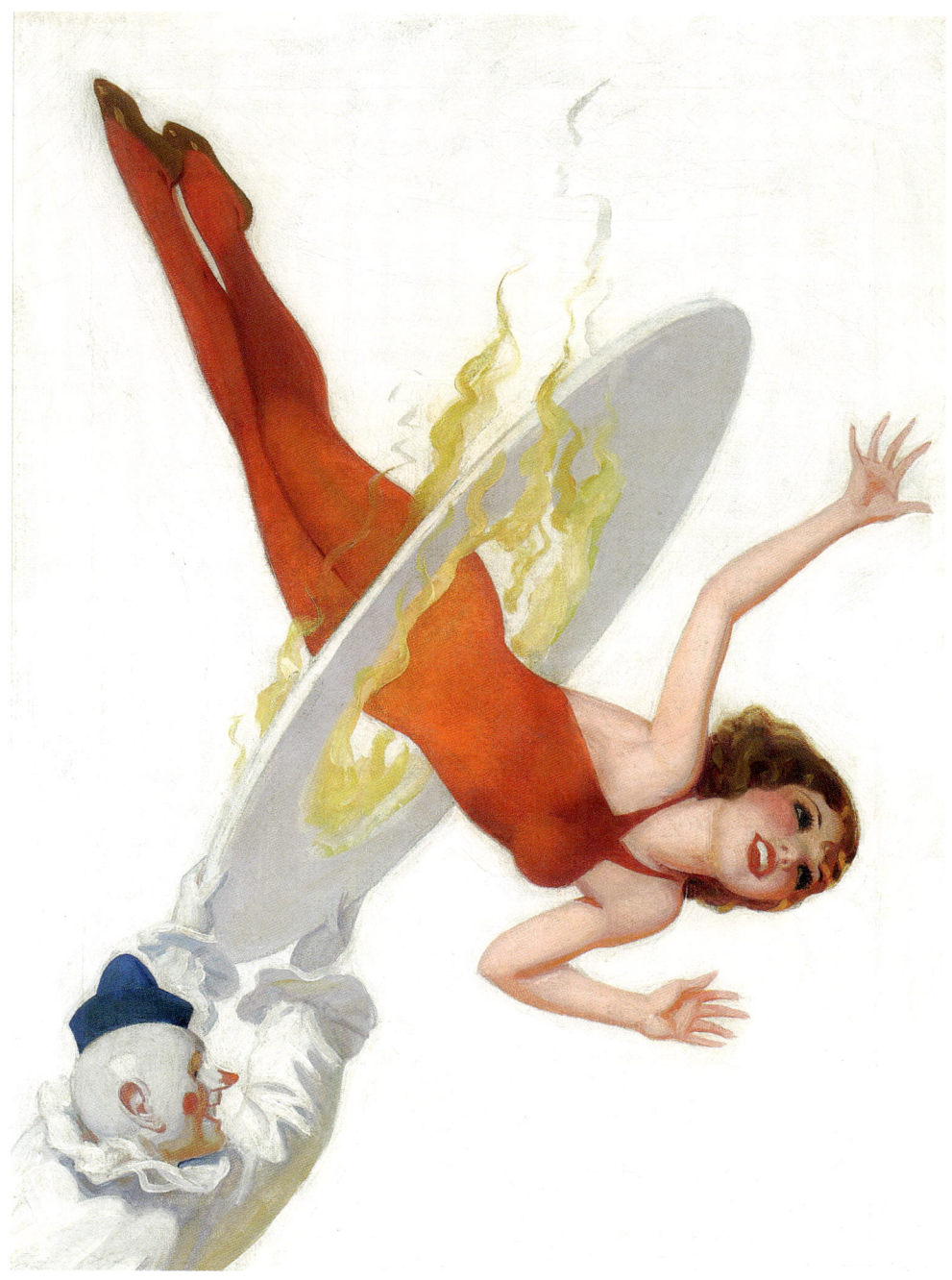

Opposite: A Bolles illustration on the film poster for *Bad Girl,* starring Sally Eilers, 1931.

Above: A Red Hot Attraction!, oil on canvas, for the cover of *Film Fun* magazine, July 1931. 24 x 18 inches.

ENOCH BOLLES

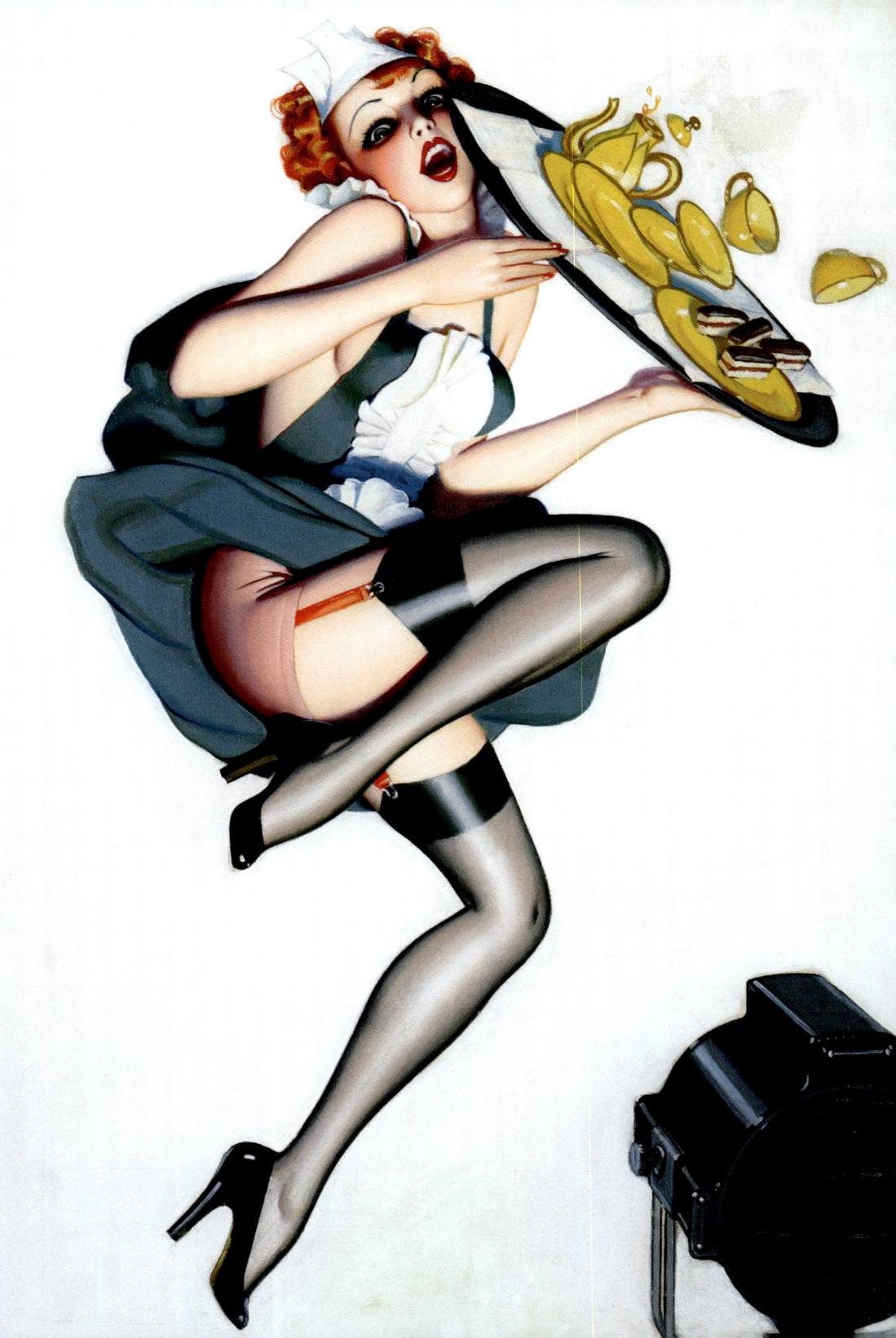

„Bolles' Titelbilder feierten eine dynamische und manchmal beunruhigende Vision des unsteten Flapper-Typs. Die *Film Fun*-Mädchen waren jung, dünn, leichtfertig und ständig in Bewegung."

Der 1883 geborene Enoch Bolles war der Spross einer gut situierten Familie, die ihre eigenen Zitrushaine in Florida bewirtschaftete. Als er zehn Jahre alt war, zwangen der plötzliche Tod seines Vaters und Großvaters und eine verheerende Kältewelle, die die Orangenkulturen zerstörte, die Familie Bolles, in den Norden zu ziehen, wo sie – mittlerweile verarmt – bei Verwandten unterkam. Die meiste Zeit lebte der heranwachsende Bolles nun in Mietwohnungen in New York City und in Newark, New Jersey. Die abrupte Veränderung – erst ein Leben in guten Verhältnissen im ländlichen Süden, dann der tägliche Überlebenskampf in dicht besiedelten, bunten Städten im Norden – löste jenen merkwürdigen Taumel aus, der Bolles' Werk erfüllte.

1903 heiratete Bolles Clara Kaufman und arbeitete die nächsten vier Jahre immer wieder als Händler, um seine Mutter, seine Schwester, seine Frau und sein Kind durchzubringen. Die

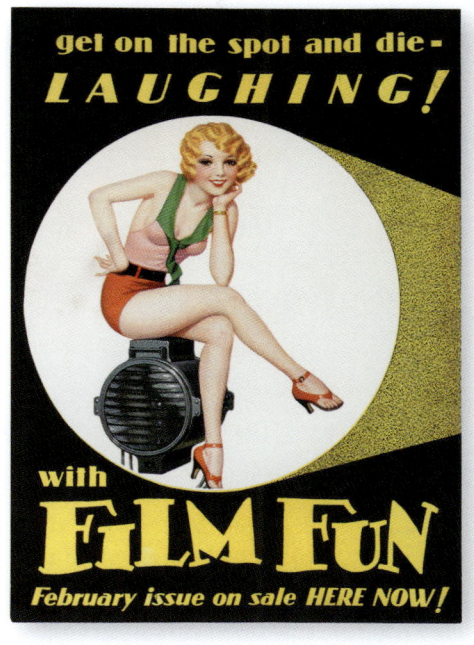

Angaben zu dem Geburtsdatum des ersten Kindes sind in den offiziellen Unterlagen widersprüchlich: Entweder wurde es kurz vor der Heirat oder drei Jahre danach geboren. Wie auch immer, das Paar sollte noch sieben weitere Kinder bekommen. Auf der Suche nach einem festen Einkommen schrieb sich der junge Vater 1907 an einer Kunstschule ein und fand Arbeit als Illustrator für Werbung auf Straßenbahnwagen. Später setzte er seine Studien unter Robert Henri fort, einem bekannten Mitglied der Ashcan-Schule, einer Kunstbewegung des frühen 20. Jahrhunderts, die sich vor allem mit den düsteren Schattenseiten der wachsenden Städte befasste. Der verstörende, kraftvolle Realismus dieser Schule beeinflusste Bolles. Seine frühen Titelbilder für Zeitschriften wie *Judge* und *Puck* erinnern an die burlesken Gemälde des Ashcan-Künstlers Everett Shinn, und selbst als Bolles bereits seinen eigenen, innovativen Stil entwickelt

Opposite: The Hottest Thing on the Menu!, oil on canvas, for the May 1937 cover of *Film Fun*. 30 x 22 inches.

Above: A 15.75-by-11.75-inch point-of-purchase poster for *Film Fun*'s February 1932 issue. It was around this time that Bolles's waifish flappers started putting on weight, growing more substantial with each subsequent issue.

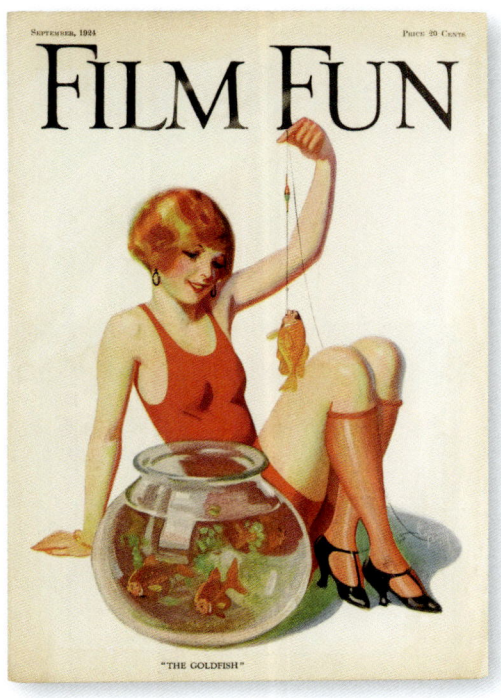

SEPTEMBER, 1924

FILM FUN

PRICE 20 CENTS

"THE GOLDFISH"

hatte, blieb er von der Schönheit geprägt, die selbst in ärmsten Lebensverhältnissen zu finden ist. 1923 wurde Bolles mit der künstlerischen Gestaltung der Titelseiten der Zeitschrift *Film Fun* betraut. Das Magazin zeigte aufreizende Stills aus Hollywood-Filmen und war ein Vorläufer der Männermagazine. Seine Tätigkeiten für *Film Fun* reichten allerdings nicht, um seine Familie zu ernähren. Doch wurde er durch seine Arbeiten für die Zeitschrift als Künstler wahrgenommen. In den 1920er-Jahren feierten Bolles' Titelbilder eine dynamische und manchmal beunruhigende Vision des unsteten Flapper-Typs. Die *Film Fun*-Mädchen waren jung, dünn, leichtfertig und ständig in Bewegung. Als die unbekümmerte Jazz-Ära in die Jahre wirtschaftlicher Depression schlitterte und Bolles mit zunehmender Arbeitsbelastung kämpfte, um über die Runden zu kommen, wurden die Frauen, die er malte, immer fülliger und bedrohlicher. Die 1930er-Jahre waren für amerikanische Männer eine schrecklich beklemmende

Zeit, oft waren sie darauf angewiesen, dass ihre Frauen und Mütter sie unterstützten. Die übermenschlichen Superweiber auf den *Film Fun*-Titelseiten der 1930er-Jahre – sie zähmten Bären, ritten auf Kanonen, verkleideten sich gar als Santa Claus (St. Nikolaus ist sicher der bedeutendste Ernährer in der Geschichte) – reflektieren das Gefühl des amerikanischen Mannes, von selbstständigen Frauen überholt zu werden. Ihre Haut, hell und leuchtend, verstärkt den Eindruck, dass Bolles' Frauen eine vollkommen neue Spezies darstellen. Die Titelseiten, die Bolles für weitaus unseriösere Pulp-Magazine schuf, ließen diese neue Sexualität noch gefährlicher, aggressiver erscheinen. In seinen Arbeiten für *Bedtime Stories* und *Stolen Sweets* kehrte Bolles zum Wagemut des Burlesken zurück und stellte kokette Frauen mit Zigaretten und zwinkernden, stark geschminkten Augen dar. Das zunehmend Rauschhafte und Düstere seines Werks spiegelte Bolles' eigenen Gemütszustand. 1938 war Bolles zum ersten Mal in Greystone Park, einer staatlichen Psychiatrie in New Jersey. Bis 1943 lieferte er weiterhin Titelbild-Entwürfe für die verschiedensten Pulp-Magazine, malte sowohl in einem Atelier, das ihm die Anstalt zur Verfügung stellte, als auch während seiner zwischenzeitlichen Aufenthalte zu Hause. Doch seine Produktion wurde mit der Zeit spärlicher und immer uninspirierter. Die meiste Zeit in den nächsten 30 Jahren blieb er in der Anstalt und musste sich den damals populären, invasiven Methoden unterziehen, mit denen Schizophrenie – so die ihm gestellte Diagnose – behandelt wurde. 1969, als derartige Heilmethoden aus der Mode kamen, wurde Bolles entlassen und von seiner Familie gepflegt. Er starb 1976 im Alter von 93 Jahren.

Above: The Goldfish, September 1924 cover of *Film Fun*, continues Bolles's theme of men as toys and victims of the adventurous flapper.

Opposite: Knots to You!, for the cover of *Spicy Stories*, December 1937. Oil on canvas, 1937, 30 x 22 inches. Courtesy Heritage Auctions.

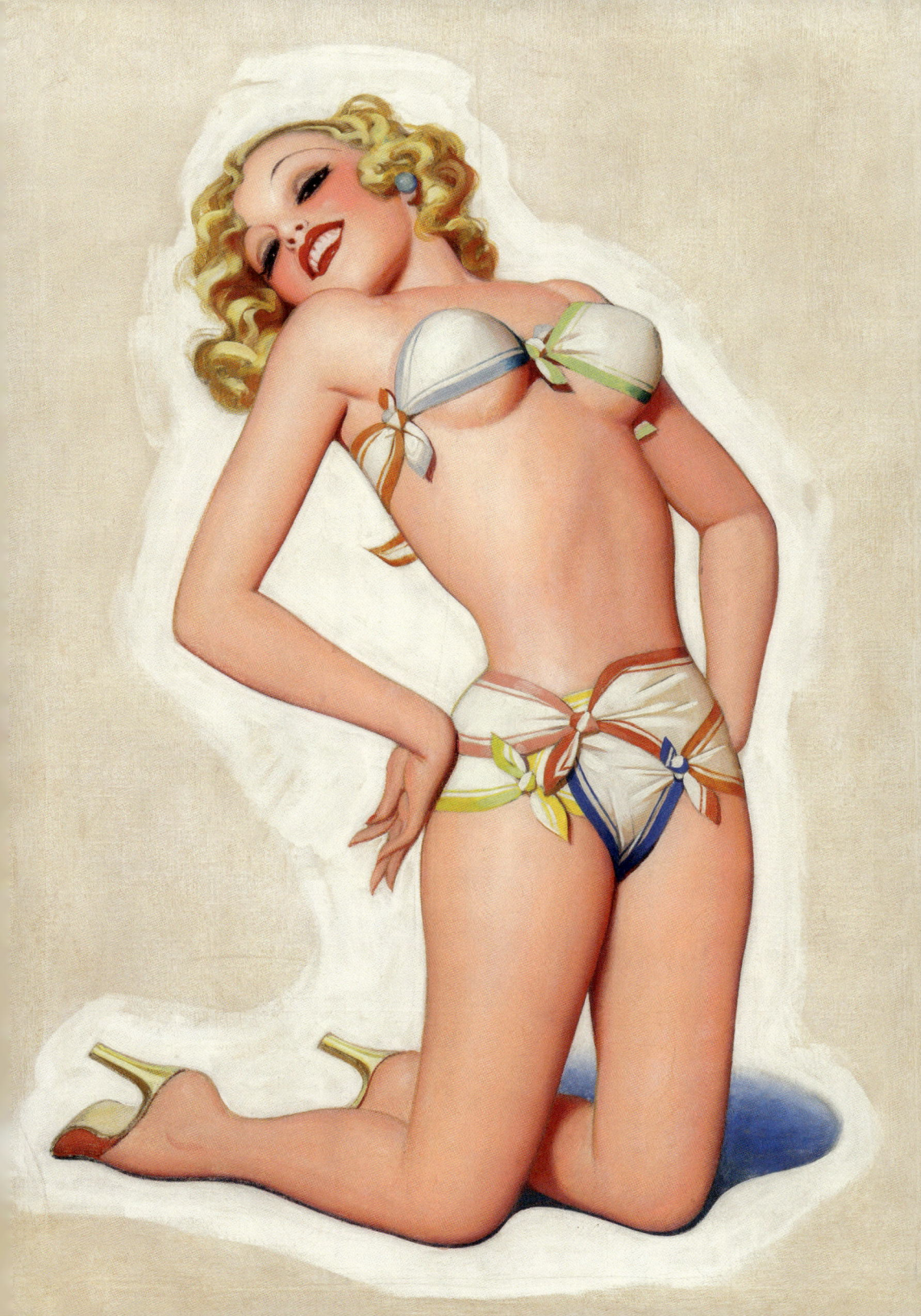

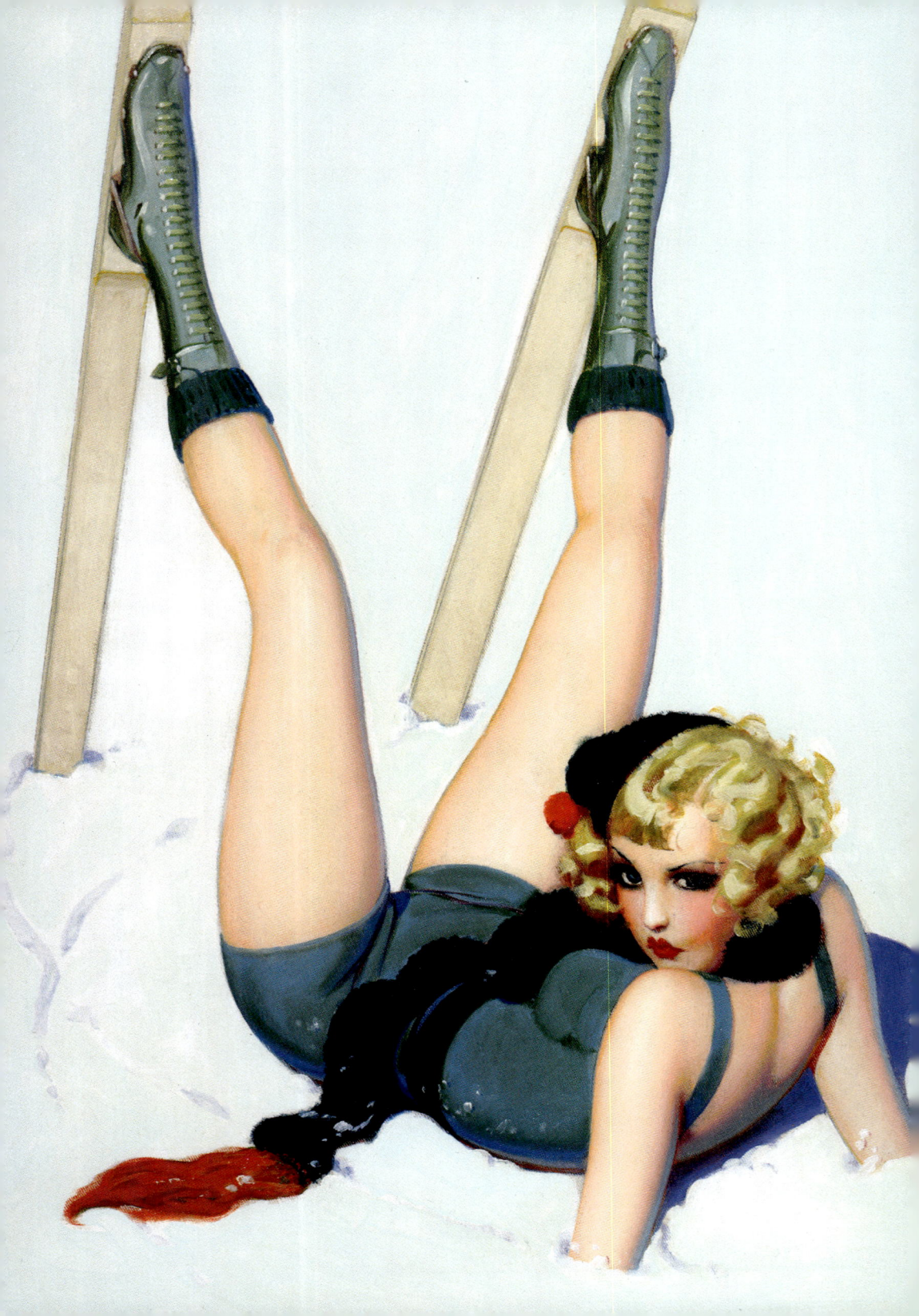

« Les couvertures de Bolles célébrèrent une vision dynamique
et parfois dérangeante de la garçonne issue des bas quartiers.
Les filles de *Film Fun* étaient jeunes, minces, insouciantes
et toujours en mouvement. »

Né en 1883, Enoch Bolles passa sa petite
enfance au sein d'une famille aisée qui
possédait des plantations d'agrumes dans le
centre de la Floride. Son père et son grand-
père moururent soudainement alors qu'il
avait dix ans. Parallèlement, un terrible gel
eut des effets dévastateurs sur la culture des
oranges et contraignit les Bolles à émigrer
plus au nord, où ils furent recueillis par des
membres de la famille comme des parents
pauvres. Bolles passa le reste de son adolescence dans des appartements miteux à New
York puis à Newark, dans le New Jersey.
Ce changement traumatique entre une vie
stable dans le Sud rural et une existence
précaire au jour le jour dans le Nord urbain
densément peuplé et infiniment plus hétéro-
gène explique le vertige particulier que l'on
retrouve dans toute son œuvre.

En 1903, Bolles épousa Clara
Kaufman. Au cours des années suivantes, il
effectua toutes sortes de petits boulots afin
de subvenir aux besoins de sa mère, de sa
sœur, de son épouse et de leur enfant. Les

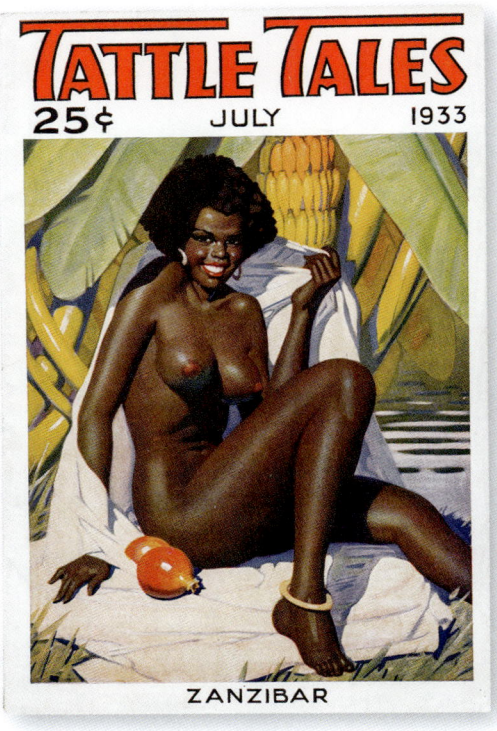

sources divergent quant à la date de naissance de leur aîné. Elle eut lieu immédiatement après
leur mariage ou trois ans plus tard ; quoi qu'il en soit, le couple eut ensuite sept autres enfants.
À la recherche d'un emploi stable, le jeune père s'inscrivit dans une école d'art en 1907 et
trouva un travail d'illustrateur de publicités pour des tramways. Il étudia ensuite avec Robert
Henri, membre éminent de l'Ashcan School, un mouvement artistique du début du XXᵉ siècle
s'intéressant aux bas-fonds des villes émergentes. Son réalisme énergique et dérangeant in-
fluença Bolles. Ses premières couvertures pour les magazines *Judge* et *Puck* évoquent les peintures burlesques d'Everett Shinn, membre du même mouvement. Même après avoir développé

Opposite: Slipping Beauty!, oil on canvas, for the
cover of *Film Fun,* February 1935. 25 x 20 inches.

Above: An extremely rare early pinup cover featuring
a Black woman. *Tattle Tales,* July 1933. Courtesy
Heritage Auctions.

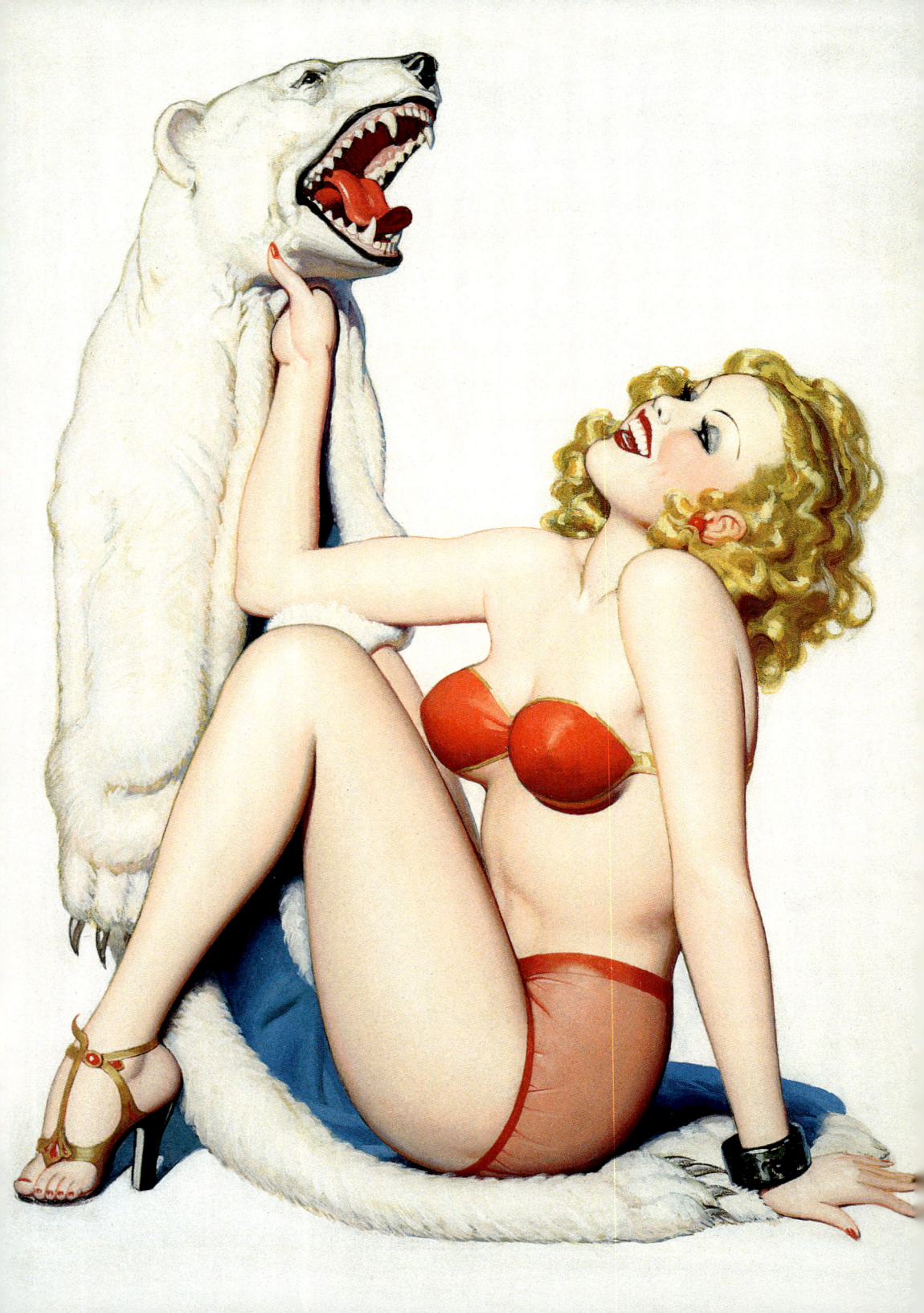

son propre style novateur, Bolles resta fasciné par la beauté cachée du monde de ceux qui menaient une vie dure. En 1923, Bolles devint l'illustrateur exclusif des couvertures de *Film Fun*, un précurseur kitsch des revues de charme rempli d'images olé olé de films hollywoodiens. Ce travail ne fut jamais assez lucratif pour nourrir pleinement sa famille, mais, au fil du temps, son association avec le magazine le définit en tant qu'artiste. Tout au long des années 1920, ses couvertures célébrèrent une vision dynamique et parfois dérangeante de la garçonne issue des bas quartiers. Les filles de *Film Fun* étaient jeunes, minces, insouciantes et toujours en mouvement. Lorsque la Grande Dépression sonna le glas des années folles, alors que Bolles multipliait les commandes afin de joindre les deux bouts, ses femmes se firent plus plantureuses et menaçantes. Les années 1930 furent une période de profonde angoisse pour l'homme

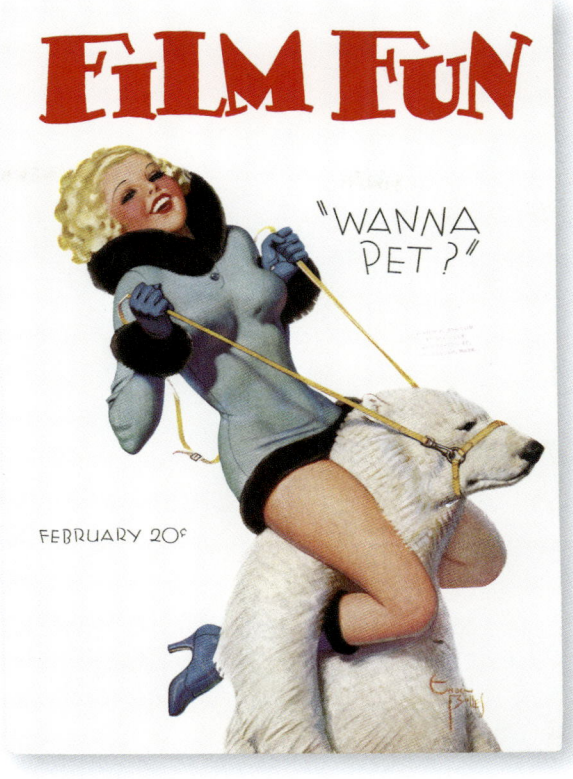

américain, qui devait souvent compter sur une épouse ou une mère pour survivre. Les walkyries de Bolles pour *Film Fun*, domptant des ours, chevauchant des canons ou se déguisant même en Père Noël (le généreux donateur par excellence) reflètent l'impression des mâles américains d'être dépassés par les femmes indépendantes. Leur peau, brillante et lisse comme du plastique, renforce l'idée qu'il s'agit là d'une toute nouvelle espèce. Les couvertures qu'il réalisa pour d'autres *pulps* encore moins respectables que *Film Fun* accentuent encore cette nouvelle sexualité agressive et dangereuse. Pour *Bedtime Stories* et *Stolen Sweets*, il renoua avec l'essence du cabaret grivois des années 1920, peignant des allumeuses coquettes aux yeux bordés de khôl et fumant des cigarettes. Son travail de plus en plus frénétique et sombre reflétait l'état mental de l'artiste. En 1938, il effectua son premier séjour au Greystone Park, un asile psychiatrique géré par l'État du New Jersey. Il continua à réaliser des couvertures pour différents *pulps* jusqu'en 1943, travaillant dans l'atelier de l'asile et à l'occasion de retour chez lui, mais son travail devint plus sporadique et moins inspiré. Il passa près d'une trentaine d'années dans cette institution, subissant les traitements médicaux agressifs alors préconisés pour la schizophrénie, un trouble dont il n'est pas certain qu'il ait vraiment souffert. En 1969, ce type de traitement étant passé de monde, il fut confié aux soins de sa famille. Il mourut en 1976 à l'âge de 93 ans.

Opposite: Ideal for a Hunting Lodge!, oil on canvas, for the cover of *Film Fun*, December 1936. 30.25 x 22 inches.

Above: Wanna Pet?, February 1933 cover of *Film Fun* magazine.

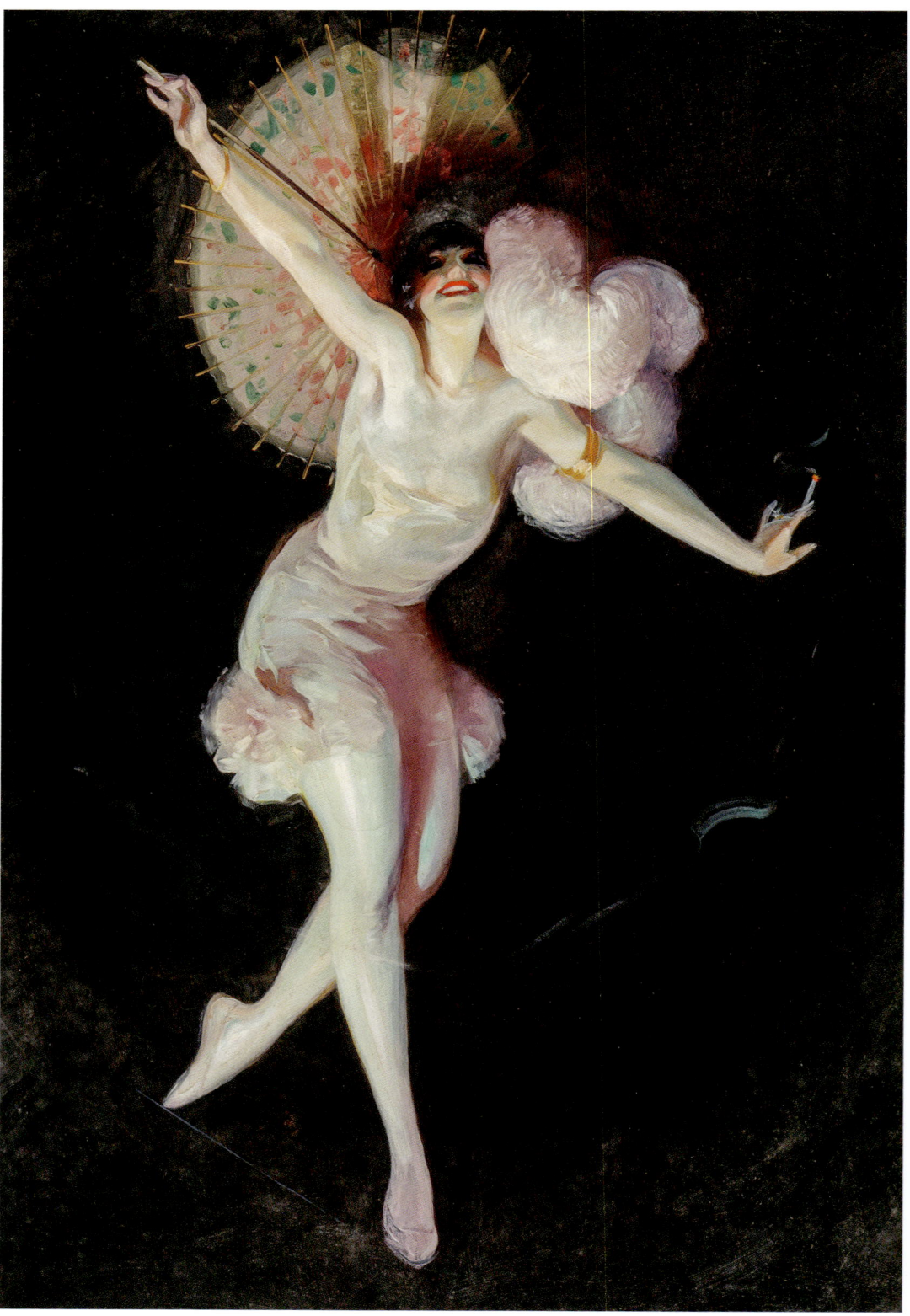

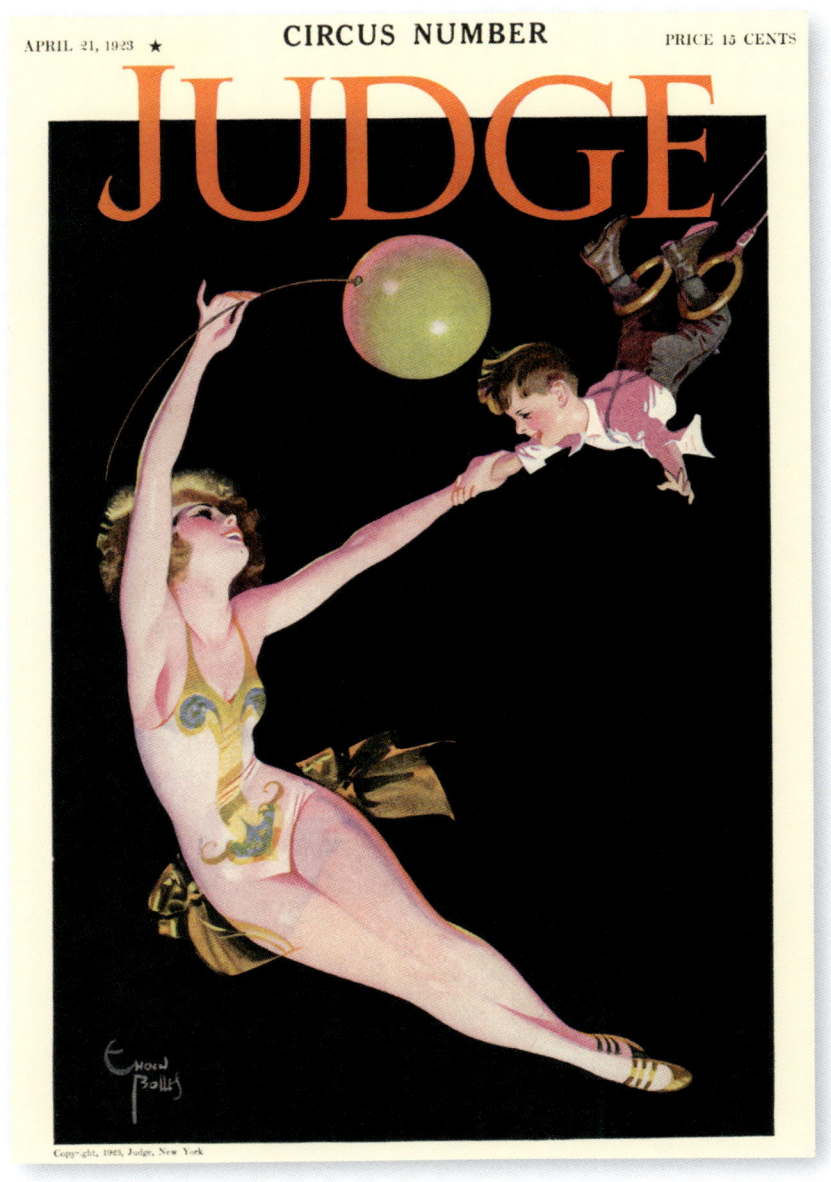

CIRCUS NUMBER

PRICE 15 CENTS

JUDGE

Copyright, 1923, Judge, New York

Opposite: Steady Work describes what Bolles hoped for when he was hired to paint this first cover for *Judge* magazine, October 31, 1914. Ten years of cover work for the humor magazine followed. Bolles expert Jack Raglin thinks this was the first American magazine cover to show a woman with a lit cigarette. The image was so popular it was subsequently made into a poster, and it served as the springboard for Bolles's career. Oil on canvas, 1914, 36 x 30 inches. Courtesy Heritage Auctions.

Above: Judge, April 21, 1923.

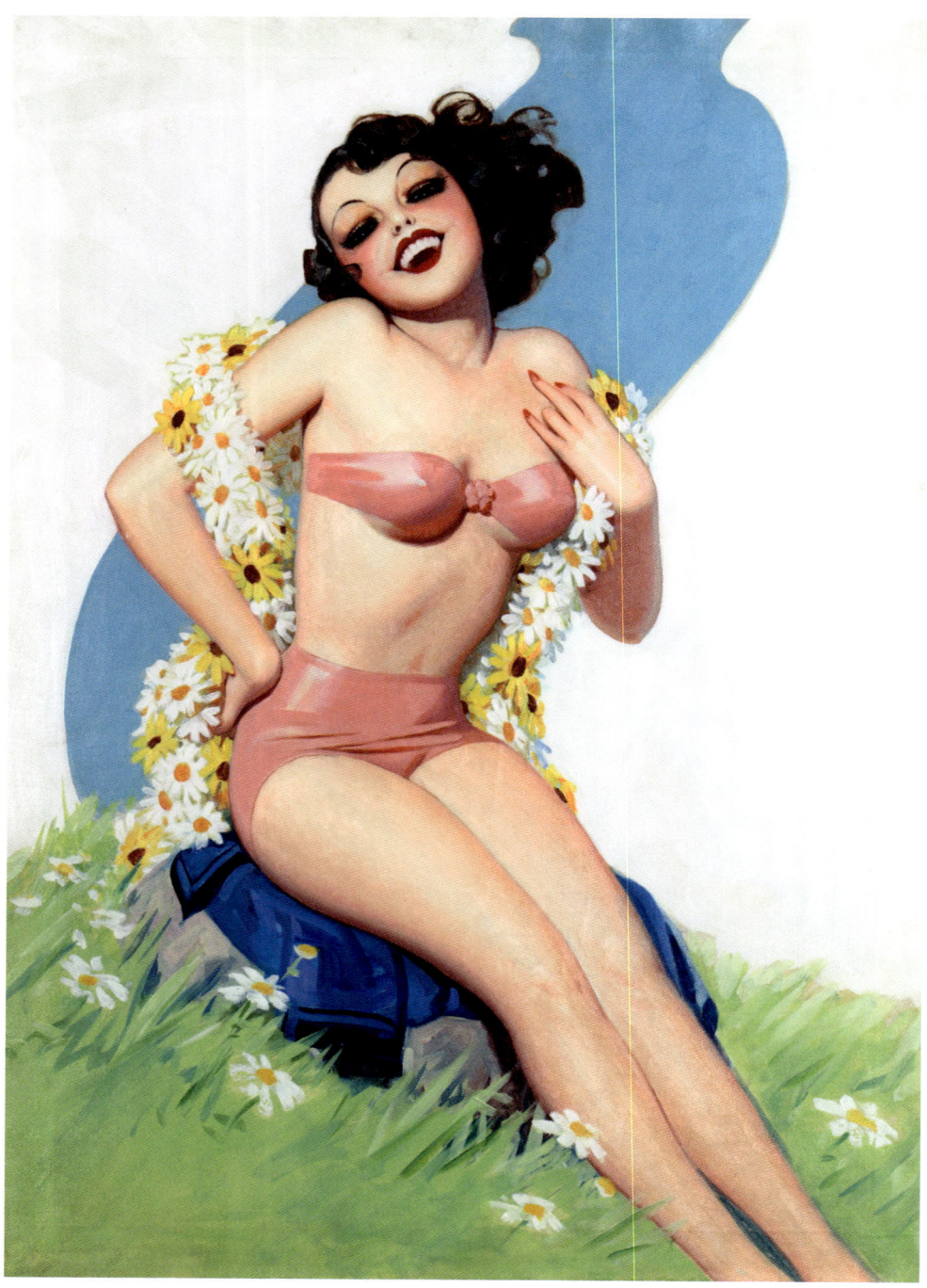

Above: Oil on canvas, circa 1935; later used for the June 1945 cover of *Breezy Stories*. 35 x 27 inches. Collection of Michael and Gail Guglielmino

Opposite: Oil on canvas for a probable *Breezy Stories* cover, circa 1935. 30 x 22 inches.

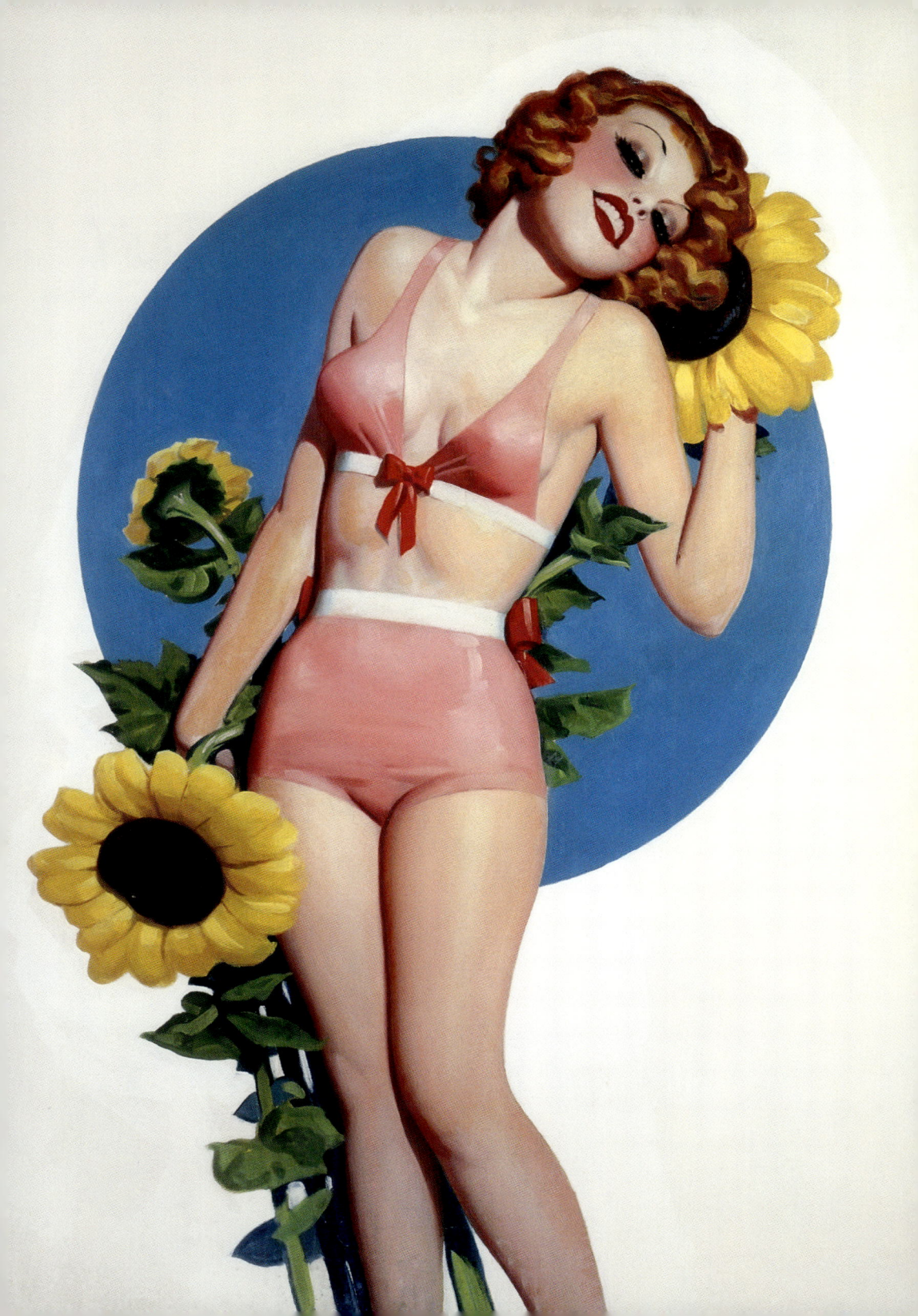

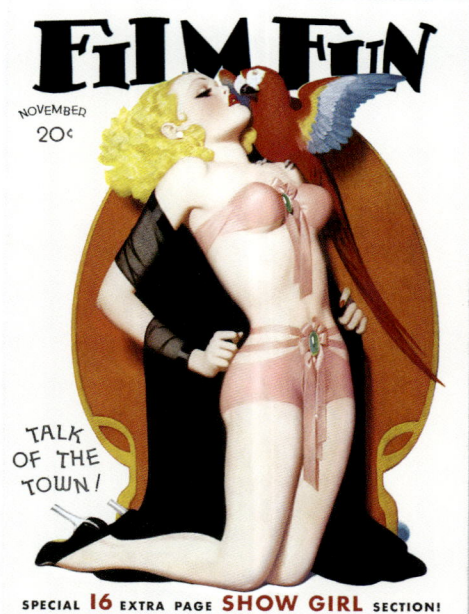

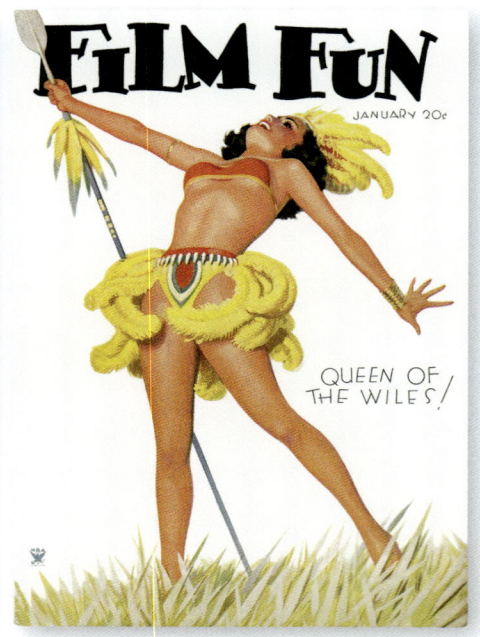

Above left: Talk of the Town!, November 1936
cover of *Film Fun*.

Above right: Queen of the Wiles!, January 1934
cover of *Film Fun*.

Opposite: Easy to Get Stuck On!, oil on board, for the
August 1937 cover of *Film Fun*. 29.5 x 22 inches.

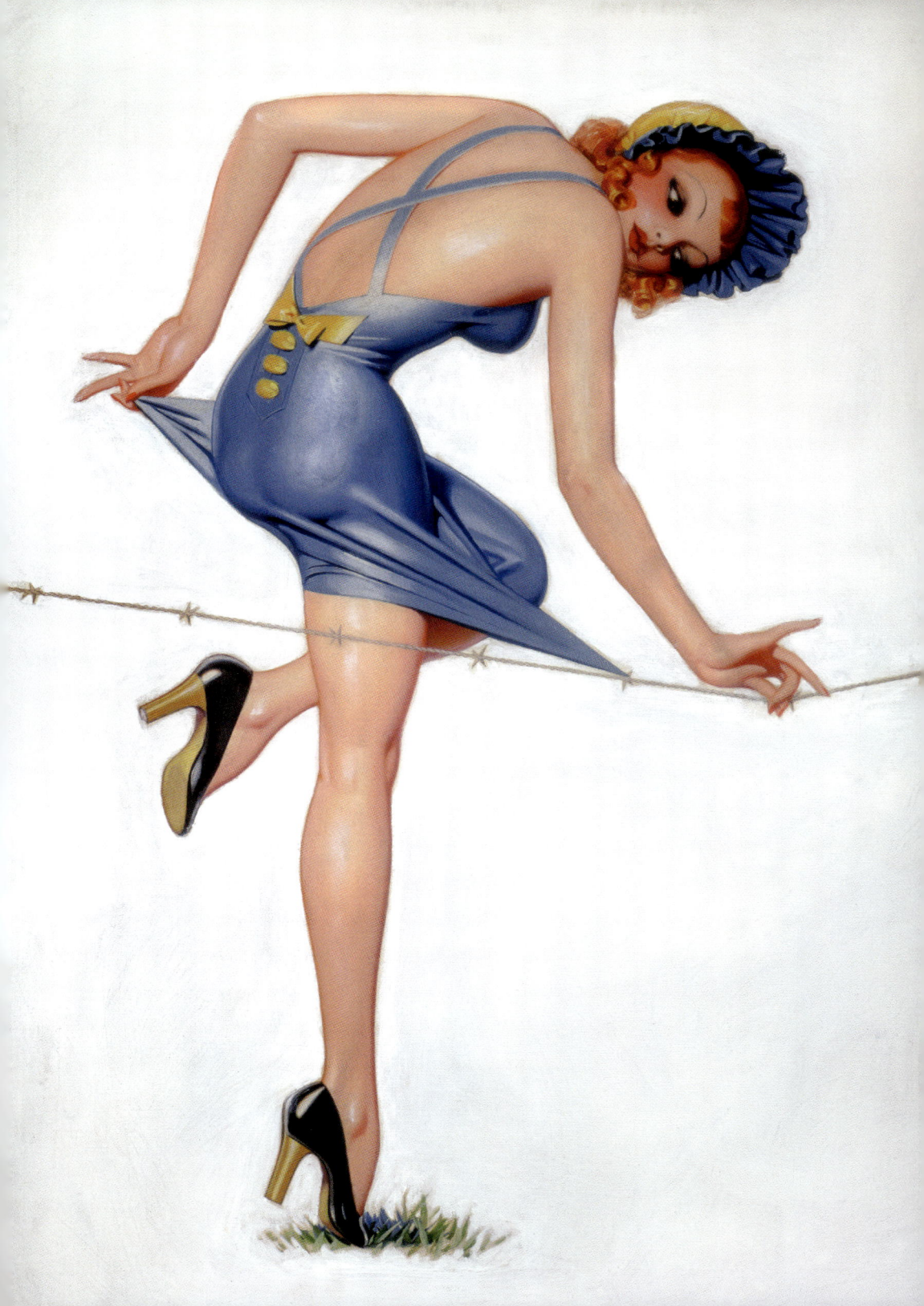

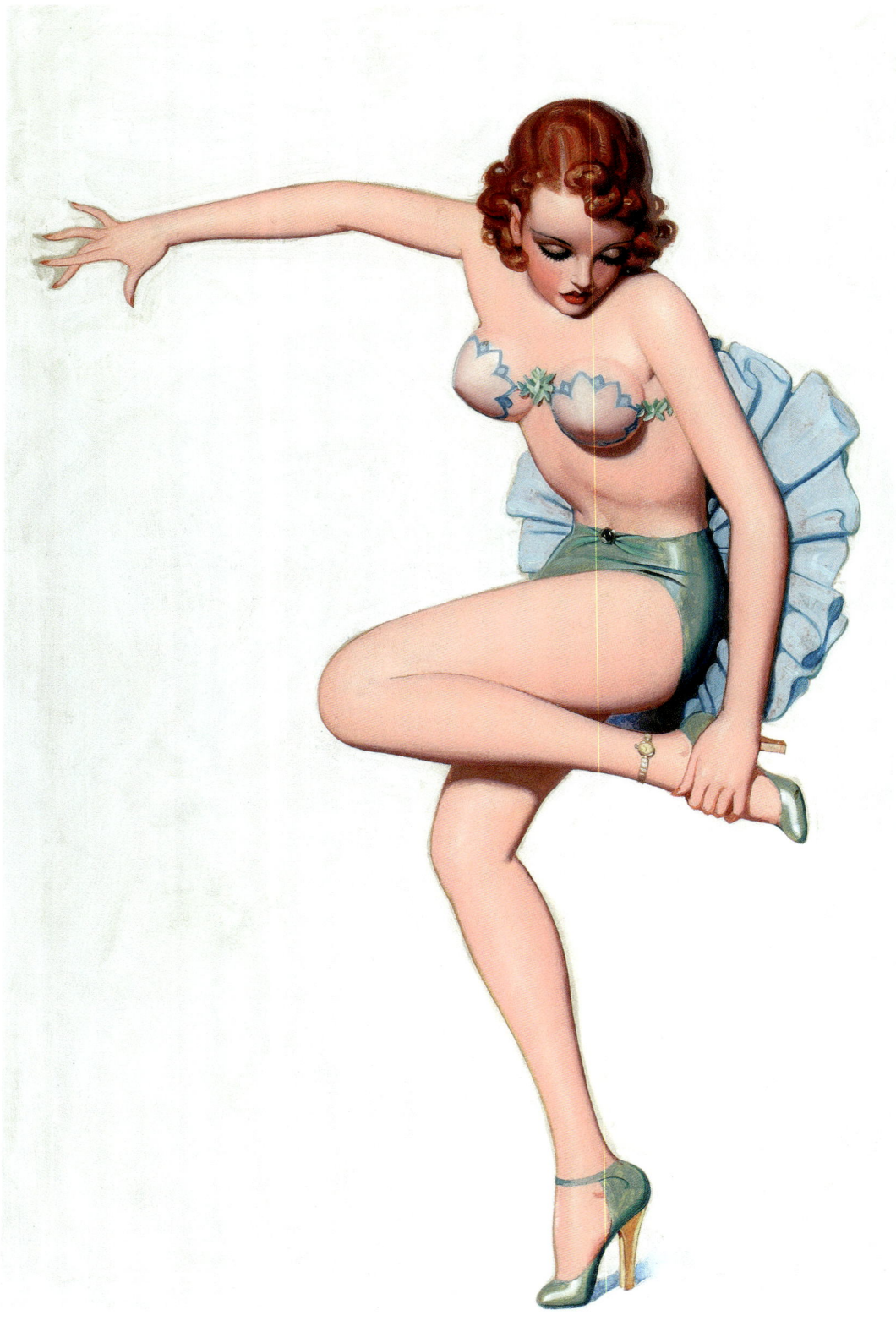

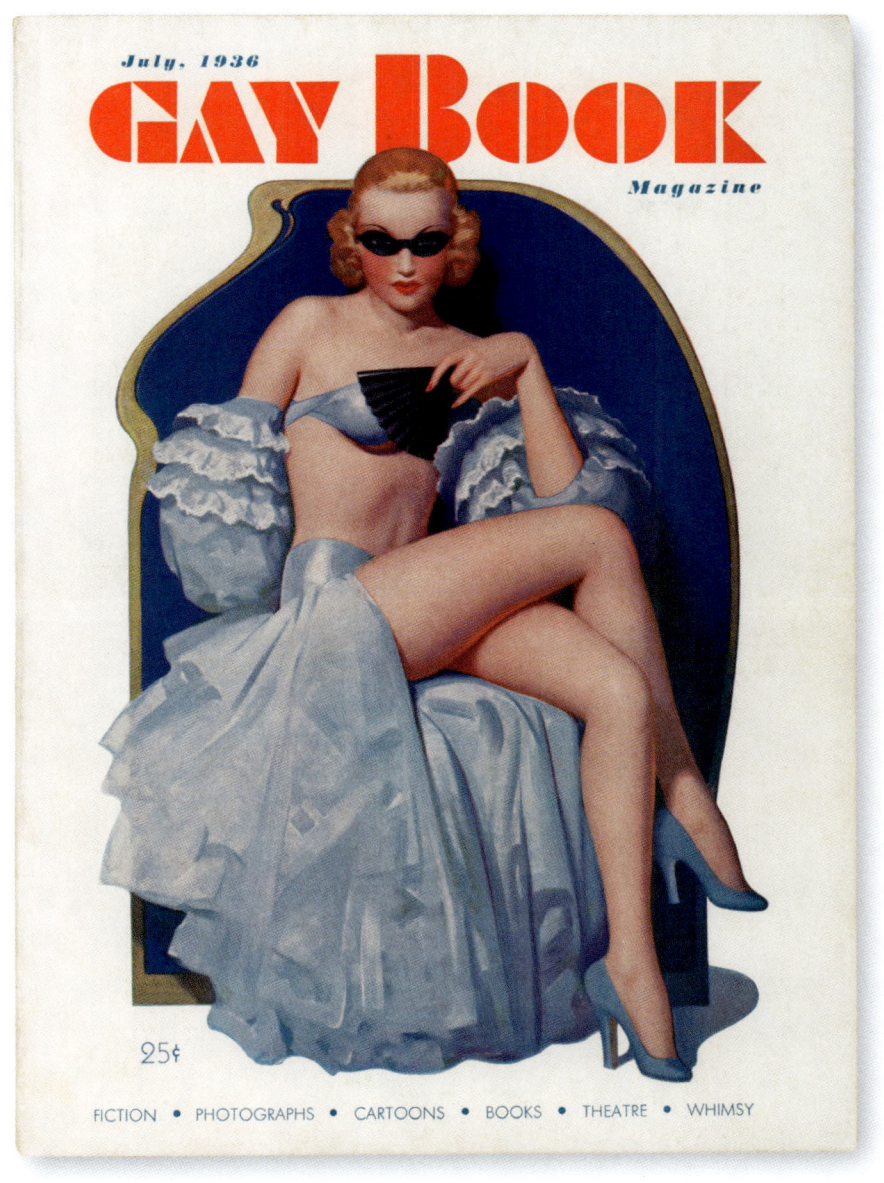

Opposite: Oil on canvas, for cover of *Spicy Stories*, September 1937. 30 x 22 inches. Courtesy Heritage Auctions.

Above: A beautiful cover for the July 1936 issue of *Gay Book*. In the 1920s and '30s, "gay" was a euphemism for "sexy." As I'm sure many think it is today.

ENOCH BOLLES

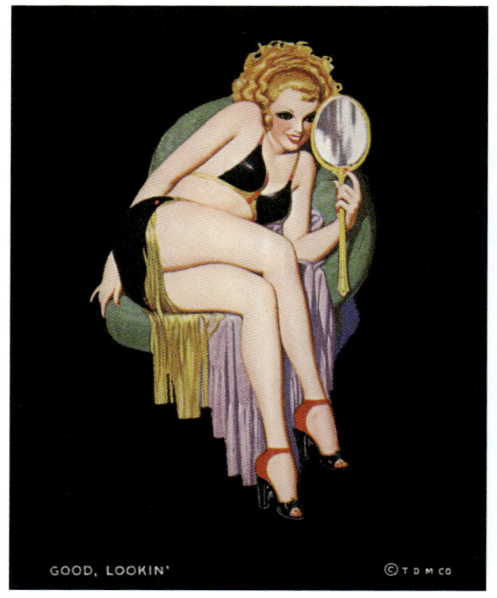

GOOD, LOOKIN'   ©T D M CO

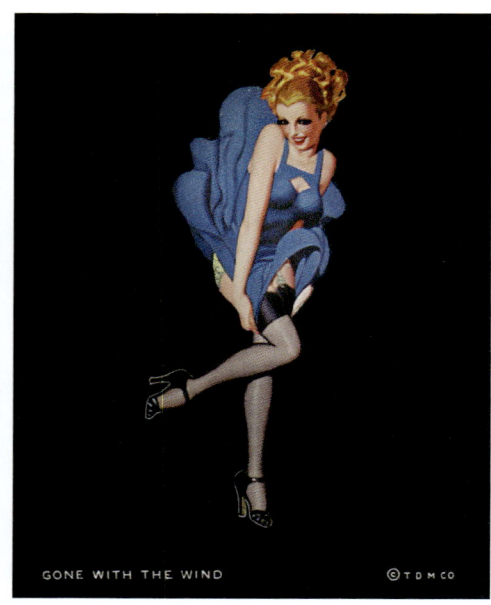

GONE WITH THE WIND   ©T D M CO

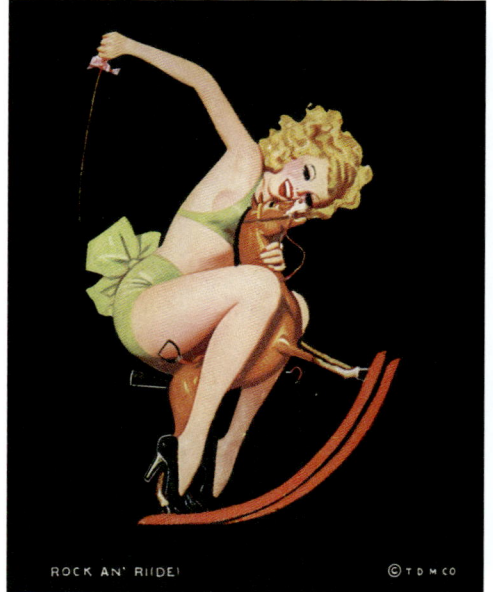

ROCK AN' RIIDE!   ©T D M CO

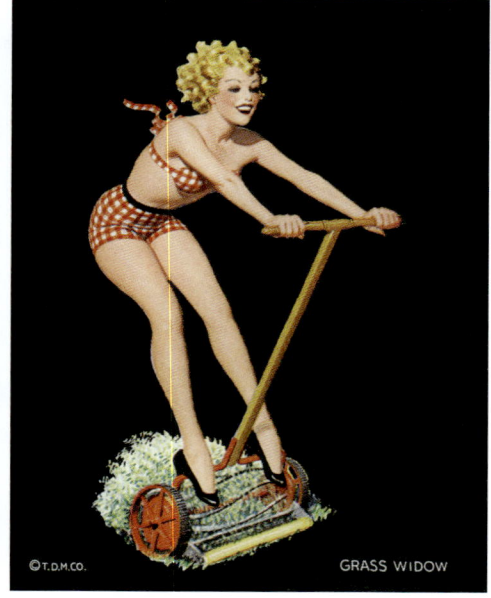

©T.D.M.CO.   GRASS WIDOW

Above: Four blotters produced by Brown & Bigelow, circa 1940, with Bolles images, clockwise from top left, for the November 1937 cover of *Film Fun*; the April 1937 cover of *Film Fun*; the August 1938 cover of *Film Fun*; and the September 1936 cover of *Spicy Stories*.

Opposite: Nice to Have a Drag With, oil on canvas, for the cover of *Film Fun*, February 1937. 30 x 22 inches. Courtesy Heritage Auctions.

THE ART OF PIN-UP

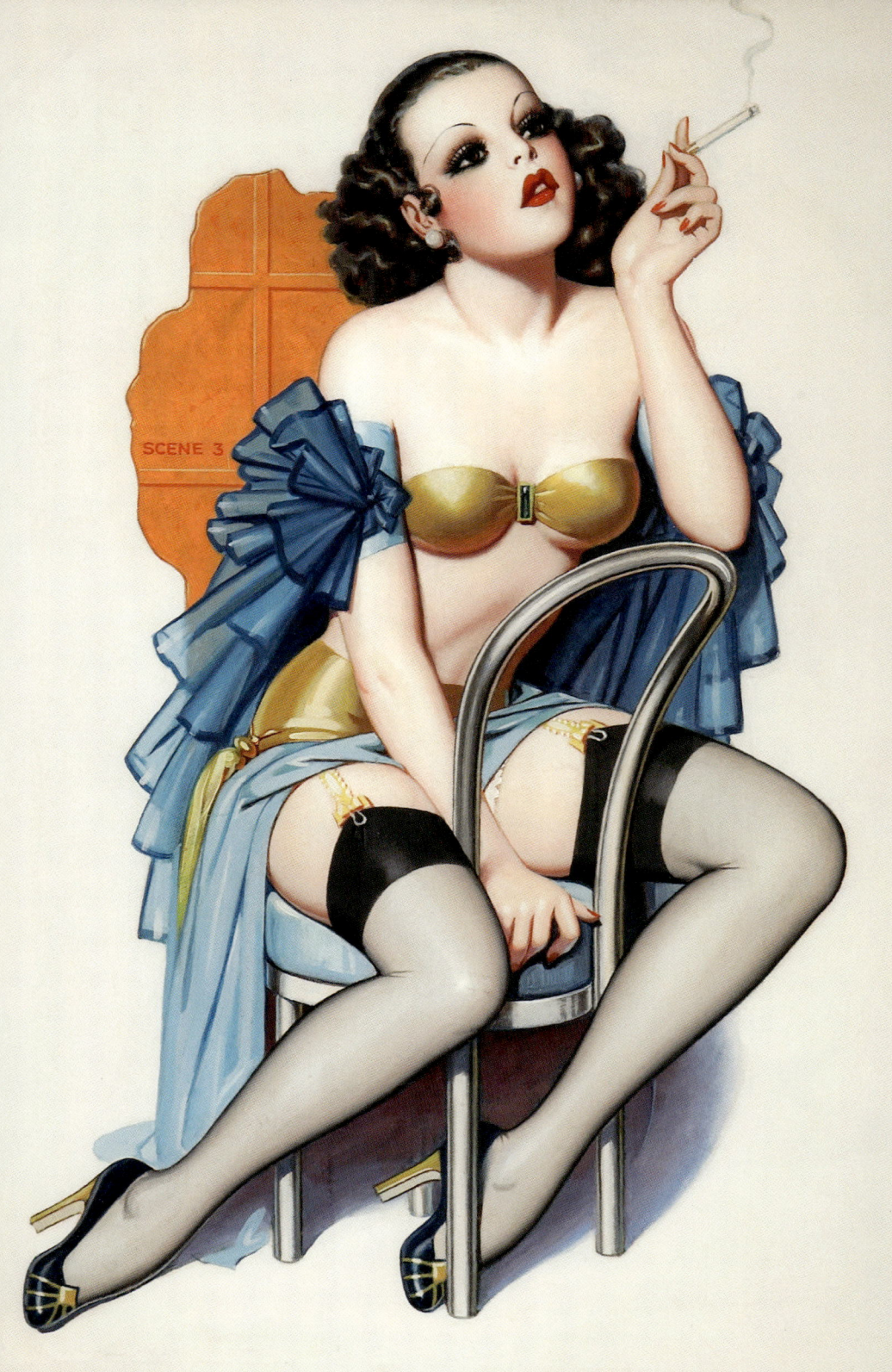

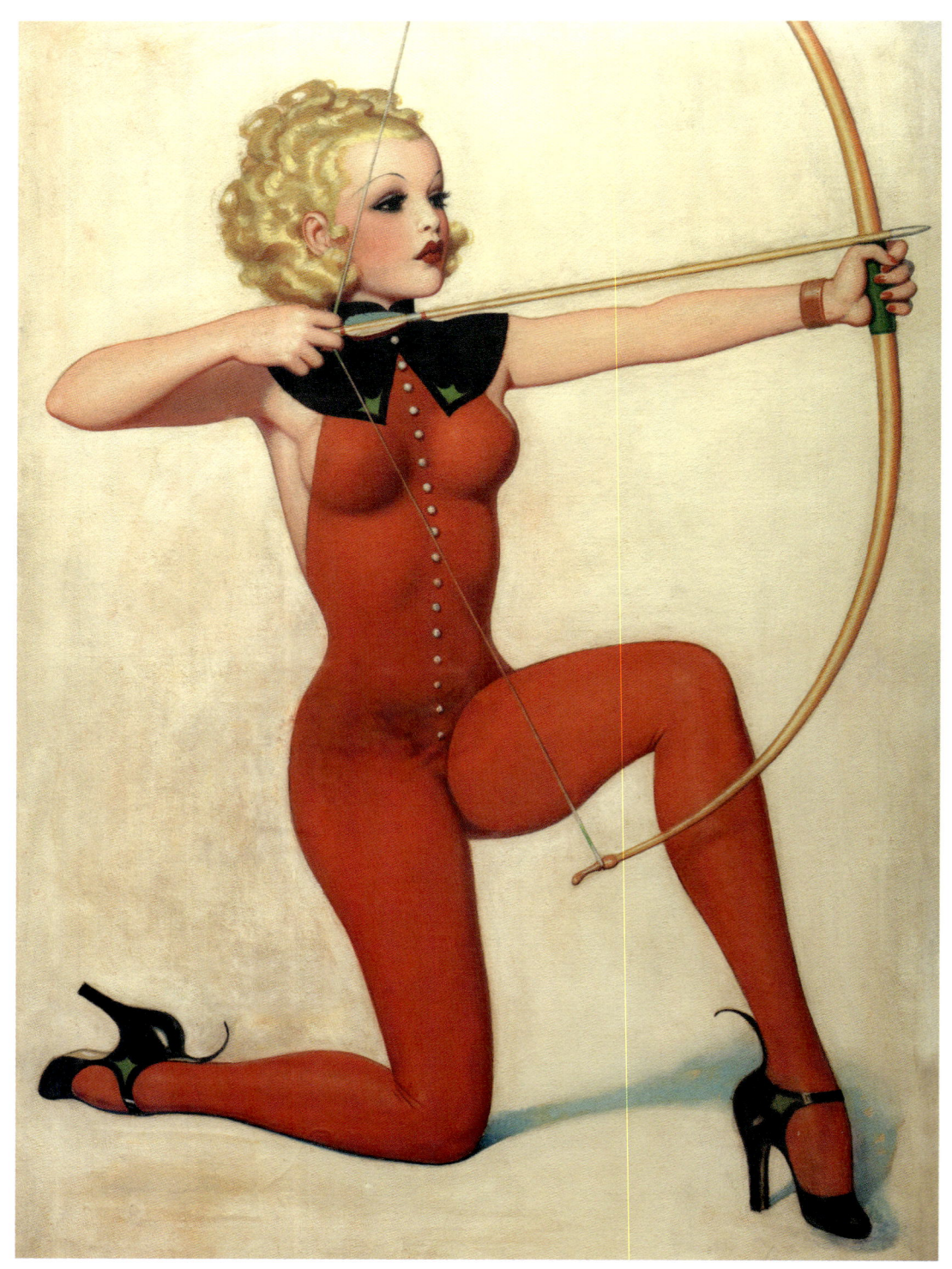

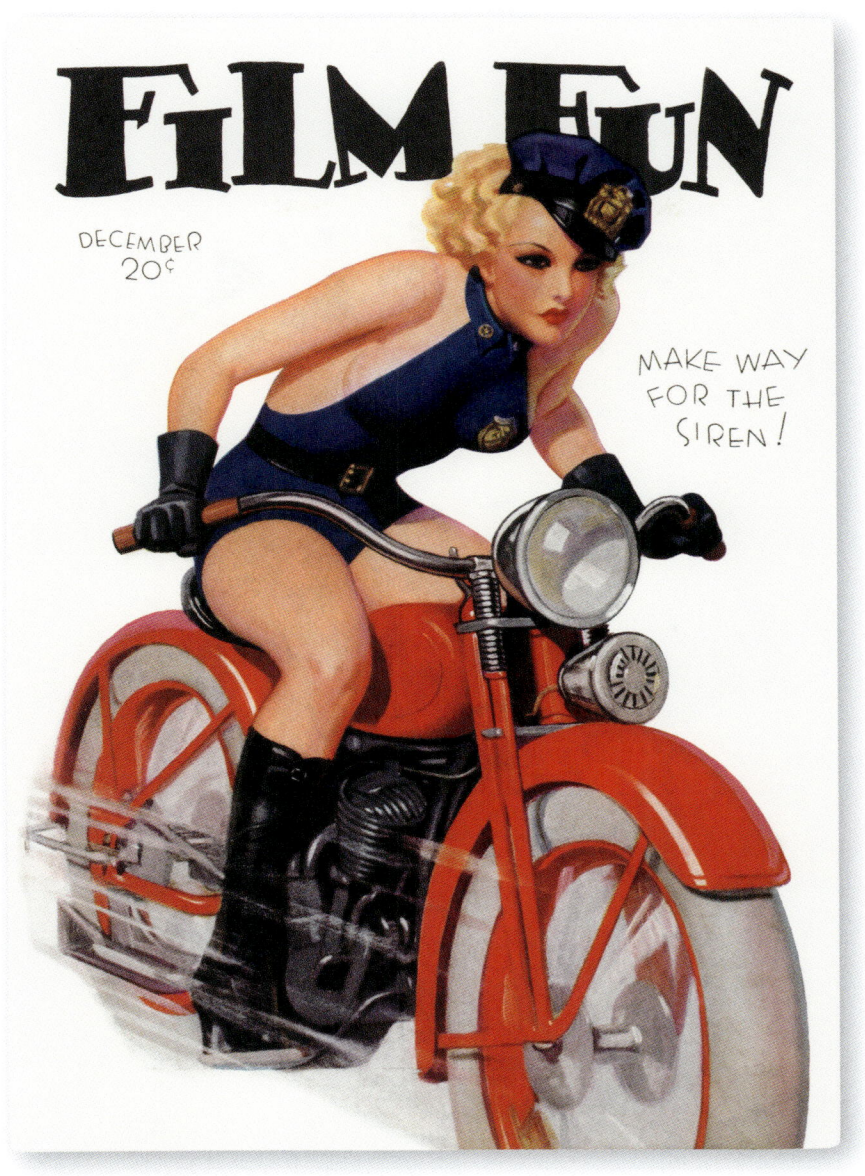

Opposite: *She Aims to Please*, oil on canvas, for cover of *Film Fun*, March 1937. 30 x 22 inches. A repair is visible above the figure's right hip. Apocryphally, Bolles destroyed many of his paintings following his nervous breakdown in 1938. Most were slashed across the crotch, this is a rare survivor.

Above: *Make Way For the Siren!*, December 1934 cover of *Film Fun*.

ENOCH BOLLES

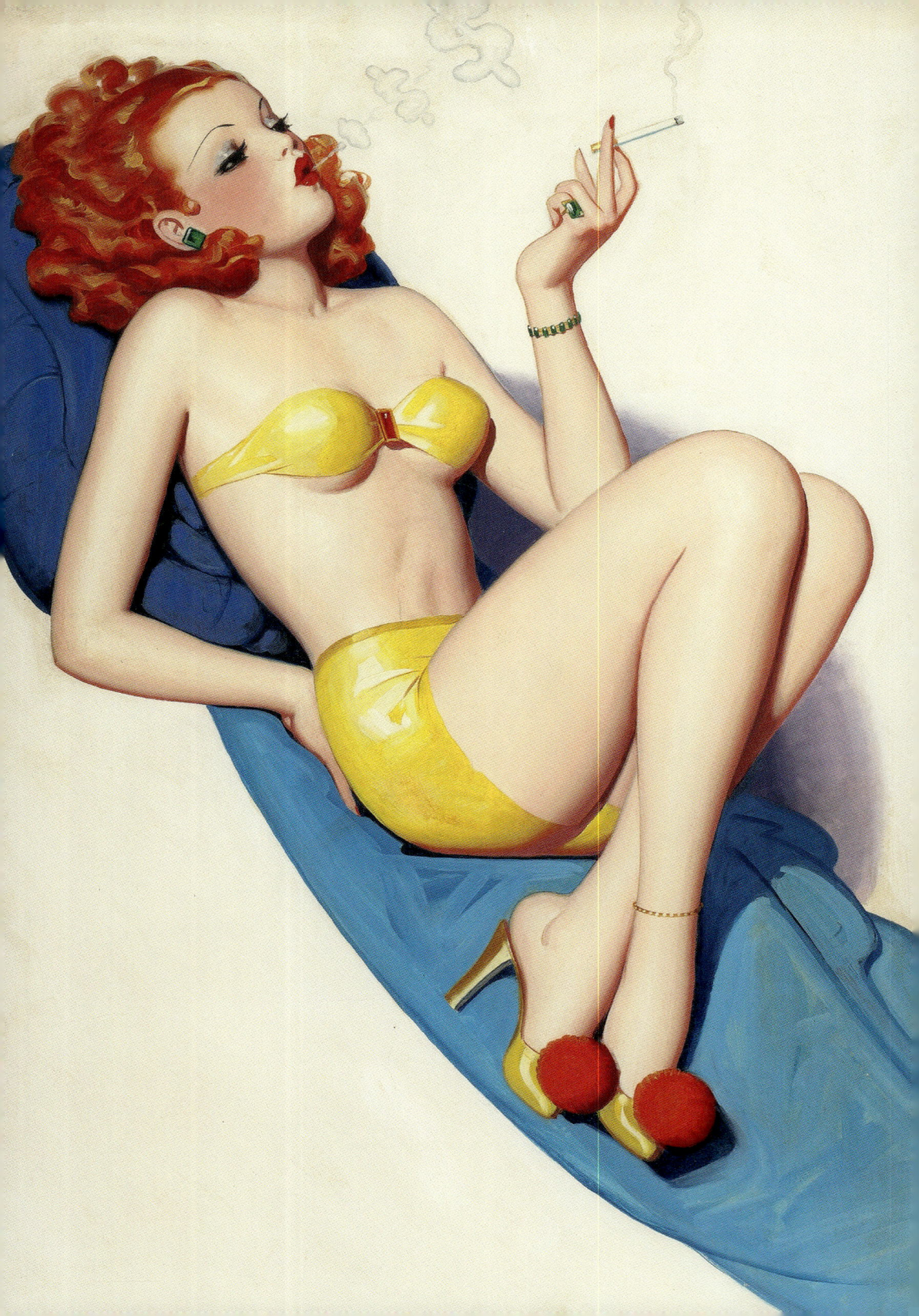

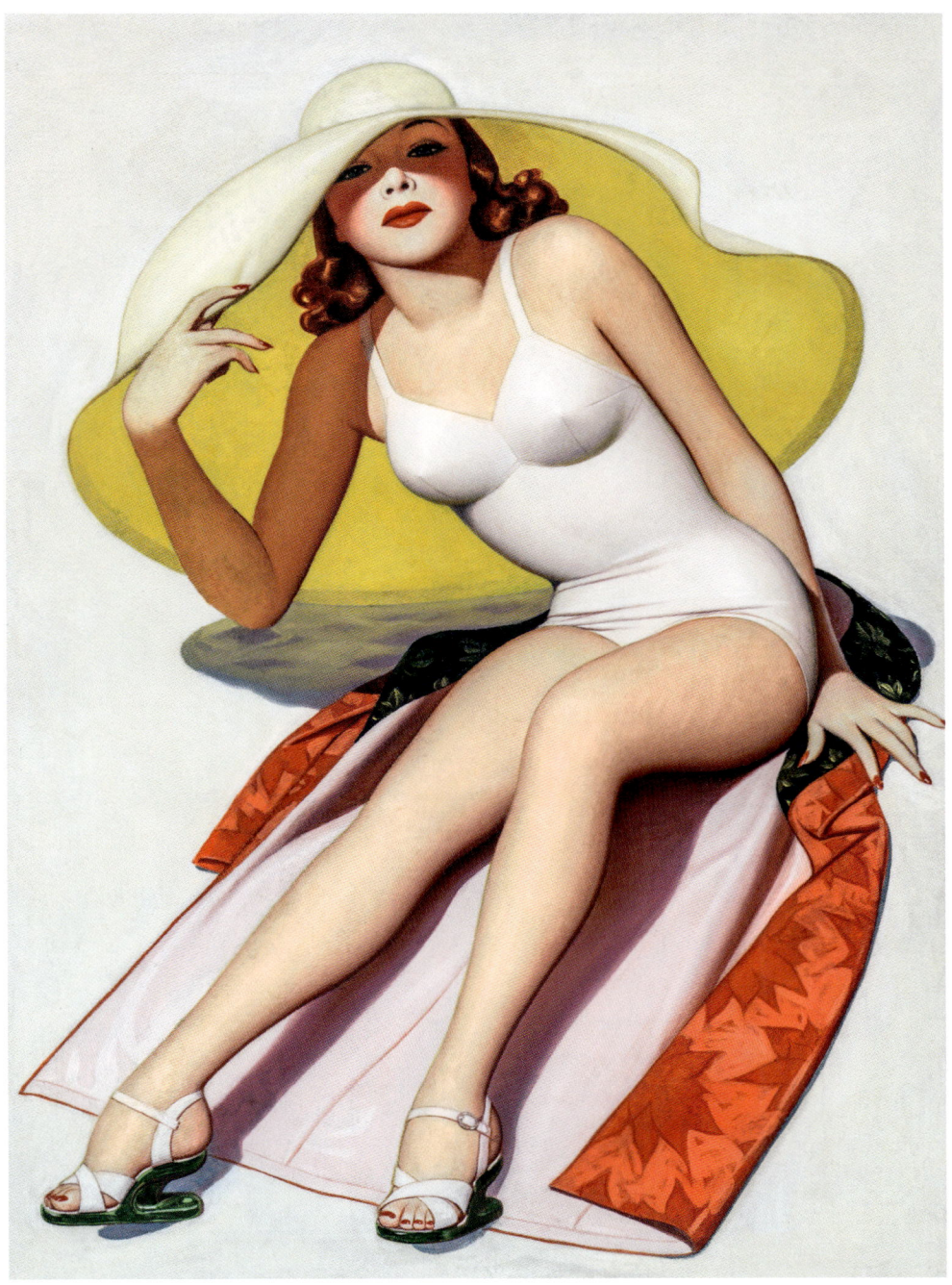

Opposite: Oil on canvas, 1936, for the March 1937 cover of *Spicy Stories*. 30 x 22 inches. Courtesy Heritage Auctions.

Above: Peek of the Season, oil on canvas, 1940, for the June 1940 cover of *Film Fun.* 30 x 22 inches.

ENOCH BOLLES

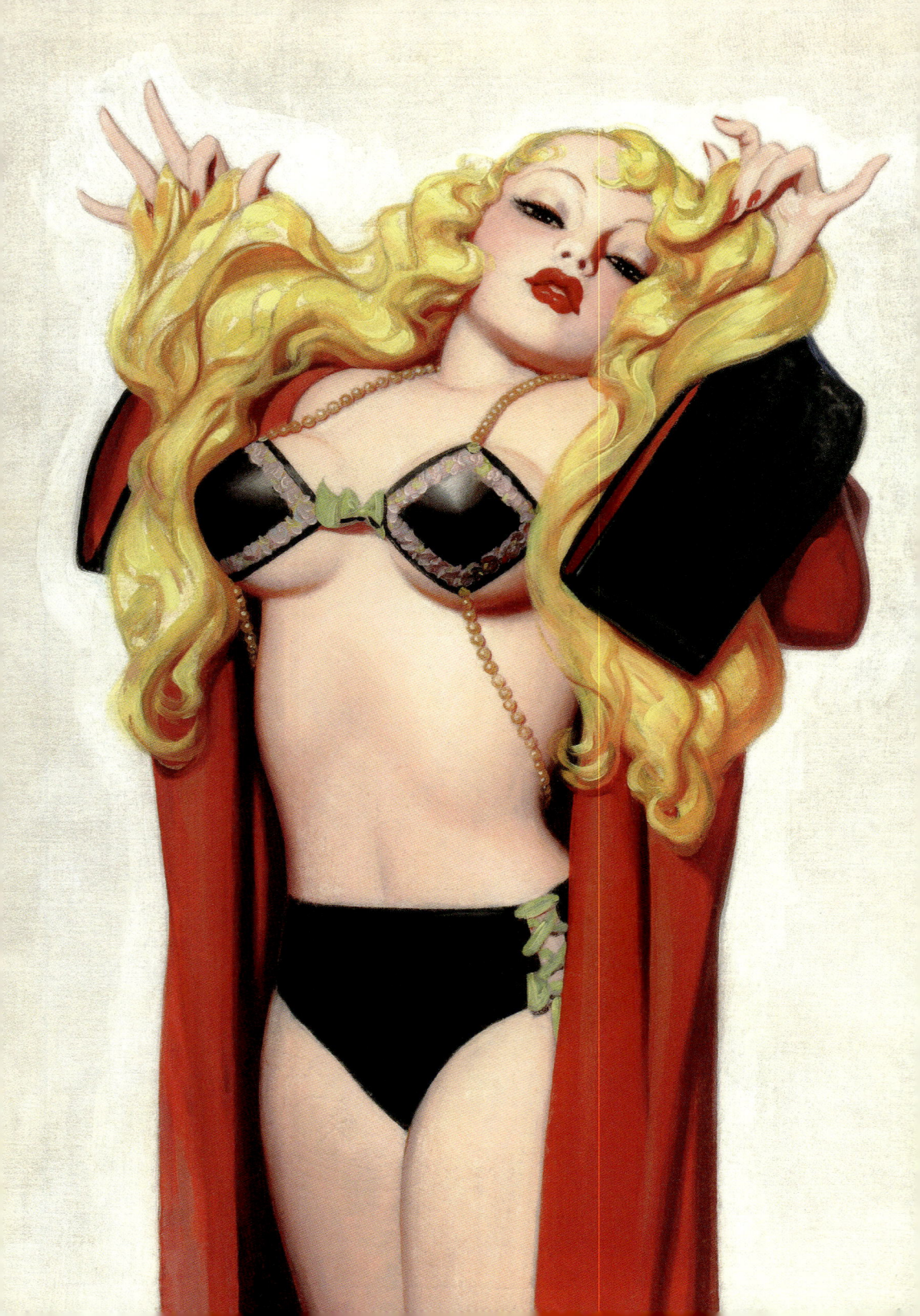

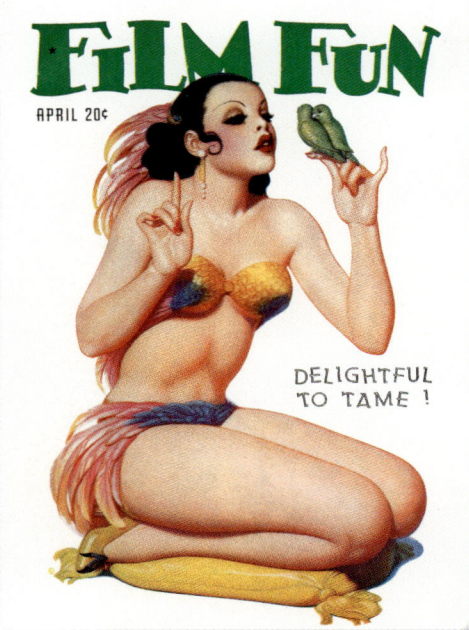

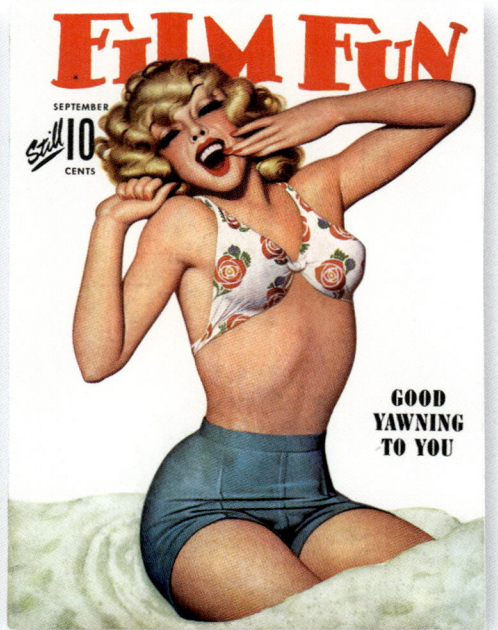

Opposite: Oil on canvas, 1937, for the March 1938 cover of *Spicy Stories*. As Bolles matured, his women got larger and were more often painted from a low angle, looking down on the artist. 30 x 22 inches. Courtesy Heritage Auctions.

Above left: This oil on canvas was first painted for the April 1938 cover of *Film Fun* as a sort of befeathered harem girl, with the title *Delightful to Tame!* It was painted over for the April 1939 cover and retitled *When You Gotta Coo, You Gotta Coo!*

Above right: Bolles's last cover for *Film Fun*, September 1942, makes for a perfect 21-year run with the magazine.

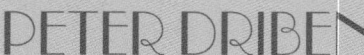

PETER DRIBEN

PETER DRIBEN-

1903–1968

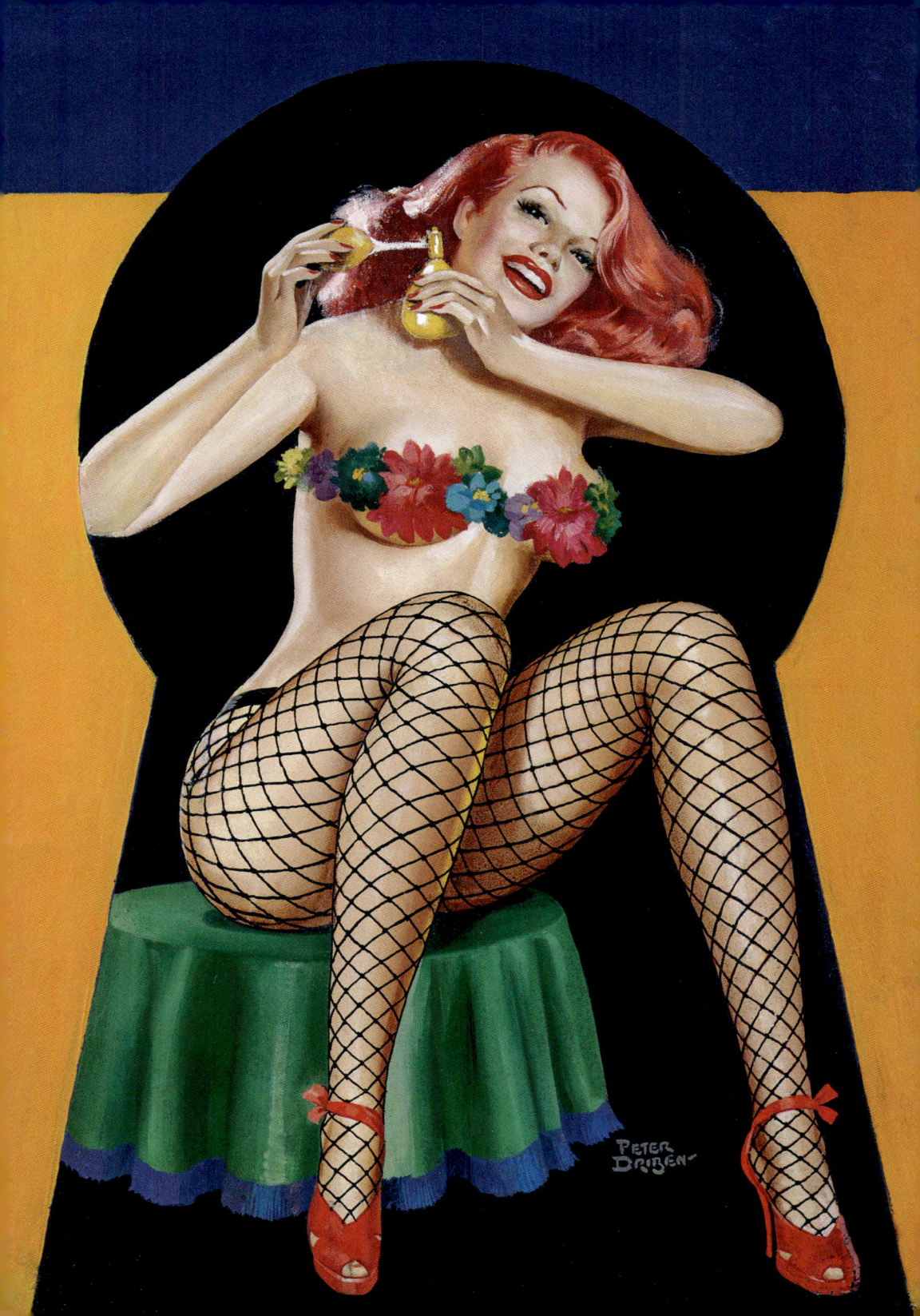

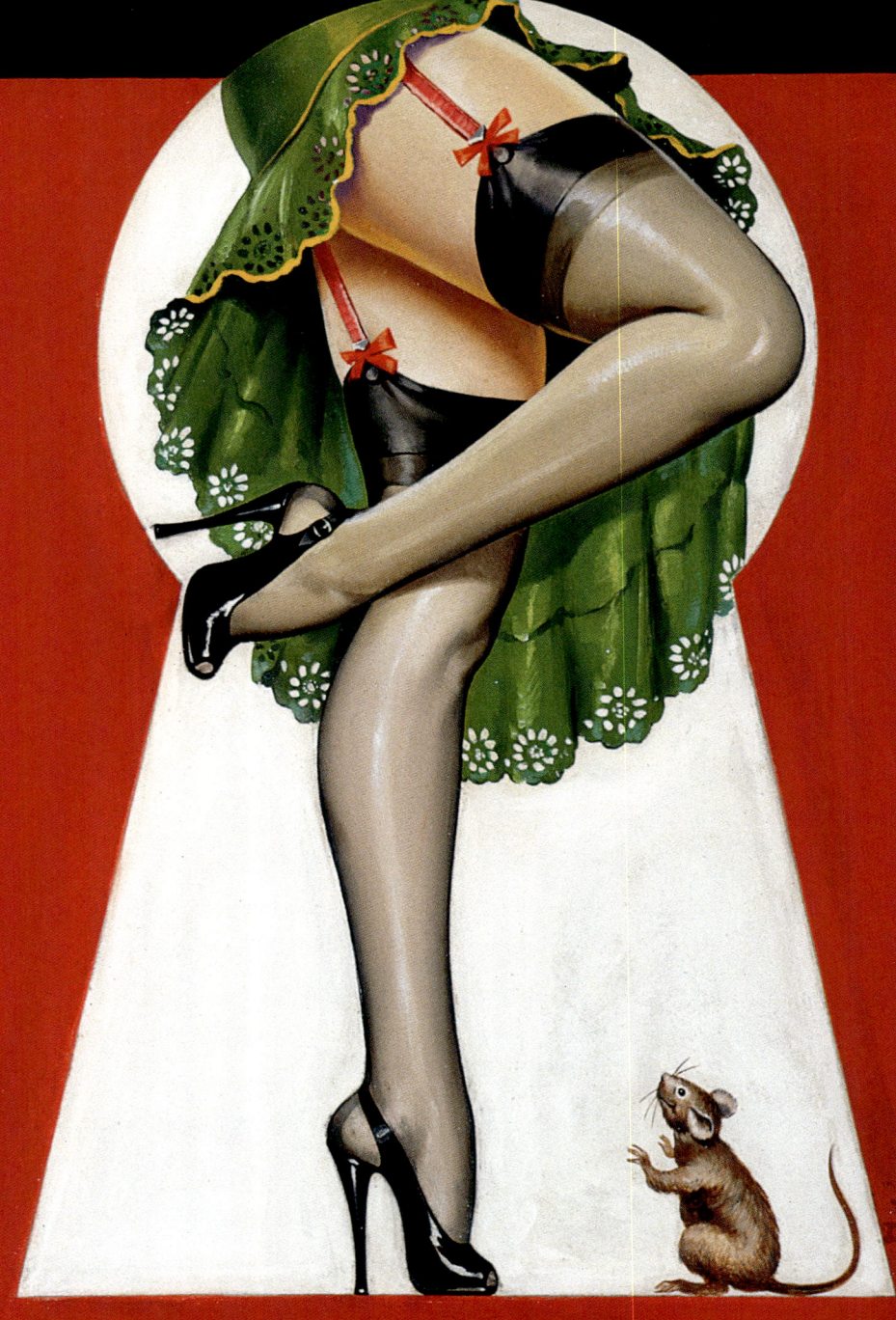

"Driben's girls couldn't really be called 'good.' Their costumes were consciously trashy, their heels whorishly high, and their thighs just far too voluptuous."

Pin-ups were split into two categories: calendars and magazines. Magazine art was further split into covers and centerfolds. Petty and Vargas were centerfold artists whereas Peter Driben was a cover man, perhaps the most prolific in the history of pin-up.

His motivation was perpetual poverty, even when doing five or 10 commissions a month. The family suspected his wife, known as crazy Aunt Louise, was behind the money problems—what with her failed acting career and "beatnik causes"—the two of them living in that filthy apartment in New York, with two dogs and all that distasteful art. In reality, no one knew what the problem was—just that Driben was driven to produce, and his drive resulted in some of the most distinctive art ever made. His big 27-by-35-inch flamboyant cover paintings for *Beauty Parade*, *Eyeful*, *Titter*, *Wink*, *Whisper*, and *Flirt*, all done in bright primary-color oils, looked like nothing else on the newsstand. In keeping with the magazines' tawdry burlesque contents, Driben's girls

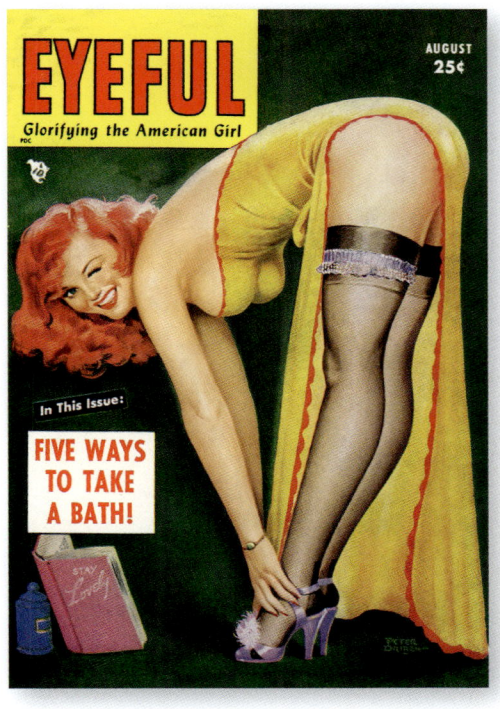

couldn't really be called "good." Their costumes were consciously trashy, their heels whorishly high, and their thighs just far too voluptuous. Only George Petty, with his toe-shoe obsession, brought a similar fetish element to pin-up, and his was much more subtle.

But then, *Esquire* was a world apart from *Eyeful*.

Driben's parents came from Russia and Lithuania sometime in the 1890s, settling in the Boston, Massachusetts, suburb of Chelsea. Peter, their first child, was born in 1903. Seven more quickly followed. The family was poor and poorly educated, but in 1925 Driben entered an art contest of the kind found on matchbook covers with the headline "Draw the Pirate and Win a

Opposite: Oil on board, 1949, for the November 1949 cover of *Whisper*. 34 x 26.5 inches. This was the magazine's first keyhole cover, based on its motto "Thru the Keyhole." The top bands of color in each keyhole painting were to accomodate the title.

Above: The August 1952 cover of *Eyeful* magazine.

Page 165: Oil on board, circa 1948, for a cover of *Whisper*.

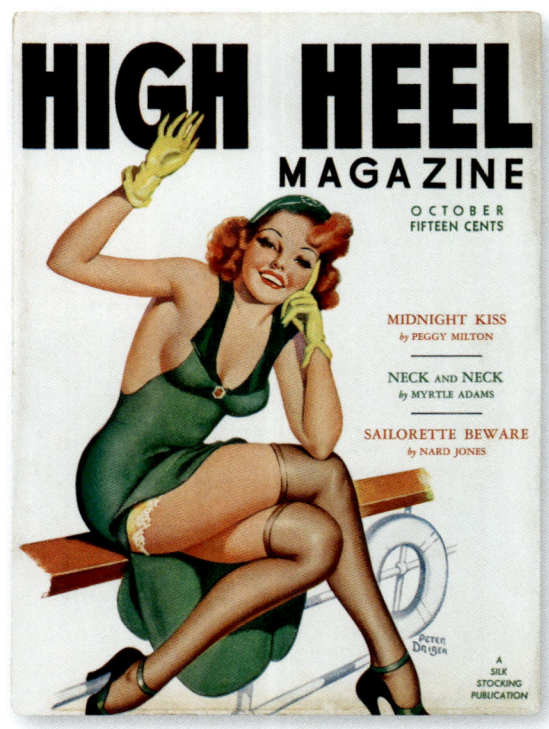

Scholarship." In Driben's case the come-on paid off: He won a full scholarship to the Vesper George School of Art in Boston. His family was not pleased. Old World tradition demanded that the oldest son help support the family, and art classes didn't seem like the quickest route to wealth. When Driben decamped to Paris following his studies at Vesper George for further instruction at the Sorbonne, his irate father reportedly disowned him.

It's not known precisely how Driben spent his years in Paris, but several sketches of Parisian showgirls survive.

In 1933 Adolf Hitler became chancellor of Germany, and Driben wisely perceived it was time for a young American Jew to get out of Europe. He did not return to his father's home and went instead to New York City, center of American magazine publishing. He got work within the year, his first pin-up appearing on the March 1934 cover of *La Paree Stories*, one of many spicy fiction digests of the era. A year later he'd had covers on *Pep Stories*, *Snappy*, *New York Nights*, and *French Night Life*, all of the same genre and possibly from the same publisher. Certainly *Bedtime Stories*, which he illustrated in 1937 and '38, was from the same publisher as *Pep Stories* and *Snappy*, as was *La Paree Stories*, where he contributed a run of 16 covers in the late '30s. Those same years he had covers on the full-size girlie titles *High Heel Magazine*, *Silk Stocking Stories*, *Modern Girl Book*, and *Gay Book*, and on the spicy film magazines *Movie Merry-Go-Round*, *Movie Humor*, and *Real Screen Fun*. All of these titles were monthlies, meaning that in 1938, his most productive year, Driben produced up to 10 paintings a month, displacing Earle Bergey, the original *Tattle Tales*, *Snappy*, and *Pep Stories* artist, giving *Film Fun* cover artist Enoch Bolles his first competition, and stealing jobs from *Movie Humor* regular George Quintana.

On top of all this painting, Driben was creating die-cut window displays for Philco radios, Cannon bath towels, and the Weber baking company, yet still going around with newspaper padding the holes in his shoes. Adding to his financial woes, sometime around 1940 he met and married the artist/actress/figure model Louise. Petite, raven-haired, and Bohemian, she became the model for most of Driben's dark-haired pin-ups and the reputed drain on their bank account with her "way out" causes. Driben kept working the magazines, doing covers for the humor

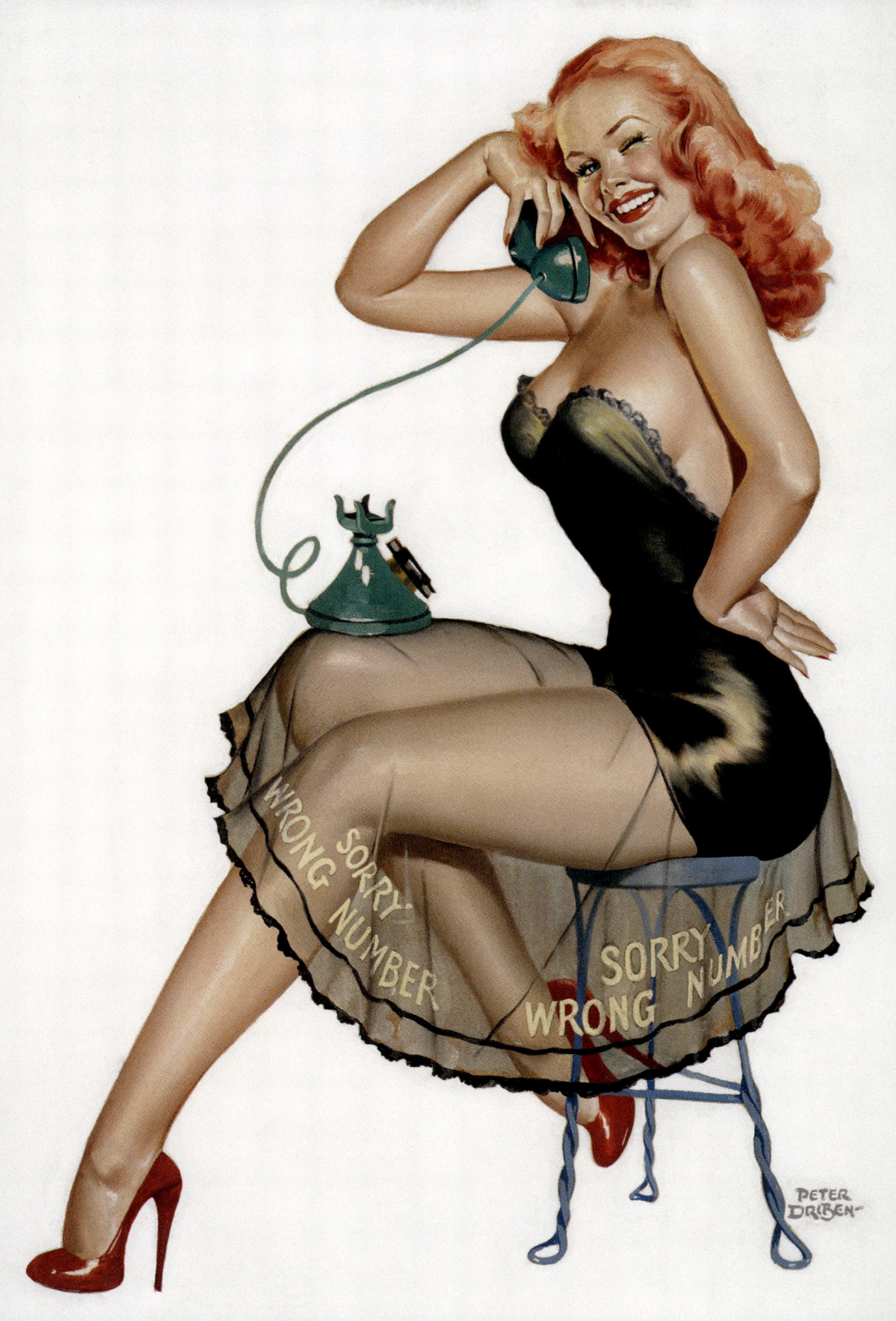

SORRY WRONG NUMBER

SORRY WRONG NUMBER

PETER DRIBEN

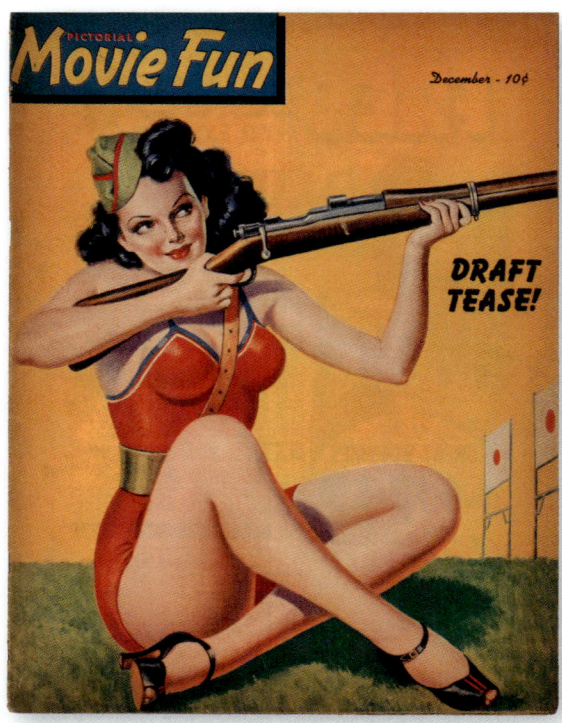

magazine *Joker* and for the detective magazines *Expose Detective* and *Special Detective* in 1942; this was also the year that Robert Harrison launched his first magazine, *Beauty Parade*, but it wasn't until November 1943 that Driben came onboard.

Earl Moran was originally tapped to paint the covers for *Beauty Parade*, but after one signed "Moran" and three signed "Steffa," he found he had no time for the work or the low pay. Harrison brought in Merlin Enabnit, then Billy DeVorss, before finding his perfect fit with Peter Driben. Strangely, the same process was repeated with each new Harrison title: *Eyeful* started with a couple Steffas, seven DeVorsses, and then Driben; *Titter* somehow got a Bolles and several DeVorsses, then Driben; *Wink* got to Driben after three DeVorsses; leaving only *Whisper* to launch with Driben, using his detective-magazine style.

Today Driben is so identified with Harrison magazines that few remember the other artists. While he painted five to eight covers a month, he still managed to serve as art director for the New York *Sun* newspaper from 1944 until 1946 — and be too broke to attend his nephew's bar mitzvah in '46.

Harrison began experimenting with photographic covers in 1950 and in 1953, but with work dwindling, the Dribens moved to Miami. Driben still did a few covers for Harrison until the magazines went under in 1955, then he sat in hotel lobbies and propositioned passersby for portrait commissions. He painted a picture of then-President Eisenhower and sent it to him, receiving back a treasured letter of thanks — but no money. In the early '60s he tried painting flesh over the clothing on some of his Harrison cover girls, hoping to cash in on the new morality, and then, like most old pin-up artists, he settled in to painting clowns that he sold in his studio.

In 1968 Driben developed bone cancer. He suspected the prognosis was bad when his father and two brothers came to visit. He asked why they'd come, and they said for the Republican convention. That's when he knew he was dying: There were no Republicans in the Driben family.

After Driben's death in 1968, it's said that Louise sold his paintings off for $10 each, 12 for $100. Even in death, poor Peter Driben couldn't earn a decent buck.

Above: Oil on board cover of December 1941 *Pictorial Movie Fun* magazine. *Pictorial Movie Fun* used a larger format than *Film Fun, Movie Merry-Go-Round, Movie Humor,* and the other spicy film magazines of the 1930s and '40s, measuring a full 13 x 10 inches. Driben was a frequent cover artist between 1935 and 1942.

Opposite: The Lady Is Willing to Die!, oil on board, 1945, for the May 1945 cover of *Special Detective* magazine. The head and bust of this painting was later used as a cover for the pulp novel *Unwilling Bride.* 27 x 22 inches.

THE ART OF PIN-UP

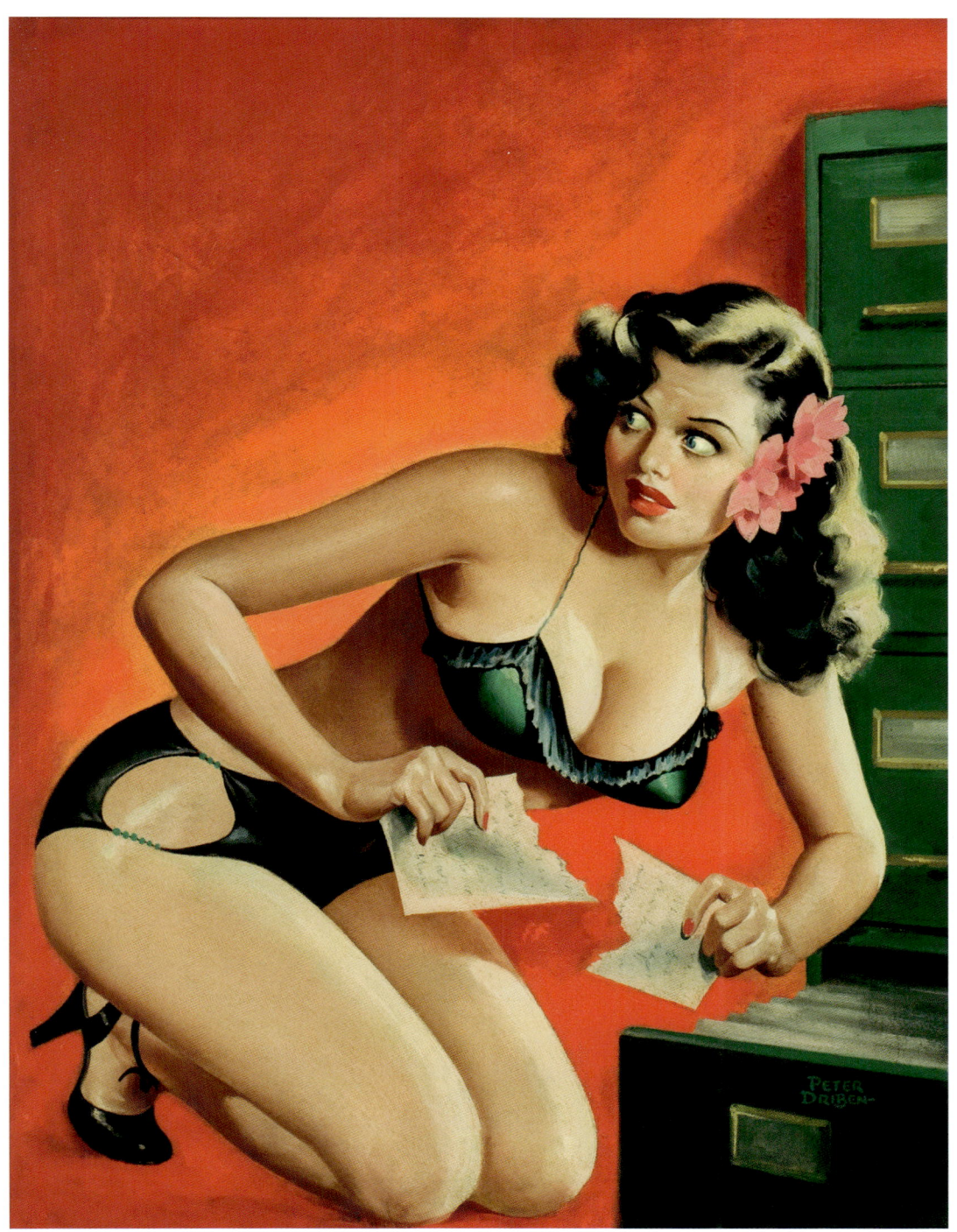

PETER DRIBEN

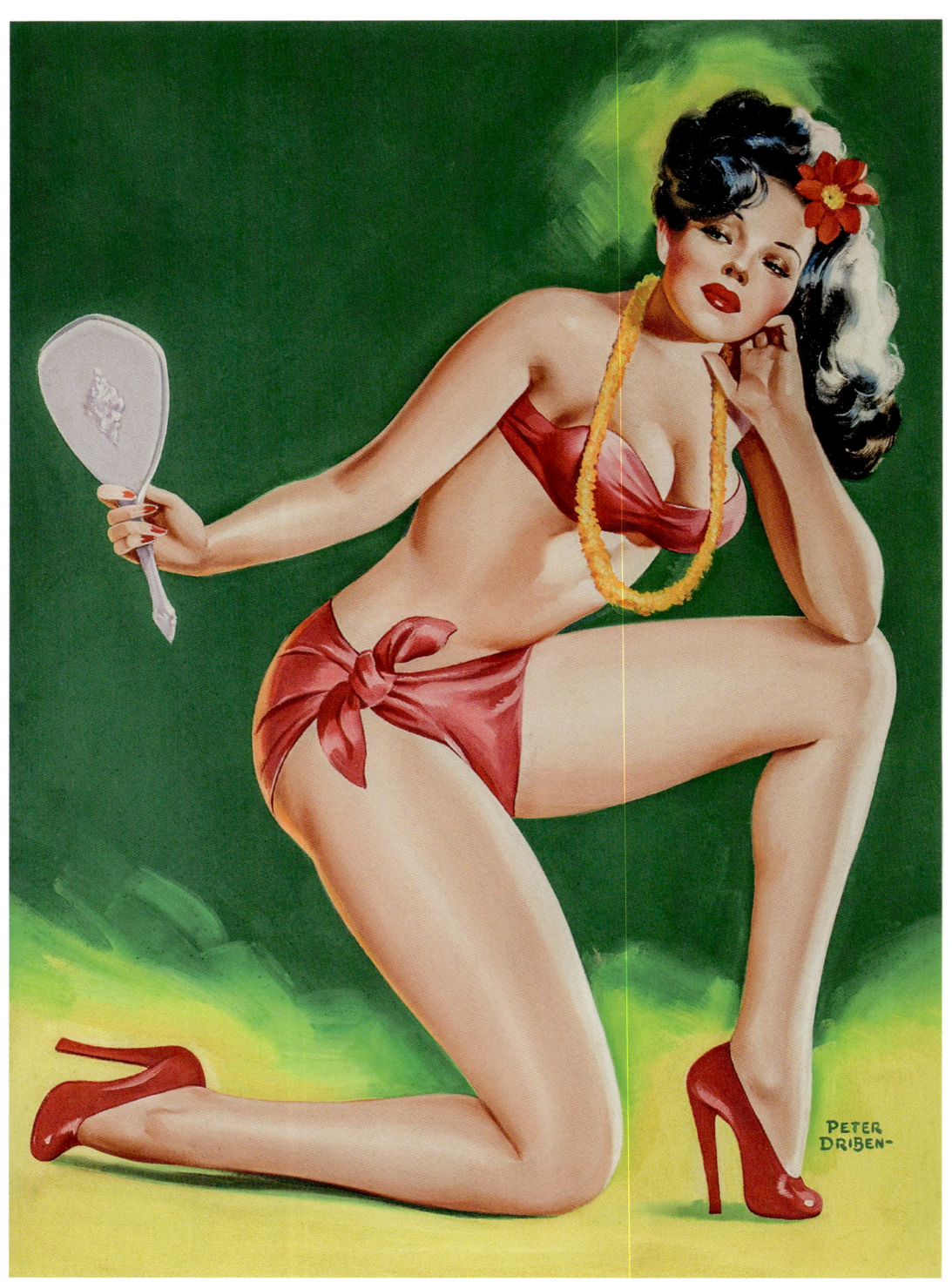

„Man konnte Dribens Mädchen nicht unbedingt als ‚brav' bezeichnen.
Ihre Klamotten waren bewusst trashig gehalten, die Absätze ihrer
Pumps hurenhaft hoch und ihre Schenkel schlicht allzu verlockend."

Pin-ups wurden in zwei Kategorien unter-
teilt: Kalender und Zeitschriften. Bei den
Bildern für Zeitschriften unterschied man
wiederum Arbeiten für Titelseiten und solche für das Ausklappbild im Innenteil. Petty
und Vargas waren auf Ausklappbilder spezia-
lisiert, während Peter Driben Titelbilder
machte, vermutlich die erfolgreichsten in
der Geschichte des Pin-ups.

Seine wichtigste Motivation war
permanente Geldnot, selbst wenn er fünf
oder zehn Aufträge pro Monat ausführte.
Die Familie vermutete, dass hinter den
Geldsorgen Peter Dribens Frau steckte,
die als die verrückte Tante Louise bekannt
war, und dass die Situation etwas mit
ihrer gescheiterten Schauspielkarriere und
einem gewissen Beatnik-Lebensstil zu
tun hatte; denn das Paar hauste mit zwei
Hunden, umgeben von dieser „geschmack-
losen" Kunst, in einer versifften Wohnung
in New York. In Wirklichkeit wusste niemand, was das Problem war – nur, dass
Driben immerfort unter Produktionsdruck

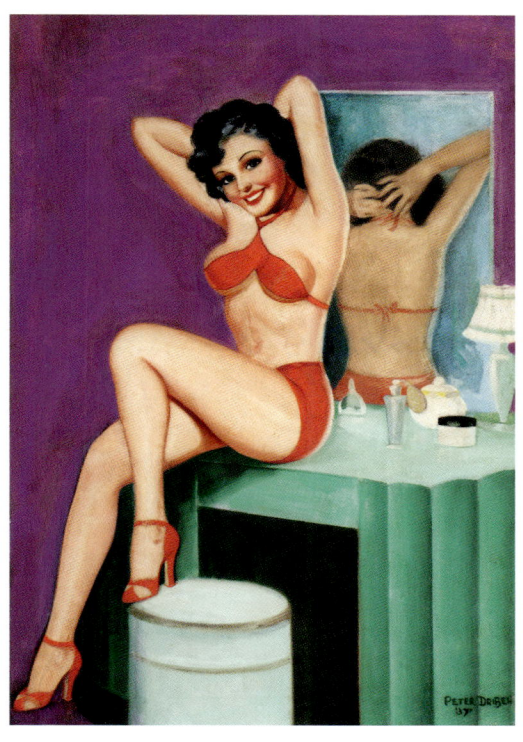

stand und dass diesem Antrieb einige unverwechselbare Kunstwerke dieses Genres entsprangen.
Seine 68,5 x 89 cm großen Bilder für die Titelseiten von *Beauty Parade*, *Eyeful*, *Titter*, *Wink*,
Whisper und *Flirt*, alle in leuchtenden Acrylfarben ausgeführt, waren einzigartig. Den trivialen,
burlesken Inhalten jener Magazine entsprechend konnte man Dribens Mädchen nicht unbe-
dingt als „brav" bezeichnen. Ihre Klamotten waren bewusst trashig gehalten, die Absätze ihrer
Pumps hurenhaft hoch und ihre Schenkel schlicht allzu verlockend. Nur George Petty mit
seiner Obsession für Schuhe, die die Zehen frei ließen, bezog in Pin-ups ein vergleichbares
Fetischelement ein, allerdings sehr viel subtiler. Aber der *Esquire* war eben eine ganz andere
Welt als *Eyeful*.

Opposite: Oil on board, 1946, for the November 1946
cover of *Titter*. *Titter* was Robert Harrison's third magazine, launched in 1943.

Above: Baby, Be Good!, oil on board, 1937, for the cover
of *Bedtime Stories*, May 1938. This is Driben's oldest
known surviving pin-up illustration. 37 x 24 inches.

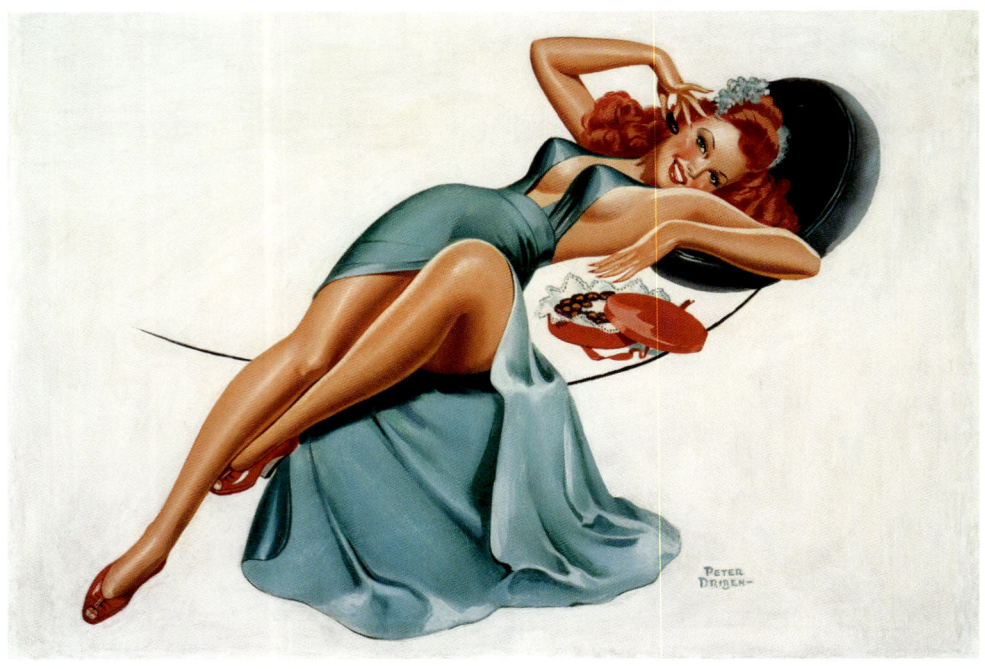

Dribens Eltern waren in den 1890er-Jahren von Russland und Litauen in die USA aus-
gewandert und ließen sich in Chelsea, einem Vorort von Boston, Massachussetts, nieder. Peter,
ihr erstes Kind, wurde 1903 geboren. In schneller Folge kamen sieben Geschwister hinzu. Die
Familie war arm und kaum gebildet, doch 1925 nahm Peter an einem Kunstwettbewerb jener
Art teil, wie man ihn auf Streichholzbriefchen findet: „Zeichne den Piraten und gewinne ein
Stipendium." In Peters Fall lohnte sich die Teilnahme: Er gewann ein Stipendium für die Vesper
George School of Art in Boston. Seine Familie war davon nicht besonders angetan, denn sie
erwartete, dass der älteste Sohn die Familie unterstützte. Kunstunterricht schien dabei nicht der
beste Weg zu sein. Als Peter nach dem Besuch der Vesper George an die Sorbonne nach Paris
ging, um dort weiterzustudieren, soll ihn sein erzürnter Vater verstoßen haben.

    Es ist nicht genau bekannt, wie Driben seine Jahre in Paris verbracht hat, doch einige erhaltene
Zeichnungen von Pariser Showgirls lassen vermuten, dass seine Karriere früh vorgezeichnet war.

    1933 wurde Adolf Hitler Reichskanzler, und Driben erkannte, dass es für einen jungen
amerikanischen Juden an der Zeit war, Europa zu verlassen. In sein Elternhaus kehrte er nicht
zurück, stattdessen ging er nach New York City, dem Zentrum der amerikanischen Zeitschrif-
tenverlage. Er hatte im ersten Jahr schon Aufträge, sein erstes Pin-up erschien 1934 auf der
Titelseite der März-Ausgabe von *La Paree Stories*, einem von vielen Heften jener Ära, die pikante
Geschichten veröffentlichten. Ein Jahr später konnte er bereits Titelbilder für *Pep Stories*, *Snappy*,
New York Nights und *French Night Life* vorweisen, alles Zeitschriften des gleichen Genres und
wohl auch vom gleichen Verleger publiziert. *Bedtime Stories*, die er 1937 und 1938 illustrierte,
erschien im selben Verlag wie *Pep Stories* und *Snappy*, genauso wie *La Paree Stories*, für das er

Above: A rare Driben horizontal oil on board,
1942, for *Stag* magazine.

Opposite: Oil on board for the August 1951 cover
of *Wink* magazine. 34.25 x 26.5 inches.

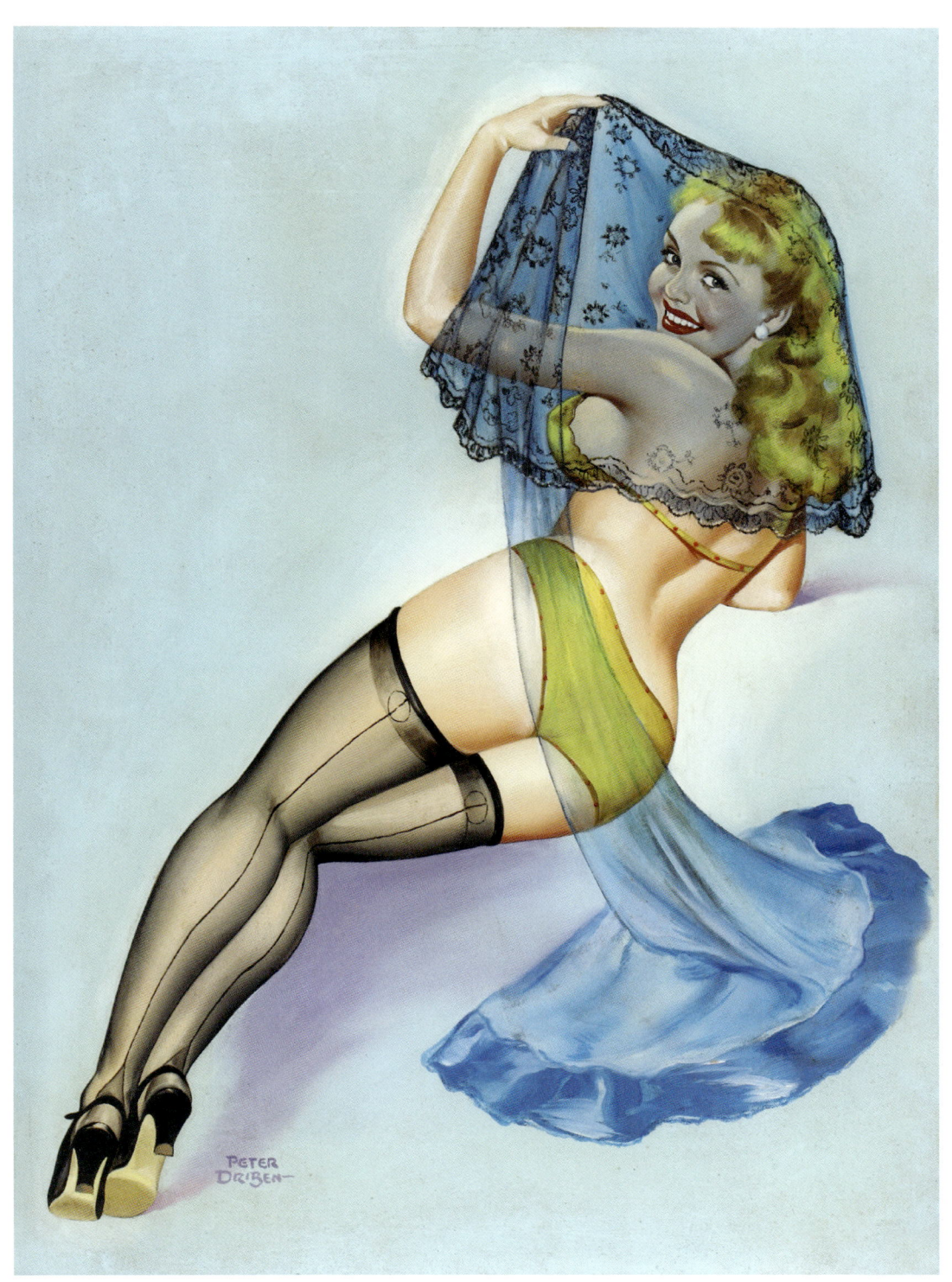

PETER DRIBEN

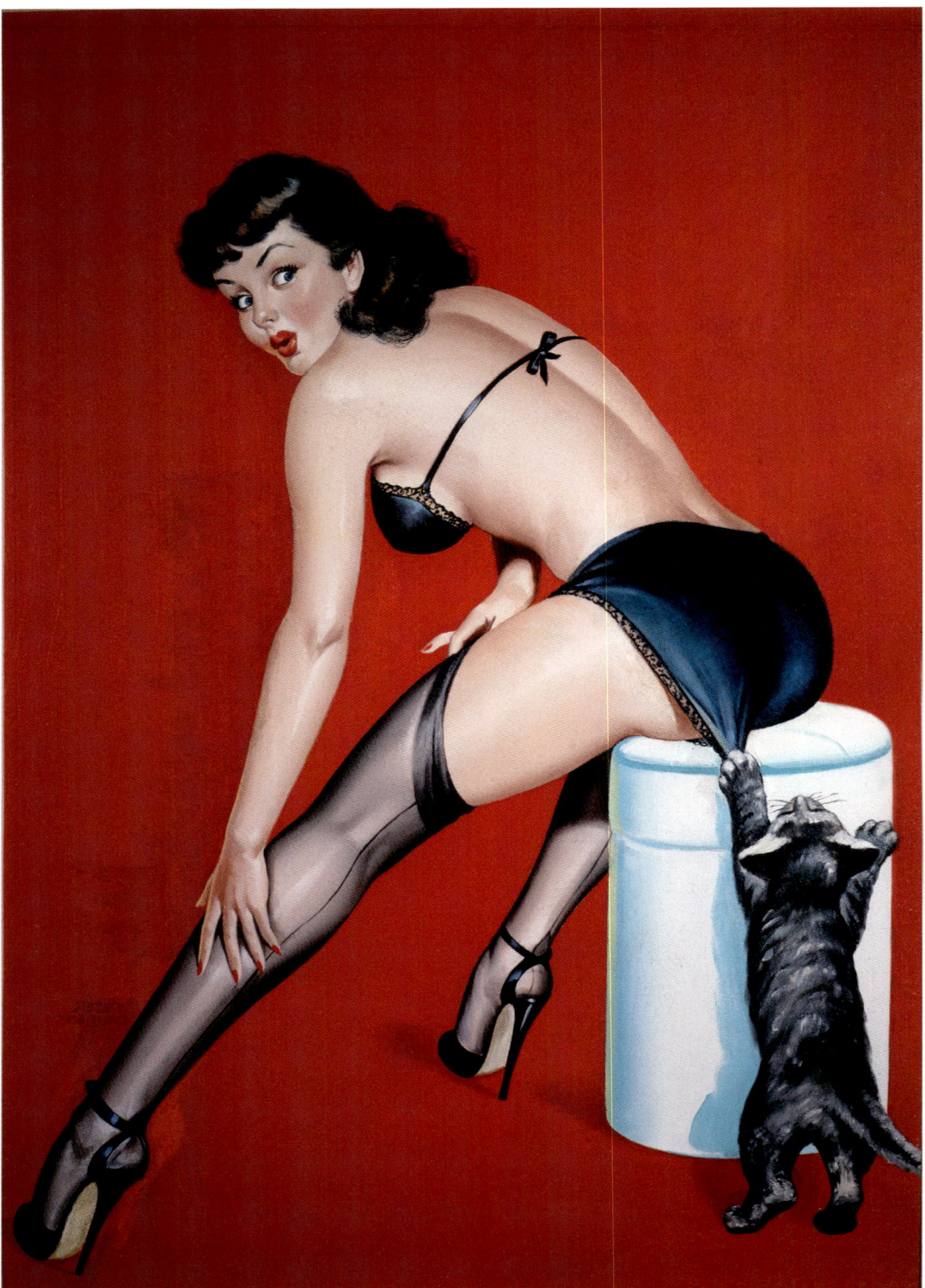

Ende der 1930er-Jahre eine Serie von 16 Titelbildern gestaltete. In dieser Zeit zeichnete er auch Cover für die Titel *High Heel, Silk Stocking Stories, Modern Girl Book* und *Gay Book* sowie für die pikanten Filmmagazine *Movie Merry-Go-Round, Movie Humor* und *Real Screen Fun*. All diese Titel erschienen monatlich, was bedeutet, dass Driben 1938, in seinem produktivsten Jahr, pro Monat bis zu zehn Bilder fertigstellte und damit Earle Bergey, den eigentlichen Hauskünstler bei *Tattle Tales, Snappy* und *Pep Stories*, ausstach, den für die Titelbilder von *Film Fun* zuständigen Künstler Enoch Bolles erstmals unter Konkurrenzdruck setzte und dem bis dahin regelmäßig für *Movie Humor* tätigen George Quintana Aufträge wegschnappte.

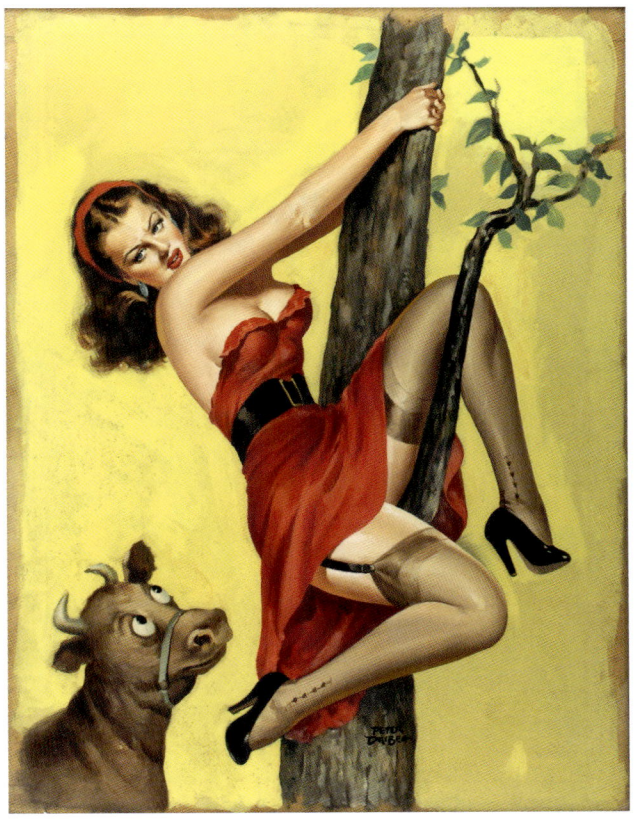

Damit nicht genug, neben diesen Malereien entwarf Driben ausgestanzte Schaufensterdisplays für Philco-Radios, Cannon-Badehandtücher und den Backbetrieb Weber. Trotzdem lief er noch mit Schuhen herum, deren Löcher er mit Zeitungspapier stopfte. Zu den finanziellen Nöten kam dann um 1940 noch die Bekanntschaft mit Louise hinzu, die er heiratete. Das zierliche Boheme-Mädchen mit rabenschwarzem Haar, das als Künstlerin, Schauspielerin und Modell tätig war, stand dem Künstler für die meisten der dunkelhaarigen Pin-ups Modell. Angeblich war sie auch für den steten Abfluss des Geldes vom Bankkonto des Paares verantwortlich.

Driben arbeitete weiterhin für Zeitschriften, malte Titelbilder für das Humormagazin *Joker*, 1942 ebenso für die Krimihefte *Expose Detective* und *Special Detective*; 1942 brachte auch Robert Harrison seine erste Zeitschrift, *Beauty Parade*, auf den Markt, doch Driben war erst im November 1943 mit an Bord.

Ursprünglich sollte Earl Moran die Titelbilder für *Beauty Parade* malen, nachdem er allerdings eine mit „Moran" und drei mit „Steffa" signierte Arbeiten abgeliefert hatte, war er der Meinung, keine Zeit mehr dafür zu haben oder zu schlecht bezahlt zu werden. Harrison versuchte es nun mit Merlin Enabnit, dann mit Billy DeVorss, bis er schließlich mit Peter Driben den perfekten Mitarbeiter fand. Seltsamerweise wiederholte sich das Gleiche mit jedem neuen

Opposite: Oil on board, 1949, for the April 1950 cover of *Flirt*. 30 x 23 inches.

Above: Oil on board, 1952, for the June 1952 cover of *Eyeful*. 34.5 x 26.5 inches.

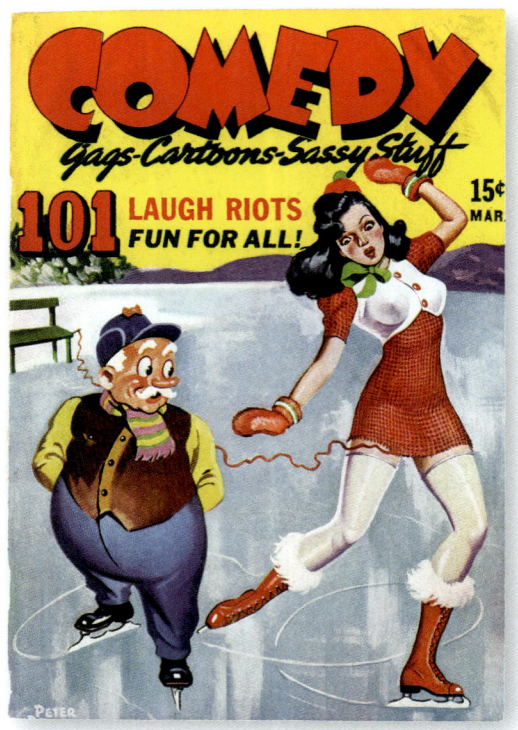

Harrison-Titel: *Eyeful* startete mit ein paar
Steffas, sieben DeVorss-Bildern, danach kam
Driben; *Titter* präsentierte einen Bolles auf
dem Cover und ein paar DeVorss, danach
war wieder Driben an der Reihe; bei *Wink*
kam Driben bereits nach drei Bildern von
DeVorss zum Einsatz; und dann gab es noch
Whisper, die einzige Zeitschrift, die von
Beginn an mit Driben-Cover im Stil seiner
Krimiheftbilder erschien.

Heute wird Driben so stark mit
Harrisons Zeitschriften identifiziert, dass
sich nur wenige daran erinnern, dass
auch andere Künstler für die Zeitschriften
tätig waren. Während Driben jeden Monat
fünf bis acht Titelbilder malte, schaffte er es
auch noch, von 1944 bis 1946 als Artdirector für *New York Sun* zu arbeiten. Dennoch
hatte er 1946 kein Geld, um bei der Bar
Mitzwa seines Neffen dabei zu sein.

1950 begann Harrison, mit Fotos für
die Cover zu experimentieren, und 1953,
als die Aufträge immer weniger wurden,
zogen die Dribens nach Miami. Ein paar
Titelbilder für Harrison produzierte Peter noch, bis der Verleger mit seinen Zeitschriften 1955
pleiteging. Fortan trieb sich Driben in Hotellobbys herum und bot Gästen an, sie zu porträtieren. Er malte ein Bild des damaligen Präsidenten Eisenhower, schickte es ihm und erhielt darauf
einen gut gehüteten Dankesbrief – aber kein Geld. In den frühen 1960er-Jahren versuchte
er sogar, in der Hoffnung, die neue Moralauffassung in bare Münze verwandeln zu können, die
Kleidung einiger seiner für Harrison produzierten Pin-ups mit nacktem Fleisch zu übermalen.
Schließlich begnügte er sich wie die meisten früheren Pin-up-Künstler damit, Clowns zu malen
und sie zu verkaufen.

1968 erkrankte Driben an Knochenkrebs. Als sein Vater und zwei Brüder zu Besuch kamen,
ahnte er, dass die Prognose schlecht war. Er fragte, warum sie gekommen seien. Als sie erklär-
ten, dass sie den Parteikongress der Republikaner sehen wollten, wusste er, dass er bald sterben
würde – unter den Dribens gab es keine Republikaner.

Louise soll Peters Gemälde nach seinem Tod 1968 für zehn Dollar das Bild und zwölf Bilder
für 100 Dollar verkauft haben. Selbst als toter Mann kam Peter Driben einfach nicht auf einen
grünen Zweig.

Above: Comedy featured a mix of cartoons and jokes
printed on pulp paper with an alluring pin-up cover.
It was read largely by enlisted men during the 1940s.
Driben was a regular cover contributor.

Opposite: The model for this painting was reputedly
Driben's wife, the woman known to his family as crazy
Aunt Louise. Oil on board for the October 1947 cover
of *Titter* magazine. 35 x 26.5 inches.

THE ART OF PIN-UP

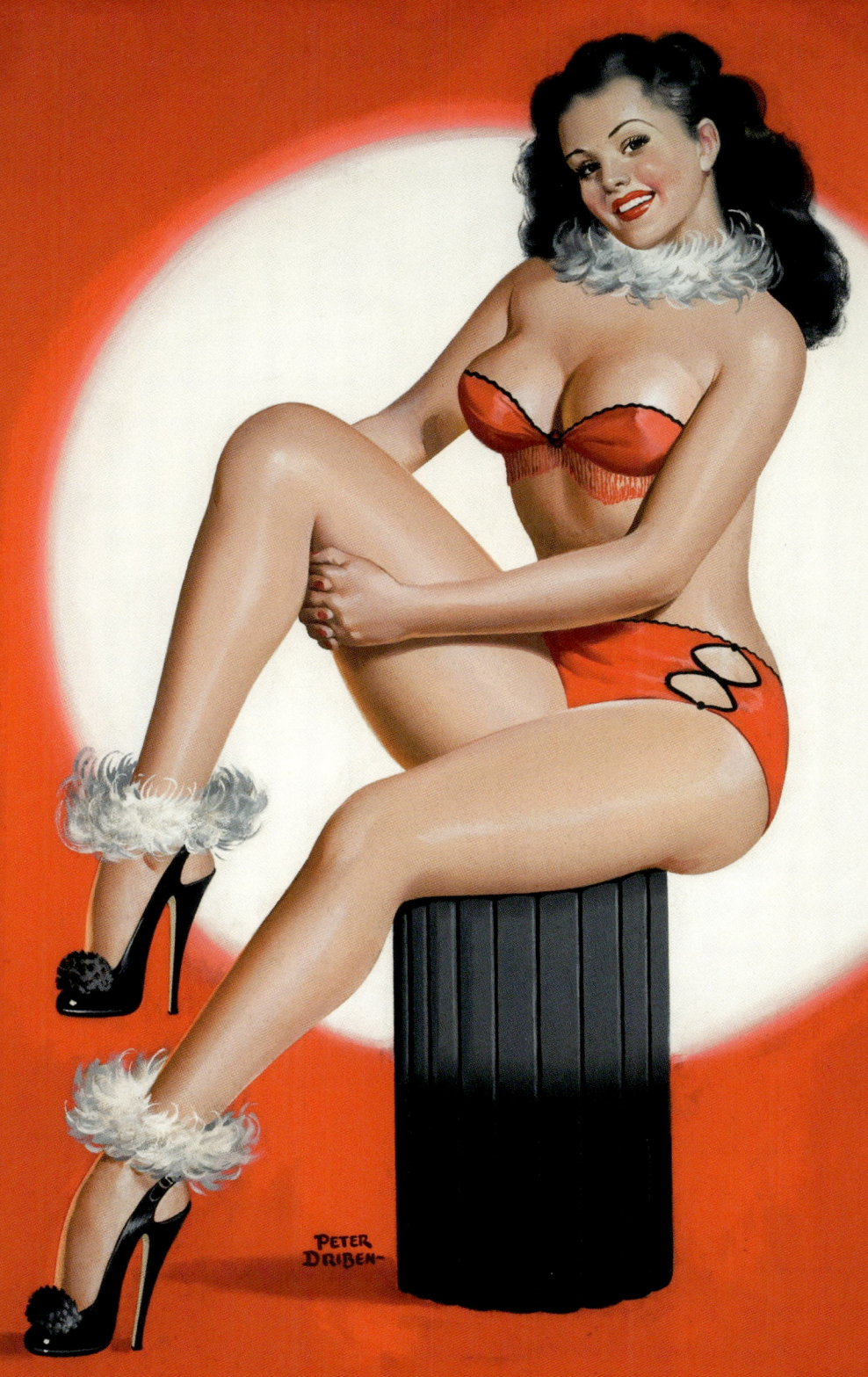

PETER
DRIBEN

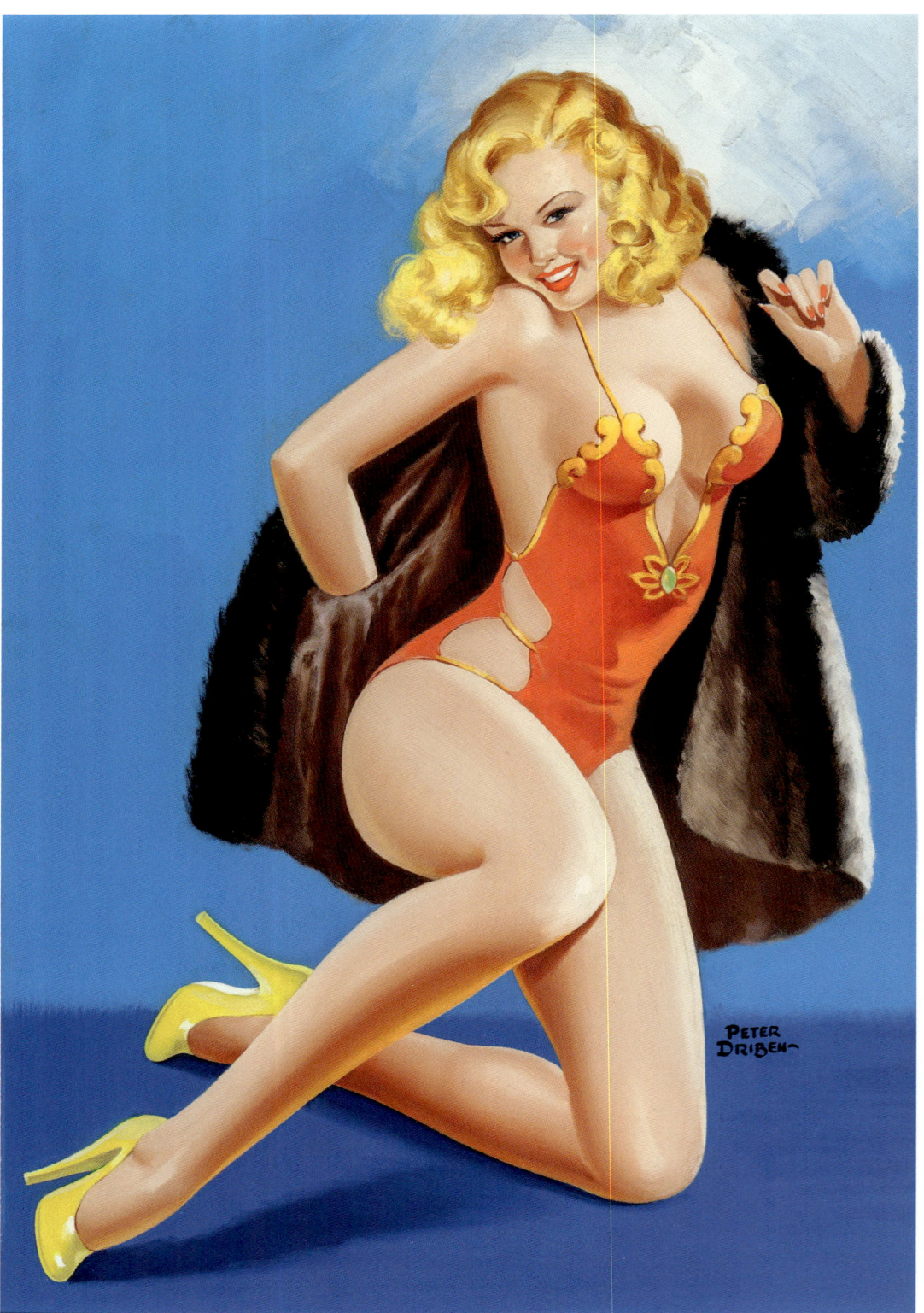

« Les girls de Driben n'étaient pas "sages". Perchées sur des talons vertigineux, elles portaient des tenues d'une vulgarité calculée qui mettaient en valeur leurs cuisses voluptueuses. »

Il y avait deux types de pin-up : celles des calendriers et celles des magazines. Cette dernière catégorie était encore divisée en deux, entre celles de la couverture et celles des pages centrales dont Petty et Vargas étaient des spécialistes. Peter Driben était un homme de couverture, sans doute le plus prolifique de l'histoire de la pin-up.

Il était perpétuellement sans le sou, même quand il réalisait cinq ou dix commandes par mois. Sa famille soupçonnait sa femme, « tante Louise la foldingue », d'en être la cause avec ses prétentions d'actrice et ses « causes beatniks ». En outre, le couple vivait dans un appartement miteux à New York, avec deux chiens et tout cet « art de mauvais goût ». En réalité, personne ne savait d'où venait le problème, mais Driben était contraint de produire toujours plus et cette contrainte se traduisit par les pin-up les plus caractéristiques jamais réalisées. Ses grandes peintures (68,5 x 89 cm) aux vives couleurs primaires pour les cou-

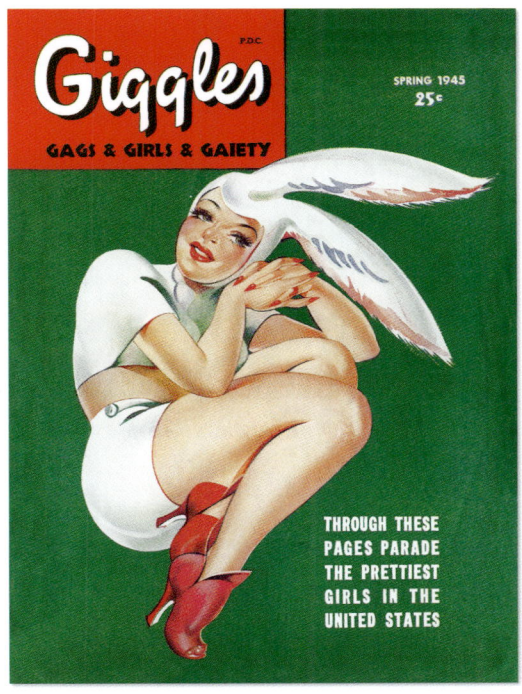

vertures de *Beauty Parade*, *Eyeful*, *Titter*, *Wink*, *Whisper* et *Flirt*, peintes à l'acrylique (parce qu'il séchait plus vite), sautaient aux yeux sur les rayonnages des marchands de journaux. Conformément au contenu salace de ces magazines, les girls de Driben n'étaient pas « sages ». Perchées sur des talons vertigineux, elles portaient des tenues d'une vulgarité calculée qui mettaient en valeur leurs cuisses voluptueuses. Seul George Petty insinua un élément fétichiste similaire dans ses pin-up avec son obsession pour les pointes, mais plus subtilement.

D'un autre côté, *Esquire* n'était pas *Eyeful*.

Originaires de Russie et de Lituanie, les parents de Driben s'installèrent à Chelsea, dans la banlieue de Boston, dans les années 1890. Peter, leur aîné, naquit en 1903, suivi rapidement par

Opposite: Oil on board, 1946, for the February 1947 issue of *Eyeful*, Robert Harrison's second magazine, launched in 1943. 30.5 x 22 inches.

Above: One can only guess that the quarterly *Giggles* paid poorly, as all Driben's covers for the wartime joke magazine were crudely executed. Spring 1945.

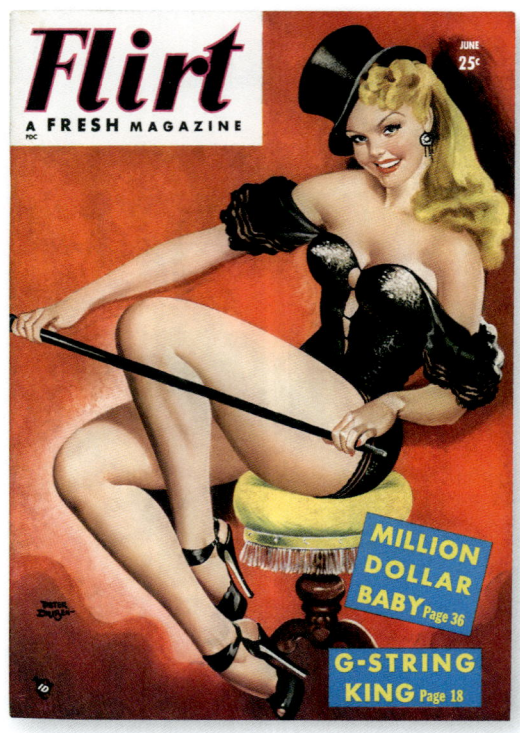

sept autres enfants. La famille était pauvre et peu instruite. En 1925, Peter gagna un concours d'art (du genre proposé sur les boîtes d'allumettes : « Dessine un pirate et remporte une bourse ») et remporta une bourse pour la Vesper George School of Art, au grand dam de ses parents. La tradition voulait que le fils aîné subvienne aux besoins de la famille et la peinture n'était pas le chemin le plus rapide vers la fortune. Il paraît que, lorsque Peter fila ensuite à Paris pour étudier à la Sorbonne, son père le renia.

On ignore ce qu'il fit à Paris mais plusieurs de ses dessins de danseuses de revues ont survécu, laissant entendre qu'il avait trouvé sa vocation.

En 1933, Adolf Hitler devint chancelier d'Allemagne. L'Europe n'était plus l'endroit rêvé pour un jeune juif américain. Driben partit pour New York et trouva du travail dans l'année. Sa première pin-up parut en couverture du numéro de mars 1934 de *La Paree Stories*, l'un des nombreux digests de fiction de l'époque. Un an plus tard, il illustrait les couvertures de *Pep Stories*, *Snappy*, *New York Nights* et *French Night Life*, toutes des publications du même acabit et sans doute du même éditeur. Il illustra également *Bedtime Stories* en 1937 et 1939 et réalisa 16 couvertures d'affilée pour *La Paree Stories* à la fin des années 1930. Parallèlement, il travailla pour des revues de charme grand format telles que *High Heel*, *Silk Stocking Stories*, *Modern Girl Book*, *Gay Book*, ainsi que pour les magazines de cinéma égrillards *Movie Merry-Go-Round*, *Movie Humor* et *Real Screen Fun*. Tous ces titres étaient mensuels, ce qui signifie qu'en 1939, son année la plus productive, Driben réalisait jusqu'à dix peintures par mois, délogeant Earle Bergey, l'artiste qui officiait avant lui chez *Tattle Tales*, *Snappy* et *Pep Stories,* concurrençant sérieusement Enoch Bolles chez *Film Fun*, et donnant du fil à retordre à George Quintana qui contribuait régulièrement à *Movie Humor*.

Outre ses peintures, Driben créa des silhouettes publicitaires en carton pour les radios Philco, les serviettes de bain Cannon et les pains Weber. Pourtant, il continuait de colmater les trous dans ses chaussures avec du papier journal. Pour ne rien arranger à sa situation financière, vers 1940 il rencontra et épousa Louise, artiste, actrice et modèle. La petite brune au tempérament bohème devint le modèle de la plupart de ses pin-up brunes.

En 1942, Peter Driben réalisait toujours des couvertures de magazines, qu'ils soient humoristiques comme *Joker* ou d'enquêtes policières comme *Expose Detective* et *Special Detective*.

Above: Cover of the June 1949 issue of *Flirt*, Harrison's sixth magazine, launched in 1947. The image was subsequently recycled for the November 1953 cover of *Beauty Parade*.

Opposite: Cover of the October 1946 issue of *Wink*.

THE ART OF PIN-UP

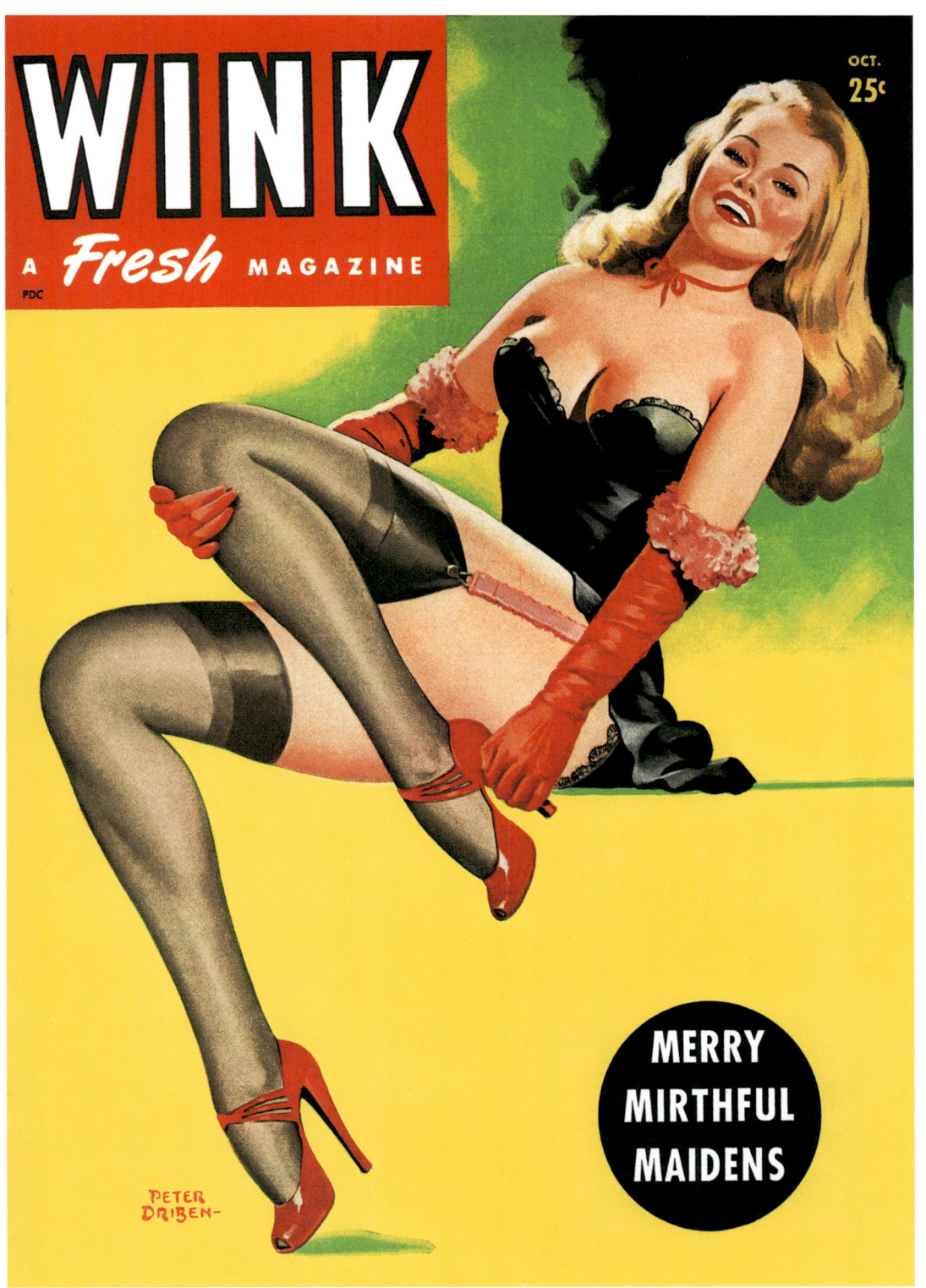

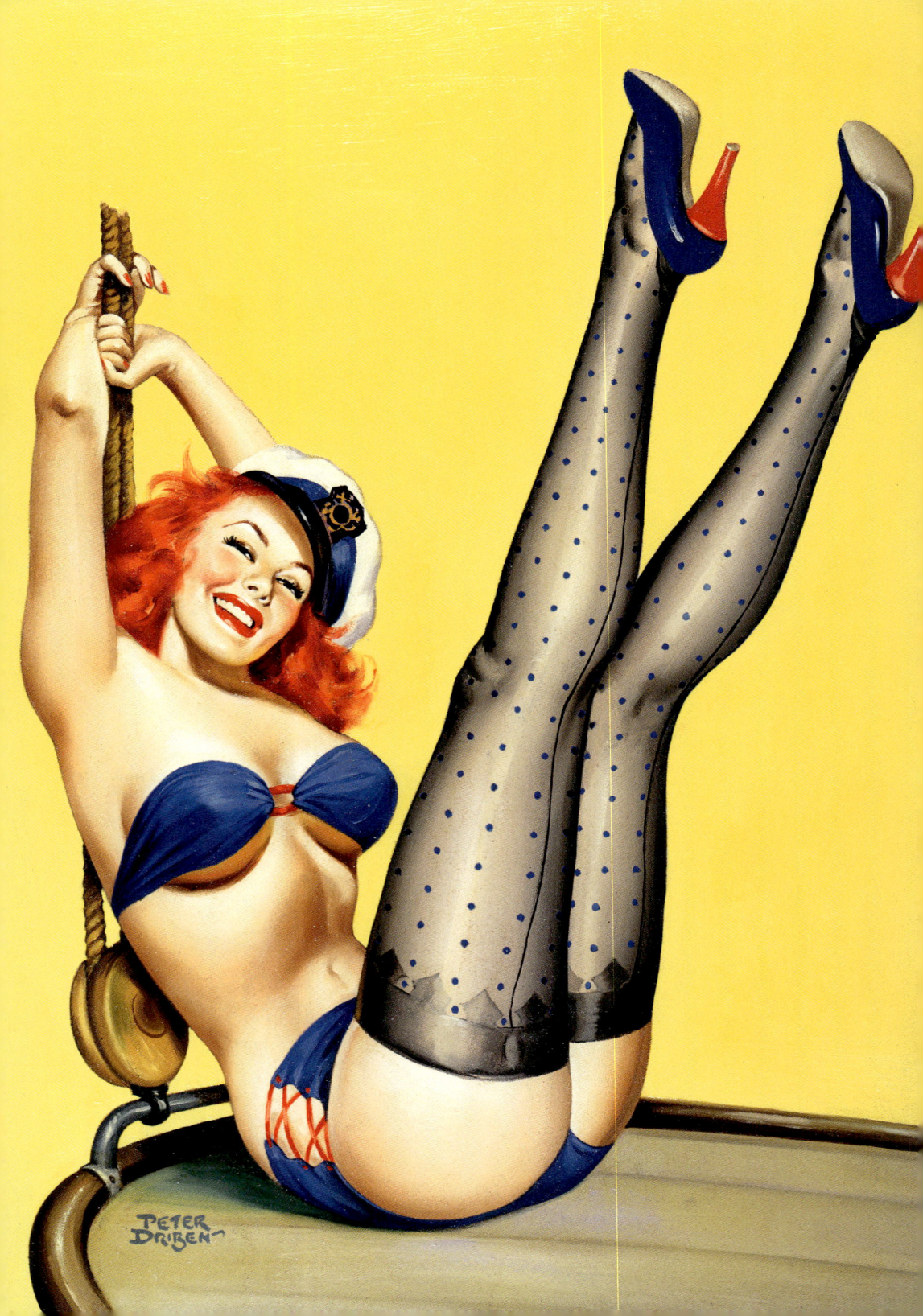

Cette année-là, Robert Harrison lança son premier titre, *Beauty Parade*, mais il ne fit appel à Driben qu'en 1943.

Les premières couvertures de *Beauty Parade* furent réalisées par Earl Moran, qui signa la première Moran, puis les trois suivantes Steffa avant de capituler faute de temps ou parce qu'il était trop mal payé. Il fut remplacé par Merlin Enabnit, puis Billy DeVorss avant que Driben ne prenne la relève. Étrangement, il en alla de même avec chacune des nouvelles publications d'Harrison : *Eyefull* débuta avec deux Steffa, sept DeVorss, puis Driben ; *Titter* avec un Bolles et plusieurs DeVorss, puis Driben ; *Wink*, avec trois DeVorss, puis Driben. Seul *Whisper* démarra directement avec Driben.

Aujourd'hui, Driben est tellement associé aux magazines d'Harrison qu'on oublie que

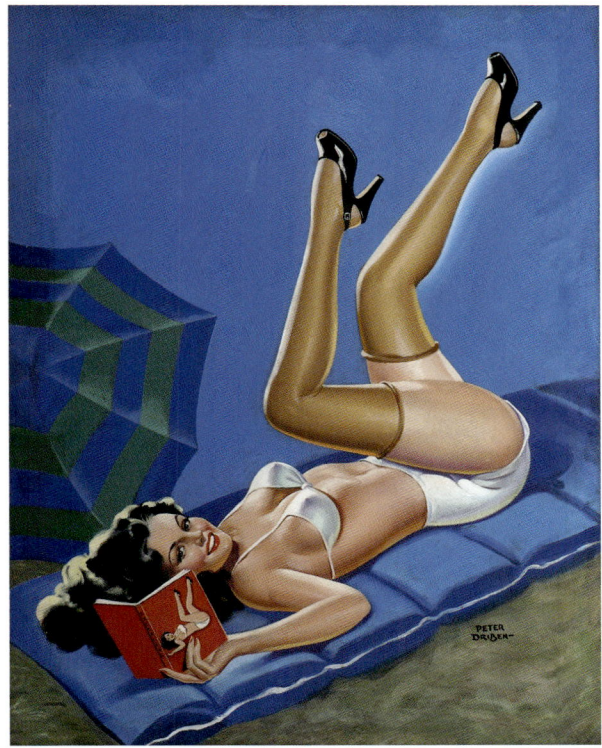

d'autres artistes sont passés avant lui. Tout en peignant cinq à huit couvertures par mois, il trouva encore le temps d'être directeur artistique du quotidien *New York Sun* de 1944 à 1946, mais était encore trop fauché pour assister à la bar-mitsvah de son neveu en 1946.

En 1950, Harrison commença à expérimenter les photographies en couverture. Les commandes diminuant, les Driben déménagèrent à Miami où Peter réalisa encore quelques couvertures avant qu'Harrison ne mette la clef sous la porte en 1955. Puis il s'assit dans les halls d'hôtel et proposa aux clients de faire leur portrait. Il réalisa un portrait du président Eisenhower et le lui envoya. Il reçut une lettre de remerciement, mais pas un sou. Au début des années 1960, il s'essaya à peindre de la chair par-dessus les tenues de ses pin-up faites pour Harrison, espérant profiter du relâchement des mœurs, puis, comme la plupart des ex-créateurs de pin-up, il peignit des clowns qu'il vendait dans son atelier/galerie.

En 1968, Driben fut atteint d'un cancer des os. Il devina que son pronostic était grave quand son père et deux de ses frères vinrent le voir. Il leur demanda la raison de leur visite et, quand ils répondirent qu'ils étaient venus pour la convention républicaine, il sut qu'il allait mourir. Il n'y avait pas de républicains chez les Driben.

Après la mort de Peter Driben survenue à la fin de l'année 1968, Louise aurait vendu ses peintures 10 dollars pièce, douze pour 100 dollars. Même dans la tombe, le pauvre Driben était sous-payé.

Opposite: Oil on board for the April 1953 cover of *Flirt* magazine. 33 x 25 inches.

Above: Oil on board for the March 1946 cover of *Wink*. 33.5 x 27 inches.

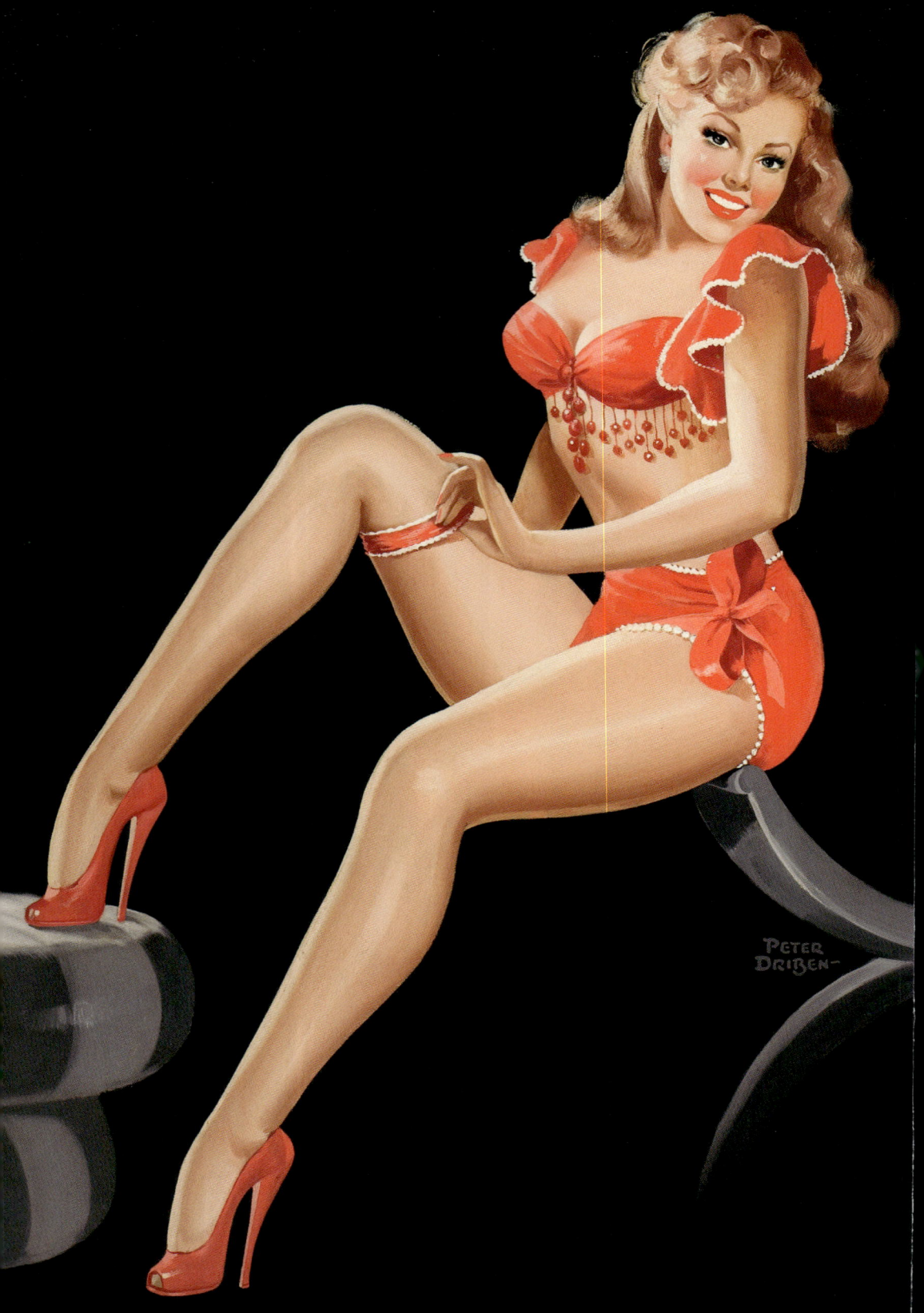

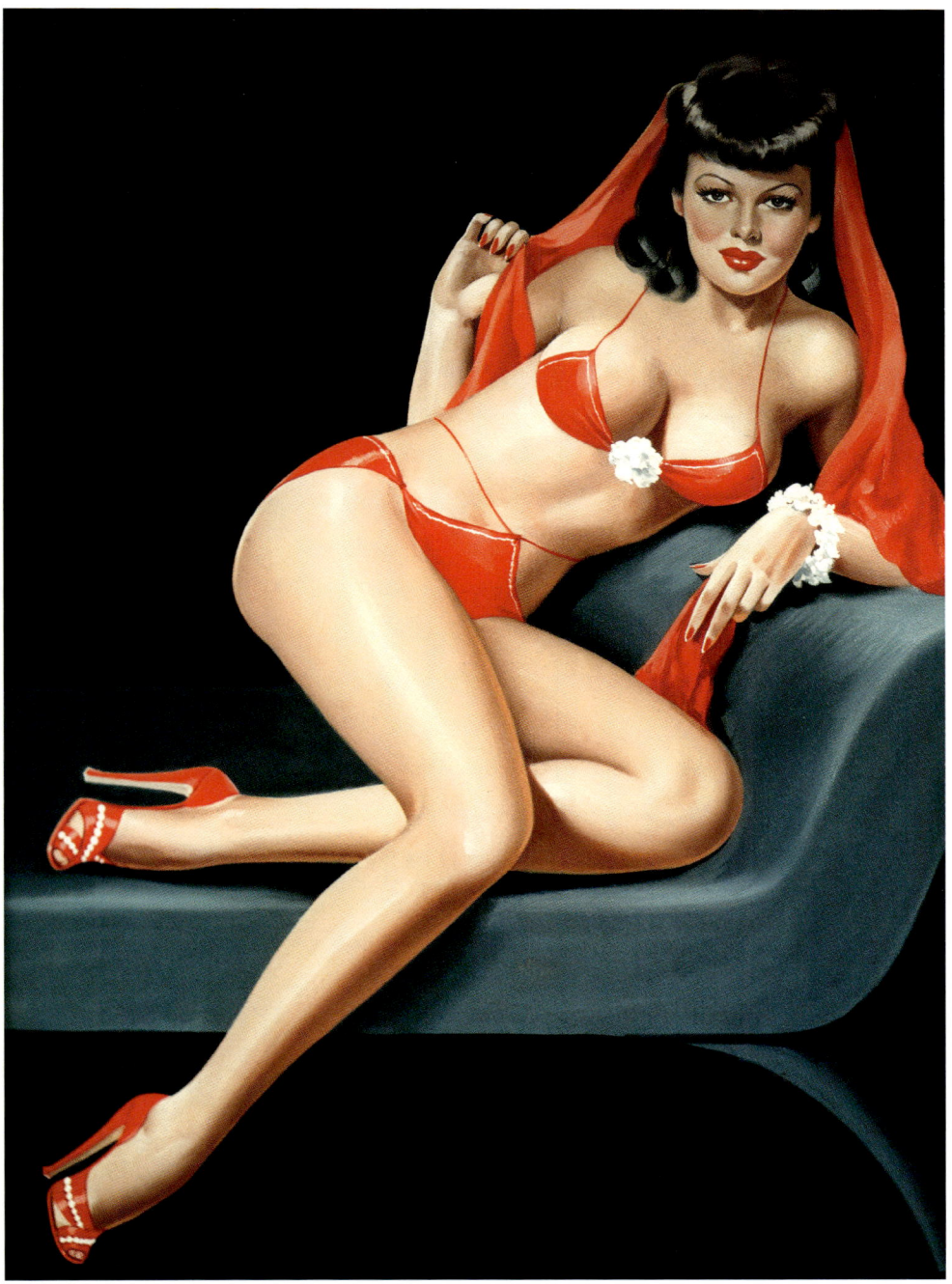

Opposite: Oil on board for the June 1948
cover of *Eyeful*. 31.75 x 23.5 inches.

Above: Oil on board for the December 1947 cover
of *Beauty Parade*. 34 x 26 inches.

PETER DRIBEN

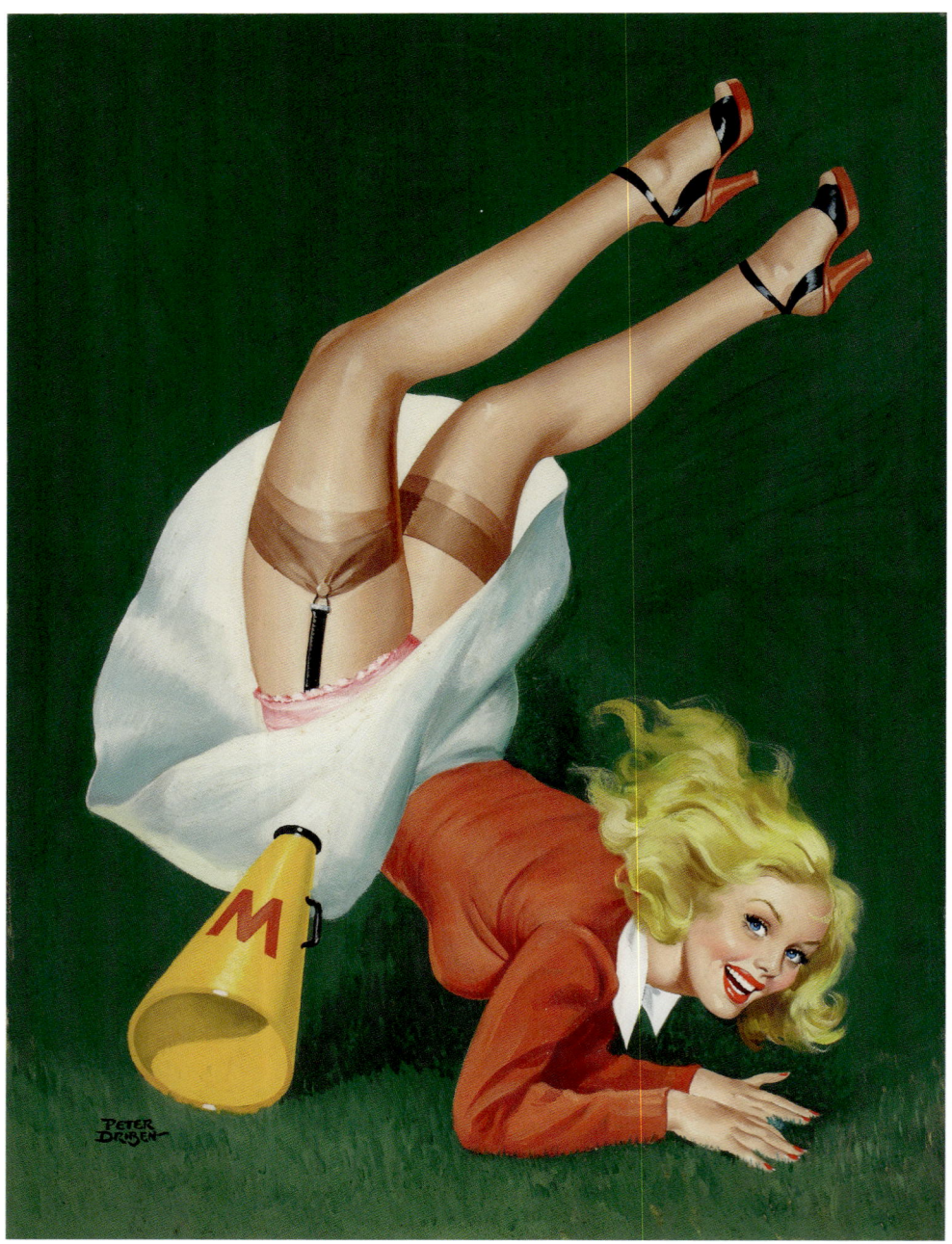

Above: Oil on board, 1951, for the December 1951 cover of *Titter*. 34 x 26.5 inches.

Opposite: Oil on board for the April 1953 cover of *Wink*. 34 x 26 inches.

Following left: Oil on board for the April 1955 cover of *Wink*. 34 x 26 inches.

Following right: Oil on board for the September 1952 cover of *Beauty Parade*. 35 x 24.5 inches.

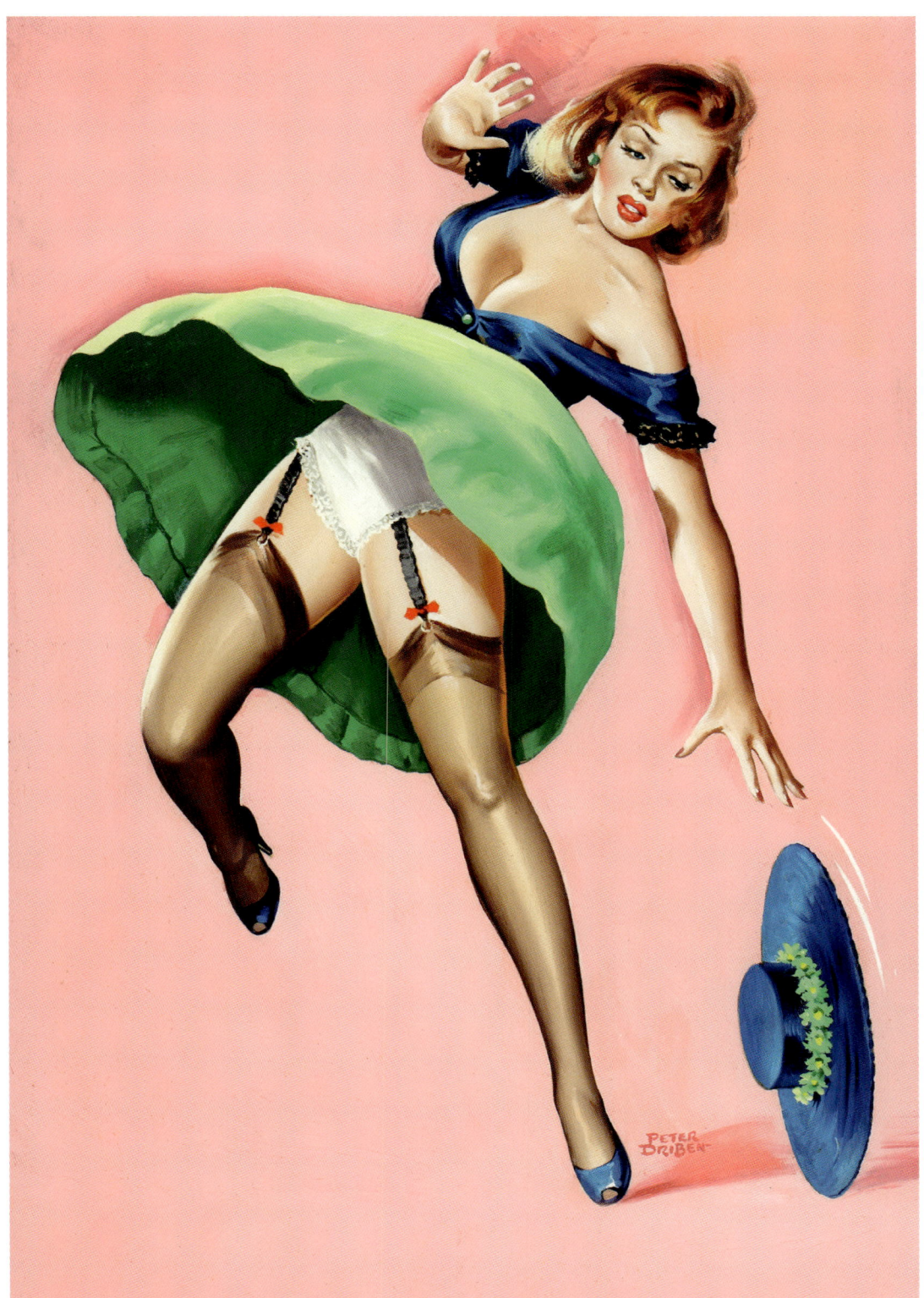

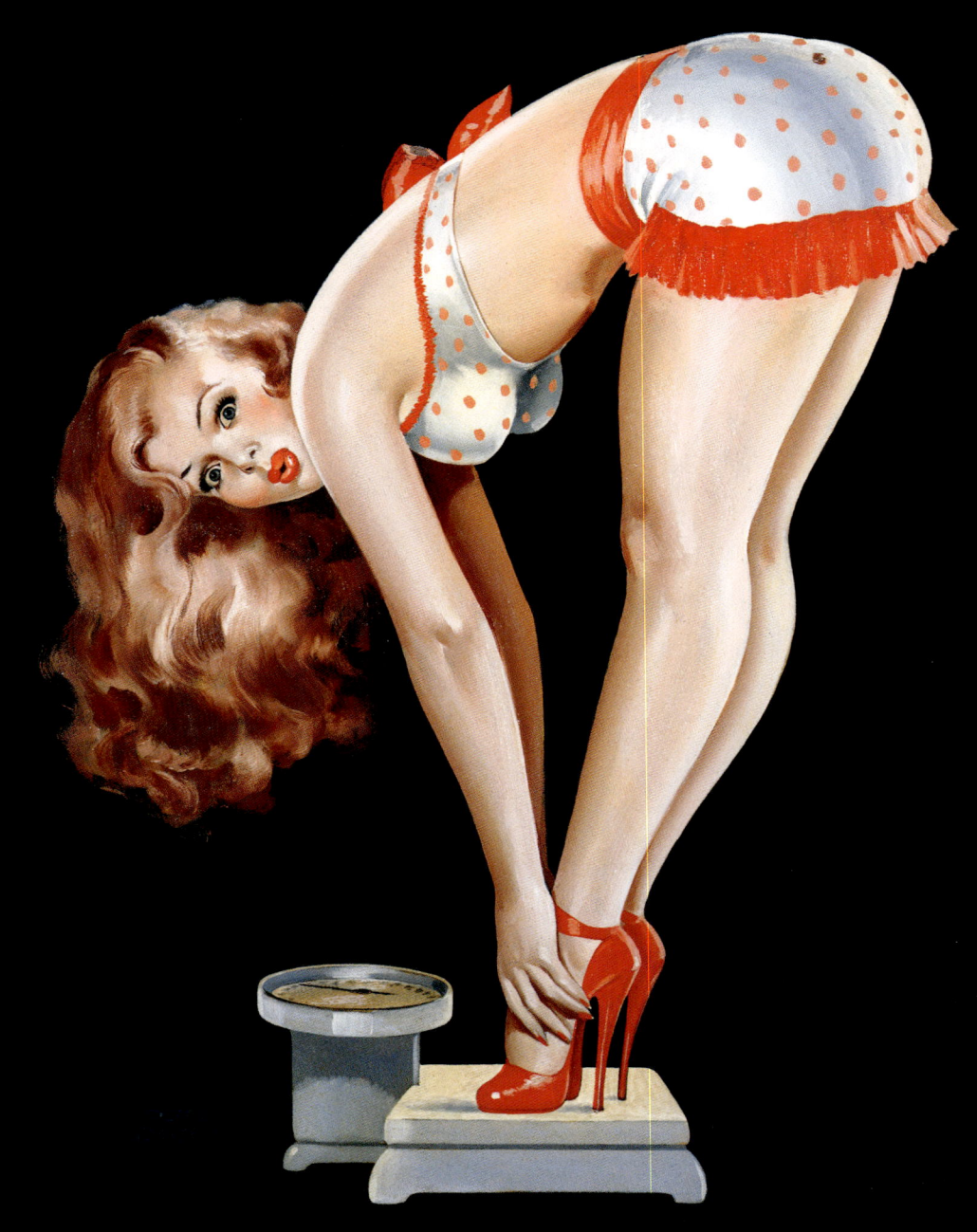

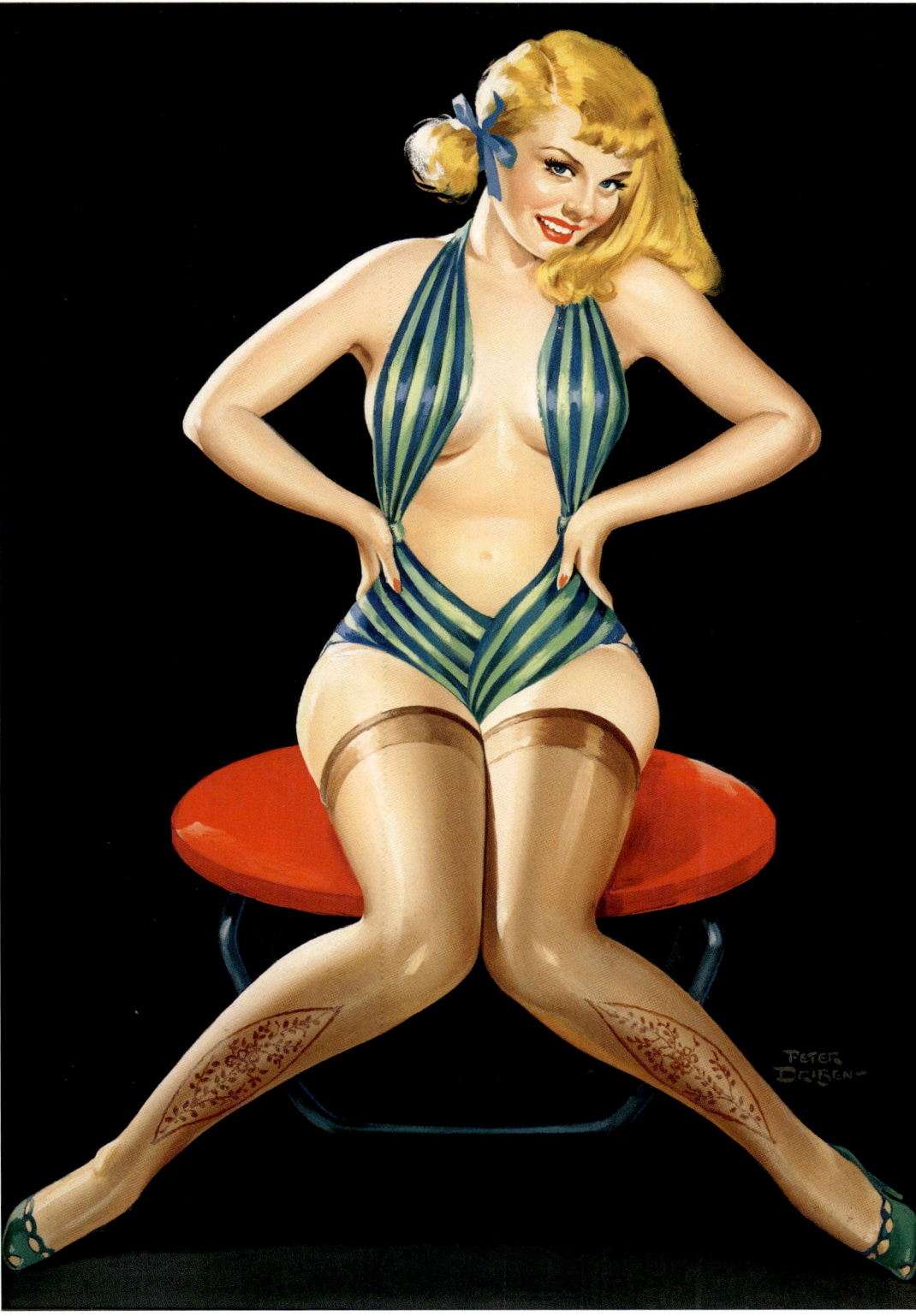

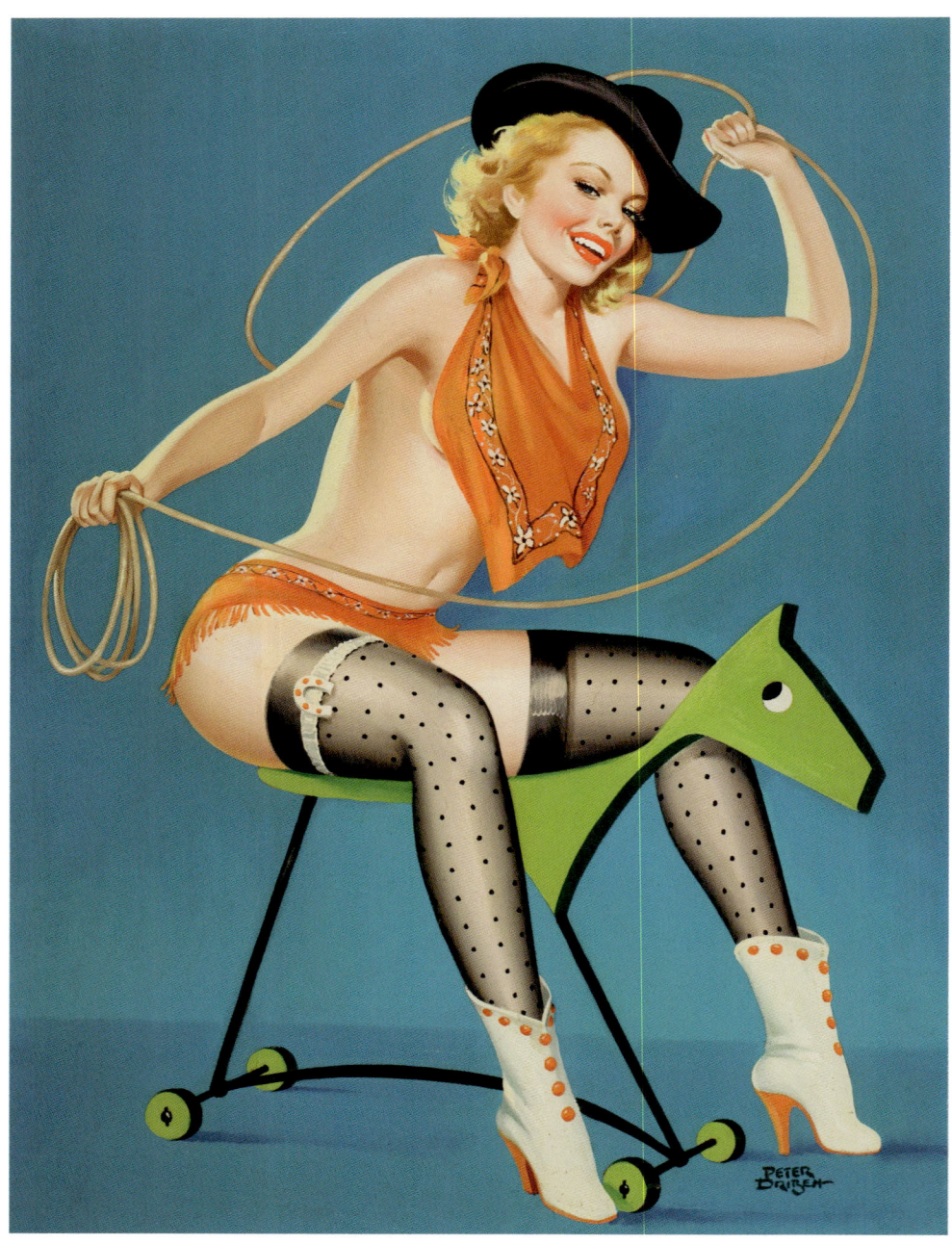

Above: Oil on board for the October 1952 cover of *Flirt*. 34 x 26.5 inches.

Opposite: Oil on canvas, 1950, for the June 1950 cover of *Wink*. Driben occasionally included a wink in the artwork he did for *Wink* covers. More often, he had no idea where a painting would end up and didn't bother.

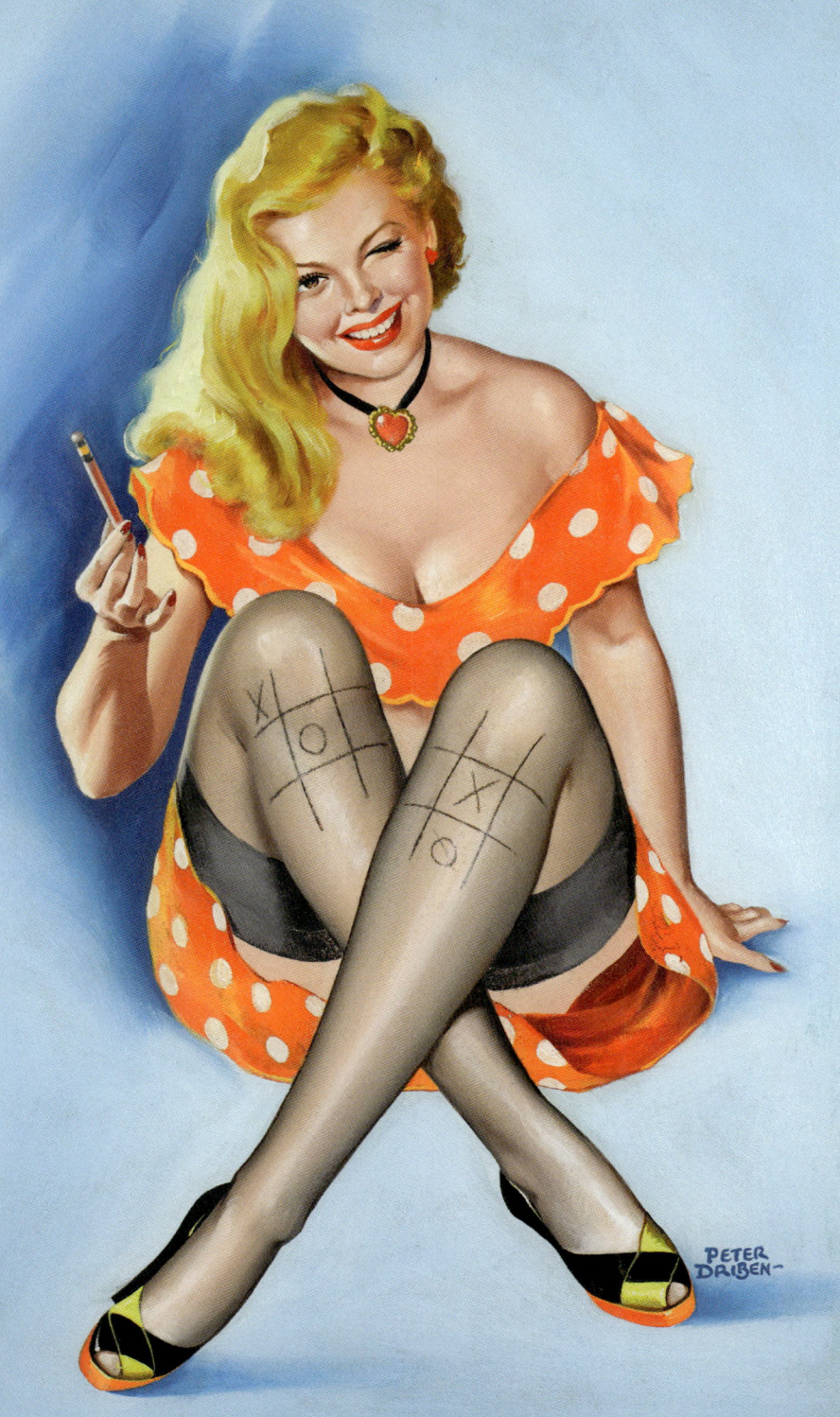

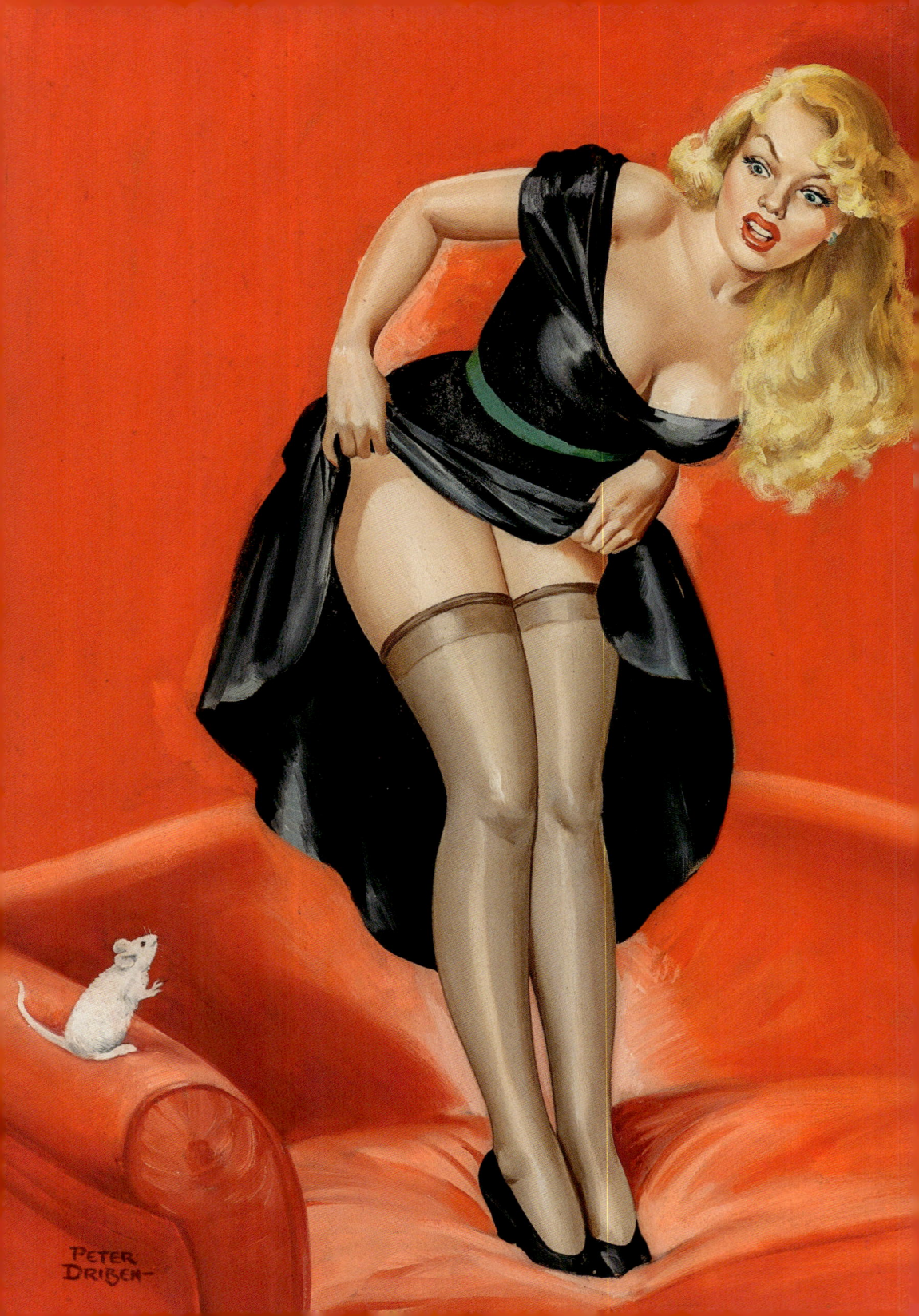

PETER
DRIBEN—

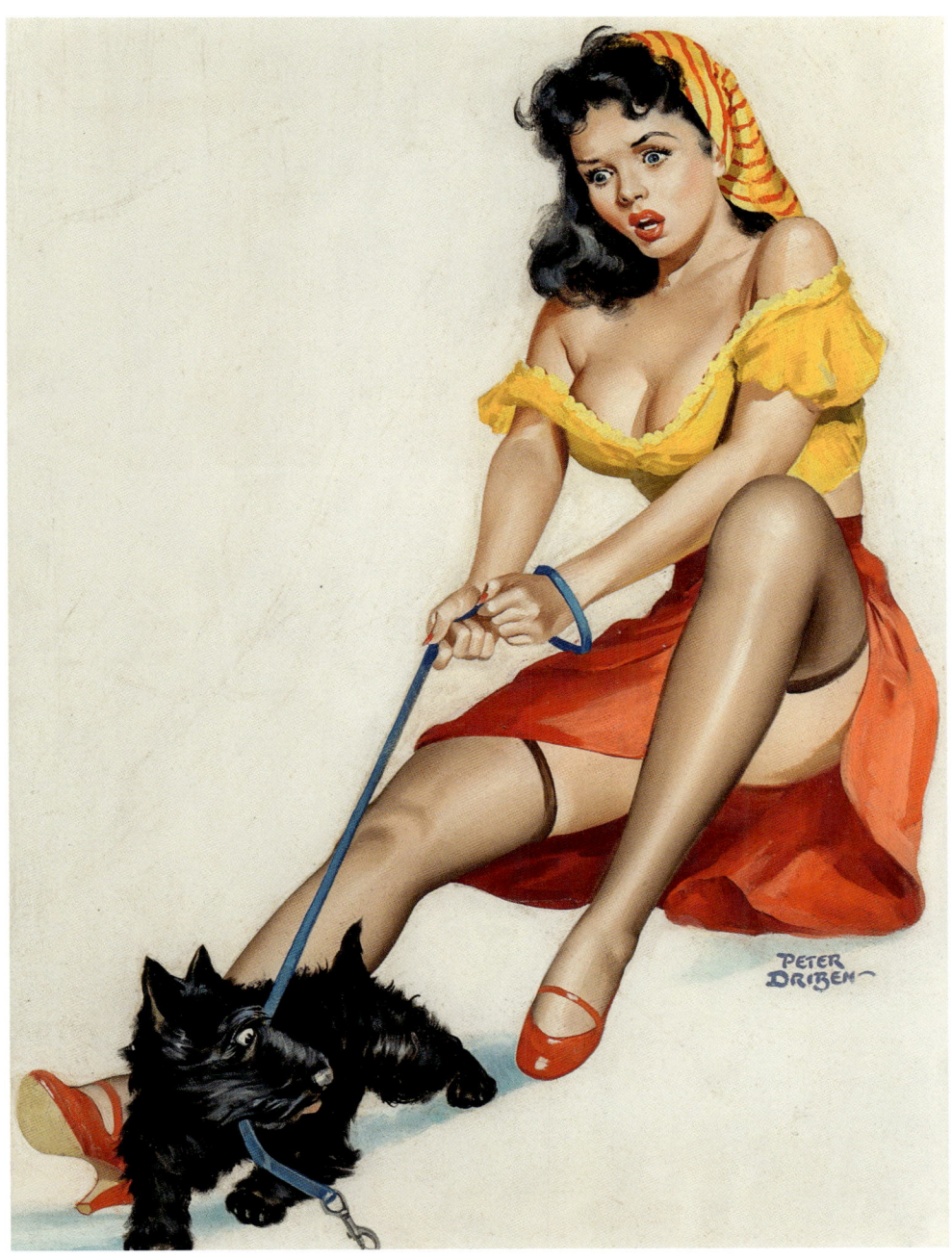

Opposite: Oil on board for the June 1951 cover of *Wink*. 33 x 24 inches. Courtesy Heritage Auctions.

Above: Oil on board for the October 1951 cover of *Flirt*. 30.5 x 22.5 inches. Courtesy Heritage Auctions.

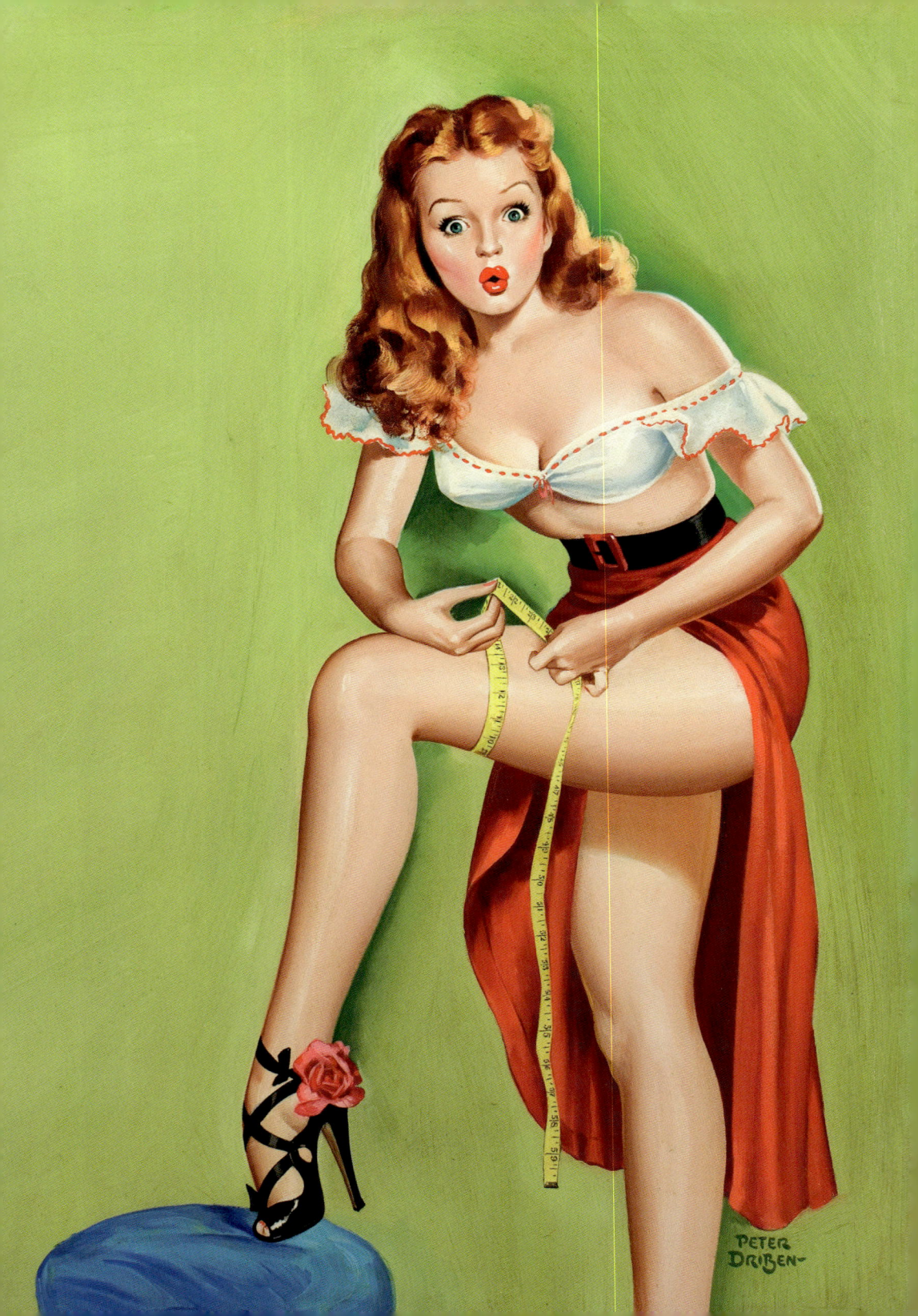

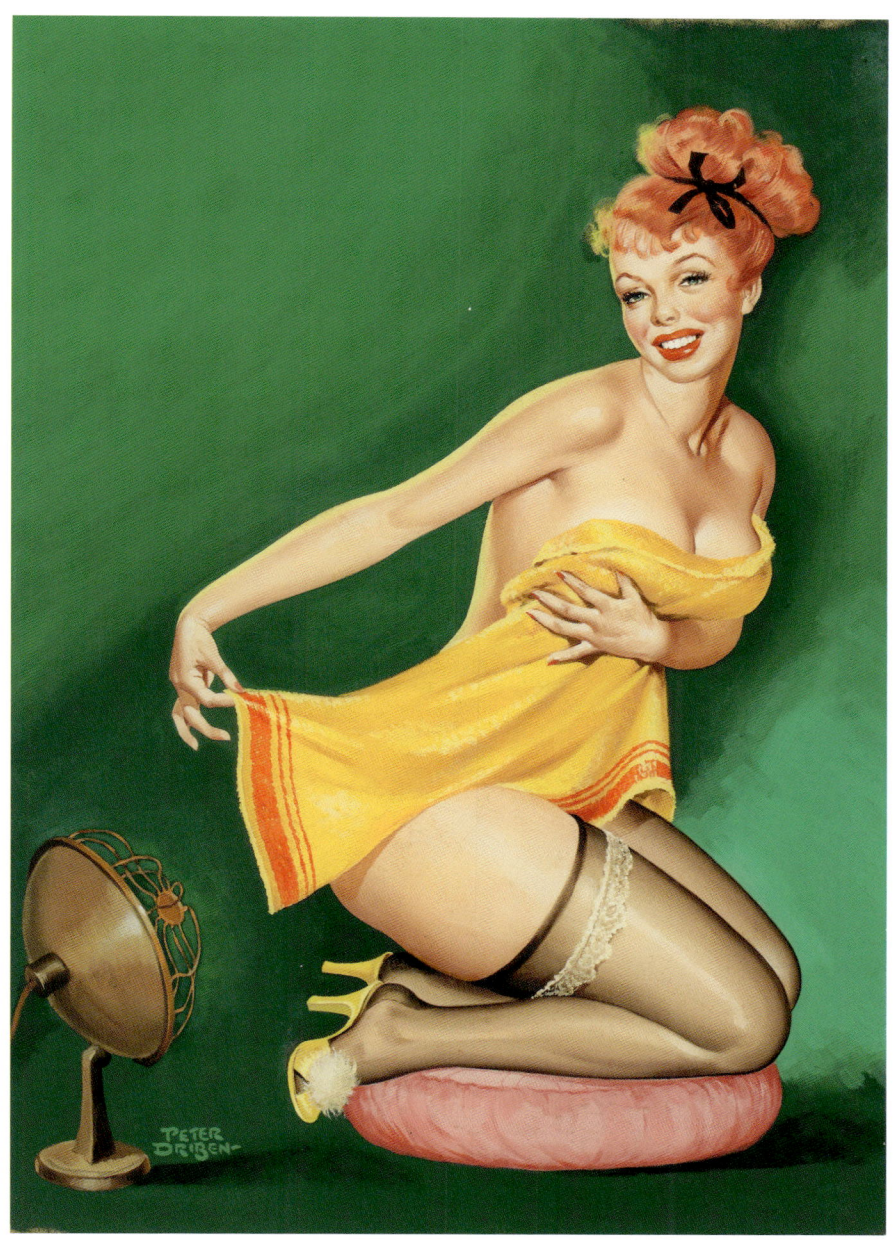

Opposite: Oil on board, 1949, for the December 1949 cover of *Wink*. Legs dominated sexual fantasy in the 1940s, and certainly dominated Driben's pin-ups. A large thigh measurement was, in 1949, as stimulating as a large bust was in 1959. 35 x 27 inches.

Above: Oil on board for the March 1952 cover of *Beauty Parade*. 33.5 x 26.5 inches.

PETER DRIBEN

GILLETTE "GIL" ELVGREN

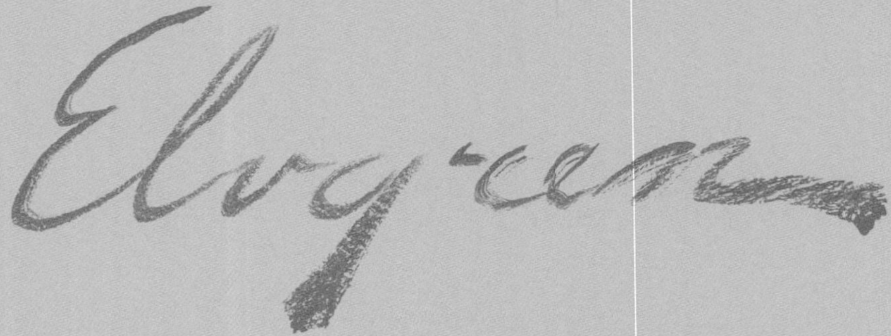

Elvgren

1914–1980

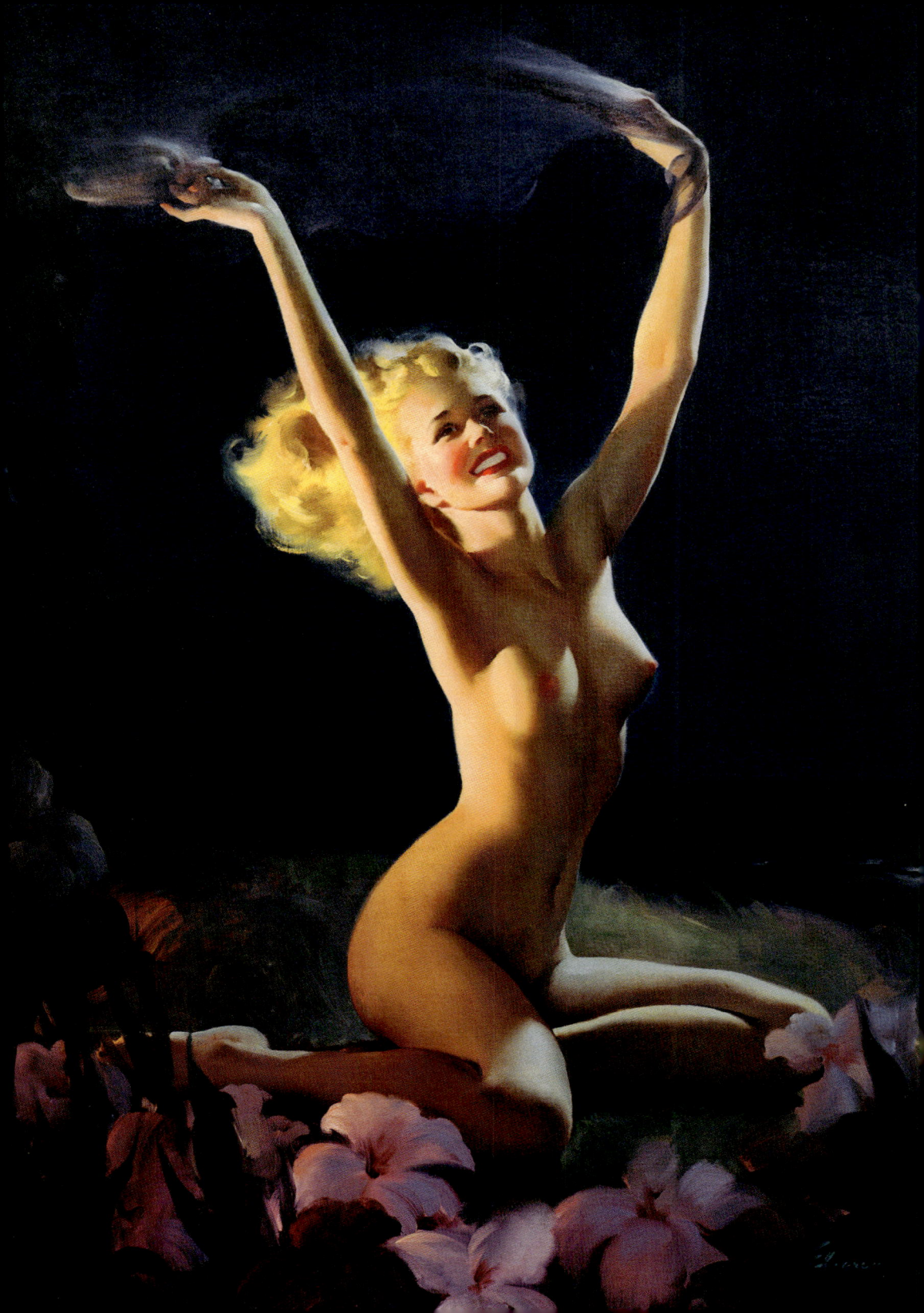

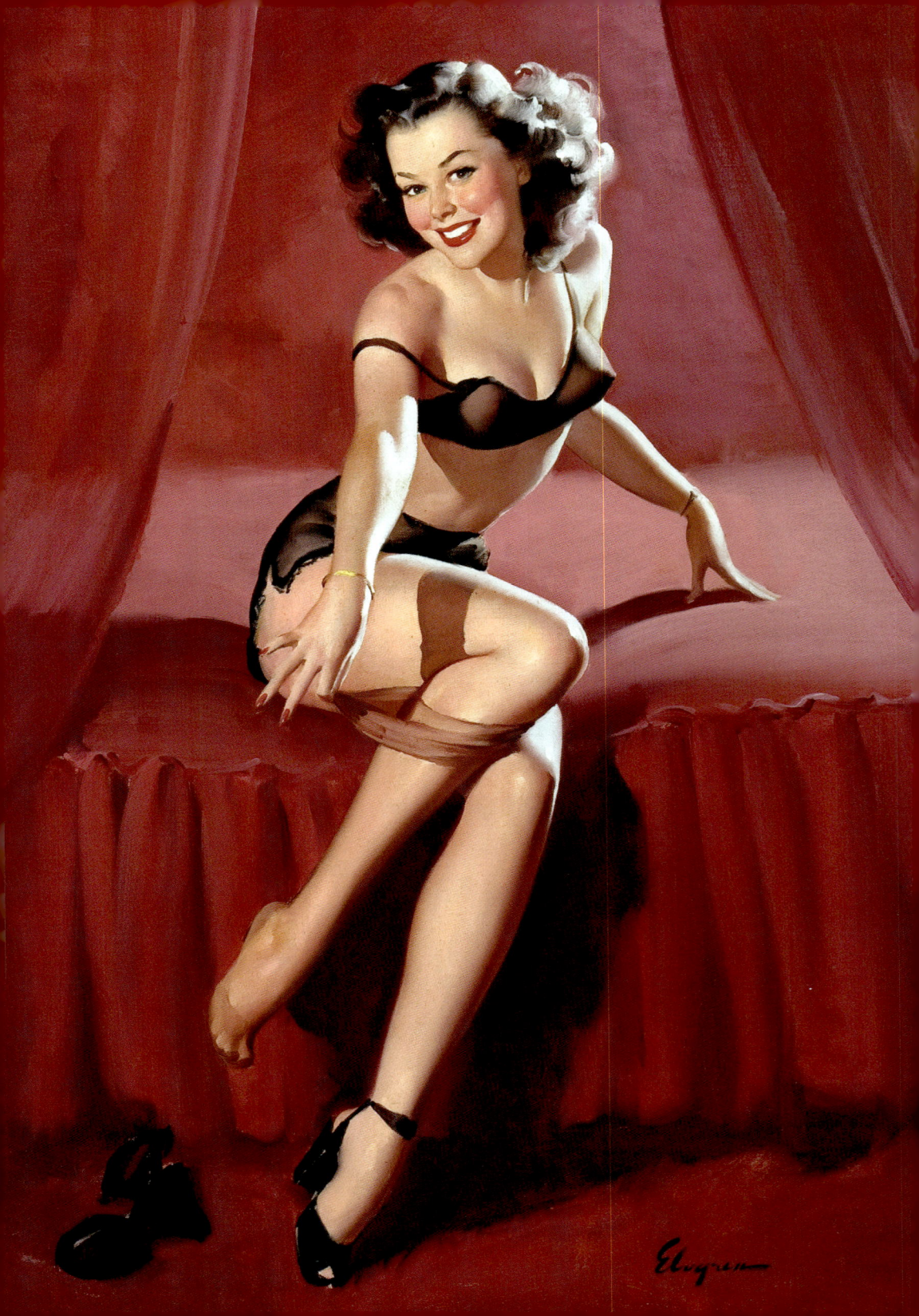

"No pin-up artist painted more iconic images than Elvgren, whose oeuvre is estimated at some 700 works, created over a 44-year career."

America's greatest glamour-girl artist, Gil Elvgren, painted women in the 1940s, '50s, and '60s who defined the genre of pin-up art. He was one of the most successful and sought-after illustrators of his time, with universal talents that were recognized by the advertising and calendar industries even in his youth, allowing him to perfect his style and technique while making the best salary in the business. No pin-up artist painted more iconic images than Elvgren, whose oeuvre is estimated at some 700 works, created over a 44-year career.

Born in St. Paul, Minnesota, in 1914, where his family founded Elvgren Paint Supply Co., Elvgren enrolled in summer courses at the Minneapolis Art Institute as a teenager, which inspired him to attend Chicago's American Academy of Art in 1934. He graduated after only two years and, with his wife, Janet Cummins, moved back to St. Paul to start his first solo studio in 1936.

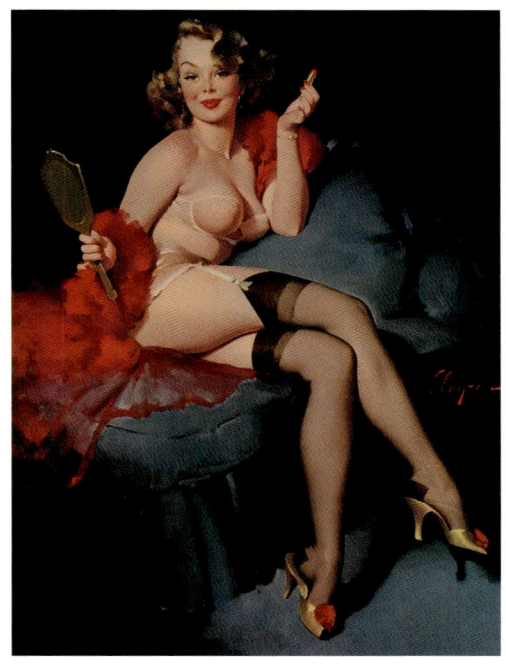

Shortly thereafter he caught his big break with a commission to paint the Dionne quintuplets for Brown & Bigelow, the nation's largest calendar company.

It's hard today to imagine the frenzy over history's first surviving quintuplets. The seeming miracle of five identical little girls born at the same time leavened the hardships of the Depression, and Gil Elvgren's illustration made him an overnight success. He was signed by America's second-largest calendar company, Louis F. Dow—not to paint more children, but to create pin-ups.

Page 199: This 1946 Gil Elvgren nude titled *Gay Nymph*, produced for Brown & Bigelow as a 1948 calendar illustration, was sold for $286,800 by Heritage Auctions in 2011, the highest price ever paid at auction for a pin-up painting. Oil on canvas, 36 x 25 inches.

Opposite: I'm Not Shy, I'm Just Retiring, oil on canvas, 1947, for a 1949 Brown & Bigelow calendar. Elvgren's style changed dramatically in his first years at Brown & Bigelow, where he was driven to produce more realistic and detailed paintings by demanding company president Charlie Ward. 30 x 24 inches.

Above: Gina, 1959, on a 1961 Brown & Bigelow calendar. Calendar measures 33 x 16 inches.

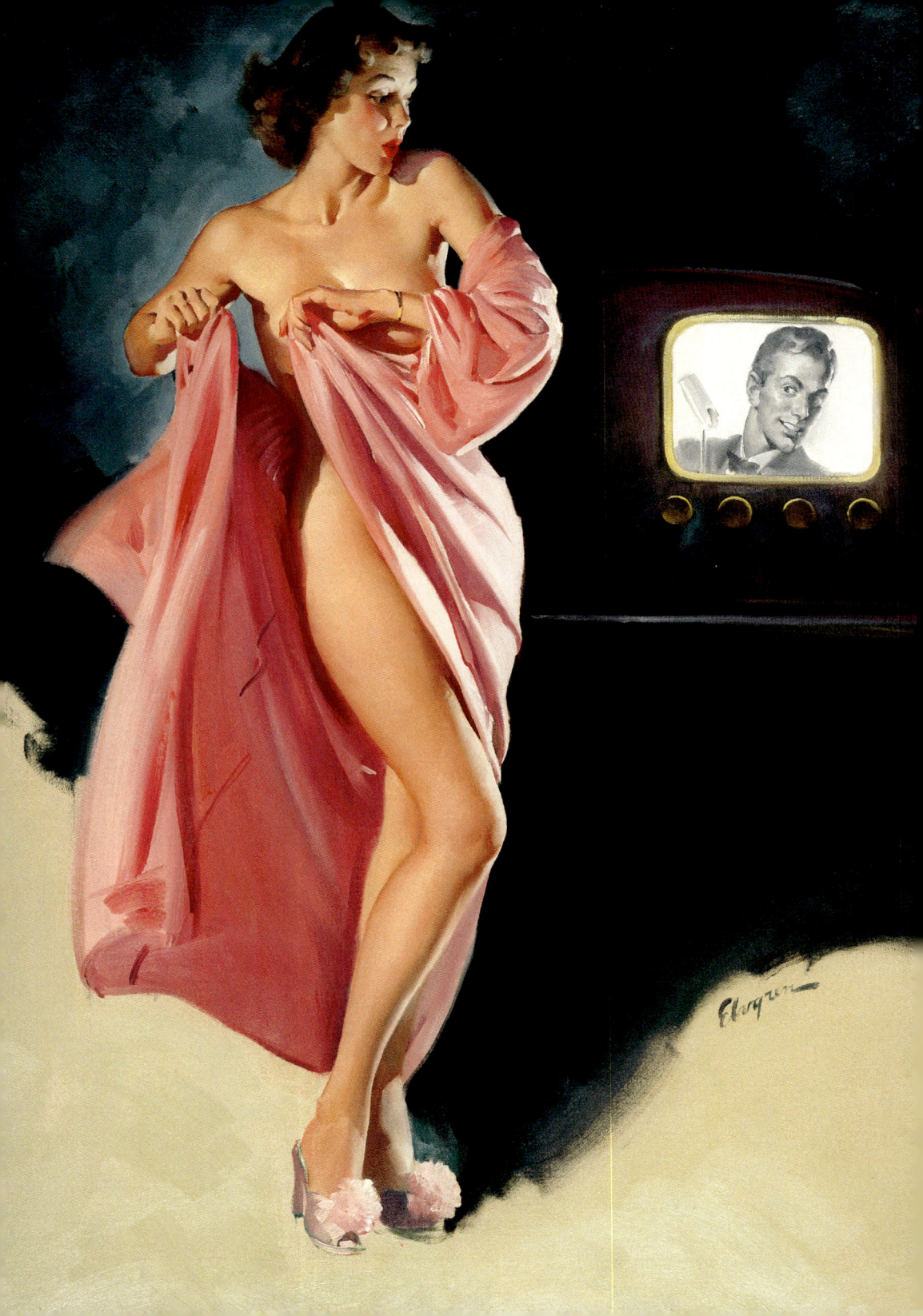

This ongoing commission continued until 1944, even as Elvgren moved his family back to Chicago in 1940 to work at the Stevens-Gross advertising studio, where he met Haddon Sundblom, who would become his life-long mentor. Elvgren's future artistic success owed much to Sundblom's wide colorful brushstrokes, carefully selected subject matter, lively compositional layouts and important industry contacts. Elvgren ultimately stayed at this studio — among trusted peers, mentors and students — for 16 years, receiving illustration commissions from magazines including *Cosmopolitan*, *Good Housekeeping*, *McCall's*, *Redbook*, *The Saturday Evening Post* and *Woman's Home Companion*, and ad work from Schlitz beer, Sealy mattresses, General Electric, General Tire and, most importantly, Coca-Cola. His connection with Coke would last 25 years, and gain Gil much recognition and respect in the advertising world, but it would not make him famous. What elevated Elvgren to mass recognition, and pushed the value of his paintings into the quarter-million-dollar range, were pretty girls — perhaps the most desirable ever created with oil on canvas.

Elvgren's rise to the top began in 1944, when he accepted a position as staff artist at Brown & Bigelow, a career-defining job he would hold for the next 30 years. His first B&B pin-up contract, negotiated through Stevens-Gross, was for a painting titled *We're Back in the Saddle Again!* He was paid an unprecedented $2,000, even more than Rolf Armstrong, whose 1944 contract guaranteed him $30,000 for 19 paintings. In 1947 Elvgren's *Gay Nymph* became the best-selling nude calendar in B&B's history, further reinforcing his value. Sixty-four years later, in 2011, *Gay Nymph* sold for $286,800 through Heritage Auctions, proving Elvgren's value continues to grow.

Elvgren was painting about 24 pin-ups a year for B&B calendars, blotters and assorted promotional items in the late '40s, and his images soon defined the genre — coveted by men and women alike. His style improved dramatically once he switched from Dow to B&B, a change

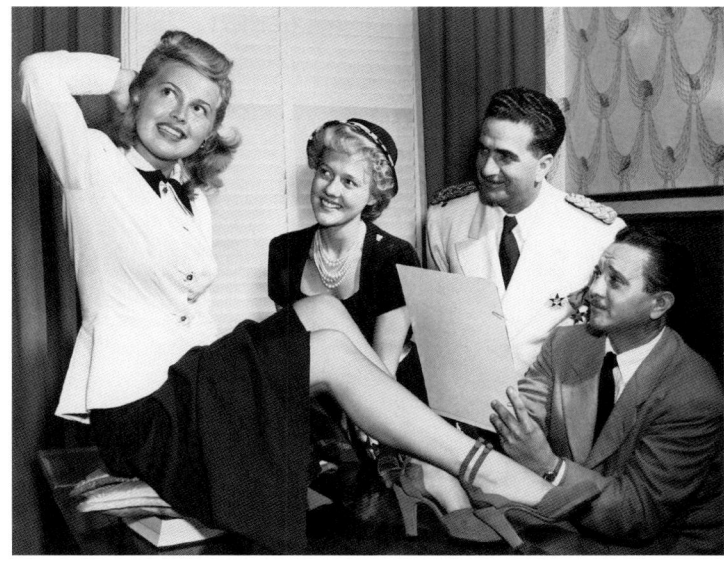

often credited to the way Brown & Bigelow president Charlie Ward drove his artists to perform. Whatever the reason, the beautiful women he painted from 1944 on were provocative, yet innocent, seeming to come to life on canvas in the humorous circumstances Elvgren created for them. Rather than painting structured nudes, he cleverly devised real-life mishaps in which

Opposite: Fresh!, oil on canvas, 1949, for a 1951 Brown & Bigelow calendar. 30 x 24 inches.

Above: Gil Elvgren, far right, sketches the winner of a St. Paul, Minnesota, beauty pageant at the Brown & Bigelow offices in 1948. Part of the pageant's advertised booty for the winner was to be painted as a pin-up by Elvgren.

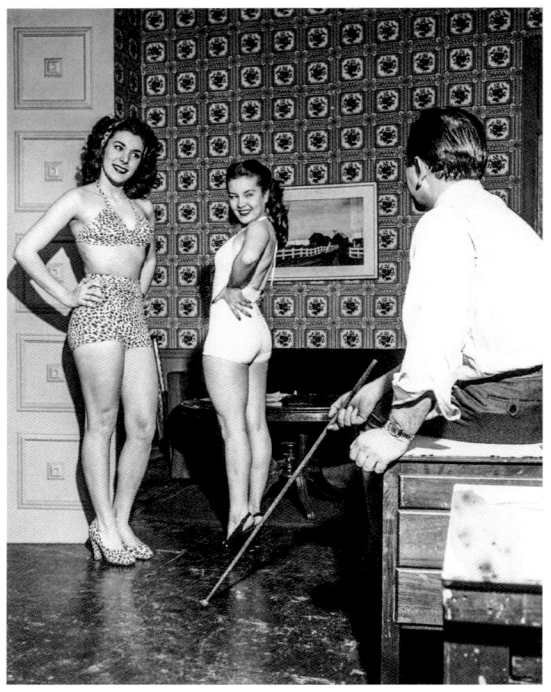

his women would unintentionally reveal their legs, stocking tops and lingerie, to the delight of the viewer. His completed images were always reinforced by a witty title: *A Knockout* (beautiful young woman in a boxing ring); *Thar She Blows* (lawn sprinkler spraying water up a billowing skirt); *Kneeding a Lift* (girl reveals her right knee while hitching a ride).

By the 1950s Elvgren was in high demand to illustrate anything requiring a pretty girl to help sales. He was averaging $2,500 per illustration from Brown & Bigelow, and his additional freelance commissions made him one of America's highest paid illustrators. In 1956 Elvgren and his family moved to Siesta Key Beach in Sarasota, Florida, where he established his own studio with every desired resource. He remained there until his death in 1980, comforted by a former model, Marjorie Shuttleworth, after his wife's death in 1966.

Myrna Hansen modeled for Elvgren from age 13, chaperoned by her mother, and opines that he had a warm face with a kindly gentleman's manner and a perpetual twinkle in his eye. He never actually painted her as a live model, but he used photographs choreographed with the aid of his studio assistants, Bobby Toombs and Peter Darro. He told her that lighting was the most important element to set the scene; and every finger and toe had to be in exactly the right position, perfectly lit, before he took the photo with his Rollei camera.

Myrna says that Elvgren knew exactly what each assignment required to produce his captivating special effects. His studio was well stocked with virtually thousands of dresses, sporting outfits, holiday costumes, vintage clothing, and shoes, as well as a great number of props, which, unlike the dresses, were in rather bad condition.

Elvgren apocryphally described the ideal model as having a 15-year-old's face on a 20-year-old's body. Myrna confirms that Elvgren sometimes glued a photo of a younger model's face to a photo of an older model's body, for he felt that the younger head made the older body look more wholesome. He also believed that younger models had more expressive faces, particularly those special few who could raise their eyebrows very high in surprised response to whatever silly situation he'd contrived to send their skirts flying.

Such opinions may strike many as inappropriate today, but in the 1940s, '50s, and '60s almost everyone responded to Elvgren's pin-ups. Women wanted to be those classically beautiful American women, and men dreamed of having such a beauty for their very own. Quite simply, Elvgren gave his audience what it wanted most, and his image of wholesome, lively beauty still resonates today. Consequently, his paintings bring the highest prices in the pin-up art world and are unlikely to ever be topped.

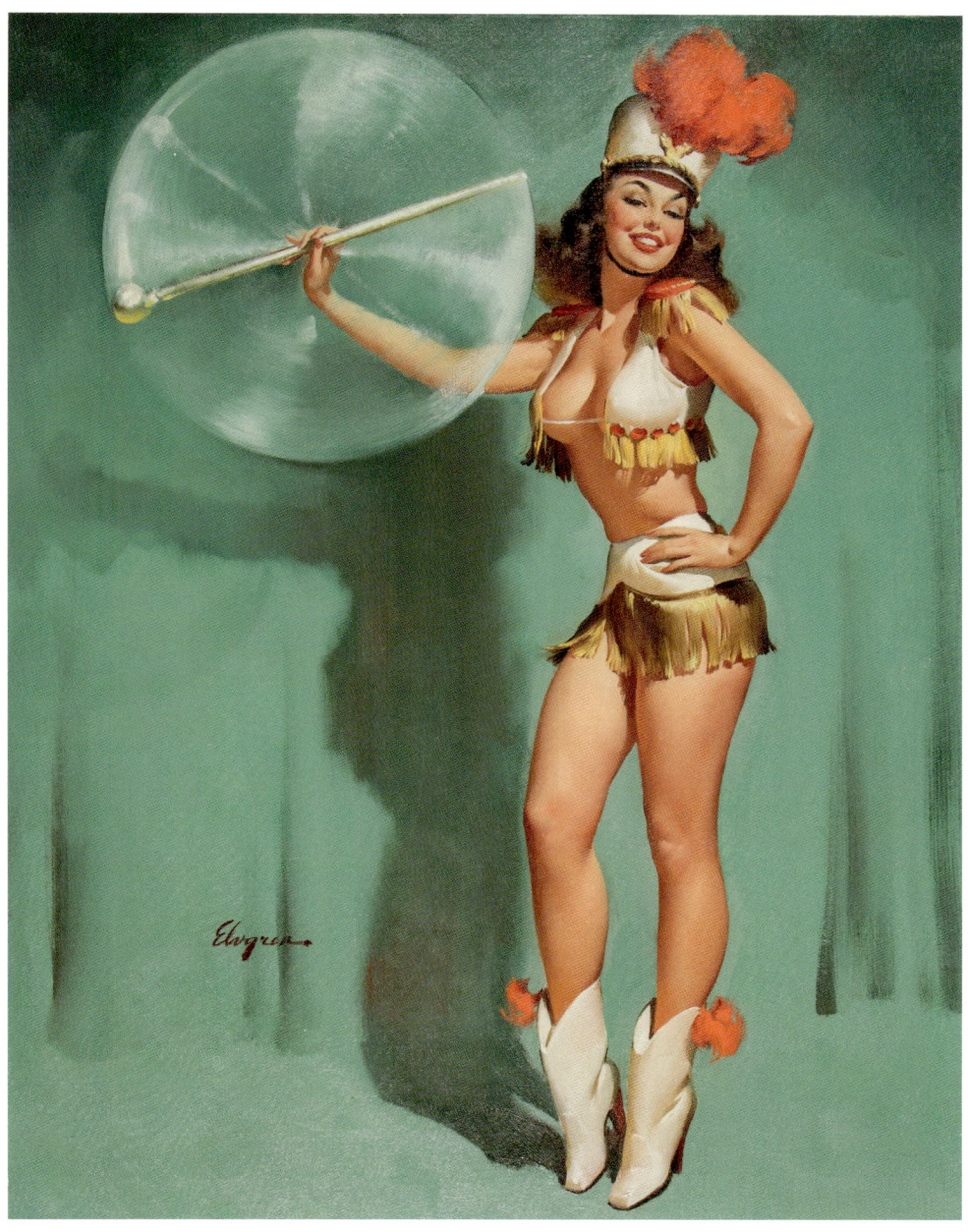

Opposite: Elvgren posing Dayl Rodney and an unknown model, posing stick in hand, 1947.

Above: Baton Twirler for a Brown & Bigelow calendar. Oil on canvas, circa 1955, 30 x 24 inches. Courtesy Heritage Auctions.

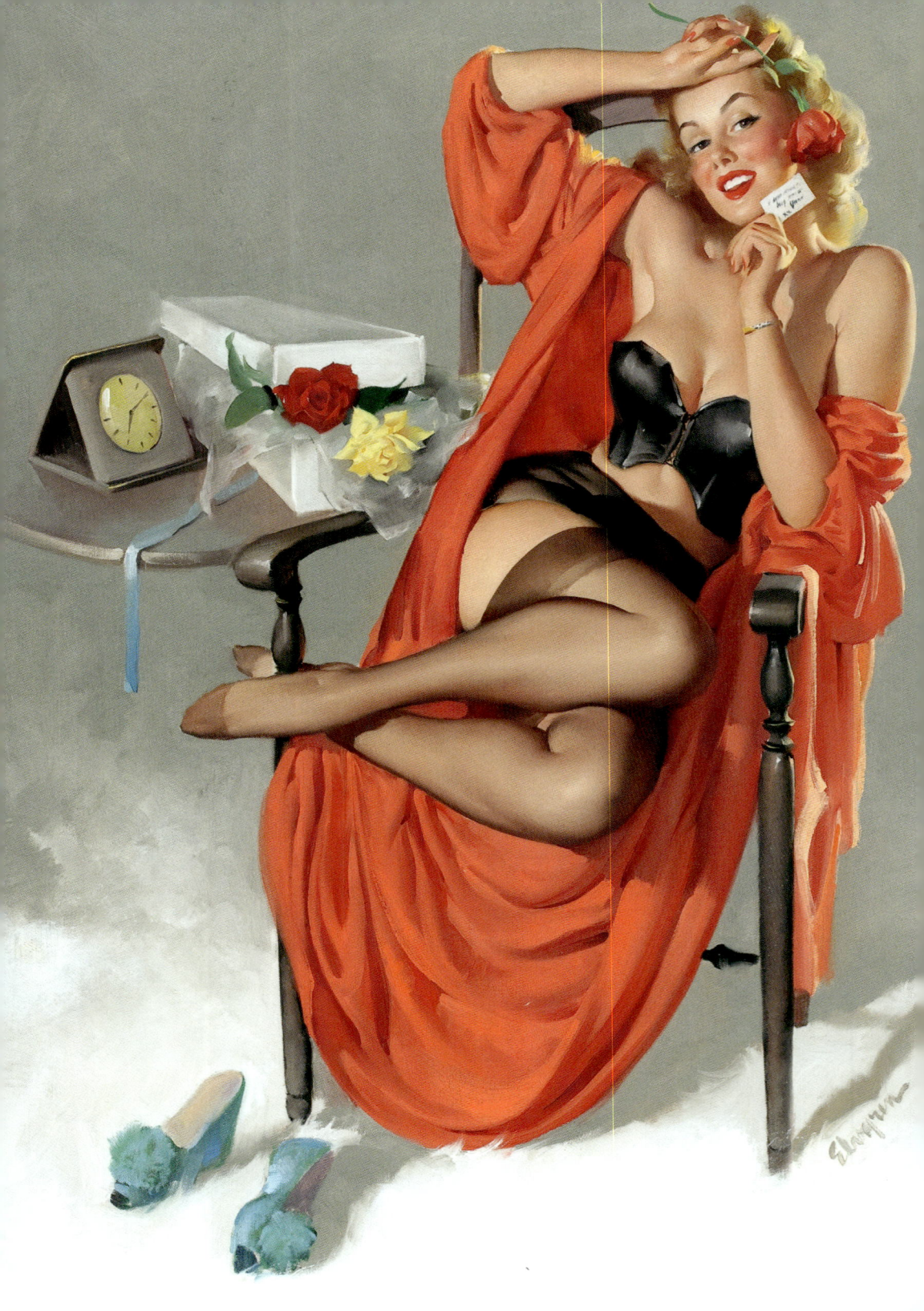

„Kein Pin-up-Künstler malte mehr legendäre Bilder als Elvgren, dessen Werk auf rund 700 Arbeiten geschätzt wird, die er im Laufe seiner 44-jährigen Karriere geschaffen hat."

Amerikas bedeutendster Glamour-Girl-Künstler, Gil Elvgren, malte in den 1940er-, 1950er- und 1960er-Jahren Bilder von Frauen, die das Pin-up-Genre prägten. Er war einer der erfolgreichsten und gefragtesten Illustratoren seiner Zeit. Seine Begabung wurde schon in seiner Jugend von der Werbeindustrie und den Kalenderverlagen erkannt, was ihm ermöglichte, seinen Stil und seine Technik früh zu perfektionieren und dabei bereits die höchsten Honorare der Branche zu beziehen. Kein Pin-up-Künstler malte mehr legendäre Bilder als Elvgren, dessen Werk auf rund 700 Arbeiten geschätzt wird, die er im Laufe seiner 44-jährigen Karriere geschaffen hat.

Gil Elvgren wurde 1914 in St. Paul, Minnesota geboren, wo seine Familie die Elvgren Paint Supply Co, einen Malerbedarfhandel, gegründet hatte. Er belegte als Teenager Sommerkurse am Minneapolis Art Institute und schrieb sich 1934 an der American Academy of Art in Chicago ein.

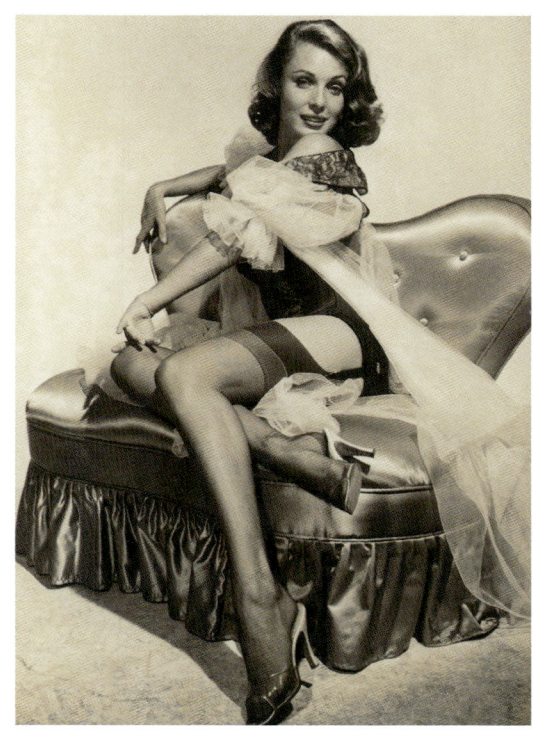

Zwei Jahre später hatte er bereits seinen Abschluss in der Tasche und zog mit seiner Frau Janet Cummins zurück nach St. Paul, um 1936 sein erstes eigenes Atelier zu eröffnen. Kurz darauf hatte er bereits seinen großen Durchbruch, als er von Brown & Bigelow, dem größten Kalenderverlag des Landes, den Auftrag erhielt, die Dionne-Fünflinge zu malen.

Heute ist es schwer, sich vorzustellen, welchen Rummel die ersten überlebenden Fünflinge der Geschichte damals auslösten. Das Wunder, dass fünf identische kleine Mädchen gleichzeitig geboren wurden, ließ die Nöte der Weltwirtschaftskrise für eine Weile vergessen, und Elvgrens Bilder sorgten dafür, dass er sozusagen über Nacht erfolgreich war. Louis F. Dow, Amerikas

Opposite: Hope He Mrs. Me, oil on canvas, 1949, for a 1951 Brown & Bigelow calendar. 30 x 24 inches.

Above: The model study photo for *Mona*, 1959, which first appeared on a 1961 Brown & Bigelow calendar.

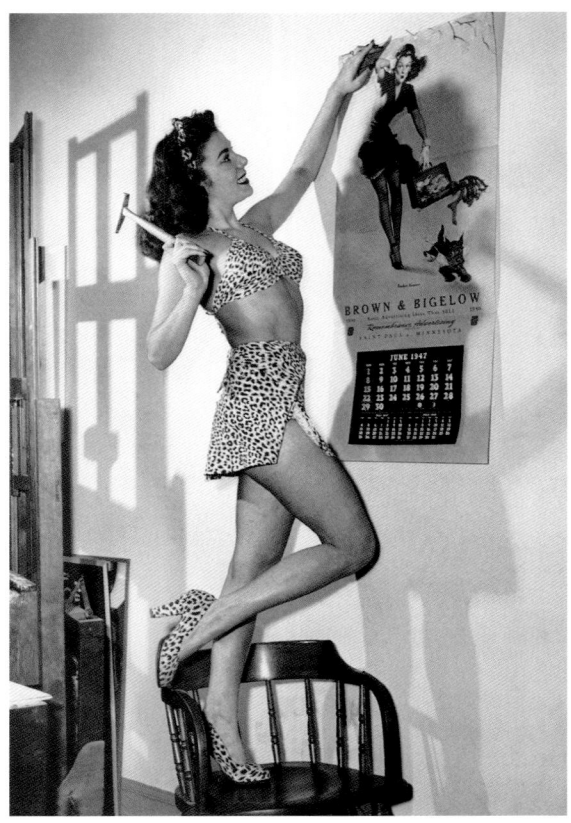

zweitgrößter Kalenderverlag, nahm ihn unter Vertrag, nicht um Kinder zu porträtieren, sondern um Pin-ups zu malen.

Dieser Tätigkeit ging Elvgren bis 1944 nach, sogar noch nachdem er 1940 mit seiner Familie nach Chicago gezogen war, um im Atelier Stevens-Gross zu arbeiten. Dort lernte er Haddon Sundblom kennen, der schließlich lebenslang sein Mentor wurde. Elvgren verdankte seinen künstlerischen Erfolg stark Sundbloms breitem, farbkräftigem Pinselstrich, dessen sorgfältig ausgewählten Motiven, den lebendig komponierten Entwürfen und wichtigen Branchenkontakten. 16 Jahre blieb Elvgren – unter vertrauten Kollegen, Mentoren und Studenten – in diesem Studio und erhielt Aufträge für Illustrationen, die in Zeitschriften wie *Cosmopolitan*, *Good Housekeeping*, *McCall's*, *Redbook*, *Saturday Evening Post* und *Woman's Home Companion* erschienen, sowie Anzeigenaufträge von Schlitz-Bier, Sealy-Matratzen, General Electric, General Tire und vor allem von Coca-Cola. Seine Zusammenarbeit mit Coke sollte 25 Jahre währen und Gil viel Anerkennung und Respekt in der Werbeindustrie verschaffen. Berühmt wurde er dadurch jedoch nicht. Was Elvgren die Anerkennung des breiten Publikums einbrachte und den Wert seiner Gemälde bis auf 250 000 Dollar hochtrieb, waren hübsche Mädchen – vermutlich die begehrenswertesten, die je mit Öl auf Leinwand geschaffen wurden.

Elvgrens Aufstieg an die Spitze begann 1944, nachdem er Hauskünstler bei Brown & Bigelow wurde, ein Job, der seine Karriere prägte und den er in den nächsten 30 Jahren behielt. Der erste von Stevens-Gross ausgehandelte Vertrag mit B & B betraf ein Gemälde mit dem Titel *We're Back in the Saddle Again*. Für dieses Bild erhielt er unerhörte 2 000 Dollar, mehr sogar als Rolf Armstrong, dessen Vertrag von 1944 ihm 30 000 Dollar für 19 Gemälde garantierte. 1947 erwies sich Elvgrens *Gay Nymph* als der bis dahin meist verkaufte Aktkalender in der Firmengeschichte von B & B, was seinen Wert als Künstler weiter steigerte. 64 Jahre später, 2011, wurde *Gay Nymph* über Heritage Auctions für 286 800 Dollar verkauft, was zeigt, dass Elvgrens Wert noch immer steigt.

Above: A Brown & Bigelow publicity photo shows Elvgren model Dayl Rodney hanging the 1947 B&B calendar *Finders Keepers*, painted in 1945, for which she posed.

Opposite: Mona, 1959, on a 1961 Brown & Bigelow calendar. Calendar measures 33 x 16 inches.

THE ART OF PIN-UP

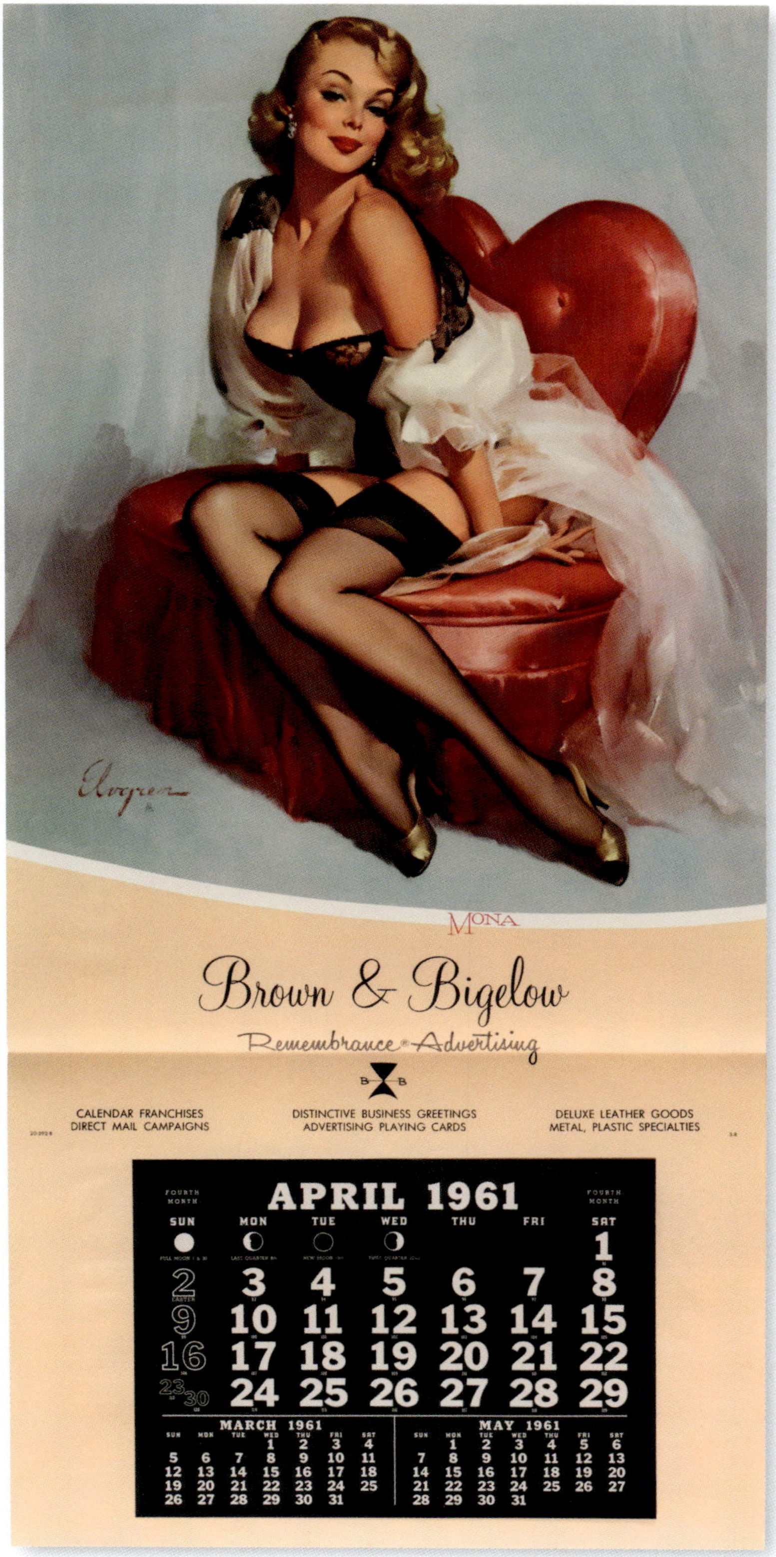

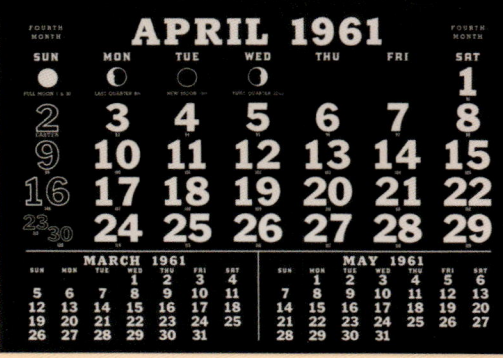

MONA

Brown & Bigelow

Remembrance • Advertising

B⧗B

CALENDAR FRANCHISES
DIRECT MAIL CAMPAIGNS

DISTINCTIVE BUSINESS GREETINGS
ADVERTISING PLAYING CARDS

DELUXE LEATHER GOODS
METAL, PLASTIC SPECIALTIES

FOURTH MONTH	APRIL 1961					FOURTH MONTH
SUN	**MON**	**TUE**	**WED**	**THU**	**FRI**	**SAT**
● FULL MOON 1 & 31	◑ LAST QUARTER 8H	● NEW MOON 15	◐ FIRST QUARTER 23H			**1**
2 EASTER	**3**	**4**	**5**	**6**	**7**	**8**
9	**10**	**11**	**12**	**13**	**14**	**15**
16	**17**	**18**	**19**	**20**	**21**	**22**
23 **30**	**24**	**25**	**26**	**27**	**28**	**29**

MARCH 1961							MAY 1961						
SUN	MON	TUE	WED	THU	FRI	SAT	SUN	MON	TUE	WED	THU	FRI	SAT
			1	2	3	4		1	2	3	4	5	6
5	6	7	8	9	10	11	7	8	9	10	11	12	13
12	13	14	15	16	17	18	14	15	16	17	18	19	20
19	20	21	22	23	24	25	21	22	23	24	25	26	27
26	27	28	29	30	31		28	29	30	31			

In den späten 1940er-Jahren malte Elvgren rund 24 Pin-ups pro Jahr für Kalender und diverse Werbematerialien von B & B, und bald legten seine Bilder – bei Männern wie bei Frauen begehrt – die Maßstäbe des Genres fest. Nachdem er von Dow zu B & B gewechselt war, verbesserte sich sein Stil erheblich, ein Umstand, der oft auf die Art zurückgeführt wird, wie Charlie Ward, der Direktor von B & B, seine Künstler zu Höchstleistungen ermunterte. Was auch immer der Grund für diesen Wandel war – die schönen Frauen, die Elvgren von 1944 an malte, wirkten provozierend, doch unschuldig und schienen durch die humorvollen Situationen, in denen Elvgren sie auf der Leinwand darstellte, lebendig zu werden. Statt einfach nur ausgetüftelte Akte zu malen, ersann er raffinierte Pannen, in denen die Frauen unbeabsichtigt und zum Vergnügen des Betrachters viel Bein, Strumpfbänder und Unterwäsche zeigten. Geistreiche Titel verstärkten noch die Wirkung seiner perfekten Bilder: *A Knockout* (schöne junge Frau in einem Boxring); *Thar She Blows* (Rasensprenger spritzt Wasser unter einen hochgewehten Rock); *Kneeding a Lift* (Mädchen zeigt beim Trampen das rechte Knie).

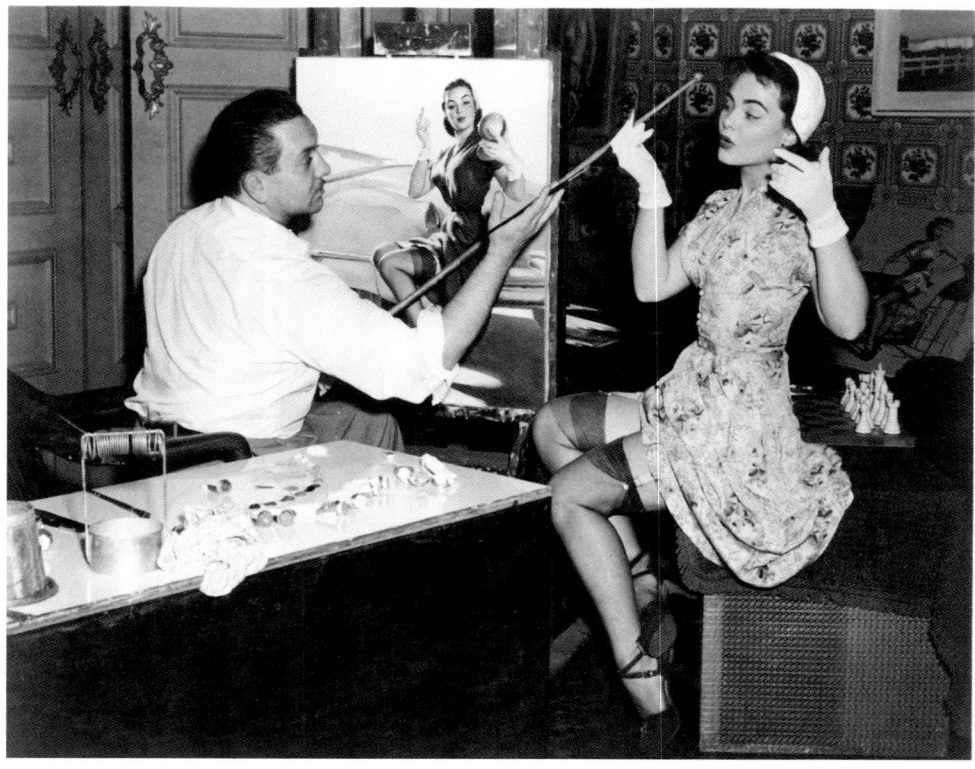

Above: In another B&B publicity photo, Elvgren directs Myrna Hansen with his posing stick, which he used to nudge models into position to avoid touching sensitive body parts with his hands. The finished painting on his easel is *Jill Needs Jack*, 1950. Hansen went on to an acting career, appearing in 17 films and on a number of television shows, including *Hawaiian Eye* and *77 Sunset Strip*.

Opposite: Jill Needs Jack, oil on canvas, 1950, for a 1952 Brown & Bigelow calendar. 30 x 24 inches.

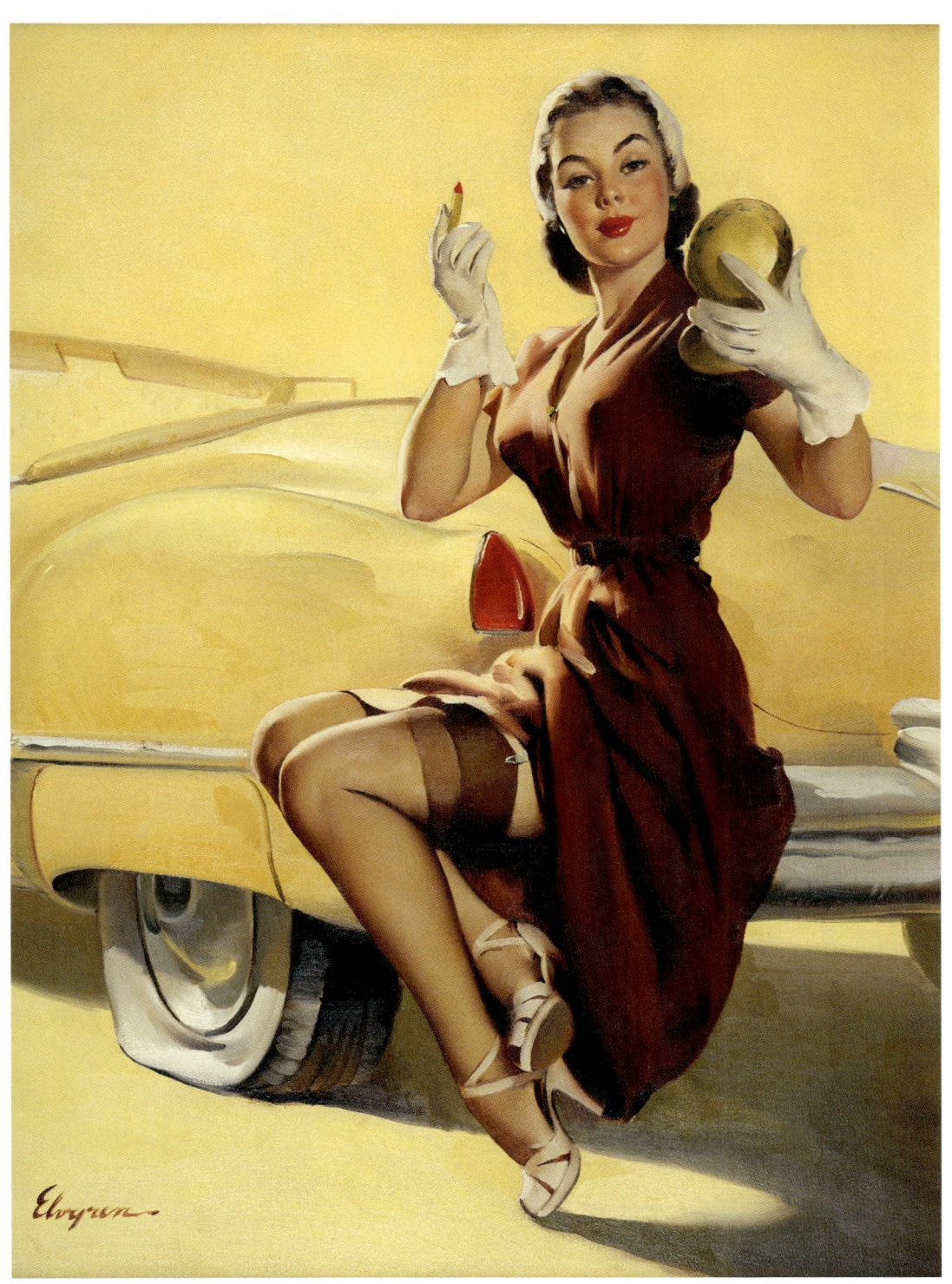

GILLETTE "GIL" ELVGREN

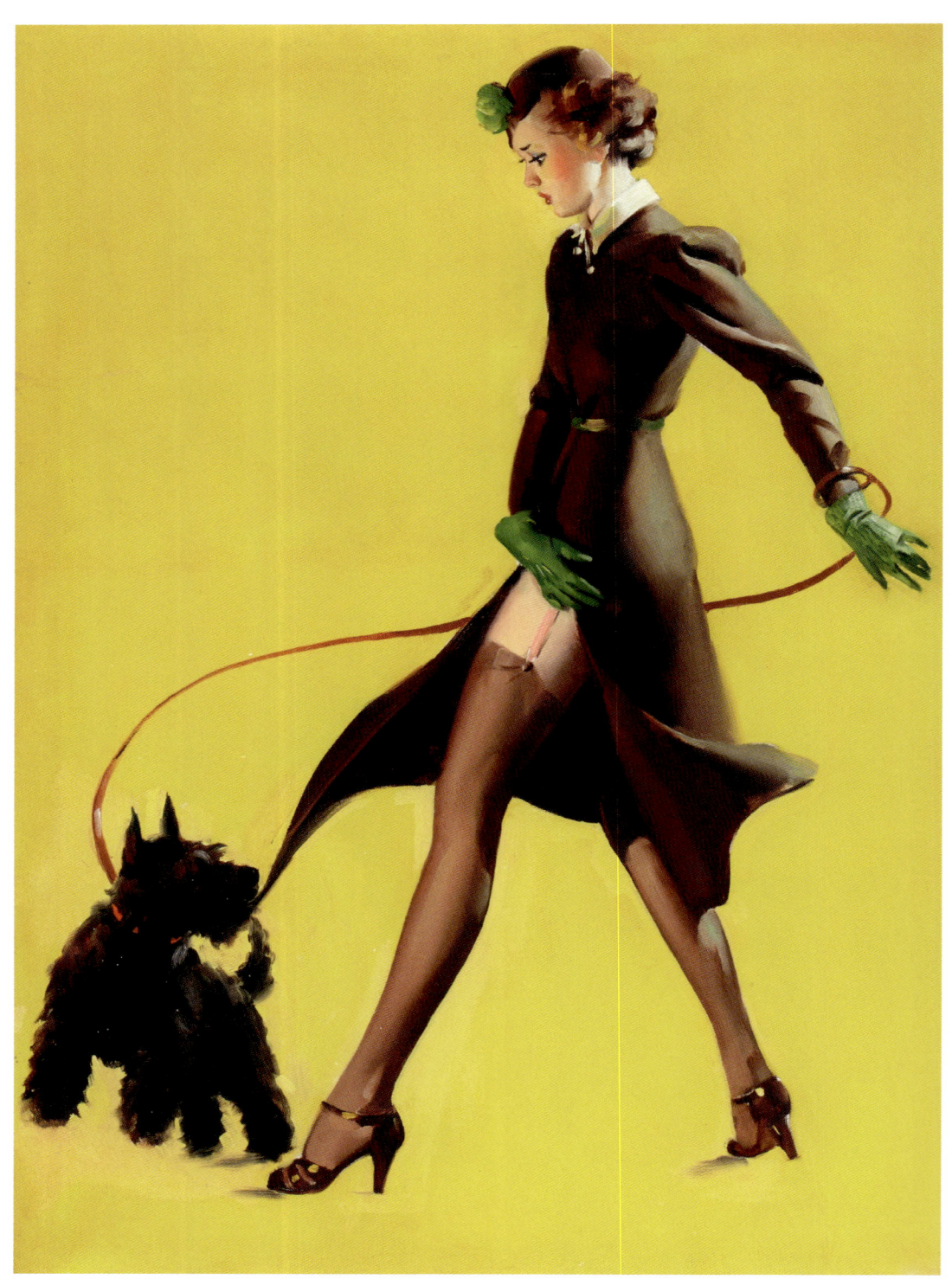

In den 1950er-Jahren war Elvgren immer dann gefragt, wenn das Bild eines hübschen Mädchens den Verkauf eines Produkts fördern sollte. Von Brown & Bigelow erhielt er für jedes Bild im Durchschnitt 2.500 Dollar. Zusammen mit den Honoraren für freie Aufträge war er damit einer der bestbezahlten Illustratoren Amerikas. 1956 zog Elvgren mit seiner Familie nach Siesta Key Beach in Sarasota, Florida. Er richtete sich sein eigenes Atelier mit allen erdenklichen Hilfsmitteln ein. Hier lebte er bis zu seinem Tod 1980 und heiratete nach dem Tod seiner ersten Frau 1966 Marjorie Shuttleworth, ein ehemaliges Modell.

Myrna Hansen saß, begleitet von ihrer Mutter, seit ihrem 13. Lebensjahr für Elvgren Modell. Sie erzählte, er habe ein gütiges Gesicht gehabt, die Manieren eines Gentlemans an den Tag gelegt und in seinen Augen sei stets ein Funkeln zu sehen gewesen. Tatsächlich hat er sie nie direkt gemalt, sondern Fotografien benutzt, die er unter Mitwirkung seiner Ateliergehilfen Bobby Toombs und Peter Darro sorgfältig inszenierte. Er erklärte Myrna, das wichtigste Element der Inszenierung sei das Licht. Jeder Finger und jeder Zeh musste in genau der richtigen Position und perfekt ausgeleuchtet sein, bevor er schließlich die Aufnahme mit seiner Rollei-Kamera machte.

Myrna erklärt, Elvgren habe genau gewusst, was für jeden Auftrag notwendig sei, um die gewünschten faszinierenden Effekte zu erlangen. Sein Atelier war mit nahezu Tausenden von Kleidern, Sportsachen, Freizeitklamotten, Vintagemode und Schuhen ausgestattet sowie einer Vielzahl von Requisiten, die allerdings – anders als die Kleider – in einem ziemlich erbärmlichen Zustand waren.

Elvgren beschrieb apokryphisch das ideale Modell als ein Mädchen mit dem Gesicht einer 15-Jährigen und dem Körper einer 20-Jährigen. Myrna bestätigt, dass Elvgren manchmal die Gesichtsaufnahme eines jüngeren Modells auf die Körperaufnahme eines älteren Modells klebte, denn er war der Meinung, der jüngere Kopf lasse den älteren Körper besser erscheinen. Auch war er der Ansicht, jüngere Modelle hätten ausdrucksvollere Gesichter, vor allem jene wenigen Mädchen, die ihre Augenbrauen erstaunt über eine von Elvren ausgedachte alberne Situation besonders hochziehen konnten.

Solche Ansichten mögen heute viele als unangemessen empfinden, doch in den 1940er-, 1950er- und 1960er-Jahren fühlte sich fast jeder von Elvgrens Pin-ups angesprochen. Frauen wollten wie eine dieser klassisch schönen Amerikanerinnen sein, und Männer träumten davon, eine solche Schönheit für sich zu haben. Elvgren bot seinem Publikum schlicht das, was es am meisten begehrte, und sein Bild einer lebhaften Schönheit findet noch heute Anklang. Daher erzielen seine Gemälde bei Auktionen von Pin-up-Kunst die höchsten Preise, und es ist unwahrscheinlich, dass er je übertroffen wird.

Opposite: Man's Best Friend, oil on canvas, 1937, for a Louis F. Dow calendar. Elvgren began his flying skirt theme for Dow, but on less voluptuous models. It's not known if B&B encouraged him to paint fuller figures or if they simply freed him to follow his own impulse in this regard. 31 x 25 inches.

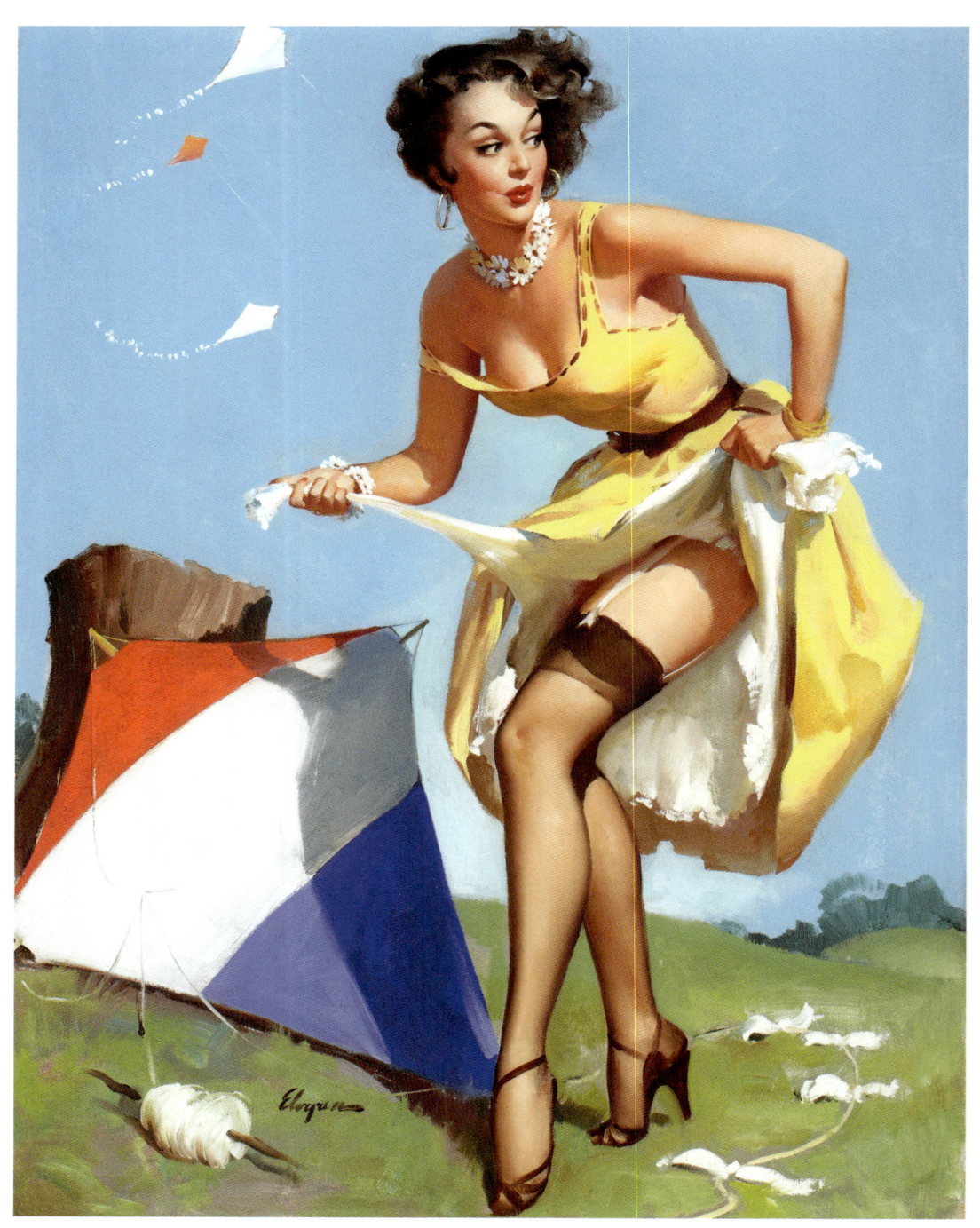

« Aucun autre artiste n'a créé autant d'images de pin-up restées célèbres. On estime qu'il en a peint environ 700 au cours d'une carrière s'étalant sur quarante-quatre ans. »

Gil Elvgren fut le plus grand artiste glamour américain. Ses femmes peintes dans les années 1940, 1950 et 1960 ont défini le genre de la pin-up. Il fut l'un des illustrateurs les plus demandés de son temps. Son talent fut reconnu par le monde de la publicité et des calendriers dès ses débuts, ce qui lui permit de perfectionner son style et sa technique tout au long de sa carrière et d'être le mieux payé du secteur. Aucun autre artiste n'a créé autant d'images de pin-up restées célèbres. On estime qu'il en a peint environ 700 au cours d'une carrière s'étalant sur quarante-quatre ans.

Né en 1914 à St. Paul dans le Minnesota, où sa famille avait fondé la Elvgren Paint Supply Co., Gil Elvgren suivit des cours d'été au Minneapolis Art Institute dans son adolescence, puis s'inscrivit à l'American Academy of Art à Chicago en 1934. Il acheva son cursus en deux ans puis, avec sa femme Janet Cummins, rentra à St. Paul pour ouvrir son premier atelier en 1936. Il décrocha rapidement sa première commande importante, une peinture des quintuplées Dionne pour Brown & Bigelow, le plus grand éditeur de calendriers du pays.

On imagine mal aujourd'hui le retentissement qu'eurent les premières quintuplées à survivre au-delà de la petite enfance, ce qui fut perçu comme un vrai miracle dans les rigueurs de la Grande Dépression. L'illustration d'Elvgren remporta un succès immédiat. Il fut recruté par Louis F. Dow, le deuxième éditeur de calendrier après B&B, non pas pour peindre des enfants, mais des pin-up.

Cette collaboration dura jusqu'en 1944, même quand Elvgren repartit vivre à Chicago avec sa famille en 1940 pour rejoindre l'atelier

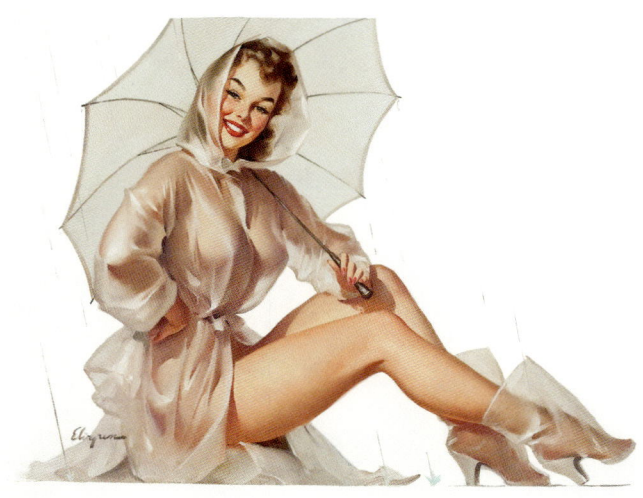

Opposite: The Final Touch, also known as *Keep 'Em Flying,* oil on canvas, 1954, for a 1956 Brown & Bigelow calendar. 30 x 24 inches.

Above: Oil on canvas commission for Simoniz car polish, circa 1960, 43.25 x 24 inches. This and a second Simoniz painting were found in an abandoned house by a lucky construction worker and brought a combined $107,550 at a Heritage auction.

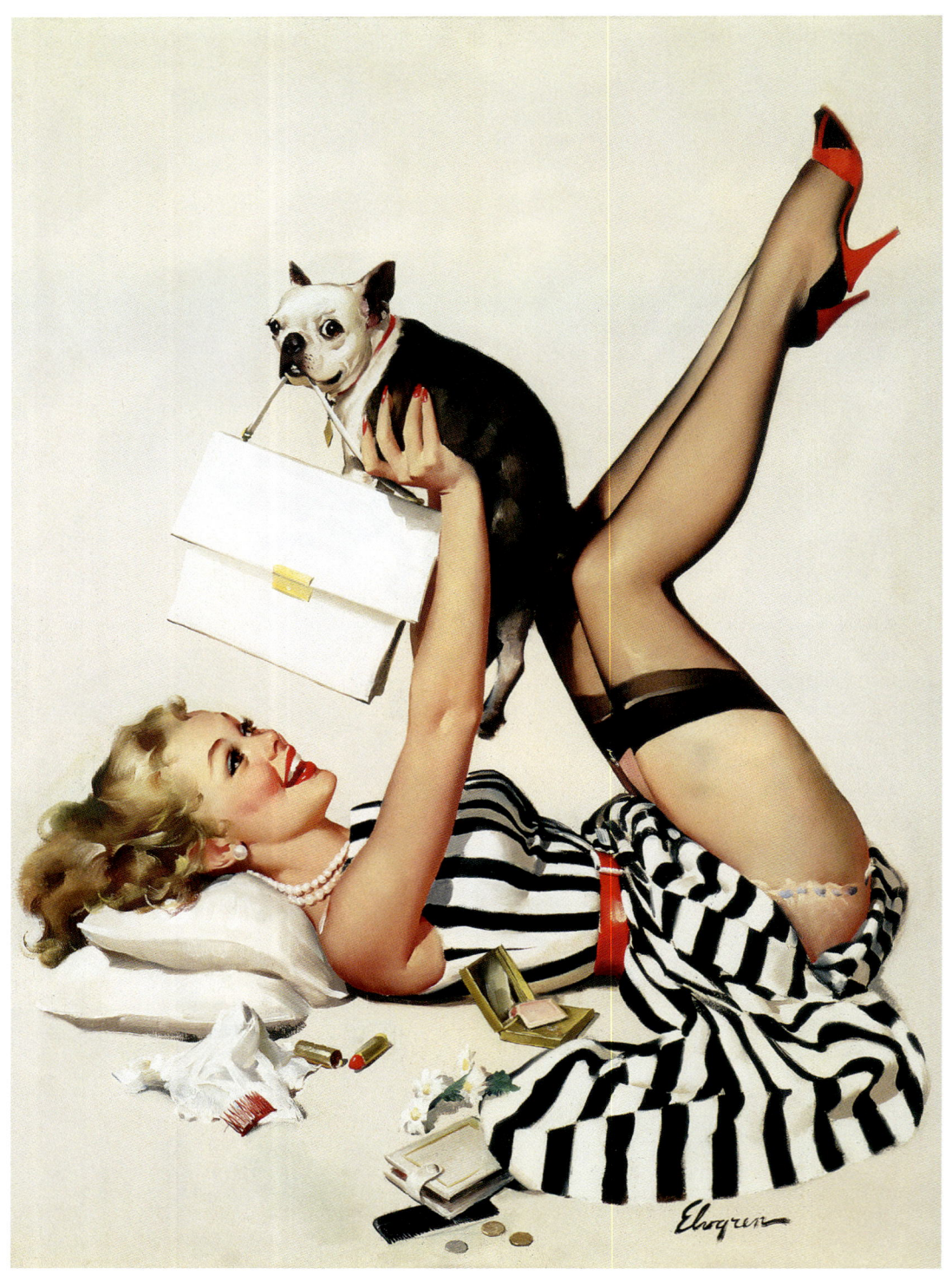

Stevens-Gross. Là, il rencontra Haddon Sundblom qui deviendrait son mentor. L'évolution du style et la réussite d'Elvgren durent beaucoup à Sundblom, avec ses grands coups de pinceau colorés, ses sujets méticuleusement choisis, ses compositions dynamiques et ses nombreux contacts. Elvgren resta seize ans dans cet atelier, entouré de ses pairs, mentors et élèves, recevant des commandes de magazines tels que *Cosmopolitan*, *Good Housekeeping*, *McCall's*, *Redbook*, *The Saturday Evening Post* et *Woman's Home Companion*, ainsi que d'annonceurs comme les bières Schlitz, les matelas Sealy, General Electric, les pneus General Tire et, surtout, Coca-Cola. Son travail pour cette firme, étalé sur vingt-cinq ans, lui valut la reconnaissance et le respect du monde de la publicité. Ce ne fut toutefois pas à Coca-Cola qu'il dut sa célébrité mais à ses jolies filles, sans doute les plus désirables jamais peintes à l'huile sur toile. Elles le firent connaître du grand public et hissèrent la valeur de ses œuvres autour du quart de million de dollars.

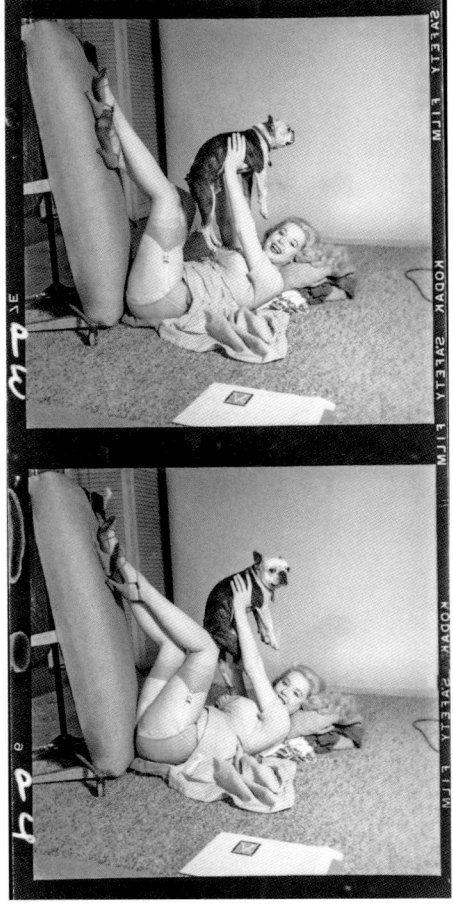

L'ascension d'Elvgren débuta en 1944, quand il entra dans l'écurie de B&B, un poste déterminant pour sa carrière et qu'il occuperait pendant trente ans. Son premier contrat avec B&B, négocié par l'intermédiaire de Stevens-Gross, était pour la pin-up *We're Back in the Saddle Again*. Il fut payé la somme sans précédent de 2 000 dollars, dépassant Rolf Armstrong dont le contrat de 1944 lui garantissait 30 000 dollars pour 19 peintures. En 1947, *Gay Nymph* devint le calendrier de nus le plus vendu de l'histoire de B&B, asseyant encore sa notoriété. En 2011, soixante-quatre ans plus tard, *Gay Nymph* fut vendu 286 800 dollars par Heritage Auctions, preuve que la valeur d'Elvgren continue d'augmenter.

À la fin des années 1940, Elvgren peignait environ 24 pin-up par an pour les calendriers, buvards et divers articles publicitaires de B&B. Ses images, appréciées par les hommes et les femmes, définirent rapidement le marché. Chez B&B, il peaufina considérablement son style, un changement que l'on attribue généralement à la manière dont Charlie Ward, président de B&B, dirigeait ses artistes. En effet, à partir de 1944, ses pin-up devinrent plus provocantes tout en restant innocentes. Elles prenaient vie sur la toile dans les circonstances amusantes qu'Elvgren créait pour elles. Il inventait des mésaventures de la vie quotidienne au cours desquels ses femmes révélaient accidentellement leurs jambes et leurs dessous, pour le plus grand plaisir des voyeurs. Il accompagnait généralement ses images d'un titre humoristique reposant sur un jeu de mots.

Opposite: Lucky Dog, also known as *Dog Gone Robber*, oil on canvas, 1958, for a 1960 Brown & Bigelow calendar. 30 x 24 inches.

Above: A proofsheet from the model session for the painting *Lucky Dog*, also known as *Dog Gone Robber*, 1958.

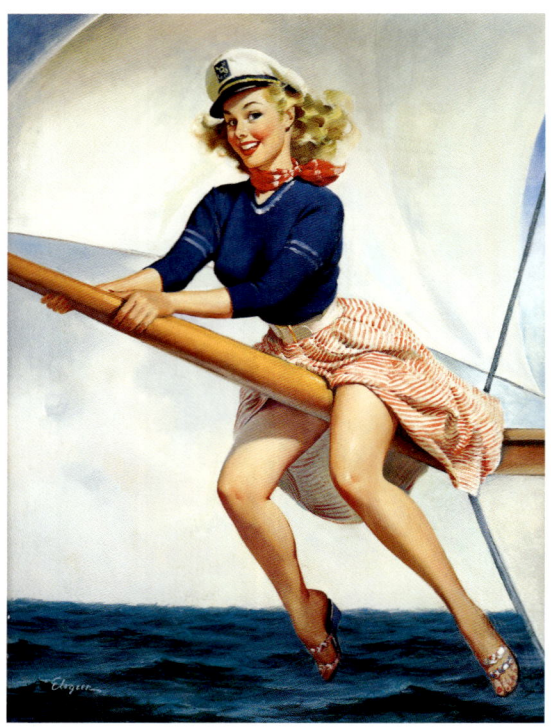

Dans les années 1950, on faisait appel à lui pour illustrer tout ce qui pouvait être vendu à l'aide d'une jolie fille. B&B le payait 2500 dollars par illustration et, avec ses commandes parallèles en free-lance, il était l'un des illustrateurs les mieux payés des États-Unis. En 1956, il emménagea avec sa famille à Siesta Key Beach à Sarasota, en Floride, où il créa son propre atelier équipé de toutes les ressources nécessaires. Il y vécut jusqu'à sa mort en 1980, se remariant avec un ancien modèle, Marjorie Shuttleworth, après le décès de sa première épouse en 1966.

Myrna Hansen posa pour lui dès l'âge de 13 ans, chaperonnée par sa mère. Elle le décrit avec un visage chaleureux, des manières de gentleman et toujours une étincelle dans le regard. Il ne la peignit jamais d'après nature, mais la mettait en scène avec l'aide de ses assistants Bobby Toombs et Peter Drabo, puis la photographiait. Il lui expliqua que la lumière était un élément essentiel, que chaque doigt et orteil devait être à la bonne place, parfaitement éclairé, avant qu'il n'appuie sur le déclencheur de son Rollei.

Selon Myrna, Elvgren savait exactement ce qu'il fallait à chaque commande pour obtenir les meilleurs effets. Son atelier regorgeait de milliers de robes, tenues de sport, costumes de fête et de diverses époques, ainsi que d'innombrables accessoires qui, contrairement aux vêtements, étaient en piteux état.

Elvgren aurait déclaré que son modèle idéal avait un visage de 15 ans sur un corps de 20 ans. Myrna confirme qu'il lui arrivait de coller le visage d'une adolescente sur la photo d'un corps plus mûr, car il trouvait que cela donnait une allure plus saine. Il considérait également que les visages jeunes étaient plus expressifs, notamment celui des adolescentes pouvant hausser très haut leurs sourcils d'un air surpris en réaction aux situations farfelues qu'il inventait pour faire voler leur jupe.

Ce genre d'opinion peut paraître déplacé aujourd'hui, mais, dans les années 1940, 1950 et 1960, tout le monde aimait les pin-up d'Elvgren. Les femmes voulaient ressembler à ces beautés classiques américaines et les hommes rêvaient de les posséder. Elvgren donnait à son public ce qu'il désirait le plus et ses images d'une beauté saine et enjouée trouvent encore un écho aujourd'hui. Cela explique que ses peintures sont les plus prisées dans le monde de la pin-up, atteignant des prix dépassant ceux de tous ses confrères.

Above: *Bow Spirit*, oil on canvas, 1960s, for a Brown & Bigelow calendar, reportedly never published because the model straddling the phallic stem of the ship's bow was considered too racy. 30 x 24 inches.

Opposite: *A Fast Takeoff*, 1954, for a 1956 Brown & Bigelow calendar, oil on canvas, 30 x 24 inches. Courtesy Heritage Auctions.

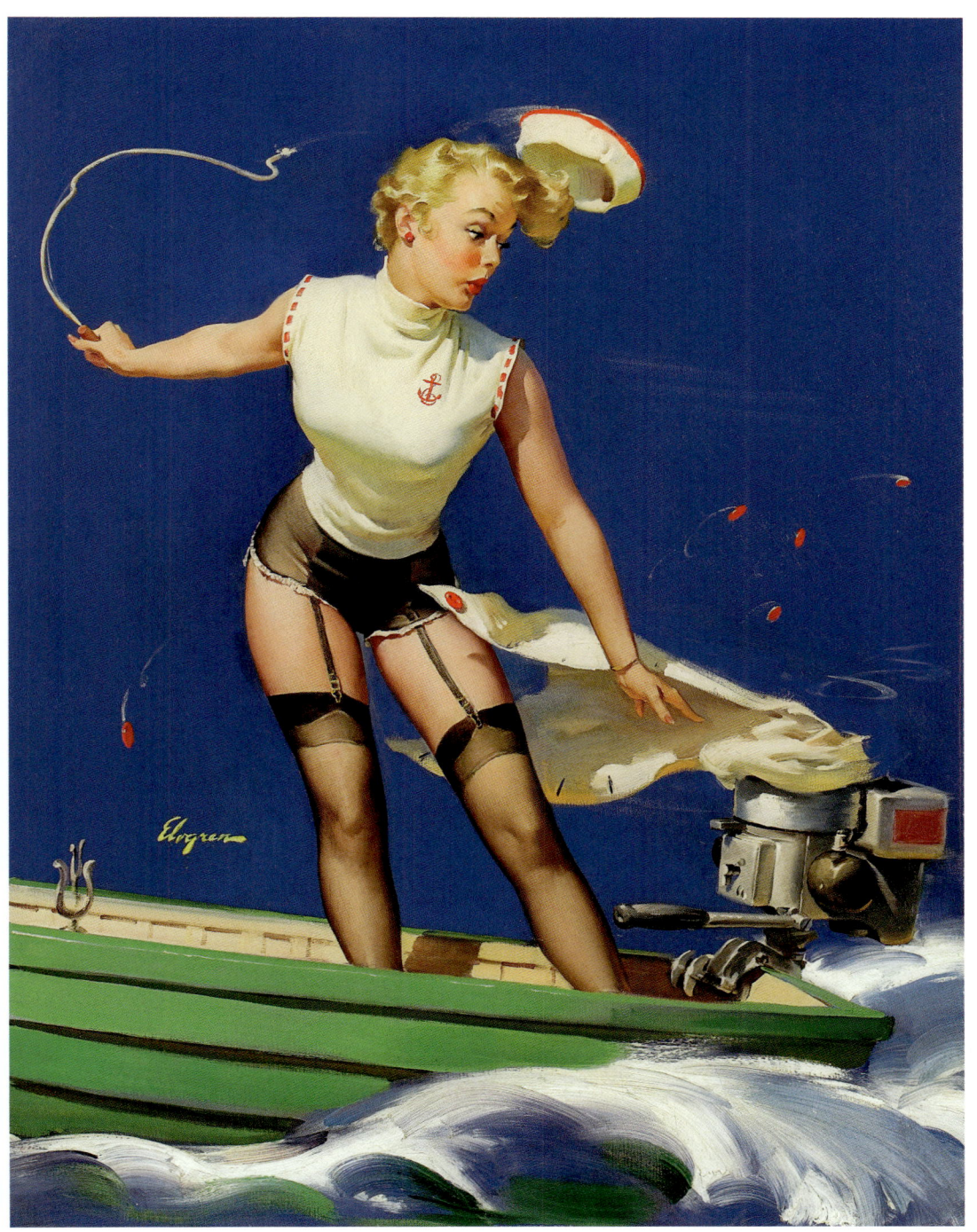

GILLETTE "GIL" ELVGREN

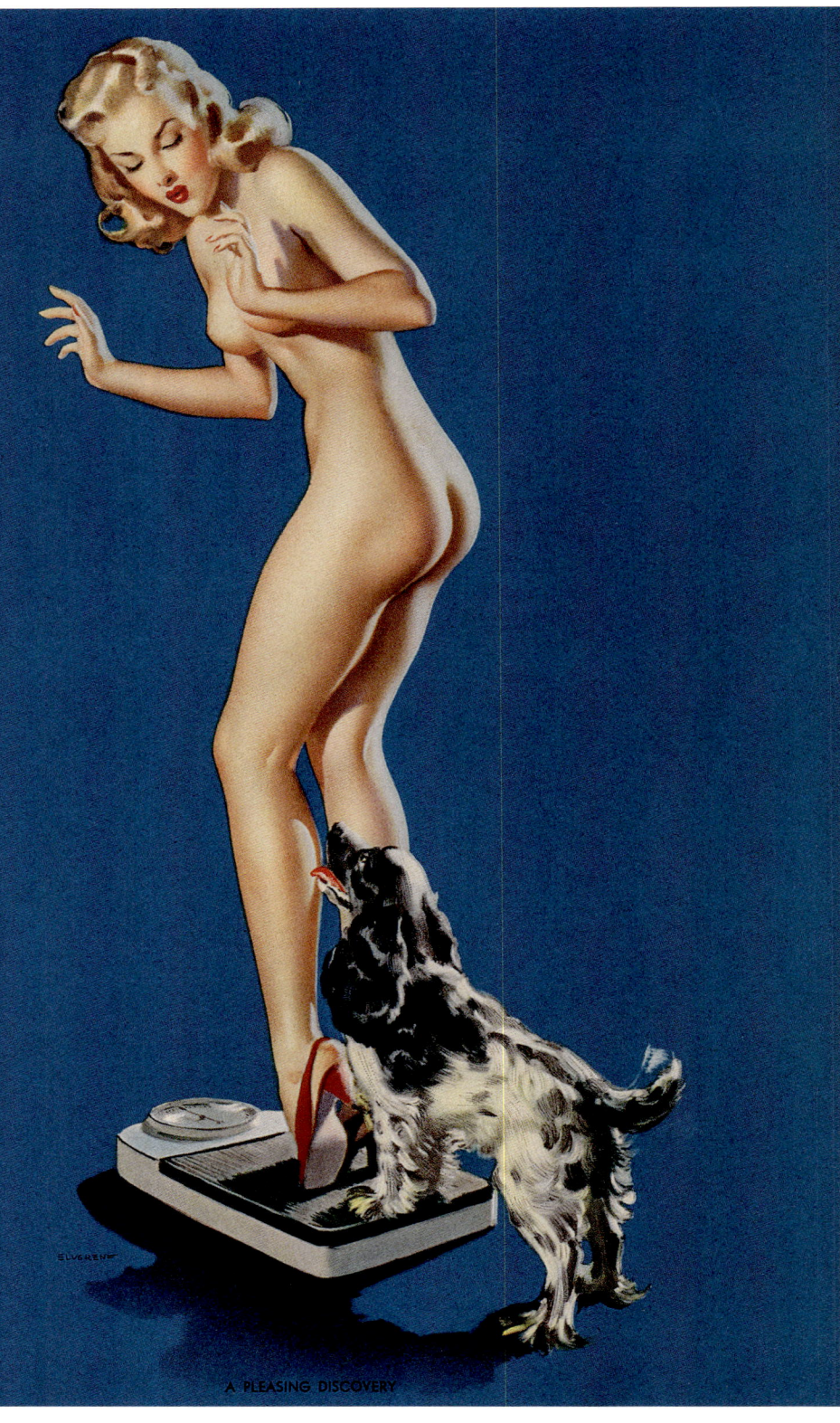

A PLEASING DISCOVERY

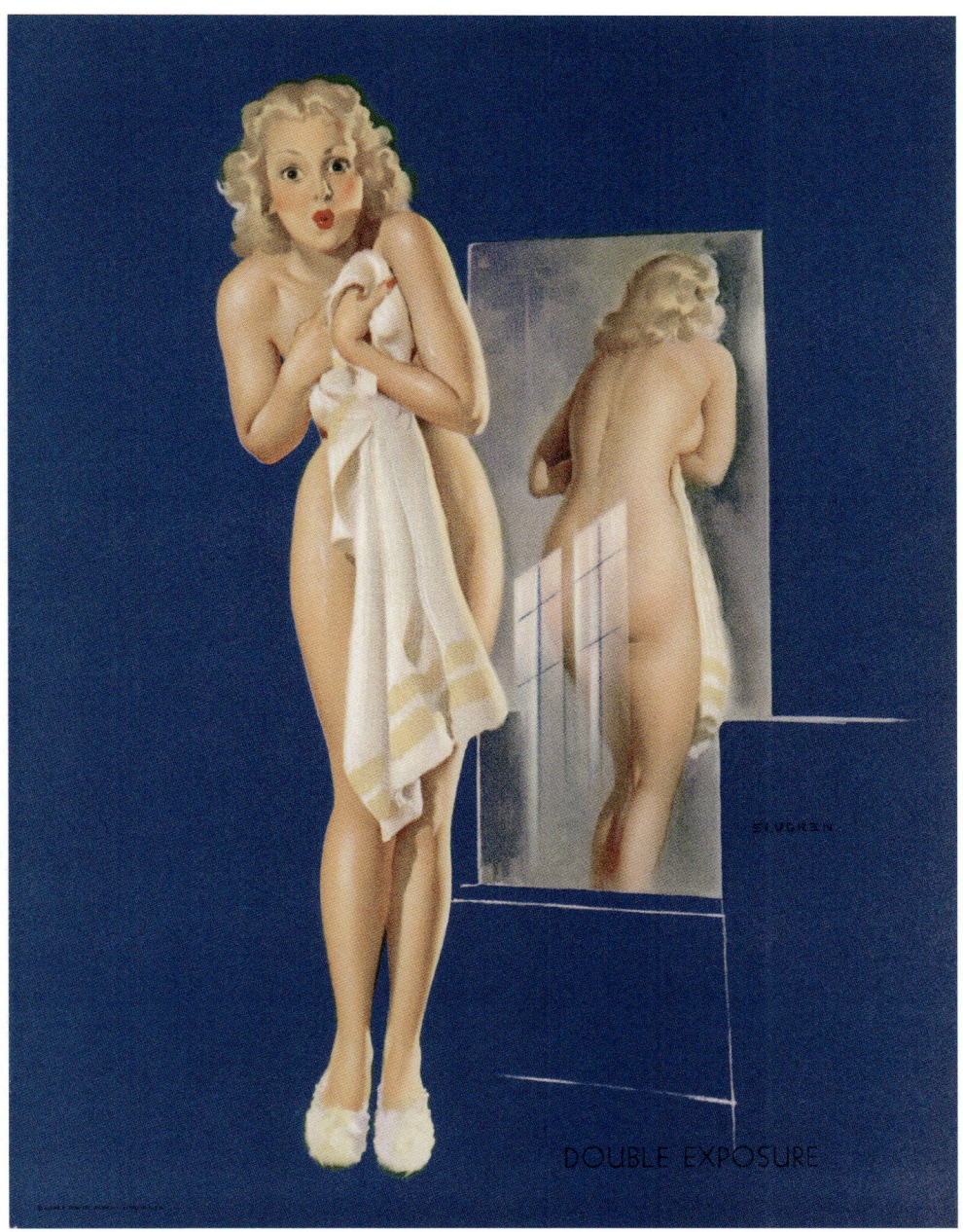

DOUBLE EXPOSURE

Opposite: A Pleasing Discovery, 1942, on a Louis F. Dow calendar. Elvgren produced one nude calender a year for Louis F. Dow from 1940 through 1944. The first three, two seen here, were all bathroom themed. All the originals, including this elegant beauty, were subsequently overpainted.

Above: Double Exposure, 1940, as a calender lithograph for Louis F. Dow.

GILLETTE "GIL" ELVGREN

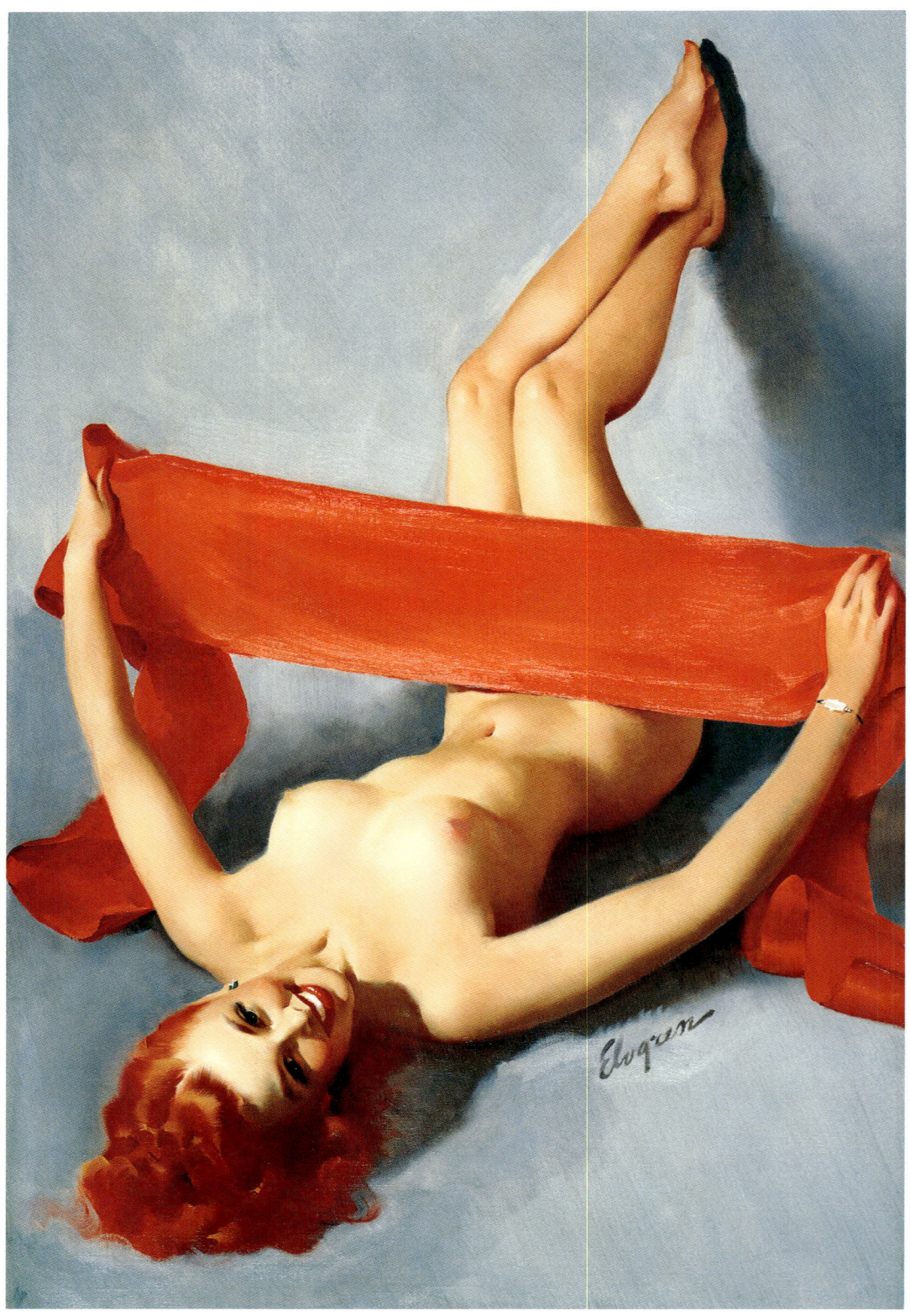

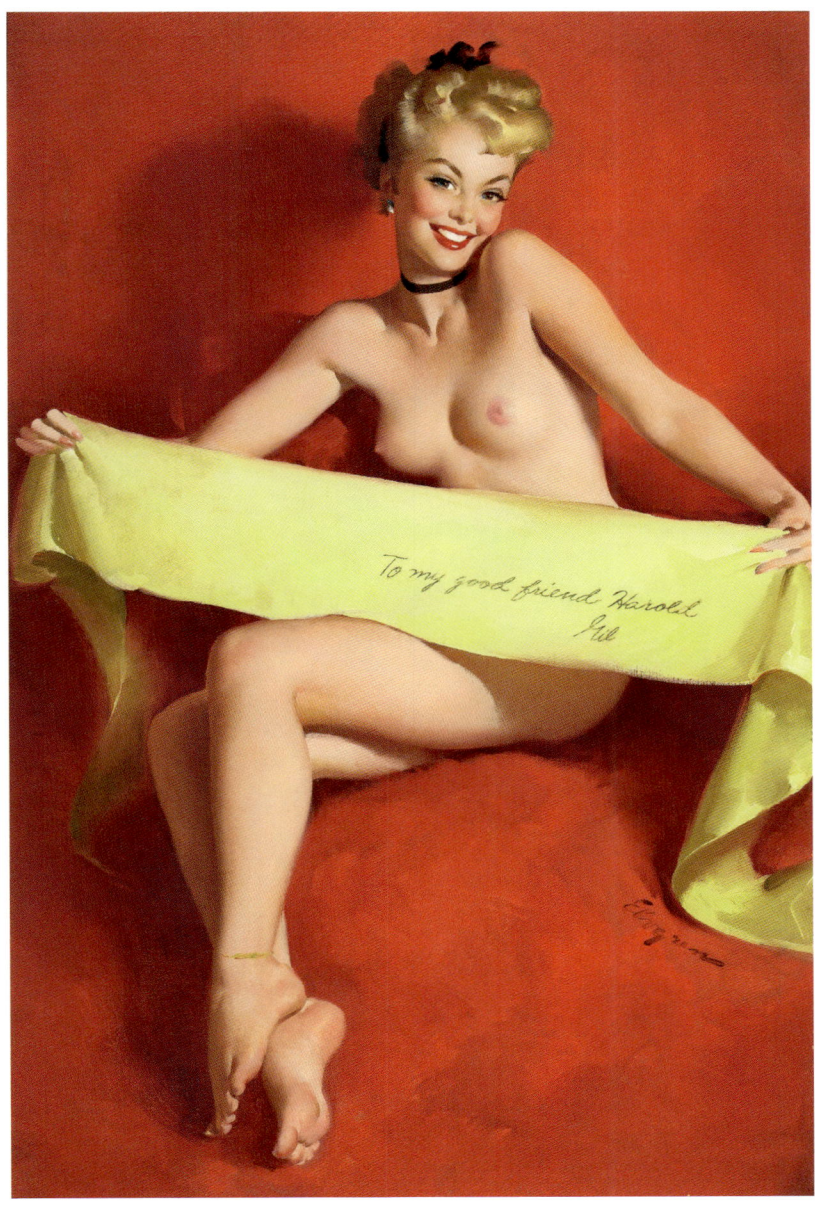

Opposite: Cee Bee (To Have), oil on canvas, 1951, is the painting for the second deck of the Fascinating Figures playing card boxed set. Elvgren painted a wisp of a bra on the model and then seemed to change his mind and left it unfinished. These two Cee Bee paintings were proportioned for playing cards, and thus are narrower than all of Elvgren's calendar pin-ups. 27 x 18 inches.

Above: Cee Bee (To Hold), oil on canvas, 1951, for the two-deck Fascinating Figures playing card set released in 1953. The inscription is to film star Harold Lloyd, who befriended Elvgren around 1950 and introduced him to his hobby of 3D color photography, often of nude pin-ups. 27 x 18 inches.

GILLETTE "GIL" ELVGREN

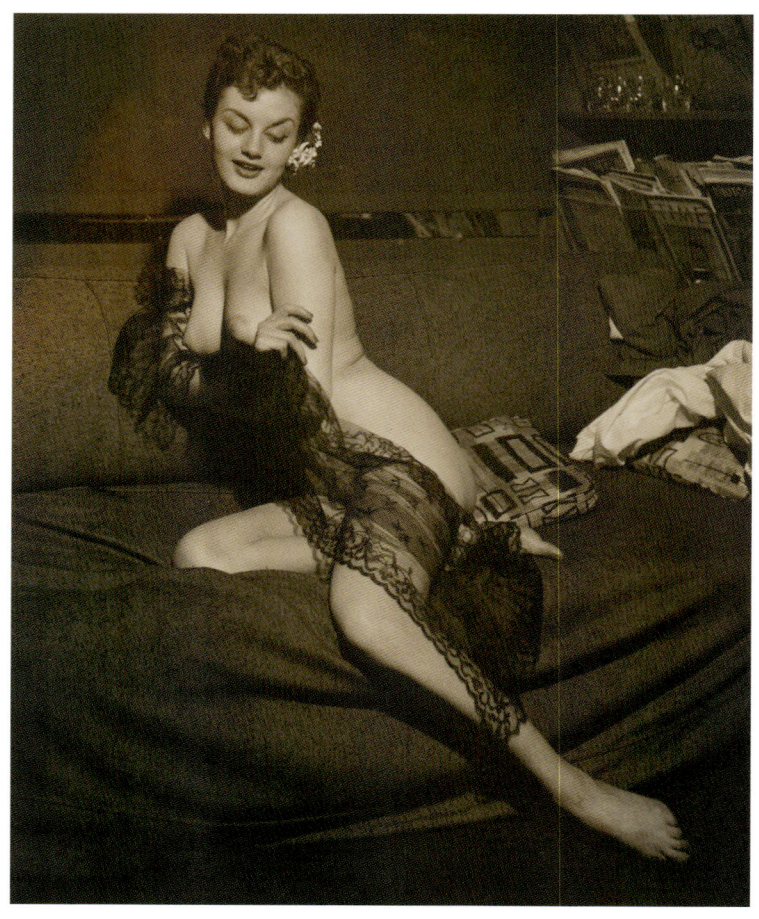

Above: The preliminary photograph for *Fascination* shows how closely Elvgren followed his model photos—and how much he improved on nature by whittling the model's waist and lifting her breasts.

Opposite: Fascination, oil on canvas, 1952, for a 1954 Brown & Bigelow calendar. 30 x 24 inches.

THE ART OF PIN-UP

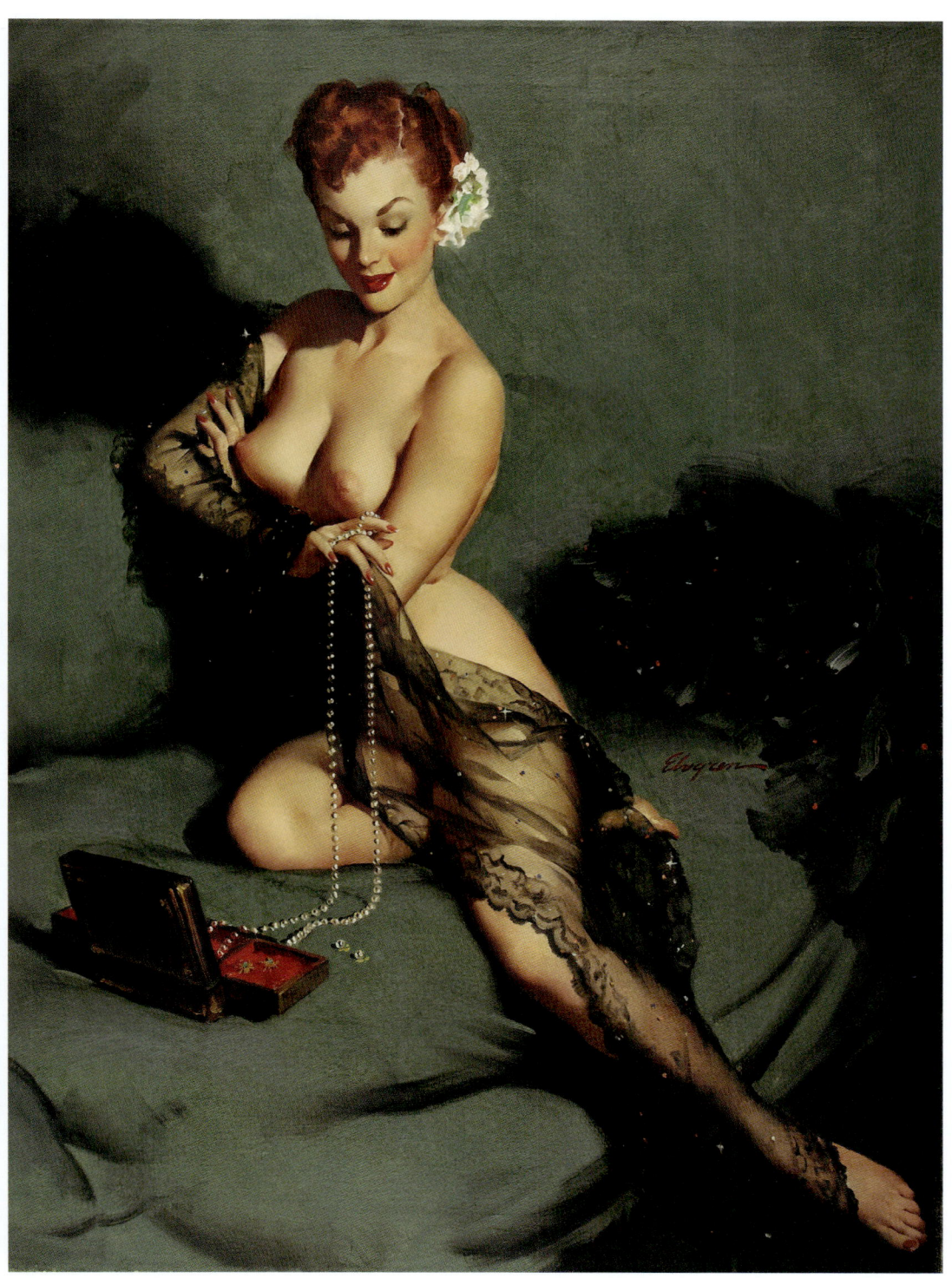

GILLETTE "GIL" ELVGREN

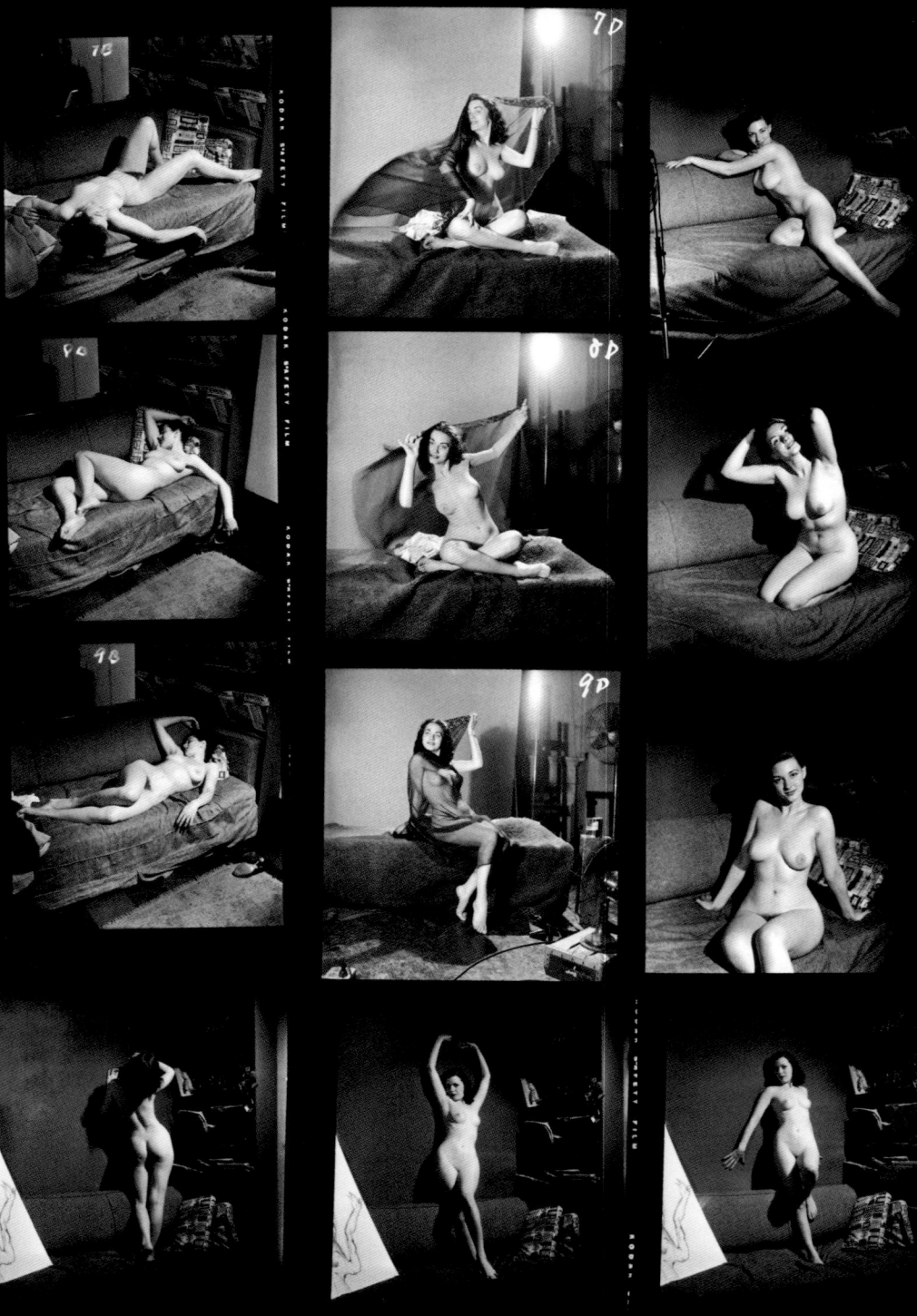

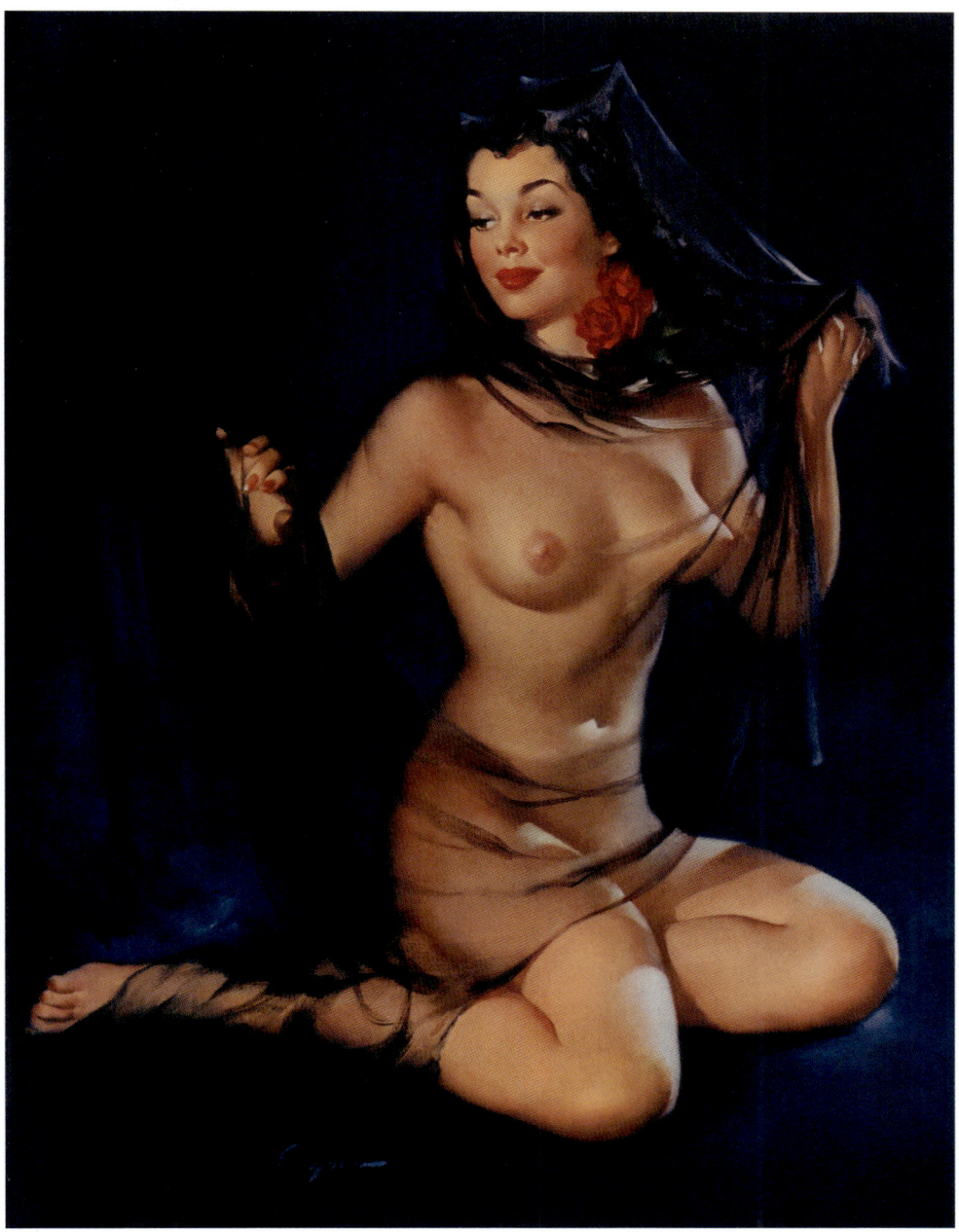

Opposite: Left to right, Elvgren photographic proof sheets for an unknown painting, circa 1955; for *Elegance*, 1950, in which a Spanish señorita is clothed in only a sheer black veil; and for *Bewitching*, 1955. The pose used for *Bewitching* is seen at top.

Above: Elegance, 1950, on a 1952 Brown & Bigelow sample calendar. Calendar measures 46 x 22 inches.

GILLETTE "GIL" ELVGREN

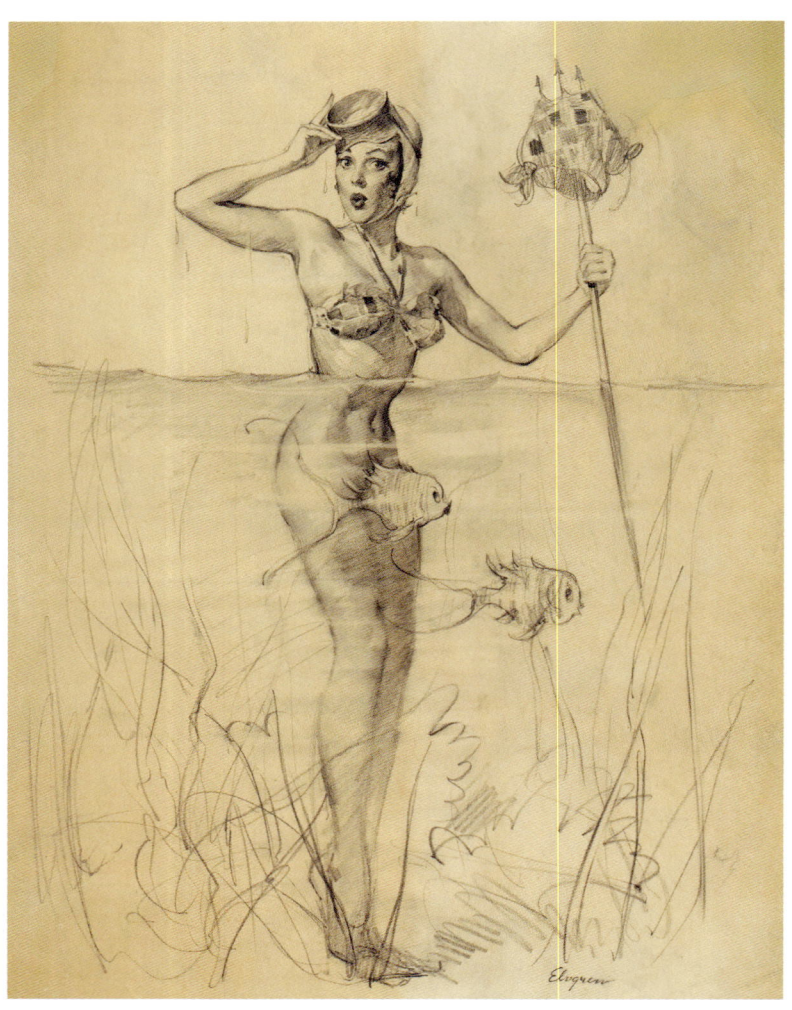

Above: A pencil on vellum preparatory sketch for *Surprising Catch*, 1951, shows Elvgren first considered having the fish serve as foil for the forbidden zone, but realized having them ogle her predicament was funnier. 22.75 x 17.75 inches.

Opposite: Surprising Catch, oil on canvas, 1952, for a 1954 Brown & Bigelow calendar. 30 x 24 inches.

THE ART OF PIN-UP

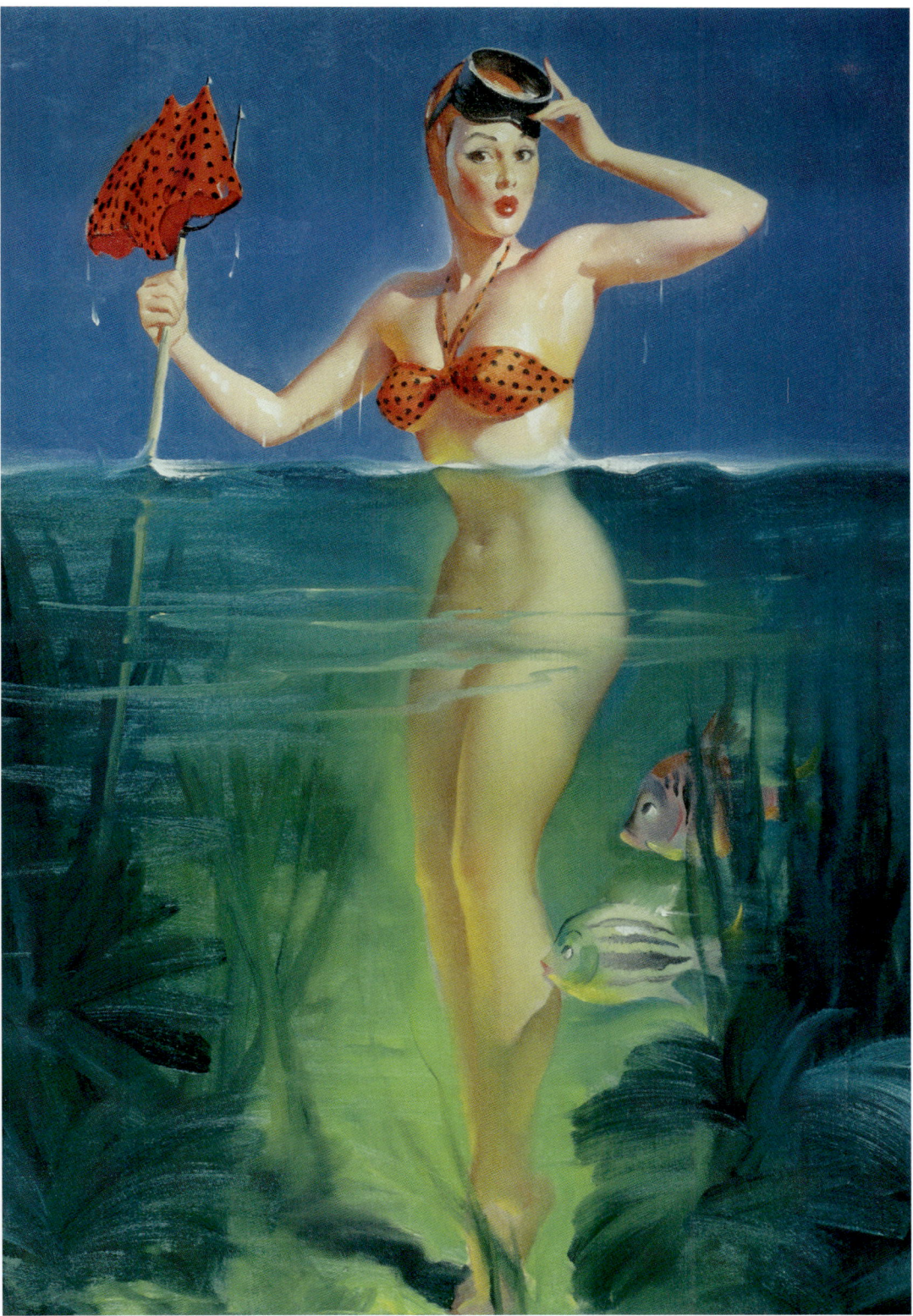

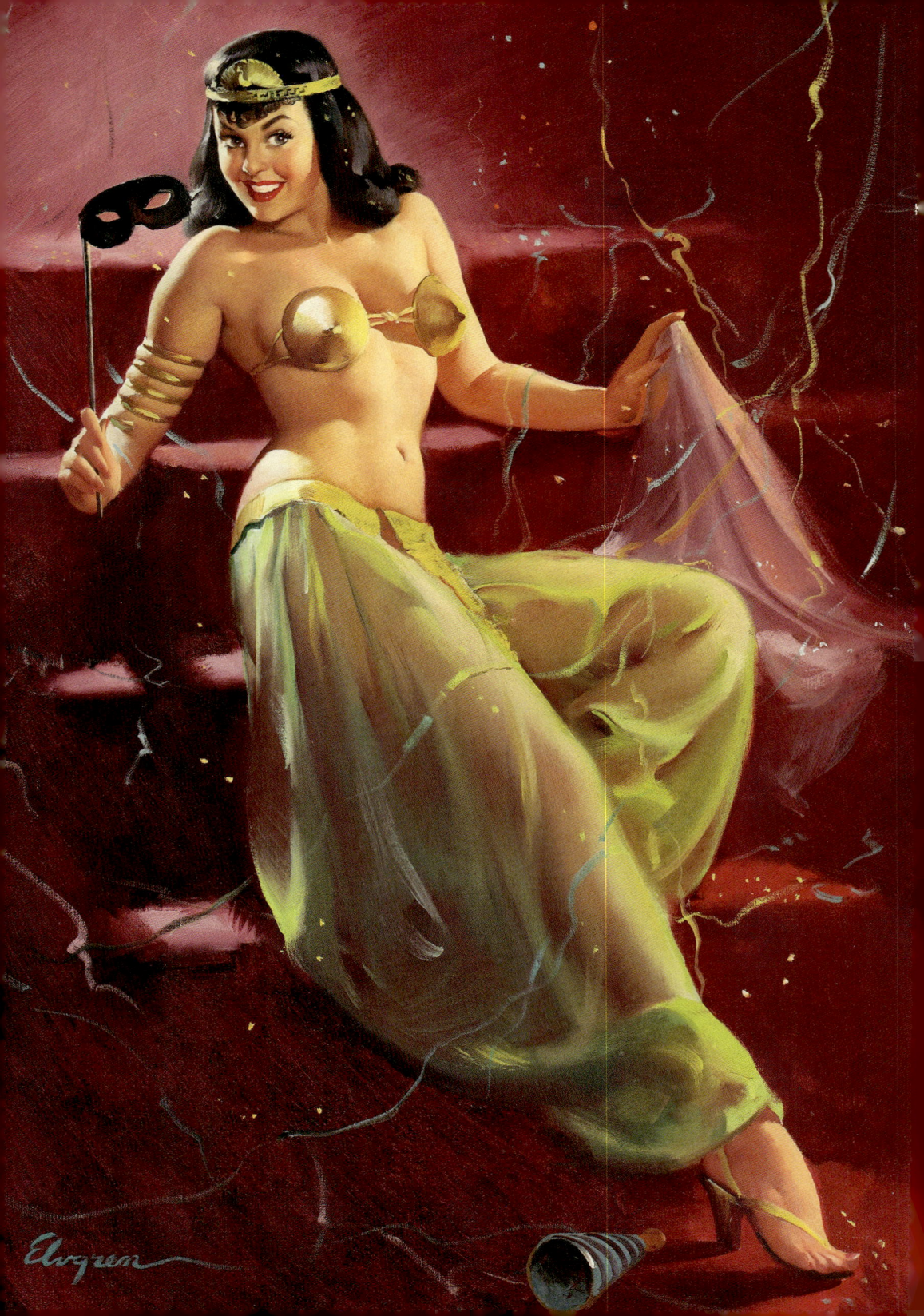

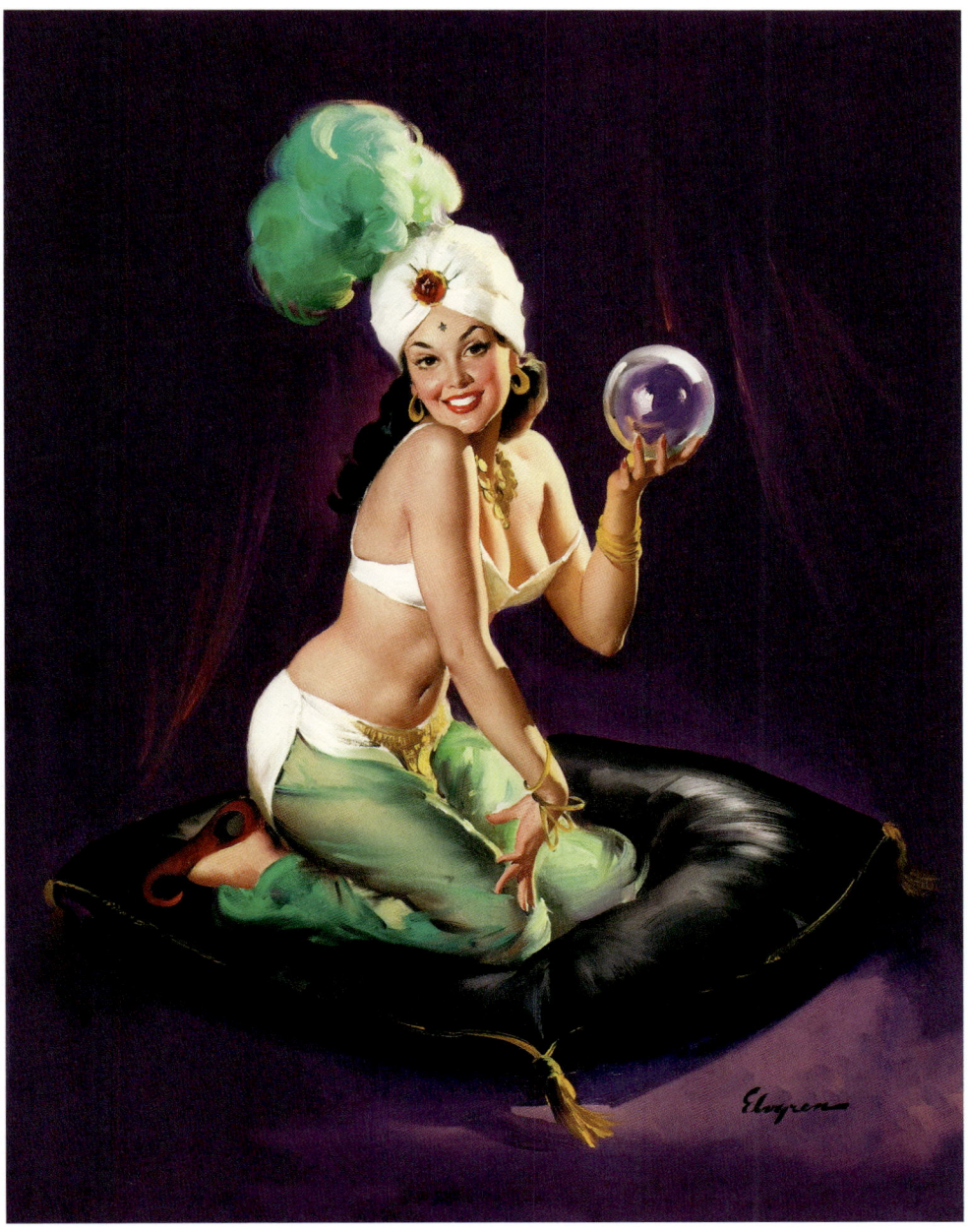

Opposite: Did You Recognize Me by My Voice?,
oil on canvas, 1948, for a 1950 Brown & Bigelow calendar.
30 x 24 inches.

Above: I'm a Happy Medium, also known as *And Find
Out How the Future Looks*, oil on canvas, 1947, for a 1949
Brown & Bigelow calendar. 30 x 24 inches.

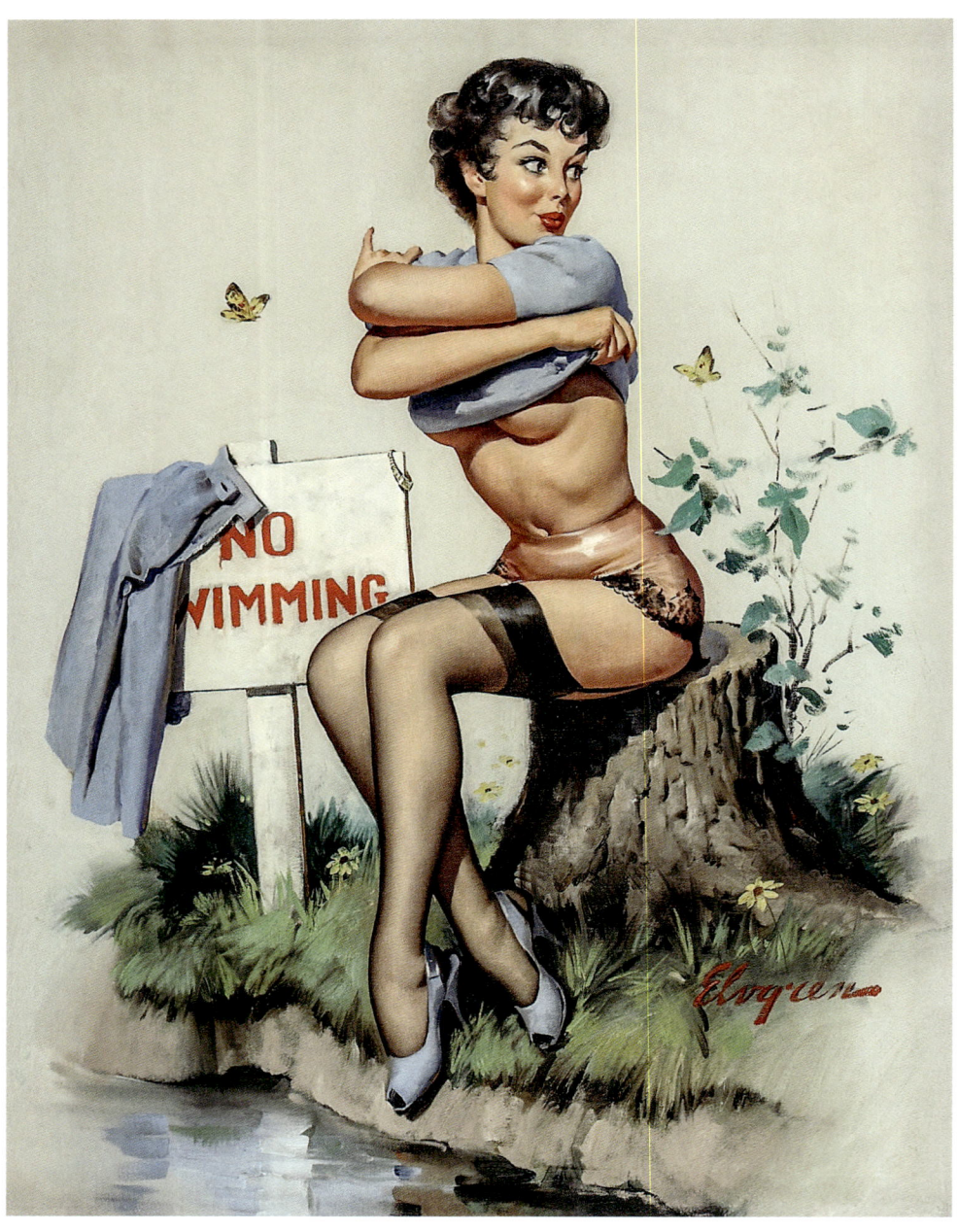

Above: Taking a Chance, also known as *No Bikini a Toll*, oil on canvas, 1962, for a 1964 Brown & Bigelow calendar. 30 x 24 inches.

Opposite: Bare Essentials, oil on canvas, 1957, for a 1959 Brown & Bigelow calendar. 30 x 24 inches.

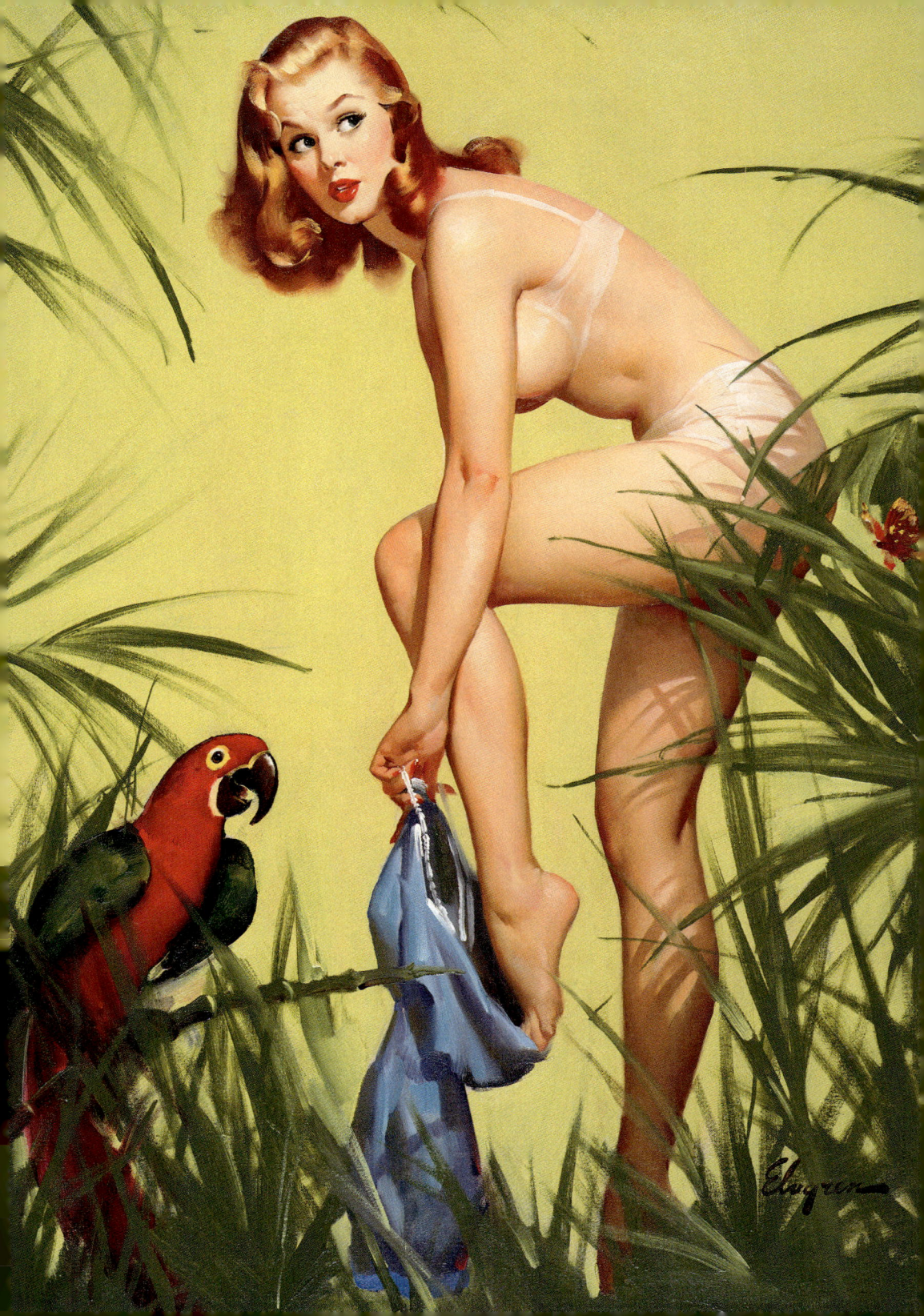

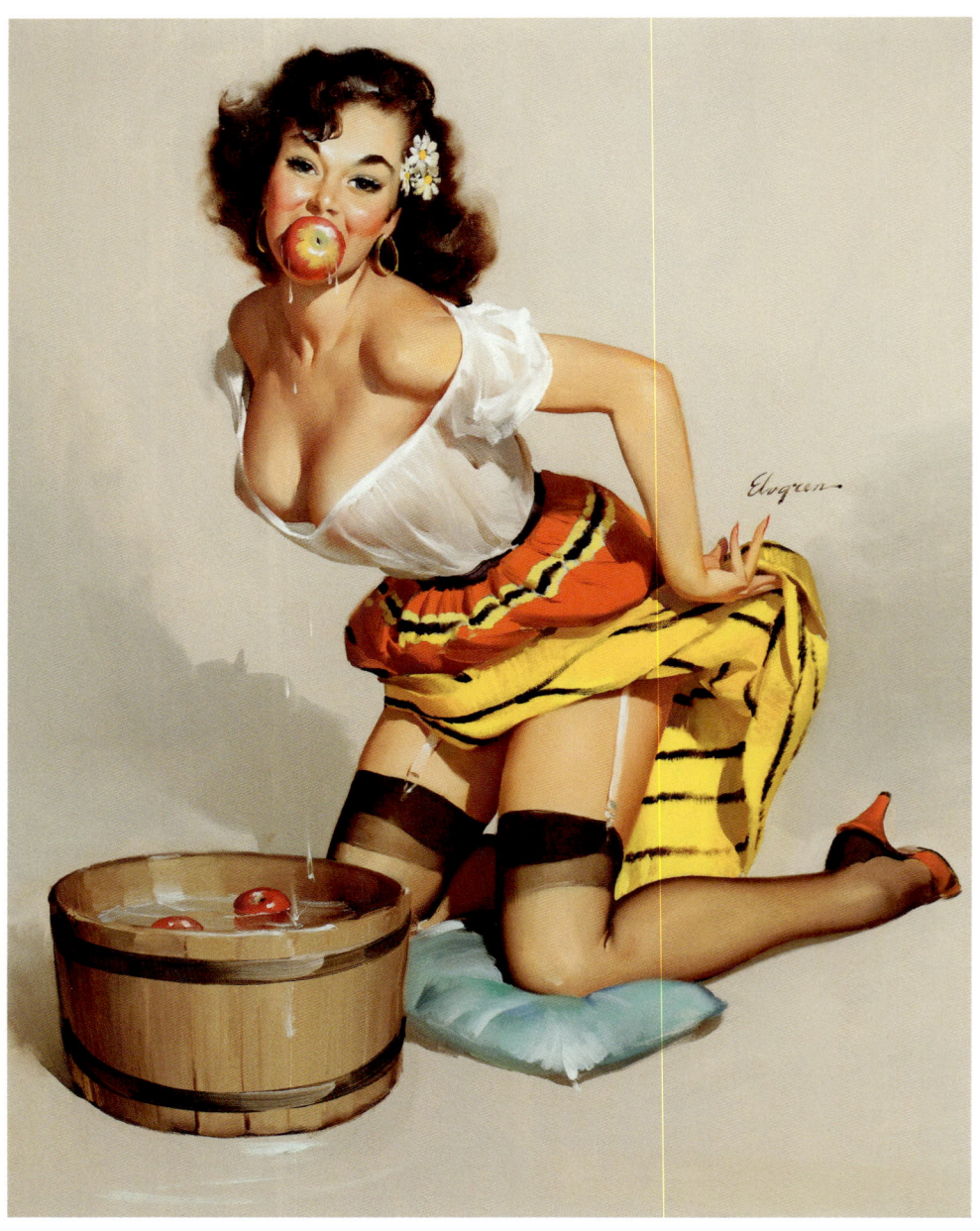

Above: The Winner!, also known as *A Fair Catch!*,
oil on canvas, 1957, for a 1959 Brown & Bigelow calendar.
30 x 24 inches.

Opposite: Neat Trick, oil on canvas, 1953, for a 1955
Brown & Bigelow calendar. 30.5 x 24 inches.

THE ART OF PIN-UP

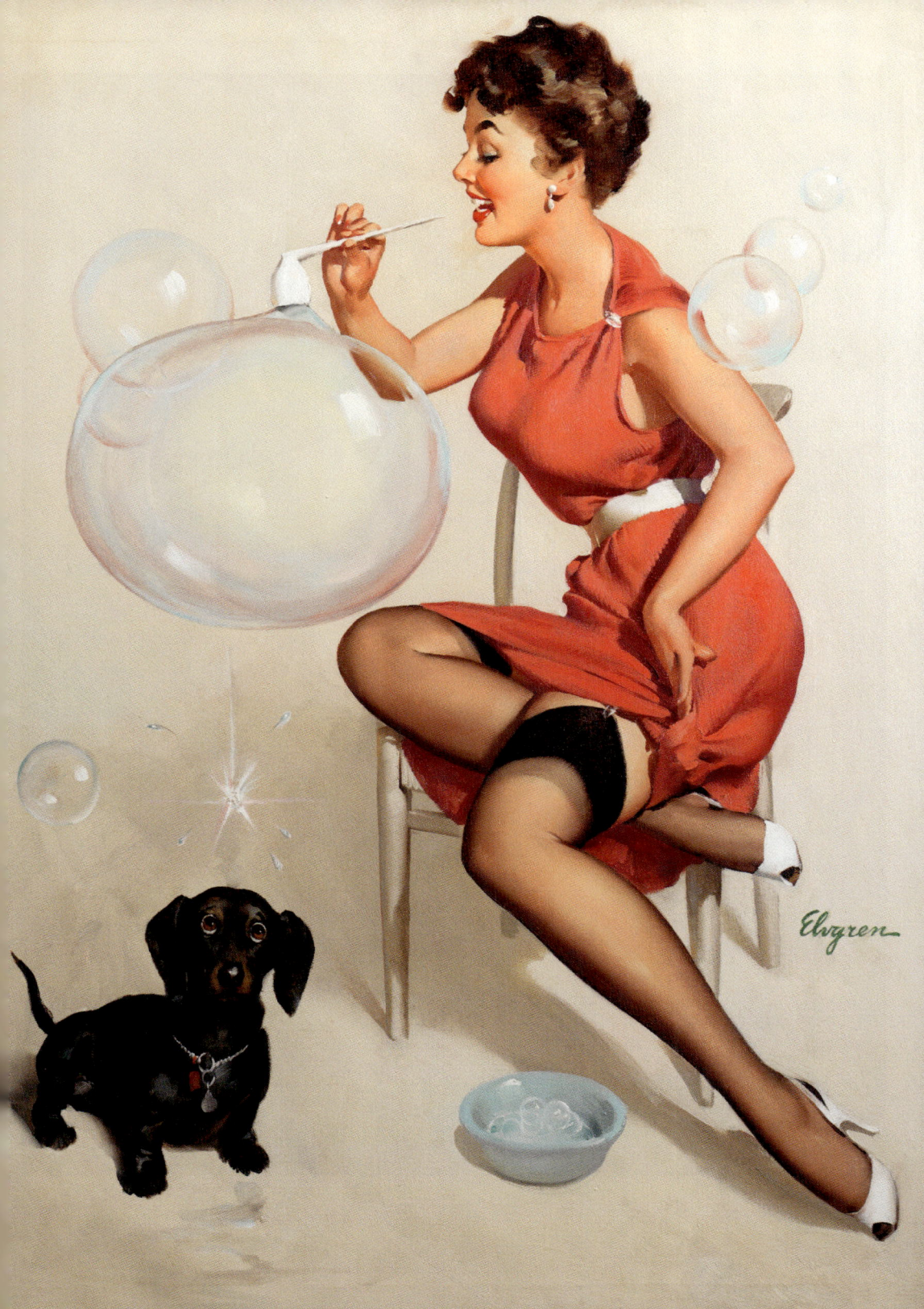

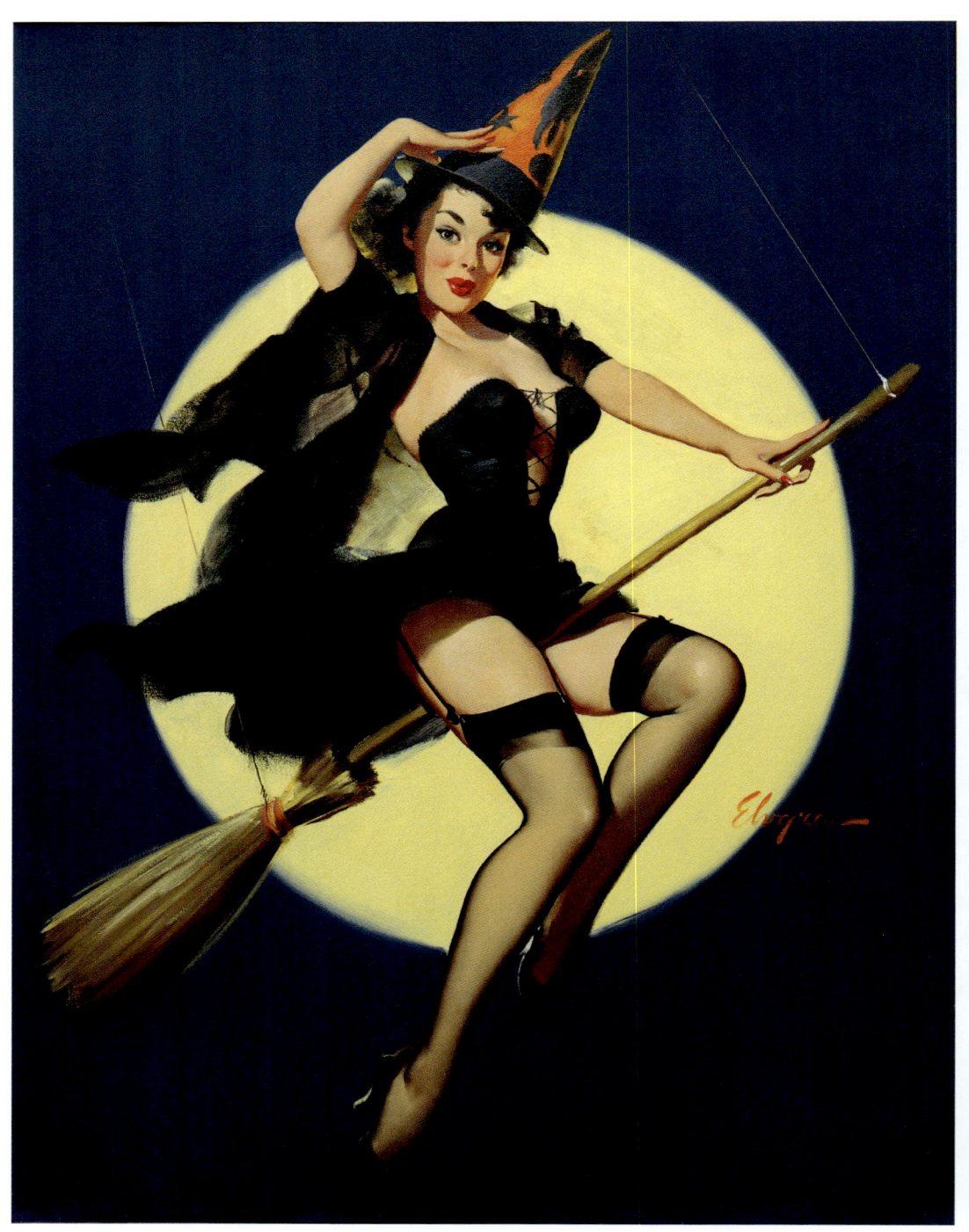

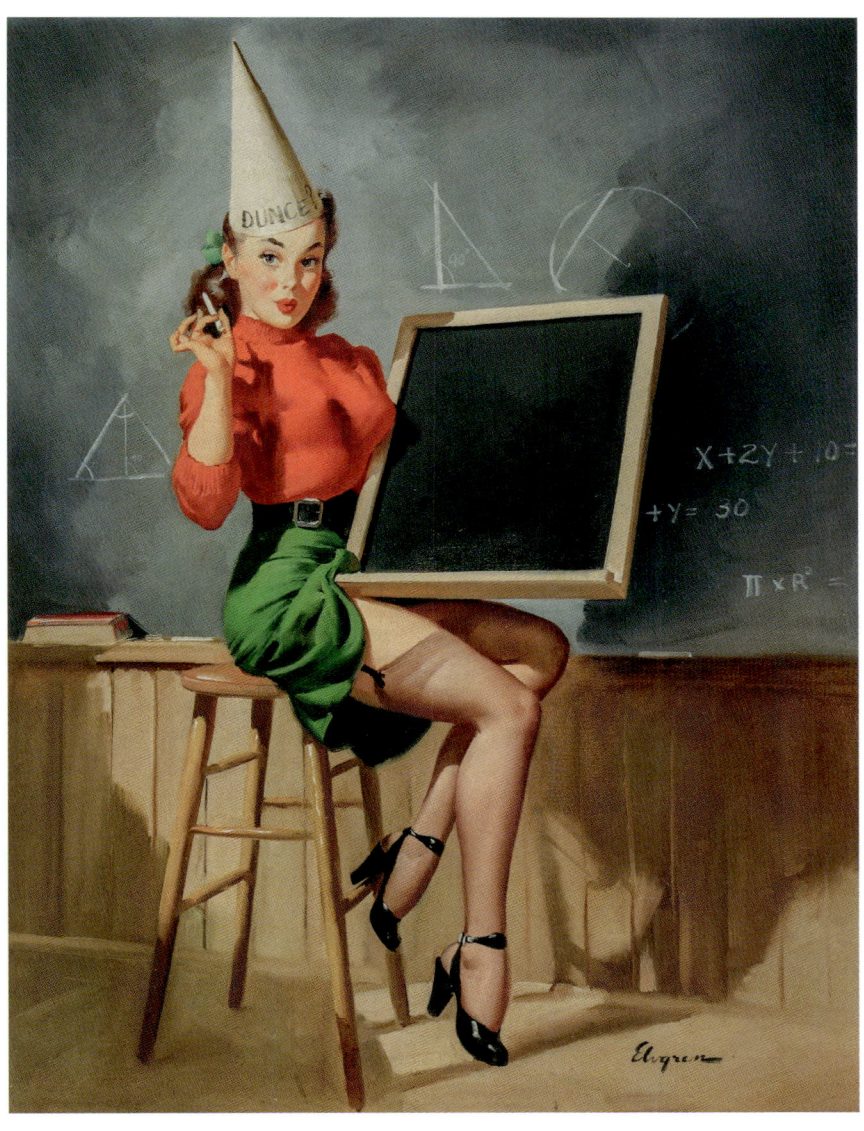

Opposite: Riding High, oil on canvas, 1958, for a 1960 Brown & Bigelow calendar. 30 x 24 inches.

Above: Is This the Right Angle, Professor?, also known as *Dunce?* Oil on canvas, circa 1948, 30 x 24 inches. Courtesy Heritage Auctions.

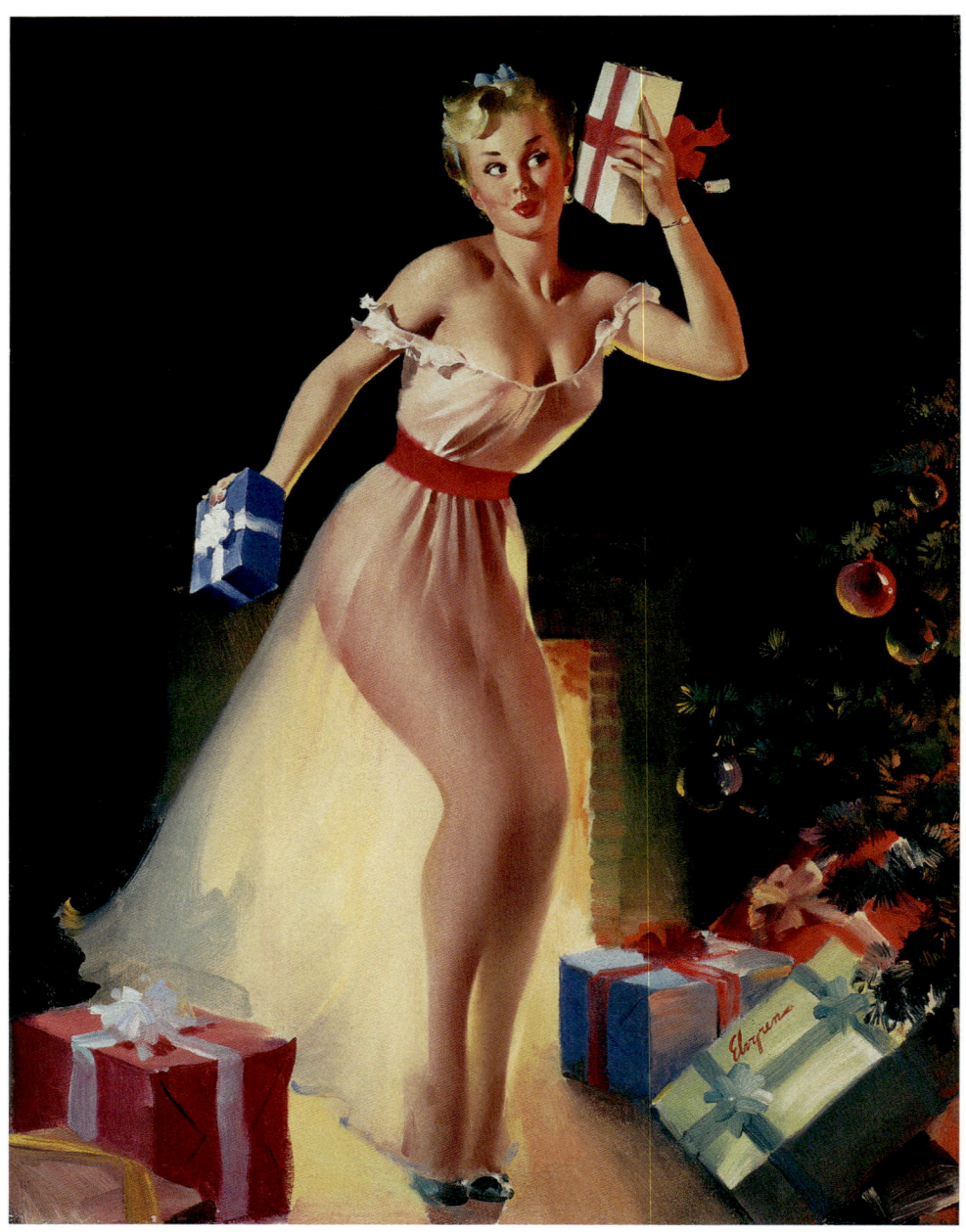

Above: A Christmas Eve, also known as *Waiting for Santa*, oil on canvas, 1954, for a 1956 Brown & Bigelow calendar. 30 x 24 inches.

Opposite: Sheer Delight, also known as *This Soots Me*, oil on canvas, 1948 for a 1950 Brown & Bigelow calendar. 30 x 24 inches.

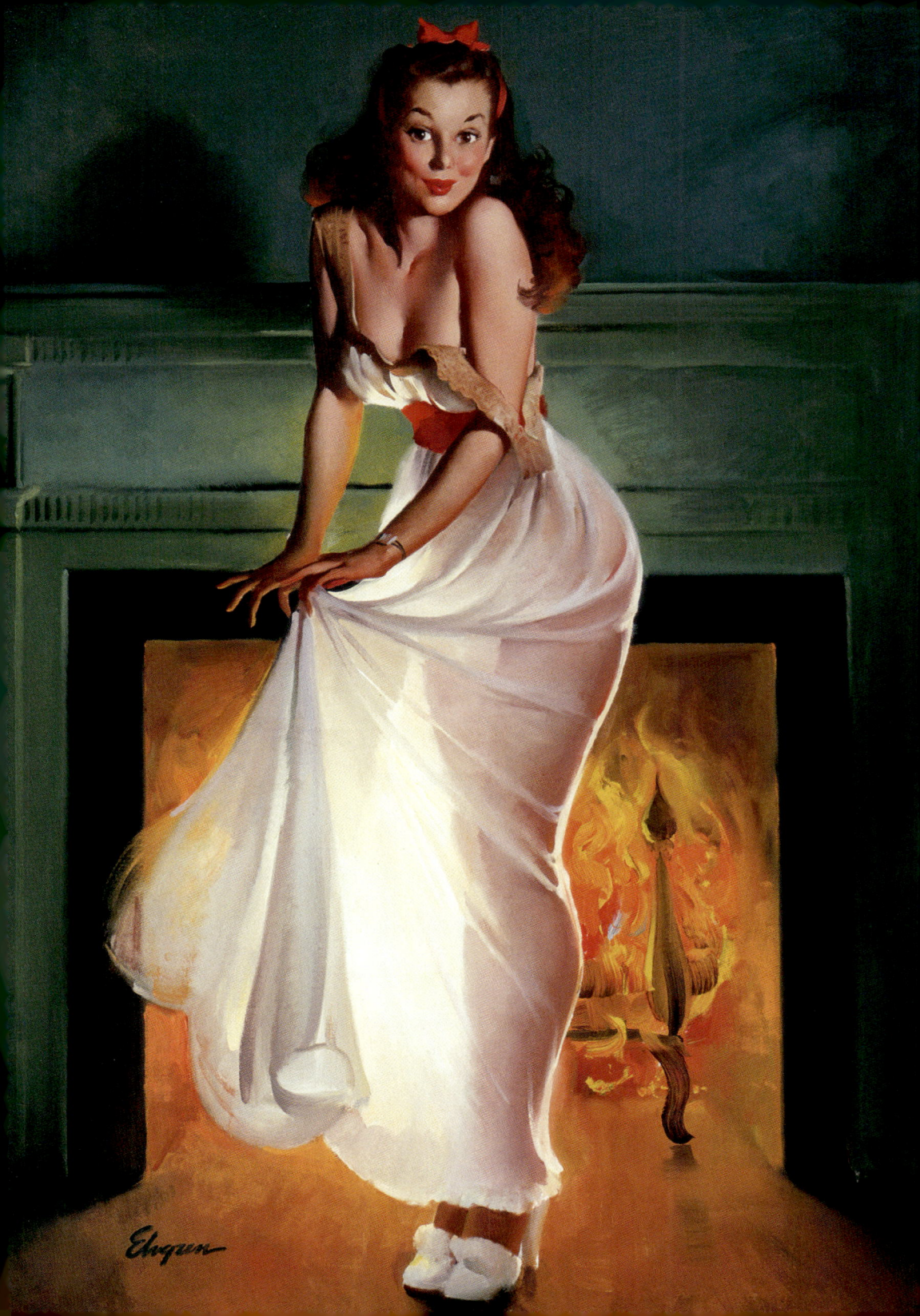

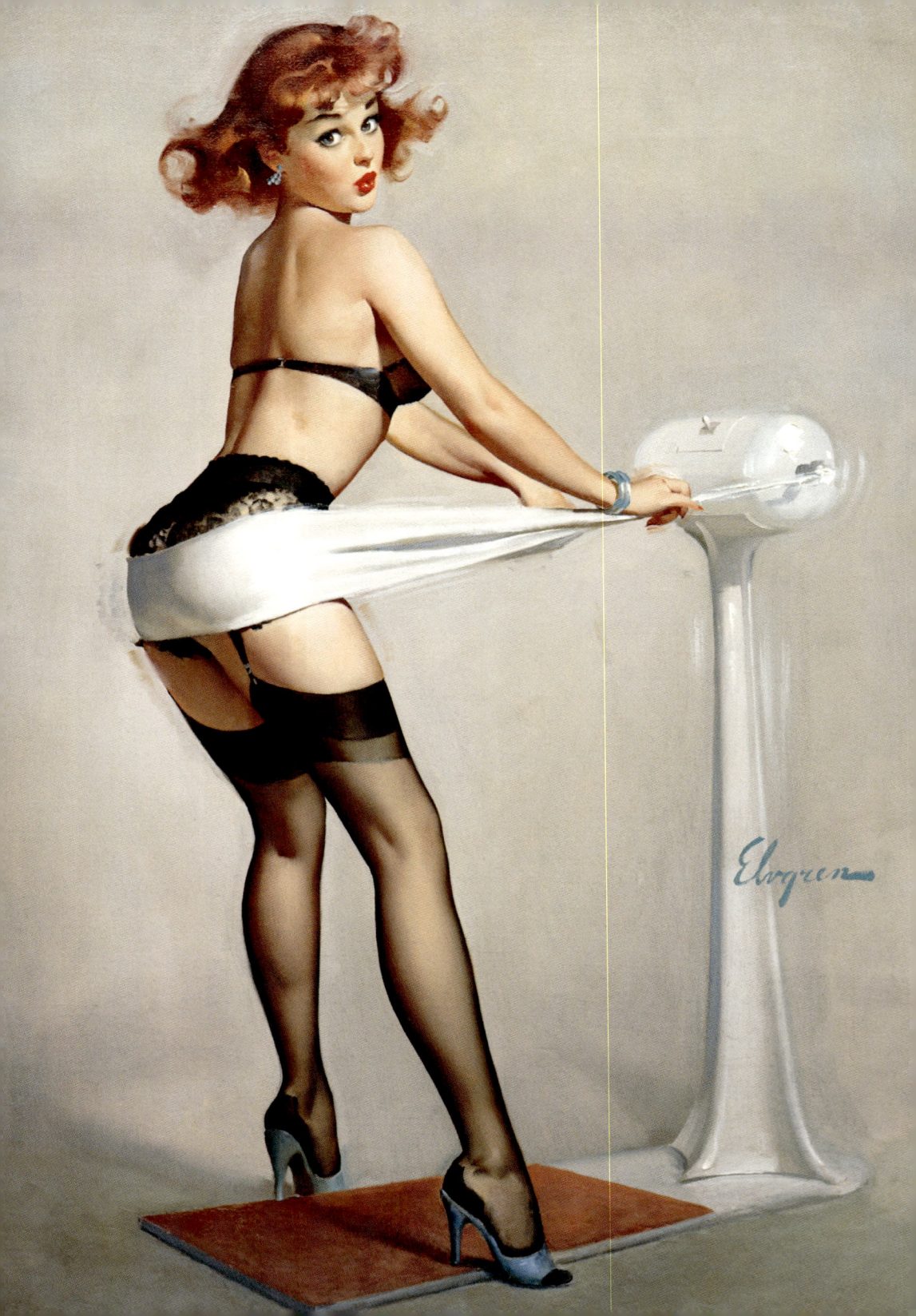

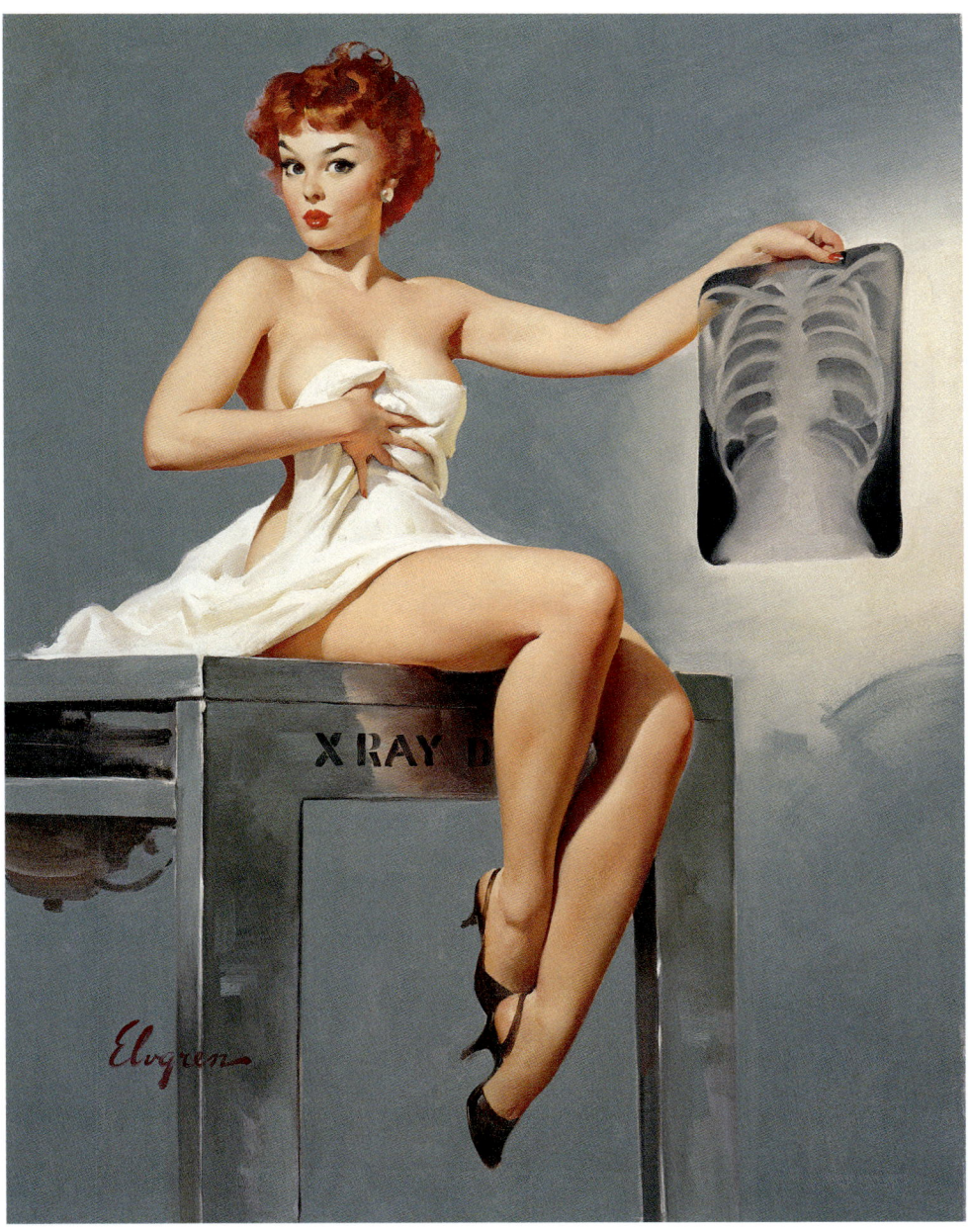

Opposite: Weighty Problem, also known as *Starting at the Bottom*, oil on canvas, 1962, for a 1964 Brown & Bigelow calendar. 30 x 24 inches.

Above: Inside Story, also known as *Over-Exposure*, oil on canvas, 1959, for a 1961 Brown & Bigelow calendar. 30 x 24 inches.

GILLETTE "GIL" ELVGREN

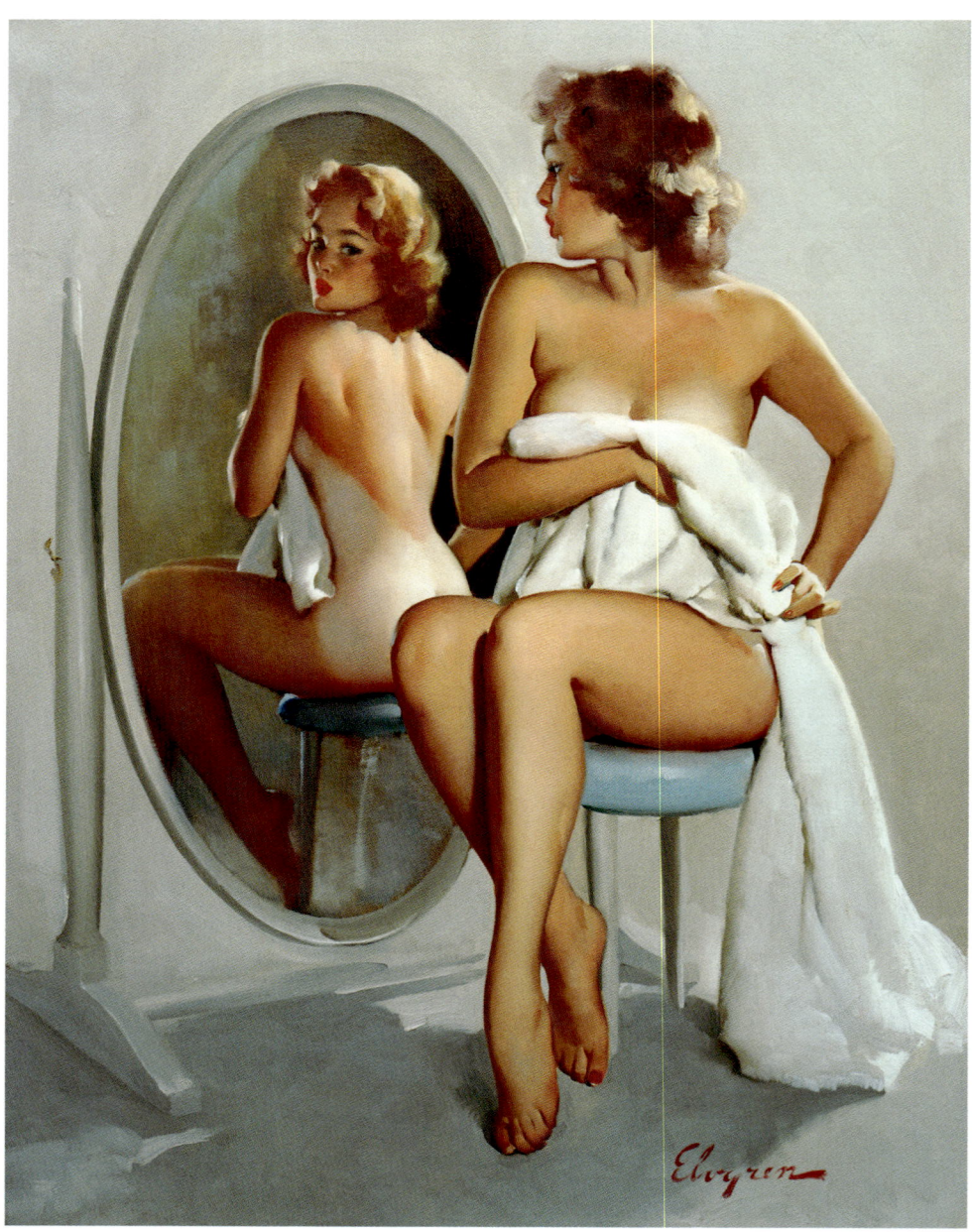

Above: Partial Coverage, also known as *Flashback* and *Sunnyside Up*, oil on canvas, 1960, for a 1962 Brown & Bigelow calendar. 30 x 24 inches.

Opposite: Shell Game, also known as *Shell Shocked*, oil on canvas, 1959, for a 1961 Brown & Bigelow calendar. 30 x 24 inches.

Following left: Something New, oil on canvas, 1957, for a 1959 Brown & Bigelow calendar. 30 x 24 inches. The client's contact information would be printed on the hatbox.

Following right: Lucky Chaps, oil on canvas, 1962, for a 1964 Brown & Bigelow calendar. 30 x 24 inches.

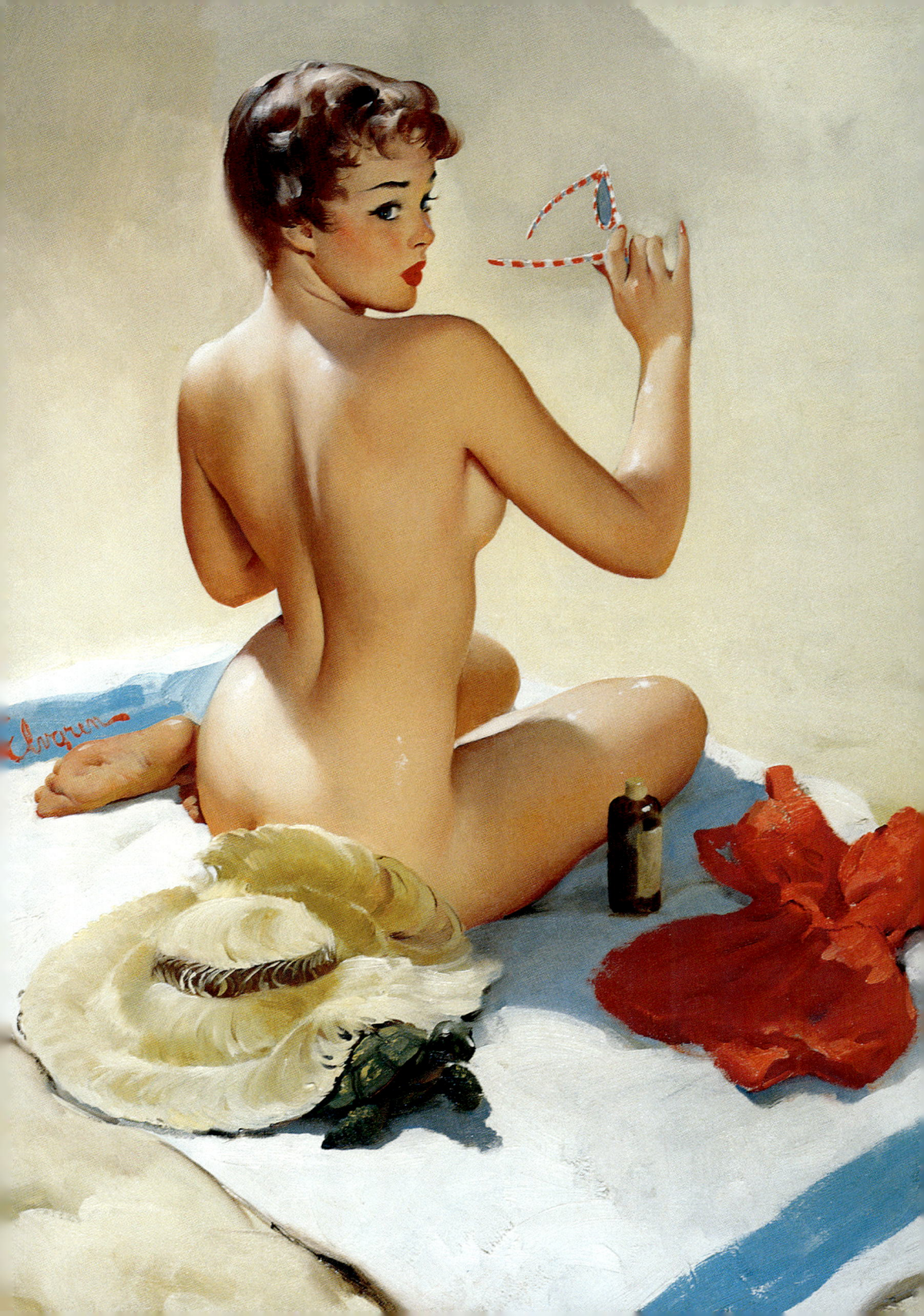

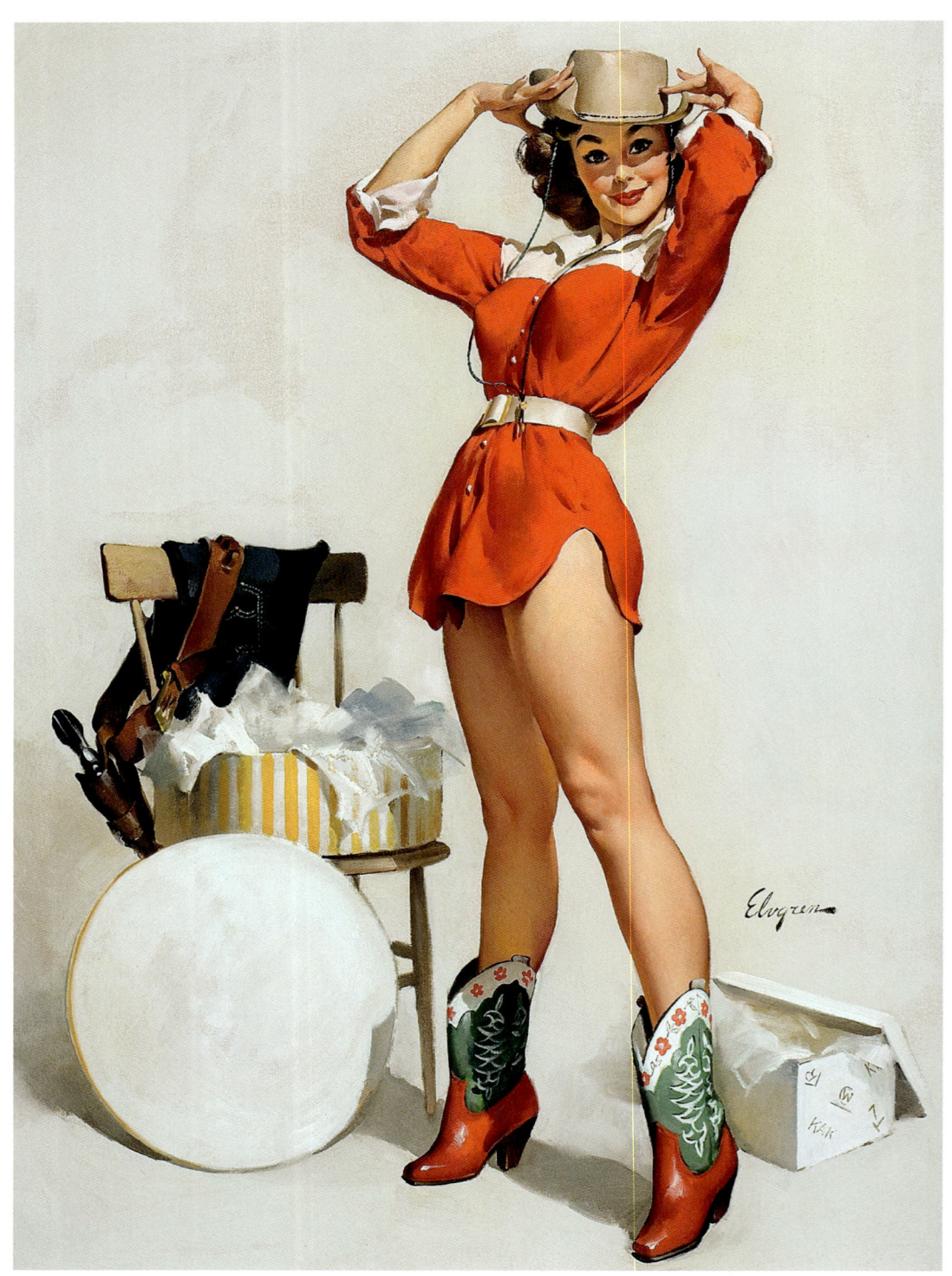

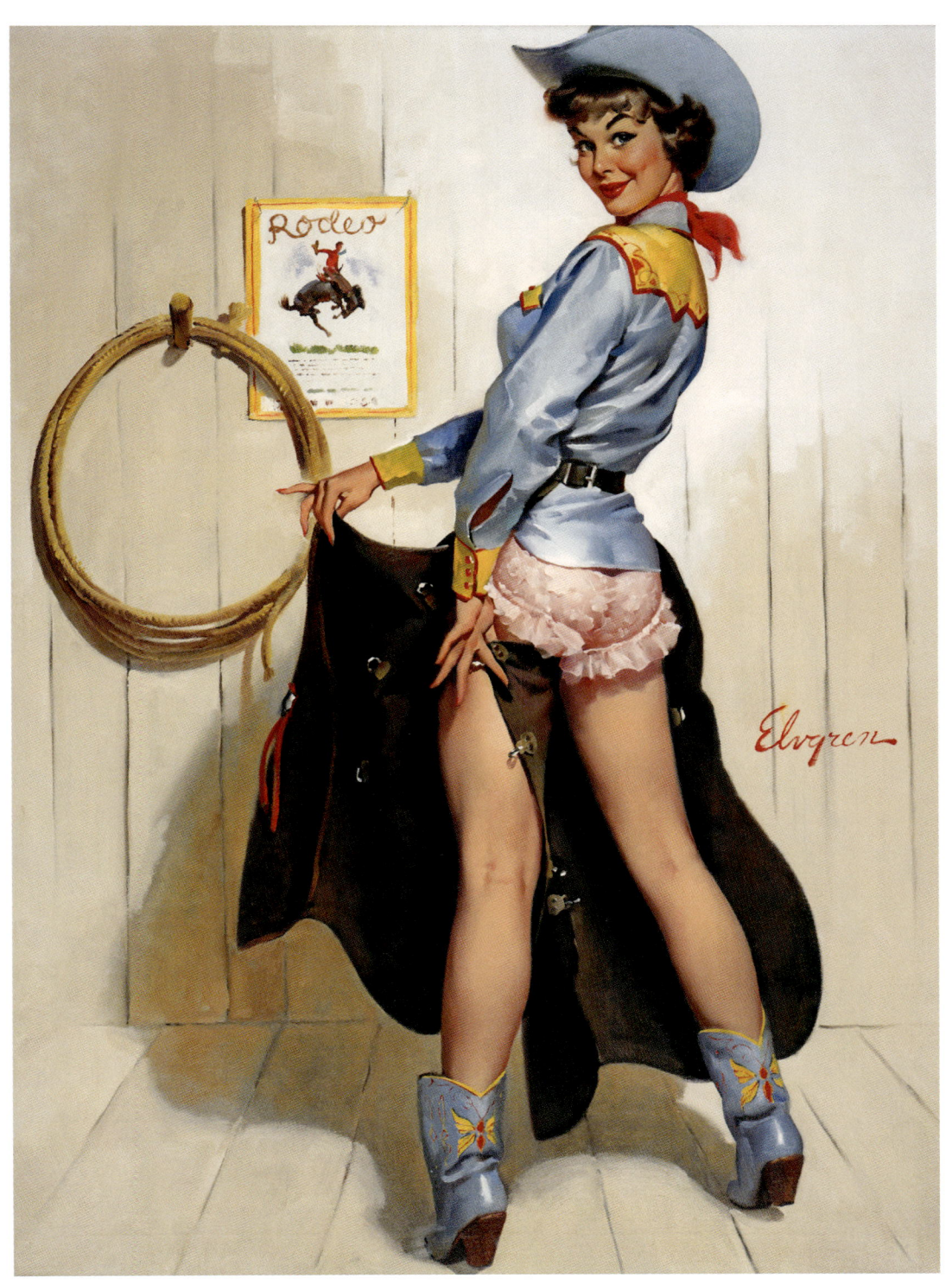

GILLETTE "GIL" ELVGREN

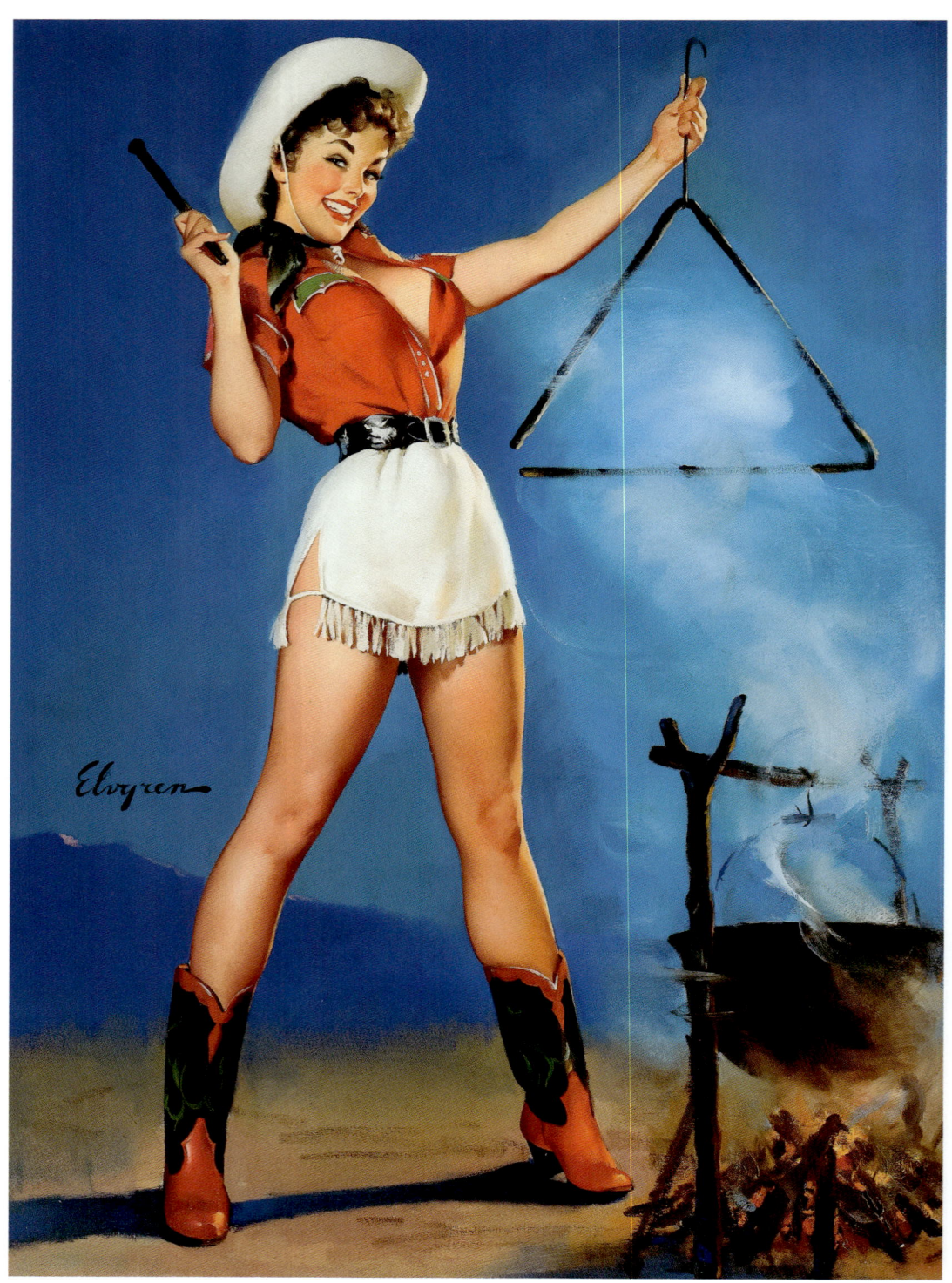

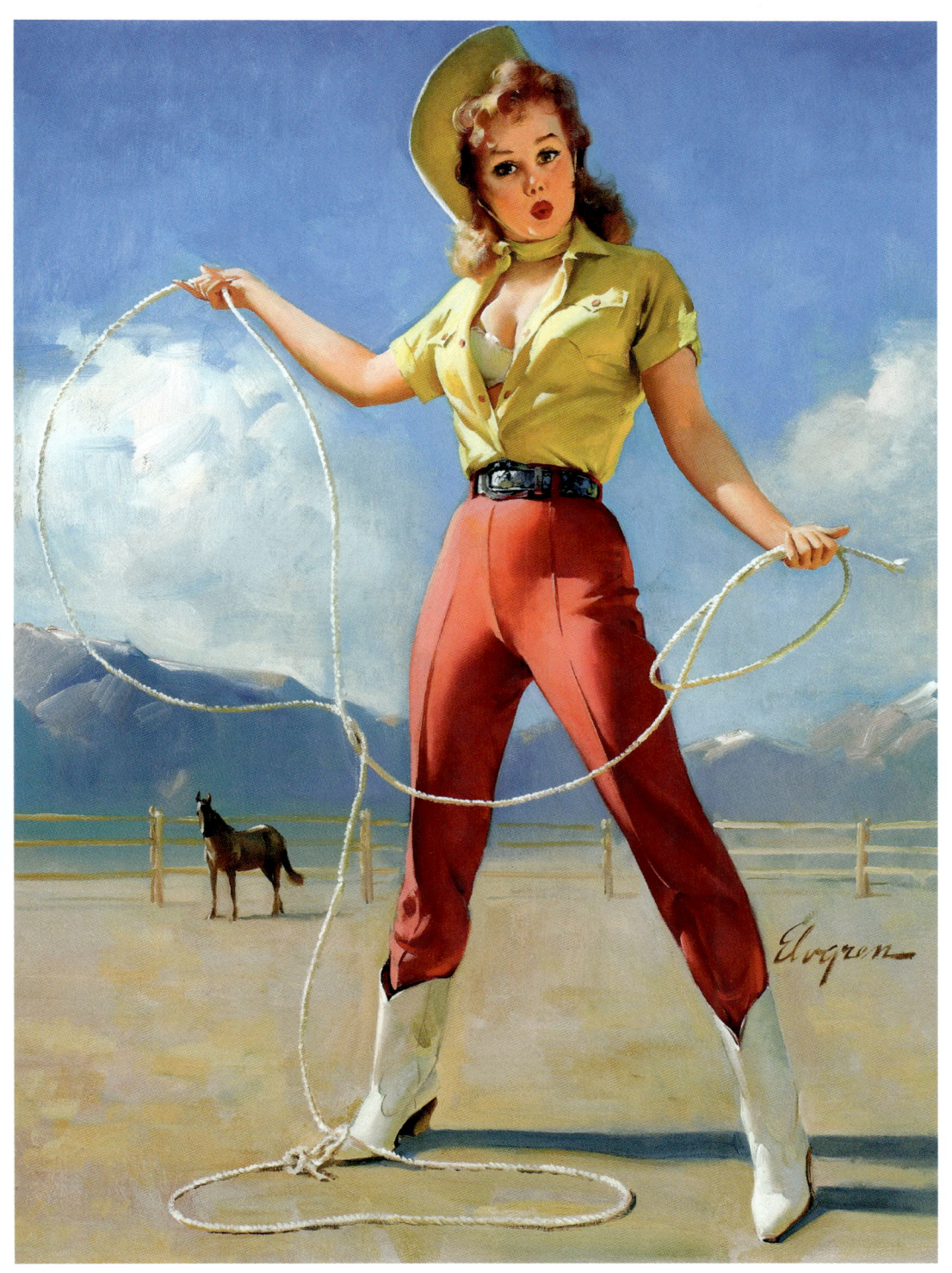

GILLETTE "GIL" ELVGREN

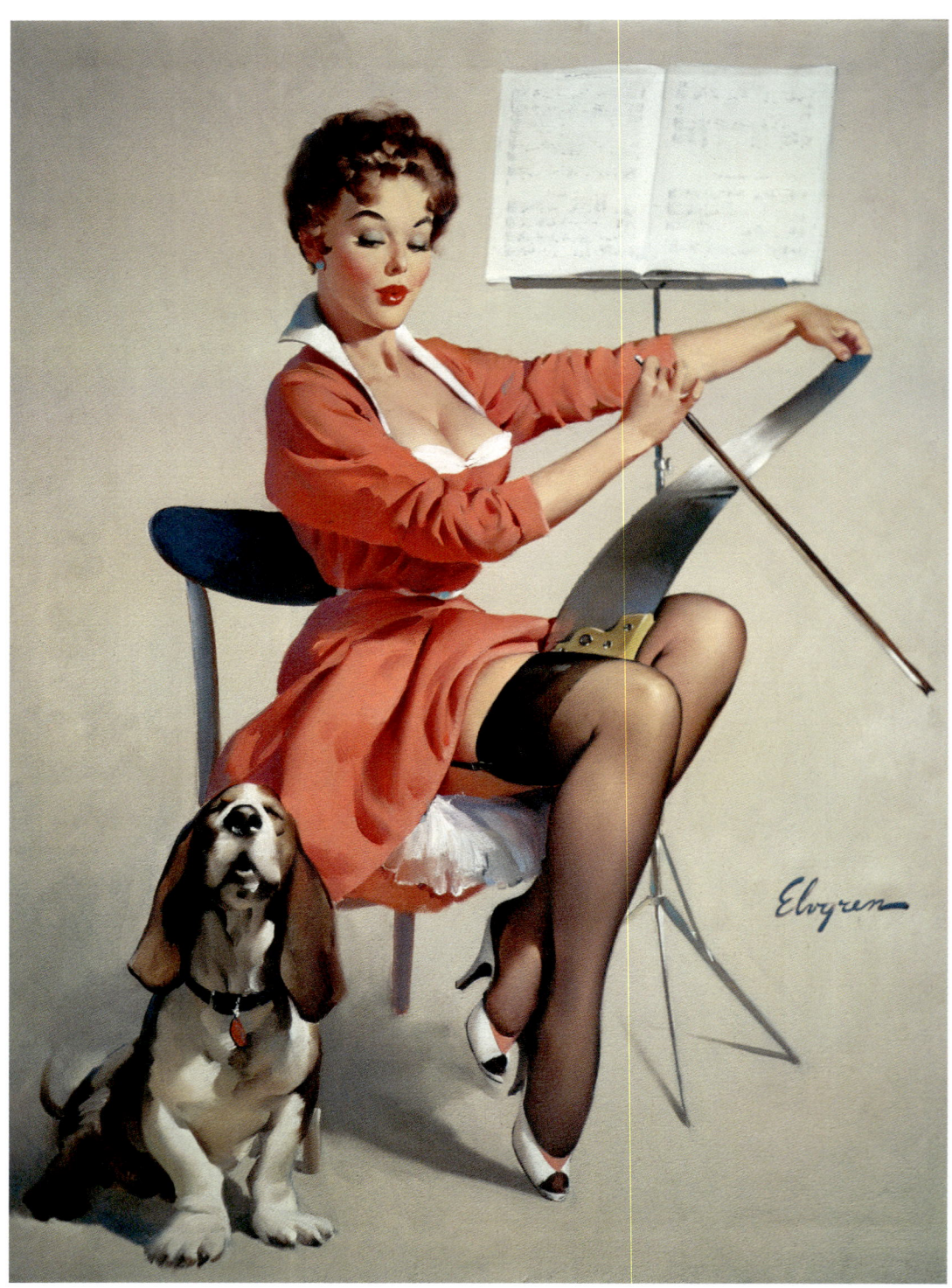

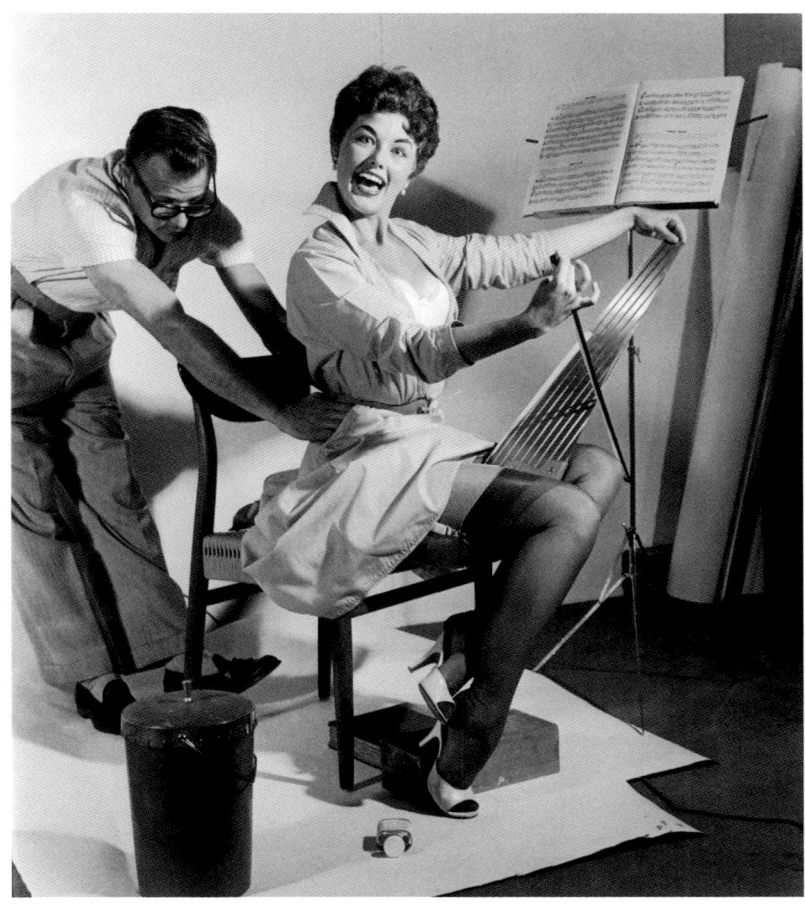

Previous left: Come and Get It, oil on canvas, 1959, for a 1961 Brown & Bigelow calendar. 30 x 24 inches.

Previous right: Perfect Form, oil on canvas, 1968, for a 1970 Brown & Bigelow calendar. 30 x 24 inches.

Opposite: Doggone Good, also known as *Puppy Love,* oil on canvas, 1959, for a 1961 Brown & Bigelow calendar. 30 x 24 inches.

Above: Elvgren assistant Bobby Toombs, a pin-up artist in his own right, positions favorite Elvgren model Myrna Hansen in the photographic study for *Doggone Good,* 1959.

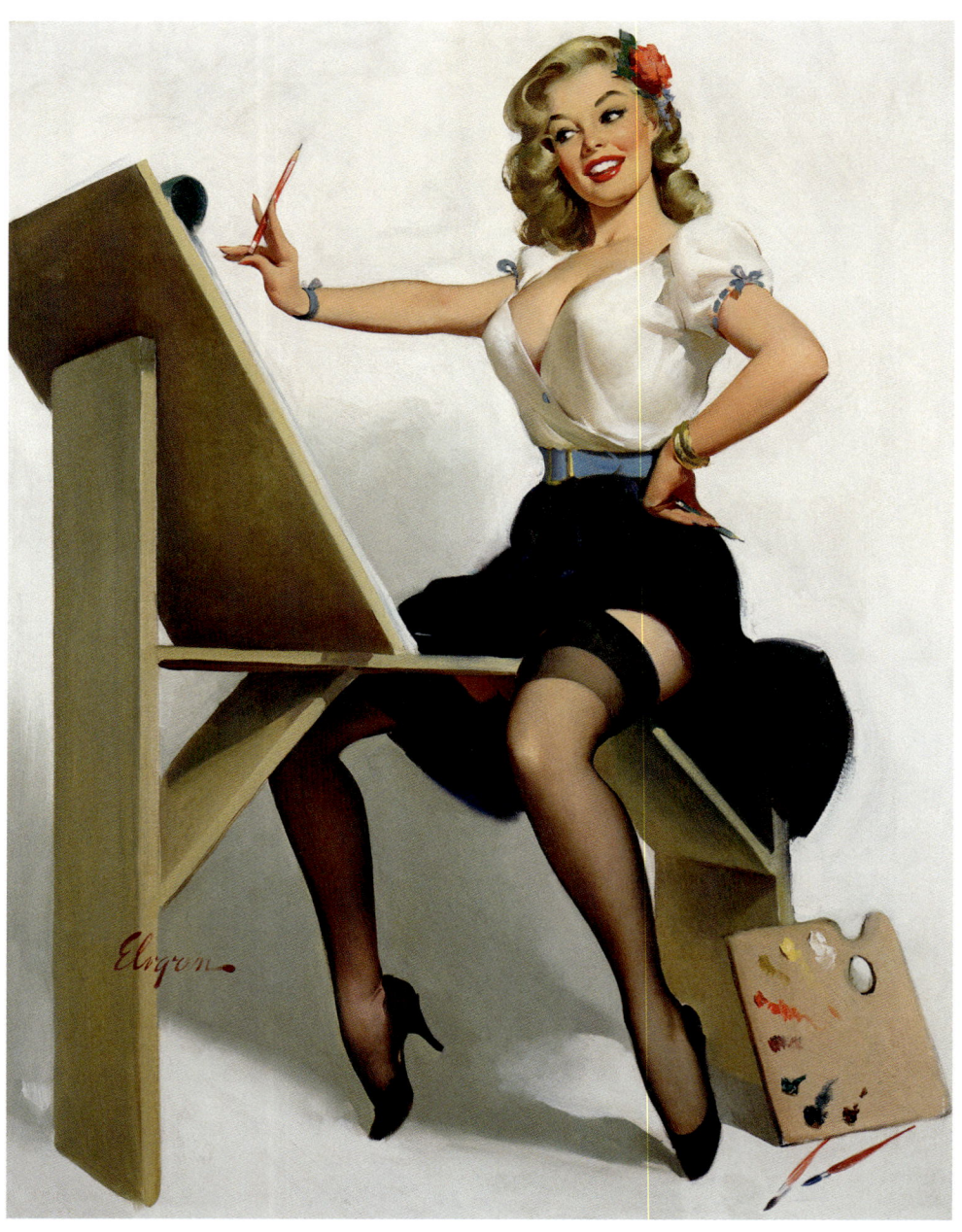

Above: The Right Touch, oil on canvas, 1958, for a 1960
Brown & Bigelow calendar. 30 x 24 inches.

Opposite: Your Choice, also known as *Me???*,
oil on canvas, 1962, for a 1964 Brown & Bigelow calendar.
30 x 24 inches.

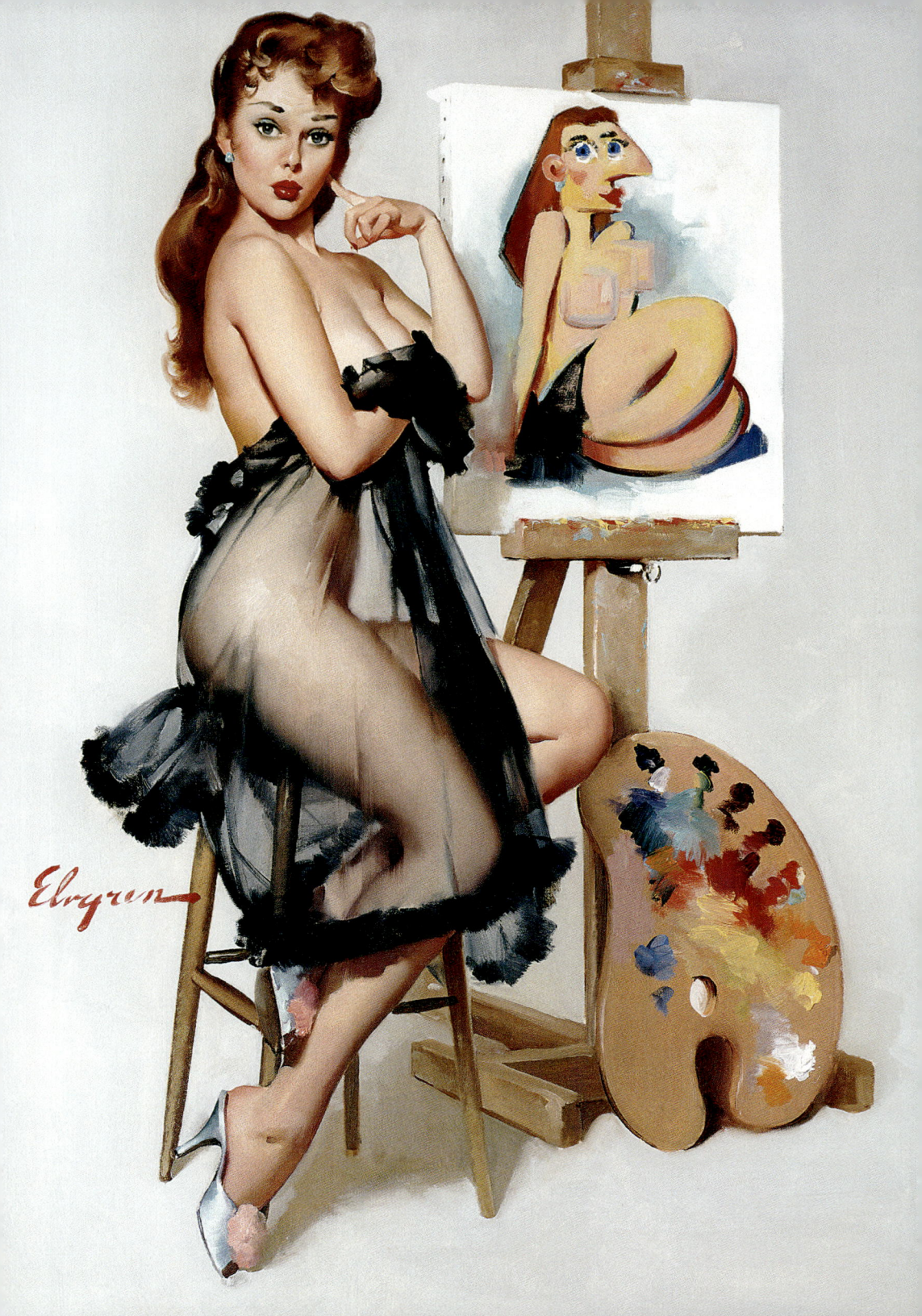

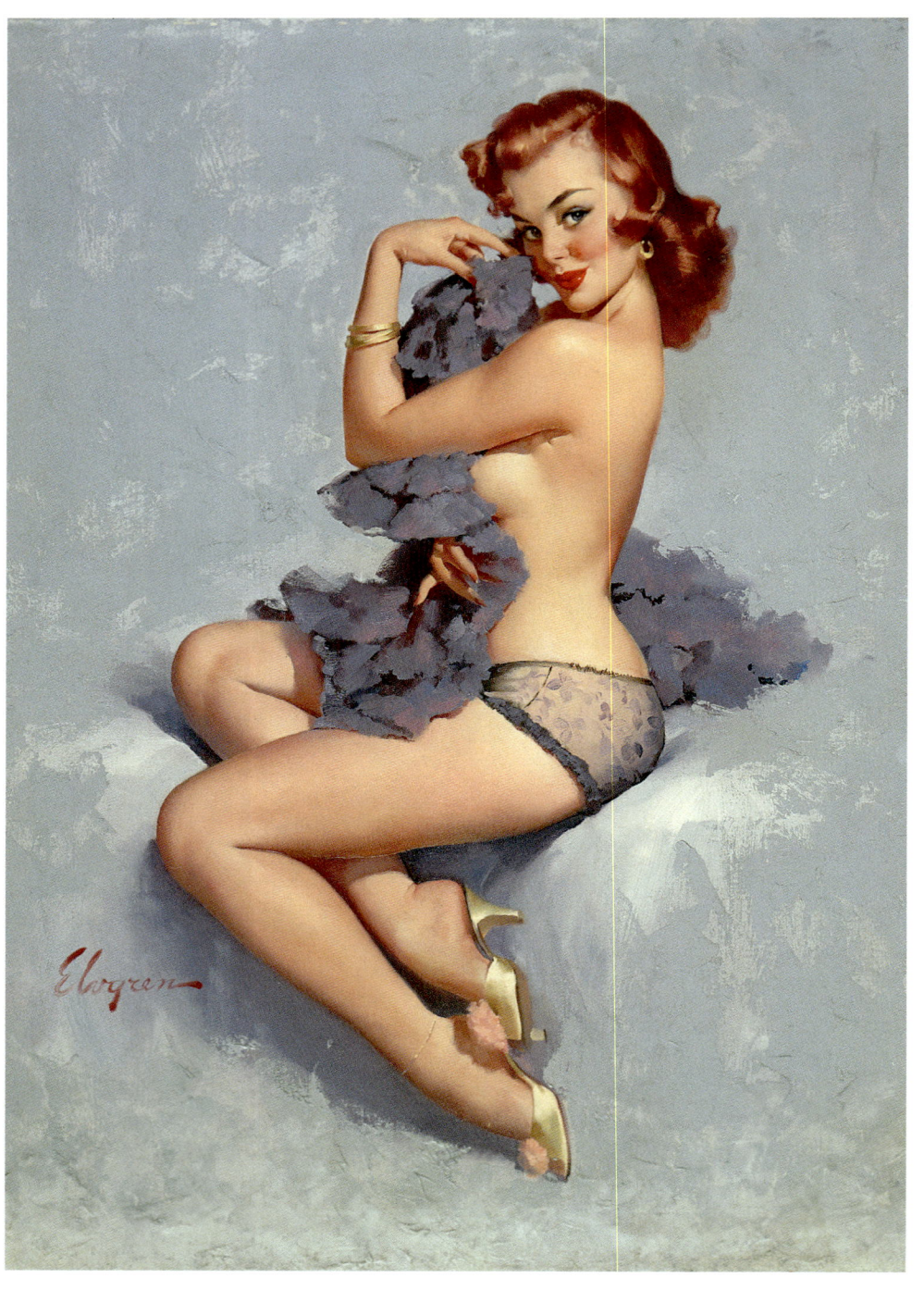

Above: Roxanne, oil on canvas, 1960, for a 1962
Brown & Bigelow calendar. 30 x 24 inches.

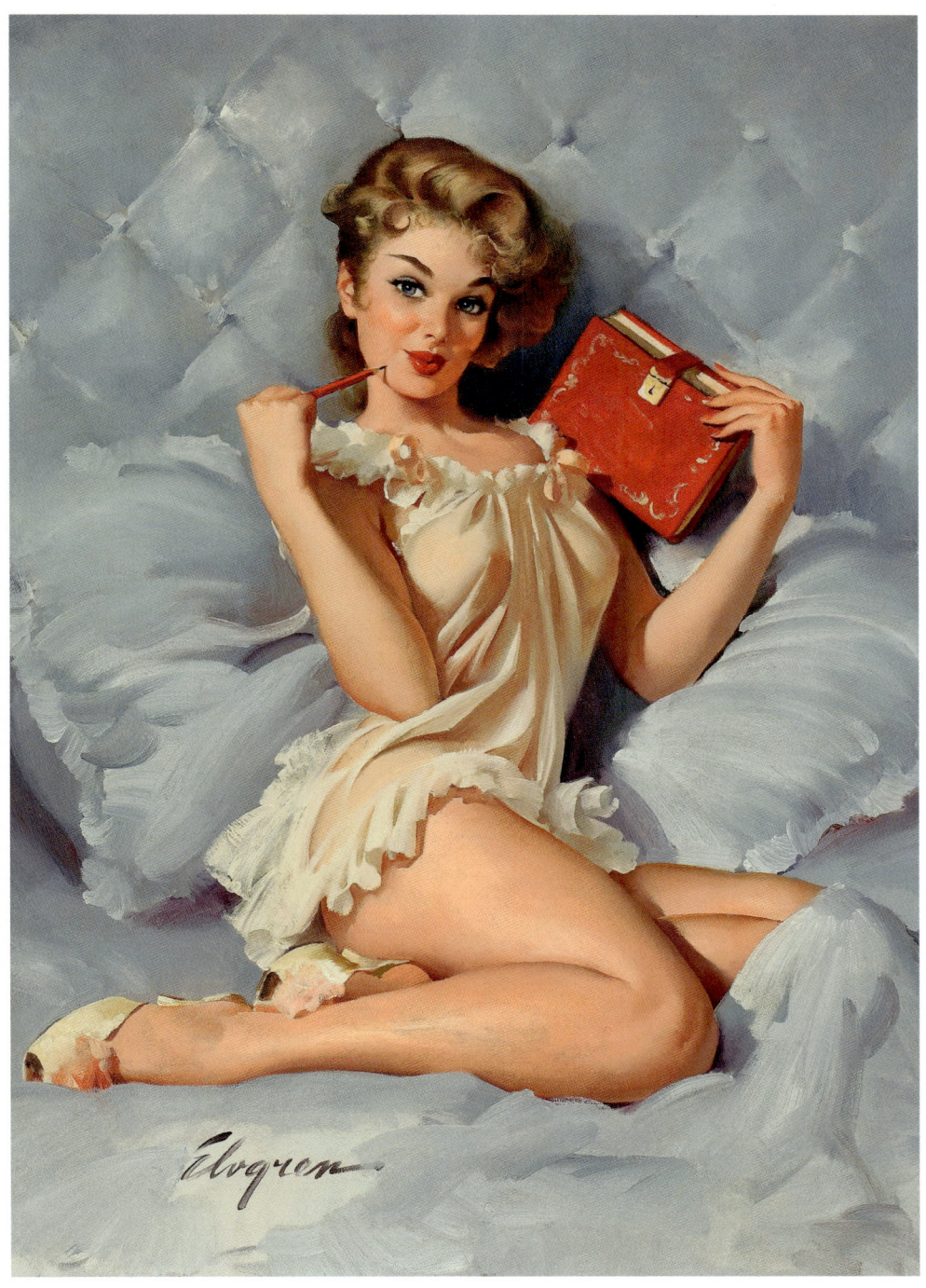

Above: *Thinking of You*, also known as *Retirement Plan*,
1962, for a 1964 Brown & Bigelow calendar. 30 x 24 inches.

GILLETTE "GIL" ELVGREN

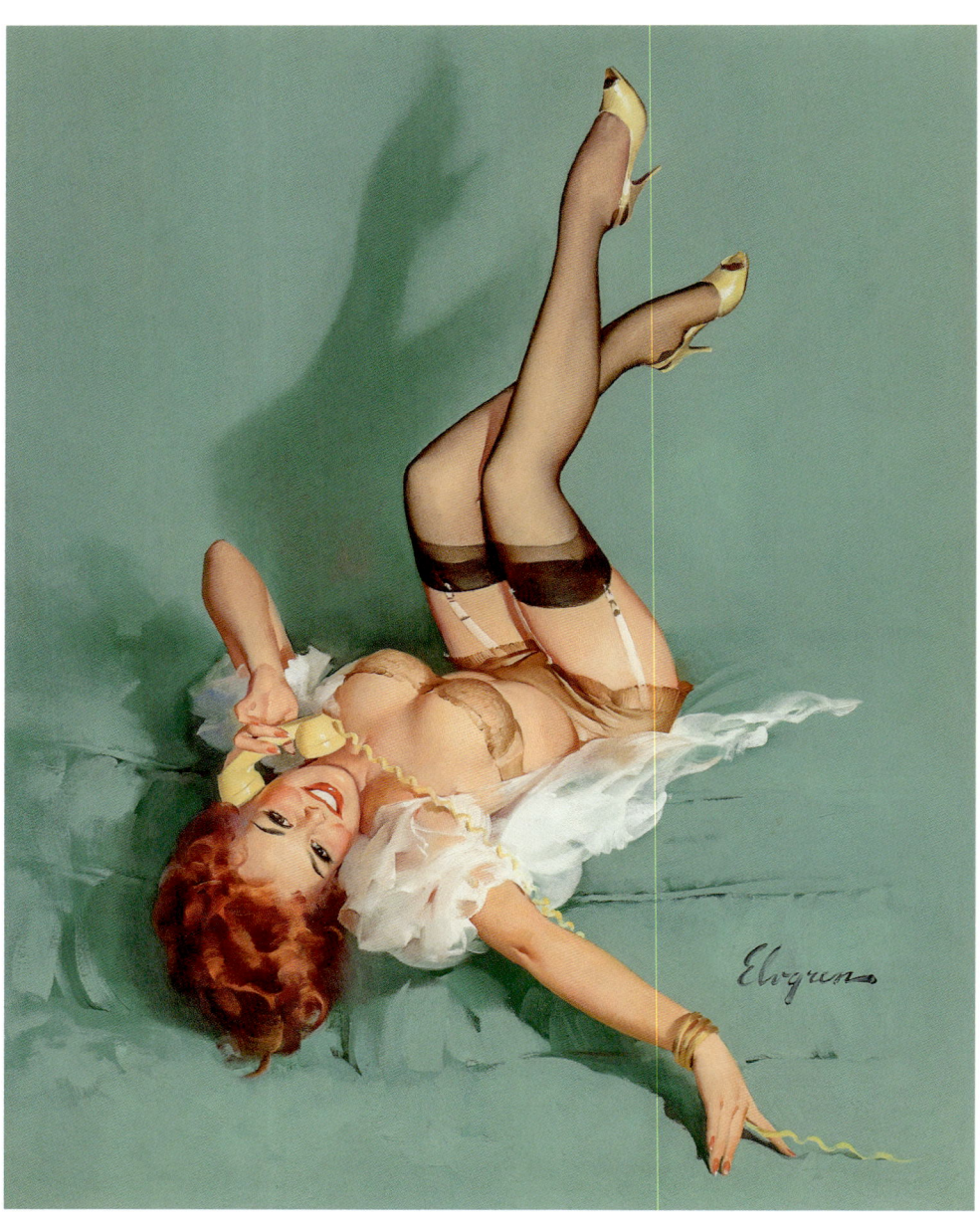

Above: The Right Number for a Brown & Bigelow calendar. Oil on canvas, 1961, 30.25 x 24.25 inches. Courtesy Heritage Auctions.

Opposite: Sheer Comfort, oil on canvas, 1959, for a 1961 Brown & Bigelow calendar. 30 x 24 inches.

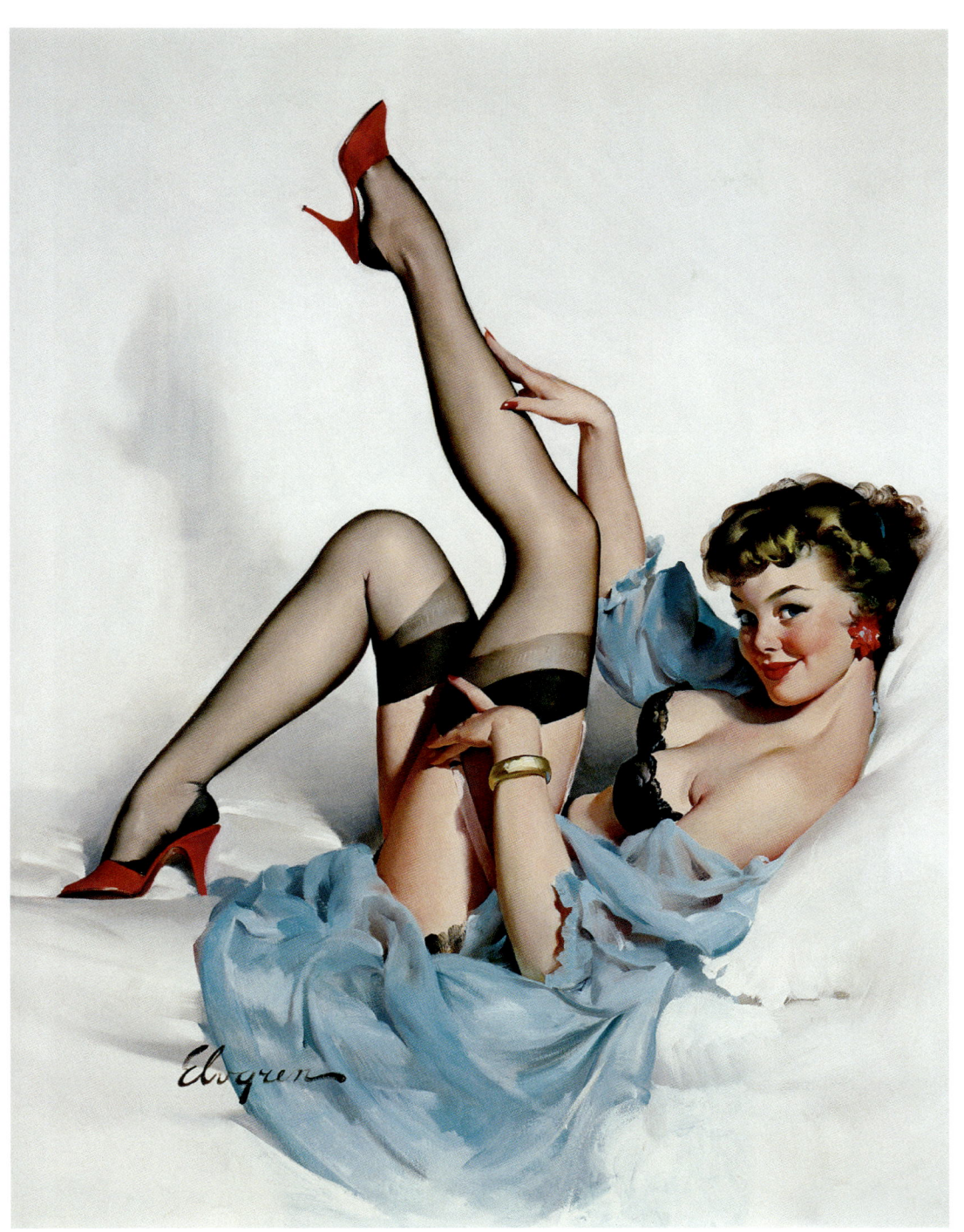

GILLETTE "GIL" ELVGREN

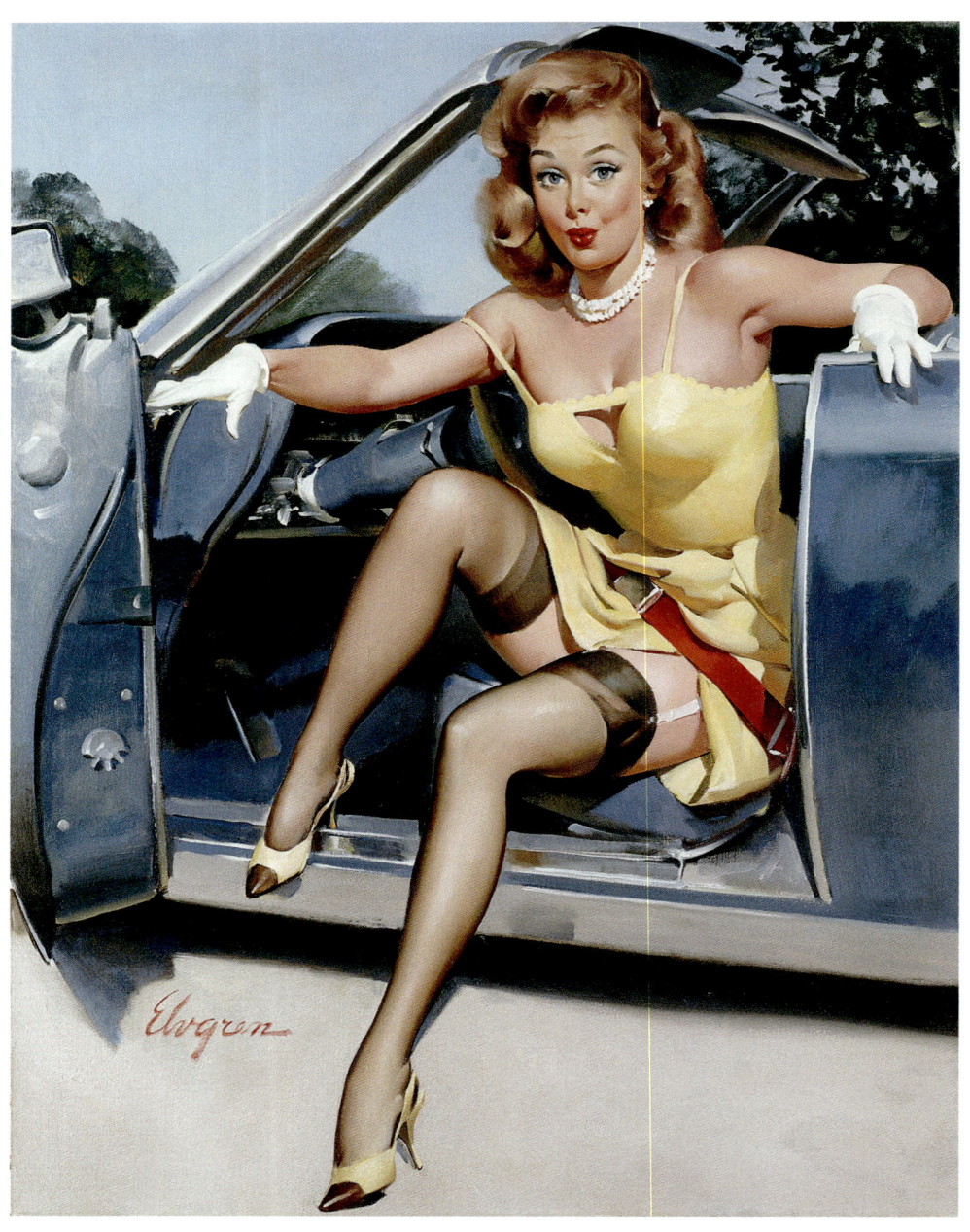

Above: Stepping Out, also known as *Stepping High*,
oil on canvas, circa 1958. 30 x 24 inches.

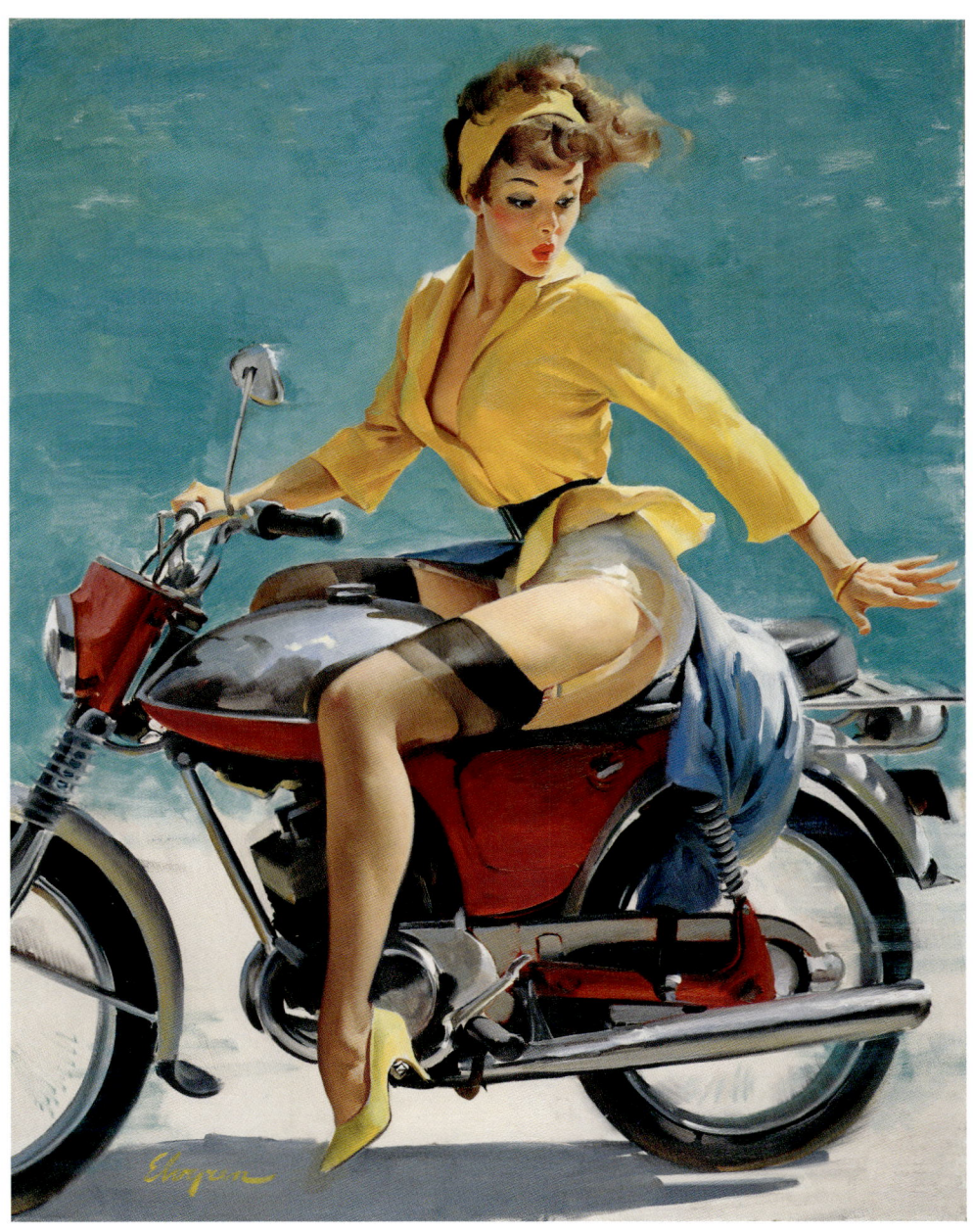

Above: Skirting the Issue, oil on canvas, 1956, for a 1958
Brown & Bigelow calendar. 30 x 24 inches.

GILLETTE "GIL" ELVGREN

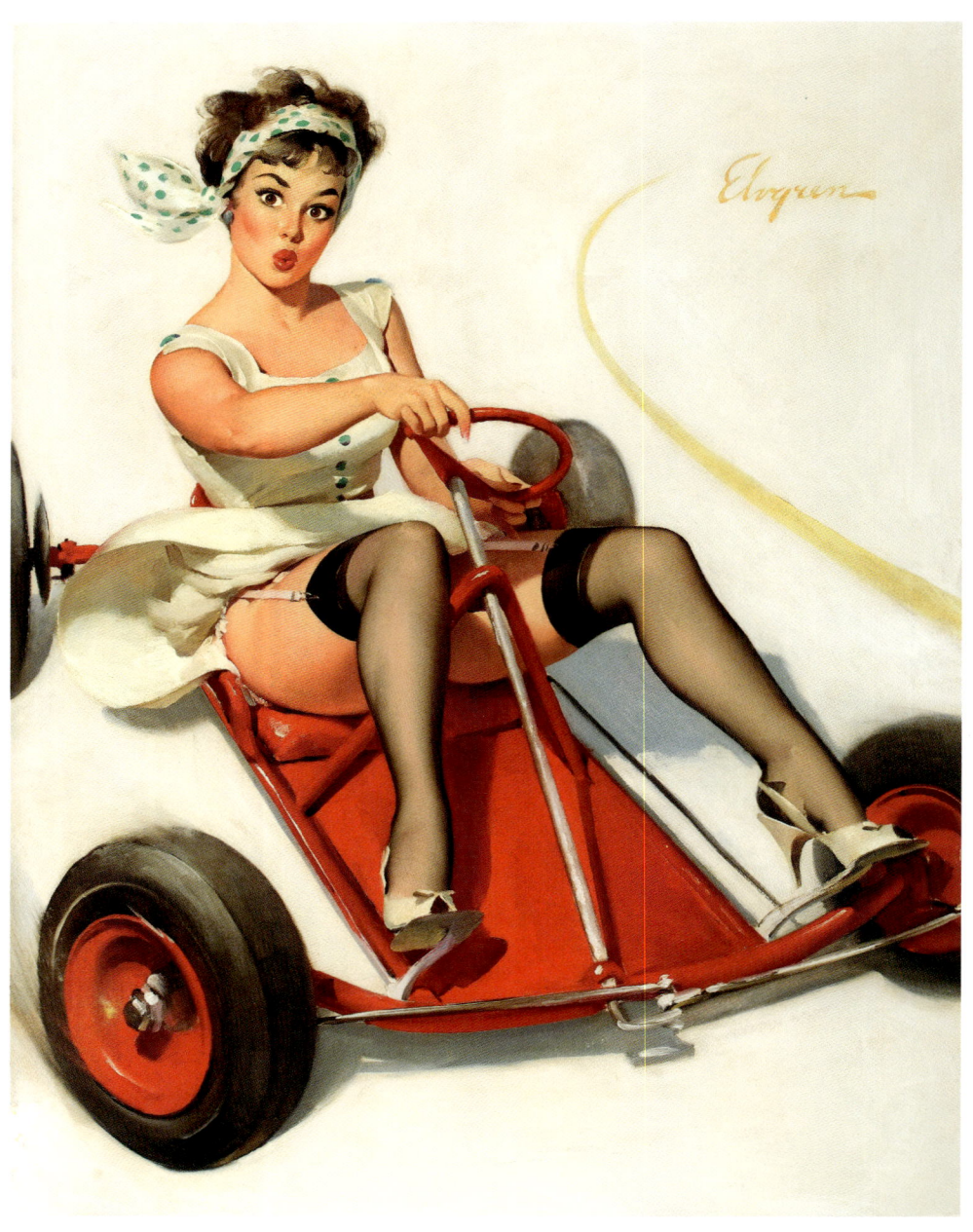

Above: Curving Around, also known as *Sharp Curves,*
oil on canvas, 1960, for a 1962 Brown & Bigelow calendar.
30 x24 inches. Mitchell Mehdy collection.

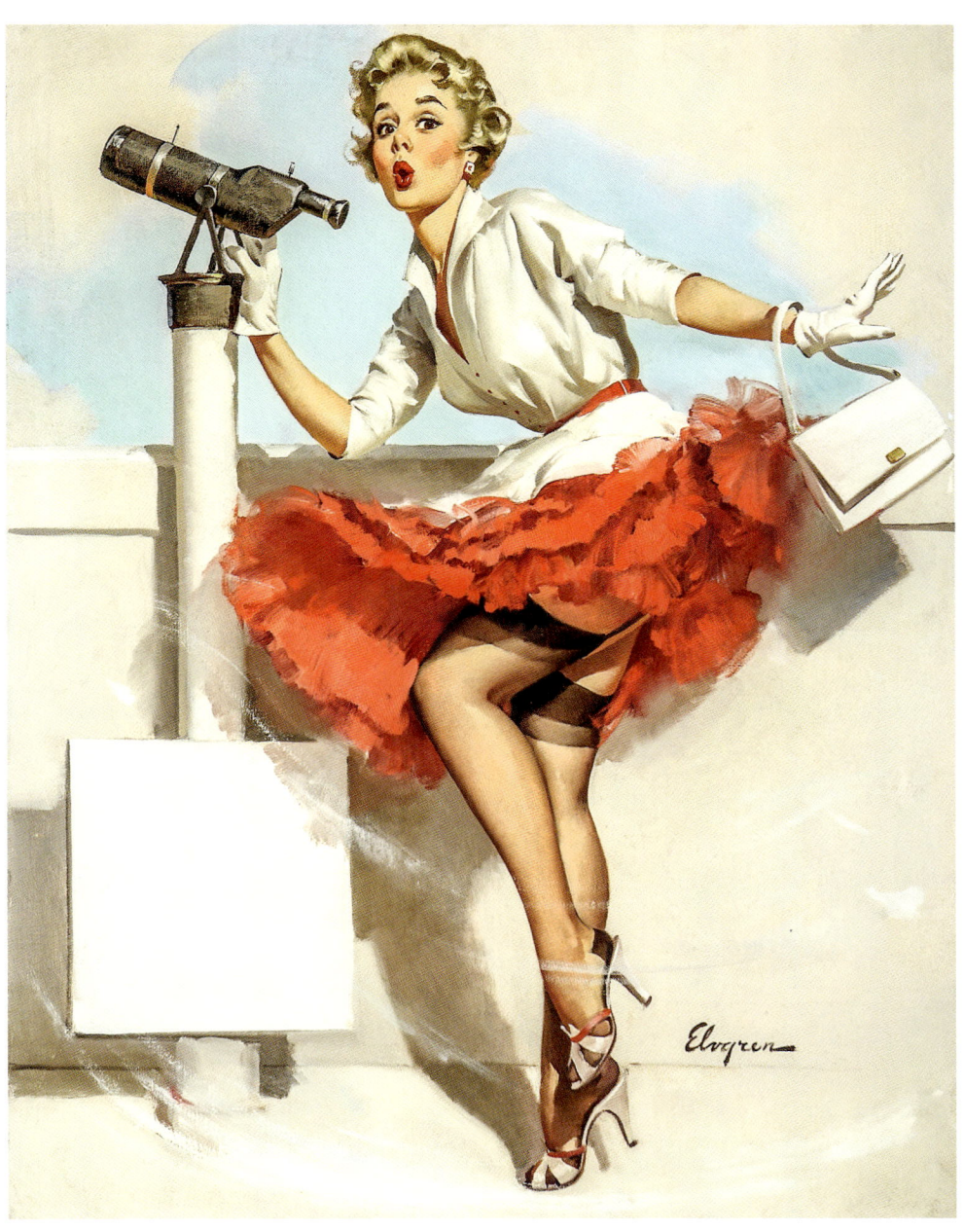

Above: What a View, oil on canvas, 1957,
for a 1959 Brown & Bigelow calendar. 30 x 24 inches.

GILLETTE "GIL" ELVGREN

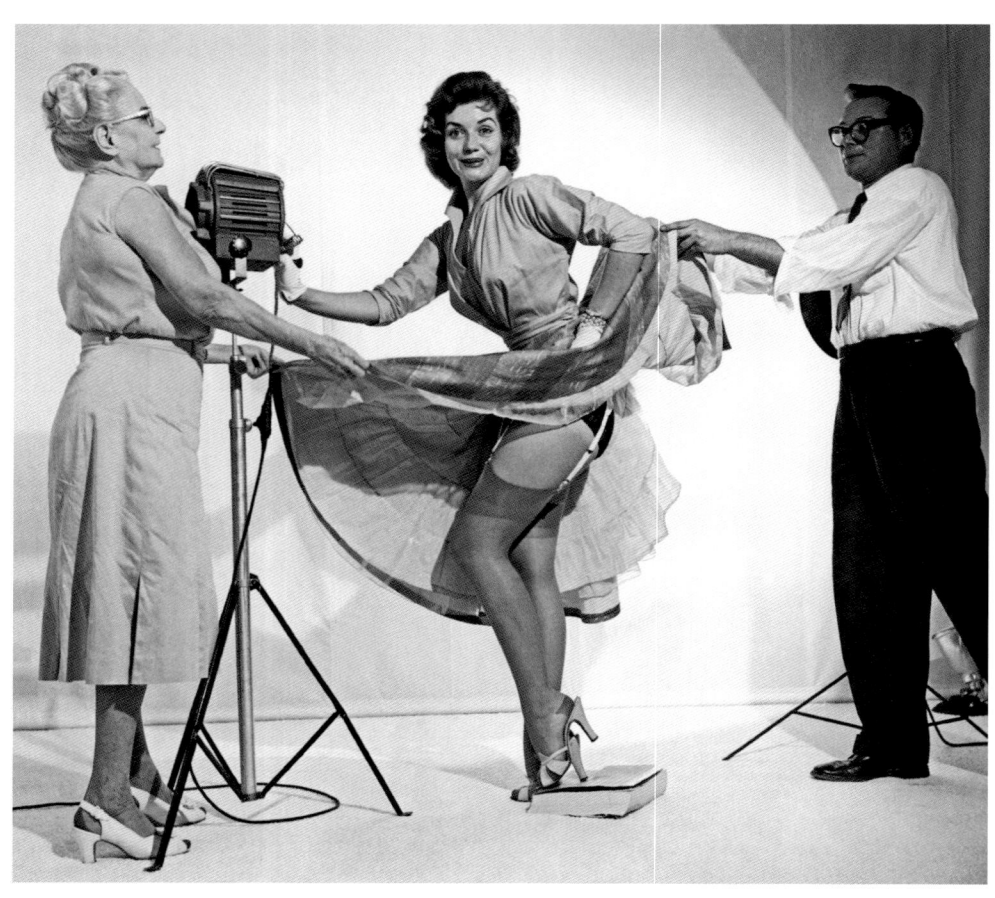

Above: Model Myrna Hansen gets help arranging her flying skirts from her mother and Elvgren assistant Bobby Toombs, for the painting *What a View*, 1957.

Opposite: Unexpected Lift, also known as *A Nice Catch*, oil on canvas, 1961, for a 1963 Brown & Bigelow calendar. 30 x 24 inches.

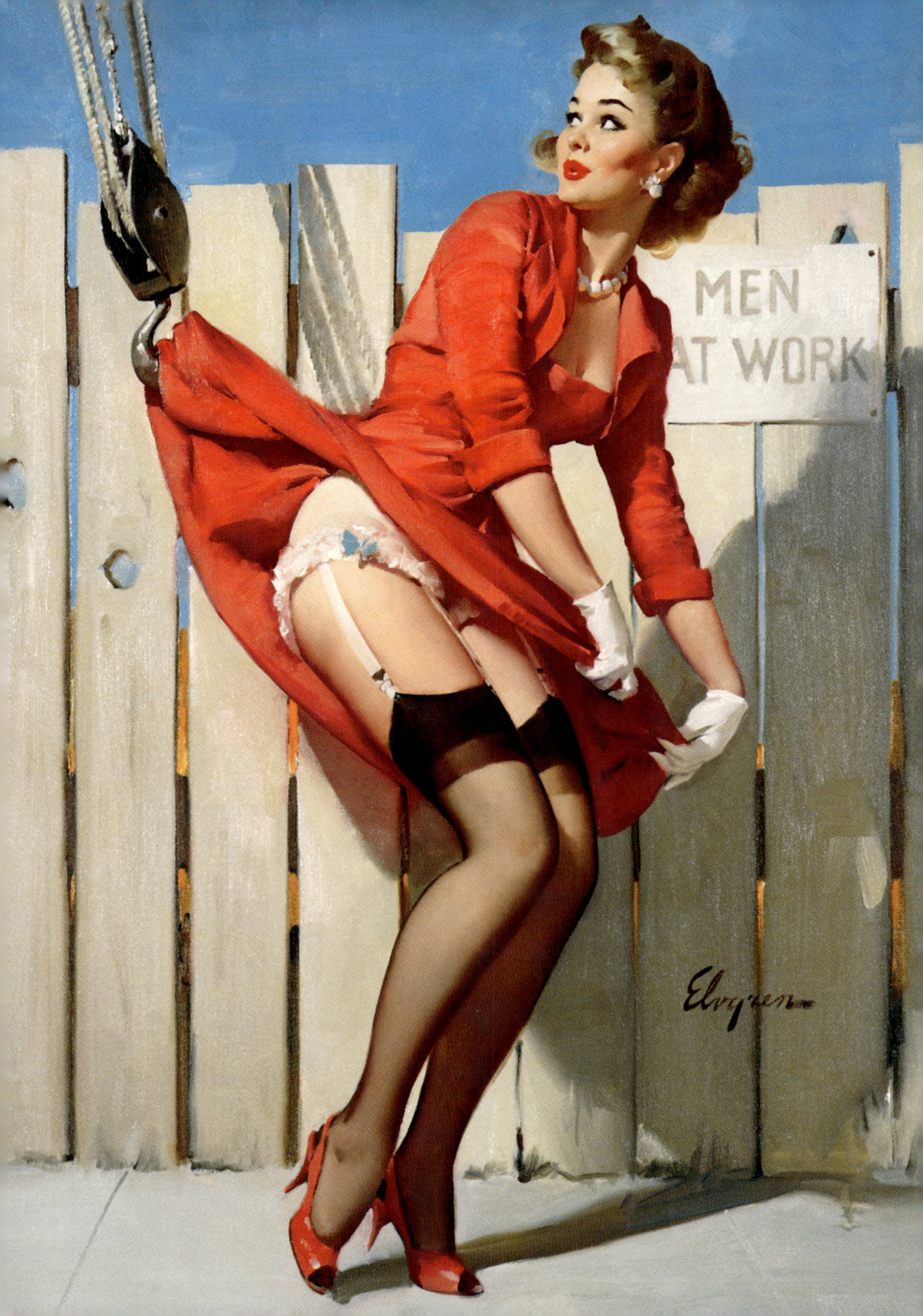

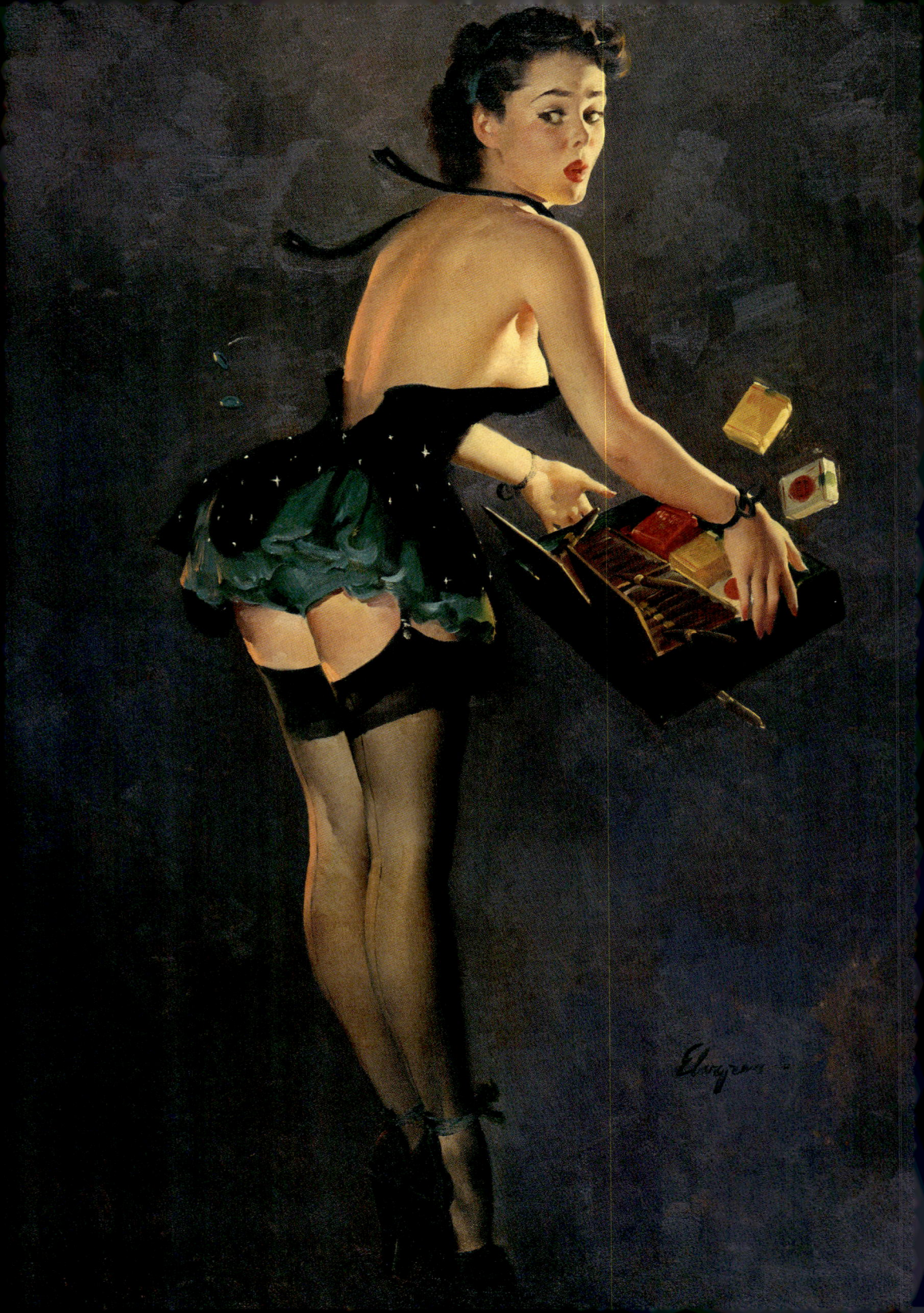

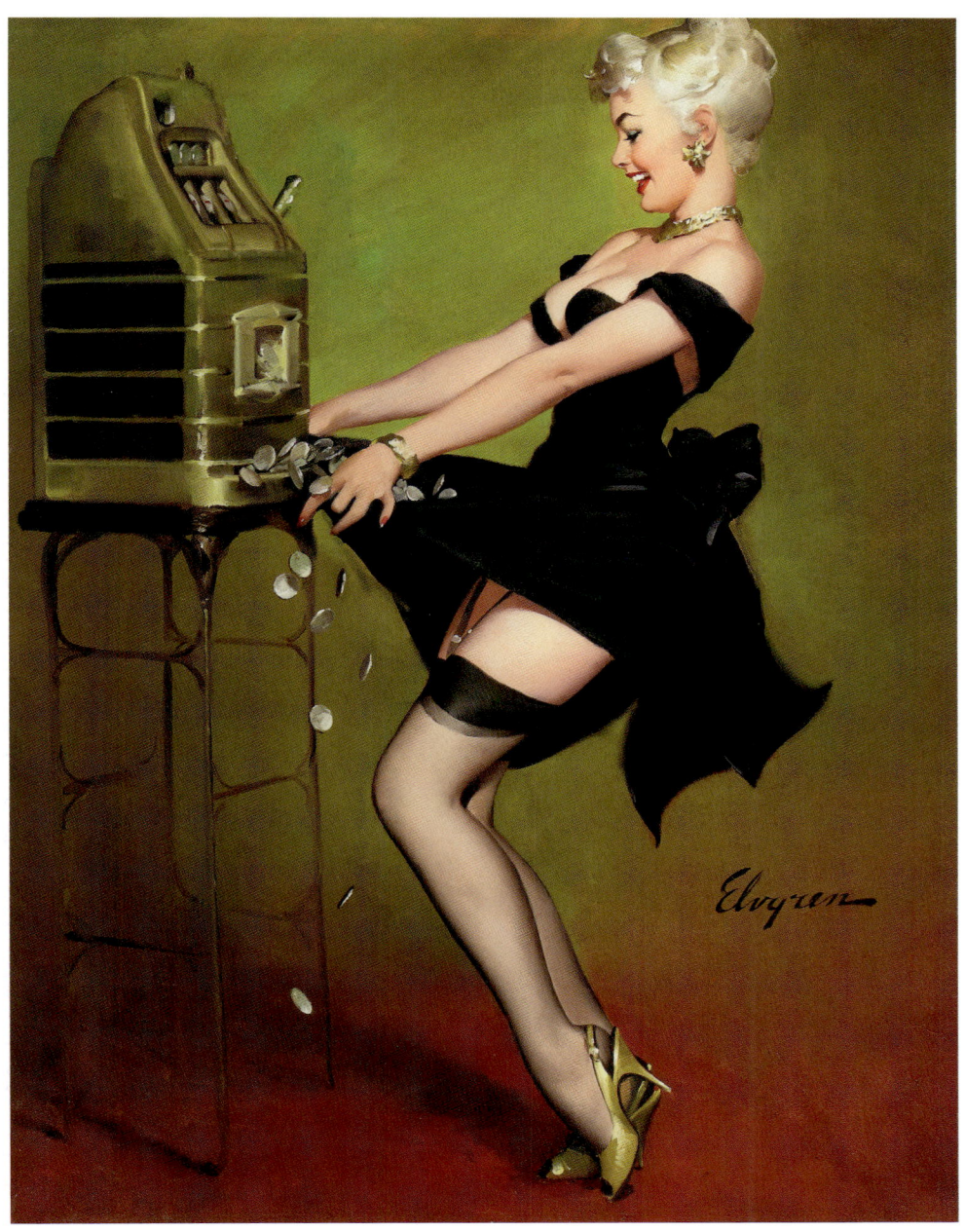

Opposite: Parting Company, oil on canvas, 1950,
for a 1952 Brown & Bigelow calendar. 30 x 24 inches.

Above: Pot Luck, oil on canvas, 1961, for a 1963
Brown & Bigelow calendar. 30 x 24 inches.

GILLETTE "GIL" ELVGREN

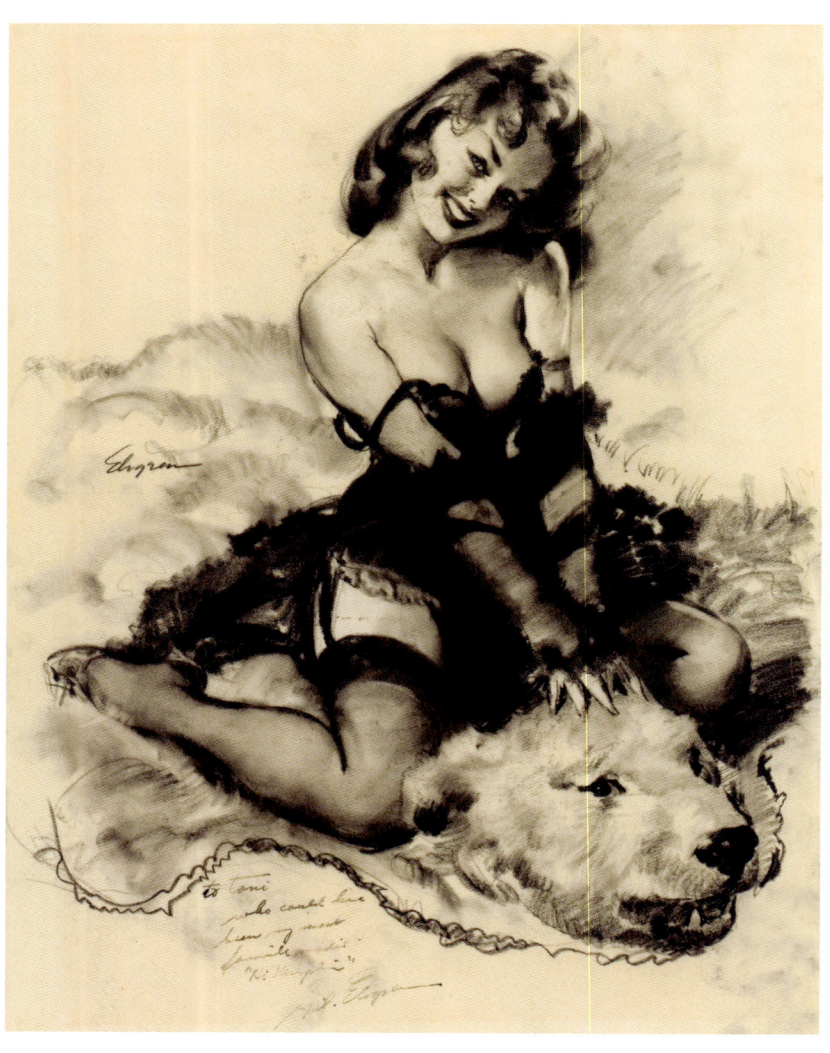

Above: A charcoal on paper preliminary sketch for *Bear Facts*, 1962. 24 x 19 inches.

Opposite: Bear Facts, oil on canvas, 1962, for a 1964 Brown & Bigelow calendar. 30 x 24 inches.

THE ART OF PIN-UP

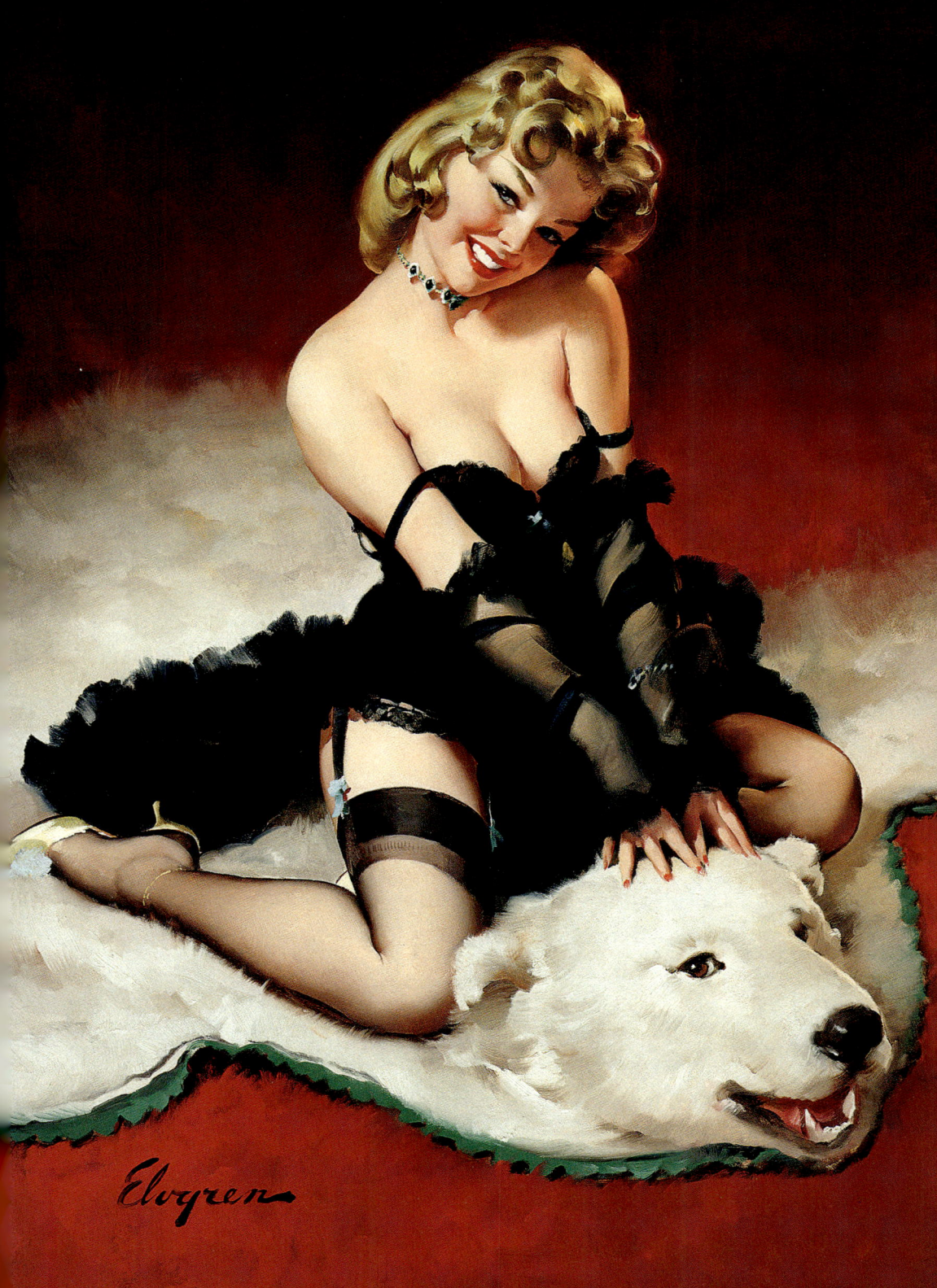

Elvgren

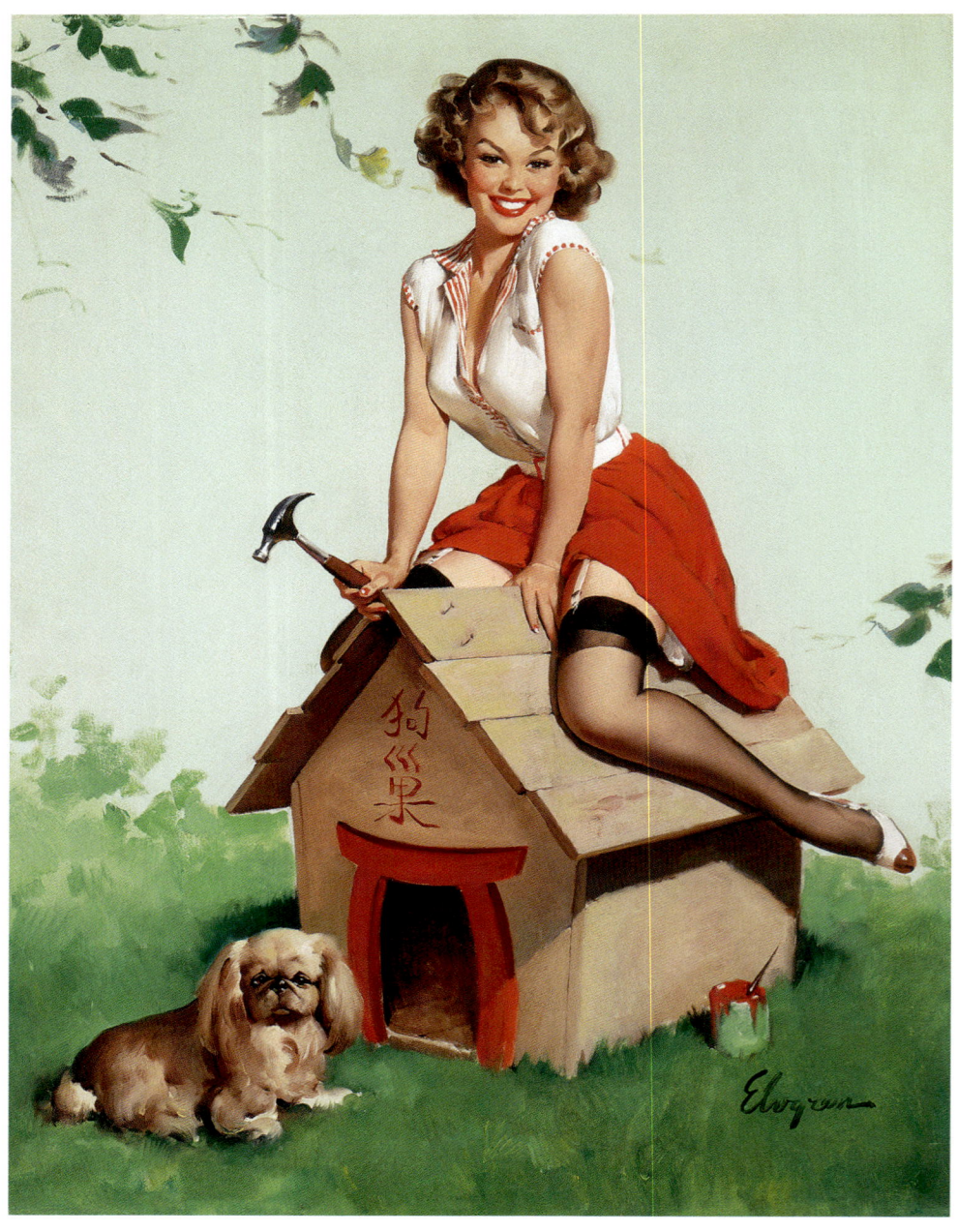

Above: Well Built, also known as *R-R-Roof!,*
oil on canvas, 1961, for a 1963 Brown & Bigelow calendar.
30 x 24 inches.

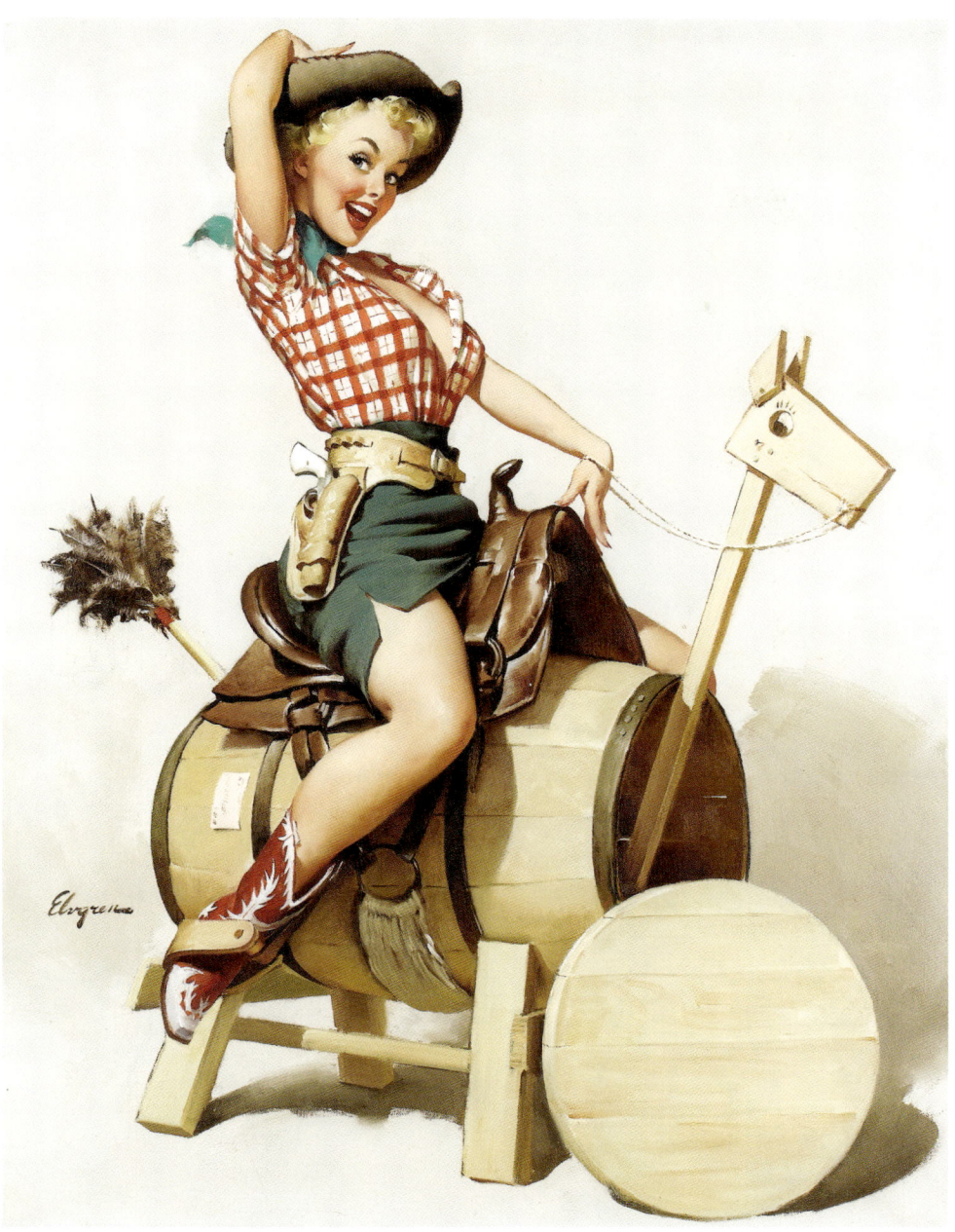

Above: Sitting Pretty, also known as *Lola*, oil on canvas, 1955, for a 1957 Brown & Bigelow calendar, and featured in Norman Rockwell's *New Year Look*. 31 x 24.5 inches. Rockwell lamented his inability to paint sexy women, and admired Elvgren all the more for his mastery of the subject.

GILLETTE "GIL" ELVGREN

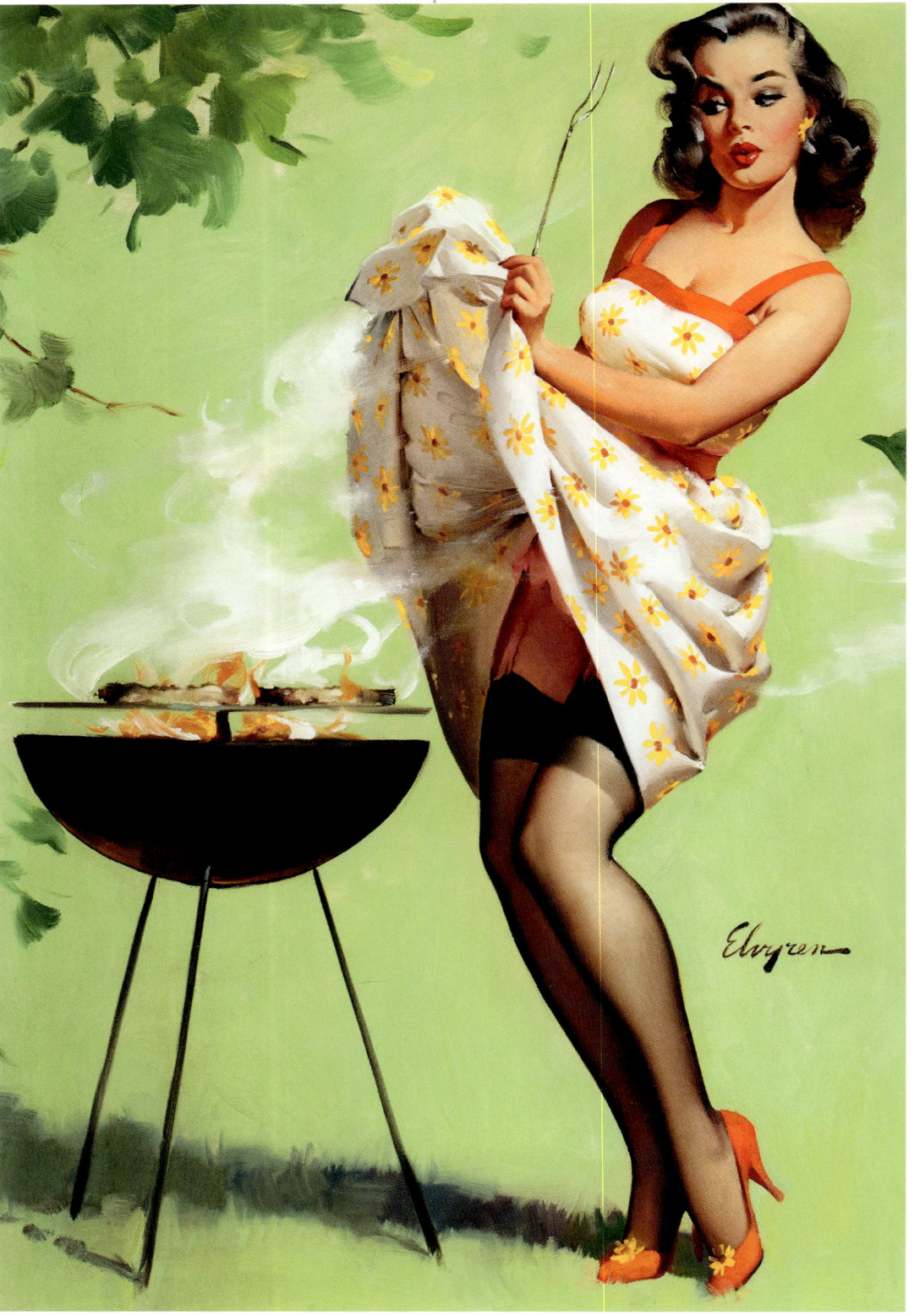

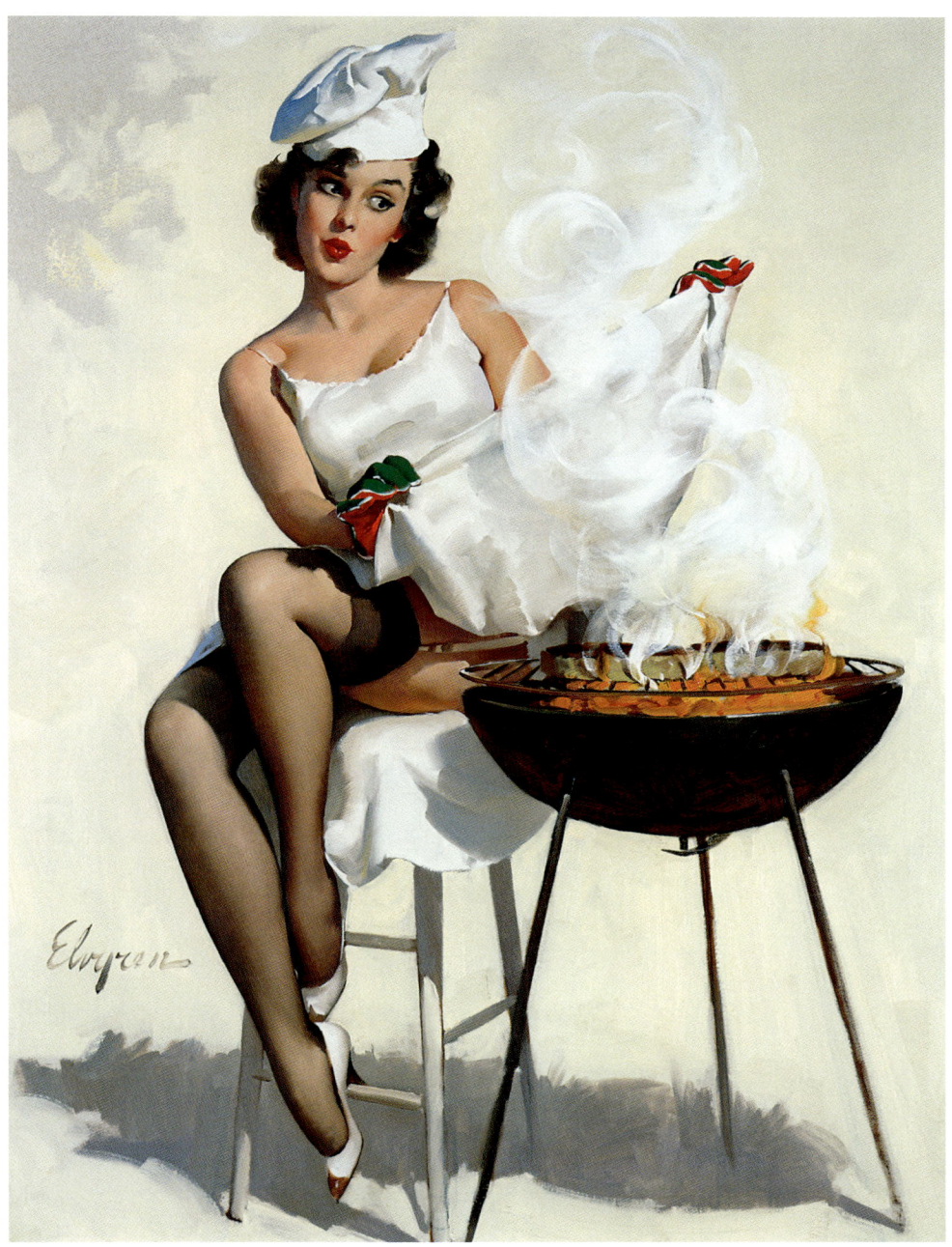

Opposite: Smoke Screen, oil on canvas, 1958, for a 1960
Brown & Bigelow calendar. 30 x 24 inches.

Above: Barbacutie, also known as *Rare Treat*,
oil on canvas, 1965, for a 1967 Brown & Bigelow calendar.
30 x 24 inches.

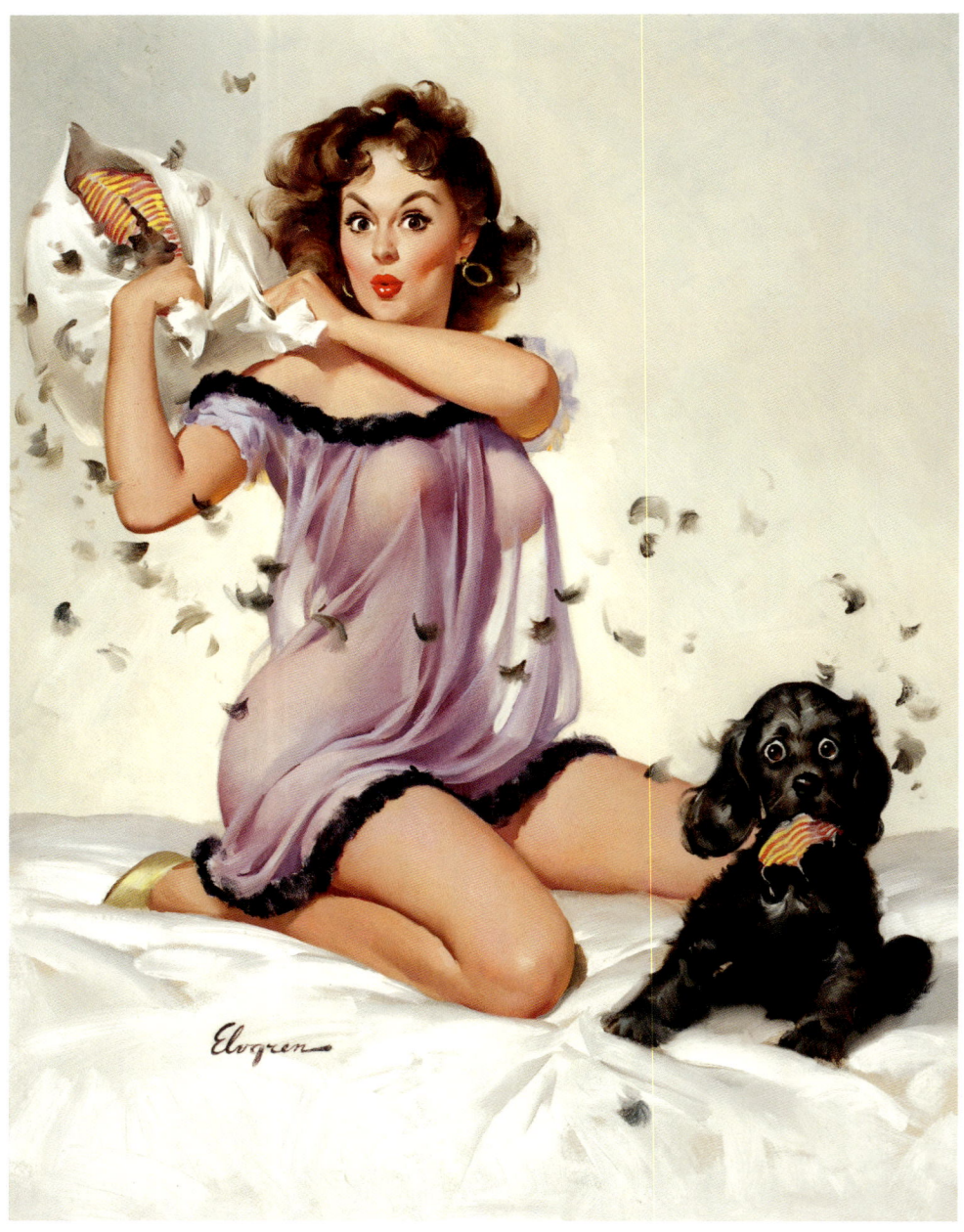

Above: Ticklish Situation, oil on canvas, 1957, for a 1959 Brown & Bigelow calendar. 30.25 x 24.25 inches.

Opposite: No You Don't!, also known as *Time for Decision*, oil on canvas, 1956, for a 1958 Brown & Bigelow calendar. 30 x 24 inches.

THE ART OF PIN-UP

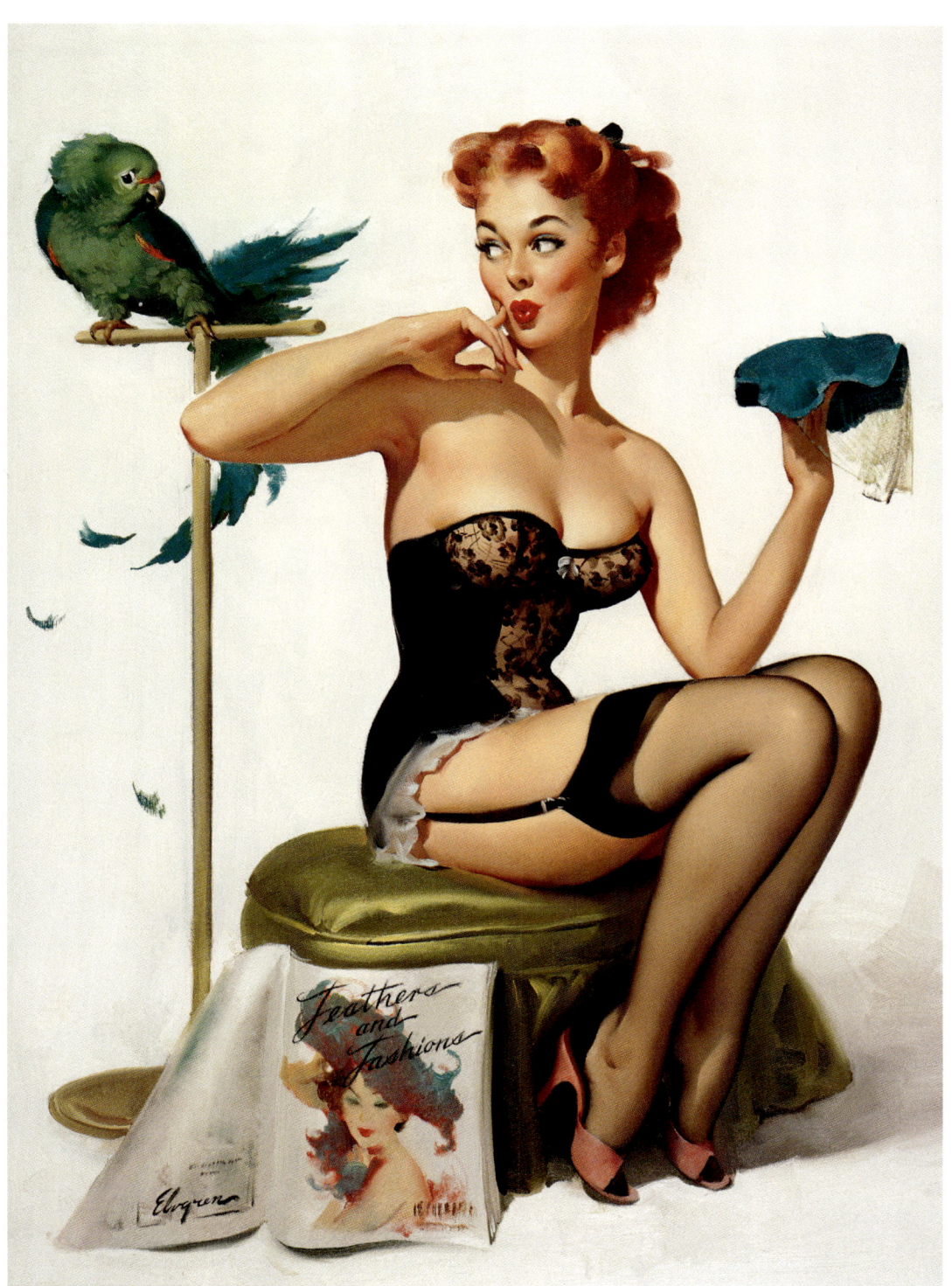

GILLETTE "GIL" ELVGREN

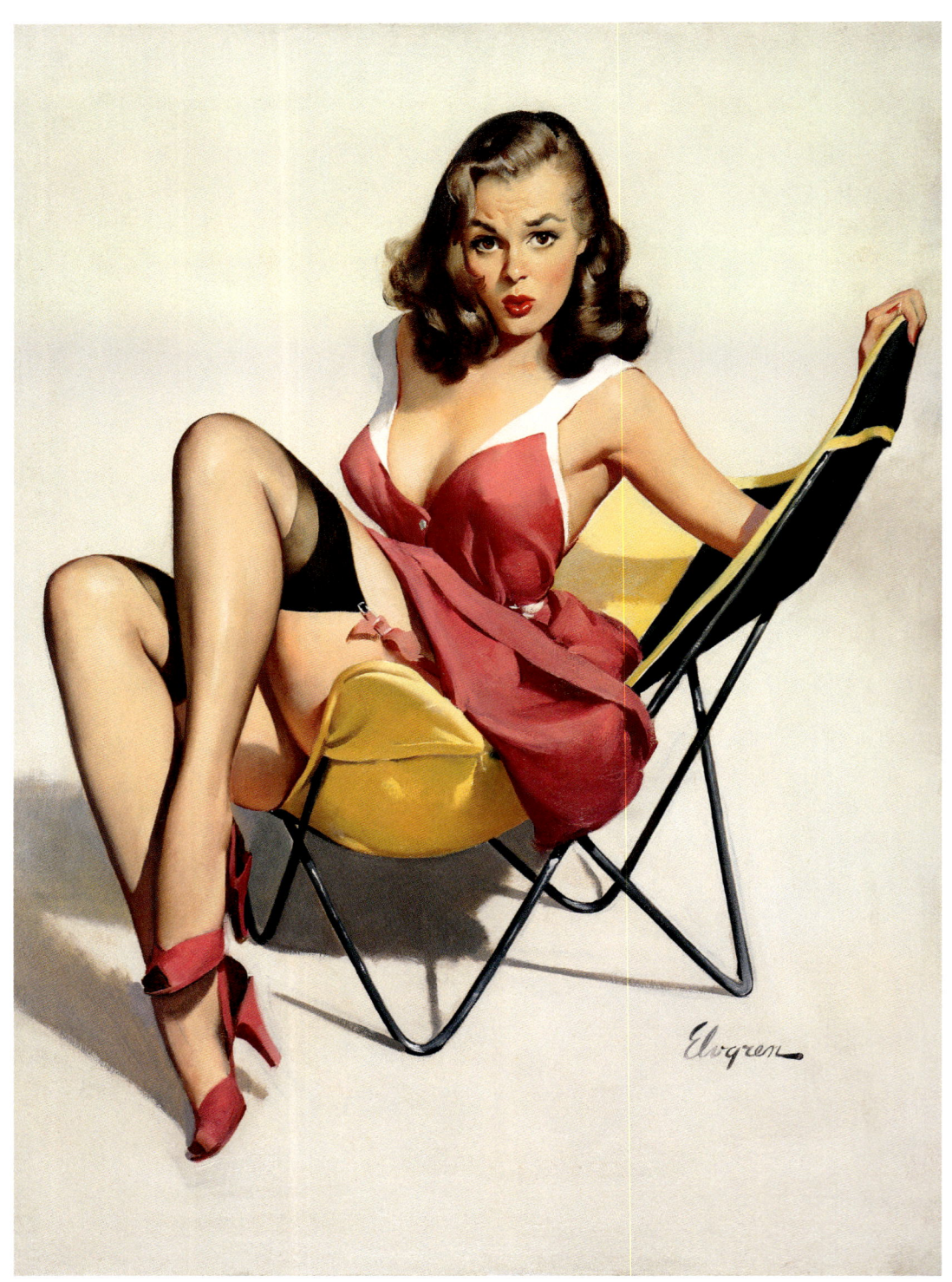

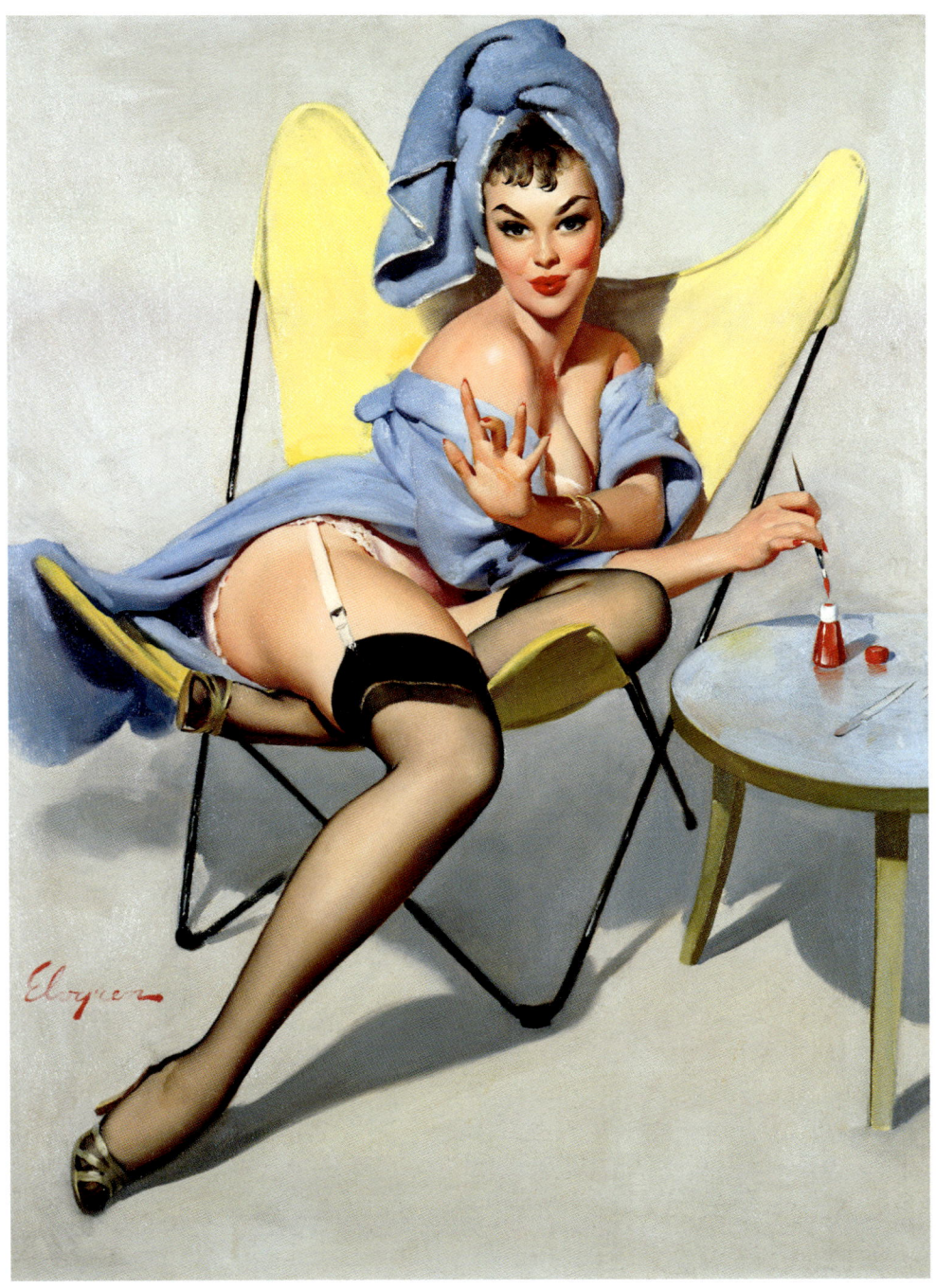

Opposite: That Low-Down Feeling, also known as *Who, Me?*, oil on canvas, 1957, for a 1959 Brown & Bigelow calendar. 30 x 24 inches.

Above: The Finishing Touch, also known as *Polished Performance*, oil on canvas, 1960, for a 1962 Brown & Bigelow calendar. 30 x 24 inches.

GILLETTE "GIL" ELVGREN

ARTHUR "ART" FRAHM

art frahm

1906–1981

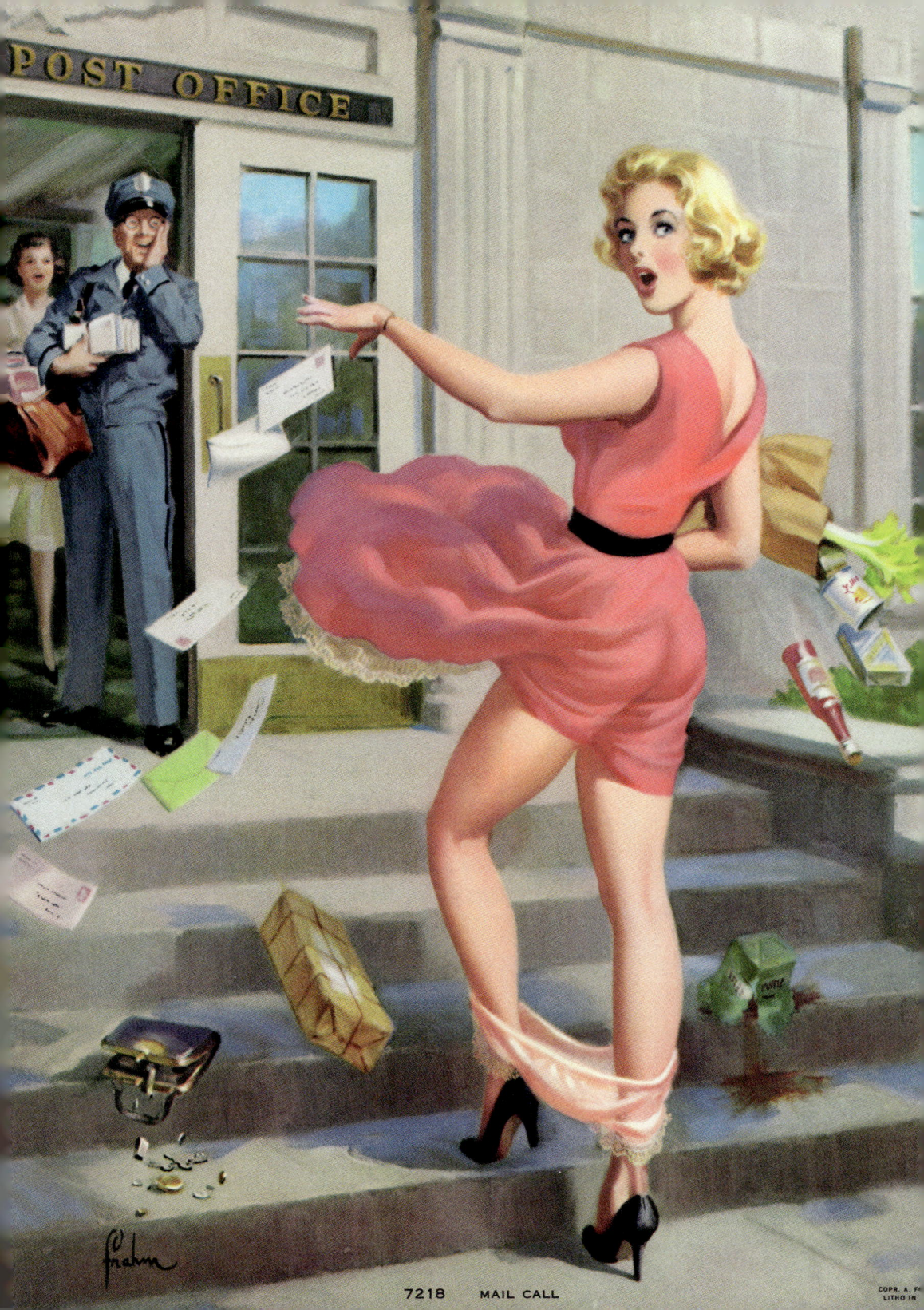

POST OFFICE

7218   MAIL CALL

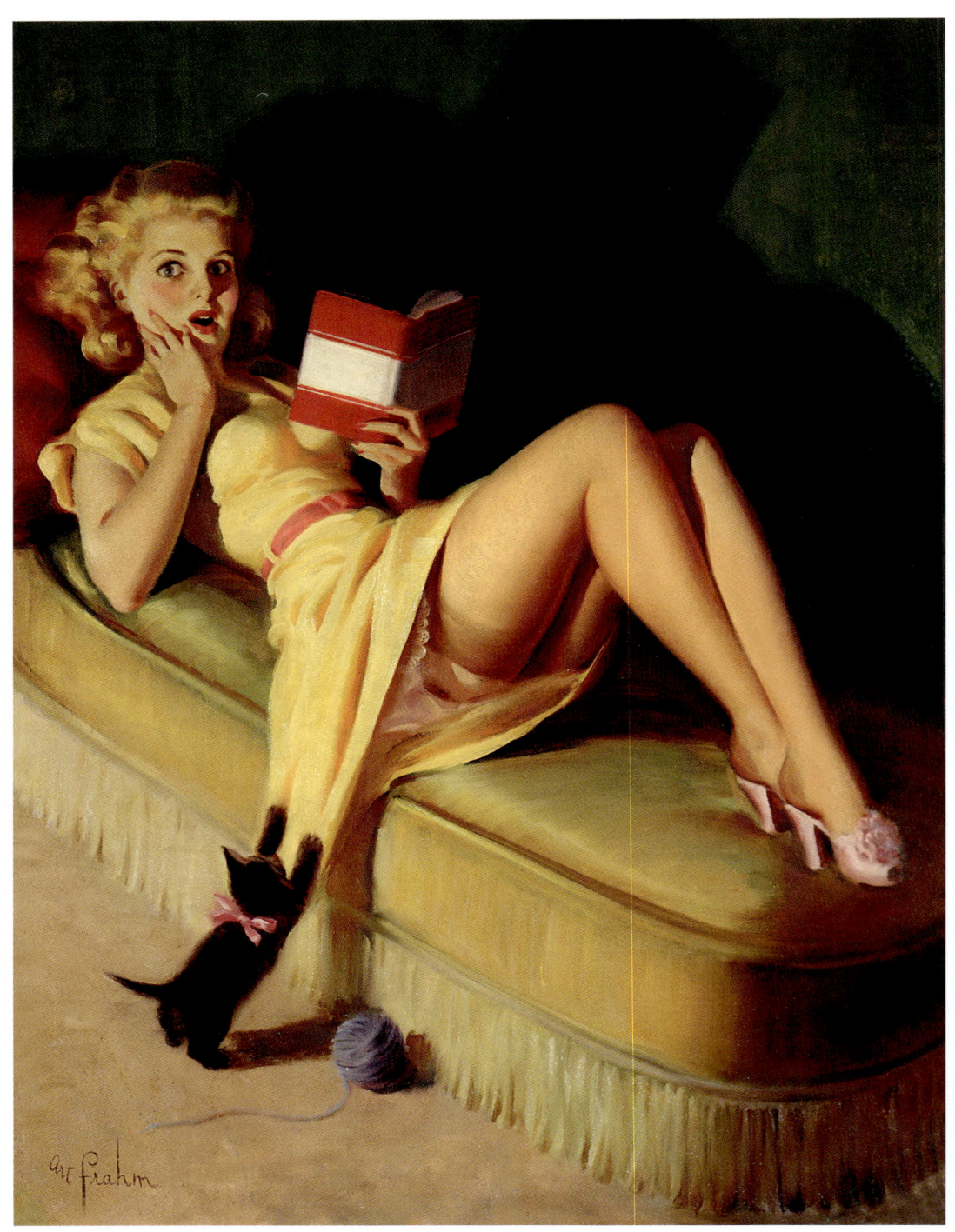

"His gleefully fanciful genre features fresh-faced young wives trying to make their way through the world, only to find their panties around their ankles."

Art Frahm was born in 1906, in an immigrant community of Chicago, to a German-born mother and a bartender father, who was later to become a machinist. After art school, Frahm closely followed the template for illustrators in the region: He apprenticed to Haddon Sundblom, assisting in his freelance assignments, and went on to join the stable at Stevens-Gross, working alongside other notable pin-up illustrators such as Joyce Ballantyne and Gil Elvgren.

The Louis F. Dow Company commissioned Frahm's earliest pin-ups. As one of many hopeful "next Elvgrens," Frahm created stand-alone pin-up images intended for V-mail to servicemen stationed overseas during World War II. In 1943 he switched from painting pin-up girls to receiving them when he enlisted in the army at age 37. Upon his return to civilian life, he began charting his own course in the pin-up world. Using the sunshiny palette and heavy, swirling

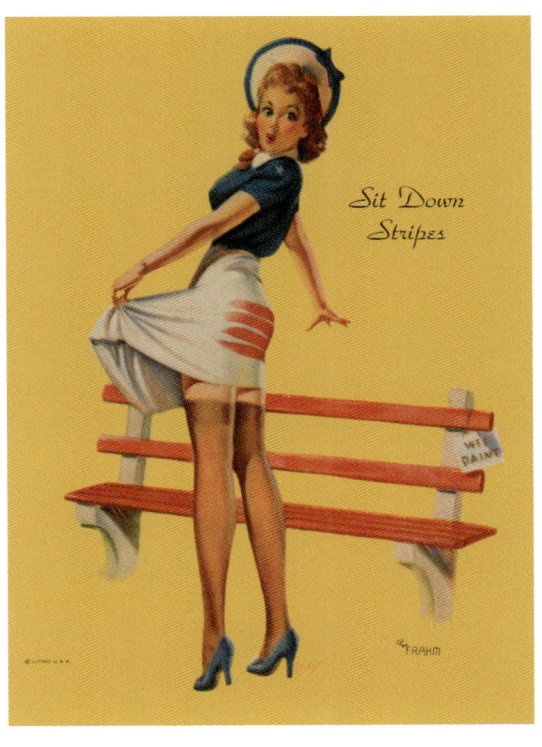

Sit Down Stripes

"mayonnaise" style of oil-on-canvas favored by the Chicago school, Frahm made a name for himself with what would come to be known as the "embarrassment series."

Working for Brown & Bigelow's lower-brow rival Joseph C. Hoover & Sons, Frahm homed in on the postwar conflict between servicemen who returned to America expecting to be king of the castle, and women who had traded their aprons for welding helmets. His gleefully fanciful

Page 275: *Mail Call*, 1960, on a 1962 Joseph C. Hoover & Sons calendar for Joesph J. Mack Exterminating Service. Art Frahm launched his "embarrassment series" for Hoover in 1952, producing a total of 12 images over 14 years. Many from the series were released as calendar prints bearing the confusing inscription "A. Fox Litho Corp." A. Fox was simply the Hoover employee in charge of acquiring copyrights between 1951 and 1964.

Opposite: *Playful Kitten*, oil on canvas, 1941, for a Louis F. Dow calendar. 36.5 x 34 inches.

Above: *Sit Down Stripes*, calendar lithograph, circa 1942. Frahm's work in this period is nearly indistinguishible from early Elvgren. 6.75 x 5 inches.

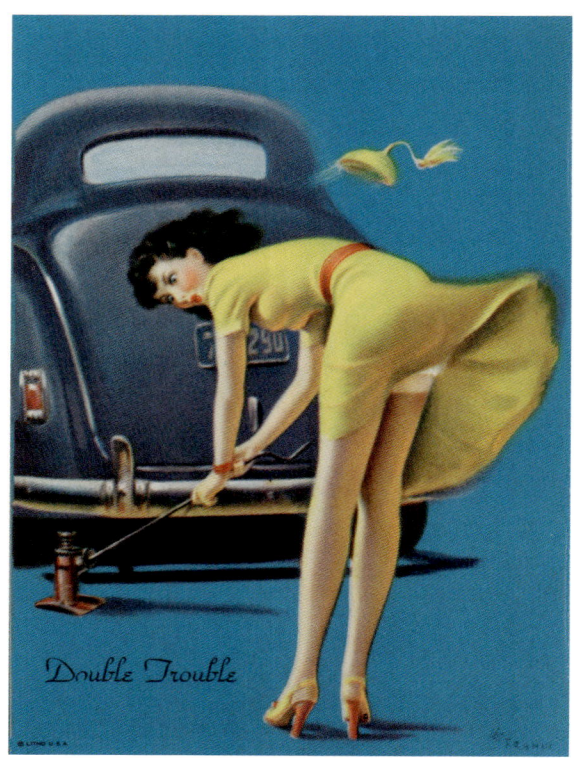

Double Trouble

genre features fresh-faced young wives trying to make their way through the world, only to find their panties around their ankles. Grocery bags are their undoing; each struggles with a full sack, or sacks, generally packed with luxuriant stalks of celery intended for a husband's dinner, that prohibit them from catching their underwear on the way down. The shocked look on their faces—the "ooh face," as it is known—evokes that liminal space between the public and private spheres. More shock than actual embarrassment, the look asks, "What just happened here?" as the male onlookers—stand-ins for the pin-ups' working-class male audience—gaze in wonder and delight. The universal astonishment stems as much from the presence of sexy housewives in the world of work—Frahm's pin-ups interrupt men driving buses, manning jackhammers, and operating elevators—as it does from the failure of nylon, of which Frahm was no fan. He could paint a leg better than anyone of his day, but he could not paint hosiery to save his life. In his lingerie pin-ups, legs become matronly rather than enticing, the stockings a muddy brown without tension or shine—the vision of a down-on-her-luck Gypsy Rose Lee.

Frahm didn't favor strippers or screen sirens, though, or even the cigarette girls who typified his native Chicago. His idealized world was Mayberry R.F.D. In his more wholesome calendars, featuring scenes of lovable police officers or sunlit fishing holes, where a blonde pin-up might bashfully step out for a skinny dip, Frahm delivered what returning vets had dreamed about while overseas. Gil Elvgren often said that the perfect pin-up had the face of a girl on the body of a woman, but Frahm painted womanly lives, with girlish attitudes. Here his young housewife spent forever getting ready for her big day out, only to suffer this embarrassing mishap. Still, it's all okay: That nice fatherly policeman will save her.

By the early 1960s fantasies had shifted, and Frahm got out of illustration. Enjoying a simpler life in retirement, he relocated with his wife, Ruth, and their daughter, Diana, to South Carolina, where he occasionally painted society notables. He remained there until his death in 1981.

Above: Double Trouble, 1935, on a small 1936 calendar lithograph from Joseph C. Hoover & Sons, under the company's A. Fox imprint, displaying Frahm's most popular theme: female embarrassment at public exposure.

Opposite: A Sudden Letdown!, Hoover & Sons calendar lithograph, 1959, from a 1958 painting.

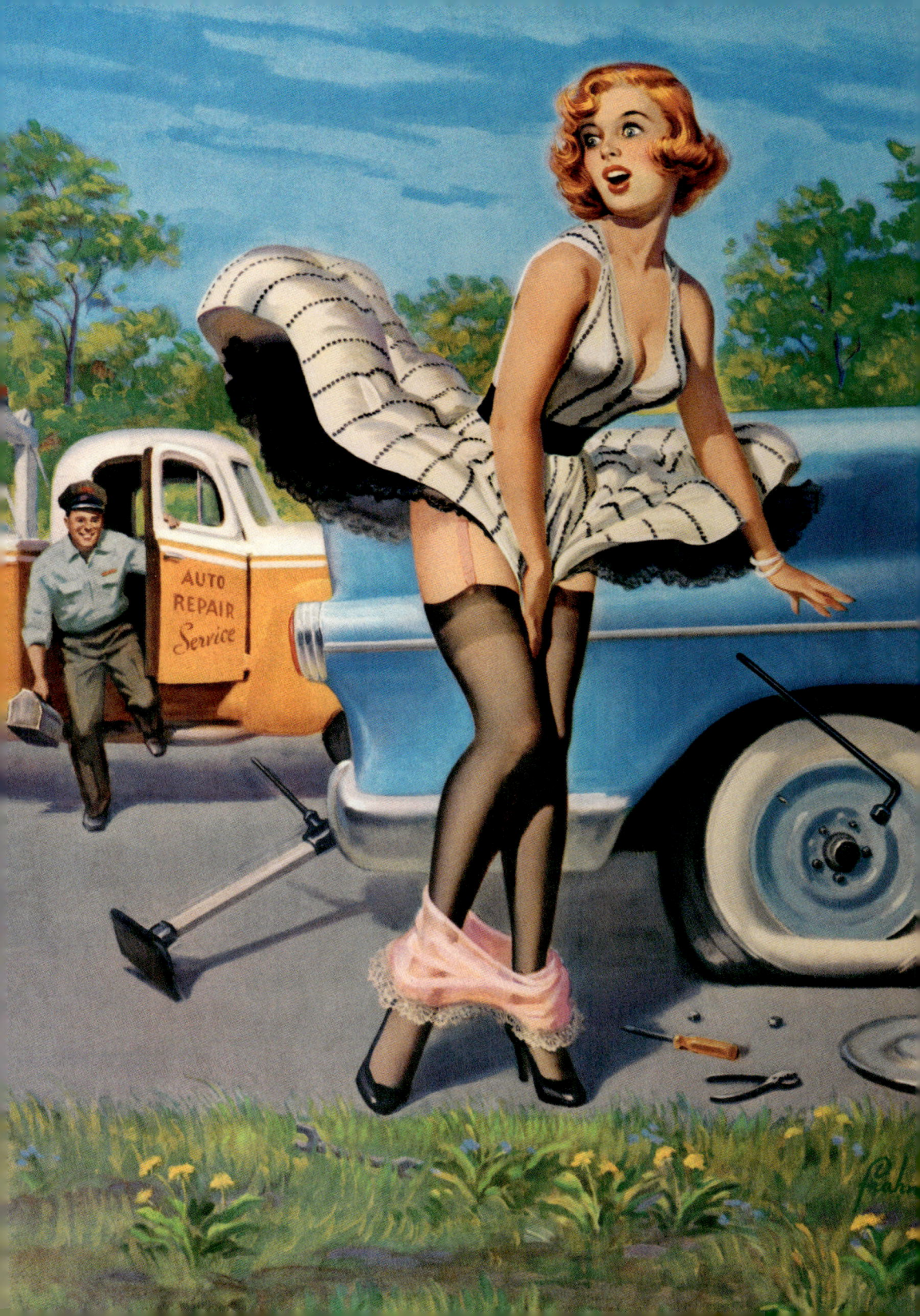

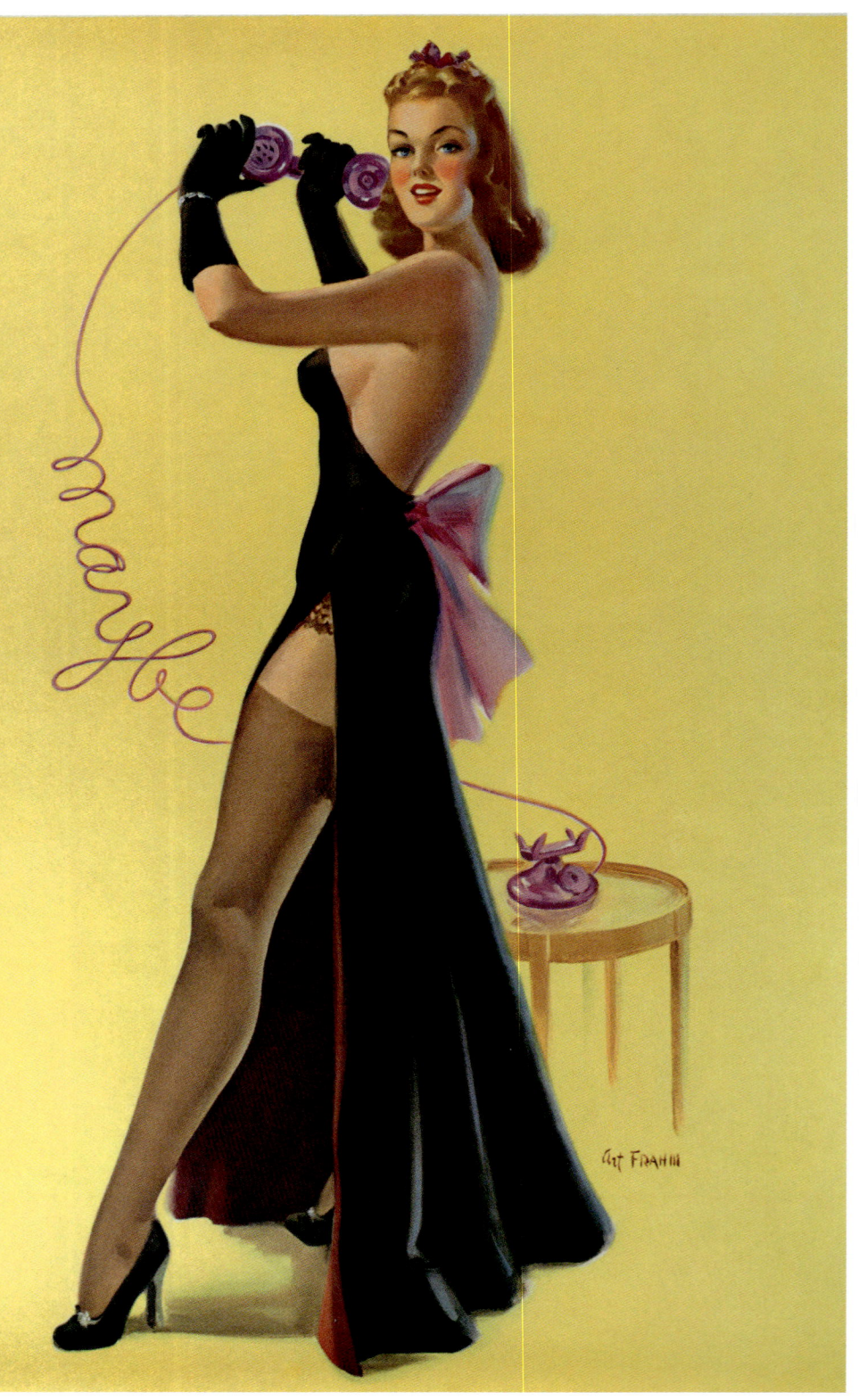

„Seine fröhlich-abstrusen Genredarstellungen zeigen
junge Ehefrauen, die versuchen, ihren Weg durch
die weite Welt zu machen, doch dabei rutschen ihnen
plötzlich die Schlüpfer bis an die Fußknöchel."

Art Frahm kam als Sohn einer aus
Deutschland stammenden Mutter und
eines Vaters, der zuerst als Barmixer,
später als Maschinenschlosser arbeitete,
in einer Einwanderergemeinde in
Chicago zur Welt. Nach dem Besuch
der Kunstakademie hielt sich Frahm an
den in der Region üblichen Werdegang
für Illustratoren: Er fing bei Haddon
Sundblom an und assistierte dem frei-
schaffenden Künstler bei seinen Auf-
trägen, dann schloss er sich der Truppe
bei Stevens-Gross an und arbeitete an
der Seite anderer bedeutender Pin-up-
Künstler wie Joyce Ballantyne und
Gil Elvgren.

Frahms früheste Pin-ups hatte die
Louis F. Dow Company in Auftrag
gegeben. Als einer von zahlreichen viel-
versprechenden „nächsten Elvgrens"
schuf er eigenständige Pin-up-Bilder,
die während des Zweiten Weltkriegs

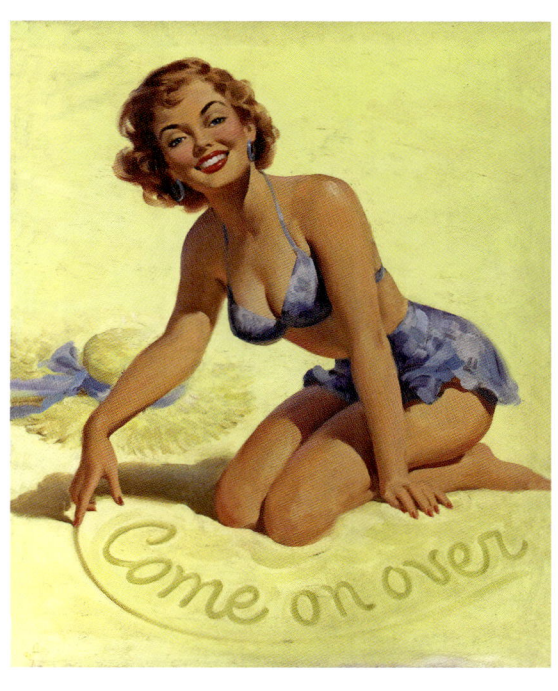

für die in Übersee stationierten Soldaten vorgesehen waren. 1943 wechselte er die Seiten, als er
mit 37 Jahren in die Armee eingezogen wurde: Er malte keine Pin-ups mehr, sondern erhielt
welche. Nach seiner Rückkehr ins Zivilleben begann er, seinen eigenen Weg in der Pin-up-Welt
einzuschlagen. Seine Ölgemälde waren gekennzeichnet von sonnigen Farben und einem schweren, wirbelnden Farbauftrag, dem sogenannten Mayonnaise-Stil, ganz in der bevorzugten Manier
der Chicagoer Schule. Frahm machte sich so mit einer Reihe von Bildern einen Namen, die
unter der Bezeichnung „Verlegenheitsserie" bekannt werden sollten.

Bei seinen Arbeiten für die anspruchsloseren Konkurrenten von Brown & Bigelow, wie
Joseph C. Hoover and Sons, stürzte sich Frahm auf die Probleme zwischen den zurückgekehr-
ten Soldaten, die erwarteten, nun wieder Herr im Hause zu sein, und ihren Frauen, die ihre
Schürzen gegen Schutzhelme ausgetauscht hatten. Seine fröhlich-abstrusen Genredarstellungen

Opposite: Maybe Girl, calendar lithograph,
circa 1948.

Above: Come On Over, oil on board, circa 1950.
24 x 19.5 inches.

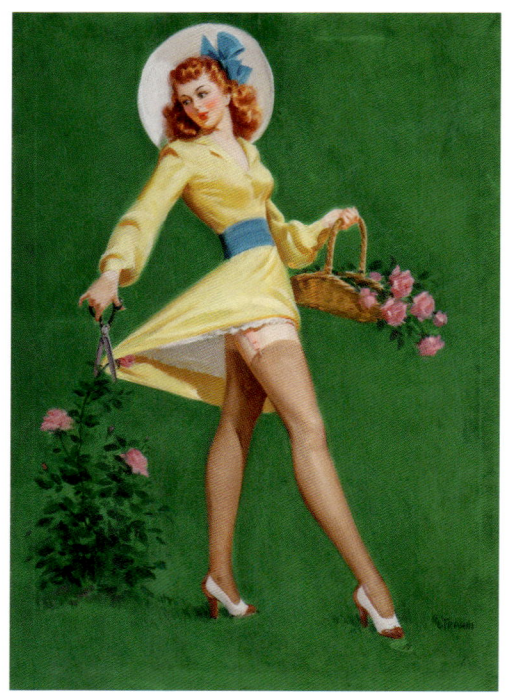

zeigen junge Ehefrauen, die versuchen, ihren Weg durch die weite Welt zu machen, doch dabei rutschen ihnen plötzlich die Schlüpfer bis an die Fußknöchel. Einkaufstüten sind ihr Verderben; jede dieser Frauen plagt sich mit einer oder mehreren Tüten herum, die in der Regel mit üppig gewachsenen – für das Abendessen des Gatten besorgten – Selleriestangen vollgepackt sind. So können sie nicht verhindern, dass ihnen das Höschen herunterrutscht. Der entsetzte Gesichtsausdruck verweist auf den Grenzbereich zwischen privater und öffentlicher Sphäre. Eher mit Schrecken als echter Verlegenheit fragt dieser Blick: „Huch, was ist denn hier passiert?" Währenddessen gaffen die männlichen Zuschauer auf den Pin-ups – in der Regel Vertreter der Arbeiterschicht – neugierig und entzückt auf das Ereignis. Die stete Verwunderung rührt ebenso stark von der Anwesenheit der sexy Hausfrauen in der Welt der Arbeit – auf Frahms Pin-ups werden Männer, die einen Bus steuern, einen Presslufthammer oder einen Aufzug bedienen, bei der Arbeit unterbrochen – wie vom Fehlen der Nylonstrümpfe, die Frahm nicht besonders mochte. Beine konnte er besser malen als jeder andere in seiner Zeit, doch mit Strümpfen hatte er Probleme. In seinen Dessous-Pin-ups sind Beine eher matronenhaft als verführerisch, die Strümpfe sind von einem schmuddeligen Braun, ohne jeden Reiz oder Glanz, und entsprechen eher der Vorstellung einer vom Glück verlassenen Gypsy Rose Lee, der berühmten amerikanischen Burlesktänzerin.

Frahm hatte allerdings weder für Stripperinnen noch Leinwandsirenen eine Vorliebe, nicht einmal für die Zigarettenmädchen, die so typisch für seine Heimatstadt Chicago waren. Frahms idealisierte Welt entsprach der der Fernsehserie *Mayberry R.F.D.* In seinen Kalenderbildern mit einem liebenswürdigen Polizisten oder einem blonden Pin-up, das nach dem Nacktbaden schüchtern einem Angelteich entsteigt, lieferte Frahm das, wovon die heimkehrenden Veteranen in Europa träumten. Gil Elvgren meinte oft, das perfekte Pin-up habe das Gesicht eines Mädchens und ansonsten den Körper einer Frau, Frahm jedoch malte Szenen weiblichen Lebens mit mädchenhaftem Verhalten. Auf diesen Bildern bereitet sich die junge Hausfrau stets darauf vor, mal auszugehen – und erleidet prompt ein peinliches Missgeschick. Aber macht nichts: Dieser nette, väterliche Polizist rettet sie ja.

Anfang der 1960er-Jahre hatten sich die Fantasien verändert, und Frahm zog sich aus dem Geschäft zurück. Im Ruhestand genoss er ein einfacheres Leben und ging mit seiner Frau Ruth und Tochter Diana nach South Carolina, wo er ab und an Honoratioren der dortigen Gesellschaftskreise malte. Er blieb in South Carolina bis zu seinem Tod 1981.

Above: Nipped in the Bud, undated, oil on canvas, 30 x 22 inches. Courtesy Heritage Auctions.

Opposite: A Grand Slam, oil on canvas, circa 1948, for a Goes Litho calendar. 35 x 28 inches.

THE ART OF PIN-UP

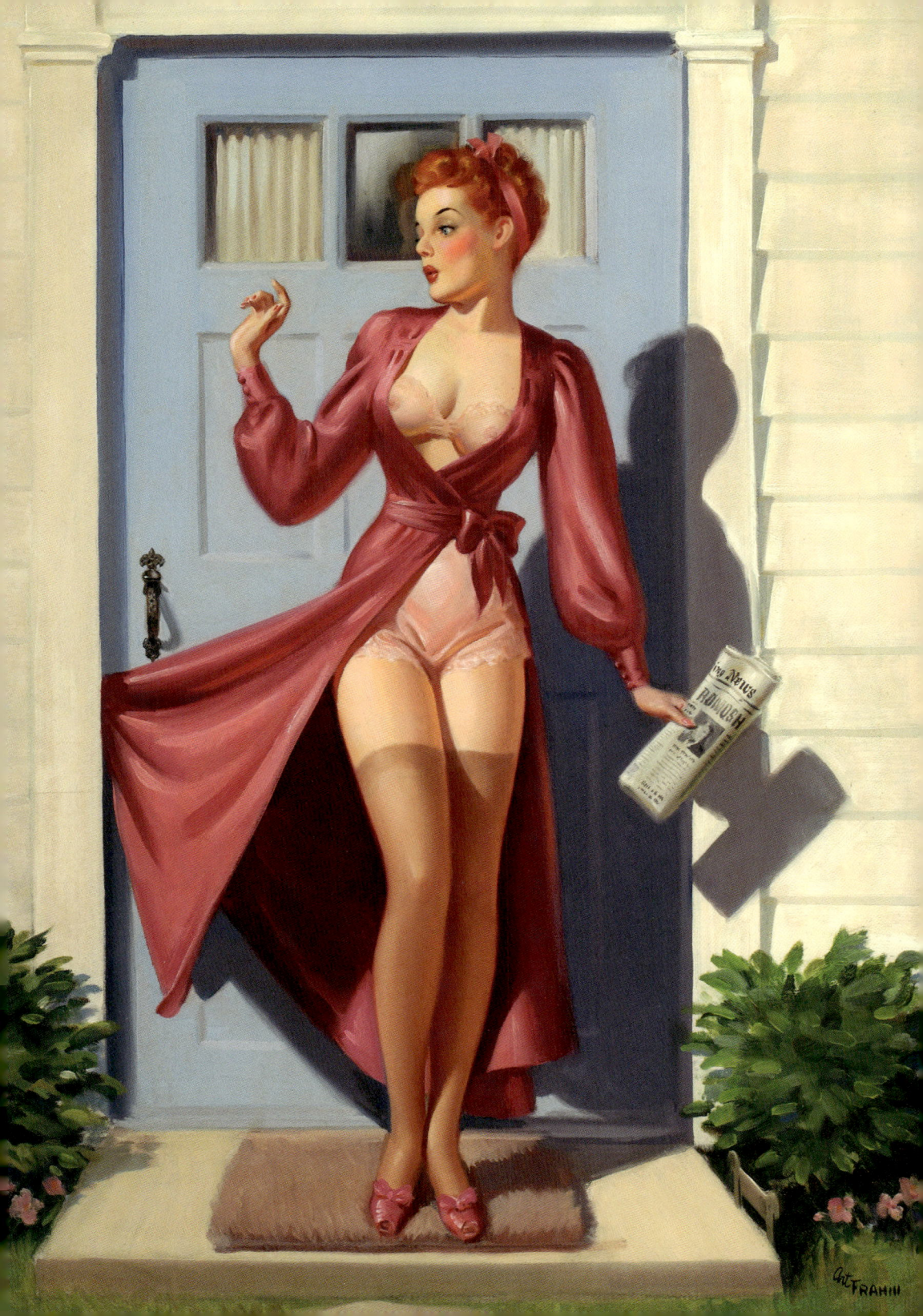

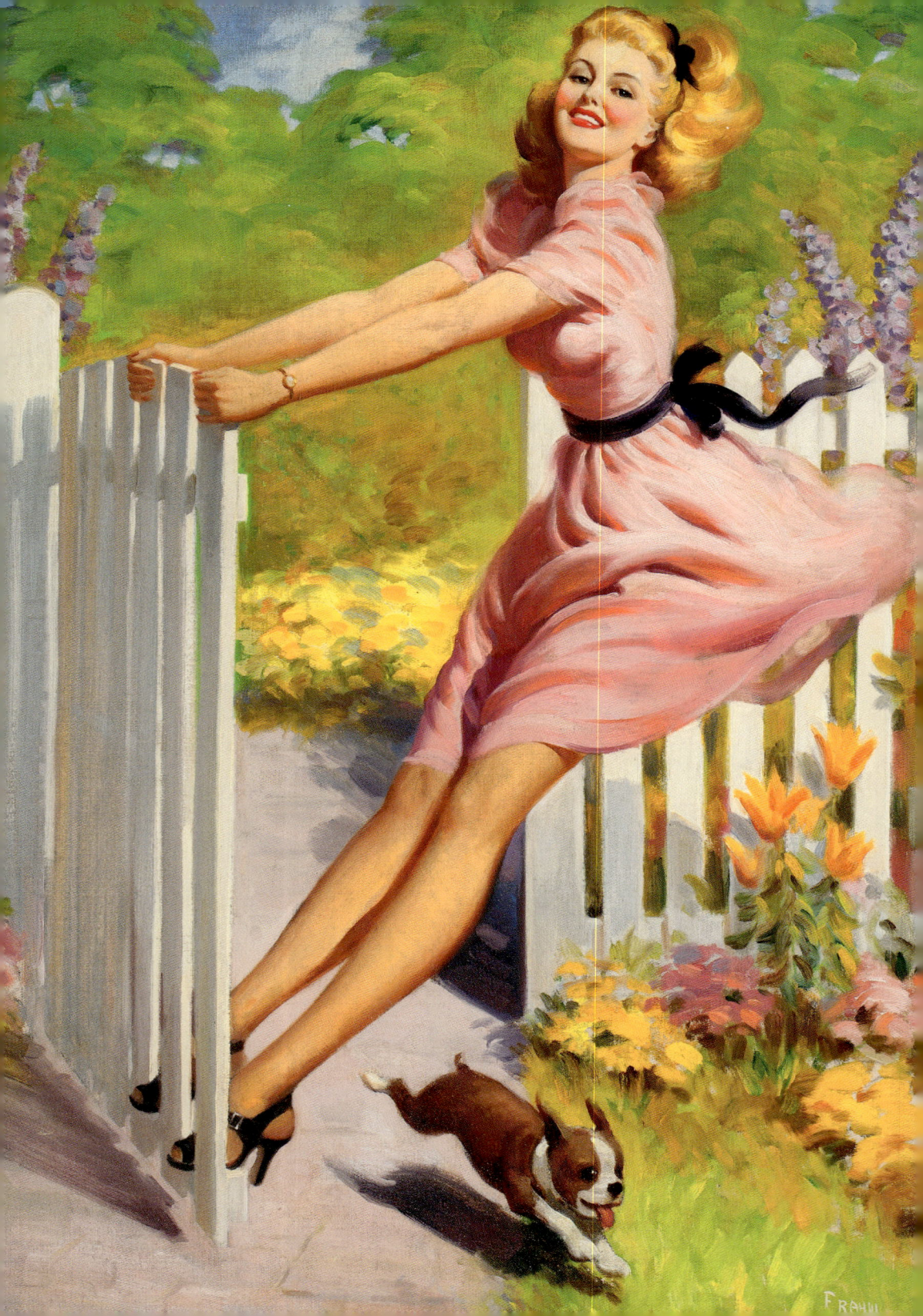

« Il dépeignait de charmantes jeunes épouses vaquant
à leurs occupations et se retrouvant avec leur culotte
autour des chevilles. »

Art Frahm naquit en 1906 dans
une communauté d'immigrants
à Chicago, d'une mère allemande et
d'un père barman, qui devint plus
tard machiniste. Après des études
d'art, il suivit le parcours habituel
des illustrateurs de la région : il fit
son apprentissage chez Haddon
Sundblom, puis rejoignit l'écurie
de Stevens-Gross, travaillant aux
côtés de sommités de l'art de la
pin-up telles que Joyce Ballantyne
et Gil Elvgren.

Ce fut Louis F. Dow qui lui
commanda ses premières pin-up.
Comme de nombreux illustrateurs rêvant de devenir le prochain
Elvgren, il peignit de jolies filles sur
un fond uni destinées à être ache-
minées par courrier militaire aux
soldats postés à l'étranger durant la
guerre. En 1943, alors âgé de 37 ans,
il s'enrôla et se trouva à son tour
récipiendaire de pin-up. De retour
à la vie civile, il adopta la palette

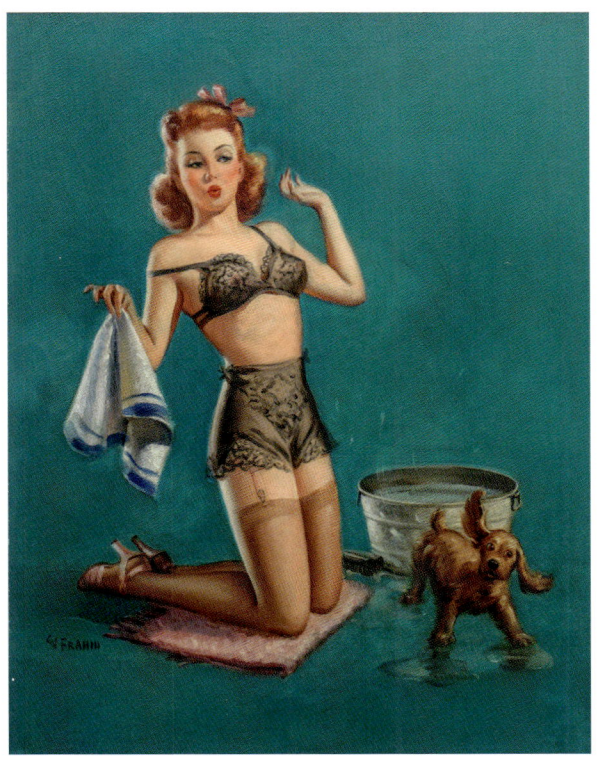

ensoleillée et les épaisses couches de peinture étalées en volutes de l'école de Chicago, se faisant
un nom avec ses « demoiselles en détresse ».

Travaillant pour la Goes Lithograph Company, rival plus modeste de B&B, Frahm jouait
sur l'antagonisme entre les soldats qui étaient rentrés au pays en s'attendant à être traités comme
des rois et les femmes qui avaient échangé leur tablier contre un masque de soudeur. Il dépeignait de charmantes jeunes épouses vaquant à leurs occupations et se retrouvant avec leur culotte
autour des chevilles. Le plus souvent, elles ont les bras chargés de sacs de course d'où sortent
de généreuses branches de céleri pour le dîner de leur mari, ce qui les empêche de rattraper le

Opposite: Swinging into Summer, oil on canvas, 1947,
for a 1949 Goes Litho calendar. 33 x 24 inches.

Above: Oil on canvas, circa 1945, for a Joseph C. Hoover
& Sons calendar. 29 x 23 inches.

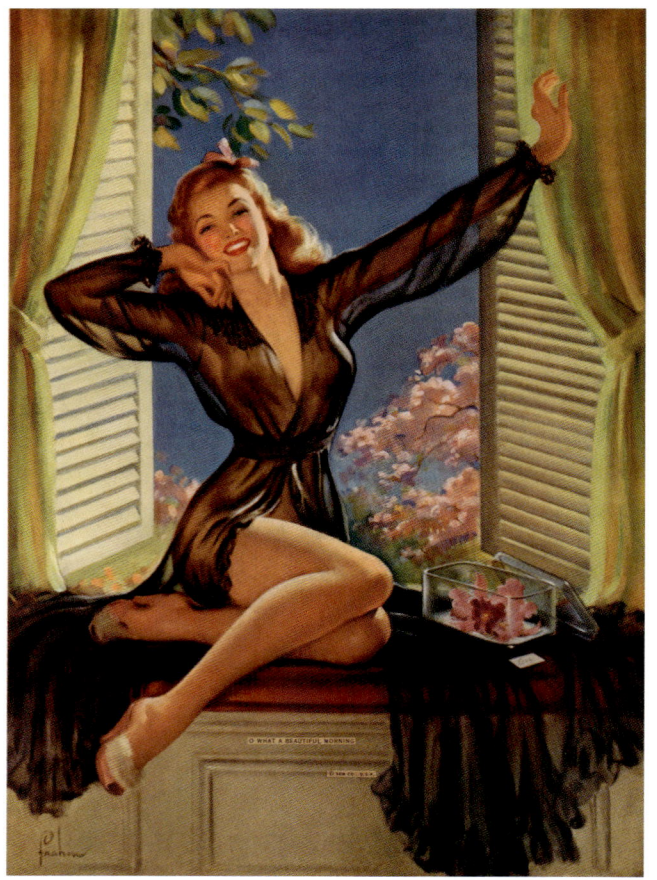

sous-vêtement. Leur expression en « oooh », tenant plus du choc que de la honte, évoque cet espace liminal entre les sphères publique et privée. Elles semblent se demander ce qui leur arrive tandis que des témoins (des hommes de la classe ouvrière, substituts du public masculin des pin-up) assistent à la scène, émerveillés et ravis. La stupeur vient autant de l'irruption de ménagères sexy dans le monde du travail (les pin-up interrompent des chauffeurs de bus, des terrassiers et des liftiers), que des inconvénients du nylon, que Frahm n'appréciait guère. Il n'avait pas son pareil pour peindre une jambe, à condition qu'elle soit nue. Ses pin-up en collant ont de grosses jambes qui n'ont rien de sexy : leurs bas sont d'un brun boueux, sans tension ni lustre, rappelant une danseuse légère sur le retour.

Frahm n'était pas un fan des strip-teaseuses, des déesses de l'écran ni même des vendeuses de cigarettes qui personnifiaient sa ville natale de Chicago. Son monde idéal était celui d'une petite ville de province. Dans ses calendriers remplis de gentils policiers et d'étangs ensoleillés d'où sortait parfois timidement une pin-up blonde et nue, il offrait à voir ce dont les soldats avaient rêvé quand ils étaient sur le front. Gil Elvgren disait souvent que la pin-up idéale avait un visage d'adolescente sur un corps de femme, mais Frahm dépeignait des femmes actives avec des attitudes d'adolescentes. La jeune épouse se préparait des heures durant pour sa sortie en ville, pour subir cette embarrassante déconvenue. Toutefois, rien de grave : le brave policier paternel lui porterait secours.

Au début des années 1960, les fantasmes changèrent et Frahm abandonna l'illustration. Souhaitant jouir d'une retraite tranquille, il s'installa en Caroline du Sud avec son épouse Ruth et leur fille Diana, où il réalisait parfois des portraits de notables locaux. Il y mourut en 1981.

Above: Oh What a Beautiful Morning calendar lithograph from the Goes Litho Company, circa 1950.

Opposite: Gossamer Girl, oil on canvas on board, circa 1955. 25 x 18 inches.

THE ART OF PIN-UP

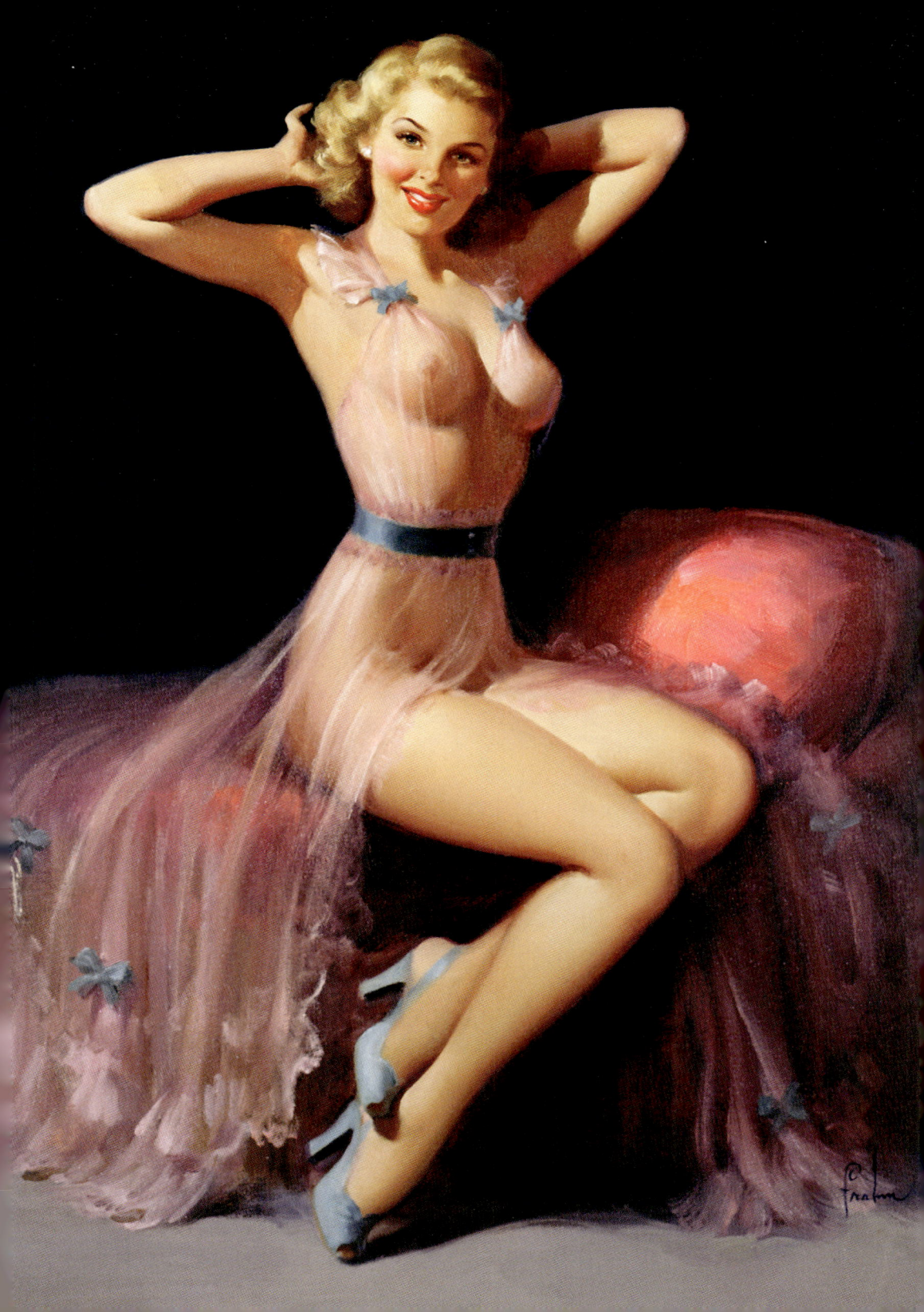

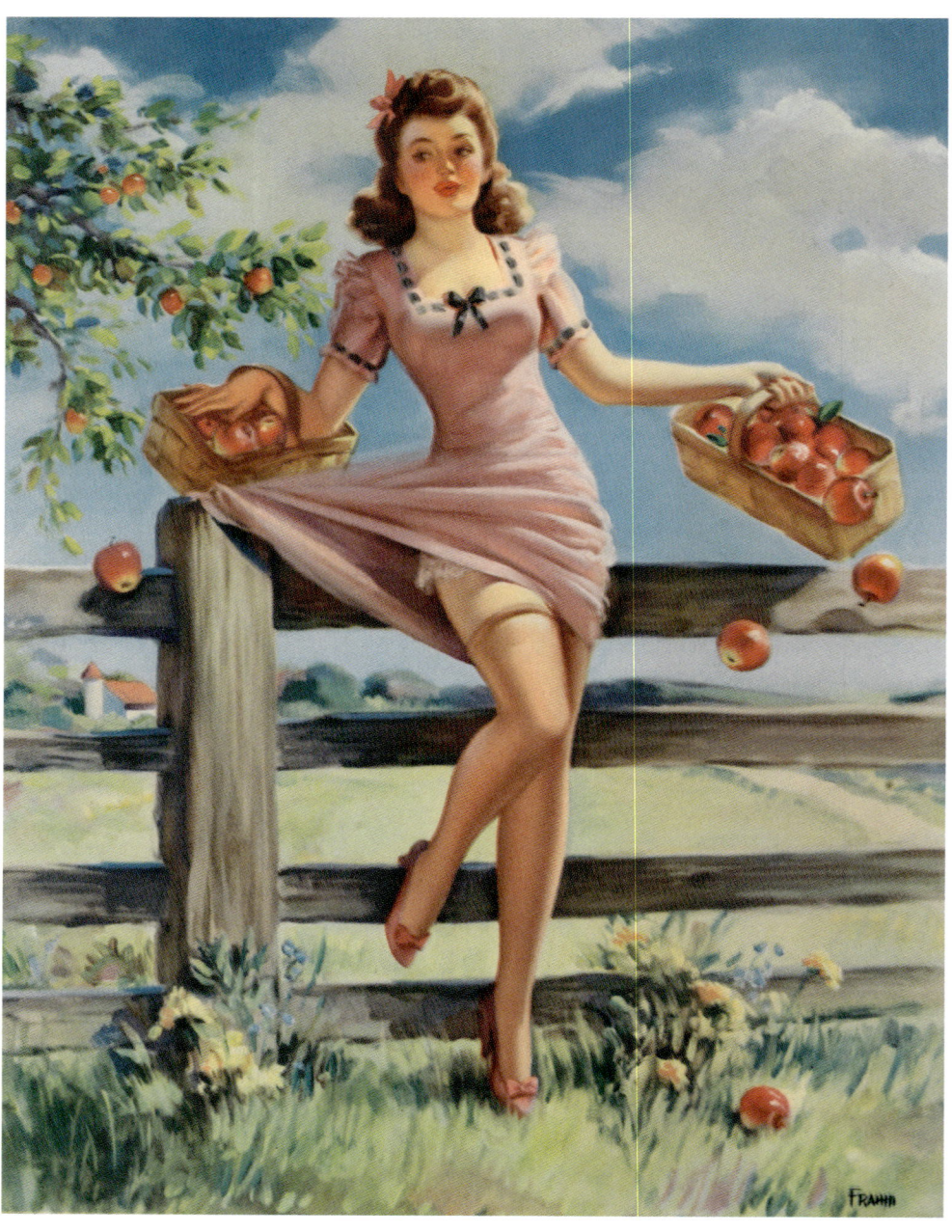

Above: The Farmer's Daughter, 1945, for a six-page 1947 Kemper-Thomas Co. calendar.

Opposite: Ostrich Feathers, oil on board, circa 1948, for a Shaw-Barton calendar. 28.5 x 22.75 inches.

THE ART OF PIN-UP

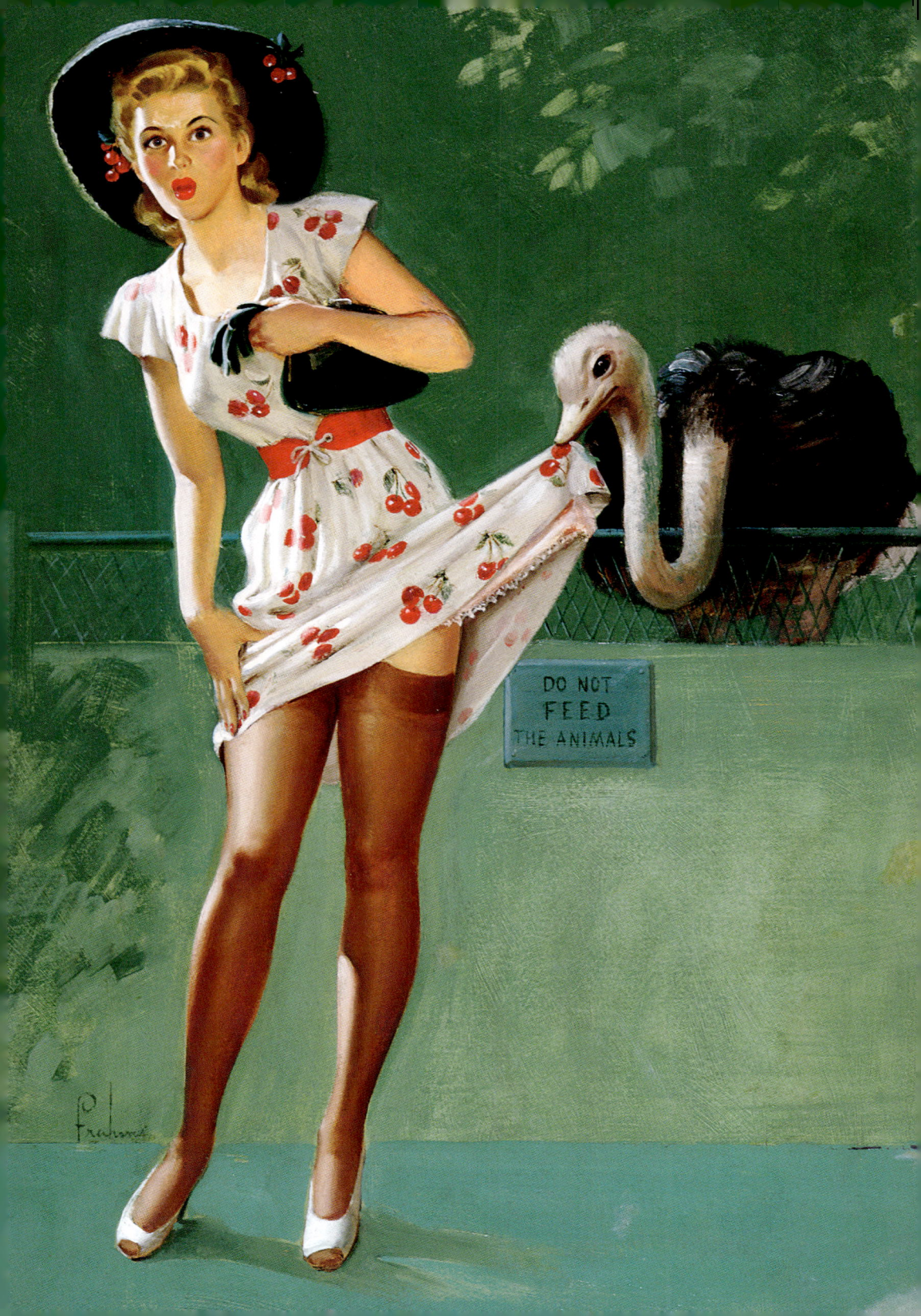

DO NOT
FEED
THE ANIMALS

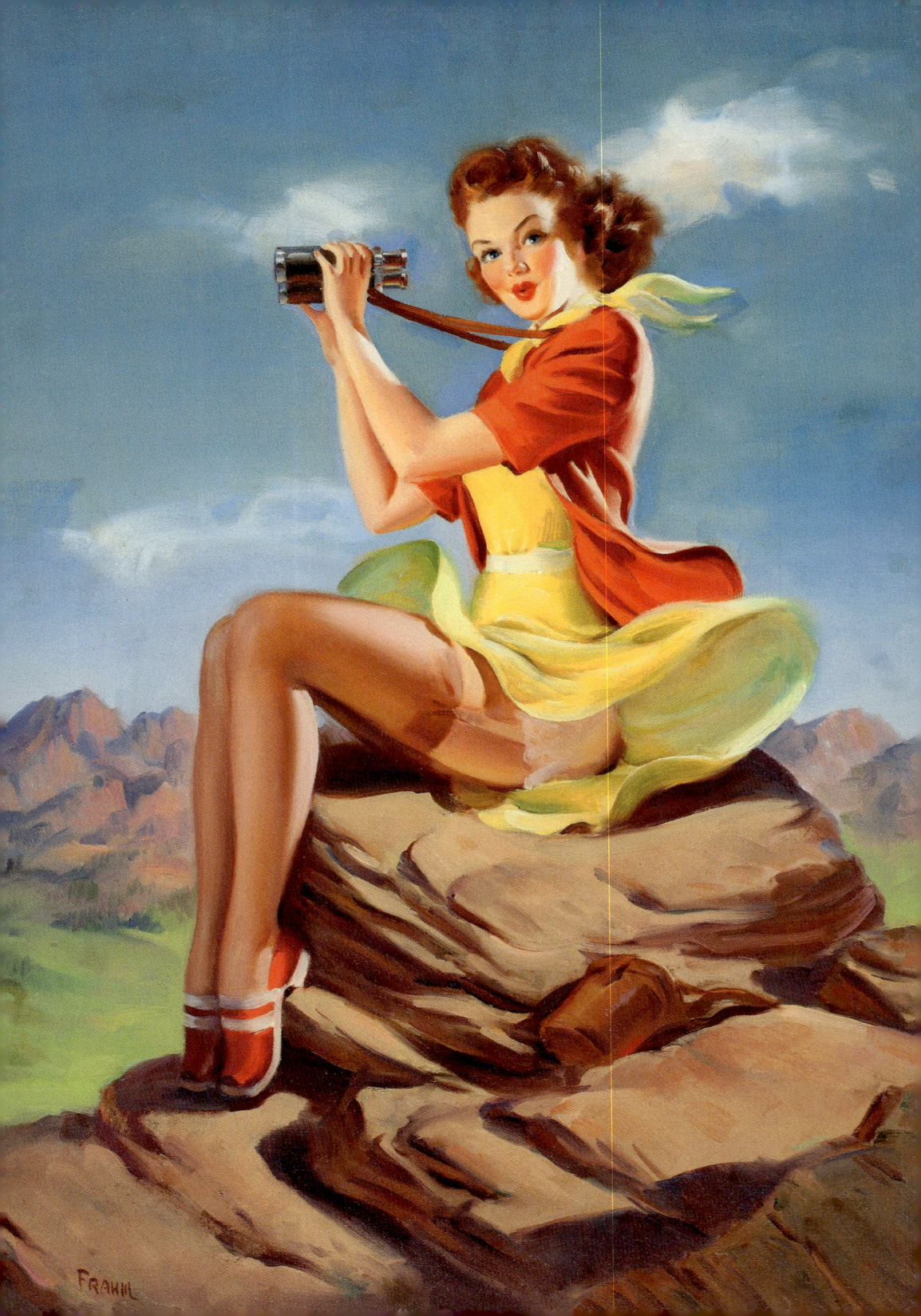

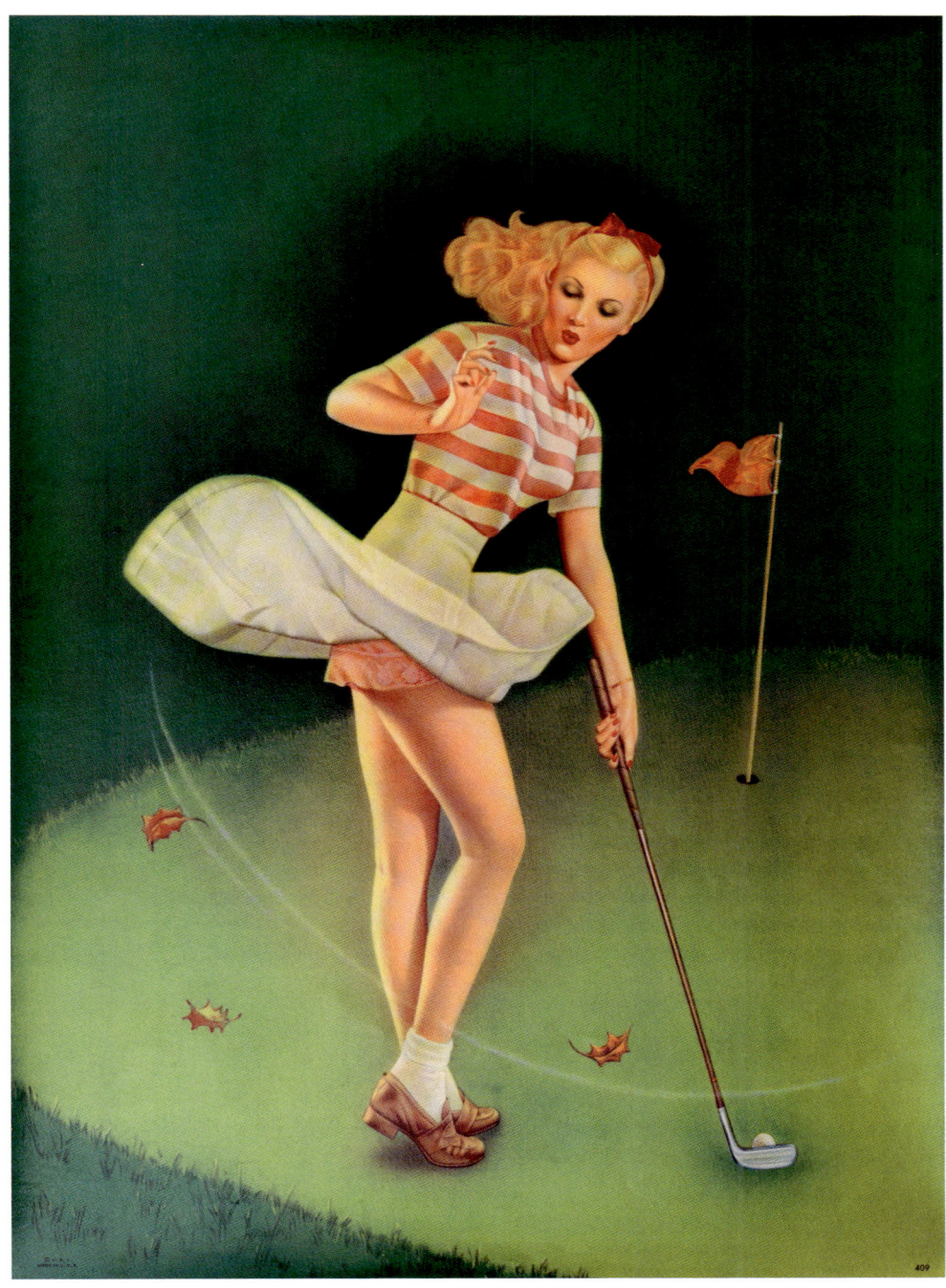

Opposite: The Look Out, oil on canvas on board, circa 1950. 30 x 24 inches.

Above: Joseph C. Hoover & Sons calendar lithograph, circa 1945.

ARTHUR "ART" FRAHM

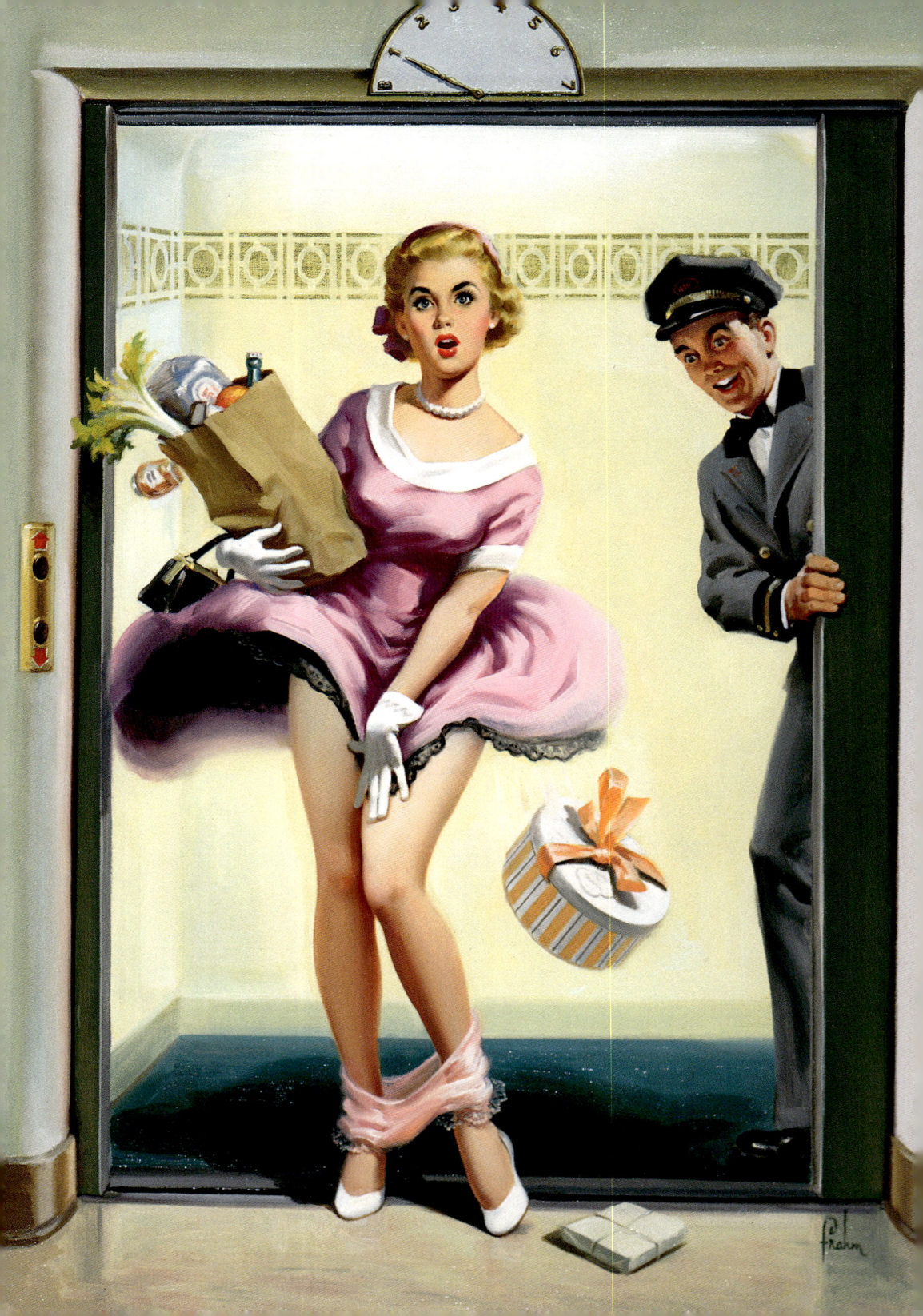

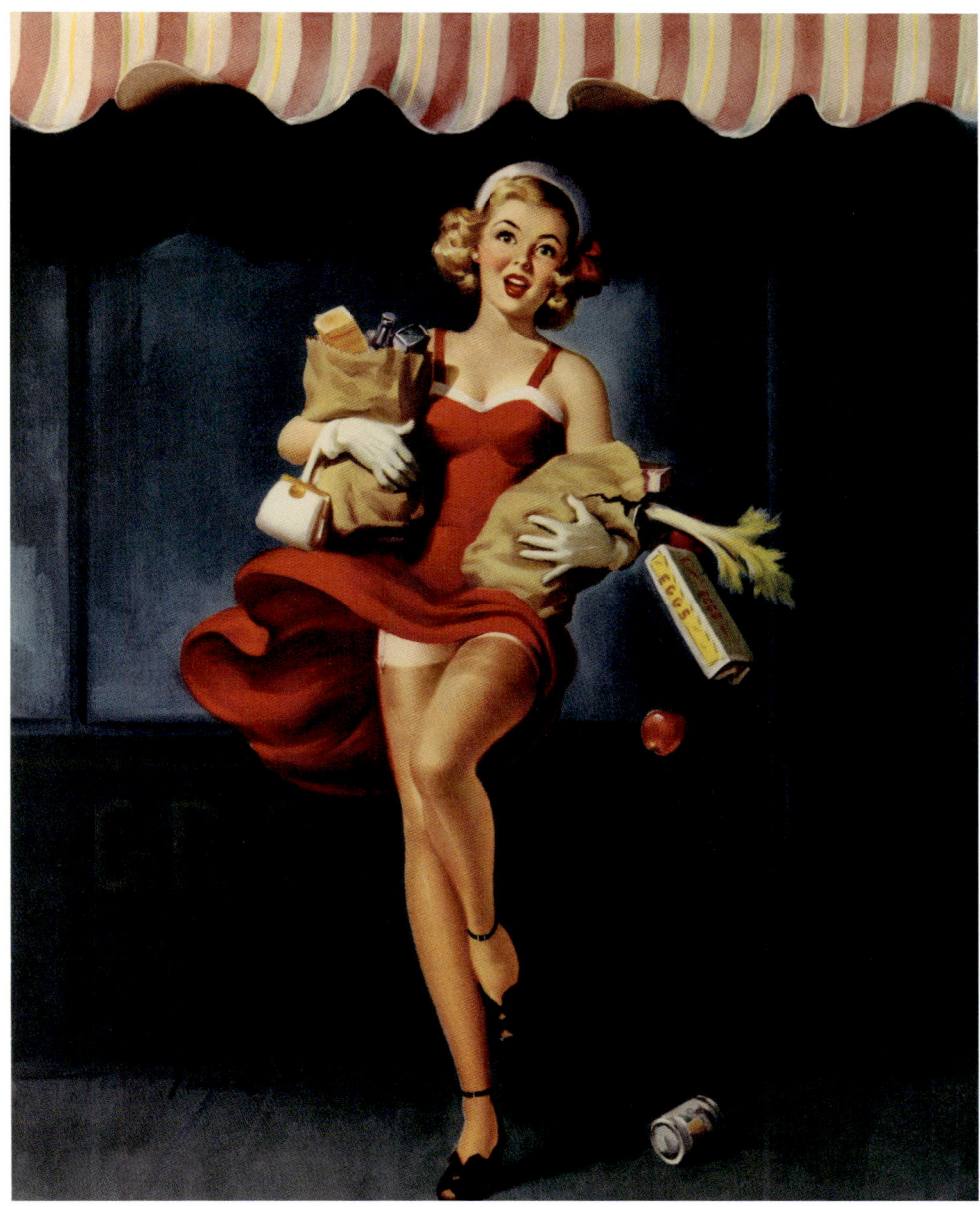

Opposite: Going Down, oil on canvas, 1956, for a 1959 Joseph C. Hoover & Sons calendar. 33 x 26 inches.

Above: A Joseph C. Hoover & Sons calendar lithograph, circa 1949. This illustration is the direct precurser of Frahm's embarrassment series. All the elements are in place: blowing skirt, public space, bags of groceries preventing the woman from exercizing clothing control, even the celery—everything but the panty drop.

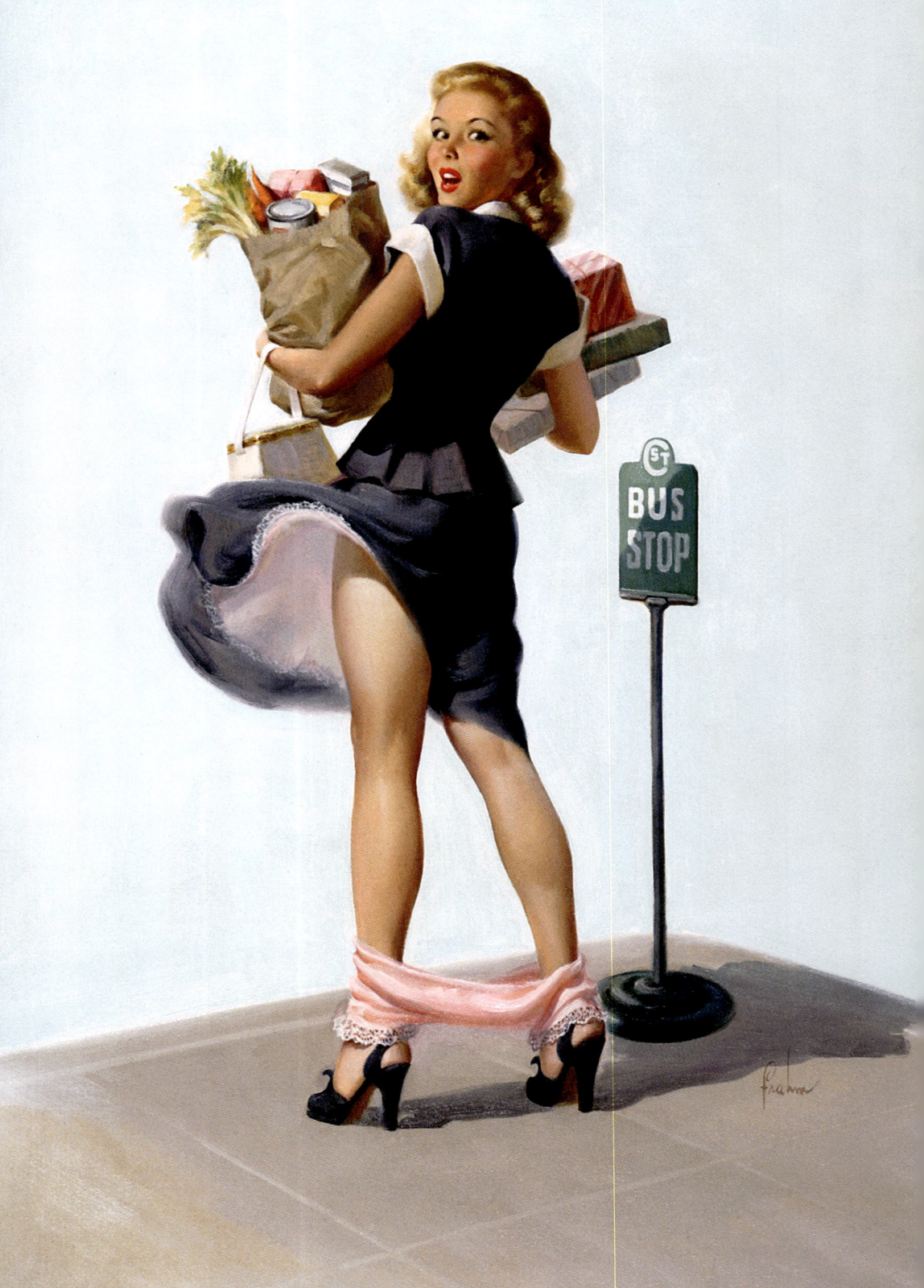

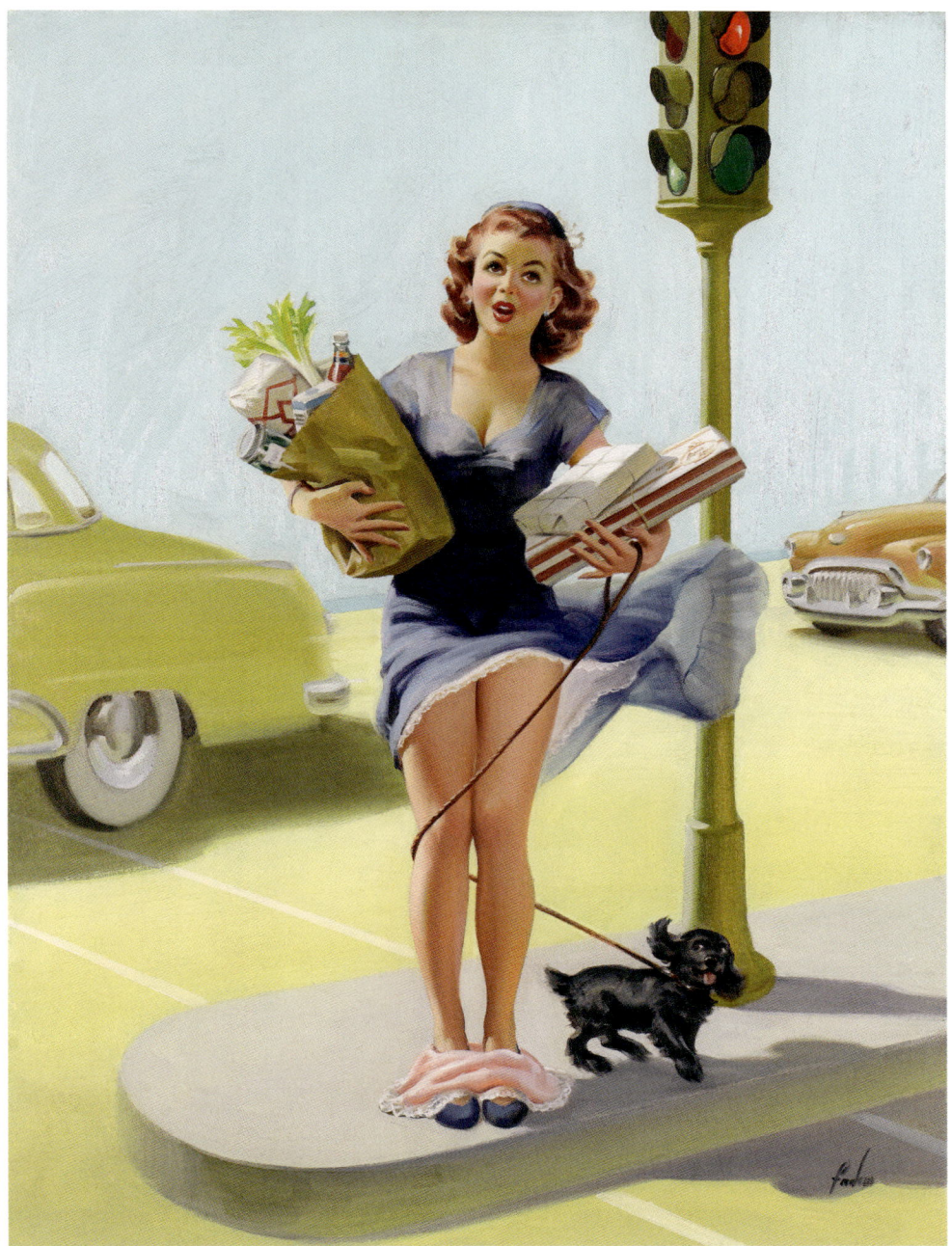

Opposite: O-Ooh!, oil on canvas, 1950, for a 1952 Joseph C. Hoover & Sons calendar. Here in Frahm's first of 12 panty drop paintings we have the basic elements for his entire "embarrassment" series: a young woman in public, her arms full of packages—most often grocery bags sprouting stalks of celery—is suddenly attacked by a playful breeze at the exact moment her panty elastic fails. "O-Ooh!" 32 x 24 inches.

Above: No Time to Go, oil on canvas, 1954, for a 1955 Joseph C. Hoover & Son calendar.

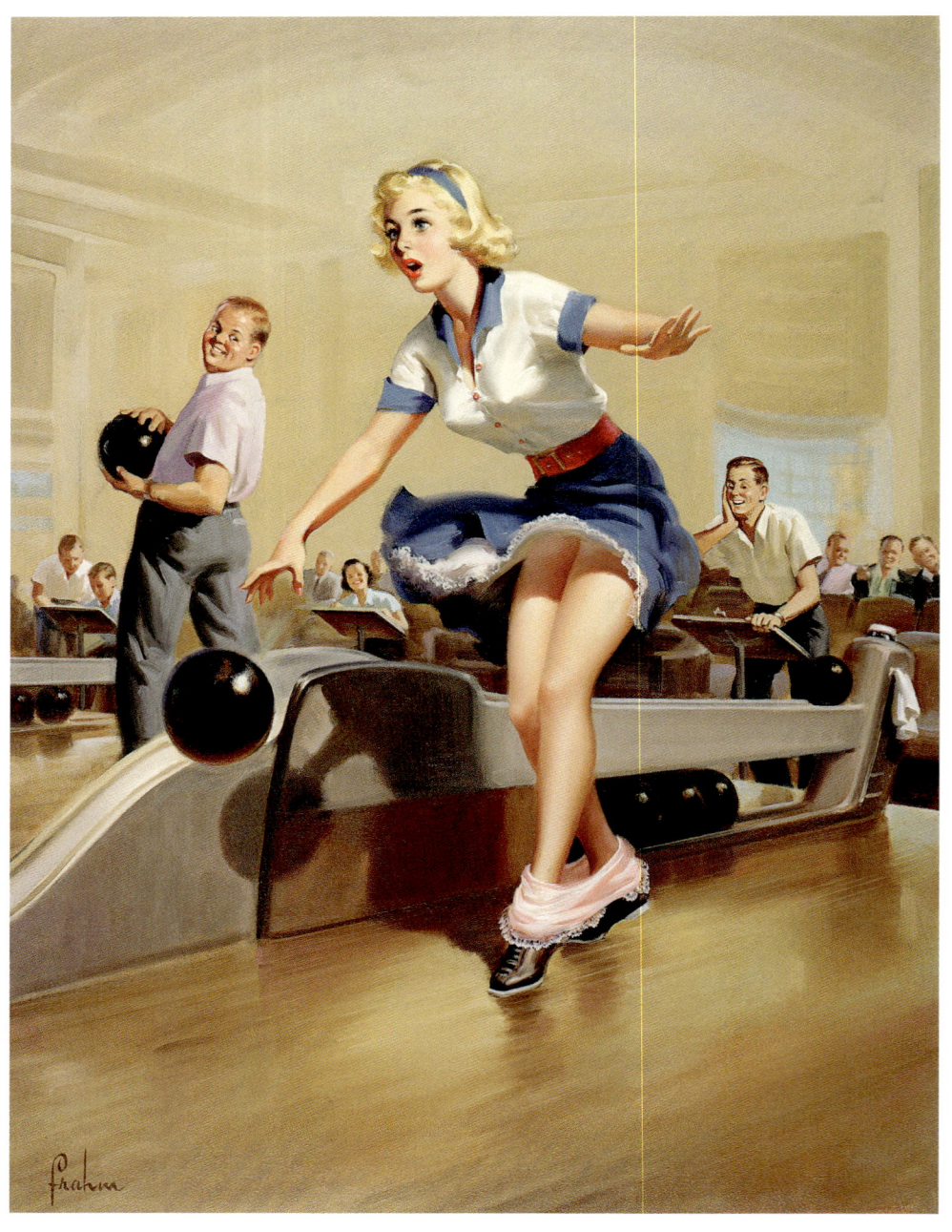

Above: Spare, oil on canvas, 1952, for a 1953
Joseph C. Hoover & Sons calendar. 30 x 24 inches.

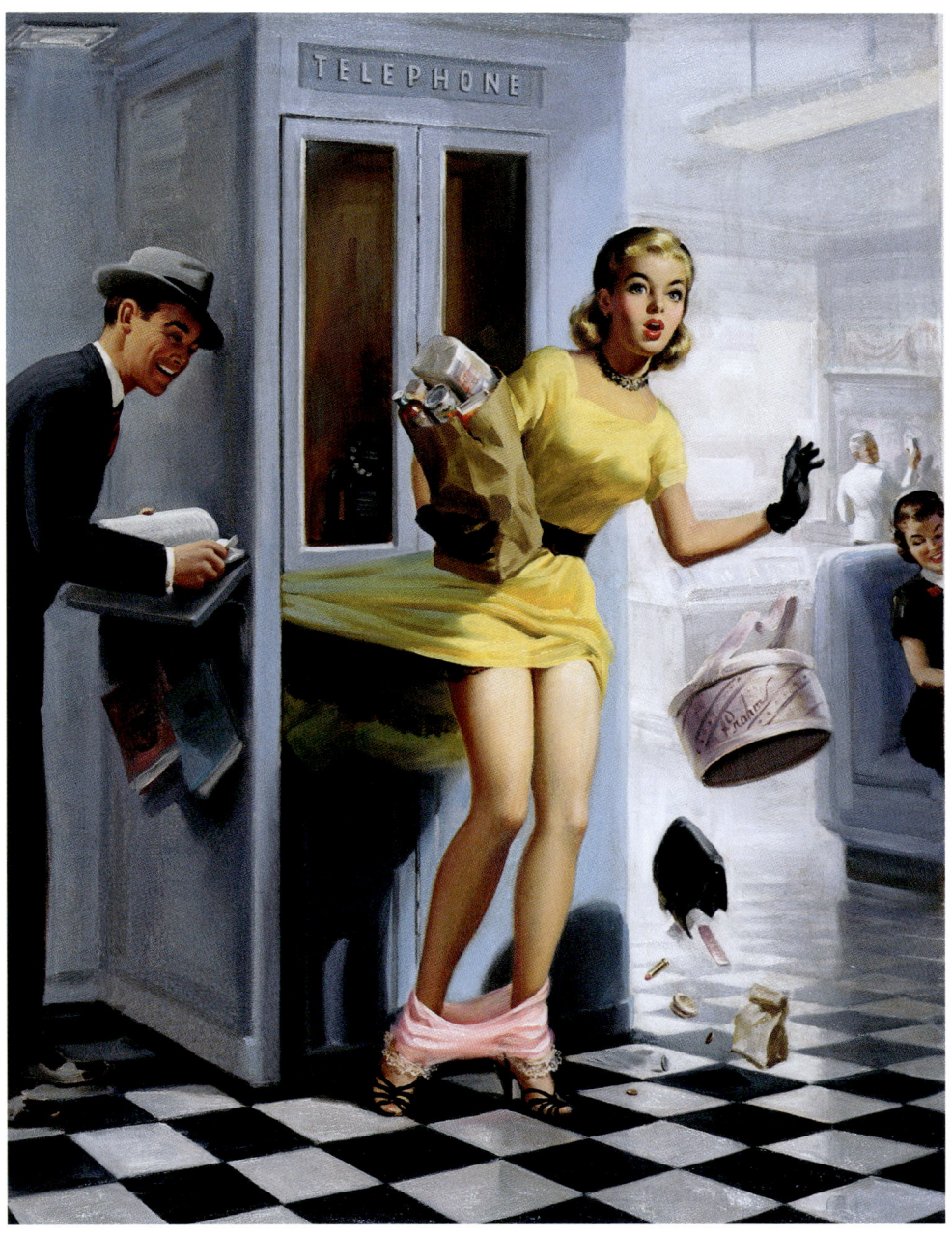

Above: Number Please, oil on canvas, 1957, for a 1958
Joseph C. Hoover & Sons calendar. 30 x 24 inches.

ARTHUR "ART" FRAHM

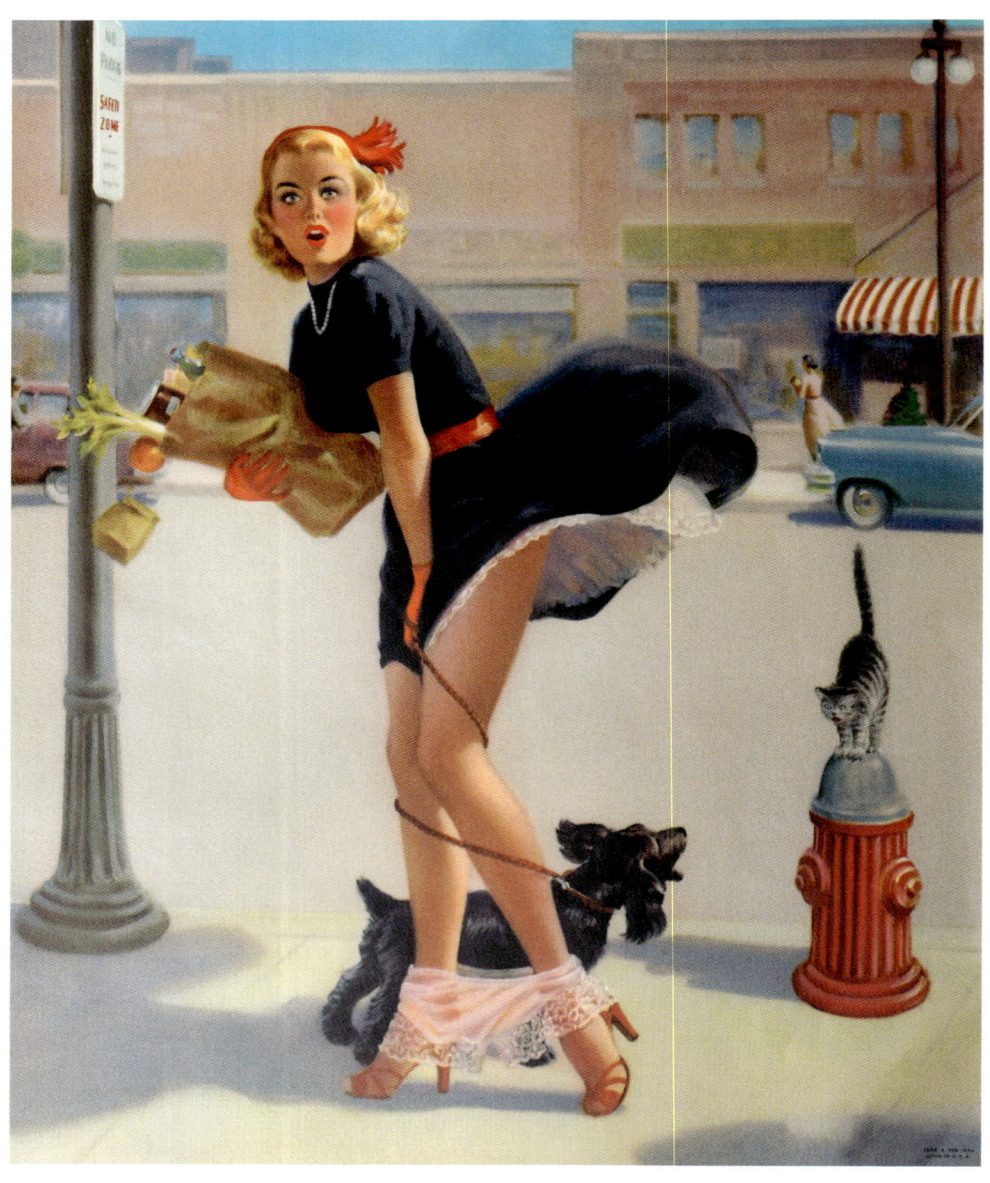

Above: Hold Everything, Joseph C. Hoover & Sons
calendar lithograph, 1954, from a 1953 painting.

THE ART OF PIN-UP

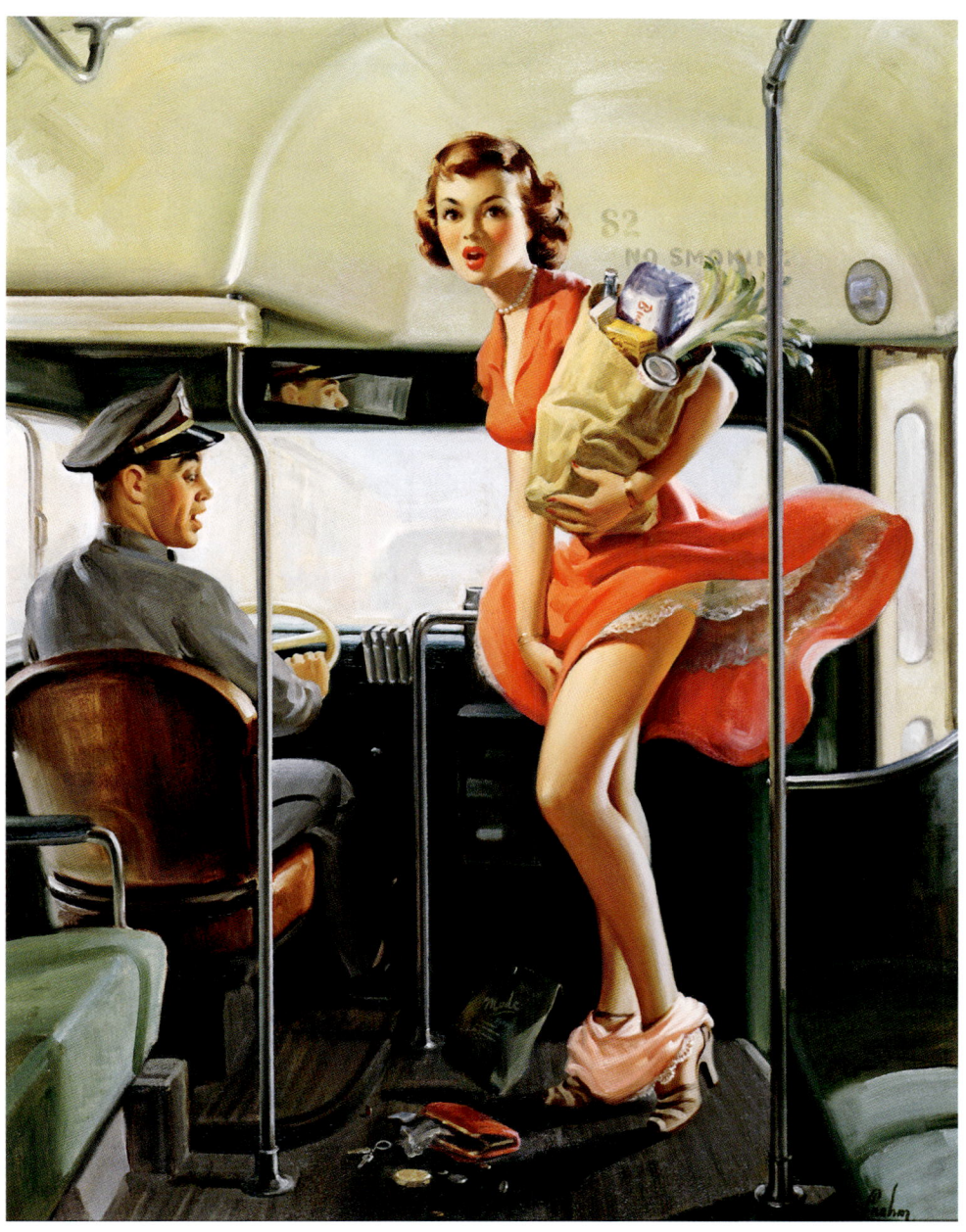

Above: A Fare Loser, oil on canvas, circa 1951,
for a Joseph C. Hoover & Sons calendar.

ARTHUR "ART" FRAHM

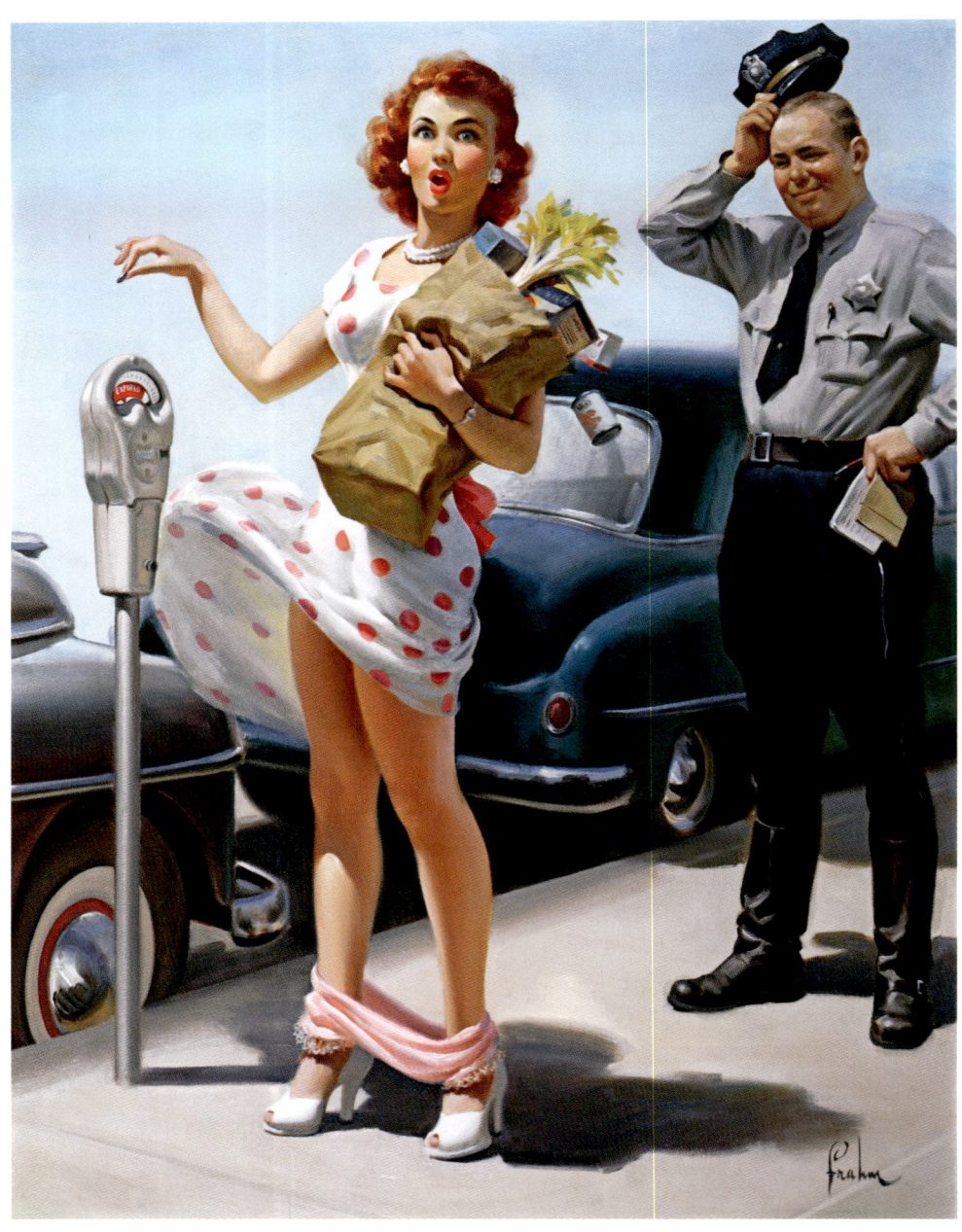

Above: No Time To Lose, oil on canvas, circa 1959, for
a Joseph C. Hoover & Sons calendar. 29.5 x 23.75 inches.

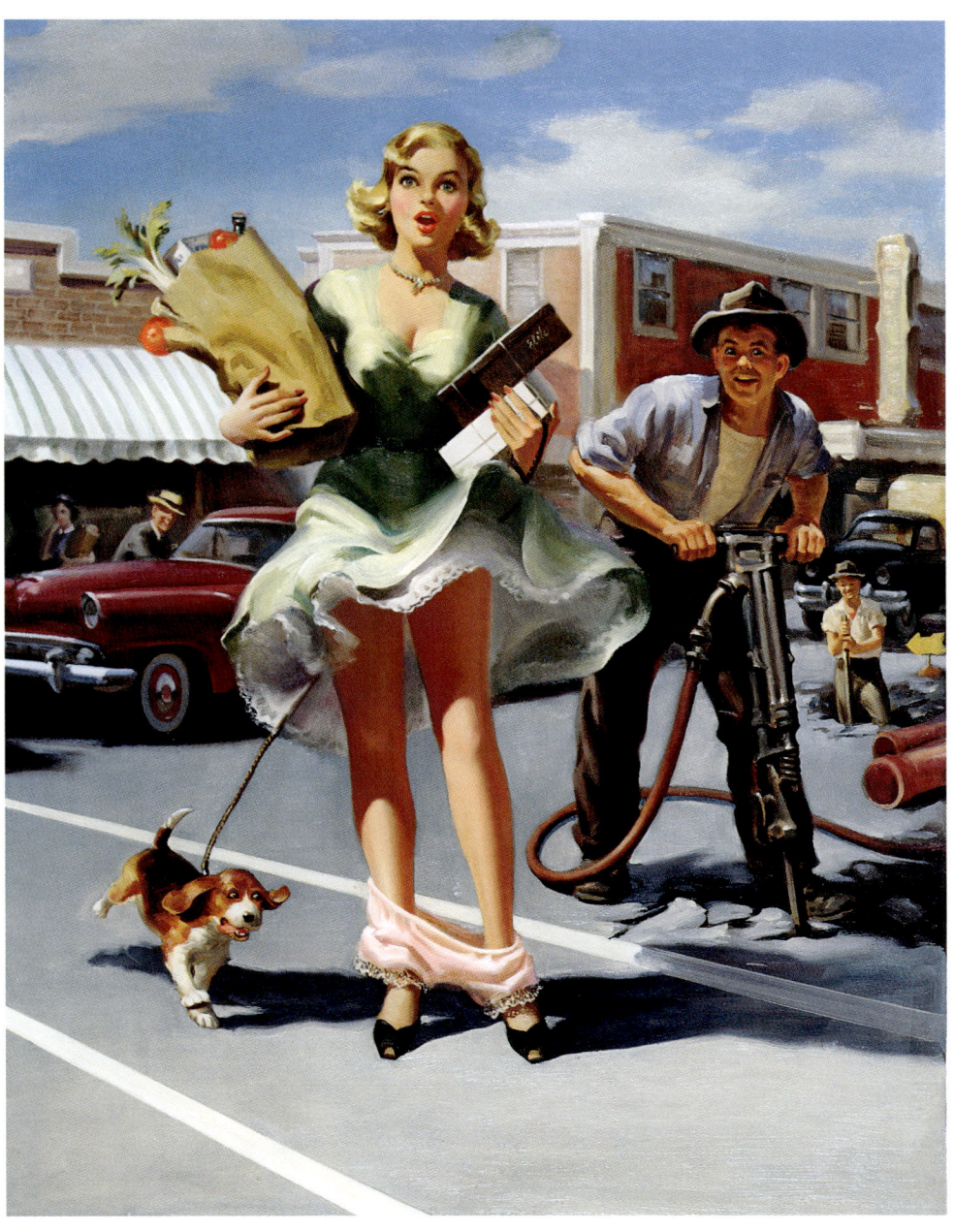

Above: The Shake-Down, oil on board, 1955, for a 1957
Joseph C. Hoover & Sons calendar. 30.5 x 24.5 inches.

WILLIAM "BILL" MEDCALF

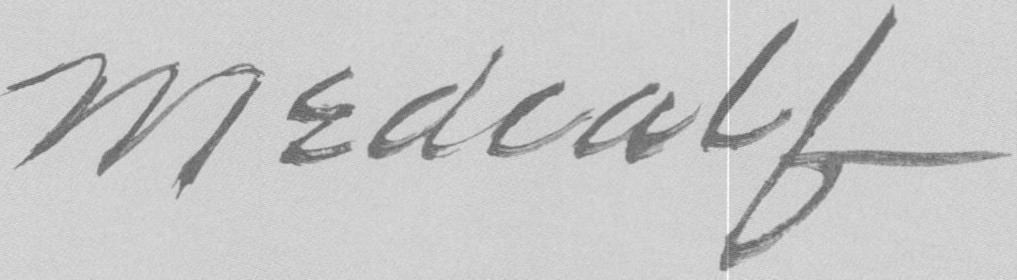

Medcalf

1920–2005

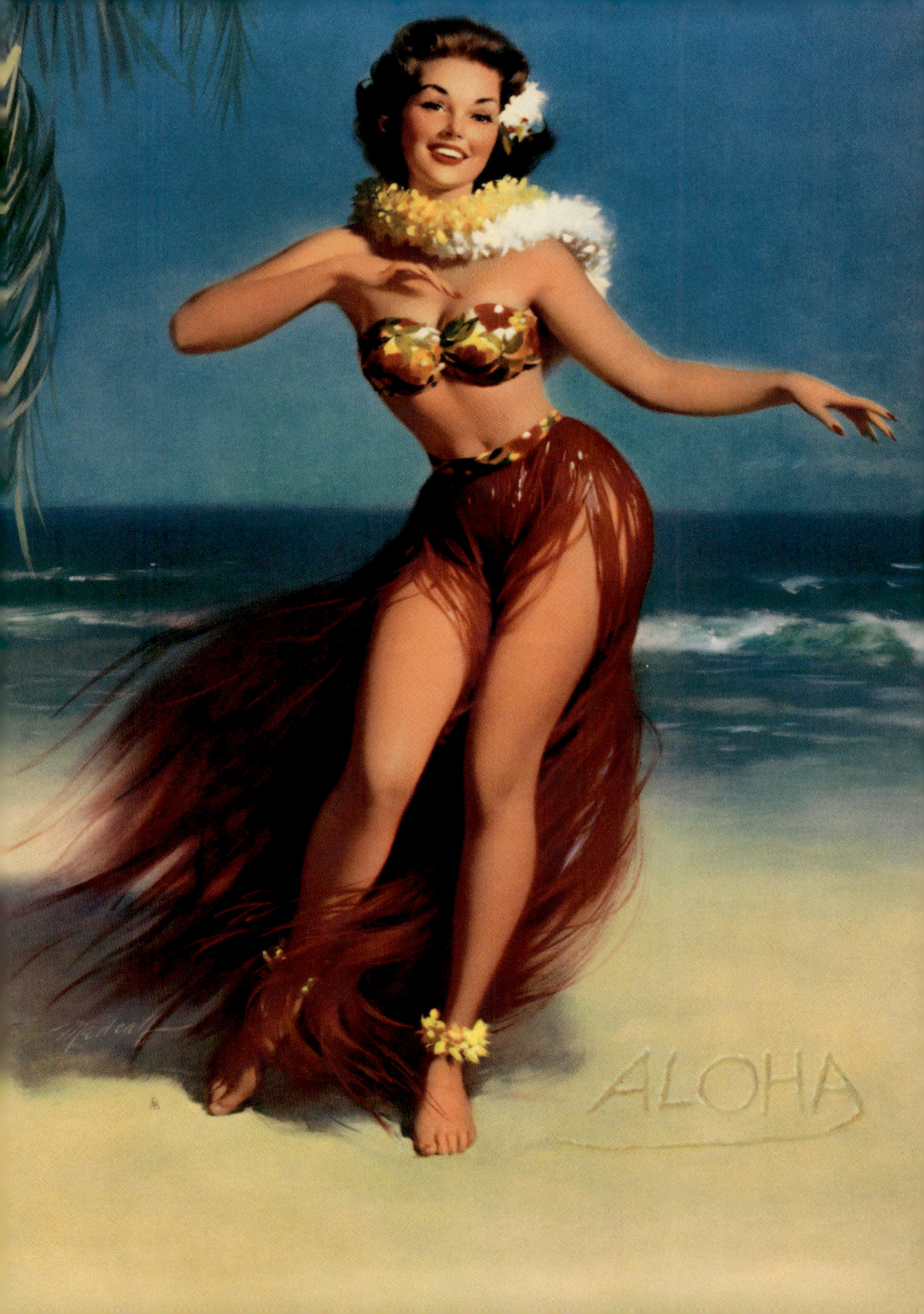

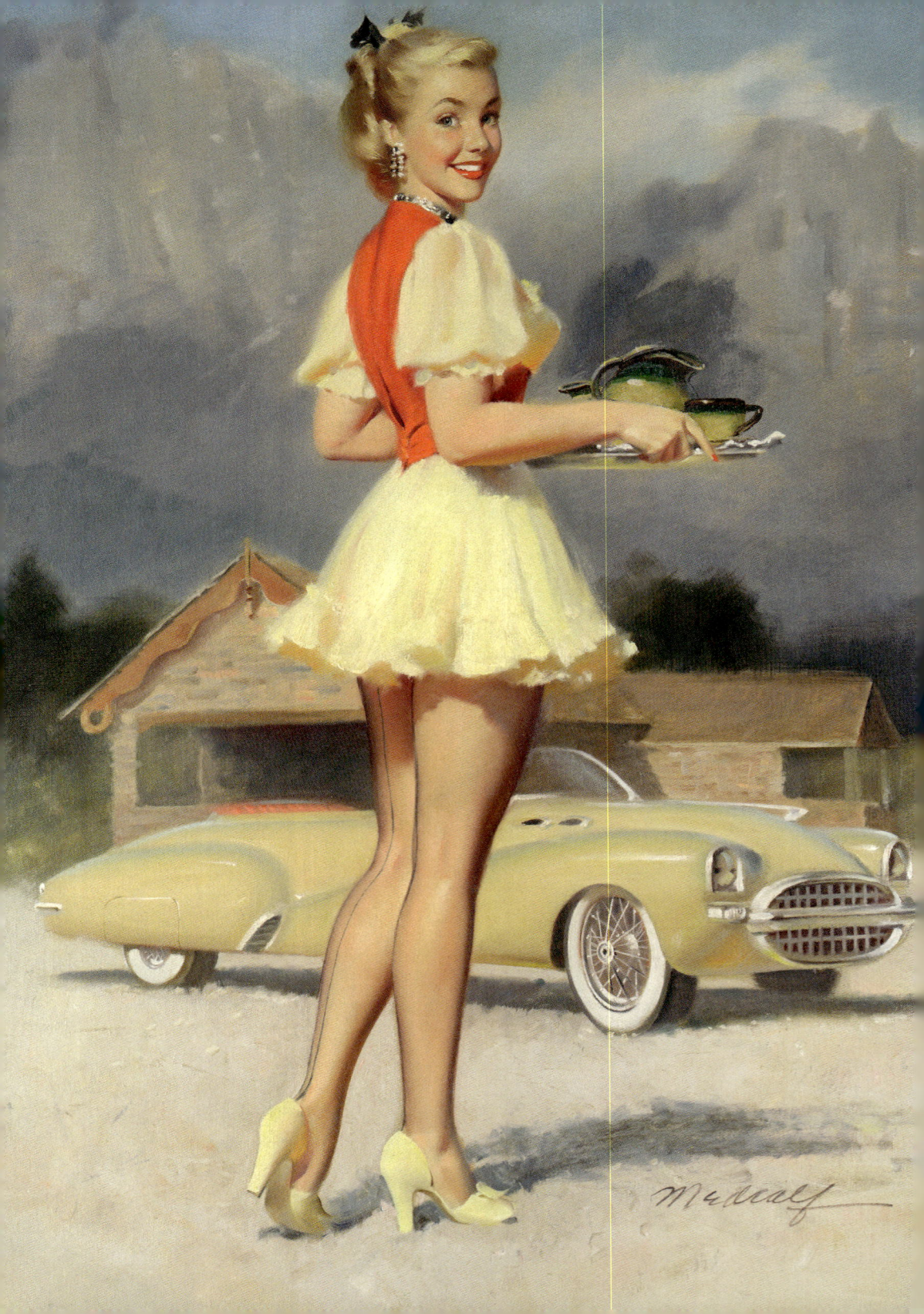

"The artist once described his perfect model as 'someone's sweet sister,' and his favored model for many years was his own wife, Henriette."

William Medcalf was born in St. Paul, Minnesota, in 1920 and remained a resident of the state for all his long life. After studying at the Minnesota School of Art (now Minnesota College of Art and Design) under Cameron Booth and Stan Fenelle, Medcalf took a job working for the U.S. Treasury's Bureau of Engraving. During World War II he served as a naval gunner's mate, then signed on with Brown & Bigelow after settling back into civilian life at war's end. His first commission was creating a specialty calendar for Kelly-Springfield's Celebrity Tires, and this high-profile assignment put him among the ranks of pin-up's most important artists. His many automotive-themed calendars — for Ditzler, NAPA, and Victor — bring gas-guzzling America to life, with the gleaming, richly chromed sports cars painted

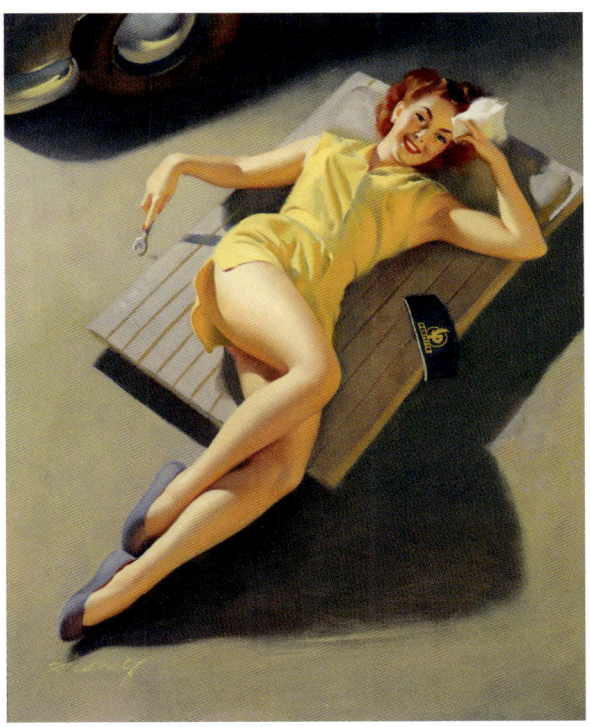

so seductively that viewers forget their plans to get the dream girl in the foreground into the backseat. His work for Sylvania Electric, starring a number of demure "Miss Sylvanias," perfectly evokes the company's claim to clean and modern lighting through use of sparkling backgrounds.

Essentially, Medcalf was the perfect company man. His entire career was spent with B&B, and during those years he worked for pretty much all of their signature lines — pin-up girls, both

Page 303: Aloha, 1960, on a 1962 Brown & Bigelow calendar. Calendar measures 46 x 22 inches.

Opposite: Oil on canvas, circa 1950, for a Kelly-Springfield Celebrity Tires calendar. 54 x 26 inches.

Above: Oil on board, circa 1955. Medcalf was skilled at rendering automobiles as well as pin-ups, and he handled many of Brown & Bigelow's auto parts calendar accounts. He created the yellow-jumpsuit-clad "Vicki" girl for Victor automotive products, though this girl has a Permite cap, indicating some crossover with Permite aluminum-based paint. 40 x 30 inches.

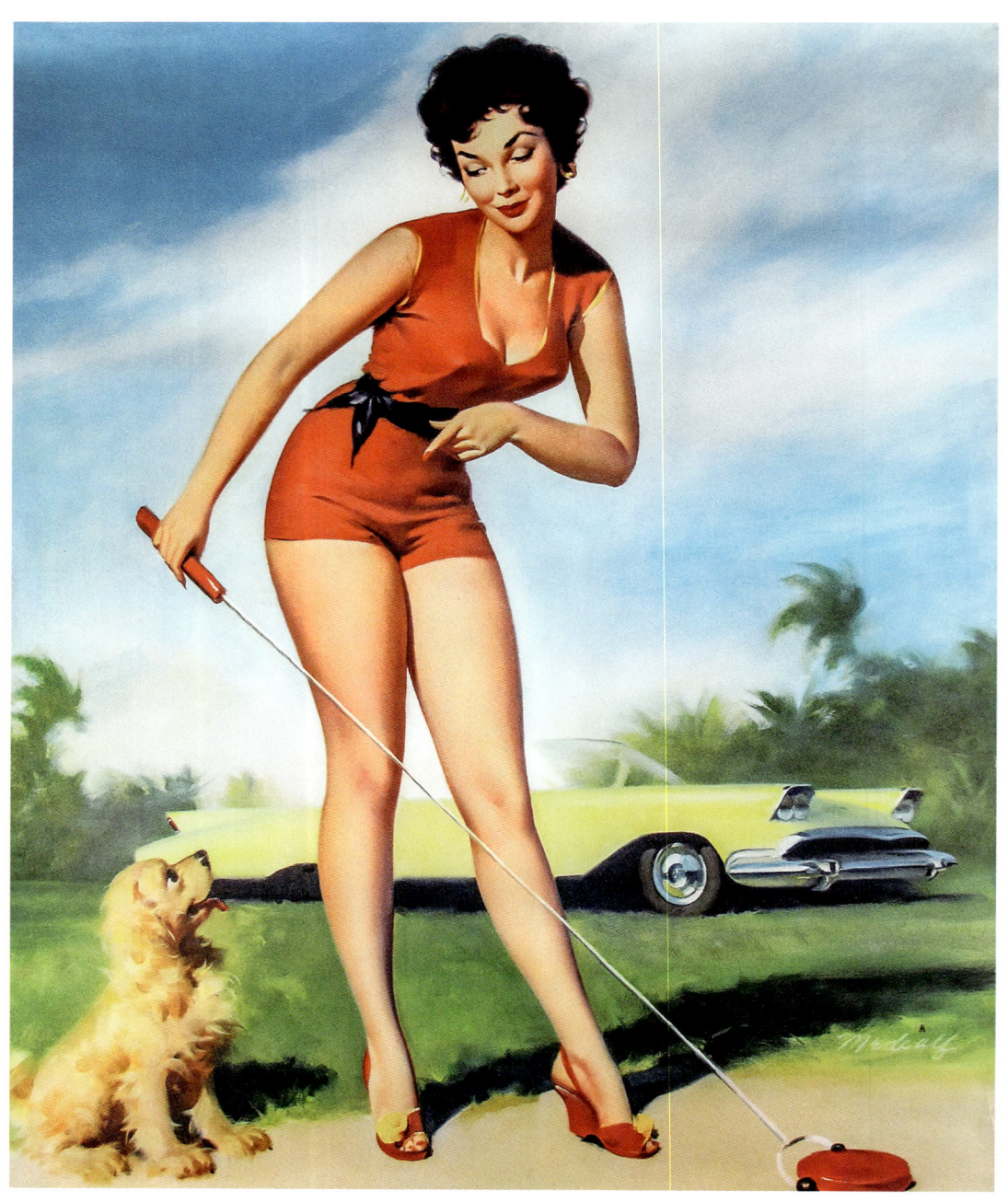

glamorous and risqué; sports, primarily baseball; the Boy Scouts and other cute kids; plus custom imagery for any and all clients. His work, done in oils on board or canvas, was as technically proficient as any of the illustrators' on salary at Brown & Bigelow, but he executed it with an ego-free precision. He was known for his voluminous preliminary sketches, which gave the art directors he worked with ample opportunity to suggest changes to theme and detailing, and by virtue of simple proximity he remained close with the department. Even after he moved his day-to-day painting from the company headquarters to a basement studio in his family home, he was a frequent visitor to Brown & Bigelow art director Clair Fry. The two socialized outside work as well, and Medcalf kept a close circle of friends among the local illustrators.

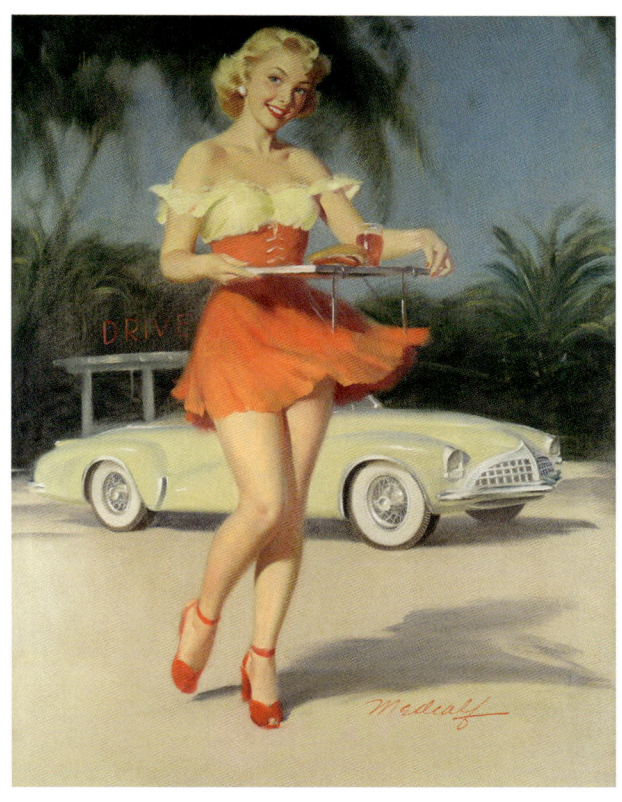

His soft, often pastel color palette, and rounded, thick-hipped figures lend femininity to much of his work, as do his preferred poses. Most Medcalf models stand upright or sit proudly erect, never contorting into the provocative and gymnastic poses favored by some colleagues. Not that they couldn't if they wanted to. Medcalf's beauties are all unusually boneless, pneumatically plump, with flesh that seems as smooth and supple as Silly Putty. The artist once described his perfect model as "someone's sweet sister," and his favored model for many years was his own wife, Henriette. His depictions reflect this sort of familial reverence, and by all accounts Medcalf was a devoted family man. He and Henriette raised two children and remained in the family home where, down in his basement studio, Medcalf continued to paint regional landscapes until his death in 2005.

Opposite: A calendar lithograph, circa 1960, for one of Medcalf's automotive advertising clients.

Above: Oil on canvas, circa 1950, for a Kelly-Springfield Celebrity Tires calendar. 54 x 26 inches. This huge canvas and the one on page 304 were created for oversized calendars designed to be displayed in garages.

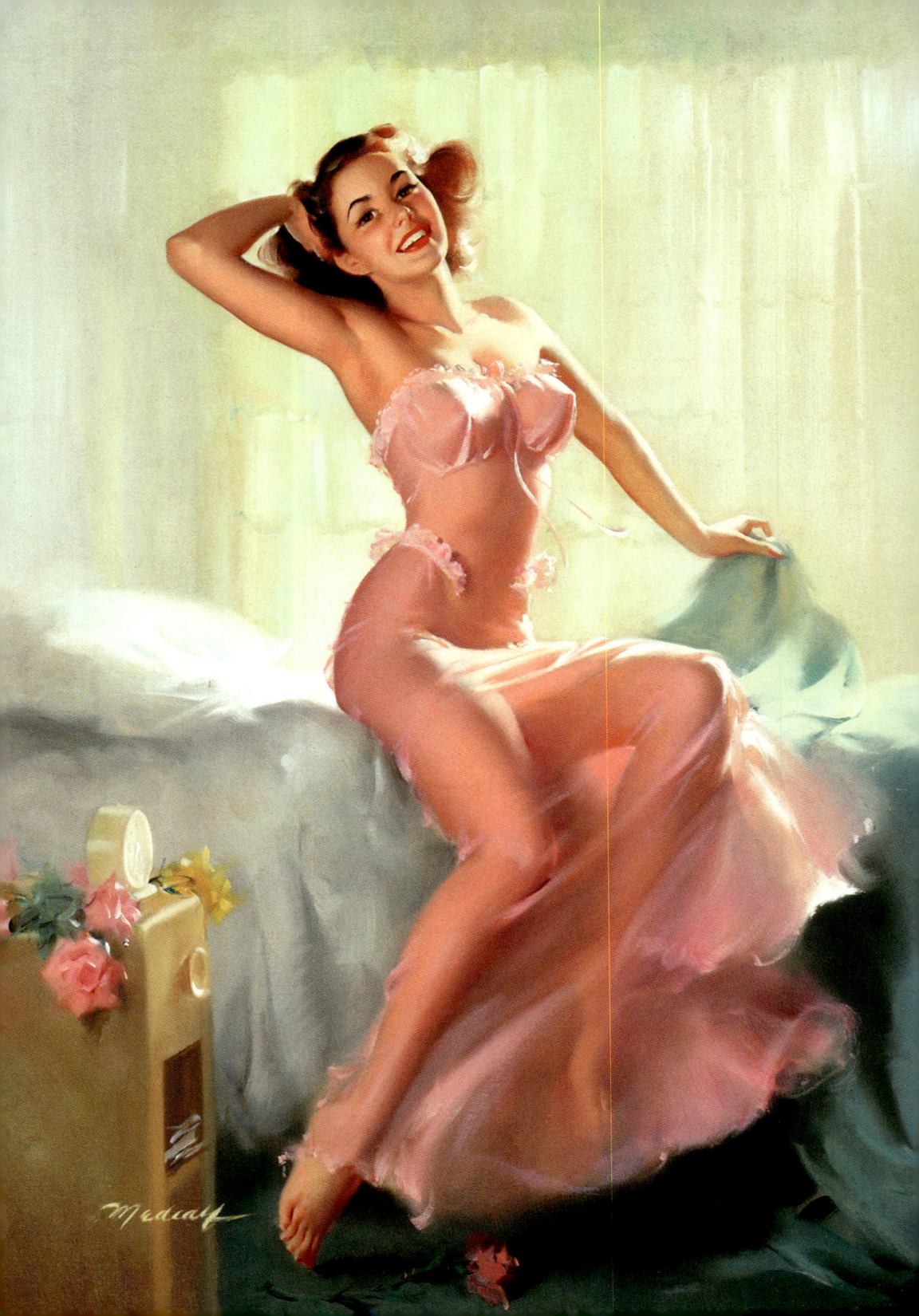

„Der Künstler beschrieb einmal sein perfektes Modell als ‚niedliche Schwester von jemandem', und über viele Jahre war seine Frau Henriette sein Lieblingsmodell."

William Medcalf wurde 1920 in St. Paul, Minnesota, geboren und blieb diesem Bundesstaat sein ganzes langes Leben treu. Nachdem er bei Cameron Booth und Stan Fenelle an der Minnesota School of Art (heute Minnesota College of Art and Design) studiert hatte, nahm Medcalf eine Beschäftigung beim U.S.-Schatzamt für Gravierungen auf. Im Zweiten Weltkrieg diente er als Gehilfe eines Bordkanoniers der Marine. Nach dem Krieg unterschrieb er einen Vertrag bei Brown & Bigelow. Gleich zu Anfang wurde er mit der Gestaltung eines besonderen Kalenders für die Celebrity-Reifen von Kelly-Springfield beauftragt, und mit dieser anspruchsvollen Aufgabe schaffte er es sofort in die Reihen der bedeutendsten Pin-up-Künstler. Ob er diesen Auftrag erhielt, weil er für seine viel gerühmte Fähigkeit bekannt war, den Frauen ein ganz spezielles Leuchten zu verleihen, oder weil Kelly-Springfield auf

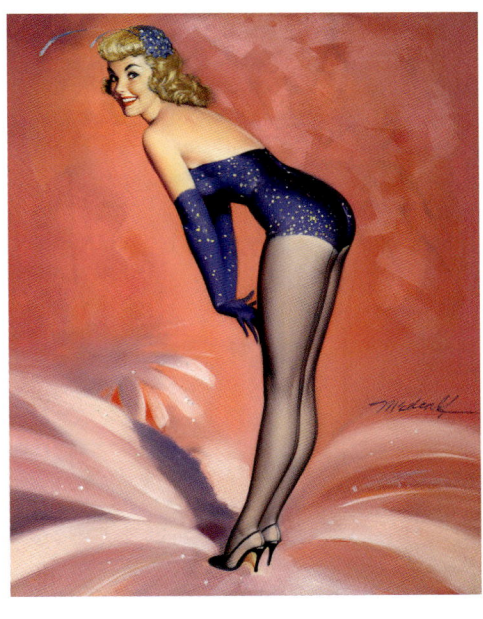

dem Kalender Elvgren-Mädchen haben wollte, ohne jedoch Elvgrens Honorare dafür zahlen zu müssen, bleibt offen. Seine zahlreichen Kalender rund um das Thema Auto – für Ditzler, NAPA und Victor – lassen das Sprit fressende Amerika aufleben: Medcalfs glänzende, reich verchromte Sportwagen sind so verführerisch gemalt, dass der Betrachter völlig vergisst, das im Vordergrund wartende Traumgirl auf den Beifahrersitz zu komplimentieren. Seine Arbeiten für Sylvania Electric dagegen, in deren Mittelpunkt diverse sittsame Mädchen vor funkelnden Hintergründen stehen, gibt auf perfekte Weise den Anspruch des Unternehmens wieder, saubere und moderne Beleuchtung zu liefern.

Medcalf ging in seinem Job vollständig auf. Seine gesamte berufliche Laufbahn verbrachte er bei B & B, und während all dieser Jahre arbeitete er an praktisch allen Themen des Verlags mit – glamouröse und gewagte Pin-ups, Sport (vor allem Baseball), Pfadfinder, niedliche Kinder oder besondere Kundenaufträge. Seine in Öl auf Karton oder Leinwand ausgeführten Werke waren technisch so versiert wie die Bilder jedes anderen Künstlers, der in den Diensten von Brown &

Opposite: What a Beautiful Morning, oil on canvas, 1950, for a 1952 Brown & Bigelow calendar. 40 x 30 inches.

Above: Blue Glitter, oil on canvas, circa 1950.

WILLIAM "BILL" MEDCALF

Bigelow stand, doch mit uneitler Präzision. Er war bekannt für seine umfangreichen Vorskizzen, die jedem Artdirector, mit dem er zusammenarbeitete, die Möglichkeit gab, noch Änderungen beim Thema oder bei Details vorschlagen zu können. Und weil er stets in der Nähe war, blieb er seiner Abteilung auch eng verbunden. Selbst als er seine Alltagsarbeit aus der Verlagszentrale in ein Atelier im Kellergeschoss seines Wohnhauses verlegte, besuchte er häufig Clair Fry, den Artdirector von Brown & Bigelow. Auch außerhalb der Arbeit waren die beiden oft zusammen, und Medcalf pflegte seine freundschaftlichen Verbindungen zu einem kleinen Kreis von Künstlern vor Ort.

Medcalfs weiche, oft pastellige Farbpalette und die gerundeten, breithüftigen Figuren seiner Pin-ups verleihen vielen seiner Arbeiten eine gewisse Weiblichkeit. Dies gilt auch für die von ihm bevorzugten Posen. Die meisten Modelle von Medcalf stehen aufrecht, oder sie sitzen stolz in aufrechter Haltung. Nie drehen sie ihre Körper in jene provokativen oder fast schon gymnastischen Posen, die manche seiner Kollegen bevorzugten. Nicht dass sie nicht konnten, sie wollten nicht. Medcalfs Schönheiten sind alle ungewöhnlich knochenlos, pneumatisch rund und so weich und schmiegsam wie ein Silikonpüppchen. Der Künstler beschrieb einmal sein perfektes Modell als „niedliche Schwester von jemandem", und über viele Jahre war seine Frau Henriette sein Lieblingsmodell. Seine Darstellungen spiegeln dieses Familiäre seiner Kunst wider, und nach übereinstimmenden Berichten war Medcalf – im Gegensatz zu Armstrong, MacPherson, Moran, Mozert und anderen – ein hingebungsvoller Familienmensch. Mit Henriette zog Medcalf zwei Kinder groß und blieb bis zu seinem Tode 2005 auch im gemeinsamen Haus, wo er in seinem Kelleratelier Landschaften der Umgebung malte.

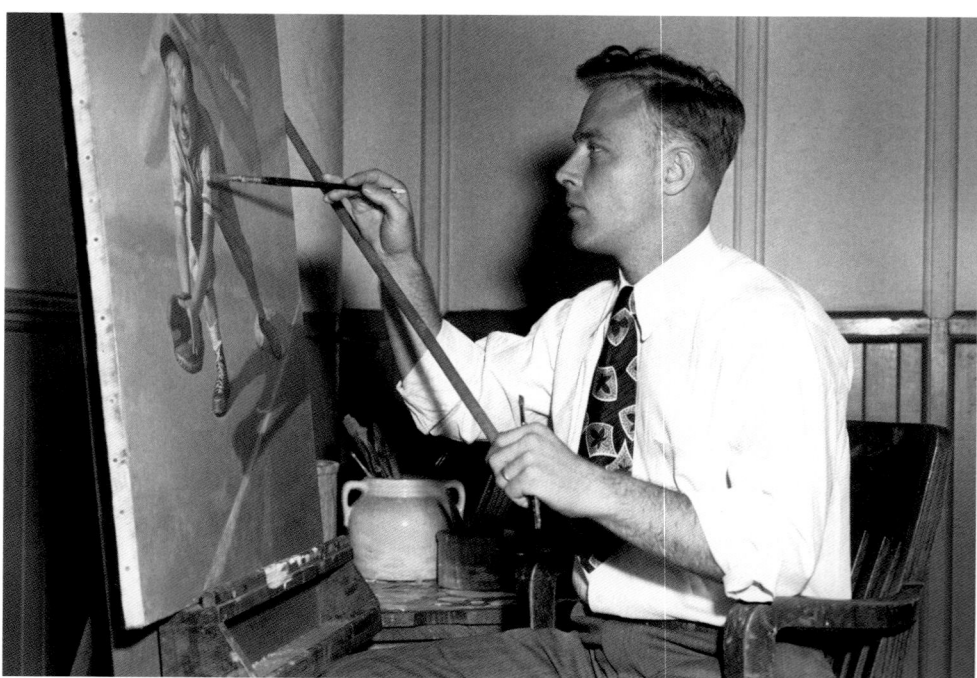

Above: Bill Medcalf working on a baseball calendar illustration in his Brown & Bigelow studio, circa 1948. He was actually better known for his maudlin paintings of Little League athletes than for pin-ups.

Opposite: Oil on board, circa 1952. 40 x 30 inches.

THE ART OF PIN-UP

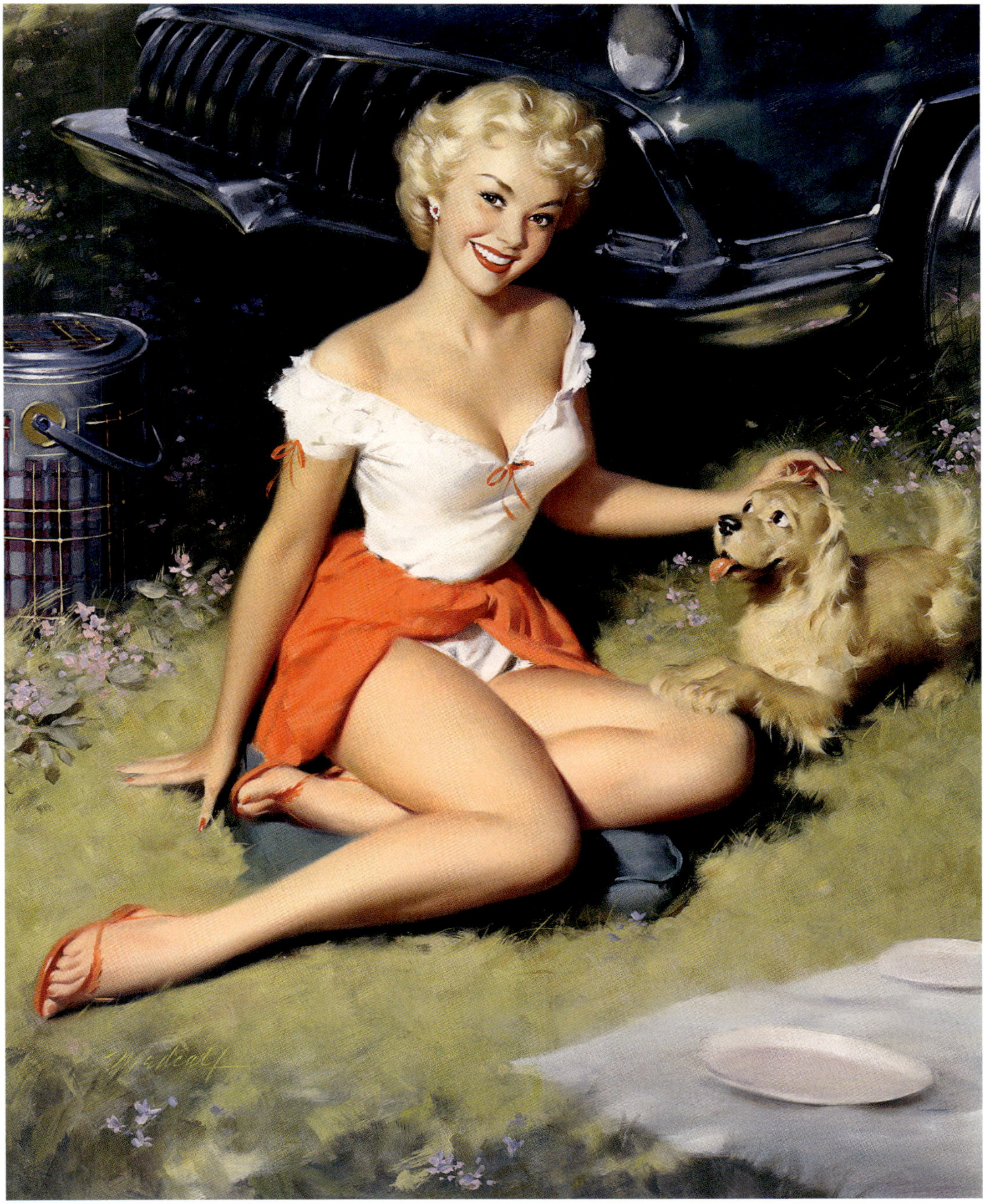

WILLIAM "BILL" MEDCALF

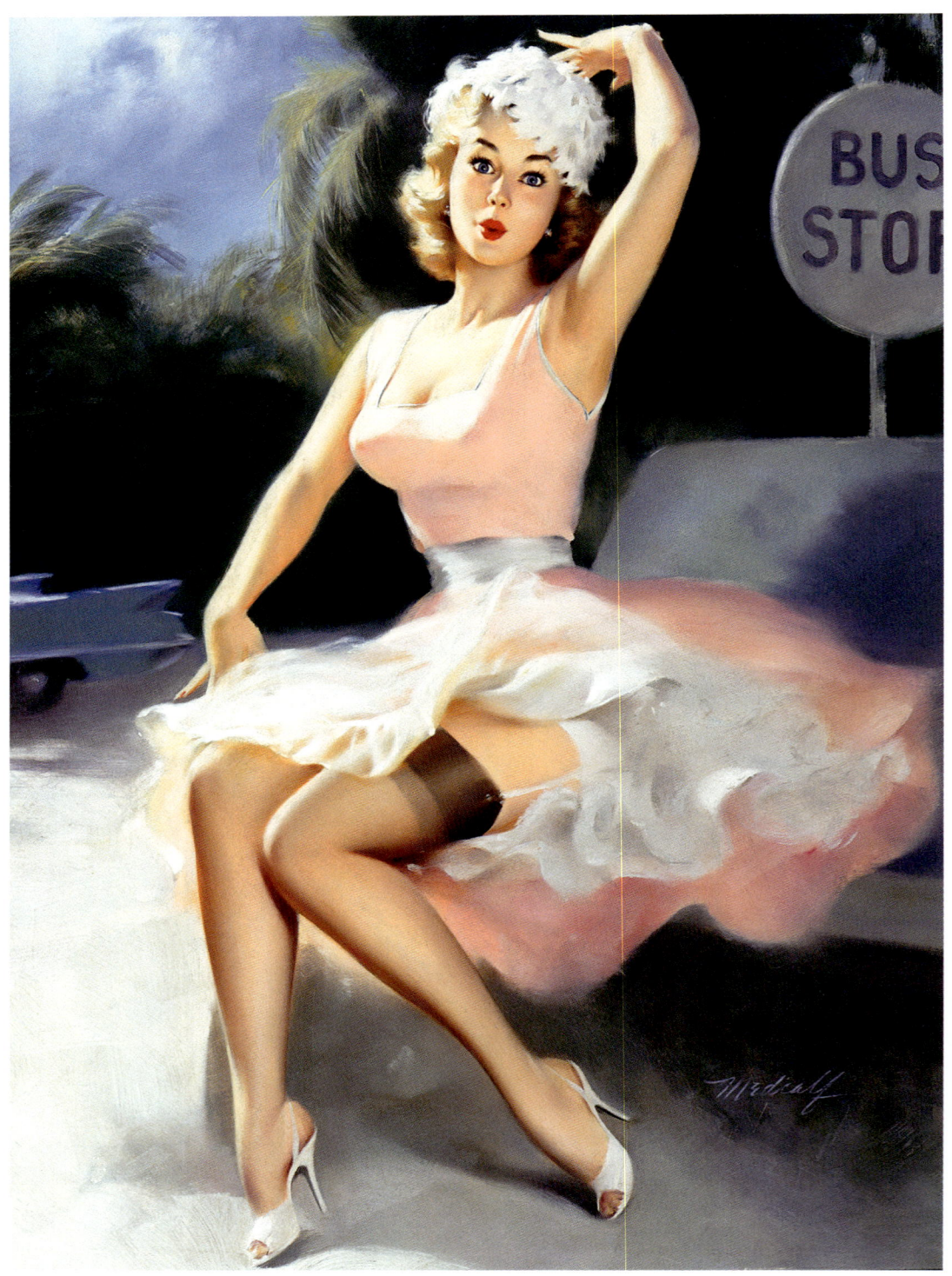

« Medcalf décrivit un jour son modèle idéal comme
"la petite sœur d'un ami", et, pendant de longues années,
fit poser sa femme Henriette. »

William « Bill » E. Medcalf naquit en
1920 à St. Paul, dans le Minnesota, où il
vécut toute sa vie. Après avoir été l'élève
de Cameron Booth et de Stan Fenelle à
la Minnesota School of Art (aujourd'hui
le Minnesota College of Art and Design),
il trouva un travail au service des gravures
du ministère des Finances.

Durant la Seconde Guerre mondiale,
il fut aide-canonnier, puis, de retour à la
vie civile, fut recruté par l'éditeur Brown
& Bigelow, basé à St. Paul. Sa première
mission fut un calendrier pour le fabricant de pneus Kelly-Springfield's Celebrity Tires, une commande prestigieuse
qui lui valut d'être rapidement classé parmi les artistes de pin-up les plus importants. On ignore si cette tâche lui fut
confiée en raison de son don pour rendre
ses femmes lumineuses, ou parce que
Kelly-Springfield cherchait un Elvgren
à moindres frais.

Ses nombreux calendriers centrés sur
le thème de l'automobile, pour Ditzler,

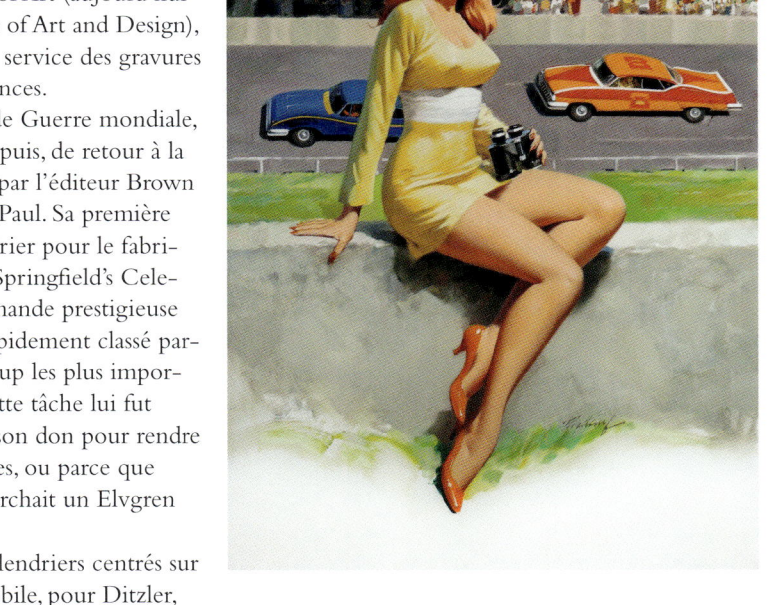

NAPA et Victor, font revivre une Amérique grande consommatrice d'essence, ses belles voitures
de sport aux chromes rutilants faisant oublier au spectateur son envie d'attirer la créature de rêve
au premier plan sur la banquette arrière. De même, avec leurs arrière-plans étincelants, ses sages
Miss Sylvania réalisées pour Sylvania Electric, reflètent parfaitement la promesse de la compagnie
de fournir un éclairage propre et moderne.

Medcalf était l'artiste maison idéal. Il passa toute sa carrière chez Brown & Bigelow travaillant dans tous les genres qui firent sa renommée : les pin-up bien évidemment, tant glamour que
plus osées ; le sport, principalement du base-ball ; les boy-scouts et autres charmants bambins ;
sans compter toutes sortes d'images sur mesure et sur commande pour toutes sortes de clients.

Opposite: Coming My Way?, oil on canvas, circa 1955,
for a Brown & Bigelow calendar. 40 x 30 inches.

Above: See You at the Finish Line, oil on board,
circa 1955, 40 x 30 inches. Courtesy Heritage Auctions.

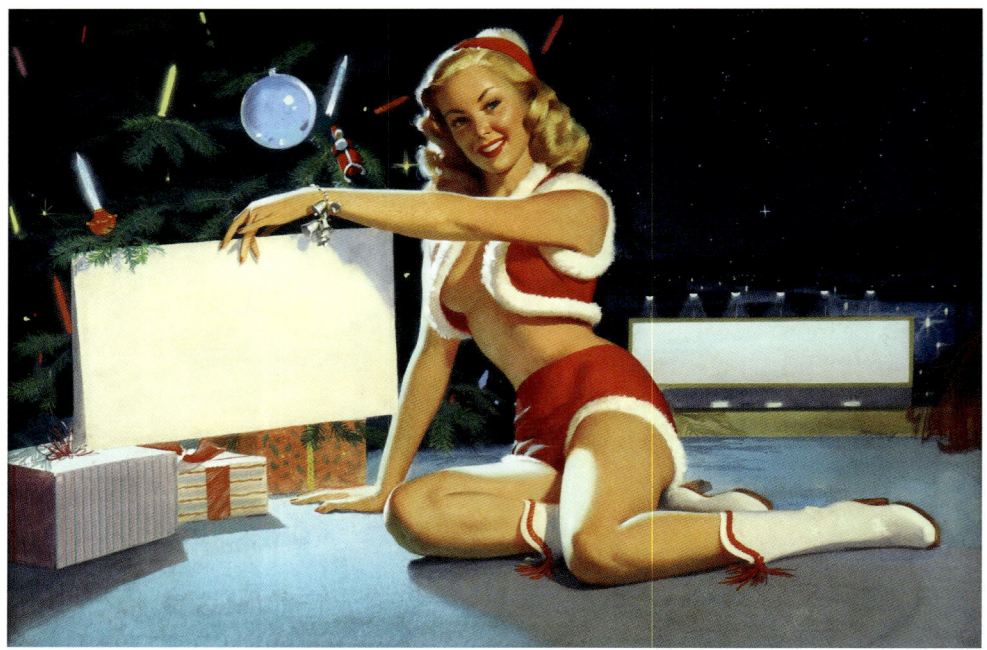

Son travail, à l'huile sur carton ou toile, était aussi maîtrisé que celui de tout autre illustrateur salarié de B&B, mais ce qui le démarquait était sa précision dépourvue de vanité. Il réalisait de nombreuses esquisses préliminaires afin que les directeurs artistiques puissent suggérer des modifications tant sur le thème que sur les détails. Comme il vivait dans le voisinage, il conserva longtemps des liens avec le service artistique. De fait après avoir déplacé son atelier des bureaux de la société d'édition au sous-sol de sa maison, il rendait encore souvent visite à Clair Fry, le directeur artistique. Ils se voyaient par ailleurs régulièrement en dehors du travail ; Medcalf fréquentait également un groupe d'amis proches qui étaient tous des illustrateurs locaux.

Sa palette douce de couleurs pastel et ses silhouettes rondes aux hanches généreuses conféraient beaucoup de féminité à ses œuvres, tout comme ses poses préférées. Ses pin-up se tiennent droites ou assises fièrement, ne se contorsionnant jamais dans les poses provocantes et acrobatiques qu'appréciaient certains de ses collègues. Pourtant, elles auraient pu, tant elles paraissent souples, toutes en courbes aérodynamiques, avec une chair aussi lisse et malléable que de la pâte à modeler. Medcalf décrivit un jour son modèle idéal comme « la petite sœur d'un ami », et, pendant de longues années, fit poser sa femme Henriette.

Ses images reflètent son amour de la famille, à la différence de, à en croire les rumeurs, Armstrong, MacPherson, Moran, Mozert et bien d'autres. Henriette et lui élevèrent leurs deux enfants et prirent leur retraite dans la même maison où, dans son atelier au sous-sol, Medcalf continua de peindre des paysages jusqu'à sa mort en 2005.

Above: Oil on board, circa 1960, for a National Automotive Parts Association (NAPA) calendar. 29 x 23 inches.

Opposite: Oil on board, circa 1962, for a Brown & Bigelow calendar.

THE ART OF PIN-UP

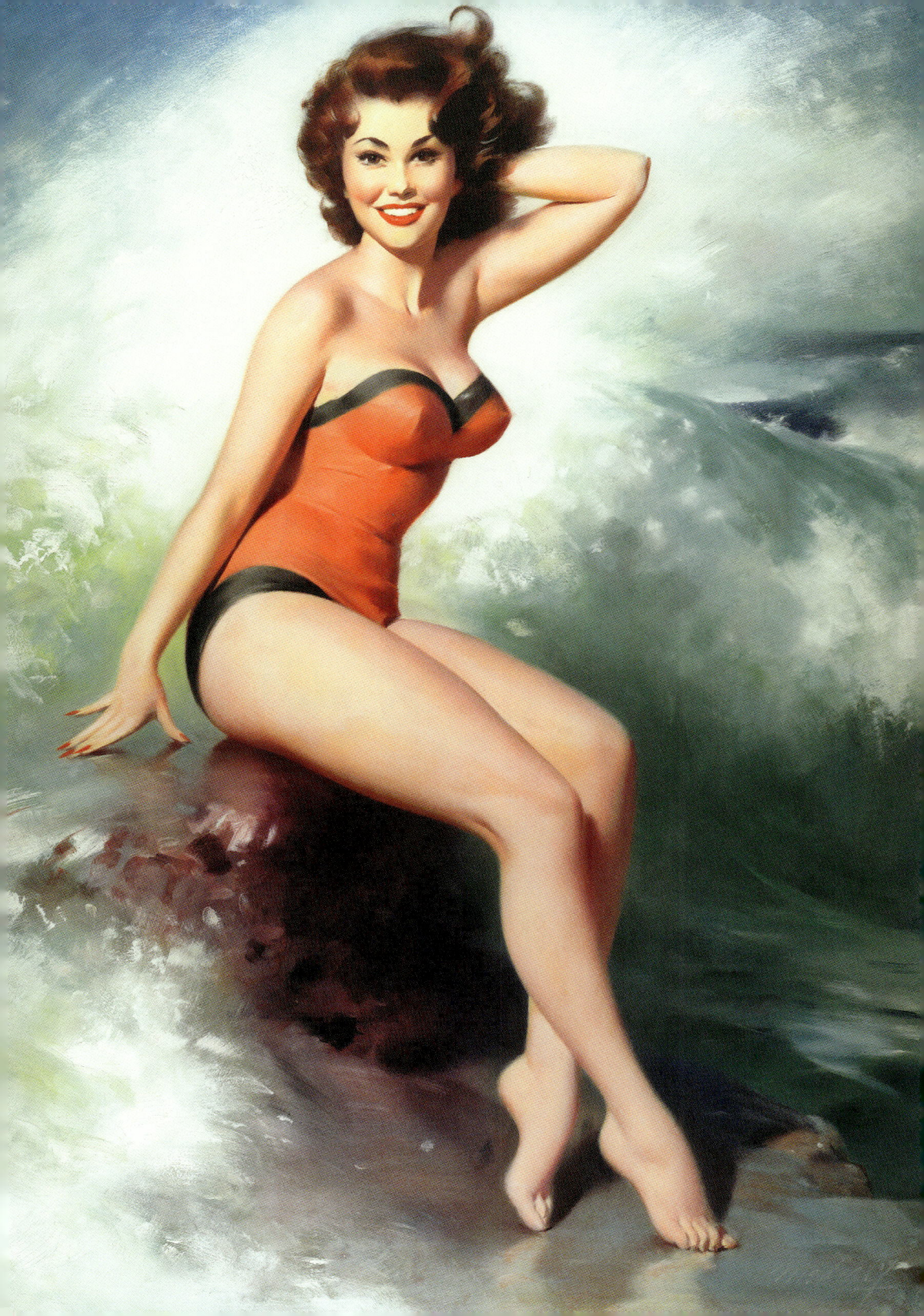

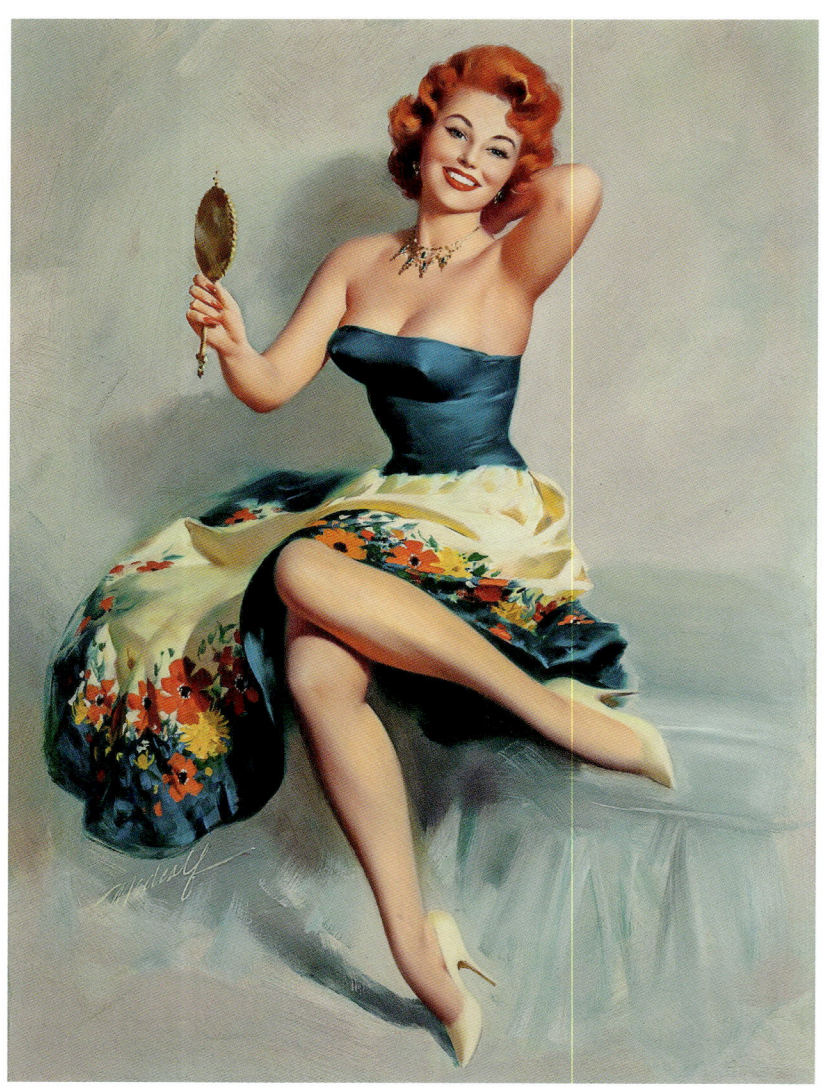

Above: Blossoming Beauty for a Brown & Bigelow calendar. Oil on board, undated, 40 x 30 inches. Courtesy Heritage Auctions.

Opposite: Miss Sylvania, for a Sylvania light bulb ad. Oil on board, circa 1962, 30 x 24 inches.

Following left: A Sudden Breeze, oil on canvas, undated, 30 x 24.75 inches. Courtesy Heritage Auctions.

Following right: On the Carnival Ride, oil on Masonite, undated, 40 x 30 inches. Courtesy Heritage Auctions.

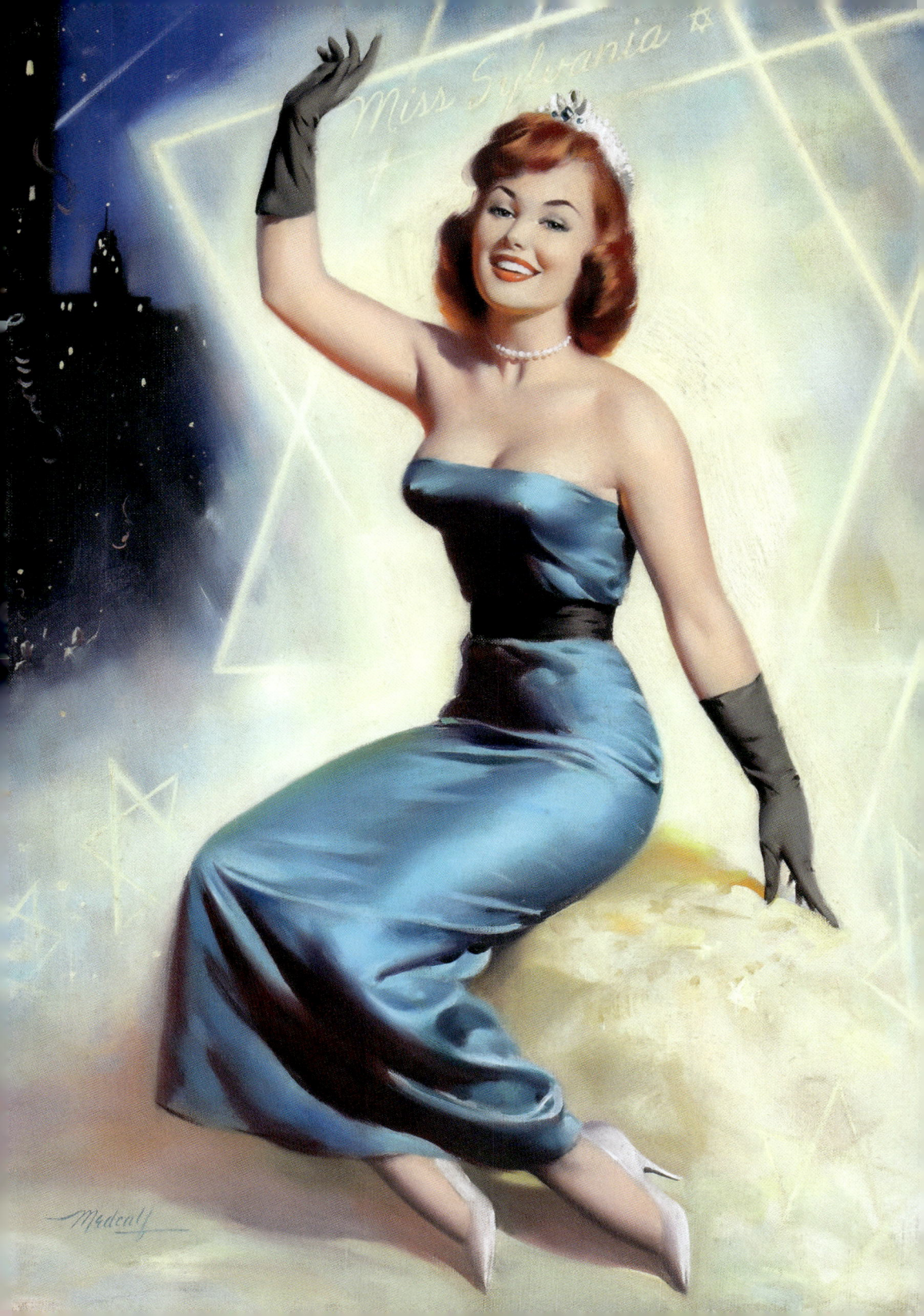

Miss Sylvania

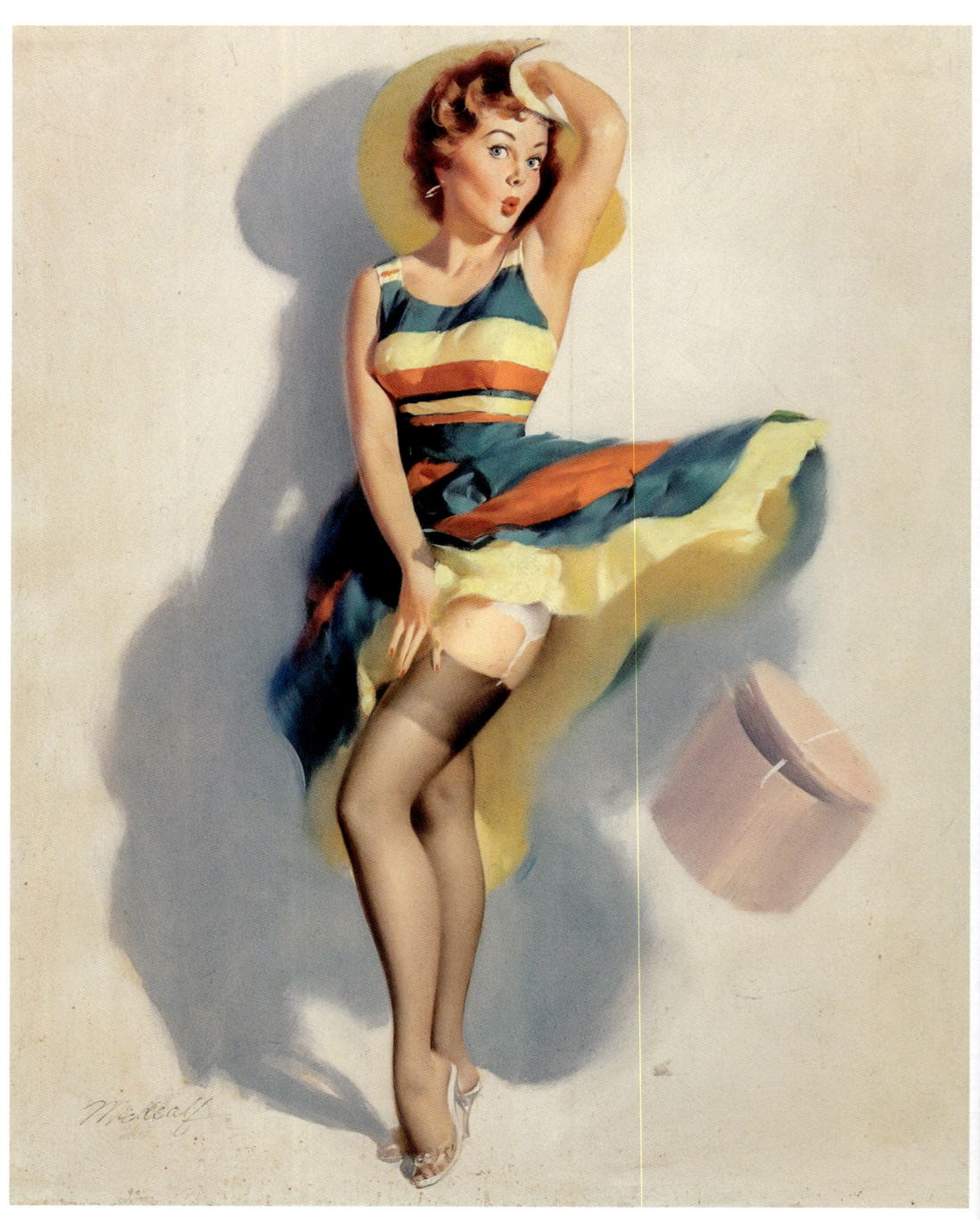

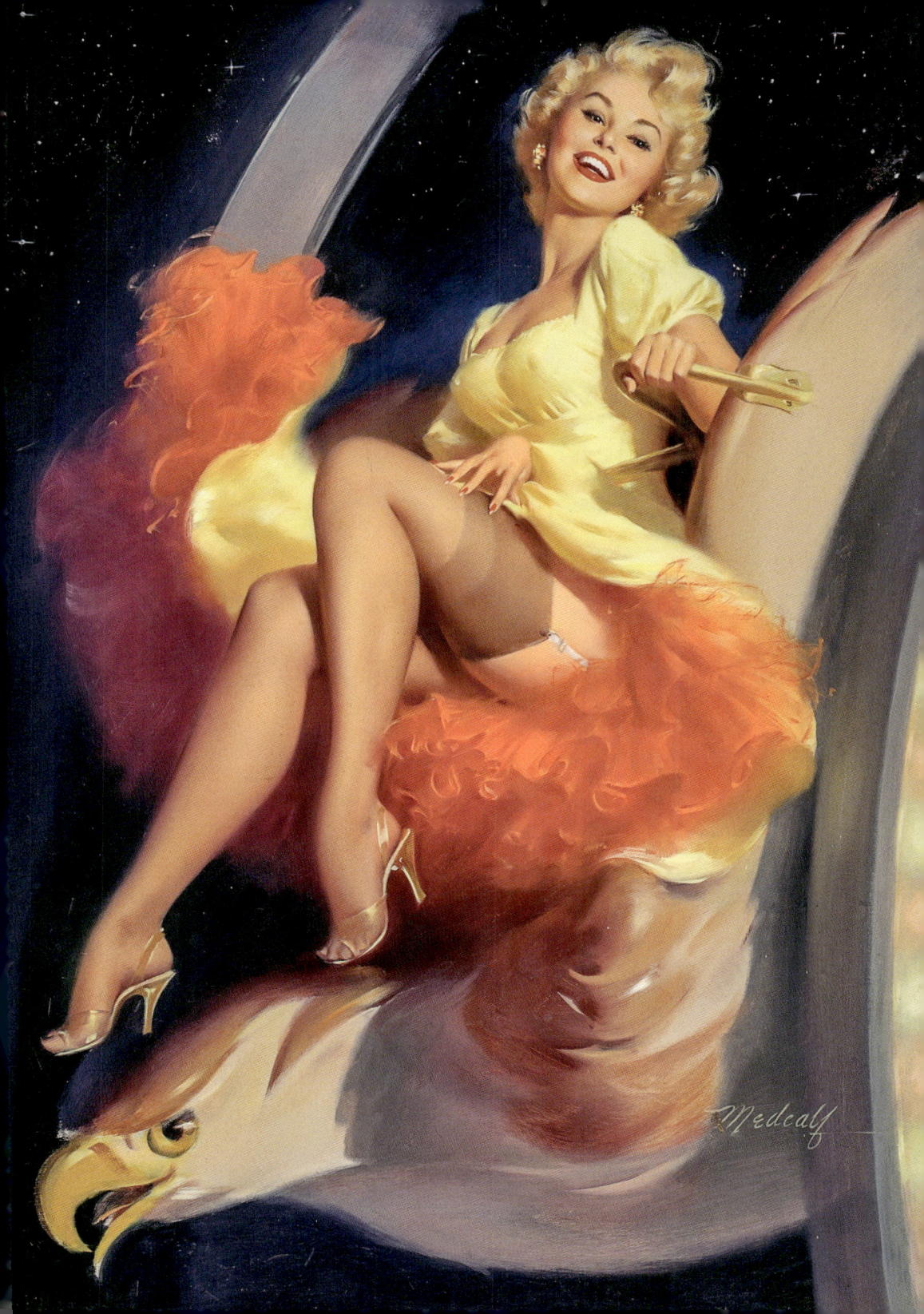

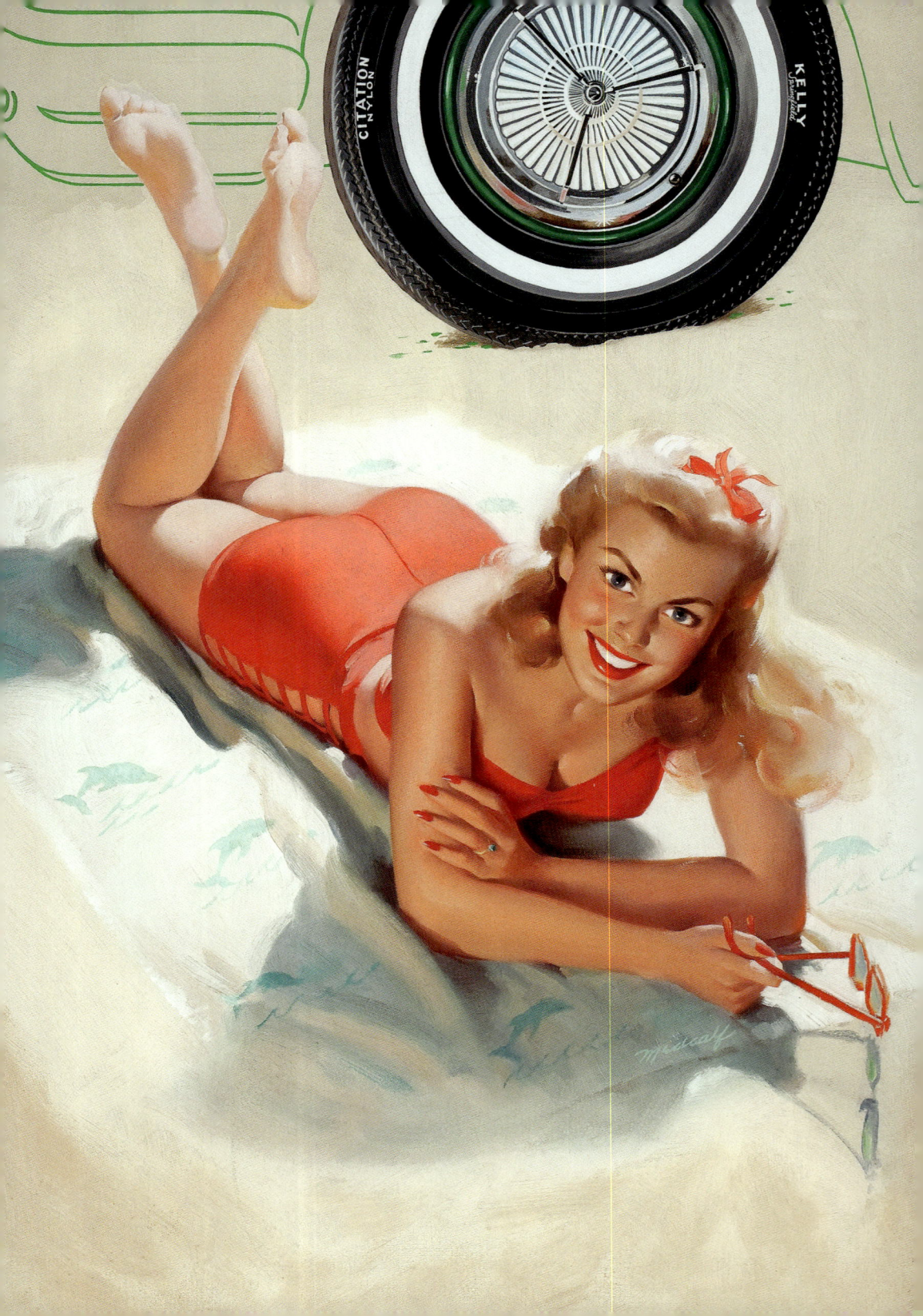

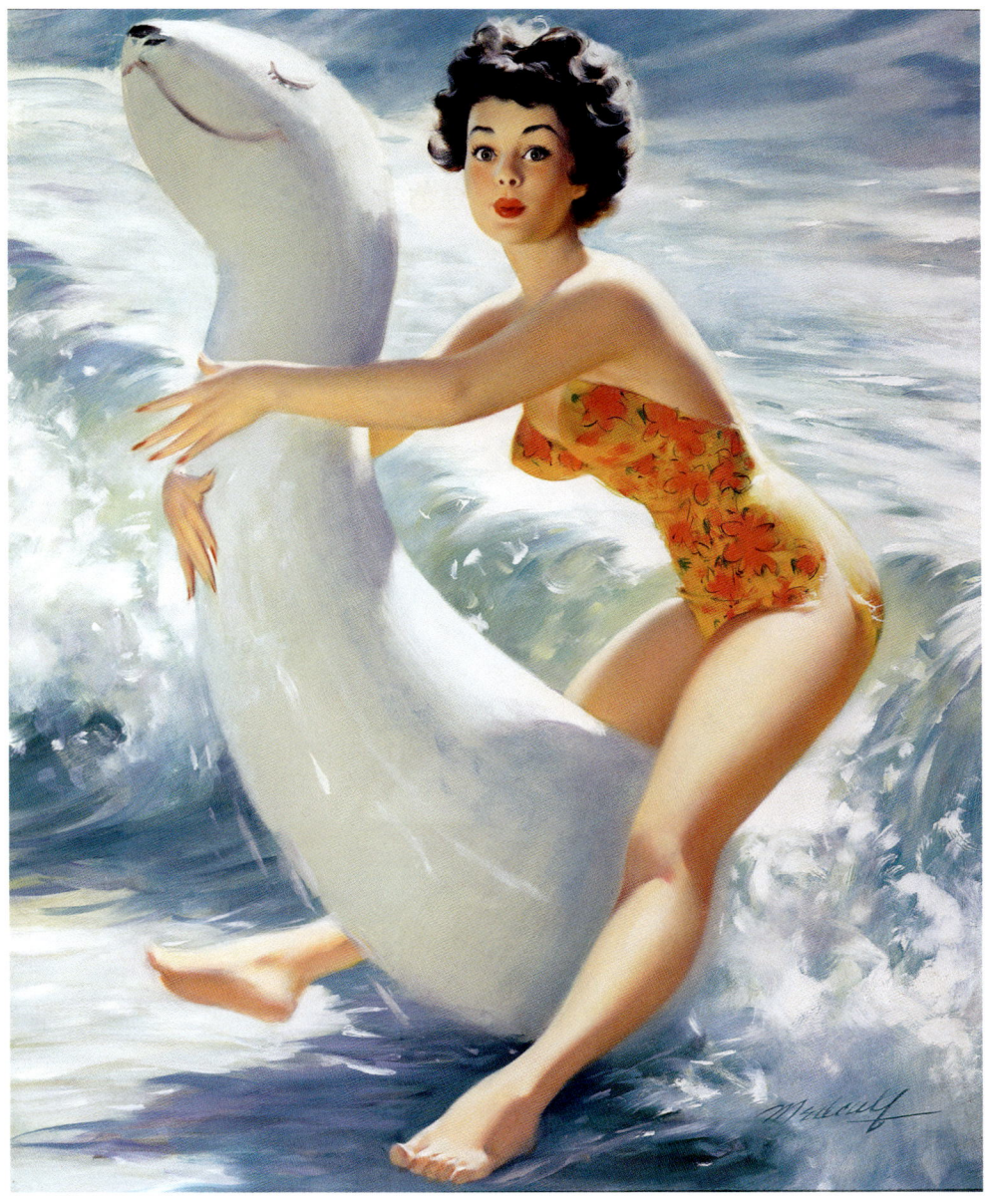

Opposite: A Kelly Girl, oil on canvas, circa 1962, for a Kelly-Springfield Celebrity Tires calendar. 30.5 x 21.5 inches.

Above: Oil on board, circa 1958, for a Brown & Bigelow calendar. 35.5 x 30 inches.

WILLIAM "BILL" MEDCALF

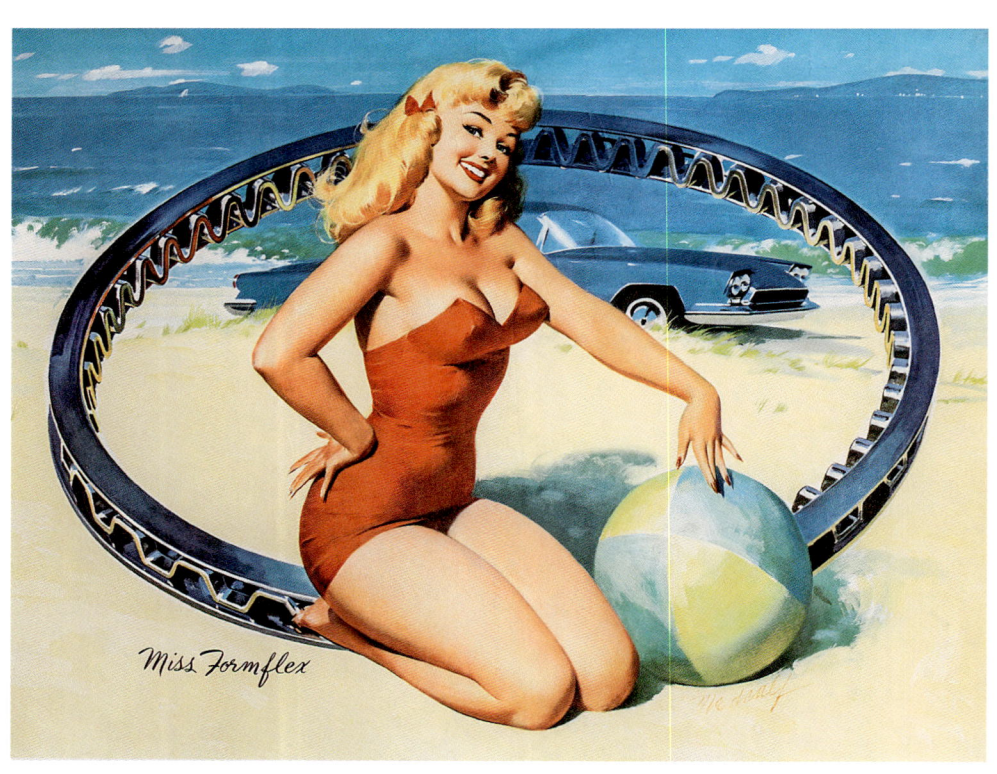

Above: Miss Formflex calendar lithograph, circa 1962, for a 1964 Gould-National Batteries calendar.

Opposite: Oil on board, circa 1960, for a Kelly-Springfield Celebrity Tires calendar. 40 x 30 inches.

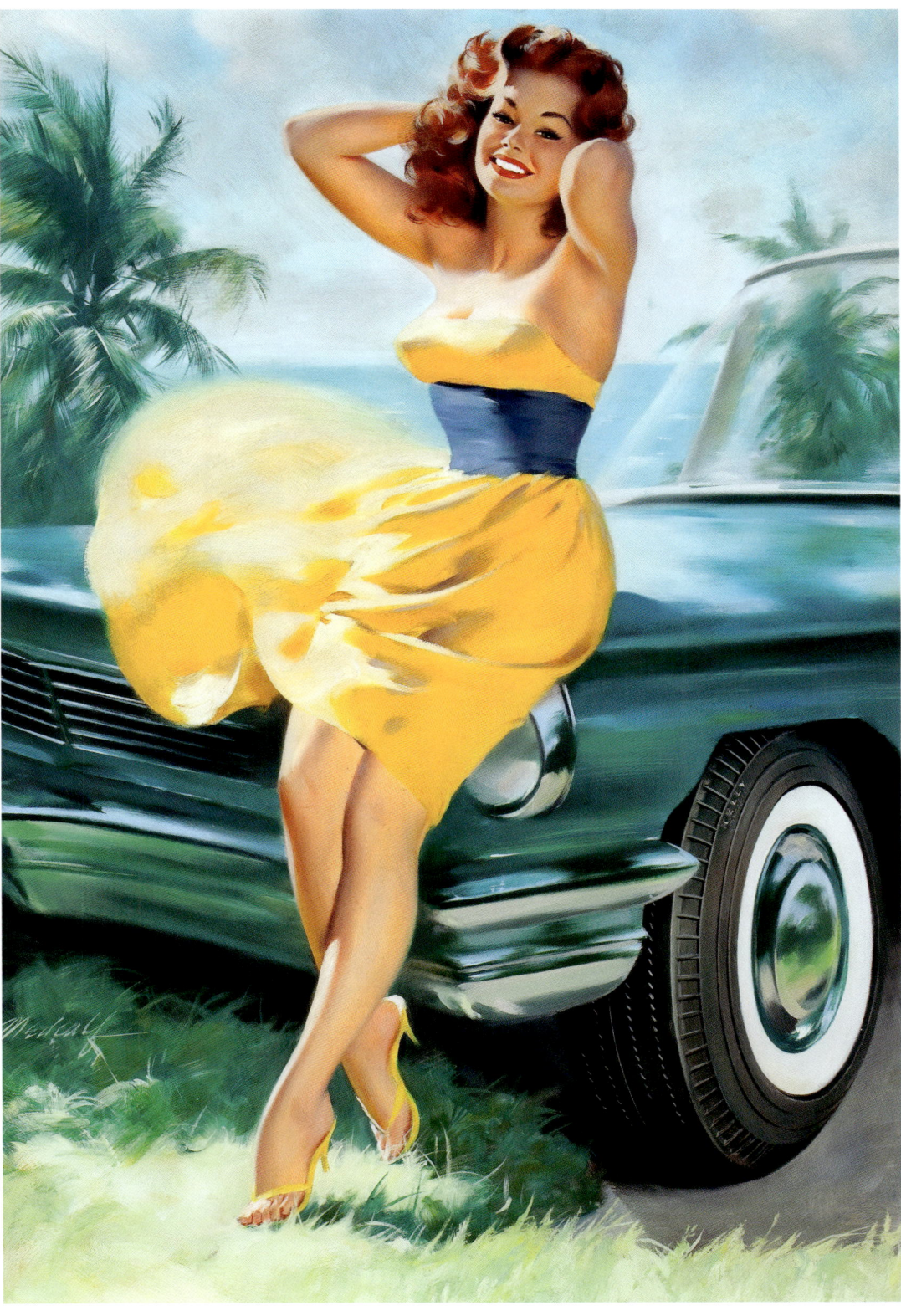

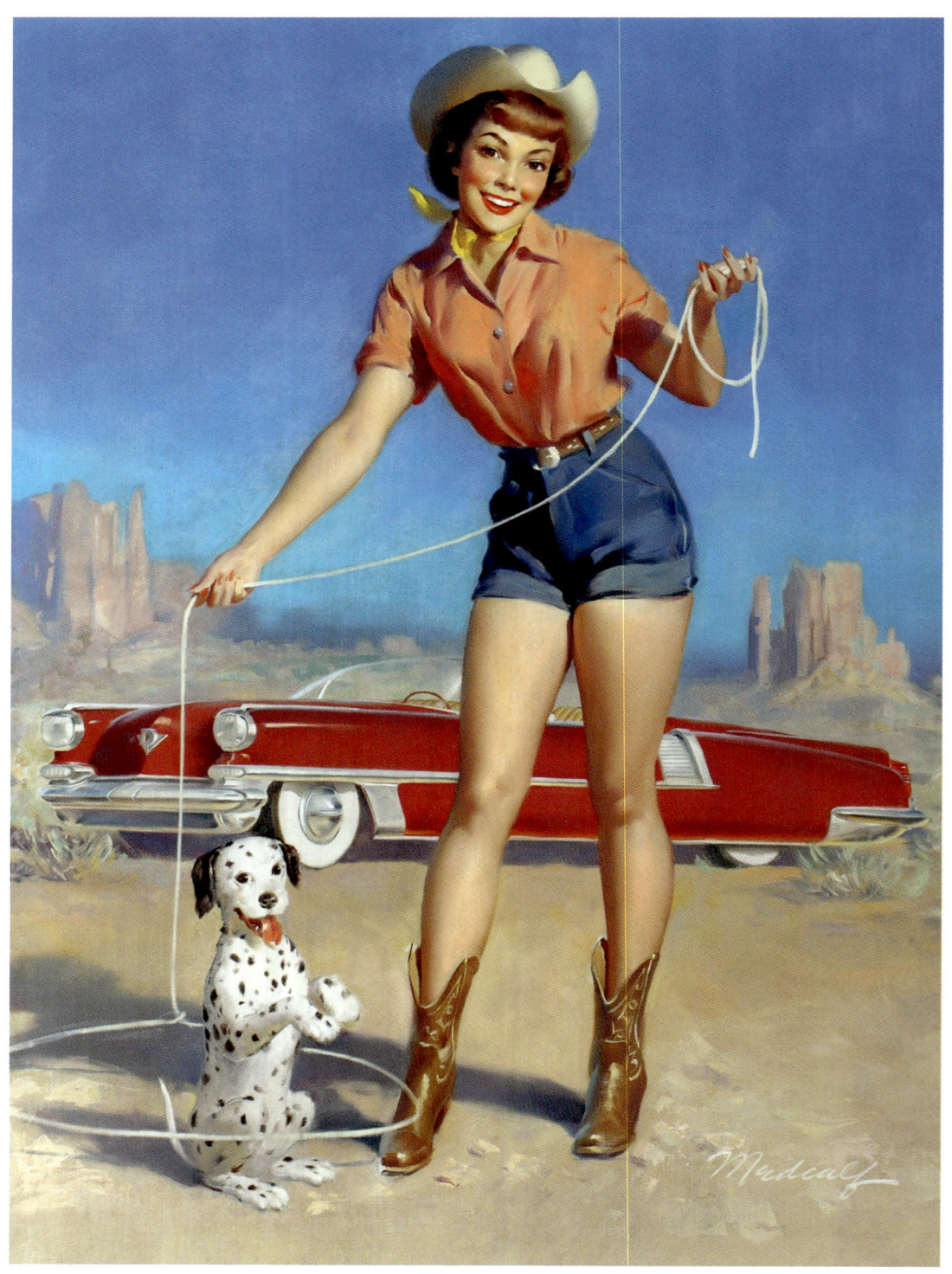

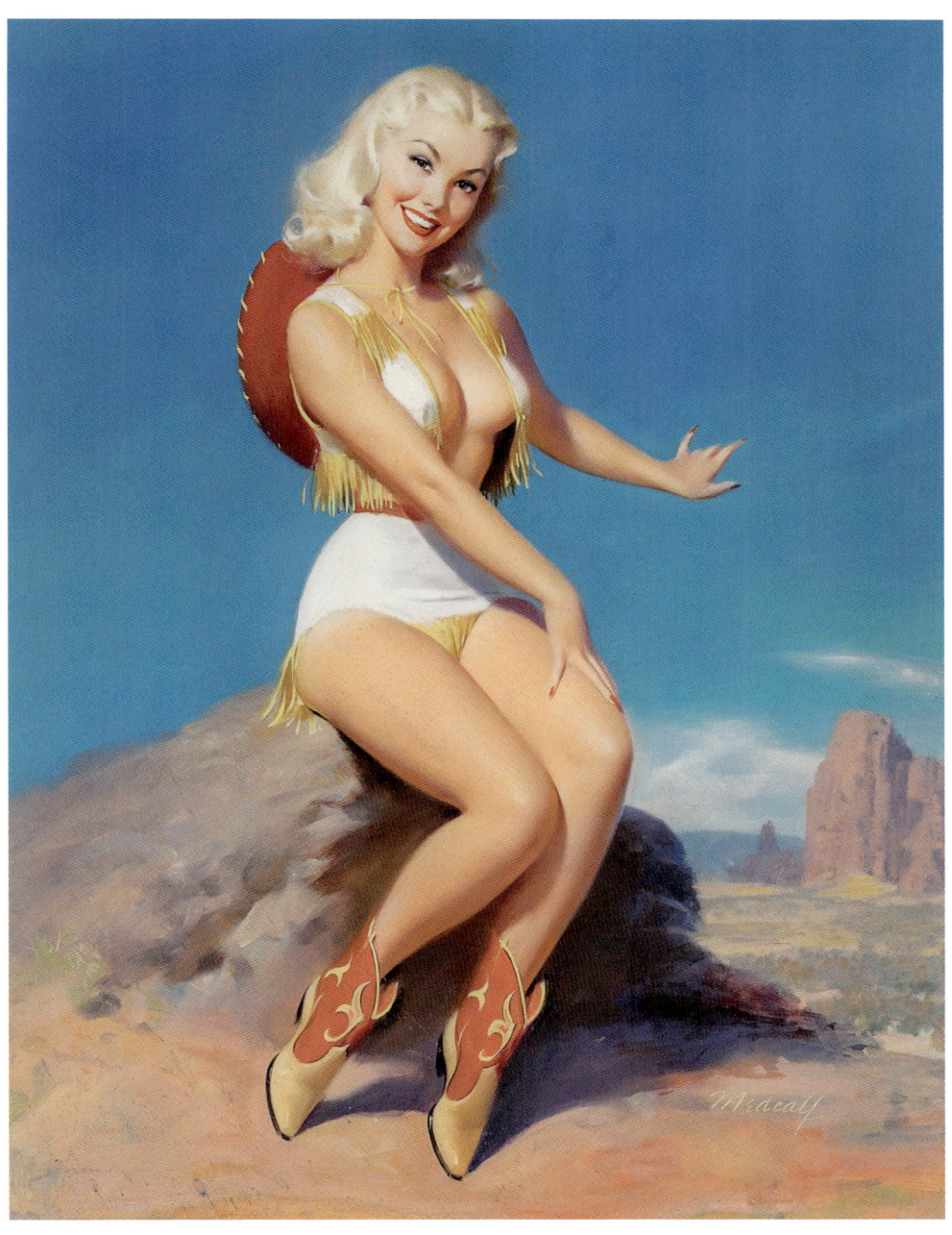

Opposite: Oil on canvas, circa 1954, for a Kelly-Springfield Celebrity Tires calendar. 36 x 29 inches.

Above: Ropin' a Cowgirl, oil on Masonite, circa 1955, 30 x 24.5 inches. Courtesy Heritage Auctions.

WILLIAM "BILL" MEDCALF

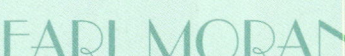

EARL MORAN

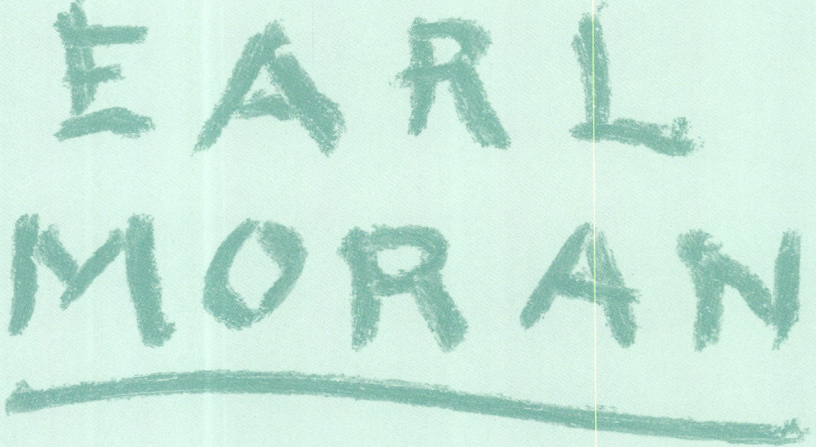

1893–1984

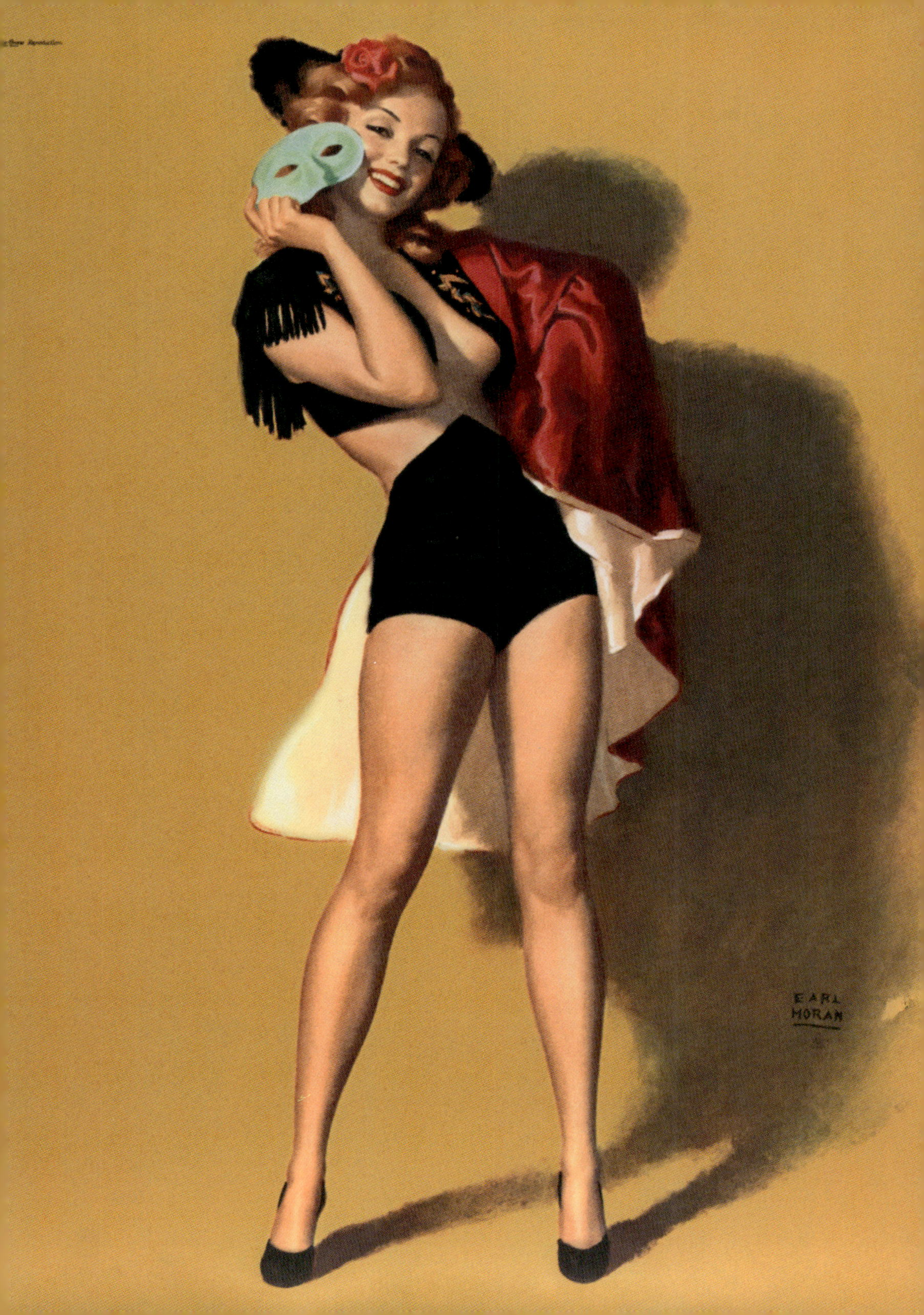
EARL MORAN

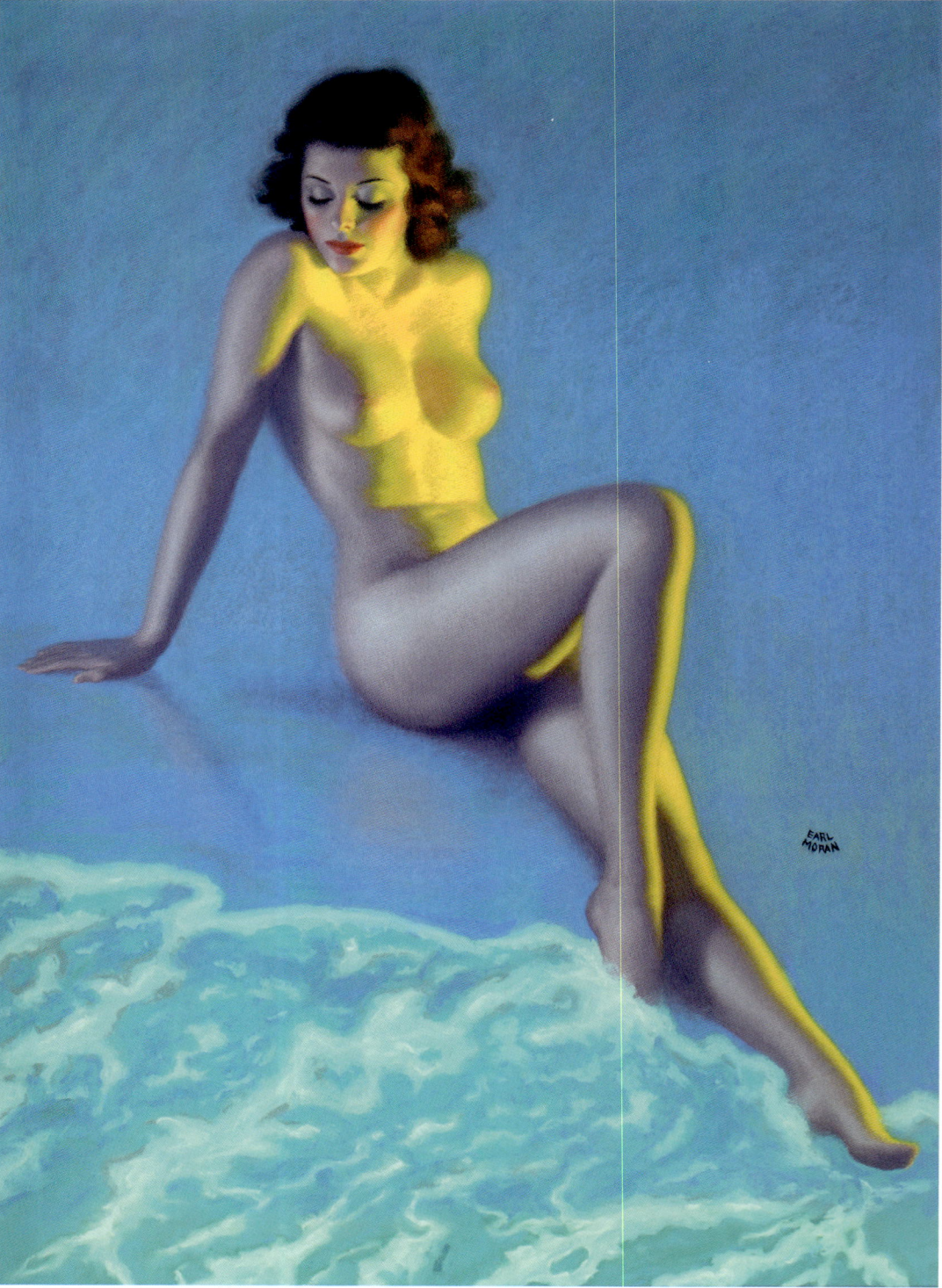

> "His star didn't rise in the field of illustration until age 40, though his devotion to the more poetic trappings of the artistic life — wanderlust and chronic infidelity — developed early."

In 1944, after nearly 10 years as a Brown & Bigelow star artist, Earl Moran was awarded an honorary BSA — Bachelor of Sex Appeal. The calendar giant used this publicity stunt to capitalize on Moran's personal sex scandal and impending bachelorhood. The previous year, having had enough of the artist's "outrageous flirting and indecent dancing, hugging, and kissing," Mura — the third Mrs. Moran — filed for divorce. She claimed to have seen the famous World War II pin-up model Chili Williams with Moran in his studio, without a camera, a canvas, or their clothes. The controversy made headlines for years, as Chili — the Polka Dot Girl — tried to protect her reputation, while Mura sought a large financial settlement and Moran moved on to yet another young model.

Like many on Brown & Bigelow's roster, Moran had a backstory as entertaining as his work, a delicate tapestry of fact and fiction. Half Clark Gable, half Horatio Alger, Moran was born in Belle Plaine, Iowa, in 1893, and spent the first

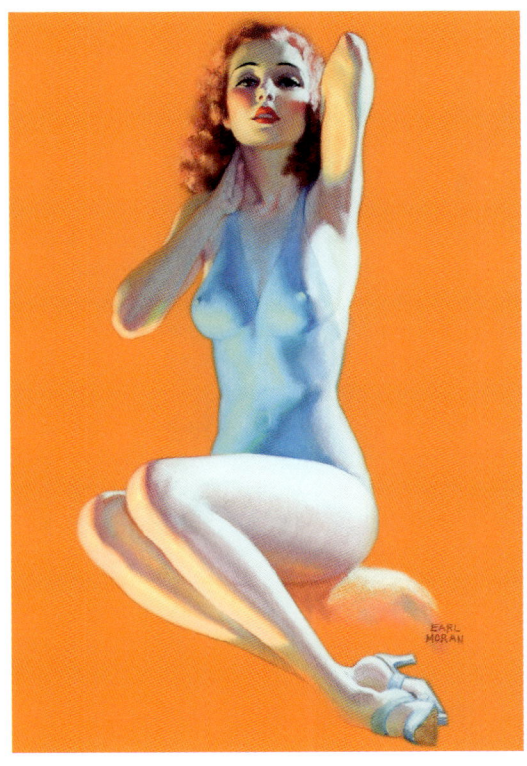

20 years of his adult life making art when there was money in it and driving delivery trucks when there wasn't. His star didn't rise in the field of illustration until age 40, though his devotion to the more poetic trappings of the artistic life — wanderlust and chronic infidelity — developed early. This fable of workingman-made-good was a source of identification

Page 327: Cansentida Del Carnaval, on this Spanish language calendar, was known as *The Spanish Girl* on the English version. The 1949 pastel created for this 1951 Brown & Bigelow calendar was actually based on a photograph of Marilyn Monroe. Calendar measures 33 x 16 inches.

Opposite: A Mere Maid, pastel on board, circa 1938, for a Brown & Bigelow calendar. The image was later licensed to Arrow Beer for its Earl Moran poster series. 38 x 29 inches.

Above: Golden Hours, pastel on board, 1932, was Moran's first pin-up, created in his spare time while illustrating men's fashion catalogs. 38.5 x 27.5 inches.

for all the businessmen who bought and sold his "Hotcha Girl" calendars and lent a certain grit to his masterful, lushly colored artwork. As the story goes, bored of his low-paying, low-status work as a commercial illustrator of men's fashion catalogs in 1932, Moran created two large-format bathing beauty pastels in his spare time. Both featured a voluptuous blonde who seemed nude despite her swimsuit, and both were accepted for publication but by rival calendar companies. Then, before the Thomas D. Murphy Company could commission any more of Moran's groundbreaking pin-ups, Brown & Bigelow signed him to an exclusive contract.

It's likely that his move toward calendar art was motivated as much by his need to support two ex-wives and three children during the Great Depression as by personal whimsy, but Brown & Bigelow never publicized that. In 1918 Moran had married Louise, a modern dancer in New York City, and the couple had two children in quick succession with plans to raise them in Chicago. His daughter Peggy Moran would go on to become a pin-up girl in her own right and one of Hollywood's early scream queens, starring in *The Mummy's Hand* and *Horror Island*. Moran often boasted about his beautiful daughter when her career took off, but he had little hand in raising her after the divorce in 1923. He had another daughter with second wife, Mary, before joining Brown & Bigelow and moving to a penthouse studio in New York, where he hosted constant parties for showgirls and celebrities. There, he took up with Mura, the model who was the mother of his youngest child and the source of so much drama and grief. Moran simply loved women, and despite his receding hairline, narcissism, and ever-present pipe, they loved him back. Brown & Bigelow could not outwardly market the artist as a playboy in the 1930s and '40s, but his intense sexuality became an integral part of his success.

Moran broke ground for B&B with the sheer eroticism of his pin-ups. The blonde bombshell was his erotic ideal, though he knew to change her hair color occasionally for other viewers' tastes, and he kept up with fashion just enough that his work never seemed dated. Though the company made him produce wholesome pin-ups as well, his knack was for mining the categories they otherwise couldn't approach. His chiaroscuro nudes—widely considered his most artistic efforts—were created for B&B between 1935 and 1940. Ironically, as calendar companies helped pin-up cross over into mainstream culture, nudes became off-limits. Moran then became Brown & Bigelow's answer to Hollywood.

While most of B&B's artists claimed that professional models lacked natural charm, Moran was a casting couch for the pros. He judged beauty pageants in New York and then used the winners as models, and after moving to Los Angeles, he employed actresses Joi Lansing, Barbara Nichols, Marie Wilson, Jayne Mansfield, and, most famously, Marilyn Monroe, at $10 an hour. He first met Monroe in 1946, when she was still Norma Jeane Baker and he was renting a studio from Henry Clive, illustration's other famous raconteur. She would go on to model for him throughout the '40s, and the many photographs that have emerged, both costumed and nude, give credence to Brown & Bigelow's claim that Moran's skill with a camera set him apart in capturing the moment of abandon calendar buyers wanted to see.

No matter who his model was, Moran's preferred pose had his subject leaning back to extend her legs and accentuate her high-heeled feet. This angle offers a more direct invitation to the viewer than seen in most pin-ups. Reinforcing this boldness, he avoided the girl next door, instead showing heroines of naughty fables, strippers, and chorus line refugees. Even his more demure images have the sitters busting out of their low-cut, peekaboo necklines. His formula was clear: a minimum of clothes, a maximum of leg and breast, and the minimum number of assignments to earn a living. Moran confessed late in life that he took up illustration "knowing how little the idea of work appealed" to him but wanting to "live as an artist." Compared

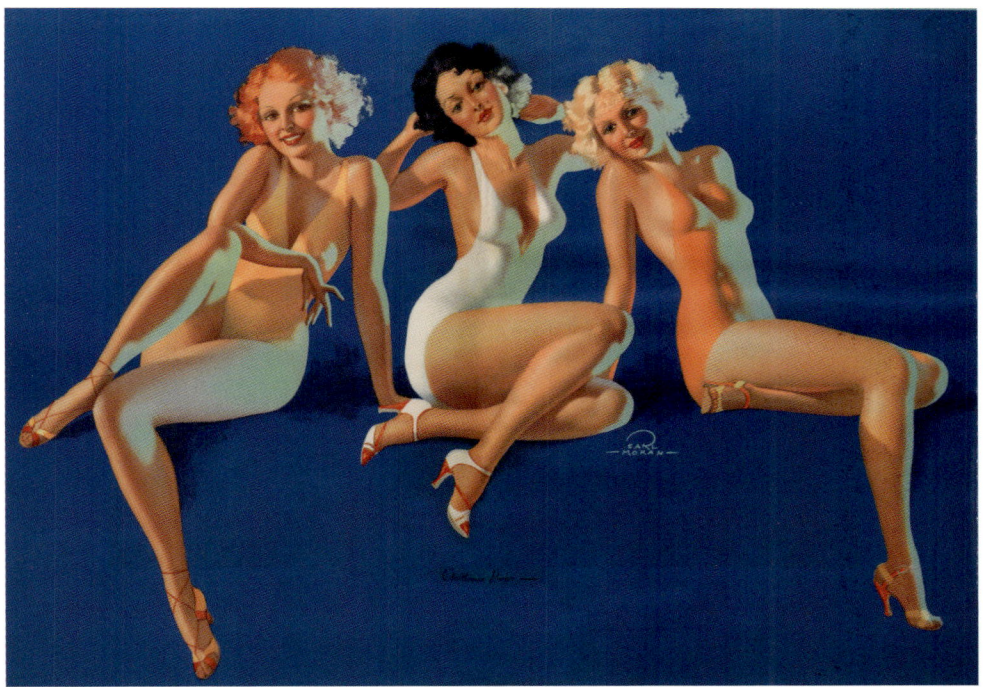

to his workhorse contemporaries, he did live more, and work less, leaving behind few sideline projects to complement his calendar art. These include a handful of risqué advertising pieces created in the 1930s and a brief partnership with the publisher Robert Harrison in 1942 to cocreate his first girlie magazine, *Beauty Parade*. In later years, Moran said he quit the magazine because the pressures were too much, but he continued to supply the first cover illustrations for each of Harrison's subsequent publications, signing them Steffa, his middle name.

After retiring from calendar work, Moran moved to Las Vegas with his fourth wife, Gloria, to live what has been described as a "fast life." In his final years he created a series of nude boudoir paintings, many of which evoke his then-deceased friend and favorite model, Marilyn Monroe.

For all his wild living, Moran lived to the age of 91—dying on January 17, 1984.

Above: Gentlemen Prefer — , a 1938 Brown & Bigelow calendar lithograph from a 1936 original. This blonde, brunette and redhead are wearing the signature "nuder than nude" swimsuits that got Moran his exclusive contract with Brown & Bigelow. His trick was to paint a *realistic nude,* and then add a bit of tint inside a swimsuit outline, so that the woman still appeared nude, while being legally covered.

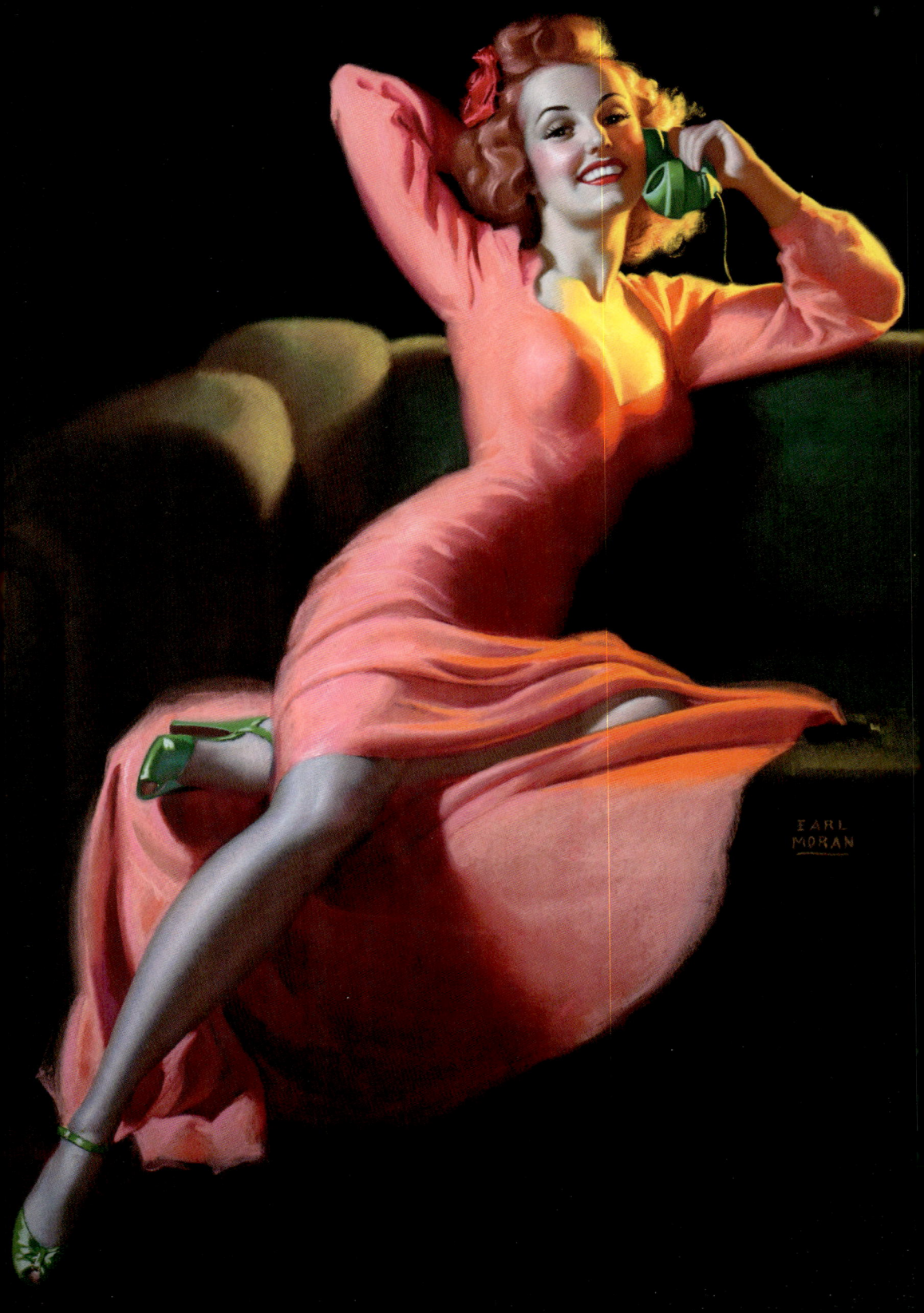

„Sein Stern als Illustrator begann erst aufzugehen, als er bereits 40 war, seine Hingabe an die poetischeren Verführungen eines Künstlerdaseins — Reiselust und chronische Untreue — war allerdings früh entwickelt."

1944, nach fast zehn Jahren als Starkünstler von Brown & Bigelow, wurde Earl Moran ein besonderer Ehrentitel zuteil — er wurde als BSA, Bachelor of Sex Appeal, ausgezeichnet. Der Kalenderverlag nutzte diesen Gag, um aus Morans privatem Sexskandal Kapital zu schlagen. Im Jahr zuvor hatte Mura — die dritte Mrs. Moran — die Scheidung eingereicht, weil sie vom „unverschämten Flirten und anstößigen Tanzen, Umarmen und den Küssereien" des Künstlers die Nase voll hatte. Sie behauptete, sie habe das im Zweiten Weltkrieg berühmte Pin-up-Modell Chili Williams mit Moran in dessen Atelier gesehen, ohne Kamera, ohne Leinwand und ohne Kleidung. Jahrelang sorgte diese Auseinandersetzung noch für Schlagzeilen, denn Chili — das Mädchen mit dem gepunkteten Bikini — versuchte, ihren Ruf zu wahren, während es Mura um eine

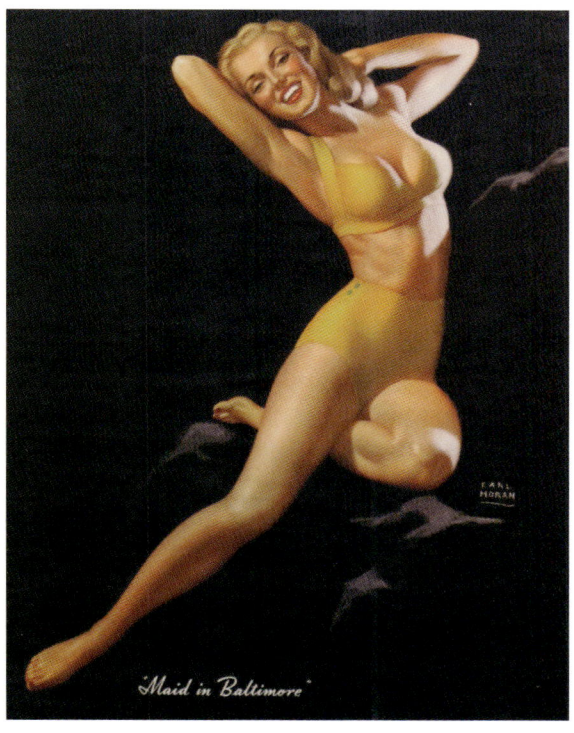

'Maid in Baltimore'

üppige finanzielle Abfindung ging und Moran schon bei einem anderen jungen Modell war.

Wie bei vielen anderen aus der Truppe von Brown & Bigelow waren die Geschichten, die sich um Moran rankten, ein heikles Gespinst aus Dichtung und Wahrheit, genauso unterhaltsam wie seine Werke. Earl Moran — halb Typ Clark Gable, halb Horatio Alger — wurde 1893 in Belle Plaine, Iowa, geboren und verbrachte die ersten 20 Jahre seines Berufslebens nur dann

Opposite: Remember Me?, pastel on board, 1947, for a 1949 Brown & Bigelow calendar. Some things just don't translate to the modern era, such as the erotic allure of a woman talking on the phone. It all began with George Petty, who did a series of cartoons of women on the phone telling unseen friends scandalous tidbits about their lives. 34 x 27 inches.

Above: Maid in Baltimore lithograph from a pastel of Monroe. The defining feature of all *Maid in Baltimore* pastels is the yellow two-piece bathing suit.

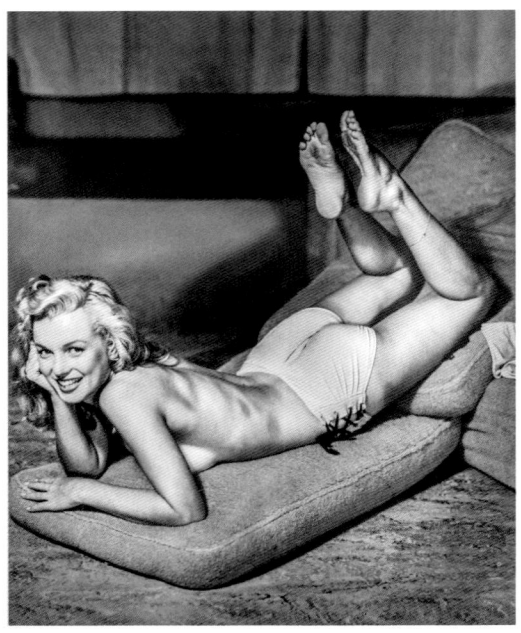

mit Kunstproduktion, wenn sich daraus Geld schlagen ließ. Wenn nicht, war er als Lkw-Fahrer unterwegs. Sein Stern als Illustrator begann erst aufzugehen, als er bereits 40 war, seine Hingabe an die poetischeren Verführungen eines Künstlerdaseins – Reiselust und chronische Untreue – war allerdings früh entwickelt. Morans märchenhafte Geschichte vom einfachen Mann, der sein Glück machte, bot all jenen Geschäftsleuten, die seine *Hotcha Girl*-Kalender kauften oder verkauften, die Möglichkeit, sich damit zu identifizieren. Es wird erzählt, Moran habe 1932, weil ihn sein schlecht bezahlter Job als Werbeillustrator für Herrenmodekataloge anödete, in seiner Freizeit zwei großformatige Pastelle mit badenden Schönheiten gezeichnet. Auf beiden Bildern war eine sinnliche Blondine dargestellt, die trotz ihres Badeanzugs nackt zu sein schien, und beide

Bilder wurden – allerdings von zwei konkurrierenden Kalenderverlagen – für eine Veröffentlichung angenommen. Doch dann, noch bevor die Thomas D. Murphy Company weitere dieser originellen Pin-ups bei Moran in Auftrag geben konnte, angelten sich Brown & Bigelow den Künstler mit einem Exklusivvertrag.

Vermutlich hat Morans Orientierung hin zur Kalenderkunst sowohl mit seinen Verpflichtungen – er musste in Zeiten der Weltwirtschaftskrise zwei Ex-Frauen und drei Kinder unterstützen – als auch mit seinen privaten Vorlieben zu tun, doch dazu äußerte sich Brown & Bigelow nie. 1918 hatte Moran Louise geheiratet, die als Ausdruckstänzerin in New York City auftrat. Kurz hintereinander bekam das Paar zwei Kinder, und man beschloss, sie in Chicago aufzuziehen. Ihre Tochter Peggy Moran sollte später aus eigenem Antrieb Pin-up-Girl werden und in *The Mummy's Hand* und *Horror Island* als eine der ersten Kreischköniginnen Hollywoods Karriere machen. Als sich die ersten beruflichen Erfolge seiner Tochter abzeichneten, prahlte Moran oft mit ihrer Schönheit, doch nach seiner Scheidung 1923 hatte er sich kaum um die Heranwachsende gekümmert. Bevor er für Brown & Bigelow tätig war und sich in einem Penthouse-Atelier in New York einrichtete, in dem er ständig Partys für Revuegirls und Prominente gab, wurde seine zweite Tochter von seiner zweiten Frau Mary geboren. Bei einer dieser Partys bändelte er mit dem Modell Mura an, der Mutter seines jüngsten Kindes, die später für jenes Trennungsdrama und den Ärger sorgte. Moran war Frauen schlicht zugetan, und trotz seiner schwindenden Haarpracht, seines Narzissmus und seiner stets präsenten Pfeife erwiderten sie diese Zuneigung. In den 1930er- und 1940er-Jahren konnte Brown & Bigelow seinen Künstler

Above: One of several photos Moran took of Marilyn Monroe in 1946 as reference for his second *Maid in Baltimore* painting, previous page. Notice her trunks match those in the original painting, opposite. Courtesy Heritage Auctions.

Opposite: The first, pre-Marilyn *Maid in Baltimore*, pastel on board, circa 1942. Moran created at least two variations on this theme, all titled *Maid in Baltimore*, with the later pastels based on photos of Monroe. 38.5 x 25.5 inches.

THE ART OF PIN-UP

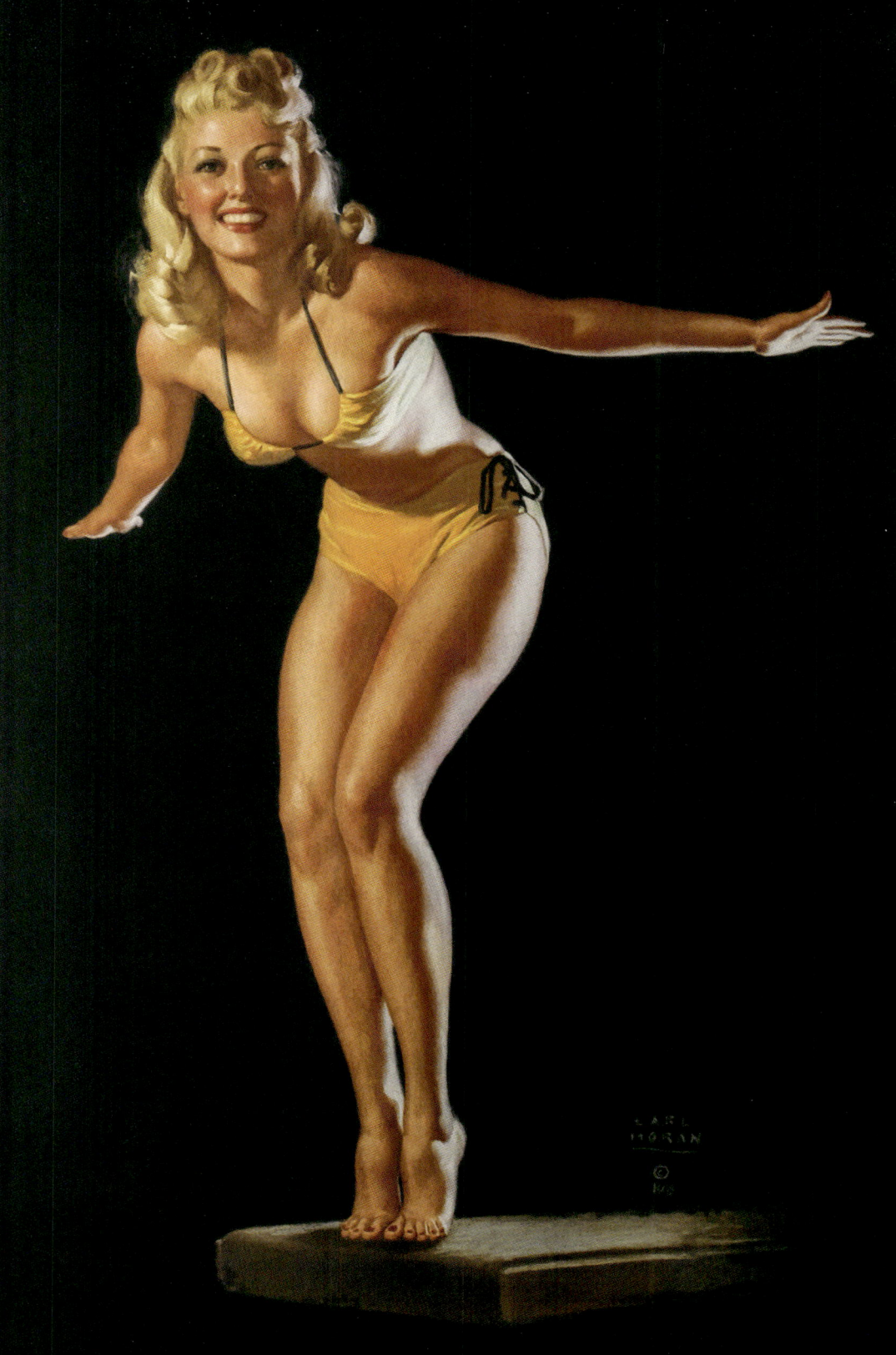

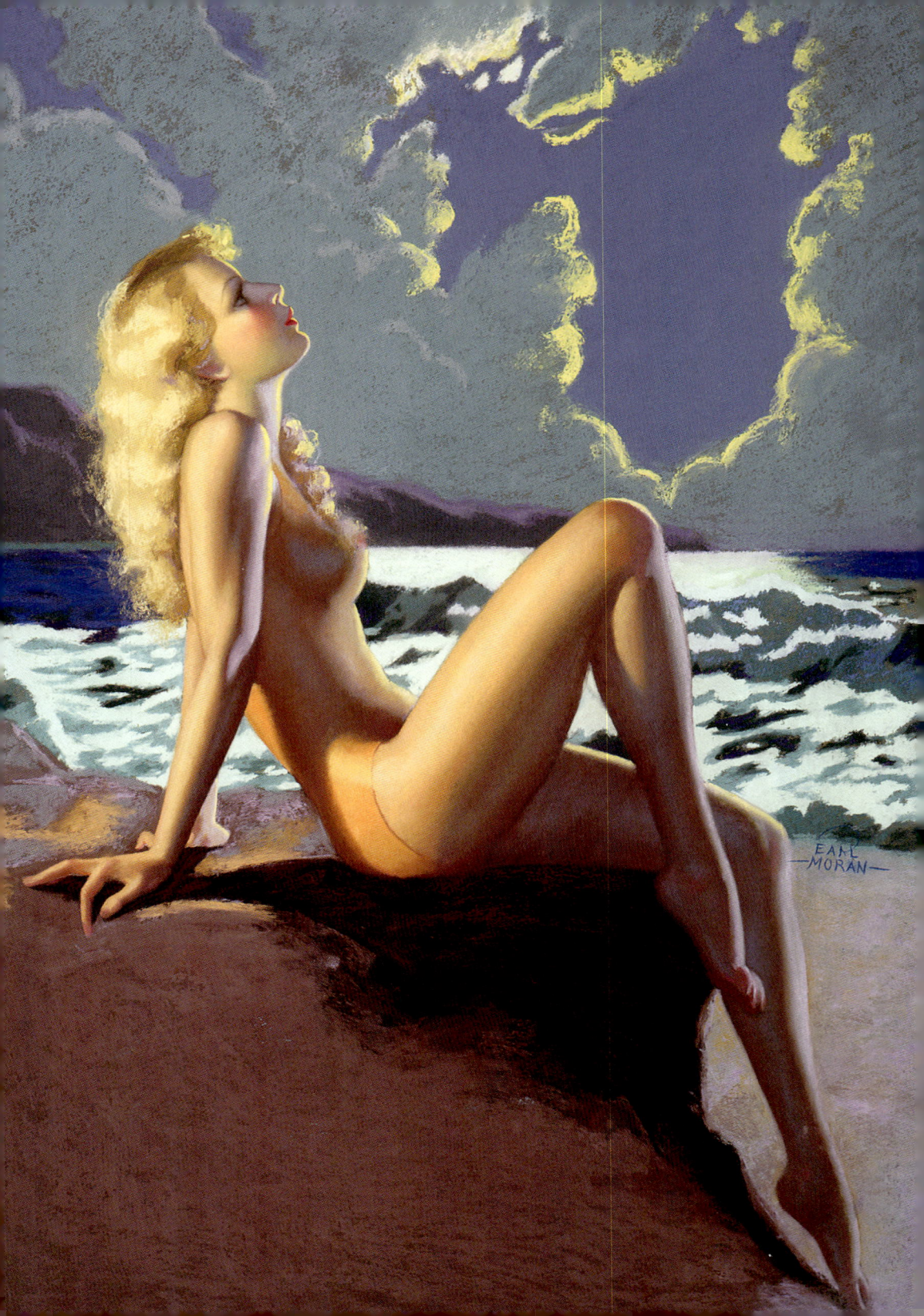

nach außen hin nicht offen als Playboy vermarkten, doch Morans munteres Sexleben wurde zu einer festen Größe für seinen Erfolg.

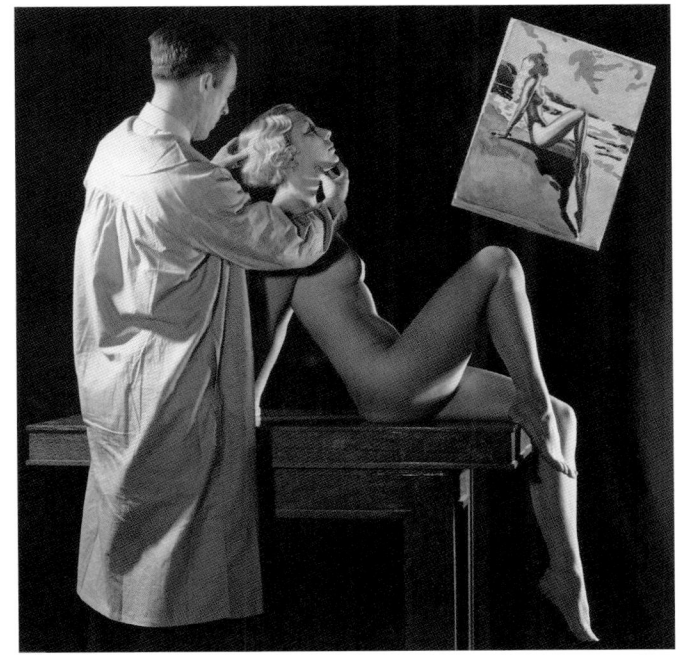

Earl Moran leistete mit der puren Erotik seiner Pin-ups für Brown & Bigelow Bahnbrechendes. Sein erotisches Ideal war die blonde Sexbombe, allerdings wusste er auch genau, dass er die Haarfarbe, um dem Geschmack anderer Betrachter entgegenzukommen, ab und an ändern musste. Und in Sachen Mode hielt er sich zumindest so weit auf dem Laufenden, dass seine Bilder nie veraltet wirkten. Obgleich ihn B & B auch mit der Produktion schicklicher Pin-ups beauftragte, zeigte er besonderes Talent für andere Gattungen, die das Unternehmen sonst nicht hätte angehen können. Morans Helldunkelakte, die als seine künstlerisch anspruchsvollsten Arbeiten gelten, entstanden zwischen 1935 und 1940 für B & B. Kalenderverlage sorgten zwar dafür, dass Pin-ups allmählich zur Mainstreamkultur gehörten, doch waren Akte ironischerweise tabu. So wurde Moran schließlich Brown & Bigelows Antwort auf Hollywood.

Während die meisten Künstler von B & B meinten, professionellen Modellen fehle der Charme, castete Moran Profis. In New York gehörte er einer Jury für Schönheitswettbewerbe an, die Gewinnerinnen setzte er dann als Modelle ein. Als er nach Los Angeles zog, engagierte er für zehn Dollar pro Stunde Schauspielerinnen wie Joi Lansing, Barbara Nichols, Marie Wilson, Jayne Mansfield und auch Marilyn Monroe.

Als er 1946 Monroe kennenlernte, hieß sie noch Norma Jeane Baker, und Moran mietete ein Atelier von Henry Clive an, einem der berühmten Geschichtenerzähler unter den Illustratoren. Monroe stand ihm die ganzen 1940er-Jahre Modell, und die vielen Fotografien der bekleideten wie auch der nackten Marilyn, die dabei entstanden, unterstreichen die Behauptung von Brown & Bigelow, Morans talentierter Umgang mit der Kamera, jenen Moment der Hingabe einzufangen, den die Käufer der Kalender sehen wollen, zeichne ihn ganz besonders aus.

Wer auch immer sein Modell war – Moran bevorzugte bei den von ihm Dargestellten eine Pose, in der sich die Frau zurücklehnte, ihre Beine weit ausstreckte und in der ihre in High Heels steckenden Füße betont wurden. Eine solche Ansicht lädt den Betrachter viel direkter

Opposite: Pastel on board, circa 1935. Though the figure appears to be nude, this is another of Moran's oh-so-subtle bathing suits.

Above: In this 1930s Brown & Bigelow publicity shot, Moran poses a model to match the painting at right.

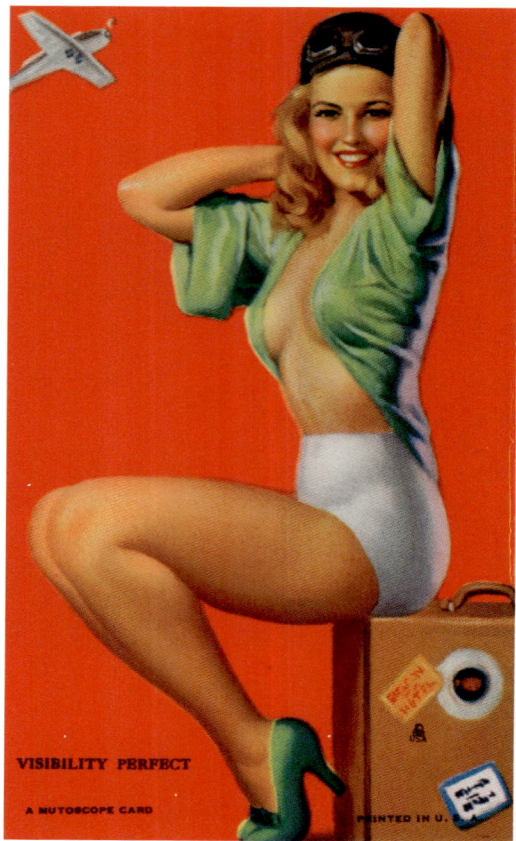

VISIBILITY PERFECT

A MUTOSCOPE CARD

PRINTED IN U.

dazu ein hinzuschauen als die meisten anderen Pin-ups. Moran verstärkte diese Ausdruckskraft noch, indem er nicht das „Mädchen von nebenan", sondern Heldinnen schmutziger Fantasiegeschichten, Stripperinnen und gescheiterte Revuegirls präsentierte. Selbst auf seinen züchtigeren Bildern quillt den Modellen der Busen, ein wahrer Hingucker, aus dem tief geschnittenen Dekolleté. Morans Rezept war eindeutig: ein Minimum an Kleidung, ein Maximum an Bein und Busen, und all das mit einem Minimum an vertraglichen Verpflichtungen, um den Lebensunterhalt zu sichern. Im hohen Alter gestand er einmal, er habe sich dem Malen von Bildern zugewandt, weil ihm klar war, „wie wenig ihn die Vorstellung von Arbeit reizte" und er darüber hinaus „wie ein Künstler leben wollte". Verglichen mit den Arbeitstieren unter seinen Kollegen, lebte er intensiver und arbeitete weniger – abgesehen von seinen Kalenderbildern widmete er sich nur wenigen anderen Projekten. Zu diesen zählen ein paar pikante Anzeigenmotive, die er in den 1930er-Jahren schuf, und eine kurze Partnerschaft mit dem Verleger Robert Harrison, dessen erstes Girlie-Magazin *Beauty Parade* er 1942 mit konzipierte. In späteren Jahren erklärte Moran, er habe die Mitarbeit an diesem Zeitschriftenprojekt aufgegeben, weil ihm der Druck zu groß gewesen sei, doch er lieferte weiterhin die ersten Titelbilder für jede der noch folgenden neuen Publikationen Harrisons und signierte die Arbeiten mit Steffa, seinem zweiten Vornamen.

Nachdem er keine Kalenderbilder mehr malte, zog Moran mit seiner vierten Frau, Gloria, nach Las Vegas, um dort das auszuleben, was er als „flottes Leben" beschrieb. In seinen letzten Lebensjahren schuf er eine Serie von Boudoir-Akten, von denen viele an seine damals bereits verstorbene Freundin, sein Lieblingsmodell Marilyn Monroe, erinnerten.

Trotz seines wilden Lebens wurde Earl Moran 91 Jahre alt. Er starb am 17. Januar 1984.

Above: *Visibility Perfect,* Mutoscope card, circa 1943. 5.25 x 3.25 inches.

Opposite: *"Don't Try Any Pincer Movements on Me,"* pastel on board, circa 1942. Though this is an original artwork, Moran painted the ad copy directly onto the board.

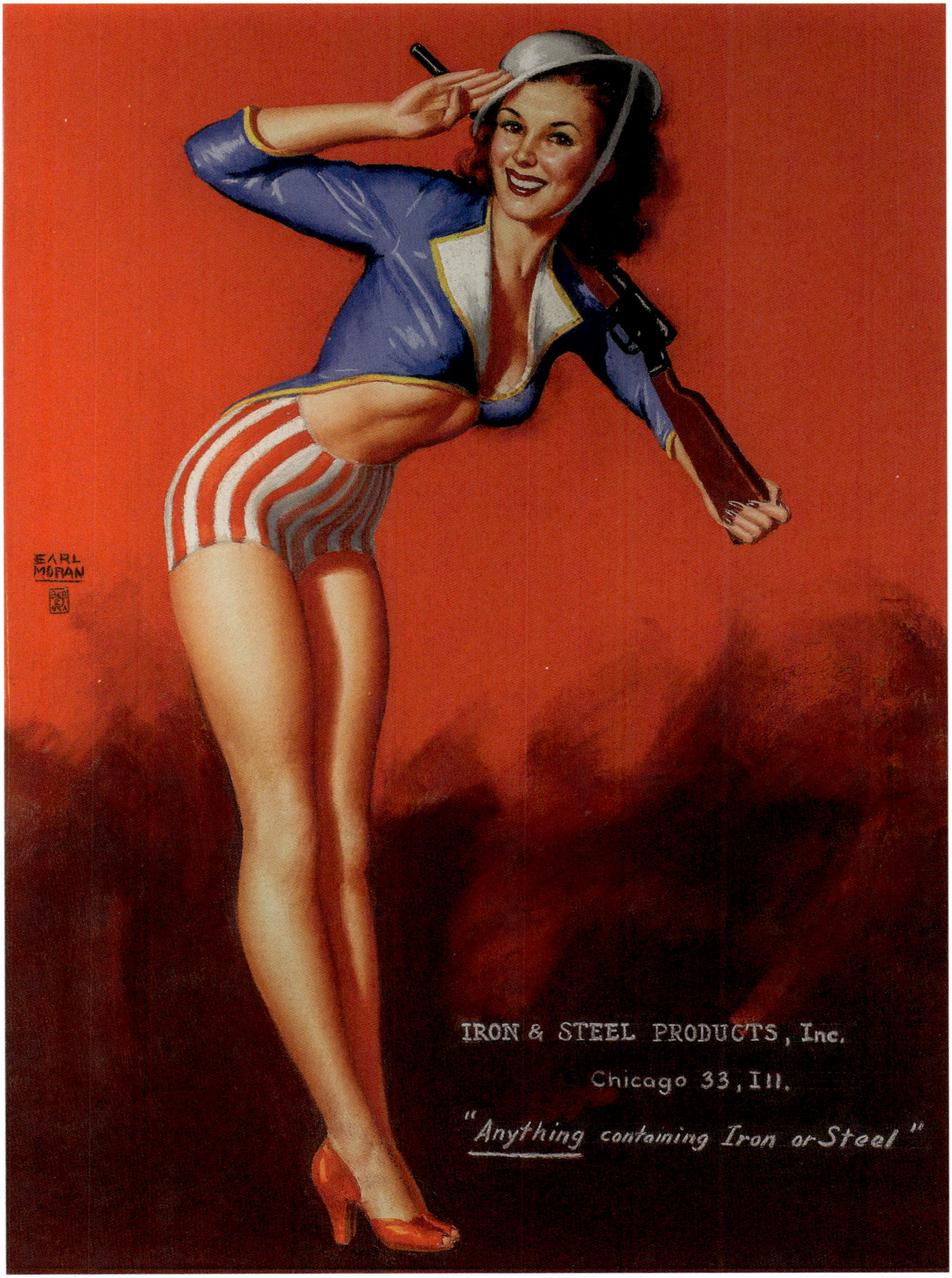
EARL MORAN
IRON & STEEL PRODUCTS, Inc.
Chicago 33, Ill.
"Anything containing Iron or Steel"

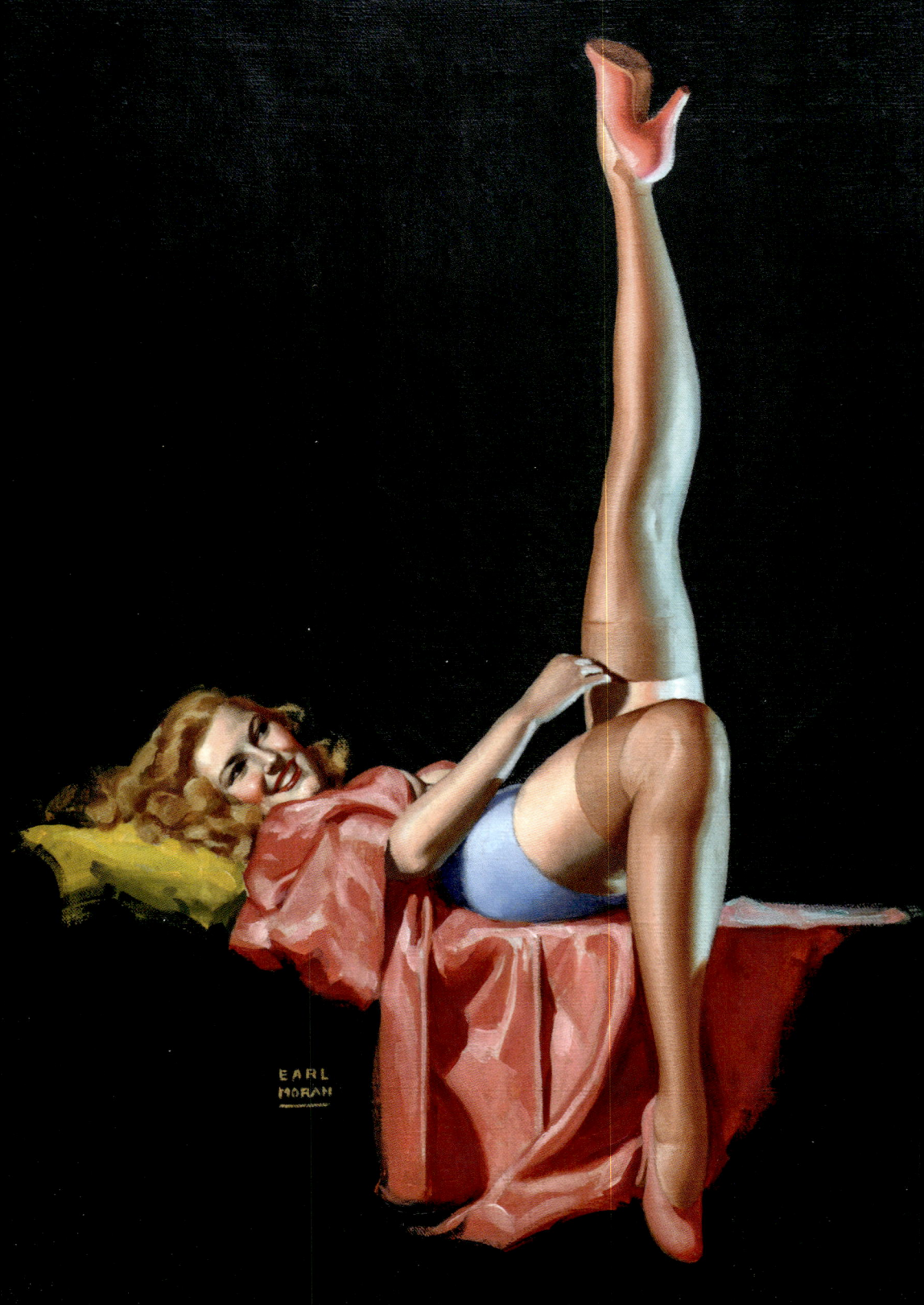

« Il ne perça dans le monde de l'illustration qu'à la quarantaine,
même s'il développa très tôt un goût pour la vie
de bohème (surtout l'esprit nomade et l'infidélité chronique). »

En 1944, alors qu'il était depuis près de dix ans l'illustrateur vedette de Brown & Bigelow, Moran reçut le titre de « licencié ès sex-appeal ». Pour l'éditeur de calendriers, c'était un coup publicitaire visant à exploiter le dernier scandale sexuel de Moran et son retour à la vie de célibataire. L'année précédente, excédée de le voir « flirter, danser, tripoter et embrasser de manière indécente », Mura, la troisième Mme Moran, avait demandé le divorce. Elle affirmait avoir surpris Chili Williams, la célèbre « pin-up aux petits pois » de la Seconde Guerre mondiale, dans l'atelier de son mari, avec ce dernier dans le plus simple appareil, sans pinceaux ni appareil photo. La presse s'en donna à cœur joie durant des années tandis que Chili tentait de sauver sa réputation et que Mura réclamait une grosse compensation financière. Entre-temps, Moran s'était entiché d'un autre modèle.

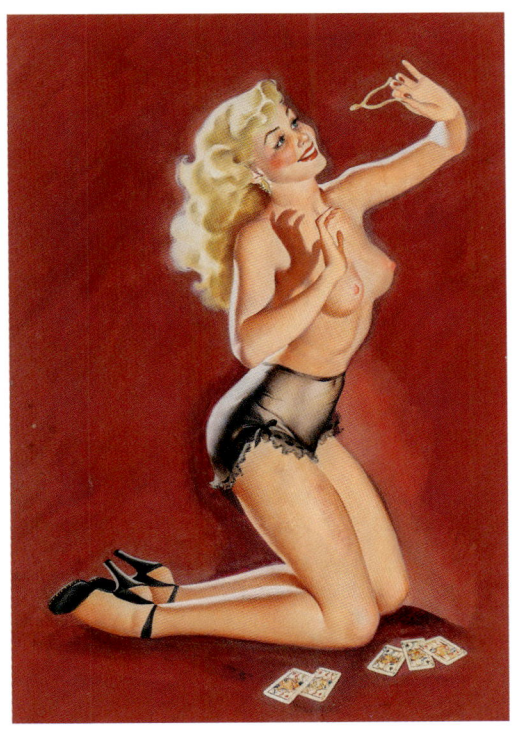

Comme de nombreux illustrateurs employés par B&B, l'histoire de Moran était aussi haute en couleur que ses œuvres, formant un tissu de vérités et d'inventions. Earl Moran naquit en 1893 à Belle Plaine, dans l'Iowa, et passa les vingt premières années de sa vie à peindre quand cela rapportait de l'argent, et à conduire des camions quand ce n'était pas le cas. Il ne perça dans le monde de l'illustration qu'à la quarantaine, même s'il développa très tôt un goût pour la vie de bohème (surtout l'esprit nomade et l'infidélité chronique). Sa fable du prolétaire qui a réussi séduisait les hommes d'affaires qui achetaient et vendaient ses calendriers *Hotcha Girl*, et donnait un certain piment

Opposite: *Stocking Up On Sugar*, oil on canvas, 1944, for a Brown & Bigelow calendar. Perhaps Moran's best-known, best-loved image. Zoë Mozert produced a similar pastel titled *A Run on Sugar* at the same time, possibly as part of the competition between B&B contract artists. 24.25 x 19.25. Mitchell Mehdy collection.

Above: *Wishbone*, oil on board, circa 1950, 19.5 x 13.5 inches. Courtesy Heritage Auctions.

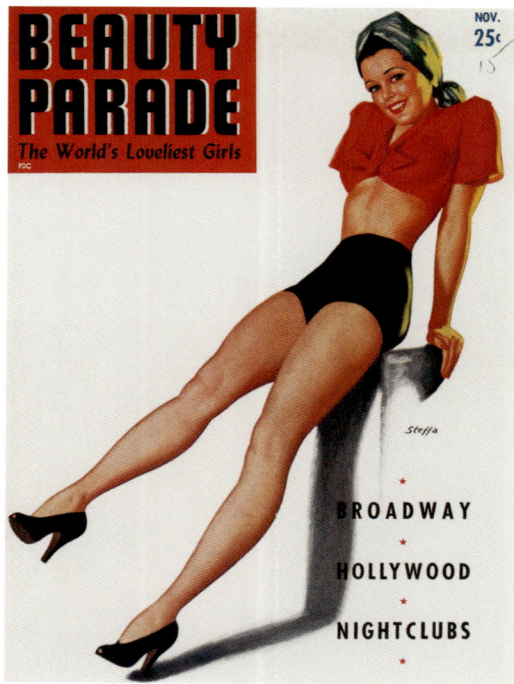

à ses œuvres virtuoses et somptueusement colorées. Selon la légende, en 1932, lassé d'être mal payé et mal considéré comme illustrateur de catalogues de mode masculine, Moran peignit au pastel deux belles baigneuses grand format. Les blondes voluptueuses paraissaient nues en dépit de leur maillot de bain et furent toutes deux acceptées par des éditeurs de calendriers concurrents. Avant que Thomas D. Murphy n'ait pu lui en commander d'autres, B&B lui fit signer un contrat d'exclusivité.

Sa décision de travailler pour les calendriers était également motivée par la nécessité de subvenir aux besoins de deux ex-femmes et de trois enfants durant la Grande Dépression. Moran avait épousé Louise, une danseuse de New York, en 1918. Ils eurent rapidement deux enfants qu'ils projetaient d'élever à Chicago. Sa fille Peggy Moran devint elle-même pin-up et reine des films d'horreur à Hollywood, jouant dans *La Main de la momie* et dans *Horror Island*. Moran était très fier d'elle, s'enorgueillissant de sa carrière même s'il n'avait pas beaucoup participé à son éducation après son divorce en 1923. Il eut un autre enfant avec sa deuxième épouse, Mary, avant d'être recruté par B&B et de s'installer dans un atelier en penthouse à New York, où il donnait constamment des fêtes pour des danseuses de revue et des célébrités. Il y rencontra Mura, sa troisième épouse et la mère de son quatrième enfant. Moran aimait les femmes et, malgré son front dégarni, son narcissisme et sa pipe omniprésente, elles l'aimaient en retour. Dans les années 1930 et 1940, B&B ne pouvait mettre en avant le côté playboy de l'artiste, mais son appétit sexuel devint partie intégrante de sa popularité.

Earl Moran apporta à B&B l'érotisme de ses pin-up. Son idéal était la bombe blonde, même s'il changeait parfois la couleur de ses cheveux pour satisfaire tous les goûts et suivait la mode, juste assez pour que ses créations ne paraissent jamais démodées. L'éditeur lui fit également réaliser des pin-up plus sages mais Moran avait le don d'explorer des domaines que, sans lui, B&B n'aurait pas osé aborder. Ses nus en clair-obscur (considérés comme ses plus artistiques) furent créés pour B&B entre 1935 et 1940. Malheureusement, à mesure que les éditeurs de calendriers s'efforçaient de séduire un public toujours plus large, les nus devinrent trop risqués.

Alors que la plupart des artistes de B&B se plaignaient du manque de charme des modèles professionnels, Moran, lui, les appréciait à plus d'un titre. Il officiait comme juge dans des concours de beauté à New York, puis utilisait les lauréates comme modèles. Une fois établi à Los Angeles, il fit poser les actrices Joi Lansing, Barbara Nichols, Marie Wilson, Jayne Mansfield et, la plus célèbre, Marilyn Monroe, pour 10 dollars de l'heure.

Above: Moran signed many of his magazine covers with his middle name, Steffa. This is *Beauty Parade*, November 1942.

Opposite: Pastel on board, circa 1945, for a Brown & Bigelow calendar.

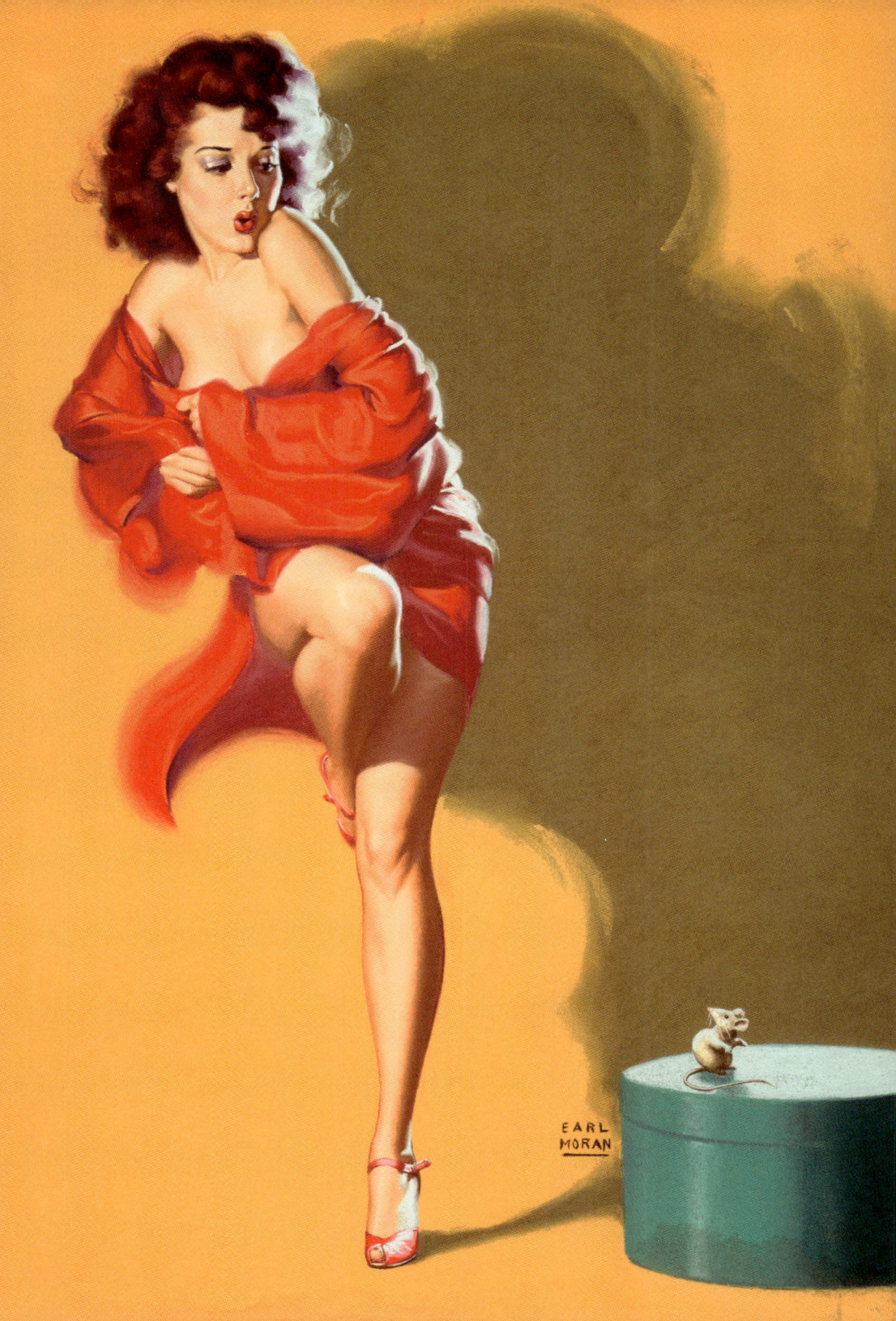

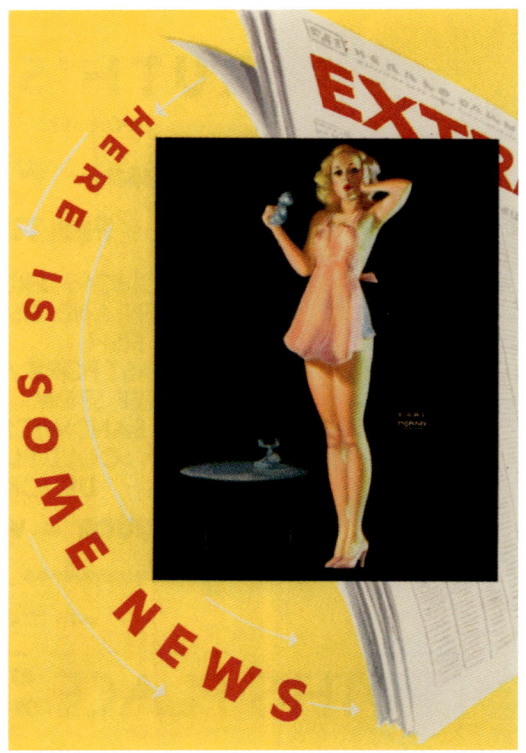

Il rencontra Monroe en 1946 alors qu'elle s'appelait encore Norma Jeane Baker et qu'il louait un atelier à Henry Clive, un autre illustrateur célèbre pour ses frasques amoureuses. Elle continua de poser pour lui jusqu'à la fin des années 1940. En regardant les nombreuses photos issues de ces séances, on est tenté de croire B&B quand la compagnie déclarait que c'était grâce à son œil de photographe que Moran parvenait à capturer ce moment d'abandon tant recherché par les acheteurs de calendriers.

Indépendamment du modèle, Moran avait une pose de prédilection : le sujet penché en arrière et étirant ses jambes en accentuant l'arc du pied. Cette pose invite le regard d'une manière plus directe que la plupart des autres images de pin-up. En outre, à la « fille d'à côté », il préférait les héroïnes de contes salaces, les effeuilleuses et les girls de revue. Même dans ses images les plus sages, les décolletés plongeants semblent sur le point d'exploser. Sa formule était claire : limiter les vêtements au maximum, insister sur les jambes et les seins, en faire le moins possible. Moran avoua plus tard qu'il avait choisi l'illustration car « l'idée de travailler ne lui plaisait pas beaucoup, mais qu'il aimait la vie d'artiste ». Comparé à ses confrères qui se tuaient à la tâche, il est vrai qu'il profitait davantage de la vie. Il accepta néanmoins quelques commandes parallèles. Parmi elles, une série de publicités osées dans les années 1930 et une brève association avec l'éditeur Robert Harrison en 1942 pour cofonder sa première revue de charme, *Beauty Parade*. Plus tard, il déclara qu'il avait quitté le magazine car la pression était trop forte, mais il continua d'illustrer la première couverture de chaque nouvelle publication de Harrison, signant Steffa, son deuxième prénom.

Après avoir cessé d'illustrer des calendriers, Moran s'installa à Las Vegas avec sa quatrième épouse, Gloria, pour mener une existence qualifiée par certains de « dissolue ». Au cours des dernières années de sa vie, il peignit une série de nus artistiques, dont bon nombre rappellent son amie disparue et son modèle préféré, Marilyn Monroe.

Après une vie bien remplie, Earl Moran s'éteignit le 17 janvier 1984 à l'âge de 91 ans.

Above: A greeting card produced by Brown & Bigelow, 1943, using a cover image from the late 1930s.

Opposite: Is My Face Red?, pastel on board, 1946, for Brown & Bigelow's *Nifty Numbers 1948* 12-page calendar. This pastel was given as a retirement gift to a B&B employee and survives in pristine condition. 24 x 19 inches.

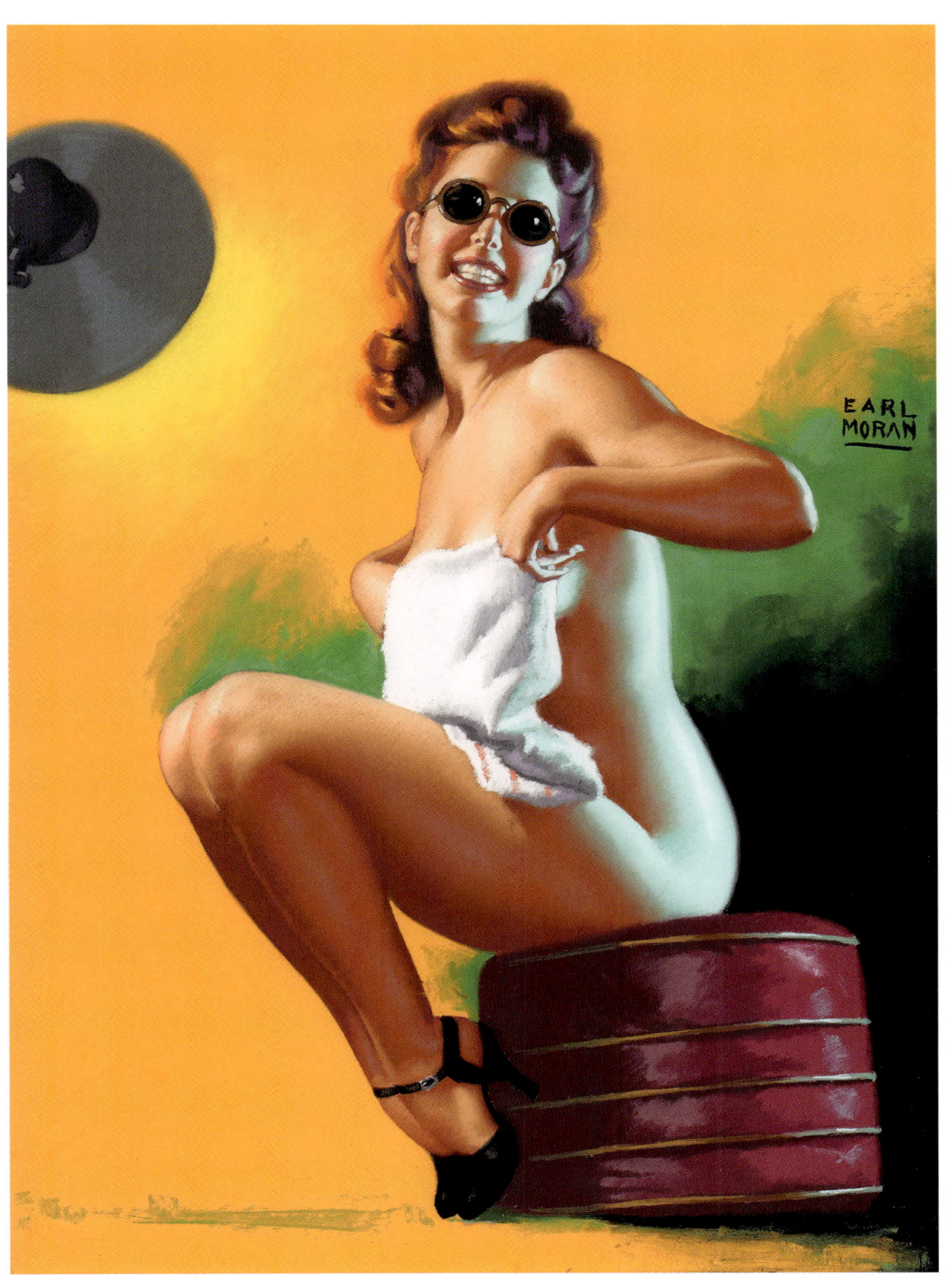

EARL MORAN

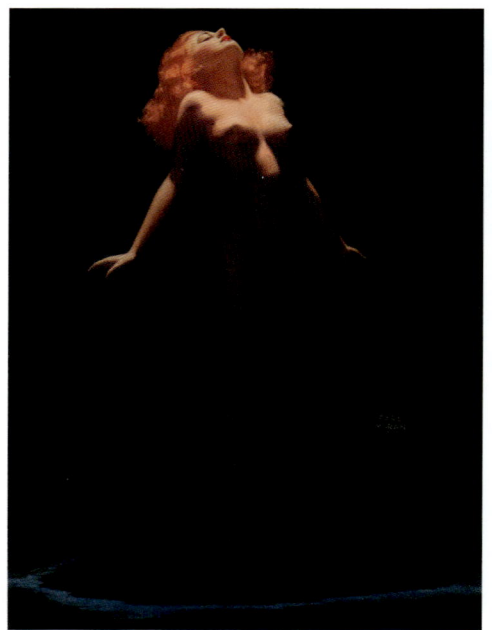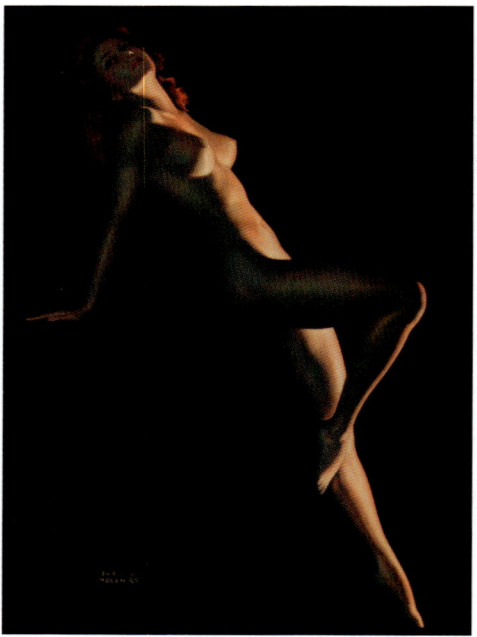

This and following spread: Arounc 1942 Brown & Bigelow produced a limited edition of 500 portfolios containing six Earl Moran lithographs, all nudes in the light & shadow style he explored in the late '30s. Titled *Running Into Six Figures*, it featured works created between 1937 and 1940 and was distributed to the company's most lucrative business accounts. *Star Bright* and *The Dancer* appear above, *Matchless Body* and *Work of Art* on the following spread. All prints are 14.5 x 11 inches.

Opposite: Tomorrow's Star, also known as *Show Girl*, pastel on board, circa 1938. The model for this large pastel, included in *Running Into Six Figures*, is reputed to be Jean Harlow. 38 x 29 inches. Collection of Michael and Gail Guglielmino.

THE ART OF PIN-UP

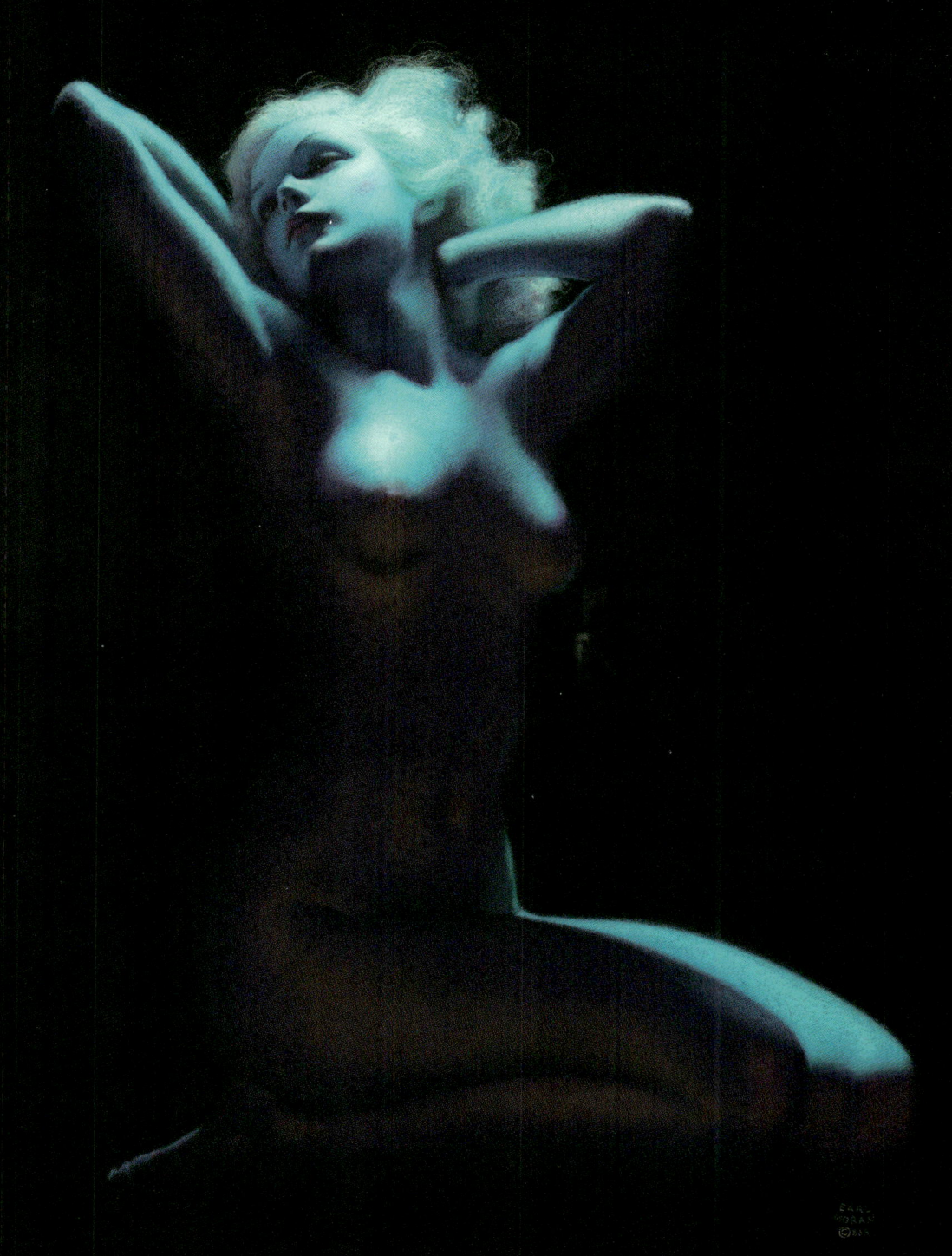

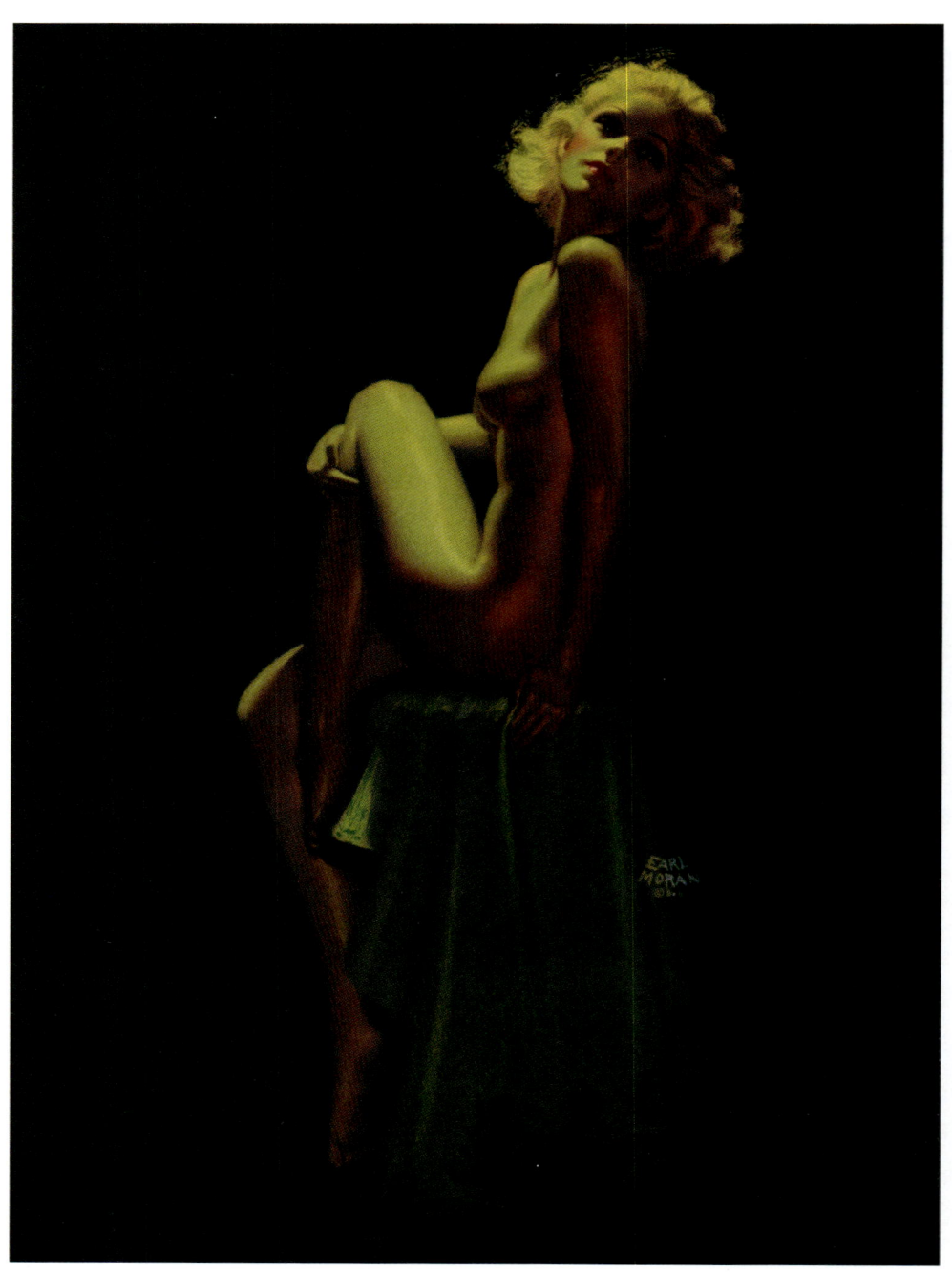

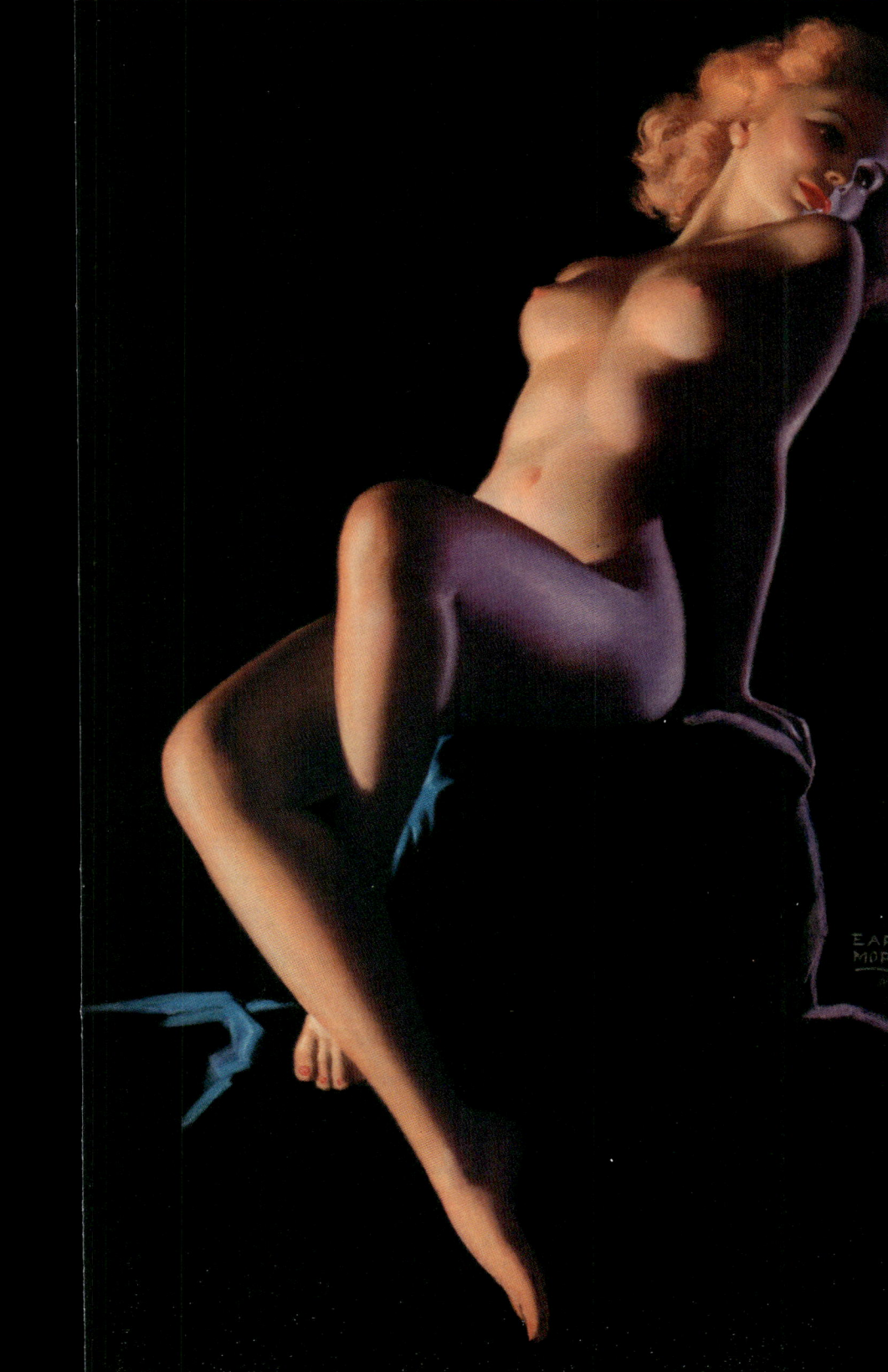

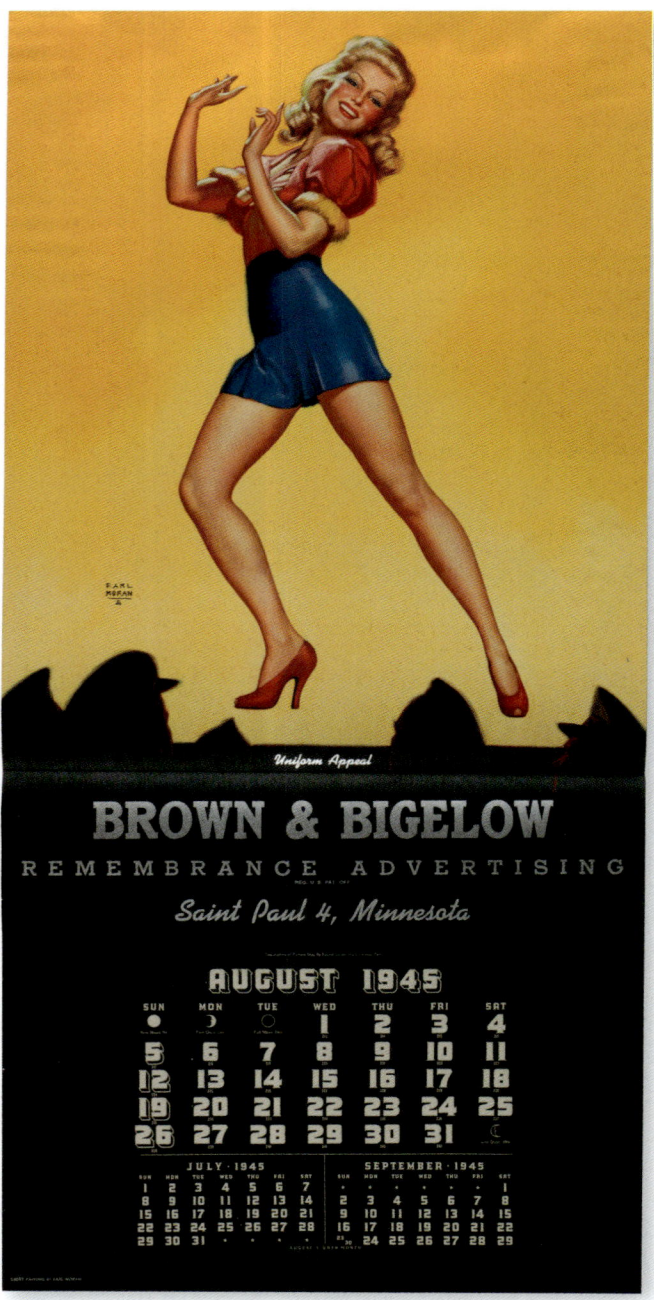

Above: *Uniform Appeal*, 1943, on a patriotic-themed 1945 Brown & Bigelow calendar. Calendar measures 46 x 22 inches.

Opposite: *Call Again*, pastel on board, 1946, for a Brown & Bigelow calendar. 32 x 26 inches.

THE ART OF PIN-UP

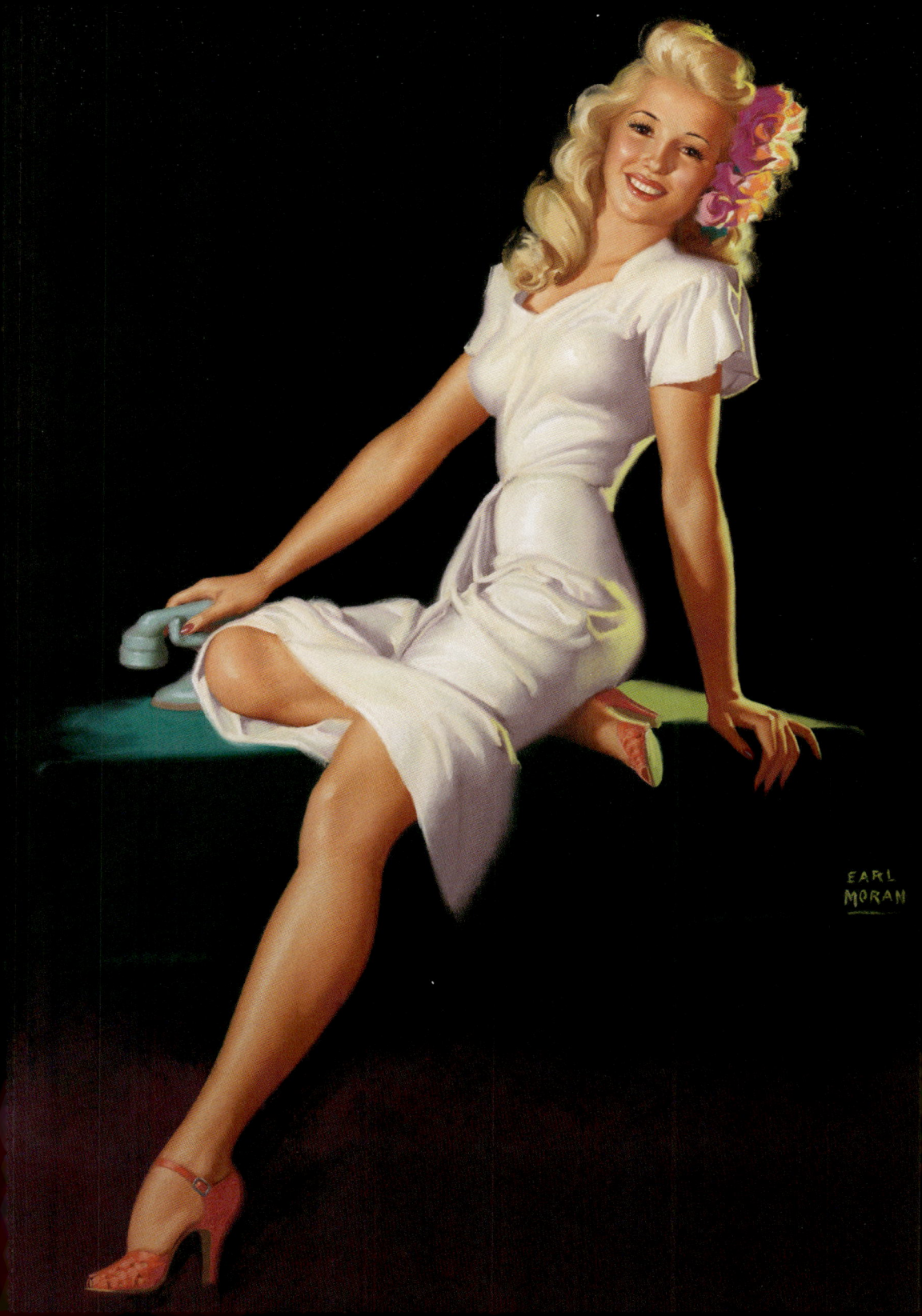

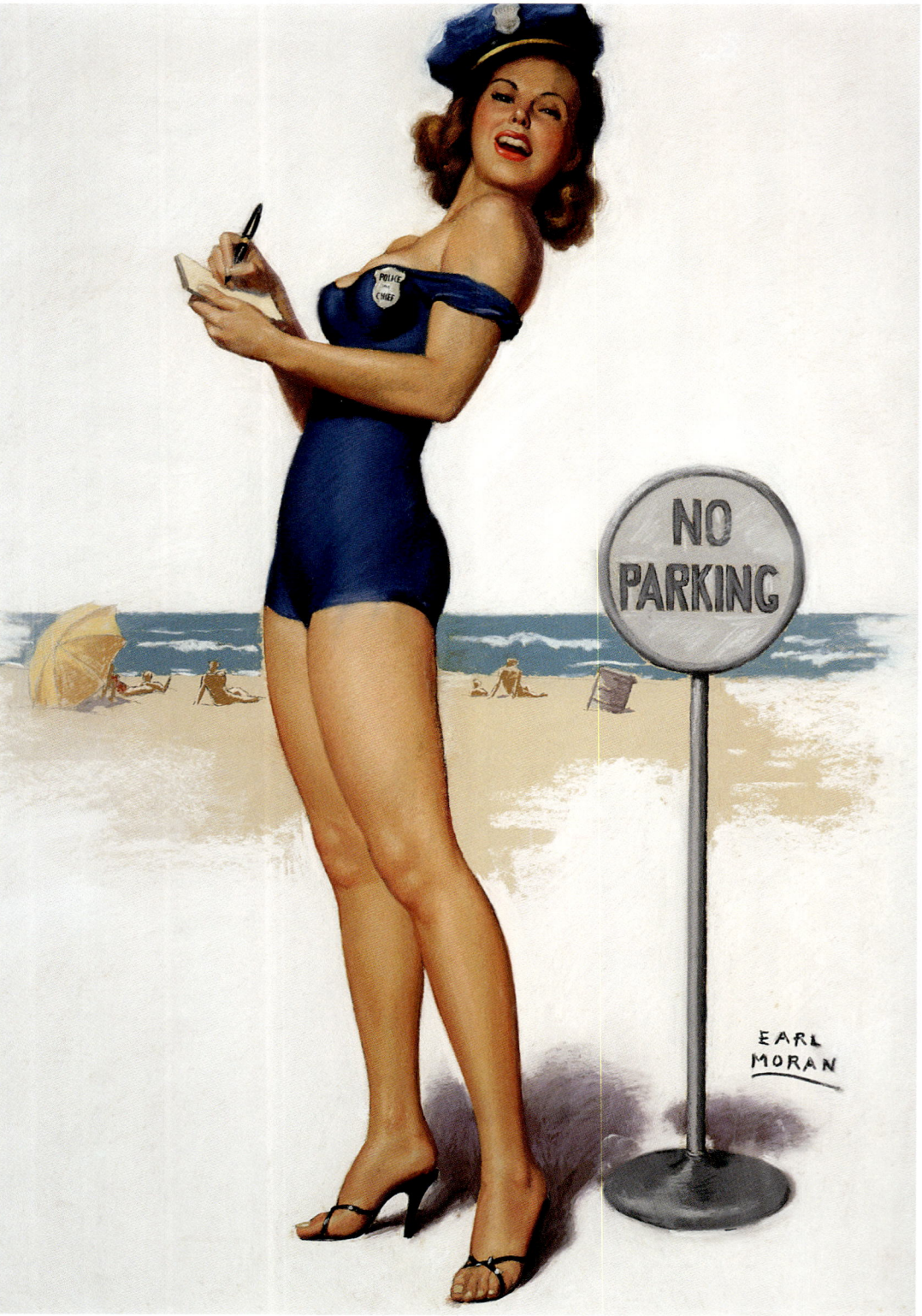

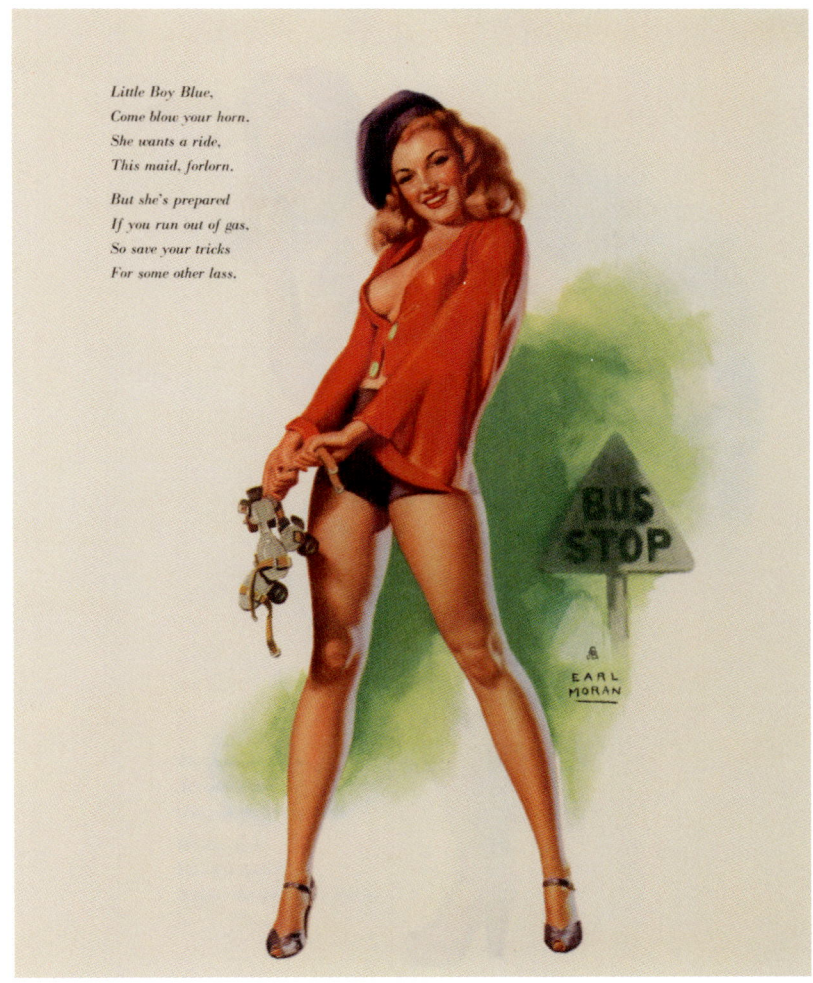

Little Boy Blue,
Come blow your horn.
She wants a ride,
This maid, forlorn.

But she's prepared
If you run out of gas,
So save your tricks
For some other lass.

Opposite: Now I'll Do the Whistling, pastel on board, 1950, for a Brown & Bigelow calendar. 27 x 19.5 inches.

Above: Little Boy Blue lithograph from the 12-page calendar *Girls of 1950*, with Marilyn Monroe as model. Since the images were always produced two years before the release date of the calendar, this year contained many pastels of Marilyn Monroe, derived from her 1946 photo sessions with Moran. Calendar measures 14.5 x 8.5 inches.

Following left: Marilyn, pastel on board, circa 1955, is yet another Moran portrait of Marilyn Monroe. This series of pastels on brown board was another experiment with media and light play. 30.75 x 22.5 inches.

Following right: Lookin' Good, pastel on board, circa 1955, for a Brown & Bigelow calendar. 30 x 22.5 inches.

EARL MORAN

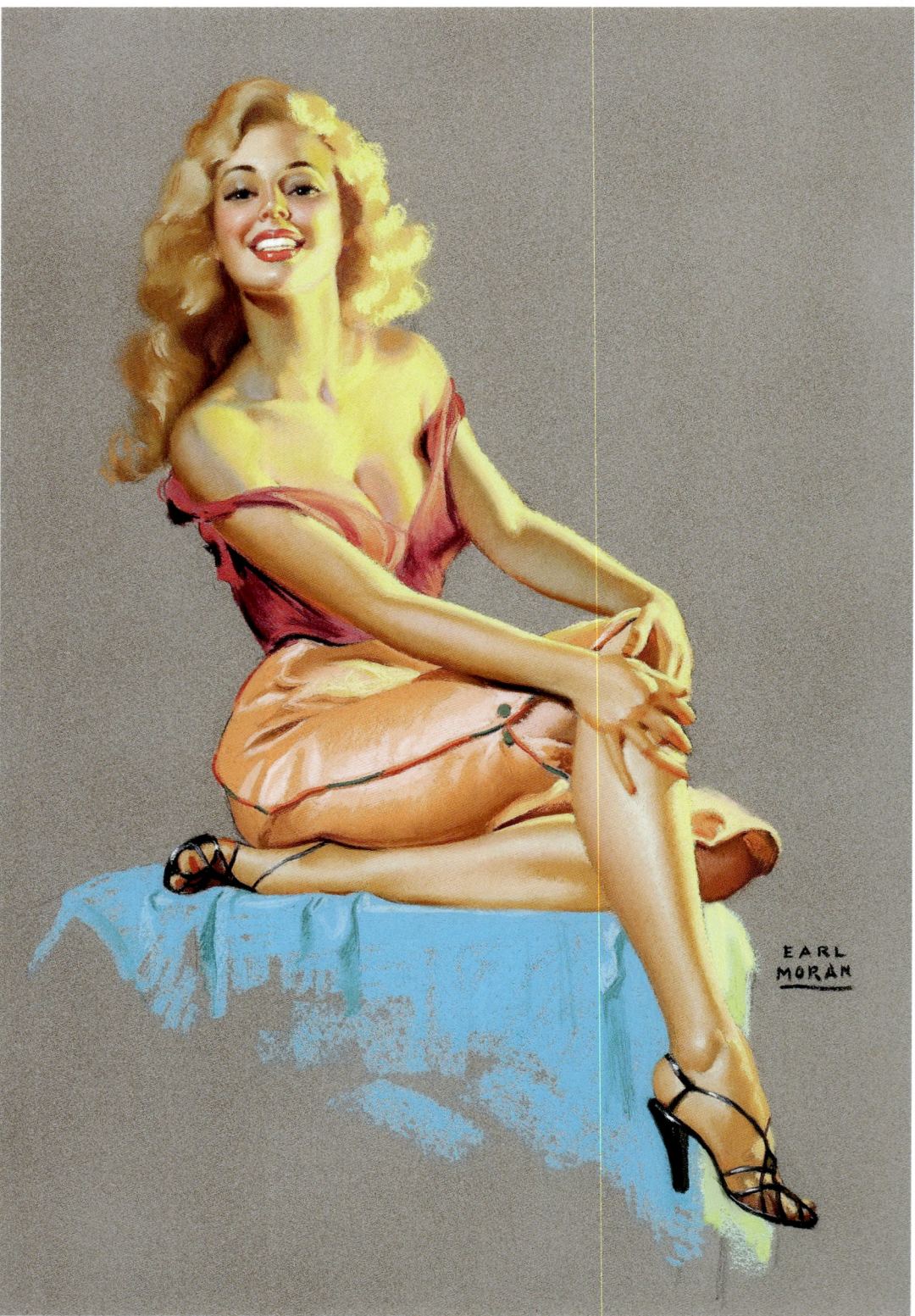

EARL
MORAN

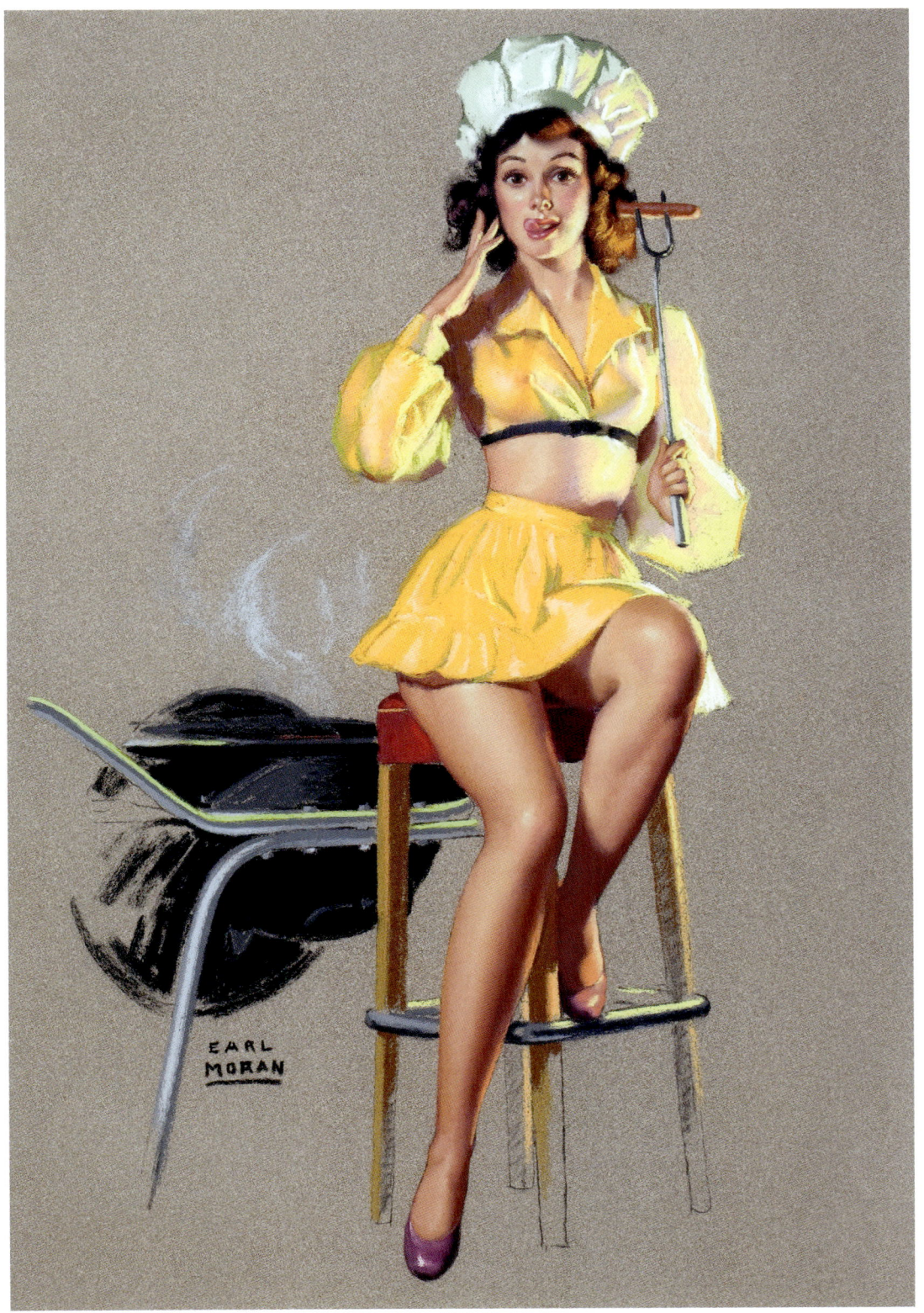

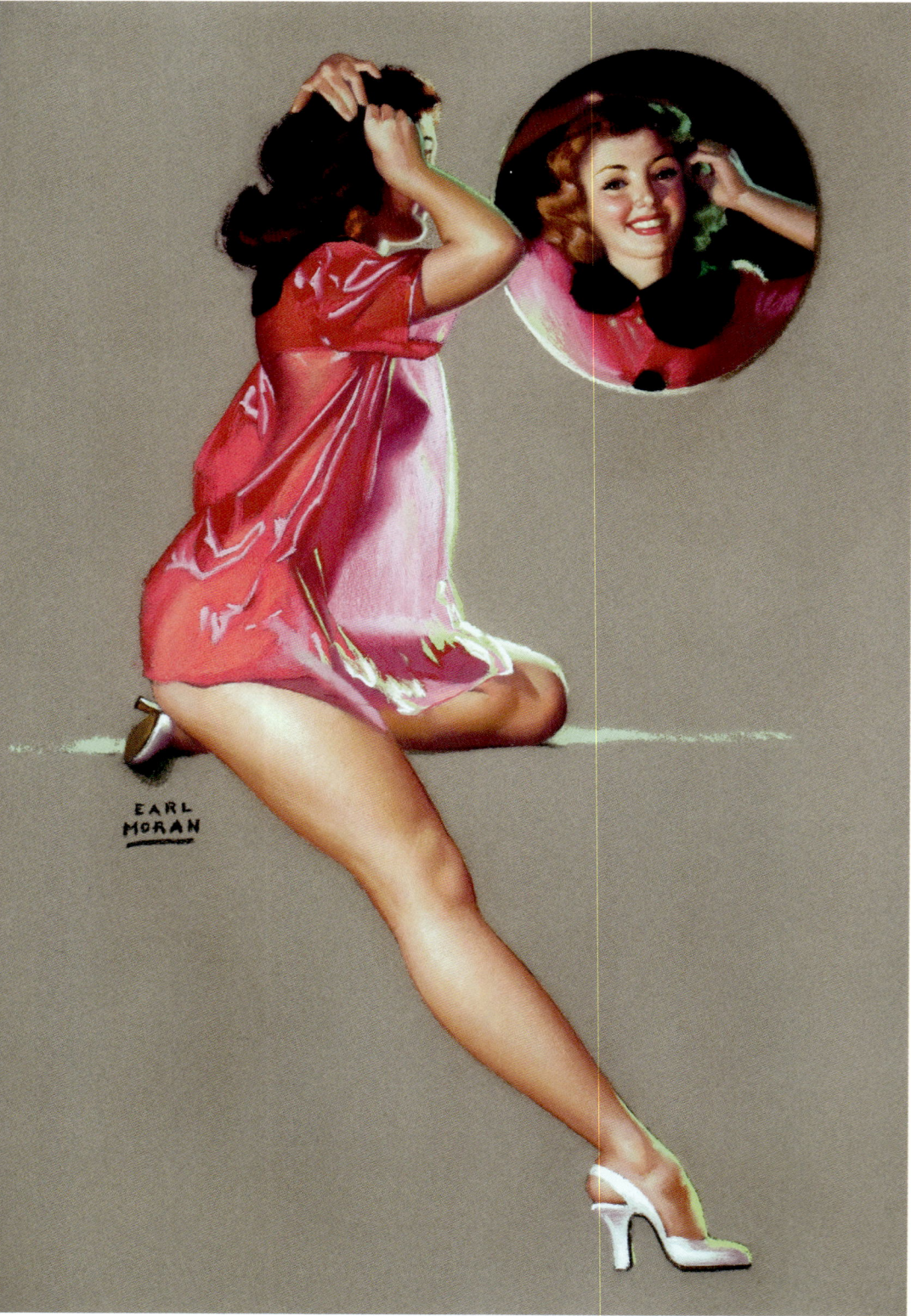

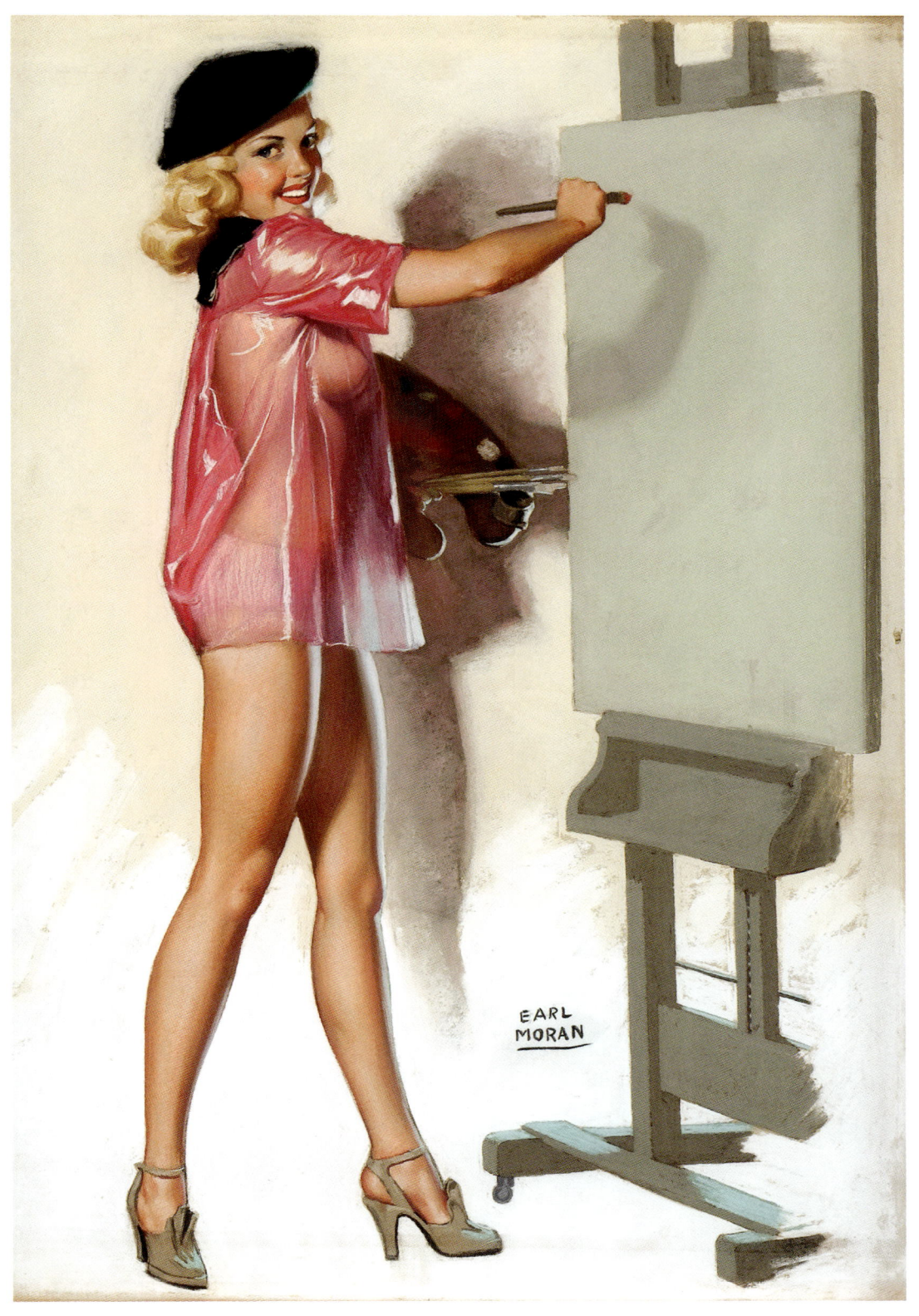

EARL
MORAN

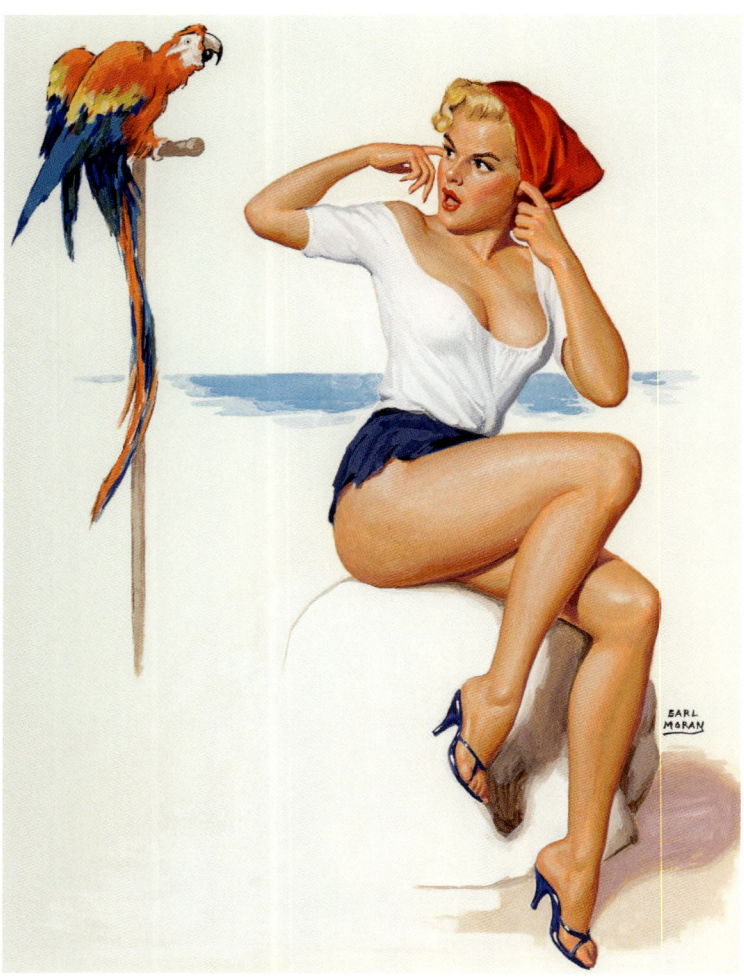

Previous left: It Was a Terrific Date with You, pastel on board, 1955. 31 x 23.5 inches.

Previous right: Pastel on board, circa 1954, for a Brown & Bigelow calendar. 28 x 20 inches.

Above: Parrot Call, watercolor and gouache on board, undated, 20 x 15.75 inches. Courtesy Heritage Auctions.

Opposite: I Don't Bite, oil on canvas, undated, 28 x 22 inches. Courtesy Heritage Auctions.

THE ART OF PIN-UP

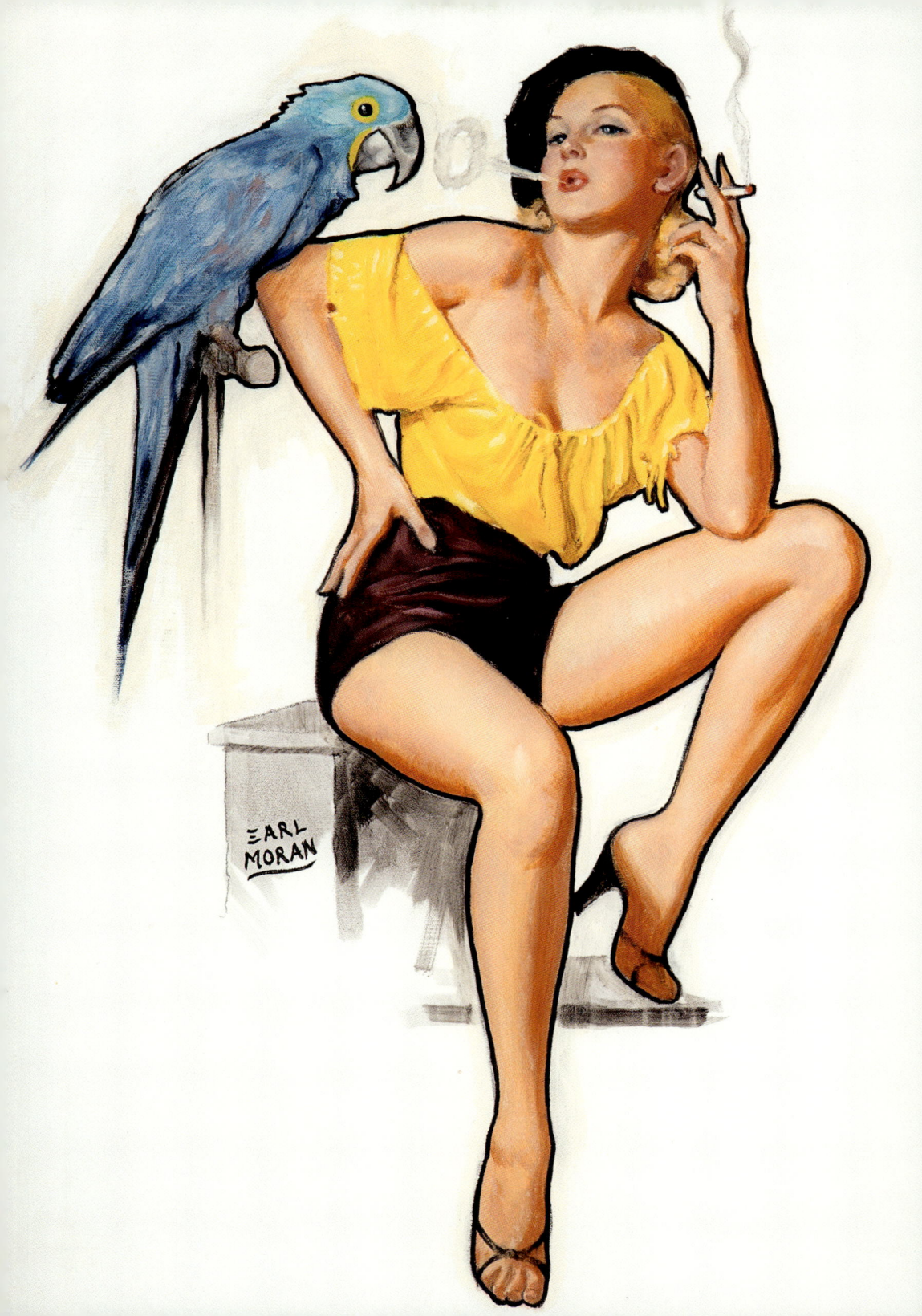

ZOË MOZERT

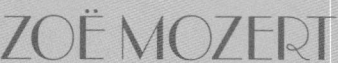

1907–1993

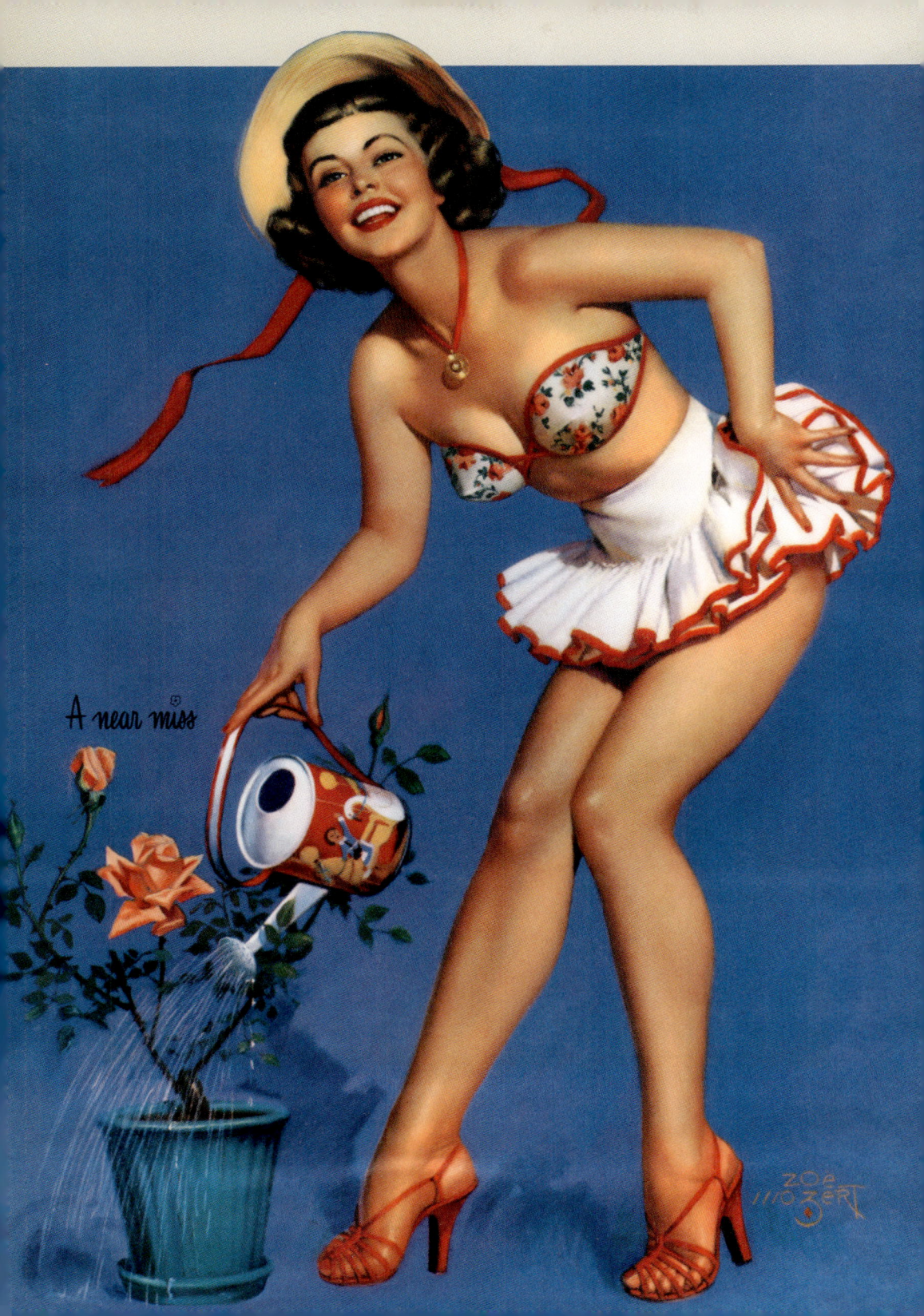

A near miss

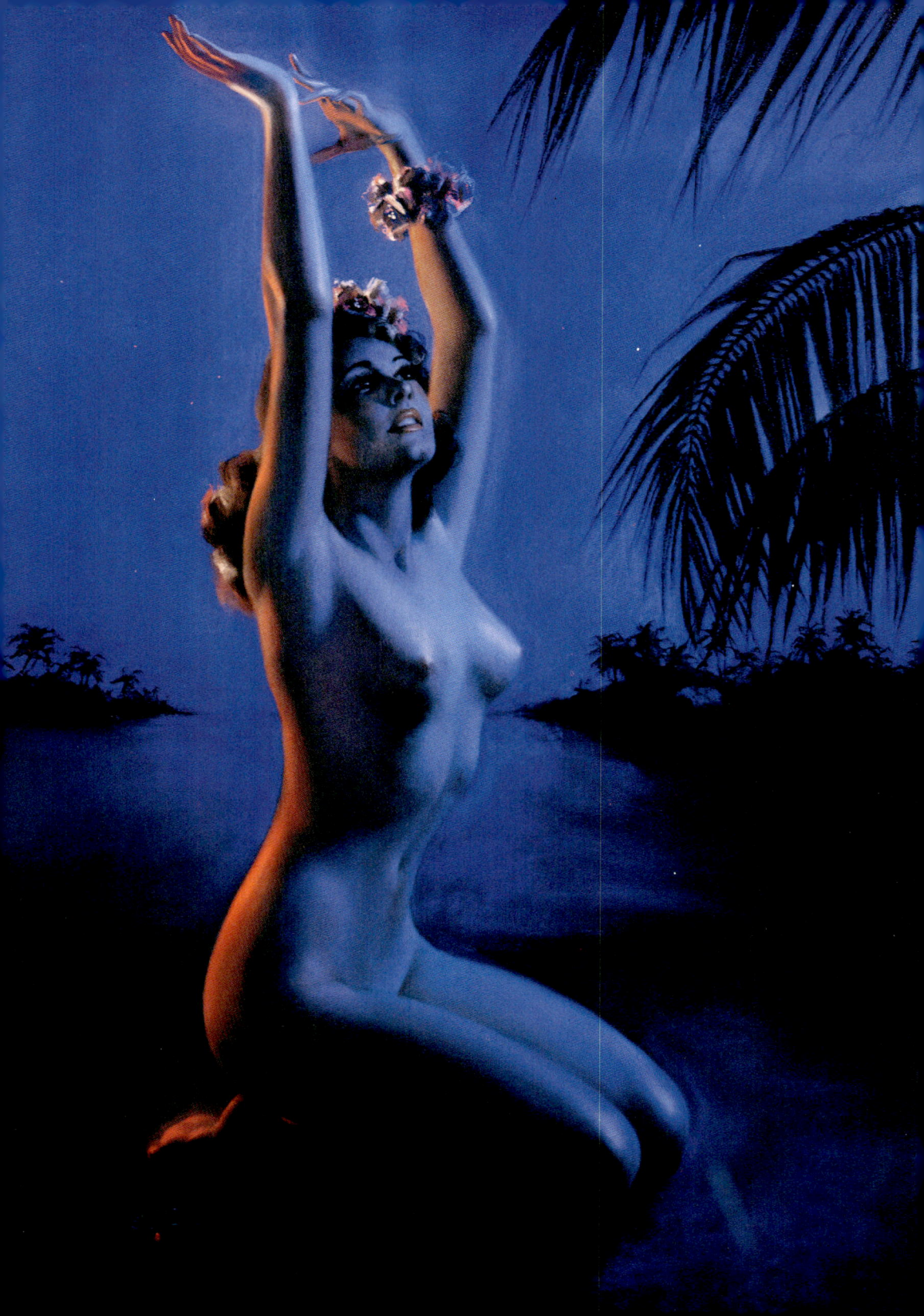

> "Supposedly there were complaints that her pin-ups were too sexy, and try as she might she couldn't tame them sufficiently."

Zoë Mozert claimed her career path was fixed at age two, when her mother put a Bible, a silver dollar, and a pencil before her. Mozert went for the pencil and made her first mark. The dollars would come later, as she rose to become America's top female pin-up artist. As for the Bible, with her smart mouth, four husbands, and fondness for the fast life, there wasn't much time for prayer.

Mozert was born Alice Adelaide Moser on April 27, 1907, in Colorado Springs, Colorado. She grew up in Ohio and Pennsylvania, attended finishing school in Virginia, and then won a scholarship to the Philadelphia School of Industrial Art. In 1926, in her third year of school, with the Jazz Age swinging and hemlines high, Mozert posed nude for art classes at a nearby women's college and lost her scholarship. In 1928, aged 21, she met and married a 17-year-old hitchhiker, establishing a lifelong taste for younger

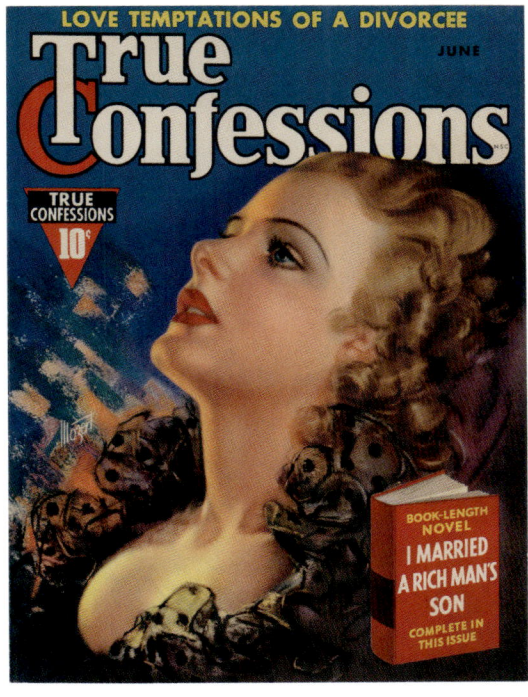

men and brief marriages: In two months Mozert was divorced and back with her parents in Scranton, Pennsylvania, painting portraits at $3 per work.

Scranton couldn't hold her long. In 1933 Mozert went to New York City, took a room at the YWCA, and headed straight to the offices of Bernarr Macfadden, publisher of high-quality lowbrow magazines. Macfadden paid $75 for a pastel of her sister Marcia and put it on the cover of his confession magazine, *True Story*. Mozert thought she'd soon be rich, but she didn't sell

Page 361: A Near Miss, 1953, on a 1955 Brown & Bigelow calendar. Mozert is the model. Calendar measures 33 x 16 inches.

Opposite: Reaching for the Stars, also known as *Starry Night*, pastel on board, 1942, for a 1944 Brown & Bigelow calendar. This was not only one of Mozert's first works for B&B, but it was licensed to Arrow Beer, reprinted as

a poster, and served as inspiration for Gil Elvgren's 1947 *Gay Nymph*. 37 x 27.5 inches.

Above: A pastel cover of *True Confessions*, June 1937. Mozert illustrated magazine covers from 1933, turning to pin-up production after Brown & Bigelow signed her to an exclusive contract in 1941. She was the company's first female artist.

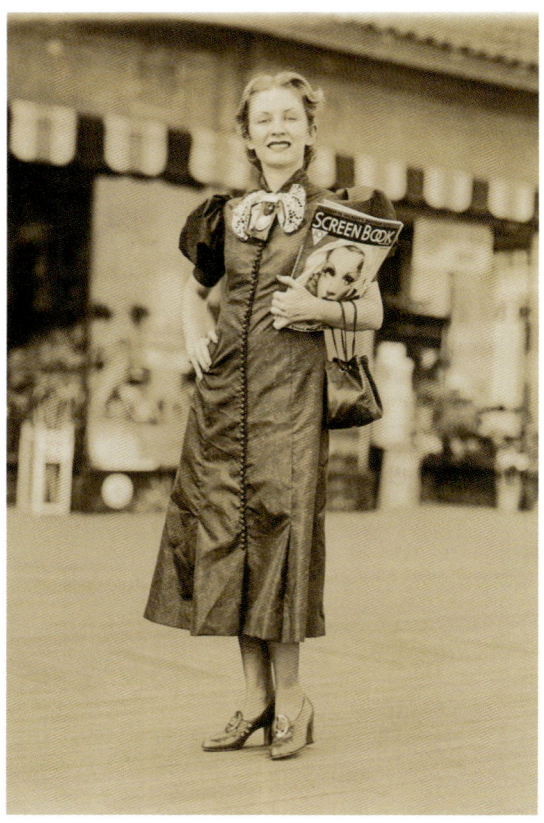

anything else for six months and had to fall back on figure modeling to pay her rent. This was when she reinvented herself as a bottle blonde with the more glamorous name Zoë Mozert.

The new glamour and old perseverance paid off over the next three years. In 1937 Mozert had done so many confession magazine covers, she was commissioned to do a poster of Carole Lombard for the film *True Confession*. By 1938 she'd sold over 400 covers to confession and movie magazines, painting Bette Davis, Claudette Colbert, Greta Garbo, Joan Crawford, and other top stars.

Unfortunately, 1938 was also the year magazines began switching over to photographic covers. Mozert decided to learn this new craft and traveled to Rio de Janeiro as a photographer's assistant. She might have had a photographic career, but on the ship coming home she drew her first nude in soft pastels from a photo of her friend Swann Marlowe. In '41 that nude caught the attention of Brown & Bigelow art director Orion Winford when it hung in New York's Mendelssohn Gallery. Based on this one piece, Winford offered Mozert a contract, and she became B&B's first female pin-up artist. Her debut pastel for Brown & Bigelow was *Sweet Dreams*, also based on Swann. B&B didn't print many nude figures, but they made an exception for Mozert, as she'd perfected the trick of making nudity seem more innocent than clothing. The pert, virginal breasts, modeled on her own, were part of it, but, more importantly, Mozert's nudes never made eye contact with the viewer unlike her dressed pin-ups. When a woman locks eyes with the viewer, her nudity appears seductive and deliberate, whereas a nude gazing lovingly at her horse, as in Mozert's magnificent 1949 pastel *Song of the Desert*, seems more the innocent victim of our voyeurism. Elvgren arguably learned this technique from her, as his 1947 *Gay Nymph* is an admittedly much improved copy of Mozert's *Reaching for the Stars*.

Perhaps Elvgren just wanted to put Mozert in her place, as she was famously competitive with B&B's male artists, signing her charcoal sketches "B-B," for "Beat the Boys." According to her the men started it, maintaining that women could never do pin-ups because the artist had to be a little bit in love with his model to do it right. Mozert was no lesbian, but she had taken to photographing herself as the model for most of her pin-ups, and with an ego far bigger than

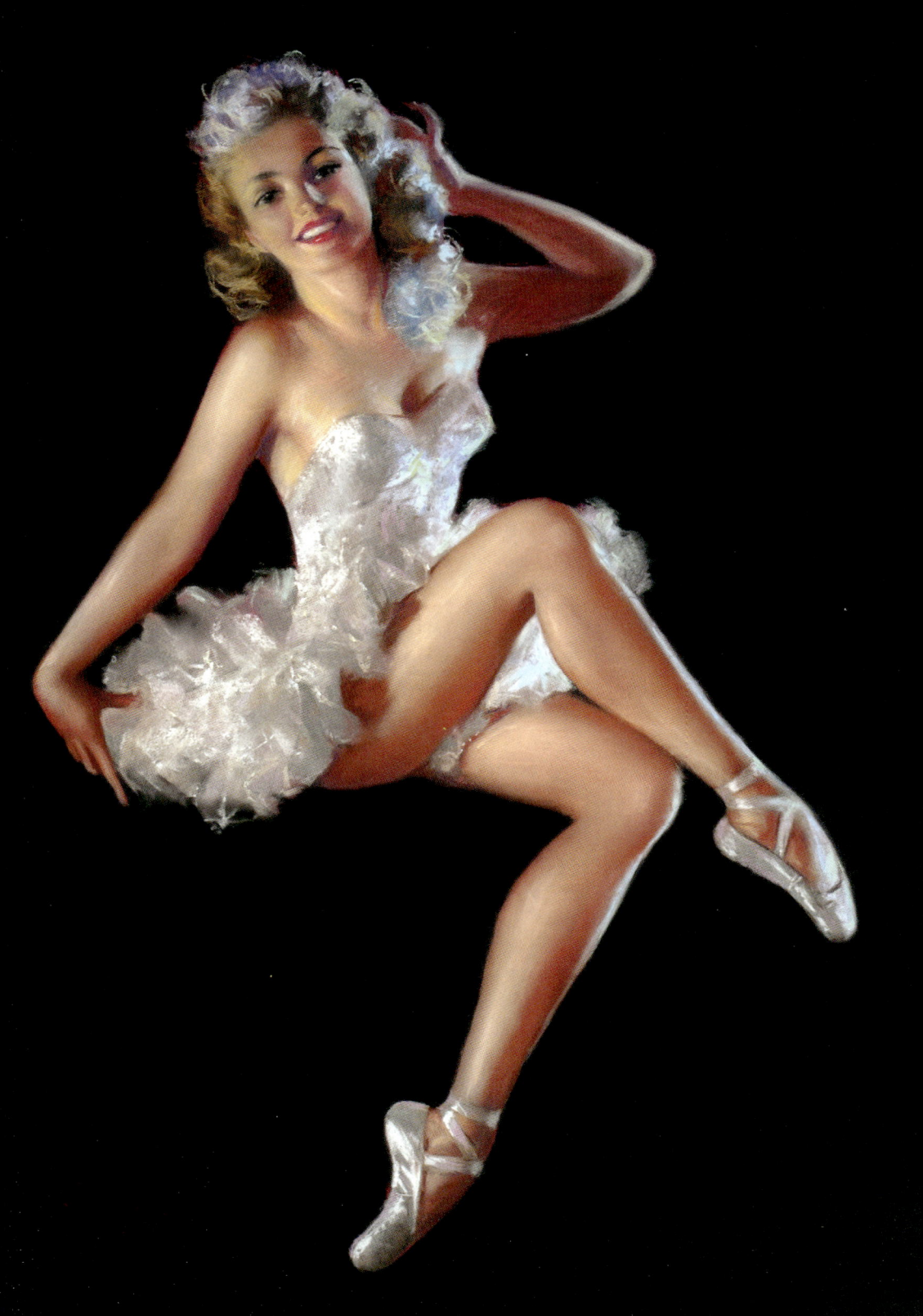

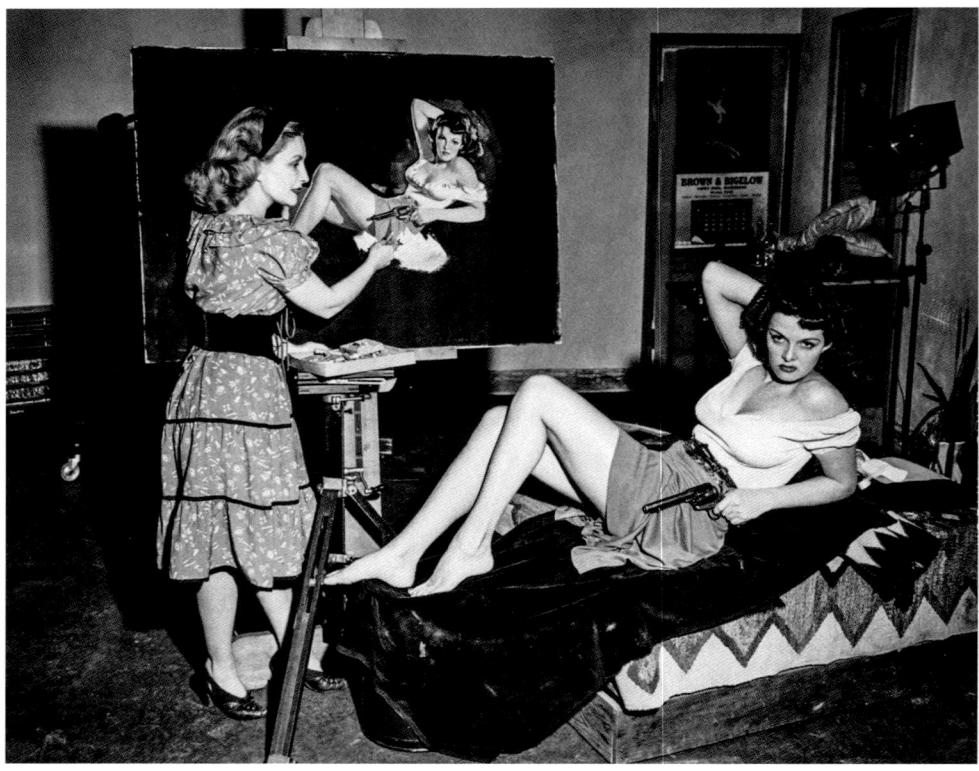

her 4-foot-11-inch, 95-pound body, there was no shortage of love. She even insisted that her other models be equally small, claiming that the anatomic structure of tall women didn't look good in pin-ups, that "little squirts" had better personalities and that men preferred the "little cuddly ones."

Men certainly liked Mozert, at least in the beginning. She married her second husband, Associated Press reporter Don Kirkley, in 1942, and hauled him out to Hollywood with plans to make it big in film. She stayed on in Hollywood, but Kirkley returned home to Washington, D.C., in 1944.

Mozert continued producing calendar girls for B&B, as well as a line of Mutoscope Victory Girls, but she also got some movie industry jobs in California. Paramount made a short feature on her for its series *Unusual Occupations* as "the pin-up girl who paints 'em too," showing her painting in front of a mirror. Then in 1945 Howard Hughes asked her to paint Jane Russell to promote his scandal-plagued film *The Outlaw*. Mozert found Russell's breasts a bit "mature"

Above: Jane Russell posing for Mozert. Mozert complained that Russell's breasts were too big to be esthetically pleasing; in her painting she lifted them and reduced their size. Howard Hughes, of course, had cast Russell specifically for the qualities Mozert criticized.

Opposite: In 1945 Mozert was contracted by Howard Hughes to create a portrait of Jane Russell to promote his film *The Outlaw*. Though completed in 1941, the film couldn't pass the Hollywood censors and didn't open until 1943, when it was quickly shut down and only saw wide release in 1946. This poster was one of several commissioned.

THE ART OF PIN-UP

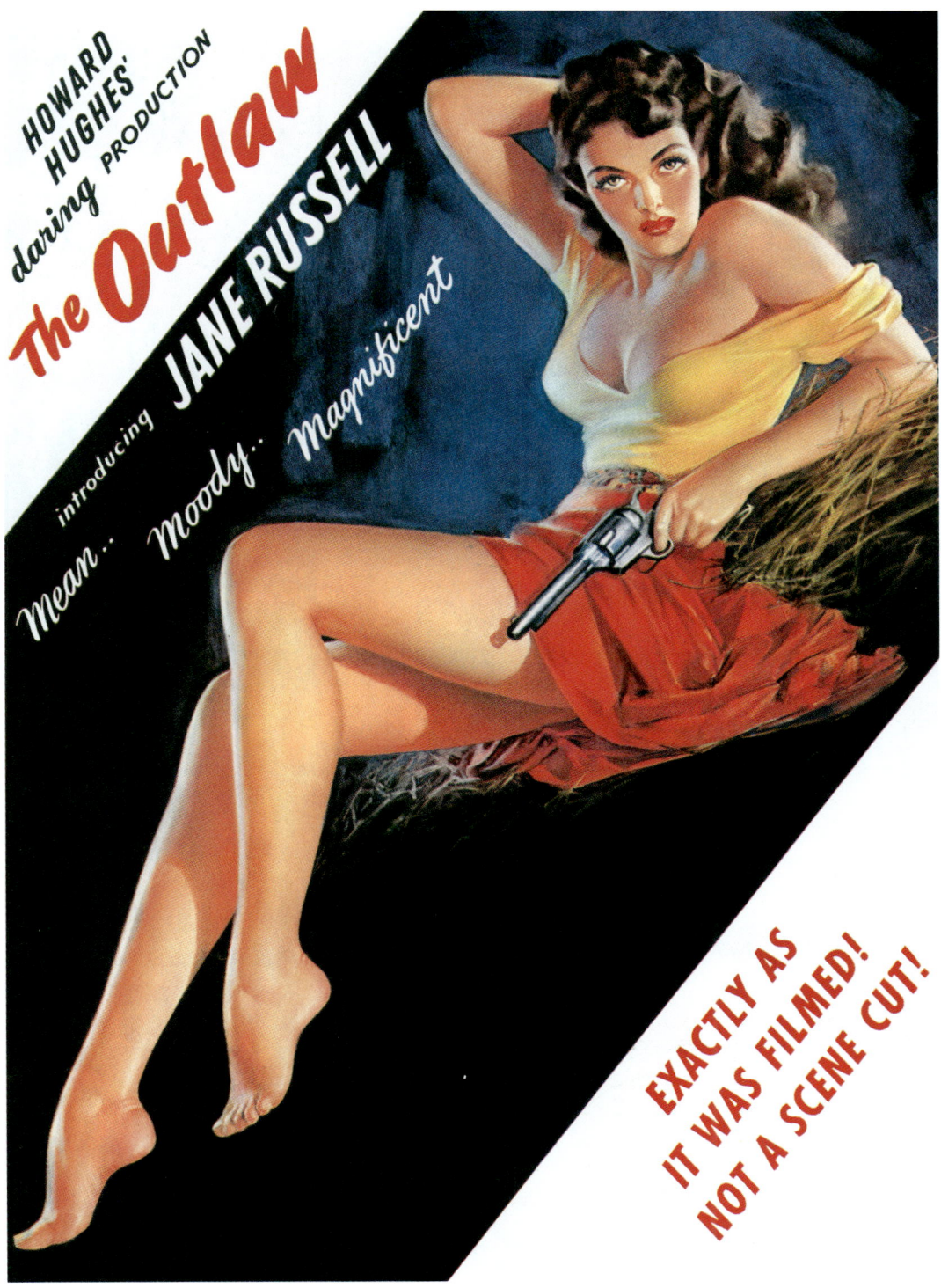

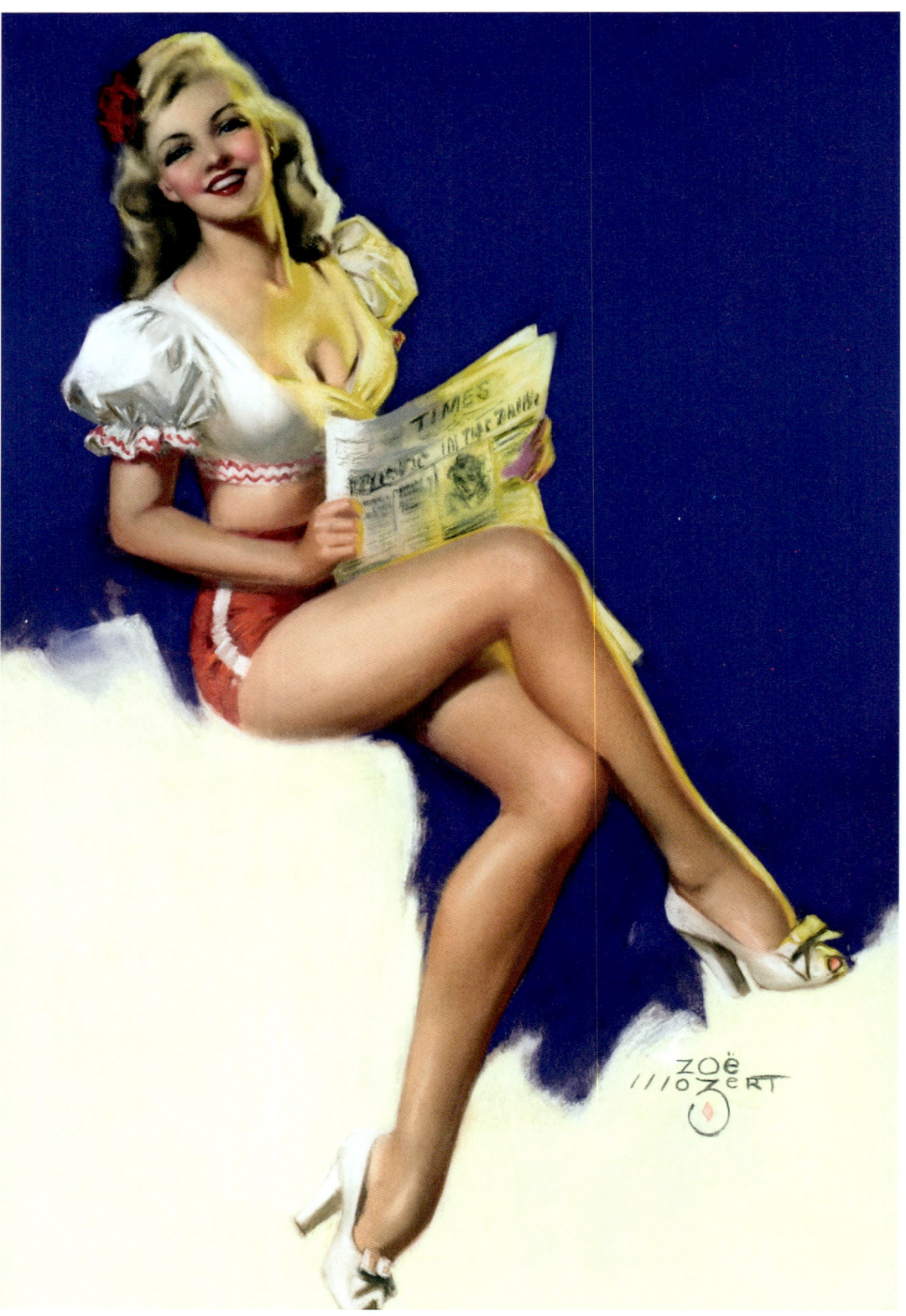

for her tastes, telling her she couldn't use models over 16 if she wanted perfect breasts (though regularly modeling her own 38-year-old bosom), and gave them a lift in the painting. The resulting poster of Russell in the hay appeared on billboards all over the country, winning more poster commissions—for *Never Say Goodbye* in '46 and *Calendar Girl* in '47.

In early 1950 Mozert, aged 42, took a third husband: six-foot-four, 25-year-old carpenter Ray "Jeep" Osterman. They divorced three years later, a record of marital longevity for the artist. Tired of California as well as Osterman, she moved to Arizona.

In 1954 Brown & Bigelow cut Mozert's contract back from 12 paintings a year to just four. Supposedly there were complaints that her pin-ups were too sexy, and try as she might she couldn't tame them sufficiently. Many works were paid for but never printed, though she remained under contract until liberal 1971.

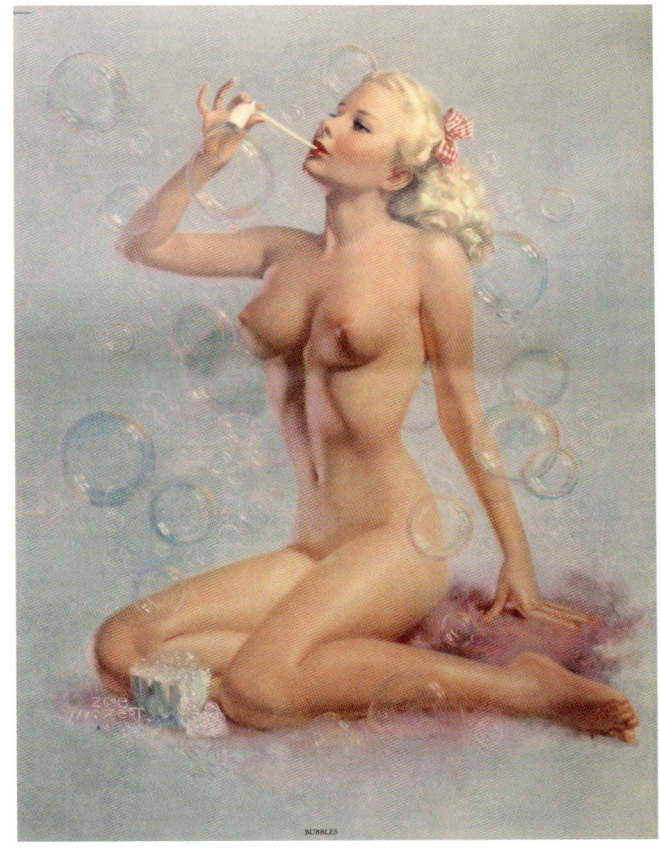

With less work, Mozert distracted herself in familiar fashion. In 1958 she married her fourth husband, painter Herbert Rhodes. Surely this marriage, to a fellow artist, would last—but no, once again Mozert left him after just two years. One stress on their time together was a commission she took in 1959 to create the world's largest reclining nude—a monumental 5.5-foot-high-by-10-foot-long oil pastel—to hang over the bar of the Red Dog Saloon in Scottsdale, Arizona. Mozert, age 52, posed for the painting and worked on it 18 hours a day in the couple's living room. *Red Dog Rosie* was displayed for only four years before the bar closed. Its whereabouts today, like most of Mozert's 1,000-plus pin-ups and magazine covers, are unknown.

Mozert gave up on husbands after Rhodes, but when interviewed by the great pin-up collector Marianne Ohl Phillips in 1990, she was once again in love with a younger man, and still painting at age 83.

Zoë Mozert died in Arizona three years later on February 1, 1993.

Opposite: "I'm Keeping Abreast of the Times," pastel on board, circa 1942, licensed for a Mutoscope card from Brown & Bigelow. 15.5 x 11 inches.

Above: Bubbles lithograph, 1947, on a 1949 Brown & Bigelow calendar.

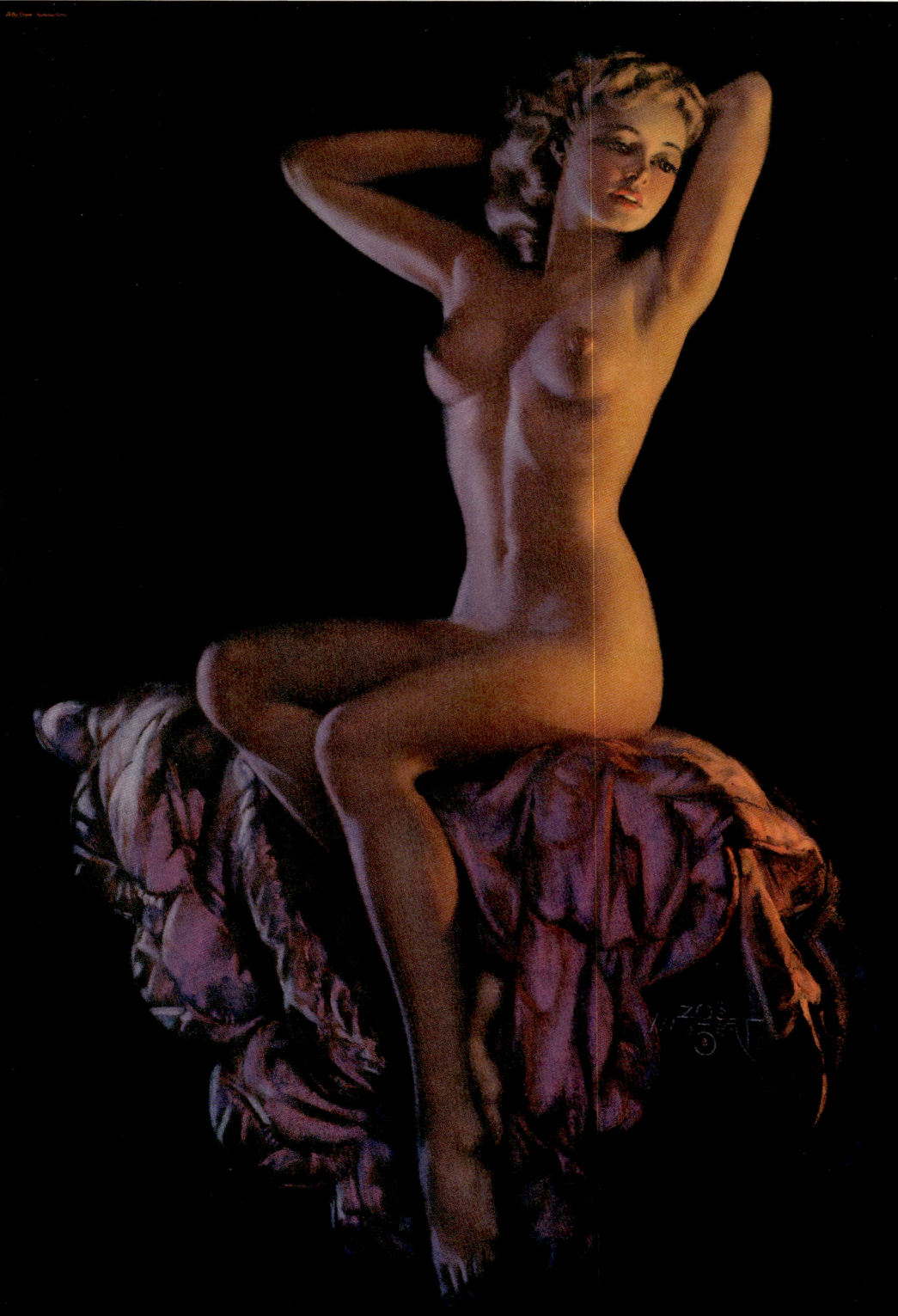

„Vermutlich gab es Beschwerden, dass ihre Pin-ups zu sexy seien, doch sie schaffte es einfach nicht, sie harmloser wirken zu lassen."

Zoë Mozert behauptete, der Grundstein für ihre Karriere sei gelegt worden, als sie zwei Jahre alt war und ihre Mutter ihr eine Bibel, einen Silberdollar und einen Stift zur Auswahl stellte. Mozert entschied sich für den Stift und zog ihren ersten Strich. Die Dollars kamen später, als sie Amerikas Topkünstlerin im Pin-up-Genre wurde. Und was die Bibel betrifft – bei ihrem losen Mundwerk, vier Ehemännern und ihrer Neigung zu einem Leben auf der Überholspur, blieb nicht viel Zeit für Gebete.

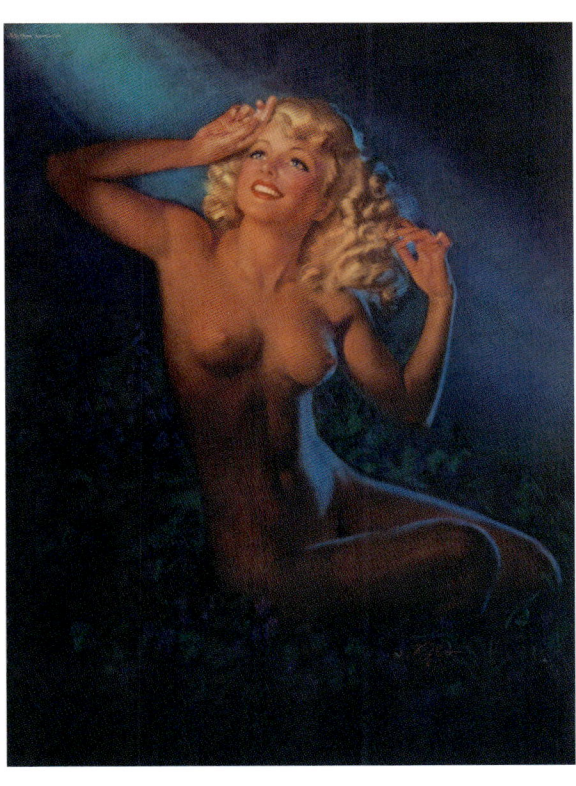

Mozert wurde am 27. April 1907 als Alice Adelaide Moser in Colorado Springs, Colorado, geboren. Sie wuchs in Ohio und Pennsylvania auf, machte ihren Schulabschluss in Virginia und bekam schließlich ein Stipendium für die Philadelphia School of Industrial Art. 1926, es war ihr drittes Jahr an dieser Institution, das Zeitalter des Jazz sorgte für Swing, und die Rocksäume rutschten hoch, posierte Alice nackt im Kunstunterricht am benachbarten Frauencollege. Daraufhin wurde ihr das Stipendium entzogen. 1928, mit 21, lernte sie einen 17 Jahre alten Tramper kennen und heiratete ihn. Es war der Beginn ihres lebenslangen Faibles für jüngere Männer und kurze Ehen: Zwei Monate später war Alice bereits wieder geschieden und zurück bei ihren Eltern in Scranton, Pennsylvania. Nun malte sie Porträts für drei Dollar pro Bild.

Opposite: Enchantment, a lithographic calendar print, circa 1945. 30 x 22 inches.

Above: Untitled lithograph, circa 1948. Mozert was a Brown & Bigelow staff artist, like Earl Moran, and like Moran had her chiaroscuro nude period. Nudes were considered more acceptable to the public if given this "art" treatment.

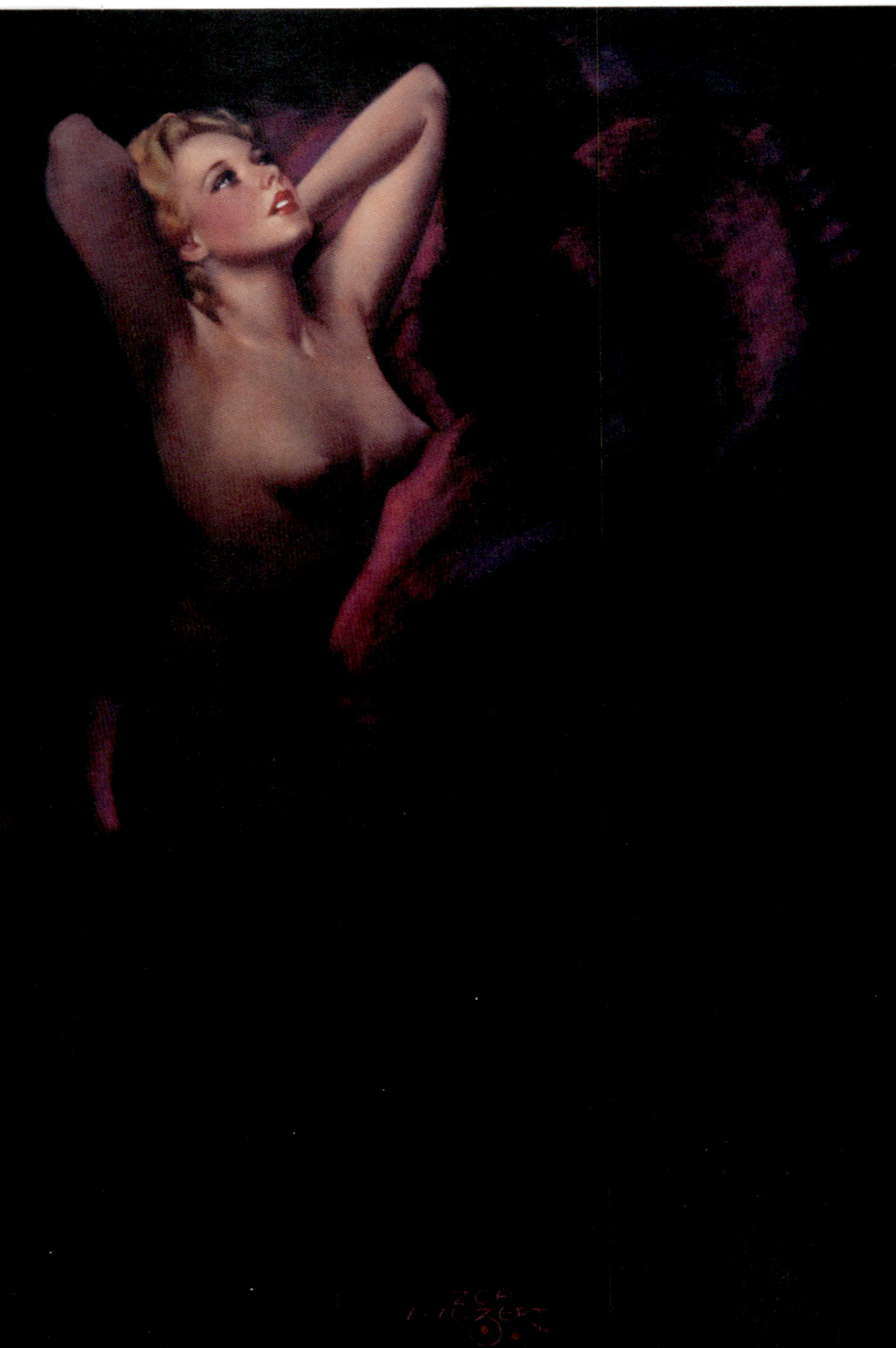

MOON GLOW

In Scranton hielt sie es nicht lange aus. 1933 ging sie nach New York City, nahm sich ein Zimmer im YMCA und machte sich schnurstracks zum Büro von Bernarr Macfadden auf, einem Verleger von Zeitschriften, die zwar anspruchslos, doch von guter Qualität waren. Macfadden zahlte ihr 75 Dollar für ein Pastell ihrer Schwester Marcia und veröffentlichte es auf der Titelseite seines Klatschblattes *True Story*. Alice meinte nun, bald sei sie reich, verkaufte dann aber sechs Monate lang nichts mehr und musste wieder als Modell arbeiten, um ihre Miete zahlen zu können. Zu dieser Zeit verpasste sie sich ein neues Äußeres als Wasserstoffblondine und gab sich den glamouröseren Namen Zoë Mozert.

Der neue Glamour und die alte Beharrlichkeit machten sich während der nächsten drei Jahre bezahlt. 1937 hatte Mozert so

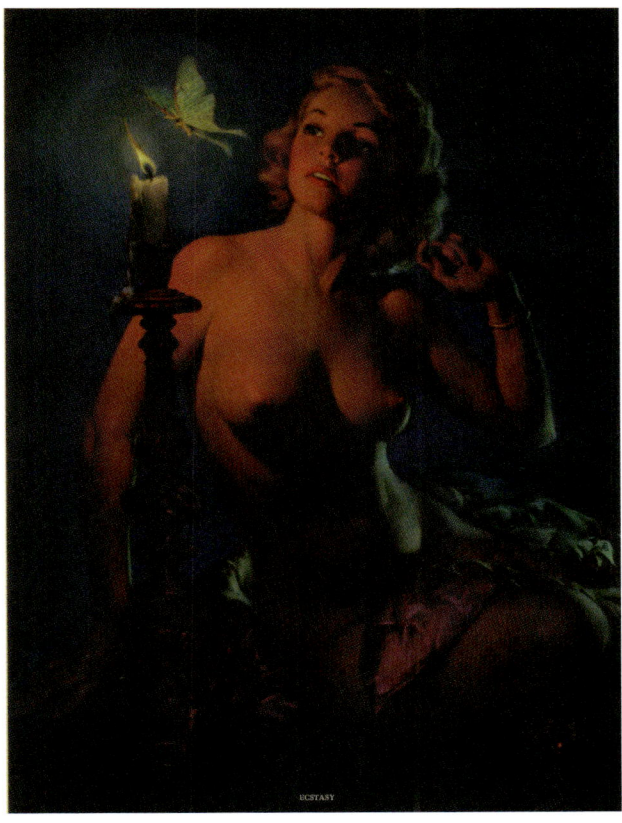

viele Titelseiten von Klatschmagazinen gestaltet, dass sie den Auftrag erhielt, für den Film *Ein Mordsschwindel* das Plakat mit Carole Lombard zu entwerfen. 1938 hatte sie bereits mehr als 400 Titelbilder für Klatsch- und Filmzeitschriften entworfen und Topstars wie Bette Davis, Claudette Colbert, Greta Garbo und Joan Crawford gemalt.

In jenem Jahr, 1938, begannen die Zeitschriften auch damit, Fotografien für Titelbilder einzusetzen. Mozert beschloss, dieses neue Handwerk zu erlernen, und reiste als Assistentin eines Fotografen nach Rio de Janeiro. Vielleicht wäre ihr ja eine Karriere als Fotografin sicher gewesen, doch auf dem Schiff, mit dem sie nach Hause reiste, zeichnete sie nach einem Foto ihrer Freundin Swann Marlowe in weichen Pastelltönen ihr erstes Aktbild. Als dieser Akt 1941 in der New Yorker Mendelssohn Gallery ausgestellt wurde, erregte er die Aufmerksamkeit von Orion Winford, dem Artdirector von Brown & Bigelow. Nur aufgrund dieses Bildes bot Winford Mozert einen Vertrag an, und so wurde sie die erste Frau unter den Pin-up-Künstlern bei B & B. Das Pastell, mit dem sie bei Brown & Bigelow debütierte, war *Sweet Dreams*, ein Bild, das ebenfalls Swann zum Modell nahm. Viele Aktbilder druckte B & B nicht, doch bei Mozert machte das Unternehmen eine Ausnahme, denn sie perfektionierte ihre Kunst, eine nackte Figur unschuldiger aussehen zu lassen als

Opposite: Moon Glow calendar lithograph, 1947, also known as *Perfection*, when reprinted as an Arrow Beer poster.

Above: Ecstasy, 1952, as a Brown & Bigelow calendar lithograph.

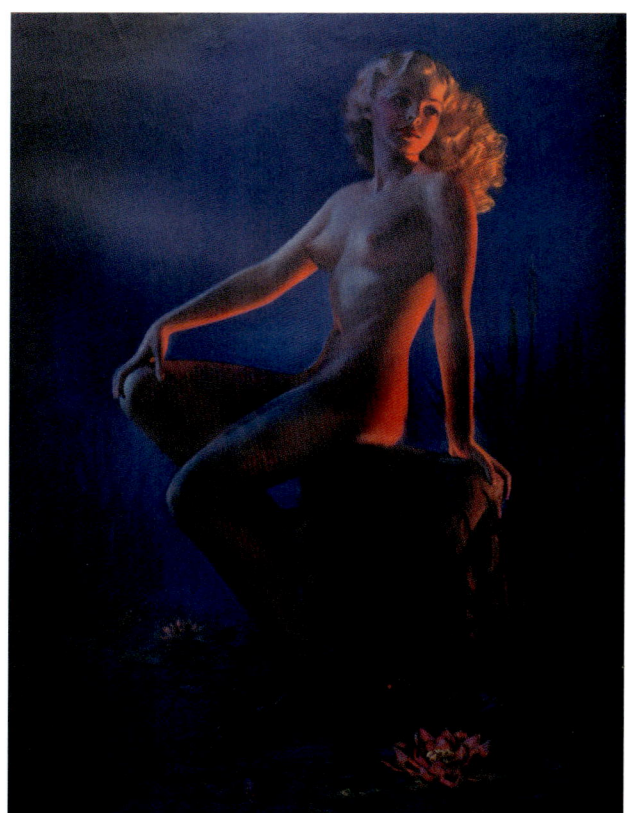

eine angezogene. Dazu gehörten die kecken, jungfräulichen Brüste, die sie nach ihrem eigenen Busen zeichnete, doch noch wichtiger war der Umstand, dass Mozerts Aktfiguren – im Gegensatz zu ihren bekleideten Pin-ups – nie den Betrachter ansah. Wenn die gemalte Frau den Betrachter direkt anblickt, erscheint ihre Nacktheit verführerisch und bewusst eingesetzt, während eine Nackte, die – wie in Mozerts großartigem Pastell *Song of the Desert* – liebevoll ihr Pferd ansieht, eher das unschuldige Opfer unseres Voyeurismus zu sein scheint. Ganz offensichtlich übernahm Elvgren diese Technik von Mozert, denn seine *Gay Nymph* von 1947, die auf einer Auktion den Rekordpreis von 286.800 Dollar erzielte, ist eine – allerdings deutlich verbesserte – Kopie von Mozerts 1944 entstandenem Bild *Reaching for the Stars.*

Vielleicht wollte Elvgren Zoë ja nur in ihre Schranken weisen, denn sie forderte die Konkurrenz der männlichen Künstler bei B & B explizit heraus, indem sie ihre Kohlezeichnungen mit „B-B" signierte, was für „Beat the Boys" stand. Mozert zufolge hatten die Männer damit angefangen, weil sie behaupteten, Frauen seien nicht in der Lage, Pin-ups zu malen. Denn der Künstler müsse schon ein bisschen in sein Modell verliebt sein, um es richtig zu malen. Zoë war keine Lesbe. Für ihre meisten Pin-ups fotografierte sie sich selbst als Modell, und ausgestattet mit einem Ego, das weit größer war als ihr knapp 1,50 m messender Körper mit seinen 43 kg Gewicht, fehlte es ihr nicht an Liebe. Sie bestand sogar darauf, dass ihre anderen Modelle genauso klein sein müssten, und behauptete, die anatomische Struktur hochgewachsener Frauen sehe auf Pin-ups nicht gut aus. Außerdem hätten die „Mäuschen" eine stärkere Persönlichkeit, und Männer würden die „kleinen Knuddelmädchen" bevorzugen.

Männer mochten Mozert sicherlich, zumindest zu Anfang. Ihren zweiten Mann, den Associated-Press-Reporter Don Kirkley, heiratete sie 1942 und schleppte ihn nach Hollywood, weil sie die Absicht hatte, beim Film groß ins Geschäft zu kommen. Sie blieb in Hollywood, doch Kirkley kehrte 1944 in seine Heimat Washington D.C. zurück.

Above: Tranquility lithograph from a 1948 Brown & Bigelow calendar.

Opposite: Sweet Dreams, 1941, on a 1943 Brown & Bigelow calendar. Calendar measures 46 x 22 inches. This was Mozert's first pastel for Brown & Bigelow.

THE ART OF PIN-UP

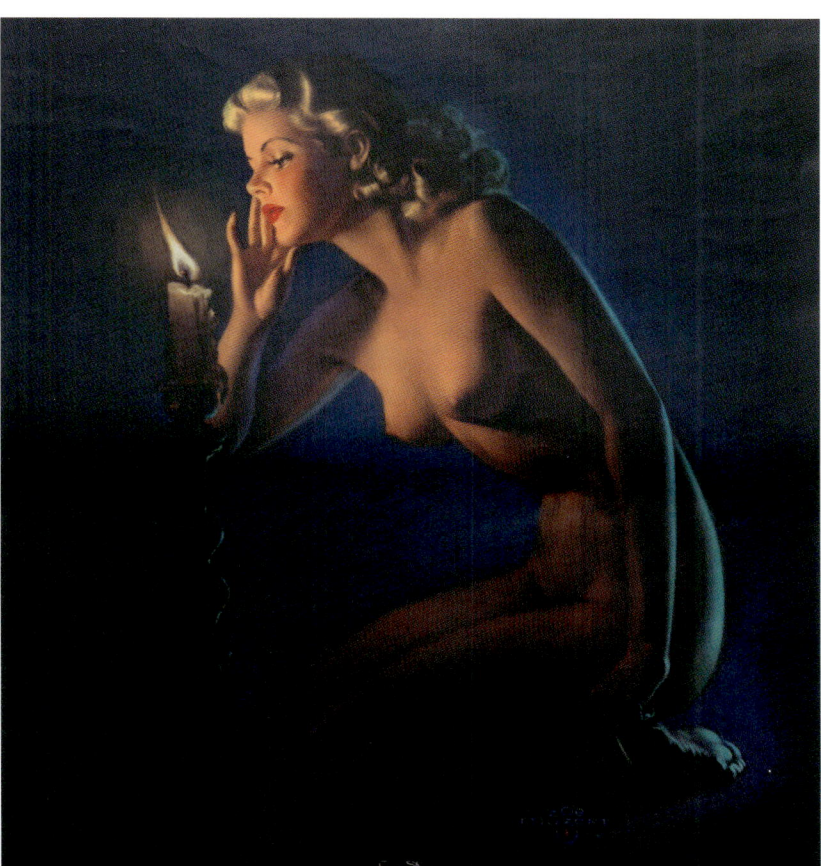

Sweet Dreams

BROWN & BIGELOW

Remembrance Advertising

REG. U.S. PAT. OFF.

SAINT PAUL   MINNESOTA

Calendars   Direct Mail   Greetings   Playing Cards   Leather   Novelties

MARCH · 1943

Sun	Mon	Tue	Wed	Thu	Fri	Sat
●	1	2	3	4	5	6
7	8	9	10	11	12	13
14	15	16	17	18	19	20
21	22	23	24	25	26	27
28	29	30	31	☽	○	☾

FEBRUARY · 1943

Sun	Mon	Tue	Wed	Thu	Fri	Sat
	1	2	3	4	5	6
7	8	9	10	11	12	13
14	15	16	17	18	19	20
21	22	23	24	25	26	27
28						

APRIL · 1943

Sun	Mon	Tue	Wed	Thu	Fri	Sat
				1	2	3
4	5	6	7	8	9	10
11	12	13	14	15	16	17
18	19	20	21	22	23	24
25	26	27	28	29	30	

MARCH—THIRD MONTH

Mozert produzierte weiterhin Kalendermädchen für B & B, auch eine Reihe von Victory-Girls für Mutoskope – 8 x 13 cm große Postkarten für Soldaten, die als V-Mail bezeichnet wurden –, aber sie erhielt auch den einen oder anderen Auftrag von der kalifornischen Filmindustrie. Für die Serie *Unusual Occupations* drehte Paramount einen kurzen Beitrag über „das Pin-up-Mädchen, das auch Pin-ups malt" und zeigte, wie sie vor einem Spiegel stehend malte. Dann, 1945, fragte Howard Hughes an, ob sie Jane Russell für ein Plakat malen wolle, mit dem sein skandalträchtiger Film *Geächtet* beworben werden sollte. Für Mozerts Geschmack war Russells Busen ein wenig zu „ausgereift". Der Schauspielerin sagte sie, mit Modellen, die älter als 16 Jahre seien, könne sie, wenn sie perfekte Brüste malen wolle, nichts anfangen (obwohl sie regelmäßig ihren eigenen 38-jährigen Busen als Modell nutzte) und hob den Busen von Russell im Bild etwas an. Das nach diesem Gemälde gedruckte Plakat von Jane im Heu war im ganzen Land zu sehen und brachte Mozert Aufträge für weitere Filmplakate ein, 1946 für *Never Say Goodbye* und 1947 für *Calendar Girl*.

Anfang 1950 heiratete die 42-jährige Mozert ihren dritten Mann, den 25-jährigen, 1,93 m großen Zimmermann Ray „Jeep" Osterman. Drei Jahre später ließen sich die beiden scheiden. Jeeps und Kaliforniens überdrüssig, zog sie schließlich nach Arizona.

1954 strich Brown & Bigelow die zwölf mit Mozert vertraglich vereinbarten Gemälde pro Jahr auf gerade mal vier Bilder zusammen. Vermutlich gab es Beschwerden, dass ihre Pin-ups zu sexy seien, doch sie schaffte es einfach nicht, sie harmloser wirken zu lassen. Viele ihrer gleichwohl bezahlten Arbeiten wurden nie gedruckt, und bis 1971 blieb sie unter Vertrag.

Da sie nun weniger zu tun hatte, vertrieb sich Mozert die Zeit mit Familienleben. 1958 heiratete sie ihren vierten Ehemann, den Maler Herbert Rhodes. Man sollte meinen, die Ehe mit einem Künstlerkollegen würde halten – aber nein, es dauerte nur zwei Jahre, bis Mozert sich von ihrem Mann trennte. Eine Sache hatte – unter anderen – während ihres Zusammenlebens für Ärger gesorgt, ein Auftrag, den sie 1959 annahm: Sie sollte den größten, sich zurücklehnenden Akt der Welt malen, ein monumentales 168 x 305 cm großes Ölkreidegemälde, das über der Bar des Red Dog Saloon in Scottsdale, Arizona, hängen sollte. Die 52-jährige Zoë posierte selbst für das Bild und arbeitete daran 18 Stunden pro Tag im Wohnzimmer des Paares. *Red Dog Rosie* hing nur vier Jahre lang an seinem Platz, dann schloss die Bar. Wo das Bild verblieb, ist, wie bei den meisten der mehr als 1000 Pin-ups von Mozert, unbekannt.

Nach Rhodes heiratete Mozert nicht mehr, doch als die Pin-up-Sammlerin Marianne Ohl Phillips sie 1990 interviewte, war Mozert gerade wieder in einen jüngeren Mann verliebt und malte mit ihren 83 Jahren noch immer.

Zoë Mozert starb drei Jahre später, am 1. Februar 1993, in Arizona.

Opposite: Mozert using her mirror image as reference for the painting on page 387. She dressed in costumes and painted idealized portraits of herself into old age.

THE ART OF PIN-UP

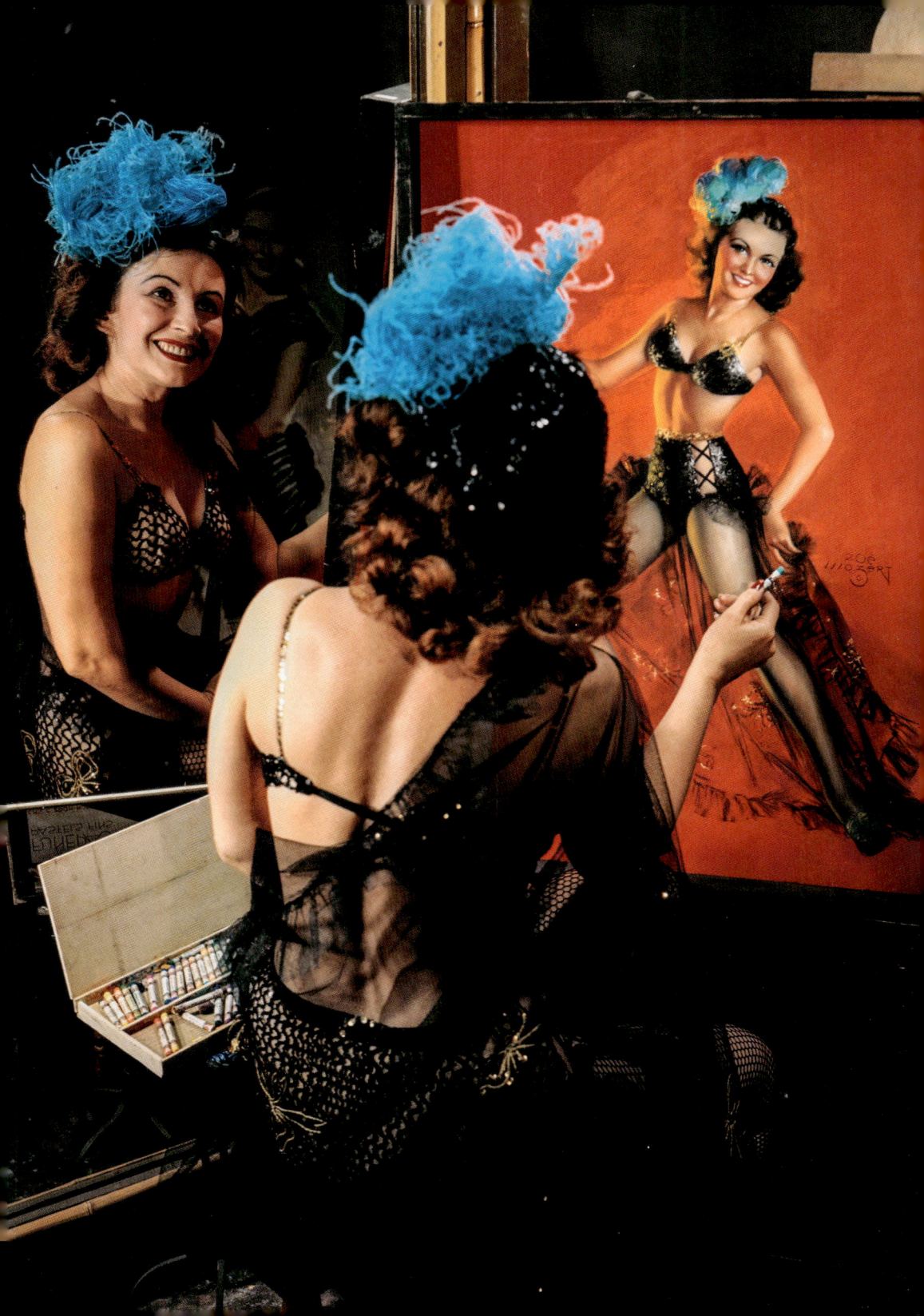

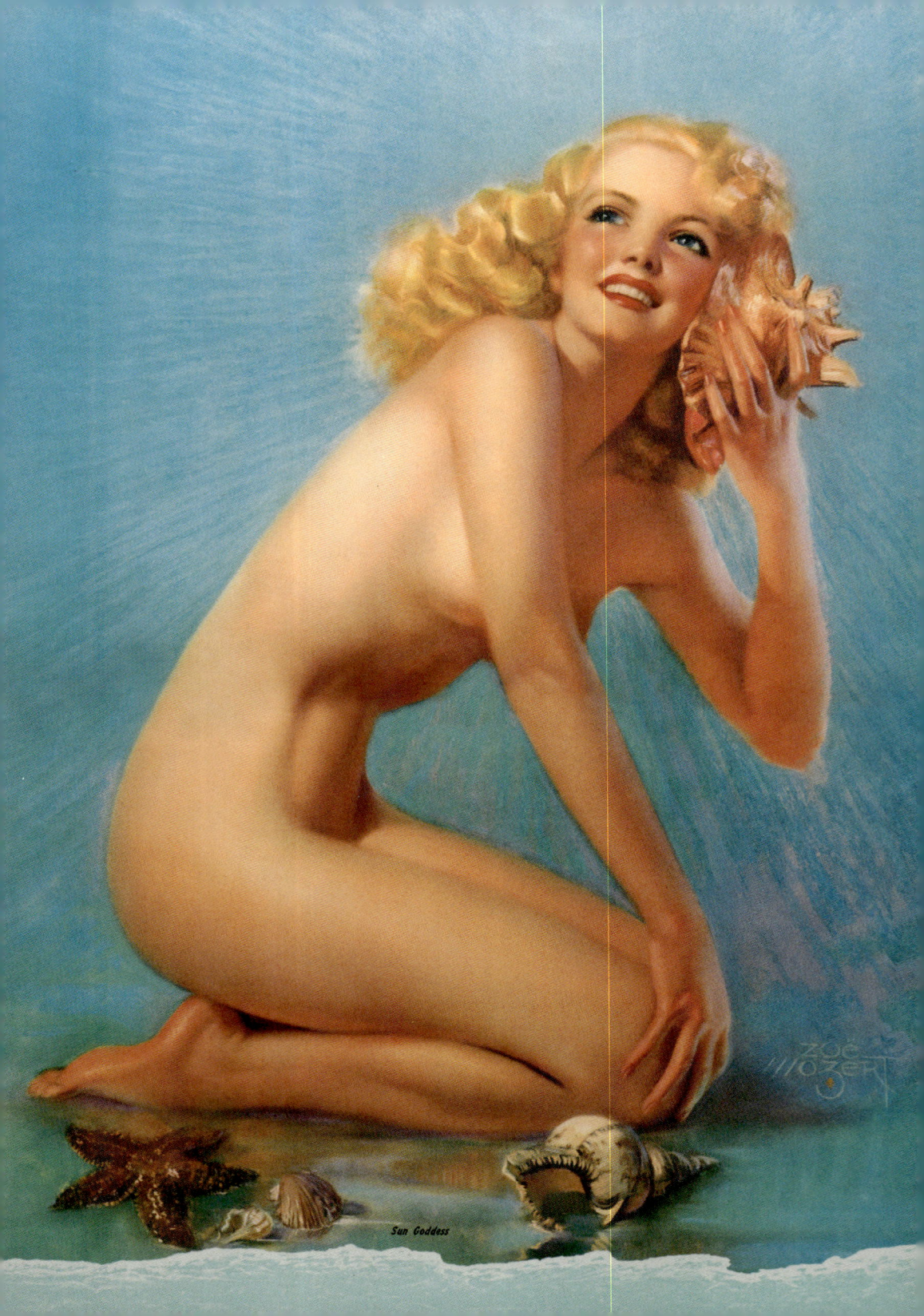

Sun Goddess

« Apparemment, ses pin-up étaient trop sexy.
Elle avait beau faire, elle ne parvenait pas à les assagir. »

Zoë Mozert affirmait avoir découvert sa vocation à l'âge de 2 ans, quand sa mère plaça devant elle une Bible, un dollar en argent et un crayon. Elle choisit le crayon. Les dollars viendraient plus tard, quand elle serait l'une des principales créatrices de pin-up. Quant à la Bible, entre sa langue acérée, ses quatre maris et son goût pour les plaisirs de la vie, il ne lui restait plus beaucoup de temps pour prier.

Née Alice Adélaïde Moser le 27 avril 1907 à Colorado Springs, elle grandit dans l'Ohio et en Pennsylvanie, fréquenta une école pour jeunes filles en Virginie puis obtint une bourse pour la Philadelphia School of Industrial Art. En 1926, au cœur des Années folles, elle posa nue dans des cours d'art d'un collège pour femmes et perdit sa bourse. En 1928, à l'âge de 21 ans, elle rencontra et épousa un auto-stoppeur de 17 ans, ayant déjà un penchant pour les hommes plus jeunes et les mariages expéditifs. Deux mois plus tard, elle divorçait et rentrait chez ses parents à Scranton, en Pennsylvanie, où elle vendit des portraits à 3 dollars pièce.

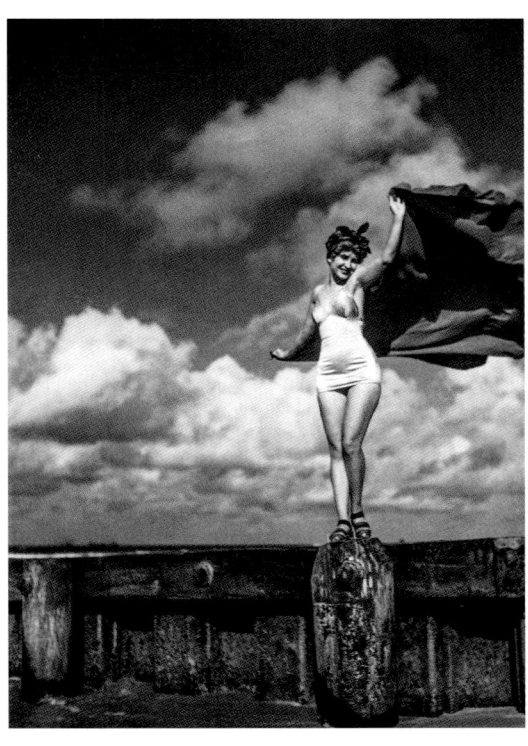

Scranton ne put la retenir longtemps. En 1933, Alice partit pour New York, prit une chambre à la YWCA et se rendit dans les bureaux de Bernarr Macfadden, éditeur de publications populaires de qualité. Il lui acheta 75 dollars un pastel de sa sœur Marcia qu'il mit en couverture de *True Story*. Alice crut qu'elle allait devenir riche mais patienta six mois avant de vendre une autre œuvre. En attendant, elle reprit son activité de modèle d'artiste et en profita pour se réinventer, se teignant en blonde et adoptant le nom plus glamour de Zoë Mozert.

Opposite: Sun Goddess, 1948, for a 1950 Brown & Bigelow calendar. Calendar measures 46 x 22 inches.

Above: Mozert posing dramatically on a sea wall in California for an unknown pin-up. All of these photos are from her personal collection, purchased after her death by pin-up collector/dealer Marianne Ohl Phillips.

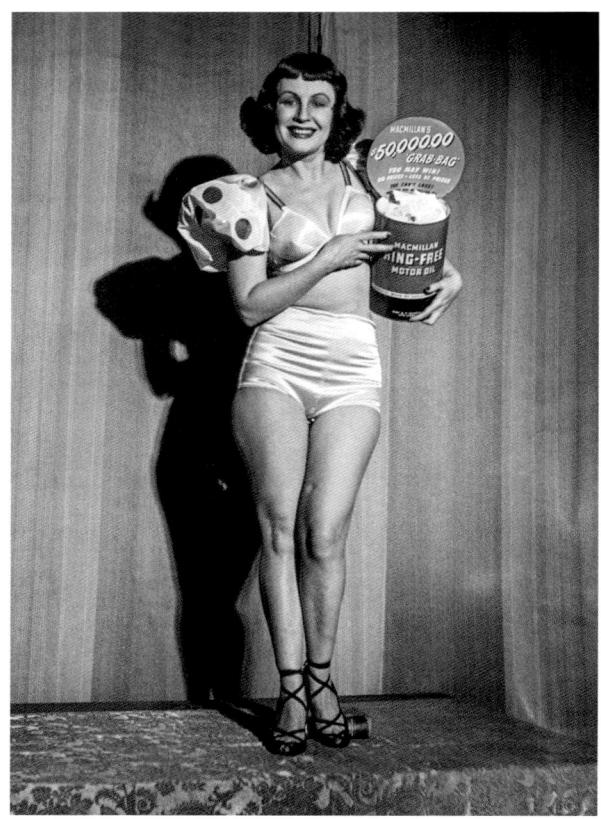

Ses efforts furent récompensés au cours des trois années suivantes. En 1937, elle avait peint tellement de couvertures de magazines de confidences qu'on lui commanda une affiche avec Carole Lombard pour le film *La Folle Confession*. En 1938, elle vendit plus de 400 couvertures pour des magazines, réalisant notamment des portraits de Bette Davis, Claudette Colbert, Greta Garbo et Joan Crawford.

Hélas, cette même année, les magazines optèrent pour les photographies en couverture. Mozert décida d'apprendre cette nouvelle discipline et partit pour Rio de Janeiro comme assistante-photographe. Elle aurait pu faire carrière dans cet art si, sur le bateau qui la ramenait à New York, elle n'avait pas réalisé son premier nu au pastel à partir d'une photo de son amie Swann Marlowe. En 1941, ce nu exposé dans la galerie Mendelssohn attira l'attention d'Orion Winford, directeur artistique chez Brown & Bigelow. Cela lui suffit pour offrir un contrat à l'artiste, faisant d'elle la première femme créatrice de pin-up de B&B. Son premier pastel pour l'éditeur fut *Sweet Dreams*, également inspiré de Swann. B&B imprimait peu de nus mais fit une exception pour Mozert car elle savait mieux que personne rendre la nudité plus innocente que les vêtements. Les seins fermes et virginaux, dessinés d'après les siens, y étaient pour quelque chose, mais, surtout, ses nus ne vous regardaient jamais dans les yeux, contrairement à ses pin-up habillées. Quand une femme regarde droit vers le spectateur, sa nudité paraît séductrice et calculée, alors que si elle contemple tendrement son cheval comme dans le magnifique *Song of the Desert* de 1950, elle devient la victime innocente de notre voyeurisme. Elle confia sans doute ce tuyau à Elvgren, dont la *Gay Nymph* de 1947, vendue 286 800 dollars en 2011, est une copie très améliorée de *Reaching for the Stars* que Mozert peignit en 1944.

Peut-être Elvgren avait-il voulu remettre Zoë à sa place, car elle cherchait toujours à rivaliser avec ses confrères de B&B, signant ses esquisses au fusain B-B, soit *Beat the Boys* (« battre les garçons »). Selon elle, les hommes avaient commencé, affirmant qu'une femme ne pourrait jamais créer des pin-up car l'artiste devait être un peu amoureux de sa créature. Zoë n'était pas

Above: Mozert, the ever-ready model, dressed in the costume used for Right This Way, *1949. She appears to be posing for a custom promotional calendar, a B&B sideline, here at age 42.*

Opposite: Right This Way, *1949, on a 1951 Brown & Bigelow calendar.*

THE ART OF PIN-UP

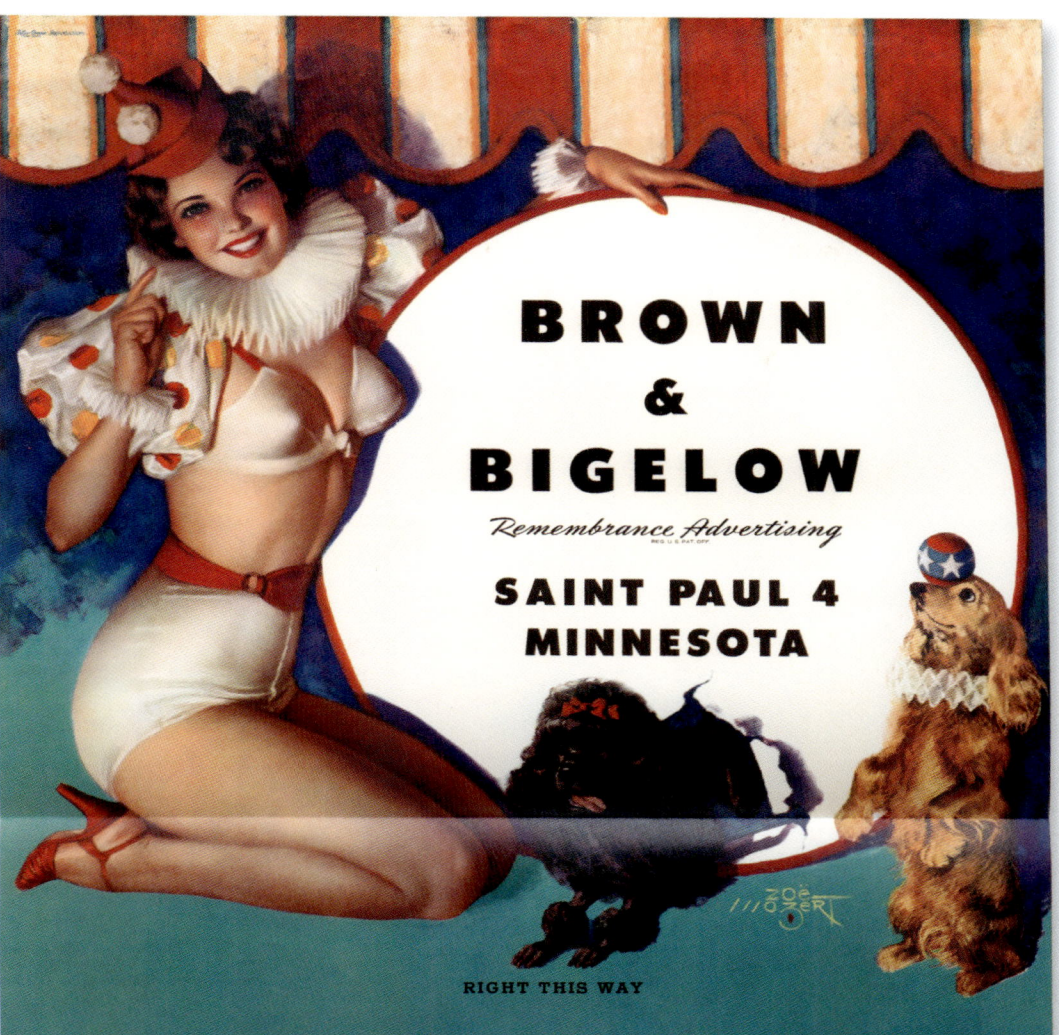

RIGHT THIS WAY

MAY 1951

SUN	MON	TUE	WED	THU	FRI	SAT
● NEW MOON 5th	☽ FIRST QUAR. 14th	1	2	3	4	5
6	7	8	9	10	11	12
13 MOTHER'S DAY	14	15	16	17	18	19
20	21	22	23	24	25	26
27	28	29	30 MEMORIAL DAY	31	○ FULL MOON 21st	☽ LAST QUAR. 27th

SUN	MON	TUE	WED	THU	FRI	SAT
		APRIL 1951				
1	2	3	4	5	6	7
8	9	10	11	12	13	14
15	16	17	18	19	20	21
22	23	24	25	26	27	28
29	30					

SUN	MON	TUE	WED	THU	FRI	SAT
		JUNE 1951				
					1	2
3	4	5	6	7	8	9
10	11	12	13	14	15	16
17	18	19	20	21	22	23
24	25	26	27	28	29	30

lesbienne mais se photographiait comme modèle de la plupart de ses pin-up. Avec un ego dépassant de loin son 1,50 mètre et ses 43 kilos, elle ne manquait donc pas d'amour. Elle tenait même à ce que ses autres modèles aient la même taille, soutenant que la structure anatomique des grandes ne convenait pas aux pin-up, que les petits gabarits avaient plus de personnalité et que les hommes préféraient les « petites câlines ».

Le fait est que les hommes aimaient Mozert, du moins au début. En 1942, elle épousa Don Kirkley, reporter à l'Associated Press, et le traîna à Hollywood. Elle y resta ; Kirkley rentra à Washington en 1944.

Mozert continua à réaliser des calendriers pour B&B, ainsi qu'une ligne de cartes postales, *Victory Girls*, destinées aux soldats. Parallèlement, l'industrie du cinéma lui passa des commandes. La Paramount réalisa un petit documentaire sur elle sous-titré « La pin-up qui en peint » pour sa série *Unusual Occupations* (« Les métiers inhabituels »), la filmant travaillant devant un miroir. En 1945, Howard Hughes lui demanda une affiche de Jane Russell pour son film sulfureux *Le Banni*. Mozert trouva les seins de Russel un peu trop « mûrs » à son goût et les peignit plus haut, lui expliquant que pour réaliser des poitrines parfaites, elle n'utilisait pas de modèles de plus de

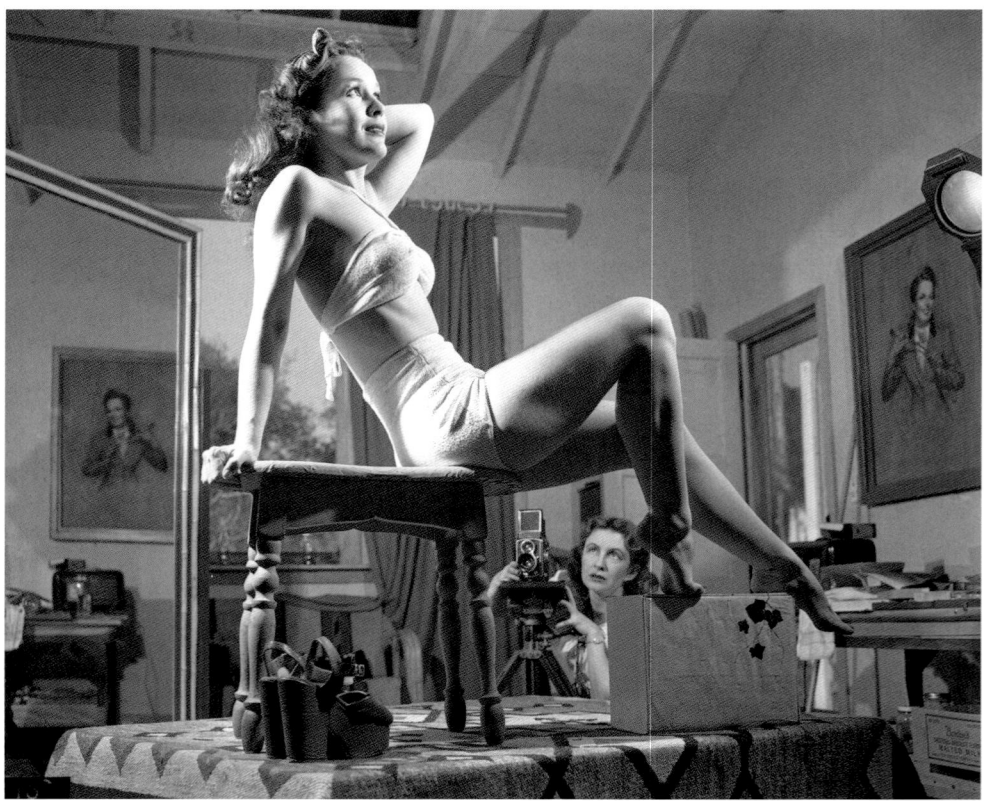

Above: Mozert photographs actress Mary Anderson in preparation for creating a pin-up, 1946. Mozert found Mary, at five-foot-two-inch, to be the perfect size for her purposes. © Bettmann/Corbis Images.

Opposite: Right You Are!, pastel on board, circa 1952, for a Brown & Bigelow calendar. Mozert, aged 45, was the model.

THE ART OF PIN-UP

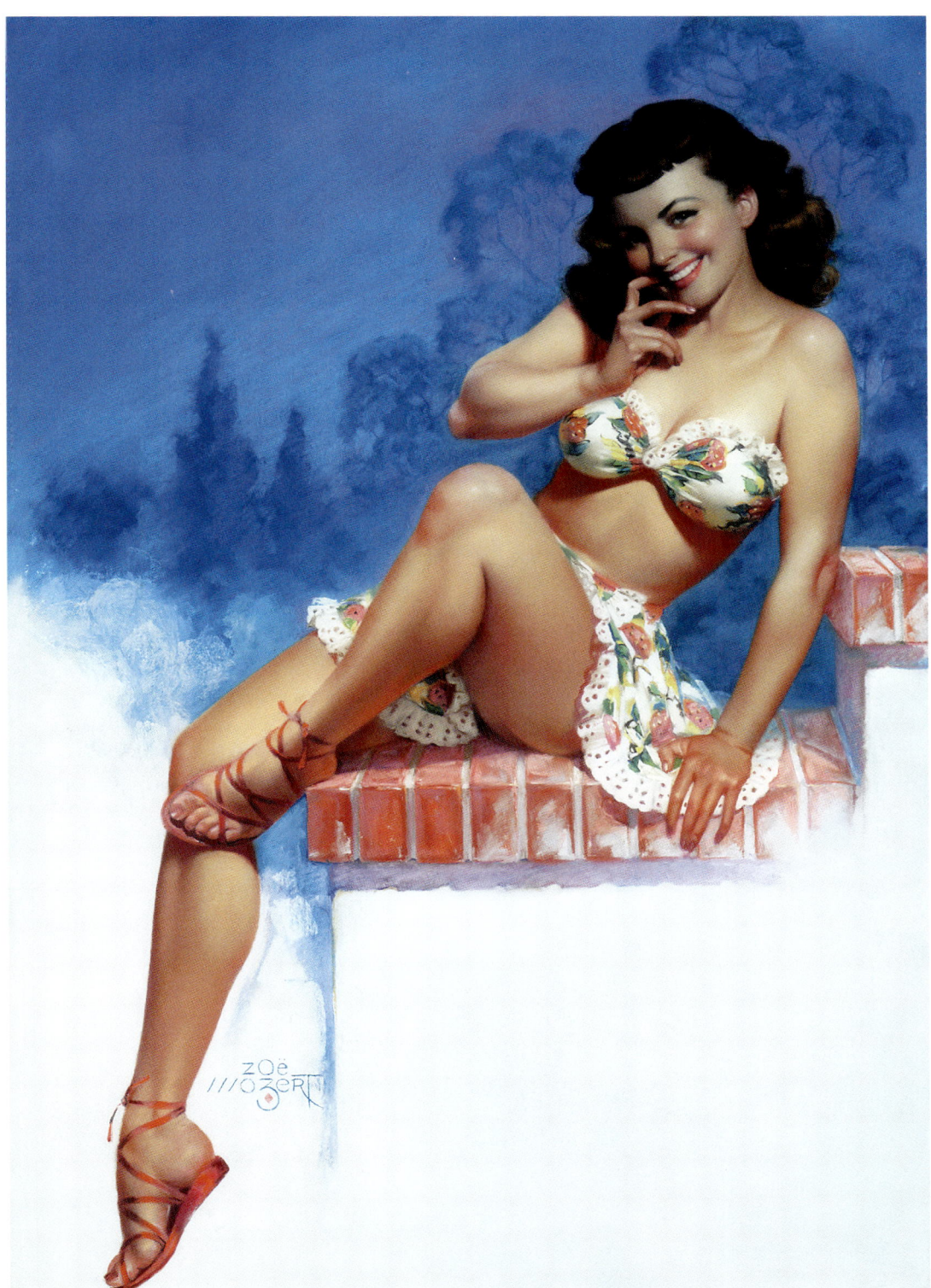

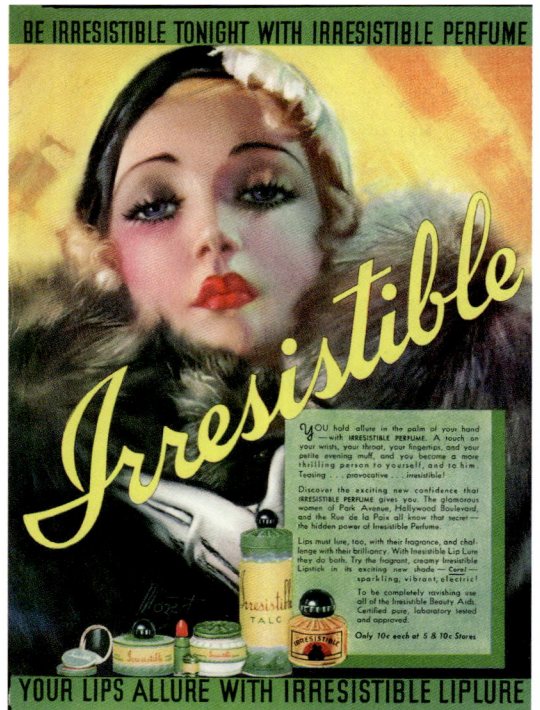

16 ans (même si elle était souvent son propre modèle à 38 ans). L'affiche de Jane Russel couchée dans le foin fut placardée dans tout le pays, lui attirant d'autres commandes, notamment pour *Ne dites jamais adieu* en 1946 et *Calendar Girl* en 1947.

En 1950, Mozert, âgée de 42 ans, prit un troisième mari : Ray « Jeep » Osterman, un menuisier de 25 ans de plus de 1,90 mètre. Ils divorcèrent trois ans plus tard, un record de longévité pour Mozert. Lassée de la Californie et de Jeep, elle déménagea en Arizona.

En 1954, B&B réduisit son contrat de douze à quatre peintures par an. Apparemment, ses pin-up étaient trop sexy. Elle avait beau faire, elle ne parvenait pas à les assagir. De nombreuses œuvres furent payées mais jamais publiées, bien que Mozert soit restée sous contrat jusqu'en 1971.

Ayant moins de travail, Mozert se tourna vers d'autres distractions. En 1958, elle épousa le peintre Herbert Rhodes. On aurait pu croire que cette union avec un confrère durerait, mais elle le quitta deux ans plus tard. Une des tensions dans leur ménage fut provoquée par la commande d'un nu couché monumental au pastel à l'huile de 1,67 x 3 m, destiné à être accroché derrière le bar du *Red Dog Saloon* à Scottsdale. Se prenant comme modèle, Zoë, âgée de 52 ans, travailla dix-huit heures par jour à sa réalisation dans le salon du couple. *Red Dog Rosie* ne fut exposé que quatre ans, puis le bar ferma. On ignore ce qu'il est devenu, tout comme la plupart de ses 1 000 pin-up et couvertures de magazine.

Après Rhodes, Mozert abandonna toute velléité de se marier mais, lorsque la collectionneuse de pin-up Marianne Ohl Phillips l'interviewa en 1990, elle était à nouveau amoureuse d'un homme plus jeune et peignait toujours. Elle avait 83 ans.

Elle mourut trois ans plus tard, le 1er février 1993, en Arizona.

Above: Mozert pastel ad for Irresistible perfume and lipstick, 1937, created at the height of her magazine illustration career.

Opposite: A Run on Sugar, pastel on board, 1941, for a 1943 Brown & Bigelow calendar. Rereleased for a 1946 calendar. 22.5 x 17 inches.

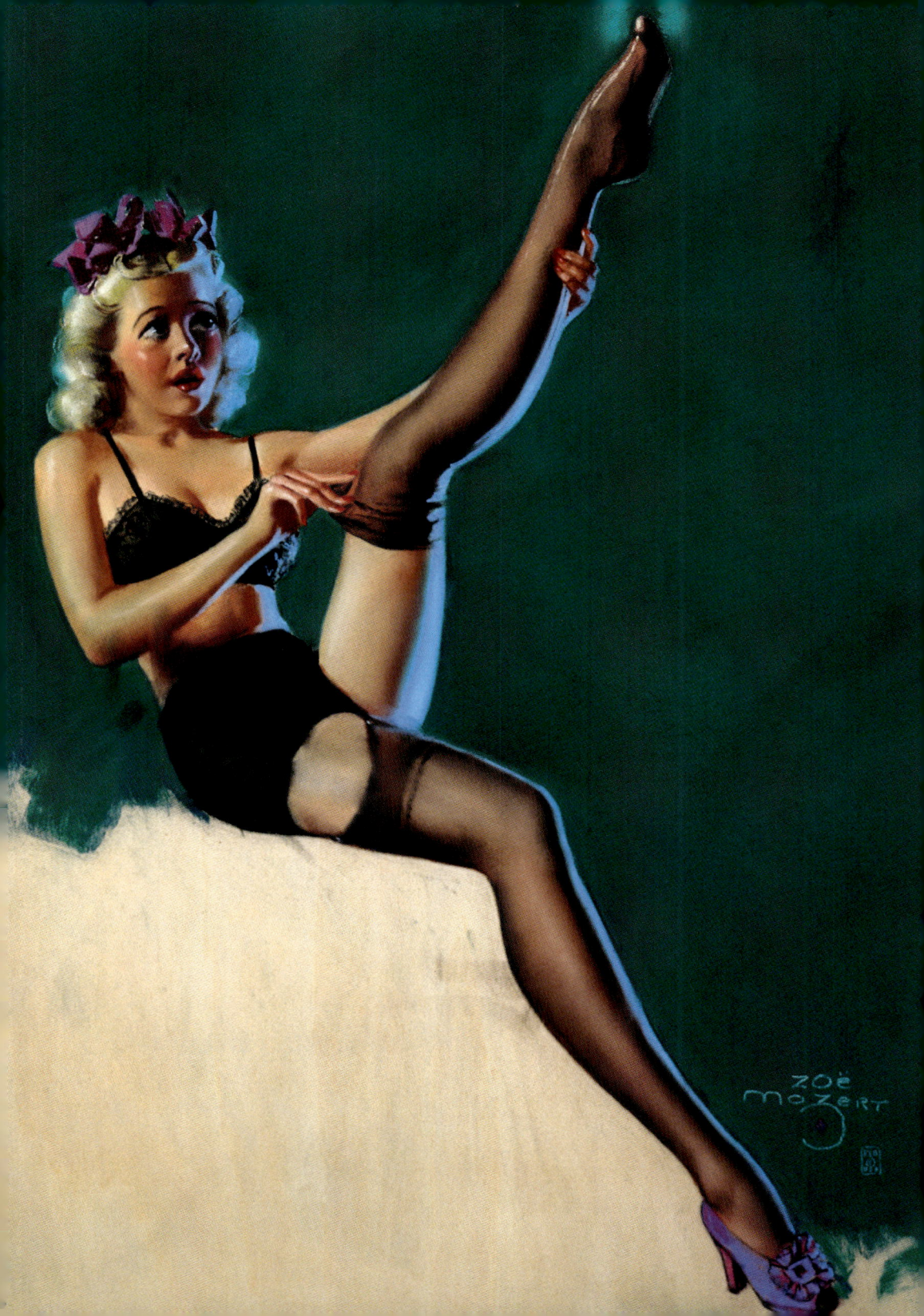

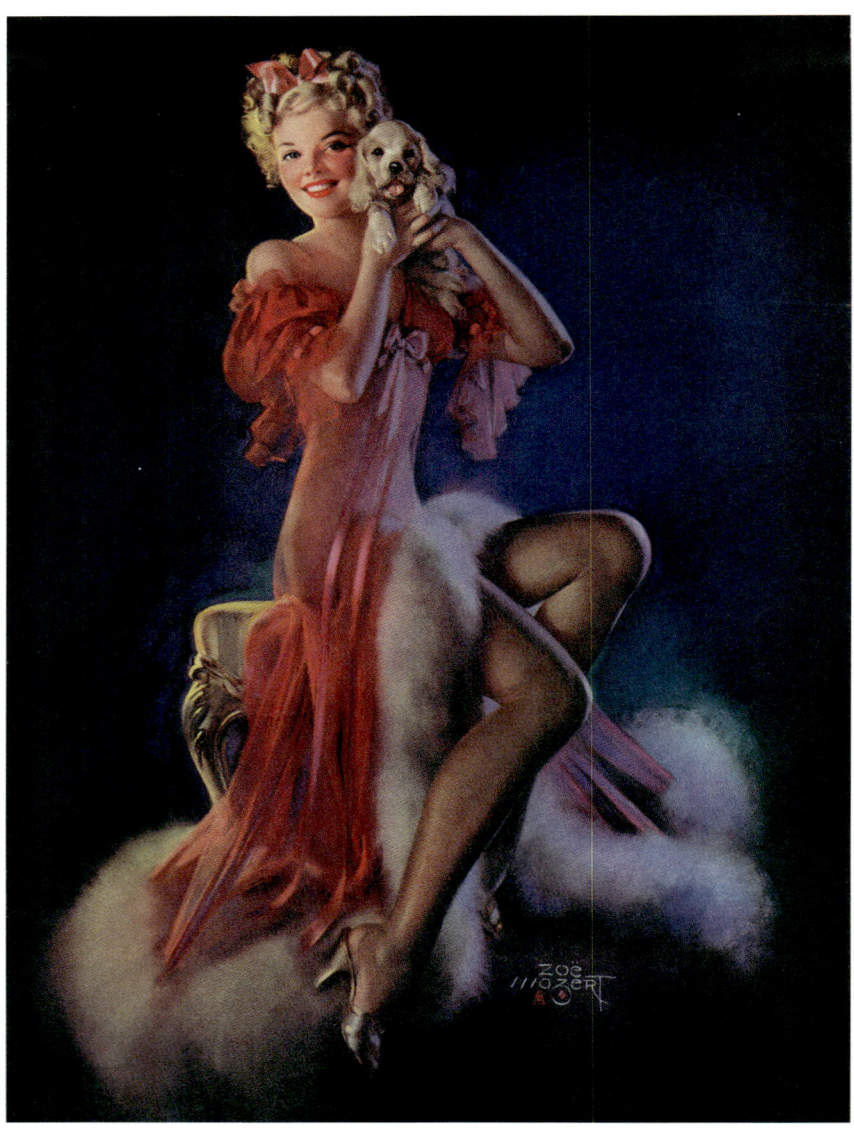

Above: Mozert was a staff artist for Brown & Bigelow at the time she painted the poster image for *Calendar Girl*. B&B therefore owned the work, and while it was never released as a calendar in the United States, it was printed as a calendar for export to B&B's Latin affiliates; this example for Cuba.

Opposite: Pastel on board, circa 1948. 32.5 x 23.5 inches.

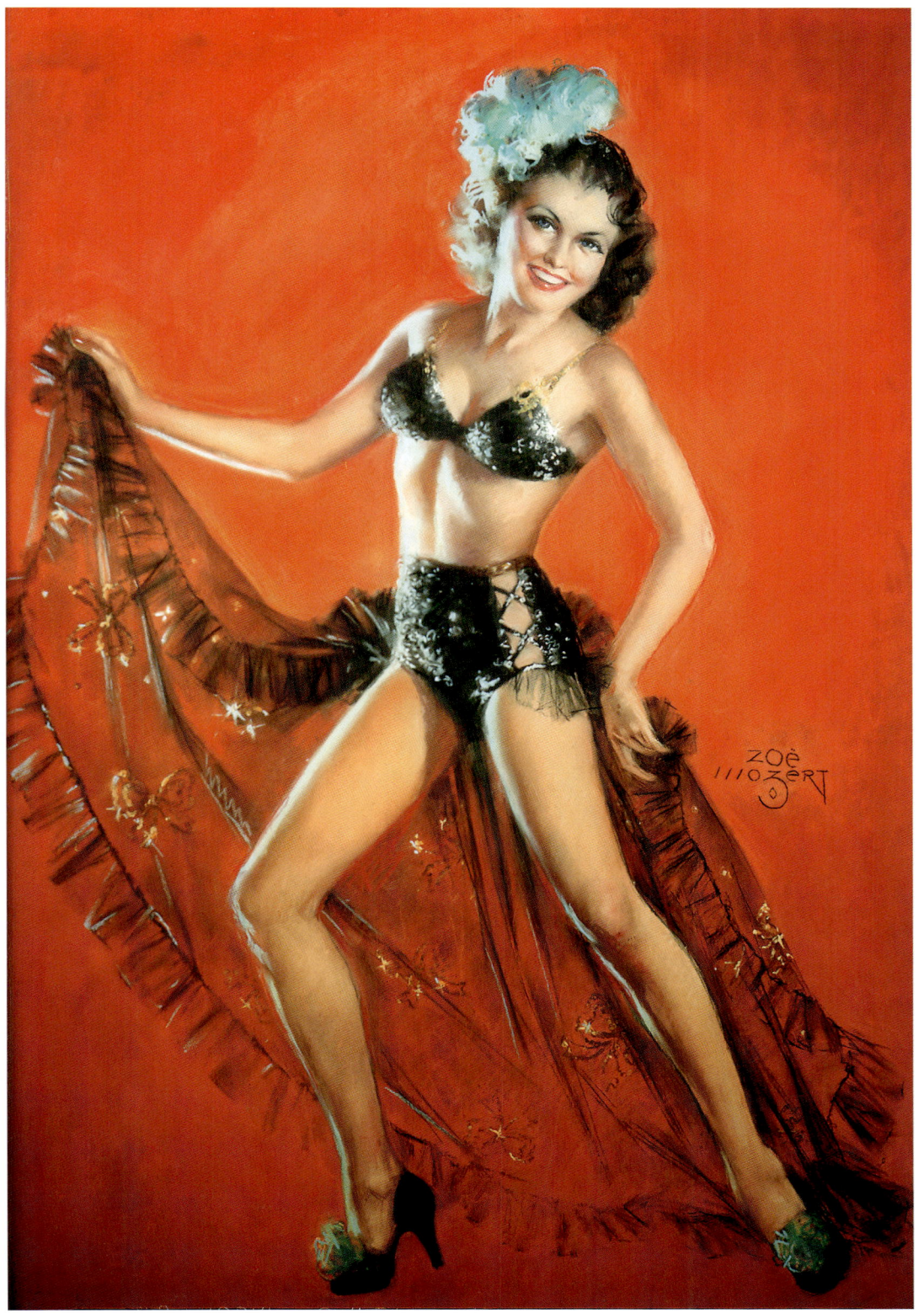

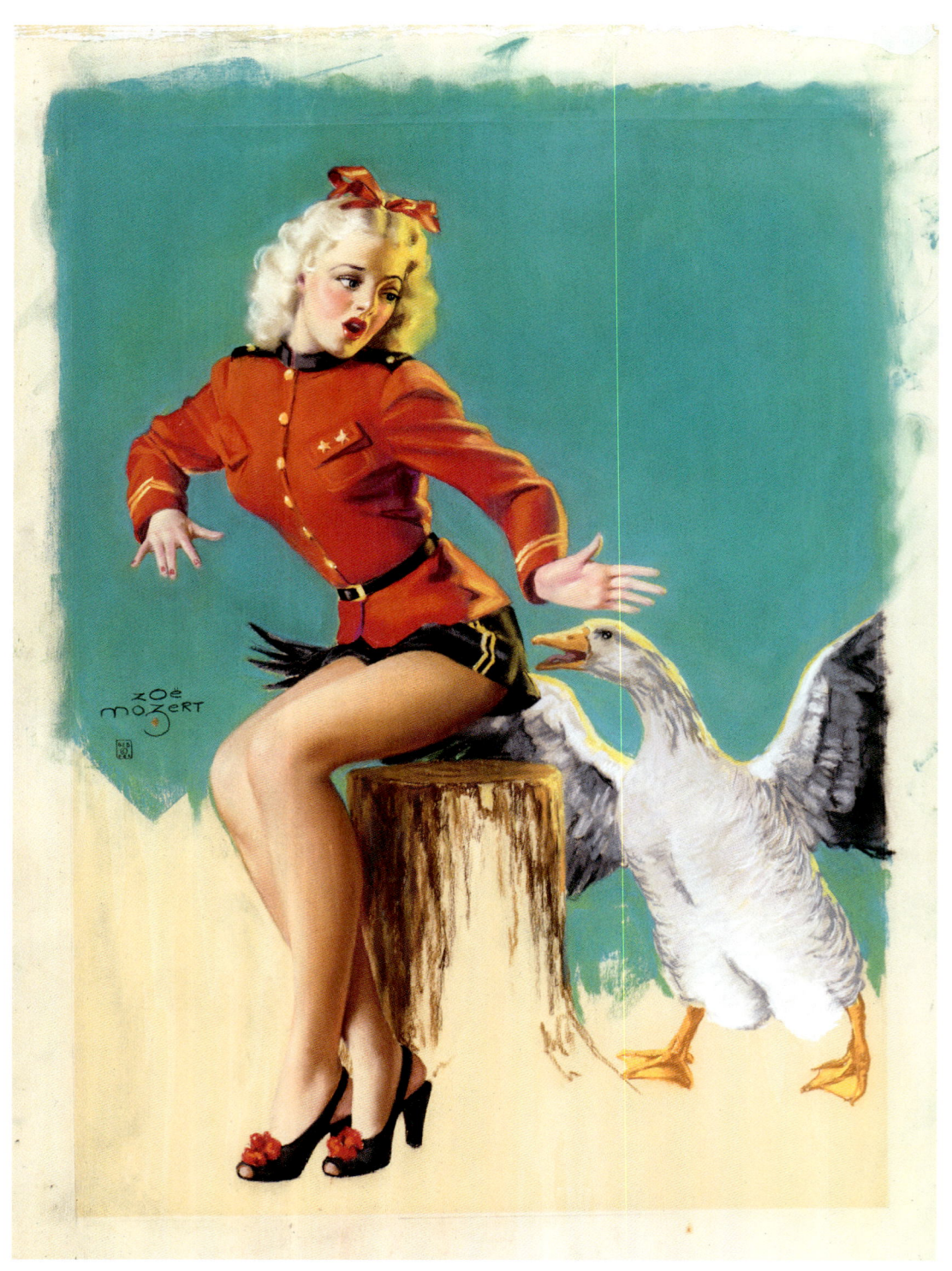

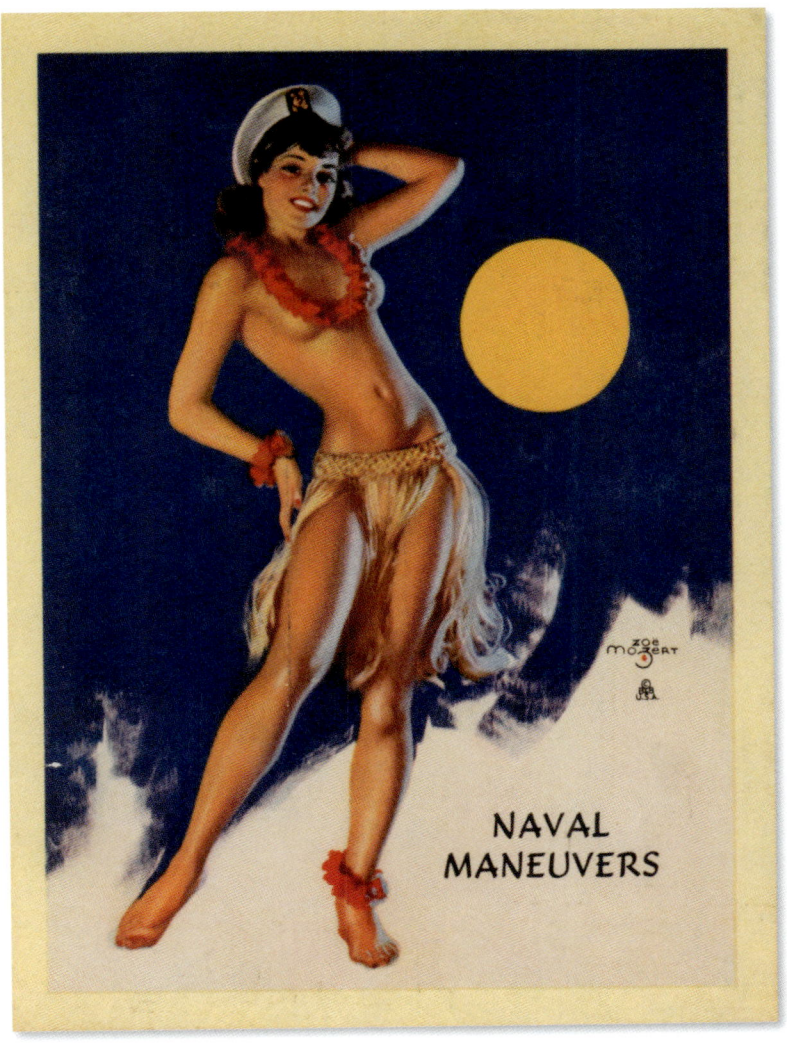

NAVAL
MANEUVERS

Opposite: Flank Attack, pastel on board, circa 1942, for a Brown & Bigelow V-Mail packet.

Above: From a 12-image series created for "V-Mail," circa 1942. The small lithographs were printed on thin paper and distributed in packs that could be shipped cheaply to servicemen anywhere in the world. The captions played on military language. Produced by Brown & Bigelow. 5.5 x 4.25 inches.

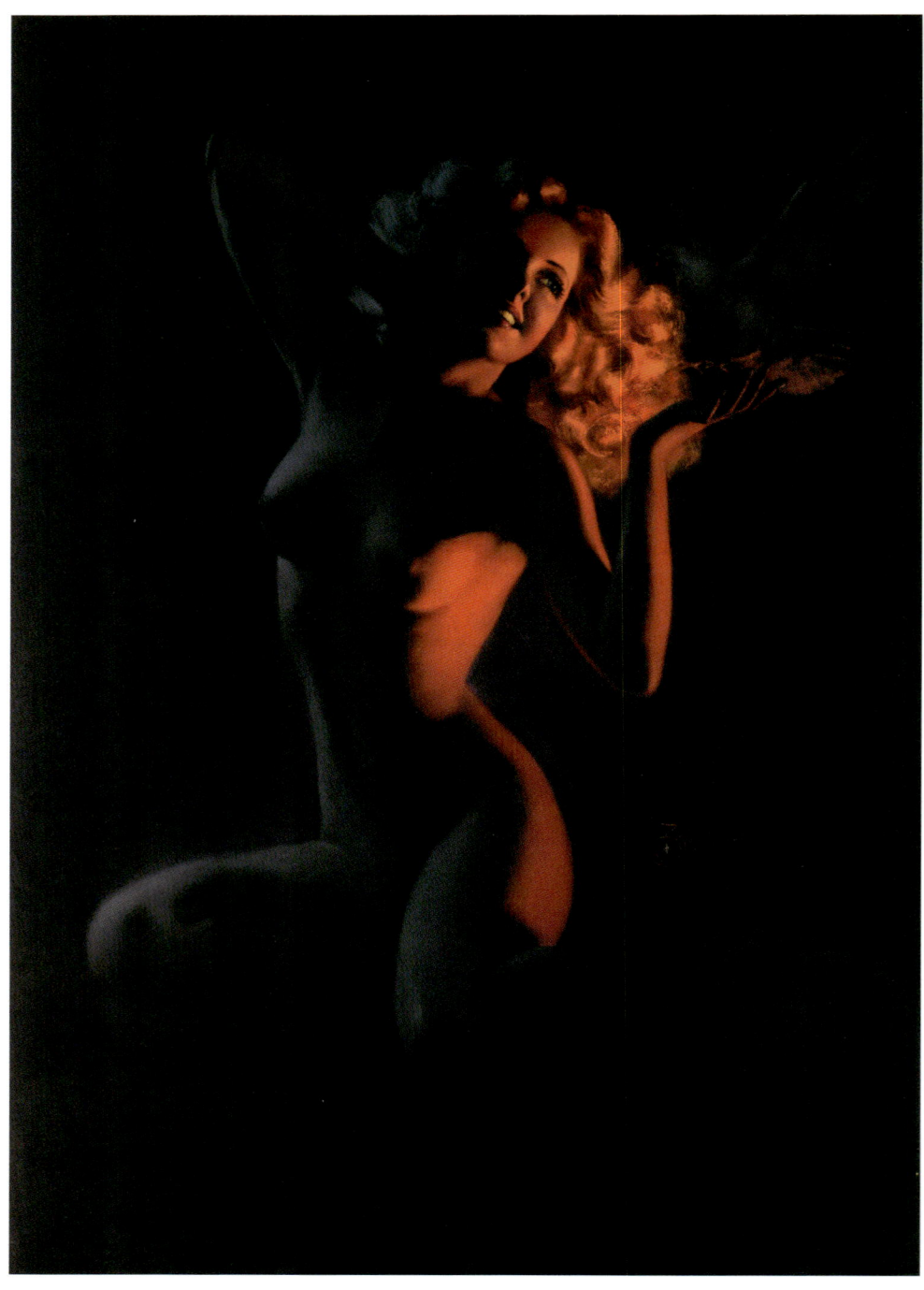

Above: The Enchantress, pastel on board, circa 1948.

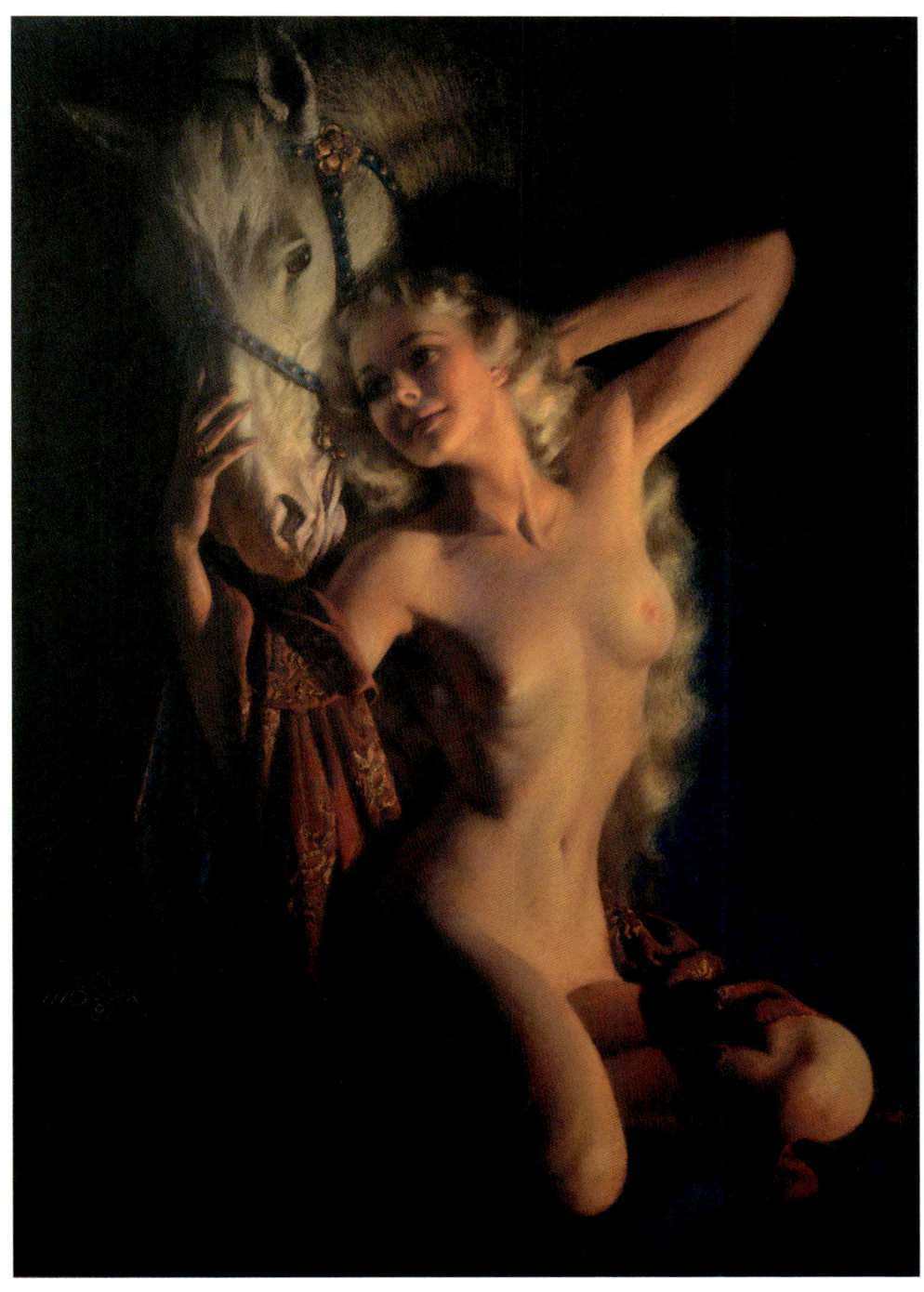

Above: Song of the Desert, pastel on paper, 1949,
for a 1951 Brown & Bigelow calendar. 38.5 x 29 inches.

ZOË MOZERT

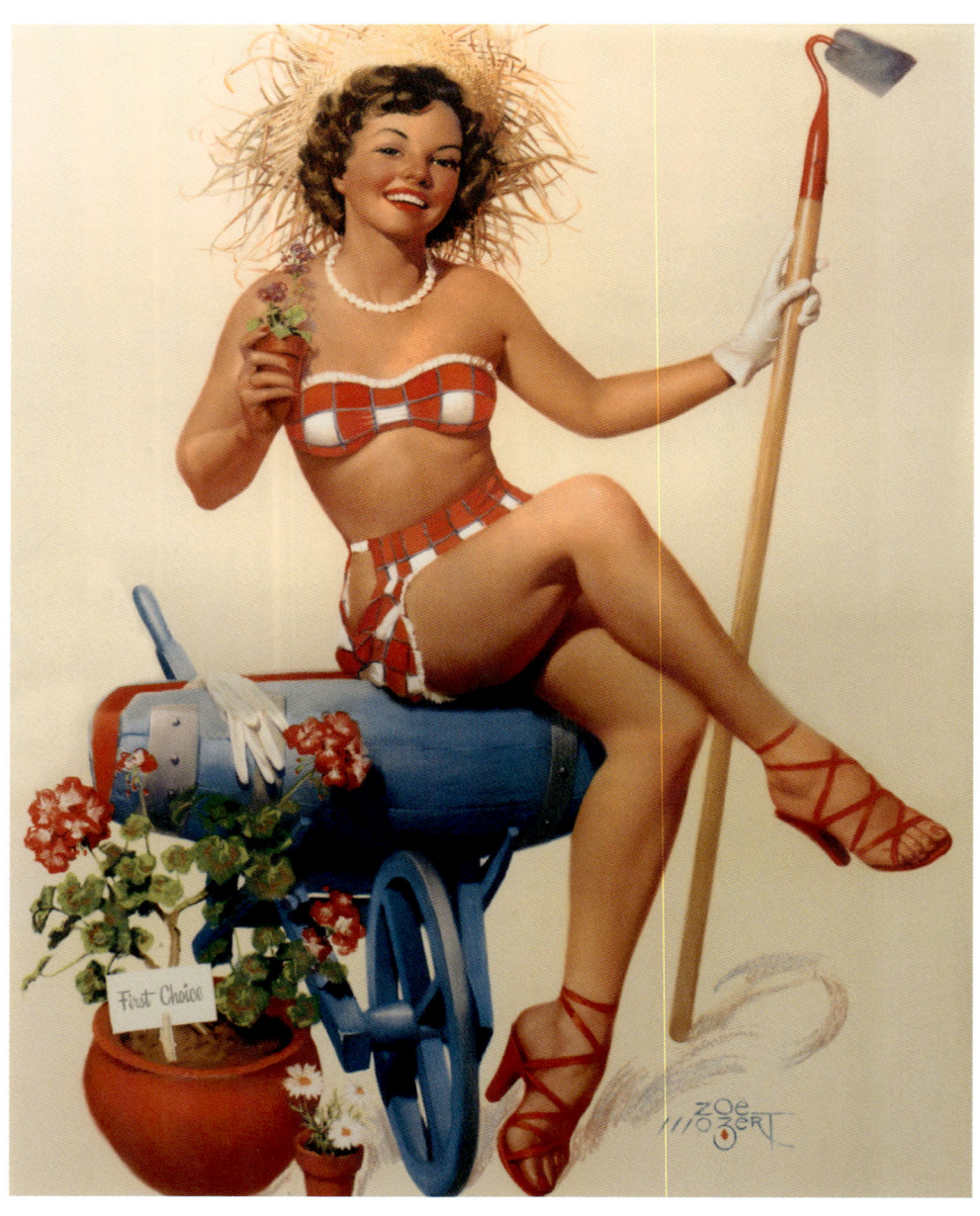

Above: First Choice, pastel on board, 1952, for a 1954
Brown & Bigelow calendar. After the war Mozert
concentrated on her light-and-shadow nudes and
on a succession of gingham-clad country girls.

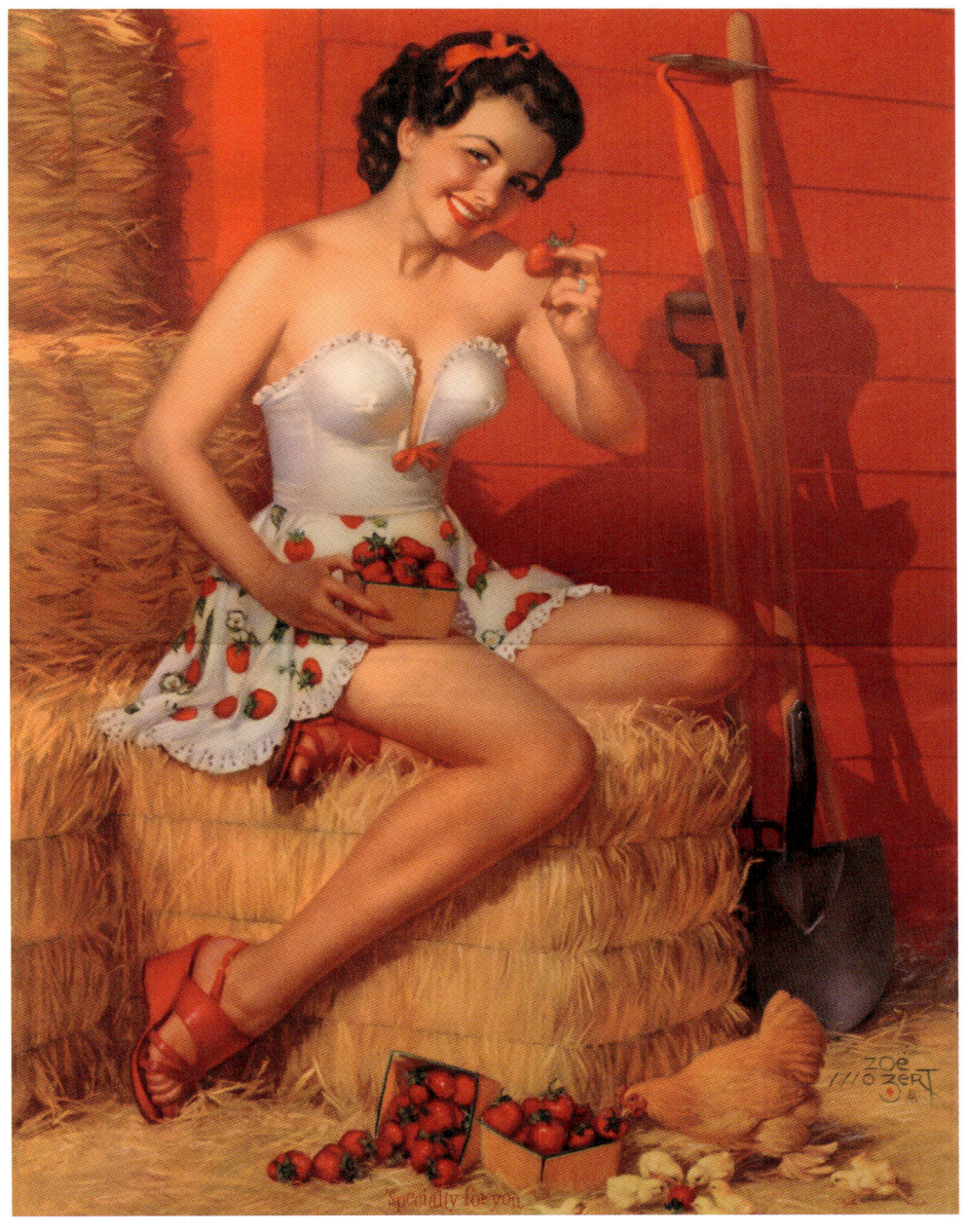

Above: Specially For You, pastel on board, 1954,
for a 1956 Brown & Bigelow calendar.

ZOË MOZERT

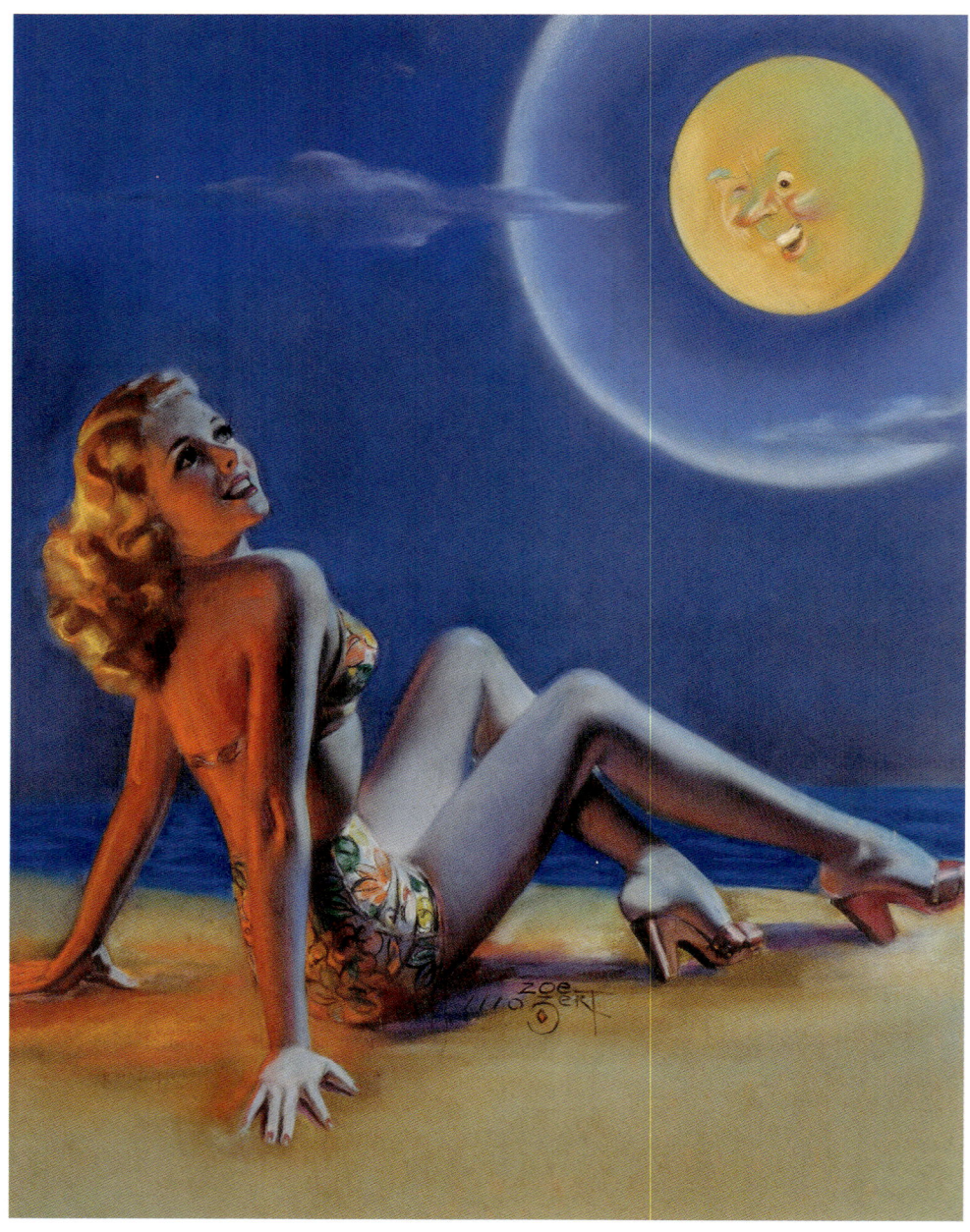

Above: *Moon Light*, pastel on board, circa 1946,
19.5 x 15.5 inches. Courtesy Heritage Auctions.

Opposite: *Morning Song*, pastel on board, 1954, for
a 1956 Brown & Bigelow calendar. B&B created an
edition of 500 24.5-by-18-inch lithographic prints of this
image in the 1970s, each hand-signed by Mozert, that
were never offered for sale. The majority remain in its
vault. 40 x 28 inches. Mitchell Mehdy collection.

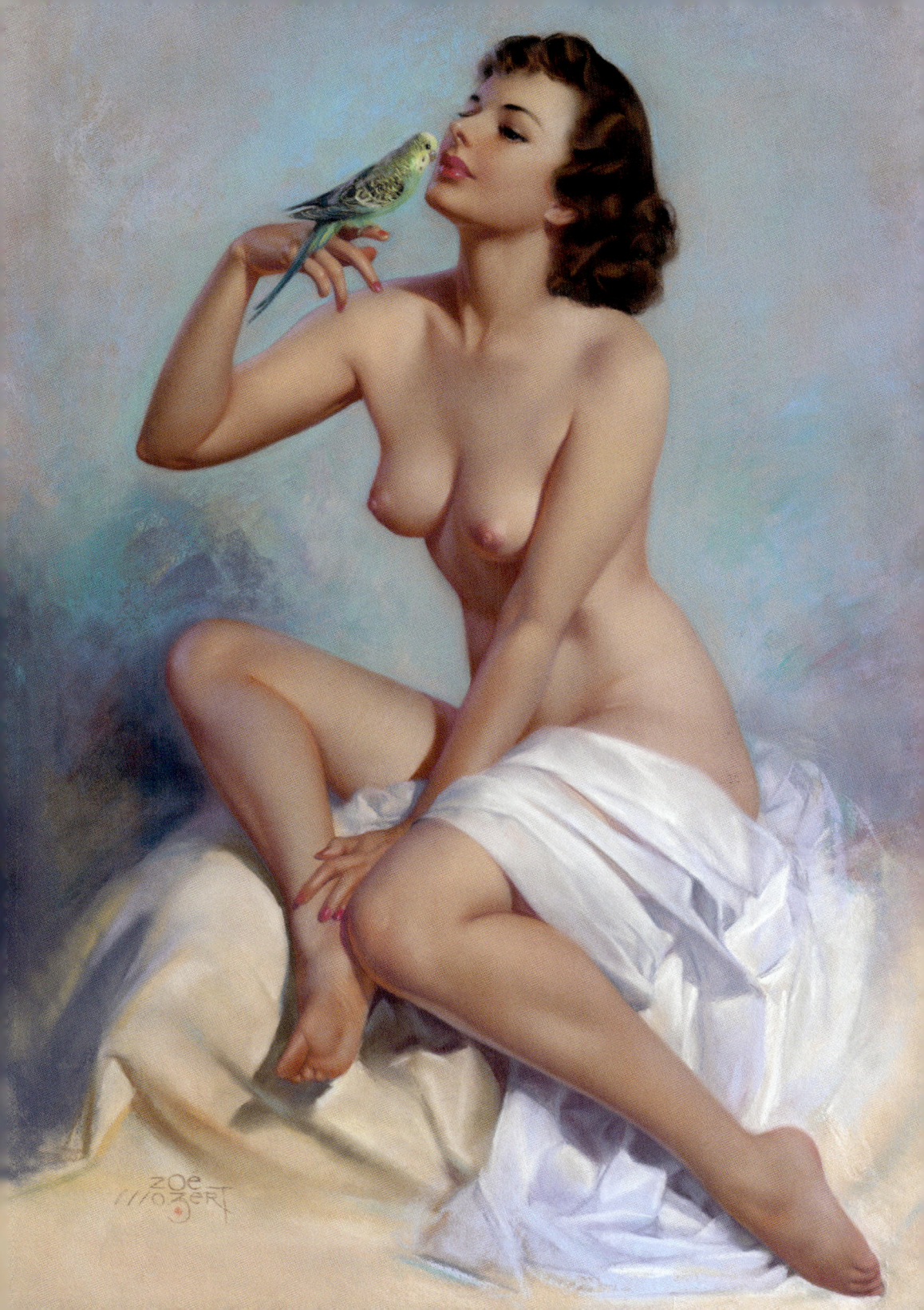

GEORGE PETTY IV

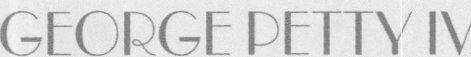

1894–1975

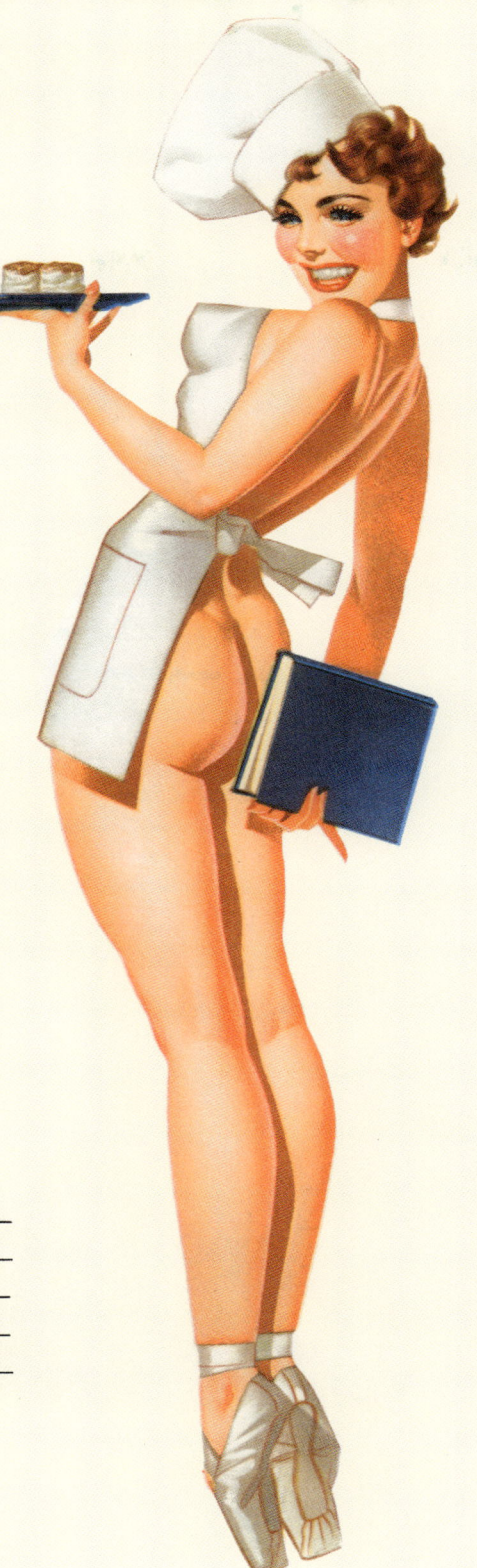

They claim the culinary art's
The quickest way to win men's hearts
So here's a dish, prepared to lure
The most discerning epicure

MARCH 1955

S	M	T	W	T	F	S
		1	2	3	4	5
6	7	8	9	10	11	12
13	14	15	16	17	18	19
20	21	22	23	24	25	26
27	28	29	30	31		

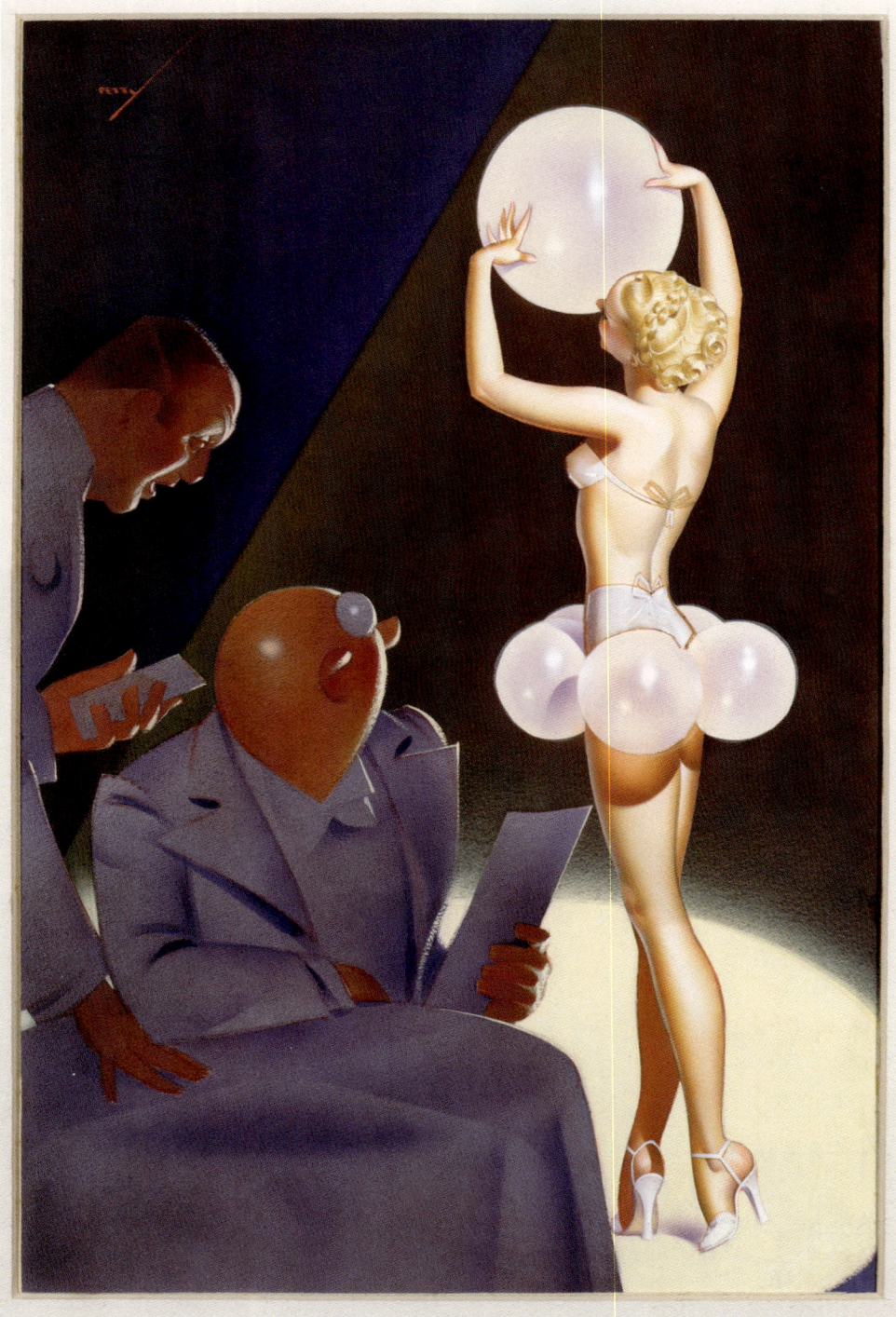

"A DRY MARTINI AND A PACKAGE OF PINS"

"What was the deal with those ballet shoes?
Unlike the telephones, which were conceived to facilitate captions,
Petty never explained."

It's hard today to fathom just how famous George Petty once was. His Petty Girl, born in the first issue of *Esquire* magazine, fall 1933, was soon everywhere: modeling Bestform bras and girdles, fondling (but never smoking) Old Gold cigarettes, strutting Jantzen swimsuits, riding Ridgid Tools, adorning the nosecones of warplanes, traveling on TWA luggage tags, and prancing across the silver screen in her own Hollywood movie.

How did this one man's work, out of so many pin-ups, come to represent our feminine ideal? And how did the man and the girl fall into such modern obscurity? True, Petty's paintings still sell in the $10,000 to $15,000 range, but this at a time when Vargas's best top $100,000 and Elvgrens are edging up to $300,000.

Perhaps Petty has not proved timeless because his pin-ups were so of their time when created—those contrived '30s hairdos; thin, penciled brows; and even in an era when legs were big, gams that pushed the boundaries of length and girth. And what *was* the deal with those ballet shoes? Unlike the telephones, which were conceived to facilitate captions, Petty never explained. Why should he? He was on top of the world and wanted by all.

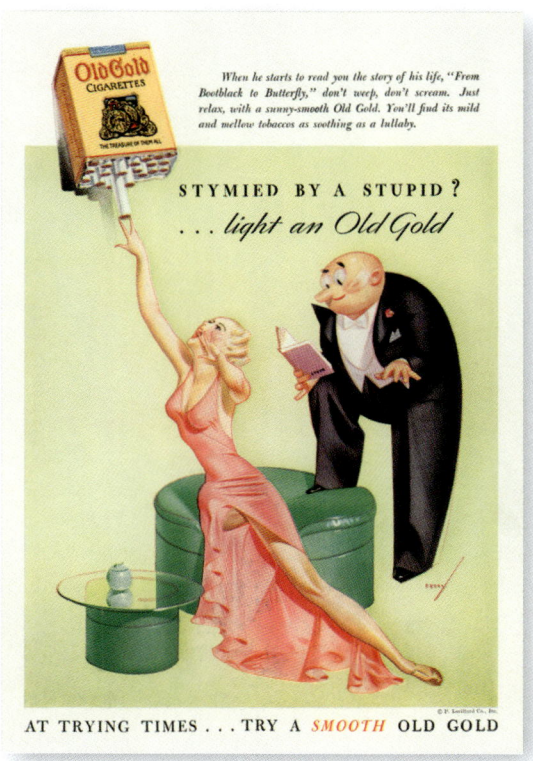

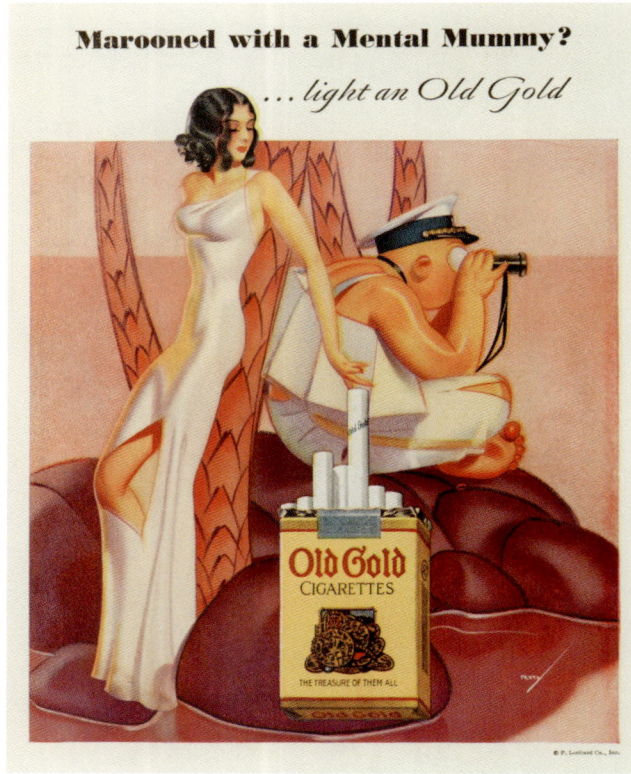

Marooned with a Mental Mummy?

...light an Old Gold

Old Gold
CIGARETTES

THE TREASURE OF THEM ALL

George Brown Petty IV was a Southern boy, born in Abbeville, Louisiana. His father, George Petty III, had a successful photo career creating hand-tinted portraits and the occasional tasteful nude. His son joined him in the studio when the family moved to Chicago, becoming an expert with the airbrush, but young Petty was not interested in photography. Inspired by the illustrations of J. C. Leyendecker, he was determined from an early age to be an artist. In 1913 his indulgent mother took him to Paris to study at Leyendecker's alma mater, the prestigious Académie Julian.

In 1916 mother and son returned to Chicago, where Petty married Julia "Jule" Donahue in 1918, joined the Ruthrauf & Ryan ad agency in 1919, and fathered two children by 1922. He struggled to establish himself in the '20s, doing catalog and magazine covers and a lot of photo retouching. His artistic breakthrough came in 1929, with a deco-style ad for a weight-loss product called the Lesser Slim Figure Bath. The nearly nude flapper in his painting was modeled after his 10-year-old daughter, Marjorie, starting a lifelong artist/model collaboration between father and daughter.

The Lesser ad fixed Petty as a "girl" artist, bringing enough work for him to leave the ad agency and, in 1933, step into the job that made him famous.

When David Smart and Arnold Gingrich were preparing to launch *Esquire* in the depth of the Depression, they couldn't afford the high-priced "girl" artist they wanted. They hired Petty instead at $25 a painting and made him work from the other artist's concepts. These were the origins of the old man/young gold digger cartoons Petty painted for his first two years at *Esquire*, which led to his first successful ad campaign, when Lorillard tobacco recycled the paintings into Old Gold cigarette ads. It was almost unknown for illustrators to hold the rights to their work at that time, but Petty insisted, and his popularity was so immediate *Esquire* didn't dare argue. Advertisers loved his smooth airbrush style, and soon Jantzen swimsuits, Bestform foundations, Vanette Hosiery, Atlantic Beer and Ale, Pontiac, and the Miss America Pageant joined Lorillard. By 1936 Petty was pulling $1,000 for a recycled image, while *Esquire* paid just $100 for the

Opposite: "What's the Idea of Handing Me Those Roses One at a Time?" watercolor on board, circa 1936, for *Esquire* magazine. Under the cap is the same old bald admirer.

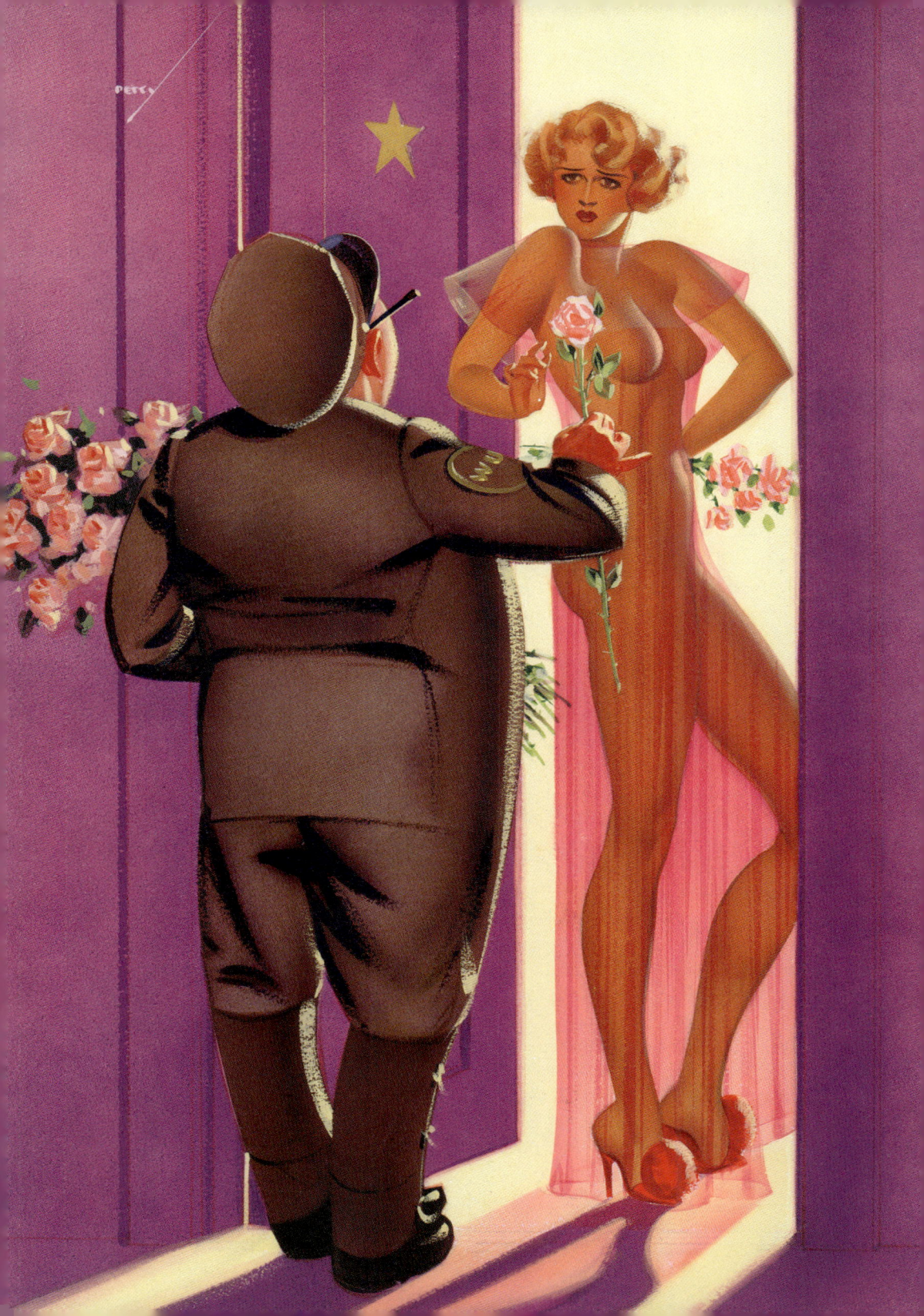

original. Consequently, he let his quality drop for the magazine, producing pin-ups that were lit-tle more than sketches. Readers complained, even as he hounded *Esquire* into producing a *Petty Portfolio* in '36 and splitting the profits with him. He also got Smart to fund big game hunting trips in '37 and '39 in exchange for coverage in the magazine.

Petty's most successful year was 1939, with more ad offers than he could accept and two Hollywood films, *Hotel for Women* and *Man About Town*, showcasing his art. Little wonder he demanded a tenfold increase in his *Esquire* fee — promising larger gatefold paintings — and a year off to fulfill his other commitments. Publisher Smart accepted the deal, then went out and found another talented airbrush artist willing to sell all rights for $75 a week: Alberto Vargas would be his new Petty.

Petty returned to *Esquire* in 1941 to find the Varga Girl touted as successor to his girl. He responded by ramping up the sexuality of his creation, making a more voluptuous girl based on daughter Marjorie's now 22-year-old figure. Fans loved the big gatefolds, and when the United States entered the war those '41 pin-ups hung in barracks for many men — be they American, English, or German. They also proved a favorite for warplane nose art. Corporal Anthony L. Starcer, who decorated 130 planes while stationed in England, was responsible for painting Miss November on the Memphis Belle, a plane that would inspire two motion pictures. Those '41s were Petty's perfect swan song; in 1942 he left *Esquire* to Vargas.

Petty donated paintings for recruitment posters through the war, began his seven-year run of program covers for Ice Capades, published a portfolio of the *Esquire* gatefolds, and produced paintings for the film *Ziegfeld Follies of 1946*. Then, just as the war ended, the Petty Girl retur-ned — not in elegant *Esquire* but in a hunting buddy's gritty *True* magazine.

The *True* centerfolds ran from 1945 to 1947. To some they represent Petty's best work; to others, the release of a long-repressed fetish better left buried. Yes, the ballet shoes. Six of Petty's *True* paintings featured toe shoes, and once unleashed, the ballet girl found her way onto Ice Capades program covers, into Ridgid Tool calendars, and even onto the poster for *The Petty Girl*, Columbia Picture's 1950 tribute to America's long-legged sweetheart. Audiences didn't seem to mind. The film triggered a new round of Petty fever, leading General Motors to commission a Petty hood ornament for its 1950 Nash, which proved so popular they ordered a more explicit design for the '53 model. In between came those incredibly collectible Ridgid Tool calendars, in '52 and '53, reminding America that the Petty Girl, ballet slippers and all, still had it 20 years after her *Esquire* debut.

But did Petty still have it? In 1954 he and Jule moved to Scottsdale, Arizona, where he offi-cially retired. Still, *Esquire* commissioned a 12-page calendar that same year and had him back for three gatefolds in 1956, while Ice Capades asked him to illustrate its 1960 through '64 programs. The work helped after Jule was killed in a car accident in 1962, but Petty was no good alone. He moved to California and quickly remarried, only to annul the marriage after a year and take a new wife.

He painted his last *Esquire* pin-up in late 1972 for the magazine's 40th anniversary issue. "The Petty Girl at Forty" appeared in the February 1973 issue, and the response was so positive Petty accepted one final job in 1974. The invitation he painted for his retirement community's annual dress ball proved he still had it. Except for her updated pumps, this final Petty Girl is indistinguishable from her 1939 sisters. George Petty died the following year on July 21, 1975.

Opposite: Watercolor on board, circa 1936,
for *Esquire* magazine.

THE ART OF PIN-UP

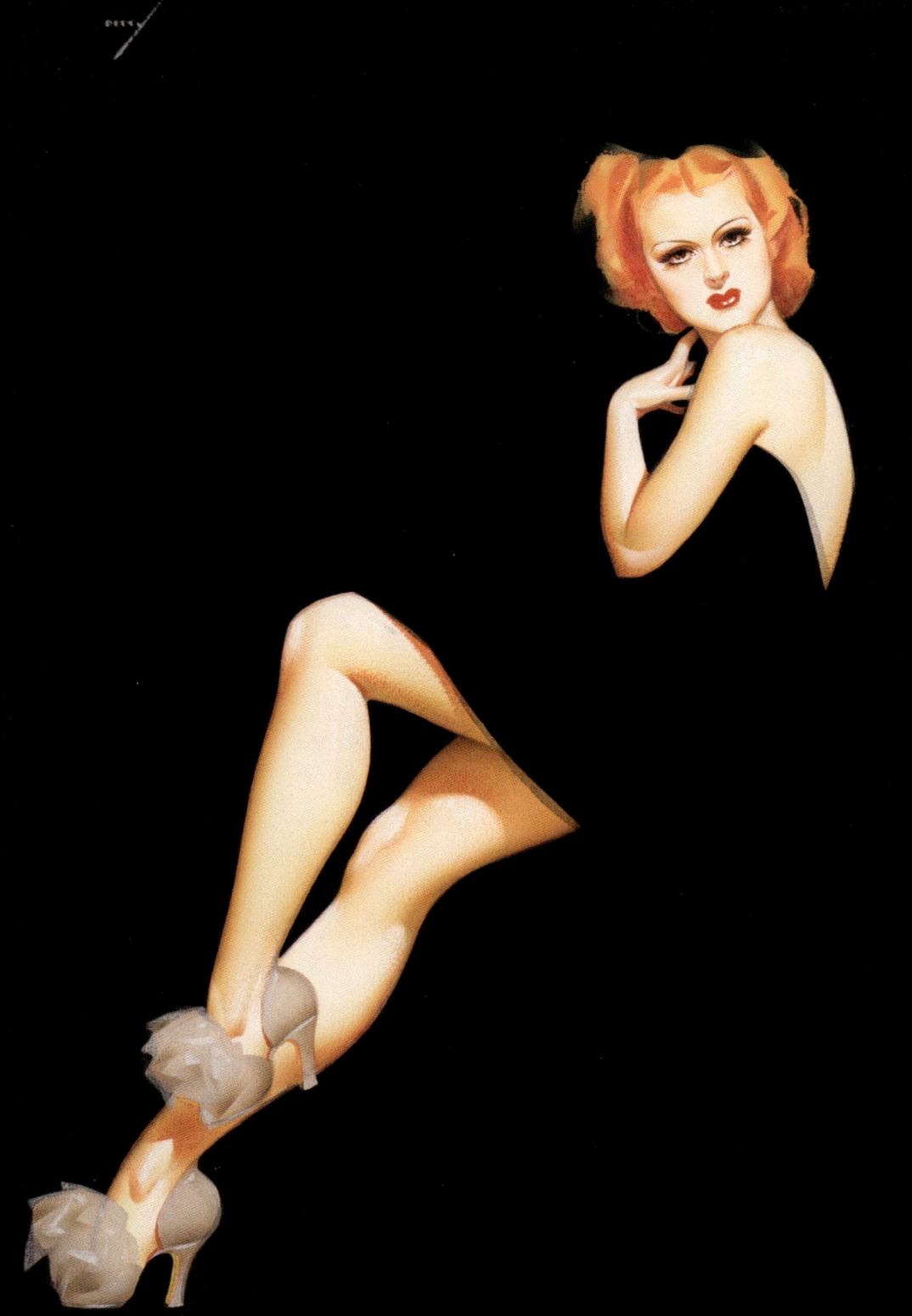

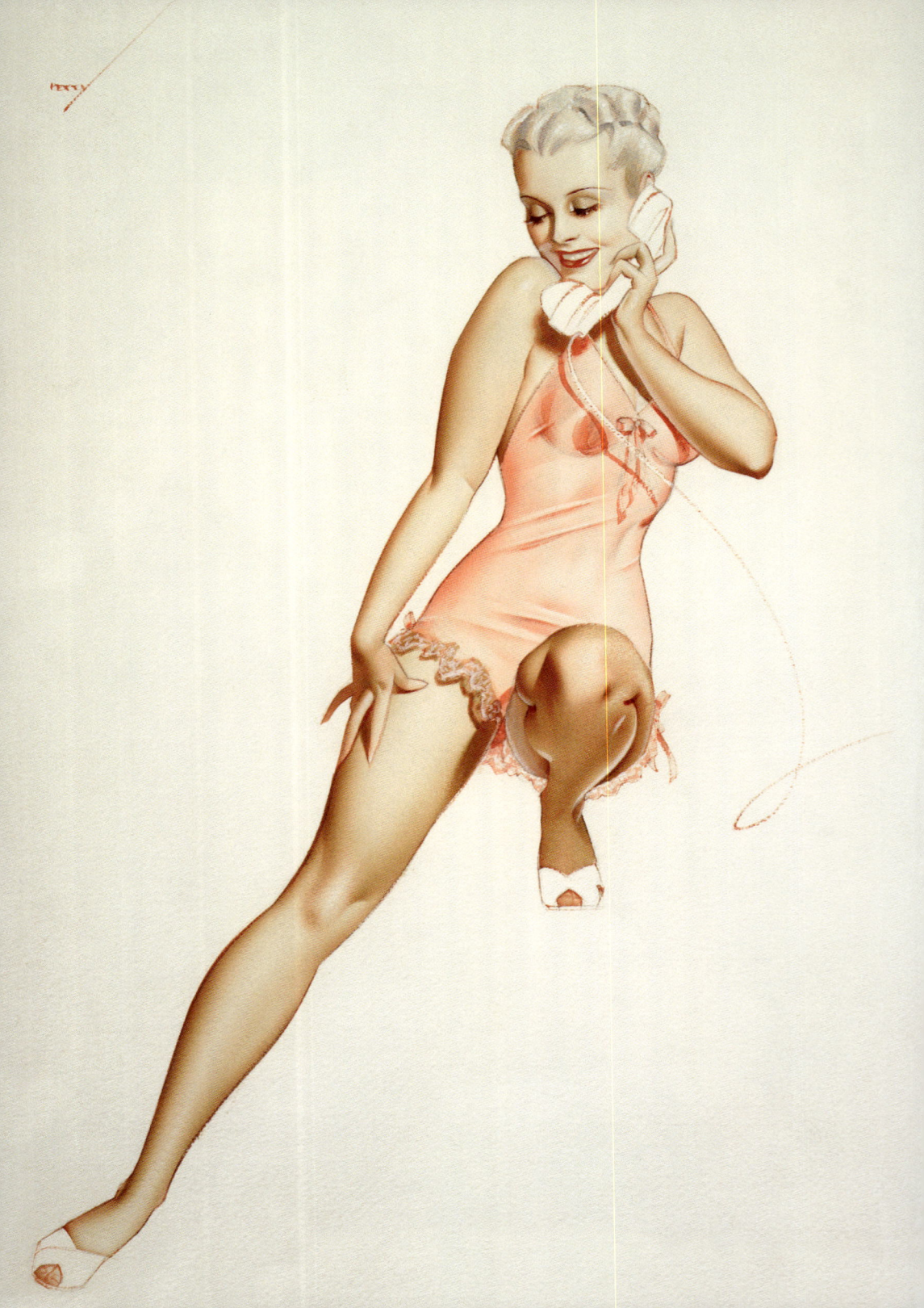

„Was hatte es mit den Ballettschuhen auf sich?
Anders als Telefone ermöglichten sie keine Bildtexte.
Petty erklärte sie nie."

Es ist heute schwer nachzuvollziehen, wie berühmt George Petty einst war. Sein mit der ersten *Esquire*-Ausgabe im Herbst 1933 geborenes Petty-Girl tauchte bald darauf überall auf: Es präsentierte „Bestform"-Büstenhalter und Mieder, berührte liebevoll Old-Gold-Zigaretten, stolzierte in Jantzen-Badeanzügen umher, hockte rittlings auf Ridgid-Werkmaschinen, zierte die Rümpfe von Kampfflugzeugen, reiste auf TWA-Gepäckaufklebern um die Welt und hüpfte in ihrem eigenen Hollywood-Film über die Kinoleinwand.

    Wie kam es, dass unter so vielen Pin-ups ausgerechnet diese eine Schöpfung das amerikanische Ideal einer Frau repräsentierte? Und wieso gerieten Künstler und Figur fast in Vergessenheit? Es ist schon richtig, Pettys Malereien erzielen noch immer zwischen 10 000 und 15 000 Dollar, doch die Preise für die besten Arbeiten von Vargas gehen bis auf 100 000 Dollar hoch, und Elvgrens Bilder erreichen sogar bis zu 300 000 Dollar.

    Vielleicht ist Petty zeitlos, weil seine Pin-ups so von der Ära geprägt sind, in der sie geschaffen wurden – mit den gekünstelten Frisuren der 1930er-Jahre, ihren dünnen, mit dem Stift gezogenen Augenbrauen und mit Beinen, die die Grenzen realistischer Körpermaße überschritten. Und was hatte es mit den Ballettschuhen auf sich? Anders als Telefone ermöglichten sie keine Bildtexte. Petty erklärte sie nie. Warum sollte er auch? Er war in aller Munde, ganz oben und begehrt.

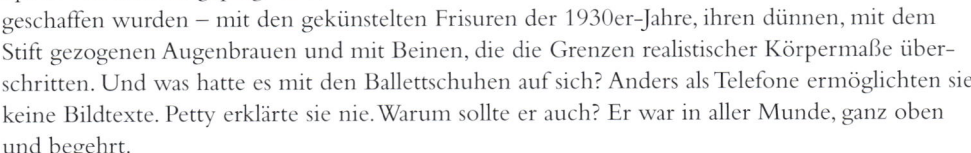

Opposite: Watercolor on board, 1937, for the February 1938 issue of *Esquire* magazine. It has been written that part of the appeal of Petty's telephone girls was that in 1937, while Americans were still sunk in the Great Depression, telephones were a rare and exotic commodity, the sort of thing that only rich men and bad women who catered to rich men could afford.

Above: "A banker? Well bring him up, I've always wanted a bank," watercolor on paper, circa 1934, of an early *Esquire* telephone girl. Golddigging girls talking on the phone would soon become Petty's pin-up signature. 18 x 12 inches.

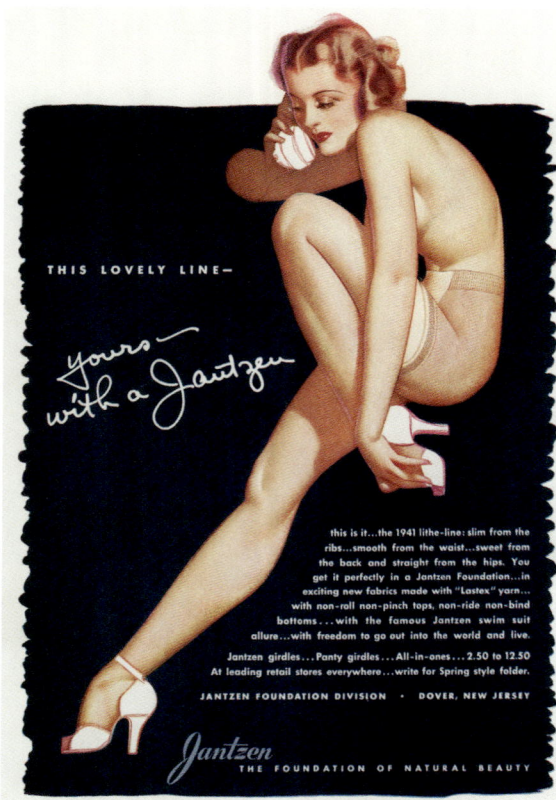

George Brown Petty IV. wurde 1894 im Süden, in Abbeville, Louisiana, geboren. Sein Vater George Petty III., ein erfolgreicher Fotograf, schuf handkolorierte Porträts und gelegentlich auch Aktaufnahmen. Als die Familie nach Chicago zog, arbeitete der Sohn im Studio seines Vaters und spezialisierte sich auf das Retuschieren, interessierte sich aber nicht für Fotografie. Schon in jungen Jahren war er, inspiriert von den Bildern J. C. Leyendeckers, entschlossen, Künstler zu werden. 1913 ging seine Mutter mit ihm nach Paris, damit er an Leyendeckers Alma Mater, der renommierten Académie Julian, studieren konnte.

1916 kehrten Mutter und Sohn nach Chicago zurück. Dort heiratete Petty 1918 Julia „Jule" Donahue, begann 1919, für die Werbeagentur Ruthrauff & Ryan tätig zu werden und wurde bis 1922 Vater von zwei Kindern. In den 1920er-Jahren versuchte er, sich als Künstler zu etablieren. So gestaltete er Katalog- und Zeitschriftencover und übernahm zahlreiche Aufträge für Fotoretuschen. Sein künstlerischer Durchbruch kam 1929 mit einer im Art-déco-Stil gehaltenen Werbeanzeige für ein Schlankheitsprodukt namens „The Lesser Slim Figure Bath". Das fast nackte Flapper-Mädchen auf seinem Bild war nach seiner zehnjährigen Tochter Marjorie gezeichnet.

Mit dieser Anzeige war Petty nun als Girl-Maler ein Begriff, was ihm so viele Aufträge einbrachte, dass er die Werbeagentur verlassen und sich 1933 in jenem Beruf selbstständig machen konnte, mit dem er berühmt wurde.

Als sich David Smart und Arnold Gingrich mitten in der Weltwirtschaftskrise an die Erstausgabe des *Esquire* machten, konnten sie sich den teuren Girl-Maler, den sie gerne wollten, noch nicht leisten. So engagierten sie stattdessen für 25 Dollar pro Bild Petty und ließen ihn im Stil der anderen Künstler arbeiten. So entstanden die Cartoons mit älteren Männern und geldgierigen jungen Frauen, die Petty in den ersten beiden Jahren beim *Esquire* schuf und die schließlich auch zur Grundlage seiner ersten erfolgreichen Anzeigenkampagne wurden:

Above: When Jantzen expanded into foundation garments in 1941, Petty put a girdle on his December 1938 *Esquire* pin-up girl and changed her hair to red. Ironically the caption for the original pin-up read: "I'm not posing for that account any longer. It seems I took the consumer's mind entirely off the product."

Opposite: Mixed media on paper, 1938. This costume design was for the harem scene in Paramount Pictures' 1939 *Man About Town*, starring Jack Benny and Dorothy Lamour. As hype for the film, Petty, then at the pinnacle of his career, was asked to choose 20 actresses to fill the harem and design their costumes. 19 x 10 inches.

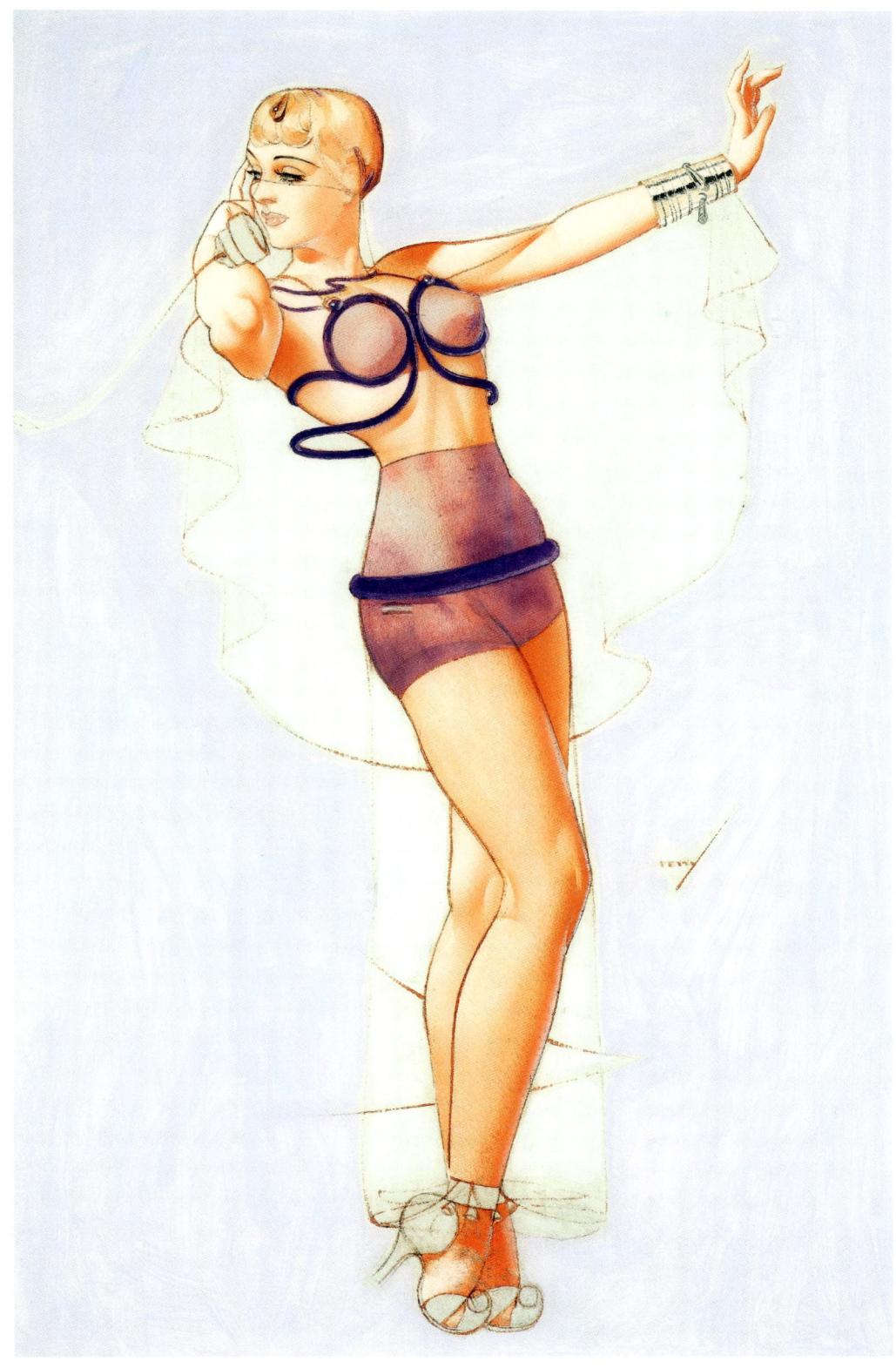

Der Tabakproduzent Lorillard setzte die Bilder in Anzeigen für seine Zigarettenmarke Old Gold ein. Damals war es noch nicht üblich, dass Illustratoren die Rechte an ihren Bildern behielten, doch Petty bestand darauf, und *Esquire* musste aufgrund seines Erfolges nachgeben. Die Anzeigenkunden mochten Pettys sanften Airbrush-Stil, und es dauerte nicht lange, da folgten Jantzen-Badeanzüge, Bestform-Miederwaren, Vanette-Strümpfe, Atlantic-Bier und -Ale, Pontiac und der Miss-America-Wettbewerb dem Beispiel von Lorillard. Um 1936 erzielte Petty für ein wiederverwendetes Bild 1 000 Dollar, während der *Esquire* für das Original gerade mal 100 Dollar zahlte. Folglich zeichnete Petty für das Magazin nur noch Pin-ups, die bessere Skizzen waren. Die Leser beklagten sich, während Petty den *Esquire* noch dazu drängte, 1936 ein *Petty Portfolio* zu produzieren, und Smart sogar dazu brachte, ihm 1937 und 1939 im Gegenzug für Magazinbeiträge Großwildjagden zu finanzieren.

1939 war Pettys erfolgreichstes Jahr: Er erhielt mehr Werbeaufträge, als er annehmen konnte, und in zwei Hollywood-Filmen, *Hotel for Women* und *Man about Town*, war seine Kunst zu sehen. So war es kaum verwunderlich, dass Petty für seine *Esquire*-Bilder nun das Zehnfache forderte, größere Aufklappbilder versprach und ein Jahr aussetzen wollte, um anderen Verpflichtungen nachkommen zu können. Verleger Smart ließ sich auf den Handel ein, machte sich jedoch umgehend auf die Suche und fand einen anderen talentierten Airbrush-Künstler, der bereit war, für 75 Dollar pro Woche sämtliche Rechte abzutreten: Sein neuer Petty hieß Alberto Vargas.

Petty kehrte 1941 zum *Esquire* zurück und musste feststellen, dass das Varga-Girl als Nachfolgerin seines Mädchens um Kunden warb. Er reagierte, indem er den Sexappeal seiner Figur erhöhte und nun ein sinnlicheres Mädchen präsentierte, dessen Figur sich an der seiner inzwischen 22 Jahre alten Tochter Marjorie orientierte. Die Fans liebten die großformatigen Ausklappbilder, und nachdem die USA in den Krieg eingetreten waren, wurden genau diese Pin-ups des Jahres 1941 aufgehängt, und zwar überall dort, wo Männer kämpfen mussten. Pettys Pin-ups waren auch als dekoratives Motiv für die Flugzeugrümpfe beliebt. Korporal Anthony L. Starcer, der 130 Flugzeuge schmückte, als er in England stationiert war, malte die Miss November von Petty auf die Memphis Belle, ein Flugzeug, das zwei Filme inspirierte. Die Pin-ups von 1941 waren Pettys perfekter Schwanengesang; 1942 überließ er *Esquire* Vargas.

Im Krieg spendete Petty Gemälde für Rekrutierungsplakate, nahm seine sieben Jahre dauernde Tätigkeit für Ice Capades auf, eine Eisrevue, für die er die Cover der Programmhefte gestaltete, veröffentlichte ein Portfolio seiner *Esquire*-Ausklappbilder und fertigte Bilder für den Film *Ziegfeld Follies* an, der 1946 gedreht wurde. Dann, der Krieg war gerade zu Ende, kehrte das Petty-Girl im draufgängerischen *True*, einer Zeitschrift, die einer von Pettys Jagdkumpels verlegte, wieder zurück.

Von 1945 bis 1947 schuf er doppelseitige Mittelbilder für *True*. Manche hielten sie für die besten Werke Pettys; andere meinten, er habe damit einen Fetisch ausgegraben, den er besser in der Versenkung belassen hätte. Ja, die Ballettschuhe. Auf sechs von Pettys Bildern für *True* sind diese Spitzentanzschuhe zu sehen, und erst einmal wieder hervorgeholt, schaffte es das Ballettmädchen nun auch auf die Cover des Programmhefts von Ice Capades, in Kalender für Ridgid-Werkzeuge und sogar auf das Filmplakat für *The Petty Girl*, eine Columbia-Pictures-Produktion von 1950, die dem langbeinigen Liebling Amerikas huldigte. Der Film läutete eine neue Runde Petty-Fieber ein, sorgte dafür, dass General Motors Petty damit beauftragte, eine Kühlerfigur für das 1950er-Modell Nash zu schaffen, die sich einer so großen Popularität erfreute, dass man für das 1953er-Modell eine weitere Figur orderte. Zwischendurch, 1952 und 1953, kamen auch noch die bei Sammlern höchst beliebten Kalender des Werkzeugherstellers Ridgid heraus, die

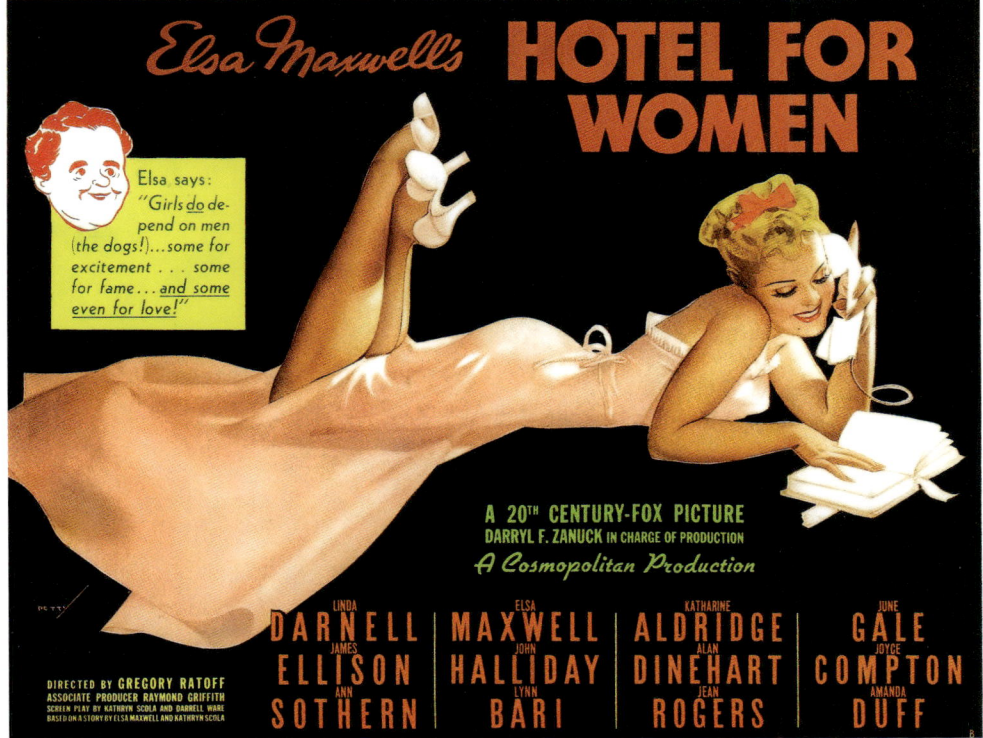

Amerika bewusst machten, dass es das Petty-Girl samt seinen Ballettschuhen 20 Jahre nach seinem Debüt im *Esquire* noch immer draufhatte.

1954 zog er sich mit seiner Frau Jule nach Scottsdale, Arizona, in den Ruhestand zurück. Doch der *Esquire* beauftragte ihn im selben Jahr noch mit der Gestaltung eines zwölfseitigen Kalenders und 1956 mit drei neuen Ausklappbildern, während Ice Capades ihn von 1960 bis 1964 die Programmhefte gestalten ließ. Die Arbeit half ihm, Jules Tod bei einem Autounfall zu verkraften. Er zog nach Kalifornien, heiratete kurz darauf erneut, ließ sich jedoch ein Jahr später scheiden und nahm sich eine neue Frau.

Ende 1972 malte er für die Ausgabe zum 40-jährigen Jubiläum des *Esquire* sein letztes Pin-up für diese Zeitschrift. „Das Petty-Girl mit vierzig" erschien im Februarheft 1973, und die Reaktionen waren so positiv, dass Petty 1974 noch einen letzten Auftrag akzeptierte. Die Einladungskarte, die er für den Kostümball seiner Seniorenresidenz malte, bewies, dass er es immer noch draufhatte. Denn abgesehen von seinen modischen hochhackigen Schuhen, ist dieses letzte Petty-Girl von seinen 1939 ins Leben gerufenen Schwestern kaum zu unterscheiden. Im Jahr darauf, am 21. Juli 1975, starb George Petty.

Above: A lobby card for 20th Century-Fox's Hotel for Women, 1939. Bradshaw Crandall and McClelland Barclay illustrated alternate posters for this romantic comedy. 14 x 11 inches.

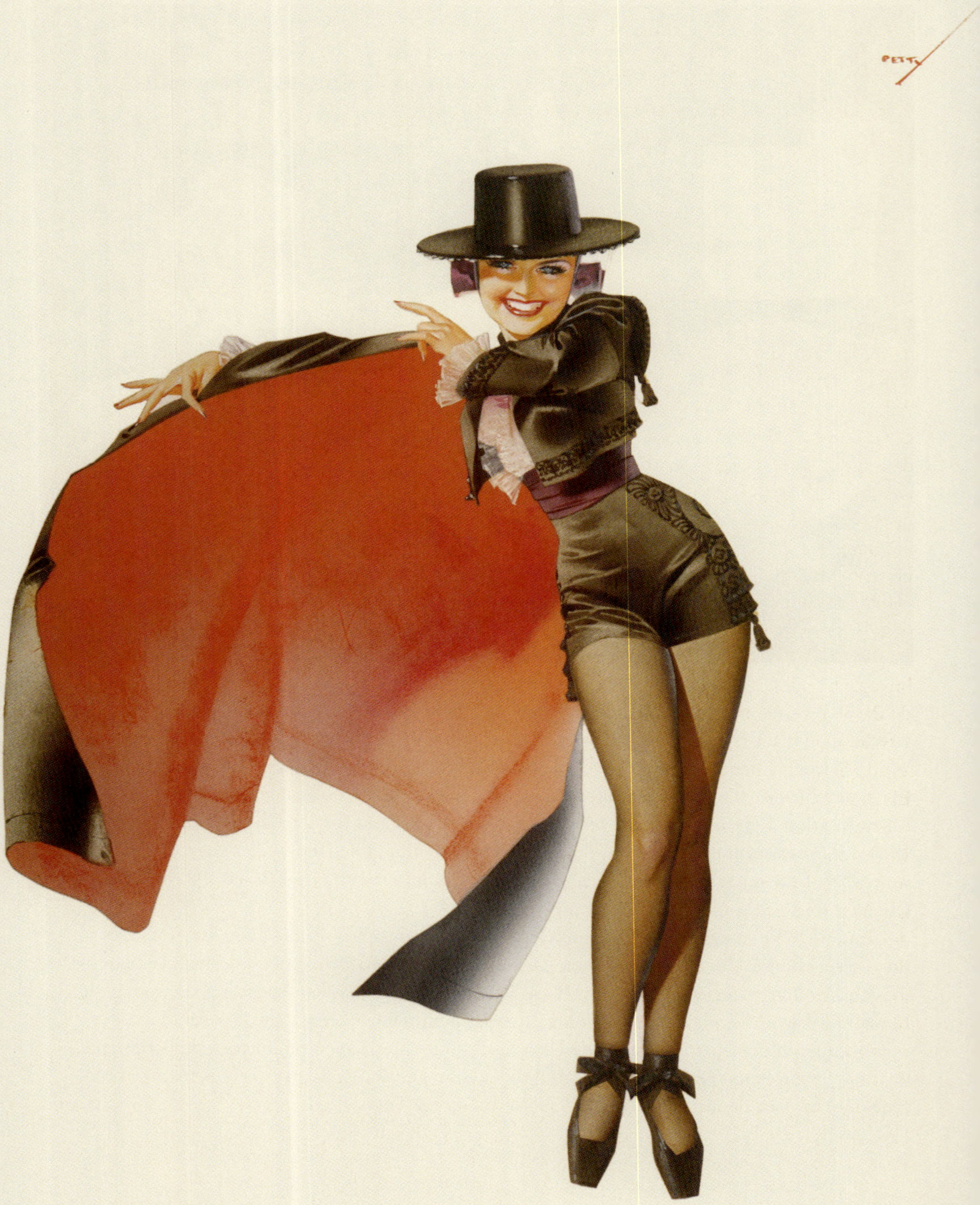

« La présence de téléphones se comprend,
car ils servaient souvent à incorporer une légende,
mais cette lubie des chaussons de danse ?
Petty ne l'expliqua jamais. »

On imagine mal aujourd'hui à quel point George Petty fut célèbre. La Petty Girl, née dans le premier numéro d'*Esquire* à l'automne 1933, était partout : posant dans des dessous Bestform, avec des cigarettes Old Gold (sans jamais les fumer), se pavanant dans des maillots de bain Jantzen, chevauchant des outils Ridgid Tools, ornant le cockpit de bombardiers, voyageant sur des étiquettes de la TWA ou sur grand écran en star d'Hollywood.

Comment ses pin-up en sont-elles venues à représenter notre idéal féminin ? Et comment cet artiste a-t-il pu sombrer dans l'oubli ? Certes, les originaux de Petty se vendent aujourd'hui entre 10 000 et 15 000 dollars, mais les meilleurs Vargas partent à 100 000 dollars et certains Elvgren avoisinent les 300 000 dollars.

Sans doute n'a-t-il pas résisté à l'épreuve du temps parce que ses pin-up étaient trop ancrées dans leur époque : coiffures alambiquées des années 1930, fins sourcils dessinés, jambes potelées d'une longueur

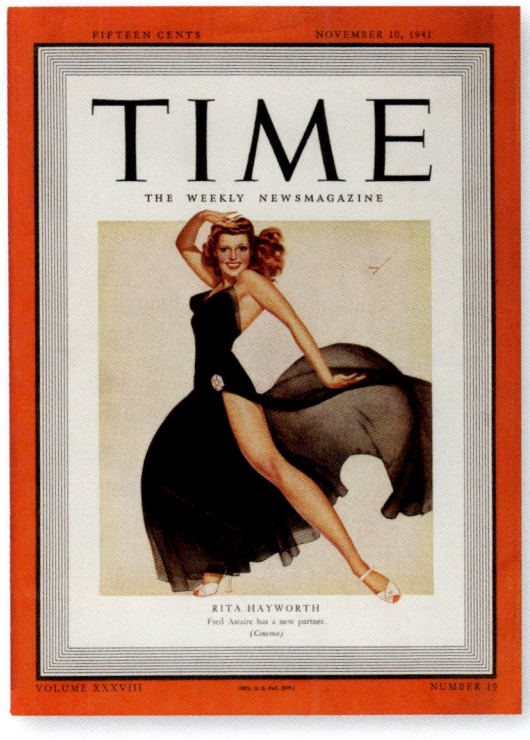

défiant la raison. La présence de téléphones se comprend, car ils servaient souvent à incorporer une légende, mais cette lubie des chaussons de danse ? Petty ne l'expliqua jamais. Il n'avait pas besoin de se justifier. Il était au sommet de la gloire et tout le monde se l'arrachait.

George Brown Petty IV est né en 1894 à Abbeville en Louisiane. Son père, George Petty III, était un photographe prospère qui réalisait des portraits teints à la main et des nus de bon goût. Lorsque la famille emménagea à Chicago, son fils travailla dans son studio où il apprit à maîtriser l'aérographe. Toutefois, la photographie ne l'intéressait pas. Inspiré par les illustrations de J. C. Leyendecker, il voulait être artiste. En 1913, sa mère l'emmena à Paris pour étudier à l'Académie Julian, par où Leyendecker était passé avant lui.

Opposite: Watercolor on board, 1954, for Petty's triumphant return to *Esquire* with the 1955 *Esquire* Girl Calendar.

Above: Rita Hayworth painted for the November 10, 1941, cover of *Time* magazine. As with all his pin-ups, Petty enlarged and elongated Hayworth's legs.

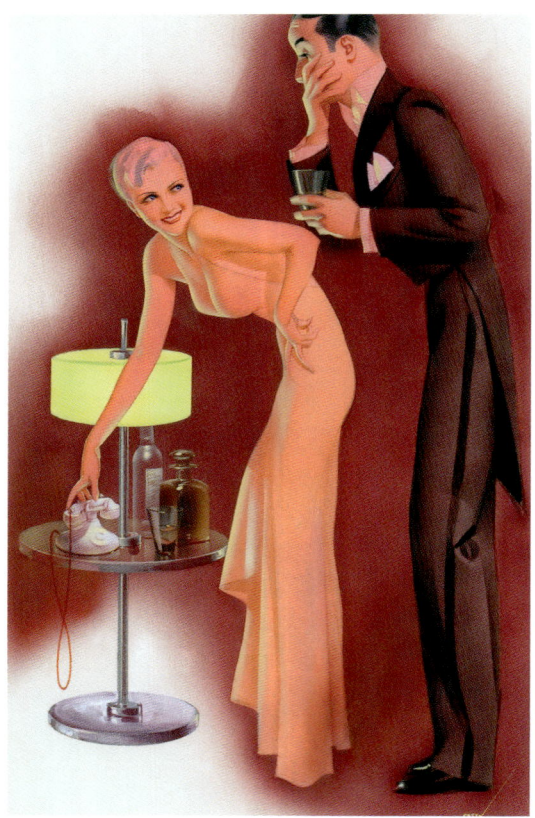

Ils rentrèrent à Chicago en 1916. Petty épousa Julia « Jule » Donahue en 1918, rejoignit l'agence publicitaire Ruthrauff & Ryan en 1919 et, en 1922, était père de deux enfants. Tout au long des années 1920, il tenta de se faire connaître, illustrant des catalogues, des couvertures de magazine et retouchant des photos. Son premier coup de maître fut pour un produit d'amaigrissement en 1929 : une garçonne presque nue de style Art déco pour laquelle il avait fait poser sa fille de 10 ans, Marjorie, le début d'une longue collaboration entre le père et la fille.

Cette publicité lui valut d'être catalogué « peintre de jolies filles » et lui apporta suffisamment de commandes pour lui permettre de quitter l'agence puis, en 1933, de se lancer dans la carrière qui le rendit célèbre.

Pendant ce temps, David Smart et Arnold Gingrich lançaient leur magazine *Esquire* en plein cœur de la dépression. Ne pouvant s'offrir les services de l'illustrateur qu'ils convoitaient, ils engagèrent Petty à 25 dollars par peinture et lui demandèrent de travailler à partir des concepts de l'autre artiste. Ainsi naquit la série humoristique mettant en scène un riche vieillard et une jeune fille que Petty réalisa pendant deux ans. Elle séduisit la société Lorillard qui lui demanda une campagne publicitaire pour ses cigarettes Old Gold. À l'époque, il était rare qu'un illustrateur détienne les droits sur ses images mais Petty insista et, devant le succès de ses Girls, *Esquire* n'osa pas refuser. Les annonceurs adoraient son style fluide à l'aérographe et, bientôt, il recevait des commandes de Jantzen, Bestform, Vanette Hosiery, Atlantic Beer and Ale, Pontiac et du concours de Miss America. En 1936, Petty était payé 1 000 dollars pour une image recyclée alors qu'*Esquire* ne lui donnait que 100 dollars pour un original. Par conséquent, il négligea son travail pour le magazine, produisant des pin-up qui étaient à peine des esquisses au grand dam des lecteurs. En 1936, il parvint néanmoins à convaincre *Esquire* d'éditer un *Petty Portfolio* en partageant les bénéfices à parts égales avec lui, puis, en 1937 et 1939, de financer deux safaris de chasse au gros gibier en échange de reportages pour le magazine.

1939 fut sa meilleure année : il était surchargé de commandes et son travail fut célébré dans deux films, *Hotel for Women* et *Man About Town*. Il n'est donc pas étonnant qu'il ait exigé d'*Esquire*

Above: Watercolor and gouache on board, 1934, for *Esquire*, September 1934. 17.5 x 11.5 inches.

Opposite: Watercolor on board, 1943, for the September 1946 issue of *True* magazine, captioned, "There's something wrong with this phone...a man called and didn't try to date me," and for the September image for *True*'s 1947 12-page calendar. 18.5 x 11 inches.

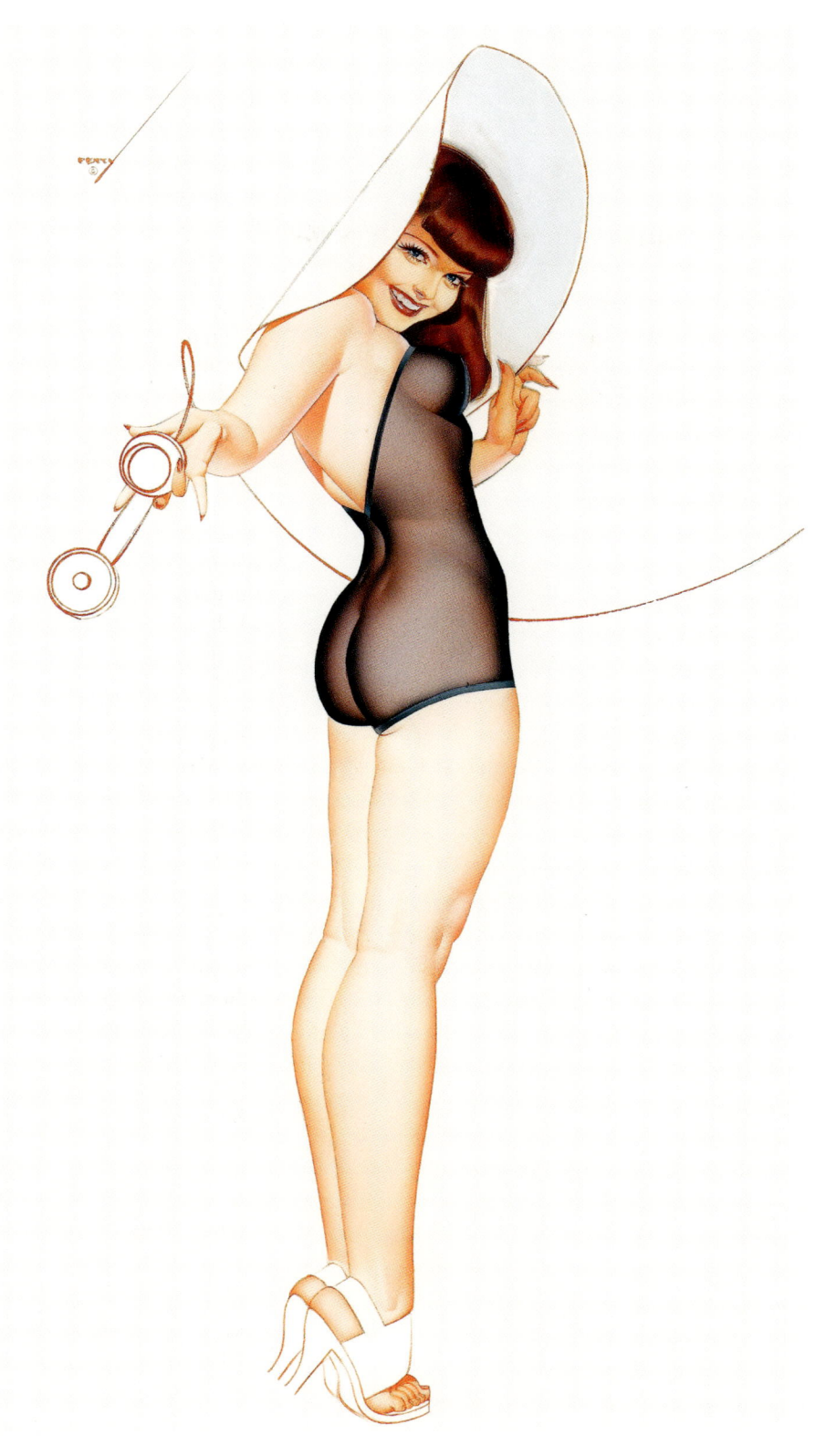

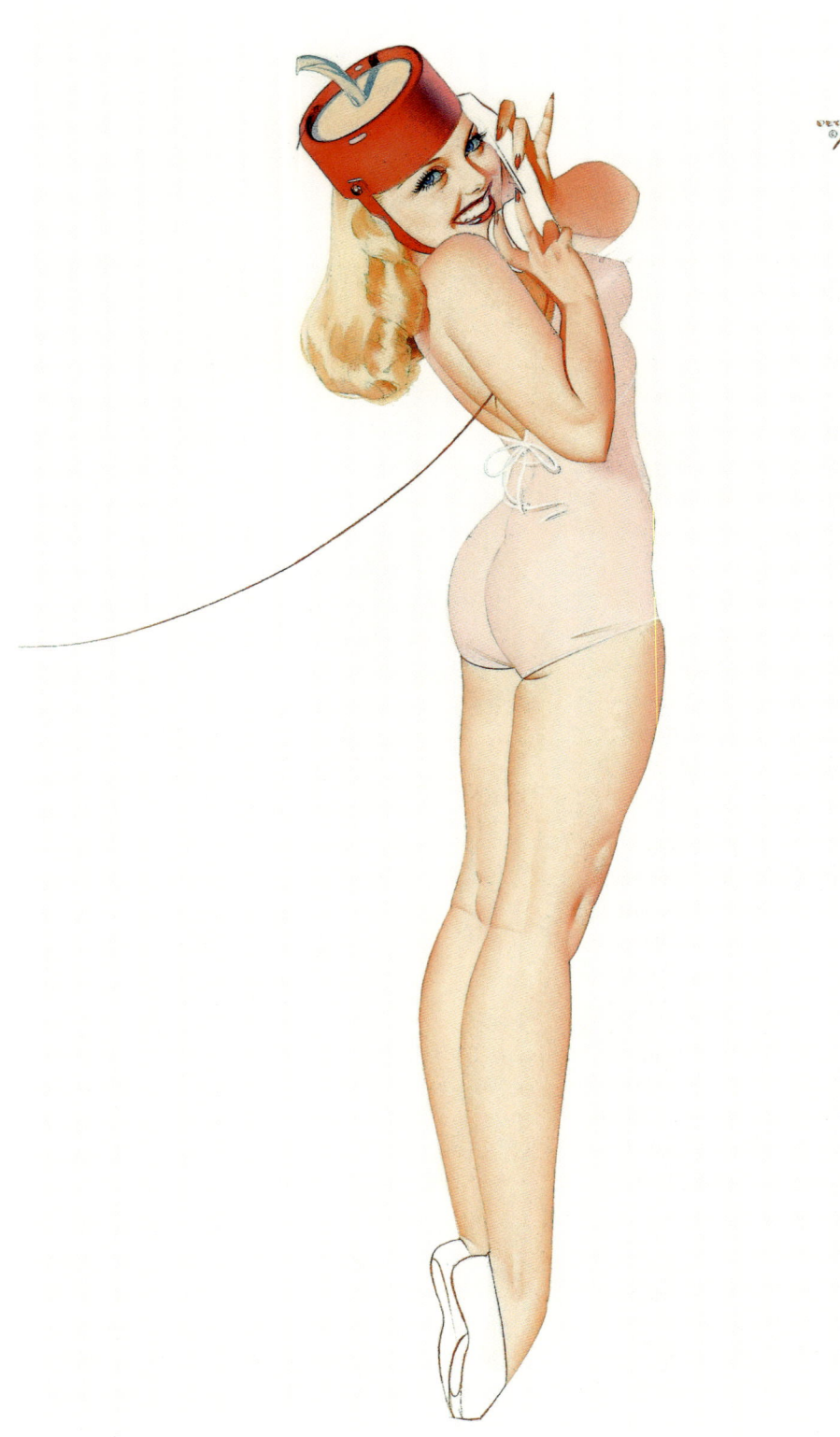

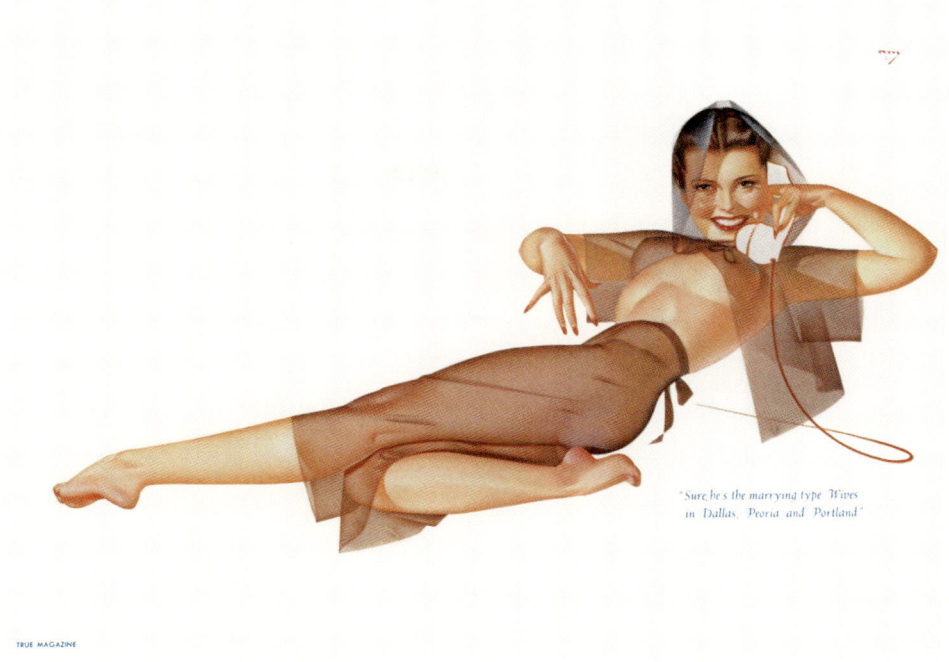

Sure, he's the marrying type. Wives in Dallas, Peoria and Portland

TRUE MAGAZINE

de décupler son salaire, promettant des peintures plus grandes pour des dépliants encartés, et qu'il ait demandé une année sabbatique afin de répondre à ses autres engagements. Smart accepta, puis alla chercher un autre maître de l'aérographe prêt à céder tous ses droits pour 75 dollars par semaine.

Lorsque Petty revint travailler pour *Esquire* en 1941, la Varga Girl avait remplacé la sienne. Il réagit en créant une Petty Girl encore plus voluptueuse inspirée de la silhouette de sa fille Marjorie, qui avait désormais 22 ans. Les fans adorèrent les grands dépliants et, quand les États-Unis entrèrent en guerre, ces pin-up de 1941 se retrouvèrent dans toutes les casernes, qu'elles soient américaines, anglaises ou allemandes. Elles devinrent également un sujet favori du *nose art*. Le caporal Anthony L. Starcer, qui décora 130 avions basés en Angleterre, peignit *Miss November* sur le Memphis Belle, un avion qui inspira deux films. Ces beautés langoureuses étaient le chant du cygne de Petty : en 1941, il abandonna *Esquire* à Vargas.

Pendant la guerre, il donna des images pour réaliser des affiches de recrutement, commença à illustrer les programmes des Ice Capades (une collaboration qui allait durer sept ans), publia un portfolio de ses dépliants pour *Esquire* et réalisa des peintures pour le film *Ziegfeld Follies* (1946). La Petty Girl fit son retour avec la paix, cette fois dans *True*, un magazine pour hommes plutôt salace.

Les posters centraux de *True* parurent de 1945 à 1947. Certains les considèrent comme le meilleur travail de Petty ; d'autres comme la libération d'un fétiche longtemps refoulé et qui aurait dû le rester. En effet, six de ses pin-up chaussent des pointes. Une fois lâchée, la ballerine

Opposite: Watercolor on board, 1946, for the July 1947 issue of *True* magazine. The image also appeared as Miss July 1948 in the annual *True* calendar. 27 x 20.5 inches.

Above: Sure, he's the marrying type. Wives in Dallas, Peoria and Portland," pin-up for the April 1947 issue of *True* magazine.

s'insinua sur les programmes d'Ice Capades, sur les calendriers Ridgid Tools et même sur l'affiche de *The Petty Girl* (1950), l'hommage de la Columbia à la chérie aux longues jambes de l'Amérique. Ce film suscita un nouvel engouement pour ses créatures. Nash Motors lui commanda un ornement de capot pour sa Rambler de 1950 qui remporta un tel succès qu'elle lui en demanda un autre encore plus sexy pour son modèle de 1953. Entre-temps, il créa les incroyables calendriers pour Ridgid Tools en 1952 et 1953, rappelant à l'Amérique que la Petty Girl n'avait rien perdu de son mordant vingt ans après ses débuts dans *Esquire*.

Pourtant, Petty commençait à fatiguer. En 1954, Jule et lui s'installèrent à Scottsdale, en Arizona, où il prit officiellement sa retraite. *Esquire* lui commanda néanmoins un calendrier de 12 pages cette année-là, puis trois autres dépliants en 1956 et Ice Capades lui demanda d'illustrer à nouveau ses programmes de 1960 à 1964. Ce travail l'aida à surmonter sa douleur quand Jule mourut dans un accident de voiture en 1962. Mais Petty ne savait pas vivre seul. Il déménagea en Californie et se remaria, pour annuler le mariage un an plus tard et se marier à nouveau.

Il peignit sa dernière pin-up fin 1972 pour le 40ᵉ anniversaire du magazine. « La Petty Girl a 40 ans » parut dans le numéro de février 1973 et remporta un tel succès que Petty accepta une dernière commande en 1974. L'invitation pour le bal masqué annuel de son village de retraités prouve qu'il n'avait rien perdu de son talent. Sa dernière Petty Girl n'a rien à envier à ses sœurs de 1939.

George Petty mourut l'année suivante, le 21 juillet 1975.

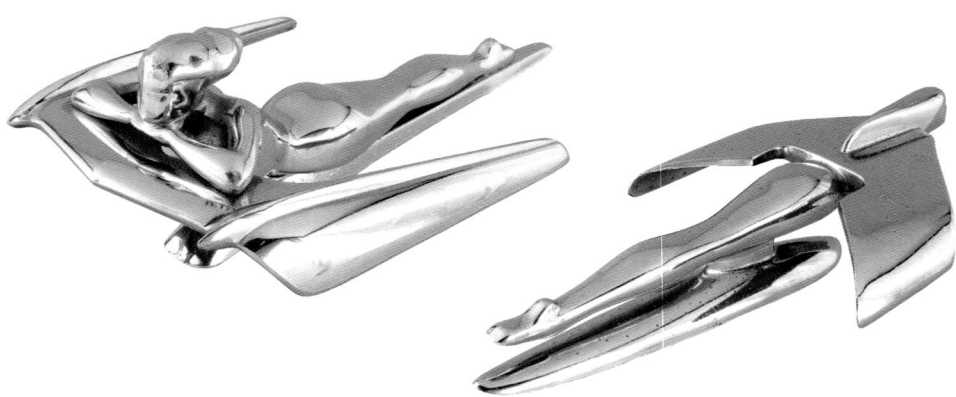

Above left: The 1951 Petty hood ornament proved so popular that Nash asked Petty to design a more anatomically detailed model for the 1954 Ambassador. Now a complete woman is represented, with full buttocks, arched back, chin resting on her hands, hair blowing in the wind. The breasts, however, are smaller and less obvious than on the 1951 model, which management pronounced too pronounced. 10.5 x 6.5 x 3 inches.

Above right: The Petty-designed 1951 Nash hood ornament. This first design, in chrome over metal, was available on the company's Ambassador and Statesman models. Though legs and breasts are clearly identifiable,

the head is represented by a sleek aerodynamic wedge, and the arms are replaced by wings. Nash advertised it as a blending of Petty Girl lines with their patented Airflyte styling. Measures 13.5 x 7 inches.

Opposite: "I will say it's her better half," watercolor on board, 1939, for the August 1939 issue of *Esquire* magazine.

Following spread: "Will you send up a dressmaker? The Bundles for Britain collector is here." Watercolor on paper, 1941, for the September 1941 *Esquire* foldout.

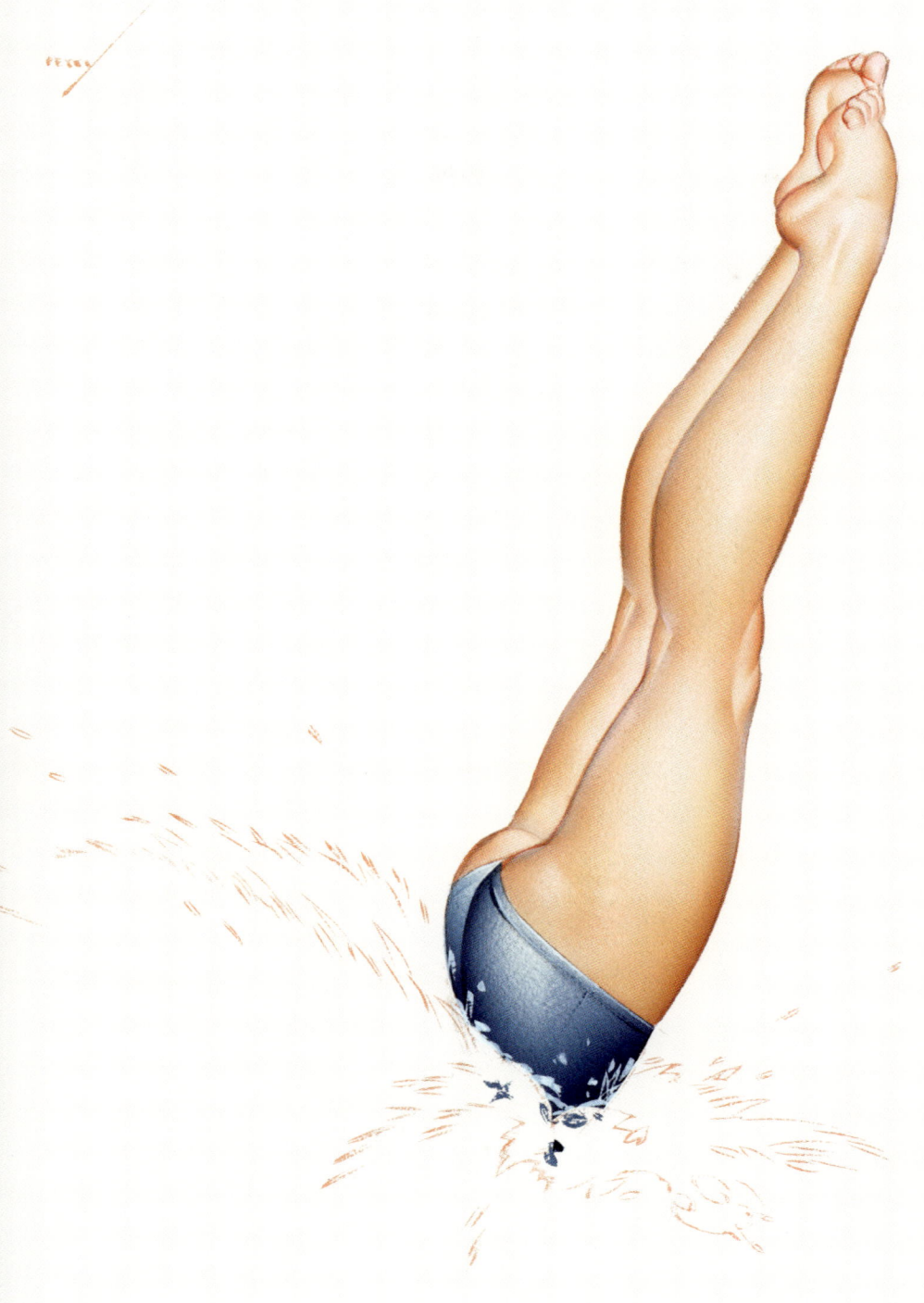

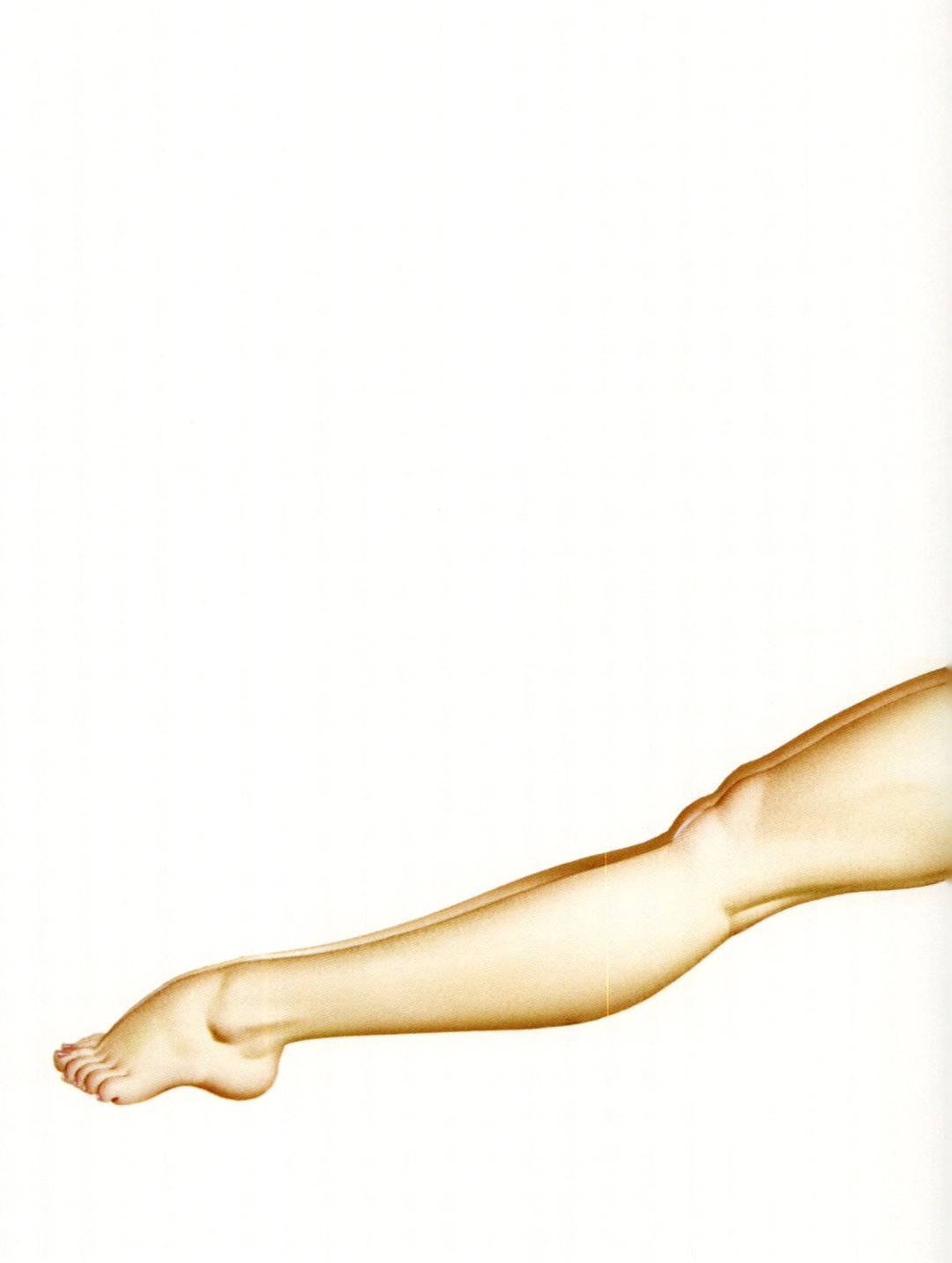

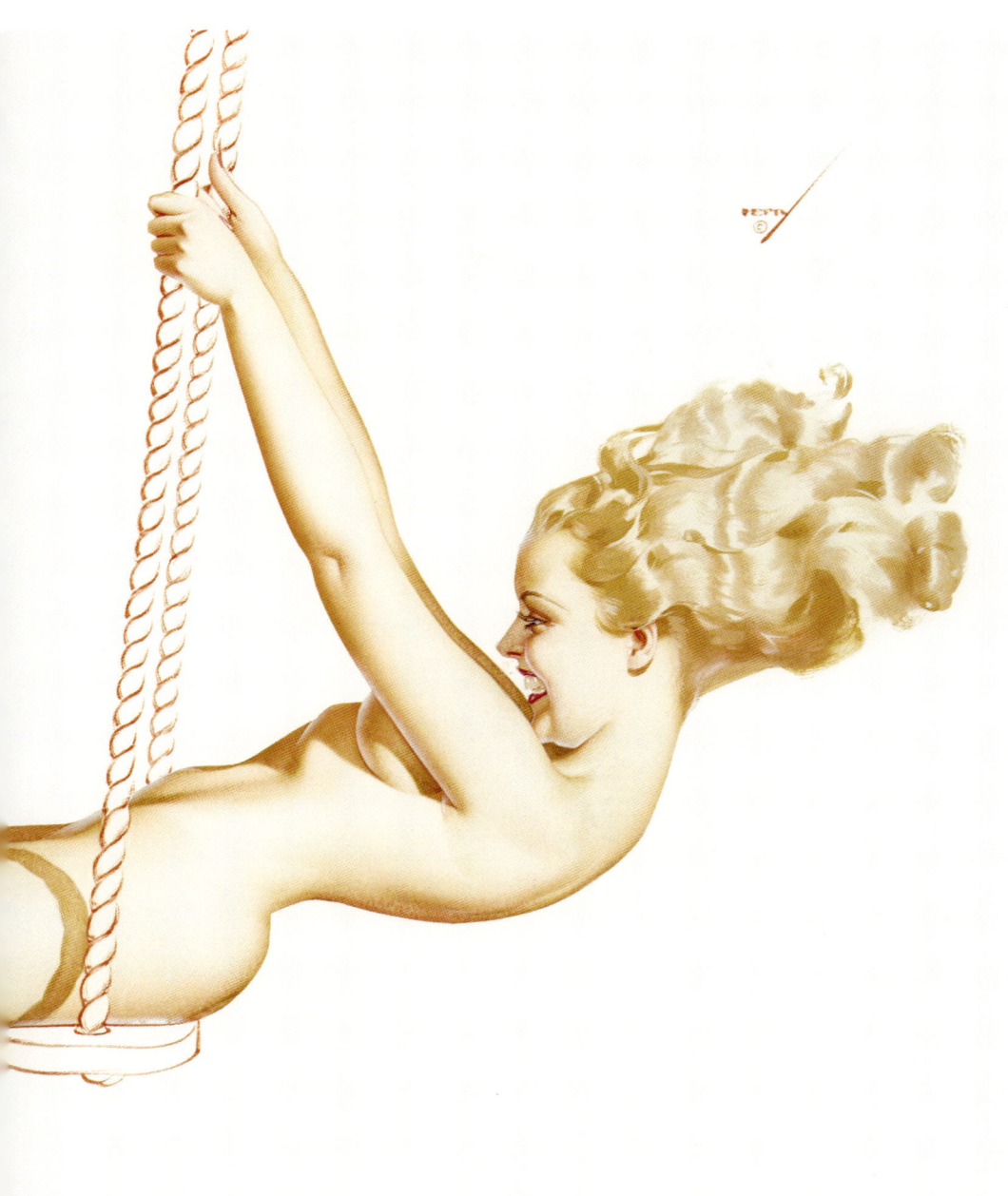

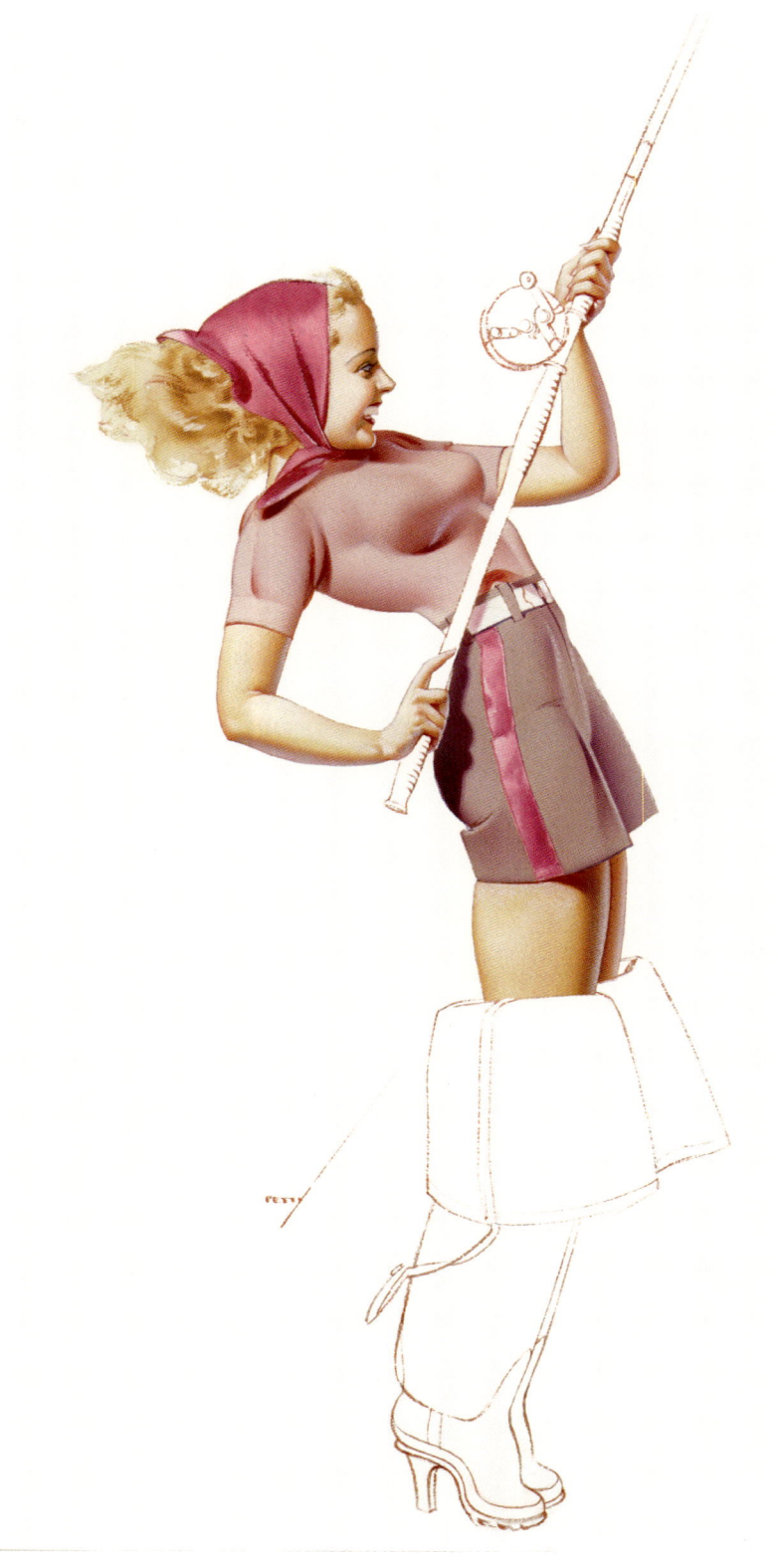

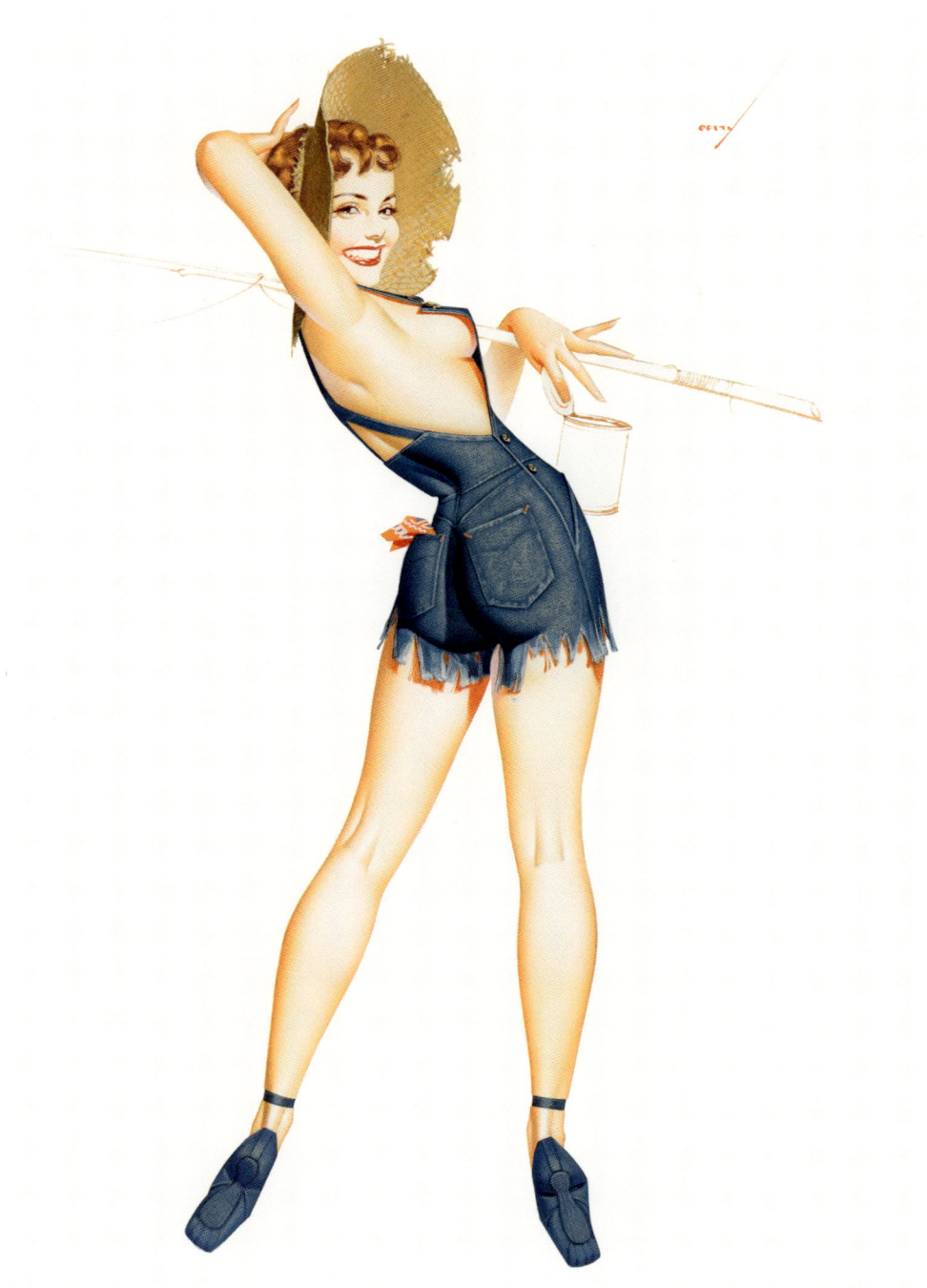

Opposite: Worth Hooking Up With!, watercolor on board, 1939, for an Old Gold cigarette ad. 22 x 13.75 inches.

Above: Mixed media on board, 1954, for the January 1955 issue of *Esquire*, and Miss June for the 12-page *1955 Esquire Girl Calendar*. 19 x 12.5 inches.

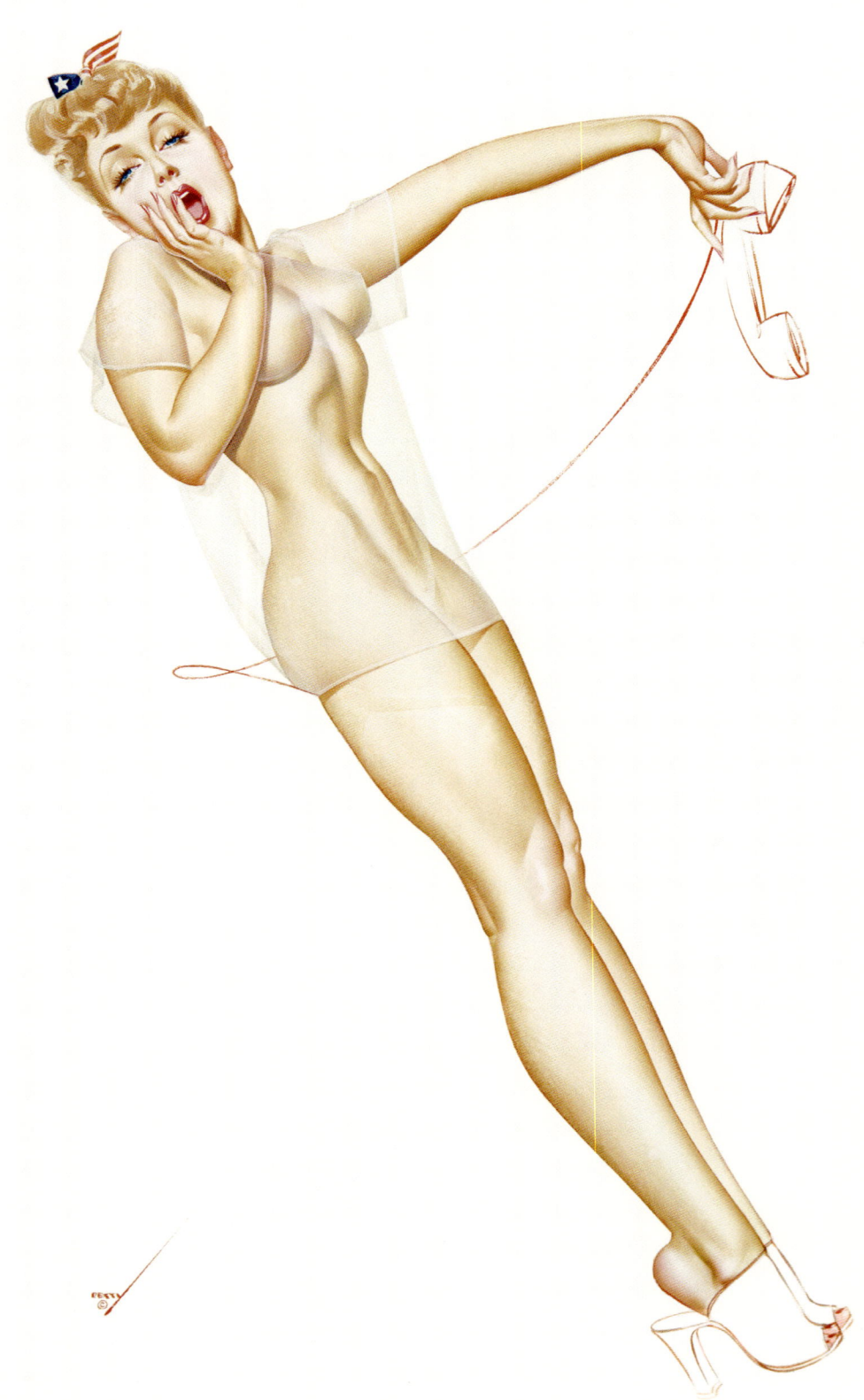

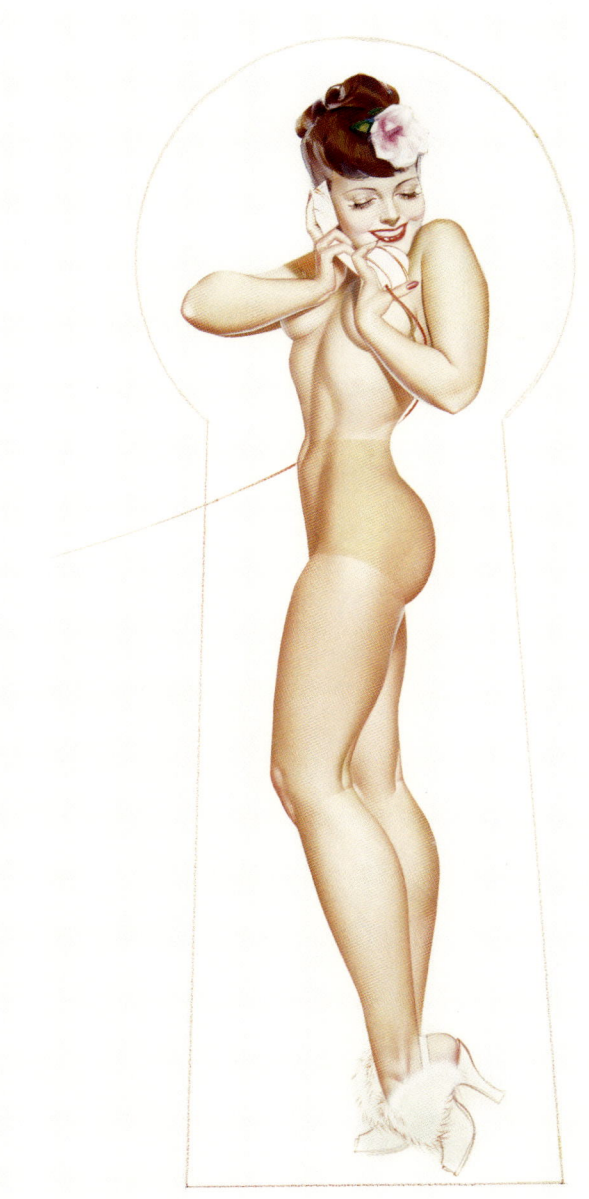

Opposite: *"Oh just another proposal from a boy whose number's up — "* watercolor on board for a 1941 *Esquire* foldout.

Above: Watercolor on board, circa 1940, for *Esquire* magazine. The image was given a new hairdo and

pink panties to appear in ads for Blue Swan's Petty Panty in 1942, one of many products that licensed the Petty name.

Following spread: Watercolor on board, 1944, for the March 1945 issue of *True* magazine.

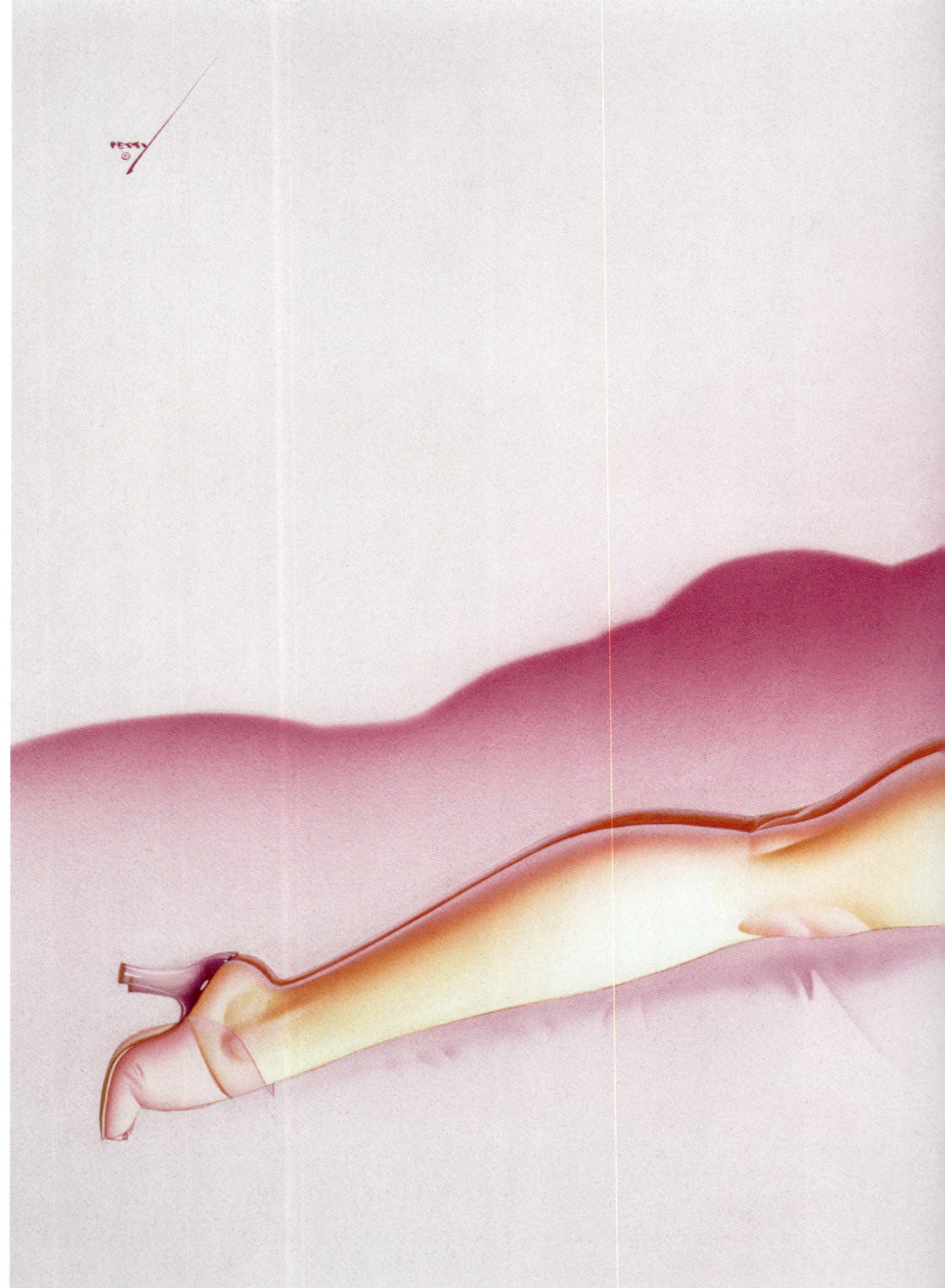

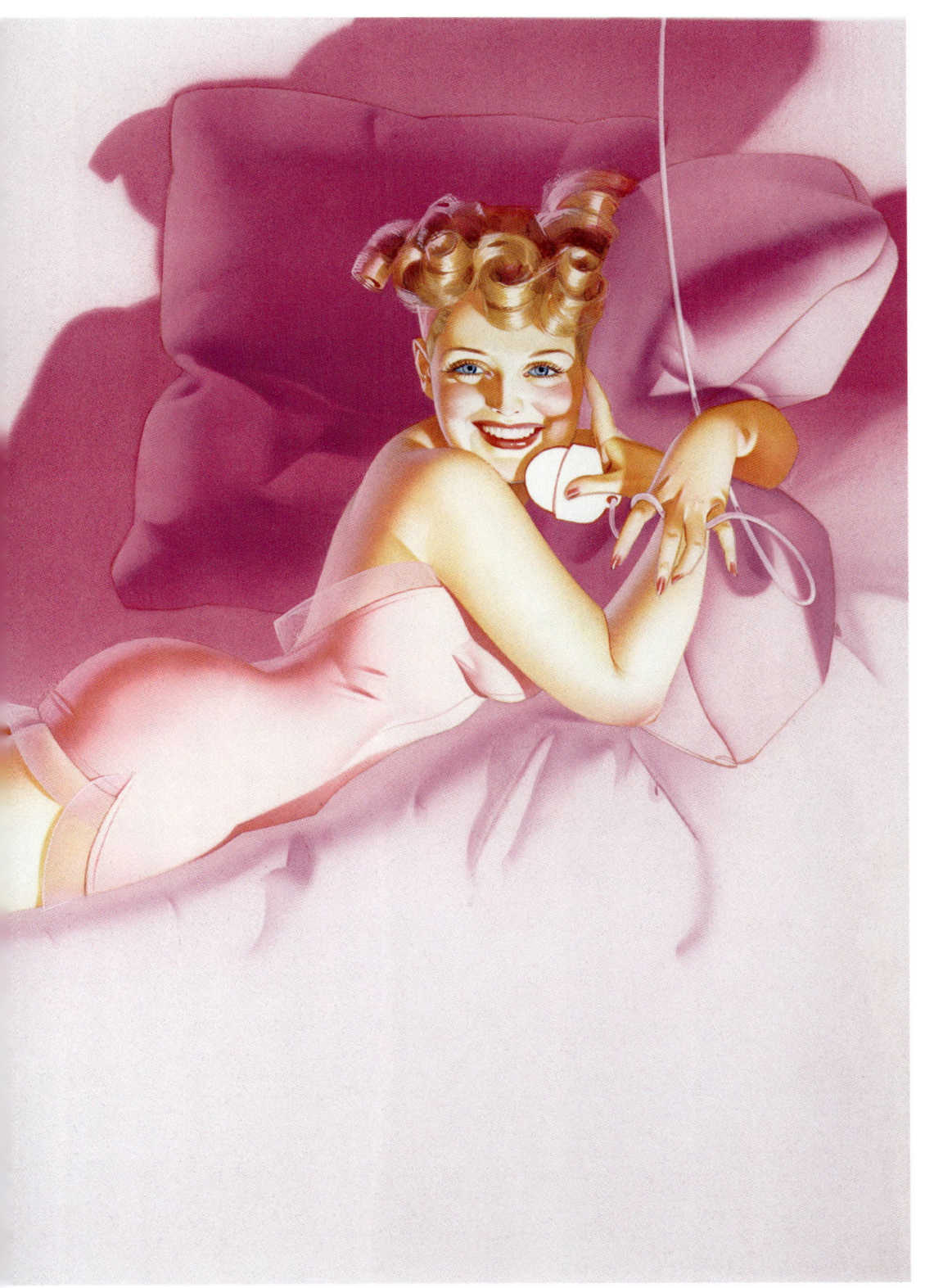

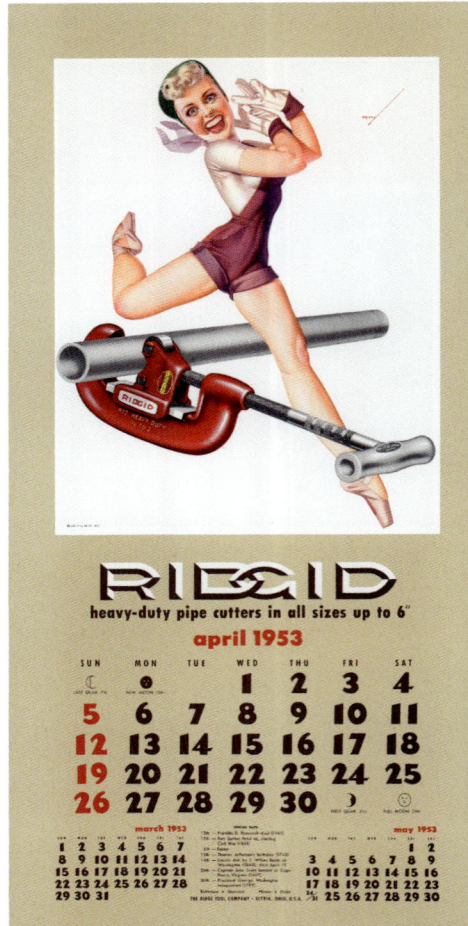

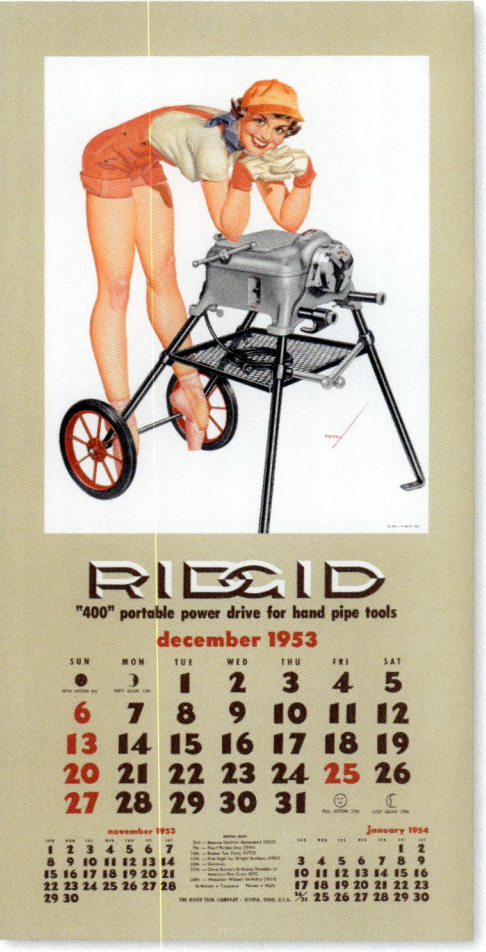

Above: The Ridge Tool Company of Elyria, Ohio, maker of RIDGID tools, released its first pin-up calendar in 1949, with images of girls fondling oversized tools by an artist identified as "West." For 1952 and '53 the company commissioned Petty to illustrate what would become two of the most collectible calendars of all time. The girls on the 1952 are mostly dressed in brief sundresses, while the 1953 girls are all in abbreviated overalls. After Petty the company released two more illustrated pin-up calendars,

one by Layne in 1955, and one by an unidentified artist in 1957, before switching to photo calendars. RIDGID discontinued its pin-up calendars in 2016, switching simply to artwork of big tools. Calendar measures 24 x 12.25 inches.

Opposite: Mixed media on board, 1951, for the 1952 RIDGID tools calender. The figure, in watercolor on paper, is pasted over the detailed rendering of sockets. 17 x 14 inches.

THE ART OF PIN-UP

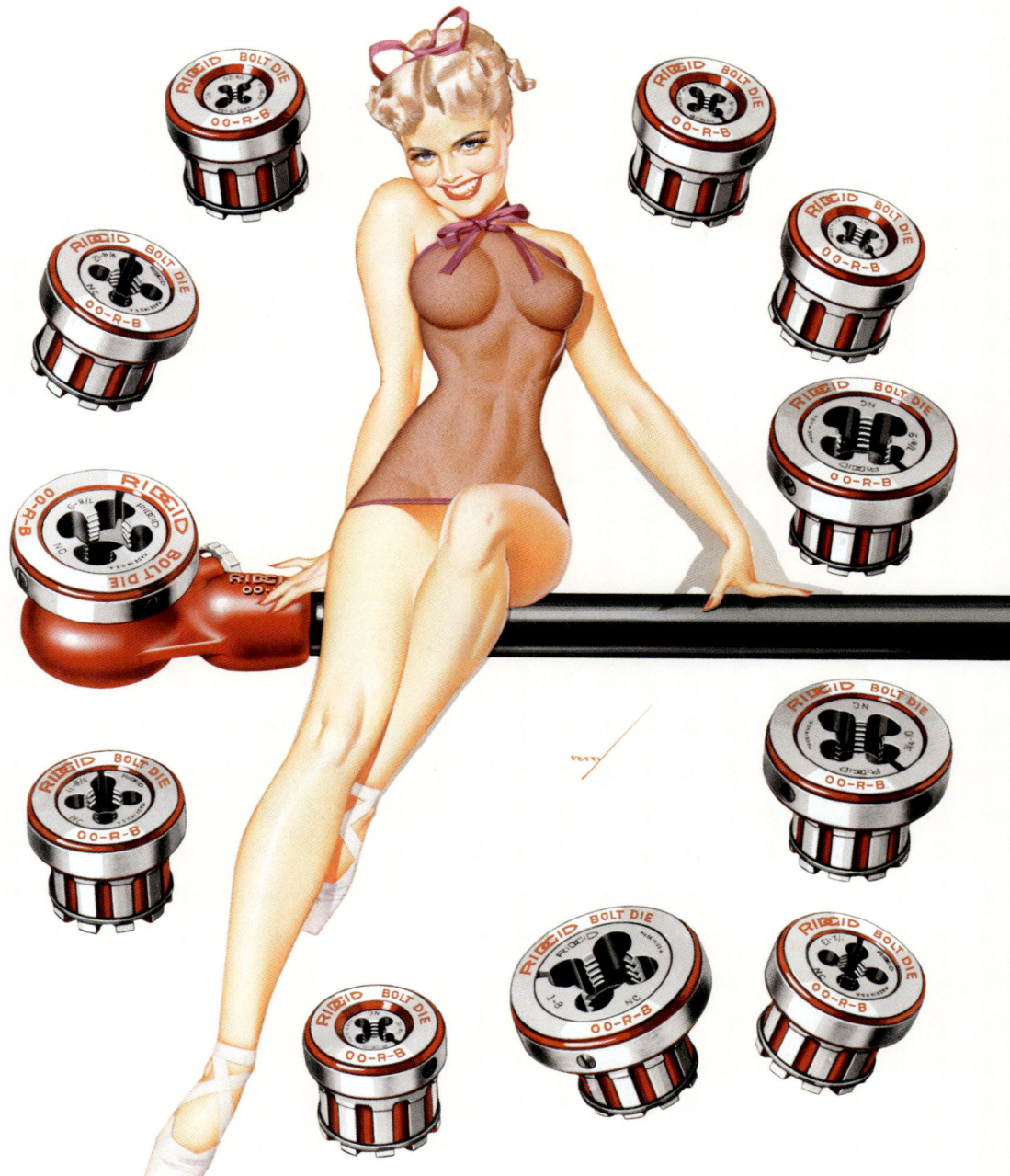

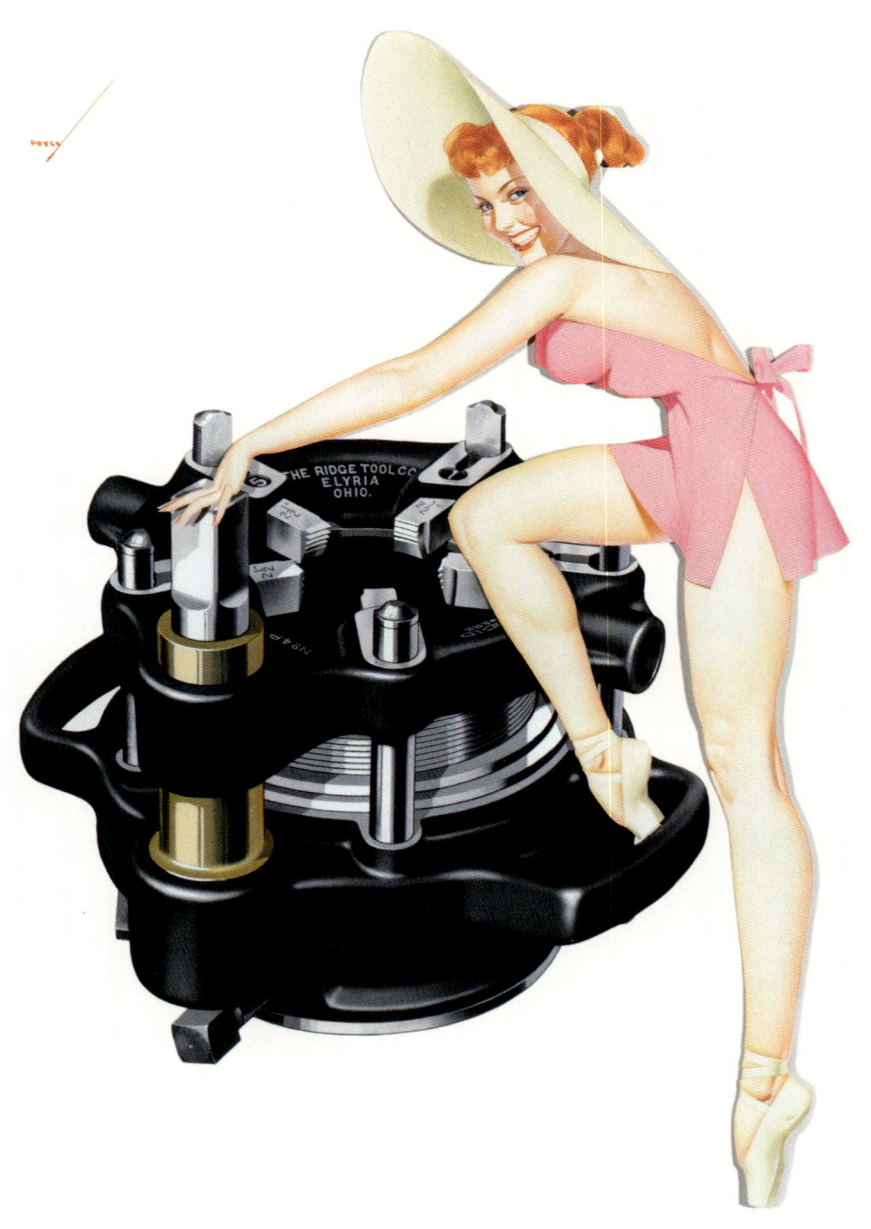

Above: Miss September, mixed media on board, 1951, for the 1952 RIDGID tools calendar.

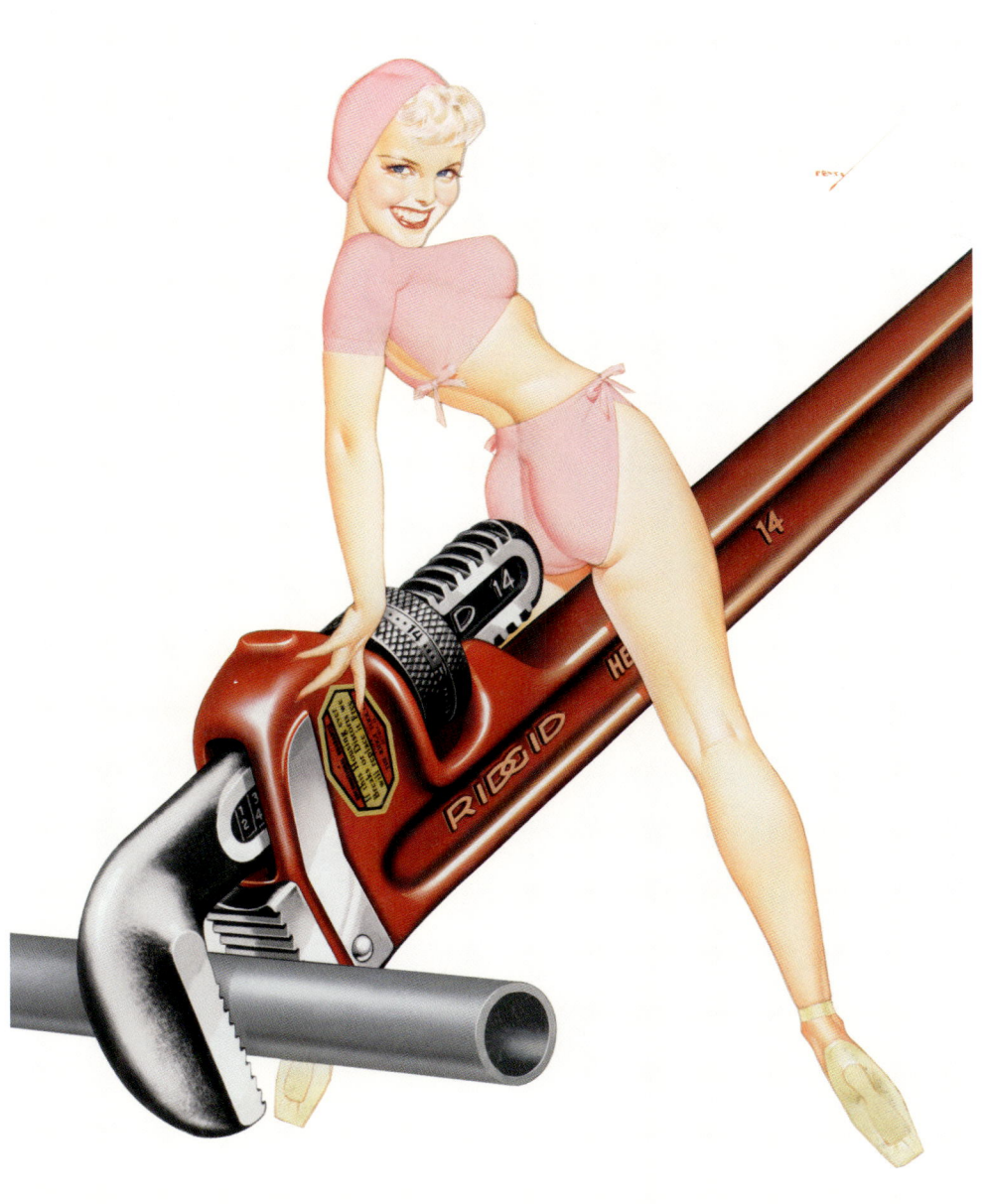

Above: Miss June, mixed media on board, 1951, for the 1952 RIDGID tools calendar.

GEORGE PETTY IV

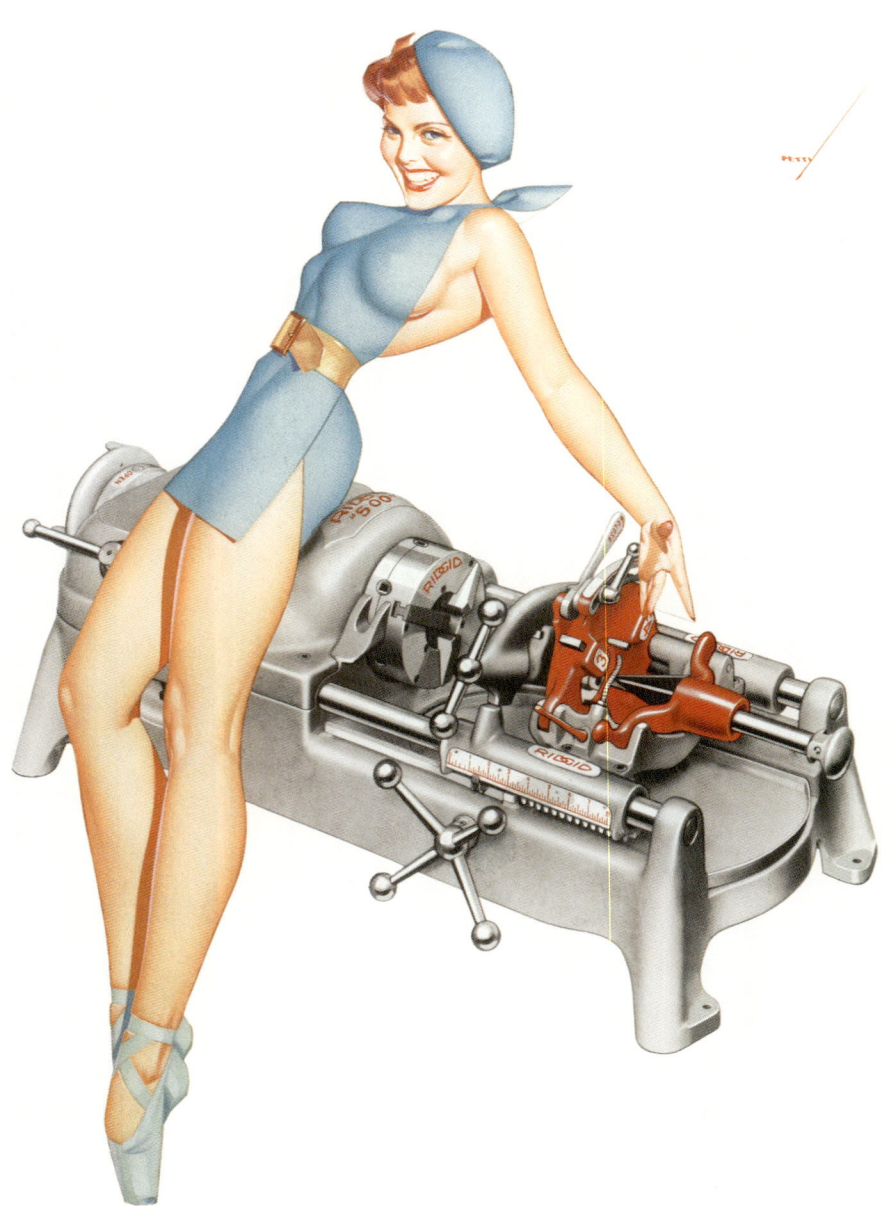

Above: Mixed media on board, 1951,
for the 1952 RIDGID tools calendar.

THE ART OF PIN-UP

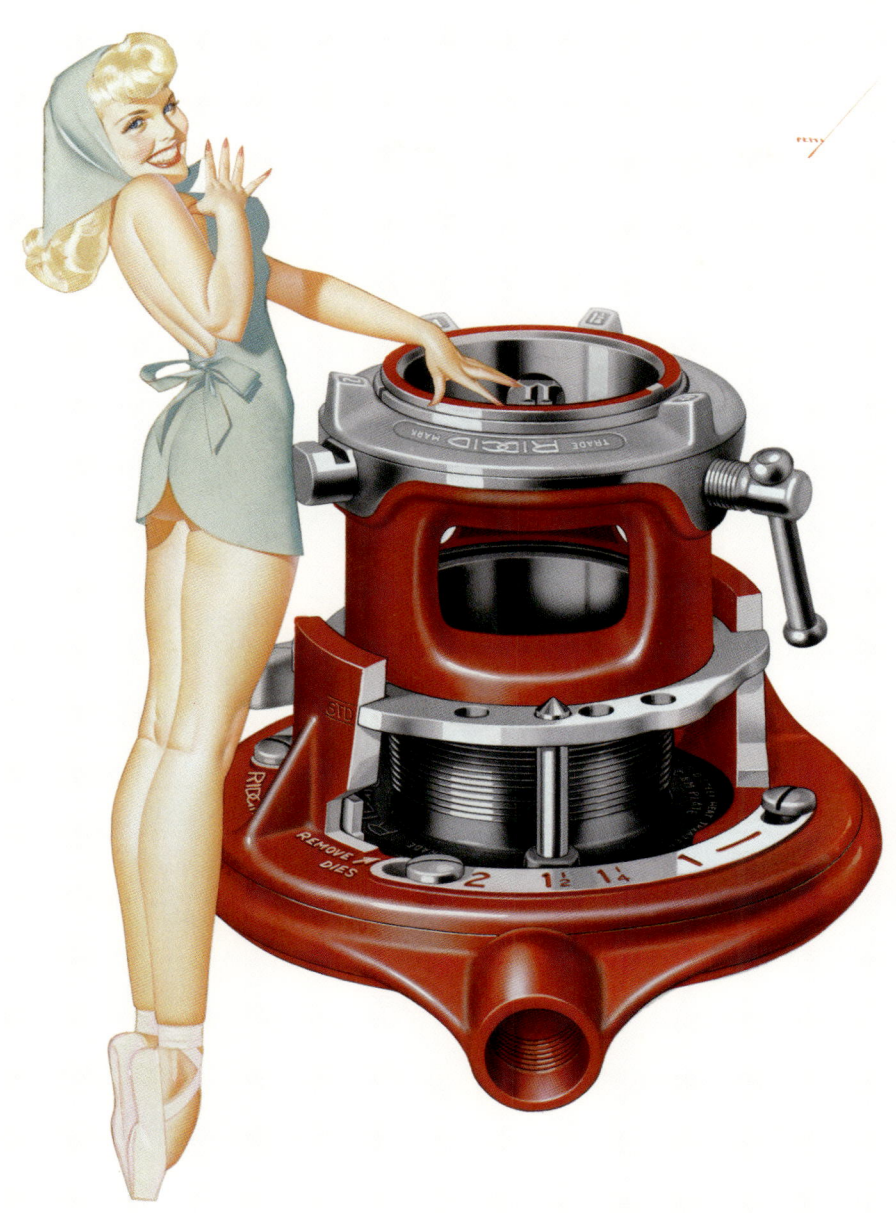

Above: Miss January, mixed media on board, 1951,
for the 1952 RIDGID tools calendar.

GEORGE PETTY IV

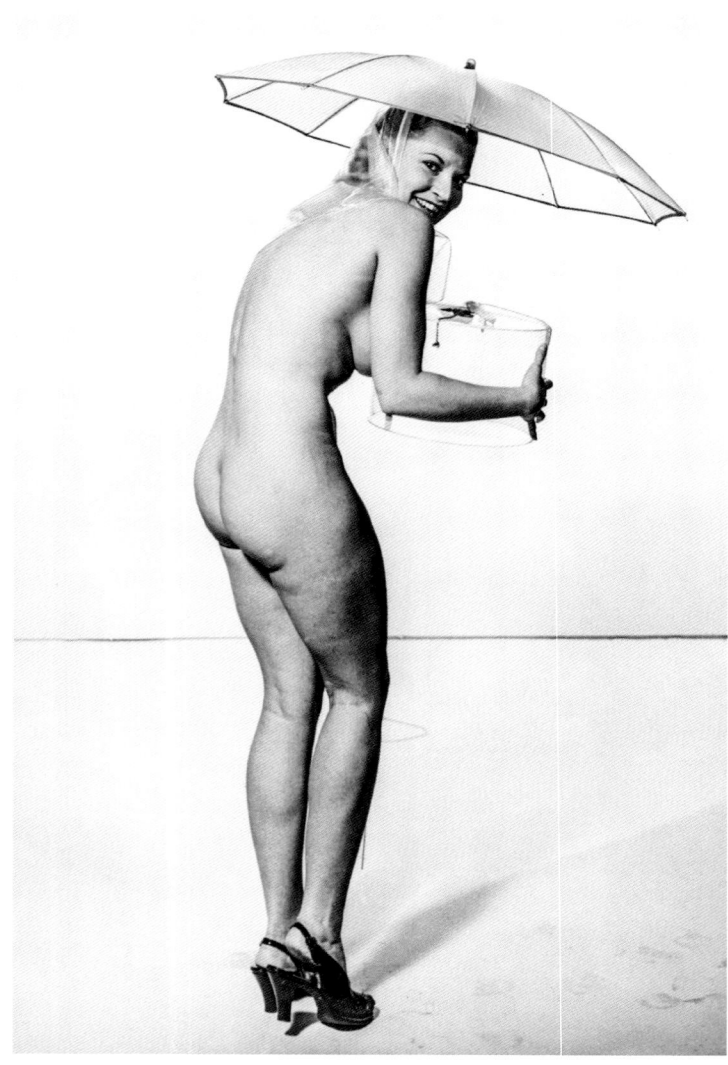

Above: Model posed for *April Showers* pin-up for the April 1946 issue of *True* magazine. Unlike most pin-up artists, who dressed their models in clothing approximating that in the finished work, Petty preferred to work from nudes and imagine the clothing.

Opposite: April Showers, watercolor on board, 1945, for the April 1946 issue of *True* magazine, and later reproduced as Miss April in the 1947 *True* calendar.

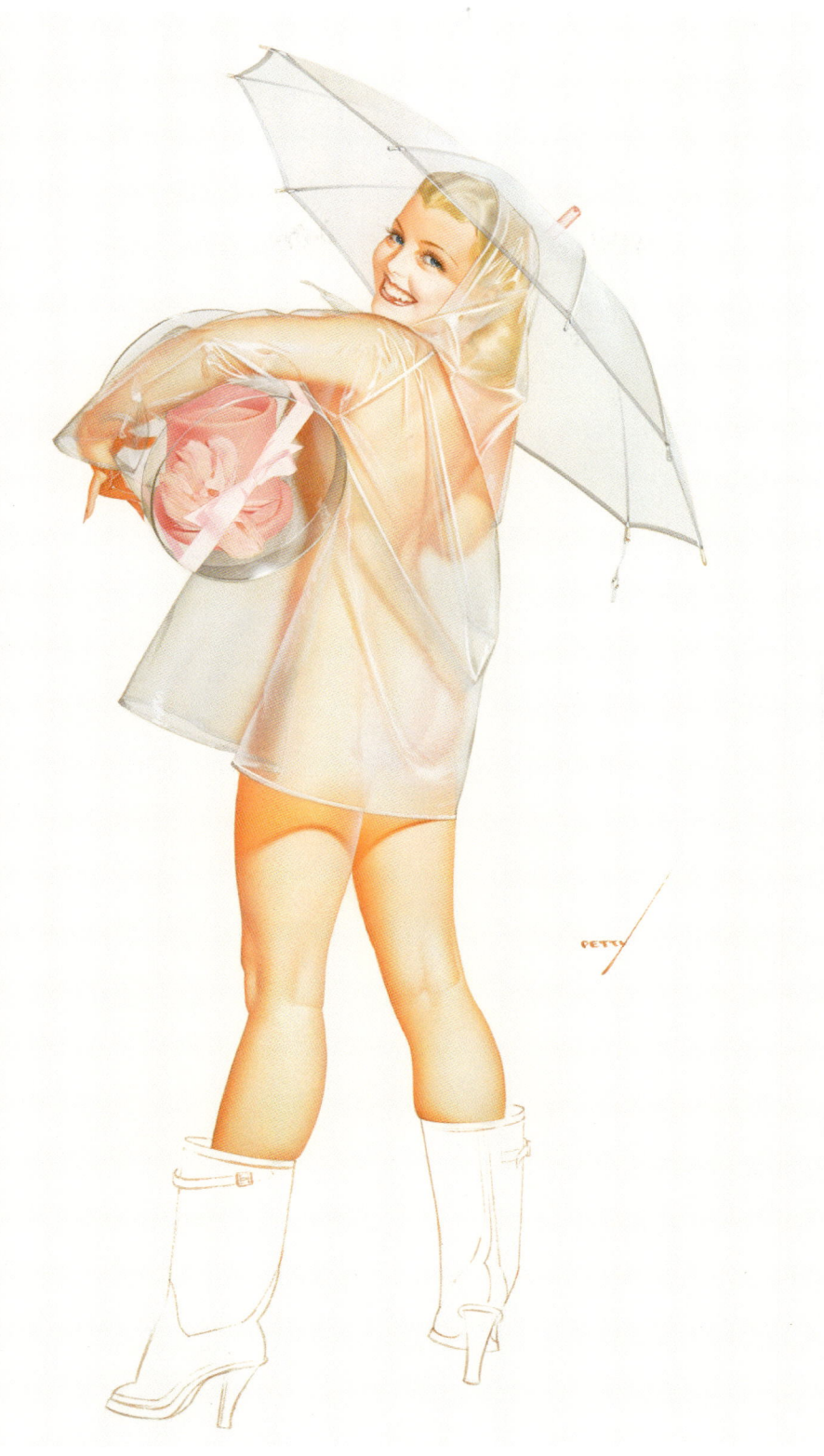

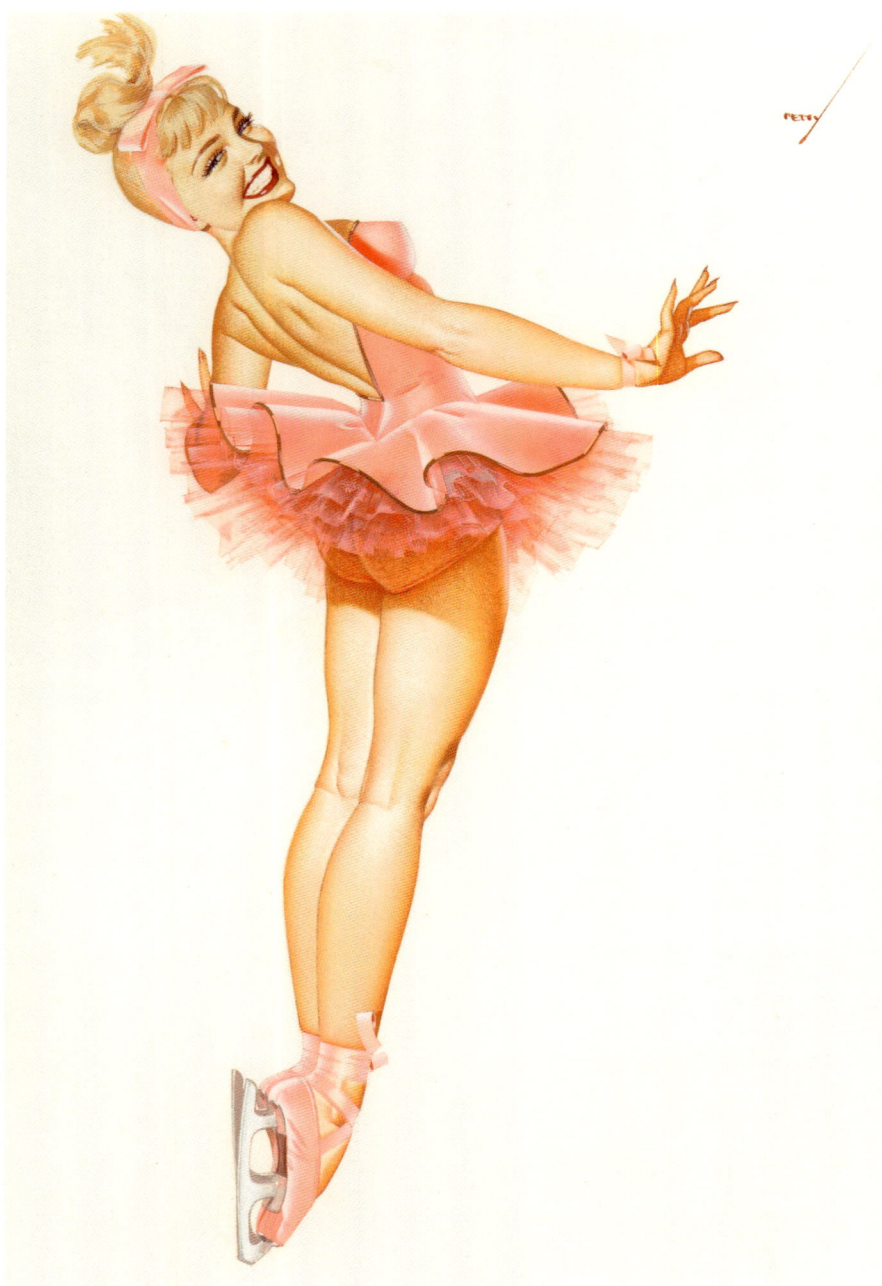

Above: Watercolor on paper for the 1962 Ice Capades program. 22.5 x 16.5 inches. Courtesy Heritage Auctions.

Opposite: Watercolor on board, 1964, created for the cover of the 1965 Ice Capade's program, but subsequently rejected. Petty was wounded and did no more covers for the ice dancing show.

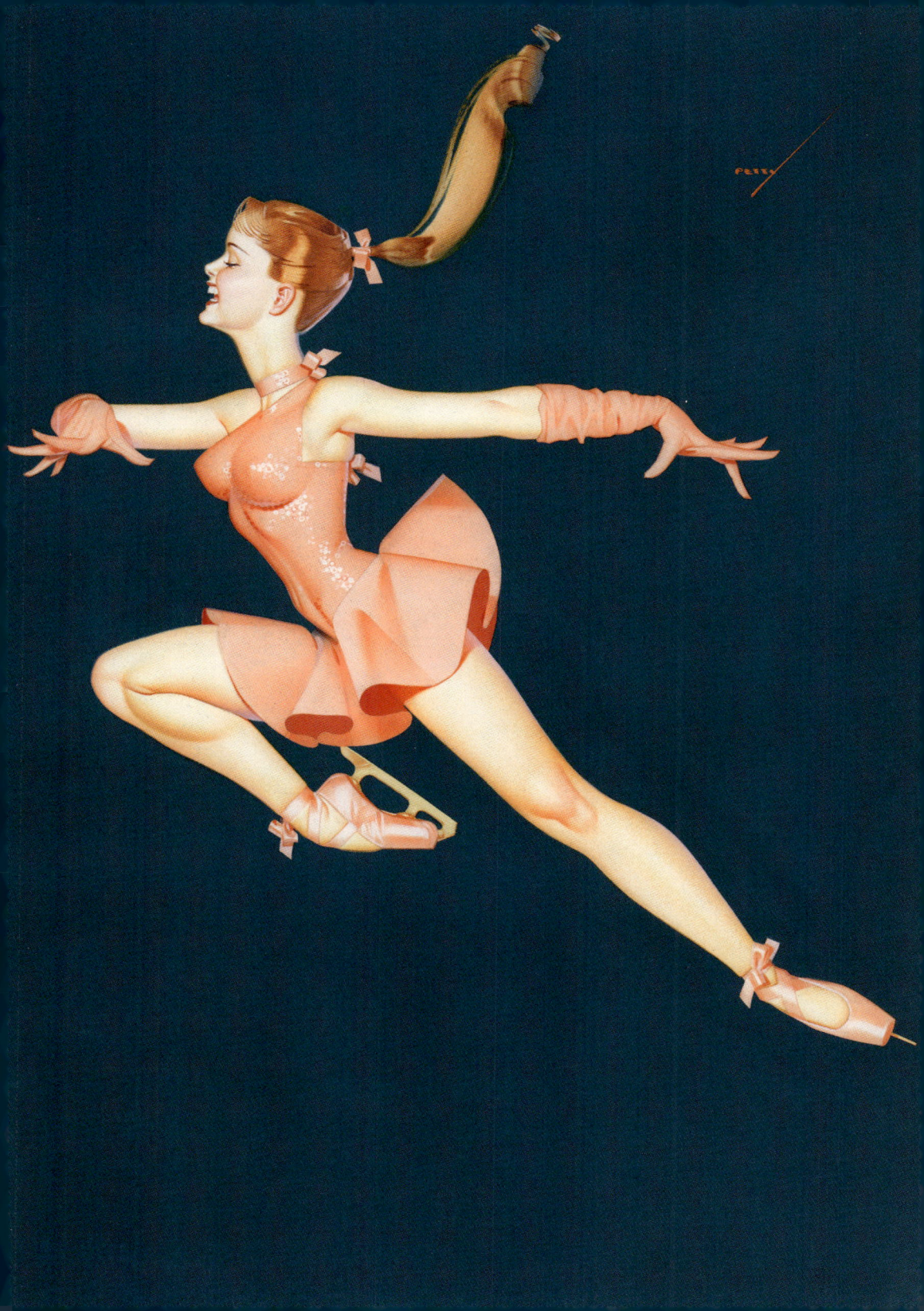

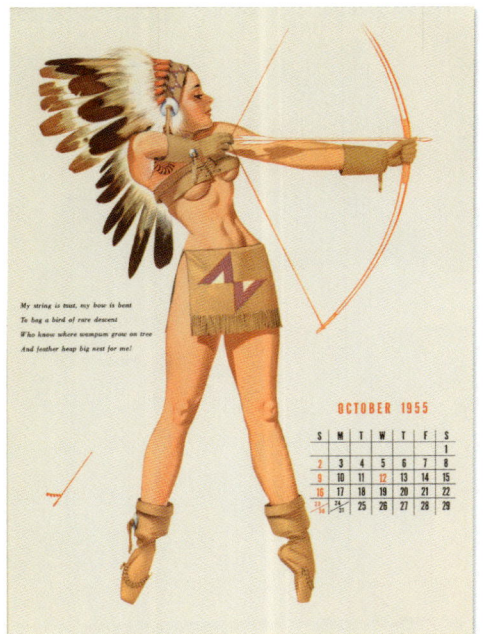

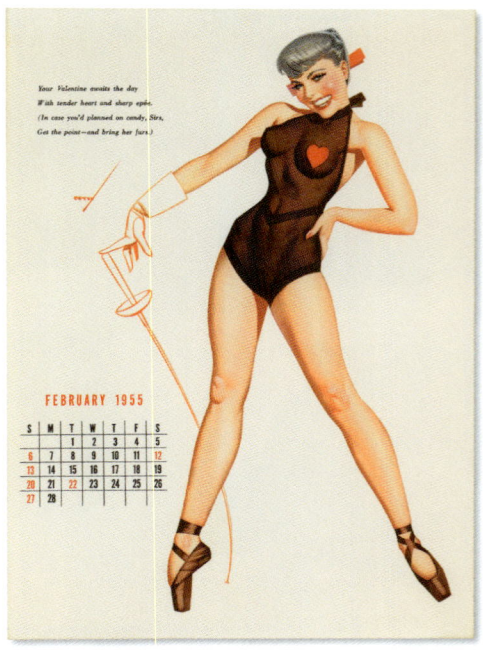

Above left: Miss October from the
1955 Esquire Girl Calendar proves that
even mocassins can be toe shoes.

Above right: Miss February from
the *1955 Esquire Girl Calendar*.

Opposite: Envelope for the *1955 Esquire Girl Calendar*.
With Petty gone 13 years from the magazine at this
point, and Vargas gone nine years, his return was
heralded with much nostalgia. Calendar measures
11 x 8.25. inches.

THE ART OF PIN-UP

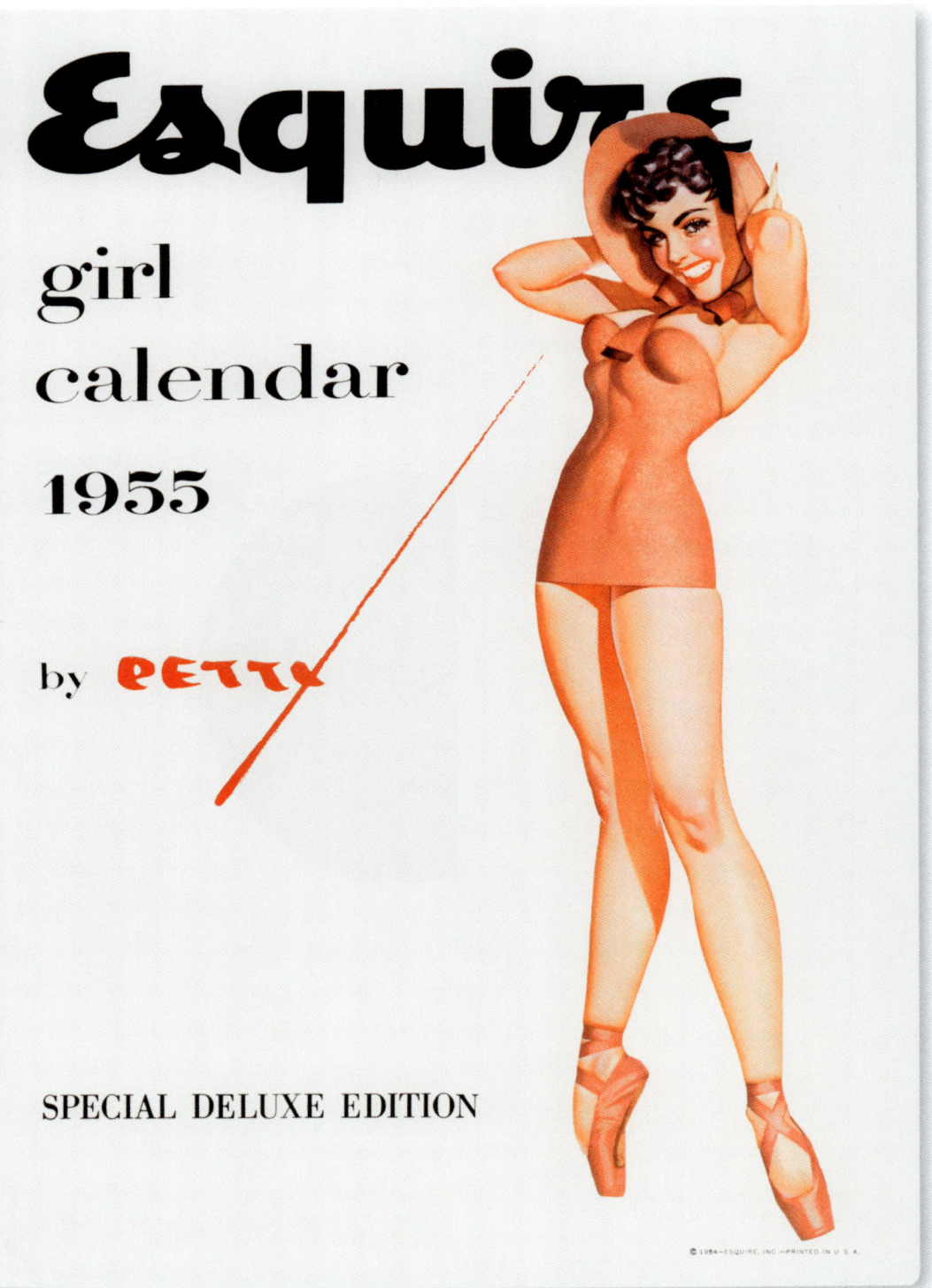

Esquire

girl

calendar

1955

by PETTY

SPECIAL DELUXE EDITION

© 1954—ESQUIRE, INC.—PRINTED IN U.S.A.

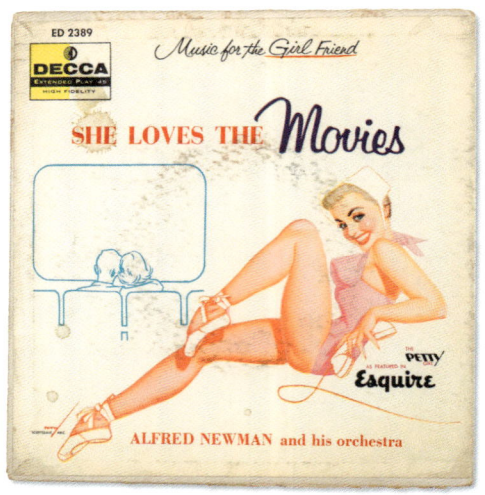

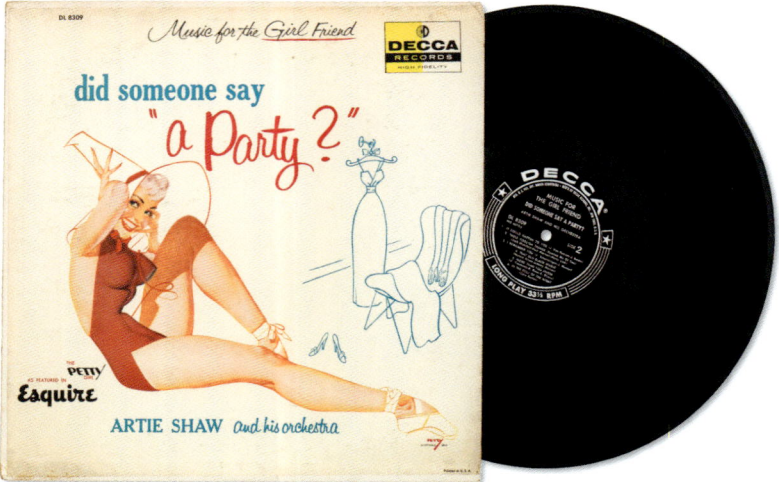

Top: Around 1958 Decca released a series of big band records, both extended-play 45 rpm singles and long-playing 33 rpms, with Petty pin-ups from the 1956 *Esquire* calendar on the covers. Four were designated Music for the Girl Friend and four Music for the Boy Friend, with *She Loves the Movies* and *did someone say "a Party?"* deemed for women, while *he likes to go dancing* and *He's a Cool Cat* were for men. The image shown here was Miss August on the 1956 calendar.

Above: *did someone say "a Party?"*, circa 1956, featured a Petty Girl on the cover and "Instrumental Fox Trots" by Artie Shaw and His Orchestra on the disc.

Opposite: Watercolor on board, 1954, for the January 1955 issue of *Esquire* and Miss May for the *1955 Esquire Girl Calendar*.

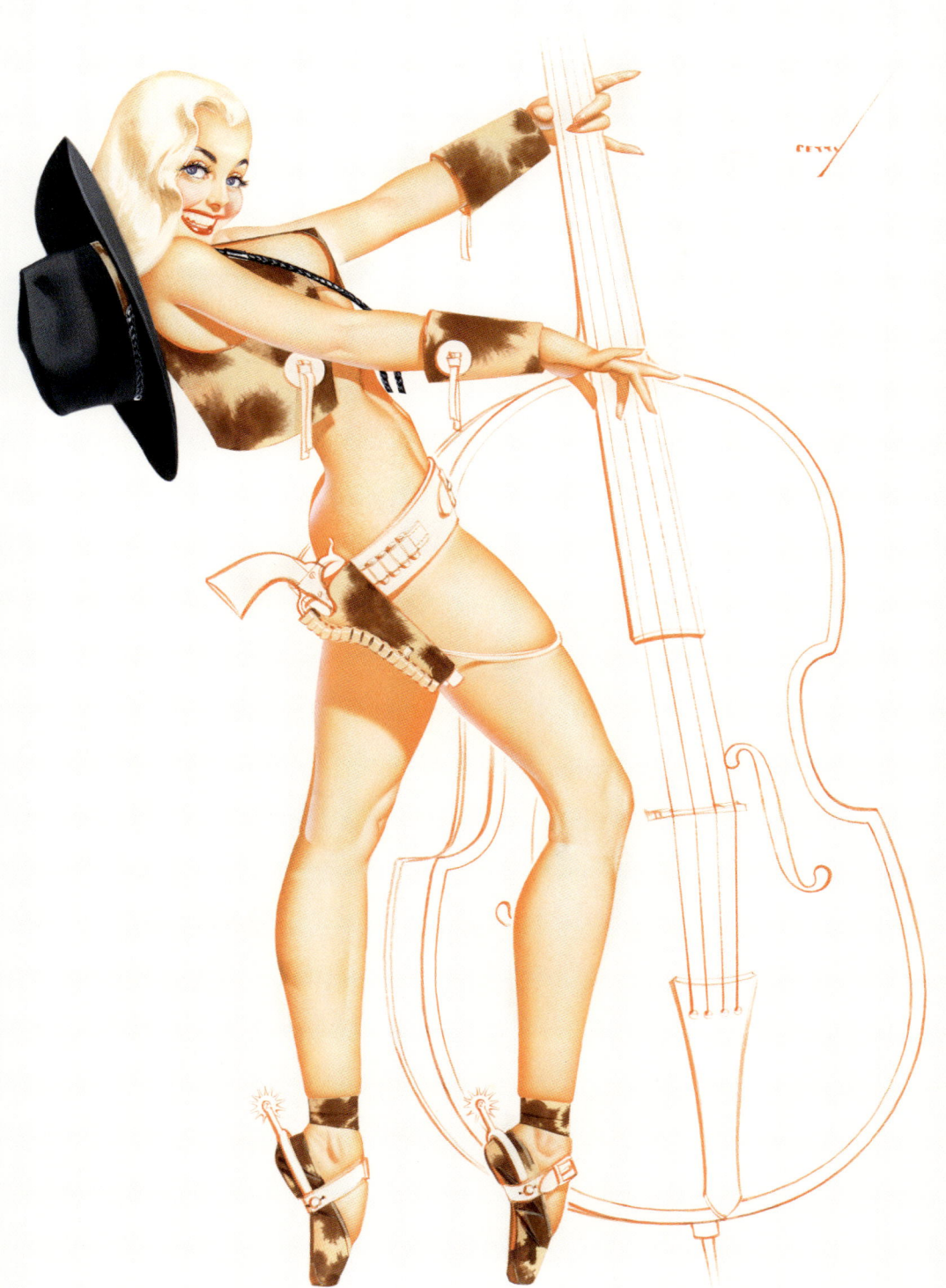

Below: Miss December, watercolor on board, 1955, for the *1956 Esquire Girl Calendar*. 15 x 13 inches.

Opposite: Watercolor on board, George Petty's final assignment: the invitation for his retirement community's annual dress ball in 1974. Petty, of course, omitted the dress and proved that even at 80 his hand was steady and his skill undiminished.

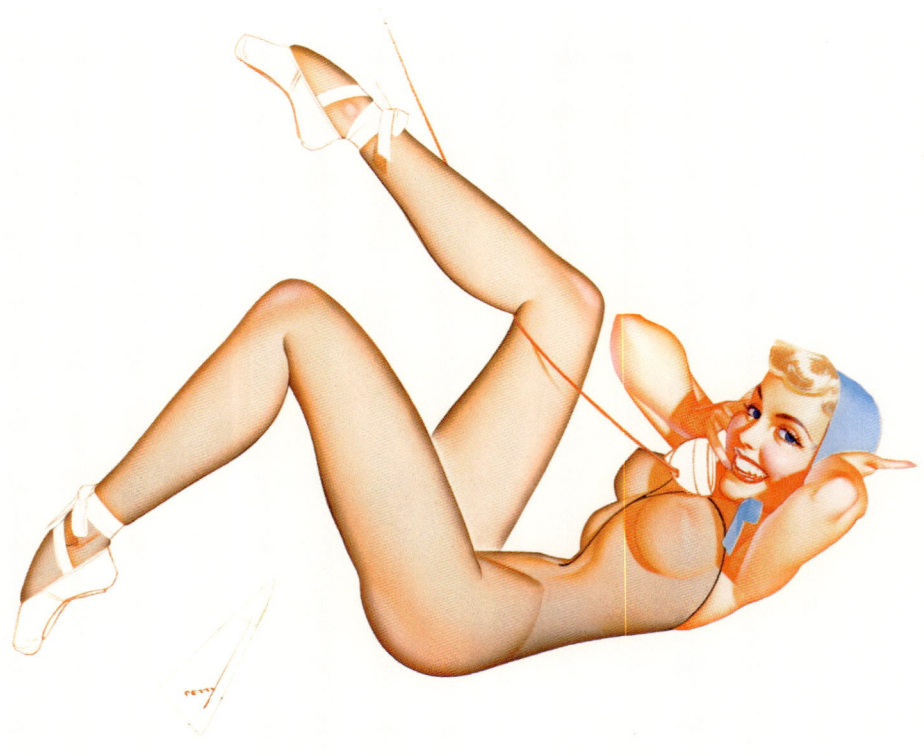

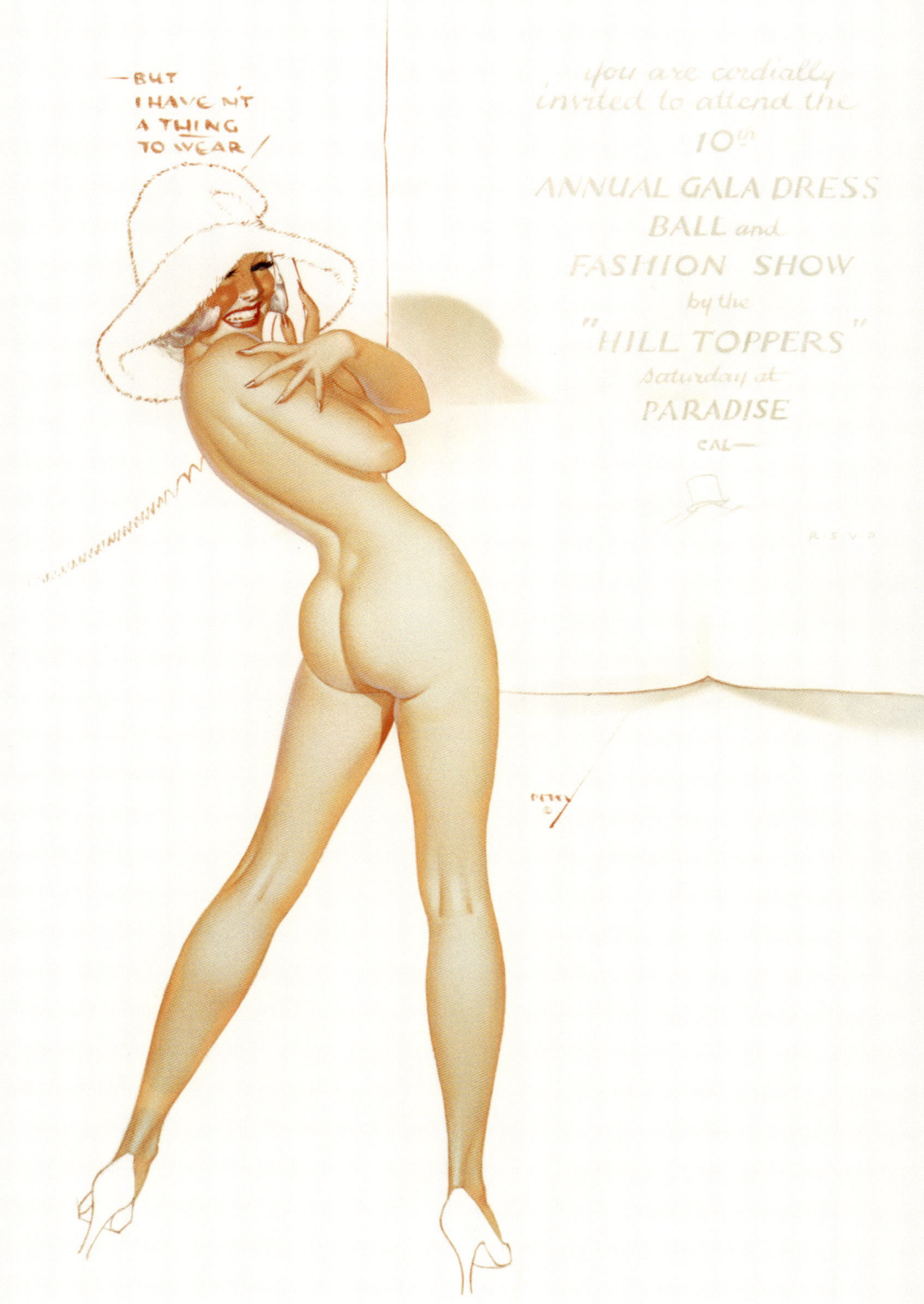

ALBERTO VARGAS

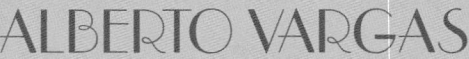

1896–1982

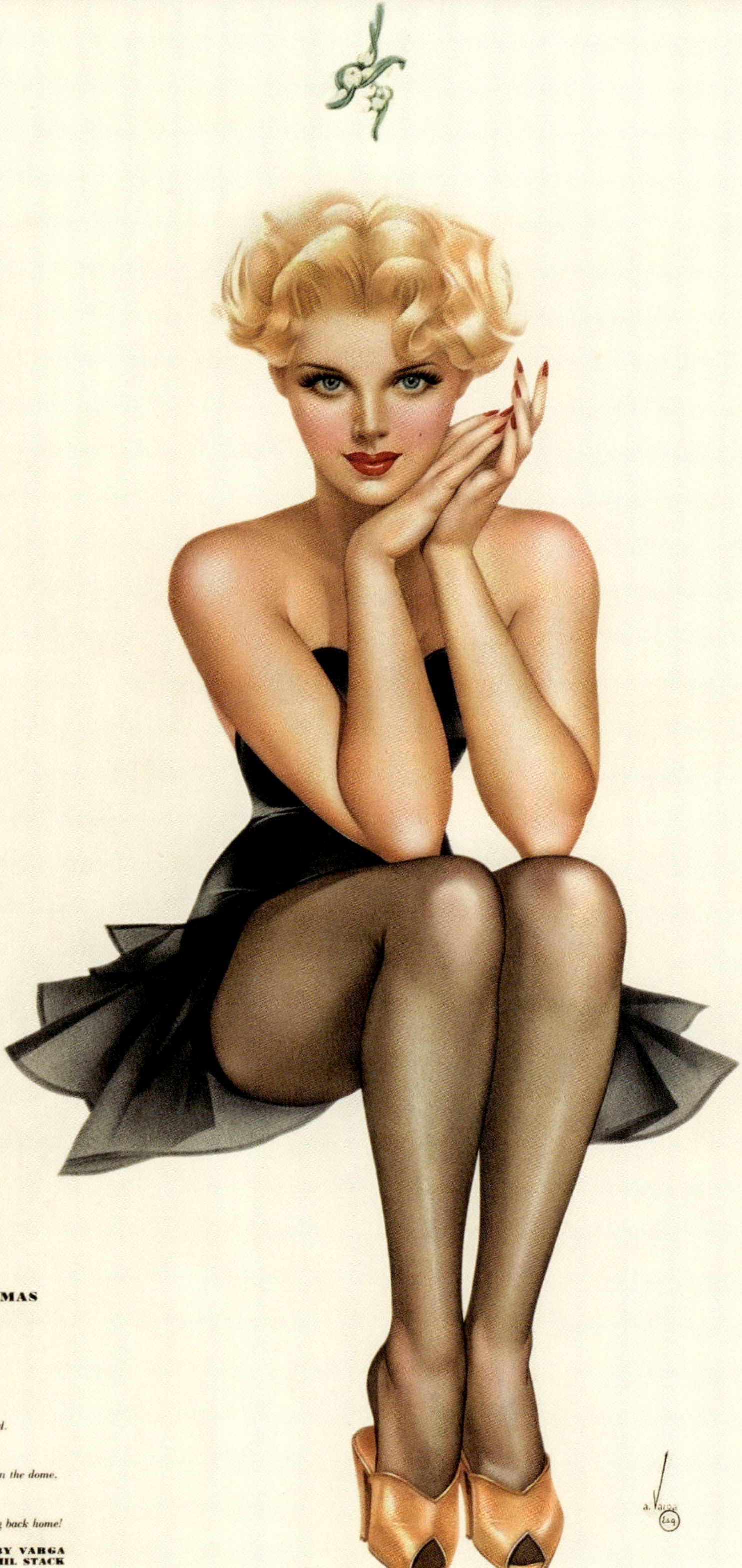

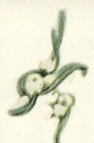

**MERRY CHRISTMAS
AND HOW!**

At this festive season
There's plenty of reason
  To get in a holiday mood.
Our enemies wither
They're all in a dither
  With plenty of reason to brood.
No wonder our guys
Were a constant surprise
  As they hammered the Hun on the dome,
For Fritz didn't know
That each Jack and each Joe
  Had a Christmas Eve waiting back home!

**PAINTING BY VARGA
VERSE BY PHIL STACK**

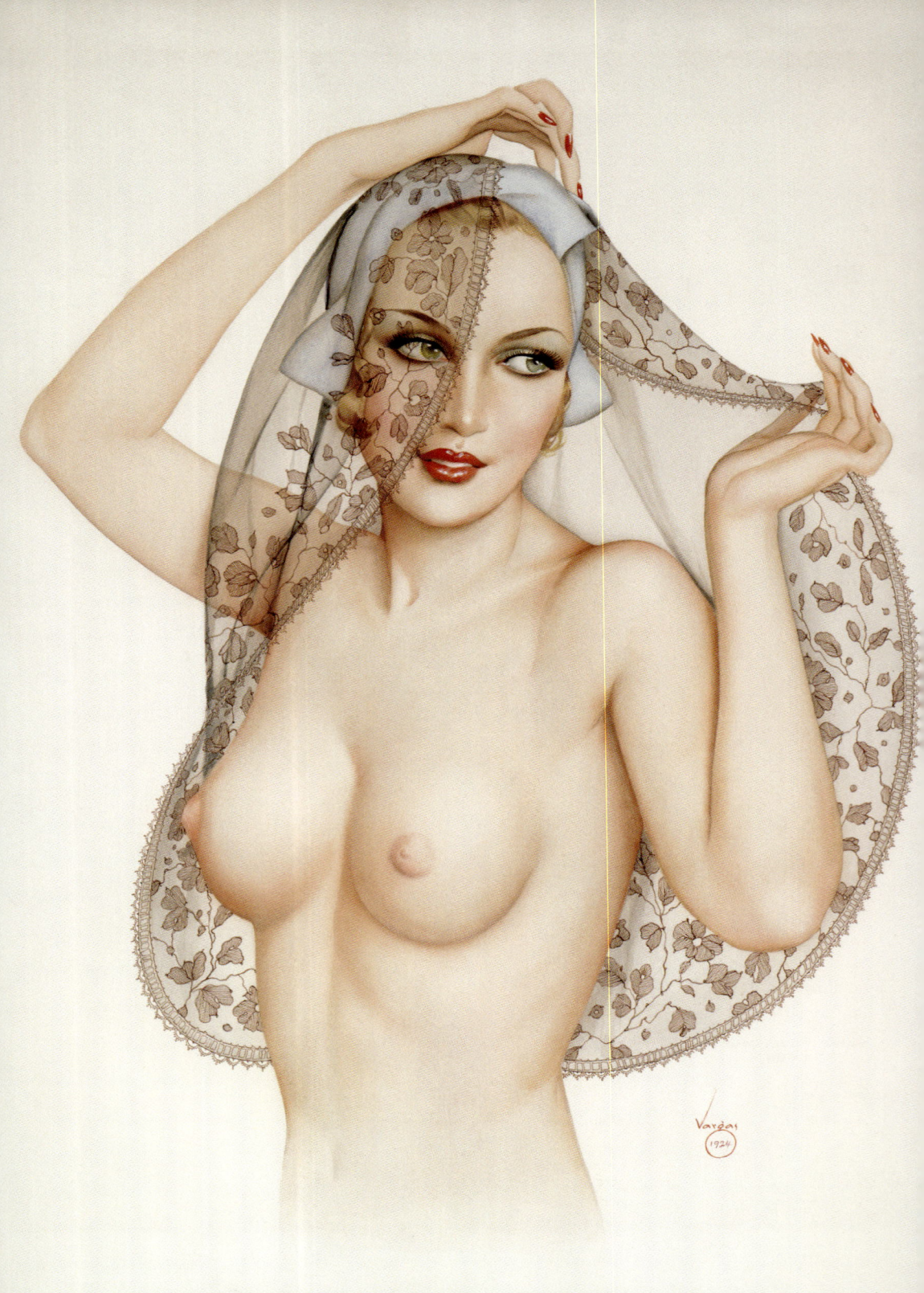

"Alberto Vargas's life was a love story. He loved his mother, he loved his wife, he loved women and he loved painting."

Though a visual artist, Alberto Vargas's life was a love story. He loved his mother, he loved his wife, he loved women, and he loved painting. Driven by this love, he captured the nuance, grace, and power of femininity for over 70 years.

The creator of the Varga Girl was born in Arequipa, Peru, on February 9, 1896, as Joaquin Alberto Vargas y Chávez. His father, Maximilian, was a successful photographer with studios in both Arequipa and La Paz, Bolivia, ensuring that Vargas and his six siblings grew up in a privileged environment. His mother, Margarita, made certain that her children received the finest educations. Vargas sketched from a young age and became skilled with the airbrush used for photo retouching in his father's studio, in much the same way as George Petty. He was a meticulous draftsman who experimented with oils and pastels before settling on watercolor as his medium of choice.

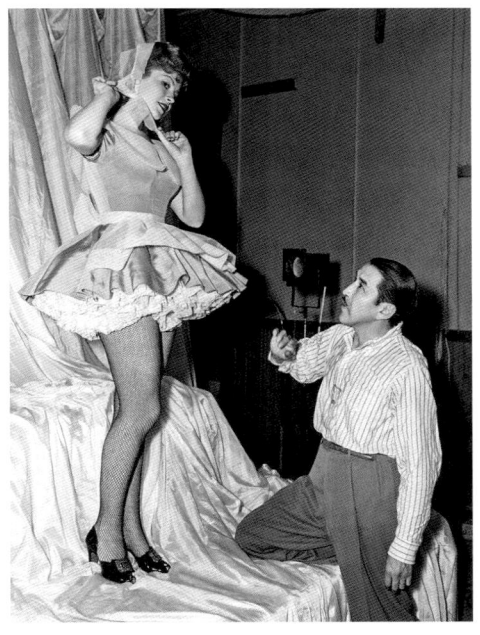

In 1911 Maximilian took his two sons to Paris, where Vargas studied art and photography, continuing his studies in Switzerland. In 1915, as war was escalating in Europe, both sons were urged by their father to leave for the United States. They arrived in New York City that same year.

During those first days in New York, Vargas was introduced to the American girl. As he walked through Union Square during lunch hour, young women came pouring out of offices and shops. "My mouth fell open and I couldn't close it again!" he said years later. "From every building came torrents of girls. Hundreds of girls with an air of self-assuredness and determination that said: 'Here I am, how do you like me?' I knew then I was not going home."

Page 443: The December 1944 Varga Girl pin-up from *Esquire* magazine.

Opposite: The Veil, watercolor on board, circa 1930. The date of 1924 was added later, and incorrectly, to this originally undated piece. The Max Vargas Collection.

Above: Alberto Vargas was invited to direct production stills of a dance number for the 1943 MGM film *Du Barry Was a Lady,* based on his *Esquire* pin-ups. Here he gives tips to "Miss November" Mary Jane French.

Vargas landed a job with a department store on 42nd Street painting portraits of live models in the store's large display window. One day the manager of the Ziegfeld Follies invited himself into the display window and said he might have a job for him. Vargas was hired to paint 12 large portraits of Ziegfeld's new stars and offered $200 per painting, launching a 12-year relationship with Ziegfeld, who provided a studio and instructed all of his stars to sit for the artist.

During this time Vargas became smitten by a young woman he "discovered" on the stage of the Greenwich Village Follies. Her name was Anna Mae Clift, from Soddy-Daisy, Tennessee. She

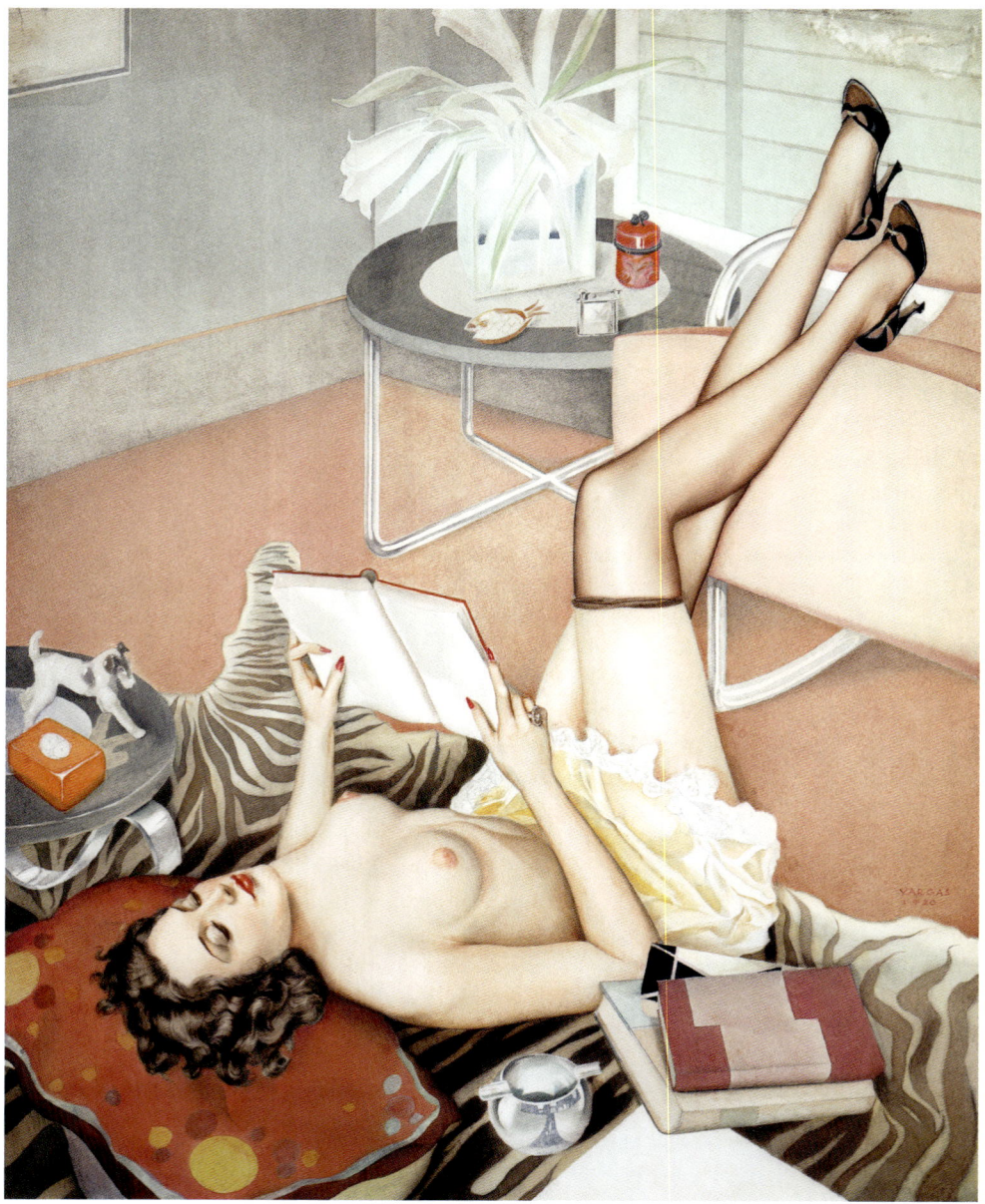

agreed to pose for him, and after that Anna Mae was his single emotional focus and favorite model. They married after a courtship of several years.

With the stock market crash of 1929, the Follies fell on hard times. Vargas was out of work. He picked up magazine illustration jobs, as well as ad assignments from various Hollywood studios. Based on the quality of this ad work, 20t Century-Fox invited him to Hollywood. With the help of Anna Mae's friend Busby Berkeley, he got set design work at Paramount and Warner Brothers, as well as Fox, and the Vargases bought their first and only home, a small bungalow in the Westwood neighborhood of Los Angeles. Marlene Dietrich, Alice Fay, Carole Lombard, and Greta Garbo were among those who sat for him in Hollywood, as well as Barbara Stanwyck, immortalized by Vargas in a poster for the 1933 film *Ladies They Talk About*.

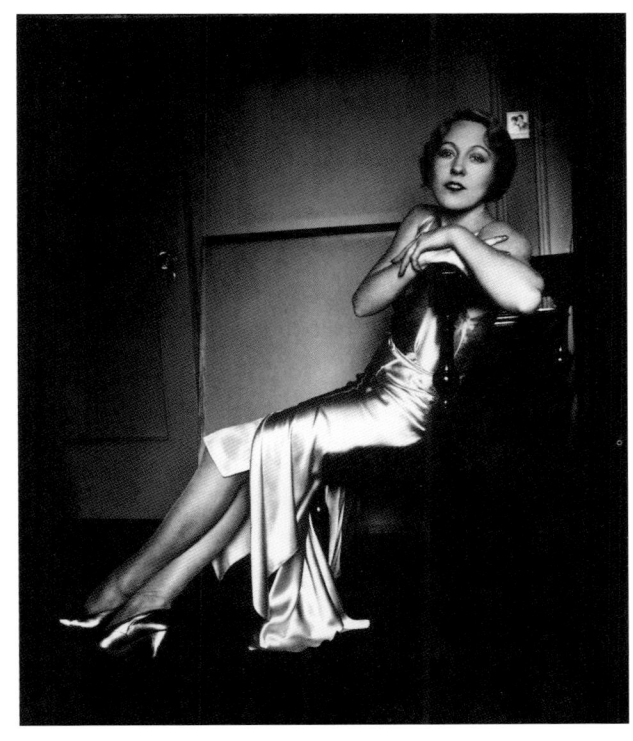

That same year *Esquire* magazine and the Petty Girl debuted.

In 1939 Vargas joined a unionized studio walkout. He was branded a communist and black-balled by the studios, so he returned alone to New York looking for work. A friend urged him to show his work to *Esquire*, where publisher David Smart was impressed with his ability—and his desperation. Petty had become increasingly difficult, demanding $1,000 per painting. Vargas offered an escape, and at only $75 a week. A three-year contract was drawn up. The Petty Girl would be replaced by the Varga Girl—removing the "s" from "Vargas," Smart insisted, made the name "more euphonious." The change seemed innocuous, but the consequences would be profound.

The first Varga Girl appeared in the October 1940 issue and was quickly embraced by readers. Vargas would later say his time with *Esquire* was both the best and the worst of his career. The first two years were the best. He had a stable income, and producing a new Varga Girl each month, along with 12 paintings a year for the *Varga Girl Calendar*, refined his skills. His first calendar, in 1941, outsold all others worldwide, and his fame soared.

When the United States entered the war, the Varga Girl was pinned up, copied, or otherwise attached near battleship bunks, in army barracks, on submarine walls, and painted on pilots' jackets

Opposite: Watercolor on board, 1920. The Max Vargas Collection.

Above: Anna Mae Vargas, nee Clift, of Soddy-Daisy, Tennessee, Greenwich Village Follies dancer, Vargas model, and the love of Vargas's life from 1919 until her death in 1974. Circa 1925.

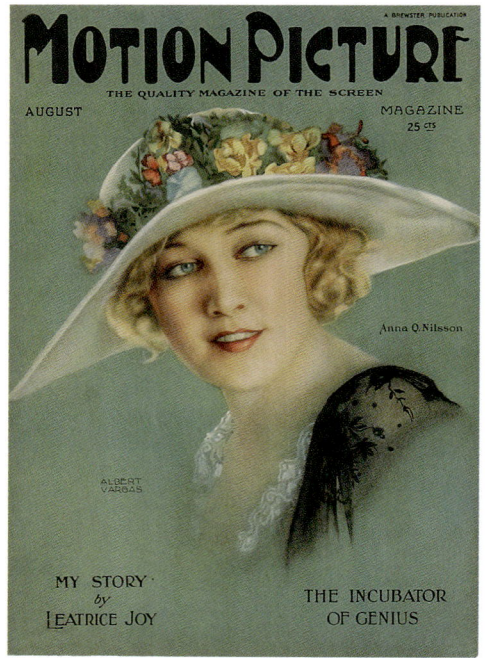

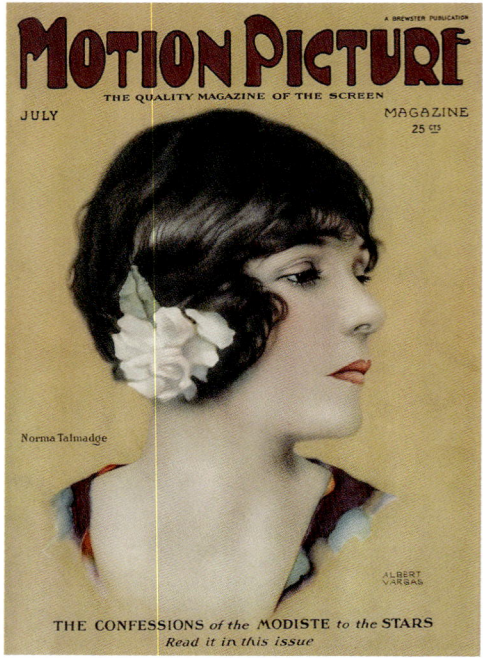

and aircraft fuselages. She was so popular that *Esquire* published free military editions of the magazine, with the Varga Girl printed on its outside back cover. Vargas began receiving letters asking him to paint special girls for individual platoons—requests he actually fulfilled as often as he could.

As Vargas's popularity grew, Smart guarded him closely. All deals had to pass through *Esquire*, including movie posters for *Something for the Boys* (1944) and MGM's *Du Barry Was a Lady* (1943). At the same time Smart pushed Vargas to produce more images for datebooks, playing cards, note cards, and, of course, calendars. Still, all was well until Smart drew up a new contract in 1943.

Smart had been a good friend, socializing with Vargas and Anna Mae, so for Vargas it was a matter of honor to trust him. He signed the contract without reading it.

Now the worst years would begin.

Vargas had essentially agreed to provide twice as many paintings to *Esquire* for roughly the same pay. When he questioned Smart, he was rudely dismissed from his office. Vargas took legal action to break the contract. He eventually won, but *Esquire* retained the right to the name Varga and to everything produced under that name.

Vargas was in his 50s and again out of work. Like Petty, he produced pin-ups for *True* magazine, a deck of playing cards with 53 unique paintings, product illustrations, matchbook covers, and even cocktail napkins, scraping along until 1957, when he was contacted by Reid Austin, an art director for *Playboy*.

Above left: Long forgotten actress Anna Q. Nilsson by Vargas on the August 1924 issue of *Motion Picture*.

Above right: Norma Talmadge on the July 1924 issue of *Motion Picture* magazine.

Opposite: The infamous six-fingered Miss November 1941 from *Esquire*. The right hand bears five visible finger tips, and no thumb. Vargas claimed he added the extra digit to see if viewers were paying attention. From the flood of mail received at the magazine, they were.

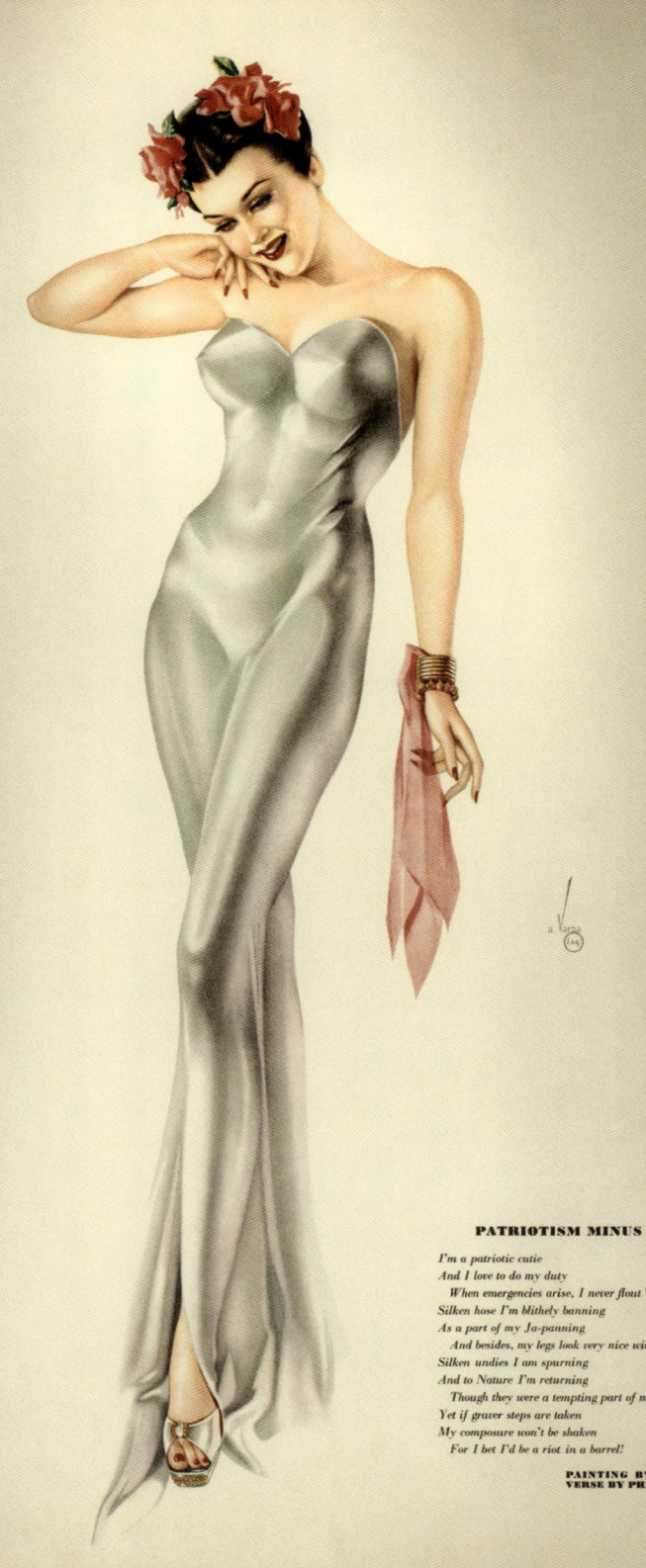

PATRIOTISM MINUS

I'm a patriotic cutie
And I love to do my duty
  When emergencies arise, I never flout 'em;
Silken hose I'm blithely banning
As a part of my Ja-panning
  And besides, my legs look very nice without 'em;
Silken undies I am spurning
And to Nature I'm returning
  Though they were a tempting part of my apparel,
Yet if graver steps are taken
My composure won't be shaken
  For I bet I'd be a riot in a barrel!

PAINTING BY VARGA
VERSE BY PHIL STACK

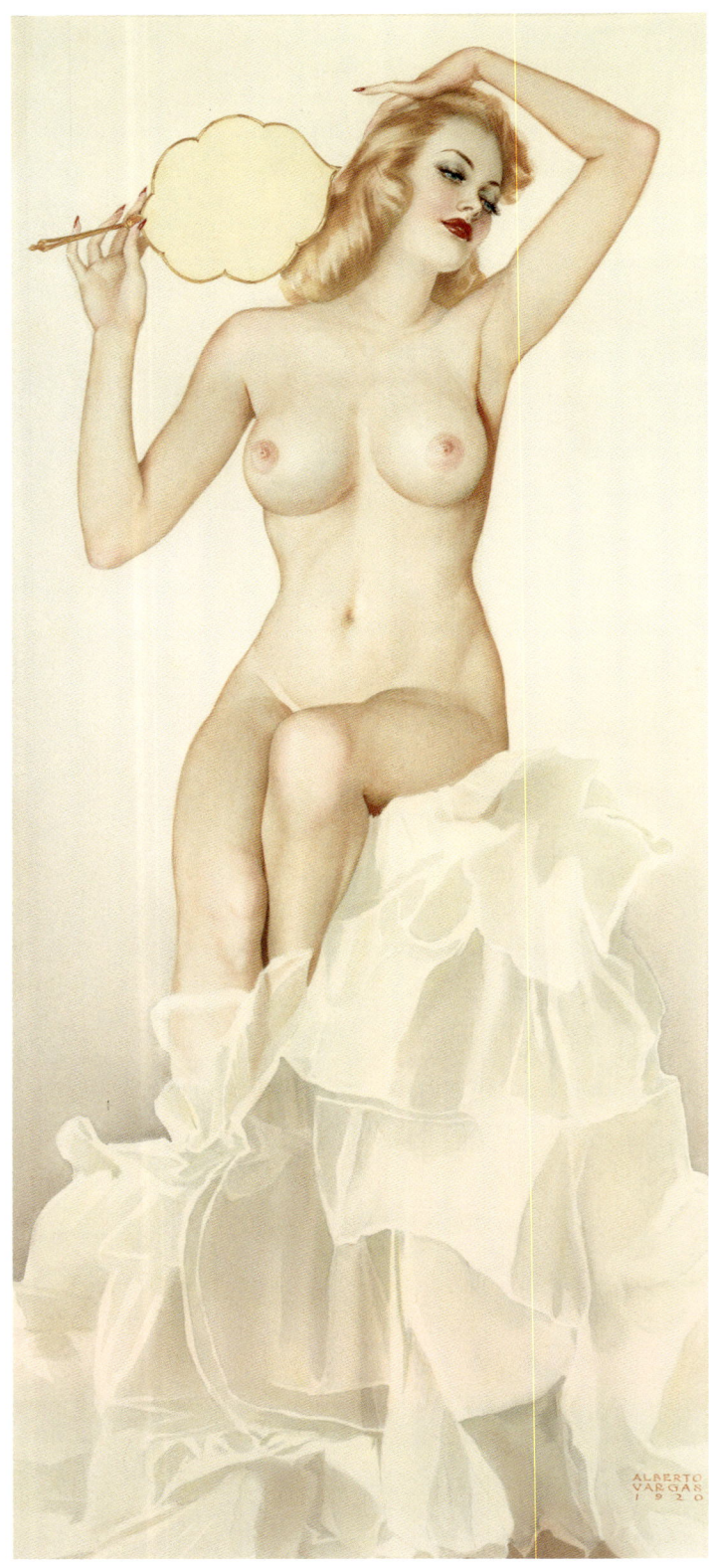

Austin was a devout fan of the Varga Girl, as was Hugh Hefner. With a handshake agreement, the Vargas Girl became a monthly feature in *Playboy*, first appearing in the September 1960 issue. Though, at times, Hef requested artistic changes Alberto found dubious, he was content, feeling he and Anna Mae finally had financial security.

Then in 1974 Alberto woke to find Anna Mae lying on the kitchen floor, suffering from a broken hip. She died in the hospital two excruciating weeks later. Vargas never accepted her death, signing Christmas cards and notes from "Anna Mae and Alberto" for the rest of his life. The couple had no children, but his niece and nephew, Astrid and Max III, helped him through this darkest period. In return, he willed them his estate, to be divided equally.

Vargas slowly returned to work, painting for *Playboy* until 1978. He created his last painting from a live model in 1979, for the cover of The Cars' album *Candy-O*, then two album covers for actress/singer Bernadette Peters. These final works show the same skill and obsessive attention to detail that he lavished on all of his paintings, a talent undiminished until the end.

Alberto Vargas died on December 30, 1982, two months before his 87th birthday.

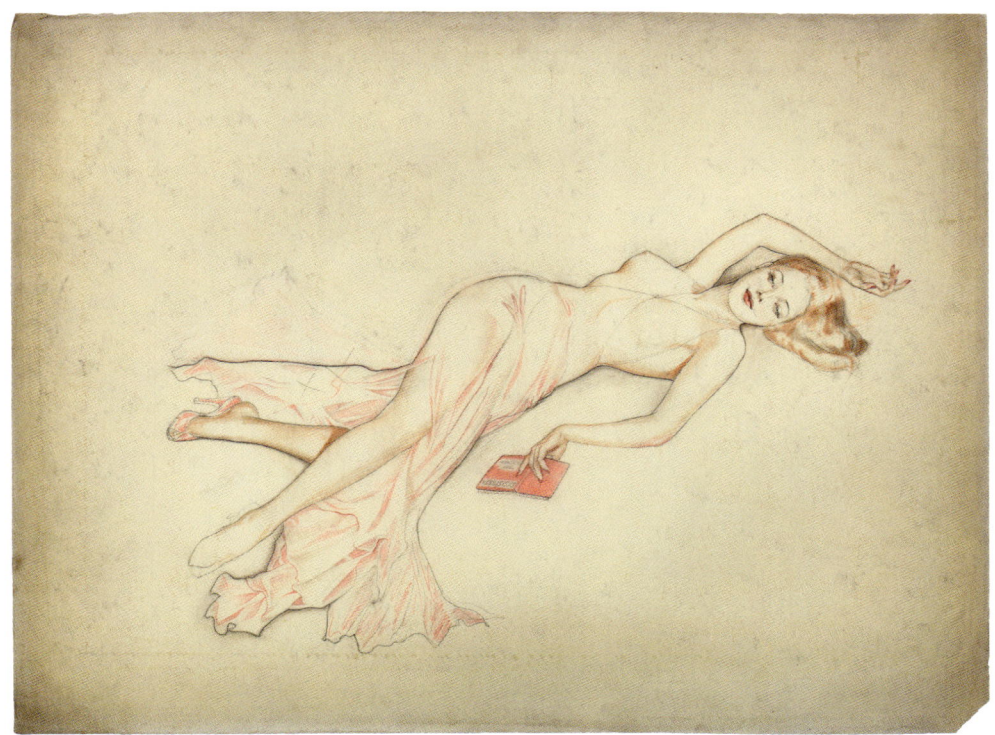

Opposite: Watercolor on board, 1920. The Max Vargas Collection.

Above: Pencil and watercolor preparatory study, circa 1950. The Max Vargas Collection.

ALBERTO VARGAS

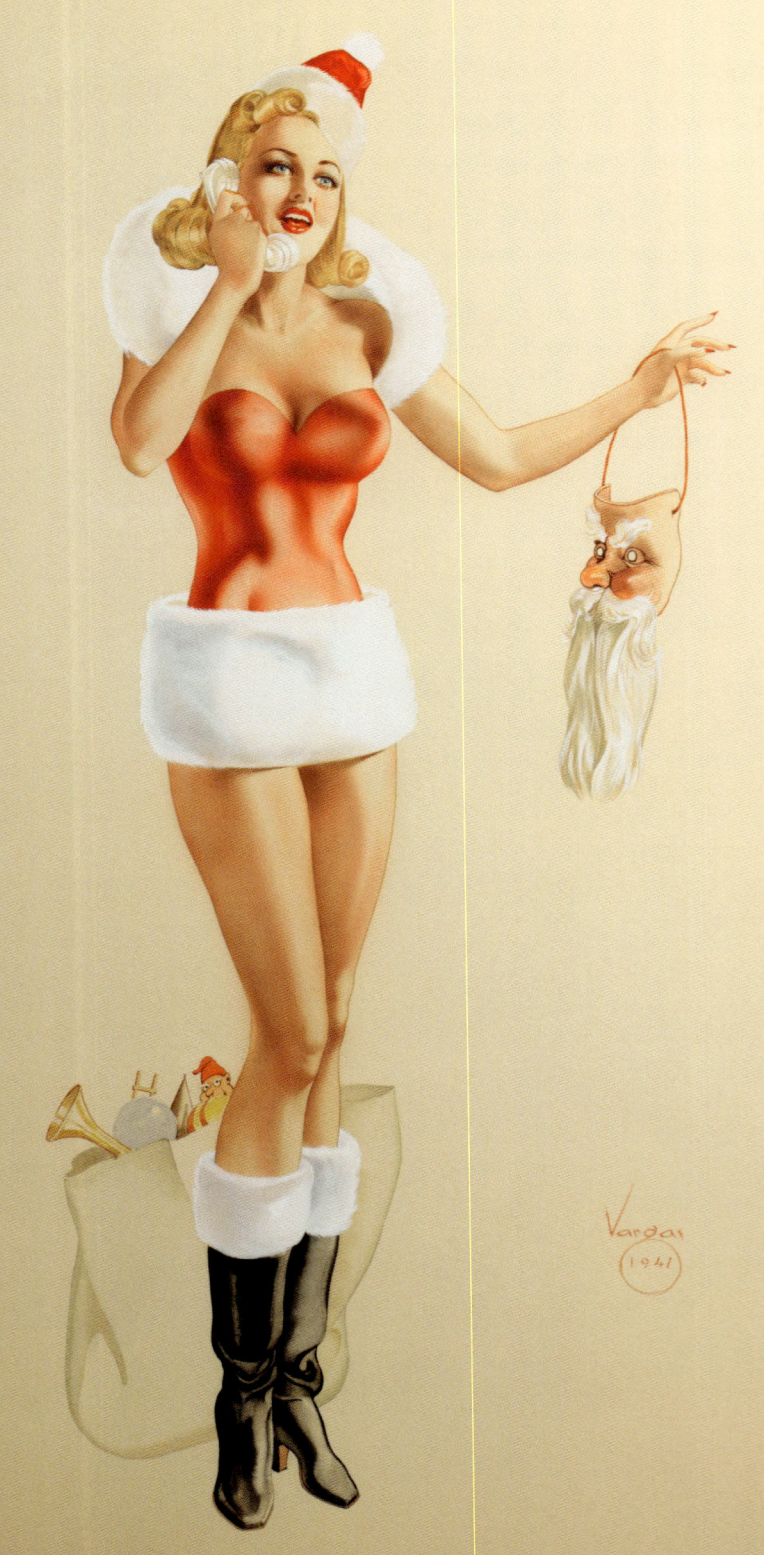

„Alberto Vargas' Leben war eine einzige Liebesgeschichte. Er liebte seine Mutter, er liebte seine Angetraute, er liebte Frauen, und er liebte das Malen."

Alberto Vargas' Leben war eine einzige Liebesgeschichte. Er liebte seine Mutter, er liebte seine Angetraute, er liebte Frauen, und er liebte das Malen. Von dieser Liebe beflügelt, malte er mehr als 70 Jahre lang alle Schattierungen von Anmut und Macht der Weiblichkeit.

Der Schöpfer des Varga-Girls wurde am 9. Februar 1896 als Joaquin Alberto Vargas y Chávez in Arequipa, Peru, geboren. Sein Vater, Maximilian, ein erfolgreicher Fotograf mit Studios in Arequipa und La Paz, Bolivien, sorgte dafür, dass Alberto und seine sechs Geschwister in einer privilegierten Umgebung aufwuchsen. Seine Mutter, Margarita, kümmerte sich darum, dass ihre Kinder die beste Ausbildung erhielten. Vargas zeichnete schon in jungen Jahren und erlernte den Umgang mit dem Airbrush, der zum Retuschieren von Fotos im Studio seines Vaters benutzt wurde, ähnlich wie George Petty. Er war ein akribischer Zeichner, der mit Ölfarbe und Pastell experimentierte, bis er sich schließlich den Aquarellfarben als bevorzugtes Medium zuwandte.

1911 brachte Maximilian seine beiden Söhne nach Paris, wo Alberto das Studium der Kunst und Fotografie aufnahm, das er dann in der Schweiz fortsetzte. Als 1915 der Krieg in Europa eskalierte, drängte der Vater die Söhne, in die Vereinigten Staaten zu reisen. Noch im gleichen Jahr trafen sie in New York City ein.

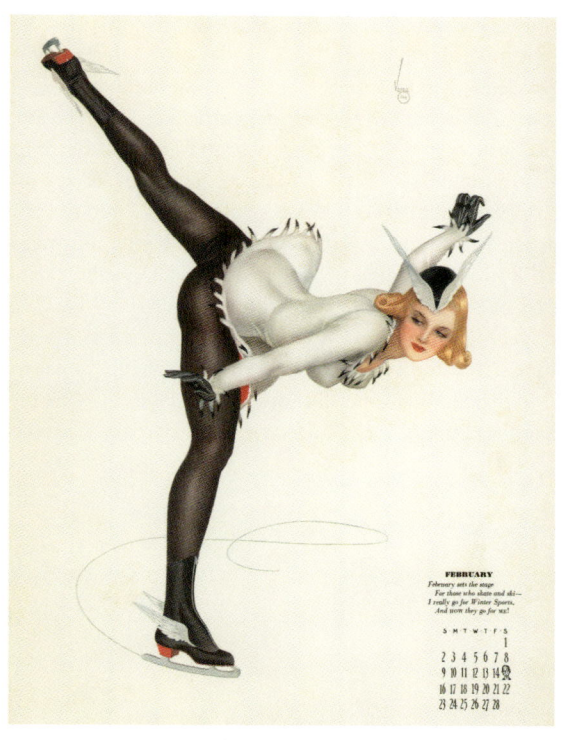

Opposite: Watercolor on board, 1940. This image was intended for the December 1940 issue of *Esquire* and was replaced at the last minute with the 1941 Vargas 12-page calendar, also released in a spiral-bound edition. Collection of Volker Morlock/© Max Vargas. 30 x 20 inches.

Above: Miss February, from *Esquire's 1941 Varga Calendar*, his first for the magazine.

Während jener ersten Tage in New York lernte Vargas die amerikanischen Mädchen kennen. Als er um die Mittagszeit über den Times Square spazierte, strömten junge Frauen aus Büros und Läden. „Mir fiel die Kinnlade runter!", erzählte er Jahre später. „Aus jedem Gebäude kamen wahre Fluten an Mädchen. Hunderte von Mädchen mit einem Ausdruck von Selbstsicherheit und Entschlossenheit, der besagte: ‚Hier bin ich, wie findest du mich?' Da wusste ich, dass ich nicht mehr nach Hause zurückkehren würde."

Vargas fand einen Job in einem Kaufhaus an der 42. Straße – er malte Porträts von Modellen im großen Schaufenster des Geschäfts. Eines Tages betrat der Manager der Ziegfeld Follies das Schaufenster und meinte, er habe vielleicht einen Job für den Künstler.

Vargas wurde engagiert, zwölf großformatige Porträts der neuen Ziegfeld-Stars zu malen, und bekam für jedes Gemälde 200 Dollar. Das war der Beginn der zwölfjährigen Zusammenarbeit mit Ziegfeld, der dem Künstler ein Atelier zur Verfügung stellte und all seine Stars bei Vargas Modell sitzen ließ. In dieser Zeit verliebte sich Vargas in eine junge Frau, die er auf der Bühne der Greenwich Village Follies „entdeckte": Anna Mae Clift stammte aus Soddy-Daisy, Tennessee, und war bereit, für ihn zu posieren. Fortan kreiste Vargas' Gefühlswelt nur noch um dieses Lieblingsmodell. Nachdem er mehrere Jahre um sie geworben hatte, heirateten sie schließlich.

Nach dem Börsenkrach von 1929 brachen für die Follies harte Zeiten an. Vargas war nun arbeitslos. Er nahm Aufträge für Zeitschriftenillustrationen und Werbebilder verschiedener Hollywood-Studios an. Angetan von der Qualität seiner Arbeiten, lud ihn die Twentieth Century Fox nach Hollywood ein. Mithilfe von Anna Maes Freund Busby Berkeley erhielt er nun Aufträge von Paramount, Warner Brothers und Fox für Bühnenbilder. Das Ehepaar Vargas kaufte sich sein erstes und einziges Haus, einen kleinen Bungalow im Westwood-Viertel von Los Angeles.

Zu den Stars, die ihm nun Modell saßen, gehörten Marlene Dietrich, Alice Fay, Carole Lombard und Greta Garbo wie auch Barbara Stanwyck, die Vargas auf einem Plakat für den

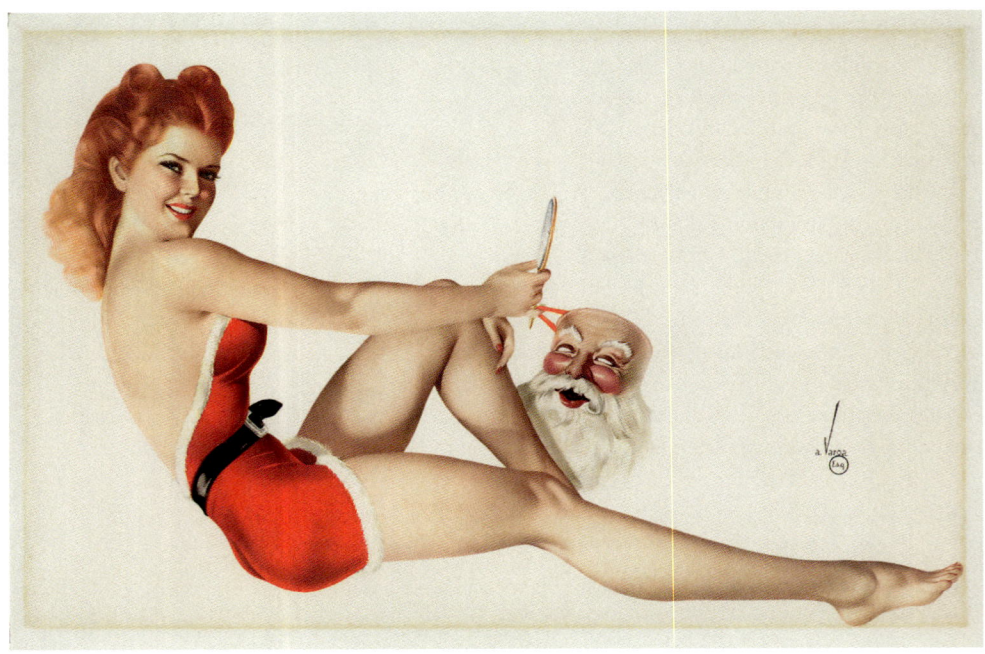

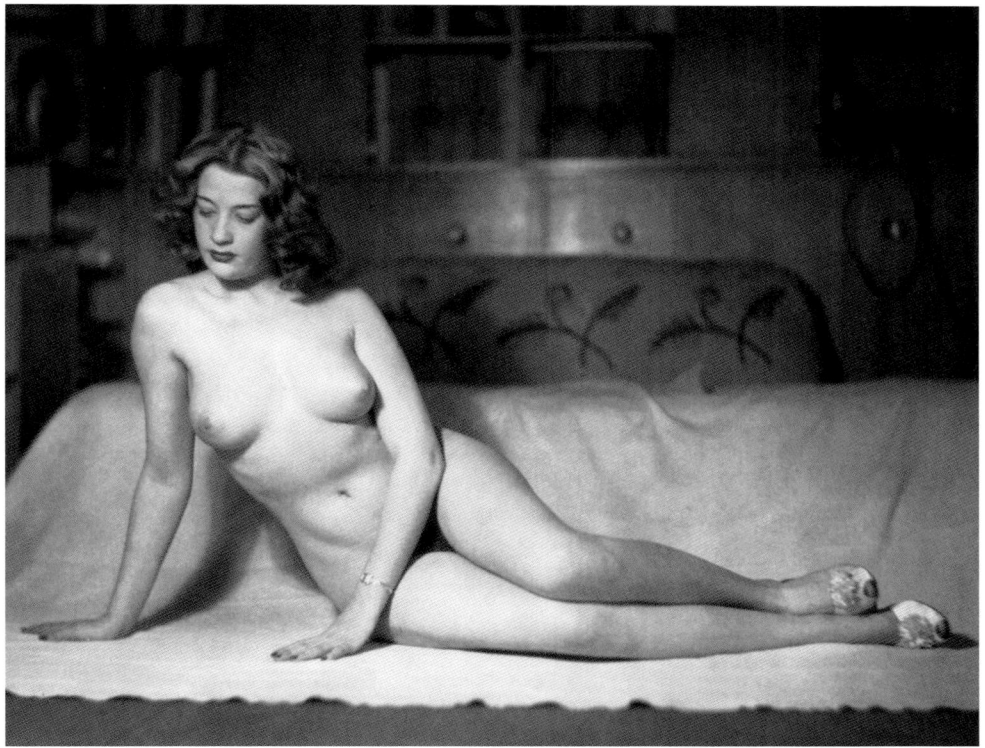

1933 entstandenen Film *Ladies They Talk About* verewigte. Im gleichen Jahr erschien die erste Ausgabe des *Esquire* mit einem Petty-Girl.

    1939 schloss sich Vargas einem gewerkschaftlich organisierten Streik der Studiomitarbeiter an. Daraufhin wurde er als Kommunist abgestempelt und fortan von den Studios gemieden. Allein machte er sich auf den Weg nach New York, um sich Arbeit zu suchen. Ein Freund drängte ihn, seine Arbeiten dem *Esquire* vorzulegen. Der Verleger David Smart war nicht nur von Vargas' Fähigkeiten, sondern auch von dessen Verzweiflung beeindruckt. Die Zusammenarbeit mit Petty, der pro Bild 1 000 Dollar forderte, gestaltete sich zunehmend schwierig. Vargas bot eine Alternative – für gerade mal 75 Dollar pro Woche. Man einigte sich auf einen Dreijahresvertrag. Das Petty-Girl wurde nun durch das Varga-Girl ersetzt – das „s" bei Vargas wurde gestrichen. Darauf hatte Smart bestanden, weil der Name so angeblich „wohlklingender" war. Diese Namensänderung schien unverfänglich zu sein, doch die Konsequenzen sollten weit reichen.

    Das erste Varga-Girl erschien in der Oktober-Ausgabe 1940 und wurde von den Lesern begeistert angenommen. Vargas sagte später, die Zeit bei *Esquire* sei die beste und zugleich die schlimmste seiner Karriere gewesen. Die ersten beiden Jahre waren die besten. Er hatte ein festes Einkommen, und während er jeden Monat ein neues Varga-Girl malte und zwölf Bilder pro

Opposite: Miss December from *Esquire's 1943 Calendar Yearbook.* The image originally appeared in the December 1942 issue of *Esquire.*

Above: Like most pin-up artists, Vargas created his own photo reference materials. Though famously shy, he photographed many models nude in his little bungalow in Los Angeles. This unknown model posed circa 1938.

Jahr für den Varga-Girl-Kalender, konnte er seine Fähigkeiten weiterentwickeln. Die Verkaufs-zahlen seines ersten, 1941 erschienenen Kalenders übertrafen weltweit alle anderen, und sein Ruhm wuchs.

Als die USA in den Krieg eintraten, wurde das Varga-Girl in Schlafkojen von Schlachtschif-fen, in Armeekasernen oder in U-Booten an Wände gepinnt, kopiert oder sonst wie befestigt sowie auf Pilotenjacken und Flugzeugrümpfe gemalt. Das Varga-Girl war so populär, dass *Esquire* kostenlose Militärauflagen druckte, die das Mädchen auf der Umschlagrückseite zeigten. Vargas erhielt nun Briefe, in denen er gebeten wurde, besondere Mädchen für einzelne Militäreinheiten zu malen – Anfragen, denen er so oft wie möglich nachkam.

Mit Alberto Vargas' steigender Popularität kontrollierte ihn sein Verleger Smart auch zuneh-mend. Sämtliche Vereinbarungen mussten über *Esquire* laufen, auch Aufträge für Kinoplakate wie für *Moon Over Miami* (1941) mit Betty Grable und den von MGM produzierten Streifen *Du Barry Was a Lady* (1943). Gleichzeitig drängte Smart Vargas, noch mehr Bilder für Agenden, Spielkarten, Karteikarten und – natürlich – für Kalender zu produzieren. Alles war in bester Ordnung, bis Smart 1943 einen neuen Vertrag aufsetzte.

Smart war mit Alberto und Anna befreundet, Alberto vertraute ihm also und unterschrieb den Vertrag, ohne ihn zu lesen. Damit begannen die schlimmsten Jahre. Vargas hatte im Wesent-lichen zugestimmt, *Esquire* die doppelte Anzahl an Bildern für fast das gleiche Geld zu liefern. Als er Smart deshalb zur Rede stellte, warf ihn dieser grob aus seinem Büro. Vargas klagte auf

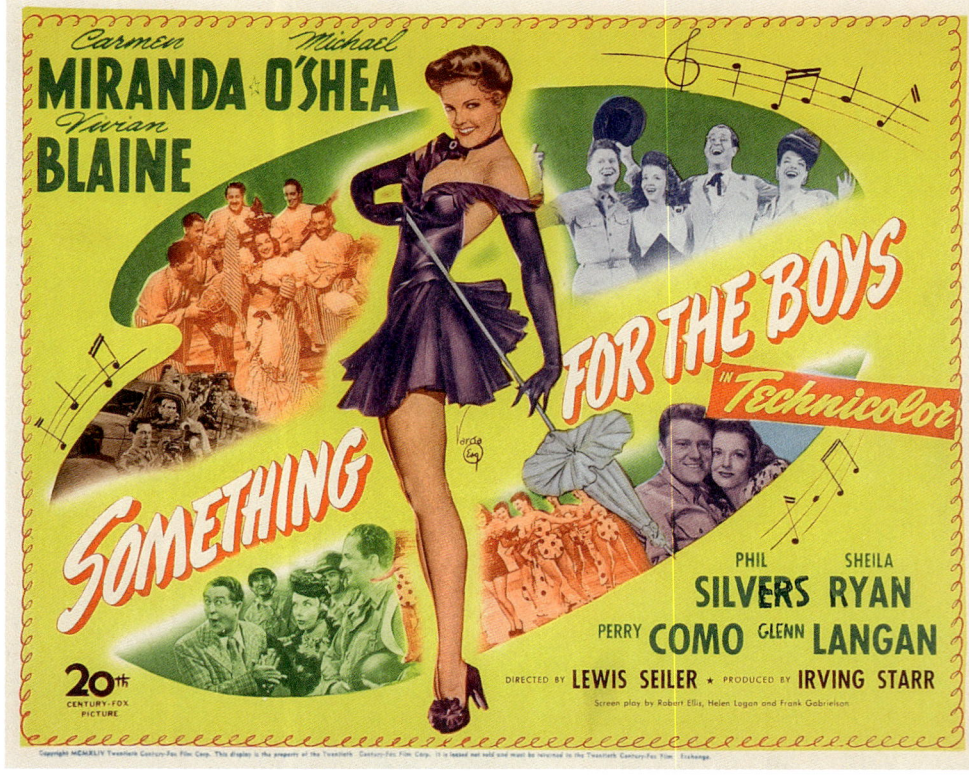

Auflösung des Vertrags. Zwar gewann er die gerichtliche Auseinandersetzung, doch *Esquire* wurde das Recht am Namen Varga und an allem, was unter dieser Bezeichnung produziert wurde, zugesprochen.

Vargas war bereits über 50 und wieder arbeitslos. Wie Petty produzierte er nun Pin-ups für das Magazin *True*, ein Kartenset aus 53 einzelnen Bildern, Produktillustrationen, Abbildungen für Streichholzbriefchen, er malte sogar Motive für Cocktailservietten und schlug sich so bis 1957 durch. In jenem Jahr kontaktierte ihn Reid Austin, der Artdirector von *Playboy*.

Austin war, genau wie Hugh Hefner, ein echter Fan des Varga-Girls. Per Handschlag wurde für das Vargas-Girl jeden Monat ein Platz im *Playboy* eingeräumt. Das erste Mädchen erschien in der September-Ausgabe 1960. Obgleich Hef gelegentlich um künstlerische Veränderungen bat, die Vargas als fragwürdig empfand, war er zufrieden und hatte das Gefühl, dass er und Anna Mae endlich finanzielle Sicherheit hatten.

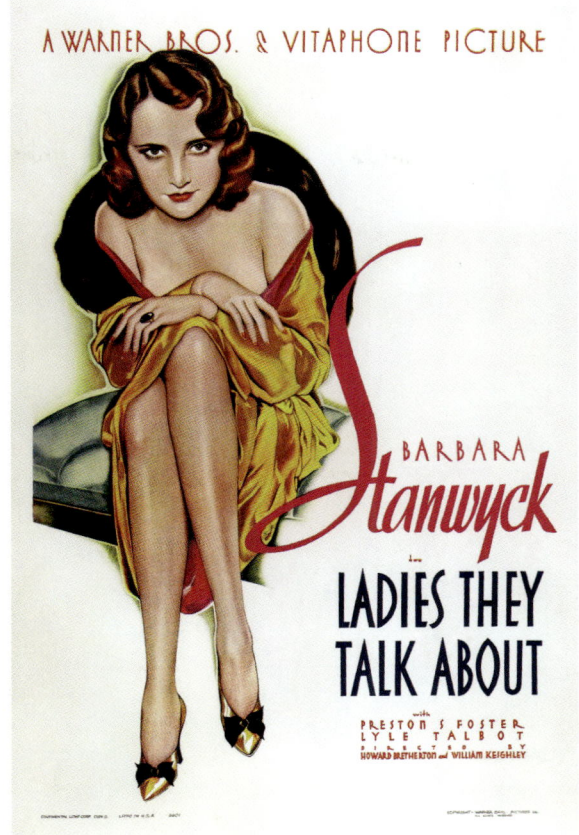

Eines Tages im Jahr 1974 fand Alberto Anna Mae auf dem Küchenboden liegend. Sie hatte sich die Hüfte gebrochen. Zwei qualvolle Wochen später starb sie im Krankenhaus. Ihren Tod akzeptierte Vargas nie. Für den Rest seines Lebens unterzeichnete er Weihnachtskarten und andere Nachrichten mit „Anna Mae und Alberto". Das Paar hatte keine Kinder, doch Albertos Nichte und Neffe, Astrid und Max III., halfen ihm, diese dunkelste Zeit zu überstehen. Er hinterließ ihnen dafür, zu gleichen Teilen, seine Besitztümer.

Nach dem Tod von Anna Mae kehrte Vargas nur langsam wieder zur Arbeit zurück. Er malte noch bis 1978 für den *Playboy*. Sein letztes Bild, das er nach einem Modell schuf, war 1979 ein Cover für das Album *Candy-O* der Rockband *The Cars*. Danach gestaltete er noch zwei Albumcover für die Schauspielerin und Sängerin Bernadette Peters. Diese letzten Arbeiten zeigen das gleiche Können und die gleiche Liebe zum Detail, die alle Vargas-Arbeiten auszeichnen.

Alberto Vargas starb am 30. Dezember 1982, zwei Monate vor seinem 87. Geburtstag.

Opposite: A Vargas painting on the lobby card for the wartime musical *Something for the Boys,* 1944. Earl Moran was the artist for the larger one-sheet poster. 28 x 22 inches.

Above: Vargas illustration on a film poster for *Ladies They Talk About,* 1933.

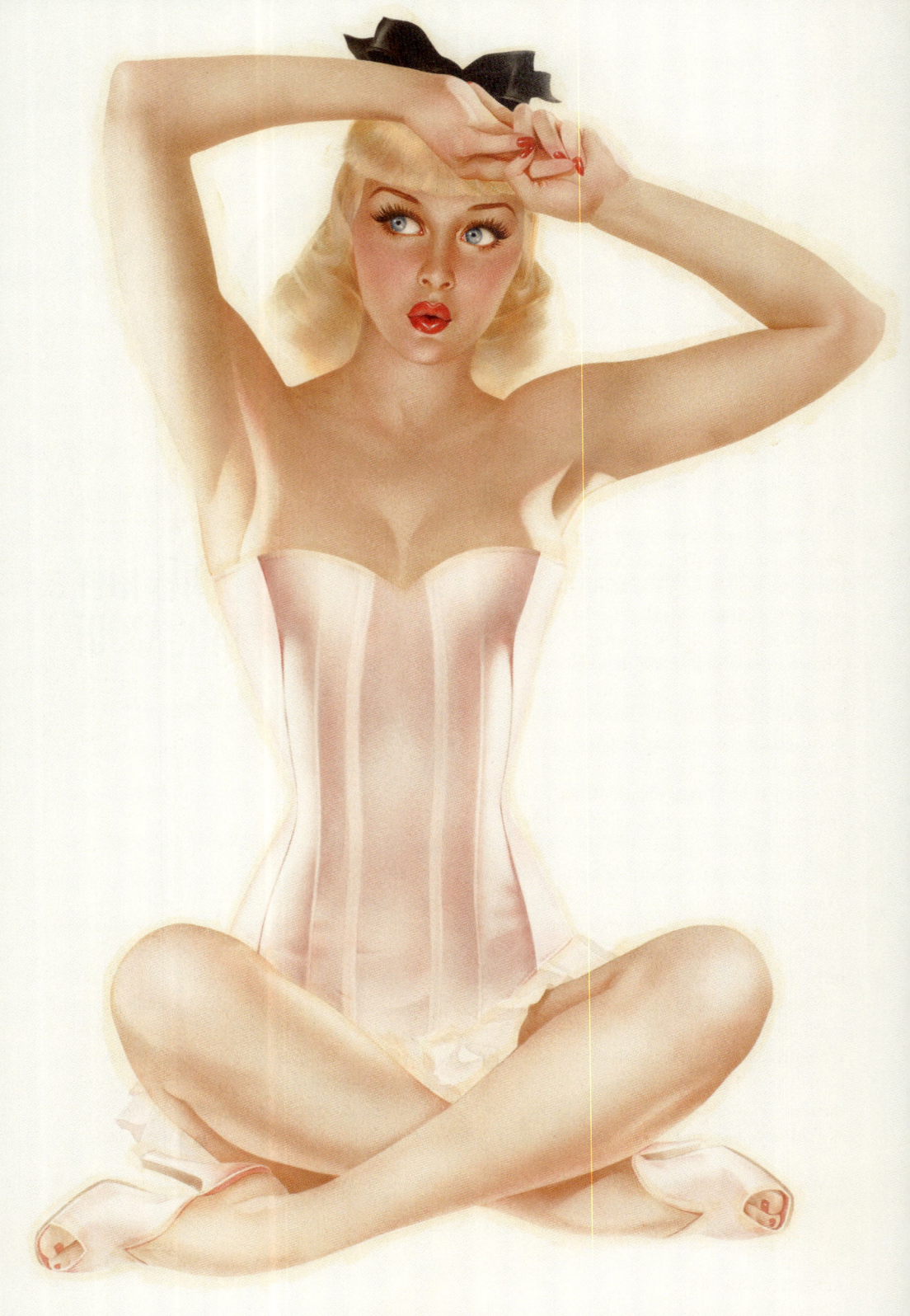

« La vie d'Alberto Vargas, artiste peintre, est une histoire d'amour.
Il aimait sa mère, sa femme, les femmes et la peinture. »

La vie d'Alberto Vargas, artiste peintre, est
une histoire d'amour. Il aimait sa mère, sa
femme, les femmes et la peinture. Animé
par tout cet amour, il captura les nuances,
la grâce et la puissance de la féminité
durant plus de soixante-dix ans.

Joaquin Alberto Vargas y Chávez est
né à Arequipa, au Pérou, le 9 février 1896.
Son père, Maximilien, était un photographe
prospère qui possédait des studios à Arequipa et à La Paz, en Bolivie. Alberto et ses
six frères et sœurs grandirent dans un environnement privilégié. Leur mère, Margarita,
veilla à ce qu'ils reçoivent la meilleure éducation. Il commença à dessiner très jeune
et maîtrisa rapidement l'aérographe utilisé
pour retoucher les photos dans le studio de
son père (comme George Petty). Dessina-
teur méticuleux, il expérimenta avec l'huile
et le pastel avant d'adopter l'aquarelle
comme matériau de prédilection.

En 1911, Maximilien emmena ses deux
fils à Paris. Alberto y étudia l'art et la photographie avant de poursuivre ses études
en Suisse. En 1915, devant l'escalade de la

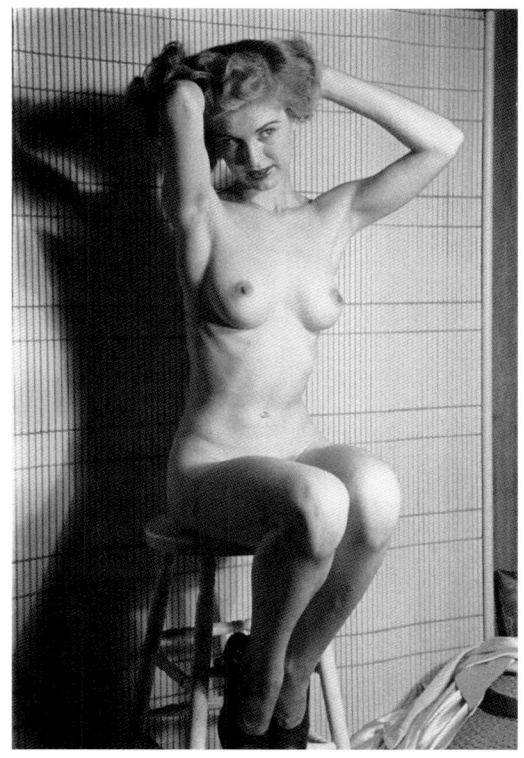

guerre, le père poussa ses deux fils à partir pour les États-Unis. Ils débarquèrent à New York la
même année.

Dès son arrivée, Vargas découvrit les « jeunes Américaines ». En traversant Time Square
à l'heure du déjeuner, il les voyait sortir des bureaux et des boutiques. Des années plus tard, il
a raconté : « J'en suis resté la bouche ouverte et ne pouvais plus la refermer. Chaque building
déversait un flot de filles. Elles étaient des centaines, avec une assurance et une détermination
qui disaient : Me voici, je vous plais ? J'ai su alors que je ne rentrerai pas au pays. »

Opposite: Watercolor on board, 1943, for the
November 1943 Varga Girl in *Esquire* magazine.

Above: A model photographed by Vargas, circa 1938; one
of about 100 model photographs rescued from a dum-
pster on the lot of a Hollywood studio where Vargas
photographed young starlets before he was blacklisted.

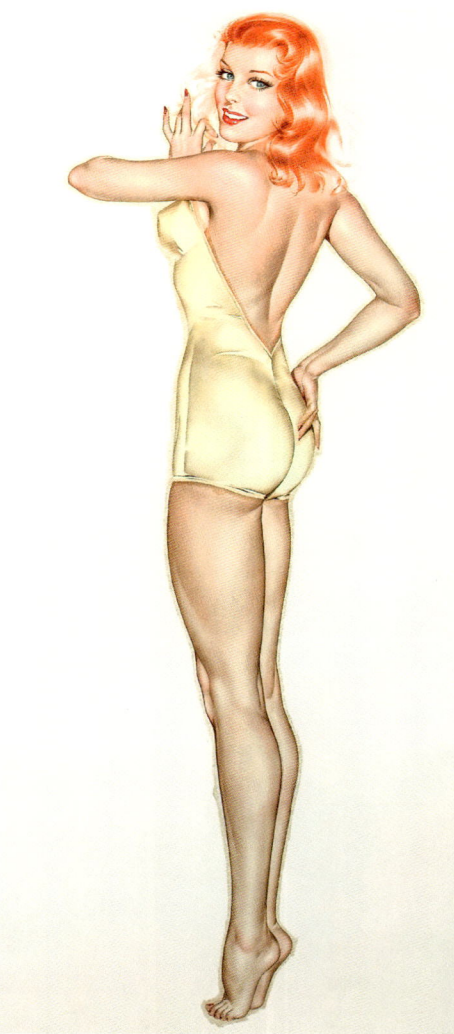

Vargas fut engagé par un grand magasin de la 42ᵉ Rue pour peindre des portraits derrière la vitrine. Un jour, le directeur des Ziegfeld Follies passa par là et lui proposa un travail.

Il lui commanda douze grands portraits des nouvelles stars de la revue. Chaque toile était payée 200 dollars. Ce fut le début d'une relation de douze ans avec Ziegfeld, qui lui fournit un atelier et demanda à toutes ses vedettes de poser pour lui.

Durant cette époque, Vargas « découvrit » une jeune femme sur la scène des Greenwich Village Follies. Elle s'appelait Anna Mae Clift et venait de Soddy-Daisy, dans le Tennessee. Elle accepta de poser pour lui et devint bientôt son modèle favori ainsi que le centre de toutes ses attentions. Il lui fit la cour durant plusieurs années avant de la demander en mariage.

Le krach de 1929 affecta durement les Follies et Vargas se retrouva sans travail. Il reçut plusieurs commandes d'illustrations pour des magazines et réalisa plusieurs publicités pour divers studios d'Hollywood. La qualité de son travail attira l'attention de la Twentieth Century Fox qui le fit venir à Hollywood. Avec l'aide de Busby Berkeley, un ami d'Anna Mae, il travailla sur des décors pour la Paramount, Warner Brothers ainsi que la Fox. Les Vargas purent bientôt acheter leur première et unique maison, un petit pavillon dans le quartier de Westwood à Los Angeles. Marlene Dietrich, Alice Fay, Carole Lombard, Greta Garbo et bien d'autres posèrent pour lui, tout comme Barbara Stanwyck, qu'il immortalisa en 1933 sur l'affiche du film *Ladies They Talk About*.

La même année, la Petty Girl fit ses débuts dans le magazine *Esquire*.

En 1939, Vargas participa à une grève syndicale. Il fut catalogué communiste et évincé par les studios. Il rentra seul à New York pour chercher du travail. Un ami le poussa à présenter son

Above: Watercolor on board, 1945, for the January 1946 issue of *Esquire*. This long narrow pin-up was printed as a triple foldout, equal to four normal magazine pages. 32 x 17.25 inches.

Opposite: Woman of Tomorrow, watercolor on board, 1955, created for the Seventh Annual California Hobby Show to "dramatize art as a hobby." This figure

represented Vargas's fantasy of the woman of 2005, a golden apple in one hand and a lasso in the other. An accompanying fact sheet described this woman as taller, leaner, and stronger than the woman of 1955, wearing fewer clothes, and so outnumbering the man of the future that she is in constant pursuit of males, thus her tempting apple and lasso.

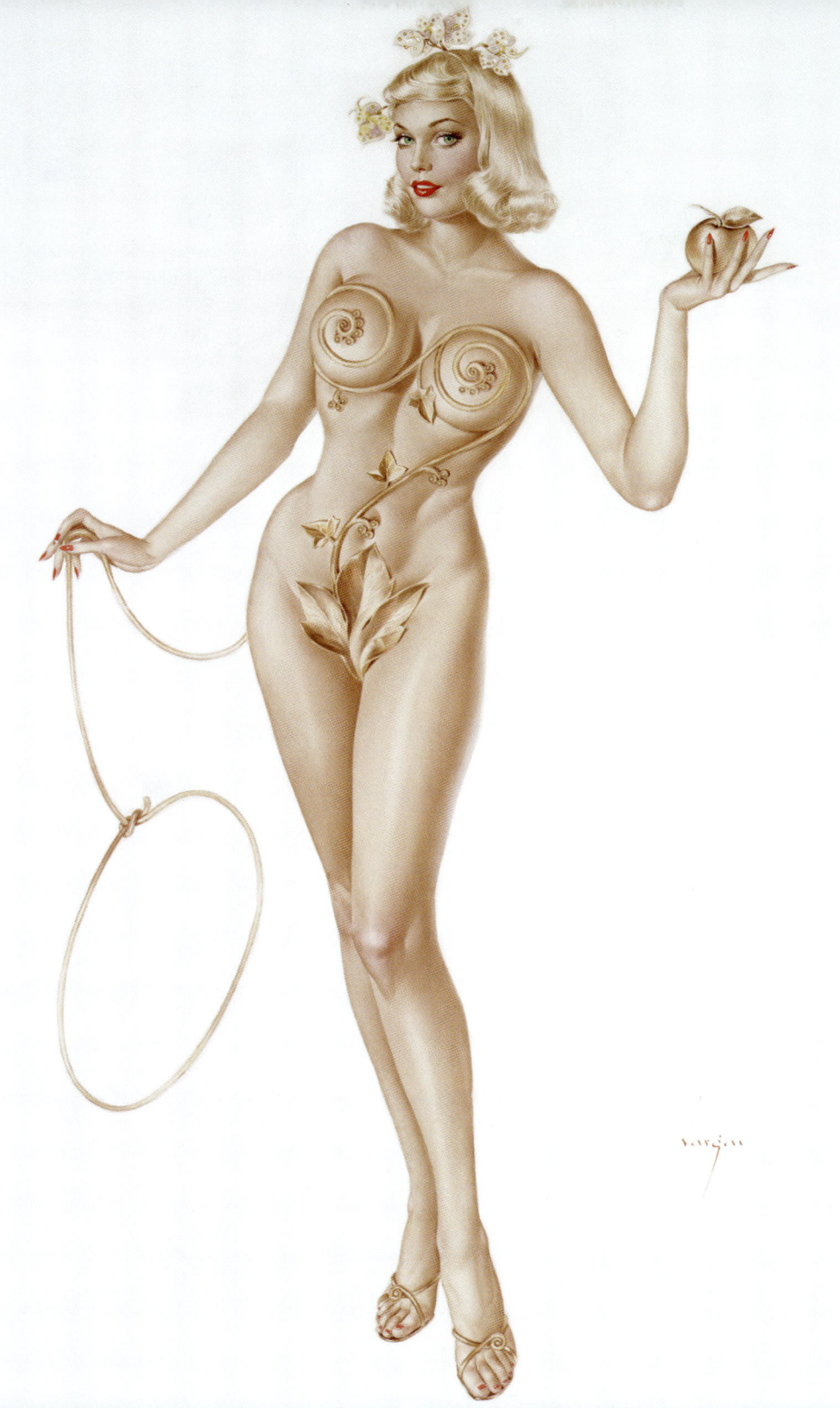

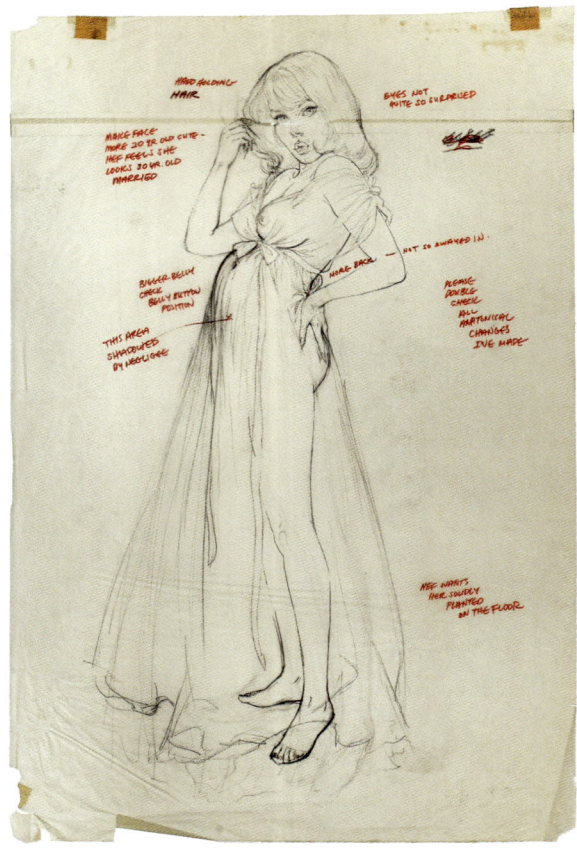

travail à *Esquire*. L'éditeur, David Smart, fut impressionné par son talent et touché par sa situation. Petty commençait à devenir ingérable, réclamant 1 000 dollars par toile. Vargas, lui, ne demandait que 75 dollars par semaine. Un contrat de trois ans fut rédigé. La Petty Girl céda la place à la Varga Girl. Smart insista pour qu'il laisse tomber le « s » final afin de rendre son nom plus « euphonique », un changement en apparence anodin mais qui devait avoir de profondes répercussions.

La première Varga Girl parut dans le numéro d'octobre 1940 d'*Esquire* et fut rapidement adoptée par les lecteurs. Vargas déclara plus tard que sa période chez *Esquire* avait été la pire et la meilleure de sa carrière. Les deux premières années furent les meilleures : il avait un revenu stable et le fait de produire une nouvelle Varga Girl chaque mois, plus douze tableaux par an pour le calendrier, affina sa patte. Son premier calendrier, paru en 1941, battit des records de vente dans le monde entier et le rendit célèbre.

Lorsque les États-Unis entrèrent en guerre, la Varga Girl se retrouva punaisée dans les chambrées des cuirassés, des casernes et des sous-marins. Elle fut peinte sur le blouson des aviateurs et les fuselages. Elle était tellement appréciée qu'*Esquire* publia des éditions spéciales gratuites pour les militaires avec une pin-up au dos de la couverture. Vargas recevait des lettres lui demandant de créer des girls personnalisées pour des bataillons, des requêtes auxquelles il répondait aussi souvent qu'il le pouvait.

Face à une telle popularité, David Smart ne lâchait pas Vargas d'un pouce. Toutes ses commandes devaient passer par *Esquire*, y compris celles pour des affiches de cinéma comme *Soirs de Miami* (1941) avec Betty Grable, et *La Du Barry était une dame* (MGM, 1943). Parallèlement, l'éditeur poussait son illustrateur à produire toujours plus d'images pour des agendas, des cartes à jouer, des carnets et, naturellement, des calendriers. Tout alla bien jusqu'à ce que Smart rédige un nouveau contrat en 1943.

Vargas considérait Smart comme un ami, le recevant régulièrement chez lui. Lui faire confiance était une question d'honneur. Il signa le contrat les yeux fermés.

Alors commencèrent les pires années.

Vargas avait accepté sans le savoir de fournir deux fois plus d'images à *Esquire* pour plus ou moins la même somme. Lorsqu'il interrogea Smart, ce dernier le chassa de son bureau. Vargas l'attaqua en justice et finit par gagner son procès, mais *Esquire* conserva les droits du nom Varga et de tout ce qui était produit sous ce nom.

Vargas avait la cinquantaine et se retrouva une nouvelle fois sans travail. À l'instar de Petty, il créa des pin-up pour le magazine *True*, 53 images originales pour un jeu de cartes, des illustrations pour des publicités, des boîtes d'allumettes et même des serviettes de cocktail, survivant tant bien que mal jusqu'en 1957, quand il fut contacté par Reid Austin, un directeur artistique de *Playboy*.

Austin était un grand admirateur des Varga Girls, tout comme Hugh Hefner. Après un accord de principe, le magazine publia tous les mois une Vargas Girl, commençant avec le numéro de septembre 1960. Bien qu'Hefner lui demandât parfois des changements qui lui paraissaient douteux, Vargas était satisfait, estimant qu'Anna Mae et lui étaient enfin à l'abri du besoin.

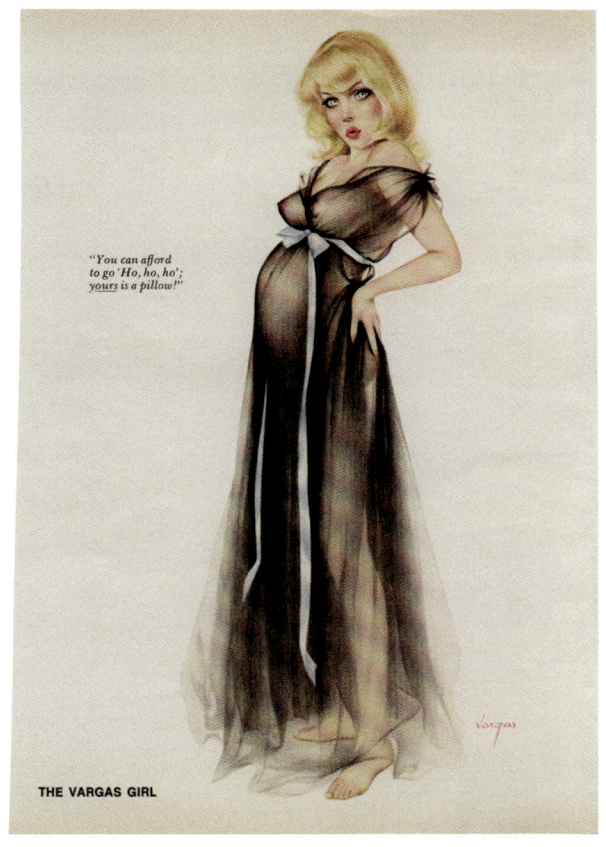

"You can afford to go 'Ho, ho, ho'; yours is a pillow!"

THE VARGAS GIRL

En se réveillant un matin de 1974, Alberto découvrit Anna Mae gisant sur le sol de la cuisine, la hanche cassée. Elle mourut à l'hôpital deux semaines plus tard. Vargas ne s'en remit jamais. Jusqu'à la fin de sa vie, il signa ses cartes de vœux et son courrier « Anna Mae et Alberto ». Le couple n'avait pas d'enfants, mais sa nièce et son neveu, Astrid et Max III, le soutinrent durant cette période la plus sombre de sa vie. En retour, il leur légua tous ses biens.

Vargas se remit lentement au travail, peignant pour *Playboy* jusqu'en 1978. Il créa sa dernière toile d'après un modèle vivant en 1979 pour la pochette de l'album *Candy-O* des *Cars*, puis illustra deux disques pour l'actrice et chanteuse Bernadette Peters. Ces dernières œuvres montrent qu'il n'avait rien perdu de son art ni de son soin du détail. Son talent demeura intact jusqu'au bout.

Alberto Vargas s'éteignit le 30 décembre 1982, deux mois avant son 87e anniversaire.

Opposite: Pencil on tissue preliminary sketch, 1974, for the December 1976 issue of *Playboy*. This image was purportedly made for a planned 1974 humor issue of *Playboy*. Hefner canceled the issue but liked the concept and encouraged Vargas to complete it — but only after he made the many changes marked in red. Hefner's vision of what was appropriate for *Playboy* was always at odds with Vargas's, yet Vargas never argued for fear of losing his job. The Max Vargas Collection.

Above: The completed pregnant pin-up as it appeared in the December 1976 issue of *Playboy*, incorporating all of Hefner's demands.

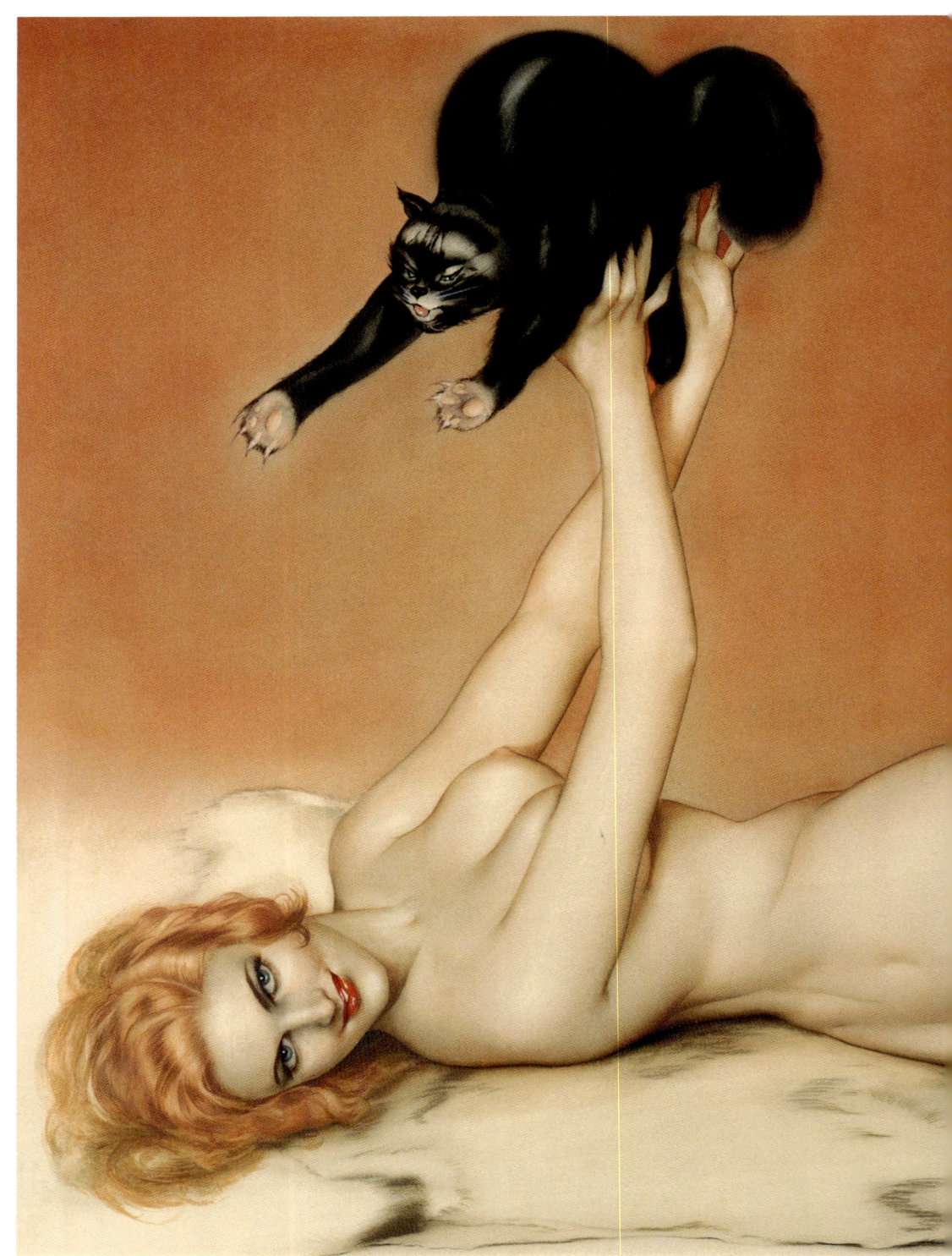

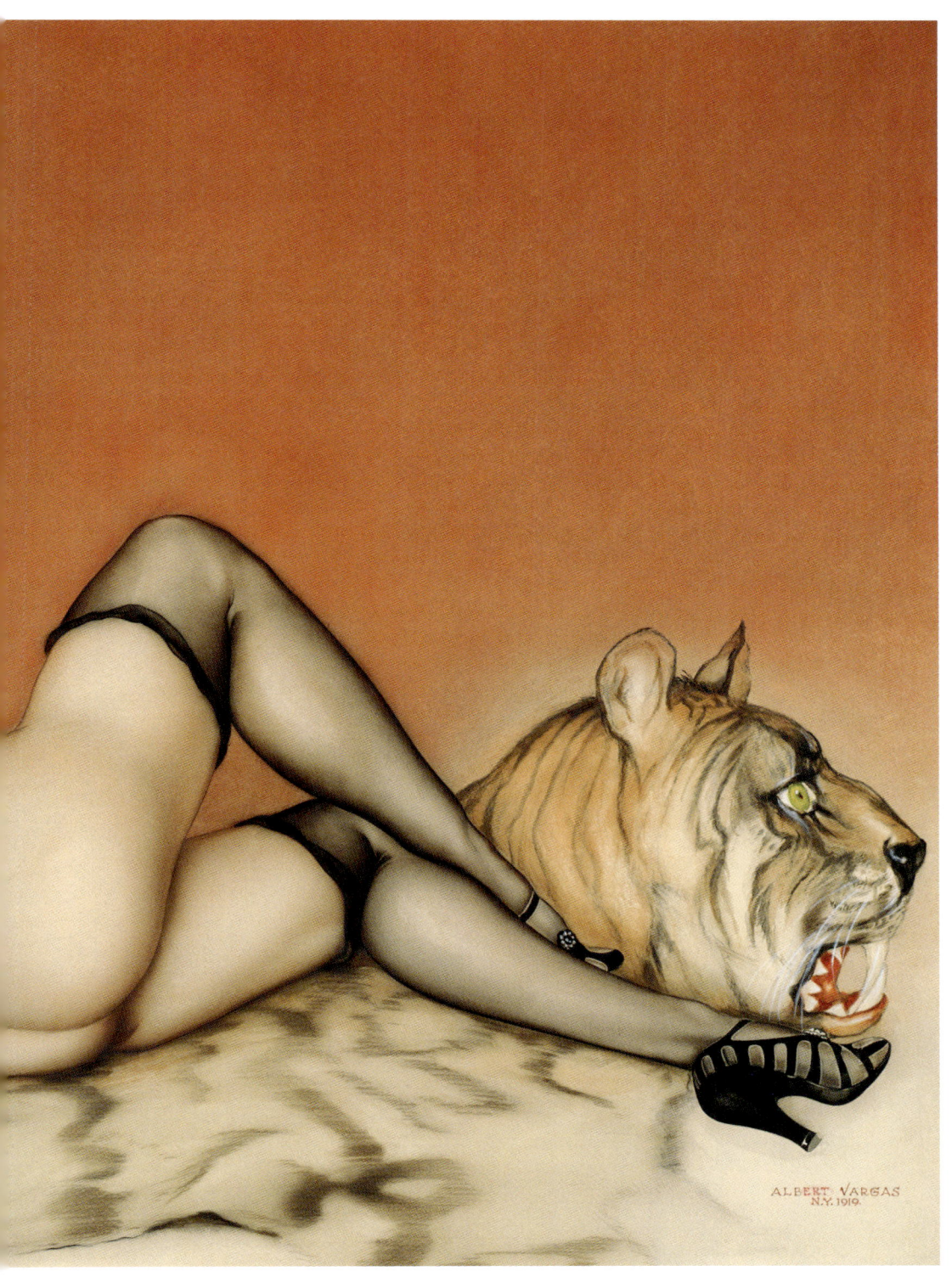

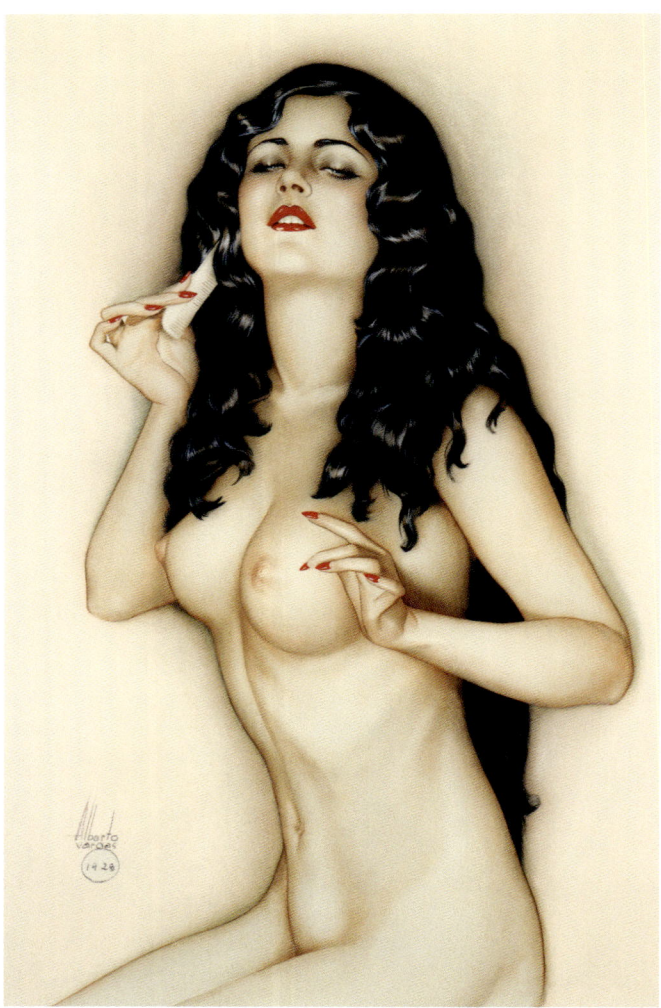

Previous spread: Watercolor on paper, 1919. A preliminary sketch exists for this piece dated 1915, suggesting that Vargas waited four years before deciding to bring this spectacular piece to completion. There's a strong element of deco Orientalism in the rendering of the cat, whose peculiar paws suggest that Vargas was more familiar with human than feline anatomy. The Max Vargas Collection.

Above: Broadway Showgirl, watercolor on paper, 1928; the subject was probably a Ziegfeld Follies dancer. 30 x 20 inches.

Opposite: Memories of Olive, watercolor on board, 1920, commemorates Ziegfeld Follies dancer turned Hollywood actress Olive Thomas. Now long forgotten, Olive was to the 1910s what Marilyn Monroe was to the 1950s. She started as a model in 1914, then became a lead dancer in Ziegfeld's private, and more risqué, Midnight Frolic show. She left for Hollywood in 1916, where she starred in films including *Madcap Madge* and *Indiscreet Corrine* — and married Mary Pickford's brother, Jack. In 1920 the couple was partying in Paris and returned, heavily intoxicated, to their hotel room, where Thomas drank a flask of mercury bichloride, which Jack used as topical treatment for his chronic syphilis. She reportedly thought it was either alcohol or a sleeping potion and died five days later of kidney failure. Her death was the first great Hollywood scandal. 24 x 18 inches.

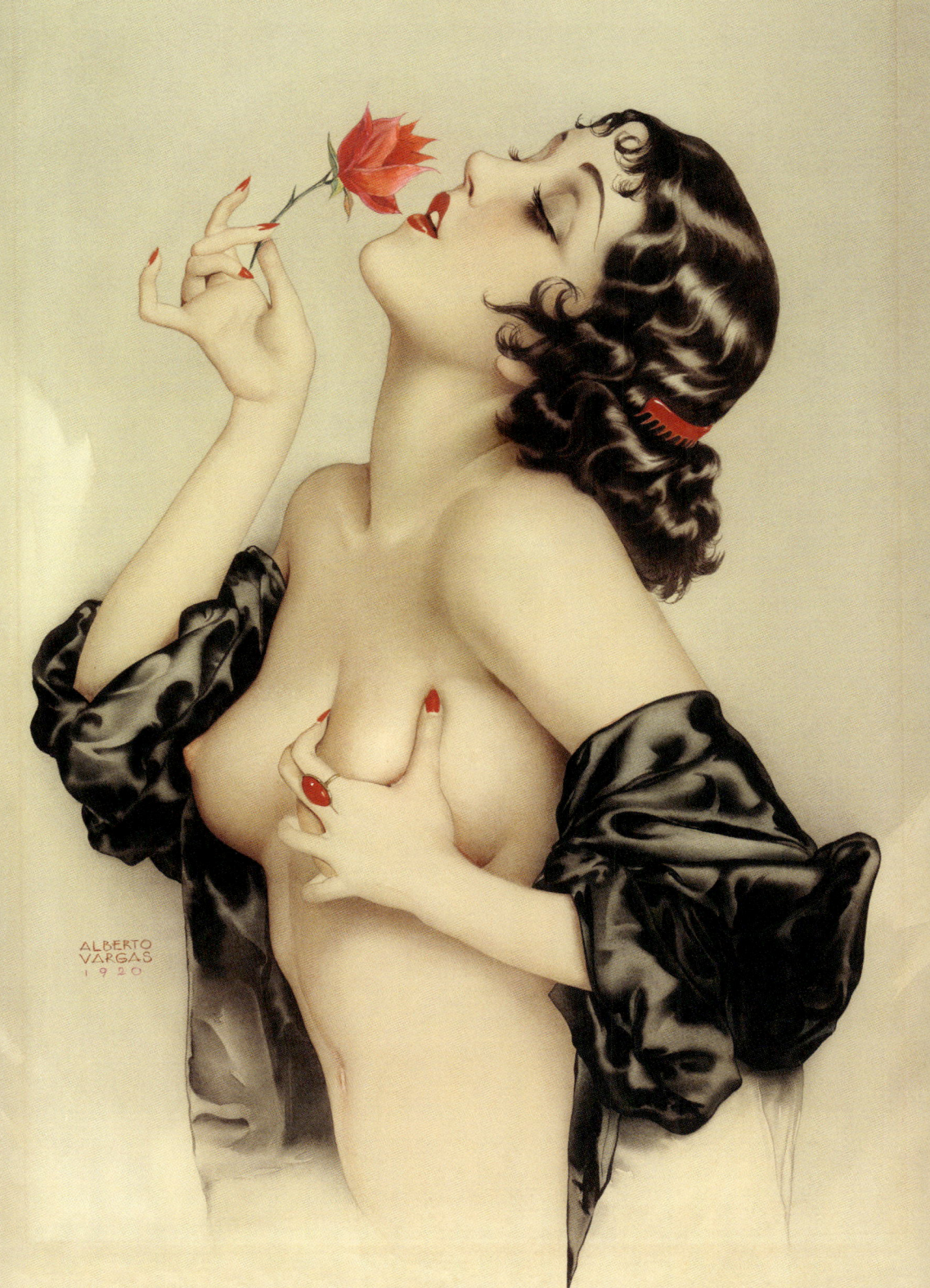

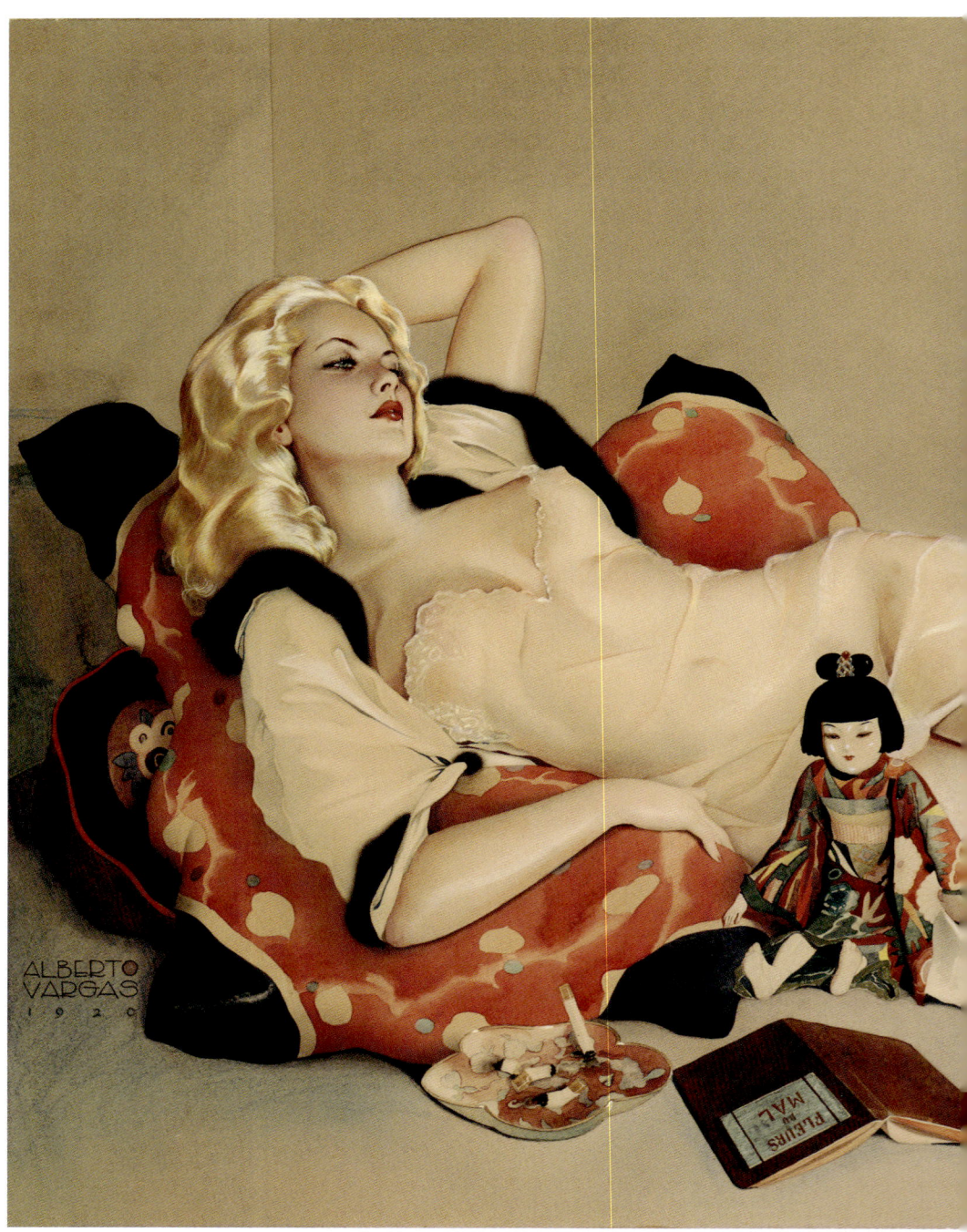

Above: Fleurs du Mal, watercolor on paper, 1920. Though originally painted as a nude, Vargas added the slip at the request of Paramount Pictures, which licensed the painting to promote a film starring actress Miriam

Hopkins sometime around 1930 (no evidence of this exists in posters for her films). When the painting was returned to Vargas, he repainted it again with a raised hem. The Max Vargas Collection.

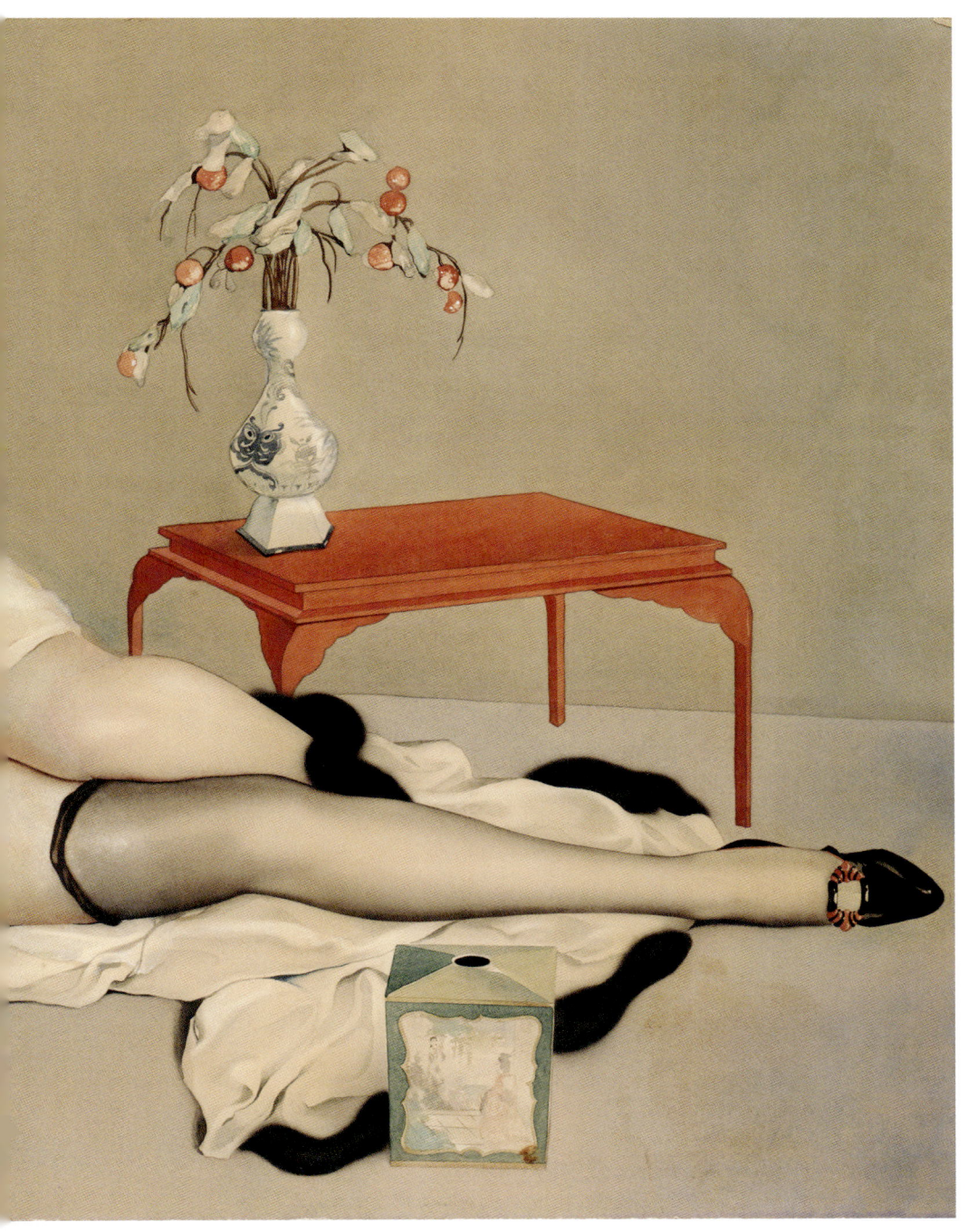

ALBERTO VARGAS

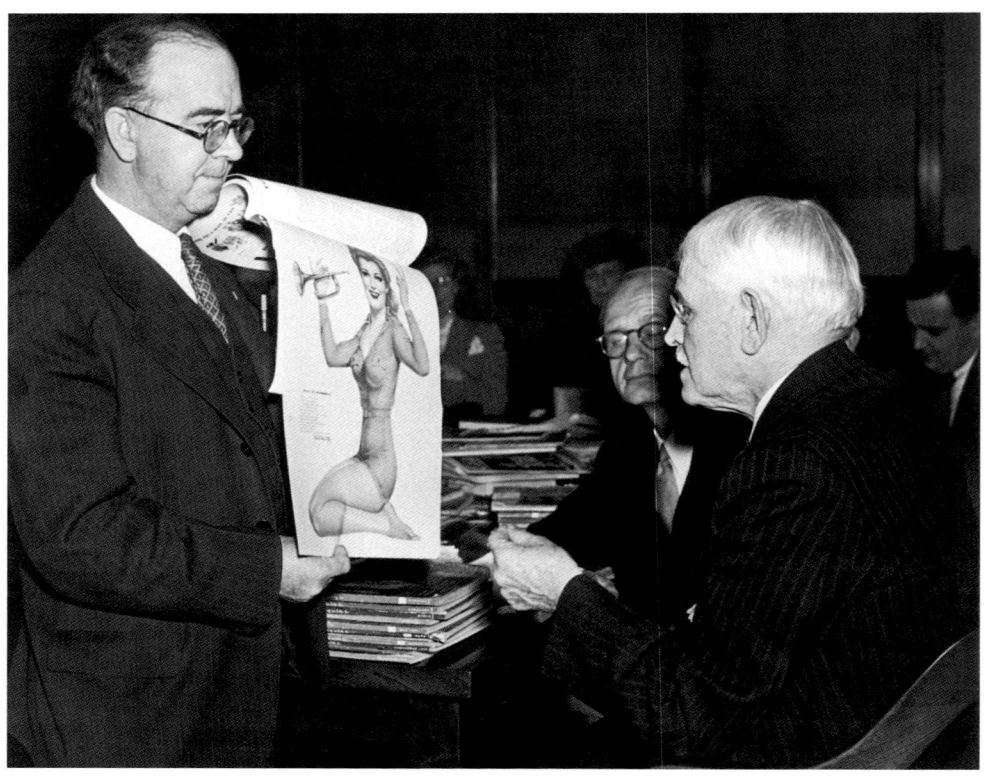

Above: Post office attorney William C. O'Brien, left, shows Bishop Edwin Hughes, Methodist resident bishop of Washington, D.C., the April 1943 *Esquire* Varga Girl. When asked what he thought of the picture, the bishop remarked: "I wouldn't care to exhibit this in my Sunday school." *Esquire* had been charged with disseminating obscenity for the supposed explicit nature of the pin-up in its September 1943 issue. © Bettmann/ Corbis Images.

Opposite: Peace, It's Wonderful! is the title of the poem accompanying this optimistic foldout from the April 1943 issue of *Esquire*. This is perhaps the first link between what was then the victory sign with the peace sign of the 1960s. 17.75 x 14 inches.

Following spread: Watercolor on board, 1942, for the January 1943 issue of *Esquire*. 29.75 x 19.75 inches. The Spencer Museum of Art.

THE ART OF PIN-UP

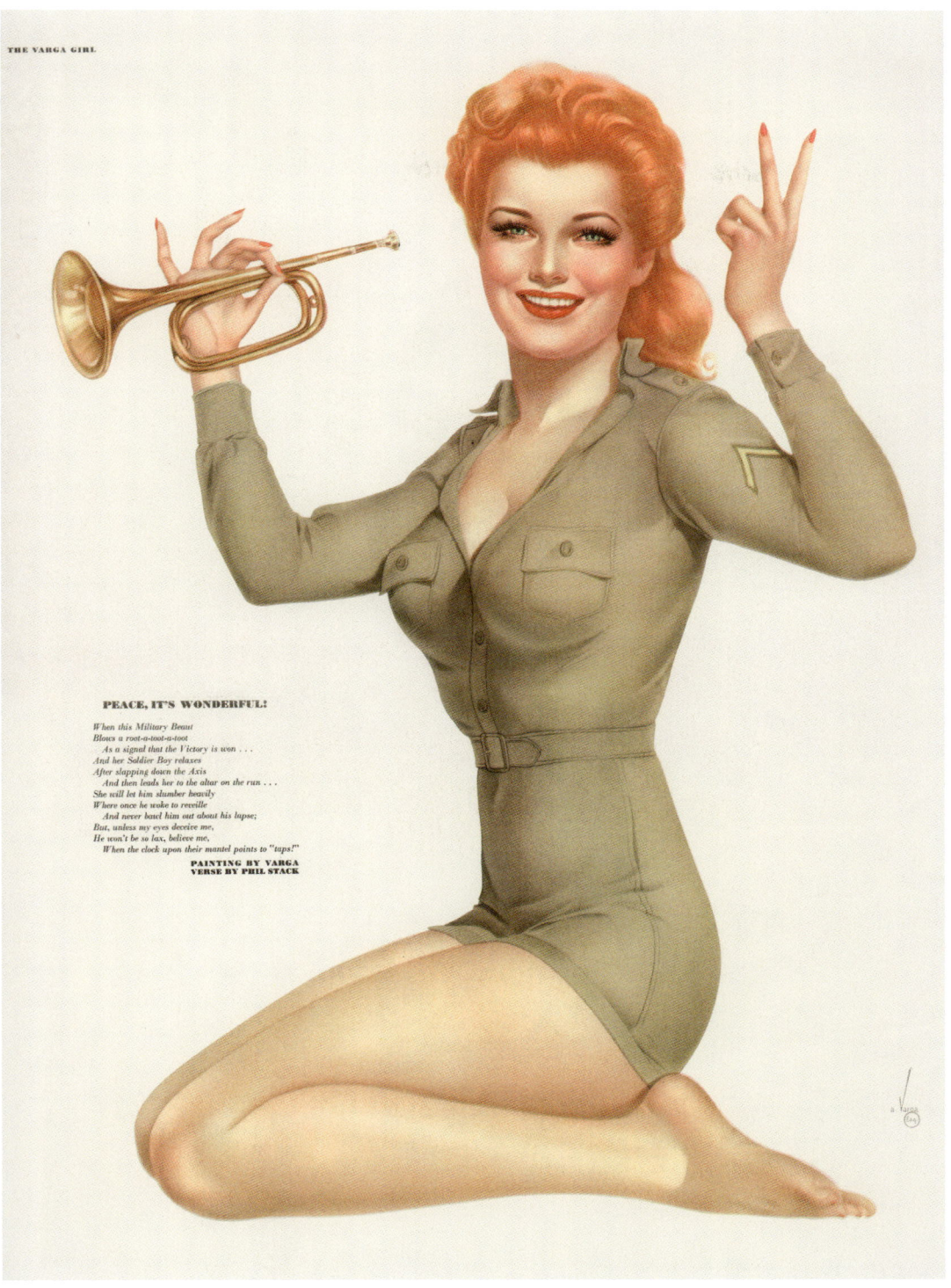

PEACE, IT'S WONDERFUL!

When this Military Beaut
Blows a root-a-toot-a-toot
As a signal that the Victory is won . . .
And her Soldier Boy relaxes
After slapping down the Axis
And then leads her to the altar on the run . . .
She will let him slumber heavily
Where once he woke to reveille
And never bawl him out about his lapse;
But, unless my eyes deceive me,
He won't be so lax, believe me,
When the clock upon their mantel points to "taps!"

PAINTING BY VARGA
VERSE BY PHIL STACK

ALBERTO VARGAS

471

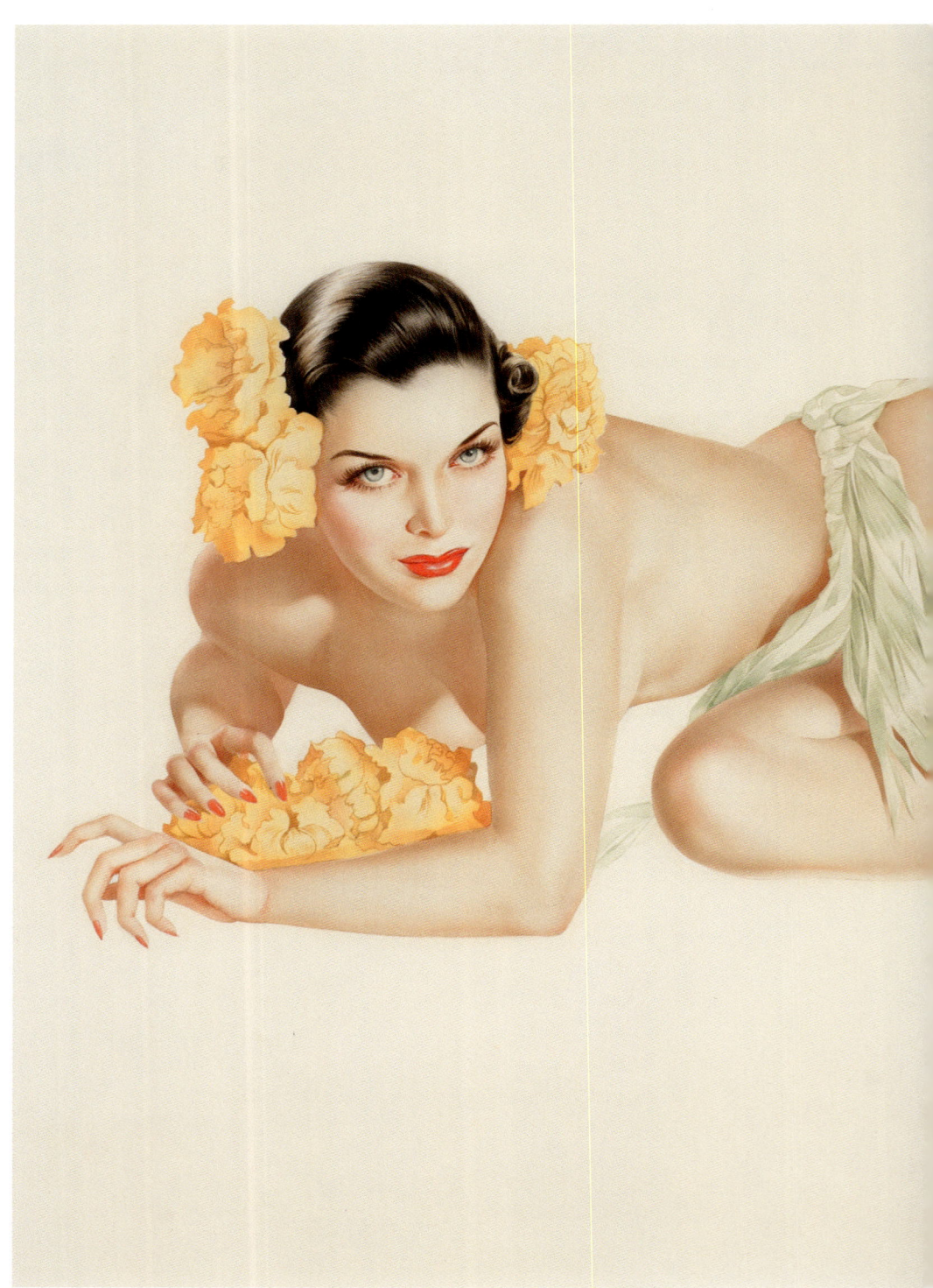

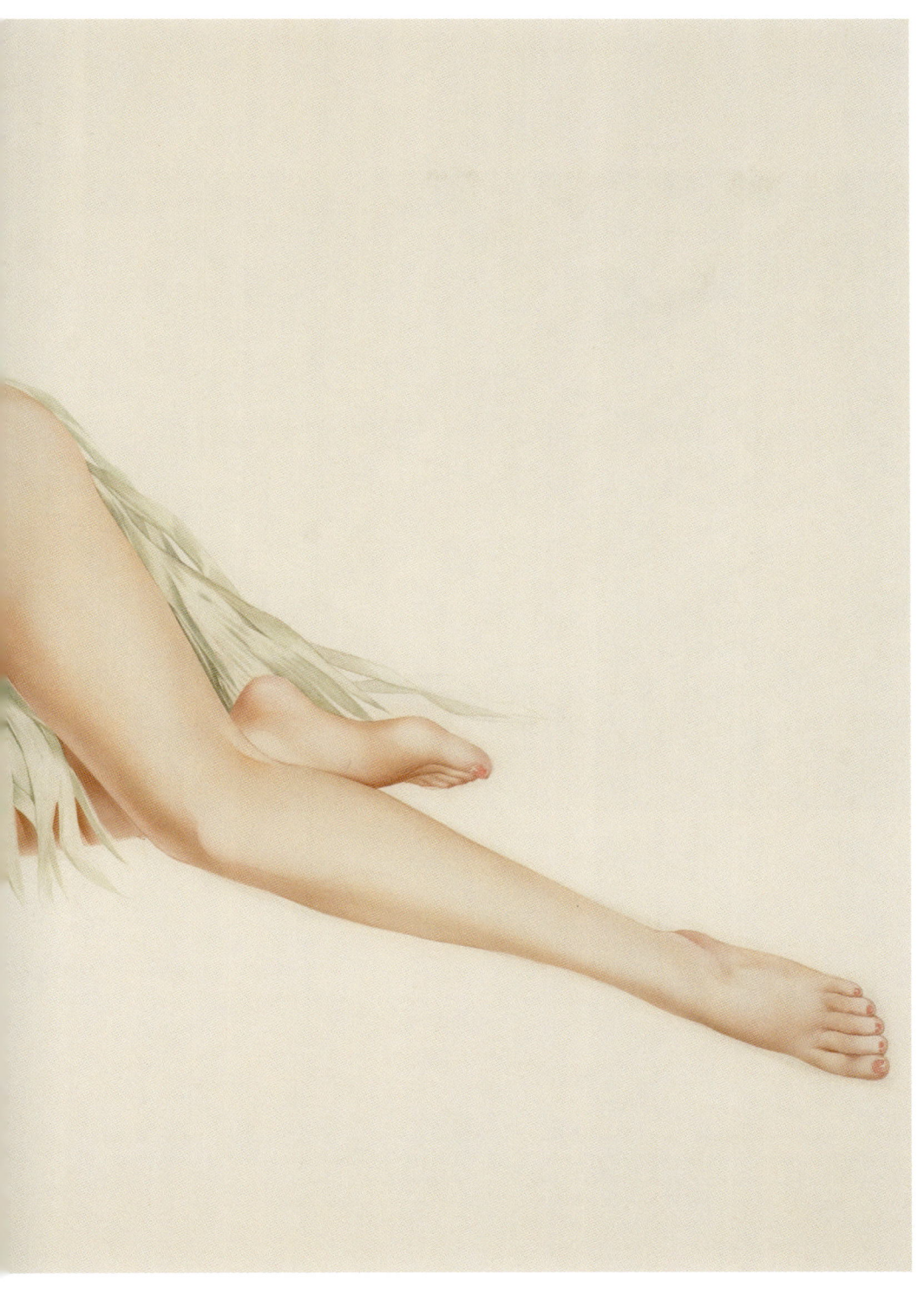

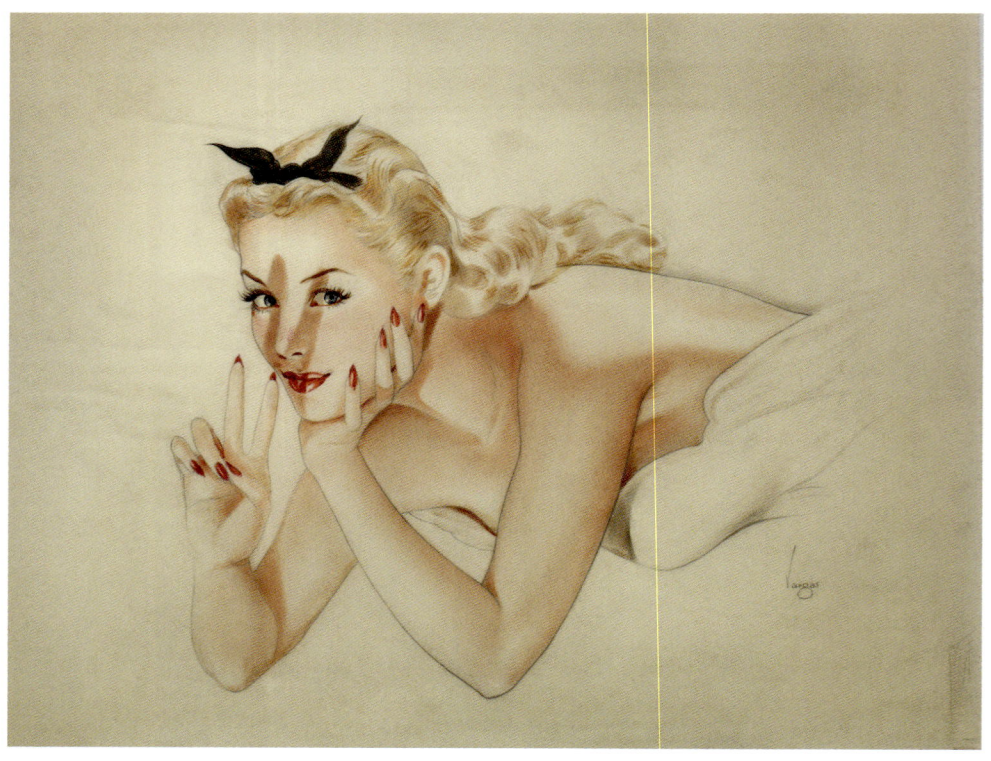

Above: A pencil-and-watercolor variation sketch of an assignment for Jergen's Face Powder, 1943. In the ad, the model is dressed in a white blouse and holding an airman's wings in her hand. The "V" for victory sign, shadowed on her face, is unique in Vargas' work, and her expression is more seductive here than in the finished ad. The Max Vargas Collection.

Opposite: Pencil-and-watercolor preparatory sketch on tissue, 1943, for *The American Weekly*'s Sweethearts of the Armed Forces. This pin-up was for the tank division. The Max Vargas Collection.

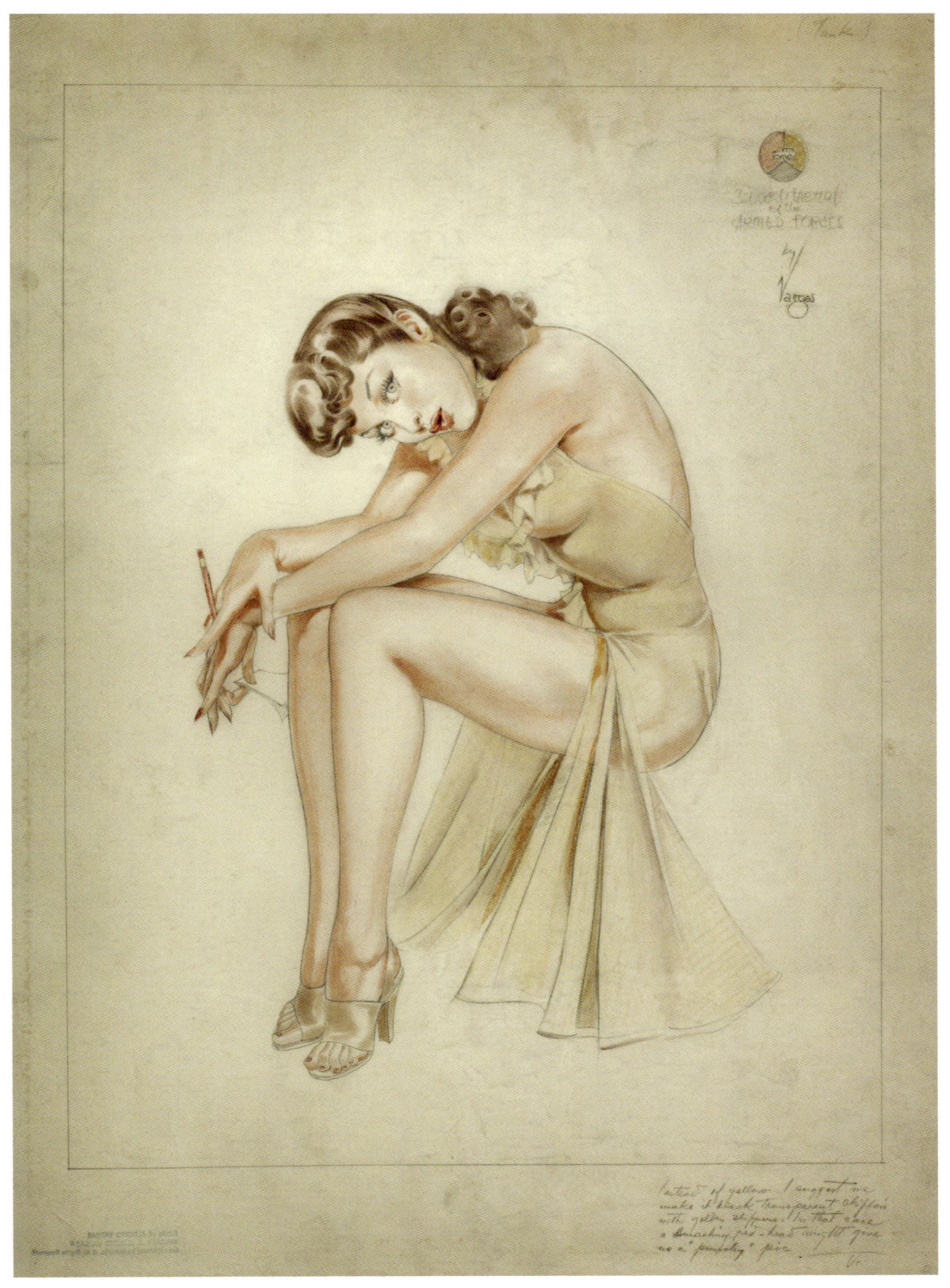

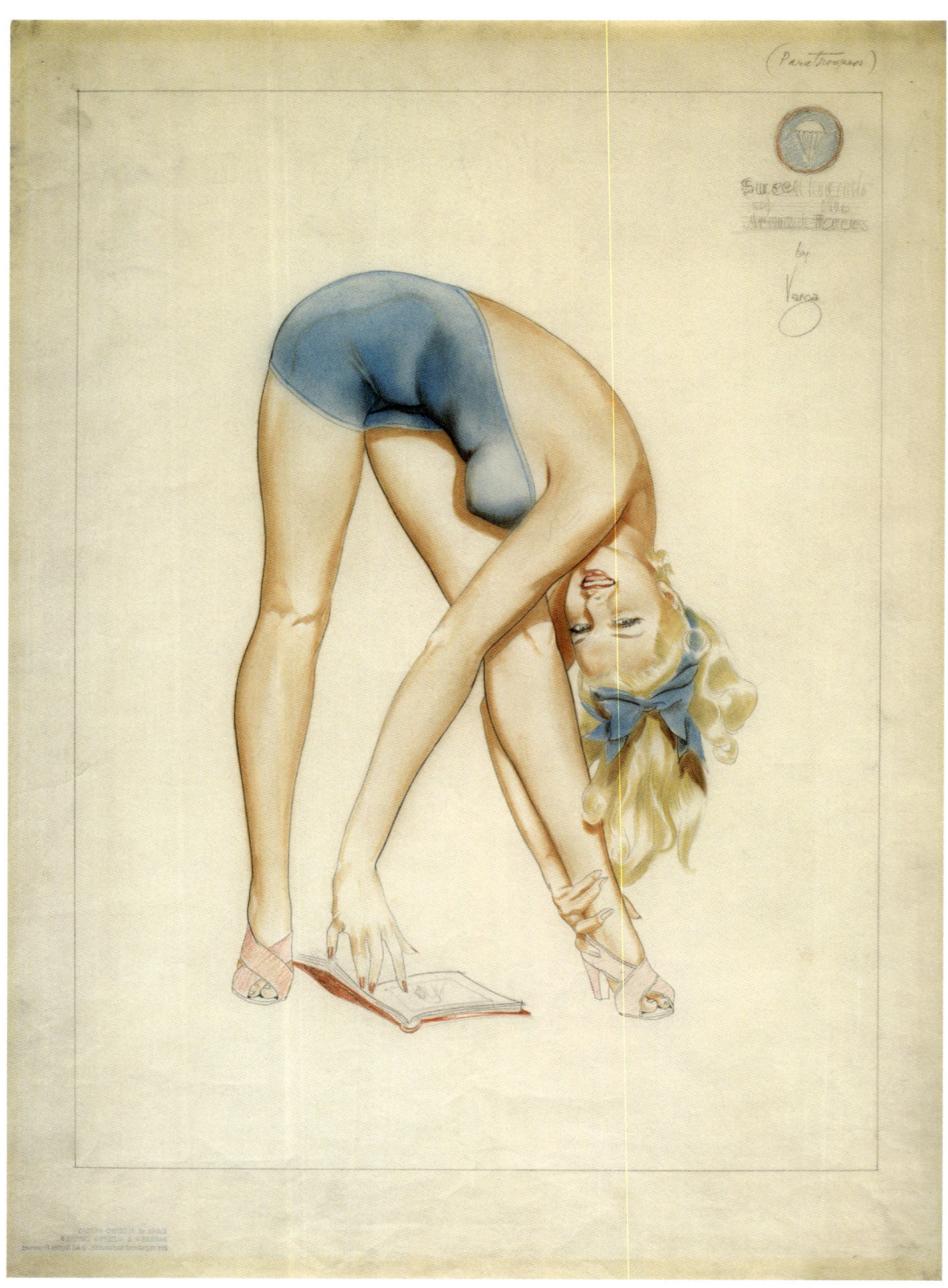

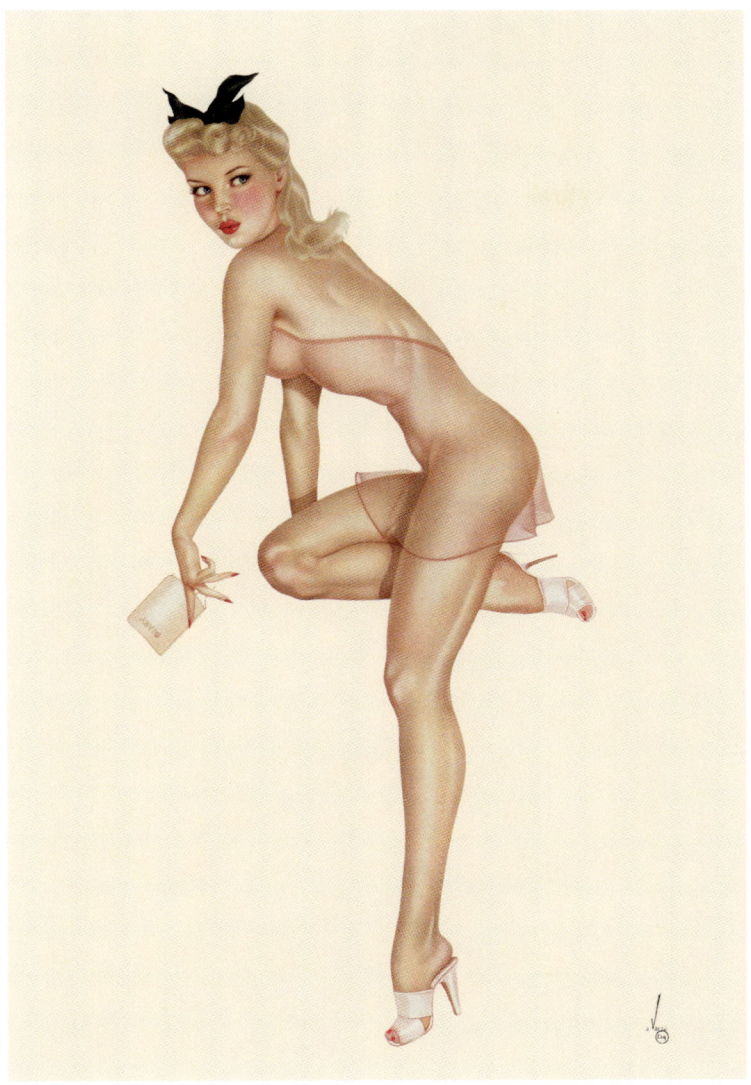

Opposite: Pencil-and-watercolor preparatory study on tissue, 1943, for *The American Weekly*'s Sweethearts of the Armed Forces. Each image was for a different military specialty—this one paratroopers—and included a graphic symbol representing the specialty. Some of the pin-ups created for this series subsequently appeared in the *1945 Esquire Varga Calendar*, sans symbol and designation. This did not. The Max Vargas Collection.

Above: The American postmaster general declared this September 1943 Vargas foldout obscene and sued *Esquire*. In response to the news a navy lieutenant in the Pacific theater wrote his congressman that "*Esquire* magazine is an aid to morale among fighting men." He went on to detail the death of a young man under his command who was shot in his foxhole still clutching an *Esquire* foldout of a Varga girl. "He had not wanted to risk leaving his picture in his tent for fear the enemy would get it." The case was ultimately dismissed.

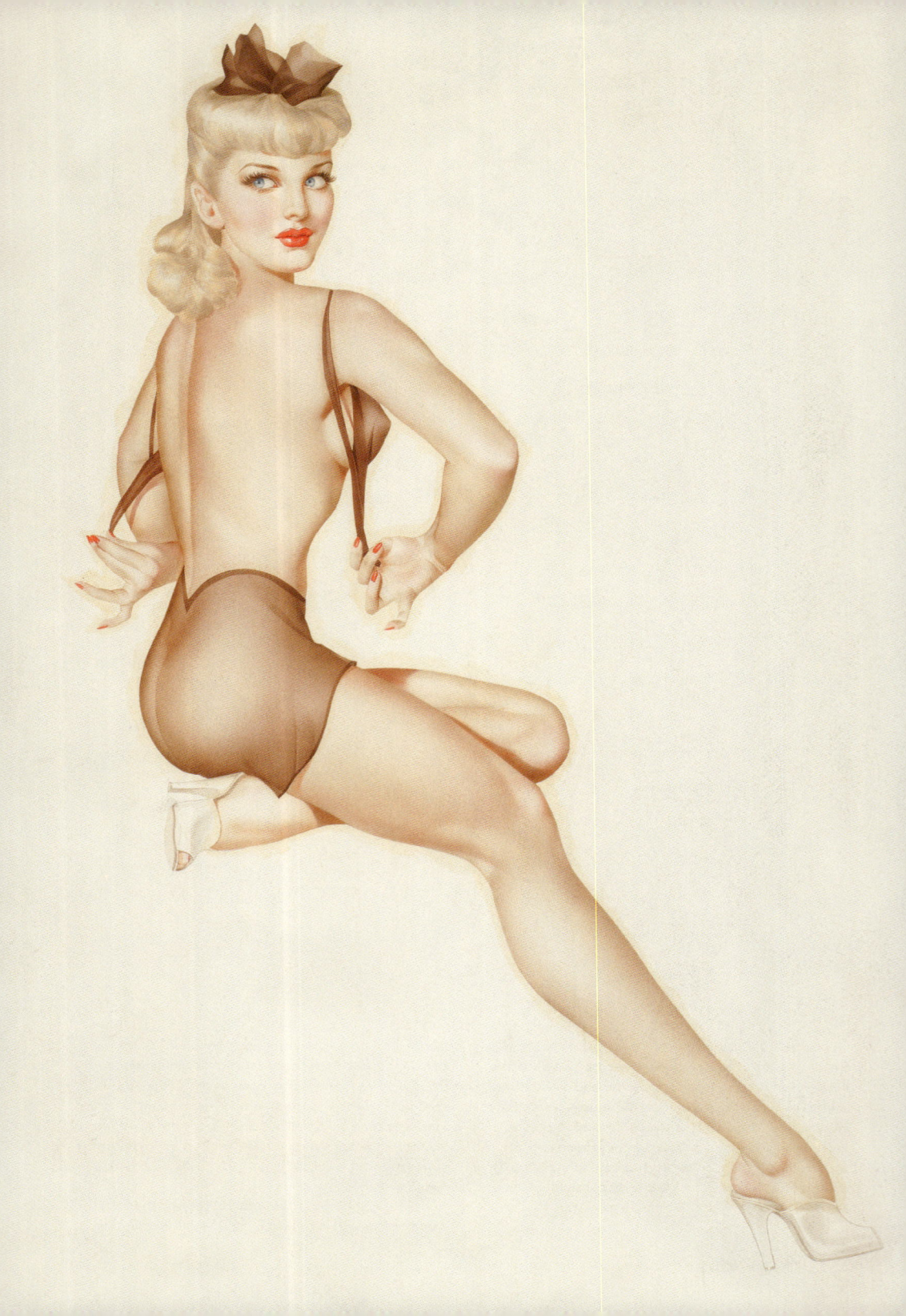

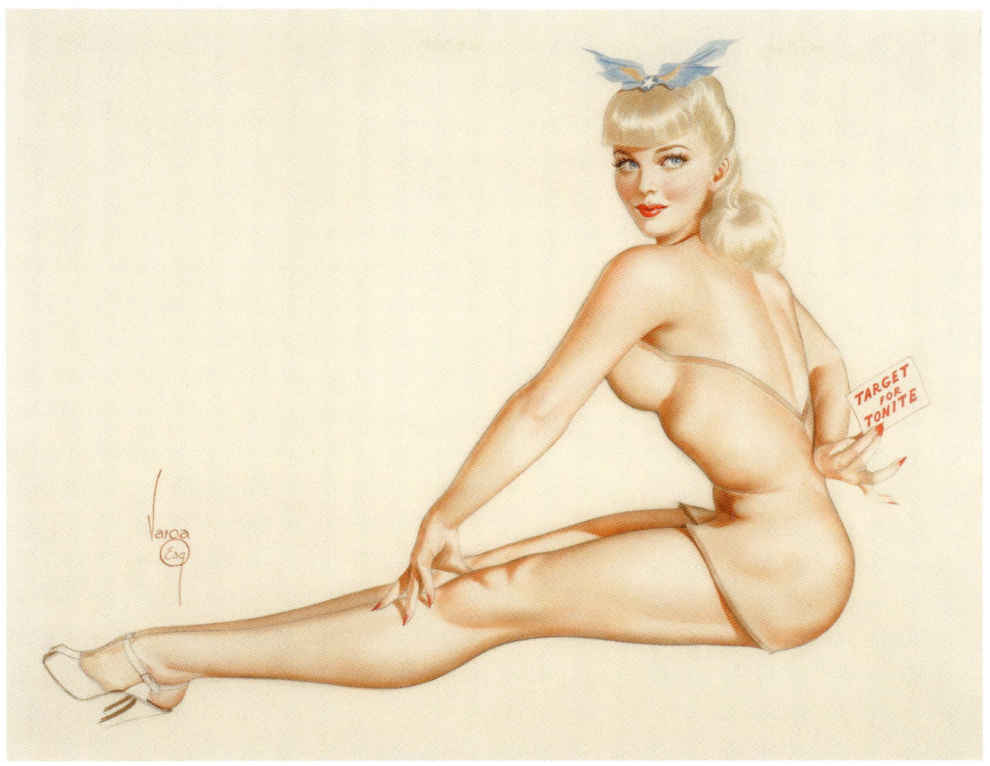

Opposite: Watercolor on paper, 1943, for Miss January, 1944 *Esquire* calendar. Feminist, writer and activist Andrea.Dworkin visited the Spencer Museum of Art at the University of Kansas, where this and all other Vargas images belonging to *Esquire* magazine now reside, and wrote that the work, collectively, is "some lazy, fetishistic view of white women, pale women, usually blonde." 26 x 22 inches. The Spencer Museum of Art.

Above: Watercolor on board, 1943, for the back cover of the March 1944 military edition of *Esquire*. This is the first of 19 original back cover pin-ups created by Vargas for *Esquire*'s military editions — regular issues printed with no advertising and distributed free to troops. 30 x 19/75 inches.

Following spread: Watercolor on board, 1944, for the August 1944 issue of *Esquire*. The Spencer Museum of Art.

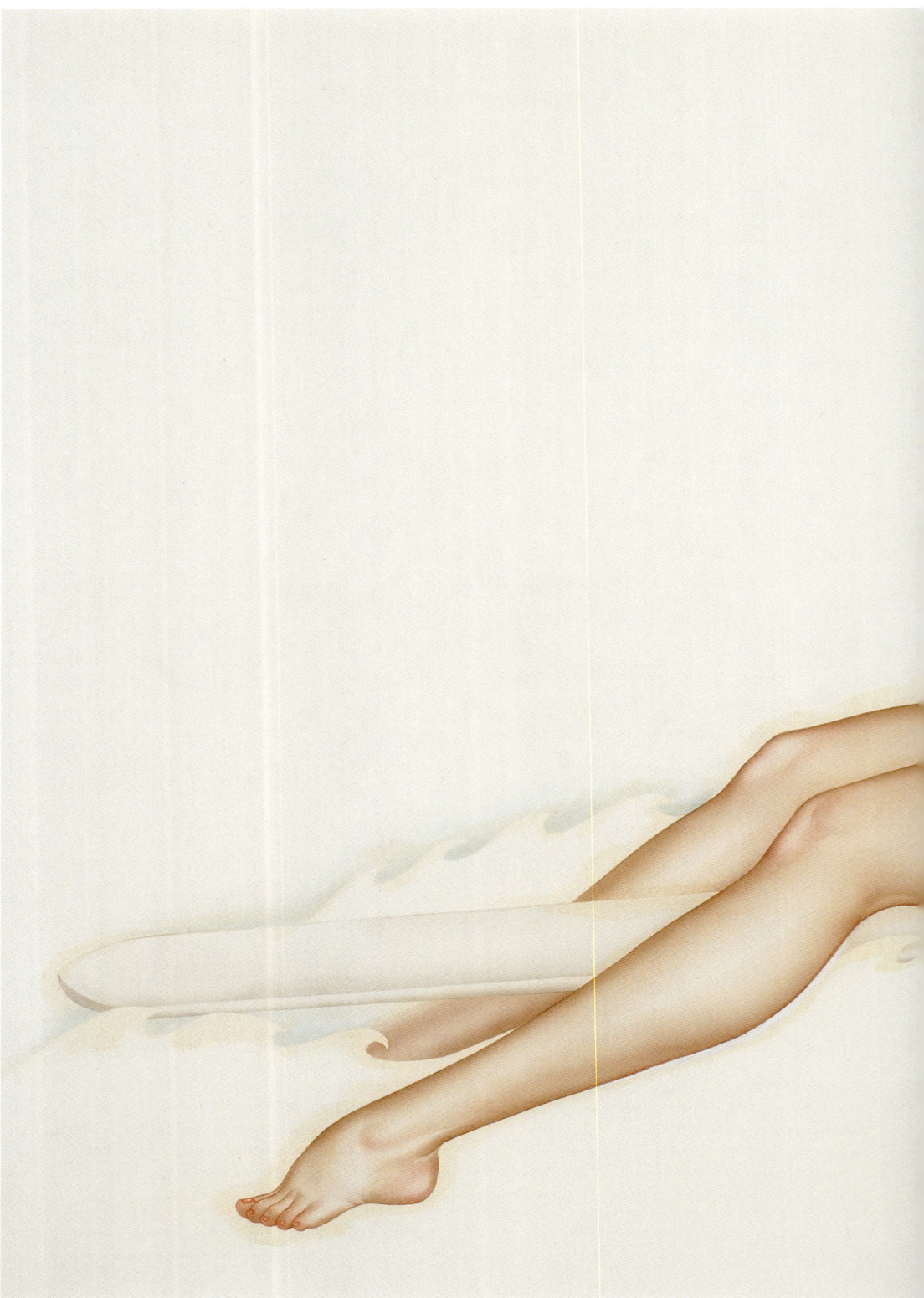

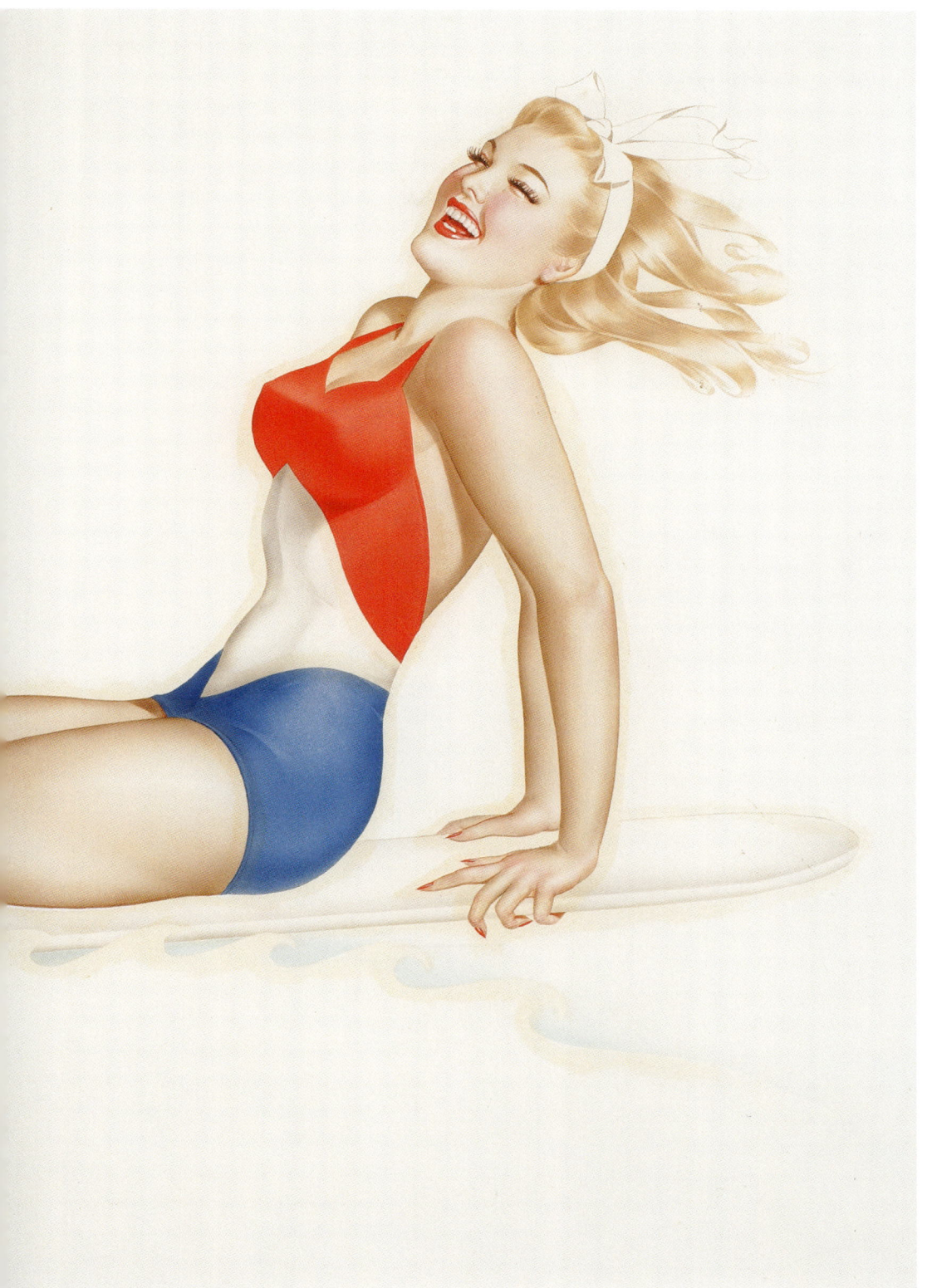

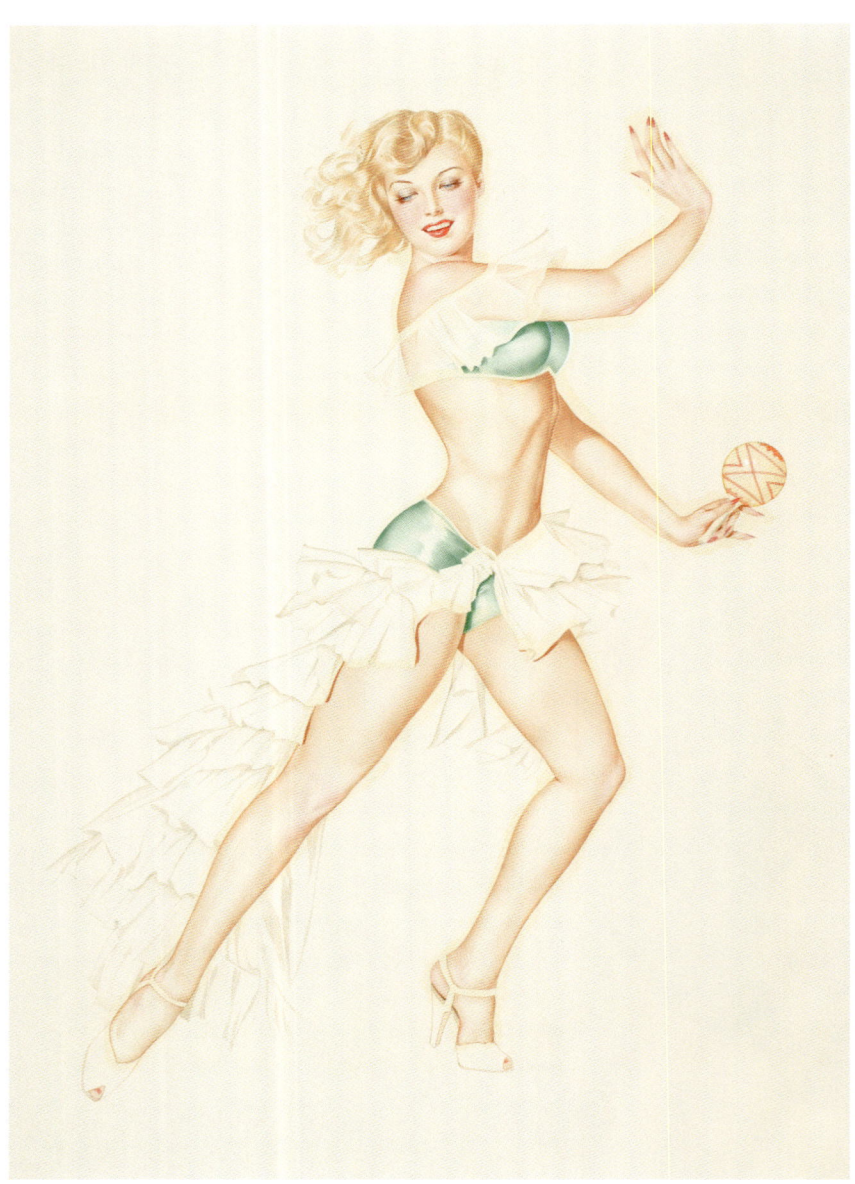

Above: Watercolor on board, 1945, for the October 1945 issue of *Esquire*. 30 x 21.75 inches. The Spencer Museum of Art.

Opposite: Watercolor on board, 1944, for the March 1945 issue of *Esquire*. 25 x 16 inches.

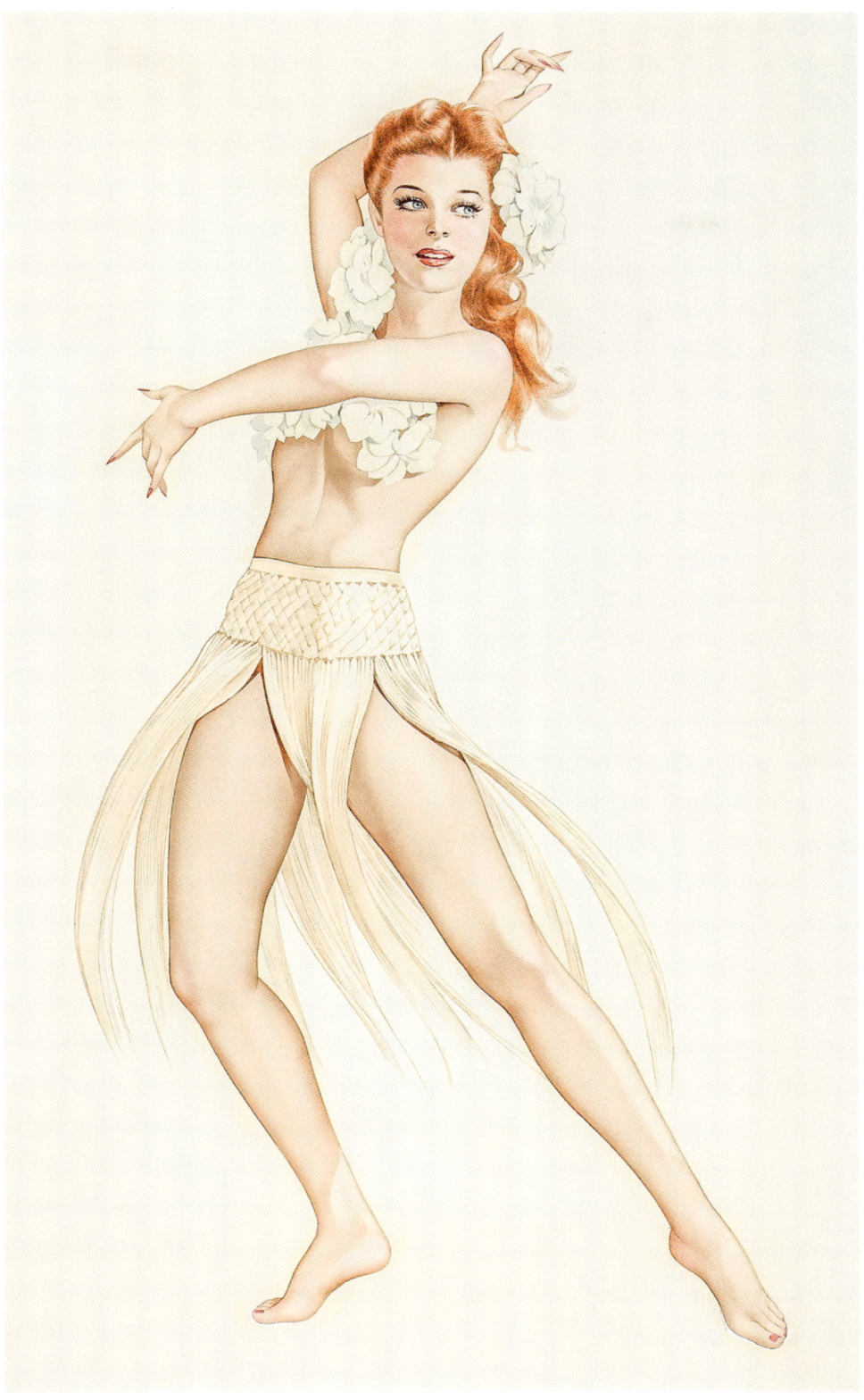

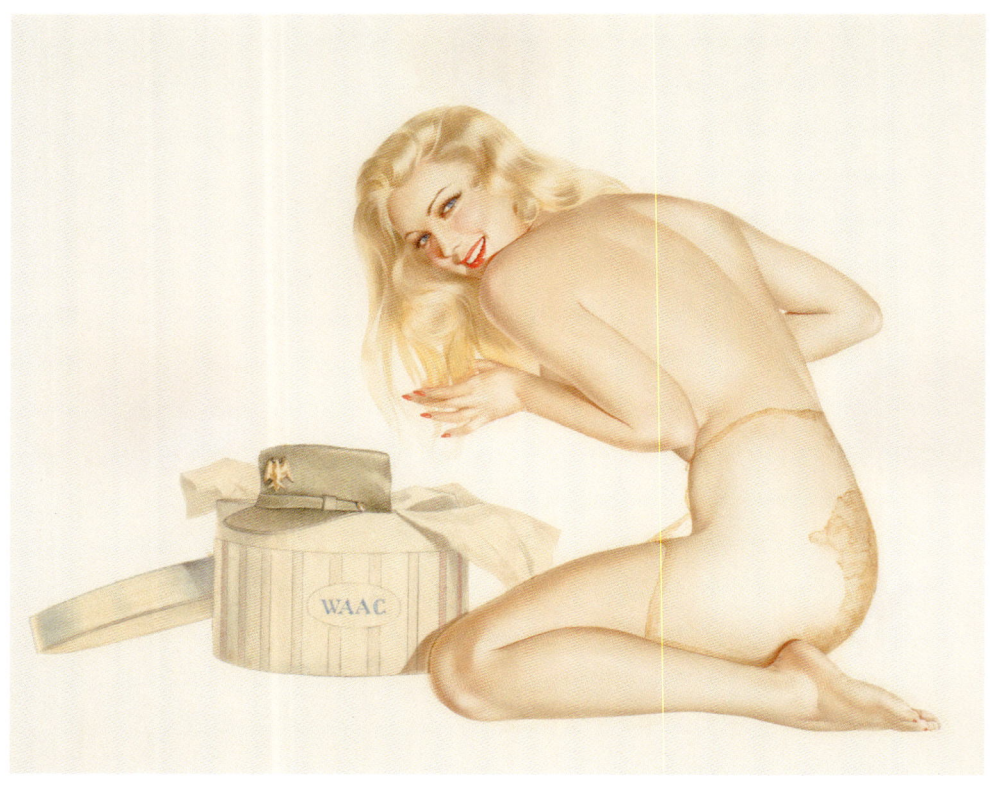

Above: Watercolor on board, 1943, for Miss December in the *1943 Esquire Varga Calendar*. The stain at the waist, thigh, and hip is glue that originally held on a paper sarong. It was Vargas's habit to paint his figures nude and add the clothing later. 30 x 23 inches. The Spencer Museum of Art.

Opposite: Watercolor on board, 1945, for the March 1946 Varga Girl in *Esquire*. 30 x 21.25 inches. The Spencer Museum of Art

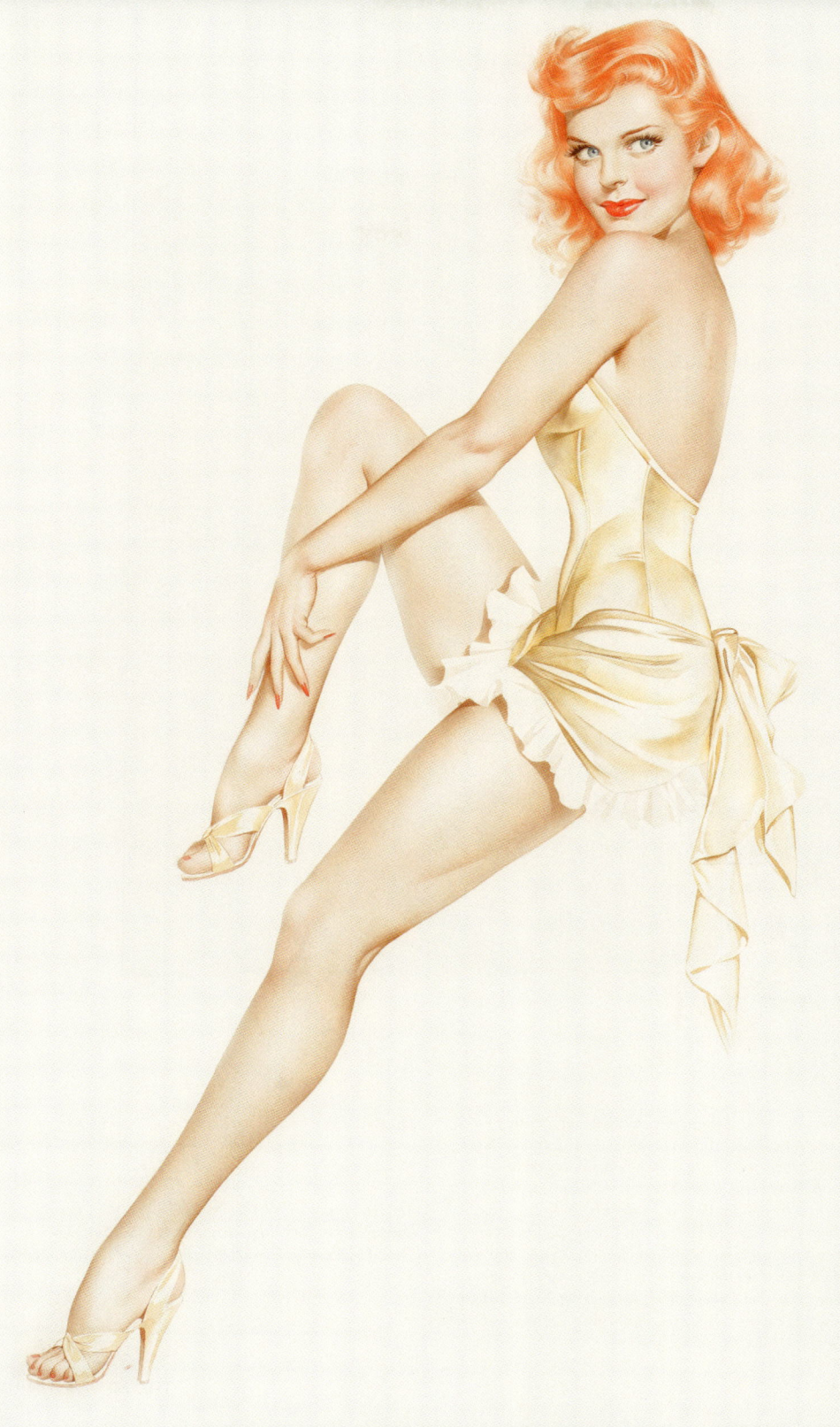

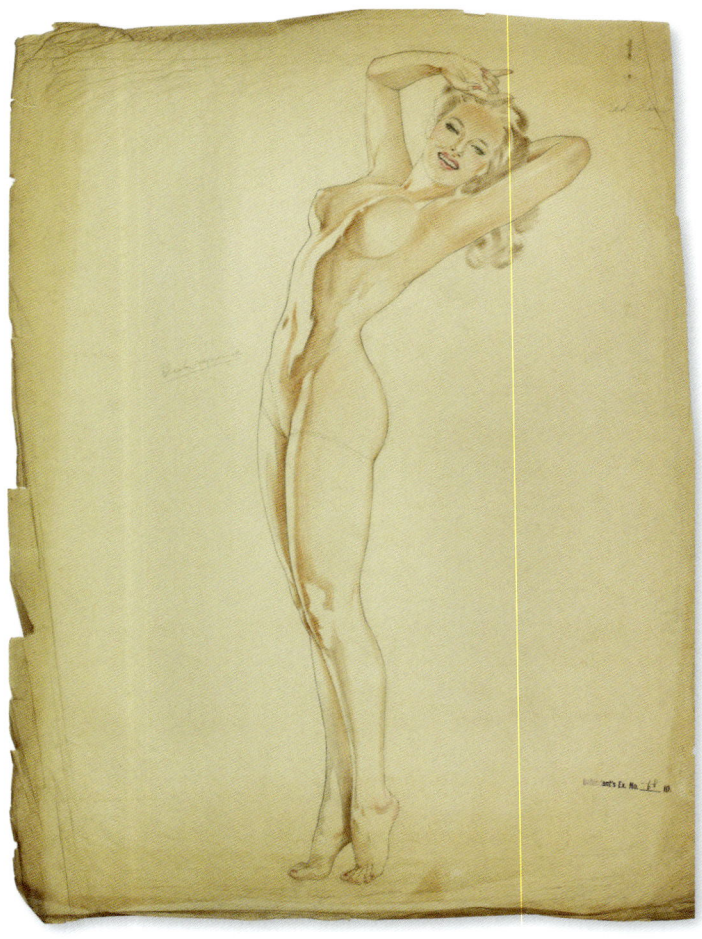

Above: Pencil-and-watercolor preparatory study on tissue, 1945, for the August 1945 issue of *Esquire*. Vargas made three preliminary sketches for every completed pin-up. First came a quick sketch on cheap paper, followed by a more detailed work on 36-by-24-inch tracing paper, as seen here. This tracing paper sketch was submitted to his editor for comments and changes before a final sketch was completed in chalk on heavy vellum. For anatomic realism, Vargas sketched this figure nude, adding the bathing suit only after perfecting her figure. The Max Vargas Collection.

Opposite: Watercolor on board, 1945, for the August 1945 issue of *Esquire* magazine. 26 x 21.75 inches. The Spencer Museum of Art.

Following spread: Watercolor on board, 1943, for the December 1943 issue of *Esquire*. 39.75 x 25 inches. The Spencer Museum of Art.

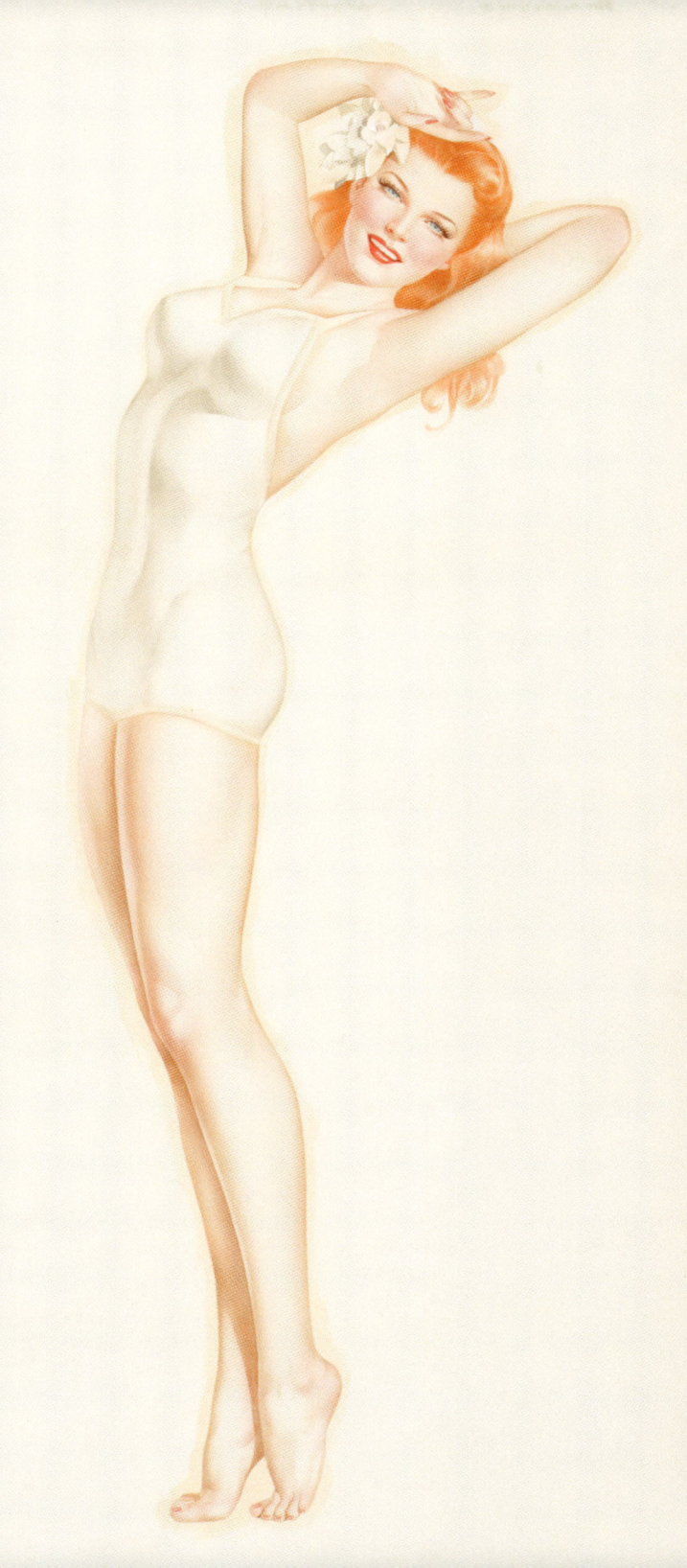

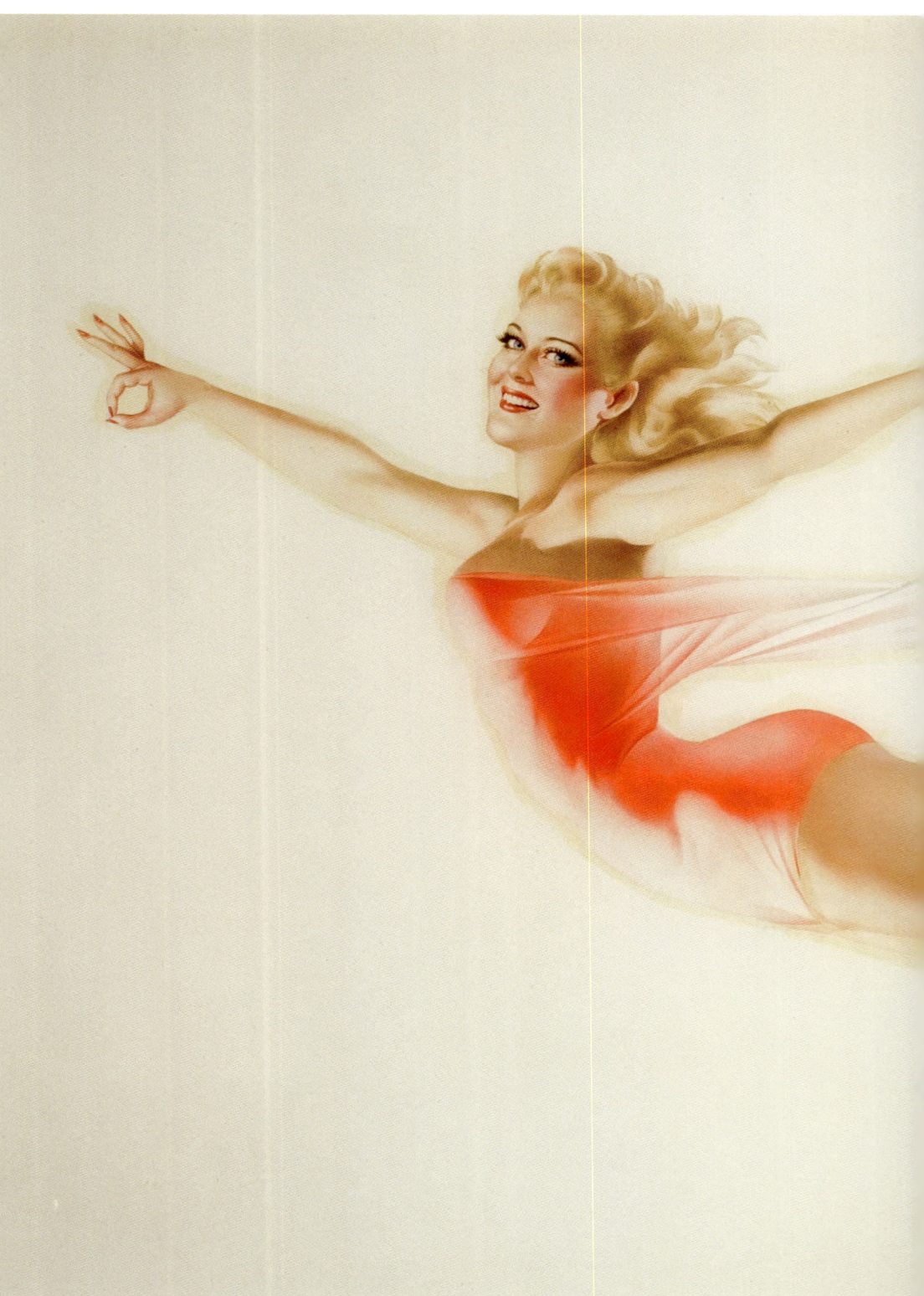

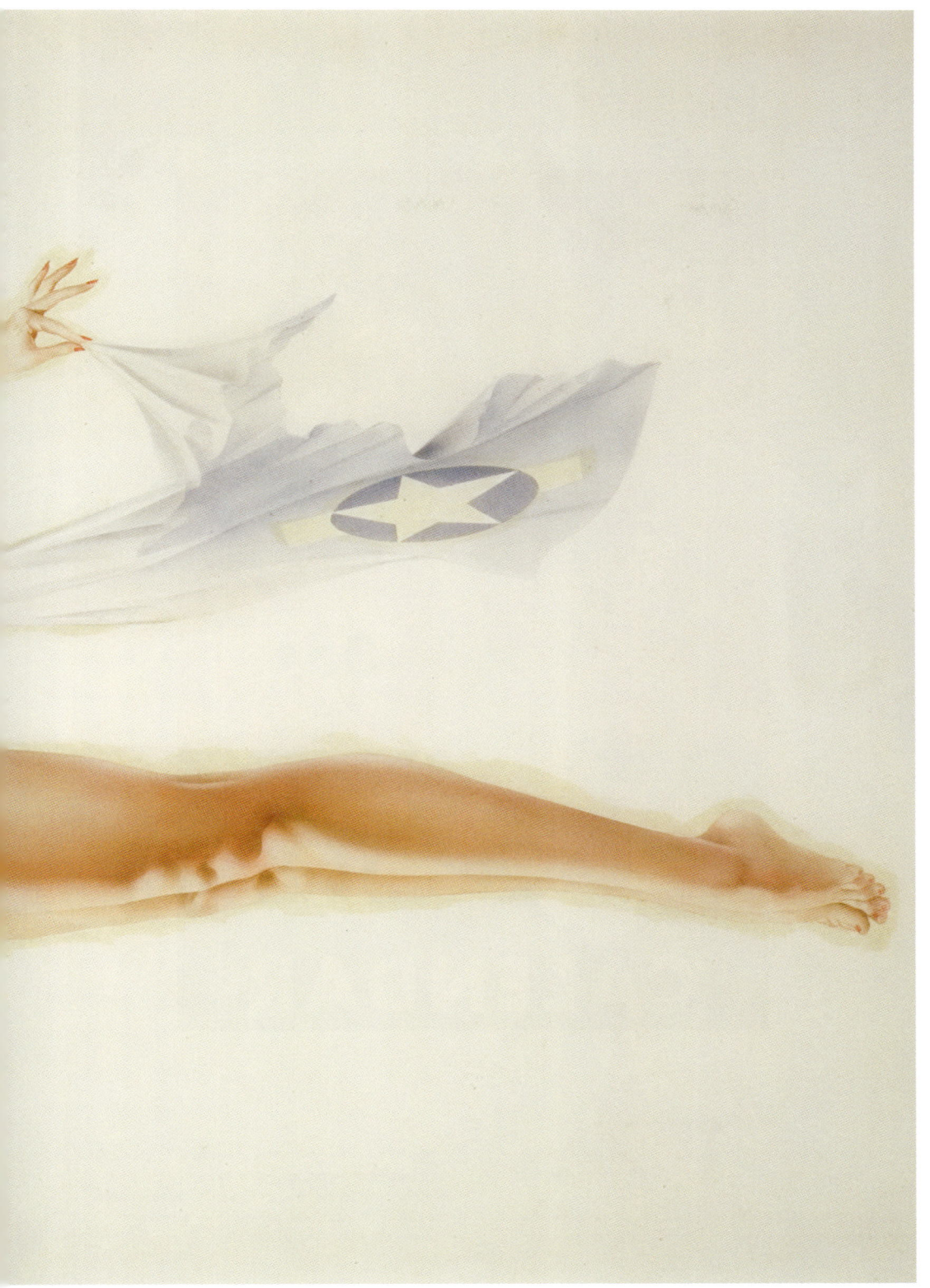

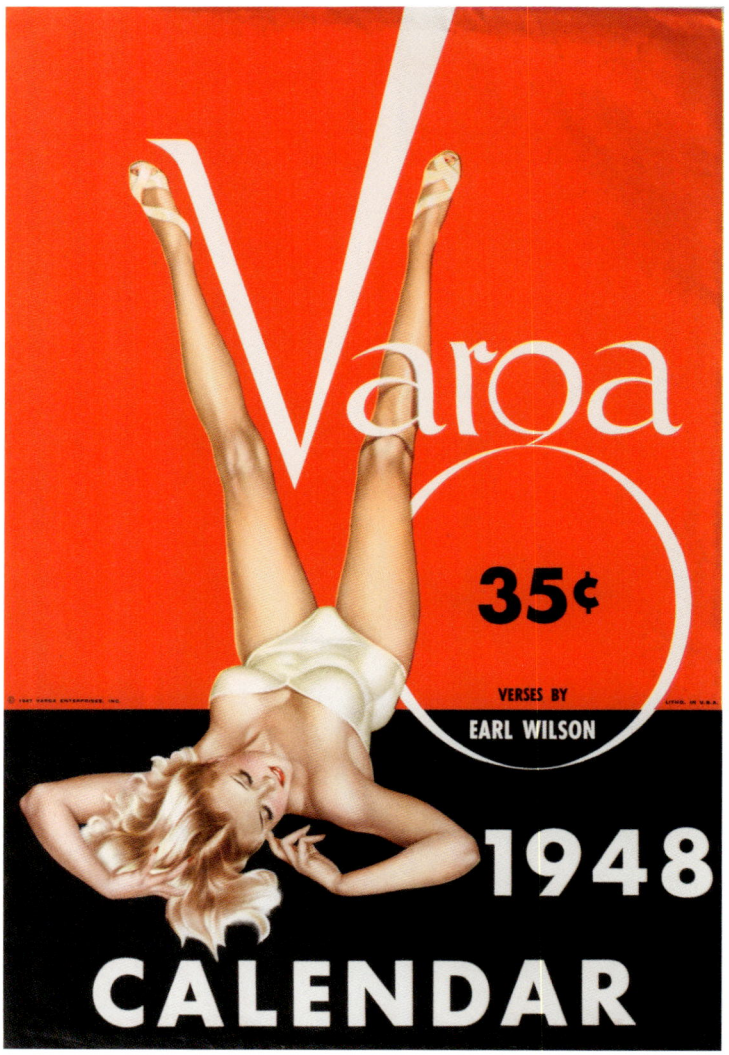

Varga

35¢

VERSES BY
EARL WILSON

1948

CALENDAR

Above: The cover of Vargas's self-published 1948 calendar, source of an *Esquire* infringement lawsuit.

Opposite: When Vargas left *Esquire* he produced his own Varga calendar for 1948, and was promptly sued

by *Esquire* for copyright infringement by using the abbreviated version of his name familiar to the public—and owned by *Esquire*. He had to rebrand, so he repainted the cover of his 1948 calendar with the "s" added to his name. The Max Vargas Collection.

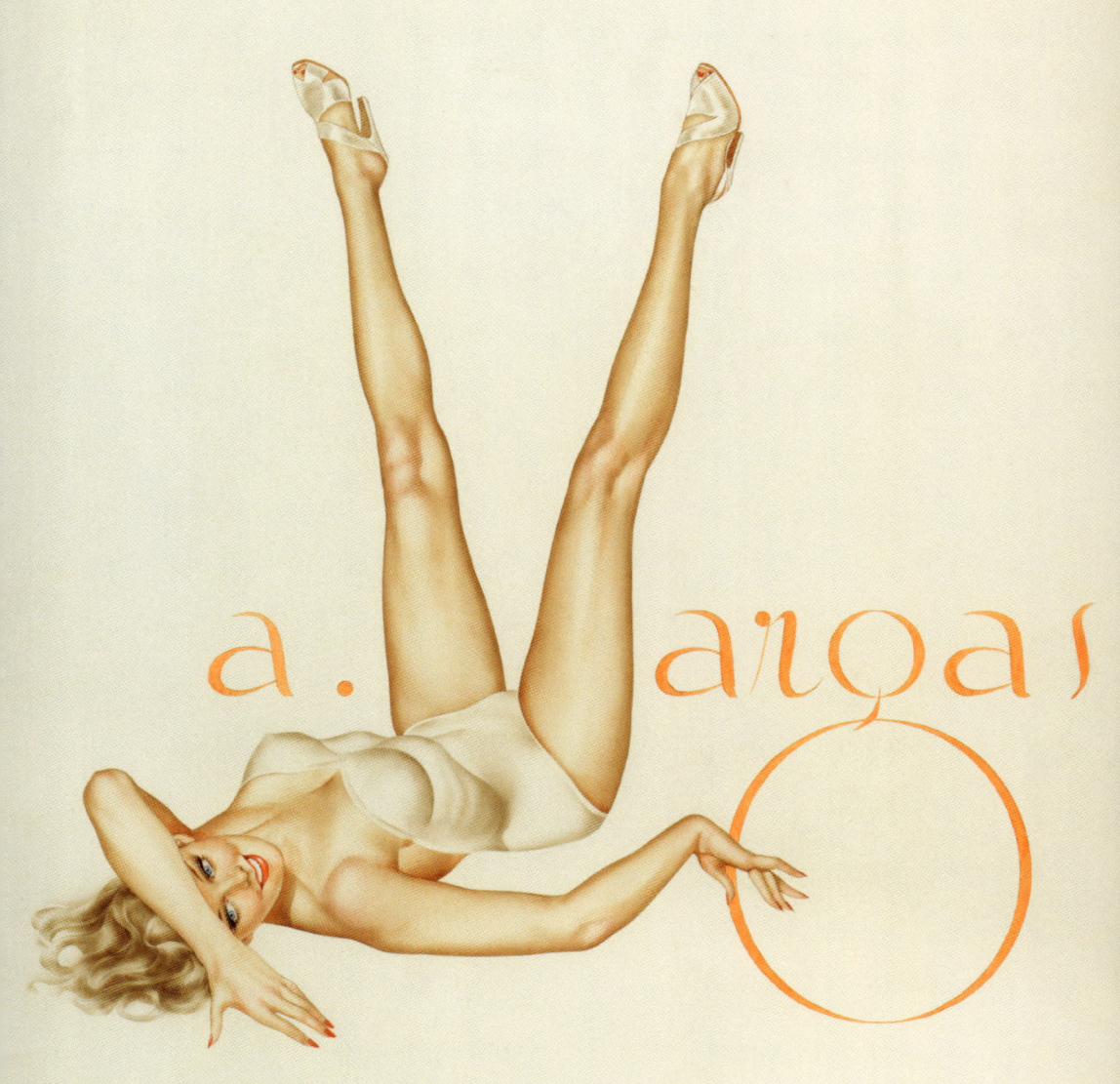

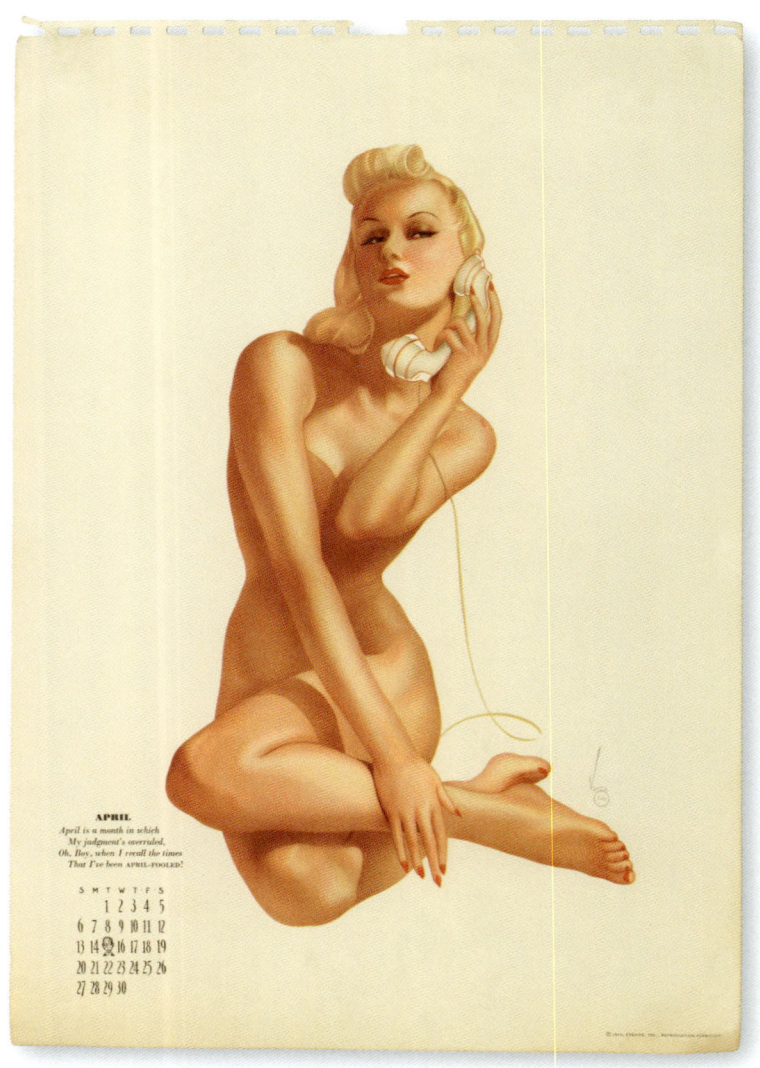

Above: Miss April from the *1941 Esquire Varga Calendar.*

Opposite: She Sells Sea Shells, Legacy Nude #12, water-color on board, 1956. Miss April from the 1941 *Esquire* calendar was a clear inspiration for this painting. Vargas was a worrier, and his biggest worry was how to support his wife in the event of his death. Thus he conceived

the Legacy Nude collection in the late 1930s: a group of 12 exquisite nudes intended to be released only after he died to support Anna Mae. The final painting, seen here, was completed in 1956. Since Anna Mae died before he did, the 12 paintings were divided between his niece and nephew upon his death. The Max Vargas Collection.

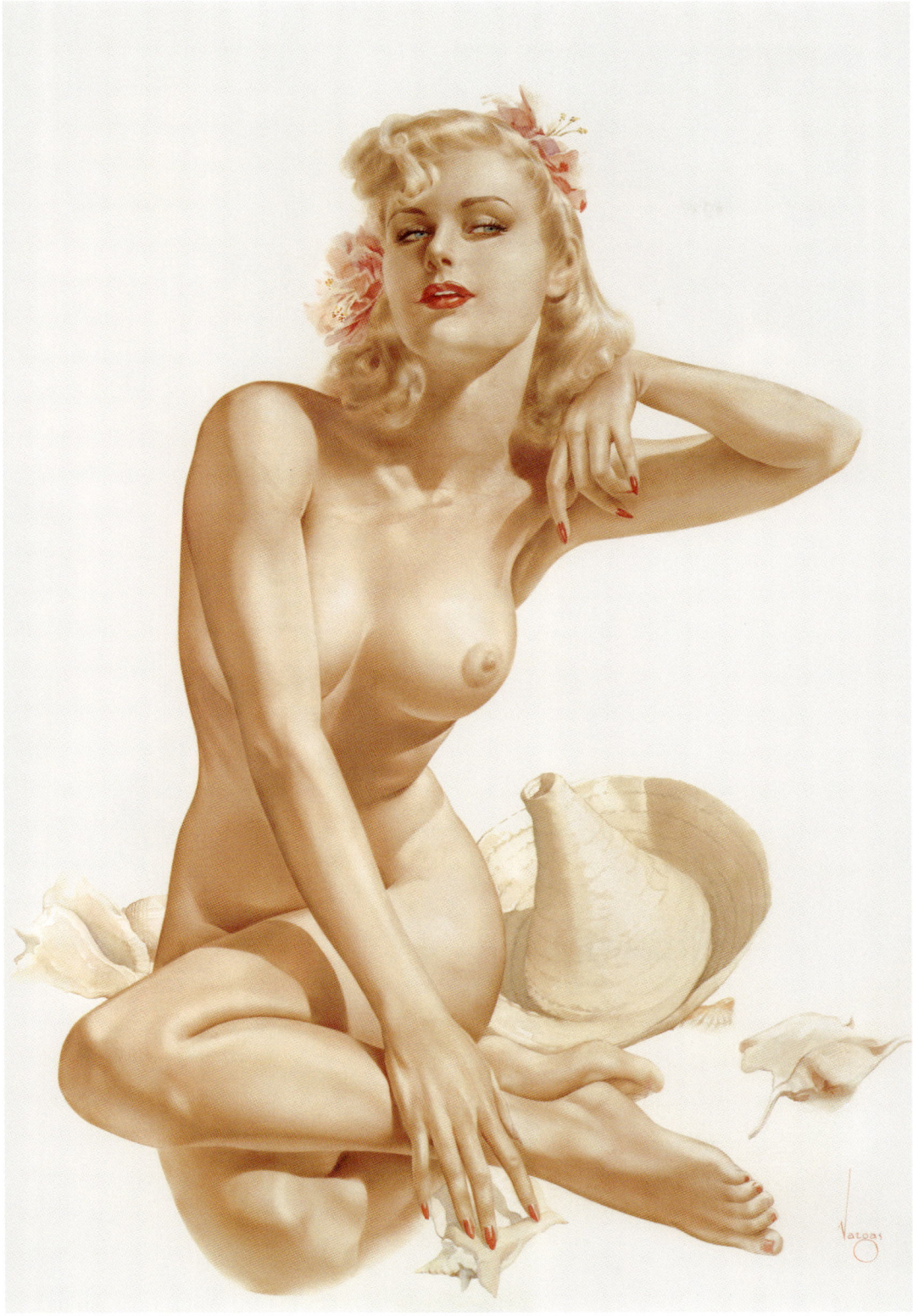

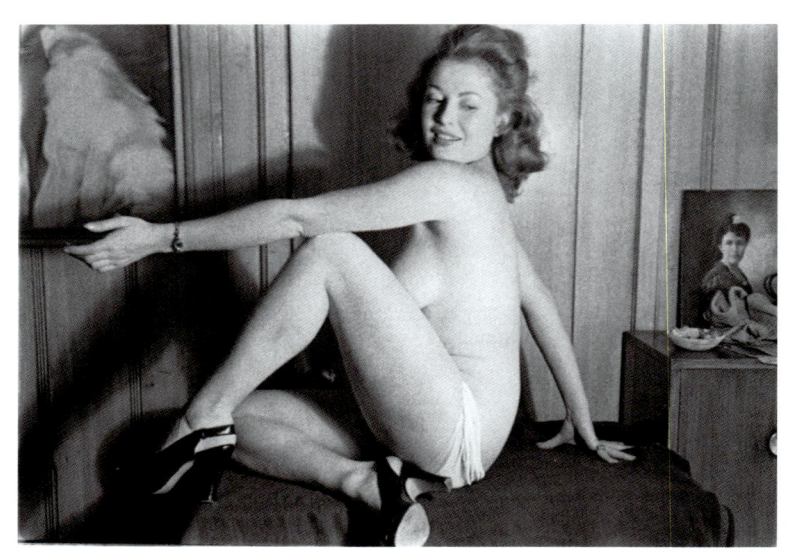

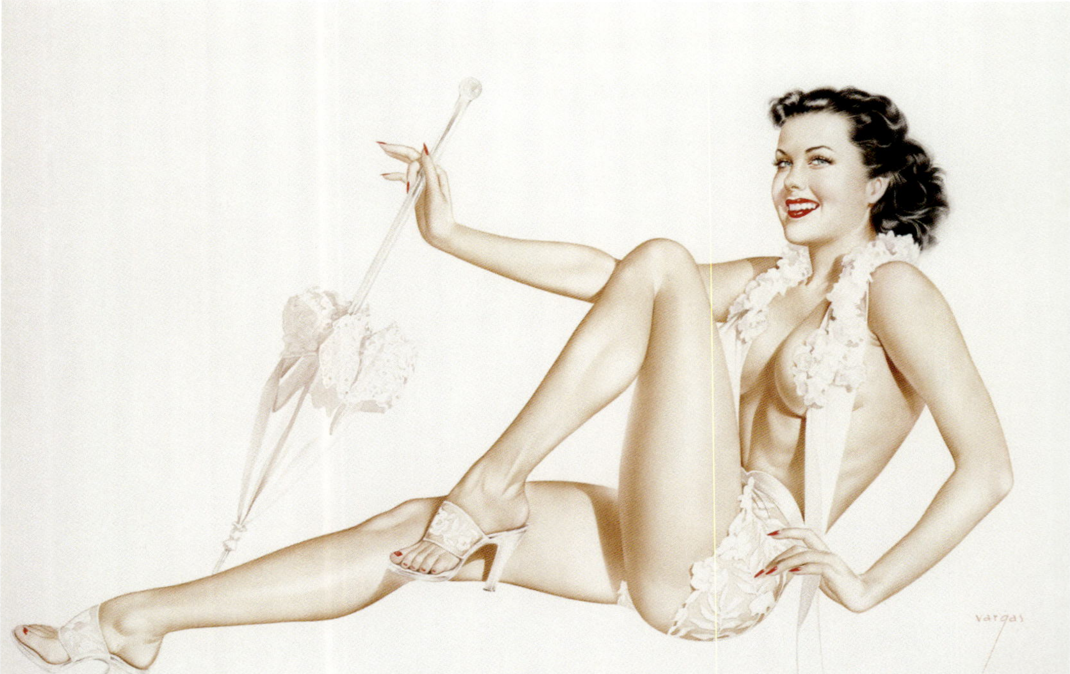

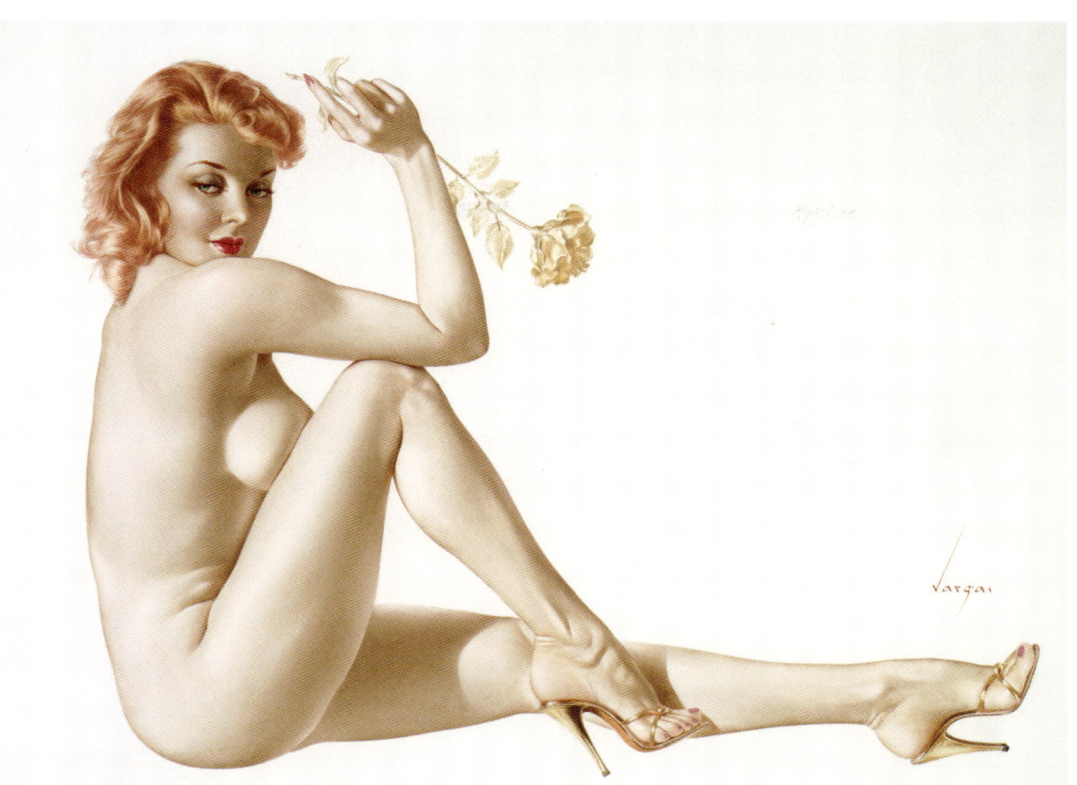

Opposite above: Model Jeanne Dean was a Vargas favorite, posing for the artist in 1941 and '42, when she was just 15 and 16, though a mature 15 and 16, as seen here. Of him she said, "He was one of the purest men I've ever known, and I don't just mean that he was intensely devoted and faithful to his wife. It was his thoughts, his gentleness. He was such a kind, soft-spoken man and so modest. He was very innocent, and I think that was translated to his pictures."

Opposite below: Miss April, watercolor on paper, circa 1954, for the Osborne calendar company's "Birthstone" calendar. The Max Vargas Collection.

Above: Gold Carnation, Legacy Nude #9, watercolor on board, circa 1950. The Max Vargas Collection.

ALBERTO VARGAS

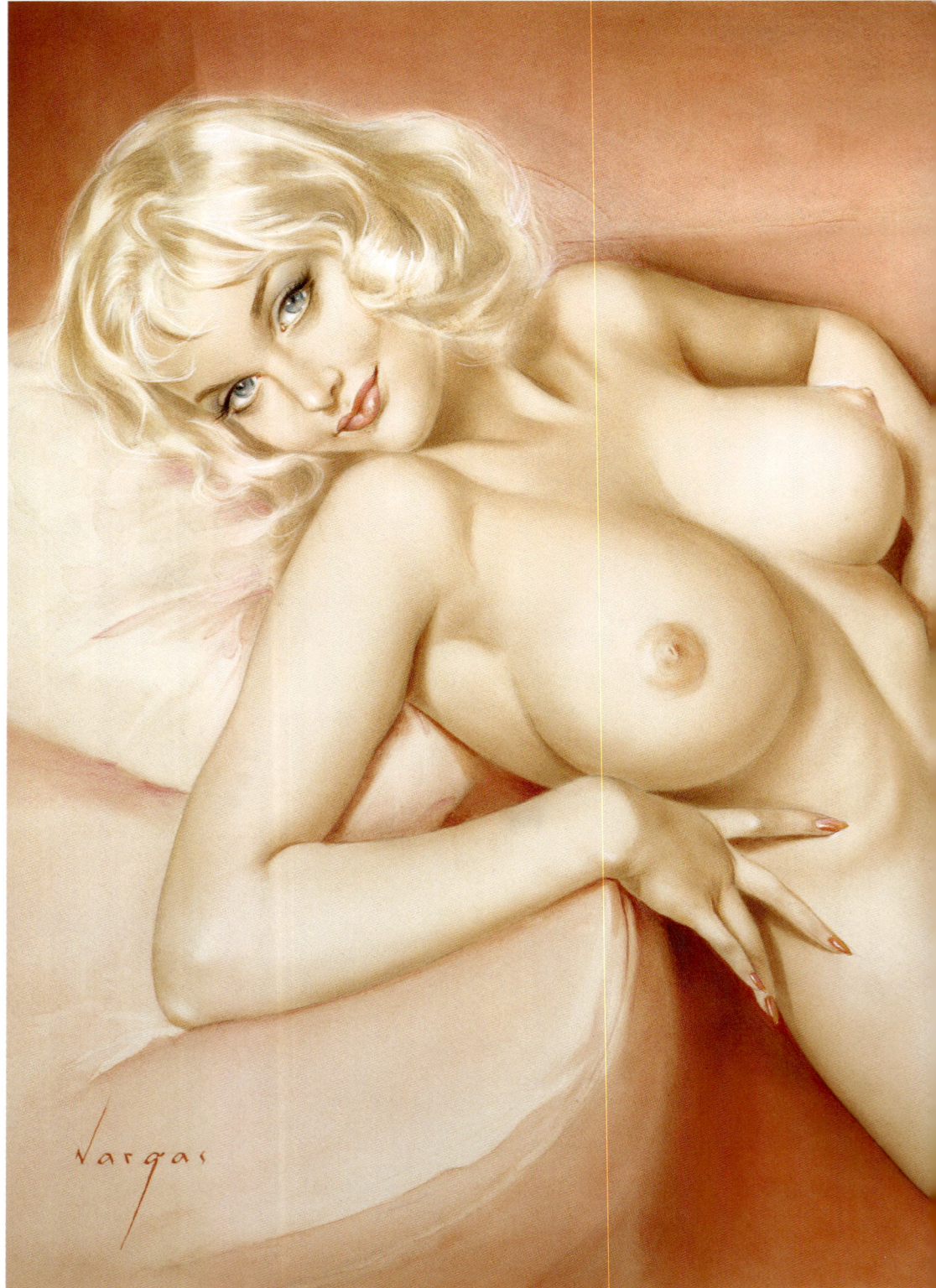

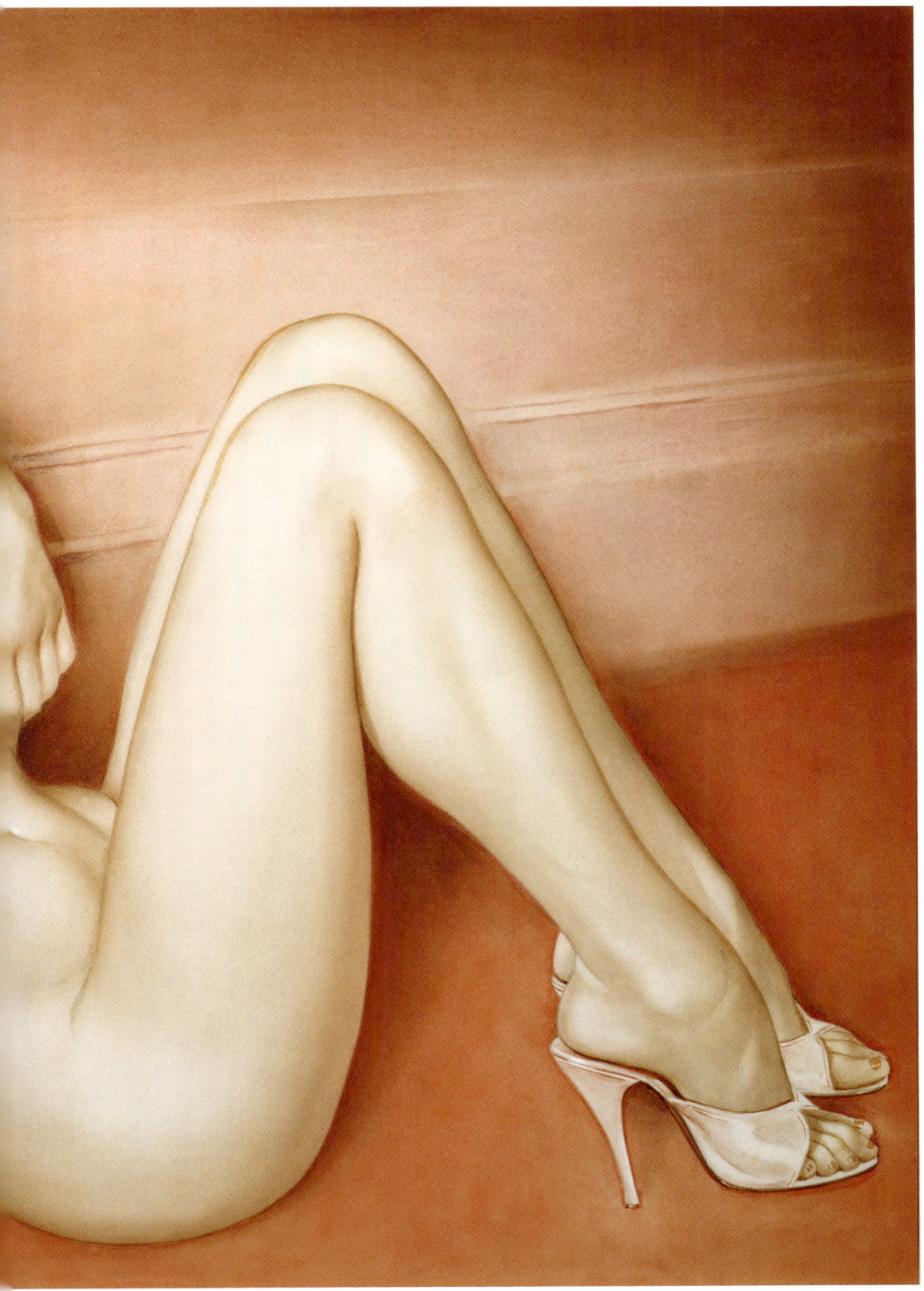

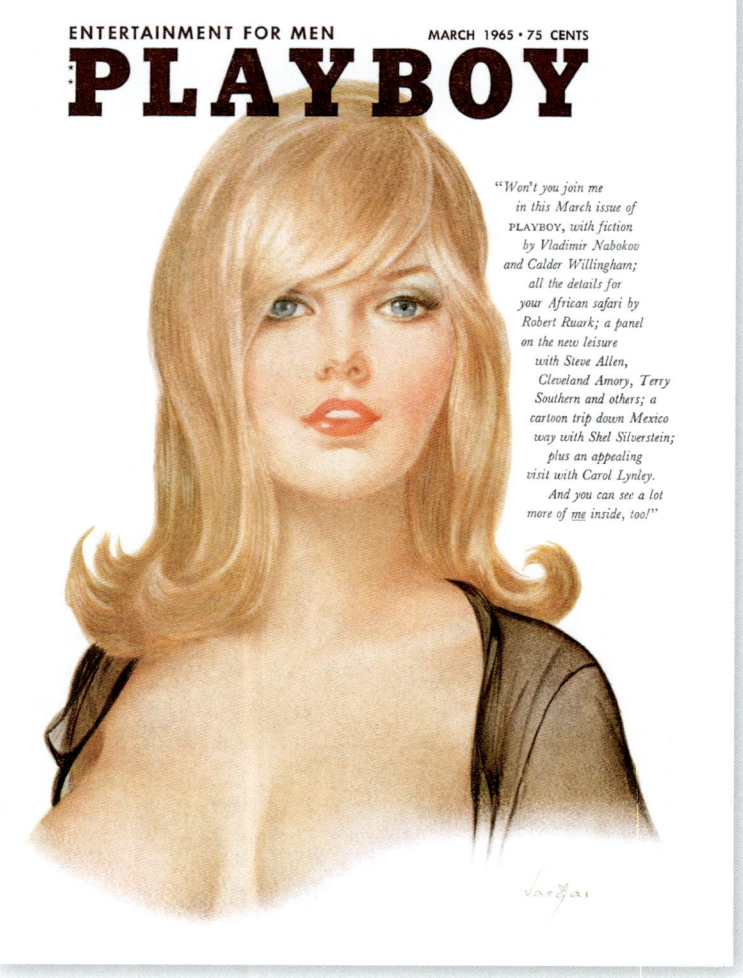

MARCH 1965 · 75 CENTS

PLAYBOY

"*Won't you join me in this March issue of* PLAYBOY, *with fiction by Vladimir Nabokov and Calder Willingham; all the details for your African safari by Robert Ruark; a panel on the new leisure with Steve Allen, Cleveland Amory, Terry Southern and others; a cartoon trip down Mexico way with Shel Silverstein; plus an appealing visit with Carol Lynley. And you can see a lot more of me inside, too!*"

Previous spread: Watercolor on board, circa 1958, but unpublished until it appeared in the December 1963 issue of *Playboy.* The Max Vargas Collection.

Above: The March 1965 issue of *Playboy* with cover by Vargas. The full figure appeared in a pin-up on the inside.

Opposite: Watercolor on board, 1960, for the October 1960 issue of *Playboy.* This was Vargas' second pin-up for the magazine. *Playboy* art director Reid Austin was a longtime fan of Vargas', and when he discovered, in 1957, that he was out of work and struggling he set up a meeting with Hefner. With a handshake agreement the Vargas Girl became a monthly feature in *Playboy.* The Max Vargas Collection.

THE ART OF PIN-UP

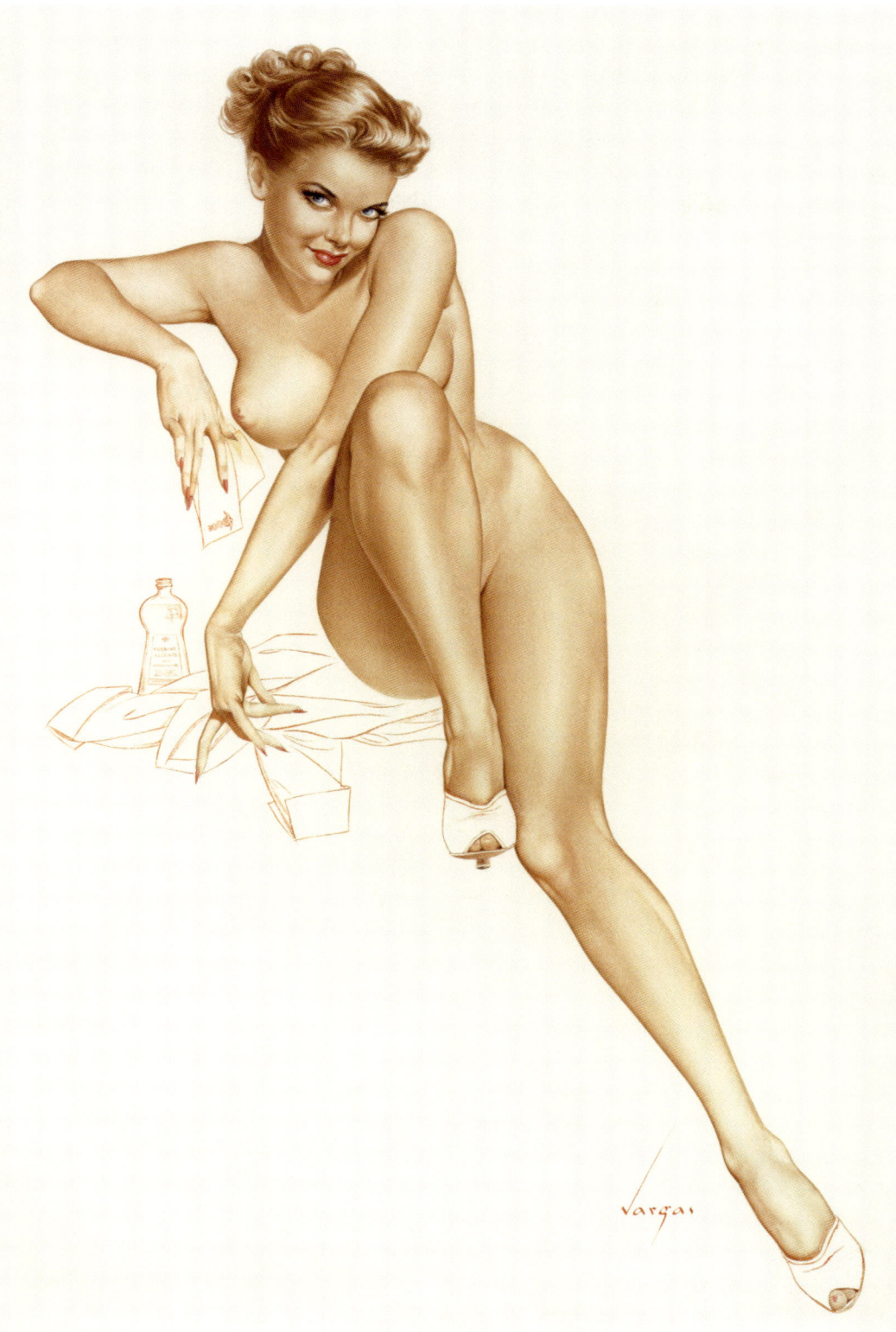

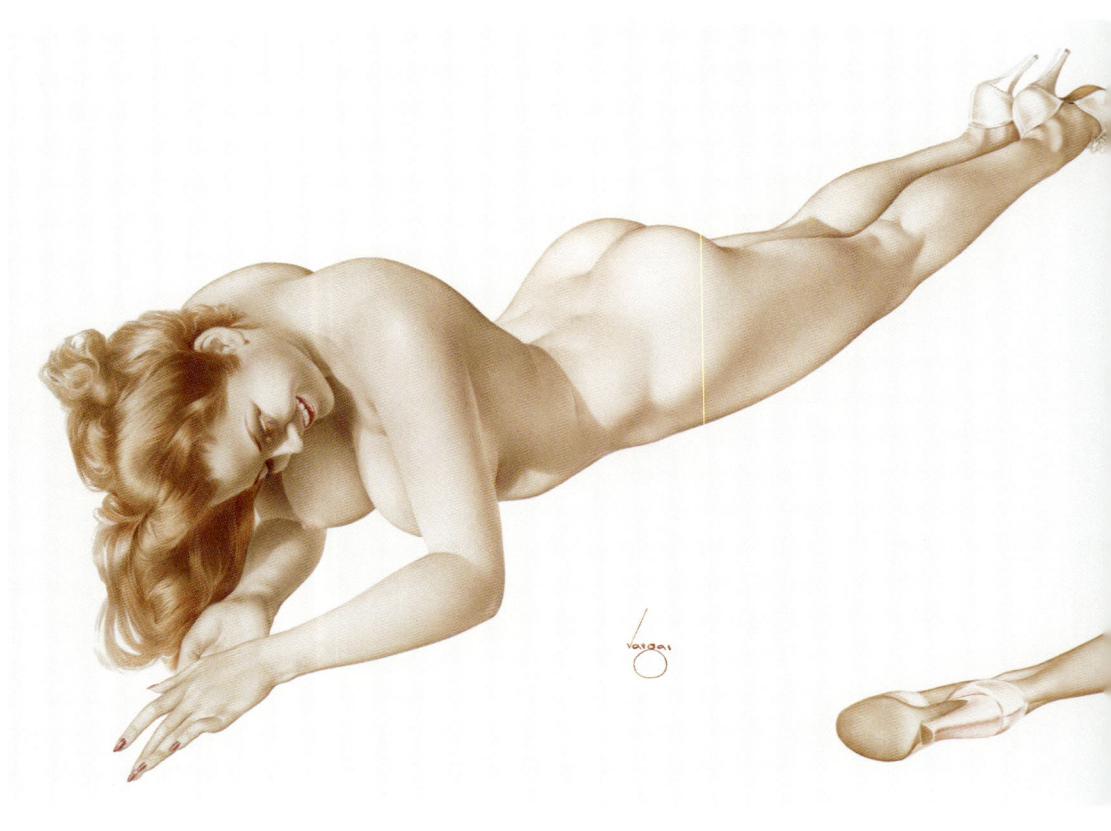

Above left: Exuberance, also known as
Cordillera de Los Andes, Legacy Nude #4,
watercolor on board, circa 1943. Posed
by Jeanne Dean. The Max Vargas Collection.

Above right: Big Blonde, Legacy Nude #6, watercolor
on board, circa 1948. The Max Vargas Collection.

THE ART OF PIN-UP

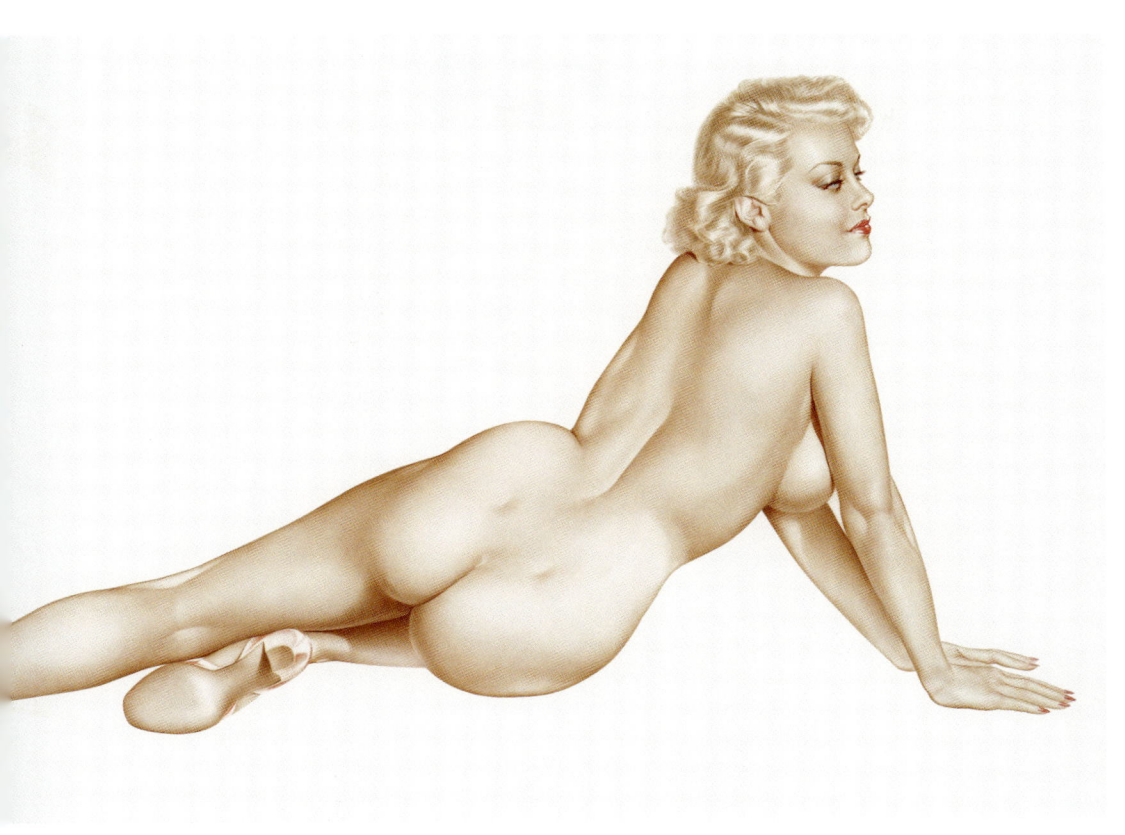

ALBERTO VARGAS

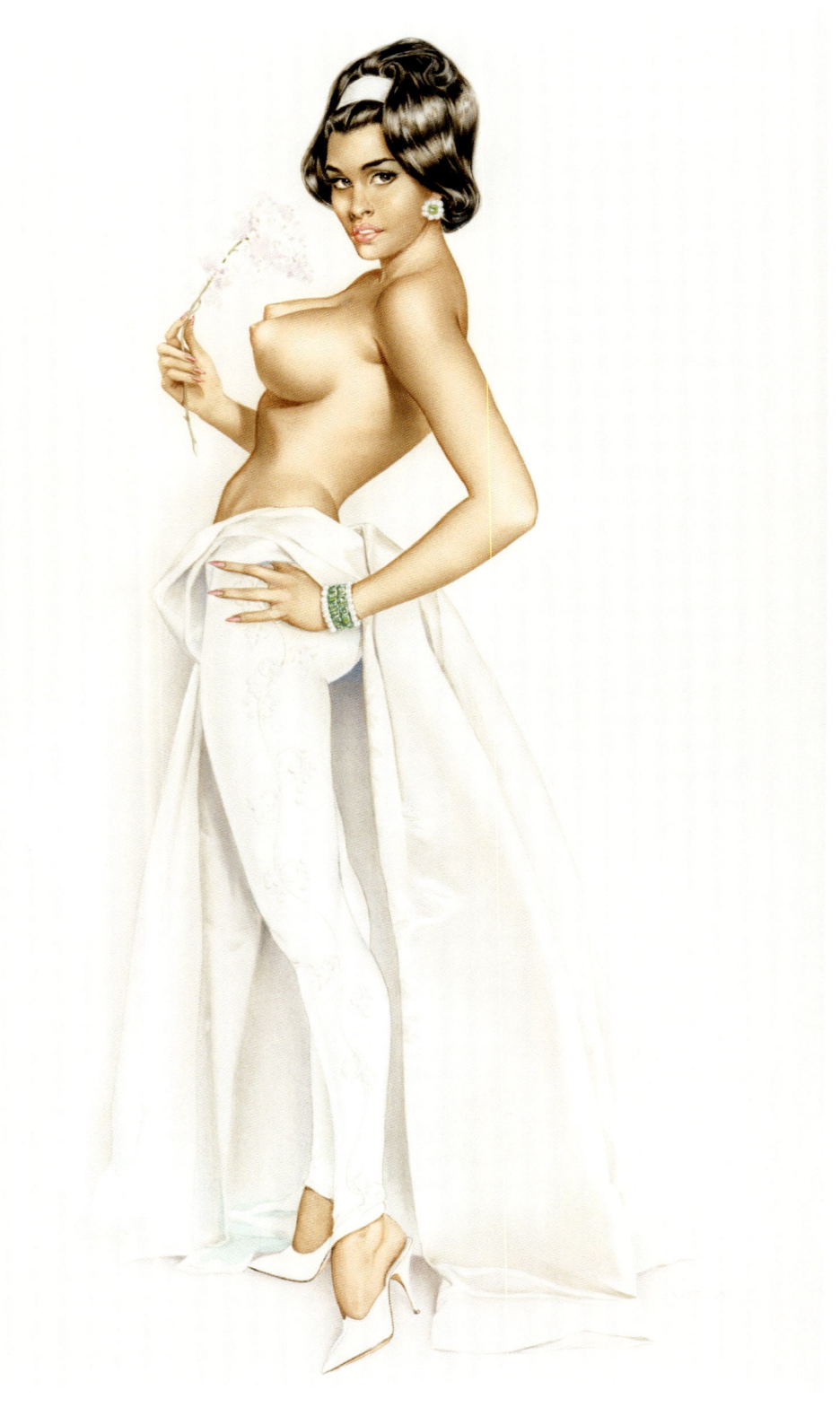

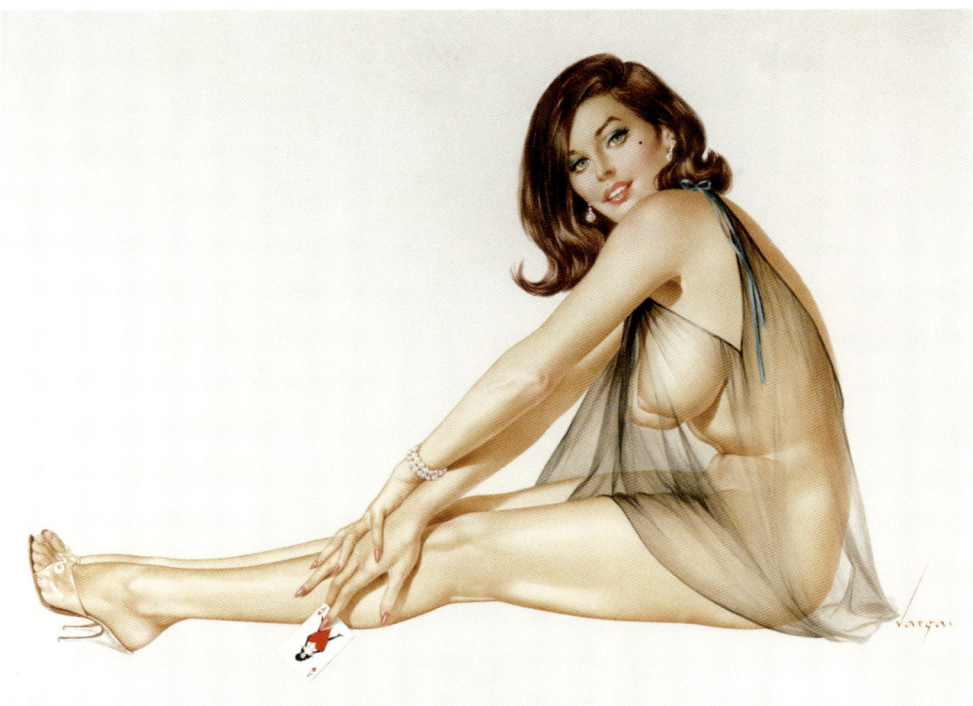

Opposite: Watercolor on board, 1963, for the March 1964 issue of *Playboy*. This is Vargas's first African American pin-up; she predated *Playboy*'s first Black Playmate of the Month, Jennifer Jackson, by exactly one year. The Max Vargas Collection.

Above: Watercolor on board, 1964, for the April 1965 issue of *Playboy*. The Max Vargas Collection.

Following spread: Alberto Vargas rivals Elvgren for the top pin-up artist spot. In recent years *Playboy* has been selling off much of its Vargas archive, bringing new work onto the market, which sells in the $20,000 to $60,000 range. This watercolor on board was done for the December 1972 issue of *Playboy*, which featured Haddon Sundblom's last pin-up on its cover.

Pages 506–507: U.S. Marine Corporal Joseph J. Perino cuts a fellow marine's hair in a quonset hut barber shop on a marine base in the Pacific, 1944. The pin-ups decorating the wall include photos of movie stars and illustrations from *Esquire*. © Bettmann/Corbis Images.

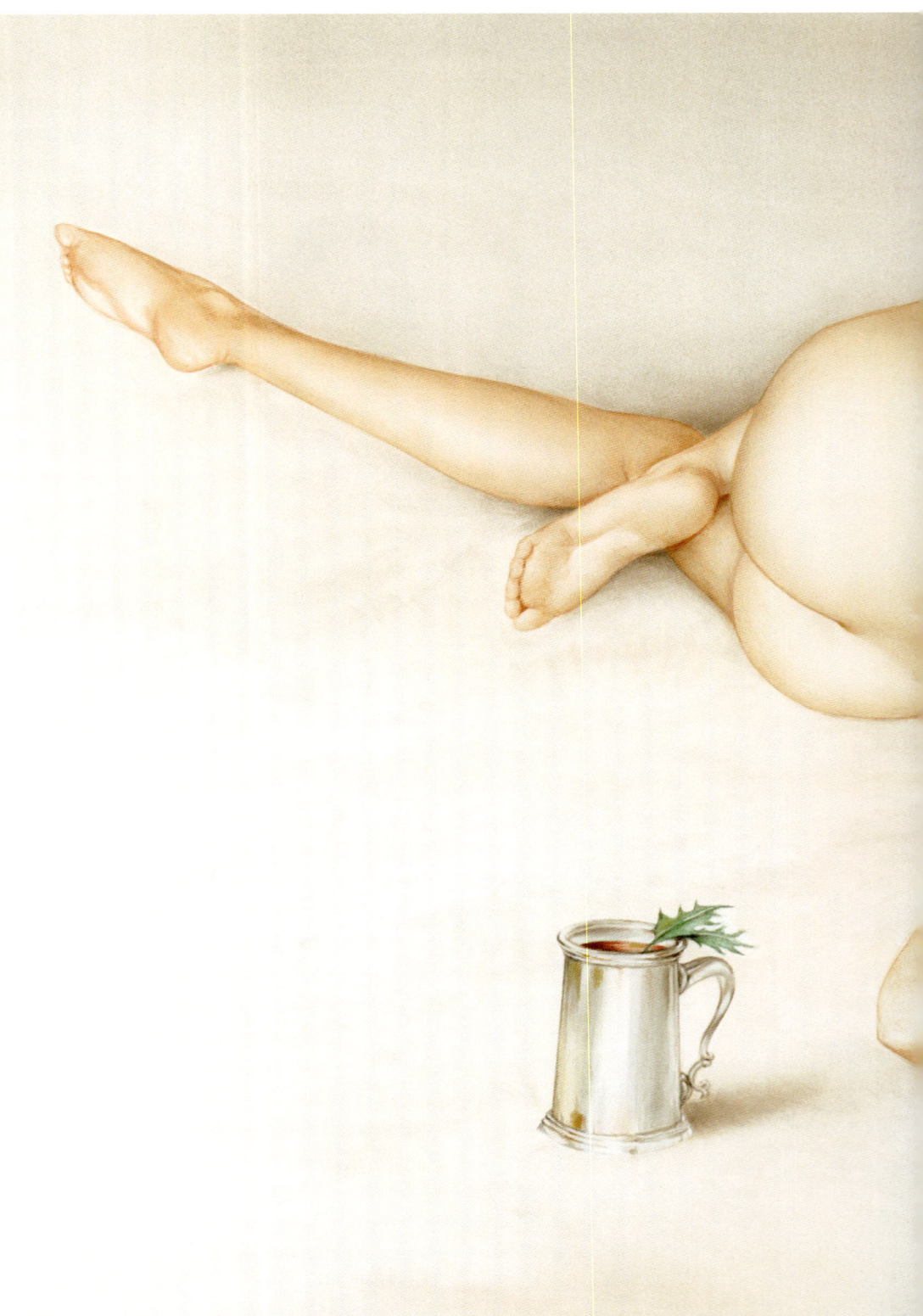

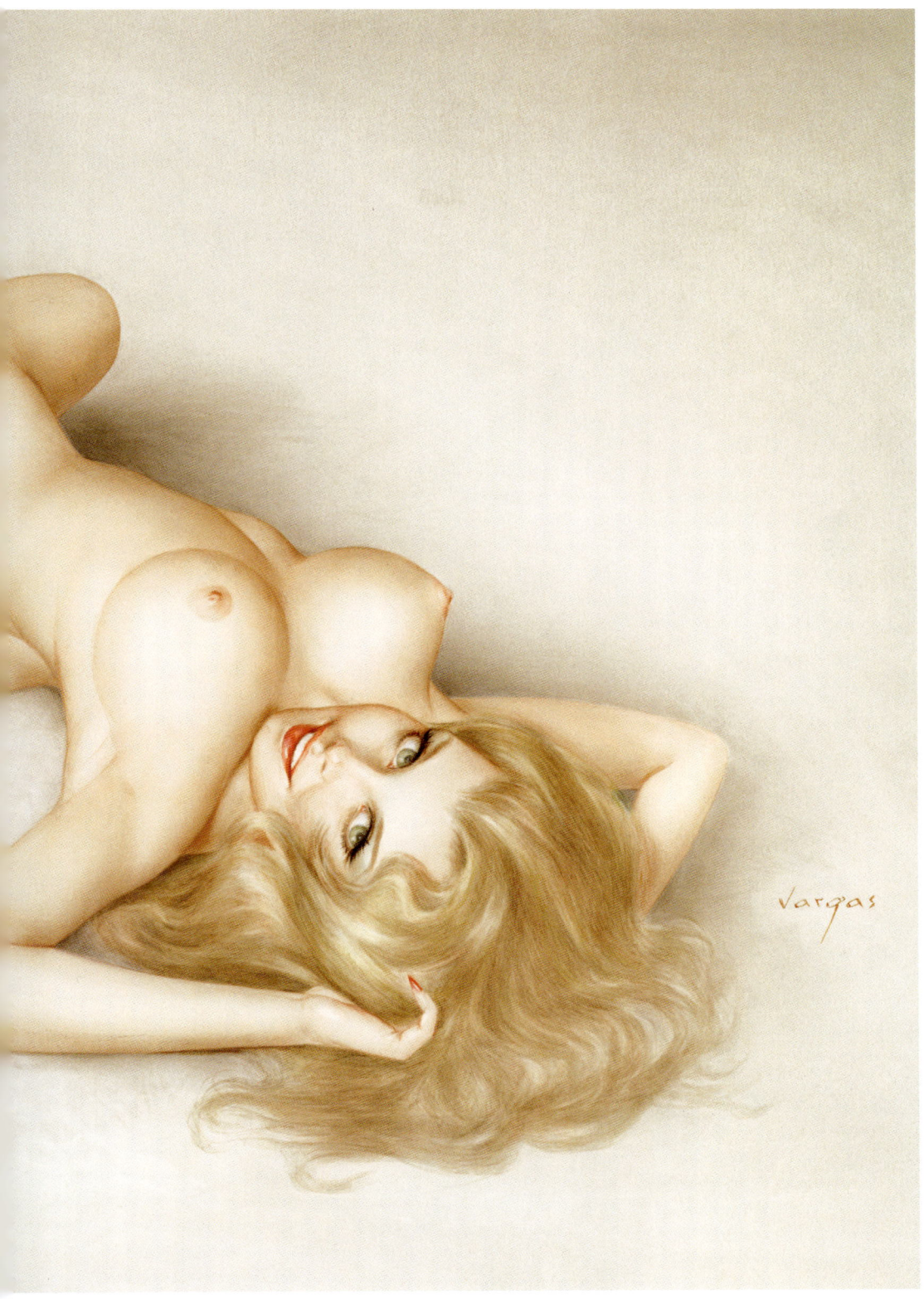

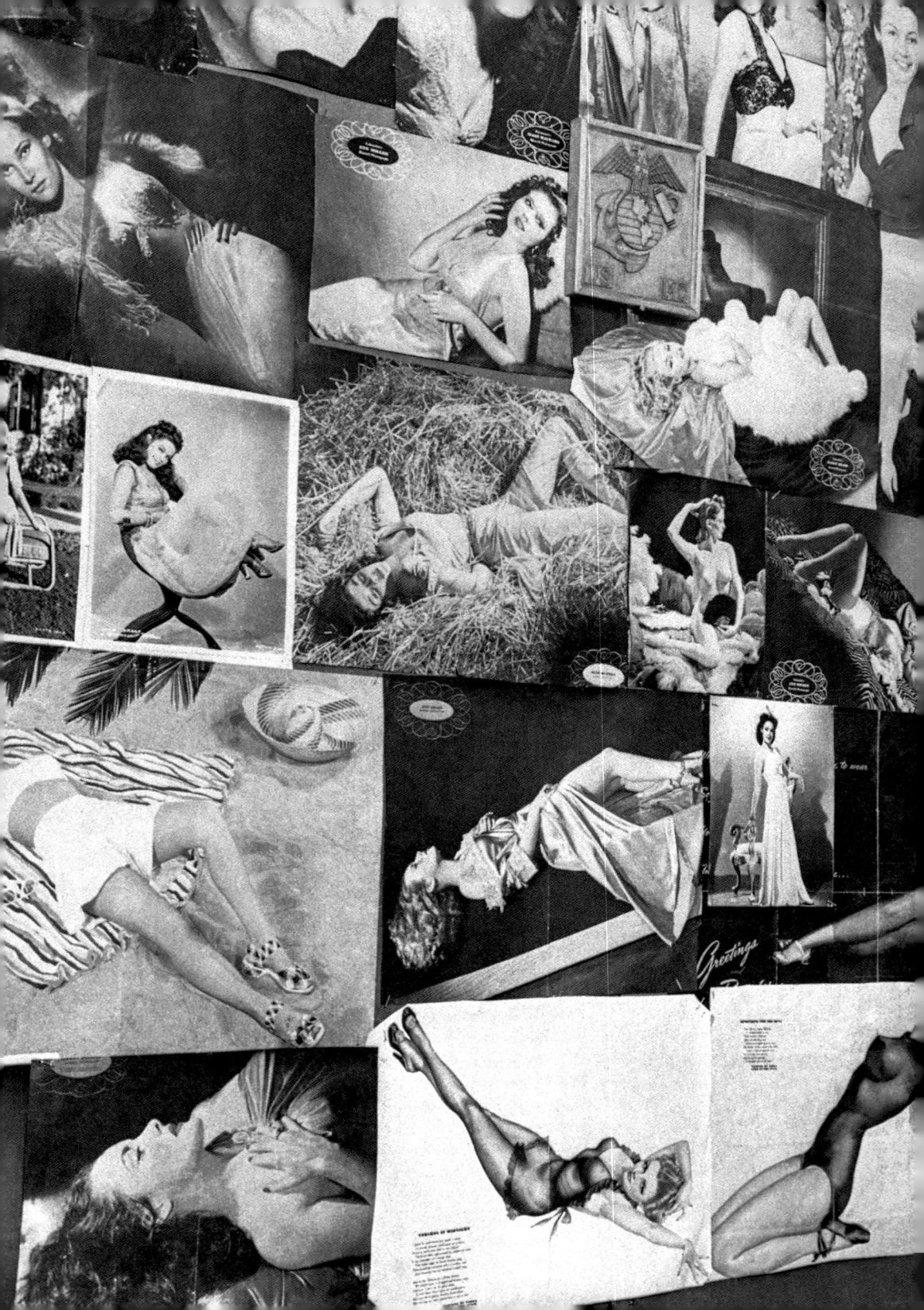

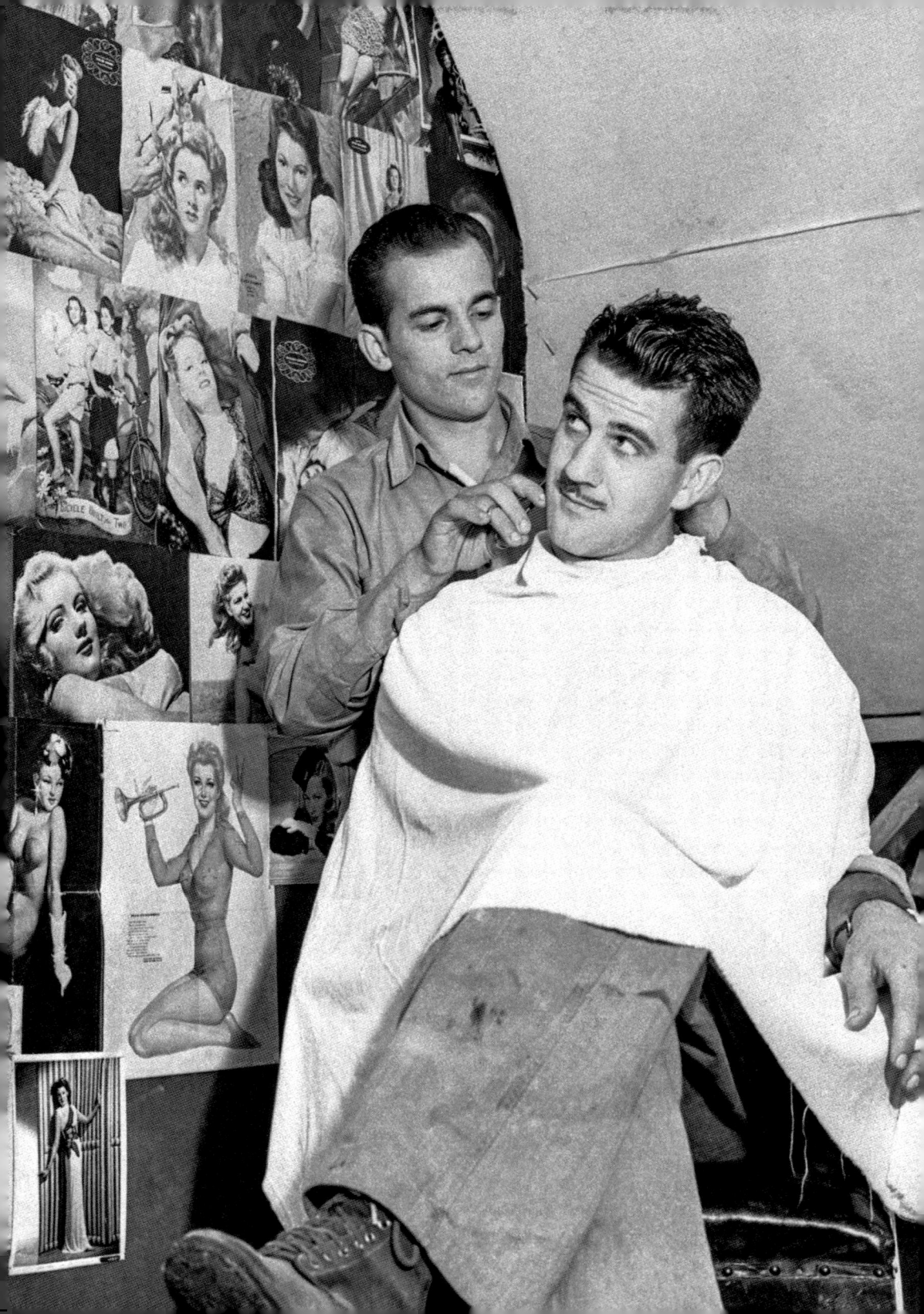

ACKNOWLEDGMENTS

Page 10, Bridgeman Art Library collection.
Pages 27, 28, 29, 30, 45, 64, 65, 103, 112, 114, 116, 119, 130, 201, 203, 210, 227, 237, 303, 310, 327, 331, 337, 344, 353, 361, 369, 372, 374, 375, 378, 381, 392, and 393, © Brown & Bigelow.
Brown & Bigelow additionally owns the copyright to all Elvgren artworks created after 1944, as well as the copyrights to many artworks by Rolf Armstrong, Al Buell, Bill Medcalf, Earl Moran, Zoë Mozert and others. Commercial use of copyright images without obtaining permission will lead to prosecution.
Pages 25, 83, 110, and 235, Jim Cook collection.
Pages 6, 9, 17, 44, 46, 50, 67, 77, 84, 89, 96, 382, 470, and 506/507, © Corbis Images.
Pages 185 and 192, Aaron Driben collection.
Pages 400, 402, 410, 417, 418/419, 420, 421, 422, 423, 424/425, 427, 428, 429, 430, 431, 433, 435, 439, and 441, courtesy of the Estate of George Petty, care of Ronald Feldman Fine Arts, New York.
Pages 18, 35, 72, 92, 93, 106, 132, 278, 338, 447, 455, 459, 490, and 494, above, Erwin and Gail Flacks collection.
Pages 31, 47, 51, 55, and 86, © Getty Images.
Pages 23, 147, 152, and 182, Eric Godtland collection.
Pages 26, 52, 53, 62, 70, 78, 81, 82, 109, 111, 120, 122, 124, 128, 133, 279, 281, 286, 291, 293, 298, 304, 306, 307, 314, 322, 332, 333, 346, 348, 349, 351, 373, 391, and 443, Grapefruit Moon Gallery collection, grapefruitmoongallery.com.
Pages 150 and 347, Michael and Gail Guglielmino collection.
Pages 7, 8, 12, 15, 23, 24, 32, 34, 38, 43, 56, 58/59, 60, 63, 66, 68, 75, 90, 100/101, 105, 141, 156, 163, 181, 183, 207, 221, 277, 288, 342, 363, 370, 371, 384, 397, 399, 400, 411, 426, left and right, 436, 437, 438, top and above, 453, 454, 463, 471, 477, 492, and 498, Dian Hanson/TASCHEN collection.

Pages 37, 54, 56, 61, 71, and 74, Jim Heimann collection.
Pages 4, 11, 17, below left, 16, 20, 22, 30, 34, 36, 39, 41, 69, 80, 83, 85, 91, 94, 95, 97, 106, 127, 129, 131, 139, 154, 157, 160, 162, 163, 167, 171, 172, 173, 175, 178, 179, 180, 186, 188, 189, 192, 196, 197, 200, 206, 212, 214, 215, 223, 225, 228, 230, 231, 232, 234, 246, 247, 253, 259, 260, 263, 264, 267, 268, 270, 281, 283, 284, 290, 314, 317, 320, 323, 324, 328, 329, 335, 345, 355, 356, 357, 365, 368, 405, 406, 409, 412, 413, 414, 416, 438, 448, 456, 457, 460, 483, and 511 courtesy of Heritage Auctions/HA.com.
Pages 14, 161, 258, 285, 340, and 395, Mitchell Mehdy collection.
Pages 2, 40, 42, 99, 104, 118, 123, 125, 126, 136, 140, 144, 147, 151, 153, 166, 176, 184, 187, 190, 191, 199, 202, 211, 216, 218, 220, 222, 229, 233, 236, 238, 239, 240, 241, 242, 243, 244, 245, 245, 248, 250, 251, 252, 255, 256, 257, 261, 262, 265, 266, 269, 271, 272, 273, 276, 287, 289, 292, 294, 295, 296, 297, 299, 300, 301, 308, 309, 311, 312, 321, 336, 339, 352, 362, 383, 384, 387, 388, 390, 404, and 432, Louis K. Meisel collection, greatamericanpinup.com.
Page 452, Volker Morlock collection.
Pages 165, 204, 208, 215, 217, 224, 226, 249, 260, 305, 343, 364, 366, 367, 379, and 380, Marianne Ohl Phillips collection, moppinup.com.
Pages 138, 142, and 148, Jack Raglin collection.
Pages 459, 472/473, 478, 479, 480/481, 482, 484, 485, 487, and 488/489, The Spencer Museum of Art, University of Kansas, Gift of Esquire, Inc.
Pages 98, 444, 446, 449, 450, 451, 461, 462, 464/465, 466, 467, 468/469, 474, 475, 476, 486, 490, 492, 493, 494, below, 495, 496/497, 499, 500/501, 502, 503, and 504/505, The Max Vargas collection.
Pages 20, 155, 159, 168, and 170, Alan Wrobel collection.
Page 158, Terry Zwigoff collection.

Front cover: Sheet Comfort, oil on canvas,
by Gil Elvgren, 1959. 30 x 24 inches.

Back cover: Oil on board by Peter Driben for
the October 1950 cover of *Wink* magazine.

Page 1: Ten of Hearts, oil on canvas, undated,
by Earle Bergey. 29 x 24 inches.

Page 2: Charmaine, oil on canvas, 1957,
by Gil Elvgren. 30 x 24 inches.

Page 4: Watercolor-and-gouache on board
by George Petty, for the May 1947 issue of
True magazine; later Miss January in *True*'s 1948
Petty calendar. 21.5 x 16 inches.

Page 511: Miss January, 1946, by George Petty
for *True* magazine's 1947 calendar.

Page 512: Peek-a-View for a Louis F. Dow
calendar. Oil on canvas, 1940, 29 x 23 inches.

SPECIAL THANKS TO

Grapefruit Moon photographer Jan Albrecht; Bill Smith, Craig Smith, and Barbara Strom at Brown & Bigelow; collector Jim Cook; collector/dealer Leroy Darwin; Aaron Driben; Drake Elvgren; Petty connection Ronald Feldman Fine Arts; collector/character Erwin Flacks; Sarahjane Blum and Danny Murphy of Grapefruit Moon Gallery; collectors Michael and Gail Guglielmino; collector Jim Heimann; the great Heritage Auctions; Theron Kabrich of the San Francisco Art Exchange; collector Mitchell Mehdy; collector/dealer Louis K. Meisel; collector Volker Morlock; TASCHEN photographer Jennifer Patrick; collector/dealer Marianne Ohl Phillips; Bolles expert Jack Raglin; Jonathon Vargas of The Max Vargas Collection; magazine collector/dealer Alan Wrobel; and the inimitable Terry Zwigoff.

EACH AND EVERY TASCHEN BOOK PLANTS A SEED!
Each year, we offset our annual carbon emissions with carbon credits at the Instituto Terra, a reforestation program in Minas Gerais, Brazil, founded by Lélia and Sebastião Salgado. To find out more about this ecological partnership, please check:
www.taschen.com/institutoterra.
Inspiration: unlimited. Carbon footprint: (almost) zero.

Want to see more? Visit taschen.com to view our current publications, browse our latest magazine, and subscribe to our newsletter.

© 2025 TASCHEN GmbH
Hohenzollernring 53, D–50672 Köln
www.taschen.com

Original edition © 2014 TASCHEN GmbH

Edited by Dian Hanson, Los Angeles
German translation by Egbert Baqué, Berlin
French translation by Philippe Safavi, Paris

Printed in Bosnia-Herzegovina
ISBN 978-3-8365-8811-9

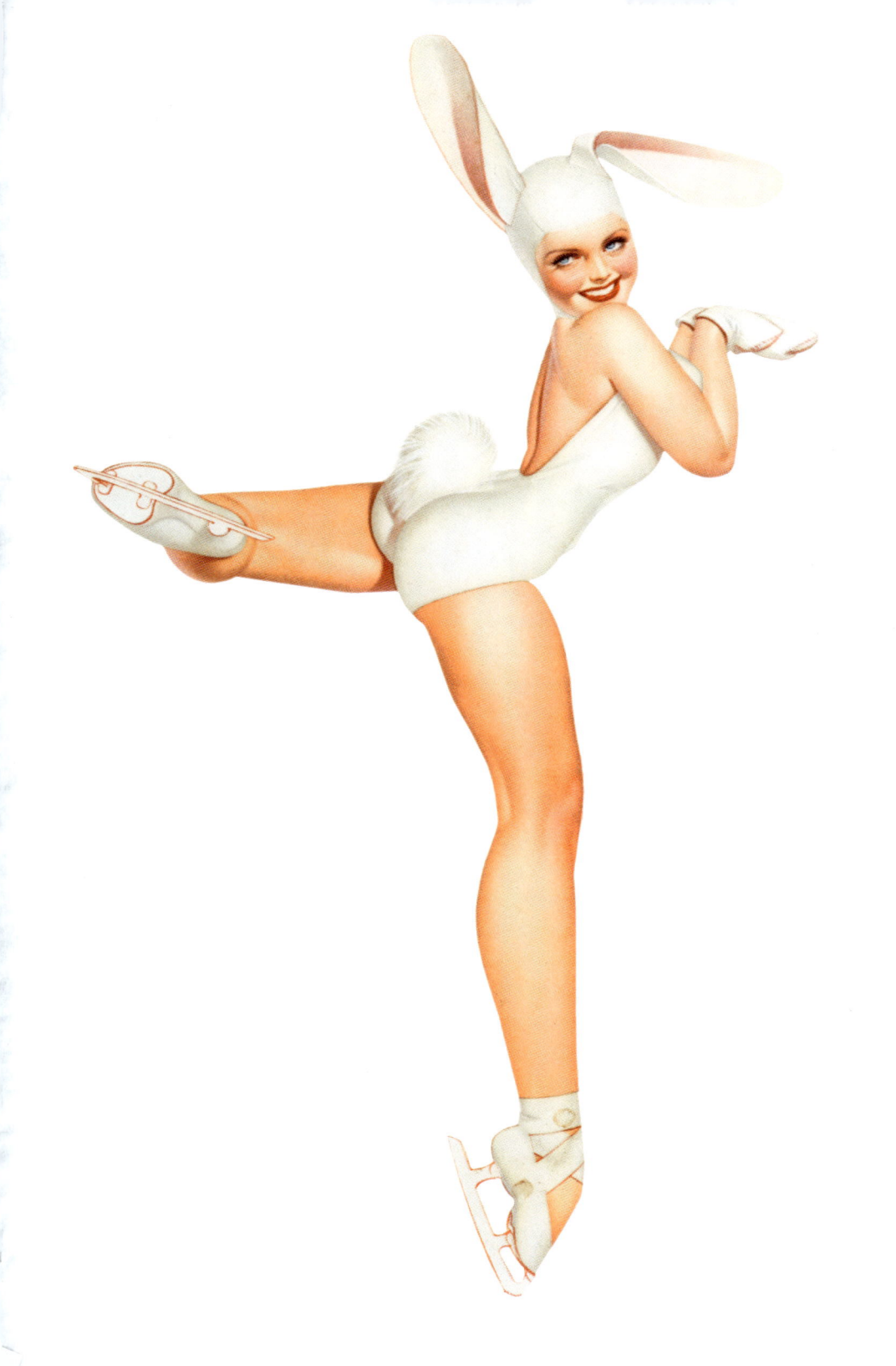

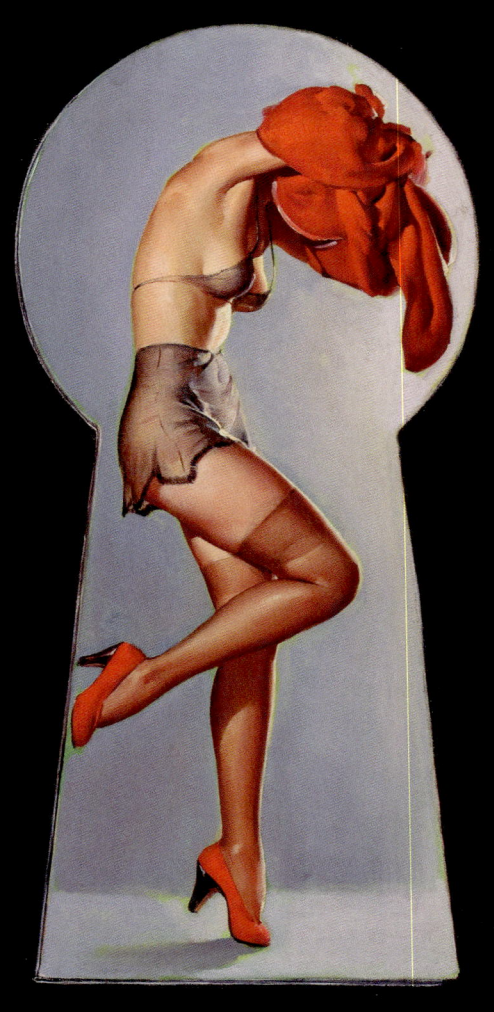

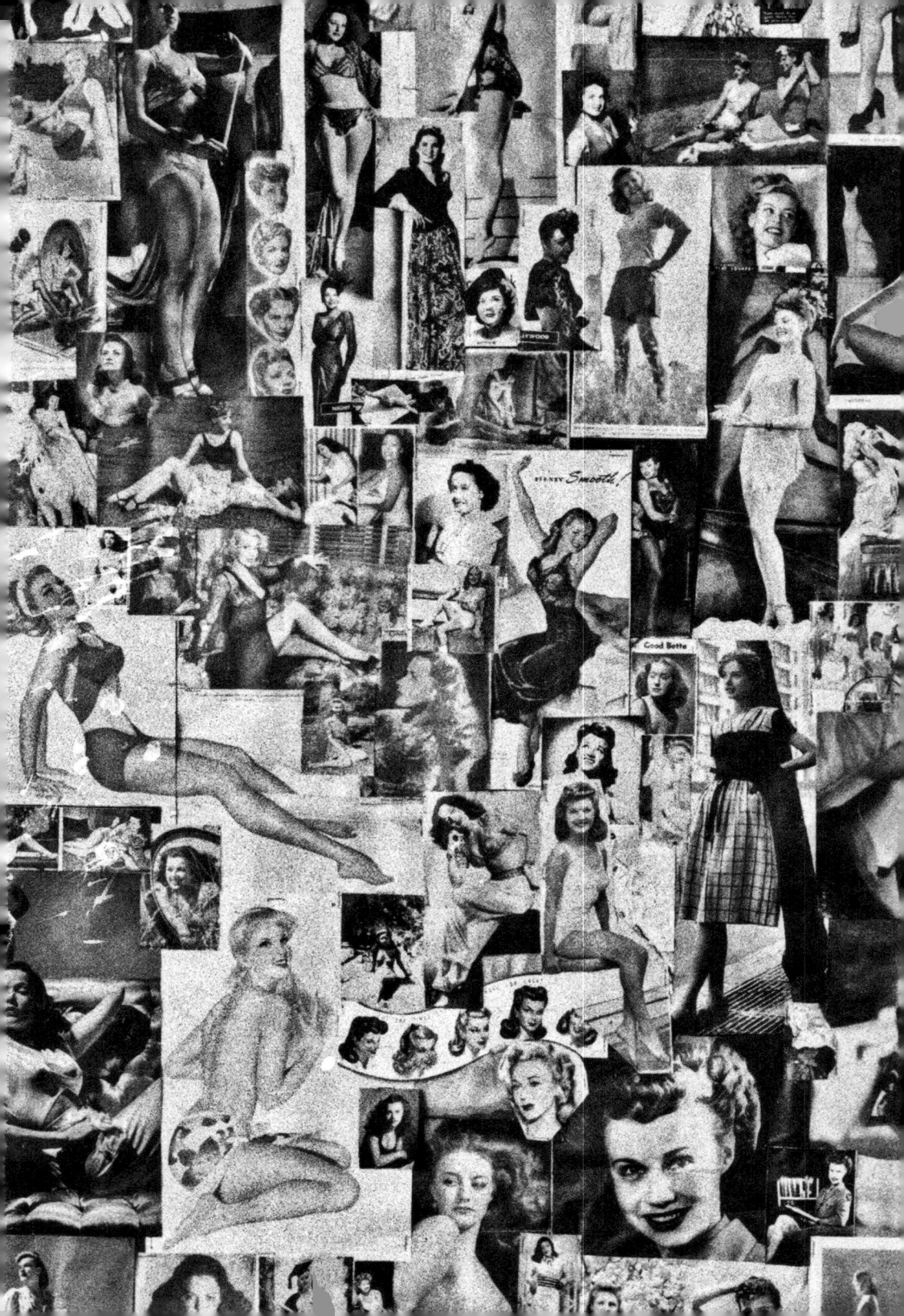